I0879836

Library of America, a nonprofit organization, champions our nation's cultural heritage by publishing America's greatest writing in authoritative new editions and providing resources for readers to explore this rich, living legacy.

H. L. MENCKEN

H. L. Mencken

PREJUDICES: FOURTH, FIFTH, AND SIXTH SERIES

Marion Elizabeth Rodgers, *editor*

THE LIBRARY OF AMERICA

H. L. MENCKEN: PREJUDICES: FOURTH, FIFTH, AND SIXTH SERIES

Volume compilation, notes, and chronology copyright © 2010 by Literary Classics of the United States, Inc., New York, N.Y.
All rights reserved.
No part of this book may be reproduced in any manner whatsoever without the permission of the publisher, except in the case of brief quotations embodied in critical articles and reviews.

Published in the United States by Library of America.
Visit our website at www.loa.org.

Prejudices: Fourth Series, Fifth Series, and Sixth Series copyright © 1924, 1926, 1927 by Alfred A. Knopf, Inc., renewed 1952, 1954, 1955 by H. L. Mencken. Reprinted by arrangement with Alfred A. Knopf, an imprint of the Knopf Doubleday Publishing Group, a division of Random House, Inc.

Permission to quote H. L. Mencken has been granted by the Enoch Pratt Free Library, Baltimore, in accordance with the terms of the bequest of H. L. Mencken.

This paper exceeds the requirements of ANSI/NISO Z39.48–1992 (Permanence of Paper).

Distributed to the trade in the United States by Penguin Random House Inc. and in Canada by Penguin Random House Canada Ltd.

Library of Congress Control Number: 2010924447
ISBN 978–1–59853–075–9

Third Printing
The Library of America—207

Manufactured in the United States of America

H. L. Mencken's
Prejudices
is published with a gift in honor of

JAY CARL PENSKE

on his 30th birthday
from his parents,

Kathryn & Roger Penske

Contents

PREJUDICES
FOURTH SERIES

I.
The American Tradition

I

EVER since Dr. William Crary Brownell, *de l'Académie Américaine*, published his little volume, "Standards," in 1917, a vast hullabaloo has been going on among the native, white, Protestant *Gelehrte* of the Republic, particularly in the great open spaces of the South and Middle West, in favor of what they call the American tradition in letters. Perhaps I libel Brownell, a worthy if somewhat gummy man, by hinting that he started this whooping; it may be that its actual generator was George Creel, the Rev. Dr. Newell Dwight Hillis, the Hon. James M. Beck, the Hon. A. Mitchell Palmer or some other such master-mind of that patriotic and intelligent era. Whatever its parentage, it was at least born in the holiest of wedlock, and to the applause of all right-thinking men; and if I now presume to pull its ear I surely hope that no one will suspect that I thereby question its legitimacy. It is, in fact, absolutely and irrefragably American from snout to *os calcis*, not only in outward seeming and demeanor, but also in inner essence, and anyone who flouts it also flouts everything that is most sacred in the spirit of Americanism. To that business I herewith address myself briefly.

What, then, is the spirit of Americanism? I precipitate it conveniently into the doctrine that the way to ascertain the truth about anything, whether in the realms of exact knowledge, in the purple zone of the fine arts or in the empyrean reaches of metaphysics, is to take a vote upon it, and that the way to propagate that truth, once it has been ascertained and proclaimed by lawful authority, is with a club. This doctrine, it seems to me, explains almost everything that is indubitably American, and particularly everything American that is most puzzling to men of older and less inspired cultures, from American politics to American learning, and from the lush and unprecedented American code of morals to the amazing and almost fabulous American code of honor. At one end it explains the archetypical buffooneries of the Ku Klux Klan, the American Legion, the Anti-Saloon League, the Department of Justice and all other such great engines of cultural propaganda, and at the other end it explains the amusing theory that the limits of the nation's æsthetic adventures are to be fixed by a vague and self-appointed camorra of rustic Ph.D.'s, and that any artist, indigenous or imported, who dares to pass them is not only a sinner against the beautiful but also a traitor to the flag, and that he ought, shall and must be throttled by the secular arm. Patriotism thus gathers in æsthetics and gives it suck, as it has already given suck to ethics. There are artists who are worthy of the boon of freedom, and there are artists who are criminal and must be put down, as anarchists and polygamists are put down. The fancies of the poet in his velvet coat, the vast soarings and grapplings of the metaphysician in his damp cell, the writhings of the logician chained to his rock, become either right or wrong, and whatever is right in them is American and whatever is wrong is not American.

How far this last notion goes under the Constitution is best shown, not in the relatively *pianissimo* pronunciamentoes of such suave and cautious dons as Brownell, who are themselves often sadly polluted by foreign ideas, despite their heroic struggle to remember Valley Forge and San Juan Hill, but in the far more frank and passionate bulls of their followers in the seminaries of the cow States, where every male of *Homo sapiens* has copious *vibrissæ* on his chest and Nordic blue eyes in his head, and is a red-blooded, go-getting, up-and-coming he-man. I introduce at once a perfect speciman, Doughty of Texas—a savant but little known in the diabetic East, but for long a favorite expert in comparative morals in the university at Austin—not a professor, alas, for he lacks the Ph.D., but *amicus curiæ* to the other professors, as befits his trade of jurisconsult, and a frequent author of critical papers. Doughty has passion but he also has diligence: a combination not too common. Unlike the lean and slippered Beers, of Yale, who once boasted that he had read none of the books he was denouncing, Doughty is at pains to look into even the most subversive, as a dutiful Censor Librorum looks into even "Science and Health" and the works of Dr. Marie C. Stopes. Some time ago, determined to get at and expose the worst, he plowed magnificently through a whole library—through all the new poetry from Carl Sandburg to "The Spoon River Anthology," and all the new novels from Dreiser to Waldo Frank, and all the vast mass of immoral criticism accompanying them, from that in the *Dial* and the *Nation* to that in the *Little Review*, *S4N* and the Chicago *Literary Times.* "For many months now," he reported when he emerged at last, "there has passed before me the whole ghastly array. . . . I have read the 'books'; the 'fiction' and the 'verse'; the 'drama,' the 'articles' and 'essays'; the 'sketches' and the 'criticisms,' and whatever else is squeaked and gibbered by these unburied and not-to-be-handled dead. . . . It is this unnamable by-product of congenital deficiency, perverted dissipation and adulterated narcotics . . . which I refer to as 'modern [American] literature.' "

And what is the Texas Taine's verdict upon this modern American literature? The verdict, in brief, of all other right-thinking, forward-looking he-men, North, East, South, West—the verdict of every American who truly loves the flag, and knows congenitally what is right and what is wrong. He not only finds that it is, in itself, nothing but "swept-up rottenness and garbage—the dilute sewage of the sordid mental slums of New York and Chicago"; he also finds that the ladies and gentlemen who compose it are no more than "a horde of chancre-laden rats," that they constitute a "devil's crew of perverted drug-addicts," that they are engaged unanimously upon a "flabby and feeble assault . . . upon that ancient decency that for unnumbered generations of the white Northern races of mankind, at least, has grown and strengthened as a seed cast upon kindly soil," and, finally, that "no one of the 'writers' of this unhappy array was in the service of the United States in the Great War"—in brief, that the whole movement is no more than a foul conspiracy to tear down the flag, uproot the Republic and exterminate the Nordic Blond, and that, in consequence, it is the duty of every American who is a member "of a white Nordic race, save the Teutonic," to come sliding down the pole, grab the tarpot, and go galloping to the alarm. So concluding and stating in rich Texan phrases, the Doughty proceeds to rend specifically a typical book by one of these immigrant foes to "the heritage of American and English men." . . . The one he chooses is "Jurgen," by James Branch Cabell, of Virginia!

2

This long-horned policeman of letters, I admit, is more exuberant than most. There are no soothing elms on the campus at Austin; instead there is only the cindered *plaza de toros* of the Ku Klux Klan. Patriotism, down there, runs wilder than elsewhere. Men have large hands and loud voices. The sight of the flag makes their blood leap and boil; when it is affronted they cannot control themselves. Nevertheless, the doctrine thus stated in harsh terms by the dreadful Doughty, is, in its essence, precisely the doctrine of his more urbane colleagues—of Brownell *de l'Académie Américaine*, of Brander Matthews *de l'Académie Américaine*, of Sherman *de l'Académie Américaine*, of Erskine *de l'Institut National*, of Boynton, of old Beers, of all the rest. It is a doctrine, as I have said, that is thoroughly American—as American, indeed, as Prohibition, correspondence schools, the Knights of Pythias or chewing-gum. But by the same token it is a doctrine that has no more fundamental sense or dignity than the politics of a Coolidge or the theology of a Billy Sunday. It is, to come to the bald fact at once, mere drivel—an endless series of false assumptions and *nonsequiturs*—bad logic piled recklessly upon unsound facts. It is the product of men who, drilled beyond their capacity for taking in ideas and harrowed from infancy by harsh and unyielding concepts of duty, have borrowed the patriotic philosophy of surburban pastors and country schoolmarms, and now seek to apply it to the consideration of phenomena that are essentially beyond their comprehension, as honor is beyond the comprehension of a politician. It is rural Fundamentalism in the black gown and disarming whiskers of *Wissenschaft*; its inevitable fruit is what Ernest Boyd has aptly called Ku Klux Kriticism.

The simple truth, of course, is that the standards and traditions these sublimated Prohibition enforcement officers argue for so eloquently have no actual existence in the first-line literature of the American people—that what they demand is not a lofty fidelity to a genuine ideal, but only an artificial and absurd subservience to notions that were regarded with contempt by every American of the civilized minority even when they prevailed. In other words, what they argue for is not a tradition that would take in Poe, Hawthorne, Emerson, Whitman and Mark Twain, but a tradition that would pass over all these men to embrace Cooper, Bryant, Donald G. Mitchell, N. P. Willis, J. G. Holland, Charles Dudley Warner, Mrs. Sigourney and the Sweet Singer of Michigan. Even Longfellow, I daresay, must be left out, for didn't he drink of green and terrible waters in Paris as a youth and didn't Poe accuse him of stealing from the Spanish and the German? Certainly even Longfellow, to go back to Doughty's interdict, "simmered in the devil's cauldron of central Europe" and was "spewed out of Italy and France." Could Bryant himself qualify? Didn't he trifle with strange tongues and admire enemy aliens? And what of Lowell? His Dante studies surely had a sinister smack; one can't imagine a Texas Grand Goblin approving them. Bayard Taylor I refrain from mentioning at all. His translation of "Faust" came to a just judgment at last when it was hurled from the shelves of every American university patronized by the issue of 100 per cent. Americans. Its incineration on a hundred far-flung campuses, indeed, was the second great patriotic event of the *annus mirabilis* which saw the launching of Brownell's "Standards" and the entrance of the Ku Klux Klan into literary criticism.

How little the patriot-pedagogues know of the verist elements of American literary history was shown very amusingly some time ago when one of them, a specialist in the Emerson tradition, got himself into a lather denouncing some Greenwich Village Brandes for arguing that beauty was independent of morals and its own sufficient justification—only to be confronted by the disconcerting fact that Emerson himself had argued the same thing. Can it be that even pedagogues are unaware that Emerson came to fame by advocating a general deliverance from the stupid and flabby tradition his name is now evoked to support, that his whole system of ideas was an unqualified protest against hampering traditions of every sort, that if he were alive today he would not be with the professors but unalterably against them? And Emerson was surely not alone. Go through the list of genuinely first-rate men: Poe, Hawthorne, Whitman, Mark Twain. One and all they stood outside the so-called tradition of their time; one and all, they remained outside the tradition that pedants try so vainly to impose upon a literature in active being today. Poe's poems and tales not only seemed strange to the respectable dolts of his time; they seemed downright horrible. His criticism, which tells us even more about him, was still worse: it impinged upon such dull fellows as Griswold exactly as "Jennie Gerhardt" impinged upon the appalled tutors in the alfalfa colleges. And what of Hawthorne? Hawthorne's onslaught upon the Puritan ethic was the most formidable and effective ever delivered, save only Emerson's. And Whitman? Whitman so staggered the professors that it is only within the last few years that they have begun to teach him at all; those who flourished in 1870 avoided all mention of him as carefully as their successors of today avoid mention of Dreiser or Cabell. And Mark Twain? I put a professor on the stand, to wit, my Christian friend, Phelps of Yale. Go to Phelps' "Essays on Modern Novelists," and you will find a long and humorous account of the efforts of unintelligent pedagogues to read Mark out of the national letters altogether—and go to Van Wyck Brooks' "The Ordeal of Mark Twain" and you will discover what great damage that imbecility did to the man himself. Phelps printed his book in 1910. It was the first book by a doctor of beautiful letters to admit categorically that Mark was an artist at all! All the other professors, even in 1910, were still teaching that Washington Irving was a great humorist and Mark a mere clown, just as they are teaching now that the criticism of Howells and Lowell was superior to the criticism of Huneker, and that Henry van Dyke is a great artist and Cabell a bad one.

Historically, there is thus nothing but folly and ignorance in all the current prattle about a restoration of the ancient American tradition. The ancient American tradition, in so far as it was vital and productive and civilized, was obviously a tradition of individualism and revolt, not of herd-morality and conformity. If one argues otherwise, one must inevitably argue that the great men of the Golden Age were not Emerson, Hawthorne, Poe and Whitman, but Cooper, Irving, Longfellow and Whittier. This nonsense, no doubt, is actually argued in the prairie seminaries; it even has its prophets, perhaps, in backwaters of the East; certainly one finds little in controversion of it in the prevailing text-books. But it remains nonsense all the same. The fact that it has been accepted for years explains the three great disgraces of American letters: the long neglect of Whitman, Melville and Mark Twain. And the fact that it is now challenged actively—that practically all young Americans of any appreciable intelligence now rebel against it—that the most significant sign of the times, in many ways, is the open revolt of the new generation against the teaching of their elders—this fact explains the new vigor that has got into American literature, and its consequent running amok. That running amok, to be sure, is leading to excesses—but so did the running amok of Whitman lead to excesses; so did the timorous running amok of Mark Twain. In order to get the rest of "Leaves of Grass" we must somehow manage to survive "A Woman Waits for Me"; in order to get "Huckleberry Finn" we must swallow the buffooneries of "The Innocents Abroad." In brief, we must be willing to pay a price for freedom, for no price that is ever asked for it is half the cost of doing without it.

3

It so happens that many of the men and women who have sought to exercise this freedom in our time have been of stocks other than the so-called Anglo-Saxon, either wholly or in part—that they have represented the newer stocks which threaten, not only in the fine arts but in practically all departments of human activity, including even business, to oust the Anglo-Saxon from his old hegemony. The fact, in a day of increasing racial consciousness, has greatly colored the whole controversy and made it extraordinarily bitter. The doctrine gradually set up between 1914 and 1917, and given the full force of law in the latter year, that a citizen of German blood, or suspected of German blood, stood on a plane inferior to that occupied by a citizen of British blood, and had a less valid claim to the equal protection of the Constitution and the laws—this doctrine was extended, in the post-war years of terror, to all Americans not specifically Anglo-Saxon. How seriously it has been taken in the more remote parts of the Republic is well displayed by the strophes that I have quoted from good Doughty—a gentleman who seems quite as content to take his anthropology from Madison Grant and Gertrude Atherton as he is to take his manners from the cattle-herders of his native steppes. Even more ludicrous attempts to set up Ku Klux criteria in letters might be dredged from the writings of more urbane, and, in theory, more intelligent and civilized critics—for example, Brander Matthews. The rancorous animosity that has pursued such men as Dreiser is certainly not wholly æsthetic, or even moral; it is, to a very large extent, racial. The man is obviously not an Anglo-Saxon; *ergo*, there is something sinister about him, and he must be put down. The more solid becomes his position as a man of letters, the more offensive he becomes to the colonial mind. His crime, indeed, is that he has made headway—that a new American tradition, differing radically from the old one that pedagogues preach, tends to grow up around him—that in European eyes, and even in English eyes, he becomes more typical of America than any of the literary Knights of Pythias who are pitted against him. It thus becomes a matter of self-preservation to dispose of him, and when it turns out to be difficult to do so by logical means then there is a quick and easy recourse to evangelistic means.

The effects of this holy war, alas, have differed greatly from those intended. Far from alarming and stampeding the non-Anglo-Saxons upon whom it has been waged, it has actually forced them, despite their differences, into a certain common action, and so made them far more formidable than they were when it began. And far from establishing any superiority in the Anglo-Saxon, it has only spread the suspicion that, for all his pretensions, he must be a very inferior fellow at bottom, else he would not be so eager to call in the mob to help him in a purely literary feud. As one who has stood on the battlements for years, and smelt the powder of every salvo, I can only report that I have come to believe in this inferiority thoroughly, and that it seems to me to be most obvious in those who most vociferously uphold the so-called American tradition. They are, in the main, extremely stupid men, and their onslaughts are seldom supported by any formidable weight of metal. What they ask the rest of us to do, in brief, is simply to come down voluntarily and irrationally to their own cultural level—the level of a class that easily dominated the country when it was a series of frontier settlements, but that has gradually lost leadership as civilization has crept in. The rest of us naturally refuse, and they thereupon try to make acquiescence a patriotic matter, and to alarm the refractory with all sorts of fantastic penalties. But it must be obvious that they fail far more often than they succeed—and their failure is a melancholy proof of their intrinsic inferiority. The current of thought in the United States, at least among the relatively civilized minority, is not actually toward the abject colonialism that they advocate; it is against that colonialism. We are further from sweetness and light today than we ever were before, and we are further from cultural slavery to the harassed and care-worn Motherland. With overwhelming numbers on their side, and every form of external authority, and all the prevailing shibboleths, the spokesmen of Anglo-Saxon domination come to grief every time they tackle the minority, or even any minority within the minority, and at no time do they come to grief more dramatically than when they prepare for battle, in the traditional Anglo-Saxon manner, by first trying to tie their opponents' hands.

When I speak of Anglo-Saxons, of course, I speak inexactly and in the common phrase. Even within the bounds of that phrase the American of the prevailing stock is Anglo-Saxon only partially, for there is probably just as much Celtic blood in his veins as Germanic, and his norm is to be found, not South of the Tyne and west of the Severn, but on the bleak Scotch hills. Among the first English colonists there were unquestionably many men of purely Teutonic stock from the East and South of England, and their influence is yet visible in many characteristic American folkways, in certain traditional American ideas—some of them now surviving only in national hyprocrisies—, and, above all, in the fundamental peculiarities of the American dialect of English. But their Teutonic blood was early diluted by Celtic strains from Scotland, from the North of Ireland and from the West of England, and today those Americans who are regarded as being most thoroughly Anglo-Saxons—for example, the mountaineers of the Appalachian slopes from Vermont to Georgia—are obviously far more

Celtic than Teutonic, not only physically but also mentally. They are leaner and taller than the true English, and far more given to moral obsessions and religious fanaticism. A Methodist revival is not an English phenomenon; it is Scotch. So, fundamentally, is Prohibition. So is the American tendency, marked by every foreign student of our history, to turn all political combats into moral crusades. The English themselves, of course, have been greatly polluted by Scotch, Irish and Welsh blood during the past three centuries, and for years past their government has been largely in the hands of Celts, but though this fact, by making them more like Americans, has tended to conceal the difference that I am discussing, it has certainly not sufficed to obliterate it altogether. Such a man as Lloyd George, in all his ways of thinking, is almost precisely like an American—but the English notion of humor remains different from the American notion, and so does the English view of personal liberty, and on the same level of primary ideas there are many other obvious differences.

But though I am thus convinced that the American Anglo-Saxon wears a false label, and grossly libels both of the great races from which he claims descent, I can imagine no good coming of trying to change it. Let him call himself whatever he pleases. Whatever he calls himself, it must be plain that the term he uses designates a genuinely distinct and differentiated race—that he is separated definitely, in character and habits of thought, from the men of all other recognizable strains—that he represents, among the peoples of the earth, almost a special species, and that he runs true to type. There is, indeed, very little tendency to variation in him—that is, in the mass. The traits that he developed when the first mixture of races took place in colonial days are the traits that he still shows; despite the vast changes in his material environment, he is almost precisely the same, in the way he thinks and acts, as his forefathers were. Some of the other great races of men, during the past two centuries, have changed very noticeably—for example, think of the complete dying out of adventurousness in the Spaniards and its sudden appearance in the Germans—but the American Anglo-Saxon has stuck to his hereditary guns. Moreover, he tends to show much less variation than other races between man and man. It is an axiom that, when five Russians or Germans meet, there are four parties in conflict, but it is equally an axiom that, among a hundred Americans, at least ninety-five will be found to hold exactly the same views upon all subjects that they can grasp at all, and may be trusted to react exactly alike to all ordinary stimuli. No other race, save it be the Chinese, is so thoroughly solid, or so firmly unresponsive to ideas from without.

4

The good qualities of this so-called Anglo-Saxon are many, and I am certainly not disposed to question them, but I here pass them over without apology, for he devotes practically the whole of his literature and fully a half of his oral discourse to celebrating them himself, and so there is no danger that they will ever be disregarded. No other known man, indeed, is so violently the blowhard, save it be his English kinsman; even the Frenchman, by comparison, is relatively modest and reticent. In this fact lies the first cause of the ridiculous figure he commonly cuts in the eyes of other people: he brags and blusters so incessantly that, if he actually had the combined virtues of Socrates, the Cid and the Twelve Apostles, he would still go beyond the facts, and so appear a mere Bombastes Furioso. This habit, I believe, is fundamentally English, but it has been exaggerated in the Americano by his larger admixture of Celtic blood. In late years in America it has taken on an almost pathological character, and is to be explained, perhaps, only in terms of the Freudian necromancy. Braggadocio, in the 100 per cent American—"we won the war," "it is our duty to lead the world," "the land of the free and the home of the brave," the "Americanization" movement, and so on—is probably no more than a protective mechanism erected to conceal an inescapable sense of inferiority.

That this inferiority is real must be obvious to any impartial observer. Whenever the Anglo-Saxon, whether of the English or of the American variety, comes into sharp conflict with men of other stocks, he tends to be worsted, or, at best, to be forced back upon extraneous and irrelevant aids to assist him in the struggle. Here in the United States his defeat is so palpable that it has filled him with vast alarms, and reduced him to seeking succor in grotesque and extravagant devices. In the fine arts, in the sciences and even in the more complex sorts of business the children of the later immigrants are running away from the descendants of the early settlers. To call the roll of Americans eminent in almost any field of human endeavor beyond that of mere dull money-grubbing is to call a list of strange and often outlandish names; even the panel of Congress presents a startling example. Of the Americans who have come into notice during the past fifty years as poets, as novelists, as critics, as painters, as sculptors and in the minor arts, less than half bear Anglo-Saxon names, and in this minority there are few of pure Anglo-Saxon blood. So in the sciences. So in the higher reaches of engineering and technology. So in philosophy and its branches. So even in industry and agriculture. In those areas where the competition between the new and the old blood-streams is most sharp and clear-cut, say in New York, in seaboard New England and in the farming States of the upper Middle West, the defeat of the Anglo-Saxon is overwhelming and unmistakable. Once his predominance everywhere was actual and undisputed; today, even where he remains heavily superior numerically, it is largely sentimental and illusory.

The descendants of the later immigrants tend generally to move upward; the descendants of the first settlers, I believe, tend plainly to move downward, mentally, spiritually and even physically. Civilization is at its lowest mark in the United States precisely in those areas where the Anglo-Saxon still presumes to rule. He runs the whole South—and in the whole South there are not as many first-rate men as in many a single city of the mongrel North. Wherever he is still firmly in the saddle, there Ku Kluxery flourishes and Fundamentalism, and lynching, and Prohibition, and all the other stupid and anti-social crazes of inferior men. It is not in the big cities, with their mixed population, that the death-rate is highest, and politics most corrupt, and religion nearest to voodooism, and every decent human aspiration suspect; it is in the areas that the recent immigrations have not penetrated, where "the purest Anglo-Saxon blood in the world" still flows. I could pile up evidences, but they are not necessary. The fact is too plain to be challenged. One testimony will be sufficient: it comes from two inquirers who made an exhaustive survey of a region in Southeastern Ohio, where "the people are more purely Americans than in the rest of the State":

> Here gross superstition exercises strong control over the thought and action of a large proportion of the people. Syphilitic and other venereal diseases are common and increasing over whole counties, while in some communities nearly every family is afflicted with inherited or infectious disease. Many cases of incest are known; inbreeding is rife. Imbeciles, feeble-minded, and delinquents are numerous, politics is corrupt, and selling of votes is common, petty crimes abound, the schools have been badly managed and poorly attended. Cases of rape, assault, and robbery are of almost weekly occurrence within five minutes walk of the corporation limits of one of the county seats, while in another county political control is held by a self-confessed criminal. Alcoholic intemperance is excessive. Gross immorality and its evil results are by no means confined to the hill districts, but are extreme also in the towns.

As I say, the American of the old stock is not unaware of this steady, and, of late, somewhat rapid degeneration—this gradual loss of his old mastery in the land his ancestors wrung from the Indian and the wild cat. He senses it, indeed, very painfully, and, as if in despair of arresting it in fact, makes desperate efforts to dispose of it by denial and concealment. These efforts often take grotesque and extravagant forms. Laws are passed to hobble and cage the citizen of newer stocks in a hundred fantastic ways. It is made difficult and socially dangerous for him to teach his children the speech of his fathers, or to maintain the cultural attitudes that he has inherited from them. Every divergence from the norm of the low-cast Anglo-Saxon is treated as an *attentat* against the commonwealth, and punished with eager ferocity. On the level of the country Ku Kluxers the thing goes to the length of downright assault; a man in Arkansas or Mississippi who ventured to speak a foreign language, or to concern himself publicly with such of the fine arts as country Methodists cannot comprehend, or to let it be known that he was a member of the Roman Catholic Church would run some risk of being tarred and feathered by his neighbors or of having his house burned down over his head. Worse, there is scarcely less pressure in the higher reaches of the so-called intellect. The demand for a restoration of what is called the American tradition in letters is nothing more or less, at bottom, than a demand for a supine and nonsensical conformity—a demand that every American, regardless of his racial character and his natural way of thinking, force all his thoughts into the low-caste Anglo-Saxon mold. It is bound to fail of effect, of course, and in that very fact lies the best of imaginable proofs of the mental poverty of those who voice it. It is not brought forward in an effort at persuasion; it is issued as an order, raucously and absurdly—and every time it is flouted the Anglo-Saxon slips another inch down the hill. He cannot prevail in fair competition, and, for all his bellicose flourishes, he cannot prevail by force and intimidation. There remains for him the rôle of martyr, and in this he already begins to display himself affectingly. The music of Americans, we are told gravely, is barred out of our concert halls and opera houses because their managers and conductors are all accursed foreigners. American painters and sculptors have to struggle against a dense tide of immigrants. American criticism has become so anti-American that poets and novelists of the old stock are on a sort of blacklist, and cannot get justice. Only in the colleges does the Anglo-Saxon intellectual hold his own, and even there he is now menaced by swarms of Jews, and must devise means of putting them down or perish with his brothers of the fine arts.

5

It so happens that I am myself an Anglo-Saxon—one of far purer blood, indeed, than any of the half-bleached Celts who pass under the name in the United States and England. I am Angle and I am Saxon, and I am very little else, and that little is all safely white, Nordic, Protestant and blond. Thus I feel free, without risk of venturing into bad taste, to regard frankly the *soi-disant* Anglo-Saxon of this incomparable Republic and his rather less dubious cousin of the Motherland. How do the two appear to me, after a quarter of a century spent largely in accumulating their disfavor? What are the characters that I discern most clearly in the so-called Anglo-Saxon type of man? I may answer at once that two stick out above all others. One is his curious and apparently incurable incompetence—his congenital inability to do any difficult thing easily and well, whether it be isolating a bacillus or writing a sonata. The other is his astounding susceptibility to fears and alarms—in short, his hereditary cowardice.

To accuse so enterprising and successful a race of cowardice, of course, is to risk immediate derision; nevertheless, I believe that a fair-minded examination of its history will bear me out. Nine-tenths of the great feats of derring-do that its sucklings are taught to venerate in school—that is, its feats as a race, not the isolated exploits of its extraordinary individuals, most of them at least partly of other stocks—have been wholly lacking in even the most elementary gallantry. Consider, for example, the events attending the extension of the two great empires, English and American. Did either movement evoke any genuine courage and resolution? The answer is plainly no. Both empires were built up primarily by swindling and butchering unarmed savages, and after that by robbing weak and friendless nations: Mexico, Spain, the Boer republics. Neither produced a hero above the average run of those in the movies; neither exposed the folks at home to the slightest danger of reprisal. The battles of Omdurman and Manila Bay were typical of these great swarmings of the Anglo-Saxon—the first a bald massacre, and the second a combat at odds of at least fifty to one. They produced highly typical Anglo-Saxon heroes—Kitchener, an Irishman, and Dewey, largely French. Almost always, indeed, mercenaries have done the Anglo-Saxon's fighting for him—a high testimony to his common sense, but scarcely flattering, I fear, to the truculence he boasts of. The British empire was won mainly by Irishmen, Scotchmen and native allies, and the American empire, at least in large part, by Frenchmen and Spaniards. Moreover, neither great enterprise cost any appreciable amount of blood; neither presented grave and dreadful risks; neither exposed the conqueror to the slightest danger of being made the conquered. The British won most of their vast dominions without having to stand up in a single battle against a civilized and formidable foe, and the Americanos won their continent at the expense of a few dozen puerile skirmishes with savages. All the Indian wars in American history, from the days of John Smith to those of Custer, did not bring down as many men as the single battle of

Tannenberg. The total cost of conquering the whole area from Plymouth Rock to the Golden Gate and from Lake George to the Everglades, including even the cost of driving out the French, Dutch, English and Spaniards, was less than the cost of defending Verdun.

So far as I can make out there is no record in history of any Anglo-Saxon nation entering upon any great war without allies, nor upon any war at all when there was the slightest danger of getting beaten, or even of suffering serious damage. The French have done it, the Dutch have done it, the Germans have done it, the Japs have done it, and even such inferior nations as the Danes, the Spaniards, the Boers and the Greeks have done it, but never the English or Americans. Can you imagine the English taking such a chance as the Germans took in 1914, or as the Turks took in 1922, or as the French prepare to take today? Can you imagine the United States resolutely facing a war in which the odds against it were as huge as they were against Spain in 1898? It seems to me that the facts of history are wholly against any such fancy. The Anglo-Saxon always tries to take a gang with him when he goes to war, and even when he has it behind him he is very uneasy, and prone to fall into panic at the first threat of genuine danger. Here I put an unimpeachably Anglo-Saxon witness on the stand, to wit, Dr. Charles W. Eliot, of Harvard. I find him saying, in an article quoted with approbation by the *Congressional Record*, that during the Revolutionary War the colonists now hymned so eloquently in the school-books "fell into a condition of despondency from which nothing but the steadfastness of Washington and the Continental army *and the aid from France* saved them," and that "when the War of 1812 brought grave losses a considerable portion of the population experienced a moral collapse, from which they were rescued only by the exertions of a few thoroughly patriotic statesmen and the exploits of three or four American frigates on the seas"—to say nothing of an enterprising Corsican gentleman, Bonaparte by name. In both these wars the Americans had enormous and obvious advantages, in terrain, in allies and in men; nevertheless, they fought, in the main, very badly, and from the first shot to the last a majority of them stood in favor of making peace on almost any terms. The Mexican and Spanish Wars I pass over as perhaps too obscenely ungallant to be discussed at all; of the former, General U. S. Grant, who fought in it, said that it was "the most unjust war ever waged by a stronger against a weaker nation." Who remembers that, during the Spanish War, the whole Atlantic Coast trembled in fear of the Spaniards' feeble fleet—that all New England had hysterics every time a strange coal-barge was sighted on the sky-line, that the safe-deposit boxes of Boston were emptied and their contents transferred to Worcester, and that the Navy had to organize a patrol to save the coast towns from depopulation? Perhaps those Reds, atheists and pro-Germans remember it who also remember that during the World War the entire country went wild with fear of an enemy who, without the aid of divine intervention, obviously could not strike it a blow at all—and that the great moral victory was gained at last with the assistance of twenty-one allies at odds of eight to one.

But the American Civil War remains? Does it, indeed? The almost unanimous opinion of the North, in 1861, was that it would be over after a few small battles; the first soldiers were actually enlisted for but three months. When, later on, it turned unexpectedly into a severe struggle, recruits had to be driven to the front by force, and the only Northerners remaining in favor of going on were Abraham Lincoln, a few ambitious generals and the profiteers. I turn to Dr. Eliot again. "In the closing year of the war," he says, "large portions of the Democratic party in the North *and of the Republican party* advocated surrender to the Confederacy, *so down-hearted were they*." Down-hearted at odds of two to one! The South was plainly more gallant, but even the gallantry of the South was largely illusory. The Confederate leaders, when the war began, adopted at once the traditional Anglo-Saxon device of seeking allies. They tried and expected to get the aid of England, and they actually came very near succeeding. When hopes in that direction began to fade (*i.e.*, when England concluded that tackling the North would be dangerous), the common people of the Confederacy, the progenitors of the chivalric Ku Kluxers of today, threw up the sponge, and so the catastrophe, when it came at last, was mainly internal. The South failed to bring the quaking North to a standstill because, to borrow a phrase that Dr. Eliot uses in another connection, it "experienced a moral collapse of unprecedented depth and duration." The folks at home failed to support the troops in the field, and the troops in the field began to desert. Even so early as Shiloh, indeed, many Confederate regiments were already refusing to fight.

This reluctance for desperate chances and hard odds, so obvious in the military record of the English-speaking nations, is also conspicuous in times of peace. What a man of another and superior stock almost always notices, living among so-called Anglo-Saxons, is (*a*) their incapacity for prevailing in fair rivalry, either in trade, in the fine arts or in what is called learning —in brief, their general incompetence, and (*b*) their invariable effort to make up for this incapacity by putting some inequitable burden upon their rivals, usually by force. The Frenchman, I believe, is the worst of chauvinists, but once he admits a foreigner to his country he at least treats that foreigner fairly, and does not try to penalize him absurdly for his mere foreignness. The Anglo-Saxon American is always trying to do it; his history is a history of recurrent outbreaks of blind rage against peoples who have begun to worst him; hence Know Nothingism, Ku Kluxery, American Legionism, and all the rest of it. Such movements would be inconceivable in an efficient and genuinely self-confident people, wholly assured of their superiority, as a Frenchman is of his or a German of his, and they would be equally inconceivable in a truly gallant and courageous people, disdaining unfair advantages and overwhelming odds. Theoretically launched against some imaginary inferiority in the non-Anglo-Saxon man, either as patriot, as democrat or as Christian, they are actually launched at his general superiority, his greater fitness to survive in the national environment. The effort is always to penalize him for winning in fair fight, to handicap him in such a manner that he will sink to the general level of the Anglo-Saxon population, and, if possible, even below it. Such devices, of course, never have the countenance of the Anglo-Saxon minority that is authentically superior, and hence self-confident and tolerant. Of that minority I do not speak here. It is serene in peace as it is brave in war. But in the United States, at least, it is pathetically small, and it tends steadily to grow smaller and feebler. The communal laws and the communal *mores* are made by the folk, and they offer all the proof that is necessary, not only of its general inferiority, but also of its alarmed awareness of that inferiority. The normal American of the "pure-blooded" majority goes to rest every night with an uneasy feeling that there is a burglar under the bed, and he gets up every morning with a sickening fear that his underwear has been stolen.

6

It is difficult, I submit, to admire such a people unreservedly, despite the good qualities that I have passed over. They lack the ease and tolerance, the fine adventurousness and love of hazard which go with a sense of firm security—in other words, with a sense of genuine superiority. The Anglo-Saxon of the great herd is, in many important respects, the least civilized of men and the least capable of true civilization. His political ideas are crude and shallow. He is almost wholly devoid of æsthetic feeling; he does not even make folk-lore or walk in the woods. The most elementary facts about the visible universe alarm him, and incite him to put them down. Educate him, make a professor of him, teach him how to express his soul, and he still remains palpably third-rate. He fears ideas almost more cravenly than he fears men. His blood, I believe, is running thin; perhaps it was not much to boast of at the start; in order that he may exercise any functions above those of a trader, a pedagogue or a mob orator, it needs the stimulus of other and less exhausted strains. Poe, Whitman, Mark Twain—these were typical products of such crosses. The fact that they increase is the best hope of the intellect in America. They shake the old race out of its spiritual lethargy, and introduce it to disquiet and experiment. They make for a free play of ideas. In opposing the process, whether in politics, in letters or in the ages-long struggle toward the truth, the prophets of Anglo-Saxon purity and tradition only make themselves ridiculous. Under the absurd *Kultur* that they advocate Agassiz would have been deported and Whitman would have been hanged, and the most eminent literati flourishing in the Republic today would be Edgar Guest and Dr. Frank Crane.

The success of these so-called Anglo-Saxons in the world, I am convinced, has been due, not so much to their merits but to their defects—and especially to their high capacity for being alarmed and their aversion to what may be called romance—in other words, to their harshly practical minds, their disdain of intellectual enterprise, their dull common sense. They have saved their hides and their money while better sportsmen were taking chances. But the bitter must go with the sweet. Such qualities belong to *Lumbricus terrestris* rather than to *Homo sapiens.* They may be valuable, but they are not pretty. Today, at the height of his triumph in the world, the Anglo-Saxon somehow looks shabby—England trembling before one-legged and bankrupt France, the United States engaged in a grotesque *pogrom* against the wop, the coon, the kike, the papist, the Jap, the what-not—worse, engaged in an even more grotesque effort to put down ideas as well as men—to repeal learning by statute, regiment the arts by lynch-law, and give the puerile ethical and theological notions of lonely farmers and corner grocers the force and dignity of constitutional axioms. As I stand on the side-lines, observing the show, I find it very hard to admire. But, save when ethyl alcohol in dilute aqueous solution has dulled my native pity, I find it even harder to laugh.

II.

The Husbandman

A READER for years of the *Congressional Record*, I have encountered in its dense and pregnant columns denunciations of almost every human act or idea that is imaginable to political pathology, from adultery to Zionism, and of all classes of men whose crimes the legislative mind can grasp, from atheists to Zoroastrians, but never once, so far as I can recall, has that great journal shown the slightest insolence, direct or indirect, to the humble husbandman, the lonely companion of *Bos taurus*, the sweating and persecuted farmer. He is, on the contrary, the pet above all other pets, the enchantment and delight, the saint and archangel of all the unearthly Sganarelles and Scaramouches who roar in the two houses of Congress. He is more to them day in and day out, than whole herds of Honest Workingmen, Gallant Jack Tars and Heroic Miners; he is more, even, than a platoon of Unknown Soldiers. There are days when one or another of these totems of the statesman is bathed with such devotion that it would make the Gracchi blush, but there is never a day that the farmer, too, doesn't get his share, and there is many a day when he gets ten times his share—when, indeed, he is completely submerged in rhetorical vaseline, so that it is hard to tell which end of him is made in the image of God and which is mere hoof. No session ever begins without a grand assault at all arms upon his hereditary foes, from the boll-weevil and the San José scale to Wall Street and the Interstate Commerce Commission. And no session comes to an end without a huge grist of new laws to save him from them—laws embodying the most subtle statecraft of the most daring and ingenious body of lawmakers ever assembled under one roof on the habitable globe. One might almost argue that the chief, and perhaps even only aim of legislation in These States is to succor and secure the farmer. If, while the bombs of goose-grease and rockets of pomade are going off in the two Chambers, certain evil men meet in the basement and hook *banderillas* into him—say, by inserting jokers into the chemical schedule of a new tariff bill, or by getting the long-haul rules changed, or by manipulating the loans of the Federal Reserve Banks,—then the crime is not against him alone; it is against the whole American people, the common decency of Christendom, and the Holy Ghost. Horn a farmer, and you stand in contumacy to the platforms of all known parties, to the devout faith of all known statesmen, and to God. *Laborantem agricolam oportet primum de fructibus percipere.*

Paul wrote to the Bishop of Ephesus, at the latest, in the year 65 A.D.; the doctrine that I have thus ascribed to the Mesmers and Grimaldis of our politics is therefore not a novelty of their contrivance. Nor is it, indeed, their monopoly, for it seems to be shared by all Americans who are articulate and devote themselves to political metaphysics and good works. The farmer is praised by all who mention him at all, from archbishops to zoölogists, day in and day out. He is praised for his industry, his frugality, his patriotism, his altruistic passion. He is praised for staying on the farm, for laboriously wringing our bread and meat from the reluctant soil, for renouncing Babylon to guard the horned cattle on the hills. He is praised for his patient fidelity to the oldest of learned professions, and the most honorable, and the most necessary to all of us. He takes on, in political speeches and newspaper editorials, a sort of mystical character. He is no longer a mundane laborer, scratching for the dollar, full of staphylococci, smelling heavily of sweat and dung; he is a high priest in a rustic temple, pouring out his heart's blood upon the altar of Ceres. The farmer, thus depicted, grows heroic, lyrical, pathetic, affecting. To murmur against him becomes a sort of sacrilege, like murmuring against the Constitution, Human Freedom, the Cause of Democracy. . . . Nevertheless, being already doomed, I herewith and hereby presume to do it. More, my murmur is scored in the manner of Berlioz, for ten thousand trombones *fortissimo*, with harsh, cacophonous chords for bombardons and ophicleides in the bass clef. Let the farmer, so far as I am concerned, be damned forevermore! To hell with him, and bad luck to him! He is, unless I err, no hero at all, and no priest, and no altruist, but simply a tedious fraud and ignoramus, a cheap rogue and hypocrite, the eternal Jack of the human pack. He deserves all that he suffers under our economic system, and more. Any city man, not insane, who sheds tears for him is shedding tears of the crocodile.

No more grasping, selfish and dishonest mammal, indeed, is known to students of the Anthropoidea. When the going is good for him he robs the rest of us up to the extreme limit of our endurance; when the going is bad he comes bawling for help out of the public till. Has anyone ever heard of a farmer making any sacrifice of his own interests, however slight, to the common good? Has anyone ever heard of a farmer practising or advocating any political idea that was not absolutely self-seeking—that was not, in fact, deliberately designed to loot the rest of us to his gain? Greenbackism, free silver, government guarantee of prices, all the complex fiscal imbecilities of the cow State John Baptists—these are the contributions of the virtuous husbandmen to American political theory. There has never been a time, in good seasons or bad, when his hands were not itching for more; there has never been a time when he was not ready to support any charlatan, however grotesque, who promised to get it for him. Why, indeed, are politicians so polite to him—before election, so romantically amorous? For the plain and simple reason that only one issue ever interests or fetches him, and that is the issue of his own profit. He must be promised something definite and valuable, to be paid to him alone, or he is off after some other mountebank. He simply cannot imagine himself as a citizen of a commonwealth, in duty bound to give as well as take; he can imagine himself only as getting all and giving nothing.

Yet we are asked to venerate this prehensile moron as the *Ur*-burgher, the citizen *par excellence*, the foundation-stone of the state! And why? Because he produces something that all of us must have—that we must get somehow on penalty of death. And how do we get it from him? By submitting helplessly to his unconscionable blackmailing—by paying him, not under any rule of reason, but in proportion to his roguery and incompetence, and hence to the direness of our need. I doubt that the human race, as a whole, would submit to that sort of high-jacking, year in and year out, from any other necessary class of men. When the American railroad workman attempted it, in 1916, there was instant indignation; when a certain small squad of the *Polizei* tried it, a few years later, there was such universal horror that a politician who denounced the crime became President of the United States. But the farmers do it over and over again, without challenge or reprisal, and the only thing that keeps them from reducing us, at intervals, to actual famine is their own imbecile knavery. They are all willing and eager to pillage us by starving us, but they can't do it because they can't resist attempts to swindle each other. Recall, for example, the case of the cotton-growers in the South. They agreed among themselves to cut down the cotton acreage in order to inflate the price—and instantly every party to the agreement began planting *more* cotton in order to profit by the abstinence of his neighbors. That abstinence being wholly imaginary, the price of cotton fell instead of going up—and then the entire pack of scoundrels began demanding assistance from the national treasury—in brief, began demanding that the rest of us indemnify them for the failure of their plot to blackmail us!

The same demand is made almost annually by the wheat farmers of the Middle West. It is the theory of the zanies who perform at Washington that a grower of wheat devotes himself to that banal art in a philanthropic and patriotic spirit—that he plants and harvests his crop in order that the folks of the cities may not go without bread. It is the plain fact that he raises wheat because it takes less labor than any other crop—because it enables him, after working sixty days a year, to loaf the rest of the twelve months. If wheat-raising could be taken out of the hands of such lazy *fellahin* and organized as the production of iron or cement is organized, the price might be reduced by a half, and still leave a large profit for *entrepreneurs.* It vacillates dangerously today, not because speculators manipulate it, but because the crop is irregular and undependable—that is to say, because those who make it are incompetent. The worst speculators, as everyone knows, are the farmers themselves. They hold their wheat as long as they can, borrowing our money from the country banks and hoping prayerfully for a rise. If it goes up, then we pay them an extra and unearned profit. If it goes down, then they demand legislation to prevent it going down next time. Sixty days a year they work; the rest of the time they gamble with our bellies. It is probably the safest gambling ever heard of. Now and then, true enough, a yokel who plunges too heavily comes to grief, and is ingested by the county-town mortgage-shark; now and then a whole county, or State or even larger area goes bankrupt, and the financial dominoes begin falling down all along the line from Saleratus Center to New York. But such catastrophes are rare, and they leave no scars. When a speculator goes broke in Wall Street it is a scandalous matter, and if he happens to have rooked anybody of importance he is railroaded to jail. But when a speculator goes broke in the great open spaces, there is a great rush of political leucocytes to the scene, and presently it is made known that the sin was not the speculator's at all, but his projected victims', and that it is the prime duty of the latter, by lawful order upon the Treasurer of the United States, to reimburse him his losses and set him up for a new trial.

The notion that wheat would be much cheaper and the supply far more dependable if it were grown, not by a motley horde of such puerile loafers and gamblers, but by competent men intelligently organized is not mine; I borrow it from Henry Ford, a busted seer. Since he betrayed them to Dr. Coolidge for a mess of pottage, the poor Liberals, once so enamored of his sagacity, denounce Ford as an idiot and a villain; nevertheless, the fact remains that his discussion of the wastefulness of our present system of wheat-growing, in the autobiography which he didn't write, is full of a powerful plausibility. Ford was born and brought up on a farm—and it was a farm, as farms go, that was very competently managed. But he knows very well that even the most competent farmer is but seldom more adept than a chimpanzee playing the violin. The Liberals, indeed, cannot controvert his judgment; they have been thrown back upon belaboring his political morals. What he proposes, they argue, is simply the enslavement of the present farmer, now so gloriously free. With capitalism gradually absorbing his fields, he would have to go to work as a wage-slave. Well, why not? For one, I surely offer no objection. All the rubber we use today is raised by slave labor; so is all the morphine consumed at Hollywood. Our children are taught in school by slaves; our newspapers are edited by slaves. Wheat raised by slave labor would be just as nutritious as wheat raised by men earning $10,000 a year, and a great deal cheaper. If the business showed a good profit, the political clowns at

Washington would launch schemes to confiscate it, as they now launch schemes to make good the losses of the farmers. In any case, why bother about the fate of the farmer? If wheat went to $10 a bushel tomorrow, and all the workmen of the cities became slaves in name as well as in fact, no farmer in this grand land of freedom would consent voluntarily to a reduction of as much as 1/8 of a cent a bushel. "The greatest wolves," say E. W. Howe, another graduate of the farm, "are the farmers who bring produce to town to sell." Wolves? Let us not insult *Canis lupus.* I move the substitution of *Hyæna hyæna.*

Meanwhile, how much truth is in the common theory that the husbandman is harassed and looted by our economic system, that the men of the cities prey upon him—specifically, that he is the chronic victim of such devices as the tariff, railroad regulation, and the banking system? So far as I can make out, there is none whatever. The net effect of our present banking system, as I have already said, is that the money accumulated by the cities is used to finance the farmers, and that they employ it to blackmail the cities. As for the tariff, is it a fact that it damages the farmer, or benefits him? Let us turn for light to the worst Tariff Act ever heard of in human history: that of 1922. It put a duty of 30 cents a bushel on wheat, and so barred out Canadian wheat, and gave the American farmer a vast and unfair advantage. For months running the difference in the price of wheat on the two sides of the American-Canadian border—wheat raised on farms not a mile apart—ran from 25 to 30 cents a bushel. Danish butter was barred out by a duty of 8 cents a pound—and the American farmer pocketed the 8 cents. Potatoes carried a duty of 50 cents a hundredweight—and the potato growers of Maine, eager, as the phrase has it, to mop up, raised such an enormous crop that the market was glutted, and they went bankrupt, and began bawling for government aid. High duties were put, too, upon meats, upon cheese, upon wool—in brief, upon practically everything that the farmer produced. But his profits were taken from him by even higher duties upon manufactured goods, and by high freight rates? Were they, indeed? There was, in fact, no duty at all upon many of the things he consumed. There was no duty, for example, upon shoes. The duty upon woolen goods gave a smaller advantage to the manufacturer than the duty on wool gave to the farmer. So with the duty on cotton goods. Automobiles were cheaper in the United States than anywhere else on earth. So were all agricultural implements. So were groceries. So were fertilizers.

But here I come to the brink of an abyss of statistics, and had better haul up. The enlightened reader is invited to investigate them for himself; they will bring him, I believe, some surprises, particularly if he has been reading the *Congressional Record* and accepting it gravely. They by no means exhaust the case against the consecrated husbandman. I have said that the only political idea he can grasp is one which promises him a direct profit. It is, alas, not quite true: he can also grasp one which has the sole effect of annoying and damaging his enemy, the city man. The same mountebanks who get to Washington by promising to augment his gains and make good his losses devote whatever time is left over from that enterprise to saddling the rest of us with oppressive and idiotic laws, all hatched on the farm. There, where the cows low through the still night, and the jug of Peruna stands behind the stove, and bathing begins, as at Biarritz, with the vernal equinox—there is the reservoir of all the nonsensical legislation which now makes the United States a buffoon among the great nations. It was among country Methodists, practitioners of a theology degraded almost to the level of voodooism, that Prohibition was invented, and it was by country Methodists, nine-tenths of them actual followers of the plow, that it was fastened upon the rest of us, to the damage of our bank accounts, our dignity and our ease. What lies under it, and under all the other crazy enactments of its category, is no more and no less than the yokel's congenital and incurable hatred of the city man—his simian rage against everyone who, as he sees it, is having a better time than he is.

That this malice is at the bottom of Prohibition, and not any altruistic yearning to put down the evils of drink, is shown clearly by the fact that most of the State enforcement acts—and even the Volstead Act, as it is interpreted at Washington—permit the farmer himself to make cider as in the past, and that every effort to deprive him of that astounding immunity has met with the opposition of his representatives. In other words, the thing he is against is not the use of alcohol *per se*, but simply the use of alcohol in its more charming and romantic forms. Prohibition, as everyone knows, has not materially diminished the consumption of alcohol in the cities, but it has obviously forced the city man to drink decoctions that he would have spurned in the old days—that is, it has forced him to drink such dreadful stuff as the farmer has always drunk. The farmer is thus content with it: it brings his enemy down to his own level. The same animus is visible in innumerable other moral statutes, all ardently supported by the peasantry. For example, the Mann Act. The aim of this amazing law, of course, is not to put down adultery; it is simply to put down that variety of adultery which is most agreeable. What got it upon the books was simply the constant gabble in the rural newspapers about the byzantine debaucheries of urban Antinomians—rich stockbrokers who frequented Atlantic City from Friday to Monday, vaudeville actors who traveled about the country with beautiful mistresses, and so on. Such aphrodisiacal tales, read beside the kitchen-stove by hinds condemned to monogamous misery with stupid, unclean and ill-natured wives, naturally aroused in them a vast detestation of errant cockneys, and this detestation eventually rolled up enough force to attract the attention of the quacks who make laws at Washington. The result was the Mann Act. Since then a number of the cow States have passed Mann Acts of their own, usually forbidding the use of automobiles "for immoral purposes." But there is nowhere a law forbidding the use of barns, cow-stables, hayricks and other such familiar rustic ateliers of sin. That is to say, there is nowhere a law forbidding yokels to drag virgins into infamy by the technic practised since Tertiary times on the farms; there are only laws forbidding city youths to do it according to the technic of the great municipalities.

Here we come to the limits of bucolic moral endeavor. It never prohibits acts that are common on the farms; it only prohibits acts that are common in the cities. In many of the Middle Western States there are statutes forbidding the smoking of cigarettes, for cigarette-smoking, to the louts of those wastes, bears the aspect of a citified and levantine vice, and if they attempted it themselves they would be derided by their fellows and perhaps divorced by their wives, just as they would be derided and divorced if they bathed every day, or dressed for dinner, or attempted to play the piano. But chewing tobacco, whether in public or in private, is nowhere forbidden by law, for the plain reason that nine-tenths of all husbandmen practise it, as they practice the drinking of raw corn liquor. The act not only lies within their tastes; it also lies within their means, and hence within their *mores.* As a consequence the inhabitants of the towns in those remote marches are free to chew tobacco all they please, even at divine service, but are clapped into jail the instant they light cigarettes. The same consideration gets into comstockery, which is chiefly supported, like Prohibition, by farmers and chiefly aimed at city men. The Comstock Act is very seldom invoked against newspapers, for the matter printed in newspapers lies within the comprehension of the peasantry, and hence within their sphere of enjoyment. Nor is it often invoked against cheap books of a frankly pornographic character—such things as "Night Life in Chicago," "Adventures on a Pullman Sleeper" and "The Confessions of an ex-Nun"—for when yokels read at all, it is commonly such garbage that they prefer. But they are hot against the infinitely less gross naughtiness of serious books, including the so-called classics, for these books they simply cannot read. In consequence the force of comstockery is chiefly directed against such literature. For one actually vile book that it suppresses it attempts to suppress at least a dozen good ones.

Now the pious husbandman shows signs of an itch to proceed further. Not content with assaulting us with his degraded and abominable ethics, he begins trying to force upon us his still worse theology. On the steppes Methodism has got itself all the estate and dignity of a State religion; it becomes a criminal offense to teach any doctrine in contempt of it. No civilized man, to be sure, is yet actually in jail for the crime; civilized men simply keep out of such bleak parking spaces for human Fords, as they keep out of Congress and Franz Josef Land. But the long arm of the Wesleyan revelation now begins to stretch forth toward Nineveh. The mountebank, Bryan, after years of preying upon the rustics on the promise that he would show them how to loot the cities by wholesale and *à outrance*, now reverses his collar and proposes to lead them in a *jehad* against what remains of American intelligence, already beleaguered in a few walled towns. We are not only to abandon the social customs of civilization at the behest of a rabble of peasants who sleep in their underclothes; we are now to give up all the basic ideas of civilization and adopt the gross superstitions of the same mob. Is this fanciful? Is the menace remote, and to be disregarded? My apologies for suggesting that perhaps you are one of the multitude who thought that way about Prohibition, and only half a dozen years ago. Bryan is a protean harlequin, and more favored by God than is commonly assumed. He lost with free silver but he won with Prohibition. The chances, if my mathematics do not fail, are thus 1 to 1 that he will win, if he keeps his health, with Fundamentalism—in his own phrase, that God will be put into the Constitution. If he does, then *Eoanthrophus* will triumph finally over *Homo sapiens.* If he does, then the humble swineherd will drive us all into his pen.

Not much gift for Vision is needed to imagine the main outlines of the ensuing *Kultur.* The city man, as now, will bear nine-tenths of the tax burden; the rural total immersionist will make all the laws. With Genesis firmly lodged in the Testament of the Fathers he will be ten times as potent as he is now and a hundred times as assiduous. No constitutional impediment will remain to cripple his moral fancy. The Wesleyan code of Kansas and Mississippi, Vermont and Minnesota will be forced upon all of us by the full military and naval power of the United States. Civilization will gradually become felonious everywhere in the Republic, as it already is in Arkansas. What I sing, I suppose, is a sort of Utopia. But it is not the Utopia of bawdy poets and metaphysicians; it is not the familiar Utopia of the books. It is a Utopia dreamed by simpler and more virtuous men—by seven millions of Christian bumpkins, far-flung in forty-eight sovereign States. They dream it on their long journeys down the twelve billion furrows of their seven million farms, up hill and down dale in the heat of the day. They dream it behind the egg-stove on Winter nights, their boots off and their socks scorching, Holy Writ in their hands. They dream it as they commune with *Bos taurus, Sus scrofa, Mephitis mephitis*, the Methodist pastor, the Ford agent. It floats before their eyes as they scan the Sears-Roebuck catalogue for horse liniment, porous plasters and Bordeaux mixture; it rises before them when they assemble in their Little

Bethels to be instructed in the word of God, the plots of the Pope, the crimes of the atheists and Jews; it transfigures the chautauquan who looms before them with his Great Message. This Utopia haunts and tortures them; they long to make it real. They have tried prayer, and it has failed; now they turn to the secular arm. The dung-fork glitters in the sun as the host prepares to march. . . .

Well, these are the sweet-smelling and altruistic agronomists whose sorrows are the *leitmotif* of our politics, whose votes keep us supplied with Bryans and Bleases, whose welfare is alleged to be the chief end of democratic statecraft, whose patriotism is the so-called bulwark of this so-called Republic!

III.
High and Ghostly Matters

I
The Cosmic Secretariat

THE argument by design, once the bulwark of Christian apologetics, is so full of holes that it is no wonder that it has had to be abandoned. The more, indeed, the theologian seeks to prove the wisdom and omnipotence of God by His works, the more he is dashed by evidences of divine incompetence and stupidity. The world is not actually well run; it is very badly run, and no Huxley was needed to labor the obvious fact. The human body, very adeptly designed in some details, is cruelly and senselessly bungled in other details, and every reflective first-year medical student must notice a hundred ways to improve it. How are we to reconcile this mixture of finesse and blundering with the concept of a single omnipotent Designer, to whom all problems are equally easy? If He could contrive so efficient and durable a machine as the human hand, then how did He come to make such botches as the tonsils, the gall-bladder, the uterus and the prostate gland? If He could perfect the hip joint and the ear, then why did He boggle the teeth?

Having never encountered a satisfactory—or even a remotely plausible—answer to such questions, I have had to go to the trouble of devising one myself. It is, at all events, quite simple, and in strict accord with all the known facts. In brief, it is this: that the theory that the universe is run by a single God must be abandoned, and that in place of it we must set up the theory that it is actually run by a board of gods, all of equal puissance and authority. Once this concept is grasped all the difficulties that have vexed theologians vanish, and human experience instantly lights up the whole dark scene. We observe in everyday life what happens when authority is divided, and great decisions are reached by consultation and compromise. We know that the effects at times, particularly when one of the consultants runs away with the others, are very good, but we also know that they are usually extremely bad. Such a mixture, precisely, is on display in the cosmos. It presents a series of brilliant successes in the midst of an infinity of failures.

I contend that my theory is the only one ever put forward that completely accounts for the clinical picture. Every other theory, facing such facts as sin, disease and disaster, is forced to admit the supposition that Omnipotence, after all, may not be omnipotent—a plain absurdity. I need toy with no such nonsense. I may assume that every god belonging to the council which rules the universe is infinitely wise and infinitely powerful, and yet not evade the plain fact that most of the acts of that council are ignorant and foolish. In truth, my assumption that a council exists is tantamount to an *a priori* assumption that its acts are ignorant and foolish, for no act of any conceivable council can be otherwise. Is the human hand perfect, or, at all events, practical and praiseworthy? Then I account for it on the ground that it was designed by some single member of the council—that the business was handed over to him by inadvertence or as a result of an irreconcilable difference of opinion among the others. Had more than one member participated actively in its design it would have been measurably less meritorious than it is, for the sketch offered by the original designer would have been forced to run the gauntlet criticisms and suggestions from all the other councillors, and human experience teaches us that most of these criticisms and suggestions would have been inferior to the original idea—that many of them, in fact, would have had nothing in them save a petty desire to maul and spoil the original idea.

But do I here accuse the high gods of harboring discreditable human weaknesses? If I do, then my excuse is that it is impossible to imagine them doing the work universally ascribed to them without admitting their possession of such weaknesses. One cannot imagine a god spending weeks and months, and maybe whole geological epochs, laboring over the design of the human kidney without assuming him to have been moved by a powerful impulse to express himself vividly, to marshal and publish his ideas, to win public credit among his fellows—in brief, without assuming him to be egoistic. And one cannot assume him to be egoistic without assuming him to prefer the adoption of his own ideas to the adoption of any other god's. I defy anyone to make the contrary assumption without plunging instantly into clouds of mysticism. Ruling it out, one comes inevitably to the conclusion that the inept management of the universe must be ascribed to clashes of egos, *i.e.*, to petty spites and revenges, among the gods, for any one of them alone, since we must assume him to be infinitely wise and powerful, could run it perfectly. We suffer from bad stomachs simply because the god who first proposed making a stomach aroused thereby the ill-nature of those who had not thought of it, and because they proceeded instantly to wreak that ill-nature upon him by improving, *i.e.*, botching, his work. We must reproduce our species in the familiar arduous, uneconomic, embarrassing and almost pathological manner because the god who devised the excellent process prevailing among the protozoa had to be put in his place when he proposed to extend it to the Primates.

2
The Nature of Faith

Many years ago, when I was more enterprising intellectually than I am to-day, I proposed the application of Haeckel's celebrated biogenetic law—to wit, that the history of the individual rehearses the history of the species—to the domain of human ideas. So applied, it leads to some superficially startling but probably quite sound conclusions, for example, that an adult poet is simply an individual in a state of arrested development—in brief, a sort of moron. Just as all of us, *in utero*, pass through a stage in which we are tadpoles, and almost indistinguishable from the tadpoles which afterward become frogs, so all of us pass through a stage, in our nonage, when we are poets. A youth of seventeen who is not a poet is simply an ass: his development has been arrested even anterior to the stage of the intellectual tadpole. But a man of fifty who still writes poetry is either an unfortunate who has never developed, intellectually, beyond his teens, or a conscious buffoon who pretends to be something that he isn't—something far younger and juicier than he actually is—, just as the late Richard Mansfield, in Schiller's play, pretended, by the use of a falsetto voice and a girlish skip, to be the eighteen-year-old Don Carlos.

Something else, of course, may enter into it. The buffoonery may be partly conscious and deliberate, and partly Freudian. Many an aging man keeps on writing poetry simply because it gives him the illusion that he is still young. For the same reason, perhaps, he plays tennis, wears green cravats, and tries to convince himself that he is in love.

It is my conviction that no normal man ever fell in love, within the ordinary meaning of the term, after the age of thirty. He may, at forty, pursue the female of his species with great assiduity, and he may, at fifty, sixty or even seventy, "woo" and marry a more or less fair one in due form of law, but the impulse that moves him to these follies at such ages is never the complex of illusions and hallucinations that poets describe as love. This complex is quite natural to all males between adolescence and the age of, say, twenty-five, when the kidneys begin to disintegrate. For a youth to reach twenty-one without having fallen in love in an abject and preposterous manner would be for doubts to be raised as to his normalcy. But if he does it after his wisdom teeth are cut, it is no more than a sign that they have been cut in vain—that he is still in his teens, whatever his biological and legal age. Love, so-called, is based upon a view of women that is impossible to any man who has had any experience of them. Such a man may, to the end of his life, enjoy their society vastly, and even respect them and admire them, but, however much he respects and admires them, he nevertheless sees them more or less clearly, and seeing them clearly is fatal to the true romance. Find a man of forty who heaves and moans over a woman in the manner of a poet and you will behold either a man who ceased to develop intellectually at twenty-four or thereabout, or a fraud who has his eye on the lands, tenements and hereditaments of the lady's deceased first husband. Or upon her talents as nurse, cook, amanuensis and audience. This, no doubt, is what George Bernard Shaw meant when he said that every man over forty is a scoundrel.

As I say, my suggestion has not been adopted by psychologists, who, in the main, are a very conservative and unimaginative body of men. If they applied the biogenetic law in the field of religion they might make some interesting observations. The chances are, indeed, that religion belongs exclusively to an extremely early stage of human development, and that its rapid decay in the world since the Reformation is evidence of a very genuine progress. Reduced to its logical essence, every religion now advocated in Christendom is simply the doctrine that there are higher powers, infinitely wise and virtuous, which take an active interest in the sordid everyday affairs of men, and not infrequently intervene in them. This doctrine is not purely romantic and *a priori*; it is based upon what is regarded by its subscribers as objective evidence. But it must be plain that that evidence tends to go to pieces as human knowledge widens—that it appears massive and impressive in direct proportion as the individual impressed is ignorant. A few hundred years ago practically every phenomenon of nature was ascribed to superhuman intervention. The plague, for example, was caused by God's anger. So was war. So was lightning. Today no enlightened man believes anything of the kind. All these phenomena are seen to be but links in an endless chain of amoral causation, and it is known that, given a certain quite intelligible and usually inevitable combination of causes, they will appear infallibly as effects. Thus religion gradually loses its old objective authority, and becomes more and more a mere sentimentality. An enlightened man's view of it is almost indistinguishable from his view of the Spirit of 1776, the Henty books, and the rosewood casket containing his grandmother's false teeth.

Such a man is not "dead" to religion. He was not born with a congenital inaptitude for it. He has simply outgrown it, as he has outgrown poetry, Socialism and love. At adolescence practically all individuals have attacks of piety, but that is only saying that their powers of perception, at that age, outrun their knowledge. They observe the phenomenon, but cannot account for it. Later on, unless their development is arrested, they gradually emerge from that romantic and spookish fog, just as they emerge from the hallucinations of secular romance. I speak here, of course, of individuals genuinely capable of education—always a small minority. If, as the Army tests of conscripts showed, nearly 50 per cent. of American adult males never get beyond the mental development of a twelve-year-old child, then it must be obvious that a much smaller number get beyond the mental development of a youth at the end of his teens. I put that number, at a venture, at 5 per cent. The remaining 95 per cent. never quite free themselves from religious superstitions. They may no longer believe it is an act of God every time an individual catches a cold, or sprains his ankle, or cuts himself shaving, but they are pretty sure to see some trace of divine intervention in it if he is struck by lightning, or hanged, or afflicted with leprosy or syphilis. That God causes wars has been believed by all the Presidents of the United States, save Grover Cleveland, since Jefferson's time. During the late war the then President actually set aside a day for praying to God to stop what He had started as soon as possible, and on terms favorable to American investments. This was not done, remember, by a voodoo man in the Congo forest, but by a sound Presbyterian, a Ph.D. of Johns Hopkins University, and the best-dressed professor ever seen at Princeton.

I have said that all modern religions are based, at least on their logical side, on this notion that there are higher powers which observe all the doings of man, and constantly take a hand in them. It should be added that a corollary is almost always appended, to the effect that these higher powers also pronounce ethical judgments upon such human acts as happen to be performed without this intervention, and are themselves animated by a lofty and impeccable morality. Most religions, of course, also embrace a concept of higher powers that are not benign, but malignant—that is, they posit the existence of demons as well as of gods. But there are very few in which the demons are regarded as superior to the gods, or even as their full equals. The great majority of creeds, East and West, savage and so-called civilized, put the gods far above the demons, and teach that the gods always wish the good of man, and that man's virtue and happiness run in direct ratio to his obedience to their desires. That is, they are all based upon the doctrine of what is called the goodness of God. This is true pre-eminently of the chief oriental faiths: Buddhism, Brahminism and Confucianism. It is true even of Christianity, despite its luxuriant demonology. No true Christian can believe that God ever deliberately and wantonly injures him, or could conceivably wish him ill. The slings and arrows of God, he believes, are brought down upon him by his own ignorance and contumacy. He believes that if he could be like God he would be perfect.

This doctrine of the goodness of God, it seems to me, is no more, at bottom, than an evidence of arrested intellectual development. It does not fit into what we know of the nature and operations of the cosmos today; it is a survival from a day of universal ignorance. That it is still given credit in the Far East is not surprising, for the intellectual development of the Far East, despite all the nonsense that is talked about Indian and Chinese "philosophy," is really no further advanced than that of Europe was in the time of St. Louis. The most profound Hindoo or Chinese "philosopher" believes, as objective facts, things that would make even a Georgia Fundamentalist snicker, and so his "philosophy" is chiefly worthless, as was that of the Greeks. The Greeks sometimes guessed right, just as the swamis and yogis of Los Angeles sometimes guess right, but in the main their speculations, being based upon false observations, were valueless, and no one would pay any attention to them today if it were not for the advertising they get from theologians, who find them to their taste, and professional "philosophers," who make a living trying to teach them to sophomores. But if the belief in the goodness of God is natural to misinformed orientals, as it was natural to the singularly ignorant Greeks, it is certainly *not* natural to the enlightened races of the West today, for all their science is simply a great massing of proofs that God, if He exists, is neither good nor bad, but simply indifferent—an infinite Force carrying on the operation of unintelligible processes without the slightest regard, either one way or the other, for the comfort, safety and happiness of man.

Why, then, does this belief survive? Largely, I am convinced, because it is supported by another hoary relic from the adolescence of the race, to wit, the weakness for poetry. The Jews fastened their religion upon the Western world, not because it was more reasonable than the religions of their contemporaries —as a matter of fact, it was vastly less reasonable than many of them—, but because it was far more poetical. The poetry in it was what fetched the decaying Romans, and after them the barbarians of the North; not the so-called Christian evidences. For the Jews were poets of a truly colossal eloquence, and they put their fundamental superstitions into dithyrambs of such compelling loveliness that they disarmed the common sense even of skeptical Romans, and so knocked out all other contemporary religions, many of which were in far closer accord with what was then known of the true operations of the universe. To this day no better poetry has ever been written. It is so powerful in its effects that even men who reject its content in toto are more or less susceptible to it. One hesitates to flout it on purely æsthetic grounds; however dubious it may be in doctrine, it is nevertheless almost perfect in form, and so even the most violent atheist tends to respect it, just as he respects a beautiful but deadly toadstool. For no man, of course, ever quite gets over poetry. He may seem to have recovered from it, just as he may seem to have recovered from the measles of his school-days, but exact observation teaches us that no such recovery is ever quite perfect; there always remains a scar, a weakness and a memory.

Now, there is reason for maintaining that the taste for poetry, in the process of human development, marks a stage measurably later than the stage of religion. Savages so little cultured that they know no more of poetry than a cow have elaborate and often very ingenious theologies. If this be true, then it follows that the individual, as he rehearses the life of the species, is apt to carry his taste for poetry further along than he carries his religion—that if his development is arrested at any stage before complete intellectual maturity that arrest is far more likely to leave him with poetical hallucinations than it is to leave him with theological hallucinations. Thus, taking men in the mass, there are many more natural victims of the former than of the latter—and here is where the talent of the ancient Jews does its execution. It holds countless thousands to the faith who are actually against the faith, and the weakness with which it holds them is their weakness for poetry, *i.e.*, for the beautiful but untrue. Put into plain, harsh words most of the articles they are asked to believe would revolt them, but put into sonorous dithyrambs the same articles fascinate and overwhelm them. It is not the logical substance of the Old Testament that continues to hold the mind of modern man, for that logical substance must often revolt him, even when he is of sub-normal intelligence; it is the sonorous strophes of the ancient bards and prophets. And it is not the epistemology, or the natural history, or the ethical scheme, or the system of jurisprudence of the New Testament that melts his heart and wets his eyes; it is simply the poetical magic of the Sermon on the Mount, the exquisite parables, and the incomparable story of the Child in the Manger.

This persistence of the weakness for poetry, no doubt, explains the great growth of ritualism in an age of skepticism. Almost every day theology gets another blow from science. So badly has it been battered during the past century, indeed, that educated men now give it little more credence than they give to sorcery, its ancient ally. But squeezing out the logical nonsense does no damage to the poetry; on the contrary, it frees, and, in a sense, dignifies the poetry. Paul's chief doctrines, clearly stated, offend the intelligence intolerably, but clothed and concealed by the gorgeous vestments of the mass they separate themselves from logic entirely and take on something of the witchery of beauty. Thus there is a constant movement of Christians, and particularly of newly-intellectual Christians, from the more literal varieties of Christian faith to the more poetical varieties. The normal Babbitt, in the United States, is born a Methodist or a Baptist, but when he begins to lay by money he and his wife tend to go over to the American branch of the Church of England, which is not only more fashionable but also less revolting to the higher cerebral centers. His daughter, when she emerges from the finishing-school, is very High Church; his grand-daughter, if the family keeps its securities, will probably go over to Rome.

In view of all this, I am convinced that the Christian church, as a going concern, is quite safe from danger, despite the rapid growth of agnosticism. The theology it merchants is full of childish and disgusting absurdities; practically all the other religions of civilized and semi-civilized man are more plausible. But all of these religions, including even Moslemism, contain the fatal defect that they appeal primarily to the reason. Christianity will survive not only Modernism but also Fundamentalism, a much more difficult business. It will survive because it makes its first and foremost appeal to that moony sense of the poetic which is in all men—to that elemental sentimentality which, in men of arrested mental development, which is to say, in the average men of Christendom, passes for the passion to seek and know beauty.

3
The Devotee

If religion is thus charming to the more enlightened modern Christian only in proportion as it is poetical, *i.e.*, as it is regarded as not literally true, it is charming to the enlightened spectator only when it is formal and hence more or less insincere. A devotee on her knees in some abysmal and mysterious cathedral, the while solemn music sounds, and clouds of incense come down the wind, and priests in luxurious, levantine costumes busy themselves with stately ceremonials in a dead and not too respectable language—this is unquestionably beautiful, particularly if the devotee herself be sightly. But the same devotee aroused to hysterical protestations of faith by the shrieks and contortions of a Methodist dervish in the costume of a Southern member of Congress, her knees trembling with the fear of God, her hands clenched as if to do combat with Beelzebub, her lips discharging hosannas and hallelujahs—this is merely obscene.

4
The Restoration of Beauty

I have said that the poetry which safeguards Christianity from destruction today was borrowed from the ancient Jews, authors of the two Testaments. But there was a long period during which it was overshadowed by purely logical ideas, many of them of a sort that would be called bolshevistic today. The principal Christians of the apostolic age were almost exactly like the modern Calvinists and Wesleyans—men quite without taste or imagination, whoopers and shouters, low vulgarians, cads. So far as is known, their public worship was wholly devoid of the sense of beauty; their sole concern was with the salvation of their so-called souls. Thus they left us nothing worth preserving—not a single church, or liturgy, or even hymn. The objects of art exhumed from the Catacombs are inferior to the drawings and statuettes of Crô-Magnon man. All the moving beauty that adorns the corpse of Christianity today came into being long after the Fathers had perished. The faith was centuries old before Christians began to build cathedrals, and nearly a thousand years old before they learned how to build good ones. It was twelve hundred years old before they invented mariolatry—the prime cause of the appearance of a purely Christian poetry. We think of Christmas as the typical Christian festival, and no doubt it is; none other is so generally kept by Christian sects, or so rich in charm and beauty. Well, Christmas, as we now have it, was almost unknown in Christendom until the Eleventh Century, when the relics of St. Nicholas of Myra, originally the patron of pawnbrokers, were brought from the East to Italy. At this time the Universal Church was already torn by controversies and menaced by schisms, and the shadow of the Reformation was plainly discernible in the West. Religions, in fact, like castles, sunsets and women, never reach their maximum of beauty until they are touched by decay.

5
End-Product

Christendom may be defined briefly as that part of the world in which, if any man stands up in public and solemnly swears that he is a Christian, all his auditors will laugh.

6
Another

At the end of one millennium and nine centuries of Christianity, it remains an unshakable assumption of the law in all Christian countries and of the moral judgment of Christians everywhere that if a man and a woman, entering a room together, close the door behind them, the man will come out sadder and the woman wiser.

7
Holy Clerks

Around no class of men do more false assumptions cluster than around the rev. clergy, our lawful commissioners at the Throne of Grace. I proceed at once to a crass example: the assumption that clergymen are necessarily religious. Obviously, it is widely cherished, even by clergymen themselves. The most ribald of us, in presence of a holy clerk, is a bit self-conscious, reticent and awed. I am myself given to criticizing Divine Providence somewhat freely, but in the company of the rector of my parish, even at the *Biertisch*, I tone down my animadversions to a level of feeble and polite remonstrance. I know the fellow too well, of course, to have any actual belief in his piety. He is, in fact, rather less pious than the average right-thinking Americano, and I doubt gravely that the sorceries he engages in professionally every day awaken in him any emotion more lofty than boredom. I have heard him pray for Coolidge, for the heathen and for rain, but I have never heard him pray for himself. Nevertheless, the public assumption that he is highly devout, though I dispute it, colors all my intercourse with him, and deprives him of hearing some of my most searching and intelligent observations.

All that is needed to expose the hollowness of this ancient delusion is to consider the chain of causes which brings a young man to taking holy orders. Is it, in point of fact, an irresistible religious impulse that sets him to studying exegetics, homiletics and the dog-Greek of the New Testament, and an irresistible religious impulse only, or is it something quite different? I believe that it is something quite different, and that that something may be described briefly as a desire to shine in the world without too much effort. The young theologue, in brief, is commonly an ambitious but somewhat lazy and incompetent fellow, and he studies theology instead of medicine or law because it offers a quicker and easier route to an assured job and public respect. The sacred sciences may be nonsensical bores, but they at least have the vast virtue of short-circuiting, so to speak, the climb up the ladder of security. The young doctor, for a number of years after he graduates, either has to work for nothing or to content himself with the dregs of practise, and the young lawyer, unless he has unusual influence or complete atrophy of the conscience, often teeters on the edge of actual starvation. But the young divine is a safe and distinguished man the moment he is ordained; indeed, his popularity, especially among the faithful who are fair, is often greater at that moment than it ever is afterward. His livelihood is assured instantly. At one stroke, he becomes a person of dignity and importance, eminent in his community, deferred to even by those who question his magic, and vaguely and pleasantly feared by those who credit it.

These facts, you may be sure, are not concealed from ambitious young men of the sort I have mentioned. Such young men have eyes, and even a certain capacity for ratiocination. They observe the nine sons of the police sergeant: one a priest at twenty-five, with a fine house to live in, invitations to all christenings and birthday parties for miles around, and plenty of time to go to the ball-game on Summer afternoons; the others struggling desperately to make their livings as piano-movers, tin-roofers, motormen or bootleggers. They observe the young Methodist dominie in his Ford sedan, flitting about among the women while their husbands labor down in the yards district, a clean collar around his neck, a solid meal of fried chicken in his gizzard, and his name in the local paper every day. They observe the Baptist dervish in his white necktie, raiding saloons, touring the bawdy-houses and raising hell generally, his tabernacle packed every Sunday night, a noble clink of silver in his collection-plates, and a fat purse for him now and then from the Ladies' Aid or the Ku Klux Klan. Only crazy women ever fall in love with young doctors or lawyers, but every young clergyman, if he is so inclined, may have a whole harem, and with infinitely less danger than a struggling lawyer, a bootlegger or a bank clerk runs every day. Even if he is celibate, the gals bathe him in their smiles; in truth, the more celibate he is, the more attention he gets from them. No wonder his high privileges and immunities propagate the sin of envy! No wonder there are still candidates for the holy shroud, despite the vast growth of atheism among us!

It seems to me that the majority of the young men who are thus sucked into holy orders are not actually pious at all, but rather somewhat excessively realistic—that genuine piety is far more apt to keep a youth out of the pulpit than to take him into it. The true devotee, frequenting the sacred edifice constantly, becomes too familiar with the daily duties of a clergyman to see any religious satisfaction in them. In the main, they have nothing to do with religion at all, but are basically social or commercial. In so far as a clergyman works at all, he works as the general manager of a corporation, and only too often it is in financial difficulties and rent by factions among the stockholders. His specifically religious duties are of a routine and monotonous nature, and must needs depress him mightily, as a surgeon is depressed by the endless snaring of tonsils and excision of appendices. He debases spiritual exaltation by reducing it to a hollow and meaningless formality, as a politician debases patriotism and a lady of joy debases love. He becomes, in the end, quite anæsthetic to religion, and even hostile to it. The fact is made distressingly visible by the right rev. the bench of bishops. For a bishop to fall on his knees spontaneously and begin to pray to God would make almost as great a scandal as if he mounted his throne in a bathing-suit. The piety of the ecclesiastic, on such high levels, becomes wholly formal and theoretical. The servant of God has been lifted so near to the saints and become so familiar with the inner workings of the divine machinery that the sense of awe and wonder has oozed out of him. He can no more undergo a genuine religious experience than a veteran scene-shifter can laugh at the wheezes of the First Gravedigger. It is, perhaps, well that this is so. If the higher clergy were actually religious some of their own sermons and pastoral epistles would scare them to death.

IV.
Justice Under Democracy

I

PERHAPS the chief victims of Prohibition in the Republic, in the long run, will turn out to be the Federal judges. I do not argue here, of course, that drinking bootleg liquors will kill them bodily; I merely suggest that enforcing the unjust and insane provisions of the Volstead Act will rob them of all their old dignity. A dozen years ago a Federal judge was perhaps the most dignified and respected official yet flourishing under our democracy. The plain people, many years before that, had lost all respect for lawmakers, whether Federal, State or municipal, and save for the President himself, they had very little respect left for the gentlemen of the executive arm, high or low. More, they had begun to view the judiciary of the States very biliously, and showed no sign of surprise when a member of it was taken in judicial adultery. But for the Federal judges they still continued to have a high veneration, and for plain reasons. *Imprimis*, the Federal judges sat for life, and thus did not have to climb down from their benches at intervals and clamor obscenely for votes. Secondly, the laws that they were told off to enforce, and especially the criminal laws, were few in number, simple in character, and thoroughly in accord with almost universal ideas of right and wrong. No citizen in his right mind had much sympathy for the felons who were shipped to Atlanta each morning by the marshals of the Federal courts—chiefly counterfeiters, fraudulent bankrupts, adulterators of food and drugs, get-rich-quick swindlers, thieving letter-carriers, crooked army officers, and so on. Public sentiment was almost unanimously behind the punishment of such rogues, and it rejoiced that that punishment was in the hands of men who carried on the business in an austere and elevated manner, without fear and without favor. It was, in those days, almost unheard of for a petit jury in a Federal court to acquit a prisoner whose guilt was plain; the percentage of convictions in some jurisdictions ran beyond ninety per cent. For guilt of the kind then dealt with by those courts met with the reprehension of practically all men not professional criminals themselves—and Federal juries, petit and grand, were picked with some care, as Federal judges themselves were picked.

I describe a Golden Age, now lamentably closed. The Uplift in its various lovely forms has completely changed the character of the work done by a Federal judge. Once the dispenser of varieties of law that only scoundrels questioned, he is now the harassed and ludicrous dispenser of varieties of law that only idiots approve. It was the Espionage Act, I suppose, that brought him to this new and dreadful office, but it is Prohibition—whether of wine-bibbing, of drug-taking, of interstate week-ending, or of what not—that has carried him beyond the bounds of what, to most normal men, is common decency. His typical job today, as a majority of the plain people see it, especially in the big cities, is simply to punish men who have refused or been unable to pay the bribes demanded by Prohibition enforcement officers. In other words, he is now chiefly apprehended by the public, not as a scourge of rascals, but as an agent of rascals and a scourge of peaceable men. He gets a great deal more publicity than he used to get in his palmy days, but it is publicity of a sort that rapidly undermines his dignity. Unfortunately for him, but perhaps very fortunately for what remains of civilized government among us, the plain people have never been able to grasp the difference between law and justice. To them the two things are one—or ought to be. So the fact that the judge is bound by law to enforce all the intolerable provisions of the Volstead Act, including even its implicit provision that men wearing its badges shall get a fair percentage upon every transaction in bootlegging—this fact does not relieve the judge himself of responsibility for the ensuing injustice. All that the vulgar observe is that justice has departed from his courtroom. Once the equal of an archbishop, he is now the equal of a police captain; once respected, he is now distrusted and disliked.

If this were all, of course, it might be possible to dismiss the whole matter on the ground that the public is an ass. That men of the highest worth are not always respected, even when they wear official robes, is a commonplace. But in the present case there is more to it than merely that. Not a few of the Federal judges have begun to show signs that the noisome work that has been forced upon them has begun to achieve its inevitable subjective effects; in other words, not a few begin to attack their sneaking sense of its lack of dignity and good repute by bedizening it with moral indignation. The judicial servant of the Anti-Saloon League thus takes on some of the neo-Christian character of the League's own dervishes and sorcerers. He is not content to send some poor yokel to jail for an artificial crime that, in the view of at least eighty per cent. of all even half-civilized Americans, is no crime at all; he must also denounce the culprit from the bench in terms fit for a man accused of arson or mayhem. Here the Freudians, perhaps, may have something to say; the great masses of the innocent and sinful, knowing nothing of Freud, observe only that the learned jurist is silly as well as unjust. There issues from that observation a generally bilious view of his office and his person. He slides slowly down a fatal chute. His day of arctic and envied eminence passes. A few sensitive judges quietly retire from the bench. But the legal mind is usually tougher than that. It can almost always find justification for doing, as agent of the law, what would be inconceivable privately to a man of honor.

2

The truth is, indeed, that the decline in dignity from which the Federal judges now suffer is not wholly due to the external fact of Prohibition; it is due quite as much to their own growing pliancy and lack of professional self-respect. All that Prohibition does to them is to make brilliantly plain, even to the meanest understanding, their lamentable departure from that high integrity of purpose, that assiduous concern for justice, that jealous watchfulness over the rights of man which simple men, at all times and everywhere, like to find in the judges set over them, and which the simple men of the United States, not so long ago, saw or thought they saw in the learned ornaments of the Federal bench. Before ever Volstead emerged from the Christian Endeavor belt with his preposterous Act, confidence had begun to shake. The country had seen Federal judges who were unmistakably mountebanks; it had seen some who were, to the naked eye, indistinguishable from rascals. It had seen one step down from the highest court in the land to engage in an undignified stumping-tour, soliciting the votes of the rabble. It had seen another diligently insinuate himself into the headlines of the yellow press, in competition with Jack Dempsey and Babe Ruth. It had seen others abuse their powers of equity in the frank interest of capital, and deny the commonest justice to poor men in their clutches. And during the war it had grown accustomed to seeing the Federal bench converted into a sort of rival to the rostrum of Liberty Loan orators, with judges hurling pious objurgations at citizens accused of nothing worse than speaking their minds freely, and all pretense to fair hearings and just punishments abandoned.

Of late the multiplication of such Dogberries has gone on apace as the best of the old-time judges have retired from the bench. These new jurisconsults, rejecting justice openly and altogether, have even begun to reject the Constitution and the law. A judicial process before them is indistinguishable from a bull-fight, with the accused, if he is unpopular enough, as the bull. It is their theory, apparently, that the sole function of a judge is to fill the jails. If the accused happens to be guilty or to be reasonably suspected of guilt, well and good. But if, as in the Chicago Socialist trials, he is obviously innocent, to hell with him anyhow. True enough, a majority of the Federal judges, high and low, still stand clear of such buffooneries. Even in the midst of the worst hysteria of the war there were plenty who refused to be run amok by Palmer, Burleson and company; I need cite only Hand, J., and Rose, J., as admirable examples of a number of judges who preserved their dignity 'mid the rockets' red glare. But the headlines in the newspapers had nothing to say about such judges; their blackest ink was reserved for the other kind. That other kind gradually established a view of the Federal bench that still persists, and that is growing more and more fixed as the farce of Prohibition enforcement unrolls. It is a view which, in brief, holds that the Federal bench is no longer the most exalted and faithful protector of the liberties of the citizen, but the most relentless and inordinate foe of them—that its main purpose is not to dispense justice at all, but to get men into jail, guilty or not guilty, by fair means or foul—that to this end it is willing to lend itself to the execution of any law, however extravagant, and to support that execution with a variety of casuistry that is flatly against every ordinary conception of common sense and common decency. The Espionage Act cases, the labor injunction cases, the deportation cases, the Postal Act cases, the Mann Act cases, and now the Prohibition cases—all of these, impinging in rapid succession upon a people brought up to regard the Bill of Rights as a reality and liberty as a precious thing, have bred suspicion of the Federal courts, including especially the Supreme Court, and, on the heels of that suspicion, a positive and apparently ineradicable distrust. I doubt that the Radical fanatics who dodge about the land have ever converted any substantial body of Americans to their crazy doctrines; certainly there is not the slightest sign today of the Revolution that they were predicting for last year, and the year before. But when they have denounced the Federal courts and produced the overwhelming evidence, their shots have gone home.

Now and then a judge has argued, defending himself against some manifestation of popular discontent, that he is helpless—that he is the agent, not of justice, but of law. Even in the heyday of the Espionage Act a few were moved to make that apology from the bench, including, if I remember rightly, the judge who sentenced Debs. The distinction thus set up is one that seems clear to lawyers, but, as I have said, it seldom gets a hospitable hearing from plain men. If the latter believe anything at all it is that law without justice is an evil thing—that such law, indeed, leads inevitably to a contradiction in terms—that the highest duty of the judiciary is not to enforce it pedantically, but to evade it, vitiate it, and, if possible, destroy it. The plain man sees plenty of other sorts of law destroyed by the courts; he can't help wondering why the process is so seldom applied to statutes that violate, not merely legal apothegms, but the baldest of common sense. Thus when he beholds a Federal judge fining a man, under a constitutional amendment prohibiting the sale of intoxicating beverages, for selling a beverage that is admittedly not intoxicating, or jailing another man who has got before the bar, as everyone knows, not because he ran a still but because he refused to pay the bribe demanded by the Prohibition enforcement officer, or issuing against a third an injunction whose sole and undisguised purpose is to deprive him, by a legal swindle, of his constitutional right to a trial by jury of his peers—when he observes such monkey-shines going on in the name of the law, is it any wonder that he concludes dismally that the law is an ass, and its agent another? In ordinary life men cannot engage in such lunatic oppressions of their fellow-men without paying a penalty for it; even a policeman must be measurably more plausible and discreet. If a judge is bound by his oath to engage in them, then so much the worse for the judge. He can no more hope to be respected than a hangman can hope to be respected.

The truth is, of course, that the judges are by no means under the compulsion that is alleged. The injunction clause of the Volstead Act actually has no constitutional mandate behind it; the only constitutional mandate that I can find, bearing upon it at all, is against it. That is to be found in the Fifth and Sixth Amendments. The first of these amendments provides that "no person shall be held to answer for a capital or otherwise infamous crime unless on a presentment or indictment of a grand jury"; the second requires that "in all criminal prosecutions the accused shall enjoy the right to a speedy and public trial by an impartial jury of the State and district wherein the crime shall have been committed." It must be obvious to everyone that the aim of the injunction clause is simply and solely to deprive the accused of these safeguards—to rob him of his clear right to a trial by a jury of his peers. The history of the clause reveals the fact clearly. It was first heard of in Iowa in the early years of the century, and it was invented there, not by Prohibitionists, but by the frantic vice-crusaders who then raged and roared in the hinterland, inflaming the pious with gaudy yarns about white slave traders, seducers armed with hypodermic syringes, and other such phantasms. In Iowa these vice-crusaders specialized in the harassing of the sort of poor women who keep cheap lodging-houses. When such a woman, by ignorance or inadvertance, admitted a lady no longer a lady to her establishment, they raided her, dragged her to jail, and charged her with keeping a bawdy-house. This was good sport, and the rev. pastors urged it on every Sunday. But after the first uproar, it began to develop defects, and the chief of these defects was that juries refused to convict. Now and then a man of sense and self-respect got upon the panel and spoiled the show. Perhaps he found it impossible to believe the sworn testimony of the vice-crusaders. Perhaps he concluded that the accused, though guilty, had been punished enough by the raid. Whatever his motive, he hung the jury and killed the hunting.

It was then that Christian lawyers came to the rescue of pious and baffled men. They did it by the simple process of throwing the whole responsibility upon the judge. Juries were hard to intimidate; there was always apt to be at least one juror who didn't care a hoot what was said against him from the sacred desk—some hell-cat who positively rejoiced in the indignation of the knock-'em-down-and-drag-'em-out clergy. But judges were tenderer. Some of them were candidates for re-election to the bench; all of them were solicitous about their dignity, and did not care to face ecclesiastical curses, pious whispers, suggestive winks. So the Iowa lawyers amended the law by inventing and inserting the injunction clause. This clause flatly abolished the right of trial by jury. When the vice-crusaders found a likely victim they simply got a friendly judge to issue an injunction against her, restraining her from using her premises for immoral purposes. Then they watched her closely. The moment they detected a dubious female entering her door they raided her again, dragged her before the same judge—and he jailed her for contempt of court, an offense punishable summarily and without a jury trial. Nine times out of ten, perhaps, a jury would have acquitted her, but the judge was already safely against her.

This scheme gave the vice-crusaders a new lease of life and greatly increased their takings in the Sunday-schools. Naturally enough, the Prohibitionists, who were, in most cases, none other than the vice-crusaders themselves, instantly borrowed it, and so it got into the Prohibition acts of all the dry States. Volstead, as a country State's attorney on the Minnesota steppes, employed it diligently and to vast effect. He put it into the Volstead Act as a matter of course. There it stands to-day, a dishonest and disgraceful blemish upon American law. Its deliberate aim is to take away from the citizen accused of crime his constitutional right to a jury trial; no imaginable argument in favor of it can dodge that plain fact. When it is invoked, as under the Volstead Act, against a man who has been found guilty of one violation of the act, it not only punishes him doubly for that violation; it also punishes him in advance for a second offense that he has admittedly not committed, and deprives him of his constitutional means of defense in case he is subsequently accused. He is, in brief, put absolutely at the mercy of the judge—and the judge is already obviously suspicious of him, and may be a senile sadist or Prohibitionist demagogue to boot. The constitutional provision that a man accused of crime may throw himself upon a jury of plain men like himself, sworn to regard only the evidence actually before them—that if he is able to convince only one of the twelve that he is innocent, or not proved guilty beyond a doubt, he shall go free—this fundamental guarantee of the citizen, this most sacred of all human rights under Anglo-Saxon jurisprudence, is specifically nullified and made a mock of in order to satisfy the frenzy of a minority of fanatics!

That contempt of court should be an offense standing outside the purview of the Fifth and Sixth Amendments—that a judge should have the power to punish summarily all deliberate floutings of his dignity—this may be reasonably argued, though there are many sound considerations against it. But that it should be lawful to convert some other and wholly unrelated offense into contempt of court by a legal fiction, and so get around the Fifth and Sixth Amendments by a swindle—this is surely more than any sensible man would soberly maintain. When it is maintained, it is only by persons who are trying to put men into jail by processes that any average jury would revolt against—mill owners eager to get rid of annoying labor leaders, coal operators bent upon making slaves of their miners, Prohibitionists lusting for the punishment of their opponents. The injunction in strike cases has been a stench for years; it is, indeed, so bad that a large number of Federal judges refuse absolutely to employ it. It is a worse stench in Prohibition cases, for here it is becoming a formidable and favorite weapon, not merely in the hands of property-owners who want to put down strikes, but in the hands of criminal Prohibition agents who seek to wring blackmail from their victims. In brief, it has become a dishonest means of oppression for men who are even more dishonest than it is. Certainly it is idle to talk of respect for the laws when such devices have legislative and judicial sanction. No reasonable man, save he be ignorant of their nature and purpose, can conceivably respect them. If, on the ground that whatever is in the law should be given full faith and credit, he maintains that they should not be resisted, then he maintains that the Bill of Rights is no more than a string of empty phrases, and that any shyster who invents a way to evade and abrogate it is a jurist as dignified as John Marshall.

3

Is a judge bound to lend himself to such gross and dishonest attacks upon the common rights of the citizen? I am no lawyer, but I presume to doubt it. There were judges in 1918 who did not think themselves obliged to sacrifice the Bill of Rights to the Espionage Act, and who resolutely refused to do so, and yet, so far as I know, nothing happened to them; at least one of them, to my knowledge, has been since promoted to a circuit. Why should any judge enforce the injunction clause of the Volstead Act? Its enforcement is surely not an automatic act; it involves deliberation and decision by the judge; he may refuse his injunction without offering any explanation to anyone. What would follow if he arose one day in his high pulpit, and announced simply that his court was purged of all such oblique and dishonest enactments henceforth—that he had resolved to refuse to lend himself to the schemes of blackmailers with badges, or to harass and punish free citizens in violation of their fundamental constitutional rights and their plain dignity as human beings, or, in brief, to engage in any other enterprise as a judge that he would shrink from engaging in as a good citizen and a man of honor? Would the result be impeachment? I should like to meet a Congressman insane enough to move the impeachment of such a judge! Would it be a storm of public indignation? . . . Or would it be a vociferous yell of delight?

It seems to me, indeed, that the first judge who rises to such a rebellion will be the first judge ever to become a popular hero in the Republic—that he will be elevated to the Supreme Court by a sort of acclamation, even if it is necessary to get rid of one of the sitting justices by setting fire to his gown. But even imagining him so elevated, the remaining eight justices will still function, and all of us know what they think of the Bill of Rights. Wouldn't such a rebel judge succumb to the system of which he was a discreet particle? Couldn't the other eight judges nullify and make a mock of his heroic defiance? Could they, indeed? Then how? If a judge, high or low, actually called in justice to rescue a citizen from the law, what precisely could the Supreme Court do about it? I know of no appeal by the District Attorney in criminal cases, once the accused has been put in jeopardy; I know only of impeachment for judges who forget the lines of the solemn farce to which they are sworn. But try to imagine the impeachment of a judge charged with punching a hole in the Volstead Act, and letting in some common justice and common decency!

So far, no such rambunctious and unprecedented judge has been heard of,—none, that is, has objected to the injunction clause in toto and head on—nor do I specifically predict his advent. He may come, but probably he won't. The law is a curse to all of us, but it is a curse of special virulence to lawyers. It becomes for them a sort of discreditable vice, a stealthy and degrading superstition. It robs them of all balance, of all capacity for clear thought, of all imagination. Judges tend to show this decay of the faculties in an exaggerated form; they become mere automata, bound by arbitrary rules, precedents, the accumulated imbecilities of generations of bad logic; to their primary lack of sense as lawyers they add the bombastic manner of bureaucrats. It is thus too much to hope for a judge showing any originality or courage; one Holmes in an era of Hardings and Coolidges is probably more than a fair allotment. But while the judges of the District Courts go on driving wild teams of jackasses through the Bill of Rights, and the rev. seniors of the Supreme Court give their approval to the business in solemn form, sometimes but not always with Holmes, J., and Brandeis, J., dissenting—while all this is going on, there are black clouds rolling up from the hinterland, where the Constitution is still taught in the schools and even Methodists are bred to reverence Patrick Henry. The files of Congress already show the way the wind is blowing—constitutional amendments to drag down and denaturize the Supreme Court, simple acts to the same end, other acts providing for the election of Federal judges, yet others even more revolutionary. I know of no such proposal that has any apparent merit. Even the best of them, hamstringing the courts, would only augment the power of a Congress that is ten times worse. But so long as judges pursue fatuously the evil business of converting every citizen into a subject, demagogues will come forward with their dubious remedies, and, soon or late, unless the bench pulls up, some of these demagogues will get themselves heard.

V.
Reflections on Human Monogamy

I
The Eternal Farce

As every attentive patron of the drama is well aware, it is difficult for even the most skillful actors to keep Ibsen's "Hedda Gabler" from degenerating to farce in the performance. The reason is certainly not occult. It lies in the plain fact that such transactions as the dramatist here deals with—a neurotic woman's effort to be heavily romantic, her horror when romance is followed by pregnancy, the manœuvres of a satanic and idiotic lover, the cuckolding of a husband wearing whiskers—are intrinsically and incurably farcical. *All* love affairs, in truth, are farcical—that is, to the spectators. When one hears that some old friend has succumbed to the blandishments of a sweet one, however virtuous and beautiful she may be, one does not gasp and roll one's eyes; one simply laughs. When one hears, a year or two later, that they are quarreling, one laughs again. When one hears that the bride is seeking consolation from the curate of the parish, one laughs a third time. When one hears that the bridegroom, in revenge, is sneaking his stenographer to dinner at an Italian restaurant, one laughs a fourth time. And so on. But when one goes to the theatre, the dramatist often asks one to wear a solemn frown when he displays the same puerile and ludicrous phenomena—that is, while he depicts a fat actress as going crazy when she discovers that her husband, an actor with a face like the abdomen of a ten-pin, has run off to Asbury Park, N.J., with another actress who pronounces all French words in the manner of the Texas Christian University.

The best dramatists, of course, make no such mistake. In Shakespeare love is always depicted as comedy—sometimes light and charming, as in "Twelfth Night," but usually rough and buffoonish, as in "The Taming of the Shrew." This comic attitude is plainly visible even in such plays as "Hamlet" and "Romeo and Juliet." In its main outlines, I suppose, "Hamlet" is properly looked upon as a tragedy, but if you believe that the love passages are intended to be tragic then all I ask is that you give a sober reading to the colloquies between Hamlet and Ophelia. They are not only farcical; they are downright obscene; Shakespeare, through the mouth of Hamlet, derides the whole business with almost intolerable ribaldry. As for "Romeo and Juliet," what is it but a penetrating burlesque upon the love guff that was fashionable in the poet's time? True enough, his head buzzed with such loveliness that he could not write even burlesque without making it beautiful—compare "Much Ado About Nothing" and "Othello"—but nevertheless it is quite absurd to say that he was serious when he wrote this tale of calf-love. Imagine such a man taking seriously the spasms and hallucinations of a *Backfisch* of fourteen, the tinpot heroics of a boy of eighteen! Shakespeare remembered very well the nature of his own amorous fancies at eighteen. It was the year of his seduction by Ann Hathaway, whose brothers later made him marry her, much to his damage and dismay. He wrote the play at forty-five. Tell it to the Marines!

I have a suspicion that even Ibsen, though he seldom permitted himself overt humor, indulged in some quiet spoofing when he wrote "A Doll's House," "Hedda Gabler," "The Lady From the Sea" and "Little Eyolf." The whole last act of "Hedda Gabler" could be converted into burlesque by changing ten words; as I have said, it is almost always burlesque as bad actors play it. In the cases of "Ghosts" and "The Master-Builder" there can be no doubt whatever. The former is a piece of buffoonery designed to make fun of the fools who were outraged by "A Doll's House"; the latter is a comic piece founded upon personal experience. At the age of sixty Ibsen amused himself with a flirtation with a girl of sixteen. Following the custom of her sex, she took his casual winks and cheek-pinchings quite seriously, and began hinting to the whole neighborhood that the old boy was hopelessly gone on her, and that he intended to divorce Fru Ibsen and run off with her to Italy. All this gave entertainment to Ibsen, who was a sardonic man, and he began speculating as to what would happen to a man of his age who actually yielded to the gross provocations of such a wench. The result was "The Master-Builder." But think of the plot! He makes the master-builder climb a church-steeple, and then jump off! Imagine him regarding such slap-stick farce seriously!

The world has very little sense of humor. It is always wagging its ears solemnly over elaborate jocosities. For 600 years it has gurgled over the "Divine Comedy" of Dante, despite the plain fact that the work is a flaming satire upon the whole Christian hocus-pocus of heaven, purgatory and hell. To have tackled such nonsense head-on, in Dante's time, would have been to flout the hangman; hence the poet clothed his attack in an irony so delicate that the ecclesiastical police were baffled. Why is the poem called a comedy? I have read at least a dozen discussions of the question by modern pedants, all of them labored and unconvincing. The same problem obviously engaged the scholars of the poet's own time. He called the thing simply "comedy"; they added the adjective "divine" in order to ameliorate what seemed to them to be an intolerable ribaldry. Well, here is a "comedy" in which human beings are torn limb from limb, boiled in sulphur, cut up with red-hot knives, and filled with molten lead! Can one imagine a man capable of such a poem regarding such fiendish imbecilities seriously? Certainly not. They appeared just as idiotic to him as they appear to you or me. But the Federal judiciary of the day made it impossible to say so in plain language, so he said so behind a smoke-screen of gaudy poetry. How Dante would have roared if he could have known that six hundred years later an illiterate President of the United States, a good Baptist with money in the bank, married happily to a divorcée—would take the whole thing with utter seriousness, and deliver a nonsensical harangue upon the lessons in it for American Christians!

The case of Wagner's "Parsifal" is still more remarkable. Even Nietzsche was deceived by it. Like the most maudlin German fat woman at Baireuth, he mistook the composer's elaborate and outrageous burlesque of Christianity for a tribute to Christianity, and so denounced him as a jackass and refused to speak to him thereafter. To this day "Parsifal" is given with all the trappings of a religious ceremonial, and pious folks go to hear it who would instantly shut their ears if the band began playing "Tristan und Isolde." It has become, in fact, a sort of "'Way Down East" or "Ben Hur" of music drama—a bait for luring patrons who are never seen in the opera-house otherwise. But try to imagine such a thumping atheist as Wagner writing a religious opera seriously! And if, by any chance, you succeed in imagining it, then turn to the Char-Freitag music, and play it on your victrola. Here is the central scene of the piece, the moment of most austere solemnity—and to it Wagner fits music that is so luscious and so fleshly—indeed, so downright lascivious and indecent—that even I, who am almost anæsthetic to such provocations, blush every time I hear it. The Flower Maidens do not raise my blood-pressure a single ohm; I have actually snored through the whole second act of "Tristan." But when I hear that Char-Freitag music all of my Freudian suppressions begin groaning and stretching their legs in the dungeons of my unconscious. And what does Char-Freitag mean? Char-Freitag means Good Friday!

2
Venus at the Domestic Hearth

One inclines to the notion that women—and especially homely women—greatly overestimate the importance of physical beauty in their eternal conspiracy against the liberty of men. It is a powerful lure, to be sure, but it is certainly not the only one that fetches the game, nor even, perhaps, the most effective one. The satisfaction that a man gets out of conquering—which is to say, out of succumbing to—a woman of noticeable pulchritude is chiefly the rather banal one of parading her before other men. He likes to show her off as he likes to show his expensive automobile or his big door-knob factory. It is her apparent costliness that is her principal charm. Her beauty sets up the assumption that she was sought eagerly by other men, some of them wealthy, and that it thus took a lot of money or a lot of skill to obtain the monopoly of her.

But very few men are so idiotic that they are blind to the hollowness of such satisfactions. A husband, after all, spends relatively few hours of his life parading his wife, or even contemplating her beauty. What engages him far more often is the unromantic business of living with her—of listening to her conversation, of trying to fathom and satisfy her whims, of detecting and counteracting her plots against his ego, of facing with her the dull hazards and boredoms of everyday life. In the discharge of this business personal beauty is certainly not necessarily a help; on the contrary, it may be a downright hindrance, if only because it makes for the hollowest and least intelligent of all forms of vanity. Of infinitely more value is a quality that women too often neglect, to wit, the quality of simple amiability. The most steadily charming of all human beings, male or female, is the one who is tolerant, unprovocative, good-humored, kind. A man wants a show only intermittently, but he wants peace and comfort every day. And to get them, if he is sagacious, he is quite willing to sacrifice scenery.

3
The Rat-trap

Much of the discontent with modern marriage centers in the fact that the laws which condition it and safeguard it all assume that its purpose is the founding of a family. This was unquestionably its purpose when those laws were devised, say three thousand years ago, but that purpose, at least among the civilized minority, is now almost forgotten. Very few educated men of today, it seems to me, have any notion of founding a family in mind when they marry. Their vanity takes different forms; moreover, they have rejected the old doctrine that they have any duty in the premises; the *Stammhalter* has pretty well disappeared from their visions. Most of them, it is probable, marry without any intelligible purpose whatever. Women flatter them, mark them down and lure them to the holy altar: everything else is afterthought. Many an American man finds himself on the brink of marriage without ever having given any sober thought even to so important a matter as the probable charm of his bride-elect as mistress. This explains many connubial calamities.

As things stand, the only legal relief from uncomfortable marriages is afforded by divorce. Every other workable device is frowned upon, and most of them are punished. The chief purpose of legal divorce, of course, is to protect the children of the marriage, *i.e.*, to safeguard the family. But the scheme is clumsy, expensive and cruel. To employ it is to cut off a leg in order to cure what may be, after all, merely a barked shin—worse, what may be no injury at all. Suppose there *are* no children? Suppose the marriage is entered upon with the clear understanding that there *shall* be no children? In the latter case it is obviously insane to surround it with safeguards for the family that will never exist. As well insure a pile of bricks against fire. What is needed is legal recognition of such marriages—recognition that will establish decorum and fair play within their actual limits, but that will not seek to burden them with conditions that look quite outside their limits. Human inertia and sentimentality, of course, will be a long while countenancing any such change. Until quite recently a marriage without children was utterly impossible, save as an act of God, and so the inevitable, by a familiar process, was converted into the creditable. This nonsense survives, despite the disappearance of the excuse for it. It is still believed, by the great majority of human beings, that there is something mysteriously laudable about achieving viable offspring. I have searched the sacred and profane scriptures for many years, but have yet to find any logical ground for this notion. To have a child is no more creditable than to have rheumatism—and no more discreditable. Ethically, it is absolutely meaningless. And practically, it is mainly a matter of chance.

4
The Love Chase

The notion that man is the aggressor in love is frequently supported by old-fashioned psychologists by pointing to the example of the lower animals. The lion, it appears, stalks the lioness to her shame and undoing; the amorous cock pursues the reluctant and virtuous hen. Granted. But all that this proves, giving the analogy all the value asked for it, is that man is the aggressor as *lover*, pure and simple, *i.e.*, as seducer. Is he also the aggressor as suitor and husband? To ask the question is almost to answer it. . . . Well, it is precisely his rôle of husband that differentiates man from lion and cock. And once he is thus differentiated, all his previous likeness disappears. . . . In civilized societies, there is a double stalking: for mistresses and for husbands. The fact that the majority of women retain their virtue to the altar and that the majority of men, soon or late, are married—this offers a capital indication of the relative enthusiasm and pertinacity with which the two varieties of aggression are carried on.

5
Women as Realpolitiker

Women in general are far too intelligent to have any respect for so-called ideas. One seldom hears of them suffering and dying for any of the bogus Great Truths that men believe in. When a woman is on good terms with her husband she is quite willing to accept his idiotic theorizings on any subject that happens to engage him, whether theological, economic, epistemological or political. When one hears of a Republican man who has a Democratic wife, or *vice versa*, it is always safe to assume that she has her eye on a handsomer, richer or more docile fellow, and is thinking of calling up a lawyer.

6
Footnote for Suffragettes

The double standard of morality will survive in this world so long as a woman whose husband has been debauched is favored with the sympathetic tears of other women, and a man whose wife has run away with an actor is laughed at by other men.

7
The Helpmate

The notion that a true and loving (and, let us hope, amiable and beautiful) wife inspires a man to high endeavor is largely illusory. Every sane woman knows instinctively, as a matter of fact, that the highest aspirations of her husband are fundamentally inimical to her, and that their realization is apt to cost her her possession of him. What she dreams of is not an infinitely brilliant husband, but an infinitely "solid" one, which is to say, one bound irretrievably by the chains of normalcy. It would delight her to see him get to the White House, for a man in the White House is as relentlessly policed as an archbishop.

But it would give her a great deal of disquiet to see him develop into a Goethe or a Wagner.

I have known in my time a good many men of the first talent, as talent is reckoned in America, and most of them have been married. I can't recall one whose wife appeared to view his achievements with perfect ease of mind. In every case the lady was full of a palpable fear—the product of feminine intuition, *i.e.*, of hard realism and common sense—that his rise shook her hold upon him, that he became a worse husband in proportion as he became a better man. In the logic I can discern no flaw. The ideal husband is surely not a man of active and daring mind; he is the man of placid and conforming mind. Here the good business man obviously beats the artist and adventurer. His rewards are all easily translated into domestic comfort and happiness. He is not wobbled by the admiration of other women, none of whom, however much they may esteem his virtues as a husband, are under any illusion as to his virtues as a lover. Above all, his mind is not analytical, and hence he is not likely to attempt any anatomizing of his marriage—the starting point for the worst sort of domestic infelicity. No man, examining his marriage intelligently, can fail to observe that it is compounded, at least in part, of slavery, and that he is the slave. Happy the woman whose husband is so stupid that he never launches into that coroner's inquest!

8
The Mime

The fundamental objection to actors, stripping the business of all mere sophistry and snobbery, is that they give away the idiotic vanity of the whole male sex. An actor is simply a man who, by word and strut, says aloud of *him*self what all normal men think of *them*selves. Thus he exposes, in a highly indiscreet and disconcerting manner, the full force of masculine vanity. But I doubt that he exaggerates it. No healthy male is ever actually modest. No healthy male ever really thinks or talks of anything save himself. His conversation is one endless boast—often covert, but always undiluted. His politics is a mere sneering at what he conceives to be inferiors; his philosophy is simply an exposure of asses; he cannot imagine himself save as superior, dominating, the center of situations. Even his theology is seldom more than a stealthy comparison of himself and God, to the disadvantage of God. . . . The youngest flapper knows all this. Feminine strategy, in the duel of sex, consists almost wholly of an adroit feeding of this vanity. Man makes love by braggadocio. Woman makes love by listening. . . . Once a woman passes a certain point in intelligence she finds it almost impossible to get a husband: she simply cannot go on listening without snickering.

9
Cavia Cobaya

I find the following in Theodore Dreiser's "Hey-Rub-a-Dub-Dub";

> Does the average strong, successful man confine himself to one woman? Has he ever?

The first question sets a insoluble problem. How are we, in such intimate matters, to say what is the average and what is not the average? But the second question is easily answered, and the answer is, He has. Here Dreiser's curious sexual obsession simply leads him into absurdity. His view of the traffic of the sexes remains the naïve one of an ex-Baptist nymph in Greenwich Village. Does he argue that Otto von Bismarck was not a "strong, successful man"? If not, then let him remember that Bismarck was a strict monogamist—a man full of sin, but always faithful to his Johanna. Again, there was Thomas Henry Huxley. Again, there was William Ewart Gladstone. Again, there was Robert Edward Lee. Yet again, there were Robert Schumann, Felix Mendelssohn, Johann Sebastian Bach, Ulysses S. Grant, Andrew Jackson, Louis Pasteur, Martin Luther, Helmuth von Moltke, Stonewall Jackson, Lyof Tolstoi, Robert Browning, Henrik Ibsen, William T. Sherman, Carl Schurz, old Sam Adams, . . . I could extend the list to pages. . . . Perhaps I am unfair to Dreiser. His notion of a "strong, successful man" may be, not such a genuinely superior fellow as Bismarck or Bach, but such a mere brigand as Shonts, Yerkes or Jim Fisk. If so, he is still wrong. If so, he still runs aground on John D. Rockefeller.

10
The Survivor

Around every bachelor of more than thirty-five legends tend to congregate, chiefly about the causes of his celibacy. If it is not whispered that he is damaged goods, and hence debarred from marriage by a lofty concept of Service to the unborn, it is told under the breath that he was insanely in love at the age of twenty-six with a beautiful creature who jilted him for an insurance underwriter and so broke his heart beyond repair. Such tales are nearly always moonshine. The reason why the average bachelor of thirty-five remains a bachelor is really very simple. It is, in brief, that no ordinarily attractive and intelligent woman has ever made a serious and undivided effort to marry him.

11
The Veteran's Disaster

The tragedy of experience is that a man no longer believes it when a woman shows all the orthodox signs of having been flustered by him. In youth it gives him immense delight to discover that he has made a mash, but when he gets into the middle years the thing merely annoys him. He is irritated that yet another female Cagliostro should try to floor him with the immemorial mumbo-jumbo, and so make a fool of him. The girl he succumbs to is the one who tells him frankly that her heart is buried in France, but that she admires him tremendously and would esteem it a singular honor to be the wife of so meritorious a fellow. This helps to explain, perhaps, why aging men so often succumb to flappers.

12
Moral Indignation

The ill-fame of the Turks in the English-speaking world is not due to their political medievalism, as is usually alleged, but to their practise of polygamy. That practise inevitably excites the erotic imagination of men doomed to monogamy, and particularly of men doomed to monogamy with despotic, prudish and unappetizing wives, which is to say, the normal, typical men of England and the United States. They envy the Turk his larger and more charming joys, and hence hate him. Every time Reuter reports him dragging a fresh herd of dark-eyed, voluptuous Georgian or American women into his seraglio, they hate him the more. The way to arouse a Puritan to his highest pitch of moral indignation is not to burn down an orphan-asylum; the way to do it is to grab a pretty girl around the waist and launch with her into the lascivious measures of a Wiener Walz. Men always hate most what they envy most.

13
The Man and His Shadow

Every man, whatever his actual qualities, is credited with and judged by certain general qualities that are supposed to appertain to his sex, particularly by women. Thus man the individual is related to Man the species, often to his damage and dismay. Consider my own case. I am by nature one of the most orderly of mortals. I have a place for every article of my personal property, whether a Bible or a cocktail-shaker, an undershirt or an eye-dropper, and I always keep it where it belongs. I never drop cigar-ashes on the floor. I never upset a waste-basket. I am never late for trains. I never run short of collars. I never go out with a purple necktie on a blue shirt. I never fail to appear in time for dinner without telephoning or telegraphing. Yet the women who are cursed by God with the care of me maintain and cherish the fiction that I am an extremely careless and even hoggish fellow—that I have to be elaborately nursed, supervised and policed—that the slightest relaxation of vigilance over my everyday conduct would reduce me to a state of helplessness and chaos, with all my clothes mislaid, half my books in the ash-can, my mail unanswered, my face unshaven, and my office not unlike an I.W.W. headquarters after a raid by the *Polizei*. It is their firm theory that, unaided by superior suggestion, I'd wear one shirt six weeks, and a straw hat until Christmas. They never speak of my workroom save in terms of horror, though it is actually the most orderly room in my house. Weekly I am accused of having lost all my socks and handkerchiefs, though they are in my clothes-press all the while. At least once a month formal plans are discussed for reorganizing my whole mode of life, that I may not sink into irremediable carelessness, inefficiency and barbarism.

I note that many other men lie under the same benign espionage and misrepresentation—in fact, nearly all men. But it is my firm belief that very few men are really disorderly. The business of the world is managed by getting order into it, and the feeling for discipline thus engendered is carried over into domestic life. I know of very few men who ever drop ashes on the dining-room rug, or store their collars in their cigar-box, or put on brown socks with their dress-clothes, or forget to turn off the water after they have bathed, or neglect to keep dinner engagements—and most of these few, I am firmly convinced, do it because their women-folk expect it of them, because it would cause astonishment and dismay if they refrained. I myself, more than once, have deliberately hung my hat on an electrolier, or clomped over the parquetry with muddy shoes, or gone out in a snowstorm without an overcoat, or come down to dinner in a ragged collar, or filled my shirt-box with old copies of the *Congressional Record*, or upset a bottle of green ink, or used Old Dutch Cleanser for shaving, or put olives into Jack Rose cocktails, or gone without a haircut for three or four weeks, or dropped an expensive beer *Seidel* upon the hard concrete of my cellar floor in order to give a certain necessary color to the superstition of my oafishness. If I failed to do such things now and then I'd become unpopular, and very justly so, for nothing is more obnoxious than a human being who is always challenging and correcting the prevailing view of him. Even now I make no protest; I merely record the facts. On my death-bed, I daresay, I shall carry on the masquerade. That is to say, I shall swallow a clinical thermometer or two, upset my clam-broth over my counterpane, keep an ouija board and a set of dice under my pillow, and maybe, at the end, fall clumsily out of bed.

14
The Balance-Sheet

Marriage, as everyone knows, is chiefly an economic matter. But too often it is assumed that economics concerns only the wife's hats; it also concerns, and perhaps more importantly, the husband's cigars. No man is genuinely happy, married, who has to drink worse gin than he used to drink when he was single.

15
Yearning

Ah, that the eugenists would breed a woman as capable of laughter as the girl of twenty and as adept at knowing when not to laugh as the woman of thirty-five!

VI.
The Politician

HALF the sorrows of the world, I suppose, are caused by making false assumptions. If the truth were only easier to ascertain the remedy for them would consist simply of ascertaining it and accepting it. This business, alas, is usually impossible, but fortunately not always: now and then, by some occult process, half rational and half instinctive, the truth gets itself found out and an ancient false assumption goes overboard. I point, in the field of the social relations, to one which afflicted the human race for millenniums: that one, to wit, which credited the rev. clergy with a mysterious wisdom and awful powers. Obviously, it has ceased to trouble all the superior varieties of men. It may survive in those remote marches where human beings go to bed with the cows, but certainly it has vanished from the cities. Asphalt and the apostolic succession, indeed, seem to be irreconcilable enemies. I can think of no clergyman in any great American city today whose public dignity and influence are much above those of an ordinary Class I Babbitt. It is hard for even the most diligent and passionate of the ancient order to get upon the first pages of the newspapers; he must make a clown-show, discreditable to his fraying cloth, or he must blush unseen. When bishops begin launching thunderbolts against heretics, the towns do not tremble; they laugh. When elders denounce sin, sin only grows more popular. Imagine a city man getting a notice from the ordinary of his diocese that he had been excommunicated. It would trouble him far less, I venture, than his morning *Katzenjammer*.

The reason for all this is not hard to find. All the superior varieties of men—and even the lowest varieties of city workmen are at least superior to peasants—have simply rid themselves of their old belief in devils. Hell no longer affrights and palsies them, and so the magic of those who profess to save them from it no longer impresses them. That profession, I believe, was bogus, and its acceptance was therefore a false assumption.

Being so, it made men unhappy; getting rid of it has delivered them. They are no longer susceptible to ecclesiastical alarms and extortions; *ergo*, they sleep and eat better. Think of what life must have been under such princes of damnation as Cotton Mather and Jonathan Edwards, with even bartenders and metaphysicians believing in them! And then compare it to life under Bishop Manning and the Rev. Dr. John Roach Straton, with only a few half-wits believing in them! Or turn to the backwoods of the Republic, where the devil is still feared, and with him his professional exterminators. In the country towns the clergy are still almost as influential as they were in Mather's day, and there, as everyone knows, they remain public nuisances, and civilized life is almost impossible. In such Neolithic regions nothing can go on without their consent, on penalty of anathema and hell-fire; as a result, nothing goes on that is worth recording. It is this survival of sacerdotal authority, I begin to believe, and not hookworm, malaria or the event of April 9, 1865, that is chiefly responsible for the cultural paralysis of the late Confederate States. The South lacks big cities; it is run by its country towns—and in every country town there is some Baptist *mullah* who rules by scaring the peasantry. The false assumption that his pretensions are sound, that he can actually bind and loose, that contumacy to him is a variety of cursing God—this false assumption is what makes the yokels so uneasy, so nervous, and hence so unhappy. If they could throw it off they would burn fewer Aframericans and sing more songs. If they could be purged of it they would be purged of Ku Kluxry too.

The cities got rid of that false assumption half a century ago, and have been making cultural progress ever since. Somewhat later they got rid of its brother, to wit, respect for government, and, in particular, respect for its visible agents, the police. That respect—traditional, and hence irrational—had been, for years, in increasingly unpleasant collision with a great body of obvious facts. The police, by assumption austere and almost sacrosanct, were gradually discovered to be, in reality, a pack of rogues and but little removed, save by superior impudence and enterprise, from the cut-throats and purse-snatchers they were set to catch. When, a few decades ago, the American people, at least in the big cities, began to accept them frankly for what they were—when the old false assumption of their integrity and public usefulness was quietly abandoned and a new and more accurate assumption of their roguery was adopted in its place—when this change was effected there was a measurable increase, I believe, in the public happiness. It no longer astonished anyone when policemen were taken in evildoing; indignation therefore abated, and with it its pains. If, before that time, the corps of Prohibition enforcement officers—*i.e.*, a corps of undisguised scoundrels with badges—had been launched upon the populace, there would have been a great roar of wrath, and much anguished gnashing of teeth. People would have felt themselves put upon, injured, insulted. But with the old false assumption about policemen removed from their minds, they met the new onslaught calmly and even smilingly. Today no one is indignant over the fact that the extortions of these new *Polizei* increase the cost of potable alcohol. The false assumption that the police are altruistic agents of a benevolent state has been replaced by the sound assumption that they are gentlemen engaged assiduously, like the rest of us, in finding meat and raiment for their families and in laying up funds to buy Liberty Bonds in the next war to end war. This is human progress, for it increases human happiness.

So much for the evidence. The deduction I propose to make from it is simply this: that a like increase would follow if the American people could only rid themselves of another and worse false assumption that still rides them—one that corrupts all their thinking about the great business of politics, and vastly augments their discontent and unhappiness—the assumption, that is, that politicians are divided into two classes, and that one of those classes is made up of good ones. I need not argue, I hope, that this assumption is almost universally held among us. Our whole politics, indeed, is based upon it, and has been based upon it since the earliest days. What is any political campaign save a concerted effort to turn out a set of politicians who are admittedly bad and put in a set who are thought to be better? The former assumption, I believe, is always sound; the latter is just as certainly false. For if experience teaches us anything at all it teaches us this: that a good politician, under democracy, is quite as unthinkable as an honest burglar. His very existence, indeed, is a standing subversion of the public good in every rational sense. He is not one who serves the common weal; he is simply one who preys upon the commonwealth. It is to the interest of all the rest of us to hold down his powers to an irreducible minimum, and to reduce his compensation to nothing; it is to his interest to augment his powers at all hazards, and to make his compensation all the traffic will bear. To argue that these aims are identical is to argue palpable nonsense. The politician, at his ideal best, never even remotely approximated in practise, is a necessary evil; at his worst he is an almost intolerable nuisance.

What I contend is simply that he would be measurably less a nuisance if we got rid of our old false assumption about him, and regarded him in the cold light of fact. At once, I believe, two-thirds of his obnoxiousness would vanish. He would remain a nuisance, but he would cease to be a swindler; the injury of having to pay freight on him would cease to be complicated by the insult of being rooked. It is the insult and not the injury that makes the deeper wounds, and causes the greater permanent damage to the national psyche. All of us have been trained, since infancy, in putting up with necessary evils, plainly recognized *as* evils. We know, for example, that the young of the human species commonly smell badly; that garbage men, bootblacks and messenger boys commonly smell worse. These facts are not agreeable, but they remain tolerable because they are universally assumed—because there is no sense of having been tricked and cozened in their perennial discovery. But try to imagine how distressing fatherhood would become if prospective fathers were all taught that the human infant radiates an aroma like the rose—if the truth came constantly as a surprise! Each fresh victim of the deception would feel that he had been basely swindled—that his own child was somehow bogus. Not infrequently, I suppose, he would be tempted to make away with it in some quiet manner, and have another—only to be shocked again. That procedure would be idiotic, admittedly, yet it is exactly the one we follow in politics. At each election we vote in a new set of politicians, insanely assuming that they are better than the set turned out. And at each election we are, as they say in the Motherland, done in.

Of late the fraud has become so gross that the plain people

begin to show a great restlessness under it. Like animals in a cage, they trot from one corner to another endlessly seeking a way out. If the Democrats win one year, it is a pretty sure sign that they will lose the next year. State after State becomes doubtful, pivotal, skittish; even the solid South begins to break. In the cities it is still worse. An evil circle is formed. First the poor taxpayers, robbed by the politicians of one great party and then by those of the other, turn to a group of free-lance rogues in the middle ground—non-partisan candidates, Liberals, reformers or what not: the name is unimportant. Then, flayed and pillaged by these gentry as they never were by the old-time professionals, they go back in despair to the latter, and are flayed and pillaged again. Back to Bach! Back to Tammany! Tammany reigns in New York because the Mitchel outfit was found to be intolerable—in other words, because the reformers were found to be even worse than the professionals. Is the fact surprising? Why should it be? Reformers and professionals are alike politicians in search of jobs; both are trying to bilk the taxpayers. Neither ever has any other motive. If any genuinely honest and altruistic politician had come to the surface in America in my time I'd have heard of him, for I have always frequented newspaper offices, and in a newspaper office the news of such a marvel would cause a dreadful tumult. I can recall no such tumult. The unanimous opinion of all the journalists that I know, excluding a few Liberals who are obviously somewhat balmy—they all believed, for example, that the late war would end war,—is that, since the days of the national Thors and Wotans, no politician who was not out for himself, and for himself alone, has ever drawn the breath of life in the United States.

The gradual disintegration of Liberalism among us, in fact, offers an excellent proof of the truth of my thesis. The Liberals have come to grief by fooling their customers, not merely once too often, but a hundred times too often. Over and over again they have trotted out some new hero, usually from the great open spaces, only to see him taken in the immemorial malpractises within ten days. Their graveyard, indeed, is filled with cracked and upset headstones, many covered with ribald pencilings. Every time there is a scandal in the grand manner the Liberals lose almost as many general officers as either the

Democrats or Republicans. Of late, racked beyond endurance by such catastrophes at home, they have gone abroad for their principal heroes; losing humor as well as hope, they now ask us to venerate such astounding paladins as the Hon. Bela Kun, a gentleman who, in any American State, would not only be in the calaboose, but actually in the death-house. But this absurdity is only an offshoot of a deeper one. Their primary error lies in making the false assumption that some politicians are better than others. This error they share with the whole American people.

I propose that it be renounced, and contend that its renunciation would greatly rationalize and improve our politics. I do not argue that there would be any improvement in our politicians; on the contrary, I believe that they would remain substantially as they are today, and perhaps grow even worse. But what I do argue is that recognizing them frankly for what they are would instantly and automatically dissipate the indignation caused by their present abominations, and that the disappearance of this indignation would promote the public contentment and happiness. Under my scheme there would be no more false assumptions and no more false hopes, and hence no more painful surprises, no more bitter resentment of fraud, no more despair. Politicians, in so far as they remained necessary, would be kept at work—but not with any insane notion that they were archangels. Their rascality would be assumed and discounted, as the rascality of the police is now assumed and discounted. Machinery would be gradually developed to limit it and counteract it. In the end, it might be utilized in some publicly profitable manner, as the insensitiveness to filth of garbage men is now utilized, as the reverence of the clergy for capitalism is now utilized. The result, perhaps, would be a world no better than the present one, but it would at least be a world more intelligent.

In all this I sincerely hope that no one will mistake me for one who shares the indignation I have spoken of—that is, for one who believes that politicians can be made good, and cherishes a fond scheme for making them so. I believe nothing of the sort. On the contrary, I am convinced that the art and mystery they practise is essentially and incurably anti-social—that they must remain irreconcilable enemies of the common weal until the end of time. But I maintain that this fact, in itself, is not a bar to their employment. There are, under Christian civilization, many necessary offices that demand the possession of anti-social talents. A professional soldier, regarded realistically, is much worse than a professional politician, for he is a professional murderer and kidnaper, whereas the politician is only a professional sharper and sneak-thief. A clergyman, too, begins to shrink and shrivel on analysis; the work he does in the world is basically almost indistinguishable from that of an astrologer, a witch-doctor or a fortune-teller. He pretends falsely that he can get sinners out of hell, and collects money from them on that promise, tacit or express. If he had to go before a jury with that pretension it would probably go hard with him. But we do not send him before a jury; we grant him his hocus-pocus on the ground that it is necessary to his office, and that his office is necessary to civilization, so-called. I pass over the journalist delicately; the time has not come to turn State's evidence. Suffice it to say that he, too, would probably wither under a stiff cross-examination. If he is no murderer, like the soldier, then he is at least a sharper and swindler, like the politician.

What I plead for, if I may borrow a term in disrepute, is simply *Realpolitik*, *i.e.*, realism in politics. I can imagine a political campaign purged of all the current false assumptions and false pretenses—a campaign in which, on election day, the voters went to the polls clearly informed that the choice between them was not between an angel and a devil, a good man and a bad man, an altruist and a go-getter, but between two frank go-getters, the one, perhaps, excelling at beautiful and nonsensical words and the other at silent and prehensile deeds—the one a chautauqua orator and the other a porch-climber. There would be, in that choice, something candid, free and exhilarating. Buncombe would be adjourned. The voter would make his selection in the full knowledge of all the facts, as he makes his selection between two heads of cabbage, or two evening papers, or two brands of chewing tobacco. Today he chooses his rulers as he buys bootleg whiskey, never knowing precisely what he is getting, only certain that it is not what it pretends to be. The Scotch may turn out to be wood alcohol or it may turn out to be gasoline; in either case it is not Scotch.

How much better if it were plainly labelled, for wood alcohol and gasoline both have their uses—higher uses, indeed, than Scotch. The danger is that the swindled and poisoned consumer, despairing of ever avoiding them when he doesn't want them, may prohibit them even when he does want them, and actually enforce his own prohibition. The danger is that the hopeless voter, forever victimized by his false assumption about politicians, may in the end gather such ferocious indignation that he will abolish them teetotally and at one insane swoop, and so cause government by the people, for the people and with the people to perish from this earth.

VII.
From a Critic's Notebook

1
Progress

THE most important change that has come over American literature in my time is this: that American satire, which once aimed all of its shafts at the relatively civilized minority, now aims most of them at the imbecile majority. If a satirist of today undertook to poke fun at the paintings of Titian and the music of Richard Wagner, he would be dismissed at once as a clown strayed in from the barber-shop weeklies and the chautauquas. Yet Mark Twain did both, and to great applause. To Mark, for all his humor, there was little that was ridiculous in such American go-getters as George F. Babbitt. He looked upon one of them, Henry H. Rogers, as his best friend, and he made another the hero of "A Connecticut Yankee." What amused Mark most profoundly was precisely whatever was most worthy of sober admiration—sound art, good manners, the aristocratic ideal. And he was typical of his age. The satirists of the present age, though they may be less accomplished workmen, are at all events more civilized men. What they make fun of is not what is dignified, or noble, or beautiful, but what is shoddy, and ignoble, and ugly.

2
The Iconoclast

Of a piece with the absurd pedagogical demand for so-called constructive criticism is the doctrine that an iconoclast is a hollow and evil fellow unless he can prove his case. Why, indeed, should he prove it? Doesn't he prove enough when he proves by his blasphemy that this or that idol is defectively convincing—that at least *one* visitor to the shrine is left full of doubts? The fact is enormously significant; it indicates that instinct has somehow risen superior to the shallowness of logic, the refuge of fools. The pedant and the priest have always been the most expert of logicians—and the most diligent disseminators of nonsense and worse. The liberation of the human mind has never been furthered by such learned dunderheads; it has been furthered by gay fellows who heaved dead cats into sanctuaries and then went roistering down the highways of the world, proving to all men that doubt, after all, was safe—that the god in the sanctuary was finite in his power, and hence a fraud. One horse-laugh is worth ten thousand syllogisms. It is not only more effective; it is also vastly more intelligent.

3
The Artists' Model

The doctrine that art is an imitation of nature is full of folly. Nine-tenths of all the art that one encounters in this world is actually an imitation of other art. Fully a half of it is an imitation twice, thrice or ten times removed. The artist, in fact, is seldom an accurate observer of nature; he leaves that gross and often revolting exploration to geologists, engineers and anatomists. The last thing he wants to see is a beautiful woman in the bright, pitiless sunlight.

4
The Good Citizen as Artist

Again, there is the bad author who defends his manufacture of magazine serials and movie scenarios on the ground that he has a wife, and is in honor bound to support her. I have seen a few such wives. I dispute the obligation. . . . As for the biological by-products of this fidelity, I rate them even lower. Show me 100 head of ordinary children who are worth one "Heart of Darkness," and I'll subside. As for "Lord Jim," I would not swap it for all the children born in Trenton, N. J., since the Spanish War.

5

Definitive Judgments

The doctrine that every critic worth reading is primarily an artist—that his fundamental aim is not to ascertain the truth, or to mete out justice, or to defend the maxims of Aristotle, or the Ten Commandments, or the statutes of the Harvard Corporation, or the Harrison Anti-Narcotic Act, or the Mann Act—this doctrine seems to give a great deal of offense to pedagogues, and every time one of them mentions it he mourns. Always he makes the accusation that it relieves the critic of his most important duty, to wit, the duty of telling his readers what the thing he criticizes is, and how far it carries out its pretension, and how it relates itself to other things in the same category, or presumably in the same category. The answer here, of course, is that no such duty exists. Its existence, indeed, is no more than a delusion of pedagogues, who invariably labor under the notion that they have said something about this or that when they have given it a name. That delusion is responsible for all of the so-called "criticism" that pedagogues write—the heavy, soggy essays upon Matthew Arnold, Poe as a poet, Browning as a philosopher, the Pre-Raphaelites, Henley, Schiller, Ibsen, Whitman, Milton, Herrick, Molière —in brief, all the blowsy efforts to reach "definite judgments" that such tedious wind-jammers delight in. What is accomplished by such "definitive judgments"? Absolutely nothing. A hedge Lowell's elaborate treatise upon Joaquin Miller will never convince any intelligent man that Miller was an important writer, nor will the same professor's effort to fit Ralph Waldo Emerson into the Methodist æsthetic and gnosiology ever stop any intelligent man from reading Emerson for himself, and enjoying him more or less. Such "criticism" invariably fails of its ostensible purpose. In so far as it has any validity and significance at all, it is not as jurisprudence but as work of art. In brief, the pedagogue, when he essays criticism, becomes an artist in spite of himself. As a moral man, of course, he avoids the sin of being a good artist, but nevertheless he is, within the limits set by his superstitions, an artist.

What separates good critics from bad ones is simply the fact that the former are sound enough artists to make the matter they discuss seem charming. It is by this route that they induce their readers to look into it further, and so achieve their function. This function is not to be confused with the pedagogical. It is infinitely more urbane and expansive. Dryden was surely no schoolmaster, even *in petto*, but when he set down his views about Shakespeare in his beautiful and ingratiating prose he interested more readers in the Bard than a whole herd of pedagogues could have mustered, and so, despite the chill that often got into his enthusiasm, he probably did more than any other man to rescue the greatest of English poets from his Restoration days' neglect. What a palpable artist finds interesting is very apt to seem interesting to all persons of taste and education; what a mere birchman advocates is apt to arouse their instinctive aversion. They do not want to be told precisely what to think about the thing discussed; all they want to be told is that it is worth examining. Every effort to lay down immutable conclusions, to state impeccable principles, to instruct them in their moral and æsthetic duties—in other words, every effort to think for them, as a college tutor thinks for a sophomore, and a professor for a tutor, and a university president for a professor, and a board of trustees for a president—is bound to annoy them and chase them away. Despite all the "definitive judgments" that pedants have pronounced upon Walt Whitman, almost always unfavorably, he continues to live and to grow. And despite all their herculean efforts to hold up Howells, he is dead.

VIII.
Totentanz

I CAN think of no great city of this world (putting aside Rio de Janeiro, Sydney and San Francisco) that is set amid scenes of greater natural beauty than New York, by which I mean, of course, Manhattan. Recall Berlin on its dismal plain, Paris and London on their toy rivers, Madrid on its desert, Copenhagen on its swamp, Rome on its ancient sewer and its absurd little hills, and then glance at Manhattan on its narrow and rock-ribbed island, with deep rivers to either side and the wide bay before it. No wonder its early visitors, however much they denounced the Dutch, always paused to praise the scene! Before it grew up, indeed, New York must have been strangely beautiful. But it was the beauty of freshness and unsophistication—in brief, of youth—and now it is no more. The town today, I think, is quite the ugliest in the world—uglier, even, than Liverpool, Chicago or Berlin. If it were actually beautiful, as London, say, is beautiful, or Munich, or Charleston, or Florence, or even parts of Paris and Washington, then New Yorkers would not be so childishly appreciative of the few so-called beauty spots that it has—for example, Washington Square, Gramercy Park, Fifth avenue and Riverside drive. Washington Square, save for one short row of old houses on the North side, is actually very shabby and ugly—a blot rather than a beauty spot. The trees, year in and year out, have a mangy and sclerotic air; the grass is like stable litter; the tall tower on the South side is ungraceful and preposterous; the memorial arch is dirty and undignified; the whole place looks dingy, frowsy and forlorn. Compare it to Mt. Vernon Square in Baltimore: the difference is that between a charwoman and a grand lady. As for Gramercy Park, it is celebrated only because it is in New York; if it were in Washington or London it would not attract a glance. Fifth avenue, to me, seems to be showy rather than beautiful. What gives it its distinction is simply its spick and span appearance of wealth; it is the only New York street that ever looks well-fed and clean.

Riverside drive lacks even so much; it is second-rate from end to end, and especially where it is gaudiest. What absurd and hideous houses, with their brummagem Frenchiness, their pathetic effort to look aristocratic! What bad landscaping! What grotesque monuments! From its heights the rich look down upon the foul scars of the Palisades, as the rich of Fifth avenue and Central Park West look down upon the anemic grass, bare rocks and blowing newspapers of Central Park. Alone among the great cities of the East, New York has never developed a domestic architecture of any charm, or, indeed, of any character at all. There are neighborhoods in Boston, in Philadelphia, in Baltimore and in many lesser cities that have all the dignity and beauty of London, but in New York the brownstone mania of the Nineteenth Century brought down the whole town to one level of depressing ugliness, and since brownstone has gone out there has been no development whatever of indigenous design, but only a naïve copying of models—the skyscraper from Chicago and the dwelling-house from Paris. Along Fifth avenue, from the Fifty-ninth street corner to the upper end of Central Park, there is not a single house that looks reposeful and habitable. Along Park avenue—but Park avenue, for all its flash of creamy brick, is surely one of the most hideous streets in all the world!

But the life of the city, it must be confessed, is as interesting as its physical aspect is dull. It is, even more than London or Paris, the modern Babylon, and since 1914 it has entered upon a period of luxuriousness that far surpasses anything seen on earth since the fall of the Eastern Empire. During many a single week, I daresay, more money is spent in New York upon useless and evil things than would suffice to run the kingdom of Denmark for a year. All the colossal accumulated wealth of the United States, the greatest robber nation in history, tends to force itself at least once a year through the narrow neck of the Manhattan funnel. To that harsh island come all the thieves of the Republic with their loot—bankers from the fat lands of the Middle West, lumbermen from the Northwestern coasts, mine owners from the mountains, oil speculators from Texas and Oklahoma, cotton-mill sweaters from the South, steel magnates and manufacturers from the Black Country, blacklegs and exploiters without end—all laden with cash, all eager to spend it, all easy marks for the town rogues and panders. The result is a social organization that ought to be far more attractive to novelists than it is—a society founded upon the prodigious wealth of Monte Cristo and upon the tastes of sailors home from a long voyage. At no time and place in modern times has harlotry reached so delicate and yet so effusive a development; it becomes, in one form or another, one of the leading industries of the town. New York, indeed, is the heaven of every variety of man with something useless and expensive to sell. There come the merchants with their bales, of Persian prayer-rugs, of silk pajamas, of yellow girls, of strange jugs and carboys, of hand-painted oil-paintings, of old books, of gim-cracks and tinsel from all the four corners of the world, and there they find customers waiting in swarms, their checkbooks open and ready. What town in Christendom has ever supported so many houses of entertainment, so many mimes and mountebanks, so many sharpers and coney-catchers, so many bawds and pimps, so many hat-holders and door-openers, so many miscellaneous servants to idleness and debauchery? The bootlegging industry takes on proportions that are almost unbelievable; there are thousands of New Yorkers, resident and transient, who pay more for alcohol every year than they pay for anything else save women. I have heard of a single party at which the guests drank 100 cases of champagne in an evening—100 cases at $100 a case—and it was, as entertainments go in New York today, a quiet and decorous affair. It is astonishing that no Zola has arisen to describe this engrossing and incomparable dance of death. Upton Sinclair once attempted it, in "The Metropolis," but Sinclair, of course, was too indignant for the job. Moreover, the era he dealt was mild and amateurish; today the pursuit of sensation has been brought to a far higher degree of perfection. One must go back to the oriental capitals of antiquity to find anything even remotely resembling it. Compared to the revels that go on in New York every night, the carnalities of the West End of Berlin are trivial and childish, and those of Paris and the Côte d'Azure take on the harmless aspect of a Sunday-school picnic.

What will be the end of the carnival? If historical precedent counts for anything, it will go on to catastrophe. But what sort of catastrophe? I hesitate to venture upon a prophecy. Manhattan Island, with deep rivers all around it, seems an almost ideal scene for a great city revolution, but I doubt very much that there is any revolutionary spirit in its proletariat. Some mysterious enchantment holds its workers to their extraordinarily uncomfortable life; they apparently get a vague sort of delight out of the great spectacle that they are no part of. The New York workman patronizes fellow workmen from the provinces even more heavily than the Wall Street magnate patronizes country mortgage-sharks. He is excessively proud of his citizenship in the great metropolis, though all it brings him is an upper berth in a dog kennel. Riding along the elevated on the East Side and gaping into the windows of the so-called human habitations that stretch on either hand, I often wonder what process of reasoning impels, say, a bricklayer or a truckdriver to spend his days in such vile hutches. True enough, he is paid a few dollars more a week in New York than he would receive anywhere else, but he gets little more use out of them than an honest bank teller. In almost any other large American city he would have a much better house to live in, and better food; in the smaller towns his advantage would be very considerable. Moreover, his chance of lifting himself out of slavery to some measure of economic independence and autonomy would be greater anywhere else; if it is hard for the American workman everywhere to establish a business of his own, it is triply hard in New York, where rents are killingly high and so much capital is required to launch a business that only Jews can raise it. Nevertheless, the poor idiot hangs on to his coop, dazzled by the wealth and splendor on display all around him. His susceptibility to this lure makes me question his capacity for revolution. He is too stupid and poltroonish for it, and he has too much respect for money. It is this respect for money in the proletariat, in fact, that chiefly safeguards and buttresses capitalism in America. It is secure among us because Americans venerate it too much to attack it.

What will finish New York in the end, I suppose, will be an onslaught from without, not from within. The city is the least defensible of great capitals. Give an enemy command of the sea, and he will be able to take it almost as easily as he could take Copenhagen. It has never been attacked in the past, indeed, without being taken. The strategists of the General Staff at Washington seem to be well aware of this fact, for their preparations to defend the city from a foe afloat have always been half-hearted and lacking in confidence. Captain Stuart Godfrey, U.S.A., who contributes the note on the fortifications of the port to Fremont Rider's "New York City: A Guide to Travelers," is at pains to warn his lay readers that the existing forts protect only the narrow spaces in front of them—that "they cannot be expected to prevent the enemy from landing elsewhere," *e.g.*, anywhere along the long reaches of the Long Island coast. Once such a landing were effected, the fact that the city stands upon an island, with deep water behind it, would be a handicap rather than a benefit. If it could not be taken and held, it could at least be battered to pieces, and so made untenable. The guns of its own forts, indeed, might be turned upon it, once those forts were open to attack from the rear. After that, the best the defenders could do would be to retire to the natural bombproofs in the cellars of the Union Hill, N.J., breweries, and there wait for God to deliver them. They might, of course, be able to throw down enough metal from the Jersey heights to prevent the enemy occupying the city and reopening its theatres and bordellos, but the more successful they were in this enterprise the more cruelly Manhattan would be used. Altogether, an assault from the sea promises to give the New Yorkers something to think about.

That it will be attempted before many years have come and gone seems to me to be very likely and I have a sneaking fear that it may succeed. As a veteran of five wars and a life-long student of homicidal science, I am often made uneasy, indeed, by the almost universal American assumption that no conceivable enemy could inflict serious wounds upon the Republic—that the Atlantic Ocean alone, not to mention the stupendous prowess of *Homo americanus*, makes it eternally safe from aggression. This notion has just enough truth in it to make it dangerous. That the *whole* country could not be conquered and occupied I grant you, but no intelligent enemy would think for a moment of trying to conquer it. All that would be necessary to bring even the most intransigeant patriots to terms would be to take and hold a small part of it—say the part lying to the East and North of the general line of the Potomac river. Early in the late war, when efforts were under way to scare the American *booboisie* with the German bugaboo, one of the Allied propagandists printed a book setting forth plans alleged to have been made by the German General Staff to land an army at the Virginia capes, march on Pittsburgh, and so separate the head of the country from its liver, kidneys, gizzard, heart, spleen, bladder, lungs and other lights. The plan was persuasive, but I doubt that it originated in Potsdam; there was a smell of Whitehall upon it. One of the things most essential to its execution, in fact, was left out as it was set forth, to wit, a thrust southward from Canada to meet and support the thrust northwestward. But even this is not necessary. Any invader who emptied New York and took the line of the Hudson would have Uncle Sam by the tail, and could enter upon peace negotiations with every prospect of getting very polite attention. The American people, of course, could go on living without New York, but they could not go on living as a great and puissant nation. Steadily, year by year, they have made New York more and more essential to the orderly functioning of the American state. If it were cut off from the rest of the country the United States would be in the hopeless position of a man relieved of his medulla oblongata—that is to say, of a man without even enough equipment left to be a father, a patriot and a Christian.

Nevertheless, it is highly probable that the predestined enemy, when he comes at last, will direct his first and hardest efforts to cutting off New York, and then make some attempt to keep it detached afterward. This, in fact, is an essential part of the new higher strategy, which is based upon economic considerations, as the old strategy was based upon dynastic considerations. In the Middle Ages, the object of war was to capture and hamstring a king; at present it is to dismember a great state, and so make it impotent. The Germans, had they won, would have broken up the British Empire, and probably detached important territories from France, Italy and Russia, beside gobbling Belgium *in toto*. The French, tantalized by a precarious and incomplete victory, attempted to break up Germany, as they broke up Austria. The chances are that an enemy capable of taking and holding New York would never give it back wholly—that is, would never consent to its restoration to the Union on the old terms. What would be proposed, I venture, would be its conversion into a sort of free state—a new Dantzig, perhaps functioning, as now, as the financial and commercial capital of the country, but nevertheless lying outside the bounds politically. This would solve the problem of the city's subsistence, and still enable the conqueror to keep his hold upon it. It is my belief that the New Yorkers, after the first blush of horror, would agree to the new arrangement and even welcome it. Their patriotism, as things stand, is next to nothing. I have never heard, indeed, of a single honest patriot in the whole town; every last man who even pretends to kiss the flag is simply a swindler with something to sell. This indifference to the great heart-throbs of the hinterland is not to be dismissed as mere criminality; it is founded upon the plain and harsh fact that New York is alien to the rest of the country, not only in blood and tastes, but also in fundamental interests—that the sort of life that New Yorkers lead differs radically from the sort of life that the rest of the American people lead, and that their deepest instincts vary with it. The city, in truth, already constitutes an independent free state in all save the name. The ordinary American law does not run there, save when it has been specifically ratified, and the ordinary American *mores* are quite unknown there. What passes as virtue in Kansas is regarded as intolerable vice in New York, and *vice versa.* The town is already powerful enough to swing the whole country when it wants to, as it did on the war issue in 1917, but the country is quite impotent to swing the town. Every great wave of popular passion that rolls up on the prairies is dashed to spray when it strikes the hard rocks of Manhattan.

As a free state, licensed to prey upon the hinterland but unharassed by its Crô-Magnon prejudices and delusions, New York would probably rise to heights of very genuine greatness, and perhaps become the most splendid city known to history. For one thing, it would be able, once it had cut the painter, to erect barriers and conditions around the privilege of citizenship, and so save itself from the double flood that now swamps it—first, of broken-down peasants from Europe, and secondly and more important, of fugitive rogues from all the land West and South of the Hudson. Citizenship in New York is now worth no more than citizenship in Arkansas, for it is open to any applicant from the marshes of Bessarabia, and, still worse, to any applicant from Arkansas. The great city-states of history have been far more fastidious. Venice, Antwerp, London, the Hansa towns, Carthage, Tyre, Cnossus, Alexandria—they were all very sniffish. Rome began to wobble when the Roman franchise was extended to immigrants from the Italian hill country, *i.e.*, the Arkansas of that time. The Hansa towns, under the democracy that has been forced upon them, are rapidly sinking to the level of Chicago and Philadelphia. New York, free to put an end to this invasion, and to drive out thousands of the gorillas who now infest it—more, free from the eternal blackmail of laws made at Albany and the Methodist tyranny of laws made at Washington—could face the future with resolution and security, and in the course of a few generations it might conceivably become genuinely civilized. It would still stand as toll-taker on the chief highway of American commerce; it would still remain the premier banker and usurer of the Republic. But it would be loosed from the bonds which now tend so strenuously to drag it down to the level of the rest of the country. Free at last, it could cease to be the auction-room and bawdy-house that it is now, and so devote its brains and energy to the building up of a civilization.

IX.
Meditations in the Methodist Desert

I
The New Galahad

My agents in attendance upon the so-called moving pictures tell me that persons who frequent such shows begin to tire of Western films—that they are no longer roused to clapper-clawing by the spectacle of actors in patent-leather jack-boots murdering Indians and Mexicans. Several of the astute Ashkenazim in charge of the movie industry, noting that slackening of taste, have sought to find a new hero to replace the scout and cowboy, but so far without success. The children of today, young and old, seem to take no interest in pirates, nor are they stirred by train-robbers, safe-blowers and other such illicit adventurers. It can't be that the movie censorship is to blame, for the same thing is visible in the field of *belles lettres.* The dime novel, once so prosperous, is practically dead. The great deeds of the James brothers, known to every literate boy in my youth, are now forgotten. And so are the great deeds of Nick Carter and Old Sleuth: the detective has fallen with his prey.

What is needed, obviously, is a new hero for the infantry of the land, for if one is not quickly supplied there is some danger that the boys will begin admiring Y.M.C.A. secretaries, crooked members of the Cabinet and lecturers on sex hygiene. In this emergency I nominate the bootlegger—not, of course, the abject scoundrel who peddles bogus Scotch in clubs and office buildings, but the dashing, romantic, defiant fellow who brings the stuff up from the Spanish Main. He is, indeed, almost an ideal hero. He is the true heir, not only of the old-time Indian fighters and train-robbers, but also of the tough and barnacled deep-water sailors, now no more. He faces the perils of the high seas in a puny shallop, and navigates the worst coast in the world in contempt of wind and storm.

Think of him lying out there on wild nights in Winter, with the waves piling mountain-high and the gale standing his crazy little craft on her beam! Think of him creeping in in his motor-boat on Christmas Eve, risking his life that the greatest of Christian festivals may be celebrated in a Christian and respectable manner! Think of him soaked and freezing, facing his exile and its hardships uncomplainingly, saving his money that his old mother may escape the poor-farm, that his wife may have her operation for gall-stones, that his little children may be decently fed and clad, and go to school regularly, and learn the principles of Americanism!

This brave lad is not only the heir of Jesse James and Ned Buntline; he is also the heir of John Hancock and of all the other heroes who throttled the accursed Hun in 1776. All the most gallant among them were smugglers, and in their fragile craft they brought in, not only rum, but also liberty. The Revolution was not only against the person of the Potsdam tyrant, George III; it was also, and especially, against harsh and intolerable laws—the worst of them the abhorrent Stamp Act. But was the Stamp Act worse than Prohibition? I leave it to any fair man. Prohibition, in fact, is a hundred times as foul, false, oppressive and tyrannical. If the Stamp Act was worth a Revolution, the Prohibition is worth a massacre and an earthquake. Well, it has already bred its Hancocks, and soon or late, no doubt, it will breed its Molly Pitchers, Paul Reveres and Mad Anthony Waynes. Liberty, driven from the land by the Methodist White Terror, has been given a refuge by the hardy boys of the Rum Fleet. In their bleak and lonely exile they cherish her and keep her alive. Some day, let us hope, they will storm the coast, slit the gullets of her enemies, and restore her to her dominion, The lubbers of the land have limber necks; their blood runs pale and yellow. But on the roaring deep there are still men who are colossally he, and when the bugle calls they will not fail.

2
Optimist vs. Optimist

If these heroes *do* fail, alas, alas, then all will be lost, including honor. For there is not the slightest sign of revolt among the craven hordes who cling to the land, ignominiously dependent for their very existence as Christians upon the gallant fellows beyond the twelve-mile limit. They simply go on hoping against hope. Each successive Congress is to relieve them, rescue them, restore the liberties bequeathed to them by the Fathers. And each successive Congress does nothing of the kind. Nor, I believe, will any one coming hereafter. Congress is made up eternally of petty scoundrels, pusillanimous poltroons, highly vulnerable and cowardly men: they will never risk provoking the full fire of the Anti-Saloon League. The notion that such degraded fellows will ever rise up and put down Prohibition, so fondly cherished by the wets, is thus a snare and a mocking, and so is the notion that they will presently find a way to enforce it, cherished by the drys. Optimist eat optimist! As for me, can find no reason whatever for believing that, within the lifetime of men now living, the voluptuous consumption of alcohol will be countenanced by law in the Republic, and neither do I see any reason for believing that it will ever be stopped, nor, indeed, any reason for believing that any serious effort will be made to stop it.

It is commonly argued by the more impatient and worthy opponents of the Methodist millennium that the Eighteenth Amendment was slipped through Congress and the State legislatures against the wishes of the majority of American freemen —that the thing was accomplished by a sort of trick, partly political and partly magical. It is further argued that, had the soldiers who were then abroad, fighting for human liberty, been at home and voting, they would have piled up such majorities for wet candidates that both Houses of Congress would have been made proof against the Anti-Saloon League. It seems to me that both contentions are unsound. The Eighteenth Amendment, when it was passed, actually had a majority behind it, and I incline to think that that majority was a very substantial one. What made it so large was simply the war hysteria of the time. *Homo boobiens* was scientifically rowelled and run amok with the news that all the German brewers of the country were against the amendment; he observed himself that all German sympathizers, whether actual Germans or not, were bitter opponents of it. His nights made dreadful by dreams of German spies, he was willing to do anything to put them down, and one of the things he was willing to do was to swallow Prohibition. When he recovered from his terror, it was too late; the first article of the Methodist Book of Discipline had been read into the Constitution, and there it remains today, an unpleasant fly in imperishable amber. The soldiers, had they been at home, would have gone the way of their lay brothers. They were, if anything, even more in terror of Germans than the latter, and even more eager to floor them and so get rid of them. In every camp and cantonment Y.M.C.A. secretaries addressed the conscripts daily, instructing them in the moral nature of the crusade they were engaged in. The effects are visible today in the familiar swineries of the American Legion; its members are still down with the war psychosis. Moreover, it is not to be forgotten that large numbers of soldiers could not have voted, even if they had been at home. For example, those who were minors. Again, the Southern Negroes. Yet again, the enormous number of aliens who were rushed to the trenches by the draft boards to relieve native patriots—in New York City alone, fully 25,000, most of them Russian Jews. Finally, it is to be recalled that there was no plebiscite on Prohibition—that the men who put it into the Constitution were all safely in office at the time the test suddenly confronted them.

But what of the state of public opinion today? Isn't it a fact that hundreds of thousands of persons who were in favor of Prohibition in 1919 are now so disgusted by its colossal failure that they have turned violently against it? I doubt it. I know of no such person. I know of a great many persons who, though they voted for Prohibition when they had the chance, or, at all events, favored it, now guzzle like actors or policemen, but I believe that substantially all of them, if the thing were put up to them tomorrow, would be for it again. Whoever believes that they have changed heart is a very poor student of the Puritan psyche. What a Puritan advocates and what he does have no necessary connection. The late Anthony Comstock was a diligent collector of dirty books, and used to entertain favored callers by exhibiting his worst specimens to them. Nevertheless, Comstock was honestly in favor of suppressing such books, and would have gone to the extreme length of giving up his own recreation if he had ever been convinced that it would have helped the cause. To the Puritan, indeed, moral obligation is something quite outside personal conduct, and has very little contact with it. He may be, in private, an extremely gross and porcine fellow, and he frequently is, but that fact doesn't diminish his veneration for his ethical ideal in the slightest. Brought to the mark, he always sticks to that ideal, however absurdly his conduct clashes with it. As everyone knows, he is rather more prone than most other men to commit fornication, particularly in its more sordid and degrading forms; nevertheless, it is impossible to imagine him advocating any relaxation of the prevailing sexual taboos, however beneficial it would be. Again, as everyone also knows, he is very apt, when he drinks at all, to make a hog of himself, for the amiable drinking customs of civilized men are beyond him; nevertheless, it is impossible to imagine him admitting specifically that any man has a right to drink at all. This last fact explains something that often puzzles foreign observers: the relative smallness and impotence of anti-Prohibition organizations in America, despite the great amount of gabbling against Prohibition that goes on. It is due to the Puritan's fear of appearing on the side of the devil. He will drink in private, but he will not defend the practise in public.

It thus seems to me that so long as Puritanism remains the dominant philosophy in America—and certainly it shows no sign of relaxing its hold upon the low-caste Anglo-Saxon majority—it will be quite hopeless to look for an abandonment of Prohibition, or even for any relaxation of its extravagant and probably unconstitutional excesses. But for precisely the same reason it seems to me to be very unlikely that Prohibition will ever be enforced, or, indeed, that any honest effort will ever be made to enforce it. For the Puritan's enthusiasm for the moral law is always grounded, at least in large part, upon a keen realization that it is, after all, only an ideal—that it may be evaded whenever the temptation grows strong enough—that he himself may evade it, readily and safely. Like every other man, he likes to kick up now and then, and forget his holiest principles. He achieves this kicking up by sinning. When drinking was perfectly lawful, he got no pleasure out of it and so tried to put it down, but now that it is against the law he delights in it, and so long as he delights in it he will keep on doing it. If the Seventh Commandment were repealed tomorrow, military marriages would decrease 95 per cent. in rural America, and the great hotels at Atlantic City would be given over to the bats and owls. Let us, therefore, neither delude ourselves nor get into sweats of Puritan-like fear. Prohibition officers will continue to beat the land for stills and bribes until you and I are long gone and forgotten, and bootleggers will continue to elude them. No genuinely wet President will be elected, save by accident, in our time, and no President will ever be able to enforce Prohibition. Respect for the Constitution will be heard of in every campaign, and then it will be forgotten for four years more. It will give candidates something to talk about, but it will not give the rest of us anything to worry about.

3
Caveat for the Defense

The wets, I often think, are worse frauds than the drys. For example, consider their great current eagerness to assure everyone that they are absolutely against the saloon—that they would not revive it for an instant, even if they could. All of their spokesmen stop short dramatically after demanding the restoration of light wines and beer; they are virtuously opposed, it would appear, to all forms of hard liquor, as they are opposed to the saloon. In this position I can detect nothing respectable. Either the advocates of it are hypocrites trying to fool the Prohibitionists with pious protestations, or they have been themselves corrupted by Methodist superstitions. The plain fact is, of course, that the saloon, at its worst, was a great deal better than any of the substitutes that have grown up under Prohibition—nay, that it was a great deal better than the ideal substitutes imagined by the Prohibitionists: for example the Y.M.C.A. And it must be equally plain that light wines and beer would not always satisfy the yearning of the normal man for alcoholic refreshment—that there are times when his system, if he is sound in body, craves far stronger stuff. To say that such a normal man, at five o'clock in the afternoon, wants to drink a *Humpen* of beer, or that, on a cold Winter morning, his inner urge would be met by half a bottle of Pontet Canet is to say something so absurd that the mere statement of it is sufficient refutation. The fact is, of course, that the last chance to exile hard liquors for light wines and beer went glimmering when the Eighteenth Amendment was ratified. In 1918, perhaps, the scheme had a certain plausibility, for the American consumption of spirits had been declining for years, and very good beer, imported from Germany and Bohemia, was everywhere obtainable at low prices, and the use of wine, chiefly because of the influence of Italian restaurants and the propaganda of the California vinegrowers, was rapidly increasing. But the years of Prohibition have reconverted Americans into a nation of whiskey and gin drinkers, as they were before the Germans brought in lager beer in the fifties of the last century. Light wines and beer, I believe, would not satisfy them now, even at meals; there would be just as much bootlegging under a modified Volstead Act as there is today. Prohibition has restored the hard guzzling of Daniel Webster's day.

As for the saloon, the case against it, as voiced by both Prohibitionists and anti-Probibitionists, is chiefly based upon a recollection of what the thing was at its lowest and worst, which is just as sensible as arguing against Christianity on the ground that a certain minority of the rev. clergy are notorious swine. The utterly vicious saloons were always relatively rare, even along the waterfront, and an honest execution of the laws in force before Prohibition would have exterminated them in ten days. Their existence was a proof, not that the saloon itself was inherently evil, but simply that it could be made evil by corrupt government. To blame it for that fact would be like blaming the Constitution for the fact that Federal judges habitually violate it. The normal saloon, I am convinced, was not an evil influence in its vicinage, but a good one. It not only enabled the poor man to effect that occasional escape from wife and children which every man must make if he would remain sane; it also threw him into a society palpably better than that of his home or his workshop, and accustomed him to refinements which unquestionably improved him. The conversation of a precinct leader or of a brewery collector would make but little impression, I daresay, in the Century Club, on the Harvard campus or in the cloakrooms of the United States Senate, but in the average saloon of a poor neighborhood it took on an unmistakable dignity and authority. This collector (or *Todsäufer*, as he was called) had fresh news; he was a man of comparatively large affairs; he had an air about him of the great world; most important of all, he was professionally communicative and affable. The influence of such a man upon the customers of the place, all of whom were bidden to drink and permitted to converse with him, was necessarily for the good. He was, in every sense comprehensible to them, a better man than they were. He had the use of more money; he dressed better; he knew more; he couched his ideas in subtler and more graceful terms; he was better bathed and had better table manners. The effect of his visits, though perhaps not as massive, was comparable to the effect that would have been worked by visits by, say, Bishop Manning or Dr. Nicholas Murray Butler. In his presence discussion took on a higher tone, and he left behind him, in many a simple heart, an aspiration toward nobler things.

But it was not only the *Todsäufer* who was a missionary of light and a pattern of the amenities; so also was the saloon itself. It represented the only concept of beauty and dignity that ever entered into the lives of many of its customers. Surrounded all day by the inconceivable hideousness of the American workshop, and confronted on their return from work by the depressing ugliness of homes outfitted out of department-stores and on the instalment plan, with slatternly women and filthy children as the fauna of the scene, they found themselves, in the saloon, in a markedly superior milieu. Here some regard was given to æsthetics. Here was relatively pretentious architecture. Here were polished hardwoods, resplendent mirrors, comfortable chairs, glittering glassware and metals, innumerable small luxuries. Here, above all, was an attempt at genuine cleanliness. The poor saloons of the by-streets were not to be compared, of course, to the superb drinking-rooms of the great hotels, but they were at least much cleaner than any of the homes or factories surrounding them, and they were at least more beautiful than the adjacent livery-stables, cigar-stores, barber-shops and Methodist Little Bethels. Furthermore, they set forth an example of life upon a more urbane and charming scale. Men had to be more polite in saloons than they were at home; if they were not, they ran risks of colliding with the fists of their fellow patrons and with the bartender's Excaliburs, the bung-starter and ice-pick. The braggart and bully here met his quick doom; the unsocial fellow felt the weight of public disapproval; the ignoramus learned the bitter taste of sniffs and sneers. Life was more spacious spiritually and more luxurious physically. Instead of the nicked chinaware of his home the customer encountered shining glass; instead of spitting out of the window or on the floor he discharged himself into magnificent brass spittoons or into the brook that ran under the bar-rail; instead of the ghastly fried beefsteaks and leathery delicatessen of his wife's cuisine, he ate appetizing herring, delicate *Wienerwürste*, well-devised *Kartoffelsalat*, celery, olives, and even such exotic titbits as *Blutwurst*, *Pumpernickel*, *Bohnensalat* and caviare.

To argue that such luxuries and amenities had no effect is to argue utter nonsense. I believe fully that the rise of the latter-day saloon (a product of the financing of saloonkeepers by wealthy brewers, so much denounced by superficial sociologists) had a very benign effect upon American manners. It purged the city workmen of their old boorishness and pugnacity; it taught them the difference between mere fodder and civilized food; it shamed them into a certain cleanliness; it gave them some dim comprehension of design and ornamentation. In more than one American city the influence of the saloon is visible today in ecclesiastical architecture, and everywhere it is visible in theatre architecture. I name one thing specifically: the use of polished hardwoods. The first parquetry ever seen in America was in saloons. And so was the first tile-work. And so was the first plate-glass. Where the saloon reached its highest development there American life became richest and most expansive. The clatter against it is ignorant, unfair, philistine and disingenuous.

4
Portrait of an Ideal World

That alcohol in dilute aqueous solution, when taken into the human organism, acts as a depressant, not as a stimulant, is now so much a commonplace of knowledge that even the more advanced varieties of physiologists are beginning to be aware of it. The intelligent layman no longer resorts to the jug when he has important business before him, whether intellectual or manual; he resorts to it after his business is done, and he desires to release his taut nerves and reduce the steam-pressure in his spleen. Alcohol, so to speak, unwinds us. It raises the threshold of sensation and makes us less sensitive to external stimuli, and particularly to those that are unpleasant. It reduces and simplifies the emotions. Putting a brake upon all the qualities which enable us to get on in the world and shine before our fellows—for example, combativeness, shrewdness, diligence, ambition,—it releases the qualities which mellow us and make our fellows love us—for example, amiability, generosity, toleration, humor, sympathy. A man who has taken aboard two or three cocktails is less competent than he was before to steer a battleship down the Ambrose Channel, or to cut off a leg, or to draw up a deed of trust, or to conduct Bach's B minor mass, but he is immensely more competent to entertain a dinner party, or to admire a pretty girl, or to *hear* Bach's B minor mass. The harsh, useful things of the world, from pulling teeth to digging potatoes, are best done by men who are as starkly sober as so many convicts in the death-house, but the lovely and useless things, the charming and exhilarating things, are best done by men with, as the phrase is, a few sheets in the wind. *Pithecanthropus erectus* was a teetotaler, but the angels, you may be sure, know what is proper at 5 P.M.

All this is so obvious that I marvel that no utopian has ever proposed to abolish all the sorrows of the world by the simple device of getting and keeping the whole human race gently stewed. I do not say drunk, remember; I say simply gently stewed—and apologize, as in duty bound, for not knowing how to describe the state in a more seemly phrase. The man who is in it is a man who has put all of his best qualities into his show-case. He is not only immensely more amiable than the cold sober man; he is immeasurably more decent. He reacts to all situations in an expansive, generous and humane manner. He has become more liberal, more tolerant, more kind. He is a better citizen, husband, father, friend. The enterprises that make human life on this earth uncomfortable and unsafe are never launched by such men. They are not makers of wars; they do not rob and oppress anyone; they invent no such plagues as high tariffs, 100 per cent. Americanism and Prohibition. All the great villainies of history, from the murder of Abel to the

Treaty of Versailles, have been perpetrated by sober men, and chiefly by teetotalers. But all the charming and beautiful things, from the Song of Songs to terrapin *à la* Maryland, and from the nine Beethoven symphonies to the Martini cocktail, have been given to humanity by men who, when the hour came, turned from well water to something with color to it, and more in it than mere oxygen and hydrogen.

I am well aware, of course, that getting the whole human race stewed and keeping it stewed, year in and year out, would present formidable technical difficulties. It would be hard to make the daily dose of each individual conform exactly to his private needs, and hard to get it to him at precisely the right time. On the one hand there would be the constant danger that large minorities might occasionally become cold sober, and so start wars, theological disputes, moral, reforms, and other such unpleasantnesses. On the other hand, there would be danger that other minorities might proceed to actual intoxication, and so annoy us all with their fatuous bawling or maudlin tears. But such technical obstacles, of course, are by no means insurmountable. Perhaps they might be got around by abandoning the administration of alcohol *per ora*, and distributing it instead by impregnating the air with it. I throw out the suggestion, and pass on. Such questions are for men skilled in therapeutics, government and business efficiency. They exist today and their enterprises often show a high ingenuity, but, being chiefly sober, they devote too much of their time to harassing the rest of us. Half-stewed, they would be ten times as humane, and perhaps at least half as efficient. Thousands of them, relieved of their present anti-social duties, would be idle, and eager for occupation. I trust to them in this small matter. If they didn't succeed completely, they would at least succeed partially.

The objection remains that even small doses of alcohol, if each followed upon the heels of its predecessor before the effects of the latter had worm off, would have a deleterious effect upon the physical health of the race—that the death-rate would increase, and whole categories of human beings would be exterminated. The answer here is that what I propose is not lengthening the span of life, but augmenting its joys. Suppose we assume its duration is reduced 20 per cent. My reply is that its delights will be increased at least 100 per cent. Misled by statisticians, we fall only too often into the error of worshiping mere figures. To say that A will live to be eighty and B will die at forty is certainly not to argue plausibly that A is more to be envied than B. A, in point of fact, may have to spend all of his eighty years in Kansas or Arkansas, with nothing to eat save corn and hog-meat and nothing to drink save polluted river water, whereas B may put in his twenty years of discretion upon the Côte d'Azure, *wie Gott im Frankreich*. It is my contention that the world I picture, even assuming the average duration of human life to be cut down 50 per cent., would be an infinitely happier and more charming world than that we live in today—that no intelligent human being, having once tasted its peace and joy, would go back voluntarily to the harsh brutalities and stupidities that we now suffer, and idiotically strive to prolong. If intelligent Americans, in these depressing days, still cling to life and try to stretch it out longer and longer, it is surely not logically, but only atavistically. It is the primeval brute in them that hangs on, not the man. The man knows only too well that ten years in a genuinely civilized and happy country would be infinitely better than a geological epoch under the curses he must face and endure every day.

Moreover, there is no need to admit that the moderate alcoholization of the whole race would materially reduce the duration of life. A great many of us are moderately alcoholized already, and yet manage to survive quite as long as the blue-noses. As for the blue-noses themselves, who would repine if breathing alcohol-laden air brought them down with delirium tremens and so sterilized and exterminated them? The advantage to the race in general would be obvious and incalculable. All the worst strains—which now not only persist, but even prosper—would be stamped out in a few generations, and so the average human being would move appreciably away from, say, the norm of a Baptist clergyman in Georgia and toward the norm of Shakespeare, Mozart and Goethe. It would take aeons, of course, to go all the way, but there would be progress with every generation, slow but sure. Today, it must be manifest, we make no progress at all; instead we slip steadily backward. That the average civilized man of today is inferior to the average civilized man of two or three generations ago is too plain to need arguing. He has less enterprise and courage; he is less resourceful and various; he is more like a rabbit and less like a lion. Harsh oppressions have made him what he is. He is the victim of tyrants. . . . Well, no man with two or three cocktails in him is a tyrant. He may be foolish but he is not cruel. He may be noisy, but he is also genial, tolerant, generous and kind. My proposal would restore Christianity to the world. It would rescue mankind from moralists, pedants and brutes.

X.
Essay in Constructive Criticism

I

ONE of the defects in the American system of government, if so superb a confection of the human mind and heart may be said, without indecency, to have any defects at all, lies in the fact that it fails to provide swift and condign punishment for the special crimes of public officials. Even when their wrong-doings take the form of offenses against the ordinary criminal statutes of the realm—as, for example, embezzlement, conversion, blackmail, armed entry, kidnaping or common assault—it seems to be very difficult to bring them under the lash of justice; they enjoy, as it were, an unwritten immunity to criminal process, running with the constitutional immunity of United States Senators, who cannot be taken by the *gendarmerie*, even for adultery or bootlegging, while the Senate is in session. The thugs and perjurers of the so-called Department of Justice, during the reign of the Martyr Wilson, committed nearly all the crimes of fraud and violence on the books, and yet, so far as I know, not one of them was ever punished, or, indeed, so much as prosecuted. Several Federal district attorneys, toward the end of that festival of oppression and worse, protested against it publicly, and there were bitter yells from specialists in human liberty and from the relatives, lodge-brothers and creditors of some of the victims, but no Federal grand jury indicted any of the criminals, and no Federal judge condemned them to the hulks. To this day, if my agents are to be believed, the same thing is going on, though perhaps on a more modest scale. Prohibition enforcement officers in all parts of the country are breaking into houses without warrants, destroying property without due process of law, engaging in blackmail in a wholesale manner, and assaulting and murdering citizens almost at their will, and yet one seldom hears of them going to jail for it, and I know of none who has been hanged.

When it comes to crimes that are peculiar to public officials and that arise out of the nature of their legal status, as bigamy and wife-beating arise out of the nature of a married man's, the case is even worse. I allude here to such special offenses as dissipating the public funds, loading the public rolls with useless and pediculous job-holders, letting contracts and franchises to political and private friends, converting public property to private uses, condoning crimes against the government, and administering the laws in a partial and dishonest manner—all of them impossible to the mere citizen and taxpayer, as default in alimony is impossible to the bachelor. Here the ordinary criminal statutes are obviously ineffective, and of special statutes there are almost none. What was the late Mr. Fall guilty of? His accusers, it appears, had to fall back upon the vague charge of conspiracy, which was not unlike accusing a burglar of trespass. With the general run of official delinquents it is impossible to go even so far. Their crimes have no names, and no adequate punishments. Certain high dignitaries, when taken in gross malfeasances, may be impeached, and most lesser ones, though not all, may be cashiered. But neither punishment is harsh enough to be a deterrent, and neither is swift and sure. Since the first days of the Republic but eight Federal job-holders have been brought before the bar of the Senate on impeachment by the House of Representatives, and of these but two have been found guilty and removed from office. Both of the latter were judges; one was convicted of drunkenness on the bench and the other of corrupt dealings with litigants. Is it argued seriously by anyone that, during all those years, but two Federal judges have been guilty of such offenses? Is it argued, indeed, that the bench is wholly guiltless of them, and of all other crimes, today?

Many of the sitting Federal judges, as a matter of fact, are obviously unfit for the duties they have to perform. Some of them owe their jobs to litigants who are habitually before them, and others are admittedly beholden to such corrupt agencies as the Anti-Saloon League. Is it maintained that such dubious fellows make competent and respectable judges, or that the clumsy and enormously costly process of impeachment offers a practicable means of dealing with their frequent and flagrant peccadillos? Plainly not. Even when their obscenities upon the bench become publicly scandalous they are protected by the fact that impeachment is essentially a political, not a judicial process, and that in consequence it is excessively slow and uncertain—in other words, by the fact that it lacks the very characters which legal punishment fundamentally needs. It is, as a matter of practise, almost as safe for a Federal judge to take care of his fellow-golfers and scofflaws as it is for a Prohibition officer to blackmail a bootlegger or for an agent of the Department of Justice to manufacture perjury against so-called Reds. If he belongs to the party in control of Congress he cannot be impeached for any crime short of highway robbery or piracy on the high seas, and even if he belongs to the minority party the citizen who complains of him must be extremely influential to be heard at all, and extremely rich to meet the heavy costs of prosecuting him. In brief, the remedy against him that is offered by the Constitution and the laws is, in substance, no remedy at all. No matter how grossly he violates his oath and the decencies, he commonly remains upon the bench until some grateful litigant or syndicate of litigants offers him a better job.

Moreover, it must be plain that the punishment of impeachment and removal from office, or of removal by executive order, without impeachment, is usually grossly inadequate. When job-holders become so unbearably corrupt or incompetent that they are actually separated from their jobs, they commonly deserve hanging, or, at least, long confinement in the hoosegow. Simply to turn them out, leaving them free to aspire to other offices, is as absurd as it would be to limit a burglar's punishment to kicking him out of the house. The case of the late Denby, Secretary of the Navy, is in point. I have no opinion as to the guilt or innocence of the gentleman; I merely recall the fact that he was accused of the very grave offense of dissipating the national property and imperilling the national defense. It would be difficult to imagine anything more flagrantly anti-social, more thoroughly vicious, more damaging to the common weal; put beside it, such ordinary crimes as arson and larceny seemed relatively harmless. Nevertheless, the worst punishment that could be inflicted upon Denby was the banal one of depriving him of his office. It was impossible, for political reasons, to impeach him or even to attempt to impeach him, and he was simply turned out, with a file of high naval dignitaries saluting him as he left and a great crowd cheering him as he got home. Here cause and effect took on a disproportion that was truly colossal; it was almost as if Czolgosz had been fined $10 for dispatching McKinley. If Denby was innocent, he deserved the salute and the cheers without the loss of his job. And if he was guilty, if only of negligence, he plainly merited at least a geological epoch on Devil's Island.

2

In the effete monarchies of the continent of Europe, now happily abolished by God's will, there was, in the old days of sin, a far more intelligent and effective way of dealing with delinquent officials. Not only were they subject, when taken in downright corruption, to the ordinary processes of the criminal laws; in addition, they were liable to prosecution in special courts for such offenses as were peculiar to their offices. In this business the abominable Prussian state, though founded by Satan, took the lead. It maintained a tribunal in Berlin that devoted itself wholly to the trial of officials accused of malfeasance, corruption, tyranny and incompetence, and any citizen was free to lodge a complaint with the learned judges. The trial was public and in accordance with rules fixed by law. An official found guilty could be punished summarily and in a dozen different ways. He could be reprimanded, reduced in rank, suspended from office for a definite period, transferred to a less desirable job, removed from the rolls altogether, fined, or sent to jail. If he was removed from office he could be deprived of his right to a pension in addition, or fined or jailed in addition. He could be made to pay damages to any citizen he had injured, or to apologize publicly. All this, remember, was in addition to his liability under the ordinary law, and the statutes specifically provided that he could be punished twice for the same offense, once in the ordinary courts and once in the administrative court. Thus, a Prussian official who, imitating the daily routine of the agents of our own Treasury or Department of Justice, assaulted a citizen, invaded his house without a warrant, and seized his property without process of law, could be deprived of his office and fined heavily by the administrative court, sent to jail by an ordinary court, and forced to pay damages to his victim by either or both. Our Federal judges, as a matter of everyday practise, issue thousands of injunctions depriving citizens of their right to a jury trial, to the sanctity of domicile and to lawful assemblage, all guaranteed by the Bill of Rights. Had a Prussian judge, overcome by *kaiserliche* passion, undertaken anything of the sort in those far-off days of despotism, any aggrieved citizen might have haled him before the administrative court and recovered heavy damages from him, beside enjoying the felicity of seeing him transferred to some dismal swamp in East Prussia, to listen all day to the unintelligible perjury of Poles. The law specifically provided that responsible officials should be punished, not more leniently than ordinary offenders, but more severely. If a corrupt policeman got six months a corrupt chief of police got two years. More, these statutes were enforced with Prussian barbarity, and the jails were constantly full of errant officials.

I do not propose, of course, that such medieval laws be set up in the United States. We have, indeed, gone far enough in imitating the Prussian system already; if we go much further the moral and enlightened nations of the world will have to unite in a new crusade to put us down. Hints to that effect are not lacking even now; they are heard in England every time the Department of State revives the question of the Bahaman rum trade, and in France every time there is mention of the war debt. As a matter of fact, the Prussian scheme would probably prove ineffective in the Republic, if only because it involved setting up one gang of job-holders to judge and punish another gang. This worked very well in Prussia before the country was civilized by force of arms because, as everyone knows, a Prussian judge was trained in ferocity from infancy, and regarded every man arraigned before him as guilty *ipso facto*; in fact, any thought of a prisoner's possible innocence was abhorrent to him as a reflection upon the *Polizei*, and, hence, by inference, upon the Throne, the whole monarchic idea, and God. But in America, even if they had no other sentiment in common, which would be rarely, judge and prisoner would often be fellow-Democrats or fellow-Republicans, and hence jointly interested in protecting their party against scandal and its members against the loss of their jobs. The operations of the Department of Justice under Mr. Daugherty showed how this community of interest impedes the flow of justice even today; it would be far more obstructive, obviously, if job-holders had to execute the laws against other job-holders, and not merely against the friends of other job-holders. Moreover, the Prussian system has another plain defect: the punishments it provides are, in the main, platitudinous and banal. They lack dramatic quality, and they lack ingenuity and appropriateness. To punish a judge taken in judicial crim. con. by fining him or sending him to jail is a bit too facile and obvious. What is needed is a system (*a*) that does not depend for its execution upon the good-will of job-holders, and (*b*) that provides swift, certain and unpedantic punishments, each fitted neatly to its crime. Such a system, after due prayer, I have devised. It is simple, it is unhackneyed, and I believe that it would work. It is divided into two halves. The first half takes the detection and punishment of the crimes of job-holders away from courts of impeachment, congressional smelling committees, and other such agencies—*i.e.*, away from other job-holders—and vests it in the whole body of free citizens, male and female. The second half provides that any member of that body, having looked into the acts of a job-holder and found him delinquent, may punish him instantly and on the spot, and in any manner that seems appropriate and convenient—and that in case this punishment involves physical damage to the job-holder, the ensuing inquiry by the grand jury or coroner shall confine itself strictly to the question whether the job-holder deserved what he got. In other words, I propose that it shall be no longer *malum in se* for a citizen to pummel, cow-hide, kick, gouge, cut, wound, bruise, maim, burn, club, bastinado, flay or even lynch a job-holder, and that it shall be *malum prohibitum* only to the extent that that the punishment exceeds the job-holder's deserts. The amount of this excess, if any, may be determined very conveniently by a petit jury, as other questions of guilt are now determined. The flogged judge, or Congressman, or Prohibition officer, or other job-holder, on being discharged from hospital—or his chief heir, in case he has perished—goes before a grand jury and makes complaint, and, if a true bill is found, a petit jury is empanelled and all the evidence is put before it. If it decides that the job-holder deserved the punishment inflicted upon him, the citizen who inflicted it is acquitted with honor. If, on the contrary, it decides that this punishment was excessive, then the citizen is adjudged guilty of assault, mayhem, murder, or whatever it is, in a degree apportioned to the difference between what the job-holder deserved and what he got, and punishment for that excess follows in the usual course.

3

The advantages of this plan, I believe, are too patent to need argument. At one stroke it removes all the legal impediments which now make the punishment of a recreant job-holder so hopeless a process and enormously widens the range of possible penalties. They are now stiff and, in large measure, illogical; under the system I propose they could be made to fit the crime precisely. Say a citizen today becomes convinced that a certain judge is a jackass—that his legal learning is defective, his sense of justice atrophied, and his conduct of cases before him tyrannical and against decency. As things stand, it is entirely impossible to do anything about it. A judge could not be impeached on the mere ground that he is a jackass; the process is far too costly and cumbersome, and there are too many judges liable to the charge. Nor is anything to be gained by denouncing him publicly and urging all good citizens to vote against him when he comes up for re-election, for his term may have ten or fifteen years to run, and even if it expires tomorrow and he is defeated the chances are good that his successor will be quite as bad, and maybe even worse. Moreover, if he is a Federal judge he never comes up for re-election at all; once he has been appointed by the President of the United States, at the advice of his more influential clients and with the consent of their agents in the Senate, he is safe until he is so far gone in senility that he has to be propped on the bench with pillows. But now imagine any citizen free to approach him in open court and pull his nose! Or even, in aggravated cases, to cut off his ears, throw him out of the window, or knock him in the head with an ax! How vastly more attentive he would be to his duties! How diligently he would apply himself to the study of the law! How careful he would be about the rights of litigants before him! How polite and even suave he would become! For judges, like all the rest of us, are vain fellows: they do not enjoy having their noses pulled. Do not forget here that the ignominy resident in the operation would not be abated by the subsequent trial of the puller, even if he should be convicted and jailed. The fact would still be brilliantly remembered that at least one citizen had deemed the judge sufficiently a malefactor to punish him publicly, and to risk going to jail for it. A dozen such episodes, and the career of any judge would be ruined, even though the jails bulged with his critics. He could not maintain his dignity on the bench; even his own catchpolls would snicker at him behind their hands, especially if he showed a cauliflower ear, a black eye or a scar over his bald head. Moreover, soon or late some citizen who had at him would be acquitted by a petit jury, and then, obviously, he would have to retire. It might be provided by law, indeed, that he should be compelled to retire in that case—that an acquittal would automatically vacate the office of the complaining job-holder.

The present system, as I have said, has in late years eloquently demonstrated its ineffectiveness on a colossal scale in the great city of Washington, the seat of the First Chief of the Republic and of a hundred thousand job-holders of gradually lessening puissance, from members of the Cabinet down to janitors, messengers and bookkeepers. All efforts to impeach Daugherty failed; when he was got rid of at last it was by a blow below the belt; in the case of Denby, his fellow-Republicans of Detroit actually treated his dismissal as a martyrdom, and received him when he got home with a band of music and public prayers. If these eminent men were actually guilty of malfeasance in office they obviously deserved far more rigorous punishment; if they were guilty merely of carelessness and neglect they deserved a severe handling as public nuisances. Under the existing system they got what was virtually no punishment at all; under my system, at the most moderate guess, some bored and impatient citizen, during the long months when they were desperately hanging on to their jobs, would have at least ventured to duck them in the Potomac or set their shirt-tails afire. I doubt that any jury would have convicted him of excess, even had he held them under while he counted 100,000. The plain people could not make out just what they had done that was immoral, if anything; but there was an almost universal feeling that they were nuisances, and ought to be got rid of. Even if the citizen who, under my system, had laid hands upon them had been convicted subsequently and sent to jail, the weary newspaper readers of the land would have given three cheers for him, and he would have become a formidable candidate for the presidency on the completion of his term. Even Dr. Coolidge, I daresay, would have had a very friendly feeling for him, and perhaps might have sent him a box of cigars or some White House pies while he was in jail.

I present my system formally to the consideration of the Congress, and offer to explain it in greater detail before a joint session of both Houses at any time not in conflict with my literary engagements. I am no lawyer, to be sure. I once studied law for a space, but forgot it on closing the books. But I retain enough technic to be convinced that my scheme presents no constitutional difficulties. It violates no constitutional right that I am aware of; on the contrary, it specifically reaffirms the right to a trial by jury, now denied in a wholesale and shameless manner by the Federal courts. It sets up no new corps of corrupt and oppressive enforcement officers; it establishes no new jobs; it does not augment the already excessive powers of the police. If there is any lingering taint of injustice in it, then that injustice would be suffered by job-holders, nine-tenths of whom now rob and persecute the rest of us incessantly, and are fast habilitating the doctrine that we are *feræ naturæ* and have no rights that they are bound to respect. It is a system of criminal law that is democratic in the widest and loftiest sense. It augments the dignity and responsibility of the citizen, and tends to increase his concern with problems of government. It sets higher standards of conduct for public officers than prevail now, and makes corruption and incompetence dangerous. Above all, it breaks down the rigid and unintelligent formalism of our scheme of punishments, and makes it infinitely more pliant, appropriate and various. We have been tending for years to reduce all punishments to two: fine and imprisonment, the first usually no punishment at all, but a mere bribe to escape punishment, and the second often cruel and almost always ineffective. That this tendency is widely regarded as evil is shown by the extra-legal efforts to combat it that are made constantly by the Ku Klux Klan, the American Legion and other such agents of lynch law. My scheme would take over the rich ingenuities of these agents and give them formal legal sanction; it would restore to the art of putting down crime something of the fine bounce and gusto that it had in the Middle Ages, when tort and penalty were united by logical, and even, indeed, æsthetic bonds, and a judge who was imaginative and original was esteemed. The certainty of punishment would daunt the offender, and the uncertainty of its nature would fill him with dread. Once proceeded against, he would become enormously cautious and conscientious. A Congressman with his ears cut off, you may be sure, would not do it again. A judge, after two or three rocket flights through his court-room window, would be forced, by an irresistible psychological process, to give heed thereafter to the Constitution, the statutes, and the common rights of man. Even a police captain or a United States Senator, once floored with a bung-starter or rolled in a barrel, would begin to think.

I dedicate my plan to my country.

XI.
On the Nature of Man

I
The Animal That Thinks

THAT the great majority of human beings, even under our perfected Christian civilization, are still almost as incapable of rational thought as so many diamond-back terrapin—this is a fact to which we have all been made privy of late by the babbling of eminent psychologists. Granted. But let us not rashly assume that this infirmity is confined strictly to the nether herd—that, above the level where thinking may be said genuinely to begin, it goes on, level by level, to greater and greater heights of clarity and acumen. Nothing, indeed, of the sort. The curve goes upward for a while, but then it begins to flatten, and finally it dips very sharply. Thinking, indeed, is so recent an accomplishment phylogenetically that man is capable of it only in a narrow area, as he is capable of sight and hearing only in narrow areas. To one side lie the instinctive tropisms and intellectual peristaltic motions of the simple, rational only by a sort of pious license; to the other side lie the more complex but even more nonsensical speculations of metaphysicians. The difference between the two is vastly less than is commonly assumed; we are all misled by the sombre, portentous manner of the metaphysicians. The truth is that between a speech by a Salvation Army convert, a Southern Congressman or a Grand Goblin of the Rotary Club and a philosophical treatise by an American Neo-Realist there is no more to choose than between the puling of an infant and the puling of a veteran of the Civil War. Both show the human cerebrum loaded far beyond its Plimsoll mark; both, strictly speaking, are idiotic.

2
Veritas Odium Parit

An old human delusion, largely fostered by theologians, is the one to the effect that truth has a mysterious medicinal power—that its propagation makes the world better and man happier . . . *et cognoscetis veritatem, et veritas liberabit vos.* But is this so-called truth about truth true? It is not. The truth, nine times out of ten, is extremely disturbing and uncomfortable; if it is not grossly discreditable to someone it is apt to be painfully amazing to everyone. The masses of men are thus wise to hold it in suspicion, as they are wise to suspect that other delusion, liberty. Let us turn to an example. The most rational religious ideas held in modern times, at least among Christians, are probably those of the Unitarians; the most nonsensical are those of the Christian Scientists. Yet it must be obvious to every observer that the average Unitarian, even when he is quite healthy, which is not often, is a sour, conscience-striken and unhappy fellow, whereas, the average Christian Scientist, even when he is down with gall-stones, is full of a childish and enviable peace. The one is disquieted by his apprehension of damning facts about God and the universe; the other is lulled by his magnificent imbecilities. I have had the honor of knowing, in my time, a number of eminent philosophers, some of them intelligent. The happiest among the latter, in his moments of greatest joy, used to entertain himself by drawing up wills leaving his body to a medical college.

3
The Eternal Cripple

Man, at his best, remains a sort of one-lunged animal, never completely rounded and perfect, as a bacillus, say, is perfect. If he shows one valuable quality, it is almost unheard of for him to show any other. Give him a head, and he lacks a heart. Give him a heart of a gallon capacity, and his head holds scarcely a pint. The artist, nine times out of ten, is a dead-beat and given to the debauching of virgins, so-called. The patriot is a bigot, and, more often than not, a cad and a coward. The man of physical bravery is often on a level, intellectually, with a Baptist clergyman. The intellectual giant has bad kidneys and cannot thread a needle. In all my years of search in this world, from the Golden Gate in the West to the Vistula in the East, and from the Orkney Islands in the North to the Spanish Main in the South, I have never met a thoroughly moral man who was honorable.

4
The Test

Don't ask what delusion he entertains regarding God, or what mountebank he follows in politics, or what he springs from, or what he submits to from his wife. Simply ask how he makes his living. It is the safest and surest of all known tests. A man who gets his board and lodging on this ball in an ignominious way is inevitably an ignominious man.

5
National Characters

The character of a nation, like its mind, is always determined, not by the masses of its citizens, but by a small minority of resolute and influential men. Nothing, for example, could be more absurd than the common notion that the French, as a people, are gallant, courageous and fond of hazard. The truth is that they are mainly dull shopkeepers and peace-loving peasants, and have been driven into all their wars of conquest by their masters, who are extraordinarily prehensile and audacious. The French plain people bitterly disapproved the military enterprises of Bonaparte, and resisted his conscriptions by every means within their power. In the late war they abandoned themselves to a melodramatic despair after the first few months, frequently broke and ran under pressure, and were kept in the fight only by heroic devices. The apparent resolution of France was largely external. That is to say, it was supplied by England. Internally, it was confined to a small group of leaders, most of them professional adventurers, and many of them, such as Marshal Foch, of enemy blood. The French masses, despite the enormous military advantages on their side, were ready to quit after every losing battle, and after not a few—for example, the Verdun operations—they did quit.

The character of the Germans, as it was displayed during the war, was also foreign to the great majority of the German people. The Germans are not pugnacious by nature, nor have they any talent for organization; on the contrary, they are incurable particularists, and never meet without quarrelling. Their political history is a history of endless squabbles in the face of the enemy. Fully a half of them believed in Napoleon I at the time he was ravaging their country; in the late war millions of them were deceived by the late Woodrow's hypocritical Fourteen Points—a deliberate and successful device to divide and conquer them. The gigantic skill and resolution visible on the German side during the war were supplied by less than one per cent. of the German people, and so were the harsh, realistic theories which underlaid them. The average German was and is quite incapable of any such theories; they horrify him almost as much as they would horrify a member of the Lake Mohonk Conference. Once the one per cent. of dominating Germans had been disposed of by their heavy losses on the field, the rest of the nation turned out to be a mob of moony sentimentalists, hot for all the democratic fallacies ever heard of, and eager to put down every surviving man of genuine courage and enterprise. That mob will continue to pursue these chimeras until a new race of rulers arises—and then the world will once more mistake the ideas of those rulers for the ideas of the average German.

The English are judged just as inaccurately, and in the same way. There is, for example, the common notion that all Englishmen are good sportsmen, resolute in battle, generous in victory and calm in defeat. It would be difficult to imagine anything more ridiculous. The English masses are probably the worst sportsmen in the world, save only, perhaps, the American masses. During the war their hysterical whoops and yells deafened the universe, and after it was over the so-called khaki election brilliantly displayed the true color of their generosity. To this day, like their brethren of the Republic, they believe it to be quite honorable to pick a German's pocket or rob a German corpse. But there is in England a small minority of men, chiefly Celtic in blood, who practise good sportsmanship as a sort of substitute for religion, and these men are still influential enough to give the hue of their own character to what appears to be the general English character. Once they succumb to democracy, not even American Anglomaniacs will ever mention English sportsmanship again.

6
The Goal

The central aim of civilization, it must be plain, is simply to defy and correct the obvious intent of God, *e.g.*, that five per cent. of the people of Christendom shall die of smallpox every year, that the issue of every love affair shall be a succession of little strangers, that cows shall devote themselves wholly to nursing their calves, that it shall take longer to convey a message from New York to Chicago than it takes to convey one from New York to Newark, that the wicked shall be miserable and the virtuous happy. Has civilization a motto? Then certainly it must be "Not *Thy* will, O Lord, but *ours*, be done!"

7
Psychology at 5 A.M.

It is in the throes of sober second thought, of spiritual *Katzenjammer*, that men reveal their true souls. The Puritan always swears a bloody oath that he will never do it again. The civilized man simply resolves to be a bit more careful next time.

8
The Reward

The cadence at the end is always in the crystalline and sardonic key of C major. . . The heroic sweatings and strivings of the Knights Templar, for a whole age the marvel of Christendom, are now embalmed in a single essay by James Anthony Froude, M.A., LL.D., an historian of charming style but dubious accuracy. If it were not for that single essay, it would be difficult, if not impossible, for an inquirer of English speech to find out what their finish was, and why they perished from the earth. Their old stronghold in London is now—what? An office-building for lawyers, a roost for such rogues as they would have put to the sword at sight. And Palestine, for which they died by the thousand, is now given over to *Schnorrer* and *Meshulachim* from Grand street and the Mile End road.

9
The Altruist

A large part of altruism, even when it is perfectly honest, is grounded upon the fact that it is uncomfortable to have unhappy people about one.

This is especially true in family life. A man makes sacrifices to his wife's desires, not because he greatly enjoys giving up what he wants himself, but because he would enjoy it even less to see her cutting a sour face across the dinner table.

10
The Man of Honor

The difference between a moral man and a man of honor is that the latter regrets a discreditable act, even when it has worked and he has not been caught.

XII.
Bugaboo

ALL of the Great Thinkers of the world, East, West, North and South, have been alarming their customers, for two or three years past, with the same bugaboo. According to the New York *Times* and the Department of State, there must be a complete restoration of the capitalistic system in Russia and Mexico, or our sweet Christian civilization will go to pot. According to the masterminds of France, the Germans must first lose all their trade and then pay 10,000 cents on the dollar, or our sweet Christian civilization will go to pot. According to H. G. Wells, the Treaty of Versailles must be denounced by all parties to it, or our sweet Christian civilization will go to pot. And so on, and so on. On the main point the propagandists of all schools are unanimously agreed: that the civilization of the West teeters on the edge of an abyss, and that a few more wobbles will send it over. The barbarians once more thunder upon the gates of Rome. Let the turmoils within go on for a brief while longer, and they will burst in with their hellish cries, and every great boon and usufruct that men have sweated and died for since the days of Charlemagne, from the cathedral at Rheims to the pneumatic automobile tire, and from fiddle music to diphtheria antitoxin, and from the inferiority complex to the bichloride tablet, will vanish in one universal catastrophe. Blood drips from the moon; another general war impends. This war, according to Will H. Irwin, a soothsayer employed by the *Saturday Evening Post*, will be so colossal a butchery that there will be no survivors save a few undertakers and profiteers, and no material salvage save a few stone quarries and a couple of million bales of worthless bonds.

Personally, I should be glad to see such a war, for it seems to me that the human race has run on long enough—that the high gods would show unaccustomed sense if they dropped it into hell and so ended the farce. I know of no existing nation that deserves to live, and I know of very few individuals. But despite the fact that my wishes are thus on the side of Dr.

Irwin's thought, I find it quite impossible to follow him. In brief, I see absolutely no sign of a general *débâcle*. On the contrary, it seems to me that the thing we call civilization was never more secure than it is today, either in Europe or in America. More bloodshed, of course, is pretty certain to come; the French, to name only one people, are obviously headed for another shambles. But that is a small matter, almost a private matter. Even the complete destruction of France would not materially damage civilization, save, perhaps, in the eyes of touring American Puritans, a-search for a moral oasis. I also incline to think that England and the United States will be by the ears before many years have come and gone, and that one or the other of them, probably the United States, will get a severe beating. But they have fought before, and civilization was scarcely aware of it. Either could be wiped out utterly, and it would still be possible to buy Ford parts, Bibles, oil stocks, canned salmon, union suits, First Folio Shakespeares, hair tonics, books on sex hygiene, diamonds, coffins, dice, dog soap, glass eyes, and all the other great blessings of our Christian *Kultur*. Both could be destroyed, wholly and horribly, and men in Italy would continue to grow excellent wine, and men in Germany would continue to pursue the colloids and the cocci, and men in Scandinavia would continue to shiver and curse God through their long, grisly Winter nights, and so keep the world supplied with its normal doses of theology, metaphysics and political theory. Moreover, there are the Chinese. If the entire population of Christendom were disposed of by some cosmic delousing operation the Chinese would have a chance —a chance denied to them today, in free competition, by their superior dignity, decency and sense of honor.

The interdependence of nations, indeed, is much overestimated by sentimentalists, chiefly of the economic faculty. They permit the gyrations of foreign exchange to alarm them. But what is it to a man in Kansas, or Uruguay, or Saskatchewan, expressed in hard figures, that a million Poles have been slaughtered, or that the Turks have again ravaged Armenia, or that the British and Dutch are at odds over human liberty and the oil-wells of Mesopotamia, or that Belgrade has fallen, or that the French refuse to go back to work but propose to live hereafter by highway robbery? It is, at most, a matter of ten per cent. This is all he feels, and this is all he cares. If he shows any excitement or even any interest it is because some drive manager has played upon his credulities, as Dr. Wells seeks to play upon the credulities of all of us. For one I refuse to be alarmed. If Paris were burned tomorrow, I'd scarcely know it on my estates in Maryland, feeding upon my razor-back hams, listening to Caruso's ghost, and reading the state papers of Thomas Jefferson. Even if I tired of that idyllic life and went abroad, I'd admire the ruins quite as much as have ever admired the Trocadero or the Eiffel tower. Both, perhaps, would escape the fire—and no doubt the incendiaries would make off with the best things in the Luxembourg and the Louvre. Nor am I greatly alarmed by the current doctrine that the late war stamped out the best strains of all the contesting nations, and that they are rapidly sinking to the level of their lower classes. This alarm is raised in an inflammatory book called "Is America Safe for Democracy?" by one William McDougall, a Scotchman imported to civilize the sophomores at Harvard. The McDougall also raises and parades another hobgoblin, once a favorite of the immortal zany, Major-General Roosevelt. That is the bugaboo of race suicide, especially among the upper classes. The wops in the ditch and the Slovaks in the mining towns, it appears, breed up to the limit of human endurance, but bank presidents seldom have more than four or five legitimate children, and the great majority of poets, metaphysicians, Oxford dons, lady Ph.D.s, assyriologists and moving-picture actors are childless, and perhaps even sterile. At the present rate of reproduction, says Prof. McDougall, 1000 Harvard graduates of today will have but 50 descendants 200 years hence, whereas 1000 Rumanians will have 100,000.

But what of it? On the one hand this gay professor assumes far too readily that Harvard graduates, taking one with another, deserve to be ranked as first-rate men, and on the other hand he greatly overestimates the number of first-rate men needed to run the world, and to insure a reasonable rate of human progress. The fact is that the safeguarding and development of civilization are and always have been in the exclusive care of a very small minority of human beings of each generation, and that the rest of the human race consists wholly of deadheads. Consider, for example, the telephone, a very characteristic agent of Christian advancement. It has been invented, perfected, organized and brought to every door in our own time by less than 20 men—nay, by less than 10 men. All the others who have made it, financed and installed it have been simply trailers. All the rest of the human race has taken a free ride. The number of such first-rate men in the world is always overestimated, and it is fatuously assumed that they are identical with the wealthier minority of the population. Prof. Dr. McDougall himself falls into this last error. He proves—what everyone knew already—that the children of well-to-do parents are brighter, by pedagogical standards, than the children of poor folk, but this fact is of no significance. If it were, then pedagogues themselves would rank as first-rate men, which is an absurdity; they are, in fact, generally stupid, and seldom produce anything of value to the world. The test of a first-rate man is not to be made by the criteria of schoolmarms. It is to be made by asking the simple question: Has he ever said or done anything that was not said or done before, and is it something of positive and permanent value to the human race? If the answer is yes, then he belongs to the superior minority; if it is no, then he belongs to the mob, no matter how brilliantly he may pass examinations, and no matter how greatly he may prosper under the civilization that his superiors have fostered and developed.

The number of men who can pass this test is always extremely small—vastly smaller than the uncritical worshipers of politicians, university presidents, prima donna theologians, opera singers, lawyers, popular philosophers, successful authors and other such human Fords usually assume. How many exist at the present moment in the United States? I turn to "Who's Who in America" and find 23,443 names. But a brief inspection is sufficient to show that only a small minority are borne by first-rate men. I run over page after page and find nothing but Fords—an army general who has done absolutely nothing save obey orders and draw his pay, three authors of the eighth rate, five or six pedagogues, a theologian or two, a Federal judge—who ever heard of a Federal judge who left the world more intelligent, more virtuous or more efficient than he found it?—a publisher of bad books, two Congressmen, a bishop. I begin to despair. Finally, I find a first-rate man: Bush of the Bush Terminals. One in 35. The proportion, I think, is fair for the whole book. This makes 670 first-rate Americans in our time. Call it 700 to be safe. But race-suicide among the upper classes will make it impossible to produce even the 700 in the next generation? Nonsense! It is not necessary that *every* first-rate man leave children behind him; it is only necessary that a few of them in each generation do so. Nature will do the rest. The first-rate character may be concealed for a generation or two, but soon or late it will reveal itself, and sometimes in many individuals. This explains the common notion that first-rate men are often produced in low life, *i.e.*, the case of Lincoln. They are, but not by low-lifers. Here the devil helps the angels, and the sinfulness of man takes on a high human utility. Often the cross is concealed in forgotten generations. The good blood is apparently lost in the flood of proletarian bilge—but suddenly it begins to run red and clear, and the platitudinarians have another up-from-slavery chapter to wag their ears over. I believe fully that the first-rate men of the world constitute a distinct and separate species—that they have little, if anything, in common with the lower orders of men. But the two races, fortunately for human progress, are mutually fertile. If they ever cease to be, then God help us all! But there is absolutely no sign that they are ceasing to be. So long as they remain as they are there need be no worry about the future of civilization. The danger is that first-rate men may grow too numerous, and so arouse the hatred of the lower orders, as happened in Greece. The United States now accommodates 700. If the number rose to 1000 I fear that the churches, the newspapers, Congress and the American Legion would grow restless, and that the catastrophe dreamed of by Prof. McDougall would begin to cast its shadows before.

Meanwhile, all the current pulling of long faces is absurd. There is not the slightest sign that the basic elements of modern civilization, such as it is, are in any danger, proximately or remotely. Europe, at the moment, is a bit weary, but no actual barbarians are thundering at the gate; all the recognizable barbarians, in fact, are retreating sadly into their native jungles, with troubles of their own. There is no decline in Christian *morale*; if anything, there is far too much Christian *morale* on tap. The one thing that one may say accurately is that there is a struggle for control within the borders of civilization itself, to wit, between the masses of simple and stupid men and various minorities of extremely egoistic and determined men. But neither side is trying to destroy civilization, save in the indignant visions of the other. On the contrary, both are trying their best to preserve it, and whether one side wins or the other it will be duly preserved. Ten years hence it will be just as easy to send a picture postcard or to be beaten by a policeman as it is to-day, and wherever one may buy a picture postcard the arts are safe and wherever one may be beaten by a policeman law and order are safe, and when the arts and law and order are safe, then civilization is also safe. False analogies are at the bottom of most of the current fears—that is, when they are honest. The analogy with Rome, so often cited, is especially nonsensical. A few hundred thousand Romans were surrounded by countless millions of barbarians, and the barbarians had arms quite as good as those of the Romans. Where is any similar horde to be found today? Are the Japs dangerous? Plainly not, save perhaps to the United States. The Japs, with all of the odds on their side, took more than two years to beat the Russians; they would stand up before a European coalition no more than 10 days. The Chinese? They don't want Europe; they want only China. The blacks of Africa? Two German divisions could dispose of all of them, given a fair, stand-up battle, in two hours. Nor is any genuine fear to be deduced from the fate of the late Confederacy in America. The intellectual colapse of the Southern States after the Civil War was purely a local and geographical matter. Most of the surviving Southerners who had been civilized before the war simply moved North, leaving only a few cripples, the darkeys and a mob of poor white trash behind. But civilization in the United States was certainly not affected; in fact, the mixing of Southerners and Northerners in the North probably improved it. Today, a half century afterward, even some of the Southern poor whites are becoming relatively civilized. A book store has been opened in New Orleans, a man in Mobile has bought a violoncello, and only the other day, in Georgia, a white man was actually taken by the constabulary for killing a dozen Negroes.

What the authors of elegies mistake for the collapse of civilization is simply the internal struggle that I have mentioned—the ages-old combat between the haves and the have-nots, now rendered transiently acute by a parlous shortening of the things fought for. The ultimate issue of that struggle seems to me to be plain enough. The have-nots will be given a drubbing, and under the protection of a new and unprecedentedly vigorous and daring capitalism the thing called Christian civilization will be promoted as it has never been promoted before. My arteries harden so fast—a consequence of my constant and quixotic sacrifice of myself to the common weal—that I cannot hope to live into the full flush of that new Golden Age, but I can at least smack my lips over it in anticipation. What I see is a vast horde of inferior men broken, after a hopeless, fruitless fight, to the hard, uninspiring labor of the world—a race of slaves superbly regimented, and kept steadily in order by great brigades of propagandists, official optimists, scare-mongers, Great Thinkers and rev. clergy. And over them a minority of capitalist overlords, well-fed, well-protected, highly respected, politely envied, and lavishly supplied with endless stores of picture postcards, gasoline, silk underwear, mayonnaise, Pontet Canet, toilet soap and phonograph records.

The battle, in fact, is already half won. In France and the United States capitalism can weather any conceivable storm. In England it craftily encourages labor to a combat that will be to a finish, and with capital on top. In Italy it is already in the saddle. In Germany only the Junkers stave off the inevitable victory of money. In Russia the Bolsheviks help capital everywhere by reducing the cause of the have-nots to an absurdity. The other countries are not dogs, but mere tails. . . . The United States, I believe, will see the thing brought to its finest flower. There were no war losses here, but only profits. In all other countries, the conscripts of the war are restless, and inclined to move toward the Left. Here they are already superbly organized to serve capital, and give the final touch of felicity to the situation by serving it for nothing. On the evening of the same day that an American Legionary has his wages reduced 40 per cent. and his hours of labor increased 25 per cent., he goes out at his own risk and expense and helps to tar and feather some visionary who tries to convince him that he has been swindled. Meanwhile, the Supreme Court of New York decides formally that "the courts . . . must stand at all times as the representatives of capital," and the newspapers commend the dictum in lavish terms. . . . I sing Utopia. It is about to burst upon us.

XIII.
On Government

I

"GOVERNMENT," said William Godwin in that "Enquiry Concerning Political Justice" which got Shelley two wives and lost him £6000 a year, "can have no more than two legitimate purposes: the suppression of injustice against individuals within the community, and the common defense against external invasion." The dictum, after a hundred and thirty-one years, remains unimproved and perhaps unimprovable. Today, to be sure, with Darwin behind us, we'd make some change in its terms: what Godwin was trying to say, obviously, was that the central aim of government was to ameliorate the struggle for existence—to cherish and protect the dignity of man in the midst of the brutal strife of *Homo neanderthalensis.* But that change would be simply substituting a *cliché* of the Nineteenth Century for one of the Eighteenth. All the furious discussion of the subject that has gone on in the intervening time has not changed the basic idea in the slightest. To the plain man of today, as to the most fanatical Liberal or Socialist, government appears primarily as a device for compensating his weakness, a machine for protecting him in rights that he could not make secure with his own arm. Even the Tory holds the same view of it: its essential function, to him, is to safeguard his property against the lascivious desires of those who, if they were not policed, would be tempted to grab it. "Government," said George Washington, "is not reason, it is not eloquence—it is force." Bad government is that which is weak, irresolute and lacking in constabulary enterprise; when one has defined it, one has also defined a bad bishop, cavalry captain or policeman. Good government is that which delivers the citizen from the risk of being done out of his life and property too arbitrarily and violently—one that relieves him sufficiently from the barbaric business of guarding them to enable him to engage in gentler, more dignified and more agreeable undertakings, to his own content and profit, and the advantage, it may be, of the commonwealth.

Unfortunately, this function is performed only imperfectly by any of the forms of government now visible in Christendom, and Dr. Johnson was perhaps justified in dismissing them all as but various aspects of the same fraud. The citizen of today, even in the most civilized states, is not only secured but defectively against other citizens who aspire to exploit and injure him—for example, highwaymen, bankers, quack doctors, clergymen, sellers of oil stock and contaminated liquor, and so-called reformers of all sorts,—and against external foes, military, commercial and philosophical; he is also exploited and injured almost without measure by the government itself—in other words, by the very agency which professes to protect him. That agency becomes, indeed, one of the most dangerous and insatiable of the inimical forces present in his everyday environment. He finds it more difficult and costly to survive in the face of it than it is to survive in the face of any other enemy. He may, if he has prudence, guard himself effectively against all the known varieties of private criminals, from stockbrokers to pickpockets and from lawyers to kidnapers, and he may, if he has been burnt enough, learn to guard himself also against the rogues who seek to rob him by the subtler device of playing upon his sentimentalities and superstitions: charity mongers, idealists, soul-savers, and others after their kind. But he can no more escape the tax-gatherer and the policemen, in all their protean and multitudinous guises, than he can escape the ultimate mortician. They beset him constantly, day in and day out, in ever-increasing numbers and in ever more disarming masks and attitudes. They invade his liberty, affront his dignity and greatly incommode his search for happiness, and every year they demand and wrest from him a larger and larger share of his worldly goods. The average American of today works more than a full day in every week to support his government. It already costs him more than his pleasures and almost as much as his vices, and in another half century, no doubt, it will begin to cost as much as his necessities.

These gross extortions and tyrannies, of course, are all practised on the theory that they are not only unavoidable, but also laudable—that government oppresses its victims in order to confer upon them the great boons mentioned by Godwin. But that theory, I believe, begins to be quite as dishonest as the chiropractor's pretense that he pummels his patient's spine in order to cure his cancer: the actual object, obviously, is simply to cure his solvency. What keeps such notions in full credit, and safeguards them against destructive analysis, is chiefly the survival into our enlightened age of a concept hatched in the black days of absolutism—the concept, to wit, that government is something that is superior to and quite distinct from all other human institutions—that it is, in its essence, not a mere organization of ordinary men, like the Ku Klux Klan, the United States Steel Corporation or Columbia University, but a transcendental organism composed of aloof and impersonal powers, devoid wholly of self-interest and not to be measured by merely human standards. One hears it spoken of, not uncommonly, as one hears the law of gravitation and the grace of God spoken of—as if its acts had no human motive in them and stood clearly above, human fallibility. This concept, I need not argue, is full of error. The government at Washington is no more impersonal than the cloak and suit business is impersonal. It is operated by precisely the same sort of men, and to almost the same ends. When we say that it has decided to do this or that, that it proposes or aspires to do this or that—usually to the great cost and inconvenience of nine-tenths of us—we simply say that a definite man or group of men has decided to do it, or proposes or aspires to do it; and when we examine this group of men realistically we almost invariably find that it is composed of individuals who are not only not superior to the general, but plainly and depressingly inferior, both in common sense and in common decency—that the act of government we are called upon to ratify and submit to is, in its essence, no more than an act of self-interest by men who, if no mythical authority stood behind them, would have a hard time of it surviving in the struggle for existence.

2

These men, in point of fact, are seldom if ever moved by anything rationally describable as public sprit; there is actually no more public spirit among them than among so many burglars or street-walkers. Their purpose, first, last and all the time, is to promote their private advantage, and to that end, and that end alone, they exercise all the vast powers that are in their hands. Sometimes the thing they want is mere security in their jobs; sometimes they want gaudier and more lucrative jobs; sometimes they are content with their jobs and their pay but yearn for more power. Whatever it is they seek, whether security, greater ease, more money or more power, it has to come out of the common stock, and so it diminishes the shares of all other men. Putting a new job-holder to work decreases the wages of every wage-earner in the land—not enough to be noticed, perhaps, but enough to leave its mark. Giving a job-holder more power takes something away from the liberty of all of us: we are less free than we were in proportion as he has more authority. Theoretically, we get something for what we thus give up, but actually we usually get absolutely nothing. Suppose two-thirds of the members of the national House of Representatives were dumped into the Washington garbage incinerator tomorrow, what would we lose to offset our gain of their salaries and the salaries of their parasites? It may be plausibly argued, of course, that the House itself is necessary to our happiness and salvation—that we need it as we need trolley conductors, chiropodists and the men who bite off puppies' tails. But even if that be granted—and I, for one, am by no means disposed to grant it—the plain fact remains that all the useful work the House does might be done just as well by fifty men, and that the rest are of no more utility to the commonwealth, in any rational sense, than so many tight-rope walkers or teachers of mah jong.

The Fathers, when they launched the Republic, were under no illusions as to the nature of government. Washington's view of its inner nature I have already quoted; Jefferson it was who said sagely that "that government is best which governs least." The Constitution in its first form, perhaps, was designed chiefly to check the rising pretensions of the lower orders, drunk with the democratic fustian of the Revolutionary era, but when the Bill of Rights was added to it its guns began to point more especially at the government itself, *i.e.*, at the class of job-holders, ever bent upon oppressing the citizen to the limit of his endurance. It is, perhaps, a fact provocative of sour mirth that the Bill of Rights was designed trustfully to prohibit forever two of the favorite crimes of all known governments: the seizure of private property without adequate compensation and the invasion of the citizen's liberty without justifiable cause and due process of law. It is a fact provocative of mirth yet more sour that the execution of these prohibitions was put into the hands of courts, which is to say, into the hands of lawyers, which is to say, into the hands of men specifically educated to discover legal excuses for dishonest, dishonorable and anti-social acts. The actual history of the Constitution, as everyone knows, has been a history of the gradual abandonment of all such impediments to governmental tyranny. Today we live frankly under a government of men, not of laws. What is the Bill of Rights to a Roosevelt, a Wilson, a Palmer, a Daugherty, a Burns? Under such tin-horn Cæsars the essential enmity between government and citizen becomes only too plain, and one gets all the proof that is needed of the eternal impossibility of protecting the latter against the former. The government can not only evoke fear in its victims; it can also evoke a sort of superstitious reverence. It is thus both an army and a church, and with sharp weapons in both hands it is virtually irresistible. Its personnel, true enough, may be changed, and so may the external forms of the fraud it practises, but its inner nature is immutable.

Politics, as hopeful men practise it in the world, consists mainly of the delusion that a change in form is a change in substance. The American colonists, when they got rid of the Potsdam tyrant, believed fondly that they were getting rid of oppressive taxes forever and setting up complete liberty. They found almost instantly that taxes were higher than ever, and before many years they were writhing under the Alien and Sedition Acts. The French, when they threw off the monarchy at last, looked forward to a Golden Age of peace, plenty and freedom. They are now wrecked by war, bankrupted beyond any chance of recovery, and hag-ridden by an apparently unbreakable combination of the most corrupt and cynical politicians ever seen in the world. The experience of the Russians and Germans is even more eloquent. The former have been ruined by their saviors, and in so far as they have any power of reflection left, long for the restoration of the tyranny they once ascribed to the devil. The latter, delivered from the Hohenzollerns, now find the Schmidts and Krauses ten times as expensive and oppressive. Six months after the republic was set up a German cabinet minister, for the first time in the history of the nation, was in flight over the border, his loot under his arm. In the first flush of surprise and indignation the people took to assassinating politicians, but before long they gave it up as hopeless: Schmidt fell but Kraus still lived, and so government kept its vitality and its character. Many Germans, reduced to despair, now advocate a complete abolition of political government; if Stinnes had lived they would have tried to make him dictator of the country. But political government, *i.e.*, government by professional job-holders, would have remained in fact, despite its theoretical abolition, and its nature would have been unchanged.

If downright revolution is thus incapable of curing the disease, the ordinary reforms that men believe in sink to the level of bald quackeries. Consider, for example, the history of so-called Civil Service Reform in the United States. It came in on a wave of intense public indignation against the whole governmental imposture; it represented a violent and romantic effort to substitute an ideal of public service for the familiar harsh reality of public exploitation. For fifty years the American people had sweated and suffered under the spoils system, that lovely legacy of the "reforms" of the Jackson era. By the opening of the eighties they were ready to dispose of it by fair means or foul. The job-holder, once theoretically a freeman discharging a lofty and necessary duty, was seen clearly to be no more than a rat devouring the communal corn; his public position was indistinguishable from that of a child-stealer, a well-poisoner or a Sunday-school superintendent; and that of his brother, the government contractor and purveyor, was even lower. Many men of both classes, including some very important ones, were clapped into jail, and many others had to depart for Canada between days, along with the nightly squad of clerical seducers and absconding bank cashiers. Thereupon seers and prophets arose to lead the people out of the wilderness. A few wild ones proposed, in effect, that government be abolished altogether, but the notion outraged democratic sentiment, and so most of them followed the job-holders into jail; some, in fact, were put to death by more or less due process of law. The majority of soothsayers were less revolutionary: they proposed only that the race of job-holders be reformed by force, that government be purged and denaturized.

This was undertaken by what came to be called Civil Service Reform. The essence of Civil Service Reform was the notion that the job-holder, in return for his high prerogatives and immunities, should be compelled to do an honest day's work—that he should fit himself for it by hard effort, as a barber fits himself for cutting hair. Led by such men of Vision as E. L. Godkin, Charles J. Bonaparte and Theodore Roosevelt (that, of course, was before Roosevelt deserted the flag and became himself the archetypical job-holder), the reformers proceeded grimly toward the dreadful purpose of making the job-holder a mere slave, like a bookkeeper in a wholesale house. His pay and emoluments were cut down and his labors were increased. Once the proudest and most envied citizen of the Republic, free to oppress all other citizens to the limit of their endurance, he became at one stroke a serf groaning in a pen, with a pistol pointed at his head. If, despite the bars and artillery surrounding him, his thrift enabled him to make a show of decent prosperity, he was clapped into prison *ipso facto*, and almost without a trial. A few short years saw his fall from the dizziest height of ease to the lowest abyss of misery.

This, of course, could not go on, else politics would have tumbled into chaos and government would have lost its basic character; nay, its very life. What is more, it did *not* go on, for human ingenuity, despite the troubles of the time, was still functioning, and presently it found a remedy for the disease—a remedy so perfect, indeed, that the patient did not know he was taking it. That remedy was achieved by the simple process of making two slight changes in the ideal of Civil Service Reform itself. First the word Reform was lopped off, and then the word Civil. There remained, then, only Service. This Service saved the day for the job-holder; it gave him a new lease upon his job; it diverted public suspicion from him; it converted him from a criminal into a sort of philanthropist. It remains with us today, the heir and assign of the old spoils system, as the bootlegger is the heir and assign of the saloon-keeper.

3

The chief achievement of Service is that it has sucked reform into the governmental orbit, and so made it official and impeccable—more, highly profitable. The old-time reformer was one who got nothing for his psychic corn-cures and shin-plasters—who gave them away freely to all comers, seeking only righteousness himself—who often, indeed, took a beating into the bargain. The new reformer, safe in a government job, with a drastic and complex law behind him, is one who is paid in legal tender, unfailingly proffered, for his passionate but usually unintelligible services to humanity—a prophet of the new enlightenment, a priest at a glittering and immense shrine. He is the fellow who enforces the Volstead Act, the Mann Act, all the endless laws for putting down sin. He is the bright evangelist who tours the country teaching mothers how to have babies, spreading the latest inventions in pedagogy, road-making, the export trade, hog-raising and vegetable-canning, waging an eternal war upon illiteracy, hookworm, the white slave trade, patent medicines, the foot and mouth disease, cholera infantum, adultery, rum. He is, quite as often as not, female; he is a lady Ph.D., cocksure, bellicose, very well paid. Male or female, he represents the new governmental tyranny; he is Vision, vice the spoils system, retired. The old-time job-holder, penned in the cage of the Civil Service, is now only a peon, a brother to the ox. He has to work quite as hard as if he labored for Judge Gary or Henry Ford, and he is very much worse paid. The high prerogatives and usufructs of government have slipped out of his hands. They are exercised and enjoyed today by the apostles of Service, a horde growing daily, vastly and irresistibly, in numbers, impudence, power and pay.

Few of the groaning taxpayers of These States, indeed, realize how far this public merchandizing of buncombe has displaced the old spoils system, or how much it is costing them every year. During the Civil War an army contractor who went to Washington looking for loot announced frankly what he was after; as a result, he was constantly under suspicion, and was lucky if he got away with as much as $100,000; only a few Vanderbilts and Morgans actually stole more. During the late war he called himself a dollar-a-year-man, put on a major's uniform, took oath to die if need be for the cause of democracy—and went home with a million, at least. The job-holder has undergone a similar metamorphosis; maybe apotheosis would be a better aimed word. In the days of the spoils system he was, at best, an amateurish and inept performer. The only reason he ever offered for demanding a place at the public trough was that he deserved it—that he had done his share to elect the ticket. The easy answer to him was that he was an obvious loafer and scoundrel, and deserved nothing. But what answer is to be made to his heir and assign, the evangelist of Service, the prophet of Vision? He doesn't start off with a bald demand for a job; he starts off with a Message. He has discovered the long-sought sure cure for all the sorrows of the world; he has the infallible scheme for putting down injustice, misery, ignorance, suffering, sin; his appeal is not to the rules of a sinister and discreditable game, but to the bursting heart of humanity, the noblest and loftiest sentiments of man. His job is never in the foreground; it is concealed in his Vision. To get at the former one must first dispose of the latter. Well, who is to do it? What true-born American will volunteer for the cynical office? Half are too idiotic and the rest are too cowardly. It takes courage to flaunt and make a mock of Vision—and where is courage?

Certainly not in this imperial commonwealth of natural kneebenders and marchers in parades. Nowhere else in Christendom, save only in France, is government more extravagant, nonsensical, unintelligent and corrupt than here, and nowhere else is it so secure. It becomes a sort of crime even to protest against its villainies; all the late investigations of waste and corruption in Washington were attacked and brought to wreck in the name of duty, decorum, patriotism. The citizen objecting to felony by the agents of the sovereign state, acting in its name, found himself posted as an anarchist! There was, of course, some logic in this imbecility, as there is in everything insane. It was felt that too violent an onslaught upon the disease might do gross damage o the patient, that the attempt to extirpate what was foul and excrescent might imperil what was useful and necessary. Is government, then, useful and necessary? So is a doctor. But suppose the dear fellow claimed the right, every time be was called in to prescribe for a bellyache or a ringing in the ears, to raid the family silver, use the family tooth-brushes, and execute the *droit de seigneur* upon the housemaid? Is it simply a coincidence that the only necessary functionaries who actually perform any comparable brigandage are the lawyers—the very men who, under democracy, chiefly determined the form, policies and acts of the government?

This great pox of civilization, alas, I believe to be incurable, and so I propose no new quackery for its treatment. I am against dosing it, and I am against killing it. All I presume to argue is that something would be accomplished by viewing it more realistically—by ceasing to let its necessary and perhaps useful functions blind us to its ever-increasing crimes against the ordinary rights of the free citizen and the common decencies of the world. The fact that it is generally respected—that it possesses effective machinery for propagating and safeguarding that respect—is the main shield of the rogues and vagabonds who use it to exploit the great masses of diligent and credulous men. Whenever you hear anyone bawling for more respect for the laws, whether it be a Coolidge on his imperial throne or an humble county judge in his hedge court, you have before you one who is trying to use them to his private advantage; whenever you hear of new legislation for putting down dissent and rebellion you may be sure that it is promoted by scoundrels. The extortions and oppressions of government will go on so long as such bare fraudulence deceives and disarms the victims—so long as they are ready to swallow the immemorial official theory that protesting against the stealings of the archbishop's secretary's nephew's mistress' illegitimate son is a sin against the Holy Ghost. They will come to an end when the victims begin to differentiate clearly between government as a necessary device for maintaining order in the world and government as a device for maintaining the authority and prosperity of predatory rascals and swindlers. In other words, they will come to an end on the Tuesday following the first Monday of November preceding the Resurrection Morn.

XIV.
Toward a Realistic Æsthetic

I
The Nature of Art

THE dominating purpose of man in the world is to conquer Nature, which is to say, to defeat the plain intent of God. God and man are the eternal antagonists. Man makes progress every time he wins a new victory; if he can hold his gains his progress is real. Poetry is one device for defeating God. Its aim is to escape some of the pains of reality by denying boldly that they exist—by saying, in some form or other, that "I am the captain of my soul" and "all's well with the world." This denial gives some comfort to human hearts, particularly to the more romantic sort; it is a poor substitute, perhaps, for the actual conquest of the harsh facts, but it is nevertheless a substitute. Religion operates in precisely the same way; its primary purpose is to read an intelligible and even laudable motive into the inscrutable assaults of God. Poetry, of course, is a cut higher than religion, logically speaking. It denies the facts, but it denies them more or less speciously and sometimes almost convincingly; it seldom, if ever, has to enounce the thumping and obvious absurdities that religion relies upon. But it is nevertheless a denial of reality, and hence very deficient as an agent of progress. Science is far more effective. It does not deny the imbecilities and horrors of Nature; it sets about actually modifying them, and even abolishing them. When science conquers it is usually a conquest that is permanent. We have got rid of wolves, ghosts and yellow fever finally and almost completely; they no longer bother civilized men. In the same way we have got rid of some of the horrors that religion raised—horrors worse than those it sought to lay. Science is not only effective against Nature; it is also effective against the dangerous remedies formerly employed against Nature.

Religion and the arts are thus only second-rate means of achieving man's chief purpose in the world. They give him a lot of comfort, but they expose him to the dangers which always follow the denial of reality. The man who believes that God is personally interested in him and will save him from harm is in a far more perilous situation than the man who knows better; so, also, with the man who believes that what poetry says is true. The other arts, having less ideational content, are a good deal less menacing. The statements that architecture makes, for example, are not against the plain facts but in accord with the plain facts—for example, that St. Thomas' Church is more beautiful than the Jersey marshes or its own rector. So with music, and, to some extent, with painting, though painting is hampered by its function of representing Nature—that is, of reproducing Nature without comment, or with very feeble and ineffective comment. Painting will become a genuinely valuable art when it finally abandons representation. The portrait of an ugly woman, even though the artist tries to ameliorate her ugliness a bit, remains almost as horrible as the ugly woman herself. That is to say, the artist simply multiplies and reinforces the horror already concocted by God.

The arts that avoid representation are like science in this: that they actually improve upon Nature, and so add permanently to man's comfort and happiness in the world. The Parthenon is not a mere idle denial of the facts of life, like poetry; it is a positive improvement upon the facts of life; it makes a Greek hilltop appreciably more beautiful than it was as God made it, and so mitigates the horror of life to man. Music achieves the same thing, and even more effectively. The nine Beethoven symphonies do not deny any palpable fact; they merely create new facts that are more agreeable than those previously existing. There are no sounds in Nature comparable to the lovely sounds that Beethoven evokes. Here man shows himself definitely the superior of God. Poetry, of course, also achieves a measure of genuine and permanent beauty. But it can do so only in its character as a form of music. The blank verse of Shakespeare, as music, is as noble a creation as the symphonies of Beethoven. But all poetry, even the best, is corrupted by its logical content. It almost invariably *says* something, and that something is almost always untrue. When man speaks or believes an untruth he certainly makes no progress with his conquest of Nature. On the contrary, he plainly gives up the battle, at least for the moment. Instead of fighting resolutely and effectively, and so improving his state, he simply buries his head in the sand.

2
The One-Legged Art

To me, at all events, painting seems to be half an alien among the fine arts. Its credentials, of course, are sounder than those of acting, but they are surely not as sound as those of music, poetry, drama, sculpture and architecture. The trouble with painting is that it lacks movement, which is to say, the chief function of life. The best a painter can hope to accomplish is to fix the mood of an instant, the momentary aspect of something. If he suggests actual movement he must do it by palpable tricks, all of which belong to craftsmanship rather than to art. The work that he produces is comparable to a single chord in music, without preparation or resolution. It may be beautiful, but its beauty plainly does not belong to the highest order. The senses soon tire of such beauty. If a man stands before a given painting for more than five or ten minutes, it is usually a sign of affectation: he is trying to convince himself that he has more delicate perceptions than the general. Or he is a painter himself and thus engrossed by the technical aspects of it, as a plumber might be engrossed by the technical aspects of a bathroom. Or he is enchanted by the story that the picture tells, which is to say, by the literature that it illustrates. True enough, he may go back to a painting over and over again, just as a music-lover may strike and re-strike a chord that pleases him, but it can't hold him for long at one session—it can't move his feelings so powerfully that he forgets the real world he lives in.

Sculpture is in measurably better case. The spectator, viewing a fine statue, does not see something dead, embalmed and fixed in a frame; he sees something that moves as he moves. A fine statue, in other words, is not one statue, but hundreds, perhaps even thousands. The transformation from one to another is infinitely pleasing; one gets out of it the same satisfying stimulation that one gets out of the unrolling of a string quartette, or out of such a poem as "Atalanta in Calydon," "Heart of Darkness" or "Faust." So with architecture. It not only revolves; it also moves vertically, as the spectator approaches it. When one walks up a street past a beautiful building one certainly gets an effect beyond that of a mere chord; it is the effect of a whole procession of beautiful chords, like that at the beginning of the slow movement of the "New World" symphony or that in the well-known and much-battered Chopin prélude. If it were a painting it would soon grow tedious. No one, after a few days, would give it a glance.

This intrinsic hollowness of painting has its effects even upon those who most vigorously defend it as the queen of all the fine arts. One hears of such persons "haunting the galleries," but one always discovers, on inquiry, that it is the show-rooms that they actually haunt. In other words, they get their chief pleasure by looking at an endless succession of *new* paintings: the multitude of chords produces, in the end, a sort of confused satisfaction. One never hears of them going to a public gallery regularly, to look at this or that masterpiece. Even the Louvre seldom attracts them more than a dozen or so times in a life-time. The other arts make a far more powerful and permanent appeal. I have read "Huckleberry Finn" at least twenty times and "Typhoon" probably ten times, and yet both pleased me as much (nay, more) the last time as they did the first time. I have heard each of the first eight symphonies of Beethoven more than fifty times, and most of Mozart's, Haydn's, Schubert's and Schumann's quite as often. Yet if Beethoven's C Minor were announced for performance tonight, I'd surely go to hear it. More, I'd enjoy every instant of it. Even second-rate music has this lasting quality. Some time ago I heard Johann Strauss' waltz, "Geschichten aus dem Wiener Wald," for the first time in a long while. I knew it well in my goatish days; every note of it was still familiar. Nevertheless, it gave me exquisite delight. Imagine a man getting exquisite delight out of a painting of corresponding calibre—a painting already so familiar to him that he could reproduce it from memory!

Painters, like barbers and cigarmakers, are able to talk while they are at work, and so they commonly gabble about their art a great deal more than other artists, and the world, in consequence, has come to assume that it is very complex, and full of subtleties. This is not true. Most of its so-called subtleties are manufactured by painters who cannot paint. The genuinely first-rate painters of the world have little to say about the technique of their art, and seem to be unaware that it is difficult. Go back to Leonardo's notes and sketches: you will find him a great deal more interested in anatomy than in painting. In fact, painting was a sort of afterthought with him; he was primarily an engineer, and the engineering that fascinated him most was that of the human body. Come down, then, to Cézanne. He painted in the way that seemed most natural to him, and was greatly astonished when a group of bad painters, seeking to imitate him, began crediting him with a long string of more or less mystical theories, by the Boul' Mich' out of the article on optics in the Encyclopædia Britannica.

The earliest Paleolithic men were already accomplished painters and sculptors. H. G. Wells, in his "Outline of History," says that "they drew astonishingly well." "Paint," he goes on, "was a big fact in their lives. They were inveterate painters." These savages were so low that they had not even invented bows and arrows, usury, the gallows or the notion of baptism by total immersion, and yet they were already accomplished draftsmen. Some of their drawings on the walls of their caves, indeed, remain a great deal more competent than the average magazine illustration of today. They also carved in and modelled in clay, and no doubt they were accomplished poets, as are the lowest Zuñi Indians of our own time. Moreover, they soon began to move out of their caves into artificial houses, and the principles of architectural design that they devised at the very dawn of history have been unchanged ever since, and are poll-parroted docilely every time a sky-scraper thrusts its snout among the cherubim. True enough, they could not draw as accurately as a photographic lens, but they could certainly draw as accurately as, say, Matisse or Gauguin. It remained for modern physicists, *i.e.*, men disdainful of drawing, to improve it. All the progress that has been made in the art during the past fifty or sixty years has been based upon quiet filches from the camera, just as all the progress that has been made in painting has been based upon filches from the spectroscope. When one finds a painter who professes to disdain these scientific aids, one always beholds a painter who is actually unable to draw or paint, and who seeks to conceal his incompetence by clothing it in hocus-pocus. This is the origin of new art that regales us with legs eight feet long, complexions of olive green, and human heads related to the soap-box rather than to the Edam cheese. This is the origin of all the gabble one hears in ratty and unheated studios about cubism, vortism, futurism and other such childish follies.

I regard any human being who, with proper instruction, cannot learn to draw reasonably well as, to all intents and purposes, a moron. He is in a stage of culture actually anterior to that of the Crô-Magnons. As for a human being incapable of writing passable verse, he simply does not exist. It is done, as everyone knows, by children—and sometimes so well that their poems are printed in books and quite solemnly reviewed. But good music is never written by children—and I am not forgetting Mozart, Schubert and Mendelssohn. Music belongs to the very latest stage of culture; to compose it in the grand manner requires long and painful training, and the highest sort of natural skill. It is complex, delicate, difficult. A miraculous youth may show talent for it, but he never reaches any thing properly describable as mastery of it until he is thoroughly mature. The music that all of us think of when we think of the best was written by men a bit bent by experience; it is quite beyond the comprehension of the general. And so with prose. Prose has no stage scenery to hide behind, as poetry has. It cannot use masks and wigs. It is not naïve, but infinitely sophisticated. It is not spontaneous, but must be fabricated by thought and painstaking. Prose is the ultimate flower of the art of words. Next to music, it is the finest of all the fine arts.

To return to music, it must be plain that it is enormously handicapped as an art by the mere fact that its technique is so frightfully difficult. I do not refer, of course, to the technique of the musical executant, but to that of the composer. Any literate man can master the technique of poetry in ten days, and that of the drama—despite all the solemn hocus-pocus of the professors who presume to teach it—in three weeks, but not even the greatest genius could do sound work in the sonata form without years of preparation. To write a good string quartette is not merely an act of creation, like writing a love song; it is also an act of applied science, like cutting out a set of tonsils. I know of no other art that demands so elaborate a professional training. Perhaps the one which comes nearest to it is architecture—that is, modern architecture. As the Greeks practised it, it was relatively simple, for they used simple materials and avoided all delicate problems of stress and strain; and they were thus able to keep their whole attention upon pure design. But the modern architect, with his complex mathematical and mechanical problems, must be an engineer before he is an artist, and the sort of engineering that he must master bristles with technical snares and conundrums. The serious musician is in even worse case. Before he may write at all he must take in and coördinate a body of technical knowledge that is almost as great as the outfit of an astronomer. I say that all this constitutes a handicap on the art of music. What I mean is that it scares off many men who have sound musical ideas and would make good composers, but who have no natural talent or taste for the technical groundwork. For one Schubert who overcomes the handicap by sheer genius there must be dozens who are repelled and discouraged. There is another, and perhaps even worse disadvantage. The potential Schuberts flee in alarm, but the Professor Sawdusts march in bravely. That is to say, music is hard for musicians, but easy for pedants, grinds and examination-passers. Its constant invasion by a hollow formalism is the result. It offers an inviting playground to the bombastic jackass whose delight it is to astonish the bourgeoisie with insane feats of virtuosity.

3
Symbiosis and the Artist

In contemplating the stupendous achievements of such a man as Wagner—achievements so colossal that only a small minority of men, specially trained, can even comprehend and appreciate them—one often finds one's self wondering how much further he would have gone had he not been harassed by his two wives. His first wife, Minna Planer, was frankly and implacably opposed to his life-work, and made deliberate efforts to dissuade him from it. She regarded "Lohengrin" as nonsensical and "Tannhäuser" as downright indecent. It was her constant hope, until Wagner finally kicked her out, that he would give over such stuff, and consecrate himself to the composition of respectable operas in the manner of Rossini, her favorite composer. The only composition of his that genuinely pleased her was a set of variations for the *cornet à piston* that he wrote in Paris. She was a singer, and had the brains of one. It must be plain that the presence of such a woman—and Wagner lived with her for twenty years—must have put a fearful burden upon the man's creative genius. No man can be absolutely indifferent to the prejudices and opinions of his wife. She has too many opportunities to shove them down his throat. If she can't make him listen to them by howling and bawling, she can make him listen by snuffling. To say that he can carry on his work without paying any heed to her is equal to saying that he can carry on his work without paying any heed to his toothache, his conscience, or the boiler-factory next door. In spite of Minna, Wagner composed a number of very fine music dramas. But if he had poisoned her at the beginning of his career it is very likely that he would have composed more of them, and perhaps even better ones.

His second wife, the celebrated Cosima Liszt-von Bülow, had far more intelligence than Minna, and so we may assume that her presence in his music factory was less of a handicap upon the composer. Nevertheless, the chances are that she, too, did him far more harm than good. To begin with, she was extremely plain in face—and nothing is more damaging to the creative faculty than the constant presence of ugliness. Cosima, in fact, looked not unlike a modern woman politician; even Nietzsche, a very romantic young fellow, had to go crazy before he could fall in love with her. In the second place, there is good reason to believe that Cosima, until after Wagner's death, secretly believed that her father, Papa Liszt, was a far better musician. Men's wives almost invariably make some such mistake; to find one who can separate the man of genius from the mere husband, and then estimate the former accurately and fairly, is surely very rare. A woman usually respects her father, but her view of her husband is mingled with contempt, for she is of course privy to the transparent devices by which she snared him. It is difficult for her, being so acutely aware of the shallowness of the man, to give due weight to the dignity of the artist. Moreover, Cosima had shoddy tastes, and they played destructively upon poor Wagner. There are parts of "Parsifal" that suggest her very strongly—more strongly, in fact, than they suggest the author of "Die Götterdämmerung." I do not here decry Wagner; on the contrary, I praise him, and perhaps excessively. It is staggering to think of the work he did, with Minna and Cosima shrilling into his ears. What interests me is the question as to how much further he might have gone had he escaped the passionate affection of the two of them and of their various volunteer assistants. The thought fascinates, and almost alarms. There is a limit beyond which sheer beauty becomes unseemly. In "Tristan und Isolde," in the Ring, and even in parts of "Parsifal," Wagner pushes his music very near that limit. A bit beyond lies the fourth dimension of tone—and madness. Both Beethoven and Brahms, I believe, more than once edged over the line. Two bachelors. Had Beethoven married in 1802, as he seems to have been tempted to do by some scheming wench, it is doubtful that the world would ever have heard the Eroica. In the Eroica there is everything that startles and dismays a loving wife: brilliant novelty, vast complexity, thunderous turmoil, great bursts of undiluted genius. Even Beethoven never wrote anything more astounding than its first movement; the first movement of the C Minor is relatively elemental beside it. Nor is there anything so revolutionary in the Ninth.

The Eroica, indeed, was written precisely at the moment when Beethoven became fully conscious of his extraordinary powers—more accurately, of his singular and unchallengeable *superiority*. It is the work, not only of a man who is absolute master of his materials, but also of a man who disdains his materials, and his customers with them. In the first movement he simply spits into the face of the cosmos. Scarcely ten measures have been played before one suddenly realizes that one is in the presence of something entirely new in music—not merely new in degree, but new in kind. It differs as much from anything written before it, even by Beethoven, as a picture by Cézanne differs from a picture by an English Academician. This first movement has never been sufficiently studied and appraised: it is unutterably stupendous. In the funeral march, I believe, Beethoven descends to some rather cheap tricks, and in the scherzo he is often obvious. But in the first movement, and to a slightly less degree in the last, he takes leave of earth and disports himself among the gods. It is the composition of a colossus. And a bachelor. No normal woman could have watched its genesis without some effort to make it more seemly, more decorous and connubial, more respectable. A faithful wife, present at its first performance, would have blushed, shivered and sworn. Women hate revolutions and revolutionists. They like men who are docile, and well-regarded at the bank, and never late at meals.

XV.

Contributions to the Study of Vulgar Psychology

I

The Downfall of the Navy

FEW phenomena offer more refined and instructive entertainment to the psychic pathologist than the American navy's decline in popularity during the past twenty-five years. At the time of the Spanish-American War, as everyone sentient in those days will recall, it was easily the premier service in the popular regard, and in even the least of its exploits the great masses of the plain people took a violent and vociferous pride. They were proud, too, of the army, and its heroic efforts against the Hunnish hordes of Spain, and one of the great captains of that army was made President for his stupendous feats of blood and blather in the field; but it was the navy that they cherished most, and the popular heroes that it produced were more numerous than those of the army, and in the main they were far more fondly cherished. Even the immortal Roosevelt, it will be remembered, was half a navy man, and what got him into the White House, I believe, was less his colossal butcheries in the land battles of the war, important though they were to the cause of human liberty, than his long antecedent struggles to free the navy from the politicians, and make it fit to fight. The navy, indeed, was popular before the war began, or even threatened. The army could tackle and massacre a whole tribe of Indians without causing half the public thrill that followed the bombardment of a Venezuelan coast village by the White Squadron, with a total loss of but one blind cripple crippled in the other leg. This White Squadron, I more than suspect, was the actual cause of the war itself. From the day it first put to sea the plain people watched it with glowing pride, and longed for a sight of it in action. If it had not been so handily cruising in Latin-American waters, glittering truculently in the sunshine, there would have been a great deal less public indignation over the wrongs of the Cubeens.

So superb a fighting arm was surely not designed by God to rust in the scabbard. Thus the fashion arose of drawing it out and poking it into Caribbean and South Atlantic rat-holes. During the half dozen years before the laying of the Spanish dragon was formally undertaken, such heroes as Schley and Fighting Bob Evans carried the White Squadron into half the ports to the southward, and knocked over a few church steeples in most of them. In the end, it was just such an enterprise that took the *Maine* into Havana harbor, and provided the legal excuse for the war itself.

This was more than a quarter of a century ago. Today, it must be obvious that there is very little public pride in the navy, and almost no public interest. I doubt that one American schoolboy out of ten thousand could name its present ranking officer; between 1890 and 1900 every schoolboy knew all the admirals by face and by name, and most of the captains, and the patriotic epigrams of the more articulate of them were chalked upon every schoolyard fence in the land. I was myself a boy in those days, and remember even today such forgotten heroes of the time as Admiral Gherardi, who commanded the White Squadron in 1893 and 1894, and was retired before the Spanish War; his portrait was on the cigarette cards, along with those of Fighting Bob Evans and Lillian Russell. Later on, having grown more reflective and critical, I specialized in the Sampson-Schley controversy, and was a bitter partisan of Schley, a native of my own Maryland Free State. Dewey, Clark, Evans, Ridley, Hobson (God save us!), Ensign Bagley, Yeoman Ellis, Sigsbee, Wainright—all these eminent tars were as real to the boys of that era as John L. Sullivan or Amos Rusie. Turn now to today. When the newspapers, a year or two ago, announced that a gentleman named Admiral Sims had denied that the German U-boat commanders committed the atrocities credited to them during the late war, how many American boys recognized his name? I myself, though I am a historian by profession, boggled him at first glance, mistaking him for a British officer. For the life of me, I could not tell you the name of another American naval officer. . . . Second thought: there was Admiral Benson. But what he did in the war, save involve himself in some controversy that has been forgotten, I can't tell you. No other name occurs to me, though I scratch my head and try various mnemonic dodges. Try me on the names of the commanders who fought the celebrated Creel battle with the U-boats, and I'll have to slide down among the morons. If there was a Hobson in that war, I can't recall him. I remember many English and German commanders—von Tirpitz, von Scheer, Jellicoe, Müller of the Emden, König, and so on—but not a single American.

The fact is, of course, that the part the American navy played in the war, though it was unquestionably important, was quite devoid of the more spectacular varieties of gallantry, and so it failed to make heroes. The battles fought were fought mainly by government press-agents, not by the navy itself; the rest was dangerous but dull policing, with some uninspiring running of ferry-boats. The navy, as everyone knows, became a funk-hole for draft-dodgers. This may account, in some measure, for the present public apathy regarding it; it is not brilliant, and hence it is not charming. But its decay in popularity, I believe, really antedated the war by several years; it was in the shadows long before Admiral Sims transferred his swivel-chair from Washington to London. What caused the change? Is it that the American people have lost their old taste for the sea, and, in particular, their old delight in the sort of heroes that it produces? Or is it that the navy itself has actually lost some of its old romance and color? I incline to think that the latter explanation explains more than the former. My hazard is that the man who made the American navy unpopular was the Hon. Josephus Daniels, and that he did it by trying to convert every battleship into a chautauqua and Sunday-school. In the days when the arrival of a naval vessel in port was the signal for hot times ashore, with the saloons packed to the doors, and all the town's wicked women out *en masse*, and the streets made picturesquely perilous by squads of drunken and roaring gobs—in those days every poor but ambitious boy, when the job of tying up packages and running errands began to palsy him, let his fancy turn toward thoughts of stealing off to foreign parts, the Republic's quarter in his pocket and riotous and attractive company all about him. The sailor of that era was an obscene but highly charming fellow. A great spaciousness was in him. He bore the scars of the constabulary espantoons of distant and romantic lands. He was a wholesale lover, a three-bottle man, a well of astounding profanity. He held the admiration of every adventurous youth. He was romance in baggy breeches, hell-bent down the mysterious by-ways of the world.

Josephus changed all that. A Christian of tender conscience and a firm believer in hell for the sinful, it appalled him to observe that nine-tenths of the young men under his official charge were obviously headed for the fire. When he got his secret reports of their doings in Port Said, Callao, Singapore, Odessa, Smyrna, Vera Cruz, Norfolk, Va., and other such seaboard stews—when these lurid documents began pouring in upon him from missionaries, Y.M.C.A. secretaries and other godly men, he staggered under the horror, and was unfit for business for days afterward. Having recourse to prayer, he was presently given counsel by a voice from the burning bush. To hear was to act. First, he abolished rum from the navy, and forced even the oldest admirals, some of whom had been pickled for years and years, to go upon the dubious water of far-flung and zymotic ports. Secondly, he forbade the enlistment of young men who were fugitives from justice for dog-stealing, moonshining, window-smashing and other such felonies—the mainstays of the navy in the old days. Thirdly, he set up night schools on every battleship, in charge of Christian men like himself, and then day schools, and then schools running both day and night, and to the customary instruction in the three R's he added the whole curriculum of the Y.M.C.A., from double-entry bookkeeping to public speaking, and from show-card writing to venereal prophylaxis. Today a young man goes into the navy from his native farm with nothing in his head save a vast yearning to get away from the smell of cows—and comes out in three years an accomplished paperhanger, with some knowledge of the saxophone, electric wiring and first aid to the injured. The old enlistment posters used to show a gob in a rickshaw with a Japanese cutie; the new ones show him practising as a house and sign painter. The old navy showed the boys the world, and taught them the difference between Swedish punch and Javanese arrak; the new navy converts them into sanitary plumbers and bookkeepers, and teaches them how to lead a prayer-meeting.

Is it any wonder that it declines in popularity—that the

youth of the land is neglectful of its eminent commanders, and has to be lured into enlistments by the arts of the grind-shop auctioneer? The Y.M.C.A. already reigns universally on the dry land of the Republic; only the remotest yokel in the highest hills can hope to escape its tentacles, and even he is fetched by its sinister sister, the chautauqua. When he dreams of the sea, he dreams of a realm that is free from all this—of a realm still barbarous, unchastened and romantic—a realm of free cavorting and exhilarating adventure. But when he gets to the recruiting-office, the first thing he sees is a large lithograph showing a class of gobs being instructed in algebra, grammar and Christian doctrine. The master-at-arms who receives him hasn't got the old naked Venus tattooed on his arm; he has instead a portrait of Dwight L. Moody, and in his button-hole is a button testifying that he has recited 52 successive Golden Texts without an error and brought 20 heathen Danish sailors to the mourners' bench. Instead of the old booby-hatch for souses in this recruiting-office, there is now a gospel hall with a melodeon. The talk is not of the yellow gals in Valparaiso, the powerful red wines of Naples, the all-night shows of Marseilles, the police of Livepool and Kiel, but of the advantages of learning the trades of tin-roofer, cost accountant and hardwood finisher. The rustic candidate, his head buzzing with romance, is floored with statistics and plunged into a bath of bichloride of mercury. No wonder his stomach turns and his heart is broken! And no wonder the navy, thus purged of all its old flavors and juices, has ceased to inflame the imagination of the plain people. Suppose they heard from Hollywood that Charlie Chaplin had become a hard-shell Baptist and opened a pants-pressing parlor?

2
The Mind of the Slave

One of the forgotten divisions between men and men is that separating those who enjoy the work they have to do in the world and those who suffer it only as a necessary evil. The distinction, despite its neglect by sociologists, is probably very important—certainly far more important than the current divisions between producers and exploiters, dolichocephalic

Nordic blonds and brachycephalic Alpines, Darwinians and so-called Christians, Republicans and Democrats, Protestants and Catholics, wets and drys. A man's politics, theology and other vices engage his attention, after all, only in his moments of leisure, and the shape of his cranium has very little demonstrable influence upon what habitually goes on within it, but the nature of the work he does in the world conditions every thought and impulse of his life, and his general attitude toward it is almost indistinguishable from his general attitude toward the cosmos.

At the one extreme lies the unmitigated slave—the man who has to spend his whole life performing tasks that are incurably uninteresting, and that offer no soothing whatever to his vanity. At the other extreme is what Beethoven called the free artist—the man who makes a living, with no boss directly over him, doing things that he enjoys enormously, and that he would keep on doing gladly, even if all economic pressure upon him disappeared. To the second category belong all the happiest men in the world, and hence, perhaps, all the most useful men. For what is done with joy is always better done, whether it be fashioning a material object, thinking out a problem or kissing a pretty girl; and the man who can make the rest of humanity pay him for being happy is obviously a better man than the general, or, at all odds, a luckier one. Here luck and superiority are one and the same. The fact that Joseph Conrad could write better than I, was in a sense, a matter of pure chance. He was born with his talent; he did not earn it. Nevertheless, it was just as real as if he had got it by Christian endeavor, and his superiority to me was thus perfectly genuine.

The slave is always conscious of his slavery, and makes constant and often desperate efforts to mitigate it or to get rid of it alogether. Sometimes he seeks that mitigation in outside activities that promise to give him the sense of dignity and importance that his daily labor denies him; sometimes he tries to give a false appearance of dignity to his work itself. The last phenomenon must be familiar to every American; it is responsible for various absurd devices to pump up lowly trades by giving them new and high-sounding names. I point, for example, to those of the real-estate agent and the undertaker. Neither trade, it must be obvious, offers any stimulation to men of genuine superiority. One could not imagine a Beethoven, a Lincoln or even a Coolidge getting any joy out of squeezing apartment-house tenants or pickling Odd Fellows. Both jobs, indeed, fail to satisfy the more imaginative sort of men among those compelled to practise them. Hence these men try to dignify them with hocus-pocus. The real-estate agent, seeking to conceal his real purpose in life, lets it be known grandly that he is an important semi-public functionary, that he has consecrated himself to Service and is a man of Vision—and to prove it he immerses himself in a private office with a secretary to insult his customers, joins a Rotary Club, and begins to call himself a realtor, a word as idiotic as flu, pep or gent. The ambitious washer of the dead—until very lately a sort of pariah in all civilized societies, like the hangman, the surgeon and the dog-catcher—proceeds magnificently along the same route. At regular intervals I receive impressive literature from a trade-union of undertakers calling themselves the Selected Morticians. By this literature it appears that the members thereof are professional men of a rank and dignity comparable to judges or archbishops, and they are hot for the subtlest and most onerous kind of Service, and even eager to offer their advice to the national government. In brief, the realtor complex all over again. I do not laugh at these soaring embalmers; I merely point out that their nonsense proves how little the mere planting of martyred lodge brothers satisfies their interior urge to be important and distinguished—an urge that is in all of us.

But most of the trades pursued by slaves, of course, offer no such opportunities for self-deceptive flummery. The clerk working in the lime and cement warehouse of some remote town of the foreign missions belt cannot conceivably convince himself that his profession is noble; worse, he cannot convince anyone else. And so with millions of other men in this great Republic, both urban and rural—millions of poor fellows doomed their life long to dull, stupid and tedious crafts—the lower sort of clerks, workmen, wagon-drivers, farmers, farm-laborers, petty officials, grabbers of odd jobs. They must be downright idiots to get any satisfaction out of their work. Happiness, the feeling that they too are somebody, the sense of being genuinely alive, must be sought in some other direction. In the big cities, that need is easily met. Here there is a vast and complex machinery for taking the slave's mind off his desolateness of spirit—moving pictures to transport him into a land of romance, where men (whom he always identifies with himself) are brave, rich and handsome, and women (whom he identifies with his wife—or perchance with her younger sister) are clean, well-dressed and beautiful; newspapers to delight and instruct him with their sports pages, their comic strips and their eloquent appeals to his liberality, public spirit and patriotism; public bands and the radio to play the latest jazz for him; circuses and parades; baseball, races, gambling, harlotry and games in arenas; a thousand devices to make him forget his woes. It is this colossal opportunity to escape from life that brings yokels swarming to the cities, not any mere lust for money. The yokel is actually far more comfortable on his native soil; the city crowds and exploits him, and nine times out of ten he remains desperately poor. But the city at least teaches him how to forget his poverty; it amuses him and thrills him while it is devouring him. I once knew an old colored woman, born in Southern Maryland, who lived miserably in one room of a shack in an alley in Baltimore. When asked why she did not go back to her village, where she would have at least had better food and more air, she replied very simply that there were never any parades in the country. It was a profound and intelligent saying.

But millions of the slaves, of course, must remain in the small towns or on the land; the cities can't absorb all of them, nor even half of them. They thus confront the problem of making life bearable out of their own meagre resources. The devices that they adopt—political, religious and social—are familiar to all of us, and account fully, it seems to me, for some of the phenomena of American life that are most puzzling to foreign observers. The hoop-la Methodist revival with its psychopathological basis; the violent bitterness of rural politics; the prosperity of the Ku Klux Klan and all the other clownish fraternal orders; the persistent popularity of lynching, tarring and feathering, barbarities of a dozen other varieties—all these things are no more than manifestations of the poor hind's pathetic effort to raise himself out of his wallow, to justify and dignify his existence, to escape from the sordid realities that daily confront him. To snort and froth at a revival makes him conspicuous, prominent, a man of mark; it is therefore easy to induce him to do it. To hold a petty county office is eminence; hence he struggles for it frantically. To belong to the Ku Klux gives him a mysterious and sinister dignity, and fills him with a sense of power and consequence; he falls for it as quickly as a city intellectual falls for the *Légion d'honneur* or an LL.D. To take a hand in a concrete tarring or lynching—this instantly makes him feel that he has played an heroic rôle in the world, that he has accomplished something large and memorable—above all, that he has had a gaudy good time. In brief, all these things make him forget, transiently or permanently, that he is a miserable worm, and of little more actual importance on earth than his own hogs.

Long ago, I suggested that a good way to diminish lynching in the South would be to establish brass bands in all the country towns. The bad music, I argued, would engage and enchant both the blackamoors and the poor white trash, and so discourage the former from crime and the latter from seeking a savage satisfaction in its punishment. I now improve and embellish that suggestion. That is to say, I propose that the band scheme be shelved, and that bull-fighting be established as a substitute. Why not, indeed? Cattle have to be killed, and the Southern poor white is admittedly a savage. Why not combine the necessary slaughter of horned quadrupeds with a show that will give that savage a thrill and take his mind from his lowly lot, and so turn him from seeking escape in politics, murder and voodoo theology? Bull-fights in the South would not only diminish lynchings; they would also undermine Prohibition. A happy peasantry would have no reason to divert itself with homicide, and neither would it have any reason to belabor the rest of us with the ethical and political manias of its Baptist dervishes. The Ku Klux, it seems to me, is a good influence in the South rather than a bad one, for it tends to regulate and formalize the normal sports of the people, and so restrains excess. The trouble with lynching before the Klan took charge of it was that men of the darker races were often hanged and burned purely arbitrarily, simply because the yokels of some Christian county could not stand boredom any longer. But now rules are laid down and a sort of jurisprudence gets into it. I have heard all kinds of wild charges against the Invisible Empire, but I have never heard anyone allege that its responsible officers have ever countenanced the execution of its laws upon anyone not obviously guilty. This is an improvement. Life is safer and happier in Georgia today that it was before the Rev. Dr. Simmons heard the voice. But it would be even safer and even happier if the pure Anglo-Saxons down there could work off their steam by going weekly to a *plaza de toros*, and there see official *picadores*, *banderilleros*, and *matadors*, all of them good Democrats and baptized men, lynch and burn (or even merely geld) a reluctant and protesting male of *Bos taurus*.

3
The Art Eternal

One of the laudable by-products of the Freudian necromancy is the discovery that lying, in most cases, is involuntary and inevitable—that the liar can no more avoid it than he can avoid blinking his eyes when a light flashes or jumping when a bomb goes off behind him. At its worst, indeed, this necessity tales on a downright pathological character, and is thus as innocent as sciatica or albuminuria. It is part of the morbid baggage of hysterics and neurasthenics: their lying is simply a symptom of their compulsive effort to adjust themselves to an environment which bears upon them too harshly for endurance. The rest of us are not quite so hard pushed, but pushed we all are. In us the thing works through the inferiority complex, which no man can escape. He who lacks it entirely is actually reckoned insane by the fact: his satisfaction with his situation in the world is indistinguishable from a delusion of grandeur. The great majority of us—all, in brief, who are normal—pass through life in constant revolt against our limitations, objective and subjective. Our conscious thought is largely devoted to plans and specifications for cutting a better figure in human society, and in our unconscious the business goes on much more steadily and powerfully. No healthy man, in his secret heart, is content with his destiny. Even the late Woodrow, during his dizzy term as the peer of Lincoln and Washington, was obviously tantalized by the reflection that, in earlier ages, there had been Martin Luther, St. Ignatius Loyola and Paul of Tarsus. We are tortured by such dreams and images as a child is tortured by the thought of a state of existence in which it would live in a candy-store and have two stomachs. The more we try to put the obscene apparition away, the more it haunts and badgers us.

Lying is the product of the unconscious yearning to realize such visions, and if the policeman, conscience, prevents the lie being put into plain words, then it is at least put into more or less plausible acts. We all play parts when we face our fellow-men, as even poets have noticed. No man could bring himself to reveal his true character, and, above all, his true limitations as a citizen and a Christian, his true meannesses, his true imbecilities, to his friends, or even to his wife. Honest autobiography is therefore a contradiction in terms: the moment a man considers himself, even *in petto*, he tries to gild and fresco himself. Thus a man's wife, however realistic her view of him, always flatters him in the end, for the worst she sees in him is appreciably better, by the time she sees it, than what is actually there. What she sees, even at times of the most appalling domestic revelation and confidence, is not the authentic man at all, but a compound made up in part of the authentic man and in part of his projection of a gaudy ideal. The man who is most respected by his wife is the one who makes this projection most vivid—that is, the one who is the most daring and ingratiating liar. He can never, of course, deceive her utterly, but if he is skillful he may at least deceive her enough to make her happy.

Omnis homo mendax: thus the Psalmist. So far the Freudians merely parrot him. What is new in their gospel is the doctrine that lying is instinctive, normal, and unavoidable—that a man is forced into it by his very will-to-live. This doctrine purges the business of certain ancient embarrassments, and restores innocence to the heart. Think of a lie as a compulsion neurose, and you think of it more kindly. I need not add, I hope, that this transfer of it from the department of free will to that of determinism by no means disposes of the penalty that traditionally pursues it, supposing it to be detected and resented. The proponents of free will always make the mistake of assuming that the determinists are simply evil fellows looking for a way to escape the just consequences of their transgressing. No sense is in that assumption. If I lie on the witness-stand and am detected by the judge, I am jailed for perjury forthwith, regardless of my helplessness under compulsion. Here justice refuses absolutely to distinguish between a misfortune and a tort: the overt act is all it is concerned with. But as jurisprudence grows more intelligent and more civilized it may change its tune, to the benefit of liars, which is to say, to the benefit of humanity. Science is unflinchingly deterministic, and it has begun to force its determinism into morals. We no longer flog a child afflicted with nocturnal enuresis; we have substituted concepts of mental aberration for concepts of crime in a whole series of cases: kleptomania-shoplifting, pyromania-arson, etc.; and, in the United States at least, the old savage punishment of murderers is now ameliorated by considerations of psychiatry and even of honor. On some shining to-morrow a psychoanalyst may be put into the box to prove that perjury is simply a compulsion neurose, like beating time with the foot at a concert or counting the lamp-posts along the highway.

However, I have but small faith in millenniums, and do not formally predict this one. Nor do I pronounce any moral judgment, pro or con: moral judgments, as old Friedrich used to say, are foreign to my nature. But let us not forget that lying, *per se*, is not forbidden by the moral code of Christendom. Holy Writ dismisses it cynically, and statutes of all civilized states are silent about it. Only the Chinese, indeed, make it a penal offense. Perjury, of course, is prohibited everywhere, and also any mendacity which amounts to fraud and deprives a fellow-man of his property, but that far more common form of truth-stretching which has only the lesser aim of augmenting the liar's personal dignity and consequence—this is looked upon with a very charitable eye. So is that form which has the aim of helping another person in the same way. In the latter direction lying may even take on the stature of a positive virtue. The late King Edward VII, when Prince of Wales, attained to great popularity throughout Christendom by venturing into downright perjury. Summoned into a court of law to give expert testimony regarding some act of adultery, he lied like a gentleman, as the phrase goes, to protect a woman. The lie, to be sure, was intrinsically useless; no one believed that the lady was innocent. Nevertheless, every decent Christian applauded the perjurer for his good intentions, including even the judge on the bench, sworn to combat false witness by every resource of forensics. All of us, worms that we are, occasionally face the alternatives that confronted Edward. On the one hand, we may tell the truth, regardless of conseqences, and on the other hand we may mellow it and sophisticate it to make it humane and tolerable. It is universally held that the man who chooses the first course is despicable. He may be highly moral, but he is nevertheless a cad—as highly moral men have so curious a way of being. But if he lies boldly, then he is held to be a man of honor, and is respected as such by all other men of honor.

For the habitual truth-teller and truth-seeker, indeed, the world has very little liking. He is always unpopular, and not infrequently his unpopularity is so excessive that it endangers his life. Run your eye back over the list of martyrs, lay and clerical: nine-tenths of them, you will find, stood accused of nothing worse than honest efforts to find out and announce the truth. Even today, with the scientific passion become familiar in the world, the general view of such fellows is highly unfavorable. The typical scientist, the typical critic of institutions, the typical truth-seeker in every field is held under suspicion by the great majority of men, and variously beset by posses of relentless foes. If he tries to find out the truth about arterio-sclerosis, or surgical shock, or cancer, he is denounced as a scoundrel by the Christian Scientists, the osteopaths and the antivivisectionists. If he tries to tell the truth about the government, its agents seek to silence him and punish him. If he turns to fiction and endeavors to depict his fellow-men accurately, he has the Comstocks on his hands. In no field can he count upon a friendly audience, and freedom from assault. Especially in the United States is his whole enterprise viewed with bilious eye. The men the American people admire most extravagantly are the most daring liars; the men they detest most violently are those who try to tell them the truth. A Galileo could no more be elected President of the United States than he could be elected Pope of Rome. Both high posts are reserved for men favored by God with an extraordinary genius for swathing the bitter facts of life in bandages of soft illusion.

Behind this almost unanimous distrust of the truth-teller there is a sound and sure instinct, as there is behind every other manifestation of crowd feeling. What it shows is simply this: that the truth is something too harsh and devastating for the majority of men to bear. In their secret hearts they know themselves, and they can suffer the thought of themselves only by idealizing the facts. The more trivial, loathsome and degraded the reality, the more powerful and relentless must be the idealization. An Aristotle, I daresay, may be able occasionally to regard himself searchingly and dispassionately—but certainly not an ordinary man. Here we come back to what we began with: the inferiority complex. The truth-seeker forgets it, and so comes to grief. He forgets that the ordinary man, at bottom, is always afraid of himself, as of some horrible monster. He refuses to sanction the lie whereby the ordinary man maintains his self-respect, just as the bounder, put upon the stand, refuses to support the lie whereby a woman maintains the necessary theory of her chastity. Thus he is unpopular, and deserves to be.

Then why does he go on? Why does he kick up such a bother and suffer such barbarous contumely, all to no end—for the majority of so-called truths, it must be evident, perish as soon as they are born: no one will believe them. The answer probably is that the truth-seeker is moved by the same obscure inner necessity (in Joseph Conrad's phrase) that animates the artist. Something within him, something entirely beyond his volition, forces him to pursue his fanatical and useless quest—some impulse as blind as that which moves a puppy to chase its tail. Again the compulsion neurose! But this one differs materially from that of the liar. The latter is hygienic; it makes for peace, health, happiness. The former makes only for strife and discontent. It invades the immemorial pruderies of the human race. It breeds scandals and heart-burnings. It is essentially anti-social, and hence, by modern theories of criminology, diseased. The truth-seeker thus becomes a pathological case. The average man is happily free from any such malaise. He avoids the truth as diligently as he avoids arson, regicide or piracy on the high seas, and for the same reason: because he believes that it is dangerous, that no good can come of it, that it doesn't pay. The very thought of it is abhorrent to him. This average man, I believe, must be accepted as the normal man, the natural man, the healthy and useful man. He presents a character that is general in the race, and favorable to its security and contentment. The truth never caresses; it stings—and life is surely too short for sane men to be stinging themselves unnecessarily. One would regard it as idiotic even in a flea.

Thus the truth about the truth emerges, and with it the truth about lying. Lying is not only excusable; it is not only innocent, and instinctive; it is, above all, necessary and unavoidable. Without the ameliorations that it offers life would become a mere syllogism, and hence too metallic to be born. The man who lies simply submits himself sensibly to the grand sweep and ripple of the cosmic process. The man who seeks and tells the truth is a rebel against the inner nature of all of us.

XVI.
The American Novel

I

It is an ancient platitude of historical criticism that great wars and their sequelæ are inimical to the fine arts, and particularly to the art of letters. The kernel of truth in it lies in the obvious fact that a people engaged in a bitter struggle for existence have no time for such concerns, which demand not only leisure but also a certain assured feeling of security, well-being and self-sufficiency—in brief, the thing often called aristocratic (or sometimes intellectual) detachment. No man ever wrote good poetry with his wife in parturition in the next room, or the police preparing to raid his house, or his shirt-tail afire. He needs to be comfortable to do it, and if not actually comfortable, then at all events safe. Wars tend to make life uncomfortable and unsafe—but not, it must be observed, inevitably and necessarily, not always and invariably. A bitter and demoralizing struggle goes with wars that are lost, and the same struggle goes with wars that are won only by dint of stupendous and ruinous effort, but it certainly does not go with wars that are won easily. These last do not palsy and asphyxiate the artist, as he is palsied and asphyxiated by cholera morbus, suits for damages or marriage. On the contrary, they pump him full of ozone, and he is never more alive and lively than following them.

I point to a few familiar examples. The Civil War, as everyone knows, bankrupted the South and made life a harsh and bitter struggle for its people, and especially for the gentler and more civilized minority of its people. In consequence, the South became as sterile artistically, after Lee's surrender, as Mexico or Portugal, and even today it lags far behind the North in beautiful letters, and even further behind in music, painting and architecture. But the war, though it went on for four years, strained the resources of the North very little, either in men or in money, and so its conclusion found the Northerners very rich and cocky, and full of a yearning to astonish the world, and that yearning, in a few decades, set up a new and extremely vigorous American literature, created an American architecture of a revolutionary character, and even laid the first courses of American schools of music and painting. Mark Twain, Walt Whitman, Henry James and William Dean Howells, all of them draft dodgers in the war itself, were in a very real sense products of the war, for they emerged as phenomena of the great outburst of creative energy that followed it, and all of them, including even James, were as thoroughly American as Jay Gould, P. T. Barnum or Jim Fisk. The stars of the national letters in the years before the war had been Americans only by geographical accident. About Emerson there hung a smell of Königsberg and Weimar; Irving was simply a New York Englishman; Poe was a citizen of No Man's Land; even Hawthorne and Cooper, despite their concern with American themes, showed not the slightest evidence of an American point of view. But Mark Twain, Howells and Whitman belonged to the Republic as palpably as Niagara Falls or Tammany Hall belonged to it, and so did James, though the thought horrified him and we must look at him through his brother William to get the proof. Turn now to Europe. France, harshly used in the war of 1870–71, was sterile for a decade, but the wounds were not deep, and recovery was in full swing by 1880. Germany, injured scarcely at all, produced Nietzsche almost before the troops got home, and was presently offering an asylum and an inspiration to Ibsen, preparing the way for the reform and modernization of the theatre, and making contributions of the utmost value to practically all of the arts and sciences. Spain, after the Armada, gave the world Cervantes and then expired; England produced Shakespeare and founded a literature that is not surpassed in history.

What has thus happened over and over again in the past—and I might pile up examples for pages—may be in process of repetition today, and under our very noses. All Europe, plainly enough, is in a state of exhaustion and depression, and in no department of human activity is the fact more visible than in that of the arts. Not only are the defeated nations, Russia, Germany and Austria, producing nothing save a few extravagant eccentricities; there is also a great lowness of spirit in the so-called victorious nations, for their victory was almost as ruinous as defeat. France, as after 1870, is running to a pretentious and artificial morbidity in letters, and marking time in music and painting; Italy is producing little save psychopathological absurdities by such mountebanks as D'Annunzio and Papini; even England shows all the signs of profound fatigue. The great English writers of the age before the war are passing. Meredith is gone; Hardy has put up his shutters; Kipling went to wreck in the war itself; Conrad is dead; Shaw, once so agile and diverting, becomes a seer and prophet. Nor is there any sign of sound progress among the younger men. Arnold Bennett, a star of brilliant promise in 1913, is today a smoking smudge. Wells has ceased to be an artist and become a prophet in the Sunday supplements. Masefield has got no further than he was on August 2, 1914. The rest of the novelists are simply chasing their own tails. The Georgian poets, having emerged gloriously during the war, now disappear behind their manners. Only a few women, led by May Sinclair, and a few iconoclastic young men, led by Aldous Huxley, are still indubitably alive.

It seems to me that, in the face of this dark depression across the water, the literary spectacle on this side takes on an aspect that is extremely reassuring, and even a bit exhilarating. For the first time in history, there begins to show itself the faint shadow of a hope that, if all goes well, leadership in the arts, and especially in all the art of letters, may eventually transfer itself from the eastern shore of the Altantic to the western shore. Our literature, as I have more than once pointed out in the past, is still oppressed by various heavy handicaps, chiefly resident in the failure of the new aristocracy of money to function as an aristocracy of taste. The artist among us is still a sort of pariah, beset by public contempt on the one hand and by academic enmity on the other; he still lacks the public position that his brothers enjoy in older and more civilized countries. Nevertheless, it must be obvious to everyone that his condition tends to improve materially—that, in our own time, it *has* improved materially—that though his rewards remain meagre, save in mere money, his freedom grows steadily greater. And it must be obvious, too that he begins to show that that increasing freedom is not wholly wasted upon him—that he knows how to use it, and is disposed to do so with some gusto. What all the younger American writers have in common is a sort of new-found elasticity or goatishness, a somewhat exaggerated sense of aliveness, a glowing delight in the spectacle before them, a vigorous and naïve self-consciousness. The schoolmaster critics belabor them for it, and call it a disrespect for tradition, and try to put it down by denouncing it as due to corrupt foreign influences. But it is really a proof of the rise of nationalism—perhaps of the first dawn of a genuine sense of nationality. No longer imitative and timorous, as most of their predecessors were, these youngsters are attempting a first-hand examination of the national scene, and making an effort to represent it in terms that are wholly American. They are the pioneers of a literature that, whatever its defects in the abstract, will at least be a faithful reflection of the national life, that will be more faithful, indeed, in its defects than in its merits. In England the novel subsides into formulæ, the drama is submerged in artificialities, and even poetry, despite occasional revolts, moves toward scholarliness and emptiness. But in America, since the war, all three show the artless and superabundant energy of little children. They lack, only too often, manner and urbanity; it is no wonder that they are often shocking to pedants. But there is the breath of life in them, and that life is far nearer its beginning than its end.

The causes of all this are not far to seek. The American Legion is right: we won the war. It cost us nothing in men; it brought us a huge profit in money; as Europe has gone down, we have gone up. Moreover, it produced a vast discharge of spiritual electricity, otherwise and more injuriously dissipated in the countries more harshly beset. The war was fought ignobly; its first and most obvious effect was to raise up a horde of cads, and set them in authority as spokesmen of the nation. But out of that swinishness there was bound to come reaction, and out of the reaction there was bound to flow a desire to re-examine the whole national pretension—to turn on the light, to reject old formulæ, to think things out anew and in terms of reality. Suddenly the old houses of cards came tumbling down, and the professors inhabiting them ran about in their nightshirts, bawling for the police. The war, first and last, produced a great deal more than John Dos Passos' "Three Soldiers." It also produced Lewis' "Babbitt," and Cabell's "Jurgen," and

Fergusson's "Capitol Hill," and O'Neill's "The Emperor Jones." And, producing them, it ended an epoch of sweetness and light.

2

The young American literatus of today, with publishers ready and eager to give him a hearing, can scarcely imagine the difficulties which beset his predecessor of twenty years ago; he is, indeed, far too little appreciative of the freedom he has, and far too prone to flee from hard work to the solace of the martyr's shroud. When I first began practise as a critic, in 1908, there was yet plenty of excuse for putting it on. It was a time of almost inconceivable complacency and conformity. Hamilton Wright Mabie was still alive and still taken seriously, and all the young pedagogues who aspired to the critical gown imitated him in his watchful stupidity. This camorra had delivered a violent wallop to Theodore Dreiser eight years before, and he was yet suffering from his bruises; it was not until 1911 that he printed "Jennie Gerhardt." Miss Harriet Monroe and her gang of new poets were still dispersed and inarticulate; Miss Amy Lowell, as yet unaware of Imagism, was writing polite doggerel in the manner of a New England schoolmarm; the reigning dramatists of the nation were Augustus Thomas, David Belasco and Clyde Fitch; Miss Cather was imitating Mrs. Wharton; Hergesheimer had six years to go before he'd come to "The Lay Anthony"; Cabell was known only as one who provided the text for illustrated gift-books; the American novelists most admired by most publishers, by most readers and by all practising critics were Richard Harding Davis, Robert W. Chambers and James Lane Allen. It is hard indeed, in retrospect, to picture those remote days just as they were. They seem almost fabulous. The chief critical organ of the Republic was actually the Literary Supplement of the New York *Times*. The *Dial* was down with diabetes in Chicago; the *Nation* was made dreadful by the gloomy humors of Paul Elmer More; the *Bookman* was even more saccharine and sophomoric than it is today. When the mild and pianissimo revolt of the middle 90's—a feeble echo of the English revolt—had spent itself, the Presbyterians marched in and took possession of the works.

Most of the erstwhile revoltés boldly took the veil—notably Hamlin Garland. No novel that told the truth about life as Americans were living it, no poem that departed from the old patterns, no play that had the merest ghost of an idea in it had a chance. When, in 1908, Mrs. Mary Roberts Rinehart printed a conventional mystery story which yet managed to have a trace of sense in it, it caused a sensation. And when, two years later, Dr. William Lyon Phelps printed a book of criticism in which he actually ranked Mark Twain alongside Emerson and Hawthorne, there was as great a stirring beneath the college elms as if a naked fancy woman had run across the campus. If Hergesheimer had come into New York in 1908 with "Cytherea" under his arm, he would have worn out his pantaloons on publishers' benches without getting so much as a polite kick. If Eugene O'Neill had come to Broadway with "The Hairy Ape," he would have been sent to Edward E. Rose to learn the elements of his trade. The devilish and advanced thing, in those days, was for the fat lady star to give a couple of matinées of Ibsen's "A Doll's House."

A great many men and a few women addressed themselves to the dispersal of this fog. Some of them were imaginative writers who found it simply impossible to bring themselves within the prevailing rules; some were critics; others were young publishers. As I look back, I can't find any sign of concerted effort; it was, in the main, a case of each on his own. The more contumacious of the younger critics, true enough, tended to rally 'round Huneker, who, as a matter of fact, was very little interested in American letters, and the young novelists had a leader in Dreiser, who, I suspect, was quite unaware of most of them. However, it was probably Dreiser who chiefly gave form to the movement, despite the fact that for eleven long years he was silent. Not only was there a useful rallying-point in the idiotic suppression of "Sister Carrie"; there was also the encouraging fact of the man's massive immovability. Physically and mentally he loomed up like a sort of headland—a great crag of basalt that no conceivable assault seemed able to touch. His predecessor, Frank Norris, was of much softer stuff. Norris, had he lived longer, would have been wooed and ruined, I fear, by the Mabies, Boyntons and other such Christian critics, as Garland had been wooed and ruined before him.

Dreiser, fortunately for American letters, never had to face any such seduction. The critical schoolmarms, young and old, fell upon him with violence the moment he appeared above the horizon of his native steppe, and soon he was the storm center of a battle-royal that lasted nearly twenty years. The man himself was solid, granitic, without nerves. Very little cunning was in him and not much bellicose enterprise, but he showed a truly appalling tenacity. The pedagogues tried to scare him to death, they tried to stampede his partisans and they tried to put him into Coventry and get him forgotten, but they failed every time. The more he was reviled, sneered at, neglected, the more resolutely he stuck to his formula. That formula is now every serious American novelist's formula. They all try to write better than Dreiser, and not a few of them succeed, but they all follow him in his fundamental purpose—to make the novel true. Dreiser added something, and here following him is harder: he tried to make the novel poignant—to add sympathy, feeling, imagination to understanding. It will be a long while before that enterprise is better managed than he managed it in "Jennie Gerhardt."

Today, it seems to me, the American imaginative writer, whether he be novelist, poet or dramatist, is quite as free as he deserves to be. He is free to depict the life about him precisely as he sees it, and to interpret it in any manner he pleases. The publishers of the land, once so fearful of novelty, are now so hospitable to it that they constantly fail to distinguish the novelty that has hard thought behind it from that which has only some Village mountebank's desire to stagger the wives of Rotarians. Our stage is perhaps the freest in the world—not only to sensations, but also to ideas. Our poets get into print regularly with stuff so bizarre and unearthly that only Christian Scientists can understand it. The extent of this new freedom, indeed, is so great that large numbers of persons appear to be unable to believe in it; they are constantly getting into sweats about the taboos and inhibitions that remain, for example, those nourished by comstockery. But the importance and puissance of comstockery, I believe, is quite as much overestimated as the importance and puissance of the objurgations still hurled at sense and honesty by the provincial professors of American Idealism, the Genius of America, and other such phantasms.

The Comstocks, true enough, still raid an occasional book, particularly when their funds are running low and there is need to inflame Christian men, but that their monkeyshines ever actually *suppress* a book of any consequence I very much doubt. The flood is too vast for them. Chasing a minnow with desperate passion, they let a whole school of whales go by. In any case, they confine their operations to the single field of sex, and it must be plain that it is not in the field of sex that the hottest battles against the old American manner have been fought and won. "Three Soldiers" was far more subversive of that manner than all the stories of sex ever written in America —and yet "Three Soldiers" came out with the imprint of one of the most respectable of American publishers, and was scarcely challenged. "Babbitt" scored a victory that was still easier, and yet more significant, for its target was the double one of American business and American Christianity; it set the whole world to laughing at two things that are far more venerated in the United States than the bodily chastity of women. Nevertheless, "Babbitt" went down so easily that even the alfalfa *Gelehrten* joined in whooping for it, apparently on the theory that praising Lewis would make the young of the national species forget Dreiser. Victimized by their own craft, the *Gelehrten* thus made a foul attack upon their own principles, for if their principles did not stand against just such anarchistic and sacrilegious books, then they were without any sense whatever, as was and is, indeed, the case.

I shall not rehearse the steps in the advance from "Sister Carrie," suppressed and proscribed, to "Babbitt," swallowed and hailed. The important thing is that, despite the caterwauling of the Comstocks and the pedagogues, a reasonable freedom for the serious artist now prevails—that publishers stand ready to print him, that critics exist who are competent to recognize him and willing to do battle for him, and that there is a large public eager to read him. What use is he making of his opportunity? Certainly not the worst use possible, but also certainly not the best. He is free, but he is not yet, perhaps, worthy of freedom. He lets the popular magazine, the movie and the cheap-John publisher pull him too hard in one direction; he lets the vagaries of his politics pull him too hard in another. Back in 1908 I predicted the destruction of Upton Sinclair the artist by Upton Sinclair the visionary and reformer. Sinclair's bones now bleach upon the beach. Beside them repose those of many another man and woman of great promise—for example, Winston Churchill. Floyd Dell is on his way—one novel and two doses of Greenwich Village psychology. Hergesheimer writes novelettes for the *Saturday Evening Post.* Willa Cather has won the Pulitzer Prize—a transaction comparable to the election of Charles W. Eliot to the Elks. Masters turns to prose that somehow fails to come off. Dreiser, forgetting his trilogy, experiments rather futilely with the drama, the essay, free verse. Fuller renounces the novel for book reviewing. Tarkington is another Pulitzer prizeman, always on the verge of first-rate work but always falling short by an inch. Many of the White Hopes of ten or fifteen years ago perished in the war, as surely victims of its slaughter as Rupert Brooke or Otto Braun; it is, indeed, curious to note that practically every American author who moaned and sobbed for democracy between the years 1914 and 1919 is now extinct. The rest have gone down the chute of the movies.

But all this, after all, may signify little. The shock troops have been piled up in great masses, but the ground is cleared for those that follow. Well, then, what of the youngsters? Do they show any sign of seizing their chance? The answer is yes and no. On the one hand there is a group which, revolving 'round the *Bookman*, talks a great deal and accomplishes nothing. On the other hand there is a group which, revolving 'round the *Dial* and the *Little Review*, talks even more and does even less. But on the third hand, as it were, there is a group which says little and saws wood. There seems to be little in common between its members, no sign of a formal movement, with its *blague* and its bombast, but all of them have this in common: that they owe both their opportunity and their method to the revolution that followed "Sister Carrie." Most of them are from the Middle West, but they are distinct from the Chicago crowd, now degenerated to posturing and worse. They are sophisticated, disillusioned, free from cant, and yet they have imagination. The raucous protests of the evangelists of American Idealism seem to have no more effect upon them than the advances of the Expressionists, Dadaists and other such café-table prophets. Out of this dispersed and ill-defined group, I believe, something will come. Its members are those who are free from the two great delusions which, from the beginning, have always cursed American letters: the delusion that a work of art is primarily a moral document, that its purpose is to make men better Christians and more docile cannon-fodder, and the delusion that it is an exercise in logic, that its purpose is to prove something. These delusions, lingering beyond their time, are responsible for most of the disasters visible in the national literature today—the disasters of the radicals as well as those of the 100 per cent. dunderheads. The writers of the future, I hope and believe, will carefully avoid both of them.

XVII.

People and Things

I

The Capital of a Great Republic

THE fourth secretary of the Paraguayan legation. . . . The chief clerk to the House committee on industrial arts an expositions. . . . The secretary to the secretary to the Secretary of Labor. . . . The brother to the former Congressman from the third Idaho district. . . . The messenger to the chief of the Senate folding-room. . . . The doorkeeper outside the committee-room of the House committee on the disposition of useless executive papers. . . . The chief correspondent of the Toomsboro, Ga., *Banner* in the Senate press-gallery. . . . The stenographer to the assistant chief entomologist of the Bureau of Animal Industry. . . . The third assistant chief computor in the office of the Naval Almanac. . . . The assistant Attorney-General in charge of the investigation of postal frauds in the South Central States. . . . The former wife of the former secretary to the former member of the Interstate Commerce Commission. . . . The brother to the wife of the *chargé d'affaires* of Czecho-Slovakia. . . . The bootlegger to the ranking Democratic member of the committee on the election of President, Vice-President and representatives in Congress. . . . The acting assistant doorkeeper of the House visitors' gallery. . . . The junior Senator from Delaware. . . . The assistant to the secretary to the chief clerk of the Division of Audits and Disbursements, Bureau of Stationery and Supplies, Postoffice Department. . . . The press-agent to the chaplain of the House. . . . The commercial attaché to the American legation at Quito. . . . The chauffeur to the fourth assistant Postmaster-General. . . . The acting substitute elevator-man in the Washington monument. . . . The brother to the wife of the brother-in-law of the Vice-President. . . . The aunt to the sister of the wife of the officer in charge of ceremonials, State Department. . . . The neighbor of the cousin of the step-father of the sister-in-law of the President's pastor. . . . The superintendent of charwomen in Temporary Storehouse B7, Bureau of Navy Yards and Docks. . . . The assistant confidential clerk to the chief clerk to the acting chief examiner of the Patent Office. . . . The valet to the Chief Justice.

2
Ambassadors of Christ

Fifth avenue rectors with shining morning faces, preaching on Easter to pews packed with stockbrokers, defendants in salacious divorce suits, members of the Sulgrave Foundation and former Zionists. . . . Evangelists of strange, incomprehensible cults whooping and bawling at two or three half-witted old women and half a dozen scared little girls in corrugated iron tabernacles down near the railroad-yards. . . . Mormon missionaries pulling door-bells in Wheeling, W. Va., and Little Rock, Ark., and handing naughty-looking tracts to giggling servant girls. . . . Baptist doctors of divinity calling upon John the Baptist and John D. Rockefeller to bear witness that the unducked will sweat in hell forevermore. . . . Methodist candidates for the sacred frock, sent out to preach trial sermons to backward churches in the mail-order belt, proving magnificently in one hour that Darwin was an ignoramus and Huxley a scoundrel. . . . Irish priests denouncing the Ku Klux Klan. . . . Rabbis denouncing Henry Ford. . . . Presbyterians denouncing Flo Ziegfeld. . . . Fashionable divines officiating at gaudy home weddings, their ears alert for the popping of corks. . . . Street evangelists in Zanesville, O., trying convince a cop and five newsboys that no men will be saved unless he be born again. . . . Missionaries in smelly gospel-shops along the waterfront, expounding the doctrine of the atonement to boozy Norwegian sailors, half of them sound asleep. . . . Cadaverous high-church Episcopalians. . . . Little fat Lutherans with the air of prosperous cheesemongers. . . . Dunkards with celluloid collars and no neckties. . . . Southern Methodists who still believe in slavery. . . . Former plumbers, threshing-machine engineers and horse-doctors turned into United Brethren bishops. . . . Missionaries collecting money from the mill children in

Raleigh, N.C., to convert the Spaniards and Italians to Calvinism. . . . Episcopal archdeacons cultivating the broad English *a*. . . . Swedenborgians trying to explain the "Arcana Cœlestia" to flabbergasted newspaper reporters. . . . Polish clergymen leaping out of the windows at Polish weddings in Johnstown, Pa., hoping that the next half-dozen beer-bottles won't hit them. . . . Methodists pulling wires for bishoprics. . . . Quakers foreclosing mortgages. . . . Baptists busy among the women.

3
Bilder aus schöner Zeit

The excellent lunch that the illustrious Crispi used to serve at Delmonico's at five o'clock in the afternoon. . . . The incomparable orange blossom cocktails at Sherry's, and the plates of salted nuts. . . . The tavern cocktails at the Beaux Arts, each with its dash of absinthe. . . . The Franziskaner Mai-Bock at Lüchow's. . . . Dear old Sieg's noble Rhine wines at the Kaiserhof. . . . The long-tailed clams and Spring onions at Rogers', with Pilsner to wash them down. . . . The amazingly good American quasi-Pilsner, made by Herr Abner, on the Raleigh roof in Washington. . . . The Castel del Remy at the Brevoort, cheap but perfect. . . . The very dark Kulmbacher at the Pabst place in 125th street in the last days of civilization. . . . The burgundy from the Cresta Blanca vineyards in California. . . . Michelob on warm Summer evenings, with the crowd singing "Throw Out the Lifeline!". . . . The old-time Florestan cocktails—50 per cent. London gin, 25 per cent. French vermouth and 25 per cent. Martini-Rossi, with a dash of Angostura bitters—drink half, then drink a glass of beer, and then drink the other half. . . . That Hoboken red wine, so strangely smooth and lovely. . . . The bad red wine (but capital cooking) at the Frenchman's in Lexington avenue. . . . Del Pezzo's superb Chianti. . . . The ale at Keen's. . . . Obst's herrings, with Löwenbraü to slack them. . . . The astounding cocktail made by the head waiter at Henri's. . . . Drinking Faust all night in St. Louis in 1904. . . . The musty ale at Losekam's in Washington. . . . The draft *Helles* at Krüger's in Philadephia. . . . A Pilsner luncheon at the old Grand Union, from one to six. . . . A stray bottle of perfect sauterne found in Rahway, New Jersey. . . . A wild night drinking Swedish punch and hot water. . . . Two or three hot Scotch nights. . . . Twenty or thirty Bass' ale nights. Five or six hundred Pilsner nights. . . .

4
The High Seas

The kid who sits in the bucket of tar. . . . The buxom stewardess who comes in and inquires archly if one rang. . . . The humorous piano-tuner who tunes the grand piano in the music-room in the 15-16ths-tone scale. . . . The electric fan which, when a stray zephyr blows in through the porthole, makes a noise like a dentist's drill. . . . The alien ship's printer who, in the daily wireless paper, reports a baseball score of 165 to 3. . . . The free Christian Science literature in the reading-room. . . . The pens in the writing-room. . . . The elderly *Grosshändler* with the young wife. . . . The red-haired girl in the green sweater. . . . The retired boot-legger disguised as a stockbroker. . . . The stockbroker disguised as a United States Senator. . . . The boy who climbs into the lifeboat. . . . The chief steward wearing the No. 18¾ collar. . . . The mysterious pipes that run along the stateroom ceilings. . . . The discovery that one forgot to pack enough undershirts. . . . The night watchman who raps on the door at 3.30 A.M. to deliver a wireless message reading "Sorry missed you. Bon voyage". . . . The bartender who adds a dash of witchhazel to cocktails. . . . The wilting flowers standing in ice-pitchers and spittoons in the hallways. . . . The fight in the steerage. . . . The old lady who gets stewed and sends for the doctor. . . . The news that the ship is in Long. 43°, 41′, 16″ W, Lat. 40°, 23′, 39″ N. . . . The report that the starboard propeller has lost a blade.

5
The Shrine of Mnemosyne

The little town of Kirkwall, in the Orkney Islands, in a mid-Winter mist, flat and charming like a Japanese print. . . . San

Francisco and Golden Gate from the top of Twin Peaks. . . . Gibraltar on a Spring day, all in pastel shades, like the back-drop for a musical comedy. . . . My first view of the tropics, the palm-trees suddenly bulging out of the darkness of dawn, the tremendous stillness, the sweetly acid smell, the immeasurable strangeness. . . . The Trentino on a glorious morning, up from Verona to the Brenner Pass. . . . Central Germany from Bremen to Munich, all in one day, with the apple trees in bloom. . . . Copenhagen on a wild night, with the *Polizei* combing the town for the American who upset the piano. . . . Christiania in January, with the snow-clad statue of Ibsen looming through the gloom like a ghost in a cellar. . . . The beach at Tybee Island, with the faint, blood-curdling rattle of the land-crabs. . . . Jacksonville after the fire in 1902, with the hick militiamen firing their machine-guns all night. . . . The first inauguration of Woodrow, and the pretty suffragette who drank beer with me at the Raleigh. . . . A child playing in the yard of a God-forsaken town in the Wyoming desert. . . . Bryan's farewell speech at the St. Louis Convention in 1904. . . . Hampton Court on Chestnut Sunday. . . . A New Year's Eve party on a Danish ship, 500 miles off the coast of Greenland. . . . The little pile of stones on the beach of Watling's Island, marking the place where Columbus landed. . . . The moon of the Caribbees, seen from a 1000-ton British tramp. . . . A dull night in a Buffalo hotel, reading the American Revised Version of the New Testament. . . . The day I received the proofs of my first book. . . . A good-bye on an Hoboken pier. . . . The Palace Hotel in Madrid.

PREJUDICES
FIFTH SERIES

I.
Four Moral Causes

I
Birth Control

THE grotesque failure of the campaign to put down propaganda for birth control in the Republic has a lesson in it for those romantic optimists who believe that in the long run, by some mysterious hook or crook and perhaps with divine help, Prohibition will be enforced. They will not heed that lesson, but it is there nevertheless. Church and state combine to baffle and exterminate the birth controllers. They are threatened with penal servitude and their customers are threatened with hell fire. Yet it must be obvious that they are making progress in the land, for the national birth-rate continues to slide downhill, steadily and rapidly.

Incidentally, it is amusing and instructive to observe that it diminishes with greatest celerity among the educated and highly respectable classes, which is to say, among those who are ordinarily most law-abiding. The same thing is to be noted when one turns to Prohibition. The majority of professional criminals, now as in the old days of sin, are teetotalers, but when one comes to the good citizens who scorn them and demand incessantly that the *Polizei* butcher them and so have done with them, one comes at once upon a high density of scofflaws. I know many Americans of easy means, some of them greatly respected and even eminent. Not two per cent make any pretense of obeying the Volstead Act. And not two per cent of their wives are innocent of birth control. The reason is not far to seek. Both the Volstead Act and the statute aimed at birth control invade the sanctity of the domestic hearth. They take the roof off a man's house, and invite the world to look in. Obviously, that looking in is unpleasant in proportion as the man himself is dignified. If he is a low fellow, he doesn't care much, for he is used to such snooping by his low neighbors. But if he is one who has a high opinion of himself, and is accustomed to seeing it ratified by others, then he is outraged.

And if he has any natural bellicosity in him and resistance seems reasonably safe, he resists with great diligence and vigor.

Here, perhaps, we come upon an explanation of the fact that Prohibition and all other such devices for making men good by force are far less opposed in the country than they are in the cities. The yokel is trained from infancy to suffer espionage. He has scarcely any privacy at all. His neighbors know everything that is to be known about him, including what he eats and what he feeds his quadrupedal colleagues. His religious ideas are matters of public discussion; if he is recusant the village pastor prays for him by name. When his wife begins the sublime biological process of giving him an heir, the news flies around. If he inherits $200 from an uncle in Idaho everyone knows it instantly. If he skins his shin, or buys a new plow, or sees a ghost, or takes a bath it is a public event. Thus living like a goldfish in a glass globe, he acquires a large tolerance of snoutery, for if he resisted it his neighbors would set him down as an enemy of their happiness, and probably burn his barn. When an official spy or two are added to the volunteer pack he scarcely notices it. It seems natural and inevitable to him that everyone outside his house should be interested in what goes on inside, and that this interest should be accompanied by definite notions as to what is nice and what is not nice, supported by pressure. So he submits to governmental tyranny as he submits to the village inquisition, and when he hears that city men resist, it only confirms his general feeling that they are scoundrels. They are scoundrels because they have a better time than he has—the sempiternal human reason. The city man is differently trained. He is used to being let alone. Save when he lives in the slums, his neighbors show no interest in him. He would regard it as outrageous for them to have opinions about what goes on within the four walls of his house. If they offered him advice he would invite them to go to hell; if they tried force he would bawl for the police. So he is doubly affronted when the police themselves stalk in. And he resists them with every means at his command, and believes it is his high duty to do so, that liberty may not perish from the earth.

The birth control fanatics profit by this elemental fact. It is their great good fortune that their enemies have tried to put them down, not by refuting their ideas, but by seeking to shove them into jail. What they argue for, at bottom, remains very dubious, and multitudes of quite honest and intelligent persons are against it. They have by no means proved that a high birth-rate is dangerous, and they have certainly not shown that they know of any sure and safe way to reduce it—that is, any way not already known to every corner druggist. But when an attempt is made to put them down by law, the question whether they are wise falls into the background, and the question whether their rights are invaded comes forward. At once the crowd on their side is immensely reinforced. It now includes not only all the persons who believe in birth control, but also all the persons who believe in free ideas and free speech, and this second group, it quickly appears, is far larger than the first one, and far more formidable. So the birth controllers suddenly find themselves supported by heavy battalions, and that support is sufficient to make them almost invulnerable. Personally, I am inclined to be against them. I believe that the ignorant should be permitted to spawn *ad libitum*, that there may be a steady supply of slaves, and that those of us who are more prudent and sanitary may be relieved of unpleasant work. If the debate were open and fair, I'd oppose the birth controllers with all the subtlest devices of rhetoric, including bogus statistics and billingsgate. But so long as they are denied their plain rights—and, in particular, so long as those rights are denied them by an evil combination of theologians and politicians,—I am for them, and shall remain so until the last galoot's ashore. They have got many more allies on the same terms. And I believe that they are winning.

The law which forbids them to send their brummagem tracts through the mails is obviously disingenuous and oppressive. It is a part of the notorious Postal Act, put on the books by Comstock himself, executed by bureaucratic numskulls, and supported by every variety of witch-burner. I know of no intelligent man or woman who is in favor of the principal of such grotesque legislation; even the worst enemies of the birth controllers would not venture to argue that it should be applied generally. The way to dispose of such laws is to flout them and make a mock of them. The theory that they can be got rid of by enforcing them is nonsense. Enforcing them simply inspires the sadists who advocate them to fresh excesses.

Worse, it accustoms the people to oppression, and so tends to make them bear it uncomplainingly. Wherever, in the United States, there has been any sincere effort to enforce Prohibition, the anti-evolutionists are already on the warpath, and the Lord's Day Alliance is drumming up recruits. No, the way to deal with such laws is to defy them, and thus make them ridiculous. This is being done in the case of the Volstead Act by millions of patriots, clerical and lay. It is being done in the case of the Comstock Act by a small band, but one full of praiseworthy resolution.

Thus I deliver myself of a whoop for the birth controllers, and pass on to pleasanter concerns. Their specific Great Cause, it seems to me, is full of holes. They draw extremely questionable conclusions from a highly dubious body of so-called facts. But they are profoundly right at bottom. They are right when they argue that anyone who tries to silence them by force is the common enemy of all of us. And they are right when they hold that the best way to get rid of such opposition is to thumb the nose at it.

2
Comstockery

In 1873, when the late Anthony Comstock began his great Christian work, the American flapper, or, as she was then called, the young lady, read *Godey's Lady's Book.* To-day she reads—but if you want to find out what she reads simply take a look at the cheap fiction magazines which rise mountain-high from every news-stand. It is an amusing and at the same time highly instructive commentary upon the effectiveness of moral legislation. The net result of fifty years of Comstockery is complete and ignominious failure. All its gaudy raids and alarms have simply gone for naught.

Comstock, of course, was an imbecile; his sayings and doings were of such sort that they inevitably excited the public mirth, and so injured the cause he labored for. But it would be inaccurate, I believe, to put all the blame for its failure upon his imbecility. His successor, in New York, John S. Sumner, is by no means another such unwitting comedian; on the contrary, he shows discretion and even a certain wistful dignity.

Nevertheless, he has failed just as miserably. When he took office "Three Weeks" was still regarded as a very salacious book. The wives of Babbitts read it in the kitchen, with the blinds down; it was hidden under every pillow in every finishing-school in the land. To-day "Three Weeks" is dismissed as intolerably banal by school girls of thirteen. To make a genuine sensation it is not sufficient that a new book be naughty; it must be downright pathological.

I have been reviewing current American fiction pretty steadily since 1908. The change that I note is immense. When I began, a new novel dealing frankly with the physiology and pathology of sex was still something of a novelty. It was, indeed, so rare that I always called attention to it. To-day it is a commonplace. The surprise now comes when a new novel turns out to be chemically pure. Try to imagine an American publisher, in these days, getting alarmed about Dreiser's "Sister Carrie" and suppressing it before publication! The oldest and most dignified houses would print it without question; they print far worse every day. Yet in 1900 it seemed so lewd and lascivious that the publisher who put it into type got into a panic of fright, and hid the whole edition in the cellar. To-day that same publisher is advertising a new edition of Walt Whitman's "Leaves of Grass," with "A Woman Waits for Me" printed in full!

What ruined the cause of the Comstocks, I believe, was the campaign of their brethren of sex hygiene. The whole Comstockian case, as good Anthony himself used to explain frankly, was grounded upon the doctrine that virtue and ignorance were identical—that the slightest knowledge of sin was fatal to virtue. Comstock believed and argued that the only way to keep girls pure was to forbid them to think about sex at all. He expounded that doctrine often and at great length. No woman, he was convinced, could be trusted. The instant she was allowed to peek over the fence she was off to the Bad Lands. This notion he supported with many texts from Holy Writ, chiefly from the Old Testament. He was a Puritan of the old school, and had no belief whatever in virtue *per se*. A good woman, to him, was simply one who was efficiently policed. Unfortunately for him, there rose up, within the bounds of his own sect, a school of uplifters who began to merchant quite contrary ideas. They believed that sin was often caused by ignorance—that many a virtuous girl was undone simply because she didn't know what she was doing. These uplifters held that unchastity was not the product of a congenital tendency to it in the female, but of the sinister enterprise of the male, flowing out of his superior knowledge and sophistication. So they set out to spread the enlightenment. If all girls of sixteen, they argued not unplausibly, knew as much about the dreadful consequences of sin as the average police lieutenant or midwife, there would be no more seductions, and in accordance with that theory, they began printing books describing the discomforts of parturition and the terminal symptoms of lues. These books they broadcasted in numerous and immense editions. Comstock, of course, was bitterly against the scheme. He had no faith in the solemn warnings; he saw only the new and startling frankness, and he believed firmly that its one effect would be to "arouse a libidinous passion . . . in the mind of a modest woman." But he was spiked and hamstrung by the impeccable respectability of the sex hygienists. Most of them were Puritans like himself; some were towering giants of Christian rectitude. One of the most active, the Rev. Dr. Sylvanus Stall, was a clergyman of the first chop—a sorcerer who had notoriously saved thousands of immortal souls. To raid such men, to cast them into jail and denounce them as scoundrels, was palpably impossible. Comstock fretted and fumed, but the thing got beyond him. Of Pastor Stall's books alone, millions were sold. Others were almost as successful; the country was flooded from coast to coast.

Whether Comstock was right or wrong I don't know—that is, whether these sex hygiene books increased or diminished loose living in the Republic I don't know. Some say one thing and some another. But this I *do* know; they had a quick and tremendous influence upon the content of American fiction. In the old-time novel what are now called the Facts of Life were glossed over mellifluously, and no one complained about it, for the great majority of fiction readers, being young and female, had no notion of what they were missing. But after they had read the sex hygiene books they began to observe that what was set out in novels was very evasive, and that much of it was downright untrue. So they began to murmur, to snicker, to boo. One by one the old-time novelists went on the shelf. I could make up a long and melancholy roll of them. Their sales dropped off; they began to be laughed at. In place of them rose a new school, and its aim was to tell it all. With this new school Comstock and his heirs have been wrestling ever since, and with steadily increasing bad fortune. Every year they make raids, perform in the newspapers and predict the end of the world, but every year the average is worse than the worst of the year before. As a practicing reviewer, I have got so used to lewd and lascivious books that I no longer notice them. They pour in from all directions. The most virtuous lady novelists write things that would have made a bartender blush to death two decades ago. If I open a new novel and find nothing about Freudian suppressions in it, I suspect at once that it is simply a reprint of some forgotten novel of 1885, with a new name. When I began reviewing I used to send my review copies, after I had sweated through them, to the Y.M.C.A. Now I send them to a medical college.

The Comstocks labor against this stream gallantly, but, it seems to me, very ineptly. They can't, of course, proceed against every naughty book that comes out, for there are far too many, but they could at least choose their marks far more sagaciously than they do. Instead of tackling the books that are frankly pornographic and have no other excuse for being, they almost always tackle books that have obvious literary merit, and are thus relatively easily defended. In consequence, they lose most of their cases. They lost with "Jurgen," they lost with "The 'Genius,'" they lost with "Mlle. de Maupin," and they have lost countless other times. And every time they lose they grow more impotent and absurd. Why do they pick out such books? Simply because raiding them gets more publicity than raiding more obscure stuff. The Comstock Society, like all other such pious organizations, is chronically short of money, and the way to raise it is to make a noise in the newspapers. A raid on "Night Life in Chicago," or "Confessions of an Escaped Nun" would get but a few lines; an attack on "Jurgen" is first-page stuff for days on end. Christian virtuosi, their libido aroused, send in their money, and so the society is saved. But when the trial is called and the case is lost, contributions fall off again, and another conspicuous victim must be found.

Well, what is the Comstocks' own remedy for this difficulty? It is to be found in what they call the Clean Books Bill. The aim of this bill is to make it impossible for a publisher accused of publishing an immoral book to make any defense at all. If it ever becomes a law the Comstocks will be able to pick out a single sentence from a Dreiser novel of 10,000 pages and base their whole case upon it; the author and publisher will be forbidden to offer the rest of the book as evidence that the whole has no pornographic purpose. Under such a law anyone printing or selling the Bible will run dreadful risks. One typographical error of a stimulating character will suffice to send a publisher to jail. But will the law actually achieve its purpose? I doubt it. Such extravagant and palpably unjust statutes never accomplish anything. Juries revolt against them; even judges punch holes in them. The Volstead Act is an excellent specimen. Has it made the Republic dry?

3
Capital Punishment

Having argued against the death penalty with great heat and eloquence for more than twenty years, I hope I do not go beyond my rights when I now announce that I have begun to wobble, and feel a strong temptation to take the other side. My doubts, in all seriousness, I ascribe to the arguments of the current abolitionists. The more earnestly they set forth those arguments, the more I am harassed by suspicions that they are full of folly. A humane and Christian spirit, to be sure, is in them; but is there any sense? As I hint, I begin to doubt it. Consider the two that are oftenest heard:

1. That hanging a man (or doing him to death in any other such coldblooded way) is a dreadful business, degrading to those who have to do it and revolting to those who have to witness it.
2. That it is useless, for it does not deter others from the same crime.

The first of these arguments, it seems to me, is plainly too weak to need serious refutation. All it says, in brief, is that the work of the hangman is unpleasant. Granted. But suppose it is? It may be quite necessary to society for all that. There are, indeed, many other jobs that are unpleasant, and yet no one thinks of abolishing them. I pass over those connected with surgery, obstetrics, plumbing, military science, journalism and the sacred office, and point to one which, like that of the hangman, has to do with the execution of the laws: to wit, the post of Federal judge under Prohibition. Consider what a judge executing the Volstead Act must do nearly every day. He must assume that men whom he esteems and loves, men of his own profession, even his fellow judges—in brief, the great body of wet and enlightened Christian men—are all criminals. And he must assume that a pack of spies and blackmailers whose mere presence, in private life, would gag him—in brief, the corps of Anti-Saloon League snouters and Prohibition agents—are truth-seekers and altruists. These assumptions are obviously hard to make. Not a few judges, unable to make them, resign from the bench; at least one has committed suicide. But the remaining judges, so long as they sit, must make them as in duty bound, whatever the outrage to their feelings. Many grow callous and suffer no more. So with the hangman, and his even more disagreeable offices. A man of delicate sensibilities, confronting them, would die of horror, but there is no evidence that they are revolting to the men who actually discharge them. I have known hangmen, indeed, who delighted in their art, and practiced it proudly. I have never heard of one who threw up his job.

In the second argument of the abolitionists there is more force, but even here, I believe, the ground under them is very shaky. Their fundamental error consists in assuming that the whole aim of punishing criminals is to deter other (potential) criminals—that we hang or electrocute A simply in order to so alarm B that he will not kill C. This, I believe, is an assumption almost as inaccurate as those which must be made by a Federal judge. It confuses a part with the whole. Deterrence, obviously, is *one* of the aims of punishment, but it is surely not the only one. On the contrary, there are at least half a dozen, and some of them are probably quite as important. At least one of them, practically considered, is *more* important. Commonly, it is described as revenge, but revenge is really not the word for it. I borrow a better term from the late Aristotle: *katharsis*. *Katharsis*, so used, means a salubrious discharge of emotions, a healthy letting off of steam. A schoolboy, disliking his teacher, deposits a tack upon the pedagogical chair; the teacher jumps and the boy laughs. This is *katharsis.* A bootlegger, paying off a Prohibition agent, gives him a counterfeit $10 bill; the agent, dropping it in the collection plate on Sunday, is arrested and jailed. This is also *katharsis.* A subscriber to a newspaper, observing his name spelled incorrectly in the report of a lodge meeting, spreads a report that the editor of the paper did not buy Liberty Bonds. This again is *katharsis.*

What I contend is that one of the prime objects of judicial punishments is to afford this grateful *katharsis* (a) to the immediate victims of the criminal punished, and (b) to the general body of moral and timorous men. These persons, and particularly the first group, are concerned only indirectly with deterring other criminals. The thing they crave primarily is the satisfaction of seeing the criminal before them suffer as he made them suffer. What they want is the peace of mind that goes with the feeling that accounts are squared. Until they get that satisfaction they are in a state of emotional tension, and hence unhappy. The instant they get it they are comfortable. I do not argue that this yearning is noble; I simply argue that it is almost universal among human beings. In the face of injuries that are unimportant and can be borne without damage it may yield to higher impulses; that is to say, it may yield to what is called Christian charity. But it never so yields when the injury is serious, and gives substantial permanent satisfaction to the person inflicting it. Here Christianity is adjourned, and even saints reach for their sidearms. The better the Christian, in fact, the more violent his demand for *katharsis*—once he has unloaded the Beatitudes. At the time of the Leopold-Loeb trial in Chicago the evangelical pastors of the town bawled for blood unanimously, and even a Catholic priest joined them. On lower levels, it is plainly asking too much of human nature to expect it to conquer so natural an impulse. A keeps a store and has a bookkeeper, B. B steals $700, invests it in Texas oil stocks, and is cleaned out. What is A to do? Let B go? If he does so he will be unable to sleep at night. The sense of injury, of injustice, will keep him awake. So he turns B over to the police, and they send him to prison. Thereafter A can sleep. More, he has pleasant dreams. He pictures B chained to the wall of a dungeon a hundred feet underground, devoured by rats. It is so agreeable that it makes him forget his $700. He has got his *katharsis.*

The same thing precisely takes place on a larger scale when there is a crime which destroys a whole community's feeling of security. Every law-abiding citizen feels menaced and frustrated until the criminals have been struck down—until the communal capacity to get even with them, and more than even, has been dramatically demonstrated. Here the business of deterring others is no more than an afterthought. The main thing is to destroy the scoundrels whose act has alarmed everyone, and thus made everyone unhappy. Until they are brought to book that unhappiness continues; when the law has been executed upon them there is a sigh of relief. In other words, there is *katharsis.*

There is no public demand for the death penalty for ordinary crimes, even for ordinary homicides. Its infliction, say, for necking, for playing poker or for bootlegging would shock all men of normal decency of feeling—that is to say, practically all men save the evangelical clergy and their lay catchpolls. But for crimes involving the deliberate and inexcusable taking of human life, by men openly defiant of all civilized order—for such crimes it seems, to nine men out of ten, a just and proper punishment. Any lesser punishment leaves them feeling that the criminal has got the better of society—that he can add insult to injury by laughing. That feeling is intensely unpleasant, and no wonder! It can be dissipated only by a recourse to *katharsis*, the invention of the aforesaid Aristotle. That *katharsis* is most effectively and economically achieved, as human nature now is, by wafting the criminal to realms of bliss.

4
War

My mail is flooded with the briefs and broadsides of pacifist organizations, damning war as a curse and those who make it as scoundrels. Such literature I always read attentively, for it is full of racy satire against the military, a class of men inevitably more or less ludicrous in time of peace. But does it convert me to the pacifist cause, which, as the pacifists contend, is the cause of God? I can only report simply that it does not. I read it, enjoy it, pass it on to my pastor—and go on believing in war myself. War is the only sport, so far as I know, that is genuinely amusing. And it is the only sport that has any intelligible use.

The arguments that are brought against it are chiefly arguments, not against the thing itself, but only against its political accompaniments and consequences, most of them transient and gratuitous. They reached a high tide of obnoxiousness, revolting to all self-respecting men, during the last great moral combat. That combat was carried on, at least from this side of the fence, in a grossly hysterical, disingenuous, cowardly and sordid manner. The high participating parties were vastly alarmed by the foe, and insanely eager to keep business going as usual, and even better than usual. The result was that the thing began as a sort of Methodist revival and ended as a raid on a gentleman's winecellar, with the Prohibition agents fighting among themselves for the best jugs. The richest of them, once peace came, began sending the others extortionate bills for the brass-knuckles, Bibles and jimmies that all had used in common, and the heroes serving this usurer began demanding tips in cash. But all that swinishness, I submit, had no necessary connection with war itself. It is perfectly possible to conduct war in a gallant and honorable manner, and without using it as a mere cloak to rob noncombatants. More, the thing has been done, and many times in the history of the world. If it has been seldom done by democratic nations, then blame democracy, not war. In democratic nations everything noble and of good account tends to decay and smell badly.

War itself, in its pure form, is something quite different. It is a combat of men who believe that a short and adventurous life, full of changing scenes and high hazards, is better than a safe and dull one—in other words, that it is better to have lived magnificently than to have lived long. In this doctrine I am unable to discern anything properly describable as fallacy. If you argue that, assuming every man to embrace it, the human race would come to an end, I reply at once that you assume something wholly impossible. And if you argue that the life of a warrior is not actually magnificent, then I report that the warrior should be permitted to judge of that himself. Against all such arguments lie the plain facts that the great races of the world have always been more or less warlike, and that war has attracted the talent and satisfied the aspiration of some of their best men. I do not speak of antiquity alone; I speak of our own time. The English, the Germans and the French are all warlike, to-day as always—and if you took away the English, the Germans and the French *Homo sapiens* would be shorn of his stomach, his liver and his ductless glands. If war is immoral, then these great races are all immoral, and so are their greatest men. The pacifists, of course, do not shrink from that absurd argument. But the more they maintain it the more it becomes evident that, as logicians, they are on all fours with the Prohibitionists.

War, so conducted by warriors, is a superb business and full of high uses. It makes for resolution, endurance, enterprise, courage. It puts down the sordid yearnings of ignoble men. Does it, incidentally, shed some blood? Does it cost lives? The pacifists, discussing those lives, always enmesh themselves in the theory that, without war, they would go on forever. It is, I believe, not so. War, at worst, shortens them somewhat. But at the same stroke it speeds up their tempo. The net result is simply a matter of bookkeeping. A man killed at thirty, after six months of war, has lived far longer than a man dead of a bellyache at sixty, after forty-five years on an office stool.

But I am not on my legs to-day to sing the charms and glories of war; my purpose is to argue that, whether glorious or not, it will remain inevitable on this sad mud-pie so long as the great races of men retain the view of it that I have described, and to deduce therefrom the doctrine that pacifism, as a scheme of practical politics, is thus not only unsound but also very dangerous. All that it could conceivably accomplish, imagining it to succeed anywhere, would be to make the nation embracing it highly vulnerable—in brief, a sort of boozy idealist or unarmored butter-and-egg man, roaming the world unprotected, and so holding out irresistible temptations to less moral and more realistic nations.

War, under the sorry scheme that now passes for civilization, has been degraded—transiently only, I hope and believe—to the uses of robbery. Whoever has gold must have an army to guard it, or resign himself to losing it. Especially must he have a guard for it if his public repute is that of one with a not too fine understanding of the difference between *meum* and *tuum*.

Such a reputation, it must be manifest, is precisely that of the United States to-day. The rest of the world is so passionately convinced that it is a thief that robbing it would take on the high virtue and dignity of a constabulary act. It is not robbed because it is strong. It will not be robbed until it grows weak.

But armed strength, argue the pacifists, does not prevent war: it causes it. Who, reading history, could believe in such transparent nonsense? Let us turn to the late enemy. What kept the peace in Europe for forty-four years if it was not the mighty German army? If it had been weak, France would have struck in 1875, and again in 1882, and again in 1887, and again every two years thereafter. It took nearly half a century to roll up a force sufficient to tackle the colossus, and it took four years to bring it down even then. Our own history is full of examples to the same effect. In 1867 Napoleon III, believing that the United States was war weary and its army disbanded, prepared to move into Mexico and tear the Monroe Doctrine to tatters. He overlooked the large forces engaged in burning barns, robbing hen-roosts and raiding cellars in the late Confederacy. When General Sheridan marched upon the Rio Grande at the head of this army of heroes, Napoleon changed his mind. Three years later he was disposed of by the Germans, and the Continent settled down to forty-four years of peace.

Consider, again, the Venezuela episode. When President Cleveland sent his message to Congress on December 17, 1895, war with England became imminent overnight. What prevented it? Was it the fact that the United States had no army worthy of the name? Or the fact that the United States had a brand-new, highly effective and immensely pugnacious navy, notoriously eager to try its guns? Come, now, to 1898. Of all the nations of Europe, only England sided with us against Spain. The Germans, at Manila, went to great lengths to show their hostility. Did they refrain from attacking Dewey because his fleet was smaller and weaker than theirs, or because it was larger and stronger?

I could multiply instances, but observe the time-keeper reaching for the gong. So far as I know, there is no record in history of a nation that ever gained anything valuable by being unable to defend itself. Such nations, true enough, have sometimes managed to exist for a time—but at what cost! There is the case of Denmark to-day. It is discussing disbanding its army on the ground that any probable or even possible foe could dispose of that army in five days. But what does this mean? It means that the Danes must reconcile themselves to living by the sheer grace of their stronger neighbors—that they must be willing, when the time comes, to see their country made a battle-ground by those neighbors, and without raising a hand. Here I do not indulge in idle talk: I am quoting almost literally a member of the Danish cabinet.

I can't imagine the people of a truly great nation submitting to any such ignominious destiny. The Danes have been forced into acquiescence by their weakness. But why should the United States invite the same fate by putting off its strength?

II.
Four Makers of Tales

I
Conrad

SOME time ago I put in a blue afternoon re-reading Joseph Conrad's "Youth." A *blue* afternoon? What nonsense! The touch of the man is like the touch of Schubert. One approaches him in various and unhappy moods: depressed, dubious, despairing; one leaves him in the clear, yellow sunshine that Nietzsche found in Bizet's music. But here again the phrase is inept. Sunshine suggests the imbecile, barnyard joy of the human kohlrabi—the official optimism of a steadily delighted and increasingly insane Republic. What the enigmatical Pole has to offer is something quite different. If its parallel is to be found in music, it is not in Schubert, but in Beethoven—perhaps even more accurately in Johann Sebastian Bach. It is the joy, not of mere satisfaction, but of understanding—the profound but surely not merry delight which goes with the comprehension of a fundamental fact—above all, of a fact that has been coy and elusive. Certainly the order of the world that Conrad sets forth with such diabolical eloquence and plausibility is no banal moral order, no childish sequence of virtuous causes and edifying effects. Rather it has an atheistic and even demoniacal smack: to the earnest Bible student it must be more than a little disconcerting. The God he visualizes is no loving papa in a house-coat and carpet-slippers, inculcating the great principles of Christian ethics by applying occasional strokes *a posteriori*. What he sees is something quite different: an extremely ingenious and humorous Improvisatore and Comedian, with a dab of red on His nose and maybe somewhat the worse for drink—a furious and far from amiable banjoist upon the human spine, and rattler of human bones. Kurtz, in "Youth," makes a capital banjo for that exalted and cynical talent. And the music that issues forth—what a superb *Hexentanz* it is!

One of the curiosities of critical stupidity is the doctrine that

Conrad is without humor. No doubt it flows out of a more general error; to wit, the assumption that tragedy is always pathetic, that death itself is inevitably a gloomy business. That error, I suppose, will persist in the world until some extraordinary astute mime conceives the plan of playing "King Lear" as a farce—I mean deliberately. That it *is* a farce seems to me quite as obvious as the fact that "Romeo and Juliet" is another, this time lamentably coarse. To adopt the contrary theory—to view it as a great moral and spiritual spectacle, capable of purging and uplifting the psyche like marriage to a red-haired widow or a month in the trenches—to toy with such notions is to borrow the critical standards of a party of old ladies weeping over the damnation of the heathen. In point of fact, death, like love, is intrinsically farcical—a solemn kicking of a brick under a plug-hat—, and most other human agonies, once they transcend the physical—*i.e.*, the unescapably real—have far more of irony in them than of pathos. Looking back upon them after they have eased one seldom shivers: one smiles—perhaps sourly but nevertheless spontaneously. This, at all events, is the notion that seems to me implicit in every line of Conrad. I give you "Heart of Darkness" as the archetype of his whole work and the keystone of his metaphysical system. Here we have all imaginable human hopes and aspirations reduced to one common denominator of folly and failure, and here we have a play of humor that is infinitely mordant and searching. Turn to pages 136 and 137 of the American edition—the story is in the volume called "Youth"—: the burial of the helmsman. Turn then to 178–184: Marlow's last interview with Kurtz's intended. The farce mounts by slow stages to dizzy and breathtaking heights. One hears harsh roars of cosmic laughter, vast splutterings of transcendental mirth, echoing and reëchoing down the black corridors of empty space. The curtain descends at last upon a wild dance in a dissecting-room. The mutilated dead rise up and jig. . . .

It is curious, re-reading a thrice-familiar story, how often one finds surprises in it. I have been amazed, toward the close of "The End of the Tether," to discover that the *Fair Maid* was wrecked, not by the deliberate act of Captain Whalley, but by the machination of the unspeakable Massy. How is one to account for so preposterous an error? Certainly I thought I knew "The End of the Tether" as well as I knew anything in this world—and yet there was that incredible misunderstanding of it, lodged firmly in my mind. Perhaps there is criticism of a sort in my blunder: it may be a fact that the old skipper willed the thing himself—that his willing it is visible in all that goes before—that Conrad, in introducing Massy's puerile infamy at the end, made some sacrifice of inner veracity to the exigencies of what, at bottom, is somewhat too neat and well-made a tale. The story, in fact, belongs to the author's earlier manner; I guess that it was written before "Youth" and surely before "Heart of Darkness." But for all that, its proportions remain truly colossal. It is one of the most magnificent narratives, long or short, old or new, in the English language, and with "Youth" and "Heart of Darkness" it makes up what is probably the best book of imaginative writing that the English literature of the Twientieth Century can yet show. Conrad learned a great deal after he wrote it, true enough. In "Lord Jim," in "Victory," and, above all, in a "A Personal Record," there are momentary illuminations, blinding flashes of brilliance that he was incapable of in those days of experiment; but no other book of his seems to me to hold so steadily to so high a general level—none other, as a whole, is more satisfying and more marvelous. There is in "Heart of Darkness" a perfection of design which one encounters only rarely and miraculously in prose fiction: it belongs rather to music. I can't imagine taking a single sentence out of that stupendous tale without leaving a visible gap; it is as thoroughly *durch componiert* as a fugue. And I can't imagine adding anything to it, even so little as a word, without doing it damage. As it stands it is austerely and beautifully perfect, just as the slow movement of the Unfinished Symphony is perfect.

I observe of late a tendency to examine the English of Conrad rather biliously. This folly is cultivated chiefly in England, where, I suppose, chauvinistic motives enter into the matter. It is the just boast of great empires that they draw in talents from near and far, exhausting the little nations to augment their own puissance; it is their misfortune that these talents often remain defectively assimilated. Conrad remained the Slav to the end. The people of his tales, whatever he calls them, are always as much Slavs as he is; the language in which he describes them retains a sharp, exotic flavor. But to say that this flavor constitutes a blemish is to say something so preposterous that only schoolmasters and their dupes may be thought of as giving it credit. The truly first-rate writer is not one who uses the language as such dolts demand that it be used; he is one who reworks it in spite of their prohibitions. It is his distinction that he thinks in a manner different from the thinking of ordinary men; that he is free from that slavery to embalmed ideas which makes them so respectable and so dull. Obviously, he cannot translate his notions into terms of everyday without doing violence to their inner integrity; as well ask a Richard Strauss to funnel all his music into the chaste jugs of Prof. Dr. Jadassohn. What Conrad brought into English literature was a new concept of the relations between fact and fact, idea and idea, and what he contributed to the complex and difficult art of writing English was a new way of putting words together. His style now amazes and irritates pedants because it does not roll along in the old ruts. Well, it is precisely that rolling along in the old ruts that he tried to avoid—and it was precisely that avoidance which made him what he is. What lies under most of his alleged sins seems to me to be simple enough: he views English logically and analytically, and not through a haze of senseless traditions and arbitrary taboos. No Oxford mincing is in him. If he cannot find his phrase above the salt, he seeks it below. His English, in a word, is innocent. And if, at times, there gets into it a color that is strange and even bizarre, then the fact is something to rejoice over, for a living language is like a man suffering incessantly from small internal hemorrhages, and what it needs above all else is constant transfusions of new blood from other tongues. The day the gates go up, that day it begins to die.

A very great man, this Mr. Conrad. As yet, I believe decidedly underestimated, even by many of his post-mortem advocates. Most of his first acclaimers mistook him for a mere romantic—a talented but somewhat uncouth follower of the Stevenson tradition, with the orthodox cutlass exchanged for a Malay *kris*. Later on he began to be heard of as a linguistic and vocational marvel: it was astonishing that any man bred to Polish should write English at all, and more astonishing that a country gentleman from the Ukraine should hold a master's certificate in the British merchant marine. Such banal attitudes are now archaic, but I suspect that they have been largely responsible for the slowness with which his fame has spread in the world. At all events, he is vastly less read and esteemed in foreign parts than he ought to be, and very few Continental Europeans have risen to any genuine comprehension of his stature. When one reflects that the Nobel Prize was given to such third-raters as Benavente, Heidenstam, Gjellerup and Tagore, with Conrad passed over, one begins to grasp the depth and density of the ignorance prevailing in the world, even among the relatively enlightened. One "Lord Jim," as human document and as work of art, is worth all the works produced by all the Benaventes and Gjellerups since the time of Rameses II. It is, indeed, an indecency of criticism to speak of such unlike things in the same breath: as well talk of Brahms in terms of Mendelssohn. Nor is "Lord Jim" a chance masterpiece, an isolated peak. On the contrary, it is but one unit in a long series of extraordinary and almost incomparable works—a series sprung suddenly and overwhelmingly into full dignity with "Almayer's Folly." I challenge the nobility and gentry of Christendom to point to another Opus 1 as magnificently planned and turned out as "Almayer's Folly." The more one studies it, the more it seems miraculous. If it is not a work of absolute genius then no work of absolute genius exists on this earth.

2
Hergesheimer

This gentleman, like Conrad, has been slated very waspishly because his English is sometimes in contempt of Lindley Murray. Once, a few years back, a grammarian writing in the *New Republic* formally excommunicated him for it. A number of his offending locutions were cited, all of them, it must be admitted, instantly recognizable as pathological and against God by any suburban schoolma'm. *Soit!* The plain truth is that Hergesheimer, when it comes to the ultimate delicacies of English grammar, is an ignoramus, as he is when it comes to the niceties of Swedenborgian theology. I doubt that he could tell a noun in the nominative case from a noun in the objective.

But neither could any other man who writes as well as he does. Such esoteric knowledge is the exclusive possession of grammarians, whose pride in it runs in direct ratio to its inaccuracy, unimportance and imbecility. English grammar as a science thus takes its place with phrenology and the New Thought: the more a grammarian knows of it, the less he is worth listening to. Mastering such blowsy nonsense is one thing, and writing sound English is quite another thing, and the two achievements seem to be impossible to the same man. As Anatole France once remarked, nearly all first-rate writers write "bad French"—or "bad English." Joseph Conrad did. France himself did. Dreiser does. Henry James did. Dickens did. Shakespeare did. Thus Hergesheimer need not repine. He is sinful, but in good company. He writes English that is "bad," but also English that is curiously musical, fluent, chromatic, various and caressing. There is in even the worst of his *Saturday Evening Post* novelettes for Main Street a fine feeling for the inner savor of words—a keen ear for their subtler and more fragile harmonies. In "Cytherea," which I like beyond all his works—even beyond "The Three Black Pennys" and "Java Head"—they are handled in so adept and ingenious a way, with so much delicacy and originality, that it is no wonder they offer an intolerable affront to pedagogues.

This novel, as I say, seems to me to be the best that Hergesheimer has yet done. His best writing is in it, and his best observation. What interests him fundamentally is the conflict between the natural impulses of men and women and the conventions of the society that they are parts of. The struggles he depicts are not between heroes and villains, dukes and peasants, patriots and spies, but between the desire to be happy and the desire to be respected. It is, perhaps, a tribute to the sly humor of God that whichever way the battle goes, the result is bound to be disastrous to the man himself. If, seeking happiness in a world that is jealous of it and so frowns upon it, he sacrifices the good will of his fellow men, he always finds in the end that happiness is not happiness at all without it. And if, grabbing the other horn of the dilemma, he sacrifices the free play of his instincts to the respect of those fellow men, he finds that he has also sacrificed his respect for himself. Hergesheimer is no seer. He does not presume to solve the problem; he merely states it with agreeable variations and in the light of a compassionate irony. In "Cytherea" it takes the ancient form of the sexual triangle—old material, but here treated, despite the underlying skepticism, with a new illumination. What we are asked to observe is a marriage in which all the customary causes follow instead of precede their customary effects. To the eye of the world, and even, perhaps, to the eye of the secondary figures in it, the Randon-Grove affair is no more than a standard-model adultery, orthodox in its origin and in its course. Lee Randon, with an amiable and faithful wife, Fanny, at home in Eastlake, Pa., in the Country-Club Belt, with two charming children at her knee, goes to the hell-hole known as New York, falls in love with the sinister Mrs. Savina Grove, and forthwith bolts with her to Cuba, there to encounter a just retribution in the form of her grotesque death. But that is precisely what does *not* happen—that is, interiorly. Savina actually has little more to do with the flight of Randon than the Pullman Company which hauls him southward. It is already inevitable when he leaves Eastlake for New York, almost unaware of her existence. Its springs are to be sought in the very normalcy that it so profoundly outrages. He is the victim, like Fanny, his wife, of a marriage that has turned upon and devoured itself.

Hergesheimer was never more convincing than in his anatomizing of this *débâcle*. He is too impatient, and perhaps too fine an artist, to do it in the conventional realistic manner of piling up small detail. Instead he launches into it with a bold sagittal section, and at once the play of forces becomes comprehensible. What ails Randon, in brief, is that he has a wife who is a shade too good. Beautiful, dutiful, amiable, virtuous, yes. But not provocative enough—not sufficiently the lady of scarlet in the chemise of snowy white. Worse, a touch of stupid blindness is in her: she can see the honest business man, but she can't see the romantic lurking within him. When Randon, at a country-club dance, sits out a hoe-down with some flashy houri on the stairs, all that Fanny can see in it is a vulgar matter, like kissing a chambermaid behind the door. Even when Randon brings home the doll, Cytherea, and gives it a place of honor in their house, and begins mooning over it strangely, she is unable to account for the business in any terms save those of transient silliness. The truth is that Cytherea is to

Randon what La Belle Ettarre is to Cabell's Felix Kennaston—his altar-flame in a dun world, his visualization of the unattainable, his symbol of what might have been. In her presence he communes secretly with the outlaw hidden beneath the chairman of executive committees, the gypsy concealed in the sound Americano. One day, bent upon God's work (specifically, upon breaking up a nefarious affair between a neighboring Rotarian and a moving-picture lady), he encounters the aforesaid Savina Grove, accidentally brushes her patella with his own, gets an incandescent glare in return, discovers to his horror that she is the living image of Cytherea—and ten days later is aboard the Key West Express with her, bound for San Cristobal de la Habaña, and the fires eternal.

A matter, fundamentally, of coincidence. Savina, too, has her Cytherea, though not projected into a doll. She too has toiled up the long slope of a flabby marriage, and come at last to the high crags where the air is thin, and a sudden giddiness may be looked for. To call the thing a love affair, in the ordinary sense, is rather fantastic; its very endearments are forced and mawkish. What Randon wants is not more love, but an escape from the bonds and penalties of love—a leap into pure adventure. And what Savina wants, as she very frankly confesses, is the same thing. If a concrete lover must go with it, then that lover must be everything that the decorous William Loyd Grove is not—violent, exigent, savage, inordinate, even a bit gross. I doubt that Savina gets her wish any more than Randon gets his. Good business men make but indifferent Grand Turks, even when they are in revolt: it is the tragedy of Western civilization. And there is no deliverance from the bonds of habit and appearance, even with a mistress. Ten days after he reaches Havana, Randon is almost as securely married as he was at Eastlake. Worse, Eastlake itself reaches out its long arm and begins to punish him, and Savina with him. The conventions of Christendom, alas, are not to be spat upon. Far back in the Cuban hinterland, in a squalid little sugar town, it is a photograph of Fanny that gives a final touch of gruesomeness to the drama of Randon and Savina. There, overtaken in her sin by that banal likeness of the enemy she has never seen, she dies her preposterous death. An ending profoundly ironical. A curtain that gives a final touch of macabre humor to a tale that, from first to last, is full of the spirit of high comedy. Hergesheimer never devised one more sardonically amusing, and he never told one with greater skill.

The reviewers, contemplating it, were shocked by his hedonism in trivialities—his unctuous manner of recording the flavor of a drink, the sheen of a fabric, the set of a skirt, the furnishings of a room. In all that, I suppose, they saw something Babylonish, and against the Constitution. But this hedonism is really as essential a part of Hergesheimer as moral purpose is part of a Puritan. He looks upon the world, not as a trial of virtue, but as a beautiful experience—in part, indeed, as a downright voluptuous experience. If it is elevating to the soul to observe the fine colors of a sunset, then why is it not quite as elevating to observe the fine colors of a woman's hair, the silk of her frock, a piece of old mahogany, a Jack Rose cocktail? Here it is not actually Hergesheimer's delight in beauty that gives offense, but his inability to differentiate between the beauty that is also the good and the true, and the beauty that is simply beauty. As for me, I incline to go with him in his heresy. It constitutes a valuable antidote to the moral obsession which still hangs over American letters, despite the collapse of the Puritan *Kultur*. It still seems a bit foreign and bizarre, but that is because we have yet to achieve a complete emancipation from the International Sunday-school Lessons. In "Cytherea," as in "Java Head," it gives a warm and exotic glow to the narrative. That narrative is always recounted, not by a moralist, but by an artist. He knows how to give an episode color and reality by the artful use of words and the images that they bring up—how to manage the tempo, the play of light, the surrounding harmonies. This investiture is always as much a part of his story as his tale itself. So is his English style, so abhorrent to grammarians. When he writes a sentence that is a bit artificial and complex, it is because he is describing something that is itself a bit artificial and complex. When he varies his rhythms suddenly and sharply, it is not because he is unable to write in the monotonous sing-song of a rhetoric professor, but because he doesn't want to write that way. Whatever such a man writes is *ipso facto* good English. It is not for pedagogues to criticise it, but to try to comprehend it and teach it. The delusion to the contrary is the cause of much folly.

3
Lardner

A few years ago a young college professor, eager to make a name for himself, brought out a laborious "critical" edition of "Sam Slick," by Judge Thomas C. Haliburton, eighty-seven years after its first publication. It turned out to be quite unreadable—a dreadful series of archaic jocosities about varieties of *Homo americanus* long perished and forgotten, in a dialect now intelligible only to paleophilologists. Sometimes I have a fear that the same fate awaits Ring Lardner. The professors of his own day, of course, are quite unaware of him, save perhaps as a low zany to be enjoyed behind the door. They would no more venture to whoop him up publicly and officially than their predecessors of 1880 would have ventured to whoop up Mark Twain, or their remoter predecessors of 1837 would have dared to say anything for Haliburton. In such matters the academic mind, being chiefly animated by a fear of sneers, works very slowly. So slowly, indeed, does it work that it usually works too late. By the time Mark Twain got into the text-books for sophomores two-thirds of his compositions, as the Young Intellectuals say, had already begun to date; by the time Haliburton was served up as a sandwich between introduction and notes he was already dead. As I say, I suspect sadly that Lardner is doomed to go the same route. His stories, it seems to me, are superbly adroit and amusing; no other contemporary American, sober or gay, writes better. But I doubt that they last: our grandchildren will wonder what they are about. It is not only, or even mainly, that the dialect that fills them will pass, though that fact is obviously a serious handicap in itself. It is principally that the people they depict will pass, that Lardner's Low Down Americans—his incomparable baseball players, pugs, song-writers, Elks, small-town Rotarians and golf caddies—are flitting figures of a transient civilization, and doomed to be a puzzling and soporific, in the year 2000, as Haliburton's Yankee clock peddler is to-day.

The fact—if I may assume it to be a fact—is certain not to be set against Lardner's account; on the contrary, it is, in its way, highly complimentary to him. For he has deliberately applied himself, not to the anatomizing of the general human soul, but to the meticulous histological study of a few salient individuals of his time and nation, and he has done it with such subtle and penetrating skill that one must belong to his time and nation to follow him. I doubt that anyone who is not familiar with professional ball players, intimately and at first hand, will ever comprehend the full merit of the amazing sketches in "You Know Me, Al"; I doubt that anyone who has not given close and deliberate attention to the American vulgate will ever realize how magnificently Lardner handles it. He has had more imitators, I suppose, than any other living American writer, but has he any actual rivals? If so, I have yet to hear of them. They all try to write the speech of the streets as adeptly and as amusingly as he writes it, and they all fall short of him; the next best is miles and miles behind him. And they are all inferior in observation, in sense of character, in shrewdness and insight. His studies, to be sure, are never very profound; he makes no attempt to get at the primary springs of human motive; all his people share the same amiable stupidity, the same transparent vanity, the same shallow swinishness; they are all human Fords in bad repair, and alike at bottom. But if he thus confines himself to the surface, it yet remains a fact that his investigations on that surface are extraordinarily alert, ingenious and brilliant—that the character he finally sets before us, however roughly articulated as to bones, is so astoundingly realistic as to epidermis that the effect is indistinguishable from that of life itself. The old man in "The Golden Honeymoon" is not merely well done; he is perfect. And so is the girl in "Some Like Them Cold." And so, even, is the idiotic Frank X. Farrell in "Alibi Ike"—an extravagant grotesque and yet quite real from glabella to calcaneus.

Lardner knows more about the management of the short story than all of its professors. His stories are built very carefully, and yet they seem to be wholly spontaneous, and even formless. He has grasped the primary fact that no conceivable ingenuity can save a story that fails to show a recognizable and interesting character; he knows that a good character sketch is always a good story, no matter what its structure. Perhaps he gets less attention than he ought to get, even among the anti-academic critics, because his people are all lowly boors. For your reviewer of books, like every other sort of American, is always vastly impressed by fashionable pretensions. He belongs to the white collar class of labor, and shares its prejudices. He praises F. Scott Fitzgerald's stories of country-club flappers eloquently, and overlooks Fitzgerald's other stories, most of which are much better. He can't rid himself of the feeling that Edith Wharton, whose people have butlers, is a better novelist than Willa Cather, whose people, in the main, dine in their kitchens. He lingers under the spell of Henry James, whose most humble character, at any rate of the later years, was at least an Englishman, and hence superior. Lardner, so to speak, hits such critics under the belt. He not only fills his stories with people who read the tabloids, say "Shake hands with my friend," and buy diamond rings on the instalment plan; he also shows them having a good time in the world, and quite devoid of inferiority complexes. They amuse him sardonically, but he does not pity them. A fatal error! The moron, perhaps, has a place in fiction, as in life, but he is not to be treated too easily and casually. It must be shown that he suffers tragically because he cannot abandon the plow to write poetry, or the sample-case to study for opera. Lardner is more realistic. If his typical hero has a secret sorrow it is that he is too old to take up osteopathy and too much in dread of his wife to venture into bootlegging.

Of late a sharply acrid flavor has got into Lardner's buffoonery. His baseball players and fifth-rate pugilists, beginning in his first stories as harmless jackasses, gradually convert themselves into loathsome scoundrels. The same change shows itself in Sinclair Lewis; it is difficult, even for an American, to contemplate the American without yielding to something hard to distinguish from moral indignation. Turn, for example, to the sketches in the volume called "The Love Nest." The first tells the story of a cinema queen married to a magnate of the films. On the surface she seems to be nothing but a noodle, but underneath there is a sewer; the woman is such a pig that she makes one shudder. Again, he investigates another familiar type: the village practical joker. The fellow in one form or other, has been laughed at since the days of Aristophanes. But here is a mercilessly realistic examination of his dunghill humor, and of its effects upon decent people. A third figure is a successful theatrical manager: he turns out to have the professional competence of a chiropractor and the honor of a Prohibition agent. A fourth is a writer of popular songs: stealing other men's ideas has become so fixed a habit with him that he comes to believe that he has an actual right to them. A fourth is a trained nurse—but I spare you this dreadful nurse. The rest are bores of the homicidal type. One gets the effect, communing with the whole gang, of visiting a museum of anatomy. They are as shocking as what one encounters there—but in every detail they are as unmistakably real.

Lardner conceals his new savagery, of course, beneath his old humor. It does not flag. No man writing among us has greater skill at the more extravagant varieties of jocosity. He sees startling and revelatory likeness between immensely disparate things, and he is full of pawky observations and bizarre comments. Two baseball-players are palavering, and one of them, Young Jake, is boasting of his conquests during Spring practice below the Potomac. "Down South ain't here!" replies the other. "Those dames in some of those swamps, they lose their head when they see a man with shoes on!" The two proceed to the discussion of a third imbecile, guilty of some obscure tort. "Why," inquires Young Jake, "didn't you break his nose or bust him in the chin?" "His nose was already broke," replied the other, "and he didn't have no chin." Such wise cracks seem easy to devise. Broadway diverts itself by manufacturing them. They constitute the substance of half the town shows. But in those made by Lardner there is something far more than mere facile humor: they are all rigidly in character, and they illuminate that character. Few American novelists, great or small, have character more firmly in hand. Lardner does not see situations; he sees people. And what people! They are all as revolting as so many Methodist evangelists, and they are all as thoroughly American.

4
Masters

The case of Masters remains mysterious; more, even, than Sherwood Anderson, his fellow fugitive from a Chicago in decay, he presents an enigma to the prayerful critic. On the one hand there stands "The Spoon River Anthology," unquestionably the most eloquent, the most profound and the most thoroughly national volume of poetry published in America since "Leaves of Grass"; on the other hand stands a great mass of feeble doggerel—imitations of Byron, of Browning, of Lowell, of George H. Boker, of all the bad poets since the dawn of the Nineteenth Century. Of late he turns to prose, and with results almost as confusing. In all of his books there are fine touches, and in one of them, "Mitch Miller," there are many of them. But in all of them there are also banalities so crass and so vast that it is almost impossible to imagine a literate man letting them go by. Consider, for example, the novel, "Mirage." It seems to me to be one of the most idiotic and yet one of the most interesting American novels that I have ever read. Whole pages of it are given over to philosophical discussions that recall nothing so much as the palavers of neighboring barbers between shaves, and yet they are intermingled with observations that are shrewd and sound, and that are set forth with excellent grace and no little eloquence. Some of the characters in the book are mere stuffed dummies, creaking in every joint; others stand out as brilliantly alive as the people of Dreiser or Miss Cather. My suspicion is that there are actually two Masterses, that the man is a sort of literary diplococcus. At his worst, he is intolerably affected, arty and artificial—almost a fit companion for the occult, unintelligible geniuses hymned in the *Dial.* At his best he probably gets nearer to the essential truth about the civilization we suffer under than any other contemporary literatus.

"Mirage," I daresay, is already forgotten, though it was published only in 1924. In substance, it is the story of Skeeters Kirby's quest for the Wonder Woman that all sentimentalists seek, and that none of them finds until drink has brought him to his death-bed, and he sees the fat, affable nurse through a purple haze. Skeeters comes from the town of Mitch Miller, and when we first encounter him he is a lawyer in Chicago. Already the search for the Perfect Doll has begun to leave scars upon his psyche. First there was the sweet one who died before he could get her to the altar; then there was the naughty Alicia, his lawful wife, but, as he would say himself, a lemon. As the story opens, Alicia, divorcing him, had just blackmailed him out of $70,000, almost his whole fortune, as the price of her silence about Mrs. Becky Morris. Becky is the widow of a rich old man, and now enjoys the usufruct of his tenements and hereditaments. She has red hair and a charming manner, and is a great liar. She falsely pretends to have read Schopenhauer's "The World as Will and Idea," and passes in her circle as an intellectual on the strength of it. She tells Skeeters that she is virtuous, or, rather, that she *has* been virtuous, and all the while she is carrying on with one Delaher, a handsome frequenter of the Hotel Ritzdorf in New York. A saucy and poisonous baggage, this Becky, but Skeeters falls violently in love with her, and gladly pays Alicia the $70,000 in order to protect her from scandal. But then she leaves him, writes him a letter of farewell, and refuses flatly to marry him, and when he pursues her to New York, confronts her with her adulteries, and throws up to her the fact that he has gone broke for her, she requites him only with a dreadful slanging. I quote the exact text:

Kirby took a drink of brandy from the flask and came to her, taking her in his arms. "Tell, me, dear, what shall we do? Are we engaged?"

Becky shook her head.

"What do you wish? Shall I treat you as my bride-to-be, or shall we go on as we are now?"

"Go on as we are now!"

"You know I am free now—and it cost me, too, to be free."

"How much?"

"Seventy thousand dollars."

"That's not much."

"It's practically all I have."

"Well, *Alicia won't have such a large income out of it.*"

"And I paid it for you."

Becky opened her eyes. Her face became a bonfire of rage. Her red hair bristled like a wild animal's.

"You're just a liar to say that! And you can't say such things in my room. This is my room; *I pay for it.* And *you can be respectful to me here, or you can go.*"

Kirby did not betray his anger. He concentrated it and went on: "*I beg your pardon.*"

In a voice as soft as oil he asked:

"Did you see Delaher?"

"Yes, I did, and he's a rough-neck."

"Well?"

"None of your business!"

"None of my business, eh?" Kirby said, with a bitter intonation.
"Leave my room," Becky said.
"No, I'll not leave your room."
"*I'll have you put out.*"
"You don't dare, Becky—you don't dare!" . . .

Two pages more of this, and then Becky breaks out grandly:

"What do you want, anyway? You have had everything I have to give: my hospitality, *my bread, my wine, my couch, my affection, gift-tokens of my love*—what do you want?"

Kirby explains that he wants a wife and a soul-mate—"a mind to be the companion of my mind." But Becky refuses to marry him. Instead she goes to her bedroom and then returns with Kirby's letters:

"Here are your letters. You've stayed and had your say out. And now that you've said it, you can see for yourself that *you have no case against me*. . . . Here are your letters."
"I don't want them."
"Very well, I'll tear them up."
She proceeded to do so.
"*Now all the evidence is destroyed*," he said.

I have thrown in a few italics to point the high spots of this singular colloquy. It goes on for page after page, and the whole book is filled with dialogues like it. What is one to make of such inconceivable banality? Is there worse in "An American Tragedy"? But Masters, you may say, is trying to depict eighth-rate people—frequenters of cabarets and hotel grill-rooms, male and female Elks, dubious hangers-on upon the edges of intelligence and decency—and that is how they actually talk. It may be so, but I note at once two objections to that defense. The first is that Masters does not appear to regard Kirby as eighth-rate; on the contrary, he takes the fellow's moony drabbing quite seriously, and even tries to get a touch of the tragic into it. The second is that precisely the same hollow and meaningless fustian often appears when the author speaks in his own person. The way he tells his story is almost precisely the way it would be told by a somewhat intellectual shoe-drummer in a Pullman smoking-room. Its approach to the eternal sex question, its central theme, is exactly that of such a gentleman; its very phrases, in the main, are his phrases. He actually appears, in fact, as a sort of chorus to the drama, under the name of Bob Haydon. Bob, facing disillusion and death, favors Kirby with many cantos of philosophy. Their general burden is that the prudent man, having marked a sweet one to his taste, uses her person to his wicked ends, and then kicks her out. Kirby's agonies do not move Bob, and neither do they bore him. "Bore me!" he exclaims. "This is better than a circus!"

As I say, I have also enjoyed it myself. It is not, indeed, without its flashes of genuine sagacity; even Bob's stockbroker view of the sexual duel, given such a male as Kirby and such females as Becky, is probably more sound than not. But the chief fascination of the story, I am bound to say, lies in its very deficiencies as a human document and a work of art—in its naïve lack of humor, its elaborate laboring of the obvious, its incredible stiltedness and triteness. There are passages that actually suggest Daisy Ashford. For example: "She was biting her nails while talking to Delaher, and biting them after he left. *Then she put on white cotton gloves to prevent this nervous habit.*" Again (Kirby has abandoned Becky for another girl, Charlotte, formerly his stenographer):

> "*May I say something to you?*" she whispered at last.
> "What is it, Charlotte?"
> "I want a child, and a child with you."

Somehow, this "May I say something to you?" gives me vast delight: the respectful politeness of the perfect stenographer surviving into the most confidential of moments! No such child is achieved—Charlotte, in fact, dies before it can be born—, and so we miss her courteous request for permission to name it after its father. But she and Kirby, alas, sin the sin, and what is worse, they sin it under his mother's roof. What is still worse, they do it with her knowledge and connivance. She is greatly taken, in fact, with Charlotte, and advises Kirby to marry her. I quote her argument:

> "If Byron had mistresses he was also a rider and a fencer and a poet; and if Webster may have been a drinker, he was great as a lawyer and a speaker. If Charlotte has had extra-marital relationships, she is a capable housekeeper, a good secretary, a woman skilled in many things;

and she has all kinds of virtues, like humor and self-control, and the spirit of happiness, and an essential honesty."

I leave the rest to posterity! What will it make of Masters as novelist? When it turns from the heroic and lovely lines of "Ann Rutledge" to the astounding banalities of "Mirage" what will it say?

III.

In Memoriam: W.J.B.

HAS it been duly marked by historians that the late William Jennings Bryan's last secular act on this globe of sin was to catch flies? A curious detail, and not without its sardonic overtones. He was the most sedulous fly-catcher in American history, and in many ways the most successful. His quarry, of course, was not *Musca domestica* but *Homo neandertalensis.* For forty years he tracked it with coo and bellow, up and down the rustic backways of the Republic. Wherever the flambeaux of Chautauqua smoked and guttered, and the bilge of Idealism ran in the veins, and Baptist pastors dammed the brooks with the sanctified, and men gathered who were weary and heavy laden, and their wives who were full of Peruna and as fecund as the shad (*Alosa sapidissima*)—there the indefatigable Jennings set up his traps and spread his bait. He knew every country town in the South and West, and he could crowd the most remote of them to suffocation by simply winding his horn. The city proletariat, transiently flustered by him in 1896, quickly penetrated his buncombe and would have no more of him; the cockney gallery jeered him at every Democratic national convention for twenty-five years. But out where the grass grows high, and the horned cattle dream away the lazy afternoons, and men still fear the powers and principalities of the air—out there between the corn-rows he held his old puissance to the end. There was no need of beaters to drive in his game. The news that he was coming was enough. For miles the flivver dust would choke the roads. And when he rose at the end of the day to discharge his Message there would be such breathless attention, such a rapt and enchanted ecstasy, such a sweet rustle of amens as the world had not known since Johann fell to Herod's ax.

There was something peculiarly fitting in the fact that his last days were spent in a one-horse Tennessee village, and that death found him there. The man felt at home in such simple and Christian scenes. He liked people who sweated freely, and were not debauched by the refinements of the toilet. Making his progress up and down the Main street of little Dayton, surrounded by gaping primates from the upland valleys of the Cumberland Range, his coat laid aside, his bare arms and hairy chest shining damply, his bald head sprinkled with dust—so accoutred and on display he was obviously happy. He liked getting up early in the morning, to the tune of cocks crowing on the dunghill. He liked the heavy, greasy victuals of the farmhouse kitchen. He liked country lawyers, country pastors, all country people. He liked the country sounds and country smells. I believe that this liking was sincere—perhaps the only sincere thing in the man. His nose showed no uneasiness when a hillman in faded overalls and hickory shirt accosted him on the street, and besought him for light upon some mystery of Holy Writ. The simian gabble of the cross-roads was not gabble to him, but wisdom of an occult and superior sort. In the presence of city folks he was palpably uneasy. Their clothes, I suspect, annoyed him, and he was suspicious of their too delicate manners. He knew all the while that they were laughing at him—if not at his baroque theology, then at least at his alpaca pantaloons. But the yokels never laughed at him. To them he was not the huntsman but the prophet, and toward the end, as he gradually forsook mundane politics for more ghostly concerns, they began to elevate him in their hierarchy. When he died he was the peer of Abraham. His old enemy, Wilson, aspiring to the same white and shining robe, came down with a thump. But Bryan made the grade. His place in Tennessee hagiography is secure. If the village barber saved any of his hair, then it is curing gall-stones down there to-day.

But what label will he bear in more urbane regions? One, I fear, of a far less flattering kind. Bryan lived too long, and descended too deeply into the mud, to be taken seriously hereafter by fully literate men, even of the kind who write schoolbooks. There was a scattering of sweet words in his funeral notices, but it was no more than a response to conventional sentimentality. The best verdict the most romantic editorial writer could dredge up, save in the humorless South, was to the general effect that his imbecilities were excused by his earnestness—that under his clowning, as under that of the juggler of Notre Dame, there was the zeal of a steadfast soul. But this was apology, not praise; precisely the same thing might be said of Mary Baker G. Eddy, the late Czar Nicholas, or Czolgosz. The truth is that even Bryan's sincerity will probably yield to what is called, in other fields, definitive criticism. Was he sincere when he opposed imperialism in the Philippines, or when he fed it with deserving Democrats in Santo Domingo? Was he sincere when he tried to shove the Prohibitionists under the table, or when he seized their banner and began to lead them with loud whoops? Was he sincere when he bellowed against war, or when he dreamed of himself as a tin-soldier in uniform, with a grave reserved among the generals? Was he sincere when he denounced the late John W. Davis, or when he swallowed Davis? Was he sincere when he fawned over Champ Clark, or when he betrayed Clark? Was he sincere when he pleaded for tolerance in New York, or when he bawled for the faggot and the stake in Tennessee?

This talk of sincerity, I confess, fatigues me. If the fellow was sincere, then so was P. T. Barnum. The word is disgraced and degraded by such uses. He was, in fact, a charlatan, a mountebank, a zany without shame or dignity. His career brought him into contact with the first men of his time; he preferred the company of rustic ignoramuses. It was hard to believe, watching him at Dayton, that he had traveled, that he had been received in civilized societies, that he had been a high officer of state. He seemed only a poor clod like those around him, deluded by a childish theology, full of an almost pathological hatred of all learning, all human dignity, all beauty, all fine and noble things. He was a peasant come home to the barnyard. Imagine a gentleman, and you have imagined everything that he was not. What animated him from end to end of his grotesque career was simply ambition—the ambition of a common man to get his hand upon the collar of his superiors, or, failing that, to get his thumb into their eyes. He was born with a roaring voice, and it had the trick of inflaming half-wits. His whole career was devoted to raising those half-wits against their betters, that he himself might shine. His last battle will be grossly misunderstood if it is thought of as a mere exercise in fanaticism—that is, if Bryan the Fundamentalist Pope is mistaken for one of the bucolic Fundamentalists. There was much more in it than that, as everyone knows who saw him on the field. What moved him, at bottom, was simply hatred of the city men who had laughed at him so long, and brought him at last to so tatterdemalion an estate. He lusted for revenge upon them. He yearned to lead the anthropoid rabble against them, to punish them for their execution upon him by attacking the very vitals of their civilization. He went far beyond the bounds of any merely religious frenzy, however inordinate. When he began denouncing the notion that man is a mammal even some of the hinds at Dayton were agape. And when, brought upon Darrow's cruel hook, he writhed and tossed in a very fury of malignancy, bawling against the baldest elements of sense and decency like a man frantic—when he came to that tragic climax of his striving there were snickers among the hinds as well as hosannas.

Upon that hook, in truth, Bryan committed suicide, as a legend as well as in the body. He staggered from the rustic court ready to die, and he staggered from it ready to be forgotten, save as a character in a third-rate farce, witless and in poor taste. It was plain to everyone who knew him, when he came to Dayton, that his great days were behind him—that, for all the fury of his hatred, he was now definitely an old man, and headed at last for silence. There was a vague, unpleasant manginess about his appearance; he somehow seemed dirty, though a close glance showed him as carefully shaven as an actor, and clad in immaculate linen. All the hair was gone from the dome of his head, and it had begun to fall out, too, behind his ears, in the obscene manner of the late Samuel Gompers. The resonance had departed from his voice; what was once a bugle blast had become reedy and quavering. Who knows that, like Demosthenes, he had a lisp? In the old days, under the magic of his eloquence, no one noticed it. But when he spoke at Dayton it was always audible.

When I first encountered him, on the sidewalk in front of the office of the rustic lawyers who were his associates in the Scopes case, the trial was yet to begin, and so he was still expansive and amiable. I had printed in the *Nation*, a week or so before, an article arguing that the Tennessee anti-evolution law, whatever its wisdom, was at least constitutional—that the rustics of the State had a clear right to have their progeny taught whatever they chose, and kept secure from whatever knowledge violated their superstitions. The old boy professed to be delighted with the argument, and gave the gaping bystanders to understand that I was a publicist of parts. Not to be outdone, I admired the preposterous country shirt that he wore—sleeveless and with the neck cut very low. We parted in the manner of two ambassadors. But that was the last touch of amiability that I was destined to see in Bryan. The next day the battle joined and his face became hard. By the end of the week he was simply a walking fever. Hour by hour he grew more bitter. What the Christian Scientists call malicious animal magnetism seemed to radiate from him like heat from a stove. From my place in the courtroom, standing upon a table, I looked directly down upon him, sweating horribly and pumping his palm-leaf fan. His eyes fascinated me; I watched them all day long. They were blazing points of hatred. They glittered like occult and sinister gems. Now and then they wandered to me, and I got my share, for my reports of the trial had come back to Dayton, and he had read them. It was like coming under fire.

Thus he fought his last fight, thirsting savagely for blood. All sense departed from him. He bit right and left, like a dog with rabies. He descended to demagogy so dreadful that his very associates at the trial table blushed. His one yearning was to keep his yokels heated up—to lead his forlorn mob of imbeciles against the foe. That foe, alas, refused to be alarmed. It insisted upon seeing the whole battle as a comedy. Even Darrow, who knew better, occasionally yielded to the prevailing spirit. One day he lured poor Bryan into the folly I have mentioned: his astounding argument against the notion that man is a mammal. I am glad I heard it, for otherwise I'd never believe in it. There stood the man who had been thrice a candidate for the Presidency of the Republic—there he stood in the glare of the world, uttering stuff that a boy of eight would laugh at! The artful Darrow led him on: he repeated it, ranted for it, bellowed it in his cracked voice. So he was prepared for the final slaughter. He came into life a hero, a Galahad, in bright and shining armor. He was passing out a poor mountebank.

The chances are that history will put the peak of democracy in America in his time; it has been on the downward curve among us since the campaign of 1896. He will be remembered perhaps, as its supreme impostor, the *reductio ad absurdum* of its pretension. Bryan came very near being President. In 1896, it is possible, he was actually elected. He lived long enough to make patriots thank the inscrutable gods for Harding, even for Coolidge. Dullness has got into the White House, and the smell of cabbage boiling, but there is at least nothing to compare to the intolerable buffoonery that went on in Tennessee. The President of the United States may be an ass, but he at least doesn't believe that the earth is square, and that witches should be put to death, and that Jonah swallowed the whale. The Golden Text is not painted weekly on the White House wall, and there is no need to keep ambassadors waiting while Pastor Simpson, of Smithville, prays for rain in the Blue Room. We have escaped something—by a narrow margin, but still we have escaped.

That is, so far. The Fundamentalists, once apparently sweeping all before them, now face minorities prepared for battle even in the South—here and there with some assurance of success. But it is too early, it seems to me, to send the firemen home; the fire is still burning on many a far-flung hill, and it may begin to roar again at any moment. The evil that men do lives after them. Bryan, in his malice, started something that it will not be easy to stop. In ten thousand country towns his old heelers, the evangelical pastors, are propagating his gospel, and everywhere the yokels are ready for it. When he disappeared from the big cities, the big cities made the capital error of assuming that he was done for. If they heard of him at all, it was only as a crimp for real-estate speculators—the heroic foe of the unearned increment hauling it in with both hands. He seemed preposterous, and hence harmless. But all the while he was busy among his old lieges, preparing for a *jacquerie* that should floor all his enemies at one blow. He did his job competently. He had vast skill at such enterprises. Heave an egg out of a Pullman window, and you will hit a Fundamentalist almost everywhere in the United States to-day. They swarm in the country towns, inflamed by their *shamans*, and with a saint, now, to venerate. They are thick in the mean streets behind the gas-works. They are everywhere where learning is too heavy a burden for mortal minds to carry, even the vague, pathetic learning on tap in little red schoolhouses. They march with the Klan, with the Christian Endeavor Society, with the Junior Order of United American Mechanics, with the Epworth League, with all the rococo bands that poor and unhappy folk organize to bring some light of purpose into their lives. They have had a thrill, and they are ready for more.

Such is Bryan's legacy to his country. He couldn't be President, but he could at least help magnificently in the solemn business of shutting off the Presidency from every intelligent and self-respecting man. The storm, perhaps, won't last long, as time goes in history. It may help, indeed, to break up the democratic delusion, now already showing weakness, and so hasten its own end. But while it lasts it will blow off some roofs.

IV.

The Hills of Zion

IT was hot weather when they tried the infidel Scopes at Dayton, but I went down there very willingly, for I had good reports of the sub-Potomac bootleggers, and moreover I was eager to see something of evangelical Christianity as a going concern. In the big cities of the Republic, despite the endless efforts of consecrated men, it is laid up with a wasting disease. The very Sunday-school superintendents, taking jazz from the stealthy radio, shake their fire-proof legs; their pupils, moving into adolescence, no longer respond to the proliferating hormones by enlisting for missionary service in Africa, but resort to necking and petting instead. I know of no evangelical church from Oregon to Maine that is not short of money: the graft begins to peter out, like wire-tapping and three-card monte before it. Even in Dayton, though the mob was up to do execution upon Scopes, there was a strong smell of antinomianism. The nine churches of the village were all half empty on Sunday, and weeds choked their yards. Only two or three of the resident pastors managed to sustain themselves by their ghostly science; the rest had to take orders for mail-order pantaloons or work in the adjacent strawberry fields; one, I heard, was a barber. On the courthouse green a score of sweating theologians debated the darker passages of Holy Writ day and night, but I soon found that they were all volunteers, and that the local faithful, while interested in their exegesis as an intellectual exercise, did not permit it to impede the indigenous debaucheries. Exactly twelve minutes after I reached the village I was taken in tow by a Christian man and introduced to the favorite tipple of the Cumberland Range: half corn liquor and half coco-cola. It seemed a dreadful dose to me, spoiled as I was by the bootleg light wines and beers of the Eastern seaboard, but I found that the Dayton illuminati got it down with gusto, rubbing their tummies and rolling their eyes. I include among them the chief local proponents of the Mosaic cosmogony. They were all hot for Genesis, but their faces were far too florid to belong to teetotalers, and when a pretty girl came tripping down the Main street, which was very often, they reached for the places where their neckties should have been with all the amorous enterprise of movie actors. It seemed somehow strange.

An amiable newspaper woman of Chattanooga, familiar with those uplands, presently enlightened me. Dayton, she explained, was simply a great capital like any other great capital. That is to say, it was to Rhea county what Atlanta was to Georgia or Paris to France. That is to say, it was predominantly epicurean and sinful. A country girl from some remote valley of the county, coming into town for her semi-annual bottle of Lydia Pinkham's Vegetable Compound, shivered on approaching Robinson's drug-store quite as a country girl from up-State New York might shiver on approaching the Metropolitan Opera House or the Ritz Hotel. In every village lout she saw a potential white-slaver. The hard sidewalks hurt her feet. Temptations of the flesh bristled to all sides of her, luring her to hell. This newspaper woman told me of a session with just such a visitor, holden a few days before. The latter waited outside one of the town hot-dog and coco-cola shops while her husband negotiated with a hardware merchant across the street. The newspaper woman, idling along and observing that the stranger was badly used by the heat, invited her to step into the shop for a glass of coca-cola. The invitation brought forth only a gurgle of terror. Coca-cola, it quickly appeared, was prohibited by the country lady's pastor, as a levantine and hell-sent narcotic. He also prohibited coffee and tea—and pies! He had his doubts about white bread and boughten meat. The newspaper woman, interested, inquired about ice-cream. It was, she found, not specifically prohibited, but going into a coca-cola shop to get it would be clearly sinful. So she offered to get a saucer of it, and bring it out to the sidewalk. The visitor vacillated—and came near being lost. But God saved her in the nick of time. When the newspaper woman emerged from the place she was in full flight up the street! Later on her husband, mounted on a mule, overtook her four miles out the mountain pike.

This newspaper woman, whose kindness covered city infidels as well as Alpine Christians, offered to take me back in the hills to a place where the old-time religion was genuinely on tap. The Scopes jury, she explained was composed mainly of its customers, with a few Dayton sophisticates added to leaven the mass. It would thus be instructive to climb the heights and observe the former at their ceremonies. The trip, fortunately, might be made by automobile. There was a road running out of Dayton to Morgantown, in the mountains to the westward, and thence beyond. But foreigners, it appeared, would have to approach the sacred grove cautiously, for the upland worshipers were very shy, and at the first sight of a strange face they would adjourn their orgy and slink into the forest. They were not to be feared, for God had long since forbidden them to practice assassination, or even assault, but if they were alarmed a rough trip would go for naught. So, after dreadful bumpings up a long and narrow road, we parked our car in a little woodpath a mile or two beyond the tiny village of Morgantown, and made the rest of the approach on foot, deployed like skirmishers. Far off in a dark, romantic glade a flickering light was visible, and out of the silence came the rumble of exhortation. We could distinguish the figure of the preacher only as a moving mote in the light: it was like looking down the tube of a dark-field microscope. Slowly and cautiously we crossed what seemed to be a pasture, and then we crouched down along the edge of a cornfield, and stealthily edged further and further. The light now grew larger and we could begin to make out what was going on. We went ahead on all fours, like snakes in the grass.

From the great limb of a mighty oak hung a couple of crude torches of the sort that car inspectors thrust under Pullman cars when a train pulls in at night. In the guttering glare was the preacher, and for a while we could see no one else. He was an immensely tall and thin mountaineer in blue jeans, his collarless shirt open at the neck and his hair a tousled mop. As he preached he paced up and down under the smoking flambeaux, and at each turn he thrust his arms into the air and yelled "Glory to God!" We crept nearer in the shadow of the cornfield, and began to hear more of his discourse. He was preaching on the Day of Judgment. The high kings of the earth, he roared, would all fall down and die; only the sanctified would stand up to receive the Lord God of Hosts. One of these kings he mentioned by name, the king of what he called Greece-y. The king of Greece-y, he said, was doomed to hell. We crawled forward a few more yards and began to see the audience. It was seated on benches ranged round the preacher in a circle. Behind him sat a row of elders, men and women. In front were the younger folk. We crept on cautiously, and individuals rose out of the ghostly gloom. A young mother sat suckling her baby, rocking as the preacher paced up and down. Two scared little girls hugged each other, their pigtails down their backs. An immensely huge mountain woman, in a gingham dress, cut in one piece, rolled on her heels at every "Glory to God!" To one side, and but half visible, was what appeared to be a bed. We found afterward that half a dozen babies were asleep upon it.

The preacher stopped at last, and there arose out of the darkness a woman with her hair pulled back into a tight knot. She began so quietly that we couldn't hear what she said, but soon her voice rose resonantly and we could follow her. She was denouncing the reading of books. Some wandering book agent, it appeared, had come to her cabin and tried to sell her a specimen of his wares. She refused to touch it. Why, indeed, read a book? If what was in it was true, then everything in it was already in the Bible. If it was false, then reading it would imperil the soul. This syllogism from Caliph Omar complete, she sat down. There followed a hymn, led by a somewhat fat brother wearing silver-rimmed country spectacles. It droned on for a half a dozen stanzas, and then the first speaker resumed the floor. He argued that the gift of tongues was real and that education was a snare. Once his children could read the Bible, he said, they had enough. Beyond lay only infidelity and damnation. Sin stalked the cities. Dayton itself was a Sodom. Even Morgantown had begun to forget God. He sat down, and a female aurochs in gingham got up. She began quietly, but was soon leaping and roaring, and it was hard to follow her. Under cover of the turmoil we sneaked a bit closer.

A couple of other discourses followed, and there were two or three hymns. Suddenly a change of mood began to make itself felt. The last hymn ran longer than the others, and dropped gradually into a monotonous, unintelligible chant. The leader beat time with his book. The faithful broke out with exultations. When the singing ended there was a brief palaver that we could not hear, and two of the men moved a bench into the circle of light directly under the flambeaux. Then a half-grown girl emerged from the darkness and threw herself upon it. We noticed with astonishment that she had bobbed hair. "This sister," said the leader, "has asked for prayers." We moved a bit closer. We could now see faces plainly, and hear every word. What followed quickly reached such heights of barbaric grotesquerie that it was hard to believe it real. At a signal all the faithful crowded up to the bench and began to pray—not in unison, but each for himself! At another they all fell on their knees, their arms over the penitent. The leader kneeled facing us, his head alternately thrown back dramatically or buried in his hands. Words spouted from his lips like bullets from a machine-gun—appeals to God to pull the penitent back out of hell, defiances of the demons of the air, a vast impassioned jargon of apocalyptic texts. Suddenly he rose to his feet, threw back his head and began to speak in the tongues—blub-blub-blub, gurgle-gurgle-gurgle. His voice rose to a higher register. The climax was a shrill, inarticulate squawk, like that of a man throttled. He fell headlong across the pyramid of suppliants.

A comic scene? Somehow, no. The poor half-wits were too horribly in earnest. It was like peeping through a knothole at the writhings of people in pain. From the squirming and jabbering mass a young woman gradually detached herself—a woman not uncomely, with a pathetic homemade cap on her head. Her head jerked back, the veins of her neck swelled, and her fists went to her throat as if she were fighting for breath. She bent backward until she was like half a hoop. Then she suddenly snapped forward. We caught a flash of the whites of her eyes. Presently her whole body began to be convulsed—great throes that began at the shoulders and ended at the hips. She would leap to her feet, thrust her arms in air, and then hurl herself upon the heap. Her praying flattened out into a mere delirious caterwauling, like that of a Tom cat on a petting party. I describe the thing discreetly, and as a strict behaviorist. The lady's subjective sensations I leave to infidel pathologists, privy to the works of Ellis, Freud and Moll. Whatever they were, they were obviously not painful, for they were accompanied by vast heavings and gurglings of a joyful and even ecstatic nature. And they seemed to be contagious, too, for soon a second penitent, also female, joined the first, and then came a third, and a fourth, and a fifth. The last one had an extraordinary violent attack. She began with mild enough jerks of the head, but in a moment she was bounding all over the place, like a chicken with its head cut off. Every time her head came up a stream of hosannas would issue out of it. Once she collided with a dark, undersized brother, hitherto silent and stolid. Contact with her set him off as if he had been kicked by a mule. He leaped into the air, threw back his head, and began to gargle as if with a mouthful of BB shot. Then he loosed one tremendous, stentorian sentence in the tongues, and collapsed.

By this time the performers were quite oblivious to the profane universe and so it was safe to go still closer. We left our hiding and came up to the little circle of light. We slipped into the vacant seats on one of the rickety benches. The heap of mourners was directly before us. They bounced into us as they cavorted. The smell that they radiated, sweating there in that obscene heap, half suffocated us. Not all of them, of course, did the thing in the grand manner. Some merely moaned and rolled their eyes. The female ox in gingham flung her great bulk on the ground and jabbered an unintelligible prayer. One of the men, in the intervals between fits, put on his spectacles and read his Bible. Beside me on the bench sat the young mother and her baby. She suckled it through the whole orgy, obviously fascinated by what was going on, but never venturing to take any hand in it. On the bed just outside the light half a dozen other babies slept peacefully. In the shadows, suddenly appearing and as suddenly going away, were vague figures, whether of believers or of scoffers I do not know. They seemed to come and go in couples. Now and then a couple at the ringside would step out and vanish into the black night. After a while some came back, the males looking somewhat sheepish. There was whispering outside the circle of vision. A couple of Fords lurched up the road, cutting holes in the darkness with their lights. Once some one out of sight loosed a bray of laughter.

All this went on for an hour or so. The original penitent, by this time, was buried three deep beneath the heap. One caught a glimpse, now and then, of her yellow bobbed hair, but then she would vanish again. How she breathed down there I don't know; it was hard enough six feet away, with a strong five-cent cigar to help. When the praying brothers would rise up for a bout with the tongues their faces were streaming with perspiration. The fat harridan in gingham sweated like a longshoreman. Her hair got loose and fell down over her face. She fanned herself with her skirt. A powerful old gal she was, plainly equal in her day to a bout with obstetrics and a week's washing on the same morning, but this was worse than a week's washing. Finally, she fell into a heap, breathing in great, convulsive gasps.

Finally, we got tired of the show and returned to Dayton. It was nearly eleven o'clock—an immensely late hour for those latitudes —but the whole town was still gathered in the courthouse yard, listening to the disputes of theologians. The Scopes trial had brought them in from all directions. There was a friar wearing a sandwich sign announcing that he was the Bible champion of the world. There was a Seventh Day Adventist arguing that Clarence Darrow was the beast with seven heads and ten horns described in Revelation xiii, and that the end of the world was at hand. There was an evangelist made up like Andy Gump, with the news that atheists in Cincinnati were preparing to descend upon Dayton, hang the eminent Judge Raulston, and burn the town. There was an ancient who maintained that no Catholic could be a Christian. There was the eloquent Dr. T. T. Martin, of Blue Mountain, Miss., come to town with a truck-load of torches and hymn-books to put Darwin in his place. There was a singing brother bellowing apocalyptic hymns. There was William Jennings Bryan, followed everywhere by a gaping crowd. Dayton was having a roaring time. It was better than the circus. But the note of devotion was simply not there; the Daytonians, after listening a while, would slip away to Robinson's drug-store to regale themselves with coca-cola, or to the lobby of the Aqua Hotel, where the learned Raulston sat in state, judicially picking his teeth. The real religion was not present. It began at the bridge over the town creek, where the road makes off for the hills.

V.

Beethoven

BEETHOVEN was one of those lucky men whose stature, viewed in retrospect, grows steadily. How many movements have there been to put him on the shelf? At least a dozen in the hundred years since his death. There was one only a few years ago in New York, launched by idiot critics and supported by the war fever: his place, it appeared, was to be taken by such prophets of the new enlightenment as Stravinsky! The net result of that movement was simply that the best orchestra in America went to pot—and Beethoven survived unscathed. It is, indeed, almost impossible to imagine displacing him—at all events, in the concert-hall, where the challenge of Bach cannot reach him. Surely the Nineteenth Century was not deficient in master musicians. It produced Schubert, Schumann, Chopin, Wagner and Brahms, to say nothing of a whole horde of Dvořáks, Tschaikowskys, Debussys, Raffs, Verdis and Puccinis. Yet it gave us nothing better than the first movement of the Eroica. That movement, the first challenge of the new music, remains its last word. It is the noblest piece of absolute music ever written in the sonata form, and it is the noblest piece of program music. In Beethoven, indeed, the distinction between the two became purely imaginary. Everything he wrote was, in a way, program music, including even the first two symphonies, and everything was absolute music, including even the Battle grotesquerie. (Is the latter, indeed, as bad as ancient report makes it? Why doesn't some *Kappellmeister* let us hear it?)

It was a bizarre jest of the gods to pit Beethoven, in his first days in Vienna, against Papa Haydn. Haydn was undeniably a genius of the first water, and, after Mozart's death, had no apparent reason to fear a rival. If he did not actually create the symphony as we know it to-day, then he at least enriched the form with its first genuine masterpieces—and not with a scant few, but literally with dozens. Tunes of the utmost loveliness gushed from him like oil from a well. More, he knew how to manage them; he was a master of musical architectonics. If his music is sniffed at to-day, then it is only by fools; there are at least six of his symphonies that are each worth all the cacophony hatched by a whole herd of Schönbergs and Eric Saties, with a couple of Korngolds thrown in to flavor the pot. But when Beethoven stepped in, then poor old Papa had to step down. It was like pitting a gazelle against an aurochs. One colossal bellow, and the combat was over. Musicians are apt to look at it as a mere contest of technicians. They point to the vastly greater skill and ingenuity of Beethoven—his firmer grip upon his materials, his greater daring and resourcefulness, his far better understanding of dynamics, rhythms and clang-tints —in brief, his tremendously superior musicianship. But that was not what made him so much greater than Haydn—for Haydn, too, had his superiorities; for example, his far readier inventiveness, his capacity for making better tunes. What lifted Beethoven above the old master, and above all other men of music save perhaps Bach and Brahms, was simply his greater dignity as a man. The feelings that Haydn put into tone were the feelings of a country pastor, a rather civilized stockbroker, a viola player gently mellowed by Kulmbacher. When he wept it was with the tears of a woman who has discovered another wrinkle; when he rejoiced it was with the joy of a child on Christmas morning. But the feelings that Beethoven put into his music were the feelings of a god. There was something olympian in his snarls and rages, and there was a touch of hell-fire in his mirth.

It is almost a literal fact that there is not a trace of cheapness in the whole body of his music. He is never sweet and romantic; he never sheds conventional tears; he never strikes orthodox attitudes. In his lightest moods there is the immense and inescapable dignity of the ancient Hebrew prophets. He concerns himself, not with the puerile agonies of love, but with the eternal tragedy of man. He is a great tragic poet, and like all great tragic poets, he is obsessed by a sense of the inscrutable meaninglessness of life. From the Eroica onward he seldom departs from that theme. It roars through the first movement of the C minor, and it comes to a stupendous final statement in the Ninth. All this, in his day, was new in music, and so it caused murmurs of surprise and even indignation.

The step from Mozart's Jupiter to the first movement of the Eroica was uncomfortable; the Viennese began to wriggle in their stalls. But there was one among them who didn't wriggle, and that was Franz Schubert. Turn to the first movement of his Unfinished or to the slow movement of his Tragic, and you will see how quickly the example of Beethoven was followed—and with what genius! But there was a long hiatus after that, with Mendelssohn, Weber, Chopin and company performing upon their pretty pipes. Eventually the day of November 6, 1876, dawned in Karlsruhe, and with it came the first performance of Brahms' C minor. Once more the gods walked in the concert-hall. They will walk again when another Brahms is born, but not before. For nothing can come out of an artist that is not in the man. What ails the music of all the Tschaikowskys, Stravinskys—and Strausses? What ails it is that it is the music of shallow men. It is often, in its way, lovely. It bristles with charming musical ideas. It is infinitely ingenious and workmanlike. But it is as hollow, at bottom, as a bull by Bishop Manning. It is the music of second-rate men.

Beethoven disdained all their artifices: he didn't need them. It would be hard to think of a composer, even of the fourth rate, who worked with thematic material of less intrinsic merit. He borrowed tunes wherever he found them; he made them up out of snatches of country jigs; when he lacked one altogether he contented himself with a simple phrase, a few banal notes. All such things he viewed simply as raw materials; his interest was concentrated upon their use. To that use of them he brought the appalling powers of his unrivaled genius. His ingenuity began where that of other men left off. His most complicated structures retained the overwhelming clarity of the Parthenon. And into them he got a kind of feeling that even the Greeks could seldom match; he was preëminently a modern man, with all trace of the barbarian vanished. In his gorgeous music there went all of the high skepticism that was of the essence of the Eighteenth Century, but into it there also went the new enthusiasm, the new determination to challenge and beat the gods, that dawned with the Nineteenth.

The older I grow, the more I am convinced that the most portentous phenomenon in the whole history of music was the first public performance of the Eroica on April 7, 1805. The manufacturers of program notes have swathed that gigantic work in so many layers of childish legend and speculation that its intrinsic merits have been almost forgotten. Was it dedicated to Napoleon I? If so, was the dedication sincere or ironical? Who cares—that is, who with ears? It might have been dedicated, just as well, to Louis XIV, Paracelsus or Pontius Pilate. What makes it worth discussing, to-day and forever, is the fact that on its very first page Beethoven threw his hat into the ring and laid his claim to immortality. Bang!—and he is off! No compromise! No easy bridge from the past! The Second Symphony is already miles behind. A new order of music has been born. The very manner of it is full of challenge. There is no sneaking into the foul business by way of a mellifluous and disarming introduction; no preparatory hemming and hawing to cajole the audience and enable the conductor to find his place in the score. Nay! Out of silence comes the angry crash of the tonic triad, and then at once, with no pause, the first statement of the first subject—grim, domineering, harsh, raucous, and yet curiously lovely—with its astounding collision with that electrical C sharp. The carnage has begun early; we are only in the seventh measure! In the thirteenth and fourteenth comes the incomparable roll down the simple scale of E flat—and what follows is all that has ever been said, perhaps all that ever *will* be said, about music-making in the grand manner. What was afterward done, even by Beethoven, was done in the light of that perfect example. Every line of modern music that is honestly music bears some sort of relation to that epoch-making first movement.

The rest is Beethovenish, but not quintessence. There is a legend that the funeral march was put in simply because it was a time of wholesale butchery, and funeral marches were in fashion. No doubt the first-night audience in Vienna, shocked and addled by the piled-up defiances of the first movement, found the lugubrious strains grateful. But the *scherzo*? Another felonious assault upon poor Papa Haydn! Two giants boxing clumsily, to a crazy piping by an orchestra of dwarfs. No wonder some honest Viennese in the gallery yelled: "I'd give another kreutzer if the thing would stop!" Well, it stopped finally, and then came something reassuring—a theme with variations. Everyone in Vienna knew and esteemed

Beethoven's themes with variations. He was, in fact, the rising master of themes with variations in the town. But a joker remained in the pack. The variations grew more and more complex and surprising. Strange novelties got into them. The polite exercises became tempestuous, moody, cacophonous, tragic. At the end a harsh, hammering, exigent row of chords—the C minor Symphony casting its sinister shadow before!

It must have been a great night in Vienna. But perhaps not for the actual Viennese. They went to hear "a new grand symphony in D sharp" (*sic!*). What they found in the Theater-an-der-Wien was a revolution!

VI.

Rondo on an Ancient Theme

It is the economic emancipation of woman, I suppose, that must be blamed for the present wholesale discussion of the sex question, so offensive to the romantic. Eminent authorities have full often described, and with the utmost heat and eloquence, her state before she was delivered from her fetters and turned loose to root or die. Almost her only feasible trade, in those dark days, was that of wife. True enough, she might also become a servant girl, or go to work in a factory, or offer herself upon the streets, but all of those vocations were so revolting that no rational woman followed them if she could help it: she would leave any one of them at a moment's notice at the call of a man, for the call of a man meant promotion for her, economically and socially. The males of the time, knowing what a boon they had to proffer, drove hard bargains. They demanded a long list of high qualities in the woman they summoned to their seraglios, but most of all they demanded what they called virtue. It was not sufficient that a candidate should be anatomically undefiled; she must also be pure in mind. There was, of course, but one way to keep her so pure, and that was by building a high wall around her mind, and hitting her with a club every time she ventured to peer over it. It was as dangerous, in that Christian era, for a woman to show any interest in or knowledge of the great physiological farce of sex as it would be to-day for a presidential candidate to reveal himself in his cups on the hustings. Everyone knew, to be sure, that as a mammal she had sex, and that as a potential wife and mother she probably had some secret interest in its phenomena, but it was felt, perhaps wisely, that even the most academic theorizing had within it the deadly germs of the experimental method, and so she was forbidden to think about the matter at all, and whatever information she acquired at all she had to acquire by a method of bootlegging.

The generation still on its legs has seen the almost total collapse of that naïve and constabulary system, and of the economic structure supporting it. Beginning with the eighties of the last century, there rose up a harem rebellion which quickly knocked both to pieces. The women of the Western World not only began to plunge heroically into all of the old professions, hitherto sacred to men; they also began to invent a lot of new professions, many of them unimagined by men. Worse, they began to succeed in them. The working woman of the old days worked only until she could snare a man; any man was better than her work. But the working woman of the new days was under no such pressure; her work made her a living and sometimes more than a living; when a man appeared in her net she took two looks at him, one of them usually very searching, before landing him. The result was an enormous augmentation of her feeling of self-sufficiency, her spirit of independence, her natural inclination to get two sides into the bargaining. The result, secondarily, was a revolt against all the old taboos that had surrounded her, all the childish incapacities and ignorances that had been forced upon her. The result, tertiarily, was a vast running amok in the field that, above all others, had been forbidden to her: that of sexual knowledge and experiment.

We now suffer from the effects of that running amok. It is women, not men, who are doing all the current gabbling about sex, and proposing all the new-fangled modifications of the rules and regulations ordained by God, and they are hard at it very largely, I suppose, because being at it at all is a privilege that is still new to them. The whole order of human females, in other words, is passing through a sort of intellectual adolescence, and it is disturbed as greatly as biological adolescents are by the spouting of the hormones. The attitude of men toward the sex question, it seems to me, has not changed greatly in my time. Barring a few earnest men whose mental processes, here as elsewhere, are essentially womanish, they still view it somewhat jocosely. Taking one with another, they believe that they know all about it that is worth knowing, and so it does not challenge their curiosity, and they do not put in much time discussing it, save mockingly. But among the women, if a bachelor may presume to judge, interest in it is intense. They want to know all that is known about it, all that has been guessed and theorized about it; they bristle with ideas of their own about it. It is hard to find a reflective woman, in these days, who is not harboring some new and startling scheme for curing the evils of monogamous marriage; it is impossible to find any woman who has not given ear to such schemes. Women, not men, read the endless books upon the subject that now rise mountain-high in all the book-stores, and women, not men, discuss and rediscuss the notions in them. An acquaintance of mine, a distinguished critic, owns a copy of one of the most revolutionary of these books, by title "The Art of Love," that was suppressed on the day of its publication by the alert Comstocks. He tells me that he has already lent it to twenty-six women and that he has more than fifty applications for it on file. Yet he has never read it himself!

As a professional fanatic for free thought and free speech, I can only view all this uproar in the *Frauenzimmer* with high satisfaction. It gives me delight to see a taboo violated, and that delight is doubled when the taboo is one that is wholly senseless. Sex is more important to women than to men, and so they ought to be free to discuss it as they please, and to hatch and propagate whatever ideas about it occur to them. Moreover, I can see nothing but nonsense in the doctrine that their concern with such matters damages their charm. So far as I am concerned, a woman who knows precisely what a Graafian follicle is is just as charming as one who doesn't—just as charming, and far less dangerous. Charm in women, indeed, is a variable star, and shows different colors at different times. When their chief mark was ignorance, then the most ignorant was the most charming; now that they begin to think deeply and indignantly there is charm in their singular astuteness. But I am inclined to believe that they have not yet attained to a genuine astuteness in the new field of sex. To the contrary, it seems to me that a fundamental error contaminates their whole dealing with the subject, and that is the error of assuming that sexual questions, whether social, physiological, or pathological, are of vast and even paramount importance to mankind in general—in brief, that sex is really a first-rate matter.

I doubt it. I believe that in this department men show better judgment than women, if only because their information is older and their experience wider. Their tendency is to dismiss the whole thing lightly, to reduce sex to the lowly estate of an afterthought and a recreation, and under that tendency there is a sound instinct. I do not believe that the lives of normal men are much colored or conditioned, either directly or indirectly, by purely sexual considerations. I believe that nine-tenths of them would carry on all the activities which engage them now, and with precisely the same humorless diligence, if there were not a woman in the world. The notion that man would not work if he lacked an audience, and that the audience must be a woman, seems to me to be a hollow sentimentality. Men work because they want to eat, because they want to feel secure, because they long to shine among their fellows, and for no other reason. A man may crave his wife's approbation, or some other woman's approbation, of his social graces, of his taste, of his generosity and courage, of his general dignity in the world, but long before he ever gives thought to such things and long after he has forgotten them he craves the approbation of his fellow men. Above all, he craves the approbation of his fellow craftsmen—the men who understand exactly what he is trying to do, and are expertly competent to judge his doing of it. Can you imagine a surgeon putting the good opinion of his wife above the good opinion of other surgeons? If you can, then you can do something that I cannot.

Here, of course, I do not argue absurdly that the good opinion of his wife is nothing to him. Obviously, it is a lot, for if it does not constitute the principal reward of his work, then it at least constitutes the principal joy of his hours of ease, when his work is done. He wants his wife to respect and admire him; to be able to make her do it is also a talent. But if he is intelligent he must discover very early that her respect and admiration do not necessarily run in direct ratio to his intrinsic worth, that the qualities and acts that please her are not always the qualities and acts that are most satisfactory to the censor within him—in brief, that the relation between man and woman, however intimate they may seem, must always remain a bit casual and superficial—that sex, at bottom, belongs to comedy and the cool of the evening and not to the sober business that goes on in the heat of the day. That sober business, as I have said, would still go on if woman were abolished and heirs and assigns were manufactured in rolling-mills. Men would not only work as hard as they do to-day; they would also get almost as much satisfaction out of their work. For of all the men that I know on this earth, ranging from poets to ambassadors and from bishops to statisticians, I know none who labors primarily because he wants to please a woman. They are all hard at it because they want to impress other men and so please themselves.

Woman, plainly enough, are in a far different case. Their emancipation has not yet gone to the length of making them genuinely free. They have rid themselves, very largely, of the absolute need to please men, but they have not yet rid themselves of the impulse to please men. Perhaps they never will: one might easily devise a plausible argument to that effect on biological grounds. But sufficient unto the day is the phenomenon before us: they have got rid of the old taboo which forbade them to think and talk about sex, and they still labor under the old superstition that sex is a matter of paramount importance. The result, in my judgment, is an absurd emission of piffle. In every division there is vast and often ludicrous exaggeration. The campaign for birth control takes on the colossal proportions of the war for democracy. The venereal diseases are represented to be as widespread, at least in men, as colds in the head, and as lethal as apoplexy or cancer. Great hordes of viragoes patrol the country, instructing school-girls in the mechanics of reproduction and their mothers in obstetrics. The light-hearted monogamy which produced all of us is denounced as an infamy comparable to cannibalism. Laws are passed regulating the mating of human beings as if they were horned cattle and converting marriage into a sort of coroner's inquest. Over all sounds the battle-cry of quacks and zealots at all times and everywhere: *Veritas liberabit vos!*

The truth? How much of this new gospel is actually truth? Perhaps two per cent. The rest is idle theorizing, doctrinaire nonsense, mere scandalous rubbish. All that is worth knowing about sex—all, that is, that is solidly established and of sound utility—can be taught to any intelligent boy of sixteen in two hours. Is it taught in the current books, so enormously circulated? I doubt it. Absolutely without exception these books admonish the poor apprentice to renounce sex altogether—to sublimate it, as the favorite phrase is, into a passion for free verse, Rotary or the League of Nations. This admonition is silly, and, I believe, dangerous. It is as much a folly to lock up sex in the hold as it is to put it in command on the bridge. Its proper place is in the social hall. As a substitute for all such nonsense I drop a pearl of wisdom, and pass on. To wit: the strict monogamist never gets into trouble.

VII.

Protestantism in the Republic

THAT Protestantism in this great Christian realm is down with a wasting disease must be obvious to every amateur of ghostly pathology. The denominational papers are full of alarming reports from its bedside, and all sorts of projects for the relief of the patient. One authority holds that only more money is needed to work a cure—that if the Christian exploiters and usurers of the country would provide a sufficient slush fund, all the vacant pews could be filled, and the baptismal tanks with them. Another authority argues that the one way to save the churches is to close all other places of resort and amusement on the Sabbath, from delicatessen shops to road-houses, and from movie parlors to jazz palaces. Yet another proposes a mass attack by prayer, apparently in the hope of provoking a miracle. A fourth advocates a vast augmentation of so-called institutional effort, *i.e.*, the scheme of putting bowling alleys and courting cubicles into church cellars, and of giving over the rest of every sacred edifice to debates on the Single Tax, boxing matches, baby shows, mental hygiene clinics, lectures by converted actors, movie shows, raffles, non-voluptuous dances, and evening classes in salesmanship, automobile repairing, birth control, interior decoration, and the art and mystery of the realtor. A fifth, borrowing a leaf from Big Business, maintains that consolidation and reorganization are what is needed—that the existence of half a dozen rival churches in every American village profits the devil a great deal more than it profits God. This last scheme seems to have won a great deal of support among the pious. At least a score of committees are now trying to draw up plans for concrete consolidations, and even the Southern and Northern Methodists, who hate each other violently, have been in peaceful though vain negotiation.

On the merits of these conflicting remedies I attempt no pronouncement, but I have been at some pains to look into the symptoms and nature of the disease. My report is that it seems to me to be analogous to that malady which afflicts a star in the heavens when it splits into two halves and they go slambanging into space in opposite directions. That, in brief, is what appears to be the matter with Protestantism in the United States to-day. One half of it is moving, with slowly accelerating speed, in the direction of the Harlot of the Seven Hills: the other is sliding down into voodooism. The former carries the greater part of Protestant money with it; the latter carries the greater part of Protestant enthusiasm, or, as the word now is, pep. What remains in the middle may be likened to a torso without either brains to think with or legs to dance—in other words, something that begins to be professionally attractive to the mortician, though it still makes shift to breathe. There is no lack of life on the higher levels, where the most solvent Methodists and the like are gradually transmogrified into Episcopalians, and the Episcopalians shin up the ancient bastions of Holy Church, and there is no lack of life on the lower levels, where the rural Baptists, by the route of Fundamentalism, the Anti-Saloon League, and the Ku Klux Klan, rapidly descend to the dogmas and practices of the Congo jungle. But in the middle there is desiccation and decay. Here is where Protestantism was once strongest. Here is the region of the plain and godly Americano, fond of devotion but distrustful of every hint of orgy—the honest fellow who suffers dutifully on Sunday, pays his share, and hopes for a few kind words from the pastor when his time comes to die. He stands to-day on a burning deck. It is no wonder that Sunday automobiling begins to get him in its clutches. If he is not staggered one day by his pastor's appearance in surplice and stole, he is staggered the day following by a file of Ku Kluxers marching up the aisle. So he tends to absent himself from pious exercises, and the news goes about that there is something the matter with the churches, and the denominational papers bristle with schemes to set it right, and many up-and-coming pastors, tiring of preaching and parish work, get excellent jobs as the executive secretaries of these schemes, and go about the country expounding them to the faithful.

The extent to which Protestantism, in its upper reaches, has succumbed to the harlotries of Rome seems to be but little apprehended by the majority of connoisseurs. I was myself unaware of the whole truth until last Christmas, when, in the pursuit of a quite unrelated inquiry, I employed agents to attend all the services held in the principal Protestant basilicas of an eminent American city, and to bring in the best reports they could formulate upon what went on in the lesser churches. The substance of these reports, in so far as they related to churches patronized by the well-to-do, was simple: they revealed a head-long movement to the right, an almost precipitate flight over the mountain. Six so-called Episcopal churches held midnight services on Christmas Eve in obvious imitation of Catholic midnight masses, and one of them actually called its service a solemn high mass. Two invited the nobility and gentry to processions, and a third concealed a procession under the name of a pageant. One offered Gounod's St. Cecilia mass on Christmas morning, and another the Messe Solennelle by the same composer; three others, somewhat more timorous, contented themselves with parts of masses. One, throwing off all pretense and euphemism, summoned the faithful to no less than three Christmas masses, naming them by name—two low and one high. All six churches were aglow with candles, and two employed incense.

But that was not the worst. Two Presbyterian churches and one Baptist church, not to mention five Lutheran churches of different synods, had choral services in the dawn of Christmas morning, and the one attended by the only one of my agents who got up early enough—it was in a Presbyterian church—was made gay with candles, and had a palpably Roman smack. Yet worse: a rich and conspicuous Methodist church, patronized by the leading Wesleyan wholesalers and money-lenders of the town, boldly offered a mediæval carol service. Mediæval? What did that mean? The Middle Ages ended on July 16, 1453, at 12 o'clock meridian, and the Reformation was not launched by Luther until October 31, 1517, at 10.15 A.M. If mediæval, in the sense in which it was here used, does not mean Roman Catholic, then I surely went to school in vain. My agent, born a Methodist, reported that the whole ceremony shocked him excessively. It began with trumpet blasts from the church spire and it concluded with an Ave Maria by a vested choir! Candles rose up in glittering ranks behind the chancel rail, and above them glowed a shining electric star.

God help us all, indeed! What next? Will the rev. pastor, on some near to-morrow, defy the lightnings of Jahveh by appearing in alb and dalmatic? Will he turn his back upon the faithful? Will he put in a telephone-booth for auricular confession? I shudder to think of what old John Wesley would have said about that vested choir and that shining star. Or Bishop Francis Asbury. Or the Rev. Jabez Bunting. Or Robert Strawbridge, that consecrated man.

Here, of course, I do not venture into the contumacy of criticising; I merely marvel. A student of the sacred sciences all my life, I am well learned in the dogmas and ceremonials of the sects, and know what they affect and what they abhor. Does anyone argue that the use of candles in public worship would have had the sanction of the *Ur*-Wesleyans, or that they would have consented to *Blasmusik* and a vested choir? If so, let the sciolist come forward. Down to fifty years ago, in fact, the Methodists prohibited Christmas services altogether, as Romish and heathen. But now we have ceremonies almost operatic, and the sweet masses of Gounod are just around the corner! As I have said, the Episcopalians—who, in most American cities, are largely ex-Methodists or ex-Presbyterians, or, in New York, ex-Jews—go still further. In three of the churches attended by my agents Holy Communion was almost indistinguishable from the mass. Two of these churches, according to information placed at my disposal by the police, are very fashionable; to get into one of them is almost as difficult as ordering a suit of clothes from Poole. But the richer the Episcopalian, the more eager he is to forget that he was once baptized by public outcry or total immersion. The Low Church rectors, in the main, struggle with poor congregations, born to the faith but deficient in buying power. As bank accounts increase the fear of the devil diminishes, and there is bred a sense of beauty. This sense of beauty, in its practical effects, is identical with the work of the Paulist Fathers. To-day, indeed, even the Methodists who remain Methodists begin to wobble. Tiring of the dreadful din that goes with the orthodox Wesleyan demonology, they take to ceremonials that grow more and more stately and voluptuous. The sermon ceases to be a cavalry charge, and becomes soft and *pizzicato*. The choir abandons "Throw Out the Life-Line" and "Are You Ready for the Judgment Day?" and toys with Händel. The rev. pastor throws off the uniform of a bank cashier and puts on a gown. It is an evolution that has, viewed from a tree, a certain merit. The stock of nonsense in the world is sensibly diminished and the stock of beauty augmented. But what would the old-time circuit-riders say of it, imagining them miraculously brought back from hell?

So much for the volatilization that is going on above the diaphragm. What is in progress below? All I can detect is a rapid descent to mere barbaric devil-chasing. In all those parts of the Republic where Beelzebub is still as real as Babe Ruth or Dr. Coolidge, and men drink raw fusel oil hot from the still—for example, in the rural sections of the Middle West and everywhere in the South save a few walled towns—the evangelical sects plunge into an abyss of malignant imbecility, and declare a holy war upon every decency that civilized men cherish. First the Anti-Saloon League, and now the Ku Klux Klan and the various Fundamentalist organizations, have converted them into vast machines for pursuing and butchering unbelievers. They have thrown the New Testament overboard, and gone back to the Old, and particularly to the bloodiest parts of it. Their one aim seems to be to break heads, to spread terror, to propagate hatred. Everywhere they have set up enmities that will not die out for generations. Neighbor looks askance at neighbor, the land is filled with spies, every man of the slightest intelligence is suspect. Christianity becomes a sort of psychic cannibalism. Unfortunately, the doings of the rustic gentlemen of God who furnish steam for this movement have been investigated but imperfectly, and in consequence too little is known about them. Even the sources of their power, so far as I know, have not been looked into. My suspicion is that it has increased as the influence of the old-time country-town newspapers has declined. These newspapers, in large areas of the land, once genuinely molded public opinion. They attracted to their service a shrewd and salty class of rustic philosophers, mainly highly alcoholized; they were outspoken in their views and responded only slightly to the prevailing crazes. In the midst of the Bryan uproar, a quarter of a century ago, scores of little weeklies in the South and Middle West kept up a gallant battle for sound money and the Hanna idealism. There were red-hot Democratic papers in Pennsylvania, and others in Ohio; there were Republican sheets in rural Maryland, and even in Virginia. The growth of the big city dailies is what chiefly reduced them to puerility. As communications improved every yokel began following Brisbane, Dr. Frank Crane, and Mutt and Jeff. The rural mail carrier began leaving a 24-page yellow in every second box. The hinds distrusted and detested the politics of these great organs, but enjoyed their imbecilities. The country weekly could not match the latter, and so it began to decline. It is now in a low state everywhere in America. Half of it is boiler-plate and the other half is cross-roads gossip. The editor is no longer the leading thinker of his town; instead, he is commonly a broken and despairing man, cadging for advertisements and hoping for a political job. He used to aspire to the State Senate; now he is content with the post of town bailiff or road supervisor.

His place has been taken by the village pastor. The pastor got into public affairs by the route of Prohibition. The shrewd shysters who developed the Anti-Saloon League made a politician of him, and once he had got a taste of power he was eager for more. It came very quickly. As industry penetrated to the rural regions the new-blown Babbitts began to sense his capacity for safeguarding the established order, and so he was given the job: he became a local Billy Sunday. And, simultaneously the old-line politicians, taught a lesson by the Anti-Saloon League, began to defer to him in general, as they had yielded to him in particular. He was consulted about candidacies; he had his say about policies. The local school-board soon became his private preserve. The wandering cony-catchers of the tin-pot fraternal orders found him a useful man. He was, by now, a specialist in all forms of public rectitude, from teetotalism to patriotism. He was put up on days of ceremony to sob for the flag, vice the county judge, retired. When the Klan burst upon the peasants all of his new duties were synthetized. He was obviously the chief local repository of its sublime principles, theological, social, ethnological and patriotic. In every country town in America to-day, wherever the Klan continues to rowel the hinds, its chief engine is a clerk in holy orders. If the Baptists are strong, their pastor is that engine. Failing Baptists, the heroic work is assumed by the Methodist parson, or the Presbyterian, or the Campbellite. Without these sacerdotal props the Invisible Empire would have faded long ago.

What one mainly notices about these ambassadors of Christ, observing them in the mass, is their vast lack of sound information and sound sense. They constitute, perhaps, the most ignorant class of teachers ever set up to lead a civilized people; they are even more ignorant than the county superintendents of schools. Learning, indeed, is not esteemed in evangelical denominations, and any literate plowhand, if the Holy Spirit inflames him, is thought to be fit to preach. Is he commonly sent, as a preliminary, to a training camp, to college? But what a college! You will find one in every mountain valley of the land, with its single building in its bare pasture lot, and its faculty of half-idiot pedagogues and broken-down preachers. One man, in such a college, teaches oratory, ancient history, arithmetic and Old Testament exegesis. The aspirant comes in from the barnyard, and goes back in a year or two to the village. His body of knowledge is that of a street-car motorman or a vaudeville actor. But he has learned the clichés of his craft, and he has got him a long-tailed coat, and so he has made his escape from the harsh labors of his ancestors, and is set up as a fountain of light and learning.

It is from such ignoramuses that the lower half of American Protestantdom gets its view of the cosmos. Certainly Fundamentalism should not be hard to understand when its sources are inspected. How can the teacher teach when his own head is empty? Of all that constitutes the sum of human knowledge he is as innocent as an Eskimo. Of the arts he knows absolutely nothing; of the sciences he has never so much as heard. No good book ever penetrates to those remote "colleges," nor does any graduate ever take away a desire to read one. He has been warned, indeed, against their blandishments; what is not addressed solely to the paramount business of saving souls is of the devil. So when he hears by chance of the battle of ideas beyond the sky-rim, he quite naturally puts it down to Beezlebub. What comes to him, vaguely and distorted, is unintelligible to him. He is suspicious of it, afraid of it—and he quickly communicates his fears to his dupes. The common man, in many ways, is hard to arouse; it is a terrific job to ram even the most elemental ideas into him. But it is always easy to scare him.

That is the daily business of the evangelical pastors of the Republic. They are specialists in alarms and bugaboos. The rum demon, atheists, Bolsheviki, the Pope, bootleggers, the Jews,—all these have served them in turn, and in the demonology of the Ku Klux Klan all have been conveniently brought together. The old stock company of devils has been retired, and with it the old repertoire of private sins. The American peasant of to-day finds it vastly easier to claw into heaven than he used to. Personal holiness has now been handed over to the Holy Rollers and other such survivors from a harsher day. It is sufficient now to hate the Pope, to hate the Jews, to hate the scientists, to hate all foreigners, to hate whatever the cities yield to. These hatreds have been spread in the land by rev. pastors, chiefly Baptists and Methodists. They constitute, with their attendant fears, the basic religion of the American clodhopper to-day. They are the essence of the new Protestantism, second division, American style.

Their public effects are constantly underestimated until it is too late. I ask no indulgence for calling attention to the case of Prohibition. Fundamentalism, it may be, is sneaking upon the nation in the same disarming way. The cities laugh at the yokels, but meanwhile the politicians take careful notice; such mountebanks as Peay of Tennessee and Blease of South Carolina have already issued their preliminary whoops. As the tide rolls up the pastors will attain to greater and greater consequence. Already, indeed, they swell visibly in power and pretension. The Klan, in its earlier days, kept them discreetly under cover; they labored valiantly in the hold, but only lay go-getters were seen upon the bridge. But now they are everywhere on public display, leading the anthropoid host. The curious thing is that their activity gets little if any attention from the established publicists. Let a lone Red arise to annoy a barroom full of Michigan lumber-jacks, and at once the fire-alarm sounds and the full military and naval power of the nation is summoned to put down the outrage. But how many Americans would the Reds convert to their rubbish, even supposing them free to spout it on every street-corner? Probably not enough, all told, to make a day's hunting for a regiment of militia. The American moron's mind simply does not run in that direction; he wants to keep his Ford, even at the cost of losing the Bill of Rights. But the stuff that the Baptist and Methodist dervishes have on tap is very much to his taste; he gulps it eagerly and rubs his tummy. I suggest that it might be well to make a scientific inquiry into the nature of it. The existing agencies of sociological snooting seem to be busy in other directions. There are elaborate surveys of some of the large cities, showing how much it costs to teach a child the principles of Americanism, how often the average citizen falls into the hands of the cops, how many detective stories are taken out of the city library daily, and how many children a normal Polish woman has every year. Why not a survey of the rustic areas, where men are he and God still reigns? Why not an attempt to find out just what the Baptist dominies have drilled into the heads of the Tennesseeans, Arkansans and Nebraskans? It would be amusing, and it would be instructive. And useful. For it is well, in such matters, to see clearly what is ahead. The United States grows increasingly urban, but its ideas are still hatched in the little towns. What the swineherds credit to-day is whooped to-morrow by their agents and attorneys in Congress, and then comes upon the cities suddenly, with all the force of law. Where do the swineherds get it? Mainly from the only publicists and metaphysicians they know: the gentlemen of the sacred faculty. It was not the bawling of the mountebank Bryan, but the sermon of a mountain Bossuet that laid the train of the Scopes case and made a whole State forever ridiculous. I suggest looking more carefully into the notions that such ignoramuses spout.

Meanwhile, what is the effect of all this upon the Protestant who retains some measure of sanity, the moderate and peaceable fellow—him called by William Graham Sumner the Forgotten Man? He is silent while the bombs burst and the stink bombs go off, but what is he thinking? I believe that he is thinking strange and dreadful thoughts—thoughts that would have frozen his own spine a dozen years ago. He is thinking, *imprimis*, that there must be something in this evolution heresy after all, else Methodist bishops and other such bristling foes to sense would not be so frantically against it. And he is thinking, secondly, that perhaps a civilized man, in the last analysis, would not be worse off if Sherman's march were repeated by the Papal Guard. Between these two thoughts American Protestantism is being squeezed, so to speak, to death.

VIII.
From the Files of a Book Reviewer

I
Counter-Offensive

Is It God's Word? by Joseph Wheless. New York: *Alfred A. Knopf.* [The American Mercury, May, 1926.]

The author of this book, who is an associate editor of the *American Bar Association Journal*, was trained as a lawyer, but that training, somewhat surprisingly, seems to have left his logical powers unimpaired, and with them his capacity for differentiating between facts and mere appearances. There is no hint of the usual evasions and obfuscations of the advocate in his pages. His business is to examine calmly the authority and plausibility of Holy Writ, both as history and as revelation of the Omnipotent Will, and to that business he brings an immense and meticulous knowledge, an exact and unfailing judicial sense, and a skill at orderly exposition which is quite extraordinary. There is no vaporing of the orthodox exegetes that he is not familiar with, and none that he fails to refute, simply and devastatingly. Nine-tenths of his evidence he takes out of the mouths of his opponents. Patiently, mercilessly, irresistibly, he subjects it to logical analysis, and when he is done at last—his book runs to 494 pages of fine print—there is little left of the two Testaments save a farrago of palpable nonsense, swathed, to be sure, in a very lovely poetry. He exposes all their gross and preposterous contradictions, their violations of common sense and common decency, their grotesque collisions with the known and indubitable facts, their petty tergiversations and fraudulences. He goes behind the mellifluous rhetoric of the King James Version to the harsh balderdash of the originals, and brings it out into the horrible light of day. He exposes the prophecies that have failed to come off. He exhibits the conflicts of romantic and unreliable witnesses, most of them with something to sell. He tracks down ideas to their barbaric sources. He concocts an almost endless series of logical dilemmas. And he does it all with good manners, never pausing to rant and nowhere going beyond the strict letter of the record.

Obviously, there is room and need for such a book, and it deserves to be widely read. For in the America of to-day, after a time of quiescence, the old conflict between religion and science has resumed with great ferocity, and the partisans of the former, not content with denouncing all free inquiry as evil, have now undertaken to make it downright unlawful. Worse, they show signs of succeeding. And why? Chiefly, it seems to me, because the cause of their opponents has been badly handled—above all, because it has lacked vigorous *offensive* leadership. Even the defense is largely an abject running away. We are assured with pious snuffling that there is actually no conflict, that the domains of science and religion do not overlap, that it is quite possible for a man to be a scientist (even a biologist!) and yet believe that Jonah swallowed the whale. No wonder the whoopers for Genesis take courage, and lay on with glad, *sforzando* shouts. At one stroke they are lifted to parity with their opponents, nay, to superority. The bilge they believe in becomes something sacrosanct; its manifest absurdities are not mentioned, and hence tend to pass unnoticed. But meanwhile they are quite free to belabor science with their whole armamentarium of imbecilities. Every cross-roads Baptist preacher becomes an authority upon its errors, and is heard gravely. In brief, science exposes itself to be shot at, but agrees not to shoot back. It would be difficult to imagine any strategy more idiotic.

Or to imagine a Huxley adopting it. Huxley, in his day, followed a far different plan. When the Gladstones, Bishop Wilberforces and other such obscurantists denounced the new biology, he did not waste any time upon conciliatory politeness. Instead, he made a bold and headlong attack upon Christian theology—an attack so vigorous and so skillful that the enemy was soon in ignominious flight. Huxley knew the first principle of war: he knew that a hearty offensive is worth a hundred defensives. How well he succeeded is shown by the fact that even to-day, with theology once more on the prowl and the very elements of science under heavy attack, some of the gaudiest of the ancient theological notions are not heard of. Huxley disposed of them completely; even in Darkest Tennessee the yokels no longer give them credit. But if the Robert Andrews Millikans and other such amiable bunglers continue to boss the scientific camp you may be sure that all these exploded myths and superstitions will be revived, and that the mob will once more embrace them. For it is the natural tendency of the ignorant to believe what is not true. In order to overcome that tendency it is not sufficient to exhibit the true; it is also necessary to expose and denounce the false. To admit the false has any standing in court, that it ought to be handled gently because millions of morons cherish it and thousands of quacks make their livings propagating it—to admit this, as the more fatuous of the reconcilers of science and religion inevitably do, is to abandon a just cause to its enemies, cravenly and without excuse.

It is, of course, quite true that there is a region in which science and religion do not conflict. That is the region of the unknowable. No one knows Who created the visible universe, and it is infinitely improbable that anything properly describable as evidence on the point will ever be discovered. No one knows what motives or intentions, if any, lie behind what we call natural laws. No one knows why man has his present form. No one knows why sin and suffering were sent into this world —that is, why the fashioning of man was so badly botched. Naturally enough, all these problems have engaged the interest of humanity since the remotest days, and in every age, with every sort of evidence completely lacking, men of speculative mind have sought to frame plausible solutions. Some of them, more bold than the rest, have pretended that their solutions were revealed to them by God, and multitudes have believed them. But no man of science believes them. He doesn't say positively that they are wrong; he simply says that there is no proof that they are right. If he admitted, without proof, that they are right, he would not be a man of science. In his view all such theories and speculations stand upon a common level. In the most ambitious soarings of a Christian theologian he can find nothing that differs in any essential way from the obvious hocus-pocus of a medicine man in the jungle. Superficially, of course, the two stand far apart. The Christian theologian, confined like all the rest to the unknowable, has to be more careful than the medicine man, for in Christendom the unknowable covers a far less extensive field than in the jungle. Christian theology is thus, in a sense, more reasonable than voodooism. But it is not more reasonable because its professors know more than the voodoo-man about the unknowable; it is more reasonable simply because they are under a far more rigorous and enlightened scrutiny, and run a risk of being hauled up sharply every time they venture too near the borders of the known.

This business of hauling them up is one of the principal functions of science. Its prompt execution is the gauge of a high and progressive civilization. So long as theologians keep within their proper bounds, science has no quarrel with them, for it is no more able to prove that they are wrong than they themselves are able to prove that they are right. But human experience shows that they never keep within their proper bounds voluntarily; they are always bulging over the line, and making a great uproar over things that they know nothing about. Such an uproar is going on in the United States at the present moment. Hordes of theologians come marching down from the Southern mountains, declaring raucously that God created the universe during a certain single week of the year 4004 B. C., and demanding that all persons who presume to doubt it be handed over to the secular arm. Here, obviously, science cannot suffer them gladly, nor even patiently. Their proposition is a statement of scientific fact; it may be examined and tested like any other statement of scientific fact. So examined and tested, it turns out to be wholly without evidential support. All the known evidence, indeed, is against it, and overwhelmingly. No man who knows the facts—that is, no man with any claim to scientific equipment—is in any doubt about that. He disbelieves it as thoroughly as he believes that the earth moves 'round the sun. Disbelieving it, it is his professional duty, his first obligation of professional honor, to attack and refute those who uphold it. Above all, it is his duty to attack the false evidence upon which they base their case.

Thus an actual conflict is joined, and it is the height of absurdity for the Millikans and other such compromisers to seek to evade it with soft words. That conflict was not begun by science. It did start with an invasion of the proper field of theological speculation by scientific raiders. It started with an invasion of the field of science by theological raiders. Now that it is on, it must be pressed vigorously from the scientific side, and without any flabby tenderness for theological susceptibilities. A defensive war is not enough; there must be a forthright onslaught upon the theological citadel, and every effort must be made to knock it down. For so long as it remains a stronghold, there will be no security for sound sense among us, and little for common decency. So long as it may be used as a recruiting-station and rallying-point for the rabble, science will have to submit to incessant forays, and the same forays will be directed against every sort of rational religion. The latter danger is not unobserved by the more enlightened theologians. They are well aware that, facing the Fundamentalists, they must either destroy or be destroyed. It is to be hoped that the men of science will perceive the same plain fact, and so give over their vain effort to stay the enemy with weasel words.

2
Heretics

ALTGELD OF ILLINOIS, by Waldo R. Browne. New York: *B. W. Huebsch.* THE LAST OF THE HERETICS, by Algernon Sidney Crapsey. New York: *Alfred A. Knopf.* [The American Mercury, October, 1924.]

When I was a boy, in the early nineties of the last century, the reigning hobgoblin of the United States was John P. Altgeld, Governor of Illinois. From this distance the ill-fame that played about him seems almost fabulous. He was a sort of horrendous combination of Trotsky and Raisuli, Darwin and the German Crown Prince, Jesse James and Oscar Wilde, with overtones of Wayne B. Wheeler and the McNamara brothers. We have had, in these later years, no such communal devil. The La Follette of 1917 was a popular favorite compared to him; the Debs of the same time was a spoiled darling. What I gathered from my elders, in the awful years of adolescence, when my voice began to break and vibrissæ sprouted on my lip, was that Altgeld was a shameless advocate of rapine and assassination, an enemy alike to the Constitution and the Ten Commandments—in short, a bloody and insatiable anarchist. I was thus bred to fear him even more than I feared the anonymous scoundrels who had stolen Charlie Ross. When I dreamed, it was of catching him in some public place and cutting off his head, to the applause of the multitude.

The elders that I have mentioned were mainly business men, with a few *Gelehrte* thrown in. I learned later on, by hard experience, that the opinions of such gentlemen, particularly of public matters and public men, were not always sound. Nevertheless, I continued to have a bilious suspicion of the Hon. Mr. Altgeld, and it survived even the discovery, made much later, that men who had actually known him—for example, Theodore Dreiser—regarded him very highly. I remember very well how shocked I was when Dreiser made me privy to this fact. It made a dent, I suppose, in my old view, but it surely did not dispose of it altogether. I continued to believe that Altgeld, though perhaps not an anarchist, as alleged, was at least a blathering Socialist, and hence deserving of a few prophylactic kicks in the pantaloons. I was far gone in my forties before ever I got at the truth. Then I found it in this modest book of Mr. Browne's—a volume that is dreadfully written, but extremely illuminating. That truth may be put very simply. Altgeld was not an anarchist, nor was he a Socialist: he was simply a sentimentalist. His error consisted in taking the college yells of democracy seriously.

I do not go into the evidence, but refer you to the book. It is very completely documented, and it leaves little room for doubt, despite Mr. Browne's obvious prejudice in favor of some of Altgeld's more dubious ideas, especially the idea of government ownership. On the main points his argument is quite beyond cavil. Did Altgeld pardon the Chicago anarchists? Then it was simply because they had been railroaded to jail on evidence that should have made the very judge on the bench guffaw—as men are still railroaded in California to-day. Did he protest against Cleveland's invasion of Chicago with Federal troops at the time of the Pullman strike? Then it was because he knew only too well how little they were needed—and what sinister influences had cajoled poor old Grover into sending them. In brief, Altgeld was one of the first public men in America to protest by word and act against government by usurers and their bashi-bazouks—the first open and avowed advocate of the Bill of Rights since Jackson's time. A romantic fellow, and a firm believer in the virtues of the common people, he couldn't rid himself of the delusion that they would follow him here—that after the yell of rage there would come a resounding cheer. That belief gradually degenerated into a hope, but I doubt that it ever disappeared altogether. The common people met it by turning Altgeld out of office, swiftly and ignominiously. After they had got rid of him as Governor of Illinois, they even rejected him as mayor of Chicago. His experience taught him a lesson, but like that of the Aframerican on the gallows, it came too late.

What lesson is in his career for the rest of us? The lesson, it seems to me, that any man who devotes himself to justice and common decency, under democracy, is a very foolish fellow—that the generality of men have no genuine respect for these things, and are always suspicious of the man who upholds them. Their public relations, like their private relations, are marked by the qualities that mark the inferior man at all times and everywhere: cowardice, stupidity and cruelty. They are in favor of whoever is wielding the whip, even when their own hides must bear the blows. How easy it was to turn the morons of the American Legion upon their fellow-slaves! How heroically they voted for Harding, and then for Coolidge after him—and so helped to put down the Reds! Dog eats dog, world without end. In the Pullman strike at least half the labor unions of the United States were against the strikers, as they were against the more recent steel strikers, and helped to beat them. Altgeld battled for the under dog all his life—and the under dog bit him in the end. A pathetic career, but not without its touches of sardonic comedy. Altgeld, in error at bottom, was often also in error on the surface, and not infrequently somewhat grotesquely. He succumbed to the free silver mania. He supported Bryan—nay more, he may be said to have discovered and made Bryan. It is fortunate for him that he was dead and in hell by 1902, and so not forced to contemplate the later states of his handiwork. He was excessively romantic, but certainly no ignoramus. Imagine him listening to one of good Jennings' harangues against the elements of biology! Such men, indeed, are always happier dead. This world, and especially this Republic, is no place for idealists.

Another proof of it is offered by the career of Dr. Crapsey, whose trial for heresy entertained the damned in 1906. He is still alive as I write, and still full of steam. But I doubt that he is as sure as he used to be that common sense and common honesty pay. Many of the frauds who drove him out of the church, though they know that he was right, are bishops today, and licensed to bind and loose. Others have been called by God, and sit upon His right hand. The church itself, as it has grown more sordid and swinish, has only grown more prosperous. In New York City its income approaches that of the bootleggers and it is almost as well regarded. Every new profiteer, even before he tries to horn into the Piping Rock Club, subscribes to its articles. It is robbing the Church of Christ Scientist of all the rich Jews; they are having their sons baptized in its fonts and christened Llewellyn, Seymour and Murray. Certainly it would be difficult to imagine a more gloriously going concern. The rising spires of its steel and concrete cathedrals begin to bulge the floor of heaven; its clergy are sleek, fat and well-oiled; its bishops come next in precedence after movie stars and members of the firm of J. P. Morgan & Company. Lately it threw out another heretic—like Dr. Crapsey, one accused of putting the Sermon on the Mount above the conflicting genealogies of the Preacher. As for Crapsey himself, he has naught to console him in his old age save the thought that hell will at least be warm.

His book is extremely amusing and instructive. Like Altgeld, he confesses to foreign and poisonous blood. The *Stammvater* of the American Crapseii was a fellow named Kropps, apparently a Hessian. But his great-great grandson, the father of the heretic, married the daughter of a United States Senator, and so there is some amelioration of the horror. Like Altgeld again, Crapsey went to the Civil War as a boy scarcely out of knee breeches. Altgeld was so poor that he gladly took the $100 offered by a patriot who had been drafted and wanted a substitute; Crapsey volunteered. Both succumbed to camp fevers and were discharged. Both then took to Service among the downtrodden, Altgeld in politics and the law, and Crapsey in one of the outlying hereditaments of Trinity parish. Both were safe so long as they appeared to be fraudulent; the moment they began to show genuine belief in their doctrines they found themselves in difficulties. So Altgeld became the favorite hobgoblin of the Republic and Crapsey became its blackest heretic.

3
The Grove of Academe

THE GOOSE-STEP, by Upton Sinclair. Pasadena, Calif.: *Published by the Author*. [The Smart Set, May, 1923.]

The doctrine preached in this fat volume—to wit, that the American colleges and universities, with precious few exceptions, are run by stock-jobbers and manned by intellectual prostitutes—this doctrine will certainly give no fillip of surprise to steady readers of my critical compositions. I have, in fact, maintained it steadily since the earliest dawn of the present marvelous century, and to the support of it I have brought forward an immense mass of glittering and irrefragable facts and a powerful stream of eloquence. Nor have I engaged in this moral enterprise *a cappella*. A great many other practitioners have devoted themselves to it with equal assiduity, including not a few reformed and conscience-stricken professors, and the net result of that united effort is that the old assumption of the pedagogue's *bona fides* is now in decay throughout the Republic. In whole departments of human knowledge he has become suspect, as it were, *ex officio*. I nominate, for example, the departments of history and of what is commonly called English language and literature. If a professor in the first field shows ordinary honesty, or, in the second field, ordinary sense, it is now regarded as a sort of marvel, and with sound reason. Barring a scant dozen extraordinary men, no American professor of history has written anything worth reading since the year 1917; nearly all the genuine history published in the United States since then has come from laymen, or from professors who have ceased to profess. And so in the domain of the national letters. The professors, with a few exceptions, mainly belated rice-converts, are unanimously and furiously consecrated to vain attacks upon the literature that is in being. Either, like the paleozoic Beers, of Yale, they refuse to read it and deny that it exists, or, like the patriotic Matthews, of Columbia, they seek to put it down by launching Ku Klux anathemas against it. The net result is that the professorial caste, as a whole, loses all its old dignity and influence. In universities large and small, East, West, North and South, the very sophomores rise in rebellion against the incompetence and imbecility of their preceptors, and in the newspapers the professor slides down gradually to the level of a chiropractor, a press-agent or a Congressman.

Thus there is nothing novel in the thesis of Dr. Sinclair's book, which deals, in brief, with the internal organization of the American universities, and their abject subjection to the Money Power, which is to say, to Chamber of Commerce and Rotary Club concepts of truth, liberty and honor. But there is something new, and very refreshing, in the manner of it, for the learned author, for the first time, manages to tell a long and dramatic story without intruding his private grievances into it. Sinclair's worst weakness, next to his vociferous appetite for Remedies that never cure, is his naïve and almost actorial vanity. As everyone knows, it botched "The Brass Check." So much of that book was given over to a humorless account of his own combats with yellow journals—which, in the main, did nothing worse to him than laugh at him when he was foolish—that he left untold a great deal that might have been said, and with perfect justice and accuracy, about the venality and swinishness of American newspapers. In "The Profits of Religion" he wobbled almost as badly; the subject, no doubt, was much too vast for a single volume; the Methodists and Baptists alone, to say nothing of Holy Church, deserved a whole shelf. But in "The Goose-Step" he tells a straightforward story in a straightforward manner—simply, good-humoredly and convincingly. When he comes into the narrative himself, which is not often, he leaves off his customary martyr's chemise. There is no complaining, no pathos, no mouthing of platitude; it is a plain record of plain facts, with names and dates—a plain record of truly appalling cowardice, disingenuousness, abjectness, and degradation. Out of it two brilliant figures emerge: first the typical American university president, a jenkins to wealth, an ignominious waiter in antechambers and puller of wires, a politician, a fraud and a cad; and secondly, the typical American professor, a puerile and pitiable slave.

Such are the common and customary bearers of the torch in the Republic. Such is the usual machinery and inner nature of the higher learning among us. Its aim, briefly stated, is almost indistinguishable from the aim of the Ku Klux Klan, the American Legion, and Kiwanis. The thing it combats most ardently is not ignorance, but free inquiry; it is devoted to forcing the whole youth of the land into one rigid mold. Its ideal product is a young man who is absolutely correct in all his ideas—a perfect reader for the *Literary Digest*, the *American Magazine*, and the editorial page of the New York *Times.* To achieve this end Big Business has endowed it with unprecedented liberality; there are single American universities with more invested wealth and more income than all the universities of Germany, France or England taken together. But in order to get that ocean of money, and to pay for the piles of pseudo-Gothic that now arise all over the land, scholarship in America has had to sacrifice free inquiry to the prejudices and private interests of its masters—the search for the truth has had to be subordinated to the safeguarding of railway bonds and electric light stocks. As Sinclair shows, there is scarcely a university in the United States, whether maintained out of the public funds or privately endowed, that is not run absolutely, in all departments, by precisely the same men who run the street railways, the banks, the rolling mills, the coal mines and the factories of the country—in brief, by men who have no more respect for scholarship than an ice-wagon driver has for beautiful letters. There is scarcely an American university or college in which the scholars who constitute it have any effective control over its general policies and enterprises, or even over the conduct of their own departments. In almost every one there is some unspeakable stock-broker, or bank director, or railway looter who, if the spirit moved him, would be perfectly free to hound a Huxley, a Karl Ludwig or a Jowett from the faculty, and even to prevent him getting a seemly berth elsewhere. It is not only possible; it has been done, and not once, but scores and hundreds of times.

Sinclair is content to set forth the basic facts; his book, as it is, is very long; he neglects laboring all of the deductions and implications that flow from his thesis, some of them obvious enough. One of them is this: that the control of the universities by Mr. Babbitt is making it increasingly difficult to induce intelligent and self-respecting young men to embrace the birchman's career, and that the personnel of the teaching staffs thus tends to decline in competence, steadily and sharply. This accounts, in large measure, for the collapse of the old public influence of the scholar in America; he begins to be derided simply because he is no longer the dignified man that he once was. In certain departments, of no immediate interest to trustees and contributors, a certain show of freedom, of course, still prevails. What is taught in astronomy, or paleontology, or Greek cannot menace the nail manufacturer on the board, and so he does not issue any orders about it, nor does his agent, the university president. But what is taught in economics, or modern history, or "education," or sociology, or even literature, involves a dealing with ideas that are apt to hit him where he lives, and so he keeps a wary eye upon those departments, and at the slightest show of heresy he takes measures to protect himself. It is in these regions, consequently, that conformity is most comfortable, and that professional character is most lamentably in decay. Even here, to be sure, a few stout-hearted survivors of an earlier day hold out, but they are surely not many, and they will have no successors. The professor of tomorrow, in all departments that have to do with life as men are now living it in the world, will either be a scholastic goose-stepper or he will be out of a job. The screws are tightening every year. In the past the Babbitts have contented themselves with farming out the management of their intellectual brothels to extra-pliant professors, but now they begin to turn to yet more reliable men: army officers, lame-duck politicians, and engineers. The time will come, no doubt, when the president of Columbia will be just as frankly a partner in J. P. Morgan & Company as the head of the Red Cross or the chief vestryman of Trinity Church.

How far will this debauching of education go? Will the universities sink eventually to the level of the public-schools of such barbarous States as Texas, Arkansas and Mississippi? Here education has been reduced to a bald device for multiplying Shriners, Knights of Pythias and Rotarians—in brief, ignoramuses. In the institutions of higher learning one may reasonably look for some resistance to the process, soon or late. I doubt, however, that it will come from the professors; they are already too much cowed and demoralized, as Sinclair shows abundantly. The American Association of University Professors, an organization formed to protect pedagogues against wanton attack by the Babbitts, numbers but 5000 members; the remaining 195,000 American professors are either afraid to join, or already too much battered to want to. How far their degradation has gone was made visible during the late war, when all save an infinitesimal minority of them yielded to the most extravagant manias of the time and thousands gave astounding exhibitions of moronic sadism. The Neandertal qualities thus awakened are still visible in many directions; in the Southern States, I am informed by an exceptional professor, fully five-sixths of his colleagues became charter members of the Ku Klux Klan. It is hopeless to look for a *Freiheitskrieg* among such poor serfs. But the students remain, and in them lies some promise for the future. The American university student, in the past, has been a victim of the same process of leveling that destroyed his teacher. He has been taught conformity, obedience, the social and intellectual goose-step; the ideal held before him has been the ideal of correctness. But that ideal, it must be plain, is not natural to youth. Youth is aspiring, rebellious, inquisitive, iconoclastic, a bit romantic. All over the country the fact is bursting through the chains of repression. In scores of far-flung colleges the students have begun to challenge their professors, often very harshly. After a while, they may begin to challenge the masters of their professors. Not all of them will do it, and not most of them. But it doesn't take a majority to make a rebellion; it takes only a few determined leaders and a sound cause.

4
The Schoolma'm's Goal

THE SOCIAL OBJECTIVES OF SCHOOL ENGLISH, by Charles S. Pendleton. Nashville, Tenn.: *Published by the Author.* [The American Mercury, March, 1925.]

Here, in the form of a large flat book, eight and a half inches wide and eleven inches tall, is a sight-seeing bus touring the slums of pedagogy. The author, Dr. Pendleton, professes the teaching of English (not English, remember, but the teaching of English) at the George Peabody College for Teachers, an eminent seminary at Nashville, in the Baptist Holy Land, and his object in the investigation he describes was, in brief, to find out what the teachers who teach English hope to accomplish by teaching it. In other words, what, precisely, is the improvement that they propose to achieve in the pupils exposed to their art and mystery? Do they believe that the aim of teaching English is to increase the exact and beautiful use of the language? Or that it is to inculcate and augment patriotism? Or that it is to diminish sorrow in the home? Or that it has some other end, cultural, economic or military?

In order to find out, Prof. Pendleton, with true pedagogical diligence, proceeded to list all the reasons for teaching English that he could find. Some he got by cross-examining teachers. Others came from educators of a higher degree and puissance. Yet others he dug out of the text-books of pedagogy in common use, and the dreadful professional journals ordinarily read by teachers. Finally, he threw in some from miscellaneous sources, including his own inner consciousness. In all, he accumulated 1581 such reasons, or, as he calls them, objectives, and then he sat down and laboriously copied them upon 1581 very thin 3x5 cards, one to a card. Some of these cards were buff in color, some were blue, some were yellow, some were pink, and some were green. On the blue cards he copied all the objectives relating to the employment of English in conversation, on the yellow cards all those dealing with its use in literary composition, on the green cards all those having to do with speech-making, and so on. Then he shook up the cards, summoned eighty professional teachers of English, and asked them to sort out the objectives in the order of appositeness and merit. The results of this laborious sorting he now sets before the learned.

Don't be impatient! I won't keep you waiting. Here is the objective that got the most votes—the champion of the whole 1581:

> The ability to spell correctly without hesitation all the ordinary words of one's writing vocabulary.

Here is the runner-up:

The ability to speak, in conversation, in complete sentences, not in broken phrases.

And here is No. 7:

The ability to capitalize speedily and accurately in one's writing.

And here is No. 9:

The ability to think quickly in an emergency.

And here are some more, all within the first hundred:

The ability to refrain from marking or marring in any way a borrowed book.

An attitude of democracy rather than snobbishness within a conversation.

Familiarity with the essential stories and persons of the Bible.

And some from the second hundred:

The ability to sing through—words and music—the national anthem.

The ability courteously and effectively to receive orders from a superior.

The avoidance of vulgarity and profanity in one's public speaking.

The ability to read silently without lip movements.

The habit of placing the page one is reading so that there will not be shadows upon it.

The ability to refrain from conversation under conditions where it is annoying or disagreeable to others.

The ability to converse intelligently about municipal and district civic matters.

The ability to comprehend accurately the meaning of all common abbreviations and signs one meets with in reading.

The ability, during one's reading, to distinguish between an author's central theme and his incidental remarks.

I refrain from any more: all these got enough votes to put them among the first 200 objectives—200 out of 1581. Nor do I choose them unfairly; most of those that I have not listed were quite as bad as those I have. But, you may protest, the good professor handed his cards to a jury of little girls of eight or nine years, or to the inmates of a home for the feeble-minded! He did, in fact, nothing of the kind. His jury was very carefully selected. It consisted of eighty teachers of such professional keenness that they were assembled at the University of Chicago for post-graduate study. Every one of them had been through either a college or a normal school; forty-seven of them held learned degrees; all of them had been engaged professionally in teaching English, some for years. They came from Michigan, Nebraska, Iowa, Missouri, Wisconsin, Toronto, Leland Stanford, Chicago and Northwestern Universities; from Oberlin, De Pauw, Goucher, Beloit and Drake Colleges; from a dozen lesser seminaries of the higher learning. They represented, not the lowest level of teachers of English in the Republic, but the highest level. And yet it was their verdict by a solemn referendum that the principal objective in teaching English was to make good spellers, and that after that came breeding of good capitalizers!

I present Dr. Pendleton's laborious work as overwhelming proof of a thesis that I have maintained for years, perhaps sometimes with undue heat: that pedagogy in the United States is fast descending to the estate of a childish necromancy, and that the worst idiots, even among pedagogues, are the teachers of English. It is positively dreadful to think that the young American species are exposed day in and day out to the contamination of such dark minds. What can be expected of education that is carried on in the very sewers of the intellect? How can morons teach anything that is worth knowing? Here and there, true enough, a competent teacher of English is encountered. I could name at least twenty in the whole country. But it does not appear that Dr. Pendleton, among his eighty, found even one. There is not the lightest glimmer of intelligence in all the appalling tables of statistics and black, zig-zag graphs that he has so painfully amassed. Nor any apparent capacity for learning. The sound thing, the sane thing and the humane thing to do with his pathetic herd of A.B.'s would be to take them out in the alley and knock them in the head.

5
The Heroic Age

JEFFERSON AND HAMILTON, by Claude G. Bowers. Boston: *The Houghton Mifflin Company.* JEFFERSON AND MONTICELLO, by Paul Wilstach. Garden City, L. I.: *Doubleday, Page &*

Company. CORRESPONDENCE OF JOHN ADAMS AND THOMAS JEFFERSON, 1812–1826, selected by Paul Wilstach. Indianapolis: *The Bobbs-Merrill Company.* [The American Mercury, March, 1926.]

Jefferson, in one of his last letters to Adams, dated March 25, 1826, spoke of the time when both came into fame as the heroic age. The phrase was certainly not mere rhetoric. The two differed enormously, both in their personalities and in their ideas—perhaps quite as much as Jefferson differed from Hamilton or Adams from his cousin Sam—but in one thing at least they were exactly alike: they were men of complete integrity. As Frederick the Great said of the Prussian *Junker*, one could not buy them, and they would not lie. The fact, at times, made them bitter enemies, and the virtues of the one were cancelled by the virtues of the other, to the damage of their common country. But when they stood together, they were irresistible, for complete integrity, when it does not spend itself against itself, is always irresistible—one of the few facts, to me known, that is creditable to the human race. The masses of men, like children, are easily deceived, but in the long run, like children again, they show a tendency to yield to character. Bit by bit it conquers them. They see in it all the high values that they are incapable of reaching themselves. They see the courage that they lack, and the honesty that they lack, and the resolution that they lack. All these things were in both Adams and Jefferson. They fell, in their day, into follies, but I don't think that anyone believes they were ever *pushed* into them. Adams, no doubt, could be bamboozled, but neither he nor Jefferson could be scared.

I fear that the gallant iconoclasts who revise our history-books sometimes forget all this. Engaged upon the destruction of legends, all of them maudlin and many of them downright insane, they also, at times, do damage to facts. One of these facts, it seems to me, ought not to be forgotten, to wit, that it took a great deal of courage, in the Summer of 1776, to sign Jefferson's celebrated exercise in colonial Johnsonese. There were ropes dangling in the air, and they were uncomfortably near. There were wives and children to be considered, and very agreeable estates. However dubious their primary motives, the men who signed took a long chance, quietly, simply, and with their faces to the front. How many of their successors in our own time have ever followed their example? I find it hard to think of one. The politician of to-day lacks their courage altogether; he lacks their incorruptible integrity. He is a complete coward. The whip of the Anti-Saloon League is enough to make him leap and tremble; the shadow of the rope would paralyze him with terror. He is for sale to anyone who has anything valuable to offer him, and the day after he has sold out to A he is ready to sell out to A's enemy, B. His honor is that of a street-walker.

So far we have progressed along the highroad of democracy. The gentleman survives in our politics only as an anachronism; his day is done. Mr. Bowers, in "Hamilton and Jefferson," traces the beggining of the decline; Mr. Wilstach, in the volume of Adams-Jefferson letters, shows it in full tide. Both authors are partial to Jefferson, and present charming portraits of him, especially Mr. Wilstach, in his other book, "Jefferson at Monticello." It seems to me that they often confuse the man and his ideas, especially Mr. Bowers. Jefferson was unquestionably one of our giants. There was more in his head than there has been in the heads of all the Presidents in office since he went out. He was a man of immense intellectual curiosity, profound originality, and great daring. His integrity was of Doric massiveness. But was he always right? I don't think many reflective Americans of to-day would argue that he was. Confronting enemies of great resourcefulness and resolute determination, he was forced, bit by bit, into giving his democratic doctrine a sweep and scope that took it far beyond the solid facts. It became a religious dogma rather than a political theory. Once he was gone, it fell into the hands of vastly inferior men, and soon it had reached its *reductio ad absurdum*. Jefferson died in 1826. By 1829, when Jackson came in, it was a nuisance; by 1837, when he went out, it was a joke.

Jefferson's enthusiasm blinded him to the fact that the liberty to which he had consecrated the high days of his early manhood was a two-headed boon. There was, first, the liberty of the people as a whole to determine the forms of their own government, levy their own taxes, and make their own laws—in brief, freedom from the despotism of the King. There was, second, the liberty of the individual man to live his own life, within the limits of decency and decorum, as he pleased—in brief, freedom from the despotism of the majority. Hamilton was as much in favor of the first kind of liberty as Jefferson: he made, in fact, even greater sacrifices for it. But he saw that it was worth nothing without the second kind—that it might easily become worth less than nothing, for the King, whatever his oppressions *en gros*, at least gave some protection to the isolated subject. Monarchy might be the protector of liberty as well as the foe of liberty. It had been so, in fact, in the Prussia of Frederick. And democracy might be far more the foe than the protector. It was obviously so in the France of the Reign of Terror. Hamilton, a hard-headed man, given to figures rather than to theories, saw all this; Jefferson, a doctrinaire, even in his best moments, saw only half of it. That failure to see together was at the bottom of their difference—and their difference came very near wrecking the United States. Burr's bullet probably prevented a colossal disaster. But it also opened the way for troubles in the years to come. We are in the midst of them yet, and we are by no means near the end of them.

The shadow of Jeffersonism, indeed, is still over us. We are still bound idiotically by the battle-cries of a struggle that was over more than a century ago. We have got the half of liberty, but the other half is yet to be wrested from the implacable fates, and there seems little likelihood that it will be wrested soon. All the fears of Hamilton have come to realization—and some of the fears of Jefferson to fill the measure. Minorities among us have no rights that the majority is bound to respect; they are dragooned and oppressed in a way that would make an oriental despot blush. Yet behind the majority, often defectively concealed, there is always a sinister minority, eager only for its own advantage and willing to adopt any device, however outrageous, to get what it wants. We have a puppet in the White House, pulled by wires, but with dangerous weapons in its hands. Law Enforcement becomes the new state religion. A law is something that A wants and can hornswoggle B, C, D, E and F into giving him—by bribery, by lying, by bluff and bluster, by making faces. G and H are therefore bound to yield it respect—nay, to worship it. It is something sacred. To question it is to sin against the Holy Ghost.

I wonder what Jefferson would think if he could come out of his tomb and examine the Republic that he helped to fashion. He was a man of towering enthusiasms, but he was also sharply intelligent: he knew an accomplished fact when he saw one. My guess is that, at the first Jefferson Day dinner following his emergence, he would make a startling and scandalous speech.

6
The Woes of a 100% American

THE NEW BARBARIANS, by Wilbur C. Abbott. Boston: *Little, Brown & Company.* [The American Mercury, May, 1925.]

It would be easy to poke fun at this disorderly and indignant tract; even, perhaps, to denounce the learned author, in a lofty manner, as a mere jackass. His argument, at more than one place, is so shaky that it tempts ribaldry with a powerful lure, almost a suction. His premisses are often gratuitous and absurd; his conclusions are often fantastic. Worse, he argues in circles, and it is frequently hard to make out what he is advocating, and why. Worst of all, the urbanity suitable to a learned gentleman resident in Sparks street, Cambridge, Mass., sometimes yields to a libido far more suitable to an auctioneer, a Federal district attorney or a Methodist bishop, and he rants dreadfully. But against all this there is yet something to be said, and that something, I think, is sufficient to stay the impulse to have at him brutally, either with cackles or with invective. It is, in brief, this: that what he inveighs against, given his natural and laudable prejudices, is plentifully sufficient to excuse all his indignation, and all his incoherence, and even his occasional departures from the strict letter of the record—that it is a merit in any man, facing what he deems to be incubi and succubi, to belabor them in a hearty and vociferous manner, and without too pedantic a respect for the rules of evidence. That merit has nothing to do, at bottom, with his rightness or wrongness; it lies in his mere sincerity. Dr. Abbott is obviously full of sincerity; no fair reader can doubt it for an instant. But he has something more: he has under him a respectable body of facts, sound ones as well as shaky ones. The deductions he draws from them are often extravagant, and now and then he mingles them with assumptions that seems to me to do violence to the most elemental common sense. Nevertheless, his basic facts remain, and if I were an Anglo-Saxon as he is I suspect that they would fever me as they fever him.

What he complains of, in a few words, is the assault that has been made of late upon the old American tradition and the fundamental canons of American idealism, *i.e.*, upon the body of ideas that Americans cherish as peculiarly their own, and believe in with a romantic devotion. What he complains of, especially, is that this assault has been made, in the main, by men who are not "Anglo-Saxons" (the professor himself quotes the term: a touching concession to ethnological exactness)—that it has been largely led by men whose very Americanism, when they claim to be Americans at all, is open to question. When I say open to question, I mean, of course, by "Anglo-Saxon" Americans. Dr. Abbott seems to be firmly convinced that these are the only ones entitled to the name. They are the pure stock; their ancestors conquered the continent unaided. They alone partake of the true national spirit, and may be trusted to guard the national hearth. All other Americans are in the position of visitors, interlopers, relatives-in-law. They may become in time, if they are good, creditable assistant Americans, but they can no more enter into the full national heritage, as free equals, than they can lift themselves by their boot-straps. The American tradition, it appears, must forever remain a bit strange to them; they are the children, not of heroes, but of serfs. Thus it is no wonder that their political notions, when they make bold to state them, are exotic and subversive. They can imagine government only as a power above and beyond the citizen. If they are not in favor of kaiserism, then they are in favor of communism, which is simply kaiserism imposed from below. Their politics is essentially a slave politics. They stand opposed eternally to that self-reliant and somewhat pugnacious individualism which is the mark of the true "Anglo-Saxon." If they ever come into power the Constitution will be destroyed and freedom will perish.

Dr. Abbott's book, as I have said, is somewhat difficult; perhaps I misrepresent him in a few details. But in the main, I believe, I gather his doctrine correctly; it is, indeed, a doctrine that has grown very familiar. The Klu Klux has carried it into every hamlet in the land, and bolstered it with the authority of Holy Writ. I could, if I would, amuse myself by exhibiting the holes in it. Is it a fact, then, that the "Anglo-Saxons" conquered the continent unaided? What of the Spaniards and French? What of the Dutch and Germans? What of the Scotch-Irish? Is it a fact that they invented the American scheme of government? What of Rousseau? Is it a fact all assaults upon that scheme have been made by assistant Americans? What of Jefferson, Jackson, Robert E. Lee, Jeff Davis, Bryan? Is it a fact that all the enemies of the Constitution came from below the salt? What of the Eighteenth Amendment: does it damage the Bill of Rights more or less than the late Dr. La Follette's vaporous schemes? Such questions suggest themselves in great variety. I could roll them off until you stood agape. But I have no desire to press a professor of history unduly; his authority, in the last analysis, cannot be upset by facts. And in the present case, whatever his errors in detail, it seems to me to be quite clear that the fundamental facts are on his side. There *is* unquestionably a difference between the "Anglo-Saxon" American and the non-"Anglo-Saxon"—a difference in their primary instincts, in their reactions to common stimuli, in their ways of looking at the world. And that difference, of late years, *has* come to the estate of a conflict, with the "Anglo-Saxon" striving to keep what he has—his point of view, his cultural leadership, his political hegemony—and the non-"Anglo-Saxon" trying to take it away from him. To deny that conflict is to fall into an absurdity far worse than any Dr. Abbott is guilty of. To admit it is to admit his clear right, nay, his bounden duty, to do battle for his side, passionately, desperately, and with any weapon at hand.

This he does in his book, and up to the limit of his forensic skill, which, I regret to have to add, is not noticeably great. If, at times, he grows a bit muddled, and even maudlin, then let us not hold the fact against him, for a man performing a *pas seul* upon a red-hot stove cannot be expected to achieve an impeccable step. It seems to me that this red-hot stove, at the moment, is under every conscious "Anglo-Saxon" in our great Republic—that he must be an insensate clod, indeed, if he does not feel the heat. The cultural leadership of the country is passing out of his hands, and he is beginning to lose even his political hegemony. I sat in the Democratic National Convention in 1924 as the Hon. Al Smith rolled up his votes, and watched the Ku Kluxers on the floor. They were transfixed with horror: if it was a comedy, then pulling tonsils is also a comedy. Dr. Abbott mentions Dreiser. The influence of Dreiser upon the literature of to-morrow in this land—upon all the youngsters who are now coming to maturity in the universities, and turning away from their ordained professors—will be a hundred times as potent as that of any New Englander now alive. Who is Dreiser? When the grandfathers of the Republic were hanging witches at Salem his forbears were raising grapes on the Rhine. Dr. Abbott professes history at Harvard. During the past ten years but one professor at that great university has materially colored the stream of ideas in America. He has since escaped abroad—and is a Spaniard. Every day a new Catholic church goes up; every day another Methodist or Presbyterian church is turned into a garage. But there is no need to labor the point. The fact is too obvious that the old easy dominance of the "Anglo-Saxon" is passing, that he must be up and doing if he would fasten his notions upon the generations to come. And the fact is equally obvious that his success in that emprise, so far, has been extremely indifferent—that, despite the great advantages that he enjoys, of position, of authority, of ancient right, he is making very heavy weather of it, and not even holding his own. I am frankly against him, and believe, as I have often made known, that he is doomed—that his opponents will turn out, in the long run, to be better men than he is. But I confess that I'd enjoy the combat more if he showed less indignation and more skill.

Dr. Abbott himself reveals many characteristic "Anglo-Saxon" weaknesses. His incoherence I have mentioned. There is also a downright inconsistency, often glaring. On one page he denounces all non-"Anglo-Saxons" as opponents of democracy; on another (for example, page 242) he denounces the fundamental tenets of democracy himself. This inconsistency is visible in nine "Anglo-Saxon" gladiators out of ten. What ails them all is that they have to defend democracy, and yet do not believe in it. Has any good "Anglo-Saxon" ever believed in it? I sometimes doubt it. Did Washington? Did John Adams? Jefferson did, but wasn't there a Celtic strain in him—wasn't he, after all, somewhat dubious, a sort of assistant American? In any case, the surviving Fathers were all apparently against him. In our own time how many "Anglo-Saxons" of the educated class actually believe in democracy? I know of none, and have heard of none. The late war revealed their true faith very brilliantly and even humorously. It was a crusade for democracy, and yet one of the shining partners was the late Czar of Russia! The assault upon the Kaiser was led by Roosevelt! The chief official enemy of absolutism was Wilson! No wonder the whole thing collasped into absurdity. Dr. Abbott falls into a similar absurdity more than once. His book would be vastly more effective if he took all the idle prattle about democracy out of it, and grounded it upon the forthright doctrine that the "Anglo-Saxons," having got here first, own the country, and have a clear right to impose political disabilities upon later comers—in other words, if he advocated the setting up of an "Anglo-Saxon" aristocracy, with high privileges and prerogatives, eternally beyond the reach of the mongrel commonalty. This, in point of fact, is what he advocates, however much he may cloud his advocacy in democratic terms. I call upon him with all solemnity to throw off his false-face and come out with the bald, harsh doctrine. There is more logic in it than in his present nonsense; he could preach it more powerfully and beautifully. More, he would get help from unexpected quarters. I can speak, of course, only for one spear. I might quibble and protest, but I'd certainly be sorely tempted.

7
Yazoo's Favorite

AN OLD-FASHIONED SENATOR, by Harris Dickson. New York: *The Frederick A. Stokes Company*. [The Nation, October 14, 1925.]

Some time ago, essaying a literary survey of the Republic, I animadverted sadly upon the dreadful barrenness of the great State of Mississippi. Speaking as a magazine editor, I said that I had never heard of a printable manuscript coming out of it. Speaking as a frequenter of the Athenian grove, I said that I had never heard of it hatching an idea. Instantly there was an uproar from Iuka to Pascagoula. The vernacular press had at me with appalling yells; there were demands from the Ku Klux that I come down to Jackson and say it again; Kiwanis joined the Baptist Young People's Society in denouncing me as one debauched by Russian gold. Worse, the Mississippi intelligentsia also had at me. Emerging heroically from the crypts and spring-houses where they were fugitive from Rotary, they bawled me out as ignorant and infamous. Had I never heard, they demanded, of Harris Dickson, the Missisippi Balzac? Had I never heard of John Sharp Williams, the Mississippi Gladstone?

I had, but remained unmoved. I now continue unmoved after reading Balzac's tome on Gladstone. It is, in its small way, a tragic book. Here, obviously, is the best that Mississippi can do, in theme and treatment—and it is such puerile, blowsy stuff that reviewing it realistically would be too cruel. Here the premier literary artist of Mississippi devotes himself *con amore* to the life and times of the premier Mississippi statesman—and the result is a volume so maudlin and nonsensical that it would disgrace a schoolboy. The book is simply mush—and out of the mush there emerges only a third-rate politician, professionally bucolic and as hollow as a jug.

Yet this Williams, during his long years in Congress, passed in Washington as an intellectual. Cloak-room and barroom gossip credited him with a profound education and very subtle parts. Such ideas, when they prevail in Washington, perhaps need and deserve no investigation; the same astute correspondents who propagated this one later coupled the preposterous Coolidge with Pericles. But maybe there was some logic in it, after all; Williams, at some time in the past, had been to Heidelberg and knew more or less German and French. That accomplishment, in a Southern politician, was sufficient to set the capital by the ears. So the Williams legend grew, and toward the end it rose to the dignity of a myth, like that of Dr. Taft's eminence as a constitutional lawyer. Even the learned hero's daily speeches on Teutonic mythology during the war did not drag him out of Valhalla himself. The press-gallery gaped and huzzahed.

But the Heidelberg chapter in Mr. Dickson's book leaves the myth rather sick. It starts off, indeed, with a disconcerting couplet:

In Germany 'twas very clear
He'd leave the rapiers for beer.

And what follows is distressingly silent about cultural accretions. Young Williams' main business at Heidelberg, it appears, was putting the abominable Prussian *Junker* in their place. They naturally assumed that their American fellow-student could be thrown about with impunity. Encountering him on the sidewalk, they tried, in the manner made historic by the Creel Press Bureau, to shove him off. Presently one of these fiends in human form came melodramatically to grief. Williams challenged him, and "according to Prussian ethics," named the weapons—pistols. A shock, indeed! The monster expected sabers, at which he was diabolically expert, but Williams didn't intend "to go home with his face all slashed, and have folks jeer at him for getting his jaw cut on a beer glass." Facing cold lead, the Prussian was so scared that he fired prematurely. Worse, he so lost his wits that he addressed his antagonist as Freiherr Williams. That antagonist fired into a snowbank. Some time later, having thus got all that was of worth out of Heidelberg, he came sailing home, "full even then of his ultimate intention: he'd go in for politics, he'd become a professional politican."

A professional politician he remained for thirty years, always in office, first in the House and then in the Senate. His start was slow—he practiced law for a time—, but once he was on the payroll he stayed there until old age was upon him. For a number of years he was Democratic leader in the House; twice he got the party vote for the Speakership. In the Senate he was technically in the ranks, but on great occasions he stepped forward. His specialties, toward the end, were the divine inspiration of Woodrow Wilson, the incomparable valor of the American soldier, the crimes of the Kaiser, the superiority of the "Anglo-Saxon," the godlike bellicosity of the Confederate gentry, and the nature and functions of a gentleman. On these themes he discoursed almost every afternoon. The boys in the press-gallery liked him, and he got plenty of space. Always his rodomontades brought forth dark hints about his esoteric learning, and the news that, next after Henry Cabot Lodge, he was the most cultivated man in the Senate.

Mr. Dickson prints extracts from some of his speeches. Criticism, obviously, is an art not yet in practice in Mississippi, even among the literati. I used to read him in the *Congressional Record*; he was really not so bad as Dickson makes him out. His career, seen in retrospect, seems to have been mainly a vacuum. Once or twice he showed a certain fine dignity, strange in a Southern politician. He opposed the Prohibition frenzy. He voted against the bonus. But usually, despite his constant talk of independence, he ran with the party pack. For years a professional Jeffersonian, he brought his career to a climax by giving lyrical support to the Emperor Woodrow, who heaved the Jeffersonian heritage into the ash-can. During the La Follette uproar he was one of the most vociferous of the witch-burners. He passed out in silence, regretted for his rustic charm, but not much missed.

I commend "An Old-Fashioned Senator" to all persons who are interested in the struggle of the South to throw off its cobwebs. Both as document and as work of art the book makes it very plain why Mississippi's place in that struggle is in the last rank.

8
The Father of Service

THE LIFE STORY OF ORISON SWETT MARDEN, by Margaret Connolly. New York: *The Thomas Y. Crowell Company.* [The American Mercury, February, 1926.]

If Dr. Marden had not written his first book, said Frank A. Munsey one day, he would have been a millionaire. By Munseyan standards, praise could go no higher—and Munsey knew his man, for they were fellow-waiters in a Summer hotel back in the '70's and kept up friendly exchange until Marden's death in 1924. Both sprang from the hard, inhospitable soil of Northern New England, both knew dire poverty in youth, both got somewhere a yearning for literary exercises, and both cherished an immense respect for the dollar. But though fate brought them together when they were young, they chose different paths later on. Munsey, with "Afloat in a Great City," "The Boy Broker," and other inspirational masterworks behind him, abandoned beautiful letters for the stock market, and eventually gathered in so much money that he could afford to butcher great newspapers in sheer excess of animal spirits, as lesser men butcher clay pigeons. Marden, going the other way, abandoned the hotel business, for which he seemed to have had genius, for the pen, and devoted the last thirty years of his life to composition.

His bibliography runs to a hundred or more volumes—a colossal, relentless, overwhelming deluge of bilge. All his books have the same subject: getting on in the world. That was, to him, the only conceivable goal of human aspiration. Day in and day out, for three decades, he preached his simple gospel to all mankind, not only in his books, but also in countless pamphlets, in lectures, and in the pages of his magazine, *Success.* Its success was instantaneous and durable. His first book, "Pushing to the Front," rapidly went through a dozen editions, and was presently translated into a dozen foreign languages. It remained, to the end, his best-seller, but it had many formidable rivals. Altogether, his writings in book-form must have reached a total of 20,000,000 copies, including 3,000,000 in twenty-five tongues other than English. In Germany alone he sold more than 500,000 copies of thirty volumes. He remains to-day the most popular of American authors in Europe, and by immense odds. I have encountered translations of his books on the news-stands of remote towns in Spain, Poland and Czecho-Slovakia. In places where even Mark Twain is unknown—nay, even Jack London, Upton Sinclair and James Oliver Curwood—he holds aloft the banner of American literature.

I lack the stomach for the job myself, but I think a lot could be learned about the psychology of *Homo boobiens* through an intensive study of Marden's vast shelf of books. The few I have read seem to be exactly alike; no doubt all the rest resemble them very closely. What they preach, in brief, is the high value of hopefulness, hard work, high purpose and unflagging resolution. The appeal is to the natural discontent and vague aspiration of the common man. The remedy offered is partly practical and partly mystical—practical in its insistence upon the sound utility of the lowly virtues, mystical in its constant implication that matter will always yield to mind, that high thinking has a cash value. An evil philosophy? Surely not. A valid one? There it is not so easy to answer. Marden is full of proofs that what he preaches works—but only too often those proofs show the incredible appositeness and impeccability of patent-medicine testimonials. How many false hopes he must have raised in his day! One imagines humble hearts leaping to the gaudy tales of Judge Elbert Gary, Beethoven and Edison in the darkest reaches of Montenegro, Norway and Tennessee. Down went the dose, but was the patient actually cured? Well, perhaps, he at least *felt* better—and that was something. Marden was not to be pinned down to clinical records; he was, in his way, a poet, and even more a prophet. A religious exaltation was in him; he knew how to roll his eyes. The first article of his creed was that it was a sin to despair—that realism was a black crime against the Holy Ghost. He reduced the Beatitudes to one: Blessed are they that believe in their stars, and are up and doing.

His infuence was immense, and perhaps mainly for the good. He soothed his customers with his optimistic taffy, and made them happier. It is, indeed, small wonder that eminent figures in finance and industry admired him greatly, and gave his books to their slaves. He turned the discontents of those slaves inward; instead of going on strike and breaking windows they sat up nights trying to generate inspiration and practicing hope and patience. He was thus a useful citizen in a democratic state, and comparable to the Rev. Dr. Billy Sunday. He preached a Direct Action of a benign and laudable sort, with Service running through it. His mark shines brilliantly from the forehead of every Y.M.C.A. secretary in the land, and from the foreheads, too, of most of the editorial writers. Many lesser platitudinarians followed him—for example, Dr. Frank Crane and the Rev. Dr. Henry van Dyke—, but he kept ahead of all of them. None other could put the obvious into such mellow and caressing terms. None other could so completely cast off all doubts and misgivings. When he spit on his hands and let himself out, the whole world began to sparkle like a Christmas tree. He was Kiwanis incarnate, with whispers of the Salvation Army.

In early manhood he had cast off the demoniacal theology of his native hills, but one treasure of his Puritan heritage he retained to the end: he knew precisely and certainly what God wanted His children to be and do. God wanted them to be happy, and He wanted them to attain to happiness by working hard, saving money, obeying the boss, and keeping on the lookout for better jobs. Thus, after a hiatus of 137 years, Marden took up the torch of Poor Richard. He was, in his way, the American St. Paul. He was the pa of Kiwanis. He carried the gospel of American optimism to all the four quarters of the world.

9
A Modern Masterpiece

THE POET ASSASSINATED, by Guillaume Apollinaire, translated from the French by Matthew Josephson. New York: *The Broom Publishing Company*. [The American Mercury, March, 1924.]

Whatever may be said against the young literary lions of the Foetal School, whether by such hoary iconoclasts as Ernest Boyd or by such virginal presbyters as John S. Sumner, the saving fact remains that the boys and girls have, beneath their false faces, a sense of humor, and are not shy about playing it upon one another. Such passionate pioneers of the movement as *Broom* and the *Little Review* printed, in their day, capital parodies in every issue, many of them, I believe, deliberate and malicious—parodies of Ezra Pound by the Baroness Elsa von Freytag-Loringhoven, and of the Baroness Elsa Freytag-Loringhoven by E. E. Cummings, and of E. E. Cummings by young Roosevelt J. Yahwitz, Harvard '27. And the thing goes on to this day. Ah, that the rev. seniors of the Hypoendocrinal School were as gay and goatish! Ah, specifically, that Dr. Paul Elmer More would occasionally do a salacious burlesque of Dr. Brander Matthews, and that Dr. Matthews would exercise his forecastle wit upon the Pennsylvania Silurian, Prof. Fred Lewis Pattee!

In the present work, beautifully printed by the *Broom* Press, there is jocosity in the grand manner. For a long while past, as time goes among such neologomaniacs, the youths of the movement have been whooping up one Guillaume Apollinaire. When this Apollinaire died in 1918, so they lamented, there passed out the greatest creative mind that France had seen since the Middle Ages. He was to Jean Cocteau, even, as Cocteau was to Eugène Sue. His books were uncompromising and revolutionary; had he lived he would have done to the banal prose of the Babbitts of letters what Eric Satie has done to the art of the fugue. Such news was not only printed in the *Tendenz* magazines that come and go; it was transmitted by word of mouth from end to end of Greenwich Village. More, it percolated to graver quarters. The estimable *Dial* let it be known that Apollinaire was a profound influence on the literature and perhaps still more on the art and spirit of this modern period. Once, when Dr. Canby was off lecturing in Lancaster, Pa., his name even got into the *Literary Review*.

This electric rumor of him was helped to prosperity by the fact that specific data about him were extremely hard to come by. His books seemed to be rare—some of them, indeed, unprocurable—, and even when one of them was obtained and examined it turned out to be largely unintelligible. He wrote, it appeared, in an occult dialect, partly made up of fantastic slang from the French army. He gave to old words new and mysterious meanings. He kept wholly outside the vocabulary at the back of "College French." Even returning exiles from La Rotonde were baffled by some of his phrases; all that they could venture was that they were unprecedented and probably obscene. But the Village, as everyone knows, does not spurn the cabalistic; on the contrary, it embraces and venerates the cabalistic. Apollinaire grew in fame as he became unscrutable. Displacing Cocteau, Paul Morand, Harry Kemp, T. S. Eliot, André Salmon, Paul Valéry, Maxwell Bodenheim, Jean Giraudoux and all the other gods of that checkered dynasty, he was lifted to the first place in the Valhalla of the Advanced Thinkers. It was Apollinaire's year. . . .

The work before us is the pricking of the bladder—a jest highly effective, but somewhat barbarous. M. Josephson simply translates Apollinaire's masterpiece, adds an *apparatus criticus* in the manner of T. S. Eliot, and then retires discreetly to wait for the yells. They will make a dreadful din, or I am no literary pathologist! For what does "The Poet Assassinated" turn out to be? It turns out to be a dull pasquinade in the manner of a rather atheistic sophomore, with a few dirty words thrown in to shock the *booboisie.* From end to end there is not as much wit in it as you will hear in a genealogical exchange between two taxicab drivers. It is flat, flabby and idiotic. It is as profound as an editorial in the Washington *Star* and as revolutionary as Ayer's Almanac. It is the best joke pulled off on the Young Forward-Lookers since Eliot floored them with the notes to "The Waste Land."

M. Josephson rather spoils its effect, I believe, by rubbing it in—that is, by hinting that Apollinaire was of romantic and mysterious origin—that his mother was a Polish lady of noble name and his father a high prelate of the Catholic Church—that he himself was born at Monte Carlo and baptized in Santa Maria Maggiore at Rome. This is too much. Apollinaire was, like all Frenchmen of humor, a German Jew. His father was a respectable waiter at Appenrodt's, by name Max Spritzwasser: hence the *nom de plume.* His mother was a Mlle. Kunigunda Luise Schmidt, of Holzkirchen, Oberbayern.

10
Sweet Stuff

SIX DAYS OF THE WEEK: A BOOK OF THOUGHTS ABOUT LIFE AND RELIGION, by Henry van Dyke. New York: *Charles Scribner's Sons.* [The American Mercury, March, 1925.]

I offer a specimen:

> As living beings we are part of a universe of life.

A second:

> Unless we men resolve to be good, the world will never be better.

A third:

> Behind Christianity there is Christ.

A fourth:

> If Washington had not liberated the American Republic, Lincoln would have had no Union to save.

A fifth:

Some people say that a revolution is coming on in our own age and country. It is possible.

A sixth:

God made us all.

A seventh:

It is a well-known fact that men can lie, and that very frequently they do.

An eighth:

To be foolish is an infirmity. To fool others is a trick.

A ninth:

The Bible was not given to teach science, but religion.

A tenth:

A whole life spent with God is better than half a life.

An eleventh:

Drunkenness ruins more homes and wrecks more lives than war.

A twelfth:

Anything out of the ordinary line will attract notice.

Tupper *est mort*! *Hoch* Tupper! *Hoch, hoch! Dreimal hoch!*

IX.
The Fringes of Lovely Letters

I
Authorship as a Trade

It is my observation as an editor that most beginning authors are attracted to the trade of letters, not because they have anything apposite and exigent to say, but simply because it seems easy. Let us imagine an ambitious and somewhat gassy young gal, turned out of the public high-school down the street with good marks in English—that is, in the sort of literary composition practiced by schoolma'ms. Having read "Ulysses," "Jurgen" and "Babbitt," she is disinclined to follow her mother too precipitately into the jaws of holy monogamy—or, at all events, she shrinks from marrying such a clod as her father is, and as her brothers and male classmates will be tomorrow. What to do? The professions demand technical equipment. Commerce is sordid. The secretary, even of a rich and handsome man, get up at 7:30 A.M. Most of the fine arts are regarded, by her family, as immoral. So she pays $3 down on a second-hand typewriter, lays in a stock of copy paper, and proceeds to enrich the national literature.

It is such aspirants, I suppose, who keep the pot boiling for the schools of short-story writing and scenario writing that now swarm in the land. Certainly these schools, in so far as I have any acquaintance with them, offer nothing of value to the beginner of genuine talent. They seem to be run, in the main, by persons as completely devoid of critical sense as so many Congressmen, street railway curve-greasers or Methodist revivalists. Their text-books are masses of unmitigated rubbish. But no doubt that rubbish seems impressive enough to the customers I have mentioned, for it is both very vague and very cocksure—an almost irresistible combination. So a hundred thousand second-hand Coronas rattle and jingle in ten thousand remote and lonely towns, and the mail of every magazine editor in America is as heavy as the mail of a get-rich-quick stock-broker.

Unluckily, there is seldom anything in this mail to bulge his eyes and make his heart go pitter-pat. What he finds in it, day in and day out, is simply the same dull, obvious, shoddy stuff —the same banal and threadbare ideas set forth in the same flabby and unbeautiful words. They all seem to write alike, as, indeed, they all seem to think alike. They react to stimuli with the machine-like uniformity and precision of soldiers in a file. The spectacle of life is to all of them exactly the same spectacle. They bring no more to it, of private, singular vision, than so many photographic lenses. In brief, they are unanimously commonplace, unanimously stupid. Free education has cursed them with aspirations beyond their congenital capacities, and they offer the art of letters only the gifts suitable to the lowly crafts of the jazz-baby and the schoolma'm. They come from an intellectual level where conformity seems the highest of goods, and so they lack the primary requisite of the imaginative author: the capacity to see the human comedy afresh, to discover new relations between things, to discover new significances in man's eternal struggle with his fate. What they have to say is simply what any moderately intelligent suburban pastor or country editor would have to say, and so it is not worth hearing.

This disparity between aspiration and equipment runs through the whole of American life; material prosperity and popular education have made it a sort of national disease. Two-thirds of the professors in our colleges are simply cans full of undigested knowledge, mechanically acquired; they cannot utilize it; they cannot think. We are cursed likewise with hordes of lawyers who would be happier and more useful driving trucks, and hordes of doctors who would be strained even as druggists. So in the realm of beautiful letters. Poetry has become a recreation among us for the intellectually unemployed and unemployable: persons who, a few generations ago, would have taken it out on china-painting. The writing of novels is undertaken by thousands who lack the skill to describe a dog-fight. The result is a colossal waste of paper, ink and postage—worse, of binding cloth and gold foil. For a great deal of this drivel, by one dodge or another, gets into print. Many of the correspondence-school students, after hard diligence, learn how to write for the cheap magazines; not a few of them eventually appear between covers, and are solemnly reviewed.

Does such stuff sell? Apparently it does, else the publishers would not print so much of it. Its effect upon those who read it must be even worse than that of the newspapers and popular magazines. They come to it with confident expectations. It is pretentiously bound; *ergo*, there must be something in it. That something is simply platitude. What has been said a thousand times is said all over again. This time it must be true! Thus the standardization of the American mind goes on, and against ideas that are genuinely novel there are higher and higher battlements erected. Meanwhile, on the lower levels, where the latest recruits to letters sweat and hope, this rubbish is laboriously imitated. Turn to any of the cheap fiction magazines, and you will find out how bad it can be at its worst. No, not quite at its worst, for the contributors to the cheap fiction magazines have at least broken into print—they have as they say, made the grade. Below them are thousands of aspirants of even slenderer talents—customers of the correspondence schools, patrons of lectures by itinerant literary pedagogues, patient manufacturers of the dreadful stuff that clogs every magazine editor's mail. Here is the ultimate reservoir of the national literature—and here, unless I err, is only bilge.

The remedy? I know of none. Moreover, I do not believe in remedies. So long as the prevailing pedagogues are not found out, and the absurd effort to cram every moron with book-learning goes on in the Republic, that long there will be too much reading, and too much writing. But let us get out of the fact whatever consolation is in it: too much writing, at worst, is at least a bearable evil. Certainly it is vastly less dangerous than too much religion, and less a nuisance than too much politics. The floggers of Coronas, if they were halted by law, might take to the uplift—as, indeed, many corn-fed pedagogues are already doing, driven out of their jobs by the murrain of Fundamentalism. If I yell against them it is because, on days when the rain keeps me indoors, I am a critic. Perhaps other folks suffer less. Nevertheless, I often wonder what the genuinely competent novelists of the nation think of it—how the invasion of their craft by so many bunglers and numskulls appears to them, and affects them. Surely it must tend to narrow the audience they appeal to, and so do them damage. Who was it who said that, in order that there may be great poets, there must be great audiences too? I believe it was old Walt. He knew. Facing an audience deluged with molasses by Whittier, Felicia Hemans and Fanny Fern, he found the assumptions all against him. He was different, and hence suspicious: it took him two generations to make his way. The competent novelist, setting up shop in America to-day, is confronted by the same flood. If he is pertinacious, he may win in the end, but certainly it takes endurance. Hergesheimer, in his first book, unquestionably had something to say. Its point of view was new; there was a fine plausibility in it; it was worth attending to. But Hergesheimer drove along for eight or ten years, almost in a vacuum. I could add others: Anderson, Cabell, even Dreiser. Cabell became known to the women's clubs with his twelfth book. Meanwhile, a dozen cheesemongers had been adored, and a thousand had made good livings with their sets of rubber-stamps.

2
Authors as Persons

My trade forces me into constant association with persons of literary skill and aspiration, good and bad, male and female, foreign and domestic. I can only report, after a quarter of a century of commerce with them, that I find them, with a few brilliant exceptions, very dull, and that I greatly prefer the society of Babbitts. Is this heresy? If so, I can only offer my sincere regrets. The words are wrung from me, not by any desire to be unpleasant, but simply by a lifelong and incurable affection for what, for want of a better name, is called the truth. Nine-tenths of the literary gents that I know, indeed, are hotter for the dollar than any Babbitt ever heard of. Their talk is not about what they write, but about what they get for it. Not infrequently they get a great deal. I know a number who make more annually than honest bank presidents, even than Christian bank presidents. A few probably top the incomes of railroad purchasing-agents and nose-and-throat specialists, and come close to the incomes of realtors, lawyers and bootleggers. They practice a very profitable trade.

And no wonder, for they pursue it in the most assiduously literate country in Christendom. Our people, perhaps, seldom read anything that is good, but they at least read—day and night, weekdays and Sundays. We have so many magazines of more than 500,000 circulation that a list of them would fill this page. We have at least a dozen above 1,000,000. These magazines have immense advertising revenues, and are thus very prosperous. They can therefore pay high prices for manuscripts. The business of supplying such manuscripts has made a whole herd of authors rich. I do not object to their wealth; I simply report its lamentable effects upon them, and upon the aspirants who strive to imitate them. For those effects go down to the lowest levels. The neophyte, as I have said, seldom shows any yearning to discharge ideas, to express himself, to tackle and master a difficult enterprise; he shows only a desire to get money in what seems to him to be an easy way. Short cuts, quick sales, easy profits—it is all very American. Do we gabble about efficiency? Then the explanation is to be sought in the backwashes of Freudism. Nowhere else on earth is genuine competence so rare. The average American plumber cannot plumb; the average American cook cannot cook; the average American literary gent has nothing to say, and says it with rubber-stamps.

But I was speaking of the literati as persons. They suffer, I believe from two things. The first is what I have just described: their general fraudulence. The second springs out of the fact that their position, in the Republic, is very insecure—that they have no public dignity. It is no longer honorable *per se* to be engaged in travails of the spirit, as it used to be in the New England of the *Aufklärung*; it is honorable only if it pays. I believe that the fact discourages many aspirants who, if they went on, might come to something. They are blasted in their tender years, and so literature loses them. Too sensitive to sit below the salt, they join the hearty, red-blooded men who feast above it, admired by the national gallery. It is, indeed, not surprising that the majority of college graduates, once headed as a matter of course for the grove of Athene, now go into business—that Harvard now turns out ten times as many bond salesmen every year as metaphysicians and martyrs. Business, in America, offers higher rewards than any other human enterprise, not only in money but also in dignity. Thus it tends to attract the best brains of the country. Is Kiwanis idiotic? The answer is that Kiwanis no more represents business than Greenwich Village represents literature. On the higher levels its bilge does not flow—and on those higher levels, as I have hinted, there are shrewder fellows, and more amusing, than ever you will find in the Authors' Club. These fellows, by the strict canons of ethnology, are Babbitts, but it seems to me that they are responsible nevertheless for everything that makes life in the United States tolerable. One finds, in their company, excellent wines and liquors, and one seldom hears any cant.

I don't believe that this is a healthy state of affairs. I believe that business should be left to commonplace and insensitive minds, and that men of originality, and hence of genuine charm, should be sucked automatically into enterprises of a greater complexity and subtlety. It is done in more ancient countries; it has been done from remote antiquity under civilizations that have aged in the wood, and are free from fusel oil. But it is not yet done in These States. Only an overwhelming natural impulse—perhaps complicated by insanity—can urge an American into the writing of fugues or epics. The pull is toward the investment securities business. That pull, yielded to, leads to high rewards. The successful business man among us—and only the sheer imbecile, in such gaudy times as these, is not successful—enjoys the public respect and adulation that elsewhere bathe only bishops and generals of artillery. He is treated with dignity in the newspapers, even when he appears in combat with his wife's lover. His opinion is sought upon all public questions, including the æsthetic. In the stews and wine-shops he receives the attention that, in old Vienna, used to be given to Beethoven. He enjoys an aristocratic immunity to most forms of judicial process. He wears the *légion d'honneur*, is an LL.D. of Yale, and is received cordially at the White House.

The literary gent, however worthy, scales no such heights under our *Kultur*. Only one President since the birth of the Republic has ever welcomed men of letters at the White House, and that one, the sainted Roosevelt, judged them by their theological orthodoxy and the hair upon their chests. A few colored poets were added to make the first pages; that was all. The literati thus wander about somewhat disconsolately among us, and tend to become morose and dull. If they enjoy the princely fees of the train-boy magazines, they are simply third-rate business men—successful, perhaps, but without the Larger Vision. If they happen to be genuine artists—and now and then it *does* happen—they are as lonely as life insurance solicitors at a convention of Seventh Day Adventists. Such sorrows do not make for *Gemütlichkeit.* There is much more of it in the pants business.

3
Birth Pangs

I have just said that the typical American author, when he talks intelligibly at all, talks of money. I have said also that his aim in writing is not to rid himself of ideas that bulge and fever his skull, but to get that money in an easy way. Both statements, though true, need a certain qualification. Writing looks easier to the neophyte than any other job open to him, but once he settles down to its practice he finds that it is full of unanticipated pains. So he tends, as he grows older, to talk of those pains almost as much as he talks of their rewards in cash. Here, indeed, all the authors that I know agree, if they agree on nothing else, and in their agreement they show the greatest heat and eloquence. And the beautiful ladies of the trade reënforce and ratify the plaint of the bucks. Writing, they all say, is the most dreadful chore ever inflicted upon human beings. It is not only exhausting mentally; it is also extremely fatiguing physically. The writer leaves his desk, his day's work done, with his mind empty and the muscles of his back and neck full of a crippling stiffness. He has suffered horribly that the babies may be fed and beauty may not die.

The worst of it is that he must always suffer alone. If authors could work in large, well-ventilated factories, like cigarmakers or garment-workers, with plenty of their mates about and a flow of lively professional gossip to entertain them, their labor would be immensely lighter. But it is essential to their craft that they perform its tedious and vexatious operations *a cappella*, and so the horrors of loneliness are added to its other unpleasantnesses. An author at work is continuously and inescapably in the presence of himself. There is nothing to divert and soothe him. So every time a vagrant regret or sorrow assails him, it has him instantly by the ear, and every time a wandering ache runs down his leg it shakes him like the bite of a tiger. I have yet meet an author who was not a hypochondriac. Saving only physicians, who are always ill and in fear of death, the literati are perhaps the most lavish consumers of pills and philtres in this world, and the most willing customers of surgeons. I can scarcely think of one, known to me personally, who is not constantly dosing himself with medicines, or regularly resorting to the knife. At the head of the craft stand men who are even more celebrated as invalids than they are as authors. I know of one who——

But perhaps I had better avoid invading what, after all, may be private confidences, though they are certainly not imparted in confidential tones. The point is that an author, penned in a room during all his working hours with no company save his own, is bound to be more conscious than other men of the petty malaises that assail all of us. They tackle him, so to speak, in a vacuum; he can't seek diversion from them without at the same time suffering diversion from his work. And what they leave of him is tortured and demoralized by wayward and uncomfortable thoughts. It must be obvious that other men, even among the intelligentsia, are not beset so cruelly. A judge on the bench, entertaining a ringing in the ears, can do his work almost as well as if he heard only the voluptuous rhetoric of the lawyers. A clergyman, carrying on his degraded mummery, is not appreciably crippled by a sour stomach: what he says has been said before, and only scoundrels question it. And a surgeon, plying his exhilarating art and mystery, suffers no professional damage from the wild thought that the attending nurse is more sightly than his wife. But I defy anyone to write a competent sonnet with a ringing in his ears, or to compose sound criticism with a sour stomach, or to do a plausible love scene with a head free of private amorous fancies. These things are sheer impossibilities. The poor literatus encounters them and their like every time he enters his work-room and spits on his hands. The moment the door bangs he begins a depressing, losing struggle with his body and his mind.

Why then, do rational men and women engage in so barbarous and exhausting a vocation—for there are relatively intelligent and enlightened authors, remember, just as there are relatively honest politicians, and even bishops. What keeps them from deserting it for trades that are less onerous, and, in the eyes of their fellow creatures, more respectable? The first, and perhaps the foremost reason I have already exposed at length: the thing pays. But there is another, and it ought to be heard too. It lies, I believe, in the fact that an author, like any other so-called artist, is a man in whom the normal vanity of all men is so vastly exaggerated that he finds it a sheer impossibility to hold it in. His overpowering impulse is to gyrate before his fellow men, flapping his wings and emitting defiant yells. This being forbidden by the *Polizei* of all civilized countries, he takes it out by putting his yells on paper. Such is the thing called self-expression.

In the confidences of the literati, of course, it is always depicted as something much more mellow and virtuous. Either they argue that they are moved by a yearning to spread the enlightenment and save the world, or they allege that what steams them and makes them leap is a passion for beauty. Both theories are quickly disposed of by an appeal to the facts. The stuff written by nine authors out of ten, it must be plain at a glance, has as little to do with spreading the enlightenment as the state papers of the late Dr. Warren Gamaliel Harding. And there is no more beauty in it, and no more sign of a feeling of beauty, than you will find in a hotel dining-room or a college yell. The impulse to create beauty, indeed, is rather rare in literary men, and almost completely absent from the younger ones. If it shows itself at all, it comes as a sort of afterthought. Far ahead of it comes the yearning to make money. And after the yearning to make money comes the yearning to make a noise. The impulse to create beauty lingers far behind; not infrequently there is a void where it ought to be. Authors, as a class, are extraordinarily insensitive to beauty, and the fact reveals itself in their customary (and often incredibly extensive) ignorance of the other arts. I'd have a hard job naming six American novelists who could be depended upon to recognize a fugue without prompting, or six poets who could give a rational account of the difference between a Gothic cathedral and a Standard Oil filling-station. The thing goes even further. Most novelists, in my experience, know nothing of poetry, and very few poets have any feeling for the beauties of prose. As for the dramatists, three-fourths of them are unaware that such things as prose and poetry exist at all. It pains me to set down such inconvenient and blushful facts. They will be seized upon, I daresay, by the evangelists of Kiwanis, and employed to support the doctrine that authors are public enemies, and ought to be deported to Russia. I do not go so far. I simply say that many who pursue the literary life are less romantic and high-toned than they might be—that communion with them is anything but the thrilling thing that provincial club ladies fancy. If the fact ought to be concealed, then blame my babbling upon scientific passion. That passion, to-day, has me by the ear.

4
Want Ad

The death of William Dean Howells in 1920 brought to an end a decorous and orderly era in American letters, and issued in a sort of anarchy. One may describe the change, perhaps, by throwing it into dramatic form. Suppose Joseph Conrad and Anatole France were still alive and on their way to the United States on a lecture tour, or to study Prohibition or sex hygiene, or to pay their respects to Henry Ford. Suppose they were to arrive in New York at 2 P.M. to-day. Who would go down the bay on a revenue-cutter to meet them—that is, who in addition to the newspaper reporters and baggage-searchers—who to represent American Literature? I can't think of a single fit candidate. So long as Howells kept to his legs he was chosen almost automatically for all such jobs, for he was the dean of the national letters, and acknowledged to be such by everyone. Moreover, he had experience at the work and a natural gift for it. He looked well in funeral garments. He had a noble and ancient head. He made a neat and caressing speech. He understood etiquette. And before he came to his growth, stretching back into the past, there was a long line precisely like him—Mark Twain, General Lew Wallace, James Russell Lowell, Edmund Clarence Stedman, Richard Watson Gilder, Bryant,

Emerson, Irving, Cooper, and so on back to the dark abysm of time.

Such men performed a useful and highly onerous function. They represented letters in all public and official ways. When there was a grand celebration at one of the older universities they were present in their robes, freely visible to the lowliest sophomore. When there was a great banquet, they sat between generals in the Army and members of the firm of J. P. Morgan & Company. When there was a solemn petition or protest to sign—against fiat money, the massacres in Armenia, municipal corruption, or the lack of international copyright—they signed in fine round hands, not for themselves alone, but for the whole fraternity of American literati. Most important of all, when a literary whale from foreign parts was sighted off Fire Island, they jumped into their frock coats, clapped on their plug-hats and made the damp, windy trip through the Narrows on the revenue-cutter, to give the visitor welcome in the name of the eminent living and the illustrious dead. It was by such men that Dickens was greeted, and Thackeray, and Herbert Spencer, and Max O'Rell, and Blasco Ibáñez, and Matthew Arnold, and James M. Barrie, and Kipling, and (until they found his bootleg wife under his bed) Maxim Gorky. I name names at random. No worthy visitor was overlooked. Always there was the stately committee on the revenue-cutter, always there was the series of polite speeches, and always there was the general feeling that the right thing had been done in the right way—that American literature had been represented in a tasteful and resounding manner.

Who is to represent it to-day? I search the country without finding a single suitable candidate, to say nothing of a whole posse. Turn, for example, to the mystic nobles of the American Academy of Arts and Letters. I pick out five at random: William C. Brownell, Augustus Thomas, Hamlin Garland, Owen Wister and Henry van Dyke. What is wrong with them? The plain but dreadful fact that no literary foreigner has even heard of them—that their appearance on the deck of his incoming barge would puzzle and alarm him, and probably cause him to call for the police. These men do not lack the homely virtues. They all spell correctly, write neatly, and print nothing that is not constructive. In the five of them there is not enough sin to raise a Congressman's temperature one-hundredth of a degree. But they are completely devoid of what is absolutely essential to the official life: they have, so to speak, no stage presence. There is nothing rotund and gaudy about them. No public and unanimous reverence bathes them. What they write or say never causes any talk. To be welcomed by them, jointly or severally, would appear to Thomas Hardy or Gabriel D'Annunzio as equal to being welcomed by representatives of the St. Joe, Mo., Rotary Club. Nor do I find any better stock among their heirs and apprentices in the National Institute. Put Henry Sydnor Harrison, say, against Howells: it is a wart succeeding Ossa. Match Clayton Hamilton with Edmund Clarence Stedman: Broadway against Wall Street. Shove Robert W. Chambers or Herman Hagedorn into the coat of Lowell: he would rattle in one of its pockets.

Worse, there are no better candidates outside the academic cloister. I daresay that most literate foreigners, asked to name the principal American novelist in practice to-day, would nominate Theodore Dreiser. He would get probably seventy-five per cent of the votes, with the rest scattered among Upton Sinclair, Sinclair Lewis, Cabell, Hergesheimer and Sherwood Anderson. But try to imagine any of these gentlemen togged out in a long-tailed coat, shivering on the deck of a revenue-cutter while Gerhart Hauptman got a grip on himself aboard the *Majestic*! Try to imagine Cabell presiding at a banquet to Knut Hamsun, with Dr. A. Lawrence Lowell to one side of him and Otto Kahn to the other! Try to picture Sinclair handing James Joyce a wreath to put upon the grave of James Whitcomb Riley! The vision, indeed, is more dismal than ludicrous. Howells, the last of his lordly line, is missed tremendously; there is something grievously lacking in the official hospitality of the country. The lack showed itself the instant he was called away. A few weeks later Columbia University gave a soirée in honor of the centenary of Lowell. The president of Columbia, Dr. Nicholas Murray Butler, is a realist. Moreover, he is a member of the American Academy himself, elected as a wet to succeed Edgar Allan Poe. He was thus privy to the deficiencies of his colleagues. To conceal the flabbiness of the evening he shoved them into back seats—and invited John D. Rockefeller, Jr., Tex Rickard, General Pershing and the board of governors of the New York Stock Exchange to the platform!

I believe that, of living masters of letters, H. G. Wells was the first to feel the new chill. When he last visited the Republic he was made welcome by a committee of ship-news reporters. It was as if one of the justices of the King's Bench, landing in America, had been received by a committee of police-court lawyers from Gary, Ind. Later on American literature bestirred itself and gave Wells a banquet in New York. I was present at this feast, and a singular one it was. Not a single author read in Iowa or taught at Harvard was present. The principal literatus at the board was the late Frank A. Munsey, author of "Derringforth" and "The Boy Broker," and the principal address was made by Max Eastman, formerly editor of the *Masses*! . . .

I come to a constructive suggestion. Let the literati of America meet in their respective places of social relaxation, each gang determining the credentials of its own members, and elect delegates to a national convention. Then let the national convention, by open ballot, choose ten spokesmen and ten alternates to represent the national letters on all formal occasions—not only when an eminent foreigner is to be made welcome, but also when Columbia University holds memorial services, when a President is inaugurated, when Harvard meets Yale, when monuments are unveiled—in brief at all times of solemn public ceremonial. Let these representatives practice deportment and elocution. Let them employ good tailors and trustworthy bootleggers. I have, alas, no candidates for the committee. As I have said, there is a dreadful dearth of them. Does Dr. Frank Crane wear whiskers? If so, I nominate him.

5
Literature and the Schoolma'm

With precious few exceptions, all the books on style in English are by writers quite unable to write. The subject, indeed, seems to exercise a special and dreadful fascination over schoolma'ms, bucolic college professors, and other such pseudoliterates. One never hears of treatises on it by George Moore or James Branch Cabell, but the pedagogues, male and female, are at it all the time. In a thousand texts they set forth their depressing ideas about it, and millions of suffering high-school pupils have to study what they say. Their central aim, of course, is to reduce the whole thing to a series of simple rules—the over-mastering passion of their melancholy order, at all times and everywhere. They aspire to teach it as bridge whist, the American Legion flag-drill and double-entry bookkeeping are taught. They fail as ignominiously as that Athenian of legend who essayed to train a regiment of grasshoppers in the goose-step.

For the essence of sound style is that it cannot be reduced to rules—that it is a living and breathing thing, with something of the devilish in it—that it fits its proprietor tightly and yet ever so loosely, as his skin fits him. It is, in fact, quite as securely an integral part of him as that skin is. It hardens as his arteries harden. It has *Katzenjammer* on the days succeeding his indiscretions. It is gaudy when he is young and gathers decorum when he grows old. On the day after he makes a mash on a new girl it glows and glitters. If he has fed well, it is mellow. If he has gastritis it is bitter. In brief, a style is always the outward and visible symbol of a man, and it cannot be anything else. To attempt to teach it is as silly as to set up courses in making love. The man who makes love out of a book is not making love at all; he is simply imitating someone else making love. God help him if, in love or literary composition, his preceptor be a pedagogue!

The schoolma'm theory that the writing of English may be taught is based upon a faulty inference from a sound observation. The sound observation is that the great majority of American high-school pupils, when they attempt to put their thoughts upon paper, produce only a mass of confused and puerile nonsense—that they express themselves so clumsily that it is often quite impossible to understand them at all. The faulty inference is to the effect that what ails them is a defective technical equipment—that they can be trained to write clearly as a dog may be trained to walk on its hind legs. This is all wrong. What ails them is not a defective technical equipment but a defective natural equipment. They write badly simply because they cannot think clearly. They cannot think clearly because they lack the brains. Trying to teach them is as hopeless as trying to teach a dog with only one hind leg. Any human being who can speak English understandably has all the materials necessary to write English clearly, and even beautifully. There is nothing mysterious about the written language; it is precisely the same, in essence, as the spoken language. If a man can think in English at all, he can find words enough to express his ideas. The fact is proved abundantly by the excellent writing that often comes from so-called ignorant men. It is proved anew by the even better writing that is done on higher levels by persons of great simplicity, for example, Abraham Lincoln. Such writing commonly arouses little enthusiasm among pedagogues. Its transparency excites their professional disdain, and they are offended by its use of homely words and phrases. They prefer something more ornate and complex—something, as they would probably put it, demanding more thought. But the thought they yearn for is the kind, alas, that they secrete themselves—the muddled, highfalutin, vapid thought that one finds in their own text-books.

I do not denounce them because they write so badly; I merely record the fact in a sad, scientific spirit. Even in such twilight regions of the intellect the style remains the man. What is in the head infallibly oozes out of the nub of the pen. If it is sparkling Burgundy the writing is full of life and charm. If it is mush the writing is mush too. The late Dr. Harding, twenty-ninth President of the Federal Union, was a highly self-conscious stylist. He practiced prose composition assiduously, and was regarded by the pedagogues of Marion, Ohio, and vicinity as a very talented fellow. But when he sent a message to Congress it was so muddled in style that even the late Henry Cabot Lodge, a professional literary man, could not understand it. Why? Simply because Dr. Harding's thoughts, on the high and grave subjects he discussed, were so muddled that he couldn't understand them himself. But on matters within his range of customary meditation he was clear and even charming, as all of us are. I once heard him deliver a brief address upon the ideals of the Elks. It was a topic close to his heart, and he had thought about it at length and *con amore*. The result was an excellent speech—clear, logical, forceful, and with a touch of wild, romantic beauty. His sentences hung together. He employed simple words, and put them together with skill. But when, at a public meeting in Washington, he essayed to deliver an oration on the subject of the late Dante Alighieri, he quickly became so obscure and absurd that even the Diplomatic Corps began to snicker. The cause was plain: he knew no more about Dante than a Tennessee county judge knows about the Institutes of Justinian. Trying to formulate ideas upon the topic, he could get together only a few disjected fragments and ghosts of ideas—here an ear, there a section of tibia, beyond a puff of soul substance or other gas. The resultant speech was thus enigmatical, cacophonous and awful stuff. It sounded precisely like a lecture by a college professor on style.

A pedagogue, confronted by Dr. Harding in class, would have set him to the business of what is called improving his vocabulary—that is, to the business of making his writing even worse than it was. Dr. Harding, in point of fact, had all the vocabulary that he needed, and a great deal more. Any idea that he could formulate clearly he could convey clearly. Any idea that genuinely moved him he could invest with charm—which is to say, with what the pedagogues call style. I believe that this capacity is possessed by all literate persons above the age of fourteen. It is not acquired by studying text-books; it is acquired by learning how to think. Children even younger often show it. I have a niece, now eleven years old, who already has an excellent style. When she writes to me about things that interest her—in other words, about the things she is capable of thinking about—she puts her thoughts into clear, dignified and admirable English. Her vocabulary, so far, is unspoiled by schoolma'ms. She doesn't try to knock me out by bombarding me with hard words, and phrases filched from Addison. She is unaffected, and hence her writing is charming. But if she essayed to send me a communication on the subject, say, of Balkan politics or government ownership, her style would descend instantly to the level of that of Dr. Harding's state papers.

To sum up, style cannot go beyond the ideas which lie at the heart of it. If they are clear, it too will be clear. If they are held passionately, it will be eloquent. Trying to teach it to persons who cannot think, especially when the business is attempted by persons who also cannot think, is a great waste of time, and an immoral imposition upon the taxpayers of the nation. It would be far more logical to devote all the energy to teaching, not writing, but logic—and probably just as useless. For I doubt that the art of thinking can be taught at all—at any rate, by school-teachers. It is not acquired, but congenital. Some persons are born with it. Their ideas flow in straight channels; they are capable of lucid reasoning; when they say anything it is instantly understandable; when they write anything it is clear and persuasive. They constitute, I should say, about one-eighth of one per cent. of the human race. The rest of God's children are just as incapable of logical thought as they are incapable of jumping over the moon. Trying to teach them to think is as vain an enterprise as trying to teach a streptococcus the principles of Americanism. The only thing to do with them is to make Ph.D.'s of them, and set them to writing handbooks on style.

6
The Critic and his Job

The assumption that it may be scientific is the worst curse that lies upon criticism. It is responsible for all the dull, blowsy, "definitive" stuff that literary pedagogues write, and it is responsible, too, for the heavy posturing that so often goes on among critics less learned. Both groups proceed upon the theory that there are exact facts to be ascertained, and that it is their business to ascertain and proclaim them. That theory is nonsense. There is, in truth, no such thing as an exact fact in the whole realm of the beautiful arts. What is true therein to-day may be false to-morrow, or vice versa, and only too often the shift is brought about by something that, properly speaking, is not an æsthetic consideration at all.

The case of Whitman comes to mind at once. Orthodox criticism, in his own time, was almost unanimously against him. At his first appearance, true enough, a few critics were a bit dazzled by him, notably Emerson, but they quickly got control of their faculties and took to cover. Down to the time of his death the prevailing doctrine was that he was a third-rate poet and a dirty fellow. Any young professor who, in the seventies or even in the early eighties, had presumed to whoop for him in class would have been cashiered at once, as both incompetent and immoral. If there was anything definitively established in those days, it was that old Walt was below the salt. To-day he is taught to sophomores everywhere, perhaps even in Tennessee, and one of the most unctuously respectable of American publishing houses brings out "Leaves of Grass" unexpurgated, and everyone agrees that he is one of the glories the national letters. Has that change been brought about by a purely critical process? Does it represent a triumph of criticism over darkness? It does not. It represents, rather, a triumph of external forces over criticism. Whitman's first partisans were not interested in poetry; they were interested in sex. They were presently reënforced by persons interested in politics. They were finally converted into a majority by a tatterdemalion horde of persons interested mainly, and perhaps only, in making a noise.

Literary criticism, properly so-called, had little if anything to do with this transformation. Scarcely a critic of any recognized authority had a hand in it. What started it off, after the first furtive, gingery snuffling over "A Woman Waits for Me" and the "Calamus" cycle, was the rise of political radicalism in the early eighties, in reaction against the swinish materialism that followed the Civil War. I am tempted to say that Terence V. Powderly had more to do with the rehabilitation of Whitman than any American critic, or, indeed, than any American poet. And if you object to Powderly, then I offer you Karl Marx, with William Jennings Bryan—no less!—peeping out of his coat-pocket. The radicals made heavy weather of it at the start. To the average respectable citizen they seemed to be mere criminals. Like the Bolsheviki of a later era, they were represented by their opponents as the enemies of all mankind. What they needed, obviously, was some means of stilling the popular fear of them—some way of tapping the national sentimentality. There stood Whitman, conveniently to hand. In his sonorous strophes to an imaginary and preposterous democracy there was an eloquent statement of their own vague and windy yearnings, and, what is more, a certificate to their virtue as sound Americans. So they adopted him with loud hosannas, and presently he was both their poet and their philosopher.

Long before any professor at Harvard dared to mention him (save, perhaps, with lascivious winks), he was being read to tatters by thousands of lonely Socialists in the mining-towns. As radicalism froze into Liberalism, and so began to influence the intelligentsia, his vogue rose, and by the end of the century even school-teachers had begun to hear of him. There followed the free verse poets, *i.e.*, a vast herd of emerging barbarians with an itch to make an uproar in the world, and no capacity for mastering the orthodox rules of prosody. Thus Whitman came to Valhalla, pushed by political propagandists and pulled by literary mountebanks. The native Taines and Matthew Arnolds made a gallant defense, but in vain. In the remoter denominational colleges some of them still hold out. But Whitman is now just as respectable at Yale as Martin Tupper or Edmund Clarence Stedman.

The point is that his new respectability is just as insecure as his old infamy—that he may be heaved out, on some bright tomorrow, just as he was heaved in, and by a similar combination of purely non-literary forces. Already I hear rumors of a plan to make Dr. Coolidge King. If his conscience stays him, then the throne may go to William Wrigley, Jr., or Judge Elbert H. Gary, LL.D. Democracy, indeed, begins to sicken among us. The doctors at its bedside dose it out of a black bottle, and make sinister signals to the coroner. If it dies, then Whitman will probably die with it. Criticism, of course, will labor desperately to save him, as it once labored to dispose of him, but such struggles are nearly always futile. The most they ever accomplish is to convert the author defended into a sort of fossil, preserved in a showcase to plague and puzzle schoolboys. The orthodox literature books, used in all schools, are simply such showcases. They represent the final effort of pedants to capture zephyrs and chain torrents. They are monuments to the delusion that criticism may be definitive—that appeals to the emotions, which shift and change with every wind, may be appraised and sorted out by appeals to the mind, which is theoretically unchangeable. Certainly every reflective student of any of the fine arts should know that this is not so. There is no such thing as a literary immortality. We remember Homer, but we forget the poets that the Greeks, too, forgot. You may be sure that there were Shakespeares in Carthage, and more of them at the court of Amenophis IV, but their very names are lost. Our own Shakespeare, as year chases year, may go the same way; in fact, his going the same way is quite as certain as anything we can imagine. A thousand years hence, even five hundred years hence, he may be, like Beowulf, only a name in a literature book, to be remembered against examination day and then forgotten.

Criticism is thus anything but scientific, for it cannot reach judgments that are surely and permanently valid. The most it can do, at its best, is to pronounce verdicts that are valid here and now, in the light of living knowledge and prejudice. As the background shifts the verdict changes. The best critic is not that fool who tries to resist the process—by setting up artificial standards, by prattling of laws and principles that do not exist, by going into the dead past for criteria of the present—, but that more prudent fellow who submits himself frankly to the flow of his time, and rejoices in its aliveness. Charles Augustin Sainte-Beuve was a good critic, for he saw everything as a Frenchman of the Second Empire, and if his judgments must be revised to-day it still remains true that they were honest and intelligent when he formulated them. Professor Balderdash is a bad critic, for he judges what is done in the American Empire of 1926 in the light of what was held to be gospel in the pastoral Republic of a century ago. For the rest, the critic survives, when he survives at all, mainly as artist. His judgments, in the long run, become archaic, and may be disregarded. But if, in stating them, he has incidentally produced a work of art on his own account, then he is read long after they are rejected, and it may be plausibly argued that he has contributed something to the glory of letters. No one takes much stock in Macaulay's notions to-day. He is, in fact, fair game for any college tutor who has majored in what is called history. He fell into many gross errors, and sometimes, it is probable, he fell into them more or less deliberately. But his criticism is still read—that is, as much as any criticism is read. It holds all its old charm and address. For Macaulay, when he sat himself down to be critical, did not try fatuously to produce a scientific treatise. What he tried to do was to produce a work of art.

7
Painting and its Critics

Having emerged lately from a diligent course of reading in so-called art criticism, and especially in that variety of it which is concerned with the painters since Cézanne, I can only report that I find it windy stuff, and sadly lacking in clarity and sense. The new critics, indeed, seem to me to be quite as vague and absurd as some of the new painters they celebrate. The more they explain and expound the thing they profess to admire, the more unintelligible it becomes. Criticism, in their hands, turns into a sort of cabbalism. One must prepare for it, as one prepares for the literature of Service or of the New Thought, by acquiring a wholly new vocabulary, and a new system of logic.

I do not argue here that the new painting, in itself, is always absurd. On the contrary, it must be manifest to anyone with eyes that some of its inventions are bold and interesting, and that now and then it achieves a sort of beauty. What I argue is simply that the criticism it has bred does not adequately account for it—that no man of ordinary sense, seeking to find out just what it is about, will get any light from what is currently written about it. All he will get will be a bath of metaphysics, heated with indignation. Polemics take the place of exposition. One comes away with a guilty feeling that one is somehow grossly ignorant and bounderish, but unable to make out why. The same phenomenon is occasionally witnessed in other fields. I have mentioned the cases of Service and the New Thought. There was, a generation ago, the case of Ibsen and the symbolists. These imbeciles read such extravagant meanings into the old man's plays that he was moved, finally, to violent protests. He was not trying to compose cryptograms, he said; he was simply trying to write stage plays. In much the same way Cézanne protested against the balderdash of his earliest disciples and interpreters. He was no messiah, he said; he was only a painter who tried to reduce what he saw in the world to canvas. The Ibsen symbolists eventually subsided into Freudism and other such rubbish, but the Cézannists continue to spoil paper with their highfalutin and occult tosh. I have read nearly all of them, and I denounce all that I have read as quacks.

This tendency to degenerate into a mere mouthing of meaningless words seems to be peculiar to so-called art criticism. There has never been, so far as I know, a critic of painting who wrote about it simply and clearly, as Sainte-Beuve, say, wrote about books, or Schumann and Berlioz about music. Even the most orthodox of the brethren, when he finds himself before a canvas that genuinely moves him, takes refuge in esoteric winks and grimaces and mysterious gurgles and belches. He can never put his feelings into plain English. Always, before he is done, he is sweating metaphysics, which is to say, nonsense. Painters themselves, when they discuss their art, commonly go the same route. Every time a new revolutionist gives a show he issues a manifesto explaining his aims and achievements, and in every such manifesto there is the same blowsy rodomontadizing that one finds in the texts of the critics. The thing, it appears, is very profound. Something new has been discovered. Rembrandt, poor old boy, lived and died in ignorance of it. Turner, had he heard of it, would have yelled for the police. Even Gaugin barely glimpsed it. One can't make out what this new arcanum is, but one takes it on faith and goes to the show. What one finds there is a series of canvases that appear to have been painted with asphalt and mayonnaise, and by a man afflicted with binocular diplopic strabismus. Is this sound drawing? Is this a new vision of color? Then so is your grandmother left-fielder of the Giants. The exceptions are very few. I have read, I suppose, at least two hundred such manifestos during the past twenty years; at one time I even started out to collect them, as odd literary delicatessen. I can't recall a single one that embodied a plain statement of an intelligible idea—that is, intelligible to a man of ordinary information and sanity. It always took a special talent to comprehend them, as it took a special talent to paint the fantastic pictures they discussed.

Two reasons, I believe, combine to make the pronunciamentos of painters so bombastic and flatulent. One lies in the plain fact that painting is a relatively simple and transparent art, and that nothing much of consequence is thus to be said about it. All that is remarkable in even the most profound painting may be grasped by an educated spectator in a few minutes. If he lingers longer he is simply seeing again what he has seen before. His essential experience, in other words, is short-lived. It is not like getting shaved, coming down with the cholera morbus, or going to the wars; it is like jumping out of the way of a taxicab or getting kissed. Consider, now, the position of a critic condemned to stretch this experience into material for a column article or for a whole chapter in a book. Obviously, he soon finds it insufficient for this purpose. What, then, is he to do? Tell the truth, and then shut up? This, alas, is not the way of critics. When their objective facts run out they always turn to subjective facts, of which the supply is unlimited. Thus the art critic begins to roll his eyes inward. He begins to poetize and philosophize his experience. He indulges himself in dark hints and innuendos. Putting words together aimlessly, he presently hits upon a combination that tickles him. He has invented a new cliché. He is a made man. The painter, expounding his work, falls into the same bog. The plain fact, nine times out of ten, is that he painted his picture without any rational plan whatever. Like any other artist, he simply experimented with his materials, trying this combination and then that. Finally he struck something that pleased him. Now he faces the dreadful job of telling why. He simply doesn't know. So he conceals his ignorance behind recondite and enigmatical phrases. He soars, insinuates, sputters, coughs behind his hand. If he is lucky, he, too, invents a cliché. Three clichés in a row, and he is a temporary immortal.

Behind what is written about painting there is always, of course, the immense amount of drivel that is talked about it. No other art is so copiously discussed by its practitioners, or encrusted with so much hollow theorizing. The reason therefor —the second of the two I mentioned above—lies in the obvious fact that painters can talk while they work, and are debarred from working at least half of their waking hours. A poet, when his hormones begin to ferment, not infrequently labors all night; when there is a fog, a thunder-storm or a torch-light parade he is specially inspired. So with a musical composer. But a painter can work only while the light is good, and in the north temperate zone that is not often. So he has much time on his hands, and inasmuch as he seldom has money enough to venture into general society and is usually too ignorant to enjoy reading, he puts in that time talking. Nowhere else on this earth is there so much gabbling as you will find in painters' studios, save it be in the pubs and more or less public bed-rooms that they frequent. It begins as soon as the sun goes down, and it keeps on all night. And it is always about painting, painting, painting. No other class of artists is so self-centered. Once a youth gets a brush into his hand and turpentine in his hair, he appears to join a race apart, and is interested no longer in the general concerns of the world. Even the other arts do not commonly engage any of his attention. If he ventures into music, it is into the banal music of college boys and colored stevedores. If he reads it is only the colicky nonsense that I have been describing. Even his amours are but incidents of his trade. Now put this immense leisure and this great professional keenness against the plain fact that the problems of painting, in the main, are very simple—that very little that is new is to be said about any of them. The result is a vast dilution of ideas, a stormy battle of mere words, an infinite logomachy. And on its higher levels, embellished with all the arts of the auctioneer, it is art criticism.

8
Greenwich Village

The whole saga of Greenwich Village is in Alfred Kreymborg's autobiography, which he calls, very appropriately, "Troubadour." The story begins with an earnest and insolvent young man in a garret, fighting cockroaches and writing free verse. It ends with a respectable gentleman of passing forty, legally married to one very charming wife, and in receipt of a comfortable income in royalties from the 6000 Little Theatres which now freckle and adorn our eminent Republic, distracting the males of the Younger Married Set from the Red Peril and Service, and their wives from millinery and birth control.

Of all the motley revolutionaries who flourished in the Village in its heyday, say fifteen years ago, Kreymborg was surely one of the most engaging, as he was one of the most honest. Most of the others, for all their heroic renunciation of commercialism, were quite as hot for the *mazuma* as other literary artists. With one breath they pledged themselves to poverty—though not, surely, to chastity or obedience!—and denounced such well-heeled poets as Kipling and Shakespeare as base harlots of the marts. With the next they bargained with such editors as ventured to buy their wares like Potash tackling One-Eye Feigenbaum. From this lamentable trafficking Kreymborg held aloof, a genuine Parnassian. He composed his bad poetry and his worse novels on a diet of *Schnecken* and synthetic coffee, and paid for that meager fare by teaching Babbitts the elements of chess.

Gradually the tumult died, and Greenwich Village fell into decay. The poets moved out, and Philistines moved in; it was all over. But Kreymborg kept the faith—at all events, longer than most. He continued to write poems like a series of college yells, plays unearthly and impossible, novels that brought the Comstocks sliding down their poles like firemen. But gradually he, too, began to show change. His hair grew thin on top; his blood grew sluggish. Presently some of his plays were produced; he had at last squeezed through the proscenium arch. Then he began to accept calls to read his dithyrambs before provincial Poetry Societies. Then he became an editor and an anthologist—ten paces behind his ancient enemy, Louis Untermeyer. Then he went through two divorces, one of them legal, and married an estimable lady of Brooklyn. Now he is past forty, has an agent, and pays income-tax. *Schön ist die Jugendzeit; sie kommt nicht mehr!* As I have hinted, there was always something charming about Kreymborg, even in the days of his most raucous verse. He threw up a good job with the Aeolian Company, demonstrating mechanical-piano records, in order to become a poet, and he stuck to his dream through many a long year. The waspishness of the other Villagers was not in him, and he was happily free of their worst imbecilities. Between cantos of free verse, I suspect, he often read Swinburne and even Tennyson; in his mandolute he concealed Howells and Mark Twain.

As one who poked many heavy jocosities at it while it lasted, I hope I may now say with good grace that I believe Greenwich Village did a good service to all the fine arts in this great land, and left a valuable legacy behind it. True enough, its own heroes were nearly all duds, and most of them have been forgotten, but it at least broke ground, it at least stirred up the animals. When it began to issue smoke and flame, the youth of the country were still under the hoof of the schoolma'm; when it blew up at last they were in full revolt. Was it Greenwich Village or Yale University that cleared the way for Cabell? Was it the Village or the Philharmonic Society that made a place for Stravinsky? Was it the Village on the trustees of the Metropolitan Museum that first whooped for Cézanne? That whooping, of course, did not stop with Cézanne, or Stravinsky, or Cabell. There were whoops almost as loud for Sascha Gilhooly, who painted sunsets with a shaving brush, and for Raoul Goetz, who wrote quartettes for automobile horns and dentist's drills, and for Bruce J. Katzenstein, whose poetry was all figures and exclamation points. But all that excess did no harm. The false prophets changed from day to day. The real ones remained.

X.
Essay in Pedagogy

I

ON the purely technical side the American novel has obviously made immense progress. As ordinarily encountered, it is very adeptly constructed, and not infrequently it is also well written. The old-time amorphous novel, rambling all over the place and ending with pious platitudes, has pretty well gone out. The American novelists of to-day, and especially the younger ones, have given earnest study to form—perhaps, indeed, too much. For in concentrating their powerful intellects upon it they have lost sight of something that is far more important. I allude, of course, to the observation of character. Thus the average contemporary American novel, though it is workmanlike and well-mannered, fails to achieve its first business. It does not evoke memorable images of human beings. One enjoys reading it, perhaps, but one seldom remembers it. And when it gets beyond the estate of a mere technical exercise, it only too often descends to the even worse estate of a treatise. It attempts to prove something—usually the simple fact that its author is a clever fellow, or a saucy gal. But all a novel of genuine bulk and beam ever proves is that the proper study of mankind is man—the proper study and the most engrossing.

In brief, a first-rate novel is always a character sketch. It may be more than that, but at bottom it is always a character sketch, or, if the author is genuinely of the imperial line, a whole series of them. More, it is a character sketch of an individual not far removed from the norm of the race. He may have his flavor of oddity, but he is never fantastic; he never violates the common rules of human action; he never shows emotions that are impossible to the rest of is. If Thackeray had made Becky Sharp seven feet tall, and given her a bass voice, nine husbands and the rank of lieutenant-general in the British Army, she would have been forgotten long ago, along with all the rest of "Vanity Fair." And if Robinson Crusoe had been an

Edison instead of a normal sailorman, he would have gone the same way.

The moral of all this is not lost upon the more competent minority of novelists in practice among us. It was not necessary to preach it to Miss Cather when she set out to write "My Antonía," nor to Abraham Cahan when he tackled "The Rise of David Levinsky," nor to Sinclair Lewis when he was at work on "Babbitt." All such novelists see the character first and the story afterward. What is the story of "Babbitt"? Who remembers? Who, indeed, remembers the story of "The Three Musketeers"? But D'Artagnan and his friends live brilliantly, and so, too, I believe, will George F. Babbitt live brilliantly—at all events, until Kiwanis ceases to trouble, and his type ceases to be real. Most of the younger American novelists, alas, seem to draw no profit from such examples. It is their aim, apparently, to shock mankind with the vivacity of their virtuosity and the heterodoxy of their ideas, and so they fill their novels with gaudy writing and banal propaganda, and convert their characters into sticks. I read novel after novel without getting any sense of contact with actual human beings. I am, at times, immensely amused and sometimes I am instructed, but I seldom carry away anything to remember. When I do so, it is not an idea, but a person. Like everyone else, I have a long memory for persons. But ideas come and go.

All this becomes the more remarkable when one considers the peculiar richness of the American scene in sharply-outlined and racy characters. Our national ideas, indeed, are mainly third-rate, and some of them are almost idiotic, but taking one year with another we probably produce more lively and diverting people than all the rest of the world taken together. More, these lively and diverting people tend to cluster into types. Mark Twain put half a dozen of them into "Huckleberry Finn" and as many more into "Roughing It," a novel disguised as history. Montague Glass collared a whole flock for his Potash and Perlmutter stories, and Ring Lardner has got another flock into his studies of the American bounder. But the younger novelists, or at least the overwhelming majority of them, stick to their sticks. Thus even the most salient and arresting of American types still lack historians, and seem doomed to perish and be forgotten with the Bill of Rights. Babbitt stood around for a dozen years, waiting for Lewis; the rest of the novelists of the land gaped at him without seeing him. How long will they gape at the American politician? At the American university president? At the American policeman? At the American lawyer? At the American insurance man? At the Prohibition fanatic? At the revival evangelist? At the bootlegger? At the Y.M.C.A. secretary? At the butter-and-egg man? At the journalist?

2

I have put the politician at the top of my list. He probably embodies more typical American traits than any other; he is, within his limits, the arch-Americano. Yet how seldom he gets into a novel! And how seldom, having got there, is he real! I can recall, indeed, but one American political novel of any value whatever as a study of character, and that is Harvey Fergusson's story of Washington, "Capitol Hill"—a series of casual sketches, but all of them vivid and true. Fergusson really understands the American politician. There is, in "Capitol Hill," no division of the *dramatis personæ* between Democrats and Republicans, progressives and reactionaries, materialists and idealists, patriots and traitors; the only division is between men and women who have something, and men and women who want it. In that simple fact lies most of the book's curious reality. For the truth about Washington is that it is not a town of politics, in the conventional and romantic sense; it is, if anything, a town almost devoid of politics. The people in the industrial cities and out on the farms take political ideas seriously; what they cherish in that department they refuse passionately to surrender. But so far as I know there are not a dozen professional politicians in Washington, high or low, who would not throw overboard, instantly and gladly, every political idea they are assumed to be devoted to, including especially every political idea that has helped them into public office, if throwing it overbroad would help them to higher and gaudier and more lucrative office. I say high or low, and I mean it literally. There has not been a President of the United States for half a century who did not, at some time or other in his career, perform a complete *volte face* in order to further his career. There is scarcely a United States Senator who does not flop at least three times within the limits of a single session.

The novelists who write about Washington are partly recruited from the ranks of the Washington newspaper correspondents, perhaps the most naïve and unreflective body of literate men in Christendom, and for the rest from the ranks of those who read the dispatches of such correspondents, and take them seriously. The result is a grossly distorted and absurd picture of life in the capital city. One carries off the notion that the essential Washington drama is based on a struggle between a powerful and corrupt Senator and a sterling young uplifter. The Senator is about to sell out the Republic to the Steel Trust, J. P. Morgan or the Japs. The uplifter detects him, exposes him, drives him from public life, and inherits his job. The love interest is supplied by a fair stenographer who steals the damning papers from the Senator's safe, or by an Ambassador's wife who goes to the White House at 3 A.M., and, at the peril of her virtue, arouses the President and tells him what is afoot. All this is poppycock. There are no Senators in Washington powerful enough to carry on any such operations single-handed, and very few of them are corrupt: it is too easy to bamboozle them to go to the expense of buying them. The most formidable bribe that the average Senator receives from year's end to year's end is a bottle or two of very dubious Scotch, and that is just as likely to come from the agent of the South Central Watermelon Growers' Association as from John D. Rockefeller or the Mikado of Japan. Nor are there any sterling young uplifters in the town. The last was chased out before the Mexican War. There are to-day only gentlemen looking for something for themselves—publicity, eminence, puissance, jobs—especially jobs. Some take one line and some another. Further than that the difference between them is no greater than the difference between a Prohibition agent and a bootlegger, or tweedledum and tweedledee.

Ideas count for nothing in Washington, whether they be political, economic or moral. The question isn't what a man thinks, but what he has to give away that is worth having. Ten years ago a professional Prohibitionist had no more standing in the town than a professional astrologer, Assyriologist or wart-remover; five years ago, having proved that his gang could make or break Congressmen, he got all the deference that belonged to the Chief Justice; now, with the wet wolves chasing him, he is once more in eclipse. If William Z. Foster were elected President to-morrow, the most fanatical Coolidge men of to-day would flock to the White House the day after, and try to catch his eye. Coolidge, while Harding was living, was an obscure and impotent fellow, viewed with contempt by everyone. The instant he mounted the throne he became a Master Mind. Fergusson got all of this into "Capitol Hill," which is not the story of a combat between the True and the False in politics, but the simple tale of a typical Washingtonian's struggle to the front—a tale that should be an inspiration to every Rotarian in the land. He begins as a petty job-holder in the Capitol itself, mailing congressional speeches to constituents on the steppes; he ends at the head of a glittering banquet table, with a Senator to one side of him and a member of the Cabinet to the other—a man who has somehow got power into his hands, and can dispense jobs, and is thus an indubitable somebody. Everybody in Washington who has jobs to dispense is somebody.

This eternal struggle is sordid, but, as Fergusson has shown, it is also extremely amusing. It brings out, as the moralists say, the worst that is in human nature, which is always the most charming. It reduces all men to one common level of ignominy, and so rids them of their customary false-faces. They take on a new humanity. Ceasing to be Guardians of the Constitution, Foes to the Interests, Apostles of Economy, Prophets of World Peace, and such-like banshees, they become ordinary men, like John Doe and Richard Roe. One beholds them sweating, not liquid idealism, but genuine sweat. They hope, fear, aspire, suffer. They are preyed upon, not by J. P. Morgan, but by designing cuties. They go to the White House, not to argue for the World Court, but to hog patronage. From end to end of Fergusson's chronicle there is absolutely no mention of the tariff, or of the farmer and his woes, or of the budget system, or of the Far Eastern question. I marvel that more American novelists have not gone to this lush and delightful material. The supply is endless and lies wide open. Six months in Washington is enough to load an ambitious novelist for all eternity. (Think of what George Moore has made of his one love-affair, back in 1877!) The Washington correspondents, of course, look at it without seeing it, and so do all the Washington novelists save Fergusson. But that is saying nothing. A Washington correspondent is one with a special talent for failing to see what is before his eyes. I have beheld a whole herd of them sit through a national convention without once laughing.

Fergusson, in "Capitol Hill," keeps mainly to that end of Pennsylvania avenue which gives his book its names. I believe that the makings of a far better novel of Washington life are to be found at the other end, to wit, in and about the alabaster cage which houses the heir of Washington, Lincoln and Chester A. Arthur. Why, indeed, has no one ever put *kaiserliche Majestät* into fiction—save, of course, as a disembodied spirit, vaguely radiating idealism? The revelations in the Daugherty inquiry gave a hint of unworked riches—but there is enough dramatic and even melodramatic material without descending to scandal. A President is a man like the rest of us. He can laugh and he can groan. There are days when his breakfast agrees with him, and days when it doesn't. His eyes have the common optical properties: they can see a sweet one as far as they can see a member of the Interstate Commerce Commission. All the funnels of intrigue are aimed at him. He is the common butt of every loud-speaker. No other man in this sad vale has so many jobs to give out, or one-half so many. Try to imagine a day in his life, from dawn to midnight. Do it, and you will have the best American novel ever heard of.

3

But I am forgetting my other candidates—for example, the American university president. I mean, of course, the university president of the new six-cylinder, air-cooled, four-wheel-brake model—half the quack, half the visionary, and wholly the go-getter—the brisk, business-like, confidential, button-holing, regular fellow who harangues Rotary and Kiwanis, extracts millions from usurers by alarming them about Bolshevism, and so builds his colossal pedagogical slaughter-house, with its tens of thousands of students, its professors of cheese-making, investment securities and cheer-leading, its galaxy of football stars, and its general air of Barnum's circus. Why has this astounding mountebank not got into a book? He fairly yells for loving embalming *à la* Babbitt. He is not only stupendously picaresque and amusing in himself—the final heir, at once, of Abelard, Cagliostro, Increase Mather, the Fox sisters, Pestalozzi, Dr. Munyon, Godey of the *Lady's Book*, and Daniel Drew—; he is also thoroughly and magnificently characteristic of the great land we live in. No other country has ever produced anything quite like him. No other country, I suspect, would tolerate him. But here he lives and flourishes, a superb and perfect American—and yet our novelists all neglect him.

Worse and more incredible still, they neglect the most American of all Americans, the very *Ur-Amerikaner*—to wit, the malignant moralist, the Christian turned cannibal, the snouting and preposterous Puritan. Where is there the American novel in which he is even half limned? There are, to be sure, glimpses of him in "The Song of the Lark," by Willa Cather, and in "Babbitt," and there is a more elaborate but still incomplete sketch in E. W. Howe's "The Story of a Country Town." But Howe, unfortunately, had other fish to fry: he slapped in his bucolic wowser brilliantly, and then passed on to melodrama and the agonies of young love. So, too, with Lewis and Miss Cather. Thus, though the Puritan Father lies embalmed magnificently in the pages of Hawthorne, his heir and assign of the present day, the high-powered uplifter, the prophet of harsh and unenforceable laws, the incurable reformer and nuisance—this sweet fellow yet awaits his anatomist.

What a novel is in him! Indeed, what a shelf of novels! For he has as many forms as there are varieties of human delusion. Sometimes he is a tin-pot evangelist, sweating to transform Oklahoma City or Altoona, Pa., into the New Jerusalem. Sometimes he is a hireling of the Anti-Saloon League, sworn to Law Enforcement. Sometimes he is a strict Sabbatarian, bawling for the police whenever he detects his neighbor washing bottles or varnishing the Ford on Sunday morning. Again he is a vice-crusader, chasing the scarlet lady with fierce Christian shouts. Yet again he is a comstock, wearing out his eyes in the quest for smut. He may even be female—a lady Ph.D. in a linoleum hat, patrolling the cow towns and the city slums, handing out edifying literature, teaching poor Polish women how to have babies. Whatever his form, he is tremendously grotesque and tremendously amusing—and always he drips with national juices, always he is as thoroughly American as a bootlegger or a college yell. If he exists at all in other lands, it is only in rudimentary and aberrant forms. Try to imagine a French Wayne B. Wheeler, or a Spanish Billy Sunday, or a German William Jennings Bryan. It is as impossible as imagining a Coolidge in the Rome of Julius.

Since the earliest days, as everyone knows, American jurisprudence has been founded upon the axiom that it is the first duty of every citizen to police his neighbors, and especially those he envies, or otherwise dislikes. There is no such thing, in this grand and puissant nation, as privacy. The yokels out in Iowa, neglecting their horned cattle, have a right, it appears—nay, a sacred duty!—to peek into my home in Baltimore, and tell me what I may and may not drink with my meals. An out-at-elbow Methodist preacher in Boston sets himself up to decide what I may read. An obscure and unintelligent job-holder in Washington, inspired by God, determines what I may receive in the mails. I must not buy lottery tickets because it offends the moral sentiment of Kansas. I must keep Sunday as the Sabbath, which is in conflict with Genesis, because it is ordered by persons who believe that Genesis can't be wrong. Such are the laws of the greatest free nation ever seen on earth. We are all governed by them. But a government of laws, of course, is a mere phantasm of political theorists: the thing is always found, on inspection, to be really a government of men. In the United States, it seems to me, the tendency is for such men to come increasingly from the class of professional uplifters. It is not the bankers who run the ostensible heads of the state, as the Liberals believe, nor the so-called bosses, as the bosses themselves believe, but the wowsers. And what is a wowser? What does the word mean? It means precisely what you think of inevitably when you hear it. A wowser is a wowser. He bears a divine commission to regulate and improve the rest of us. He knows exactly what is best for us. He is what Howe calls a Good Man. So long as you and I are sinful, he can't sleep. So long as we are happy, he is after us.

I throw off the guess that there are at least forty novels in the wowser—that is, forty good ones. He has, as I have said, as many forms as the demons who ride him, and every one of them should make a competent novelist, authentically called to the vocation, leap in air with loud hosannas, and spit upon his hands. His psychology remains mysterious. The Freudians, I believe, have misunderstood him, and the psychiatrists have avoided him. What are the springs of his peculiar frenzy to harass and punish his fellow men? By what process of malign eugenics is he hatched? And what is his typical life history? Here is work for the novelist, which is to say, for the professional anatomist of character. I believe that Frank Norris, had he lived, would have tackled it with enthusiasm, and made a great success of its execution. Norris, like Dreiser after him, had a romantic and even a mystical inclination, but at bottom he was a satirist—and the American Puritan was made for satirists as catnip was made for cats. It is easy to laugh at him, but it is hard to hate him. He is eternally in the position of a man trying to empty the ocean with a tin-dipper. He will be mauled, and the chance he offers thrown away, if the novelist who attempts him in the end forgets the tragedy under his comedy. I have known many American wowsers in my time, some of them intimately. They were all intensely unhappy men. They suffered as vastly as Prometheus chained to his rock, with the buzzards exploring his liver. A novelist blind to that capital fact will never comprehend the type. It needs irony—but above all it needs pity.

4

So does another type that also awaits its Thackeray: to wit, the American journalist. Most American novelists, before they challenge Dostoevski, put in an apprenticeship on the public prints, and thus have a chance to study and grasp the peculiarities of the journalistic mind; nevertheless, the fact remains that there is not a single genuine newspaper man, done in the grand manner, in the whole range of American fiction. As in the case of the wowser, there are some excellent brief sketches, but there is no adequate portrait of the journalist as a whole, from his beginnings as a romantic young reporter to his finish as a Babbitt, correct in every idea and as hollow as a jug. Here, I believe, is genuine tragedy. Here is the matter that enters into all fiction of the first class. Here is human character in disintegration

—the primary theme of every sound novelist ever heard of, from Fielding to Zola and from Turgeniev to Joseph Conrad. I know of no American who starts from a higher level of aspiration than the journalist. He is, in his first phase, genuinely romantic. He plans to be both an artist and a moralist—a master of lovely words and a merchant of sound ideas. He ends, commonly, as the most depressing jackass in his community—that is, if his career goes on to what is called success. He becomes the repository of all its worst delusions and superstitions. He becomes the darling of all its frauds and idiots, and the despair of all its honest men. He belongs to a good club, and the initiation fee was his soul.

Here I speak by the book, for I have been in active practice as a journalist for more than a quarter of a century, and have an immense acquaintance in the craft. I could name a man who fits my specifications exactly in every American city east of the Mississippi, and refrain only on the advice of counsel. I do not say that all journalists go that route. Far from it! Many escape by failing; some even escape by succeeding. But the majority succumb. They begin with high hopes. They end with safe jobs. In the career of any such man, it seems to me, there are materials for fiction of the highest order. He is interesting intrinsically, for his early ambition is at least not ignoble—he is not born an earthworm. And he is interesting as a figure in drama, for he falls gradually, resisting all the while, to forces that are beyond his strength. If he can't make the grade, it is not because he is unwilling or weak, but because the grade itself is too steep. Here is tragedy—and here is America. For the curse of this country, as of all democracies, is precisely the fact that it treats its best men as enemies. The aim of our society, if it may be said to have an aim, is to iron them out. The ideal American, in the public sense, is a respectable vacuum.

I heave this typical American journalist to the massed novelists of the Federal Union, and invite them to lay on. There is a capital novel in him—a capital character sketch and a capital picture of the American scene. He is representative and yet he is not commonplace. People will recognize him, and yet they are not familiar with him. Let the fictioneers have at him! But let them bear in mind that, like the wowser, he is not to be done to the tune of superior sneers. He is a wreck, but he has not succumbed to the gales without resistence. Let him be done ironically, as Lewis did Babbitt, but let him be done also with pity. He is not a comedian, but a tragedian. Above all, let him be done without any mouthing of theories. His simple story is poignant enough.

Is he too difficult? Then I offer a substitute: the American policeman. Certainly it is high time for him to get into a book. I dedicate him to the novelists of the nation at once, and provide them simultaneously with all the plot they will need. A moron with an IQ of 53, despairing of ever getting a better job, goes on the force and begins pounding a beat. A chance favor to a saloonkeeper makes a sergeant of him, and thereafter he slowly mounts the ladder. At the end he is an inspector, and in charge of operations against a fabulous crime wave, imagined by the city editor of a tabloid newspaper. Isn't that enough? What a vivid and exhilarating picture of American life could be got out of it! What humors are there, and what genuine drama! Nor are the materials esoteric. Every newspaper reporter's head is stuffed with them. I myself could do such a work in ten volumes folio. Nine young journalists out of ten, I believe, aspire to the novel. Well, here is a chance to write a novel as good as "Babbitt."

XI.

On Living in Baltimore

SOME time ago, writing in an eminent Baltimore newspaper upon the Baltimore of my boyhood, I permitted myself an eloquent passage upon its charm, and let fall the doctrine that nearly all of that charm had vanished. Mere rhetoric, I greatly fear. The old charm, in truth, still survives in the town, despite the frantic efforts of the boosters and boomers who, in late years, have replaced all its ancient cobblestones with asphalt, and bedizened it with Great White Ways and suburban boulevards, and surrounded it with stinking steel plants and oil refineries, and increased its population from 400,000 to 800,000. I am never more conscious of the fact than when I return to it from New York. Behind me lies the greatest city of the modern world, with more money in it than all Europe and more clowns and harlots than all Asia, and yet it has no more charm than a circus lot or second-rate hotel. It can't show a single genuinely distinguished street. It hasn't a single park that is more lovely than a cemetery lot. It is without manner as it is without manners. Escaping from it to so ancient and solid a town as Baltimore is like coming out of a football crowd into quiet communion with a fair one who is also amiable, and has the gift of consolation for hard-beset and despairing men.

I have confessed to rhetoric, but I surely do not indulge in it here. For twenty-five years I have resisted a constant temptation to move to New York, and I resist it more easily to-day than I did when it began. I am, perhaps, the most arduous commuter ever heard of, even in that Babylon of commuters. My office is on Manhattan Island and has been there since 1914; yet I live, vote and have my being in Baltimore, and go back there the instant my job allows. If my desk bangs at 3 P.M. I leap for the 3.25 train. Four long hours in the Pullman follow, but the first is the worst. My back, at all events, is toward New York! Behind lies a place fit only for the gross business of getting money; ahead is a place made for enjoying it.

What makes New York so dreadful, I believe, is mainly the

fact that the vast majority of its people have been forced to rid themselves of one of the oldest and most powerful of human instincts—the instinct to make a permanent home. Crowded, shoved about and exploited without mercy, they have lost the feeling that any part of the earth belongs to them, and so they simply camp out like tramps, waiting for the constables to rush in and chase them away. I am not speaking here of the poor (God knows how they exist in New York at all!); I am speaking of the well-to-do, even of the rich. The very richest man, in New York, is never quite sure that the house he lives in now will be his next year—that he will be able to resist the constant pressure of business expansion and rising land values. I have known actual millionaires to be chased out of their homes in this way, and forced into apartments. In Baltimore too, the same pressure exists, to be sure, but it is not oppressive, for the householder can meet it by yielding to it half way. It may force him into the suburbs, even into the adjacent country, but he is still in direct contact with the city, sharing in its life, and wherever he lands he may make a stand. But on Manhattan Island he is quickly brought up by the rivers, and once he has crossed them he may as well move to Syracuse or Trenton.

Nine times out of ten he tries to avoid crossing them. That is, he moves into meaner quarters on the island itself, and pays more for them. His house gives way to a flat—one offering perhaps half the room for his goods and chattels that his house offered. Next year he is in a smaller flat, and three-fourths of his goods and chattels have vanished. A few years more, and he is in two or three rooms. Finally, he lands in an hotel. At this point he ceases to exist as the head of a house. His quarters are precisely like the quarters of 50,000 other men. The front he presents to the world is simply an anonymous door on a gloomy corridor. Inside, he lives like a sardine in a can. Such a habitation, it must be plain, cannot be called a home. A home is not a mere transient shelter: its essence lies in its permanence, in its capacity for accretion and solidification, in its quality of representing, in all its details, the personalities of the people who live in it. In the course of years it becomes a sort of museum of these people; they give it its indefinable air, separating it from all other homes, as one human face is separated from all others. It is at once a refuge from the world, a treasure-house, a castle, and the shrine of a whole hierarchy of peculiarly private and potent gods.

This concept of the home cannot survive the mode of life that prevails in New York. I have seen it go to pieces under my eyes in the houses of my own friends. The intense crowding in the town, and the restlessness and unhappiness that go with it, make it almost impossible for anyone to accumulate the materials of a home—the trivial, fortuitous and often grotesque things that gather around a family, as glories and debts gather around a state. The New Yorker lacks the room to house them; he thus learns to live without them. In the end he is a stranger in the house he lives in. More and more, it tends to be no more than Job No. 16432b from this or that decorator's studio. I know one New Yorker, a man of considerable means, who moves every three years. Every time he moves his wife sells the entire contents of the apartment she is leaving, and employs a decorator to outfit the new one. To me, at all events, such a mode of living would be unendurable. The charm of getting home, as I see it, is the charm of getting back to what is inextricably my own—to things familiar and long loved, to things that belong to me alone and none other. I have lived in one house in Baltimore for nearly forty-five years. It has changed in that time, as I have—but somehow it still remains the same. No conceivable decorator's masterpiece could give me the same ease. It is as much a part of me as my two hands. If I had to leave it I'd be as certainly crippled as if I lost a leg.

I believe that this feeling for the hearth, for the immemorial lares and penates, is infinitely stronger in Baltimore than in New York—that it has better survived there, indeed, than in any other large city of America—and that its persistence accounts for the superior charm of the town. There are, of course, thousands of Baltimoreans in flats—but I know of none to whom a flat seems more than a makeshift, a substitute, a necessary and temporary evil. They are all planning to get out, to find house-room in one of the new suburbs, to resume living in a home. What they see about them is too painfully not theirs. The New Yorker has simply lost that discontent. He is a vagabond. His notions of the agreeable become those of a vaudeville actor. He takes on the shallowness and unpleasantness of any other homeless man. He is highly sophisticated, and inordinately trashy. The fact no doubt explains the lack of charm that one finds in his town; the fact that the normal man of Baltimore is almost his exact antithesis explains the charm that is there. Human relations, in such a place, tend to assume a solid permanence. A man's circle of friends becomes a sort of extension of his family circle. His contacts are with men and women who are rooted as he is. They are not moving all the time, and so they are not changing their friends all the time. Thus abiding relationships tend to be built up, and when fortune brings unexpected changes, they survive those changes. The men I know and esteem in Baltimore are, on the whole, men I have known and esteemed a long while; even those who have come into my ken relatively lately seem likely to last. But of the men I knew best when I first began going to New York, twenty-five years ago, not one is a friend to-day. Of those I knew best ten years ago, not six are friends. The rest have got lost in the riot, and the friends of to-day, I sometimes fear, will get lost in the same way.

In human relationships that are so casual there is seldom any satisfaction. It is our fellows who make life endurable to us, and give it a purpose and a meaning; if our contacts with them are light and frivolous there is something lacking, and it is something of the very first importance. What I contend is that in Baltimore, under a slow-moving and cautious social organization, touched by the Southern sun, such contacts are more enduring than elsewhere, and that life in consequence is more agreeable. Of the external embellishments of life there is a plenty there—as great a supply, indeed, to any rational taste, as in New York itself. But there is also something much better: a tradition of sound and comfortable living. A Baltimorean is not merely John Doe, an isolated individual of *Homo sapiens*, exactly like every other John Doe. He is John Doe *of* a certain place—of Baltimore, of a definite *house* in Baltimore. It is not by accident that all the peoples of Europe, very early in their history, distinguished their best men by adding *of* this or that place to their names.

XII.

The Last New Englander

THE late Prof. Barrett Wendell, of Harvard, whose letters have been done into a stately volume by M. A. DeWolfe Howe, will probably go down into history as the last flower of the Puritan *Kultur.* Himself by no means a pure New Englander, for his surname was obviously Dutch, he yet had enough New England blood in him to feel himself wholly of that forlorn region, and he was accepted as a fit representative of it by all its tribal headmen. He was steeped in its tradition, and venerated its heroes. What came out of New England seemed to him to be virtuous and lovely, or, as he might have said, gentlemanly; what came out of the rest of the country was simply barbarous.

Nevertheless, Wendell was himself a walking proof that all he admired was passing into the shadows, for, try as he would, he could not, as a contemporary man, squeeze himself into the old Puritan mold. Over and over again he would make an effort to do so, but always, as he struggled with the lid, a diabolical, iconoclastic mood would overcome him, and he would leap up and emit a ribald yell. Harvard, startled and uneasy, never knew what to make of him. His principles were apparently impeccable; he was, in the current phrase, a consistent booster for the lost Golden Age, its glories and high deeds. And yet, whenever the answering cheer came back, he would make a mocking face and say something awful. The Cambridge campus is still warmed by these mockings. What saved him from downright infamy was the fact that, whenever they were actually in contempt of the Puritan mores and gnosiology, they were safely superficial—that is, they never questioned fundamentals. Wendell had a lot to say about the transient excesses and imbecilities of democracy, visible in his time, but he nevertheless believed in all the primary democratic fallacies, and even defended them eloquently. He was a tart critic of the whole educational process, and went to the length, in his own department of English, of denying it any value whatever;

nevertheless, he remained a romantic Harvard man to the end of his days, and venerated *alma mater* with the best of them. He must have seen clearly that there was little that was sound and solid left in the New England culture, that the rest of the country had little need of it and would quickly surpass it; all the same, he clung to the superstition that the preposterous theologians of its early days constituted an intellectual aristocracy, and even wrote a book eulogizing the most absurd of them, Cotton Mather.

Wendell, in fact, was two men, separate and distinct, and they were often at war. One of these men was highly intelligent (though surely not very learned); the other was a romantic under the spell of a disintegrating tradition. The latter was the more charming, but often a prey to mere lyrical fancy. The picture of the American character that Wendell presented to gaping throngs in his Sorbonne lectures was a sort of fantastic chromo of the primeval New England character, seen through nine thicknesses of amber gelatine—in brief, a thing as bizarre as the accounts of the Revolution that used to be in schoolbooks. Fundamentally, he once said somewhere else, we believe in fair play. It would be hard to imagine a more inaccurate saying. If any single quality, indeed, has marked off the Americano from all other civilized men since the start, it is his incapacity to purge combat of passion, his strong disinclination to allow any merit whatever to the other fellow;—in brief, his bad sportsmanship. Our history is a history of minorities put down with clubs. Even the duel, during the few years it flourished in America, took on a ferocity unheard of elsewhere. Gentlemen, going out at daybreak, shot to kill. Aaron Burr was a thorough American; Hamilton was an Englishman. In other fields, Wendell indulged himself in similar sentimentalities. He reacted to the shock of the late war in the correct manner of a State Street banker. He succumbed to the Coolidge buncombe far back in 1920. Yet always the sharply intelligent Wendell hauled up and stayed the orthodox romantic. The tribute to him by Prof. Kuno Francke, quoted by Mr. Howe, is a tribute not only to a gentleman, but also to a man of sense. And even in the midst of his banal speculation whether Coolidge, after all, would not turn out to be a Yankee Lincoln, he saw clearly the "small, hatchet-faced, colorless man, with a tight-shut, thin-lipped mouth"—in other words, the third-rate, small-town attorney, stuffed with copy-book platitudes and quite without imagination. He saw, too, the truth about Wilson, and stated it blisteringly in a letter to his friend R. W. Curtis.

Wendell's actual books, I believe, are now all dead, even his arbitrary and ignorant but highly amusing "Literary History of America." His volume on Shakespeare, published in 1894, is admired by Sir Arthur Quiller-Couch and Mrs. Edith Wharton, but no one else seems to remember it. His novels and dramas are long forgotten. His "English Composition" was and is a school-book; he himself, in his old age, had doubts that it had accomplished even its pedagogic purpose. His political essays, once so salacious, now read like the heresies of the Jefferson era. What remains, then, of Prof. Barrett Wendell. A.B., Litt.D.? A great deal more, I believe, than a mere ghost. When, indeed, the roll of American literati is drawn up at last, and the high deeds of each are set down, it will be found that Wendell, too, did something, and that what he did was of considerable importance. In a few words, he helped to divert criticism from books to life itself—he was one of the first to see that mere literature is, after all, mere literature—that it cannot be understood without knowing something about the society which produced it. Even Poe, masterly critic that he was, overlooked this obvious and all-important fact. His discussion of books went on in a sort of vacuum. He had brilliant (and often sound) opinions about every technical problem imaginable, and about every question of taste, but only too often he overlooked the fact that his author was also a man, and that what the author wrote the man had first to think, feel and endure. Wendell got rid of that narrow bookishness, still lingering in Lowell. He was primarily a critic, not of literary manners and postures, but of human existence under the Republic. There was no scholarly affectation about him, for all his superficial playacting, his delight in impressing sophomores. He did not bury his nose in books; he went out and looked at the world, and what he saw there amused him immensely and filled him with ideas. In Mr. Howe's index the name of Longfellow appears but once, and that of Gilder but once, and that of Aldrich not at all, but that of Blaine is there six times, and after Democracy there are twenty-two entries.

It seems to me that this break with the old American tradition had its high uses, and has left its mark upon American letters. Criticism among us is vastly less cloistered than it once was. Even professors of the loftiest tone, if they would have themselves attended to, must descend from their ivory towers and show themselves at the sea-level. The aloof and austere spirit is now viewed with suspicion. There are, I daresay, ancients who deplore the change. A natural regret, for it has made criticism vastly more difficult. But few deplore it, I believe, who know what literature really is—few, that is, who know the difference between mere intellectual prettiness and a body of living ideas.

As for Wendell's amazing contradictions and inconsistencies, his endless flounderings between orthodoxy and heresy, I believe that an adequate explanation of them is to be found in the compositions of Prof. Dr. Sigmund Freud, the Viennese necromancer. Freud, himself a Jew, discusses in one of his books the curious fact that jokes at the expense of the Jews are chiefly circulated by Jews themselves, and especially by the younger ones. Two Jewish drummers in a Pullman smoking-room fall into an exchange of such jocosities almost automatically. Why? Because, says Freud, they attain thereby to an escape from their Jewishness, which often irks them. It is not that they are ashamed of being Jews; it is that the Jewish practices of their elders are burdensome. They dare not revolt openly, for their sense of filial piety is strong, so they take it out by making jokes. By much the same psychological process, I believe, Wendell arrived at his curious mixture of contrarieties. Sentimentally and emotionally, he was moved powerfully by the New England tradition, and felt a strong impulse to defend it against the world. Intellectually, he saw clearly that it was in collapse around him—worse, that it had been full of defects and weaknesses even when, by his own doctrine, it had been strong. The result was his endless shuttling between worship and ribaldry. The last of the New Englanders, he clung pathetically to a faith which gradually succumbed to doubts. In his later years he thus stood upon a burning deck, whence all but him had fled.

Two things, for all his skepticism, he could never bring himself to admit formally, both obvious: first, that the so-called culture of Puritan New England was largely imaginary, that civilization was actually introduced into the region by anti-Puritans, and second, that when Transcendentalism came in, the leadership of Puritanism passed from New England and went to the South and Middle West. To admit the truth of either proposition was psychically impossible to a man of his romantic feelings. Each, baldly stated, seemed to flout the local Holy Ghost. And yet both were true, and their proofs were visible at a glance. The first, I daresay, will never be granted formally, or even heard patiently, by any genuine New Englander. Only a short while ago Walter Prichard Eaton, a very able Puritan, was arguing eloquently that his blue-nosed ancestors were really lovers of beauty, nay, downright artists—and offering the charming old houses on Nantucket Island as exhibits. Unfortunate examples, alas, alas! The houses on Nantucket were not built until the Puritan theocracy was completely demoralized and impotent—until Boston had a theatre, and was already two-thirds of the way to hell. And if they were actually built by Puritans at all, then it was by Puritans who had gone out into the wide, wide world and savored its dreadful and voluptuous marvels—Puritans who had come back from the Eastern seas with gaudy silks in their sea-chests, and the perfume of strange gals upon their whiskers, and a new glitter to their eyes.

Orthodox history, at least as it appears in school-books, assumes that the witch-burners and infant-damners had it all their own way in New England, even down to Revolutionary times. They actually met with sturdy opposition from the start. All of their sea-ports gradually filled up with sailors who were anything but pious Christian men, and even the back-country had its heretics, as the incessant wars upon them demonstrate. The fact that only Puritans could vote in the towns has deceived the historians; they mistake what was the law for what was really said and done. We have had proofs in our own time that that error is easy. Made by students of early New England, it leads to multiple absurdities. The fact is that the civilization that grew up in the region, such as it was, owed very little to the actual Puritans; it was mainly the product of anti-Puritans, either home-bred or imported. Even the school system, so celebrated in legend, owed whatever value was in it to what were currently regarded as criminals. The Puritans did not found their schools for the purpose of propagating what is now known as learning; they found them simply as nurseries of orthodoxy. Beyond the barest rudiments nothing of any worldly value was taught in them. The principal subject of study, first and last, was theology, and it was theology of the most grotesque and insane sort ever cherished by man. Genuine education began in New England only when the rising minority of anti-Puritans, eventually to become a majority, rose against this theology, and tried to put it down. The revolt was first felt at Harvard; it gradually converted a seminary for the training of Puritan pastors into a genuine educational institution. Harvard delivered New England, and made civilization possible there. All the men who adorned that civilization in the days of its glory—Emerson, Hawthorne and all the rest of them—were essentially anti-Puritans.

To-day, save in its remoter villages, New England is no more Puritan than, say, Maryland or Missouri. There is scarcely a clergyman in the entire region who, if the Mathers could come back to life, would not be condemned by them instantly as a heretic, and even as an atheist. The dominant theology is mild, skeptical and wholly lacking in passion. The evangelical spirit has completely disappeared. Save in a small minority of atavistic fanatics, there is a tolerance that is almost indistinguishable from indifference. Roman Catholicism and Christian Science are alike viewed amiably. The old heat is gone. Where it lingers in America is in far places—on the Methodist prairies of the Middle West, in the Baptist back-waters of the South. There, I believe, it still retains not a little of its old vitality. There Puritanism survives, not merely as a system of theology, but also as a way of life. It colors every human activity. Kiwanis mouths it; it is powerful in politics; learning wears its tinge. To charge a Harvard professor of to-day with agnosticism would sound as banal as to charge him with playing the violoncello. But his colleague of Kansas, facing the same accusation, would go damp upon the forehead, and his colleague of Texas would leave town between days.

Wendell, a sentimentalist, tried to put these facts behind him, though he must have been well aware of them. There got into his work, in consequence, a sense of futility, even when he was discussing very real and important things. He opened paths that he was unable to traverse himself. Sturdier men, following him, were soon marching far ahead of him. He will live in the history of American criticism, but his own criticism is already dead.

XIII.
The Nation

ONE often hears lamentation that the American weeklies of opinion are not as good as their English prototypes—that we have never produced anything in that line to equal, say, the *Athenæum* or the *Saturday Review*. In the notion, it seems to me, there is nothing save that melancholy colonialism which is one of the curses of America. The plain fact is that our weeklies, taking one with another, are quite as well turned out as anything that England has ever seen, and that at least two of them, the *Nation* and the *New Republic*, are a great deal better. They are better because they are more hospitable to ideas, because they are served by a wider and more various range of writers, and because they show an occasional sense of humor. Even the *New Republic* knows how to be waggish, though it also knows, especially when it is discussing religion, how to be cruelly dull. Its Washington correspondence is better than any Parliamentary stuff in any English weekly ever heard of, if only because it is completely devoid of amateur statesmanship, the traditional defect of political correspondence at all times and everywhere. The editors of the English weeklies all ride political hobbies, and many of them are actively engaged in politics. Their American colleagues, I suspect, have been tempted in that direction more than once, but happily they have resisted, or maybe fate has resisted for them.

Of all the weeklies—and I go through at least twenty each week, American and English, including the Catholic *Commonweal* and a Negro journal—I like the *Nation* best. There is something charming about its format, and it never fails to print an interesting piece of news, missed by the daily newspapers. Moreover, there is always a burst of fury in it, and somewhere or other, often hidden in a letter from a subscriber, a flash of wit—two things that make for amusing reading. The *New Republic*, I suspect, is more authoritative in certain fields, —for example, the economic—but it is also more pontifical. The *Nation* gets the air of a lark into many of its most violent crusades against fraud and folly; one somehow gathers the notion that its editors really do not expect the millennium to come in to-morrow. Of late they have shown many signs of forsaking Liberalism for Libertarianism—a far sounder and more satisfying politics. A liberal is committed to sure cures that always turn out to be swindles; a Libertarian throws the bottles out of the window, and asks only that the patient be let alone.

What the circulation of the *Nation* may be I don't know. In its sixtieth anniversary number, published in 1925, there was a hint that the number then sold each week ran far ahead of the 11,000 with which E. L. Godkin began in 1865. I have heard gabble in the saloons frequented by New York publishers that the present circulation is above 30,000. But no one, so far as I know, has ever suggested that it equals the circulation of even a third-rate daily paper. Such dull, preposterous sheets as the New York *Telegram*, the Washington *Star*, the Philadelphia *Public Ledger* and the Atlanta *Constitution* sell two or three times as many copies. Such magazines for the herd as *True Stories* and *Hot Dog* sell fifty times as many. Nevertheless, if I were a fellow of public spirit and eager to poison the Republic with my sagacity, I'd rather be editor of the *Nation* than editor of any of the other journals that I have mentioned—nay, I'd rather be editor of the *Nation* than editor of all of them together, with every other newspaper and magazine in America, save perhaps four or five, thrown in. For the *Nation* is unique in American journalism for one thing: it is read by its enemies. They may damn it, they may have it barred from libraries, they may even—as they did during the war—try to have it put down by the Postoffice, but all the while they read it. That is, the more intelligent of them—the least hopeless minority of them. It is to such minorities that the *Nation* addresses itself, on both sides of the fence. It has penetrated to the capital fact that they alone count—that the ideas sneaked into them to-day will begin to sweat out of the herd day after to-morrow.

Is the Creel Press Bureau theory of the late war abandoned? Is it impossible to find an educated man who is not ashamed that he succumbed to the Wilson buncombe? Then thank the *Nation* for that deliverance, for when it tackled Wilson it tackled him alone. Is the Coolidge Golden Age beginning to be sicklied o'er with a pale cast of green? Then prepare to thank the *Nation* again, for it began to tell the harsh, cold truth about good Cal at a time when all the daily journals of America, with not ten exceptions, were competing for the honor of shining his shoes. I often wonder, indeed, that the great success of the *Nation* under Villard has made such little impression upon American journalists—that they are so dead to the lessons that it roars into their ears. They all read it—that is, all who read anything at all. It prints news every week that they can't find in their own papers—sometimes news of the very first importance. It comments upon that news in a tart and well-informed fashion. It presents all the new ideas that rage in the world, always promptly and often pungently. To an editorial writer the *Nation* is indispensable. Either he reads it, or he is an idiot. Yet its example is very seldom followed—that is, forthrightly and heartily. Editorial writers all over the land steal ideas from it daily; it supplies, indeed, all the ideas that most of them ever have. It lifts them an inch, two inches, three inches, above the sedimentary stratum of Rotarians, bankers and ice-wagon drivers; they are conscious of its pull even when they resist. Yet very few of them seem to make the inevitable deduction that the kind of journalism it practices is better and more effective than the common kind—that they, too, might amount to something in this world if they would imitate it.

In such matters, alas, change is very slow. The whole press of the United States, I believe, is moving in the direction of the *Nation*—that is, in the direction of independence and honesty. Even such papers as the New York *Herald-Tribune* are measurably less stupid and intransigeant than they used to be, in their news if not in their opinions. But the majority of active journalists in the higher ranks were bred on the old-time party organs, and it is very difficult for them to reform their ways. They still think, not as free men, but as party hacks. On the one side they put the truth; on the other side they put what they call policy. Thus there are thousands of them who still sit down nightly to praise Coolidge—though to the best of my knowledge and belief there is not a single journalist in the whole United States who ever speaks of Coolidge in private without sneering at him. This resistance to change grows all the more curious when one observes what happens to the occasional paper which abandons it. I offer the Baltimore *Sunpaper* as an example—an especially apposite one, for the influence of the *Nation* upon it must be apparent to everyone familiar with its recent history. It was, a dozen years ago, a respectable but immensely dull journal. It presented the day's news in a formal, unintelligent fashion. It was accurate in small things, and free from sensationalism, but it seldom if ever went beyond the overt event to the causes and motives behind it. Its editorial opinions were flabby, and without influence. To-day it is certainly something far different. It must still go a long, long way, I suspect, before it escapes its old self altogether, but that must be a dull reader, indeed, who cannot see how vastly it has improved. It no longer prints the news formally; it devotes immense energy to discovering and revealing what is behind the news. In opinion it has thrown off all chains of faction and party, and is sharply and often intelligently independent. Its reaction to a new public problem is not that of a party hack, but that of a free man. It is, perhaps, sometimes grossly wrong, but no sane person believes that it is ever deliberately disingenuous.

Well, the point is that this new scheme has been tremendously successful—that it has paid in hard cash as well as in the usufructs of the spirit. There is no sign that the readers of the *Sunpaper*—barring a few quacks with something to sell—dislike its new vigor, enterprise and independence. On the contrary, there is every evidence that they like it. They have increased greatly in numbers. The paper itself rises in dignity and influence. And every other newspaper in America that ventures upon the same innovations, from the *World* in New York to the *Enquirer-Sun* down in Columbus, Ga., rises in the same way. It is my contention that the *Nation* has led the way in this reform of American journalism—that it will be followed by many papers to-morrow, as it is followed by a few to-day. Its politics are sometimes outrageous. It frequently gets into lamentable snarls, battling for liberty with one hand and more laws with the other. It is doctrinaire, inconsistent, bellicose. It whoops for men one day, and damns them as frauds the next. It has no sense of decorum. It is sometimes a bit rowdy. But who will deny that it is honest? And who will deny that, taking one day with another, it is generally right—that its enthusiasms, if they occasionally send it mooning after dreamers, at least never send it cheering for rogues—that its wrongness, when it is wrong, is at all events not the dull, simian wrongness of mere stupidity? It is disliked inordinately, but not, I believe, by honest men, even among its enemies. It is disliked by demagogues and exploiters, by frauds great and small. They have all tasted its snickersnee, and they have all good reason to dislike it.

Personally, I do not subscribe to its politics, save when it advocates liberty openly and unashamed. I have no belief in politicians: the good ones and the bad ones seem to me to be unanimously thieves. Thus I hope I may whoop for it with some grace, despite the fact that my name appears on its flagstaff. How my name got there I don't know; I receive no emolument from its coffers, and write for it very seldom, and then only in contravention of its ideas. I even have to pay cash for my annual subscription—a strange and painful burden for a journalist to bear. But I know of no other expenditure (that is, of a secular character) that I make with more satisfaction, or that brings me a better return. Most of the papers that I am doomed to read are idiotic even when they are right. The *Nation* is intelligent and instructive even when it is wrong.

XIV.

Officers and Gentlemen

HARD luck pursues the American Navy. It is the common butt, not only of political mountebanks, but also of all the brummagem uplifters and soul-snatchers who now sweat to save us. If a Mr. Secretary Denby is not permitting the Falls and Dohenys to raid its goods, a Mr. Secretary Wilbur or Josephus Daniels is trying to convert it into a Methodist Sunday-school. Worse, the Navy gets more than its fair share of the national dirty work. It is told off to put down free speech in the Virgin Islands, and it is delegated to flog, hang and butcher the poor Haitians, and so convert them into black Iowans, with money in the bank. Elsewhere in the world such disagreeable jobs are given to the Army. The British Army, for example, performs all the massacres that are necessary in India, and the French Army attends to whatever routine murders and mayhems are called for in Syria and Morocco. But the American custom puts all such Christian endeavor upon the Navy.

However, unless my agents lie, it is not the gore that revolts the more high-toned naval officers, but the new rectitude that has been thrust upon them. They are, as a class, excellent fellows, and full of pride in their uniform. As officers, they are all theoretically gentlemen, and many of them are so in fact. They have traveled widely, and are familiar with the usages of the civilized world. They know what is decent and seemly. Well, try to imagine how they must feel when they read the daily papers. One day they read that the Secretary of the Navy has ordered a group of their colleagues to prosecute a woman nurse for bringing in a couple of jugs aboard a naval collier. The next day they observe that a high officer in the Marines has filled the newspapers with a meticulous and indignant account of what went on at a table where he was a guest, in the house of one of his subordinates. Explanations of this last episode have been offered, but they certainly do not explain it away. The essential and immovable point is that one officer snitched on another, his host—that the immemorial and invariable obligations of a guest were sacrificed to Law Enforcement. What would happen to an English naval officer who made any such assault upon the code? What, indeed would happen to an honest Elk?

But I am not arguing here that any such things ought to happen; I am merely calling attention to the fact that, under democracy, it is becoming increasingly difficult for officers to be gentlemen, as the term is commonly understood in the world, and perhaps also increasingly improbable. We are, it would appear, passing through a time of changing values, and what was considered decent by our fathers will lose that quality to-morrow. The lower orders of men, having attained to political power, now proceed to force their ideas upon their betters, and some of those ideas naturally have to do with decorum. It is already unlawful in America to take a bottle of wine to a sick friend; in a few years it may also be indelicate. And simultaneously, it may become quite proper to go to the police with anything that is said or done in a friend's house. Personally, I am inclined to oppose such changes, if only in sheer hunkerousness, but I am surely under no illusion that opposing them will stop them. They flow naturally out of the character of the common man, now in the saddle, and are thus irresistible. He is extremely and even excessively moral, but the concept of what is called honor is beyond him. If, for example, he aspires to public office, he believes that it is entirely proper to abandon one conviction and take on its opposite in order to get votes. And, having got into office, he believes that it is entirely proper to hold on at any cost, even at the cost of common decency.

There is a familiar example. I allude to the Cathcart case. In that case a high officer of State found himself confronting an uncomfortable dilemma. On the one hand he was bound by an outrageous law to engage in a public and obscene chase of a woman taken in adultery. On the other hand he was bound by the code of all civilized men to refuse and refrain. What was the way out for him? The way out, obviously, was for him to resign his office—in other words, to decline flatly to perform any such ignoble and disgusting duty, and to spurn as insults the honors and emoluments offered for doing it. But, as far as I can make out, he never so much as thought of that. Instead he played the bounder—and kept his dirty job. His conduct, I believe, seemed quite proper to the overwhelming majority of his countrymen. The newspapers, in discussing it, never once suggested that a man of honor, in his boots, would resign forthwith. Instead, they simply denounced him for doing his plain duty under the law—that is, they proposed that he get out of his dilemma by violating his oath of office. The device is characteristically American. Anything is fair and decent that keeps a man his job. That has been the settled American doctrine since Jackson's time.

But it is only of late, I believe, that it has been defended openly, and its antithesis denounced as, in some mysterious fashion, inimical to democracy. We owe that change to the liberation of the lower orders which began with the Civil War. That liberation produced, on one side, an immense increase in political corruption, and, on the other, a rise in moral frenzy. All the characteristic ideas of the mob began to be reflected in public life and legislation. The typical American public officer, who had been a theorist willing to sacrifice anything, including his office, to his notions, became a realist willing to sacrifice anything, including his principles and his honor, to his job. We have him with us to-day, and he smells worse and worse as year chases year. Grover Cleveland was perhaps the last lonely survivor of the old days. He had his faults, God knows, but no one could have imagined him yielding to the mob in order to make votes. Right or wrong, he was his own man—and never more surely than when, by popular standards, he was wrong. In his successor, Dr. Coolidge, we have an almost perfect specimen of the new order. Coolidge is a professional trimmer, who has made his living at the art since his early manhood. It is impossible to imagine him sacrificing his political welfare to his convictions. He has vanity, but nothing properly describable as dignity or self-respect. One automatically pictures him doing, in the Cathcart case, precisely what his subordinate did. He performed many comparable acts during the stinking progress of the Fall case.

This general decay of honor is bound, plainly enough, to drive all the decenter sort of men out of public life among us. The process, indeed, has already gone a long way. I point to Congress. I point to the Federal judiciary. In both directions one observes an increase in trimmers and knee-benders and a decrease in independent and self-respecting men. The bench, in particular, has suffered. The better sort of judges, torn between their lawyer-like respect for all law and their inescapable conviction that many of the new laws they are called upon to enforce are unjust and dishonest, tend to throw off the ermine and go back to practice. And their places are filled by limber nonentities selected—and policed—by the Anti-Saloon League.

Until a few years ago the Army and the Navy escaped this general degradation. Their officers stood apart from the main body of public job-holders. They held office for life, and they were assumed to be innocent of politics. Having no need to curry favor with the mob, they could afford to disdain the common hypocrisies. Inheriting an austere and exact tradition of professional honor, they were what is called gentlemen. They did not blab upon one another. They had the fine tolerance of civilized men. They had dignity. It was as impossible to imagine a naval officer or an army officer playing the spy for the Anti-Saloon League as it was to imagine him using a table-napkin as a handkerchief or getting converted at a Methodist revival. But I fear those days are past. The pressure from outside, exerted through such mountebanks as Mr. Secretary Wilbur, becomes too heavy to be borne. Worse, there is disintegration within, due in part, perhaps, to the packing of the two Services with civilians from the gutter, but in part also to changes in the method of selecting candidates for Annapolis and West Point. Whatever the cause, the effects are already plain. In a few short years, perhaps, we shall see a major-general in the Army preaching Fundamentalism in Tennessee, and an admiral in the Navy going to work for the Anti-Saloon League.

XV.
Golden Age

THE rest of us, struggling onward painfully, must wait in patience for the boons and usufructs of Heaven; Judge Elbert Henry Gary, LL.D., chairman of the United States Steel Corporation, has them here and now. To few men in history, I believe, has it been given to live in a universe so nearly to their hearts' desire. Let the learned ex-jurist look East or West, he will find only scenes to content him. Let him look North or South, and his eye will be caressed and frankincense will spray his gills. The emperor and pope of all the Babbitts, he sits at the center of a Babbitts' paradise. For him and his like there dawns a Golden Age, and its hero is good Cal.

I hope I do not exaggerate. No doubt Judge Gary, in the privacy of his chamber, sweats and fumes against imperfections invisible to the rest of us. He is a man of imagination, and has, I daresay, a bold and soaring fancy. He can imagine a Republic even kinder and more osculatory than this one—that is, to Babbitts. He can even, perhaps, imagine a President more ineffable than Cal. But here we shoot into mere human weaknesses —the voluptuous, Freudian day-dreams of one who, like all of us, has his aberrant, goatish moods. Dr. John Roach Straton, I suppose, can imagine improvements in the Holy Scriptures—here a paragraph excised *pro bonos mores*, there a comma inserted to make sense. I myself have dreamed of a malt liquor better than Pilsner Bürgerbräu. But I do not sign my name to such inordinate speculations, and neither does Dr. Straton. Judge Gary, too, holds his tongue. The rest of us, contemplating him, can only envy him. A vast nation of 110,000,000 human beings, all of them alike, seems to be organized to the one end of making him happy. Whatever he wants it to do, it does. Its laws are framed to his precise taste; its public conscience approves his partisans and execrates his enemies; its high officers of state are his excellent friends, and humble and obedient servants. When he gives a feast, judges and ambassadors leap to grace it. When he would dine out, he is welcome at the White House. The newspapers fawn upon him. Labor licks his hand. His frown is dreaded in the Senate house and on the bench. Altogether, his life is happier than that of a Broadway actor, and if he is not content then it is only because contentment is physiologically impossible to *Homo sapiens.*

The United States, I believe, is the first great empire in the history of the world to ground its whole national philosophy upon business. There have been, of course, eminent trading nations in the past, but none ever went so far. Even in Carthage there was a *Junker* hierarchy that stood above the merchants; in Hannibal it actually had a Crown Prince. And even in England, the nation of shopkeepers of Napoleon's derision, there has always been an aristocracy (made up mainly of military freebooters, enterprising adulterers, the issue of the latter, and, in modern times, shyster lawyers, vaudeville magnates, and the proprietors of yellow newspapers) that has held its own against the men of trade, even at the cost of absorbing the more pugnacious of them. But here in this great Republic of the West the art of trafficking is king—and Judge Gary is its grand vizier, as Cal is its chief eunuch. No other human activity brings such great rewards in money and power, and none is more lavishly honored. The one aim of our jurisprudence is to safeguard business—to make its risks small and its profits sure. If the rights of the citizen get in the way, then the rights of the citizen must be sacrificed. Upon this point our higher courts have delivered themselves more than once, and in eloquent, ringing terms. Judge Gary and his friends prefer dry and dismal slaves to those who are stewed and happy. *Also*, to hell with the Bill of Rights! They prefer, when there is a strike, to win it rather than lose it. Out, then, with the pad of blank junctions! They sweat under criticism, and shiver under attack. To the hoosegow, constable, with the Bolsheviks!

All this, of course, was not achieved without a struggle. For years the Constitution stood in the way—the Constitution and certain national superstitions—the latter sprung from the blather of the Revolutionary stump. But all those impediments are now surmounted. The bench gave Judge Gary to business, and business has reciprocated the favor by providing sound and sane men for the bench. To-day jurisprudence is unfettered. When, a year or so ago, the Supreme Court finally got rid of the Fourth Amendment, that delayed mopping up went almost unnoticed. As I say, Judge Gary ought to be a happy man. The sun shines upon him from all four points of the compass. Congress, well rehearsed, plays soft jazz for him; bishops bring him his toddy; a straw issues from the White House and tickles him behind the ear. But never is his happiness greater, I believe, than when his thoughts turn idly upon the subject of labor, and he contemplates the state of the union movement in the Federal Union.

For this state, it is plain, he has the late Sam Gompers to thank—that great idealist and easy mark. If he sent less than ten hay-wagons of roses to Sam's funeral, then he is a niggard, indeed. For Sam got upon the back of the American labor movement when it was beginning to be dangerous, and rode it so magnificently that at the end of his life it was as tame as a tabby cat. It retains that character to-day, and will continue to do so as long as the Gompersian hierarchy lasts,—that is, so long as Judge Gary and his friends continue to appoint Sam's heirs and assigns to high-sounding committees, and to invite them to gaudy dinners. A plate of puddle duck and a chance to make a speech—that was always enough to fetch Sam. And when Sam was fetched, the 4,000,000 members of the American Federation of Labor were also fetched. Where else in the world is there a great union organization that has so long and honorable a record as a strike-breaker? Or that is so diligently devoted to keeping the lower ranks of labor in due subordination? If it had been conceived and hatched by Judge Gary himself, it could not have been more nearly perfect. Practically considered, it is not a labor organization at all; it is simply a balloon mattress interposed between capital and labor to protect the former from the latter. Gazing upon it, I daresay, Judge Gary feels a glow flickering along the periphery of his gizzard, and if he were not a Christian he would permit himself a guffaw.

I leave the sweetest to the last. The courts might be docile, Congress might be consecrated to right thought, labor might grovel and the bench of bishops might applaud, but if there were an anarchist in the White House it would all go for naught. Imagine, then, Judge Gary's joy in contemplating the incomparable Cal! It is almost as if, in New York, a bootlegger were made king. The man's merits, in the Babbitt view, are almost fabulous. He seems, indeed, scarcely like a man at all, but more like some miraculous visitation or act of God. He is the ideal made visible, if not audible—perfection put into a cutaway coat and trotted up and down like a mannequin in a cloak and suit atelier. Nor was there any long stress of training him—no season of doubt and misgiving. Nature heaved him forth full-blown, like a new star shot into the heavens. In him the philosophy of Babbitt comes to its perfect and transcendental form. Thrift, to him, is the queen of all the virtues. He respects money in each and every one of its beautiful forms—pennies, nickels, dimes, dollars, five-dollar bills, and so on *ad infinitum.* He venerates those who have it. He believes that they have wisdom. He craves the loan and use of that wisdom. He invites them to breakfast, and listens to them. The thing they revere, he reveres. The things they long for, he longs to give them.

Judge Gary is an old man—just how old I do not know, for he withholds the date of his birth from "Who's Who in America," along with the principal suffragettes. He remembers the dreadful days of Roosevelt, with bombs going off every two hours. He remembers the turmoils of the Taft administration. He remembers how *difficile* Woodrow was—how he had to be wooed, flattered, led by the nose, drenched with goose-grease. He remembers the crude carnival under the martyr Harding—Broadway sports, pug managers, small-town Elks at the trough. And then he thinks of Washington to-day, and sees it bathed in pink sunshine. There he is ever welcome. There he is *imperator in imperio.* There is good *Geschäft.* There is the Athens of the new Golden Age.

XVI.
Edgar Saltus

FORTY years ago Edgar Saltus was a shining star in the national literature, leading the way out of the Egyptian night of Victorian sentimentality. To-day he survives only as the favorite author of the late Warren Gamaliel Harding. I can recall, in the circle of Athene, no more complete collapse. Saltus plunged from the top of the world to the bottom of the sea. His books, of late, have been reissued, and his surviving third wife has printed a biography of him. But all his old following, save for a few romantic die-hards, has vanished.

The causes of the débâcle are certainly not hard to determine. They were set forth twenty-five years ago by that ingenious man, the late Percival Pollard, and you will find them in his book, "Their Day in Court." Saltus was simply a bright young fellow who succumbed to his own cleverness. The gaudy glittering phrase enchanted him. He found early in life that he had a hand for shaping it; he found soon afterward that it had a high capacity for getting him notice. So he devoted himself to its concoction—and presently he was lost. His life after that was simply one long intoxication. He was drunk on words. Ideas gradually departed from him. Day and night, for years and years, he held his nozzle against the jug of nouns, adjectives, verbs, pronouns, prepositions and interjections. Some of his phrases, of course, were good ones. There were enough of that kind in "Imperial Purple," for example, to fascinate the sainted Harding, a voluptuary in all the arts. But the rest quickly wore out—and with them Saltus himself wore out. He passed into the shadows, and was forgotten. When he died, a few years ago, all that remained of him was a vague name.

His wife's biography is encased in an orange slip-cover which announces melodramatically that it is "an extraordinary revealing life." It is, but I doubt that what it reveals will serve to recuscitate poor Saltus. The man who emerges from it is simply a silly and hollow trifler—a mass of puerile pretensions and affectations, vain of his unsound knowledge and full of sentimentalities. He began life by hawking the stale ribaldries of Arthur Schopenhauer, already dead twenty years; he departed to realms of bliss chattering the blowsy nonsense of theosophy. Mrs. Saltus, in the new and appalling fashion of literary wives, is extremely frank. Her Edgar was a handsome dog, but extremely foolish, and even childish. When he was engaged upon his rococo compositions he had to be protected like a queen bee in childbed. The slightest sound dissipated his inspiration, and set him to yelling. If a fish-peddler stopped beneath his window he was done for the day. If a cat came in and brushed his leg he was thrown into hysterics, and had to go to bed. His love affairs were highly complex, and apparently took up a great deal of his time. Early in life, while he was a student at Heidelberg, he had an affair with a lady of noble birth, and even ran away with her. The business was quickly broken up, apparently by the allied sovereigns of Europe. The bride-elect was immured in a convent, and died there "the year following." Saltus then came back to the Republic and married the daughter of a partner in J. P. Morgan & Company. "She was no small catch," but the alliance was doomed. The man was too fascinating to women. His pulchritude charmed them, and his epigrams finished them. In a few years Mrs. Saltus was suing for divorce.

There followed a series of morganatic affairs, culminating in a second marriage. This one also blew up quickly; the bride denounced Saltus as a liar, and even hinted that he had induced her to marry him by fraud. But though she soon left his bed and board, she clung resolutely to her other rights as his wife, and thereafter, for many long years, he devoted all the time he could spare from his writing to efforts to get rid of her. He moved from New York to California, in fact, mainly because the divorce laws on the Coast were easier than in the East. But they were not easy enough to free him. Finally, after endless waiting, he got news one day that the party of the second part was dead. He displayed the correct regrets, but was obviously much relieved. Meanwhile, Wife No. 3 was at call in the anteroom. She had been there, in fact, for years. When Saltus first met her she was a school-girl with her hair down her back, and his attentions to her—he was then rising forty—naturally outraged her family. But her own heart was lost, and so the effort to warn him off failed. He followed her, after that, all over the civilized world. Did she go to London, he was at her heels on the next steamer. Did she move to Los Angeles, he arrived by the next train. In the end they were married in Montreal, on a very hot day and after a pretty lovers' quarrel.

This lady is the author of the biography with the orange slip-cover. Facing page 310 there is a portrait of her showing her "sitting at the table on which her husband wrote his books, burning incense before a Siamese Buddha, and meditating on a stanza from the Bhagavad-Gita." She denies, however, that Saltus took to theosophy under her tutelage. The actual recruiting officer was certain Mr. Colville, of Pasadena, who combined the "enthusiasm of a scholar and the erudition of a sage." This Colville introduced Saltus to the theosophical elements, and later guided his faltering steps. In the end poor old Schopenhauer lost a customer and the art of epigram a gifted and diligent practitioner. Saltus passed into senility with his thoughts concentrated powerfully upon Higher Things.

A grotesque and somewhat pathetic story. The man began life with everything in his favor. His family was well-to-do and of good social position in New York; he was sent to Eton and then to Heidelberg, and apparently made useful friends at both places; he plunged into writing at the precise moment when revolt against the New England Brahmins was rising; he attracted attention quickly, and was given a lavish welcome. No American author of 1885 was more talked about. When his first novel, "The Truth About Tristrem Varick," came out in 1888 it made a genuine sensation. But the stick came down almost as fast as the rocket had gone up. His books set the nation agog for a short while, and were then quickly forgotten. He began as the hope of American letters, and ended as a writer of yellow-backs and a special correspondent for the Hearst papers. What ailed him was simply lack of solid substance. He could be clever, as cleverness was understood during the first Cleveland administration, but he lacked dignity, information, sense. His books of "philosophy" were feeble and superficial, his novels were only facile improvisations, full of satanic melodrama and wooden marionettes.

Of late I have been re-reading them—a sad job, surely, for when I was a schoolboy they were nine-day wonders, barred from all the libraries but devoured eagerly by every aspiring youth. Now their epigrams are dulled, and there is nothing else left. "The Anatomy of Negation" and "The Philosophy of Disenchantment" have been superseded by far better books; "The Truth About Tristrem Varick" reads like one of the shockers of Gertrude Atherton; "Mary Magdalen" is a dead shell; the essays and articles republished as "Uplands of Dream" are simply ninth-rate journalism. Of them all only "Imperial Purple" holds up. A certain fine glow is still in it; it has gusto if not profundity; Saltus's worst faults do not damage it appreciably. I find myself, indeed, agreeing thoroughly with the literary judgment of Dr. Harding. "Imperial Purple" remains Saltus's best book. It remains also, alas, his only good one!

XVII.
Miscellaneous Notes

1
Martyrs

To die for an idea: it is unquestionably noble. But how much nobler it would be if men died for ideas that were true! Searching history, I can find no such case. All the great martyrs of the books died for sheer nonsense—often for trivial matters of doctrine and ceremonial, too absurd to be stated in plain terms. But what of the countless thousands who have perished in the wars, fighting magnificently for their country? Well, show me one who knew precisely what the war he died in was about, and could put it into a simple and plausible proposition.

2
The Ancients

The theory that the ancient Greeks and Romans were men of a vast and ineffable superiority runs aground on the fact that they were great admirers of oratory. No other art was so assiduously practiced among them. To-day we venerate the architecture of Greece far more than we venerate its orators, but the Greeks themselves put the orators first, and so much better records of them are preserved to-day. But oratory, as a matter of fact, is the most primitive and hence the lowest of all the arts. Where is it most respected to-day? Among savages, in and out of civilization. The yokels of the open spaces flock by the thousand to hear imbeciles yawp and heave; the city proletariat glues its ears to the radio every night. But what genuinely civilized man would turn out to hear even the champion orator of the country? Dozens of the most eminent professors of the art show off their tricks every day in the United States Senate. Yet the galleries of the Senate, save when news goes out that some Senator is stewed and about to make an ass of himself, are occupied only by Negroes who have come in to get warm, and hand-holding bridal couples from rural North Carolina and West Virginia.

3
Jack Ketch as Eugenist

Has any historian ever noticed the salubrious effect, on the English character, of the frenzy for hanging that went on in England during the Eighteenth Century? When I say salubrious, of course, I mean in the purely social sense. At the end of the Seventeenth Century the Englishman was still one of the most turbulent and lawless of civilized men; at the beginning of the Nineteenth he was the most law-abiding; *i.e.*, the most docile. What worked the change in him? I believe that it was worked by the rope of Jack Ketch. During the Eighteenth Century the lawless strain was simply choked out of the race. Perhaps a third of those in whose veins it ran were actually hanged; the rest were chased out of the British Isles, never to return. Some fled to Ireland, and revivified the decaying Irish race: in practically all the Irish rebels of the past century there have been plain traces of English blood. Others went to the Dominions. Yet others came to the United States, and after helping to conquer the Western wilderness, begat the yeggman, Prohibition agents, footpads and hijackers of to-day.

The murder rate is very low in England, perhaps the lowest in the world. It is low because nearly all the potential ancestors of murderers were hanged or exiled in the Eighteenth Century. Why is it so high in the United States? Because most of the potential ancestors of murderers, in the late Eighteenth and early Nineteenth Centuries, were *not* hanged. And why did they escape? For two plain reasons. First, the existing government was too weak to track them down and execute them, especially in the West. Second, the qualities of daring and enterprise that went with their murderousness were so valuable that it was socially profitable to overlook their homicides. In other words, the job of occupying and organizing the vast domain of the new Republic was one that demanded the aid of men who, among other things, occasionally butchered their fellow men. The butchering had to be winked at in order to get their help. Thus the murder rate, on the frontier, rose to unprecedented heights, while the execution rate remained very low. Probably 100,000 men altogether were murdered in the territory west of the Ohio between 1776 and 1865; probably not 100 murderers were formally executed. When they were punished at all, it was by other murderers—and this left the strain unimpaired.

4
Heroes

Of human eminence there are obviously two varieties: that which issues out of the inner substance of the eminent individual and that which comes to him, either partially or wholly, from without. It is not difficult to recognize men at the two extremes. No sane person would argue seriously that the eminence of such a man, say, as Richard Wagner was, in any plausible sense, accidental or unearned. Wagner created "Tristan und Isolde" out of his own inherent substance. Allowing everything for the chances of his education and environment, the massive fact remains that no other man of the same general education and environment has ever created anything even remotely comparable to it. Wagner deserved the eminence that came to him quite as certainly as the Lord God Jehovah deserves that which attaches to Him. He got it by differing sharply from other men, and enormously for the better, and by laboring colossally and incessantly to make that difference visible. At the other extreme lies such a fellow, say, as young John D. Rockefeller. He is, by all ordinary standards, an eminent man. When he says anything the newspapers report it in full. If he fell ill of gallstones to-morrow, or eloped with a lady Ph.D., or fell off the roof of his house, or was taken in a rum raid the news would be telegraphed to all parts of the earth and at least a billion human beings would show some interest in it. And if he went to Washington and pulled the White House bell he would be let in infallibly, even if the Heir of Lincoln had to quit a saxophone lesson to see him. But it must be obvious that young John's eminence, such as it is, is almost purely fortuitous and unearned. He is attended to simply because he happens to be the son of old John, and hence heir to a large fortune. So far as the records show, he has never said anything in his life that was beyond the talents of a Rotary Club orator or a newspaper editorial writer, or done anything that would have strained an intelligent bookkeeper. He is, to all intents and purposes, a vacuum, and yet he is known to more people, and especially to more people of means, than Wagner, and admired and envied vastly more by all classes.

Between Wagner and young John there are infinite gradations, and sometimes it is a hard matter to distinguish between them. To most Americans, I daresay, a Harding or a Coolidge appears to enjoy an eminence that is not only more gaudy but also more solid than that of, say, an Einstein. When Einstein visited the United States, a few years ago, he was taken to see Harding as a sort of treat, and many worthy patriots, no doubt, regarded it as somewhat too rich for him, an enemy alien and a Jew. If Thomas Hardy came here to-morrow, his publisher would undoubtedly try to get an invitation to the White House for him, not merely to advertise his books but also to honor the man. Yet it must be plain that the eminence of Coolidge, however vastly it may be whooped up by gentlemen of enlightened self-interest, is actually greatly inferior to that of either Einstein or Hardy. These men owe whatever fame they have to actual accomplishments. There is no doubt whatever that what they have is wholly theirs. They owe nothing to anyone, and no conceivable series of accidents could have made them what they are. If superiority exists among men, then they are indubitably superior. But is there any sign of superiority in Coolidge? I can find none. His eminence is due entirely to two things: first, a series of accidents, and secondly, the possession of qualities that, in themselves, do not mark a superior man, but an inferior. He is a cheap, sordid and grasping politician, a seeker of jobs all his life, willing to do almost anything imaginable to get them. He has never said a word worth hearing, or done a thing requiring genius, or even ordinary skill. Put into his place and given the opportunities that have arisen before him in a long succession, any other ninth-rate lawyer in the land could have got as far as he has got.

Now for my point. It is, in brief, that the public estimation of eminence runs almost directly in inverse ratio to its genuineness. That is to say, the sort of eminence that the mob esteems most highly is precisely the sort that has least grounding in solid worth and honest accomplishment. And the reason therefor is not far to seek. The kind of eminence that it admires is simply the kind that it can understand—the kind that it can aspire to. The very puerility of a Coolidge, in fact, is one of the principal causes of the admiration he excites. What he has done in the world is within the capacities, given luck enough, of any John Smith. His merits, such as they are, are almost universal, and hence perfectly comprehensible. But what a Wagner or an Einstein does is wholly beyond the understanding of an ordinary ignoramus, and so it is impossible for the ignoramus to admire it. Worse, it tends to arouse his suspicion, and hence his animosity. He is not merely indifferent to the merits of a Wagner; he will, if any attempt is made to force them upon his attention, challenge them sharply. What he admires fundamentally, in other words, is himself, and in a Coolidge, a Harding, a baseball pitcher, a movie actor, an archbishop, or a bank president he can see himself. He can see himself, too, though perhaps more dimly, in a Dewey, a Pershing, a Rockefeller or a Jack Dempsey. But he can no more see himself in a Wagner or an Einstein than he can see himself on the throne of the Romanoffs, and so he suspects and dislikes such men, as he suspects and dislikes Romanoffs.

Unluckily, it is one thing to denounce his stupidity, and quite another thing to escape its consequences. The history of mankind is peopled chiefly, not with the genuinely great men of the race, but with the flashy and hollow fellows who appealed to the mob. Every American remembers vividly the contribution that Theodore Roosevelt made to the building of the Panama Canal—a contribution that might have been made by any other American thrown fortuitously into his place, assuming only that the substitute shared his normal American lack of a sense of honor. But who remembers the name of the man who actually designed the canal? I turn to the New International Encyclopedia and find nine whole pages about the canal, with many drawings. There is eloquent mention of Col. Goethals—who simply carried out the designer's plans. There is mention, too, of Col. Gorgas—whose sanitary work was a simple application of other men's ideas. There is ample space for Roosevelt, and his blackjacking of Colombia. But so far as I can find, the name of the designer is not there. The mob did not admire him, and so history has overlooked him.

5
An Historic Blunder

The Southern gentry made a thumping mistake when, after the Civil War, they disfranchised the blacks. Had they permitted the latter to vote, they would have retained political control of all the Southern States, for the blacks, like the peasants everywhere else, would have followed their natural masters. As it was, control quickly passed to the poor white trash, who still maintain it, though many of them have ceased to be poor. The gentry struggle in vain to get back in the saddle; they lack the votes to achieve the business unaided, and the blacks, who were ready to follow them in 1870, are now incurably suspicious of them. The result is that politics in the South remain fathomlessly swinish. Every civilized Southerner knows it and is ashamed of it, but the time has apparently passed to do anything about it. To get rid of its Bleases, Mayfields, Slemps, Peays and Vardamans, the South must wait until the white trash are themselves civilized. This is a matter demanding almost as much patience as the long vigil of the Seventh Day Adventists.

6
On Cynicism

One of the most curious of human delusions lies in the theory that cynics are unhappy men—that cynicism makes for a general biliousness and malaise. It is a false deduction, I believe, from the obvious fact that cynics make *other* men unhappy. But they are themselves among the most comfortable and serene of mammals; perhaps only bishops, pet dogs and actors are happier. For what a cynic believes, though it may be too dreadful to be put into formal words, at least usually has the merit of being true—and truth is ever a rock, hard and harsh, but solid under the feet. A cynic is chronically in the position of a wedding guest who has known the bride for nine years, and has had her confidence. He is a great deal less happy, theoretically, than the bridegroom. The bridegroom, beautifully barbered and arrayed, is about to launch into the honeymoon. But the cynic looks ahead two weeks, two months, two years. Such, to borrow a phrase fron the late Dr. Eliot, are the durable satisfactions of life.

7
Music and Sin

Among Christian workers and other intellectual cripples the delusion seems to persist that jazz is highly aphrodisiacal. I never encounter a sermon on the subject without finding it full of dark warnings to parents, urging them to keep their nubile daughters out of the jazz palaces on the ground that the voluptuous music will inflame their passions and so make them easy prey to bond salesmen, musicians and other such carnal fellows. All this seems to me to be nonsense. Jazz, in point of fact, is not voluptuous at all. Its monotonous rhythm and puerile tunes make it a sedative rather than a stimulant. If it is an aphrodisiac, then the sound of riveting is also an aphrodisiac. What fetches the flappers who come to grief in the jazz parlors is not the music at all, but the alcohol. Drinking it out of flasks in the washrooms, they fail to keep the dose in harmony with their natural resistance, and so they lose control of their faculties, and what follows is lamentable. Jazz, which came in with Prohibition, gets the blame that belongs to its partner. In the old days, when it was uncommon for refined women to get drunk at dances, it would have been quite harmless. To-day even Chopin's funeral march would be dangerous.

The truth is that jazz is probably the least voluptuous variety of music commonly heard in Christendom. There are plenty of Methodist hymns that are ten times as aphrodisiacal, and the fact is proved by the scandals that follow every camp-meeting. In most parts of the United States, indeed, the Methodists have begun to abandon camp-meetings as subversive of morality. Where they still flourish it is not unusual for even the rev. clergy to be taken in byzantine practices. But so-called good music is yet worse than the Methodist hymns. Has the world so soon forgotten James Huneker's story of the prudent opera mamma who refused to let her daughter sing Isolde, on the ground that no woman could ever get through the second act without forgetting God? That second act, even so, is much overestimated. There are piano pieces of Chopin that are a hundred times worse; if the Comstocks really had any sense, they would forbid their performance. And what of the late Puccini? If "La Bohème" is not an aphrodisiac, then what is it? Yet it is sung publicly all over the world. Only in Atlanta, Ga., is there a law against it, and even that law was probably inspired by the fact that it was written by a Catholic and not by the fact that it has brought hundreds of thousand of Christian women to the edge of the abyss.

Old Ludwig himself was not without guilt. His "Egmont" overture is a gross and undisguised appeal to the medulla oblongata. And what of his symphonies and quartettes? The last movement of his Eroica is not only voluptuous to the last degree; it is also Bolshevistic. Try to play it with your eyes on a portrait of Dr. Coolidge. You will find the thing as impossible as eating ice-cream on roast beef. At the time of its first performance in Vienna the moral sense of the community was so greatly outraged that Beethoven had to get out of town for a while. I pass over Wagner, whose "Tristan und Isolde" was probably his most decorous work, despite Huneker—think of "Parsifal"!—and come to Richard Strauss. Here I need offer no argument: his "Salomé" and "Elektra" have been prohibited by the police, at one time or another, in nearly every country in the world. I believe that "Der Rosenkavalier" is still worse, though the police leave it unmolested. Compare its first act to the most libidinous jazz ever heard of on Broadway. It is like comparing vodka to ginger-pop. No woman who hears it is ever the same again. She may remain within the law, but her thoughts are wayward henceforth. Into her ear the sirens have poured their abminable song. She has been beset by witches. There is a sinister glitter in her eye.

8
The Champion

Of the forty-eight sovereign States of this imperial Federation, which is the worst? In what one of them is a civilized man most uncomfortable? Over half the votes, if the question were put to a vote, would probably be divided between California and Tennessee. Each in its way, is almost unspeakable. Tennessee, of course, has never been civilized, save in a small area; even in the earliest days of the Republic it was regarded as barbaric by its neighbors. But California, at one time, promised to develop a charming and enlightened civilization. There was a touch of tropical balm in its air, and a touch of Latin and oriental color in its ideas. Like Louisiana, it seemed likely to resist Americanization for many years; perhaps forever. But new California, the old California, is simply extinct. What remains is an Alsatia of retired Ford agents and crazy fat women—a paradise of 100% Americanism and the New Thought. Its laws are the most extravagant and idiotic ever heard of Christendom. Its public officers, and particularly its judges, are famous all over the world for their imbecilities. When one hears of it at all, one hears that some citizen has been jailed for reading the Constitution of the United States, or that some new swami in a yellow bed-tick has got all the realtors' wives of Los Angeles by the ears. When one hears of it further, it is only to learn that some obscure movie lady in Hollywood has murdered another lover. The State is run by its Chambers of Commerce, which is to say, by the worst variety of resident shysters. No civilized man ever seems to take any part in its public life. Not an idea comes out of it—that is, not an idea beyond the grasp of a Kiwanis Club secretary, Christian Science sorcerer, or a grand goblin of the American Legion. Twice, of late, it has offered the country candidates for the presidency. One was the Hon. Hiram Johnson and the other was the Hon. William Gibbs McAdoo! Only Vermont can beat that record.

The minority of civilized Californians—who lately, by the way, sent out a call from Los Angeles for succor, as if they were beset by wolves!—commonly lay the blame for this degeneration of a once-proud commonwealth upon the horde of morons that has flowed in from Iowa, Nebraska and the other cow-States, seeking relief from the bitter climate of the steppes. The California realtors have been luring in these hinds for a generation past, and they now swarm in all the southern towns, especially Los Angeles. They come in with their savings, are swindled and sent home, and so make room for more. While they remain and have any part of their money left, they patronize the swamis, buy oil stock, gape at the movie folk, and pack the Methodist churches. Unquestionably, the influence of such vacuums has tended to degrade the general tone of California life; what was once a Spanish *fiesta* is now merely an upper Mississippi valley street-carnival. But it is not to be forgotten that the Native Sons have gone down the chute with the newcomers—that there is no more sign of intellectual vigor in the old stock than there is in the new stock. A few intransigeants hold out against the tide of 100% Americanism, but only a few. The rest bawl against the Reds as loudly as any Iowa steer-stuffer.

The truth is that it is unjust to blame Iowa for the decay of California, for Iowa itself is now moving up, not down. And so is Nebraska. A few years ago both States were as sterile, intellectually, as Spain, but both are showing signs of progress to-day, and in another generation or two, as the Prohibition lunacy passes and the pall of Methodism begins to lift, they will probably burst into very vigorous activity. Some excellent stock is in them; it is very little contaminated by what is called Anglo-Saxon blood. Iowa, even to-day, is decidedly more civilized than California. It is producing more ideas, and, more important still, it is carrying on a much less violent war *against* ideas. I doubt that any man who read the Constitution in Davenport or Des Moines would be jailed for it, as Upton Sinclair (or one of his friends) was in Pasadena. The American Legion would undoubtedly protest, but the police would probably do nothing, for the learned judges of the State would not entertain the charge.

Thus California remains something of a mystery. The whole United States, of course, has been going down hill since the beginning of the century, but why should one State go so much faster than the others? Is the climate to blame? Hardly. The climate of San Francisco is thoroughly un-Californian, and yet San Francisco is almost as dead as Los Angeles. It was there, indeed, that that California masterpiece, the Mooney case, was staged; it was here that the cops made three efforts to convict poor Fatty Arbuckle of murder in the first-degree; it was there that the late Dr. Abrams launched a quackery that went Mother Eddy one better. San Francisco, once the home of Mark Twain and Bret Harte, is now ravaged by Prohibition enforcement officers. But if the climate is not to blame, then what is? Why should a great State, lovely physically and of romantic history, so violently renounce all sense and decency? What has got into it? God alone knows!

9
Honor in America

Some time ago I enjoyed the distinguished honor of entertaining an American university professor in my house. The fellow had a resilient gullet, and in the course of the evening we got down a quart of Scotch. Made expansive by the liquor, he told me this story:

A short while before, at his university, one of the professors gave a booze party for a group of colleagues, including the president of the institution. It was warm weather, and they sat on the veranda, guzzling moonshine and ginger-ale. There was so much chatter that they didn't hear a student coming up the path. Suddenly he was on them, and they almost fainted. . . .

At this point I asked why they were alarmed.

"Well," said my visitor, "suppose the student had turned out to be a Christian? He would have babbled, and then our host would have lost his chair. The president would have been forced to cashier him."

"But the president," I argued, "was a guest in the man's house. How could he have dismissed him?"

"What else would there have been for him to do?" asked the professor.

"Resign at once," I replied. "Wasn't he under the obligations of a guest? Wasn't he *particeps criminis*? How could he separate himself from his host? How could he sit as judge upon his host, even if only formally?"

But the professor couldn't see the point. I began to fear that he was in his cups, but it soon appeared that he was quite clear. We argued for half an hour: he was still unable to see the point.

The duty of a president to enforce an unwilling and dishonest obedience to an absurd law—this duty was superior to his duty as a guest, *i.e.*, it was superior to his obligation as a man of honor! We passed on to another point.

"What of the student?" I asked. "I take it that he turned out to be a gentleman. Suppose he had been a Christian? Suppose he had blabbed? What would the other boys have done to him?"

The professor stared at me blankly.

"Nothing," he said at length. "After all, we *were* boozing."

This professor, I should add, was a man of the old American stock—in fact, a fellow very proud of his colonial ancestry. When he got back to his university he joined in signing a public statement that Prohibition was a great success there.

I proceed to another case. One day in the Summer of 1924, during the Republican National Convention at Cleveland, I met an eminent American publicist in a hotel lobby there. He told me at once that he was suffering from a dreadful bellyache. I had a jug in my room, but my own hotel was far away, so I suggested that help might be got from a journalist on the premises. We went to his room, and I introduced the publicist. The journalist promptly got out a bottle and gave him a policeman's drink. The publicist had recovered in three minutes. . . . When he got home, he joined, like the professor, in signing a public statement praising Prohibition.

10

Note in the Margin of a Treatise on Psychology

As I stoop to lace my shoe you hit me over the coccyx with a length of hickory (*Carya laciniosa*). I conclude instantly that you are a jackass. This is the whole process of human thought in little. This also is free will.

11

Definition

Democracy is that system of government under which the people, having 35,717,342 native-born adult whites to choose from, including thousands who are handsome and many who are wise, pick out a Coolidge to be head of the State. It is as if a hungry man, set before a banquet prepared by master cooks and covering a table an acre in area, should turn his back upon the feast and stay his stomach by catching and eating flies.

XVIII.
Catechism

Q. If you find so much that is unworthy of reverence in the United States, then why do you live here?

A. Why do men go to zoos?

PREJUDICES
SIXTH SERIES

I.
Journalism in America

I

ONE of the agreeable spiritual phenomena of the great age in which we live is the soul-searching now going on among American journalists. Fifteen years ago, or even ten years ago, there was scarcely a sign of it. The working newspaper men of the Republic, of whom I have had the honor to be one since the last century, were then almost as complacent as so many Federal judges, movie magnates, or major-generals in the army. When they discussed their puissant craft at all, it was only to smack their chests proudly, boasting of their vast power in public matters, of their adamantine resistance to all the less tempting varieties of bribes, and of the fact that a politician of enlightened self-interest, giving them important but inaccurate news confidently, could rely upon them to mangle it beyond recognition before publishing it. I describe a sort of Golden Age, and confess frankly that I can't do so without a certain yielding to emotion. Salaries had been going up since the dawn of the new century, and the journalist, however humble, was beginning to feel his oats. For the first time in history he was paid as well as the human cranes and steam-shovels slinging rolls of paper in the cellar. He began to own two hats, two suits of clothes, two pairs of shoes, two walking-sticks, even two belts. He ceased to feed horribly in one-arm lunch-rooms and began to dine in places with fumigated waitresses, some of a considerable pulchritude and amiability, and red-shaded table lamps. He was, as such things are reckoned, happy. But at the heart of his happiness, alas, there yet gnawed a canker-worm. One enemy remained in his world, unscotched and apparently unscotchable, to wit, the business manager. The business manager, at will, could send up a blue slip and order him fired. In the face of that menace from below-stairs his literary superiors were helpless, up to and including the editor-in-chief. All of them were under the hoof of the business manager, and all the business manager ever thought of was advertising. Let an advertiser complain that his honor had been impugned or his *clavi* abraded, and off went a head.

It was the great war for human freedom, I suspect and allege, that brought the journals deliverance from that last and most abominable hazard: he was, perhaps, one of the few real beneficiaries of all the carnage. As the struggle grew more savage on Flanders fields and business grew better and better at home, reporters of any capacity whatever got to be far too scarce to fire loosely. Moreover, the business manager, with copy pouring over his desk almost unsolicited, began to lose his old dread of advertisers, and then even some of his natural respect for them. It was a sellers' market, in journalism as in the pants business. Customers were no longer kissed; the lesser among them actually began to stand in line. The new spirit, so strange and so exhilarating, spread like a benign pestilence, and presently it began to invade even the editorial rooms. In almost every American city, large or small, some flabbergasted advertiser, his money in his hand, sweat pouring from him as if he had seen a ghost, was kicked out with spectacular ceremonies. All the principal papers, suddenly grown rich, began also to grow independent, virtuous, touchy, sniffish. No — — — — could dictate to them, God damn! So the old free reading notices of the Bon Marché and the Palais Royal disappeared, salaries continued to climb, and the liberated journalist, taking huge breaths of thrilling air, began to think of himself as a professional man.

Upon that cogitation he is still engaged, and all the weeklies that print the news of the craft are full of its fruits. He elects representatives and they meet in lugubrious conclave to draw up codes of ethics. He begins to read books dealing with professional questions of other sorts—even books not dealing with professional questions. He changes his old cynical view of schools of journalism, and is lured, now and then, into lecturing in them himself. He no longer thinks of his calling as a business, like the haberdasher's or tallow chandler's, or as a game, like the stockbroker's or faro-dealer's, but as a profession, like the jurisconsult's or gynecologist's. His purpose is to set it on its legs as such—to inject plausible theories into its practise, and rid it of its old casualness and opportunism. He no longer sees it as a craft to be mastered in four days, and abandoned at the first sign of a better job. He begins to talk darkly of the long apprenticeship necessary to master its technic, of the wide information and sagacity needed to adorn it, of the high rewards that it offers—or may offer later on—to the man of true talent and devotion. Once he thought of himself, whenever he thought at all, as what Beethoven called a free artist—a gay adventurer careening down charming highways of the world, the gutter ahead of him but ecstasy in his heart. Now he thinks of himself as a fellow of weight and responsibility, a beginning publicist and public man, sworn to the service of the born and unborn, heavy with duties to the Republic and to his profession.

In all this, I fear, there is some illusion, as there always is in human thinking. The journalist can no more see himself realistically than a bishop can see himself realistically. He gilds and engauds the picture, unconsciously and irresistibly. For one thing, and a most important one, he is probably somewhat in error about his professional status. He remains for all his dreams, a hired man—the owner downstairs, or even the business manager, though he doesn't do it very often now, is still free to demand his head—, and a hired man is not a professional man. The essence of a professional man is that he is answerable for his professional conduct only to his professional peers. A physician cannot be fired by any one, save when he has voluntarily converted himself into a job-holder; he is secure in his livelihood so long as he keeps his health, and can render service, or what they regard as service, to his patients. A lawyer is in the same boat. So is a dentist. So, even, is a horse-doctor. But a journalist still lingers in the twilight zone, along with the trained nurse, the embalmer, the rev. clergy and the great majority of engineers. He cannot sell his services directly to the consumer, but only to entrepreneurs, and so those entrepreneurs have the power of veto over all his soaring fancies. His codes of ethics are all right so long as they do not menace newspaper profits; the moment they do so the business manager, now quiescent, will begin to growl again. Nor has he the same freedom that the lawyers and the physicians have when it comes to fixing his own compensation; what he faces is not a client but a boss. Above all, he is unable, as yet, to control admission to his craft. It is constantly recruited, on its lowest levels, from men who have little professional training or none at all, and some of these men master its chief mysteries very quickly. Thus even the most competent journalist faces at all times a severe competition, easily expanded at need, and cannot afford to be too saucy. When a managing editor is fired there is always another one waiting to take his place, but there is seldom another place waiting for the managing editor.

All these things plainly diminish the autonomy of the journalist, and hamper his effort to lift his trade to professional rank and dignity. When he talks of codes of ethics, indeed, he only too often falls into mere tall talk, for he cannot enforce the rules he so solemnly draws up—that is, in the face of dissent from above. Nevertheless, his discussion of the subject is still not wholly absurd, for there remain plenty of rules that he *can* enforce, and I incline to think that there are more of them than of the other kind. Most of the evils that continue to beset American journalism to-day, in truth, are not due to the rascality of owners nor even to the Kiwanian bombast of business managers, but simply and solely to the stupidity, cowardice and Philistinism of working newspaper men. The majority of them, in almost every American city, are still ignoramuses, and proud of it. All the knowledge that they pack into their brains is, in every reasonable cultural sense, useless; it is the sort of knowledge that belongs, not to a professional man, but to a police captain, a railway mail-clerk, or a board-boy in a brokerage house. It is a mass of trivialities and puerilities; to recite it would be to make even a barber beg for mercy. What is missing from it, in brief, is everything worth knowing—everything that enters into the common knowledge of educated men. There are managing editors in the United States, and scores of them, who have never heard of Kant or Johannes Müller and never read the Constitution of the United States; there are city editors who do not know what a symphony is, or a streptococcus, or the Statute of Frauds; there are reporters by the thousand who could not pass the entrance examination for Harvard or Tuskegee, or even Yale. It is this vast and militant ignorance, this wide-spread and fathomless prejudice against intelligence, that makes American journalism so pathetically feeble and vulgar, and so generally disreputable. A man with so little intellectual enterprise that, dealing with news daily, he can go through life without taking in any news that is worth knowing—such a man, you may be sure, is lacking in professional dignity quite as much as he is lacking in curiosity. The delicate thing called honor can never be a function of stupidity. If it belongs to those men who are genuinely professional men, it belongs to them because they have lifted themselves to the plane of a true aristocracy, in learning as well as in liberty—because they have deliberately and successfully separated themselves from the great masses of men, to whom learning is an insult and liberty an agony. The journalists, in seeking to acquire that status, put the cart before the horse.

2

The facts that I here set forth are well known to every American newspaper man who rises above the ice-wagon driver level, and in those sad conferences which mark every gathering of the craft they do not go undiscussed. Even the American Society of Newspaper Editors, *i.e.*, of those journalists who have got into golf clubs and become minor Babbitts, has dealt with them at some of its annual pow-wows, albeit very gingerly and with many uneasy glances behind the door. But in general journalism suffers from a lack of alert and competent professional criticism; its slaves, afflicted by a natural inferiority complex, discountenance free speaking as a sort of treason; I have myself been damned as a public enemy for calling attention, ever and anon, to the intolerable incompetence and quackery of all save a small minority of the Washington correspondents. This struthion fear of the light is surely not to be noted in any of the actual professions. The medical men, in their trade journals, criticise one another frankly and sharply, and so do the lawyers in theirs: the latter, indeed, are not above taking occasional hacks at the very judges, their lawful fathers and patterns of grace. As for the clergy, every one knows that they devote a large part of their professional energy to refuting and damning their brethren, and that not a few of them do it on public stumps, with the laity invited. So, also, in the fine arts. It is impossible for an architect to affront humanity with a blotch without hearing from other architects, and it is impossible for a poet to print anything at all without tasting the clubs of other poets. Even dramatists, movie actors, chiropractors and politicians criticise one another, and so keep themselves on tiptoe. But not journalists. If a Heywood Broun is exasperated into telling the truth about the manhandling of a Snyder trial, or a Walter Lippmann exposes the imbecility of the Russian "news" in a New York *Times*, or an Oswald Garrison Villard turns his searchlight on a Boston *Herald* or a Washington *Star*, it is a rarity and an indecorum. The organs of the craft—and there are journals for journalists, just as there are doctors for doctors—are all filled with bilge borrowed from Rotary and Kiwanis. Reading them, one gathers the impression that every newspaper proprietor in the United States is a distinguished public figure, and every circulation manager a wizard. The editorial boys, it appears, never fall down on their jobs; they are not only geniuses, but also heroes. Some time ago, having read all such journals assiduously for years, I stopped my subscriptions to them. I found that I preferred the clip-sheet of the Methodist Board of Temperance, Prohibition and Public Morals.

But if there is thus little or no frank and open discussion of the evils that beset journalism in the Republic, there is a great deal of private discontent and soul-searching, and it shows itself in all the fantastic codes of ethics that issue from embattled professors of journalism in the great rolling-mills of learning, and from editorial associations in the cow States. In such codes, I am sorry to have to repeat, I take no stock. Most of them are the handiwork of journalists of no professional importance whatever, and, what is worse, of no apparent sense. They run the scale from metaphysical principia worthy of Rotary to sets of rules fit only for the government of a Y.M.C.A. lamasery or a State's prison. They concern themselves furiously with abuses which are not peculiar to journalism but run through the whole of American life, and they are delicately silent about abuses that are wholly journalistic, and could be remedied quickly and without the slightest difficulty. Their purpose, I believe, is largely rhetorical. They give a certain ease and comfort to the laboring patient without letting any of his blood. Nevertheless, I am glad to see them multiply, for though most of them may be hollow to-day, there is always a chance that some solid substance may get into them to-morrow. If they accomplish nothing else at the moment, they at least accustom the journalist to the notion that his craft needs an overhauling. His old romantic optimism oozes out of him. He is no longer quite happy. Out of his rising discomforts, I believe, there will issue eventually a more realistic attitude toward the problems that confront him, and on some bright day in the future he may address himself rationally to the hard business of solving them. Most of them, I believe, are clearly soluble. More, most of them can be solved by working newspaper men, without any help from experts in ethics. What they call for is not any transcendental gift for righteousness, but simply ordinary professional competence and common sense.

For example, the problem of false news. How does so much of it get into the American newspapers, even the good ones? Is it because journalists, as a class, are habitual liars, and prefer what is not true to what is true? I don't think it is. Rather, it is because journalists are, in the main, extremely stupid, sentimental and credulous fellows—because nothing is easier than to fool them—because the majority of them lack the sharp intelligence that the proper discharge of their duties demands. The New York *Times* did not print all its famous blather and balderdash about Russia because the Hon. Mr. Ochs desired to deceive his customers, or because his slaves were in the pay of Russian reactionaries, but simply and solely because his slaves, facing the elemental professional problem of distinguishing between true news and false, turned out to be incompetent. All around the borders of Russia sat propagandists hired to fool them. In many cases, I have no doubt, they detected that purpose, and foiled it; we only know what they printed, not what they threw into their wastebaskets. But in many other cases they succumbed easily, and even ridiculously, and the result was the vast mass of puerile rubbish that Mr. Lippmann later made a show of. In other words, the editors of the American newspaper most brilliantly distinguished above its fellows for its news-gathering enterprise turned out to be unequal to a job of news-gathering presenting special but surely not insuperable difficulties. It was not an ethical failure, but a purely technical failure. And so was the same eminent newspaper's idiotic misreporting of the news from China in the early part of 1927, and the grotesque paralysis of the whole American press in the face of the Miami hurricane in 1926.

Obviously, the way to diminish such failures in future is not to adopt sonorous platitudes borrowed from the realtors, the morticians, the sanitary plumbers and Kiwanis, but to undertake an overhauling of the faulty technic, and of the incompetent personnel responsible for it. This overhauling, of course, will take some intelligence, but I don't think it will make demands that are impossible. The bootlegging, legal or delicatessen professions, confronted by like demands, would quickly furnish the talent necessary to meet them; I see no reason why the profession of journalism should not measure up as well. What lies in the way of it is simply the profound, maudlin sentimentality of the average American journalist—his ingenuous and almost automatic belief in everything that comes to him in writing. One would think that his daily experience with the written word would make him suspicious of it; he himself, in fact, believes fondly that he is proof against it. But the truth is that he swallows it far more often than he rejects it, and that his most eager swallowing is done in the face of the plainest evidence of its falsity. Let it come in by telegraph, and his mouth flies open. Let it come in by telegraph *from a press association* and down it goes at once. I do not say, of course, that *all* press association news is thus swallowed by news editors. When the means are readily at hand, he often attempts to check it, and sometimes even rejects it. But when such checking presents difficulties—in other words, when deceit is especially easy, and hence should be guarded most vigilantly—he succumbs nine times out of ten, and without a struggle. It was precisely by this process that the editors of the *Times*, otherwise men of extraordinary professional alertness, were victimized by the Russian "news" that made that paper ridiculous. In the face of great improbabilities, they interpreted their inability to dispose of them as a license to accept them as truth. Journalism will be a sounder and more dignified profession when a directly contrary interpretation of the journalist's duty prevails. There will then be less news in the papers, but it will at least have the merit of being true.

Nor is the typical American journalist's credulity confined to such canards and roorbacks from far places. He is often victimized just as easily at home, despite his lofty belief that he is superior to the wiles of press agents. The plain fact is that most of the stuff he prints now emanates from press agents, and that his machinery for scrutinizing it is lamentably defective. True enough, the bold, gay liars employed by theatrical managers and opera singers no longer fool him as they used to; he has grown so suspicious of them that he often turns them out when they have real news. But what of the press agents of such organizations as the Red Cross, the Prohibition Unit, the Near-East Relief, the Chamber of Commerce of the United States, the Department of Justice, the Y.M.C.A., and the various bands of professional patriots? I do not say that the press agents of such bodies are always or necessarily liars; all I say is that, nine times out of ten, their statements are accepted as true by the newspapers without any attempt to determine accurately whether they are true or not. They may be simple statements of plain fact; they may, on the contrary, conceal highly dubious purposes, of organizations and individuals. In both cases they are set forth in the same way—solemnly and without comment. Who, ordinarily, would believe a Prohibition agent? Perhaps a Federal judge in his robes of office and full of seized evidence; I can think of no one else. Yet the American newspapers are filled every day with the dreadful boasts and threats of such frauds: it is set before the people, not as lies, but as news. What is the purpose of such rubbish? Its purpose, obviously, is to make it appear that the authors are actually enforcing Prohibition—in other words, to made them secure in their jobs. Every newspaper man in America knows that Prohibition is not being enforced—and yet it is rarely that an American newspaper comes out in these days without a gaudy story on its first page, rehearsing all the old lies under new and blacker headlines.

I do not argue here, of course, that only demonstrable facts are news. There are times and occasions when rumor is almost as important as the truth—when a newspaper's duty to its readers requires it to tell them not only what has happened, but also what is reported, what is threatened, what is merely said. What I contend is simply that such quasi-news, such half-baked and still dubious news, should be printed for exactly what it is—that it ought to be clearly differentiated from news that, by an overwhelming probability, is true. That differentiation is made easily and as a matter of course by most European newspapers of any dignity. When they print a dispatch from the Russian border they indicate its source, and not infrequently follow it with a cynical comment. If they had Prohibition agents on their hands, they would print the fulminations of those gentlemen in the same way—with plain warnings to stop, look and listen. In brief, they make every reasonable effort to make up for their own technical limitations as news-gatherers—they do the best they can, and say so frankly when it is not very good. I believe that American newspapers might imitate them profitably. If it were done, then the public's justifiable distrust of all newspapers, now rising, would tend to ebb. They would have to throw off their present affectation of omniscience, but they would gain a new repute for honesty and candor; they would begin to seem more reliable when they failed than they now seem when they succeed. The scheme I propose would cost nothing; on the contrary, it would probably save expense. It would throw no unbearable burden upon the journalistic mind; it would simply make it more cautious and alert. Best of it, it would increase the dignity of journalism without resort to flapdoodlish and unenforceable codes of ethics, by Mush out of Tosh.

3

In private communions, though seldom in public, the more conscientious and unhappy variety of journalists commonly blame the woes of the craft upon the entrance into newspaper ownership of such opulent vacuums as Cyrus H. K. Curtis and the late Frank A. Munsey. As a result of the application of chain-store methods to journalism by these amiable Vandals there are fewer papers than there used to be, and the individual journalist is less important. All the multitudinous Hearst papers are substantially identical, and so are all the Scripps-Howard papers, and all the Curtis papers, and so were the Munsey papers in the great days of that pathetic man. There is little room, on the papers of such chains, for the young man who aspires to shine. Two-thirds of their contents are produced in great factories, and what remains is chiefly a highly standardized bilge. In the early days of Hearst, when he had only a few widely-scattered papers, his staffs were manned by men of great professional enterprise and cunning, and some of them became celebrated in the craft, and even generally. But now a Hearst paper, however inflammatory, is no more than a single unit in a long row of filling-stations, and so it tends to attract only the duller and less picturesque sort of men. There is scarcely a Hearst managing editor to-day who amounts to anything professionally, or is heard of outside his own dung-hill. The platitudes of Brisbane and Dr. Frank Crane serve as pabulum for all of them. What they think is what the machines at the central factory think; what they do is determined by men they have never seen. So with the Scripps-Howard slaves, and the slaves of Cox, and those of Curtis, and all the rest. Their predecessors of a generation ago were gaudy adventurers, experimenters, artists; they themselves are golf-players, which is to say, blanks. They are well paid, but effectively knee-haltered. The rewards of trade used to come in freedom, opportunity, the incomparable delights of self-expression; now they come in money.

But the sweet goes with the bitter. The newspapers of to-day, though they may be as rigidly standardized as Uneeda biscuits, are at least solvent: they are no longer the paltry free-booters that they used to be. A Munsey, perhaps, is a jackass, but he is at least honest; no one seriously alleges that his papers are for sale; even the sinister Wall Street powers that Liberals see in the background must get what they want out of him by being polite to him, not by simply sending him orders. The old-timers, contemplating the ghastly spectacle of a New York *Sun* submerged in the Munsey swamp and an *Evening Post* descending from a Villard to a Curtis, forget conveniently how bad most of the papers they once worked for really were. In the town where I began there were five papers, and four of them were cheap, trashy, stupid and corrupt. They all played politics for what there was in it, and leaped obscenely every time an advertiser blew his nose. Every other American city of that era was full of such papers—dreadful little rags, venal, vulnerable and vile. Not a few of them made great pretensions, and were accepted by a naïve public as organs of the enlightenment. To-day, I believe, such journalistic streetwalkers are very rare. The consolidations that every old-timer deplores have accomplished at least one good thing: they have got the newspapers, in the main, out of the hands of needy men. When orders come from a Curtis or a Munsey to-day the man who gets them, though he may regard them as ill-advised and even as idiotic, is seldom in any doubt as to their good faith. He may execute them without feeling that he has been made an unwilling party to an ignominious barter. He is not condemned daily to acts whose true purpose he would not dare to put into words, even to himself. His predecessor, I believe, often suffered that dismaying necessity: he seldom had any illusions about the *bona fides* of his boss. It took the whole force of his characteristic sentimentality to make him believe in his paper, and not infrequently even that sentimentality was impotent without the aid of ethyl alcohol.

Thus there is something to be said for the new newspaper Babbitts, as reluctant as every self-respecting journalist must be to say it. And in what is commonly said against them there is not infrequently a certain palpable exaggeration and injustice. Are they responsible for the imbecile editorial policies of their papers, for the grotesque lathering of such mountebanks as Coolidge and Mellon, for the general smugness and lack of intellectual enterprise that pervades American journalism? Perhaps they are. But do they issue orders that their papers shall be printed in blowsy, clumsy English? That they shall stand against every decent thing, and in favor of everything that is meretricious and ignoble? That they shall wallow in trivialities, and manhandle important news? That their view of learning shall be that of a bartender? Has any newspaper proprietor ever issued orders that the funeral orgies of a Harding should be described in the language of a Tennessee revival? Or that helpless men, with the mob against them, should be pursued without fairness, decency or sense? I doubt it. I doubt, even, that the Babbitts turned Greeleys are responsible, in the last analysis, for the political rubbish that fills their papers—the preposterous anointing of Coolidge, the craven yielding to such sinister forces as the Ku Klux Klan and the Anti-Saloon League, the incessant, humorless, degrading hymning of all sorts of rogues and charlatans. The average newspaper proprietor, I suspect, gets nine-tenths of his political ideas from his own men. In other words, he is such an ass that he believes political reporters, and especially his own political reporters. They have, he fancies, wide and confidential sources of information: their wisdom is a function of their prestige as his agents. What they tell him is, in the long run, what he believes, with certain inconsiderable corrections by professionals trying to work him. If only because they have confidential access to him day in and day out, they are able to introduce their own notions into his head. He may have their jobs in his hands, but they have his ears and eyes, so to speak, in theirs.

Even the political garbage that emanates from Washington, and especially from the typewriters of the more eminent and puissant correspondents there resident, is seldom inspired, I am convinced, by orders from the Curtis or Munsey at home: its sources are rather to be sought in the professional deficiencies of the correspondents themselves—a class of men of almost incredible credulity. In other words, they are to be sought, not in the corruption and enslavement of the press, but in the incompetence of the press. The average Washington correspondent, I believe, is honest enough, as honesty goes in the United States, though his willingness to do press work for the National Committees in campaign time and for other highly dubious agencies at other times is not to be forgotten. What ails him mainly is that he is a man without sufficient force of character to resist the blandishments that surround him from the moment he sets foot in Washington. A few men, true enough, resist, and their papers, getting the benefit of it, become notable for their independence and intelligence, but the great majority succumb almost at once. A few months of associating with the gaudy magnificoes of the town, and they pick up its meretricious values, and are unable to distinguish men of sense and dignity from mountebanks. A few clumsy overtures from the White House, and they are rattled and undone. They come in as newspaper men, trained to get the news and eager to get it; they end as tin-horn statesmen, full of dark secrets and unable to write the truth if they tried. Here I spread no scandal and violate no confidence. The facts are familiar to every newspaper man in the United States. A few of the more intelligent managing editors, cynical of ever counteracting the effects of the Washington miasma, seek to evade them by frequently changing their men. But the average managing editor is too stupid to deal with such difficulties. He prints balderdash because he doesn't know how to get anything better—perhaps, in many cases, because he doesn't know that anything better exists. Drenched with propaganda at home, he is quite content to take more propaganda from Washington. It is not that he is dishonest, but that he is stupid—and, being stupid, a coward. The resourcefulness, enterprise and bellicosity that his job demands are simply not in him. He doesn't wear himself out trying to get the news, as romance has it; he slides supinely into the estate and dignity of a golf-player. American journalism suffers from too many golf-players. They swarm in the Washington Press Gallery. They, and not their bosses, are responsible for most of the imbecilities that now afflict their trade.

4

The journalists of the United States will never get rid of those afflictions by putting the blame on Dives, and never by making speeches at one another in annual conventions, and never by drawing up codes of ethics that most of their brethren will infallibly laugh at, as a Congressman laughs at a gentleman. The job before them—that is, before the civilized minority of them—is to purge trade before they seek to dignify it—to clean house before they paint the roof and raise a flag. Can the thing be done? It not only can be done; it *has* been done. There are at least a dozen newspapers in the United States that already show a determined effort to get out of the old slough. Any managing editor in the land, if he has the will, can carry his own paper with them. He is under no compulsion, save rarely, to employ this or that hand; it is not often that owners, or even business managers, take any interest in that business, save to watch the payroll. Is his paper trifling, ill-informed, petty and unfair? Is its news full of transparent absurdities? Are its editorials ignorant and without sense? Is it written in English full of *clichés* and vulgarities—English that would disgrace a manager of prize-fighters or a county superintendent of schools? Then the fault belongs plainly, not to some remote man, but to the proximate man—to the man who lets such drivel go by. He could get better if he wanted it, you may be sure. There is in all history no record of a newspaper owner who complained because his paper was well-edited. And I know of no business manager who objected when the complaints pouring in upon him, of misrepresentations, invasions of privacy, gross inaccuracies and other such nuisances, began to lighten.

Not a few managing editors, as I say, are moving in the right directions. There has been an appreciable improvement, during the past dozen years, in the general tone of American newspapers. They are still full of preposterous blather, but they are measurably more accurate, I believe, than they used to be, and some of them are better written. A number of them are less absurdly partisan, particularly in the smaller cities. Save in the South and in the remoter fastnesses of New England the old-time party organ has gone out of fashion. In the big cities the faithful hacks of the New York *Tribune* type have begun to vanish. With them has gone the old-time drunken reporter, and in his place is appearing a young fellow of better education, and generally finer metal. The uplifters of the craft try to make him increase, and to that end encourage schools of journalism. But these seminaries, so far, show two palpable defects. On the one hand, they are seldom manned by men of any genuine professional standing, or of any firm notion of what journalism is about. On the other hand, they are nearly all too easy in their requirements for admission. Probably half of them, indeed, are simply refuges for students too stupid to tackle the other professions. They offer snap courses, and they promise quick jobs. The result is that the graduates coming out of them are mainly second-raters—that young men and women issuing from the general arts courses make better journalistic material.

What ails these schools of journalism is that they are not yet professional schools, but simply trade schools. Their like is to be found, not in the schools of medicine and law, but in the institutions that teach barbering, bookkeeping and scenario-writing. Obviously, the remedy for their general failure is to borrow a leaf from the book of the medical men, and weed out the incompetents, not after they have finished, but before they have begun. Twenty-five years ago any yokel who had got through the three R's was free to study medicine in the United

States. In three years, and sometimes in two years, he was turned out to practice upon his fellow hinds, and once he had his license it was a practical impossibility to challenge him. But now there is scarcely a medical school in the United States that does not demand a bachelor's degree or its equivalent as a prerequisite to entrance, and the term of study in all of them is four years, and it must be followed by at least one year of hospital service. This reform was not achieved by passing laws against the old hedge schools: it was achieved simply by setting up the competition of good schools. The latter gradually elbowed the former out. Their graduates had immense advantages. They had professional prestige from the moment of their entrance into practice. The public quickly detected the difference between them and their competitors from the surviving hedge schools. Soon the latter began to disintegrate, and now all save a few of them have disappeared. The medical men improved their profession by making it more difficult to become a medical man. To-day the thing is a practical impossibility to any young man who is not of genuine intelligence.

But at least two-thirds of the so-called schools of journalism still admit any aspirant who can make shift to read and write. The pedagogues who run them cannot be expected to devote much thought or money to improving them; they are in the position of the quacks who used to run the hedge medical schools. The impulse toward improvement, if it ever comes at all, must come from the profession they presume to serve. Here is a chance for the editorial committees and societies of journalists that now spring up on all sides. Let them abandon their vain effort to frame codes of ethics and devote themselves to the nursery. If they can get together a committee on schools of journalism as wise and as bold as the Council on Medical Education of the American Medical Association they will accomplish more in a few years than they can hope to accomplish with academic codes of ethics in a half century.

All the rest will follow. The old fond theory, still surviving in many a newspaper office, that it is somehow discreditable for a reporter to show any sign of education and culture, that he is most competent and laudable when his intellectual baggage most closely approaches that of a bootlegger—this theory will fall before the competition of novices who have been adequately trained, and have more in their heads than their mere training. Journalism, compared to the other trades of literate men, is surely not unattractive, even to-day. It is more amusing than the army or the cloth, and it offers a better living at the start than either medicine or the law. There is a career in it for the young man of original mind and forceful personality—a career leading to power and even to a sort of wealth. In point of fact, it has always attracted such young men, else it would be in an even lower state than it is now. It would attract a great many more of them if its public opinion were more favorable to them—if they were less harassed by the commands of professional superiors of no dignity, and the dislike of fellows of no sense. Every time two of them are drawn in they draw another. The problem is to keep them. That is the central problem of journalism in the United States to-day.

I seem to be in a mood for constructive criticism. Let me add one more pearl of wisdom before I withdraw. I put it in the form of a question. Suppose the shyster lawyers of every town organized a third-rate club, called it the Bar Association, took in any Prohibition agent or precinct politician who could raise the dues, and then announced publicly, from the Courthouse steps, that it represented the whole bar, and that membership in it was an excellent form of insurance—that any member who paid his dues would get very friendly consideration, if he ever got into trouble, from the town's judges and district attorney. And suppose the decent lawyers of the town permitted this preposterous pretension to go unchallenged—and some of them even gave countenance to it by joining the club. How long would the legal profession in that town retain its professional honor and dignity? How many laymen, after two or three years, would have any respect left for *any* lawyer, even a judge?

Yet the journalists of the United States permit that precise thing to go on under their noses. In almost every city of the country there is a so-called Press Club, and at last three-fourths of them are exactly like the hypothetical Bar Association that I have described. They are run by newspaper men of the worst type—many of them so incompetent and disreputable that they cannot even get jobs on newspapers. They take the money of all the town grafters and rascals on the pretense that newspaper favors go with its receipt. They are the resorts of idlers and blackmailers. They are nuisances and disgraces. Yet in how many towns have they been put down? In how many towns do the decent newspaper men take any overt action against them? My proposal is very simple. I propose that they be shut up, East, West, North and South, before anything more is said about codes of newspaper ethics.

II.
From the Memoirs of a Subject of the United States

I
Government by Bounder

OF government, at least in democratic states, it may be said briefly that it is an agency engaged wholesale, and as a matter of solemn duty, in the performance of acts which all self-respecting individuals refrain from as a matter of common decency. The American newspapers supply examples every day, chiefly issuing out of Federal tribunals, judicial and administrative. The whole process of the Federal law, indeed, becomes a process of bounderism. Its catchpolls are not policemen, in any rational and ordinary sense, but simply sneaks and scoundrels with their eyes glued eternally to knot-holes. Imagine a man of ordinary decency discovering his son reading an account of the proceedings against the once celebrated Lady Cathcart, now happily forgotten? Would his exposition of the case take the form of patriotic hallelujahs, or would he caution the boy that such things are not done by gentlemen? No wonder the teaching of patriotism in the Republic is being handed over to virgin schoolma'ms, who know of honor only as an anatomical matter! The business becomes too difficult for men who must face their fellow-men daily, and therewith the ancient prejudices of the race. Those prejudices, for unnumbered centuries, have run against the man who mouths the frailties of a fair one in the market-place. But the commission of Uncle Sam, it appears, repeals that obligation of elemental honor, as it repeals every other. One sworn to uphold the Constitution becomes straightway a licentiate in swinishness, with a mandate to examine the female guests of the nation publicly, and to denounce all who are not *virgo intacta*. This mandate covers not only the lowly ruffians told off to guard the ports, but also magnificoes of ministerial rank. The Cabinet of a great Christian nation meets behind locked doors to perform a business which, if done by an honest Elk, would bring his board of governors together to kick him out.

If such obscenities were rare one might set them down to moral profit and loss, and so try to forget them. But they happen every day. If a Cathcart case is not on the front pages, then a Whitney case or a Kollontai case is there. And day in and day out the newspapers are filled with the revolting muckeries of Prohibition agents, and their attendant district attorneys and judges. The whole trend of American legislation, and with it of jurisprudence, seems to be toward such ideas of dignity and decency as prevail in remote and forlorn country villages, among the human débris of Puritanism. A court of justice, once a place where the state intervened to curb the savagery of the strong, is now an arena of savagery both cruel and cynical. The notion seems to be that any device of deceit or brutality is fair, so long as it helps to fill the jails. The government, through its authorized agents, sets itself deliberately to lure men into so-called crime, and then punishes them mercilessly for succumbing. Is there such a thing as a *contrat social*? Then certainly it is getting heavy blows in the Federal Union. For if it is not based upon the expectation that one citizen will treat another with common decency, it is based upon nothing more than a shadow—and that expectation is fast becoming vain among us. The natural confidence that every man should have in his fellows—that they will not hit below the belt, that they will not abuse his natural trust, that he may rely upon them, in a given situation, to act according to the principles of fair-play prevailing immemorially among civilized men—this confidence, when it touches American officialdom, has no longer any basis in fact. The government, under the Volstead Act, is a spy and a snitcher, just as, under the Immigration Act, it is a brute and blackguard, and under the Alien Property Act, a common thief.

Obviously, such things cannot go on without having profound effects upon the general American character. A government, though it may be worse than the average man it governs, is still made up of just such average men. If, by some process of legal decay, it is set to disgusting acts, then the consequence must be that, in the long run, they will become less disgusting. How the business has worked in other lands has been displayed with much snuffling by specialists in Americanism; unfortunately, they seem to show no interest in the phenomena when it is repeated at home. I have spoken then of the father with a son ripe for instruction in the traditional decencies. Unfecund myself, I can only imagine his difficulties, but it must be obvious that they are serious. How, indeed, is he to interpret such an inescapable transaction as the Cathcart uproar? Is it his duty to tell his son that gentlemen set their dogs upon loose women? Or is it his duty to say that the United States is not a gentleman—nay, not even a decent thug?

Such doings, it seems to me, flow quite naturally out of the democratic theory. It holds, *imprimis*, that cads make just as good governors as civilized and self-respecting men, and it holds, *secundo*, that the notions of propriety and decency held by the mob are good enough for the state, and ought, in fact, to have the force of law. Thus it becomes increasingly difficult to be a good American, as the thing is officially defined, and remain what all the other peoples of the world regard as a good citizen—that is, one who views the acts and ideas of his fellows with a tolerant and charitable eye, and wishes them to be free and happy. The whole tendency of American law, in this day, is to put down happiness wherever it is encountered, and the *mores* of the land march with the law. The doctrine seems to be that it is the highest duty of the citizen to police his fellows. What they naturally want to do is precisely what they must be kept from doing. To this business a large and increasing class of professional snouters and smellers addresses itself. How many noses it can muster, God only knows, but the number must be immensely large. In the single State of Ohio, with the Anti-Saloon League in the saddle, there are certainly at least five thousand, and every prowling village deacon and petty urban blackmailer is free to join the force as a volunteer. And in more civilized regions, where public opinion, even in the mob, runs against such putridities, the Federal government supplies the scoundrels.

This antagonism between democratic Puritanism and common decency is inherent in the nature of the two things, and leads to conflicts in all so-called "free" countries, but it is only in the United States that it has reached the stage of open and continuous war, with Puritanism sweeping the field and common decency in flight. Thus life in the Republic grows increasingly uncomfortable to men of the more urbane and seemly sort, and, despite the great material prosperity of the country, the general stock of happiness probably diminishes steadily. For the thing that makes us enjoy the society of our fellows is not admiration of their inner virtues but delight in their outward manners. It is not enough that they are headed for heaven, and will sit upon the right hand of God through all eternity; it is also necessary that they be polite, generous, and, above all, trustworthy. We must have confidence in them in order to get any pleasure out of associating with them. We must be sure that they will not do unto us as we should refuse, even for cash in hand, to do unto them. It is the tragedy of the Puritan that he can never inspire this confidence in his fellowmen. He is by nature a pedant in ethics, and hence he is by nature a mucker. With the best of intentions he cannot rid himself of the belief that it is his duty to save us from our follies—*i.e.*, from all the non-puritanical acts and whimsies that make life charming. His duty to let us be happy takes second, third or fourth. A Puritan cannot be tolerant—and with tolerance goes magnanimity. The late Dr. Woodrow Wilson was a typical Puritan—of the better sort, perhaps, for he at least toyed with the ambition to appear as a gentleman, but nevertheless a true Puritan. Magnanimity was simply beyond him. Confronted, on his death-bed, with the case of poor old Debs, all his instincts compelled him to keep Debs in jail. I daresay that, as a purely logical matter, he saw clearly that the old fellow ought to be turned loose; certainly he must have known that Washington would not have hesitated, or Lincoln. But Calvinism triumphed as his intellectual faculties decayed. In the full bloom of health, with a plug hat on his head, he aped the gentry of his wistful adoration very cleverly, but lying in bed, stripped like Thackeray's Louis XIV, he reverted to his congenital Puritanism, which is to say, bounderism.

Of such sort are the grand seigneurs of the nation—the custodians of its dignity and honor. They speak for it to the world. They set the tone of the national life at home. Is there any widespread murmuring against them? I wish I could report that there was, but I see no sign of it. Instead, there seems to be only a resigned sort of feeling that nothing can be done about it—that the swinishness of government lies in the very nature of things, and so cannot be changed. Even the popular discontent with Prohibition is not a discontent with its sneaking and knavishness—its wholesale turning loose of licensed blacklegs and blackmailers, its appalling degradation of the judiciary, its corruption of Congress, its disingenuous invasion of the Bill of Rights. What is complained of is simply the fact that Scotch is dubious and costs too much. As bootlegging grows more efficient, I suppose, even that complaint will sink to a whisper, perhaps in the form of a snigger. Of any forthright grappling with the underlying indecency there is little show. It would be difficult, in most American communities, to get signers for even the most academic protest against it. The American, played upon for years by a stream of jackass legislation, takes refuge in frank skulking. He first dodges the laws, and then he dodges the duty of protesting against them. His life becomes a process of sneaking through back-alleys, watching over one shoulder for the cop and over the other for his neighbor. Thus a-tremble (and with a weather eye open for Bolsheviks, atheists and loose women), he serves the high oath that government of the people, by the people, and for the people shall not perish from the earth.

2
Constructive Proposal

A mood of constructive criticism being upon me, I propose forthwith that the method of choosing legislators now prevailing in the United States be abandoned and that the method used in choosing juries be substituted. That is to say, I propose that the men who make our laws be chosen by chance and against their will, instead of by fraud and against the will of all the rest of us, as now. But isn't the jury system itself imperfect? Isn't it occasionally disgraced by gross abuse and scandal? Then so is the system of justice devised and ordained by the Lord God Himself. Didn't He assume that the Noachian Deluge would be a lasting lesson to sinful humanity—that it would put an end to all manner of crime and wickedness, and convert mankind into a race of Methodists? And wasn't Noah himself, its chief beneficiary, lying drunk, naked and uproarious within a year after the ark landed on Ararat? All I argue for the jury system, invented by man, is that it is measurably better than the scheme invented by God. It has its failures and its absurdities, its abuses and its corruptions, but taking one day with another it manifestly works. It is not the fault of juries that so many murderers go unwhipped of justice, and it is not the fault of juries that so many honest men are harassed by preposterous laws. The juries find the gunmen guilty: it is the judges higher up who deliver them from the noose, and turn them out to resume their butcheries. It is from judges again, and not from juries, that Volsteadian padlocks issue, and all the other devices for making a mock of the Bill of Rights. Are juries occasionally sentimental? Then let us not forget that it was their sentimentality, in the Eighteenth Century, that gradually forced a measure of decency and justice into the English Criminal Law. It was a jury that blocked the effort of the Department of Justice to railroad Senator Wheeler to prison on false charges. It was another jury that detected and baffled the same Department's perjurers in the O'Leary case, during the late war. And it was yet another jury that delivered the eminent Fatty Arbuckle from what was, perhaps, the most disingenuous and outrageous persecution ever witnessed in a civilized land.

Would any American Legislature, or Congress itself, have resisted the vast pressure of the bureaucracy in these cases? To ask the question is to answer it. The dominant character of every legislative body ever heard of, at least in this great free Republic, is precisely its susceptibility to such pressure. It not only leaps when the bureaucracy cracks the whip; it also leaps to the whip-cracking of scores of extra-legal (and often, indeed, *il*legal) agencies. The Anti-Saloon League, despite its frequent disasters, is still so powerful everywhere that four legislators out of five obey it almost instinctively. When it is flouted, as has happened in a few States under an adverse pressure yet more powerful, the thing is marvelled at as a sort of miracle. The bureaucracy itself is seldom flouted at all. When it is in a moral mood, and heaving with altruistic sobs, the thing simply never happens. Is it argued that Congress has nevertheless defied it, and Dr. Coolidge with it? Then the argument comes from persons whose studies of Washington pathology have been very superficial. At least nine-tenths of the idiocies advocated by Dr. Coolidge and his highly dubious friends have been swallowed by both Houses with no more than a few reflex gags. Even the celebrated Warren appointment was defeated in the Senate by only a few votes—and the few votes were delivered, as connoisseurs will recall, by a process indistinguishable from an act of God. It is my contention that a jury of plain men, issuing unwilling from their plumbing-shops and grocery-stores and eager to get back to work, would have rejected Warren without leaving their box, and that the same jury, confronted by such things as the World Court imbecility, would dispose of them just as quickly.

Why were the learned Senators so much less intelligent and so much less resolute? For a plain reason. Fully two-thirds of them were not thinking of Warren as they voted; they were thinking of their jobs. The problem before them was not whether elevating the preposterous Warren was a reasonable and laudable measure, likely to benefit and glorify the United States, but whether voting for Warren would augment or diminish their chance of reëlection. In other words, they were not free agents, and in consequence not honest men. They had sought their jobs on their bellies, and they were eager to keep them, even at the cost of groveling on their bellies again. Say the worst you can say against a box of twelve jurymen, and you can never say that. Not one among them sought his job. Not one among them wants to keep it. The business before them presents itself as a public duty to be done, not as an opportunity for private advantage. They are eager only to get it done decently, and go home.

So my proposal is that our Legislatures be chosen as our juries are now chosen—that the names of all the men eligible in each assembly district be put into a hat (or, if no hat can be found that is large enough, into a bathtub), and that a blind moron, preferably of tender years, be delegated to draw out one. Let the constituted catchpolls then proceed swiftly to this man's house, and take him before he can get away. Let him be brought into court forthwith, and put under a stupendous bond to serve as elected, and if he cannot furnish the bond, let him be kept until the appointed day in the nearest jail.

The advantages that this system would offer are so vast and

so obvious that I hesitate to venture into the banality of rehearsing them. It would, in the first place, save the commonwealth the present excessive cost of elections, and make political campaigns unnecessary. It would, in the second place, get rid of all the heart-burnings that now flow out of every contest at the polls, and block the reprisals and charges of fraud that now issue from the heart-burnings. It would, in the third place, fill all the State Legislatures with men of a peculiar and unprecedented cast of mind—men actually convinced that public service is a public burden, and not merely a private snap. And it would, in the fourth and most important place, completely dispose of the present degrading knee-bending and trading in votes, for nine-tenths of the legislators, having got into office unwillingly, would be eager only to finish their duties and go home, and even those who acquired a taste for the life would be unable to do anything to increase the probability, even by one chance in a million, of their reëlection.

The disadvantages of the plan are very few, and most of them, I believe, yield readily to analysis. Do I hear argument that a miscellaneous gang of tin-roofers, delicatessen dealers and retired bookkeepers, chosen by hazard, would lack the vast knowledge of public affairs needed by makers of laws? Then I can only answer (*a*) that no such knowledge is actually necessary, and (*b*) that few, if any, of the existing legislators possess it. The great majority of public problems, indeed, are quite simple, and any man may be trusted to grasp their elements in ten days who may be—and is—trusted to unravel the obfuscations of two gangs of lawyers in the same time. In this department the so-called expertness of so-called experts is largely imaginary. The masters of the tariff who sit at Washington know little about the fundamental philosophy of protection, and care less; the subject, if discussed on the floor, would send the whole House flying to the Capitol bootleggers. The knowledge that these frauds are full of is simply knowledge of how many votes an extra ten cents on aluminum dishpans may be counted on producing, and how much the National Association of Brass Cuspidor Manufacturers deserves to be given for its campaign contribution of $10,000. Such is the science of the tariff as it is practiced by the professors who now flourish. It is my contention that a House of malt-and-hop dealers, garage mechanics and trolley conductors, brought in by the common hangman, would deal with the question with quite as much knowledge, and with a great deal more honesty. It might make mistakes, but it would not, at least, be pledged to them in advance. Some of its members might sell out, but there would remain, at worst, a workable minority of honest men.

The tariff, in any case, is no longer an issue. Neither are most of the other great politico-economical puzzles that harassed the statesmen of an elder day. They have all been solved; the two great parties agree upon them, with a few wild fellows dissenting. But as economics and finance go out, morals come in. The legislation of to-day is chiefly made up of quack cure-alls, invented by fanatics and supported by the bureaucracy. Well, I ask you what sort of Legislature is the more likely to swallow these cure-alls: one made up of professionals eager to hold their jobs, or one made up of amateurs eager only to get rid of their jobs?

My scheme would have the capital merit, if it had no other, of barring the professionals from the game. They would lose their present enormous advantages as a class, and so their class would tend to disappear. Would that be a disservice to the state? Certainly not. On the contrary, it would be a service of the first magnitude, for the worst curse of democracy, as we suffer under it to-day, is that it makes public office a monopoly of a palpably inferior and ignoble group of men. They have to abase themselves in order to get it, and they have to keep on abasing themselves in order to hold it. The fact reflects itself in their general character, which is obviously low. They are men congenitally capable of ignoble acts, else they would not have got into public life at all. There are, of course, exceptions to that rule among them, but how many? What I contend is simply that the number of such exceptions is bound to be smaller in the class of professional job-seekers than it is in any other class, or in the population in general. What I contend, second, is that choosing legislators from that population, by chance, would reduce immensely the proportion of such crawling, slimy men in the halls of legislation, and that the effects would be instantly visible in a great improvement in the justice and reasonableness of the laws.

Are juries ignorant? Then they are still intelligent enough to be entrusted with your life and mine. Are they venal? Then they are still honest enough to take our fortunes into their hands. Such is the fundamental law of the Germanic peoples, and it has worked for nearly a thousand years. I have launched my proposal that it be extended upward and onward, and the mood of constructive criticism passes from me. My plan belongs to any reformer who cares to lift it.

3
The Nature of Government

What ails the world mainly, at least in the political sense, is that its governments are too strong. It has been a recurrent pest since the dawn of civilization. Government is always depicted, in the orthodox texts, as the creation of the people governed; the theory is that they created it in order to secure their own safety and promote their daily business. But no Professor Oppenheimer was needed to demonstrate that it is really something imposed from without, or, at all events, the heir and assign of something imposed from without. Its interests and those of the people it governs are the same only occasionally, and then usually accidentally. True enough, it must sometimes throw them bones, and even beefsteaks, lest they grow desperate and attempt to destroy it, but such concessions are always made grudgingly, and withdrawn very promptly the moment it looks safe.

The history of the United States would make all this plain enough, if that history were studied realistically. Consider, for example, the matter of liberty. The American people profess to esteem liberty very highly—so highly, in fact, that their common talk about it seems somewhat lyrical and excessive to the people of most other nations. They seem to believe that there is more of it on tap in the Republic than anywhere else on earth—that the Republic was actually founded for the sole purpose of giving it to them. Yet it must be obvious that their hold upon it is always precarious, and that their government tries to take it away from them whenever possible—not completely, perhaps, but always substantially. That government resisted their demand for it at the very start, and yielded only after a very severe struggle. The Bill of Rights was not in the original Constitution; it got in only as amendments. Ever since then, at every opportunity, the government has tried to weaken it. Here parties and personalities count for very little. The most successful raids upon the Bill of Rights so far recorded were made by Abraham Lincoln, a Republican and the spokesman (in theory) of the inferior man, and by Woodrow Wilson, a Democrat and the agent of what passes, in the United States, for an aristocracy.

The men who constitute the government always try to make it appear, of course, that they carry on their activities in a patriotic and altruistic way—in brief, they are full of public spirit. But that pretension deceives no one, not even *Homo boobiens.* The average man, whatever his errors otherwise, at least sees clearly that the government is something lying outside him and outside the generality of his fellow men—that it is a separate, independent and often hostile power, only partly under his control, and capable, on occasion, of doing him great harm. In his romantic moments, he may think of it as a benevolent father or even a sort of *jinn* or god, but he never thinks of it as part of himself. In times of trouble he looks to it to perform miracles for his benefit; at other times he sees it as an enemy with which he must do constant battle. Is it a fact of no significance that robbing the government is everywhere regarded as a crime of less magnitude than robbing an individual, or even a corporation? In the United States to-day it is punished only when it is complicated by some secondary, and, in the public judgment, worse offense—for example, depriving crippled war veterans of their lawful relief. Otherwise, it carries a smaller penalty and infinitely less odium than acts that are intrinsically trivial—for example, spitting on the sidewalk or marrying two wives. None of the thieves who robbed the government at Hog Island during the war has ever gone to jail. The airship contractors, though they made off with nearly a billion dollars, are still all at large. So are all the camp contractors. More, the man who broke up the feeble and abortive effort to punish these scoundrels—who denounced that effort as, in some mysterious way, an *attentat* against public morality—that man is now first in succession to the presidency of the

Republic. His indignation plainly had public sentiment behind it. He was and is an accomplished professor of the mind of man under democracy.

Other politicians, less gifted in that science, often take the other side, and so come to grief. They assume absurdly that the public conscience is opposed to robbing the government, and try to climb into popularity and high office by pursuing the gay fellows who do it. The attempt almost always fails. The great masses of the plain people, true enough, enjoy the chase, as they enjoy, indeed, *any* chase. The damning evidence, as it unrolls, delights them; they devour every accusation, however ill supported. But it usually turns out in the end that they do not care to eat the game. The minute the evidence is all in they lose interest; there is no demand from them for the jailing of the accused. On the contrary, they sympathize with the accused, and show it actively when the time comes to supply conscripts for the trial jury. Perhaps the safest men in the whole United States to-day are the gentlemen who have been indicted for robbing the government. Every such indictment is a sort of policy of insurance against going to jail.

What lies behind all this, I believe, is a deep sense of the fundamental antagonism between the government and the people it governs. It is apprehended, not as a committee of citizens chosen to carry on the communal business of the whole population, but as a separate and autonomous corporation, mainly devoted to exploiting the population for the benefit of its own members. Robbing it is thus an act almost devoid of infamy—an exploit rather resembling those of Robin Hood and the eminent pirates of tradition. When a private citizen is robbed a worthy man is deprived of the fruits of his industry and thrift; when the government is robbed the worst that happens is that certain rogues and loafers have less money to play with than they had before. The notion that they have earned that money is never entertained; to most men it would seem extremely ludicrous. They are simply rascals who, by accidents of law, have a somewhat dubious right to a share in the earnings of their fellowmen. When that share is diminished by private enterprise the business is, on the whole, far more laudable than not.

The average man, when he pays taxes, certainly does not believe that he is making a prudent and productive investment of his money; on the contrary, he feels that he is being mulcted in an excessive amount for services that, in the main, are useless to him, and that, in substantial part, are downright inimical to him. He may be convinced that a police force, say, is necessary for the protection of his life and property, and that an army and navy safeguard him from being reduced to slavery by some vague foreign kaiser, but even so he views these things as extravagantly expensive—he sees in even the most essential of them an agency for making it easier for the exploiters constituting the government to rob him. The policeman, in fact, is his symbol for a thief. The army and navy, as he sees them, are blankets for mere display, ostentation and waste—of his hard-earned money. The rest of the government is purely predatory and useless; he believes that he gets no more benefit from its vast and costly operations than he gets from the money he lends to his wife's brother. It is a power that stands over him constantly, ever alert for new chances to squeeze him. If it could do so safely it would strip him to his hide. If it leaves him anything at all, it is simply prudentially, as a farmer leaves a hen some of her eggs.

Thus he sees nothing wrong, in the sense that robbing a neighbor is wrong to him, in turning the tables upon it whenever the opportunity offers. When he steals anything from it he is only recovering his own, with fair interest and a decent profit. Two gangs thus stand confronted: on the one hand the gang of drones and exploiters constituting the government, and on the other hand the body of prehensile and enterprising citizens. The latter is certainly not made up exclusively, as the Liberals and other such romantics seem to think, of bankers, railroad stockholders, great industrialists and other such magnificoes. There is plenty of room in it for more lowly men, if only they have the courage to horn in. During the late war all the union men of the nation, by pooling their strength and so dispersing the risk, made a magnificent and successful effort to get their share: they stole almost as much, in all probability, as the dollar-a-year men. And when the war was over the soldiers, deprived of their chance while the going was good, demanded it belatedly. The chief argument for the bonus was not that the veterans of the war had leaped gallantly to the defense of democracy, for at least two-thirds of them, as everyone knows, tried their best to evade service. The chief argument was that they were forced into the army against their will and in violation of their private interests—that they didn't get their fair chance at the loot. They did not demand the punishment of those who looted while they served; they only demanded a rectification of the injustice which kept them honest themselves.

The difference between the two gangs—of professionals and of amateurs—is that the former has law on its side, and so enjoys an unfair advantage. Worse, it makes the very laws it profits by. Yet worse, it controls all the agencies which execute them, including the courts. The other gang is almost unarmored. The government is always able, when it happens to be so disposed, to single out a few of its ring-leaders and clap them into jail. Such proceedings, of course, are unpopular, but they are nevertheless possible. But the government gang is well-nigh immune to punishment. Its worst extortions, even when they are baldly for private profit, carry no certain penalties under our laws. Since the first days of the Republic less than a dozen of its members have been impeached, and only a few obscure understrappers have ever been put into prison. The number of men sitting at Atlanta and Leavenworth for revolting against the extortions of the government is always ten times as great as the number of government officials condemned for oppressing the tax-payers to their own gain. Thus the combat which goes on is not unlike that between the Anti-Saloon League and the bootleggers. The Anti-Saloon League, it must be manifest, is quite as criminal as the bootleggers; it devotes itself professionally to violating the Bill of Rights; its kept judges have pretty well disposed of all the constitutional guarantees of the citizen. But its control of the government puts it above the law. Its agents, on and off the bench, commit their crimes almost unmolested; only one of them, in fact, has ever got into jail—and that was by a sort of accident.

But public opinion is mainly on the side of the bootleggers. They represent, in the combat, the plain man, eternally oppressed and robbed by his overlords. In their popularity is to be seen the first glimmers of a revolt that must one day shake the world—a revolt, not against this or that form of government, but against the tyranny at the bottom of *all* government. Government, to-day, is growing too strong to be safe.

There are no longer any citizens in the world; there are only subjects. They work day in and day out for their masters; they are bound to die for their masters at call. Out of this working and dying they tend to get less and less. On some bright tomorrow, a geological epoch or two hence, they will come to the end of their endurance, and then such newspapers as survive will have a first-page story well worth its black headlines.

4
Freudian Footnote

That the life of man is a struggle and an agony was remarked by the Brisbanes and Dr. Frank Cranes of the remotest antiquity. The earliest philosophers busied themselves with the fact, and so did the earliest poets. It runs like a *Leitmotif* through the literature of the Greeks and the Jews alike. "Vanity of vanities," saith the Preacher, "vanity of vanities; all is vanity!" "O ye deathward-going tribes of men," chants Sophocles, "what do your lives mean except that they go to nothingness?" But not placidly, not unresistingly, not without horrible groans and gurgles. Man is never honestly the fatalist, nor even the stoic. He fights his fate, often desperately. He is forever entering bold exceptions to the rulings of the bench of gods. This fighting, no doubt, makes for human progress, for it favors the strong and the brave. It also makes for beauty, for lesser men try to escape from a hopeless and intolerable world by creating a more lovely one of their own. Poetry, as every one knows, is a means to that end—facile, and hence popular. The aim of poetry is to give a high and voluptuous plausibility to what is palpably not true. I offer the Twenty-third Psalm as an example: "The Lord is my shepherd; I shall not want." It is immensely esteemed by the inmates of almshouses, and by gentlemen waiting to be hanged. I have to limit my own reading of it, avoiding soft and yielding moods, for I too, in my way, am a gentleman waiting to be hanged, as you are. If the air were impregnated with poetry, as it is with carbon in Pittsburgh, and alcohol in Hoboken, N.J., and stale incense in Boston, the world would be a more comfortable and caressing place, but the service of the truth would be neglected. The truth is served by prose. The aim of prose is not to conceal the facts, but to display them. It is thus apt to be harsh and painful. All that the philosophers and metaphysicians of the world have accomplished, grinding away in their damp cells since man became cryptococcygeal, is to prove that *Homo sapiens* and *Equus asinus* are brothers under their skins. As for the more imaginative *prosateurs*, they have pretty well confined themselves, since the earliest beginnings of their craft, to the lugubrious chronicle of man's struggle and defeat. I know of no first-rate novel that hasn't this theme. In all of them, from "Don Quixote" to "The Brothers Karamazov" and from "Vanity Fair" to "McTeague," we are made privy to the agonies of a man resisting his destiny, and getting badly beaten.

The struggle is always the same, but in its details it differs in different ages. There was a time, I believe, when it was mainly a combat between the natural instincts of the individual and his yearning to get into Heaven. That was an unhealthy time, for throttling the instincts is almost as deleterious as breathing bad air; it makes for an unpleasant clamminess. The Age of Faith, seen in retrospect, looks somehow pale and puffy: one admires its saints and anchorites without being conscious of any very active desire to shake hands with them and smell them. To-day the yearning to get into Heaven is in abeyance, at least among the vast majority of humankind, and so the ancient struggle takes a new form. In the main, it is a struggle of man with society—a conflict between his desire to be respected and his impulse to follow his own bent. It seems to me that society usually wins. There are, to be sure, free spirits in the world, but their freedom, in the last analysis, is not much greater than that of a canary in a cage. They may leap from perch to perch; they may bathe and guzzle at their will; they may flap their wings and sing. But they are still in the cage, and soon or late it conquers them. What was once a great itch for long flights and the open spaces is gradually converted into a fading memory and nostalgia, sometimes stimulating but more often merely blushful. The free man, made in God's image, is converted into a Freudian case.

Such Freudian cases swarm in modern society; they are hidden in all sorts of unexpected places. Observing a Congressman, one sees only a gross and revolting shape, with dull eyes and prehensile hands. But under that preposterous mask there may be yearnings, and some of them may be of high voltage and laudable delicacy. There are Congressmen, I have no doubt, who regret their lost honor, as women often do in the films. Tossing in their beds on hot, sticky Washington nights, their gizzards devoured by bad liquor, they may lament the ruin that the service of Demos has brought to their souls. For Congressmen, despite their dishonorable trade, are exactly like the rest of us at bottom, and respond to the same biogenetic laws. In infancy they go to Sunday-school. Passing through adolescence, they are idealists, and dream of saving the world. Come to young manhood, they suffer the purifying pangs of love. The impulse to seek political preferment, when it arises in them, is not always, nor primarily, an impulse to grab something, to victimize and exploit the rest of us. That comes later: even Penrose and Roosevelt started out as altruists and reformers. But the rules of the game run one way, and common honesty and common decency run another. There comes a time when the candidate must surrender either his ideals or his aspirations. If he is in Congress it is a sign that he has preserved the latter.

Democracy produces swarms of such men, in politics and on other planes, and their secret shames and sorrows, I believe, are largely responsible for the generally depressing tone of democratic society. Old Freud, living in a more urbane and civilized world, paid too little heed to that sort of repression. He assumed fatuously that what was repressed was always, or nearly always, something intrinsically discreditable, or, at all events, anti-social—for example, the natural impulse to neck a pretty woman, regardless of her husband's protests. But under democracy that is only half the story. The democrat with a yearning to shine before his fellows must not only repress all the common varieties of natural wickedness; he must also repress many of the varieties of natural decency. His impulse to speak his mind freely, to tell the truth as he sees it, to be his own man, comes into early and painful collision with the democratic dogma that such things are not nice—that the most worthy and laudable citizen is that one who is most like all the rest. In youth, as every one knows, this dogma is frequently challenged, and sometimes with great asperity, but the rebellion, taking one case with another, is not of long duration. The campus Nietzsche, at thirty, begins to feel the suction of Rotary; at forty he is a sound Mellon man; at fifty he is fit for Congress.

But his early yearning for freedom and its natural concomitants is still not dead; it is merely imprisoned in the depths of his subconscious. Down there it drags out its weary and intolerable years, protesting silently but relentlessly against its durance. We know, by Freud's appalling evidence, what the suppression of the common wickednesses can do to the individual—how it can shake his reason on its throne, and even give him such things as gastritis, migraine and angina pectoris. Every Sunday-school in the land is full of such wrecks; they recruit the endless brigades of lady policemen and male wowsers. A vice-crusader is simply an unfortunate who goes about with a brothel in his own cellar; a Prohibitionist is one who has buried rum, but would have been safer drinking it. All this is now a commonplace of knowledge to every American school-girl. The wowsers themselves give the facts a universal dispersion by trying to suppress them. But so far no psychoanalyst has done a tome on the complexes that issue out of moral struggles against common decency, though they are commoner under democracy than the other kind, and infinitely more ferocious. A man who has throttled a bad impulse has at least some consolation in his agonies, but a man who has throttled a good one is in a bad way indeed. Yet this great Republic swarms with such men, and their sufferings are under every eye. We have more of them, perhaps, than all the rest of Christendom, with heathendom thrown in to make it unanimous.

I marvel that no corn-fed Freud or Adler has ever investigated the case of the learned judges among us, and especially those of the Federal rite. Prohibition, I suspect, has filled them with such repressions that even a psychoanalyst, plowing into the matter, would be shocked. Enforcing its savage and anti-social mandates, with fanatics pulling them and blacklegs pushing them, has obviously compelled them to make away with all the pruderies that are natural to men of their class and condition. There may be individuals among them, to be sure, who were born without any pruderies and hence do not suffer, just as there are individuals who were born without any capacity for affection and hence show no trace of the Œdipus complex, but such men must be very rare, even among politicians, even among lawyers. The average judge, I take it, is much like the rest of us. When he is free to do it, he does the decent thing. His natural impulse is to speak the truth as he sees it, to challenge error and imposture, to frown upon fraud. What, now, if his high and solemn duties compel him to treat fraud as if it were divine revelation? What if he must spend his days prospering rogues and oppressing honest men? What if his oath wars horribly with his conscience? No Freud was needed to argue that the effect upon him must be very evil. He cannot perform his work without assassinating his inner integrity. Putting on his black gown, he must simultaneously cram his unconscious with all the sound impulses and natural decencies that make him the noble fellow that he is.

The clinical effects are certainly not occult. One hears constantly of judges coming down with symptoms which, in ordinary men, would be accepted as proofs of inner turmoils, insusceptible to correction by the pharmacopœia. They break into hysterical tirades from the bench; they speak in unintelligible language; they deliver judgments that upset the laws of logic; they complain of buzzings in the ears, flashes before the eyes, and vague bellyaches. Two Federal judges, of late, have committed suicide. One climbed a high mountain in his motor-car, and then leaped into space: a monstrous act, and no doubt of plain significance to a Freudian adept. The other left a note saying frankly that Prohibition had wrecked him. The faculty has at such disturbances of the psyche by hunting for focal infections and pulling teeth: the whole judiciary tends to become toothless. But it would be easier and cheaper and more effective, I am convinced, to send for a psychoanalyst. The stricken judge would come out of the room cured, and the psychoanalyst would come out with a new outfit of complexes.

I speak of the judges because their sufferings are palpable. But there must be swarms of other victims in this eminent free nation. Every one of us has been under the steam-roller; every one of us, in this way or that, confirms unwillingly, and has the corpse of a good impulse belowstairs. There are probably no exceptions. Psychoanalyze a Methodist bishop, and you'll probably find him stuffed with good impulses, all of them repressed. On blue afternoons, perhaps, there sneaks out of his unconscious a civilized yearning for a decent drink; in the dark watches of the night he remembers a Catholic girl of his youth, and weeps that she was so fair; he may even, passing a public library, feel a sudden, goatish inclination to go in and read a good book. Suppressed, such appetites make him uncomfortable, unhappy, desperate, an enemy to society. Dredged up by some super-Freud, and dissipated in the sunlight, they would leave him an honest and happy man.

5
Bach to Bach!

Ah, at evening, to be drinking from the glassy pond, to have—oh, better than all marrow-bones!—the fresh illusion of lapping up the stars!

I take the thought from Patou, the forward-looking hound-dog in Rostand's "Chantecler." Let him stand as a symbol of the whole melancholy company of crib-haltered but aspiring Americans, their hands doomed to go-getting but their hearts leaping into interstellar space. Patou, lifted to his hind legs and outfitted with pantaloons, would have made a capital Rotarian. Condemned by destiny to a kennel in a barnyard, he yet had that soaring, humorless Vision which is the essence of Rotary, and the secret, no doubt, of its firm hold upon otherwise unpoetical men. For even in the paradise of Babbitt, Babbitt is vaguely uneasy and unhappy. He needs something more, he finds, than is to be found in bulging order-books; in innumerable caravans of prospects, and in belching chimneys and laden trains. He needs something more than is to be got out of blowing spitballs and playing golf. So he searches for that something in the realm of the fancy, where the husks of things fall and their inner sap is revealed. He reads the dithyrambs of Edgar Albert Guest, Arthur Brisbane, and Dr. Frank Crane. He listens to the exhortations of itinerant rhetoricians, gifted and eloquent men, specialists in what it is all about. He intones "Sweet Adeline," and is not ashamed of the tear that babbles down his nose. Thus Babbitt, too, is tantalized by a Grail; he seeks it up and down the gorgeous corridors of his Statler

Hotel, past the cigar-stand and the lair of the hat-check gal, and on to the perfumed catacombs of the lovely manicurist and the white-robed chirotonsor. *Non in solo pane vivit homo.* Man cannot live by bread alone. He must hope also. He must dream. He must yearn.

The fact explains the Rotarian and his humble brother, the Kiwanian; more, it strips them of not a little of their superficial obnoxiousness. They are fools, but they are not quite damned. If their quest is carried on in motley, they at least trail after better men. And so do all their brethren of Service, great and small—the Americanizers, the Law Enforcers, the boosters and boomers, and the endless others after their kind. At first glance, one sees in these visionaries only noisy and preposterous fellows, disturbing the peace of their betters. But a closer examination is more favorable to them. They are tortured, in their odd, clumsy fashion, by the same ringing in the ears that maddened Ludwig van Beethoven. They suffer from the same optical delusions, painful and not due to sin, that set the prophets of antiquity to howling: they look at a Harding or a Coolidge and see a Man. What lures them to their bizarre cavortings—and it is surely not to be sniffed at *per se*—is a dim and disturbing mirage of a world more lovely and serene than the one the Lord God has doomed them to live in. What they lack in common, thus diverging from the prophets, is a rational conception of what it ought to be, and might be.

It is somewhat astonishing that 100% Americans should wander so helplessly in this wilderness. For there is a well-paved road across the whole waste, and it issues, at its place of beginning, from the tombs of the Fathers, and their sacred and immemorial dust. Straight as a pistol so it runs, until at the other end it sweeps up a glittering slope to a shrine upon a high hill. This shrine may be seen on fair days for many leagues, and presents a magnificent spectacle. Its base is confected of the bones of Revolutionary heroes, and out of them rises an heroic effigy of George Washington, in alabaster. Surrounding this effigy, and on a slightly smaller scale, are graven images of Jefferson, Franklin, Nathan Hale, old Sam Adams, John Hancock and Paul Revere, each with a Bible under his arm and the Stars and Stripes fluttering over his shoulder. A bit to the rear, and without the Bible, is a statue of Thomas Paine.

Over the whole structure stretch great bands of the tricolor, in silk, satin and other precious fabrics. Red and white stripes run up and down the legs of Washington, and his waistcoat is spattered with stars. The effect is the grandiose one of a Democratic national convention. At night, in the American manner, spotlights play upon the shrine. Hot dogs are on sale nearby, that pilgrims may not hunger, and there is a free park for Fords, with running water and booths for the sale of spare parts. It is the shrine of Liberty!

But where are the pilgrims? One observes the immense parking space and the huge pyramids of hot dogs, and one looks for great hordes of worshipers, fighting their way to the altar-steps. But they are *non est.* Now and then a honeymoon couple wanders in from the rural South or Middle West, to gape at the splendors hand in hand, and now and then a schoolma'm arrives with a flock of her pupils, and lectures them solemnly out of a book. More often, perhaps, a foreign visitor is to be seen, with a *couronne* of tin bay-leaves under his arm. He deposits the *couronne* at the foot of Washington, crosses himself lugubriously, and retires to the nearest hot dog stand. But where are the Americanos? Where are the he-men, heirs to the heroes whose gilded skulls here wait the Judgment Day? Where are the Americanizers? Where are the boosters and boomers? Where are the sturdy Coolidge men? Where are the Rotarians, Kiwanians, Lions? Where are the authors of newspaper editorials? The visionaries of Chautauqua? The keepers of the national idealism? Go search for them, if you don't trust the first report of your eyes! Go search for honest men in Congress! They are simply not present. For among all the visions that now inflame forward-looking and up-and-coming men in this great Republic, there is no sign any more of the one that is older than all the rest, and that is the vision of Liberty. The Fathers saw it, and the devotion they gave to it went far beyond three cheers a week. It survived into Jackson's time, and its glow was renewed in Lincoln's. But now it is no more.

The phenomenon is curious, and deserves far more study by eminent psychologists than it has got. I may undertake that study as an amateur in a work reserved for my senility; at the moment I can only point to the fact. Liberty, to-day, not only lacks its old hot partisans and romantic fanatics in America; it has grown so disreputable that even to mention it, save in terms of a fossilized and hollow rhetoric, becomes a sort of indecorum. I know of but one national organization that advocates it with any genuine heartiness, and that organization, not long ago, was rewarded with a violent denunciation on the floor of the House of Representatives: only the lone Socialist, once in jail himself for the same offense, made bold to defend it. From the chosen elders of the nation, legislative, executive and judicial, one hears only that demanding it is treason. It is the first duty of the free citizen, it appears, to make a willing sacrifice of the Bill of Rights. He must leap to the business gladly, and with no mental reservations. If he pauses, then he is a Bolshevik.

I venture to argue that this doctrine is evil, and that renouncing it would yield a sweeter usufruct to the American people than all the varieties of Service that now prevail. Of what use is it for Kiwanis to buy wooden legs for one-legged boys if they must grow up as slaves to the Anti-Saloon League? What is the net gain to a boomed and boosted town if its people, coincidentally, lose their right to trial by jury and their inviolability of domicile? Who gives a damn for the Coolidge idealism if its chief agent and executor, even the Cabinet, is the Board of Temperance, Prohibition and Public Morals of the Methodist Episcopal Church, *i.e.*, a gang of snooty ecclesiastics, committed unanimously to the doctrines that Christ should have been jailed for the business at Cana, that God sent she-bears to "tare" forty-two little children because they had made fun of Elisha's bald head, and that Jonah swallowed the whale? Imagine an immigrant studying the new science of Americanism, and coming to the eighteen amendments to the Constitution. What will he make of the discovery that only the Eighteenth embodies a categorical imperative—that all the others must yield to it when they conflict with it—that the Fourteenth and Fifteenth are not binding upon the Prohibitionists of the South and that the First, Fourth, Fifth and Sixth are not binding upon Prohibitionists anywhere?

I preach reaction. Bach to Bach! I can't find the word Service in the Constitution, but what is there is sounder and nobler than anything ever heard of where Regular Fellows meet to slap backs and blow spitballs—or, at all events, it *was* there before January 16, 1920. The Fathers, too, had a Vision. They were, in their way, forward-lookers; they were even go-getters. What they dreamed of and fought for was a civilization based upon a body of simple, equitable and reasonable laws—a code designed to break the chains of lingering medivælism and set the individual free. The thing they imagined was a commonwealth of free men, all equal before the law. Some of them had grave doubts about it, and put off making it a reality as long as possible, but in the end the optimists won over the doubters, and they all made the venture together. I am myself no partisan of their scheme. It seems to me that there were fundamental defects in it—that some of their primary assumptions were false. But in their intention, at least, there was something exhilarating, and in it there was also something sound. That something was the premiss that the first aim of civilization is to augment and safeguard the dignity of man—that it is worth nothing to be a citizen of a commonwealth which holds the humblest citizen cheaply and uses him ill.

This is what we have lost, and not all the whooping and yelling of new messiahs can cover the fact. The government, as I have shown, becomes the common enemy of all well-disposed and decent men. It commandeers and wastes their money, it assaults and insults them with outrageous and extravagant laws, and it turns loose upon them a horde of professional blackguards, bent only upon destroying their liberties. The individual, facing this pestilence of tyranny and corruption, finds himself quite helpless. If he goes to the agents of the government itself with his protest, he gets only stupid reviling. If he turns to his fellow victims for support, he is lucky to escape jail. Worse, he is lucky to escape lynching. For the thing has gone so far that the great majority of dull and unimaginative men have begun to take it as a matter of course—almost as the order of nature. The Bill of Rights becomes a mere series of romantic dithyrambs, without solid substance or meaning—say, like the Sermon on the Mount. The school-books of the next generation will omit it. The few fanatics who remember it will keep it on the top shelf, along with the Family Doctor

Book, the scientific works of Dr. Marie Stopes, and "Only a Boy."

Against all this I protest, feebly and too late. The land swarms with Men of Vision, all pining for Service. What I propose is that they forget their brummagem Grails for one week, and concentrate their pep upon a chase that really leads uphill. Let us have a Bill of Rights Week. Let us have a Common Decency Week.

III.
The Human Mind

I
On Metaphysicians

In the Summer of the year, when the weather on my estates in the Maryland jungles is too hot for serious mental activity, I always give over a couple of weeks to a re-reading of the so-called philosophical classics, with a glance or two at the latest compositions of the extant philosophers. It is a far from agreeable job, and I undertake it sadly, as a surgeon, after an untoward and fatal hemorrhage, brushes up on anatomy; there is, somewhere down in my recesses, an obscure conviction that I owe a duty to my customers, who look to me to flatter them with occasional dark references to Aristotle, Spinoza and the categorical imperative. Out of the business, despite its high austerity, I always carry away the feeling that I have had a hell of a time. That is, I carry away the feeling that the art and mystery of philosophy, as it is practiced in the world by professional philosophers, is largely moonshine and wind-music—or, to borrow Henry Ford's searching term, bunk.

Is this anarchy and atheism? Has Russian gold got to me at last? Am I in training for the abattoir of the Department of Justice? In stay of execution I can only point to the philosophy books themselves. For three millenniums their authors have been searching the world and its suburbs for the truth—and they have yet to agree upon so much as the rules of the search. Since the dawn of time they have been trying to get order and method into the thinking of *Homo sapiens*—and *Homo sapiens*, when he thinks at all, is still a brother to the lowly ass (*Equus africanus*), even to the ears and the bray. I include the philosophers themselves, unanimously and especially. True enough, one arises now and then who somehow manages to be charming and even plausible. I point to Plato, to Nietzsche, to Schopenhauer. But it is always as poet or politician, not as philosopher. The genuine professional, sticking to his gloomy speculations, is as dull as a table of logarithms. What man in human history ever wrote worse than Kant? Was it, perhaps, Hegel? My own candidate, if I were pushed, would be found among the so-called Critical Realists of to-day. They achieve the truly astounding feats of writing worse than the New Thoughters, whom they also resemble otherwise—nay, even worse than the late Warren Gamaliel Harding.

What reduces all philosophers to incoherence and folly, soon or late, is the lure of the absolute. It tortures them as the dream of Law Enforcement tortures Prohibitionists. Now and then, when they forget it transiently, they grow relatively rational and even ingratiating, but in the long run they always resume their chase of it, and that chase carries them inevitably into the intellectual Bad Lands. For the absolute, of course, is a mere banshee, a concept without substance or reality. No such thing exists. When, by logical devices, it is triumphantly established, the feat is exactly on all fours with that of the mathematician who proved that twice two was double once two. Who believes in Kant's categorical imperatives to-day? Certainly not any student of psychology who has got beyond the first page of his horn-book. There is, in fact, no idea in any man that may be found certainly in all men. Only the philosophers seem to cling to the doctrine that there is. Functioning as theologians, for example, they still argue for the immortality of the soul on the ground that a yearning for immortal life is in all of us. But that is simply nonsense. I know scores of men in whom no such yearning is apparent, either outwardly or in their consciousness. I have seen such men die, and they passed into what they held to be oblivion without showing the slightest sign of wishing that it was something else. All the other absolutes, whether theological, ethical or philosophical in the strict sense, are likewise chimeras. On inspection it always turns out that they are no more the same to all men than a woman A or a cocktail B is the same to all men. They are even different to the same man at different times. I cherished ethical postulates at the age of twenty-one that seem puerile to me to-day, and to-day I am cherishing postulates that would have shocked me then. *Quod est veritas?* Simply something that seems to me to be so—now, and to me. It has no more objective character than the sweet and dreadful passion of love. It is as tenderly personal and private as a gallstone.

The common sense of mankind, which is immensely superior to the anæmic, camphor-smelling wisdom of philosophers, long ago revolted against the quest of the absolute. Men found back in Mousterian days that it got them nowhere, but left them, intellectually speaking, with one leg up and one leg down. So they began to set up arbitrary values, if only to get some peace. Religion is a series of such arbitrary values. Most of them are dubious, and many of them are palpably false, but the experience of the race has shown that, for certain types of mind and in certain situations, they work. So they are accepted as, if not quite true, then as true enough, and the gloomy business of rectifying them, when they need it, is turned over to theologians, who are enemies of mankind anyhow, and thus deserve and get no sympathy when they suffer. Arbitrary values of the same sort are made use of every day in all the fields of human speculation and activity. They are brilliantly visible in the field of politics and government. Here they are rammed into children in the little red schoolhouse, and questioning them later in life becomes a crime against the Holy Ghost. Is it therefore to be assumed that they are true? Not at all. Many of them are so transparently dubious that even patriots, preparing to mumble them, have to make ready for it by closing their eyes and taking long breaths. But they at least work. They at least get some semblance of order into the complicated and dangerous business of living together in society. They at least relieve the mind. And so they are cherished.

Unfortunately, human existence is not static but dynamic, and in consequence the axioms that work well to-day tend to work less well to-morrow. Now and then, as the social organization changes, certain ancient and honorable ones have to be abandoned. This is always a perilous business, and usually it is accomplished only by a letting of blood. The fact is not without its significance. In the long run, I believe, it will be found that (as the Behaviorists argue even now) human ideas come out of the liver far more often than they come out of the soul, and that changing them is a job for surgeons rather than for metaphysicians. The thought leads at once to a constructive suggestion, and in the exalted field of pedagogy. What is the present aim of education, as the professors thereof expound it? To make good citizens. And what is a good citizen? Simply one who never says, does or thinks anything that is unusual. Schools are maintained in order to bring this uniformity up to the highest possible point. A school is a hopper into which children are heaved while they are still young and tender; therein they are pressed into certain standard shapes and covered from head to heels with official rubber-stamps. Unluckily, it is a very inefficient machine. Many children, though squeezed diligently, do not take the standard shapes. Others have hides so oily that the most indelible of rubber-stamps is washed from them by the first rain, or even blown from them by the first wind.

It is my notion that surgery will one day find a remedy for this unpleasant and dangerous state of affairs. It will first perfect means of detecting such aberrant children in their early youth, and then it will devise means of curing them. The child who laughs when the Bill of Rights is read will not be stood in a corner and deprived of chewing-gum, as now; it will be sent to the operating-table, and the offending convolution, or gland, or tumor, or whatever it is will be cut out. While it is lying open all other suspicious excrescences will be removed, and so it will be returned to the class-room a normal 100% American. This scheme, if it turns out to be practicable, will add a great deal to the happiness of the American people. It will not only protect those of us who are naturally respectable from the menace of strange and disturbing ideas; it will also relieve the present agonies of those who cherish them. For the search for imaginary absolutes—*i.e.*, for the truth, that ghost—is not pleasant, as poets allege, but intensely painful. There is no record in human history of a happy philosopher: they exist only in romantic legend. Many of them have committed suicide; practically all of them have turned their children out of doors and beaten their wives. And no wonder! If you want to find out how a philosopher feels when he is engaged in the practice of his profession, go to the nearest zoo and watch a chimpanzee at the wearying and hopeless job of chasing fleas. Both suffer damnably, and neither can win.

2
On Suicide

The suicide rate, so I am told by an intelligent mortician, is going up everywhere on earth. It is good news to his profession, which has been badly used of late by the progress of medical science, and scarcely less so by the rise of cut-throat, go-getting competition within its own ranks. It is also good news to those romantic optimists who like to believe that the human race is capable of rational acts. What could be more logical than suicide? What could be more preposterous than keeping alive? Yet nearly all of us cling to life with desperate devotion, even when the length of it remaining is palpably slight, and filled with agony. Half the time of all medical men is wasted keeping life in human wrecks who have no more intelligible reason for hanging on than a cow has for mooing.

In part, no doubt, this absurd frenzy has its springs in the human imagination, or, as it is more poetically called, the human reason. Man, having acquired the high faculty of visualizing death, visualizes it as something painful and dreadful. It is, of course, seldom anything of the sort. The proceedings anterior to it are sometimes (though surely not always) painful, but death itself appears to be almost devoid of sensation, either psychic or physical. The candidate, facing it at last, simply loses his faculties. Death is no more to him than it is to a coccus. The dreadful, like the painful, is not in it. It is far more likely to show elements of the grotesque. I speak here, of course, of natural death. Suicide is plainly more unpleasant, if only because there is some uncertainty about it. The candidate hesitates to shoot himself because he fears, with some show of reason, that he may fail to kill himself, and only hurt himself. Moreover, this shooting, along with most of the other more common aids to an artificial exitus, involves a kind of affront to his dignity: it is apt to make a mess. But that objection, it seems to me, is one that is bound to disappear with the progress of science. Safe, sure, easy and sanitary methods of departing this life will be invented. Some, in truth, are already known, and perhaps the fact explains the steady increase in suicides, so satisfactory to my mortician friend.

I pass over the theological objections to self-destruction as too transparently sophistical to be worth a serious answer. From the earliest days Christianity has depicted life on this earth as so sad and vain that its value is indistinguishable from that of a damn. Then why cling to it? Simply because its vanity and unpleasantness are parts of the will of a Creator whose love for His creatures takes the form of torturing them. If they revolt in this world they will be tortured a million times worse in the next. I present the argument as a typical specimen of theological reasoning, and proceed to more engaging themes. Specifically, to my original thesis: that it is difficult, if not impossible, to discover any evidential or logical reason, not instantly observed to be full of fallacy, for keeping alive. The fact that we nevertheless do it is no more than proof that reason is mainly only a sort of afterthought. I enjoy the effects of alcohol when I am sad. *Ergo*, all Prohibitionists are fools and most of them are scoundrels. Alcohol makes me ill and killed my Uncle Emil. *Ergo*, it ought to be prohibited by law, as it is by the Holy Scriptures, though in a passage that, at the moment, I can't recall. I admire and enjoy Americans, particularly when they make asses of themselves. *Ergo*, any foreigner who essays to butcher them is a fiend from Hell. Americans fatigue me. *Ergo*, the same foreigner is a charming fellow.

But sometimes these second thoughts—and *all* thoughts are second thoughts—are unanimous, and then they become what is called universal wisdom. The universal wisdom of the world long ago concluded that life is mainly a curse. Turn to the proverbial philosophy of any race, and you will find it full of a sense of the futility of the mundane struggle. Anticipation is better than realization. Disappointment is the lot of man. We are born in pain and die in sorrow. The lucky man died a' Wednesday. He giveth His beloved sleep. I could run the list to pages. If you disdain folk-wisdom, secular or sacred, then turn to the immortal works of William Shakespeare. They drip with such pessimism from end to end. If there is any general idea in them, it is the idea that human existence is a painful futility. Out, out, brief candle!

Yet we cling to it in a muddled physiological sort of way—or, perhaps more accurately, in a pathological way—and even try to fill it with gaudy hocus-pocus. All men who, in any true sense, are sentient strive mightily for distinction and power, *i.e.*, for the respect and envy of their fellowmen, *i.e.*, for the ill-natured admiration of an endless series of miserable and ridiculous bags of rapidly disintegrating amino acids. Why? If I knew, I'd certainly not be writing books in this infernal American climate; I'd be sitting in state in a hall of crystal and gold, and people would be paying $10 a head to gape at me through peep-holes. But though the central mystery remains, it is possible, perhaps, to investigate the superficial symptoms to some profit. I offer myself as a laboratory animal. Why have I worked so hard for thirty years, desperately striving to accomplish something that remains impenetrable to me to this day? Is it because I desire money? Bosh! I can't recall ever desiring it for an instant: I have always found it easy to get all I wanted. Is it, then, notoriety that I am after? Again the answer must be no. The attention of strangers is unpleasant to me, and I avoid it as much as possible. Then is it a yearning to Do Good that moves me? Bosh and blah! If I am convinced of anything, it is that Doing Good is in bad taste.

Once I ventured the guess that men worked in response to a vague inner urge for self-expression. But that was probably a feeble theory, for some men who work the hardest have nothing to express. An hypothesis with rather more plausibility in it now suggests itself. It is that men work simply in order to escape the depressing agony of contemplating life—that their work, like their play, is a mumbo-jumbo that serves them by permitting them to escape from reality. Both work and play, ordinarily, are illusions. Neither serves any solid and permanent purpose. If work has what is called value, then it only condemns more human beings to work. But life, stripped of such illusions, instantly becomes unbearable. Man cannot sit still, contemplating his destiny in this world, without going frantic. So he invents ways to take his mind off the horror. He works. He plays. He accumulates the preposterous nothing called property. He strives for the coy eye-wink called fame. He founds a family, and spreads his curse over others. All the while the thing that moves him is simply the yearning to lose himself, to forget himself, to escape the tragi-comedy that is himself. Life, fundamentally, is not worth living. So he confects artificialities to make it so. So he erects a gaudy structure to conceal the fact that it is *not* so.

Perhaps my talk of agonies and tragi-comedies may be a bit misleading. The basic fact about human existence is not that it is a tragedy, but that it is a bore. It is not so much a war as an endless standing in line. The objection to it is not that it is predominantly painful, but that it is lacking in sense. What is ahead for the race? Even theologians, to whom devils are easily visible, can see nothing but a gray emptiness, with a burst of irrational fireworks at the end. But there is such a thing as human progress. True. It is the progress that a felon makes from the watch-house to the jail, and from the jail to the death-house. Every generation faces the same intolerable boredom.

I speak as one who has had what must be regarded, speaking statistically, as a happy life. I work a great deal, but working is more agreeable to me than anything else I can imagine. I am conscious of no vast, overwhelming and unattainable desires. I want nothing that I can't get. But it remains my conclusion, at the gate of senility, that the whole thing is a grandiose futility, and not even amusing. The end is always a vanity, and usually a sordid one, without any noble touch of the pathetic. The means remain. In them lies a secret of what is called contentment, *i.e.*, the capacity to postpone suicide for at least another day. They are themselves without meaning, but at all events they offer a way of escape from the paralyzing reality. The central aim of life is to simulate extinction. We have been yelling up the wrong rain-spout.

3
On Controversy

Any man engaged habitually in controversy, as I have been for twenty years past, must enter upon his declining days with a melancholy sense of its hollowness and futility. Especially in this great Republic, where all ideas are suspect, it tends almost inevitably to degenerate into a mere exchange of nonsense. Have you ever examined carefully the speeches made by the candidates in a Presidential campaign? If so, you know that they are of bilge and blather all compact. Now and then, true enough, one of the august aspirants to the Washingtonian breeches is goaded or misled into saying something pungent and even apposite, but not often, not deliberately. His daily stint is simply balderdash.

It is rare, indeed, to encounter a controversialist who states his own case clearly, or who shows any sign of understanding his opponent's. Turn, for example, to the current combat between the Fundamentalists and the Modernists—an academic and puerile duel in our great Sodoms and Ninevehs, but raging like an oil fire in the Bible and Hookworm Belt, where men are he and Hell yawns. Both sides wallow in pishposh. The Fundamentalists, claiming a monopoly of faith, allege that they believe the whole Bible *verbatim et literatim*, which is not true, for at least 99% of them reject Exodus XXII, 18, to say nothing of I Timothy V, 23. And the Modernists argue that there is no conflict between science and Holy Writ, which is even less true. This controversy, in fact, is almost classical in character. Neither side is able to stick to the question at issue. Each tries to dispose of the other by delivering mighty wallops below the belt—the Fundamentalists by passing laws converting the Modernists into criminals (that is, as criminality is now defined by American jurisprudence), and the Modernists by depicting the Fundamentalists as a horde of gibbering baboons, sworn to uproot civilization and not above suspicion of cannibalism.

I have had a hand in this great battle of scattered wits myself, striving in an austere and lofty manner to introduce the sublime principles of Aristotle's "Organon" into it. I have got the traditional reward of one stopping to preach in front of a house afire. The more extreme Modernists—which is to say, the professional atheists,—discontented because I haven't advocated hanging the Fundamentalists, denounce me as a Crypto-Calvinist, and hold me up to obloquy in their papers. The Fundamentalists, suspecting me of a partiality for Darwin, accuse me of trying to upset the Ten Commandments, and one of the most eminent of them lately hinted that I have personally had a bout with No. 7, and come to grief in the manner described by the late Dr. Sylvanus Stall, in his well-known work on pathology, "What Every Boy of Fourteen Should Know." This last accusation was novel, but, as they run in such affairs, very mild. The usual charge against an opponent, in the

America of to-day, is that he is a Bolshevist, and in receipt of traitor's gold. It has been leveled at me so often that probably a majority of the persons who have heard of me at all believe it, and there are even dismal days when I half believe it myself, though I have been denouncing Socialism publicly for twenty years, and am, in fact, an incurable Tory in politics. A short while ago a Boston critic, becoming aware of the latter fact by some miracle, at once proceeded to denounce me because my radicalism, as he thought he had discovered, was bogus.

During the decade 1910–1920 I was chiefly engaged in literary controversies, and so my politics were aside from the issue. But when the great wave of idealism engulfed the United States in 1917, I was at once bawled out as a German spy, and open demands were made that my purely æsthetic heresies be put down by the *Polizei*. One of my opponents, in those days, was an eminent college professor, now unhappily deceased. He not only attempted to dispose of my literary judgments by arguing that they were inspired by the Kaiser; he even made the same charge against the works of the writers I was currently whooping up. And so did many of his learned colleagues. It was not easy to meet this onslaught by logical devices; logic, in those days, was completely adjourned, along with the Bill of Rights. Moreover, there was a considerable plausibility in the general charge. So I attempted no defense; it is, indeed, against my nature to take the defensive. Instead, I launched into an elaborate effort to prove that all college professors, regardless of their politics, were hollow and preposterous asses, and to this business I brought up all the ancient and horrifying devices of the art of rhetoric.

The issue of the controversy was characteristic: thus all combats in the realm of so-called ideas end. The moment the War to End War was over there came a revulsion against its blather, and so it was no longer damaging to me to be accused of taking the money of the Hohenzollern. Thus the professor I have mentioned suddenly found his principal ammunition gone, and in an effort to unearth more he began reading the books I had been advocating. To his surprise he found that many of them were works of high merit, whereupon he began whooping for them himself, and even going beyond my loudest hurrahs. In the end he was actually searching them for evidences of Teutonic influence, and hailing it with enthusiasm when found! His poor fellow-professors, meanwhile, were the goats. I ceased to revile them, once the war was over, and devoted myself mainly to political and moral concerns, but various other controversialists took up the jehad where I left off, and in a short time it was raging from coast to coast. It got far beyond anything I had myself dreamed of. Indignant publicists, quite unknown to me, began grouping all professors with chiropractors, Congressmen and spiritualists. In dozens of colleges large and small, North, East, South and West, the students began holding meetings and flinging insults at their tutors. Scores of college papers, for flouting them in contumacious terms, had to be suppressed. In several great institutions of learning the thing actually reached the form of physical assault. When the smoke cleared away the professor, once so highly respected by every one, found himself a sort of questionable character, and he remains so to this day. In many cases, I believe, he actually is, but surely not in all. The point is that the virtuous have suffered with the guilty. Many an honest and God-fearing professor, laboriously striving to ram his dismal nonsense into the progeny of Babbitts, is bombarded with ribald spit-balls as a result of a controversy which begun quite outside his ken and speedily got far beyond the issue between the original combatants.

Such are the ways of war in the psychic field. Why they should be so I don't know, but so they are. No controversy to my knowledge has ever ended on the ground where it began. Even the historic one between Huxley and Wilberforce, two of the most eminent men of their time in England, ranged all over the landscape before the contestants had enough. It began with Huxley trying to prove that Darwin's "Origin of Species" was a sound book; it ended with Bishop Wilberforce trying to prove that Huxley's grandfather was a gorilla. What was its issue? Did Huxley convert Wilberforce? Did Wilberforce make any dent in the armor of Huxley? I apologize for wasting your time with silly rhetorical questions. Did Luther convert Leo X? Did Grant convert Lee?

4
On Faith

Some time ago I received a letter from a learned Socialist, one very active in the movement, but long since retired. It was stuffed with circulars advertising a new sure cure for all human ills, from bellyache to cancer. This invention, the Socialist assured me, was no fake. He had personally seen it snatch back men and women from the brink of the grave. It would be in use everywhere, he said, and saving hundreds of thousands of lives a year, if it were not for the hellish conspiracies of the American Medical Association.

It all seemed familiar. More, it all seemed quite natural. For who has ever heard of a Socialist who did not also believe in some other quackery? I have known all of the principal gladiators of the movement in my time, at least in America; I have yet to meet one who was not as gullible as a Mississippi darkey, nay, even a Mississippi white man. Didn't Karl Marx himself carry a madstone and believe in astrology? If not, then it was strange indeed. Didn't Debs believe that quinine would cure a cold? If not, then he was not a genuine Socialist.

The leading living Socialist of this great Republic is Upton Sinclair. Perhaps, indeed, he is the only leader the movement has left, for Debs is dead, and most of the rest leaped down the sewers during the late war. Well, Sinclair believes in so many different kinds of nonsense that he needs two thick volumes to record them. He was one of the earliest believers in the fasting cure for catarrh, and he was one of the first dupes to be roped in by the late Dr. Albert Abrams, the San Francisco swindler. I do not hold all this against Sinclair: he is a charming fellow otherwise. I merely say that such credulity is natural to Socialists. Turn to England, where one of the late heroes of the movement is young Oliver Baldwin, son of the Prime Minister. Some time ago the Associated Press was reporting from London that Oliver had taken to spiritualism and was hearing "spirit voices coming from all parts of the room in no fewer than five languages."

As I have said, practically all of the more eminent Socialists of the United States took to the sewers in 1917. When the gunmen of the Hon. A. Mitchell Palmer began rounding up the lesser comrades, and pliant Federal judges began sending them to Atlanta for five, ten and twenty years, the high-toned members of the movement saw a great light, and began to bawl and sob for the flag. Now, with the danger over, they can't get back: the surviving comrades won't have anything to do with them, and even denounce them bitterly as scabs. But if the Marxian grove is thus closed to them, there is plenty of room for them around other flambeaux, and all of them seem to be crowding up. A considerable number, in 1920, became violent Prohibitionists, and began predicting that the country would be bone-dry in two years. Others became chiropractors. Yet others announced that they were converted to the League of Nations. Many became spiritualists, and a few, I believe, followed Sinclair in succumbing to Dr. Abrams. The rest went in for free love, Fundamentalism, mental telepathy, the Harding idealism, Texas oil stocks, numerology, the poetry of T. S. Eliot, the music of Erik Satie, or the ouija board. One or two became professional sorcerers. The point is that every last one of them found some sort of satisfaction and solace for the imperative need of his nature—every one found something outlandish and preposterous to believe in. For all of them, as ex-Socialist, had believing minds. They could get rid of their Socialism, especially when helped by the *Polizei*, but they could no more get rid of their believing minds than they could get rid of the shapes of their heads. A Socialist, in brief, is simply a man suffering from an overwhelming compulsion to believe what is not true. He yearns for it as a cow yearns for the milkmaid, lowing in the cool of the evening. He pines for it as a dry Congressman pines for a drink.

Of all the things that are palpably not true Socialism is one of the most satisfying to men of that romantic kidney, and so nine-tenths of them, at one time or another in their lives, are Socialists, or, if not Socialists, then at least Progressives, or Single Taxers, or evangelists of Farm Relief. But Socialism, though it is sweet, is never enough for them, and neither is the Single Tax. They always reach out for something else. They always succumb to some other and worse Marx, with longer whiskers and dirtier finger-nails. Years ago, when the Single Taxers were still making a noise in the land, I made a roster of the princes of the movement, setting down beside each name the varieties of balderdash that its owner believed in. There was not a single name without two entries and some of them had a dozen. One of the leading Single Taxers was also president of the League for Medical Freedom, a verein of quacks organized to oppose vaccination. Another was militant anti-vivisectionist, and proposed that the Johns Hopkins Medical School be closed by the police. A third was an anthropophagous atheist of the kind that proselytes, especially among peaceable old ladies. A third was a table-tapper, and a fourth got messages from the ghosts of Martin Luther, Lucy Stone and Sitting Bull. A fifth deserted his wife for a cutie with pansy eyes, and lost, in consequence, his job as a college professor. A sixth, believing that he was Millard Fillmore, was put away by his family.

What lies beneath all this is simply an ancient fact, noted long ago by William James, and before him by Friedrich Wilhelm Nietzsche, and before him by the Greeks, and before the Greeks by the first human politicians. It is the fact that the race of men is divided sharply into two classes: those who are what James called tough-minded, and demand proofs before they will believe, and those who are what he called tender-minded, and are willing to believe anything that seems to be pleasant. It is the tender-minded who keep quacks of all sorts well-fed and active, and hence vastly augment the charm of this world. They find it wholly impossible to distinguish between what is subjectively agreeable and what is objectively true. Would it be nice if the whole world turned sober overnight, and even flappers put away the jug? If so, then there must be a quick and sure way to accomplish it. Does Prohibition promise to do so? If so, then Prohibition must be true. This is precisely the route by which Sinclair became a Prohibitionist—one of his follies that I forgot to mention above. And this is the route by which multitudes of his tender-hearted brethren and sistren followed him into the jaws of the Anti-Saloon League.

Socialism, while it was still vague and untested, appealed powerfully to all such persons. Fifteen or twenty years ago it was making immense progress in the United States, vice Free Silver, deceased. All the young college professors, in those days, were Socialists, as they are now eugenists and birth controllers. It swept and enchanted the tender-minded. Fat women wept over it, as they now weep over the Armenians. But one day it collided slambang with the harsh and horrible facts. One day it was put to the test in Russia,—and promptly blew up. Even the tender-minded could not dodge the appalling proofs. So they fled in this direction and that. Some took to spiritualism, some to chiropractic, some to Genesis. Some, like Sinclair, took to Prohibition, the Single Tax, fasting, and the electronic vibrations of Dr. Abrams. But not one, so far as I can make out, took to sense.

IV.
Clarion Call to Poets

ONE of the crying needs of the time in this incomparable Republic—the goal and despair of all other and hence lesser states—is for a suitable Burial Service for the admittedly damned. I speak as one who has of late attended the funeral orgies of several such gentlemen, each time to my æsthetic distress. The first of these gentlemen, having a great abhorrence of rhetoric in all its branches, left strict orders that not a word was to be said at his obsequies. The result was two extremely chilly and uncomfortable moments: when six of us walked into his house in utter silence and carried out his clay, and when we shoved it, in the same crawling silence, into the yawning firebox of the crematory. The whole business was somehow unnatural and even a shade indecent: it violated one of the most ancient sentiments of *Homo sapiens* to dispatch so charming a fellow in so cavalier a fashion. One felt almost irresistibly impelled to say good-by to him in some manner or other, if only, soldier fashion, by blowing a bugle and rolling a drum. Even the mortician, an eminent star of one of the most self-possessed of professions, looked a bit uneasy and ashamed.

The second funeral was even worse. The deceased had been a Socialist of the militantly anti-clerical variety, and threatened, on his death-bed, to leap from his coffin with roars if a clergyman were hired to snuffle over him. His widow accordingly asked two of his Socialist colleagues to address the mourners. They prepared for the business by resorting to a bootlegger, and in consequence both of them were garrulous and injudicious. One of them traced the career of Karl Marx in immense detail, and deduced from it a long series of lessons for ambitious American boys. The other, after first denouncing the New York *Times*, read twenty or thirty cantos of execrable poetry from the *Freethinker*. If the widow had not performed a series of very realistic sobs—leaning for support, I may add, upon a comrade who soon afterward succeeded to the rights of the deceased in her person and real estate—the ceremony would have been indistinguishable from a session of the House of Representatives.

The third funeral was conducted by Freemasons, who came in plug hats and with white aprons over their cow-catchers. They entered the house of mourning in a long file, with their hats held over their left breasts in the manner of a President reviewing an inaugural parade, and filed past the open coffin at a brisk parade march. As each passed he gave a swift, mechanical glance at the fallen brother: there was in it the somewhat metallic efficiency of an old hand. These Freemasons brought their own limousines and took a place in the funeral procession ahead of the hearse. At the cemetery they deployed around the grave, and as soon as the clergyman had finished his mumbo-jumbo, began a ceremonial of their own. Their leader, standing at the head of the grave with his plug hat on, first read a long series of quasi-theological generalities—to the general effect, so far as I could make out, that Freemasons are immune to Hell, as they are notoriously immune to hanging—, and then a brother at the foot of the grave replied. After that there was a slight pause, and in rather ragged chorus the rest of the brethren said "So mote it be!" This went on almost endlessly; I was heartily glad when it as over. The whole ceremony, in fact, was tedious and trashy. As for me, I'd rather have been planted by a Swedenborgian, whiskers and all. Or even by a grand goblin of the Ethical Culture Society.

What is needed, and what I bawl for politely, is a service that is free from the pious but unsupported asseverations that revolt so many of our best minds, and yet remains happily graceful and consoling. It will be very hard, I grant you, to concoct anything as lasciviously beautiful as the dithyrambs in the Book of Common prayer. Who wrote them originally I don't know, but whoever did it was a poet. They put the highly improbable into amazingly luscious words, and the palpably not-true into words even more caressing and disarming. It is impossible to listen to them, when they are intoned by a High Church rector of sepulchral gifts, without harboring a sneaking wish that, by some transcendental magic, they could throw off their lowly poetical character and take on the dignity and reliability of prose—in other words, that the departed could be actually imagined as leaping out of the grave on the Last

Morn, his split colloids all restored to their pristine complexity, his clothes neatly scoured and pressed, and every molecule of him thrilling with a wild surmise. I have felt this wish at the funerals of many virtuous and earnest brethren, whose sole sin was their refusal to swallow such anecdotes as the one in II Kings II, 23–24. It seems a pity that men of that sort should be doomed to Hell, and it seems an even greater pity that they should be laid away to the banal chin-music of humorless Freemasons and stewed Socialists.

But, so far as I know, no suitable last rites for them have ever been drawn up. Between the service in the Book of Common Prayer (and its various analogues, nearly all of them greatly inferior) and the maudlin mortuary dialogues of the Freemasons, Ku Kluxers, Knights of Pythias and other such assassins of beauty there is absolutely nothing. Even the professional agnostics, who are violently literary, have never produced anything worthy to be considered; their best is indistinguishable from the text of a flag-drill or high-school pageant. Thus the average American skeptic, when his time comes to return to earth, is commonly turned off with what, considering his prejudices, may be best described as a razzing. His widow, disinclined to risk scandal by burying him without any ceremonies at all, calls in the nearest clergyman, and the result is a lamentable comedy, creditable neither to honest faith nor to honest doubt. More than once, in attendance upon such an affair, I have observed a sardonic glitter in the eye of the pastor, especially when he came to the unequivocal statement that the deceased would infallibly rise again. Did he secretly doubt it? Or was he poking fun at a dead opponent, now persuaded of the truth of revelation at last? In either case there was something unpleasant in the spectacle. A suitable funeral for doubters, full of lovely poetry but devoid of any specific pronouncement on the subject of a future life, would make such unpleasantness unnecessary.

We have the poets for the job, and I incline to suspect that their private theological ideas fit them for it. Skepticism, in fact, runs with their cynical trade. Most Americans, as every one knows, give their ecclesiastical affiliations in "Who's Who in America"—especially Congressmen, pedagogues, bank presidents and uplifters. But not the poets. The sole exception, so far as I can make out, is Vachel Lindsay, who reports that he is a member of the "Christian (Disciples) Church," a powerful sect in the No-More-Scrub-Bulls Belt, with a private Hell of its own, deep and hot. Even Edgar Albert Guest is silent on the subject, though he mentions the fact that he is a 33° Mason. Frost, Robinson, Sandburg and Masters keep suspiciously mum. I suggest that they meet in some quiet saloon and draw up the ritual I advocate. Let Masters be chairman of the committee: he is a lawyer as well as a poet, and may be trusted to keep within the statutes. And let Edna St. Vincent Millay be added to give the thing a refined voluptuousness, and James Weldon Johnson to put music into it, that it may be intoned without getting the celebrant out of breath. Here Holy Church shows the way. Its funeral service is a great deal less forensic than operatic.

There is some need, too, for a Marriage Service for the damned, and at different times attempts have been made to supply it. But all such works seem to emanate from radicals showing a characteristic lack of humor—and humor is as necessary to a Marriage Service as poetry is to a Funeral Service: a fact that the astute authors of the Book of Common Prayer did not overlook. However, the need here is not pressing, for in most American States civil marriage is sufficient, and heretics may be safely united without going before a sorcerer at all. Court clerks and police magistrates perform the job, mumbling unintelligibly out of a mysterious book, perhaps only a stolen Gideon Bible, excavated to hold cigarettes. The main thing is to pay the fee. Marriages after midnight cost double, and if the bridegroom has the fumes of wine in his head, he is apt to lose his watch as well as his liberty.

As I say, the Marriage Services drawn up by antinomians for the use of unbelievers lack humor. Worse, they are full of indignation—against the common theory that a wife is bound to give some care to her husband's goods, against the convention that she shall adopt his surname, and so on. It is hard to give serious attention to such grim notions at a time immemorially viewed as festive and jocose. One hears frequently of wedding guests getting drunk and fighting—not long ago a Methodist pastor in Missouri was protesting against it publicly—, but when they are drawn into sociological controversy it is too much. Such revolutionary Marriage Services, in point of fact, have never gained much popularity. Now and then a pair of Socialists resorts to one, but even Socialists appear to prefer the harsh, mechanical offices of a court clerk.

Nor is there any active demand for a non-theological Baptismal Service. I am constantly amazed, as a bachelor, by the number of children growing up, in these iconoclastic modern days, without any formal naming at all. Not only do heretics spurn the ceremony; even professing Christians often neglect it. In my own nonage practically all babies, at least of the more respectable tribes of the race, were christened. There was a general feeling that failing to put them through the sacrament was, in some obscure way, a tort against them—that it would bring them bad luck, and perhaps lead to difficulties in after life. It is so believed to this day nearly everywhere in Europe, and for sound reasons. Whenever a citizen in those decaying lands comes into contact with the state, which is very often, its agents demand his baptismal certificate as well as his birth certificate. So far, the imbeciles at Washington have not come to that, but it must be plain that they will come to it soon or late, and when the time is finally upon us there will be trouble for all those Americanos whose naming is now trusted to acclamation. They will have to dig up senile aunts and uncles, and produce affidavits that they were known to every one as so-and-so at some date far in the past, just as they now have to get such affidavits, more often than not, when they want passports. The bureaucracy grinds slowly, but it grinds exceeding fine. Recruited from the mentally deficient, it runs to circular insanities. Let it be proved to-morrow that some John Doe, suspected of favoring the recognition of Russia, was actually baptized Johannes, and it will be sufficient excuse for a regulation requiring all of us to prove that we are legally entitled to the names we sign to checks.

But all these are side issues. The main thing is that the poets, though most of them seem to have departed from the precincts and protection of Holy Church and her schismatic colonies—since when has a first-rate American poet written a hymn?—have failed, so far, to rise to the occasion when, even among heretics, poets are most pressingly needed. I have suggested that they meet in some convenient speak-easy and remedy the lack gloriously, but I don't insist, of course, that their service for the doubting dead be wholly original. The authors of the Book of Common Prayer, though they were poets of great talent, certainly did not trust only to their private inspiration. They borrowed copiously from the old missals, and they borrowed, too, directly from Holy Writ. What they concocted finally was a composite, but it was very discreetly and delicately put together, and remains impregnable to this day, despite many furious efforts to undo it.

All I propose is that the committee of poets imitate them, but with an avoidance of strophes objectionable in doctrine. Isn't there material enough in the books? There is enough, and to spare. I point to the works of Walt Whitman, now at last passing freely through the mails—to those parts, of course, of a non-erotic and non-political nature. I point to certain memorable stanzas of William Cullen Bryant. I point to Blake, Tennyson, Milton, Shelley, Keats, even Swinburne; what gaudy stuff for the purpose is in "Ave Atque Vale," "Tristram of Lyonesse" and "Atalanta in Calydon"! There is here a sweet soothing, a healing reassurance, a divine booziness—in brief, all the stuff of A No. 1 poetry. It would bring comfort, I believe, to many a poor widow who now groans as the Freemasons intone their balderdash, or flounces her veil, fidgets and blushes as a Socialist orator denounces Omnipotence for permitting stock dividends—it would bring her a great deal more comfort, certainly, than the positive statement, made defiantly by the unwilling rector of the parish, that her departed John, having been colloidal and as the beasts, has now become gaseous and immortal. Such a libretto for the inescapable last act would be humane and valuable. I renew my suggestion that the poets spit upon their hands and confect it at once.

V.
Souvenirs of a Book Reviewer

I
The Emperor of Wowsers

ANTHONY COMSTOCK: ROUNDSMAN OF THE LORD, by Heywood Broun and Margaret Leech. New York: *Albert & Charles Boni.* [Books, March 6, 1927.]

IN an appendix to this amusing and instructive work, Mr. Broun states the case against comstockery in a neat, realistic and unanswerable manner, but the book itself is by no means a philippic against old Anthony. On the contrary, it deals with him in a very humane and even ingratiating way. And why not? He was, in point of fact, a man of manifold virtues, and even his faults showed a rugged, Berserker quality that was sneakingly charming. It is quite impossible, at this distance, to doubt his *bona fides*, and almost as difficult, despite his notorious extravagances, to question his essential sanity. Like all the rest of us in our several ways, he was simply a damned fool. Starting out in life with an idea lying well within the bounds of what most men would call the rational, he gradually pumped it up until it bulged over all four borders. But he never departed from it altogether; he never let go his hold upon logic; he never abandoned reason for mere intuition. Once his premisses were granted, the only way to escape his conclusions was to forsake Aristotle for Epicurus. Such logical impeccability, as all connoisseurs must know, is very common among theologians; they hold, indeed, almost a monopoly of it. The rest of us, finding that our ratiocination is leading us into uncomfortable waters, give it the slip and return to dry land. But not the theologians. They have horribly literal minds; they are less men than intellectual machines. I defy any one to find a logical flaw in their proofs of the existence of Hell. They demonstrate it magnificently and irrefutably. Do multitudes of wise men nevertheless deny it? Then that is only because very few wise men have any honest belief in the reality of the thing that the theologians and other logicians call truth.

Mr. Broun, in his appendix, tries to find holes in Anthony's logic, but it turns out to be far from easy: what he arrives at, in the end, is mainly only proof that a logician is an immensely unpleasant fellow. Turn, for example, to a typical and very familiar comstockian syllogism. First premiss: The effect of sexual images, upon the young, is to induce auto-erotism. Second premiss: the effects of auto-erotism are idiocy, epilepsy and locomotor ataxia. *Ergo*, now is the time for all good men to put down every book or picture likely to evoke sexual images. What is wrong with all this? Simply that Mr. Broun and you and I belong to a later generation than Anthony's, and are thus skeptical of his premisses. But let us not forget that they were true for him. His first came out of the hard, incontrovertible experience of a Puritan farm-boy, in executive session behind the barn. His second was supported, when he was getting his education, by the almost unanimous medical opinion of Christendom. And so his conclusion was perfect. We have made no progress in logic since his time; we have simply made progress in skepticism. All his grand truths are now dubious, and most of them are laughed at even by sucklings.

I think that he himself had a great deal to do with upsetting them. The service that he performed, in his grandiose way, was no more than a magnification of the service that is performed every day by multitudes of humble Y.M.C.A. secretaries, evangelical clergymen, and other such lowly fauna. It is their function in the world to ruin their ideas by believing in them and living them. Striving sincerely to be patterns to the young, they suffer the ironical fate of becoming horrible examples. I remember very well, how, as a boy of ten, I was articled to the Y.M.C.A.: the aim was to improve my taste for respectability, and so curb my apparently natural flair for the art and mystery of the highwayman. But a few months of contact with the official representatives of that great organization filled me with a vast loathing, not only for the men themselves, but also for all the ideas they stood for. Thus, at the age of eleven, I abandoned Christian Endeavor forevermore, and have been an antinomian ever since, contumacious to holy men and resigned to Hell. Old Anthony, I believe, accomplished much the same thing that the Y.M.C.A. achieved with me, but on an immeasurably larger scale. He did more than any other man to ruin Puritanism in the United States. When he began his long and brilliant career of unwitting sabotage, the essential principles of comstockery were believed in by practically every reputable American. Half a century later, when he went upon the shelf, comstockery enjoyed a degree of public esteem, at least in the big cities, half way between that enjoyed by phrenology and that enjoyed by homosexuality. It was, at best, laughable. It was, at worst, revolting.

So much did one consecrated man achieve in the short span of his life. I believe that it was no mean accomplishment. Anthony managed it, not because there was any unusual ability in him, but simply because he had a congenital talent for giving shows. The fellow, in his way, was a sort of Barnum. A band naturally followed him, playing in time to his yells. He could not undertake even so banal a business as raiding a dealer in abortifacient pills without giving it the melodramatic air of a battle with a brontosaurus. So a crowd always followed him, and when he made a colossal ass of himself, which was very frequently, the fact was bruited about. Years of such gargantuan endeavor made him one of the national clowns—and his cause one of the national jokes. In precisely the same way, I believe, such gaudy zanies as the Rev. Dr. Billy Sunday and the Rev. John Roach Straton are ruining the evangelical demonology in the Bible Belt. They make so much uproar that no one can fail to notice them. The young peasants, observing them, are gradually enlightened by them—unintentionally, but none the less surely. The men themselves are obviously charlatans; *ergo*, their ideas must be fraudulent too. What has been the net effect of the Scopes trial, with its solemn martyrdom of William Jennings Bryan? Its chief effect seems to be that societies of young atheists are now flourishing in all the Southern colleges. Has the study of Darwin been put down? Far from it. Darwin is now being read below the Potomac, and by the flower of Christian youth, as assiduously as "Only a Boy" used to be read in New York in the great days of Anthony's historic offensive against it.

Comstockery, of course, still lives, but it must be manifest that its glories have greatly faded. There is, anon, a series of raids and uproars, but they soon pass, and the work of the Devil goes on. It would be hard to imagine Anthony taking orders from district attorneys, or going into amicable conference with his enemies (and God's), or consenting to the appointment of joint committees (mainly made up of obvious anti-Puritans) to discover and protect the least dirty among the dirty plays of Broadway; he would have raided them all, single-handed and alone. His heirs and assigns are far milder men, and hence, I sometimes fear, more dangerous. Their sweet reasonableness is disarming; it tends to conceal the fact that they are nevertheless blue-noses at heart, and quite as eager to harry and harass the rest of us as Anthony was. Those opponents who now parley with them had better remember the warning against making truces with Adam-Zad. They may end by restoring to comstockery some of its old respectability, and so throw us back to where we were during the Grant administration. I sound the warning and pass on. It will take, at best, a long time, and I'll be beyond all hope or caring before it is accomplished. For Anthony's ghost still stalks the scenes of his old endeavors, to plague and palsy his successors. His name has given a term of opprobrium to the common tongue. Dead, and—as Mr. Broun and Miss Leech so beautifully suggest, an angel with harp, wings and muttonchops—he is yet as alive as Pecksniff, Chadband or Elmer Gantry.

Well, here is his story, done fully, competently, and with excellent manners. There is much in it that you will not find in the earlier biography by Charles Gallaudet Trumbull, for Trumbull wrote for the Sunday-schools, and so had to do a lot of pious dodging and snuffling. The additional facts that Mr. Broun and Miss Leech set forth are often very amusing, but I must add at once that they are seldom discreditable. Old Anthony was preposterous, but not dishonest. He believed in his idiotic postulates as devotedly as a Tennessee Baptist believes that a horse-hair put into a bottle of water will turn into a snake. His life, as he saw it, was one of sacrifice for righteousness. Born with a natural gift for the wholesale drygoods trade, he might have wrung a fortune from its practice, and so won an heroic equestrian statue in the Cathedral of St. John the Divine. Perhaps there were blue days when regret crept over him, shaking his Christian resolution. His muttonchop whiskers, the stigma and trademark of the merchant princes of his era, had a pathetic, Freudian smack. But I don't think he wobbled often. The Lord was always back of him, guiding and stimulating his fighting arm. So he was content to live in a drab suburb on the revenues of a second-rate lawyer, with his elderly, terrified wife and his half-witted foster-daughter. There was never any hint, in that humble home, of the gaudy connubial debaucheries that the modern sex hygienists describe so eloquently. Anthony had to go outside for his fun. Comstockery was his corner saloon.

I confess to a great liking for the old imbecile. He is one of my favorite characters in American history, along with Frances E. Willard, Daniel Drew and Brigham Young. He added a great deal to the joys of life in the Federal Republic. More than any other man, he liberated American letters from the blight of Puritanism.

2
Thwacks From the Motherland

THE BABBITT WARREN, by C.E.M. Joad. New York: *Harper & Brothers.* [The Nation, April 20, 1927.]

Mr. Joad, who is a philosopher by trade, prefaces his thunderous philippic against all things Yankee and accursed with a disarming quotation from the late Filippo G. Bruno, of Nola, Italy: "*Se non è vero, è ben trovato.*" He needs this plea in confession and avoidance, and very badly, for he admits frankly that he "has not had the privilege of visiting the United States," and the fact is visible on almost every page of his book. Much of the evidence he relies on, indeed, seems to have been derived from the travelers' tales of returning English actors and the confidences of the more humorous and ingenious members of the corps of cabin-stewards of the Cunard line. Thus, on page 83, he begins a long diatribe with the postulate that "the films are the literature of America"—which is to say, the *only* literature—and on page 89 he permits himself the grave announcement that the lamented J. Gordon Coogler was "the one famous Southern American poet." The one criterion of eminence in the Republic, according to the agents he appears to trust, is money. "The artist, the scientist, the musician, the statesman, and the author are held of no account unless their claims to consideration are backed by money." A rich man, regardless of his private virtue, "is king of any company he chooses to enter." This preëminence, it seems, takes on a transcendental character, and so works miracles. "Thus a rich man who had lost his eye recently purchased another from a poor man, the transfer of optics being hailed as a marvel of medical science." And no wonder!

But it is not necessary to swallow all of Mr. Joad's evidence in order to discuss his conclusions. They are, in brief, that the machine civilization which now threatens the whole world has reached its highest development in the United States, that the influence of American gold is rapidly extending it, and that if its proliferation is not checked it will destroy most the values that men have cherished for ten thousand years. I see nothing against reason here. The facts, in truth, are apparent to every one, and even some of the most startling testimony that Mr. Joad introduces, though it is not true, is at least consonant with what is. We have surely not yet come to the pass that "a rich man is king of any company he chooses to enter," but we have certainly developed a respect for bare money which goes far beyond the bounds of the seemly and ordinate. I know of no other country in which the hollow imbecilities of a Judge Gary would get the respect they got here, nor in which so preposterous a vacuum as Andy Mellon would be venerated as a great statesman. The English also bend the knee to men of money, and so do the Germans and the French, but they have not yet come to the point of mistaking them for philosophers. The English had a fair chance to venerate Otto H. Kahn, but seem to have muffed him. The Germans, I fear, if Charlie Schwab went to live and make speeches among them, would regard him as a comic character. Even the Portuguese, Serbs, Rumanians, and Greeks would probably laugh at Cal.

Thus Mr. Joad is often right in essence, even when he is wrong in his specification. It is not true, literally, that J. Gordon Cooglar was "the one famous Southern American poet," but nevertheless there is an inner plausibility in the dictum that makes it somehow disconcerting: if the majority of Southern fanciers had their way it *would* be true. Similarly, it is not true, literally, that the dreadful bilge of the movie-parlors is the only American literature now in being, but there remains an uncomfortable possibility that it may be true on some not distant to-morrow. Try to put together a list of American imaginative authors, all of the first chop, who have never taken the film shilling. I can think of Cabell and Sherwood Anderson, but there I begin to wabble; the complete roster is surely not long. The rest of the scrivening boys and girls have all submitted to the loathsome embraces of the Hollywood art-fosterers. The effects of this psychic fornication are not concealed from Mr. Joad's eyes. The movie rubber-stamp, he observes, begins to show itself upon even the swellest varieties of our national swell letters. The self-same novelists who, but a decade and a half ago, swore upon Alps of Bibles (and meant it) that they'd never yield to the foul caresses of Hamilton Wright Mabie and Anthony Comstock—these same novelists, planning their masterpieces to-day, find it a sheer impossibility to rid themselves of sneaking, Freudian thoughts of Gloria Swanson and Jack Gilbert. It is sad, but it is *vero*.

Such sadnesses fill Mr. Joad's tome—an instructive work, but extremely depressing. Purge it of all its errors of fact—some of them really shocking—and its general thesis remains defensible. More, its general thesis remains a fair statement of the view of the Republic held by civilized Europeans. That view is not only critical; it is downright indignant. We are, it appears, not only a nation of barbarians; we are actually hard to distinguish from criminals. Unless we are dissuaded from our course by remonstrance, and, if remonstrance fails, by a resort to *force majeure*, the civilization that men have been struggling for since the dawn of history will go to pot. The wisdom of the late Gary will supplant that of Plato and Aristotle; Henry Ford will displace Thucydides; Luther and St. Francis will be shelved for the Rev. Dr. Billy Sunday and the beauteous Aimée Semple McPherson; the epic and the sonnet will be alike engulfed by the scenario; and the whole world will read the *Saturday Evening Post*. I do not argue that these transformations would ruin humanity, or that they are sure to come to pass; I merely report that a fear of them is widespread in the world. Mr. Joad simply puts into a convenient book, weighing exactly one pound (it is printed on feather-weight paper), what gnaws at the hearts of hundreds of thousands of the European *intelligentsia*. One cannot pick up an English newspaper without getting some flavor of that dread and indignation. It is an ironical situation, and no doubt full of lessons for specialists in the historical and ethical sciences. The Yankee saved civilization, and now civilization damns him to Hell. He put down the accursed Hun, and now the Hun, compared to him, becomes an archangel. As a professional patriot I resent all this. But on days when my patriotism passes a dividend I confess that I am consoled by certain *pizzicato* snickers, or, as they say in the Motherland, sniggers.

3
The Powers of the Air

THE HISTORY OF WITCHCRAFT AND DEMONOLOGY, by Montague Summers. New York: *Alfred A. Knopf.* [The American Mercury, May, 1927.]

This tome is learned, honest and amusing. Its author, an English clergyman—his full name is the Rev. Alphonsus Joseph-Mary Augustus Montague, M.A.—wastes no time trying to reconcile religion and science, a folly that has brought so many American scientists, including the eminent but mushy Dr. Robert Andrews Millikan, to grief. He is in favor of religion, not of science, and with it, in the manner of a true believer, he goes the whole hog. Does Exodus XXII, 18, say flatly that witches exist, and that it is the duty of every righteous man to butcher them when found? Then Dr. Summers accepts the fact and the duty without evasion, and proceeds to elaborate on both. He can't imagine a Christian who refuses to believe in demoniacal possession, and no more can I. Marshaling an array of proofs that must shake even an atheistic archbishop, he demonstrates with fine eloquence and impeccable logic that the air is full of sinister spirits, and that it is their constant effort to enter into the bodies of men and women, and so convert good Christians, made in God's image, into witches, sorcerers, spiritualists, biologists, and other such revolting shapes. The Bible is the rock of his argument, but he also makes frequent and very effective use of the revelations vouchsafed to Holy Church. There has never been a time in Christian history, he shows, when its chief experts and wiseacres did not believe in demons. The Roman rite, accepting their existence as indubitable, provides elaborate machinery for their scotching to this day. That machinery, to be sure, is not put into effect lightly. So long as the medical faculty is convinced that the patient is suffering from nothing worse than a leaping tapeworm or delirium tremens, and hope of his cure by chemical and mechanical means is thus held out, he is resigned to the secular arm. But once it becomes manifest that a fiend or goblin has got into him, the business becomes a matter for supernatural intervention, and the subsequent proceedings must be carried on by an ordained pastor, and according to a formula set forth in the "Rituale Romanum," and in use since the pontificate of Peter I.

This formula is extremely complicated, and I suspect that using it must be somewhat fatiguing to the officiating clergyman. He must be himself a man of mature years, guiltless of anything even approaching loose living, and, according to Mr. Summers, "a systematic student, and well versed in the latest trends and developments of psychological science." He is required to make himself quite sure, before he begins his exorcism, that the patient before him is actually possessed by a demon—that he is not confronting a mere case of insanity, or, worse still, imposture. Once convinced, he proceeds with the utmost heat and diligence, never relenting until the unclean spirit takes wing, and so returns to Hell. Mr. Summers gives the words of the exorcism, translated into English; they are so terrifying that I hesitate to reprint them in a volume designed for reading aloud at the domestic hearth. The demon is denounced in words that sting like scorpions: no Baptist pastor, damning Clarence Darrow, ever scorched the air with worse. And if, at the first attack, they fail to dislodge him they are to be used again, and then again, and so on until the exorcism is completed. The patient, it appears, is apt to fall asleep while they are being intoned: making him do so is one of the Devil's favorite tricks. If it happens, then the exorcist must awaken him, and by any device that seems workable, including smart blows *a posteriori*. Ordinarily, all this must be done in a church, but if the patient is too ill to leave his bed the exorcist may visit him in his own boarding-house. Idle spectators are forbidden, but the canon requires that, as at a baptism or electrocution, a number of official witnesses, of known piety and sober mien, shall be present. No unnecessary conversation with the demon is permitted. If he speaks through the mouth of the patient, he is to be heard politely, but when he has had a sufficient say he is to be shut off. In particular, he is not to be permitted to indulge in ribaldries.

It is commonly believed that Protestantism questions the actuality of demoniacal possession, but this is not so. True enough, the Unitarians and Universalists have doubts about it, but so far as I am aware no other Protestant sect has ever formally repudiated it. There is a canon of the Church of England which forbids a priest to exorcise demons without the "license or direction (*mandatum*)" of his Bishop, but there is nothing to prevent a Bishop issuing such a *mandatum*. If Bishop Manning became convinced tomorrow that Sinclair Lewis or any other such antinomian was possessed, he could, I believe, give Dr. William N. Guthrie a *mandatum* to exorcise the invading gaseous organism. I do not allege that Dr. Manning would do it or that Dr. Guthrie would take advantage of the license; all I argue is that the transaction would lie within the confines of canon law. The Lutherans, who are very orthodox, all believe in demoniacal possession, and hence, by a necessary inference, in witches; if they did not they would have to put Martin Luther down as a liar. As for the Methodists, the Baptists and other such proletarians of the Lord, it must be obvious that doubts among them are confined to a few advanced intellectuals, debauched by reading the epicurean poetry of Edgar A. Guest. The Baptists, at least in the South, even believe in ghosts, especially the colored brethren. The colored pastors have an elaborate ceremonial for exorcising all varieties of spirits, good or evil; an important part of it is the free-will offering just before the curative anathema is launched. In my own native republic, the Saorstát Maryland, I once made an attempt to ascertain the number of people, regardless of creed, who believed in ghosts and witches. After elaborate inquiries through prudent agents, I came to the conclusion that 92% of the population believed in ghosts, and that 74% also believed in witches. In the latter group was the then Governor of the State. He believed that rheumatism was caused by witchcraft, and wore a string around his middle to ward it off. The Marylanders are a gay and liberty-loving people, and drink and drab, perhaps, somewhat more than is good for them, but atheism has never made much progress among them. At least one of the eminent professors in the Johns Hopkins Medical School, at Baltimore, has been publicly accused of believing in witches, and has never, so far as I know, made a categorical denial of it.

Dr. Summers is equally honest, and I think he deserves all praise for being so. Most ecclesiastics, when they write upon such subjects, try to evade the clear issue. They seem to be convinced—on what ground I don't know—that the old belief in demons is now dying out in the world, and to be afraid that they will be laughed at if they confess to it. All I can say is that that is a poor way to get into Heaven *post mortem*. Such duckers and skulkers, you may be sure, will have extremely unpleasant sessions with St. Peter when they reach the Gates, and Peter will be well justified in razzing them. Either the Christian religion involves a belief in disembodied powers, good and evil, or it doesn't. If it doesn't, then its Sacred Scriptures are a mass of nonsense, and even its Founder was grossly misinformed. If it does, then every one adhering to it ought to confess the fact frankly, and without ignominious equivocation. This is what Dr. Summers does. In detail, his colleagues in theology may sometimes reasonably challenge him, as when, for example, he lays down the doctrine that the heaving of tables at spiritualist séances is performed by demons from Hell. But his fundamental postulates stand beyond refutation. If he is wrong, then the whole science of Christian theology is a degraded imposture—something which no right-thinking, law-abiding, home-loving American, I am sure, will want to allege. I rejoice to find a holy man so forthright and courageous, and so irresistibly convincing. He has rescued demonology from its long neglect, and restored it to its old high place among the sacred sciences. What a knock-out he would be on an American lecture tour! I offer him $1,000 in advance for his Jackson, Miss., house, with an offer of the fattest pastorate in the town thrown in.

4

To the Glory of an Artist

LIFE AND LETTERS OF HENRY WILLIAM THOMAS, MIXOLOGIST, by Various Hands. Washington: *Privately Printed.* [The American Mercury, February, 1927.]

This entertaining and instructive work is, in form, a *Festschrift* in honor of Mr. Thomas, for many years one of the most eminent of Washington bartenders. He pontificated, in the closing days of the Bill of Rights (*selig!*), in various celebrated Washington bars, including Loehl's, Shoomaker's, Arman's, and George Driver's, and those of the Shoreham, Willard, Raleigh and Metropolitan Hotels. His longest term of service was at Driver's, which was the first really high-toned saloon encountered in Pennsylvania avenue as one left the halls of Congress. Here his clients included all the most distinguished statesmen of the Republic, and many of its heroic warriors, gifted publicists and opulent men of affairs. His acquaintance among such men was wide and intimate: he lived in an atmosphere of greatness that was denser and more exhilarating, even, than that surrounding Col. George B. M. Harvey or Dr. Otto H. Kahn. His professional or bedside manner, like that of every other salient man of his craft, was delicate, discreet and judicious. If a Congressman, coming in from a committee meeting, raced his metabolism by drinking too fast and so began to blab high matters of state, Mr. Thomas would knock him off with a reliable silencer, and save him from ruin. If a Senator came in with a constituent who seemed suspiciously Christian, Mr. Thomas would express regret at not having seen him (the Senator) for a long, long time. If even higher dignitaries began to sway dizzily and clutch the bar-rail, Mr. Thomas would summon a pair of trustworthy Negroes and have them carted home. Such thoughtfulness and humanity, when combined with a high professional competence, naturally made him popular in the town, and when the Methodist Board of Temperance, Prohibition and Public Morals supplanted Congress in the government of the District, and all the saloons were closed, and Mr. Thomas moved out to Chevy Chase, and began serving limeade and coca-cola at what was once the bar of the club there—when these events fell like thunderclaps there was widespread woe in the highest circles, and congressional funerals began to multiply. Now his surviving friends, to honor him in his declining years, print the present *Festschrift*.

It is a mellow and charming volume, and the pity is that it is printed for private circulation only, and will thus not get into the public libraries, for the instruction of future generations. Prohibition, as every one knows, has not actually cut off the supply of strong drink, nor has it diminished the consumption. On the contrary, it has made drinking more common than ever before, especially among the young. But the young miss something that their fathers enjoyed: the privilege of contact with amiable and accomplished bartenders. They drink in washrooms, surrounded by bootblacks, busboys and subway tiles; their fathers drank in front of mahogany bars, with men of the world serving them. In the more high-toned of the old-time saloons American civilization, such as it is, probably reached its highest point. The society was of the best. The most obscure man, if he were decently clad, could meet United States Senators, the Governors of great States, men distinguished in all the arts and sciences, and the principal industrial and financial heads of the nation. It was a charming and admirable school for youngsters just coming to maturity, not only in manners but also in all the ideas and fancies that engrossed the superior minority. They heard the great problems of statecraft discussed in an offhand and confidential way. They saw notable men in mufti, so to speak, with their cares laid off, and their minds functioning brilliantly. They came into contact with every class making up the world of affairs, from members of the Cabinet to champion pugilists, and from scientific men of the first caliber to the greatest artists and manufacturers of the nation. All this was especially true in Washington. The saloons of that town, during the half century before Prohibition, were the true centers of its intellectual activity. Its great men frequented them incessantly. They entertained all its eminent guests. Naturally enough, such customers would shrink from being served by roughnecks: they demanded bartenders of the highest skill and most delicate prudence. Such a bartender was Henry

William Thomas. The statesmen and others who have collaborated in the *Festschrift* in his honor do honor to themselves.

The volume is small, as befits the modesty of the man whose virtues it celebrates, but it is packed with good things. It opens with a series of quotations from the greatest authors of all time —Homer, Shakespeare, Cervantes and so on—, every one of them a conscientious wet. Lesser men are also included—Longfellow, Sheridan, Villon, Irving, Pepys, Omar, Horace, Ben Johnson and company—all of them equally wet. There follows a series of original toasts by some of the collaborators in the *Festschrift*, and after that comes a page of music and a sketch of the life and times of Mr. Thomas. Some curious details are in it, and not a few of them are pathetic. In the days of his service at Driver's, it appears, the common price of French and Italian vermouth, in case lots, was $6 a case. Absinthe cost $15 a case, and the best gins were obtainable at from $10 to $18. Scotch ran from $14 to $30, and rye from $6 to $16. Fourteen-year-old brandy cost $20, and sixty-year-old brandy $50. The booticians of to-day, though they gradually perfect their art, will never be able to offer sound goods at such prices. If, by the end of the fifth or sixth Coolidge administration, Scotch drops to $50 a case, as the public relations counsel of the New York booters lately predicted, it will still cost four times as much as the average Scotch of Mr. Thomas' prime. Moreover, it will be inferior in quality. Such bars as Driver's served only the choicest goods. They didn't buy labels, but Scotch. To-day it runs the other way. The last part of the *Festschrift* is given over to a long and voluptuous discussion of the drinks that Mr. Thomas used to compound. Many of the materials mentioned are almost unobtainable to-day. The booters bring in plenty of so-called Scotch whiskey and English gin, and immense supplies of highly dubious champagne, but it would be hard, I believe, to find one able to furnish a plausible Sloe gin, or a sound Hollands, or a genuine St. Croix rum. Such delicatessen have simply gone out of the répertoire. They have gone out with the old-time bartenders—men of fine feelings and high gifts, their lives consecrated to an art that made men happy. Of these great craftsmen Mr. Thomas was one of the best. The frontispiece of the *Festschrift* shows him as he is to-day, still vigorous and handsome, but with the light of tragedy in his eyes. He looks as Shakespeare would have looked had he (Shakespeare) lived into the bleak, sour days of the Commonwealth. He looks as Washington would have looked if he had lived to see Coolidge.

5

God Help the South!

THE ADVANCING SOUTH, by Edwin Mims. Garden City, L. I.: *Doubleday, Page & Company* [The American Mercury, August, 1926.]

Dr. Mims, who hails from Arkansas, is professor of English at Vanderbilt University, in the great Christian *Polizeistaat* of Tennessee, and a member of the Joint Hymn-Book Committee of the Methodist Episcopal Church. He has lectured at Chautauqua, N.Y., and is secretary of the Tennessee Law and Order League. He thus makes the grade, by Southern standards, as a critic of literature and life. But in the less Christian North, I suspect, there will be scoffers to cavil at him, especially when it is noted that he is very suspicious of James Branch Cabell, and in fact puts Ellen Glasgow above him. And even in the South there will be heretics to repine that a more competent and sympathetic historian was not found to tell the story of their heroic (and perhaps vain) struggle to haul the Confederacy out of its wallow. For the good Dr. Mims, despite a laudable diligence and a high degree of uplifting enthusiasm, constantly gives one the impression of a scrivener laboring valiantly with a theme that he doesn't quite understand. Perhaps I may throw some light upon his equipment by observing that, when he comes to discuss Southern journalists, he has high and sweet praises for the late Mooney of Memphis, the most passionate defender of the Bryan theological imbecilities ever heard of even in Tennessee, and not a word for Hall of Montgomery, Wright of Columbia, S.C., Jaffe of Norfolk, Dabney of Richmond, or Sanders of Mooney's own town. In brief, Dr. Mims seems to know little more about the current journalistic situation in the South, and hence about the political and cultural situation, than a somewhat advanced village schoolma'm. He has heard of Johnson of Greensboro, now that Johnson has left the South, and of Harris of Columbus, Ga., now that Harris has the Pulitzer prize, and of such women as Miss Frances Newman, Miss Nell Battle Lewis and Miss Sara Haardt, now that the North has discovered them, but one cannot escape the suspicion that they were outside his ken in the days of their first and hardest labors, as their heirs and assigns are outside his ken to-day. Call me a Union spy if you will, but I give you my solemn word that in his book of 319 pages, devoted largely, if not principally, to the renaissance of literary endeavor below the Potomac, there is absolutely no mention of Emily Clark, of Richmond, founder of the *Reviewer*! Or of Mrs. Julia Peterkin! Or of T. S. Stribling! Or of Clement Wood! Or of J. W. Krutch!

It is, perhaps, the worst of all the curses of the South that it is interpreted for the nation by just such depressing obfuscators. They love it as no Scotsman ever loved his smoky crags, and their yearning to see it go forward has all the violent passion of an evangelical religion, but they are seldom clear as to what is the matter with it, and they seldom differentiate accurately between its genuinely enlightened leaders—mainly young and extremely unpopular—and its mere windjammers. Dr. Mims, I should say in all fairness, is better than most, but he is still far too much the orthodox Southerner to see what is the matter with the South. A resident of Tennessee for a generation, he shows all the peculiar Tennessee prejudices and puerilities. For the pious Mooney, bawling for Genesis, he has high praises; for the intelligent and courageous John R. Neal he has only sneers. Where was he himself when Bryan marched in, and the hill-billies came down to drive all sense and decency out of the State? Was he in the forefront of the fray? Was he heard at Dayton, on the side of educated and self-respecting men? If so, his voice was small indeed, for I got no echo of it in the courtroom. Like all the other so-called intellectuals of the State, journalistic, legal and pedagogical, he left the heavy burden of the fight to Dr. Neal, and now all he can say of Neal is that he is "a local attorney" and "an often defeated politician." It is the tragedy of Tennessee that such men as Neal are defeated and such men as the mountebank Peay are kept in high office. It is the greater tragedy of the South that when, by some act of God, a Neal springs out of the land all the Mimses combine to cry him down.

That they succeed only too well is proved by Mims' own evidence. His book is strewn with the names of Southerners who have been forced to come North for air—Walter Hines Page, William E. Dodd, John Spencer Bassett, W. P. Trent, Woodrow Wilson, Ashby Jones. Of some of these men, especially on the political side, I am surely no romantic admirer, but they were the best that the South could produce, and the South obviously needed them. All came North—and the younger men and women of to-day are following them. Perhaps the best newspaper editorial writer that the South has produced in my time is Gerald W. Johnson: he is now in Baltimore. The best newspaper reporter is Paul Y. Anderson: he is now in St. Louis. The most promising critic of letters and life is Joseph W. Krutch: he is now in New York. The list might be lengthened almost endlessly. In particular, the names of many women are on it, for the South, despite its gabble of chivalry, still knows how to be unpleasant to a woman who is intelligent. True enough, a few hard-boiled and heroic men, their veins filled with manganese, manage to hold out: for example, W. L. Poteat, John D. Wade, Paul Green, and Howard W. Odum. But Poteat is of such years that his mere antiquity now begins to protect him, and Wade, Green and Odum, though they remain in the South to-day, will probably be on their way tomorrow. The kind of "leader" who survives down there is mainly the yellow dog kind. The Underwoods pass out and the Peays and Bleases come in. The South loses Johnson and keeps Clark Howell, Douglas Freeman, and the incredible Sullens, of Mississippi; it lets the *Reviewer* die and reads and admires the *Manufacturers' Record*. The enlightened Pastor Jones departs for Kansas City and the preposterous Bishop Candler, with his coca-cola theology, holds the fort. Who *goes* South? I recall two salient emigrants: William Jennings Bryan and the Rev. Dr. John Roach Straton.

What is to be noted in all this is that the South is by no means sterile. It still produces a very respectable annual crop of bright young men and women. Considering its backwardness in education, indeed, it probably produces more of them, relatively, than some of the States of the North—for example, New Jersey, Ohio and Vermont. The best blood of the South, I am inclined to think, is the best in the whole Republic—that is, taking account only of so-called Anglo-Saxons. But that best blood, save in a few areas, mainly along tide-water, is no longer dominant. The lower orders of Southerners, having been lifted out of poverty by the general economic rise of the region, have got the reins of political power into their hands, and through the medium of politics they are trying to force their ignorance upon their betters. Every emerging leader must pass their tests—and their tests are scarcely to be distinguished from those of the savages in the Borneo jungle. Culturally, indeed, they are precisely on the level of the anthropoid blacks surrounding them. They share the same suspicion of knowledge, they show the same primitive emotionality, and they practice the same barbaric and revolting religion. This religion, as is always the case with people only superficially civilized, colors their whole lives. The *shaman* is the principal functionary among them, and his fiats have the force of divine revelation. Nothing can be undertaken that does not meet his approval; nothing is regarded as sound, or even as decent, that violates the tenets of his hog-wallow theology. The troubles of the South, it seems to me, all revolve around that simple fact. The *shaman*, who has been reduced to innocuousness in more civilized regions, is still too powerful down there. All the Southern politicians flatter and cajole him, and he is treated with elaborate respect by practically all the Southern newspapers. No wonder he believes in his own magic! And no wonder it is difficult, in the face of his ignorance and his power, to launch a sound idea!

It seems to me that the more intelligent Southerners, rising one by one out of the general darkness, are all doomed to failure until they concentrate upon this chartered enemy of every intellectual dignity and decency, and clear him off the scene. Their error, at the moment, consists in trying to compromise with him. They are all too eager to avoid violating the pious pruderies of his victims. It is an error that is not new in the world, and wherever it has been followed it has greatly prospered *shamans*. In its final form it converts itself into the doctrine that any and every theological notion, however insane and outageous, deserves respect. I can imagine nothing more unsound. If the men of past ages had cherished that delusion we'd still be sweating under the Inquisition—nay, we'd be consulting oracles and trembling before sorcerers. In other words, the whole human race would still be on the level of the Haitian voodoo-worshipers and the Georgia Baptists. The way to get rid of such ideas is not to walk softly before them, but to attack them vigorously and with clubs. If Mims and his fellow pussy-footers had done that in Tennessee, there would have been no Scopes trial, and no ensuing disgrace of the State. I don't think the yokels themselves were to blame for that obscenity. Such of them as I met during the trial seemed to me to be decidedly above the general level of American peasants, They were not noticeably stupid; they were simply grossly misinformed. The rubbish that was preached to them four times a week by their pastors went unchallenged. The Mimses hesitated to attack it, I daresay, for fear of being accused of attacking religion. Well, why should religion *not* be attacked when it is idiotic? What gives a theological imbecility superiority over any other imbecility? Why should a moron dressed up as a Methodist preacher get any more respect than a moron behind a plow? The doctrine that there are differences here greatly burdens the South. If it is ever to have a general intellectual awakening, and not merely a series of gallant but unimportant one-man revolts, it must first get rid of its superstitious reverence for sacerdotal mountebanks. They are the common enemies of every enlightened Southerner, including such liberal but faithful churchmen as Dr. Jones and Dr. Poteat quite as much as such skeptics as Miss Newman and Cabell. No tolerant and progressive civilization will ever rise in the South with their consent.

Thus the fundamental struggle there is a *Kulturkampf* in the strictest Bismarckian sense, and soon or late its challenge must be squarely met. The question is whether the South is to be run by its educated and intelligent men, or by a rabble of hedge theologians, led by blood-sweating fanatics and followed by a docile tail of crooked politicians and boot-licking editors. As I have said, it produces plenty of admirable candidates for leadership—perhaps more, relatively, than any other American section save the Northeastern seaboard. But they are driven out almost as fast as they arise. The village pastors flush them instantly, and they are soon in full flight, with a baying pack of Ku Kluxers, Methodist bishops, Fundamentalist legislators, Daughters of the Confederacy, and professional wowsers after them. Suppose that, by some miracle, a competent biologist were produced at Vanderbilt University, at Nashville, which Dr. Mims serves as a professor. Where could he pass on his learning in Tennessee, save at Vanderbilt University? Suppose a competent journalist arose in Mississippi. What paper in that State would employ him? Certainly the same questions could not be asked in Illinois, say, or in Wisconsin, or in Maryland, or even in Pennsylvania, as dull and degraded as it is. Such States utilize their own good men. They welcome the free play of ideas. They have got beyond that elemental stage of civilization in which all questions are questions of faith. They have thrown off the tyranny of the *shaman*. The South, I believe, will some day follow them. But the road is long and full of perils, and many a head will be cracked before the end of it is reached.

6
The Immortal Democrat

JEFFERSON, by Albert Jay Nock. New York: *Harcourt, Brace & Company*. [The American Mercury, September, 1926.]

This book has a fine surface: it is the work of a subtle and highly dexterous craftsman. What publicist among us, indeed, writes better than Nock? His editorials during the three brief years of the *Freeman* set a mark that no other man of his trade has ever quite managed to reach. They were well-informed and sometimes even learned, but there was never the slightest trace of pedantry in them. In even the least of them there were sound writing and solid structure. Nock has an excellent ear. Thinking in English, he thinks in charming rhythms. There is never any cacophony in his sentences, as there is never any muddling in his ideas. One may reject his doctrines as evil and against God, but one never finds any flaws in his actual syllogisms. In the present volume he is completely at home. Jefferson has been his Baal since his nonage, and he is soaked in Jeffersoniana as the late Dr. Harding was soaked in the idealism of the Elks.

What emerges here is in no sense a formal biography, nor

even a political history. It is, rather, an elaborate psychological study of the man—an attempt to search out the origins of his chief ideas, to discern and delimit the forms that they finally took in his mind, and to estimate them in the light of the problems to which they were applied, and of the experience that has accumulated in the century since Jefferson's death. In brief, the book is a sort of critical analysis of Jeffersonism, done with constant sympathy and yet with a sharp outlook for fallacy and folly. It is accurate, it is shrewd, it is well ordered, and above all it is charming. I know of no other book on Jefferson that penetrates so persuasively to the essential substance of the man. There are no weak spots in it, and no false notes. It is overwhelmingly convincing as polemic and it is unfailingly caressing as work of art.

It goes without saying that much of Nock's attention is directed toward clearing off the vast mountain of doctrinaire rubbish that has risen above Jefferson's bones. In that Hell where politicians go the Sage of Monticello, I daresay, has suffered far more than most. Imagine his ghost contemplating Bryan, Alton B. Parker, Jimmie Cox, Al Smith, Jimmie Walker, W. G. McAdoo, Cole Blease, Ma and Pa Ferguson, John W. Davis, Tom Taggart, even Woodrow Wilson and Grover Cleveland! It is, indeed, one of the fine ironies of history that the party which professes to follow him has been led almost exclusively, for a hundred years, by leaders wholly unable to grasp the elements of his political philosophy. It stands as far from him to-day as the Methodist Board of Temperance, Prohibition and Public Morals stands from Christ. That is to say, it stands as far off as it is humanly possible to get. Its titular leader, in 1924, was the preposterous Davis: he led it to disaster, but nevertheless he led it. Well, this Davis was, and is, the perfect embodiment of everything that Jefferson distrusted and disliked. He is precisely the sort of man whose oblique doings, in the years between 1810 and 1825, tortured old Tom with his dreams of monocrats. The rest are even worse: McAdoo and his Ku Kluxers, Al Smith and his Tammany gorillas, the Southern State bosses and their tatterdemalion hordes of boozy Prohibitionists. In the whole outfit there is but one man, I suspect, who would get any politeness from Jefferson, imagining him come back to earth. That man, by a coincidence that is surely not strange, was long in formal exile from the Democratic party. He was excommunicated by the late Woodrow; in the Cox convention he was denied a seat; in the Davis convention he took no part. But he remains nearer to Jefferson than all the rest.

Of the Jeffersonian system Mr. Nock offers a clear and comprehensive account, disentangling it from the trivialities that party history has thrown about it. The essence of it, he says, is to be found in what would be called, to-day, Jefferson's class consciousness. He divided all mankind into two classes, the producers and the exploiters, and he was for the former first, last and all the time. But there is no consolation in the fact for the Marxians who now rage in the world, for to Jefferson producers meant far more than mere handworkers. A manufacturer, if he made some useful thing, was also a producer; so was a large landowner, if only he worked his land; Jefferson regarded himself as a producer, and his friend Jimmie Madison as another. Living in our own time, no doubt, he would put Henry Ford in that category; Henry, in fact, puts himself there, and with no little show of reason. The only genuine non-producer, in the Jefferson lexicon, was the speculator—that is to say, the banker, the promoter, the usurer, the jobber. It was against this class that he launched all his most awful thunderbolts of invective; it was this class that he sought to upset and destroy in the ferocious and memorable campaign of 1800. His failure was colossal. Driving that class out of the executive offices and making life very warm for it in the halls of legislation, he only shoved it into the courts, and there it has survived gloriously ever since, gradually extending and consolidating its power. Since Marshall's day the American courts have suffered many vicissitudes and entertained many heresies, but in one department, at least they have kept the faith heroically: they have always protected the virtuous and patriotic bond-holder.

Jefferson has come down in legend as the most adroit of all the early American politicians—that is, after Sam Adams. He is credited with having conjured up, almost out of the air, the party which still disgraces him. He is accused of almost fabulous feats of demagogy. I see little evidence for all this in his actual history. He was, in fact, far less the practical politician than the political philosopher. Office seems to have had few attractions for him, and he was quite devoid of the sense of party regularity. His so-called demagogy turns out, on inspection, to have been simply a realistic statement of fundamental democratic theory. There is little in even his most startling pronouncements that is not implicit in the Bill of Rights. He was far less the foe of the Federalists than of government in general. He believed that it tended inevitably to become corrupt—that it was the common enemy of all well-disposed, industrious and decent men. The less there was of it, the better he liked it, and the more he trusted it. Well, that was a century ago, and wild doctrines from the barricades were still in the air. Government has now gone far beyond anything dreamed of in Jefferson's day. It has taken on a vast mass of new duties and responsibilities; it has spread out its powers until they penetrate to every act of the citizen, however secret; it has begun to throw around its operations the high dignity and impeccability of a state religion; its agents become a separate and superior caste, with authority to bind and loose, and their thumbs in every pot. But it still remains, as it was in the beginning, the common enemy of all well-disposed, industrious and decent men.

7
Fides Ante Intellectum

A SCIENTIFIC MAN AND THE BIBLE, by Howard A. Kelly. Philadelphia: *The Sunday-School Times Company.* [The American Mercury, February, 1926.]

The author of this astounding and depressing book is professor emeritus of gynecological surgery at the Johns Hopkins, and one of the most celebrated surgeons in the United States. This is what his own university says of him in an official document:

> His contribution to the development of genito-urinary surgery for women has been unparalleled. Step by step he unraveled the diseases of the bladder, ureter and kidney. . . . His methods of examination revolutionized gynecological diagnosis.

And much more to the same effect. In brief, a medical man of the first caliber: when he speaks of himself as a scientist, as he does very often in his book, he has every right to use the word. His life has been devoted to exact observation, and that observation has been made so competently and interpreted so logically that the result has been a series of immensely valuable improvements in the healing art and craft. And yet—and yet—How am I to make you believe that such a man has actually written such a volume as this one? How am I to convince you that one of four men who laid the foundations of the Johns Hopkins Medical School—the daily associate and peer of Osler, Welch and Halsted—is here on exhibition as a Fundamentalist of the most extreme wing, compared to whom Judge Raulston, of Dayton, Tenn., seems almost an atheist?

Yet it is so—and I go, for the appalling proof, behind the book and to the man himself. I have known Dr. Kelly for twenty years, and at different times have seen a great deal of him. Hours on end I have discussed his theological ideas with him, and heard his reasons for cherishing them. They seem to me now, as they seemed when I first heard them, to be completely insane—yet Kelly himself is surely not insane. Nor is there the remotest suspicion of insincerity about him. It would be of vast benefit to him professionally to throw over his great cargo of supernatural rubbish, and trim his course as his colleagues trim theirs. If he did so, the Johns Hopkins would be illuminated with Roman candles, star shells and incandescent bock beer signs, and the very cadavers in the deadhouse would have their backs slapped. But he will not budge. He believes that God created the world in six calendar days, and rested on the seventh. He believes that God caused forty-two little children to be devoured by she-bears because they made fun of Elijah's bald head. He believes that Jonah was three days and three nights in the belly of a whale (*Physeter macrocephalus*), and then came out alive. *Medicinæ doctor* though he be, he believes that the hallucinations of John on the island of Patmos were real. An LL.D. of Aberdeen, he believes (Exodus XXII, 18) that witches exist and should be put to death. An honorary member of learned societies in Paris, Vienna, Rome, Berlin, Leipzig, Bucharest and Moscow, he believes in both the Virgin Birth (Matthew I, 18–25), and in the descent of Jesus from

David through Joseph (Matthew I, I–17). All this, and much more, he believes absolutely without reservation, as a Tennessee hind believes it. "I accept the *whole* Bible," he says, "as God's Word." And he adds something that even the hind balks at: he believes in the Second Coming—"at any moment"!

In his book Dr. Kelly offers powerful argument for his amazing credo, but I can only report that, in cold type as *viva voce*, it leaves me full of what the lawyers call reasonable doubt. His logic has a curious habit of going halfway to a plausible conclusion, and then blowing up completely. For example, he starts off, in one place, by showing how the early criticism of the Gospel of John has broken down—and then proceeds gaily to the assumption that proving an error in criticism is identical with proving the complete authenticity of the thing criticized. Again, he denounces the effort to raise up doubts of the Mosaic authorship and divine inspiration of the Pentateuch—and then clinches his case by showing that the Bible itself "claims in all its parts" that it is "the very literal Word of God." But the record of a personal experience exhibits the workings of his mind even more beautifully. Early in manhood he had to give up his medical studies on account of ill-health, and went West to recuperate. In Colorado, during a blizzard, he was beset by snow blindness, and had to take to his bed. Suddenly there came upon him "an overwhelming sense of a great light in the room." How would any ordinary medical student interpret that great light? How would any ordinary ice-wagon driver, or chiropractor, or Methodist bishop, or even catfish interpret it? Obviously, he would refer it to the violent conjunctivitis from which he was suffering—in other words, to a purely physical cause. But not Kelly. After nearly fifty years of active medical practice he still believes that the glare was due to the presence of God! This divine visitation he speaks of very simply as "the chief event" of his life! It surely was—if it was real!

What I'd like to read is a scientific review, by a scientific psychologist—if any exists—of "A Scientific Man and the Bible." By what route do otherwise sane men come to believe such inconceivable nonsense? How is it possible for a human brain to be divided into two insulated halves, one functioning normally, naturally and even brilliantly, and the other capable only of the ghastly balderdash which issues from the minds of

Baptist evangelists? Such balderdash takes various forms, but it is at its worst when it is religious. Why should this be so? What is there in religion that completely flabbergasts the wits of those who believe in it? I see no logical necessity for that flabbergasting. Religion, after all, is nothing but an hypothesis framed to account for what is evidentially unaccounted for. In other fields such hypotheses are common, and yet they do no apparent damage to those who incline to them. But in the religious field they quickly rush the believer to the intellectual Bad Lands. He not only becomes anæsthetic to objective fact; he becomes a violent enemy of objective fact. It annoys and irritates him. He sweeps it away as something somehow evil.

This little book I commend to all persons interested in the mysteries of the so-called mind of man. It is a document full of fascination, especially to the infidel and damned. There is a frankness about it that is refreshing and commendable. The author does not apologize for his notions, nor does he try to bring them into grotesque and incredible harmony with scientific facts. He believes the Bible from cover to cover, fly-specks and all, and he says so (considering his station in life) with great courage.

8

Speech Day in the Greisenheim

ACADEMY PAPERS: ADDRESSES ON LANGUAGE, by Members of the American Academy of Arts and Letters. New York: *Charles Scribners' Sons.* [The American Mercury, January, 1926.]

The contributors to this volume, with their academic dignities, and their ages at the time it was published, are as follows:

Paul Elmer More, A.B., A.M., LL.D., 3(Litt.D.)	61 years
Bliss Perry, A.B., 2(A.M.), 3(L.H.D.), Litt.D., 2(LL.D.)	64 "
Paul Shorey, A.B., Ph.D., 7(LL.D.), 2(Litt.D.)	69 "
Brander Matthews, A.B., A.M., LL.B., D.C.L., Litt.D., LL.D.	73 "
Henry van Dyke, A.M., 3(D.D.), 3(LL.D.), D.C.L.	73 "

Robert Underwood Johnson, B.S., A.M., Ph.D., L.H.D.	73	"
William M. Sloane, A.B., A.M., Ph.D., L.H.D., 2(LL.D.)	75	"
William Crary Brownell, A.B., L.H.D., Litt.D., LL.D.	75	"

This works out to an average of a little more than seventy—the age, according to Psalms xc, 10, of extreme unction. Is it surprising that the dullness of the different papers runs in almost direct ratio to the years of their authors? Surprising or not, it is a fact. Dr. More, though he has nothing to say, and seems to have noticed little about the language he writes save that the English also use it, nevertheless offers a paper that has a certain stealthy liveliness, and even a touch of sauciness. He opens it, indeed, with a quotation from "The Merchant of Venice" which, flung at them by a barbarian, would have caused the most potent, grave and reverend signiors of the Academy to wince. But youth must kick up its legs, and Dr. More of the time of his cavorting, was only sixty-one. Ten years will mellow him, and give him a softer patina.

Dr. Perry, who is three years older and has been in cold storage at Harvard for years, is also somewhat goatish. He even goes to the length of presenting three ideas, one of which is actually new. The first, apparently borrowed from the philologians of the Invisible Empire, is that the secular arm should be summoned to safeguard the mother-tongue in the Republic—that is, that the process of Americanization should be pushed by law. The second is that the Academy should establish a grand prize for diction—to be given annually, it would seem, to some English *cabotin*, for the only virtuosi of "distinguished diction" that Dr. Perry mentions are George Arliss and Edith Wynne Matthison. The third suggestion, and the only one that is original, is that the Academy should also set up rewards for those authors, apparently American in this case, whose books "are characterized by distinction of style." A good idea, but full of dynamite. How would the old boys dodge giving an occasional gold medal, or India-paper Bible, or basket of Moët et Chandon, or silk American flag, or whatever the prize was, to James Branch Cabell? And what would they do with Cabell's blistering reply, having received and read it?

Dr. Shorey comes next—and with an unfair advantage. He is not a bad author and no more, like the rest, but a professor of Greek, and denoted all his life to Plato *geb.* Aristocles. (The rest, I venture, know so little Greek that they can scarcely shine their own shoes.) His paper is that of an innocent but amiable bystander. He denies that there is an American dialect of English, and then proves very charmingly that there is. He is full of amusing anecdotes and shrewd observations. He closes with an engaging, but, I regret to have to add, far from convincing plea for the study of Latin. The day he read his paper before the Academy must have been a pleasant one for the janitor, staff surgeon, newspaper reporters, wheel-chair motormen, trained nurses and embalmers in attendance. But I guess that more than one immortal blew his nose sadly as wheeze followed wheeze, and cackles rippled through the audience. Shorey was then only sixty-nine and had lived at Bonn, Leipzig, Munich and Athens.

Over seventy Academicians jell. Dr. Matthews' paper is heavy and hollow stuff—the sort of thing he used to write for *Munsey's Magazine* in the days when he and it were ornaments to the national letters, and the Kaiser had not yet sent in such men as Cabell, Lewis and Dreiser to annoy him. Dr. Brownell contributes two dull papers in his baroque and tedious style, with occasional descents to dubious English. (See, for example, the first two lines of page 42.) Pastor van Dyke, turning aside from his combat of Golden Texts with Dr. Frank Crane, offers an essay in which he denounces Carl Sandburg and says of "The Spoon River Anthology" that "to call it poetry is to manhandle a sacred word." (Has the rev. gentleman ever come to the page containing "Ann Rutledge"?) Finally, Dr. Johnson, after joining in the butchery of Sandburg, delivers a whoop for the old-style poetry—by which, on his own showing, he means poetry full of moral purpose—and then ends with a tart reference, in execrable taste, to the poetry printed by the *Century Magazine* since his retirement as its editor.

Thus the ancients of the American Academy of Arts and Letters. Eight of them join forces to write a book of 282 pages

—and the result is sheer emptiness, signifying nothing. Their subject is the language all of them are supposed to write, not merely well but better than any other eight men in the country—and what seven of them have to say of it is simply what one would expect from a baker's half-dozen of school-ma'ms, chosen at random.

9
Professors of English

THE STANDARDS OF AMERICAN SPEECH, AND OTHER PAPERS, by Fred Newton Scott. Boston: *Allyn & Bacon.* HOW TO DESCRIBE AND NARRATE VISUALLY, by L. A. Sherman. New York: *The George H. Doran Company.* [The American Mercury, October, 1926.]

Scott is an A.B., an A.M. and a Ph.D.; he has professed at the University of Michigan since 1887 and is now professor of rhetoric and journalism there and university editor; he has been president of the Modern Language Association, of the National Council of Teachers of English, of the North Central Association of Colleges and Secondary Schools, and of the American Association of Teachers of Journalism; he is a member of the Modern Language Research Association, the American Association for the Advancement of Science, and the British Association, and represented the literati of the Republic at the Conference of American and British Professors of English at London in 1920; he is the author of many works, including an English grammar, a treatise on literary criticism and another on æsthetics, and the editor of many more, including two volumes of gems from Holy Writ. Sherman is an A.B., a Ph.D. and an LL.D.; he has professed English at the University of Nebraska since 1882, and is now dean of the graduate college there; he is a member of Phi Beta Kappa, Alpha Delta Phi and other learned lodges; he has composed a book called "What is Shakespeare?" and another called "Analytics of Literature"; his textbooks are in wide use.

Well, what have these powerfully learned and eminent men to say in their present volumes? Scott devotes a chapter to proving that "of the 10,565 lines of 'Paradise Lost,' 670, or 6.3%, contain each two or more accented alliterating vowels," another proving that in such word-groups as "rough and ready,"

68% put the monosyllable first and the dissyllable second, and 42% put the dissyllable first and the monosyllable second, and a third (very long) to developing John Stuart Mill's well-known saying that "eloquence is heard; poetry is overheard," *i.e.*, that the primary aim of prose is persuasion, whereas that of poetry is simply self-expression. So much for Scott. Sherman fills 364 pages with windy platitudes on the writing of English, and lays chief stress on the revolutionary discovery that visual images are very effective. At the end of each chapter he sets a dozen or more tests for students. I offer a few specimens:

Detail the points of exposition as gathered from some recent sermon.

Draw a character by the use of imaginative appeals of degree.

From some outgrown or discarded theme, find what sentences are not of the first or second grade of value.

Describe, by form-types, the safety chain.

Devise a new system of ten points, five of matter, five of manner, and by it evaluate three debates prepared on the same side of some live question of the hour.

Find or recall an example of summarizing narration that seems to you worthy of being told in the consecutive manner, and give reasons for your criticism.

Such are two of the great whales of literary science among us. God help the poor yokels who have to sweat through their books! God help the national letters!

VI.
Five Little Excursions

I
Brahms

MY excuse for writing of the above gentleman is simply that, at the moment, I can think of nothing else. A week or so ago, on a Baltimore Summer evening of furious heat, I heard his sextette for strings, opus 18, and ever since then it has been sliding and pirouetting through my head. I have gone to bed with it and I have got up with it. Not, of course, with the whole sextette, nor even with any principal tune of it, but with the modest and fragile little episode at the end of the first section of the first movement—a lowly thing of nine measures, thrown off like a perfume, so to speak, from the second subject:

What is the magic in such sublime trivialities? Here is a tune so slight and unassuming that it runs to but eight measures and uses but six of the twelve tones in the octave, and yet it rides an elderly and unromantic man, weighing 180 pounds and with a liver far beyond pills or prayer, as if it were the very queen of the succubi. Is it because I have a delicately sensitive ear? Bosh! I am almost tone-deaf. Or a tender and impressionable heart? Bosh again! Or a beautiful soul? *Dreimal* bosh! No theologian not in his cups would insure me against Hell for cent per cent. No, the answer is to be found in the tune, not in the man. Trivial in seeming, there is yet in it the power of a thousand horses. Modest, it speaks with a clarion voice, and having spoken, it is remembered. Brahms made many another like it. There is one at the beginning of the trio for violin, 'cello and piano, opus 8—the loveliest tune, perhaps, in the whole range of music. There is another in the slow movement of the quintette for piano and strings, opus 34. There is yet another in the double concerto for violin and 'cello, opus 102—the first subject of the slow movement. There is one in the coda of the Third Symphony. There is an exquisite one in the Fourth Symphony. But if you know Brahms, you know all of them quite as well as I do. Hearing him is as dangerous as hearing Schubert. One does not go away filled and satisfied, to resume business as usual in the morning. One goes away charged with a something that remains in the blood a long while, like the toxins of love or the pneumococcus. If I had a heavy job of work to do on the morrow, with all hands on deck and the cerebrum thrown into high, I'd certainly not risk hearing any of the Schubert string quartettes, or the incomparable quintette with the extra 'cello, or the Tragic Symphony. And I'd hesitate a long time before risking Brahms.

It seems an astounding thing that there was once a war over him, and that certain competent musicians, otherwise sane, argued that he was dull. As well imagine a war over Beauvais Cathedral or the Hundred-and-third Psalm! The contention of these foolish fellows, if I recall it aright, was that Brahms was dull in his development sections—that he flogged his tunes to death. I can think of nothing more magnificently idiotic. Turn to the sextette that I have mentioned, written in the early '60's of the last century, when the composer was barely thirty. The development section of the first movement is not only fluent and workmanlike: it is a downright masterpiece. There is a magnificent battle of moods in it, from the fieriest to the tenderest, and it ends with a coda that is sheer perfection. True enough, Brahms had to learn—and it is in the handling of thematic material, not in its invention, that learning counts. When he wrote his first piano trio, at twenty-five or thereabout, he started off, as I have said, with one of the most lovely tunes ever put on paper, but when he came to develop it his inexperience showed itself, and the result was such that years later he rewrote the whole work. But by the time he came to his piano concerto in D he was the complete master of his materials, and ever thereafter he showed a quality of workmanship that no other composer has ever surpassed, not even Beethoven. The first movement of the Eroica, I grant you, is *sui generis*: it will never be matched until the time two great geniuses collide again. But what is in the rest of the first eight symphonies, even including the Fifth and Ninth, that is clearly better than what is in the four of Brahms? The first performance of his First, indeed, was as memorable an event in the history of music as the first performance of the Eroica. Both were furiously denounced, and yet both were instantaneous successes. I'd rather have been present at Karlsruhe on November 6, 1876, I think, than at the initiation of General Pershing into the Elks, or even than at the baptism of Coolidge. And I'd rather have been present at Vienna on April 7, 1805, than at the landing of Columbus.

In music, as in all the other arts, the dignity of the work is simply a reflection of the dignity of the man. The notion that shallow and trivial men can write masterpieces is one of the follies that flow out of the common human taste for scandalous anecdote. Wagner wore a velvet cap and stole another man's wife; *ergo*, nothing is needed to write great music save the talents of a movie actor. What could be more preposterous? More than any other art, perhaps, music demands brains. It is full of technical complexities. It calls for a capacity to do a dozen things at once. But most of all it is revelatory of what is called character. When a trashy man writes it, it is trashy music.

Here is where the immense superiority of such a man as Brahms becomes manifest. There is less trashiness in his music than there is in the music of any other man ever heard of, with the sole exception, perhaps, of Johann Sebastian Bach. It was simply impossible for him, at least after he had learned his trade, to be obvious or banal. He could not write even the baldest tune without getting into it something of his own high dignity and profound seriousness; he could not play with that tune, however light his mood, without putting an austere and noble stateliness into it. Hearing Brahms, one never gets any sense of being entertained by a clever mountebank. One is facing a superior man, and the fact is evident from the first note. I give you his "Deutsches Requiem" as an example. There is no hint of what is commonly regarded as religious feeling in it. Brahms, so far as I know, was not a religious man. Nor is there the slightest sign of the cheap fustian of conventional patriotism. Nevertheless, a superb emotion is there—nay, an overwhelming emotion. The thing is irresistibly moving. It is moving because a man of the highest intellectual dignity, a man of exalted feelings, a man of brains, put into it his love for and pride in his country. Lucky the country which produces such men!

But in music emotion is only half the story. Mendelssohn had it, and yet he belongs to the second table. Nor is it a matter of mere beauty—that is, of mere sensuous loveliness. If it were, then Dvořák would be greater than Beethoven, whose tunes are seldom inspired, and who not infrequently does without them altogether. What makes great music is the thing I have mentioned: brains. The greatest musician is a man whose thoughts and feelings are above the common level, and whose language matches them. What he has to say comes out of a wisdom that is not ordinary. Platitude is impossible to him. He is the precise antithesis of Mr. Babbitt. Above all, he is a master of his craft, as opposed to his art. He gets his effects in new, difficult and ingenious ways—and they convince one instantly that they are inevitable. One can easily imagine improvements in the human eye, and in the Alps, and in the art of love, and even in the Constitution, but one cannot imagine improvements in the first movement of the Eroica. The thing is completely perfect, even at the places where the composer halts to draw breath. Any change in it would damage it. But what is inevitable is never obvious. John Doe would not and could not write thus. The immovable truths that are there —and there are truths in the arts as well as in theology —became truths when Beethoven formulated them. They did not exist before. They cannot perish hereafter.

So with Brahms. There are plenty of composers of more romantic appeal. I need mention only Schubert. Schubert, had he lived, might have been the greatest of them all, but he died before any patina had formed on him; he was still going to school in his last days. But Brahms seems to have come into the world full-blown. A few experiments, brilliant even when they failed, and he was a master beside Beethoven and Bach. In all his music done after his beard had sprouted, there is not the slightest sign of bewilderment and confusion, of trial and error, of uncertainty and irresolution. He knew precisely what he wanted to say, and he said it colossally.

2
Johann Strauss

The centenary of John Strauss the Younger passed almost unnoticed in the United States. In Berlin and in Vienna it was celebrated with imposing ceremonies, and all the German radio stations put "Wein, Weib und Gesang" and "Rosen aus dem Süden" on the air. Why wasn't it done in this great country? Was the pestilence of jazz to blame—or was it due to the scarcity of sound beer? I incline to Answer No. 2. Any music is difficult on well-water, but the waltz is a sheer impossibility. "Man Lebt Nur Einmal" would be as dreadful in a dry town as a Sousa march at a hanging.

For the essence of a Viennese waltz, and especially of a Strauss waltz, is merriment, good humor, happiness, *Gemütlichkeit.* It reflects brilliantly the spirits of a people who are eternally gay, war or no war. Sad music, to be sure, has been written in Vienna—but chiefly by foreigners: Haydn, who was a Croat; Beethoven, whose pap had been a sour Rhine wine; Brahms, who came from the bleak Baltic coast. I come upon Schubert—but all rules go to pot when he appears. As for Strauss, he was a 100% Viennese, and could no more be sad than he could be indignant. The waltz wandered into the minor keys in Paris, in the hands of the sardonic Alsatian Jew, Waldteufel. At home old Johann kept it in golden major, and so did young Johann after him. The two, taking it from Schubert and the folk, lifted it to imperial splendor. No other dance-form, not even the minuet, has ever brought forth more lovely music. And none other has preserved so perfectly the divine beeriness of the peasant dance. The best of the Strauss waltzes were written for the most stilted and ceremonious court in Europe, but in every one of them, great and little, there remains the boggy, expansive flavor of the village green. Even the stately "Kaiser" waltz, with its preliminary heel-clicks and saber-rattling, is soon swinging jocosely to the measures of the rustic *Springtanz.*

It is a curious, melancholy and gruesome fact that Johann

Strauss II was brought up to the variety of thieving known as the banking business. His father planned that he should be what in our time is called a bond salesman. What asses fathers are! This one was himself a great master of the waltz, and yet he believed that he could save all three of his sons from its lascivious allurements! Young Johann was dedicated to investment banking, Josef to architecture, and Eduard, the baby, to the law. The old man died on September 25, 1849. On September 26 all three were writing waltzes. Johann, it quickly appeared, was the best of the trio. In fact, he was the best musician who ever wrote waltzes for dancing, and one of the really first-rate musicians of his time. He took the waltz as his father left it, and gradually built it up into a form almost symphonic. He developed the introduction, which had been little more than an opening fanfare, into a complex and beautiful thing, almost an overture, and he elaborated the coda until it began to demand every resource of the composer's art, including even counterpoint. And into the waltz itself he threw such lush melodic riches, so vastly a rhythmic inventiveness and so adept a mastery of instrumentation that the effect was overwhelming. The Strauss waltzes, it seems to me, have never been sufficiently studied. That other Strauss, Richard, knows what is in them, you may be sure, for the first act of "Der Rosenkavalier" proves it, but the musical pedants and pedagogues have kept aloof. What they miss! Consider, for example, the astonishing skill with which Johann manages his procession of keys—the inevitable air which he always gets into his choice! And the immense ingenuity with which he puts variety into his bass—so monotonous in Waldteufel, and even in Lanner and Gung'l! And the endless resourcefulness which marks his orchestration—never formal and obvious for an instant, but always with some new quirk in it, some fresh and charming beauty! And his codas—how simple they are, and yet how ravishing!

Johann certainly did not blush unseen. He was an important figure at the Austrian court, and when he passed necks were craned as if at an ambassador. He traveled widely and was received with honor everywhere. His waltzes swept the world. His operettas, following them, offered formidable rivalry to the pieces of Gilbert and Sullivan. He was plastered with orders like a Doug Fairbanks or an Otto Kahn. He took in, in his time, a great deal of money, and left all his wives well provided for. More, he had the respect and a little of the envy of all his musical contemporaries. Wagner delighted in his waltzes and so did Brahms. Brahms once gave the score of one of them to a fair admirer with the inscription, "Leider *nicht* von Johannes Brahms"—Unfortunately, *not* by Johannes Brahms. Coming from so reserved a man, it was a tremendous compliment indeed,—perhaps the most tremendous recorded in history—nor was there any mere politeness in it, for Brahms had written plenty of waltzes himself, and knew that it was not as easy as it looked. The lesser fish followed the whales. There was never any clash of debate over Strauss. It was unanimously agreed that he was first-rate. His field was not wide, but within that field he was the unchallenged master. He became, in the end, the dean of a sort of college of waltz writers, centering at Vienna. The waltz, as he had brought it up to perfection, became the standard ball-room dance of the civilized world, and though it had to meet rivals constantly, it held its own for two generations, and even now, despite the murrain of jazz, it threatens to come back once more. Disciples of great skill began to appear in the Straussian wake—Ziehrer, with the beautiful "Weaner Mad'l," Lincke with "Ach, Frühling, Wie Bist Du So Schön," and many another. But old Johann never lost his primacy. Down to the very day of his death in 1899 he was *primus inter omnes.* Vienna wept oceans of beery tears into his grave. A great Viennese—perhaps the ultimate flower of old Vienna—was gone.

Now he is dead a hundred years. But surely not forgotten, despite shadows over the moon here and there. The man who makes lovely tunes has the laugh on Father Time. Oblivion never quite fetches him. He goes out of fashion now and then, but he always returns. There was a time when even Bach seemed to be forgotten. What a joke! Bach will last as long as human beings are born with ears; in the end, perhaps, he will be all that the world remembers of the Eighteenth Century. And Strauss, I suspect, will keep on bobbing up in the memory of the race so long as men have legs and can leap in 3–4 time,—at all events, so long as there is good malt liquor anywhere in the world. World-wide Prohibition, it is conceivable, may eventually kill him; in a dry universe he would be *contra bonus mores.* But jazz can do him no more permanent damage than a dog visiting his grave.

3
Poetry in America

The New Poetry Movement in America, so full of life and even of malicious animal magnetism a dozen years ago, is now obviously down with cholelithiasis, and no literary pathologist of genuine gifts would be surprised to hear, at any moment, of its death. Most of its former ornaments, indeed, begin to flee its bedside. Miss Lowell, in her last years, devoted herself to prose, and Masters goes the same way. Vachel Lindsay and Robert Frost take to college professing. Carl Sandburg has joined the minstrels. All the principal Greenwich Village poets, harassed by the morals squad, fled long ago to Paris, where landlords are less prying, and even artists may lead their own lives.

This slackening of effort is visible in all the little poetry magazines. Most of them continue to come out, and in the backwaters of the Republic, where all varieties of human progress are behind schedule, there are even occasional appearances of new ones, but there is little in any of them that is worth reading, and almost no actual poetry. What they print, in the main, is simply a series of exercises in the new prosody. It turns out, on examination, to be quite as tight and arbitrary as the old kind. For one thing that a poet of 1885 could not do there are ten things that a poet of 1927 cannot do. Thus the revolt against form expires in a new and worse formalism. The fact is most visible, of course, on the edges of the movement—that is, among the poets of Greenwich Village. What one observes in the advanced and atrabilious magazines which they publish is simply a sort of organized imbecility. The poet is strictly forbidden to make use of any of the traditional materials of his craft, or to concede anything to its traditional idioms. He must eschew all rhyme that really rhymes, he must eschew all the orthodox rhythms, and he must eschew all direct attack upon the emotions. In other words, he must eschew poetry. What he writes, it must be confessed, is sometimes very interesting, in its bizarre, unearthly way—just as a college yell, say, is interesting, or an act of Congress. But it is no more poetry than the college yell is music or the act of Congress wisdom.

The trouble with most of the new poets, whether in or out of Greenwich Village, is that they are too cerebral—that they attack the problems of a fine art with the methods of science. That error runs through all their public discussions of the business. Those discussions are full of theories, by the new psychology out of the cant of the studios, that do not work and are not true. The old-time poet did not bother with theories. When the urge to write was upon him, he simply got himself into a lather, tied a towel around his head, and then tried to reduce his feelings to paper. If he had any skill the result was poetry; if he lacked skill it was nonsense. But even his worst failure still had something natural and excusable about it—it was the failure of a man admittedly somewhat feverish, with purple paint on his nose and vine-leaves in his hair. The failure of the new poet is the far more grotesque failure of a scientist who turns out to be a quack—of a mathematician who divides 20 by 4 and gets 6, of a chiropractor who looks in the vertebrae for the cause of cross-eyes, of a cook who tries to make an omelette of china doorknobs. Poetry can never be concocted by any purely intellectual process. It has nothing to do with the intellect; it is, in fact, a violent and irreconcilable enemy to the intellect. Its purpose is not to establish facts, but to evade and deny them. What it essays to do is to make life more bearable in an intolerable world by concealing and obliterating all the harsher realities. Its message is that all will be well to-morrow, or, at the latest, next Tuesday, that the grave is not cold and damp but steam-heated and lined with roses, that serving in the trenches is far more amusing and comfortable than serving in the United States Senate, that a girl is not a viviparous mammal, full of pathogenic organisms and enlightened self-interest, but an angel with bobbed wings and a heart of gold. Take this denial of the bald and dreadful facts out of poetry—make it scientific and sensible—and it simply ceases to be what it pretends to be. It may remain good prose; it may even remain beautiful prose. But it cannot stir the blood as true poetry does; it cannot offer that soothing consolation, that escape from reality, that sovereign balm for every spiritual itch and twinge which is the great gift of poetry to man. The best poetry is always palpably untrue; it is its eloquent untruth that makes it so lovely. The other day I read of a gentleman, condemned to death in one of the Southern States, who went to the electric chair reciting the Twenty-third Psalm. It is a pity he had to die; he would have made an excellent critic, for he understood perfectly the nature and purpose of poetry.

The new poets, now passing into the shadows, not only made the mistake of trying to rationalize poetry, an enterprise comparable to trying to rationalize necking, drunkenness or the use of hasheesh; they also tried to detach themselves from the ordinary flow of American ideas, and to convert themselves into an intellectual aristocracy. Some of them, true enough, quickly found the thing impossible, and so turned back, notably Sandburg and Lindsay, but nearly all at least made the attempt. Miss Lowell, perhaps, went furthest; there was a time when even Boston felt bucolic and loutish, and hence very uneasy, in her presence. The result was that nine-tenths of the compositions the fraternity produced simply shot into space. The great heart of the folk reacted to them as feebly as it might have reacted to polemics between astronomers. When poetry fails in this way it fails all over. I do not argue that it ought to reach and soothe the nether herd, though some of the very best poetry ever written actually does—for example, the poetry in the Bible. All I contend is that it ought to reach the generality of the literate. If literary pastors are not moved by it, if it fails to supply phrases for editorial writers, if it is not quoted by stewed Congressmen at the endless memorial services on Capitol Hill, then it has obviously missed fire. Of all the stuff produced by the new poets precious little has ever gone that far. I can recall a few poems by Sandburg and Lindsay, perhaps one or two by Frost, and none other. The whole body of verse of Miss Lowell is as dead as if it had been written in Choctaw. Meanwhile, certain old-fashioned poets, notably Miss Reese and Miss Teasdale, have written things that will probably live. They will live because they are alive.

I sometimes think, indeed, that the real poetry of our era has been written, not by poets at all, but by men who would be as indignant, if you called them poets, as if you called them kidnapers, violoncellists or Socialists. I allude to the earnest rhetoricians who roam the chautauquas and the Kiwanis Clubs, waving the banner of idealism. What these fellows say is almost always nonsense, but it is at least the sort of nonsense that the American people yearn to cherish and believe in—it somehow fills their need. I point, for example, to their gabble about Service—already the source of phrases that Congressmen, clergymen, editorial writers and so on mouth every day. Here is the essential poetry of the Americano: his life is sordid, but he tries to escape from the fact by leering at the stars. It is a comprehensible impulse, and even worthy. The poets of his country have not helped him to attain his heart's desire. He has had to turn to traveling go-getters and forward-lookers.

Alas, whenever one thus discusses the nature and function of poetry—that is, whenever one tries to be realistic about it—one is sure to be accused of being an enemy to the art itself. But does this necessarily follow? I am sure it does not. The social value of poetry is not diminished in the slightest by looking at it without illusion. It still offers its old escape from reality; it still offers consolation to *Homo sapiens* in his woeful journey through this inclement vale. To denounce it out of hand would be as absurd as to denounce religion or anesthetics. The purpose of anesthetics is to get rid of the harsh torture of pain and substitute the sweet peace of sleep. The purpose of even the highest poetry is almost precisely the same. Chloroform tells a man that he is not having his leg cut off, but lying drunk on a feather-bed, with fireworks to entertain him. Poetry tells him that his girl is as beautiful as Venus and is marrying him without a single thought of his tenements and hereditaments, that his country is a Galahad among the nations and wholly devoid of the rascality prevailing everywhere else, that he himself is a noble fellow and will go to Heaven when he dies. All these things, I suspect, are false. But all of them make life more bearable. Poets are simply men who devote themselves to spreading them, often at great sacrifice of income. They are liars, but their lies, I believe, will be viewed very generously on the Resurrection Morn.

4
Victualry As A Fine Art

Some time ago, functioning as a magazine editor, I essayed to get hold of some articles on the American cuisine. At once I discovered that the number of American authors capable of writing upon the subject, charmingly and at first hand, was so small as to be substantially equal to the number of honest Prohibition agents. After six months' search, in fact, I found but three, and one of them had been living abroad for years and the other had lived there since childhood. Even the third was scarcely a 100% American, for he had traveled extensively in heathen lands, and though he was holding a public office in Washington when I found him, he confessed in the first sentence of his article that he wished the Volstead Act were repealed and the Hon. Mr. Volstead himself in Hell.

I speak here, of course, of authors competent to write of victualing as a fine art. Of cooking-school ma'ms, of course, we have a plenty, and we also have a vast and cocksure rabble of dietitians, some of them more or less scientific. But it must be obvious that the cooking-school ma'm knows very little about voluptuous eating, and that the dietitian is its enemy. The ma'm, indeed, seldom shows any sign that the flavor of victuals interests her. The thing she is primarily interested in, to borrow a term from surgery, is the cosmetic effect. In the women's magazines she prints pretty pictures of her masterpieces, often in full color. They look precisely like the dreadful tit-bits one encounters in the more high-toned sort of tea-rooms, and at wedding breakfasts. One admires them as spectacles, but eating them is something else again. Moreover, the ma'm is primarily a cook, not an epicure. She is interested in materials and processes, not in gustatory effects. When she invents a new way to utilize the hard heel of a ham, she believes that she has achieved something, though even the house-cat may gag at it. Her efforts are to the art of the *cordon bleu* what those of a house-painter are to those of a Cézanne. She is a pedagogue, not an artist. The fact that she is heeded in the land, and her depressing concoctions solemnly devoured, is sufficient proof, if any were needed, that Americans do not respect the dignity of their palates.

Why this should be so I don't know, for here in this great Republic we have the materials for the most superb victuary the world has ever seen, and our people have the money to pay for it. Even the poorest Americano, indeed, eats relatively expensive food: his wife knows nothing of the hard pinching that entertains her French sister. He has meat in abundance and in considerable variety, and a great wealth of fruits and vegetables. Yet he eats badly, gets very little enjoyment out of his meals, and is constantly taking pills. The hot dog is the *reductio ad absurdum* of American eating. The Sicilian in the ditch, though he can never be President, knows better: he puts a slice of onion between his slabs of bread, not a cartridge filled with the sweepings of the abattoir. This national taste for bad food seems all the more remarkable when one recalls that the United States, more than any other country of the modern world, has been enriched by immigrant cuisines. Every fresh wave of newcomers has brought in new dishes, and many of them have been of the highest merit. But very few of them have been adopted by the natives, and the few have been mainly inferior. From the Italians, for example, we have got only spaghetti; it is now so American that it is to be had in cans. But spaghetti is to the Italian cuisine simply what eggs are to the Spanish: a raw material. We eat it as only those Italians eat it who are on the verge of ceasing to eat at all. Of the multitudinous ways in which it may be cooked and garnished we have learned but one, and that one is undoubtedly the worst. So with the German sauerkraut—a superb victual when properly prepared for the table. But how often, in America, is it properly prepared? Perhaps once in 100,000 times. Even the Germans, coming here, lose the art of handling it as its inner nature deserves. It becomes in their hands, as in the hands of American cooks, simply a sort of stewed hay, with overtones of the dishpan. To encounter a decent dish of it in an American eating-house would be as startling as to encounter a decent soup.

What ails our victualry, principally, is the depressing standardization that ails everything else American. There was a time when every American eating-house had its specialties, and many of them were excellent. One did not expect to find the same things everywhere. One went to one place for roast goose, and to another for broiled soft crabs, and to another for oysters, and to yet another for mutton chops. Rolls made the old Parker House in Boston famous, and terrapin *à la* Maryland did the same for Barnum's and Guy's Hotels in Baltimore. This specialization still prevails in Europe. The best restaurants in Paris—that is, the best in the epicurean, not in the fashionable sense—do not profess to offer the whole range of the French cuisine. Each has its specialty, and upon that specialty the art of the chef is lavished, aided by prayer and fasting. His rivals in other places do not try to meet and best him on his own ground. They let him have his masterpiece, and devote themselves to perfecting masterpieces of their own. Thus victualing in France continues to show a great variety, and a never-failing charm. One may eat superbly every day, and never encounter a dish that is merely eatable. The Parisians look forward to dinner as a Mississippian looks forward to his evening necking of the Scriptures. But in America the public cooks have all abandoned specialization, and every one of them seems bent upon cooking as nearly as possible like all the rest. The American hotel meal is as rigidly standardized as the parts of a Ford, and so is the American restaurant meal. The local dishes, in all eating-houses pretending to any tone, are banned as low. So one hunts in vain in Boston for a decent plate of beans, and in Baltimore for a decent mess of steamed hard crabs, and in St. Louis for a decent rasher of catfish. They are obtainable, perhaps, but only along the wharves. One must take a squad of police along to enjoy them in safety.

What remains? A series of dishes fit only for diners who are hurrying to catch trains—tasteless roasts, banal beefsteaks, cremated chops, fish drenched in unintelligible sauces, greasy potatoes, and a long répertoire of vegetables with no more taste than baled shavings. The bill-of-fare is the same everywhere, and nowhere is it interesting. Within the past year I have been in the heart of New England and in the heart of the South. In both places the hotels offered the same standardized cuisine. In neither was there any culinary sign that I was not in Chicago or New York. In New England the brown bread was indistinguishable from the stuff served on railway dining-cars, and in the South there was no corn-bread at all.

I daresay that the railway diner has done much to bring in

this standardization. Distances are so great in the Federal Union that the man who does much traveling eats most of his meals on trains. So he gets used to dishes that all taste alike, whatever their ostensible contents, and ends by being unable to distinguish one from another. Thus he is indifferent to novelty, and perhaps hostile to it. The hotels give him what he wants. If he protested often enough and loudly enough, they would turn out their present crews of street-railway curve-greasers and locomotive firemen and put in cooks.

I leave the meals served on railway diners for a separate treatise, to be undertaken later in life. They are botched by the effect to give them the delusive variety of the appalling meals served in American hotels. In a kitchen two feet wide and eleven feet long, four or five honest but uninspired Aframericans try to concoct fifteen or twenty different dishes. They naturally spoil all of them. On the Continent of Europe all meals served on trains are *table d'hôte*. Their principal dishes are cooked, not on the train, but at the terminals. They are always appetizing and often excellent. Light wines and beers wash them down. The dining-cars are hideous with gaudy advertisements—one sees inside what one sees outside in America—but the chow does not insult the palate. At home I have to eat many meals in railway diners. I always order the same thing. It is impossible for even a cook traveling seventy miles an hour to spoil ham and eggs.

5
The Libido For the Ugly

On a Winter day, not long ago, coming out of Pittsburgh on one of the swift, luxurious expresses of the eminent Pennsylvania Railroad, I rolled eastward for an hour through the coal and steel towns of Westmoreland county. It was familiar ground; boy and man, I had been through it often before. But somehow I had never quite sensed its appalling desolation. Here was the very heart of industrial America, the center of its most lucrative and characteristic activity, the boast and pride of the richest and grandest nation ever seen on earth—and here was a scene so dreadfully hideous, so intolerably bleak and forlorn that it reduced the whole aspiration of man to a macabre and depressing joke. Here was wealth beyond computation, almost beyond imagination—and here were human habitations so abominable that they would have disgraced a race of alley cats.

I am not speaking of mere filth. One expects steel towns to be dirty. What I allude to is the unbroken and agonizing ugliness, the sheer revolting monstrousness, of every house in sight. From East Liberty to Greensburg, a distance of twenty-five miles, there was not one in sight from the train that did not insult and lacerate the eye. Some were so bad, and they were among the most pretentious—churches, stores, warehouses, and the like—that they were downright startling: one blinked before them as one blinks before a man with his face shot away. It was as if all the more advanced Expressionist architects of Berlin had been got drunk on *Schnapps*, and put to matching aberrations. A few masterpieces linger in memory, horrible even there: a crazy little church just west of Jeannette, set like a dormer-window on the side of a bare, leprous hill; the headquarters of the Veterans of Foreign Wars at Irwin; a steel stadium like a huge rat-trap somewhere further down the line. But most of all I recall the general effect—of hideousness without a break. There was not a single decent house within eye-range from the Pittsburgh suburbs to the Greensburg yards. There was not one that was not misshapen, and there was not one that was not shabby.

The county itself is not uncomely, despite the grime of the endless mills. It is, in form, a narrow river valley, with deep gullies running up into the hills. It is thickly settled, but not noticeably overcrowded. There is still plenty of room for building, even in the larger towns, and there are very few solid blocks. Nearly every house, big and little, has space on all four sides. Obviously, if there were architects of any professional sense or dignity in the region, they would have perfected a châlet to hug the hillsides—a châlet with a high-pitched roof, to throw off the heavy Winter snows, but still essentially a low and clinging building, wider than it was tall. But what have they done? They have taken as their model a brick set on end. This they have converted into a thing of dingy clapboards, with a narrow, low-pitched roof. And the whole they have set upon thin, preposterous brick piers. What could be more appalling? By the hundreds and thousands these abominable houses cover the bare hillsides, like gravestones in some gigantic and decaying cemetery. On their deep sides they are three, four and even five stories high; on their low sides they bury themselves swinishly in the mud. Not a fifth of them are perpendicular. They lean this way and that, hanging on to their bases precariously. And one and all they are streaked in grime, with dead and eczematous patches of paint peeping through the streaks.

Now and then there is a house of brick. But what brick! When it is new it is the color of a fried egg. When it has taken on the patina of the mills it is the color of an egg long past all hope or caring. Was it necessary to adopt that shocking color? No more than it was necessary to set all of the houses on end. Red brick, even in a steel town, ages with some dignity. Let it become downright black, and it is still sightly, especially if its trimmings are of white stone, with soot in the depths and the high spots washed by the rain. But in Westmoreland they prefer that uremic yellow, and so they have the most loathsome towns and villages ever seen by mortal eye.

I award this championship only after laborious research and incessant prayer. I have seen, I believe, all of the most unlovely towns of the world; they are all to be found in the United States. I have seen the mill towns of decomposing New England and the desert towns of Utah, Arizona and Texas. I am familiar with the back streets of Newark, Brooklyn, Chicago and Pittsburgh, and have made bold scientific explorations to Camden, N.J. and Newport News, Va. Safe in a Pullman, I have whirled through the gloomy, Godforsaken villages of Iowa and Kansas, and the malarious tide-water hamlets of Georgia. I have been to Bridgeport, Conn., and to Los Angeles. But nowhere on this earth, at home or abroad, have I seen anything to compare to the villages that huddle along the line of the Pennsylvania from the Pittsburgh yards to Greensburg. They are incomparable in color, and they are incomparable in design. It is as if some titanic and aberrant genius, uncompromisingly inimical to man, had devoted all the ingenuity of Hell to the making of them. They show grotesqueries of ugliness that, in retrospect, become almost diabolical. One cannot imagine mere human beings concocting such dreadful things, and one can scarcely imagine human beings bearing life in them.

Are they so frightful because the valley is full of foreigners——dull, insensate brutes, with no love of beauty in them? Then why didn't these foreigners set up similar abominations in the countries that they came from? You will, in fact, find nothing of the sort in Europe—save perhaps in a few putrefying parts of England. There is scarcely an ugly village on the whole Continent. The peasants, however poor, somehow manage to make themselves graceful and charming habitations, even in Italy and Spain. But in the American village and small town the pull is always toward ugliness, and in that Westmoreland valley it has been yielded to with an eagerness bordering upon passion. It is incredible that mere ignorance should have achieved such masterpieces of horror. There is a voluptuous quality in them—the same quality that one finds in a Methodist sermon or an editorial in the New York *Herald-Tribune*. They look deliberate.

On certain levels of the human race, indeed, there seems to be a positive libido for the ugly, as on other and less Christian levels there is a libido for the beautiful. It is impossible to put down the wallpaper that defaces the average American home of the lower middle class to mere inadvertence, or to the obscene humor of the manufacturers. Such ghastly designs, it must be obvious, give a genuine delight to a certain type of mind. They meet, in some unfathomable way, its obscure and unintelligible demands. They caress it as "The Palms" caresses it, or the art of Landseer, or the ecclesiastical architecture of the United Brethren. The taste for them is as enigmatical and yet as common as the taste for vaudeville, dogmatic theology, sentimental movies, and the poetry of Edgar A. Guest. Or for the metaphysical speculations of Arthur Brisbane. Thus I suspect (though confessedly without knowing) that the vast majority of the honest folk of Westmoreland county, and especially the 100% Americans among them, actually admire the houses they live in, and are proud of them. For the same money they could get vastly better ones, but they prefer what they have got. Certainly there was no pressure upon the Veterans of Foreign Wars at Irwin to choose the dreadful edifice that bears their banner, for there are plenty of vacant buildings along the trackside, and some of them are appreciably better. They might, indeed, have built a better one of their own. But they chose that clapboarded horror with their eyes open, and having chosen it, they let it mellow into its present shocking depravity. They like it as it is: beside it, the Parthenon would no doubt offend them. In precisely the same way the authors of the rat-trap stadium that I have mentioned made a deliberate choice. After painfully designing and erecting it, they made it perfect in their own sight by putting a completely impossible pent-house, painted a staring yellow, on top of it. The effect is truly appalling. It is that of a fat woman with a black eye. It is that of a Presbyterian grinning. But they like it.

Here is something that the psychologists have so far neglected: the love of ugliness for its own sake, the lust to make the world intolerable. Its habitat is the United States. Out of the melting pot emerges a race which hates beauty as it hates truth. The etiology of this madness deserves a great deal more study than it has got. There must be causes behind it; it arises and flourishes in obedience to biological laws, and not as a mere act of God. What, precisely, are the terms of those laws? And why do they run stronger in America than elsewhere? Let some honest *Privat Dozent* apply himself to the problem.

VII.
Hymn to the Truth

On December 28, 1917, in the midst of war's alarums, I printed in the New York *Evening Mail*, a journal now happily extinct, an article purporting to give the history of the bathtub. This article, I may say at once, was a tissue of somewhat heavy absurdities, all of them deliberate and most of them obvious. I alleged that the bathtub was unknown in the world until the '40's of the last century, and that it was then invented in Cincinnati by a contemporary of *Stammvater* Longworth. I described how the inventor, in the absence of running water in the town, employed Aframericans to haul it in buckets from the adjacent Ohio river. I told how a bathtub was put into the White House in the '50's, and how the intrepid Millard Fillmore, of Cayuga, N.Y., took the first presidential bath. I ended by saying that the medical faculty of the Republic opposed the new invention as dangerous to health, and that laws against it were passed by the legislators of Virginia, Pennsylvania and Massachusetts.

This article, plainly enough, was of spoofing all compact. I composed it, in fact, to sublimate and so make bearable the intolerable libido of the war for democracy, and I confess that I regarded it, when it came out in the *Mail*, with a certain professional satisfaction. It was promptly reprinted by various other great organs of the enlightenment, sometimes with credit, and after a while a stream of letters began to reach me from persons who had read it. Then, of a sudden, all my satisfaction turned to consternation. For it quickly appeared that at least nine-tenths of these readers took my idle jocosities with complete seriousness! Some of them, of antiquarian tastes, asked for further light upon this or that phase of the subject. Others offered corrections in detail. Yet others offered me corroboration! But the worst was to come. Soon I began to discover my preposterous "facts" in the writings of other men, some of them immensely earnest. The chiropractors and other such quacks collared them for use as evidence of the stupidity of medical men. They were cited by medical men as proof of the progress of public hygiene. They got into learned journals and the transactions of learned societies. They were alluded to on the floor of Congress. The editorial writers of the land, borrowing them in toto and without mentioning my begetting of them, began to labor them in their dull, indignant way. They crossed the dreadful wastes of the North Atlantic, and were discussed horribly by English uplifters and German professors. Finally, they got into the standard works of reference, and began to be taught to the young.

For a while I was alarmed; then I was amused; then I began to be alarmed again. In the early part of 1926, having undergone a spiritual rebirth and put off sin, I resolved to confess, and so put an end to the imposture. This I did formally on May 23. I admitted categorically that I had invented the whole tale, and that there was not a word of truth in it. I pointed out its obvious and multitudinous absurdities. I called upon the pedagogues of the land to cease teaching such appalling nonsense to the young, and upon the historians to take it out of their books. This confession and appeal were printed simultaneously in thirty great American newspapers, with a combined circulation, according to their sworn claims, of more than 250,000,000. One of them, and perhaps the greatest of them all, was the eminent Boston *Herald*, organ of the New England illuminati. The *Herald*, on that bright May Sunday, printed my article on a leading page of its so-called Editorial Section, under a black and beetling four-column head, and with a two-column cartoon labeled satirically "The American Public Will Swallow Anything." And then, three weeks later, on June 13, in the same Editorial Section, but promoted to page one, the same *Herald* reprinted my ten-year-old fake—soberly and as a piece of news!

Do not misunderstand me: I am not seeking to cast a stone at the *Herald*, or at its talented and patriotic editors. It is, as every one knows, one of the glories of American journalism, and is awarded Pulitzer prizes almost as often as the Pulitzer papers themselves. It labors unceasingly for public morality, the Andy Mellon idealism, and the flag. If it were suppressed by the Watch and Ward Society to-morrow New England would revert instantly to savagery, wolves and catamounts would roam in Boylston Street, and the Harvard Law School would be engulfed by Bolshevism. Little does the public reck what great sums such journals expend to establish and disseminate the truth. It may cost $10,000 and a reporter's leg to get a full and accurate list of the guests at a Roxbury wake, with their injuries. My point is that, despite all this extravagant frenzy for the truth, there is something in the human mind that turns instinctively to fiction, and that even the most gifted journalists succumb to it. A German philosopher, Dr. Hans Vaihinger, has put the thing into a formal theory, and you will find it expounded at length in his book, "The Philosophy of As If." It is a sheer impossibility, says Dr. Vaihinger, for human beings to think exclusively in terms of the truth. For one thing, the stock of indubitable truths is too scanty. For another thing, there is the instinctive aversion to them that I have mentioned. All of our thinking, according to Vaihinger, is in terms of assumptions, many of them plainly not true. Into our most solemn and serious reflections fictions enter—and three times out of four they quickly crowd out all the facts.

That this truth about the so-called truth is true needs no argument. Every man, thinking of his wife, has to assume that she is beautiful and amiable, else despair will seize him and he will be unable to think at all. Every 100% American, contemplating Dr. Coolidge, is psychically bound to admire him: the alternative is anarchy. Every Christian, viewing the clergy, is forced into a bold theorizing to save himself from Darwinism and Hell. And all of us, taking stock of ourselves, must resort to hypothesis to escape the river. What ails the bald truth is that it is mainly uncomfortable, and never caressing. What the actual history of the bathtub may be I don't know: digging it out would be an endless job, and the result, after all the labor, would probably be only a string of banalities. The fiction I concocted back in 1917 was at least better than that. It lacked sense, but it was certainly not without a certain charm. There were heroes in it, and villains. It revealed a conflict, with virtue winning. So it was embraced by mankind, precisely as the story of George Washington and the cherry-tree was embraced, and it will live, I daresay, until it is displaced by something worse—and hence better.

In other words, it was poetry, which is to say, a mellifluous and caressing statement of the certainly not true. The two elements, of untruth and of beauty, are both important, and perhaps equally. It is not sufficient that the thing said in poetry be untrue: it must also be said with a certain grace—it must soothe the ear while it debauches the mind. And it is not sufficient that it be voluptuous: it must also offer a rock and a refuge from the harsh facts of everyday. Poets, of course, protest against this doctrine. They argue that they actually deal in the truth, and that their brand of truth is of a peculiarly profound and esoteric quality—in other words, that their compositions add to the sum of human wisdom. It is sufficient answer to them to say that the chiropractors make precisely the same claim, and with exactly the same plausibility. Both actually deal in fictions. Those fictions are not truths; they are not even truths in decay. They are simply better-than-truths. They make life more comfortable and happy. They turn and dull the sharp edge of reality.

It is commonly held that the vast majority of men are anæsthetic to the poetry, as they are alleged to be anæsthetic to other forms of beauty, but this is itself a fiction, devised by poets to dignify their trade, and make it seem high-toned and mysterious. The fact is that the love of poetry is one of the most primitive of human traits, and that it appears in children almost as soon as they learn to speak and steal. I do not refer here to the love of verbal jingles, but to the love of poetry properly-so-called—that is, to the love of the agreeably not-so. A little girl who nurses a rag-doll is a poet, and so is a boy who plays at soldiers with a box of clothes-pins. Their ma is another poet when she brags about them to the neighbors, and their pa when he praises the cooking of their ma. The more simple-minded the individual, indeed, the greater his need of poetry, and hence the more steady his demand for it. No poet approved by the *intelligentsia* ever had so many customers as Edgar A. Guest. Are Guest's dithyrambs laughed at by the *intelligentsia*? Then it is not because the things they say are not so, but because the fiction in them is of a kind not satisfying to sniffish and snooty men. It is fiction suitable to persons of a less critical habit. It preaches the joys open to the humble. It glorifies their dire necessities. It cries down their lacks. It promises them happiness, and if not happiness, then at least contentment. No wonder it is popular! No wonder it is intoned every time Kiwanians get together, and the reassuring slapping of backs begins. It is itself a sort of back-slapping. And so is all other poetry. The strophes of Robert Browning elude the Kiwanian, but they are full of soothing for the young college professor, for they tell him that it is a marvelous and exhilarating thing to be as intellectual as he is. This, of course, is not true—which is the chief reason why it is pleasant. No normal human being wants to hear the truth. It is the passion of a small and aberrant minority of men, most of them pathological. They are hated for telling it while they live, and when they die they are swiftly forgotten. What remains to the world, in the field of wisdom, is a series of long-tested and solidly agreeable lies. It is out of such lies that most of the so-called knowledge of humanity flows. What begins as poetry ends as fact, and is embalmed in the history books. One recalls the gaudy days of 1914–1918.

But I am forgetting the coda to my story. On July 25, six weeks after the *Herald's* astounding *faux pas* and nine weeks after my exposure of the original fraud, I printed another article on the subject, disclosing the complete facts once more, and cackling over the joke at the *Herald's* expense. This second article got a great deal of attention: it was reprinted from end to end of the Republic, and discussed in such remote and barbarous places as Liverpool, Melbourne and Cape Town. And then, early in 1927, the distinguished *Scribner's Magazine* printed a learned article on the history of bathing, and in it all my stale nonsense was once more set forth as fact!

VIII.

The Pedagogy of Sex

It is a curious and instructive fact that in all the vast literature of so-called sex hygiene emitted from the American presses for twenty years past there is scarcely a book of any sound and practical value. I have been through, I should say, at least a hundred such volumes, and I can recall but one that was even completely honest. That one was a little pamphlet called "The Sex Side of Life," by Mrs. Mary Ware Dennett, a birth controller but an intelligent woman. Naturally enough, it was suppressed by the wowsers of the Postoffice, and is now contraband. All the rest of the expository and hortatory manuals, large and small, are full of evasions, with many descents to downright false pretenses. It is difficult to imagine such prissy rubbish deceiving the adolescents to whom it is ostensibly addressed. For youth, though it may lack knowledge, is certainly not devoid of intelligence: it sees through shams with sharp and terrible eyes. When a schoolmaster is an ass, which happens in Christendom more often than not, you may be sure that even the dullest of his pupils is well aware of it.

The teachers of sex hygiene fall almost unanimously into that melancholy category. Very few such books appear to be written by adults of worldly experience and sound sense. They are, like the school physiology books, mainly the product of authors cursed with the *furor pedagogicus*—which is to say, of authors whose yearning to teach is unaccompanied by anything properly describable as useful knowledge or civilized discretion. I have read such books that were downright idiotic, and I have read others that were palpably dangerous. What ails most of them is simply the fact that their composers, as pedagogues, are moralists first, and scientists only afterward. Dealing with a subject in which only the plain and unequivocal facts can be of any imaginable value, they swathe those facts in such endless yards of pious platitude that not even a modern puella, appalling keen though her wits may be, can be expected to penetrate to the core of wisdom that is theoretically concealed within them.

Several common defects run through these lamentable tomes. One is the thumping *non sequitur* that is in them—the gross disparity between their premisses and their conclusions. They start off with attempts to show that the phenomena of sex in the lower organisms—usually dahlias, herring or frogs—are beautiful and instructive, and they close with horrible warnings that the phenomena of sex in man are ugly and not to be mentioned. I do not forget, of course, their frequent high praise of maternity, their florid descriptions of the ineffable joys of philoprogenitiveness. But maternity, as they picture it, is scarcely more sexual than playing the piano. It is, in fact, set up as something definitely anti-sexual, and virtuous thereby, —as a sweet boon that must be forfeited if sex is yielded to. I do not know how this logical swamp is to be got around. It may present, indeed, a difficulty that no one will ever resolve. All I presume to do is to point out that the authors of the sex hygiene books have certainly not disposed of it, and that most of them seem to be happily unaware that it exists. First they describe romantically the mating of the calla-lilies and the June bugs, and then they plunge furiously into their revolting treatises upon *ophthalmia neonatorum*, lues, prostatitis, female weakness, and the fires of Hell. First they paint a picture fit for a Christmas card, and then they turn it around and show a panorama of jails, gutters and dissecting-rooms. It is the old juristic error of trying to put down crime by converting trivial misdemeanors into thumping felonies, with capital punishment. I don't believe that it works. Personally, I do not frequent adolescent society, but if those who do so are to be believed it is looser to-day than it ever was before. That is to say, the era of sex hygiene books—pouring from the presses by the million—is an era of rapidly increasing sexual recklessness. Is there any relation of cause and effect here? I incline to think that there may be. Youth, with its highly efficient eyes, sees plainly that many, at least, of the dangers described are enormously exaggerated. What more natural than for it to conclude that the rest are exaggerated, too?

There is another defect common to most of these books, and it is quite as serious as the first. It lies in their evasion of the plain fact that sex would be unimportant if it were not for its capacity to produce an overwhelming ecstasy—that the average human being seldom thinks of it in any other aspect, and almost never hears of it. This ecstasy, of course, does not have to be taught; it is known by every flapper who has been kissed by her first beau. But when, in a treatise upon the subject, it is not mentioned at all—or, if mentioned, passed over gingerly—, then it is certainly not surprising if the young reader drops the book as ignorant and fraudulent, and is lost to the moral lessons it inculcates. Only Mrs. Dennett, of all the sexual pedagogues I have read, so much as hints that the exercise of the reproductive faculty is immensely agreeable—and Mrs. Dennett, as I have said, is under the ban of the Postoffice. The rest of the sex hygienists depict it either as something inert and banal, like having one's hair cut, or as something painful and dangerous, like having one's appendix out. There is, on the one hand, the chaste and arctic philandering of the rose, and there is on the other hand a complex of pathological horrors. The average youngster, male or female, is deceived by neither picture. It is well known, even in the primary grades, that kissing is far more pleasant than gargling or sneezing, and it is unanimously suspected that what instinct suggests ought to follow is more pleasant still. Those ensuing proceedings constitute the fundamental mystery of sex, as the young confront it—and yet it is precisely there that the sex hygiene books are least illuminating. They are full of alarming news about the remotest and most improbable consequences of a phenomenon, and leave the phenomenon itself undescribed. Thus they fail to satisfy the very curiosity that ostensibly brought them into being—the very curiosity they so ineptly inflame. Is it any wonder that intelligent young readers—and even a moron, at twelve, is still intelligent—cast them aside as buncombe, and carry away nothing from them save the notion that what is so dangerous must be immensely fascinating, else the human race would have committed suicide long ago by avoiding the risk?

As I have hinted, it may be that these defects in the sex hygiene books—and I could list many more—are inescapable. It may be that the subject is inherently and incurably resistent to pedagogical science. But I prefer to take a more optimistic view. The human mind is a pliant and puissant organ. It has solved many occult and vexatious problems. Perhaps, in the long run, it will solve this one too. Perhaps, indeed, the solution would be possible to-morrow—if the higher powers of the mind were applied to it. In the sex hygiene books, so far as I can make out, only the lower powers are in action. Such books, it appears, are not ordinarily written by persons of sound information and ordinary sense. On the contrary, they seem to be mainly the product of Freudian cripples who know very little about the subject they discuss, and have nothing to say about it that is apposite and worth hearing. They are moral exhorters, not seekers of the truth. Their aim is hortatory, not scientific. They apply themselves to what ought to be, not to what is.

I believe that the remedy lies in trying to enlist performers of a better grade—that is, performers who have taken the trouble to investigate the matters they deal with, calmly and thoroughly, and who have the degree of common sense that one ordinarily looks for in a railroad conductor or an ice-man. There must be plenty of such men, not to mention women. Their writings, indeed, are already available—pursued by the wowsers, but not yet quite scotched. I have mentioned Mrs. Dennett and offer Havelock Ellis as another example. But most such authors, of course, address adults—what is more, highly sophisticated adults. What remains is for them to bring their knowledge down to the comprehension of the young. I believe that it can be done, and that on some near to-morrow it will be done. When the day comes at least nine-tenths of the sex hygiene books that now stand in the book-shops will be thrown out as rubbish.

IX.
Metropolis

It is astonishing how little New York figures in current American literature. Think of the best dozen American novels of the last ten years. No matter which way your taste and prejudice carry you, you will find, I believe, that Manhattan Island is completely missing from at least ten of them, and that in the other two it is little more than a passing scene, unimportant to the main action. Perhaps the explanation is to be sought in the fact that very few authors of any capacity live in the town. It attracts all the young aspirants powerfully, and hundreds of them, lingering on, develop into very proficient hacks and quacks, and so eventually adorn the Authors' League, the Poetry Society, and the National Institute of Arts and Letters. But not many remain who have anything worth hearing to say. They may keep quarters on the island, but they do their writing somewhere else.

Primarily, I suppose, it is too expensive for them: in order to live decently they must grind through so much hack work for the cheap magazines, the movies and the Broadway theaters that there is no time left for their serious concerns. But there is also something else. The town is too full of distractions to be comfortable to artists; it is comfortable only to performers. Its machinery of dissipation is so vastly developed that no man can escape it—not even an author laboring in his lonely room, the blinds down and chewing-gum plugging his ears. He hears the swish of skirts through the key-hole; down the area-way comes the clink of ice in tall glasses; some one sends him a pair of tickets to a show which whisper promises will be the dirtiest seen since the time of the Twelve Apostles. It is a sheer impossibility in New York to escape such appeals to the ductless glands. They are in the very air. The town is no longer a place of work; it is a place of pleasure. Even the up-State Baptist, coming down to hear the Rev. Dr. John Roach Straton tear into sin, must feel the pull of temptation. He wanders along Broadway to shiver dutifully before the Metropolitan Opera

House, with its black record of lascivious music dramas and adulterous tenors, but before he knows what has struck him he is lured into a movie house even gaudier and wickeder, to sweat before a film of carnal love with the lewd music of Tschaikowsky dinning in his ears, or into a grindshop auction house to buy an ormolu clock disgraceful to a Christian, or into Childs' to debauch himself with such victuals as are seen in Herkimer county only on days of great ceremonial.

Such is the effect of organized badness, operating upon imperfect man. But what is bad is also commonly amusing, and so I continue to marvel that the authors of the Republic, and especially the novelists, do not more often reduce it to words. Is there anything more charming and instructive in the scenes that actually engage them? I presume to doubt it. There are more frauds and scoundrels, more quacks and cony-catchers, more suckers and visionaries in New York than in all the country west of the Union Hill, N.J., breweries. In other words, there are more interesting people. They pour in from all four points of the compass, and on the hard rocks of Manhattan they do their incomparable stuff, day and night, year in and year out, ever hopeful and ever hot for more. Is it drama if Jens Jensen, out in Nebraska, pauses in his furrow to yearn heavily that he were a chiropractor? Then why isn't it drama if John Doe, prancing in a New York night club, pauses to wonder who the fellow was who just left in a taxi with Mrs. Doe? Is it tragedy that Nils Nilsen, in South Dakota, wastes his substance trying to horn into a mythical Heaven? Then why isn't it tragedy when J. Eustace Garfunkel, after years of effort, fails to make the steep grade of St. Bartholomew's Church?

New York is not all bricks and steel. There are hearts there, too, and if they do not break, then they at least know how to leap. It is the place where all the aspirations of the Western World meet to form one vast master aspiration, as powerful as the suction of a steam dredge. It is the icing on the pie called Christian civilization. That it may have buildings higher than any ever heard of, and gin enough to keep it gay, and bawdy shows enough, and door-openers enough, and noise and confusion enough—that these imperial ends may be achieved, uncounted millions sweat and slave on all the forlorn farms of the earth, and in all the miserable slums, including its own. It pays more for a meal than an Italian or a Pole pays for a wife, and the meal is better than the wife. It gets the best of everything, and especially of what, by all reputable ethical systems, is the worst. It has passed beyond all fear of Hell or hope of Heaven. The primary postulates of all the rest of the world are its familiar jokes. A city apart, it is breeding a race apart. Is that race American? Then so is a bashi-bazouk American. Is it decent? Then so is a street-walker decent. But I don't think that it may be reasonably denounced as dull.

What I marvel at is that the gorgeous, voluptuous color of this greatest of world capitals makes so little showing in the lovely letters of the United States. I am not forgetting such things as John Dos Passos' "Manhattan Transfer" and Felix Riesenberg's "East Side, West Side"—but neither am I admitting that they fill my bill. If only as spectacle, the city is superb. It has a glitter like that of the Constantinople of the Comneni. It roars with life like the Bagdad of the Sassanians. These great capitals of antiquity, in fact, were squalid villages compared to it, as Rome was after their kind, and Paris, Berlin and London are to-day. There is little in New York that does not issue out of money. It is not a town of ideas; it is not even a town of causes. But what issues out of money is often extremely brilliant, and I believe that it is more brilliant in New York than it has ever been anywhere else. A truly overwhelming opulence envelops the whole place, even the slums. The slaves who keep it going may dwell in vile cubicles, but they are hauled to and from their work by machinery that costs hundreds of millions, and when they fare forth to recreate themselves for to-morrow's tasks they are felled and made dumb by a gaudiness that would have floored John Paleologus himself. Has any one ever figured out, in hard cash, the value of the objects of art stored upon Manhattan Island? I narrow it to paintings, and bar out all the good ones. What would it cost to replace even the bad ones? Or all the statuary, bronzes, hangings, pottery, and bogus antiques? Or the tons of bangles, chains of pearls stomachers, necklaces, and other baubles? Assemble all the diamonds into one colossal stone, and you will have a weapon to slay Behemoth. The crowds pour in daily, bringing the gold wrung from iron and coal, hog and cow. It is invisible, for they carry it in checks, but it is real for all that. Every dollar earned in

Kansas or Montana finds its way, soon or late, to New York, and if there is a part of it that goes back, there is also a part of it that sticks.

What I contend is that this spectacle, lush and barbaric in its every detail, offers the material for a great imaginative literature. There is not only gaudiness in it; there is also a hint of strangeness; it has overtones of the fabulous and even of the diabolical. The thing simply cannot last. If it does not end by catastrophe, then it will end by becoming stale, which is to say, dull. But while it is in full blast it certainly holds out every sort of stimulation that the gifted literatus may plausibly demand. The shocking imbecility of Main Street is there and the macabre touch of Spoon River. But though Main Street and Spoon River have both found their poets, Manhattan is still to be adequately sung. How will the historian of the future get at it, imagining a future and assuming that it will have historians? The story is not written anywhere in official records. It is not in the files of the newspapers, which reflect only the surface, and not even all of that. It will not go into memoirs, for the actors in the melodramatic comedy have no taste for prose, and moreover they are all afraid to tell what they know. What it needs, obviously, is an imaginative artist. We have them in this bursting, stall-fed land—not many of them, perhaps—not as many as our supply of quacks—but nevertheless we have them. The trouble is that they either hate Manhattan too much to do its portrait, or are so bedazzled by it that their hands are palsied and their parts of speech demoralized. Thus we have dithyrambs of Manhattan—but no prose.

I hymn the town without loving it. It is immensely amusing, but I see nothing in it to inspire the fragile and shy thing called affection. I can imagine an Iowan loving the black, fecund stretches of his native State, or a New Englander loving the wreck of Boston, or even a Chicagoan loving Chicago, poets, Loop, stockyards and all, but it is hard for me to fancy any rational human being loving New York. Does one love bartenders? Or interior decorators? Or elevator starters? Or the head-waiters of night clubs? No, one delights in such functionaries, and perhaps one respects them and even reveres them, but one does not love them. They are as palpably cold and artificial as the Cathedral of St. John the Divine. Like it, they are mere functions of solvency. When the sheriff comes in they flutter away. One invests affection in places where it will be safe when the winds blow.

But I am speaking now of spectacles, not of love affairs. The spectacle of New York remains—infinitely grand and gorgeous, stimulating like the best that comes out of goblets, and none the worse for its sinister smack. The town seizes upon all the more facile and agreeable emotions like band music. It is immensely trashy—but it remains immense. Is it a mere Utopia of rogues, a vast and complicated machine for rooking honest men? I don't think so. The honest man, going to its market, gets sound value for his money. It offers him luxury of a kind never dreamed of in the world before—the luxury of being served by perfect and unobtrusive slaves, human and mechanical. It permits him to wallow regally—nay, almost celestially. The Heaven of the Moslems is open to any one who can pay the *couvert* charge and honorarium of the hat-check girl—and there is a door, too, leading into the Heaven of the Christians, or, at all events, into every part of it save that devoted to praise and prayer. Nor is all this luxury purely physiological. There is entertainment also for the spirit, or for what passes for the spirit when men are happy. There were more orchestral concerts in New York last Winter than there were in Berlin. The town has more theaters, and far better ones, than a dozen Londons. It is, as I have said, loaded with art to the gunwales, and steadily piling more on deck. Is it unfecund of ideas? Perhaps. But surely it is not hostile to them. There is far more to the show it offers than watching a pretty gal oscillate her hips; one may also hear some other gal, only a shade less sightly, babble the latest discoveries in antinomianism. All kinds, in brief, come in. There are parts for all in the *Totentanz*, even for moralists to call the figures. But there is, as yet, no recorder to put it on paper.

X.
Dives into Quackery

I
Chiropractic

THIS preposterous quackery is now all the rage in the back reaches of the Republic, and even begins to conquer the less civilized of the big cities. As the old-time family doctor dies out in the country towns, with no trained successor willing to take over his dismal business, he is followed by some hearty blacksmith or ice-wagon driver, turned into a chiropractor in six months, often by correspondence. In Los Angeles the damned there are more chiropractors than actual physicians, and they are far more generally esteemed. Proceeding from the Ambassador Hotel to the heart of the town, along Wilshire boulevard, one passes scores of their gaudy signs; there are even many chiropractic "hospitals." The morons who pour in from the prairies and deserts, most of them ailing, patronize these "hospitals" copiously, and give to the chiropractic pathology the same high respect that they accord to the theology of Aimée McPherson and the art of Cecil De Mille. That pathology is grounded upon the doctrine that all human ills are caused by the pressure of misplaced vertebra upon the nerves which come out of the spinal cord—in other words, that every disease is the result of a pinch. This, plainly enough, is buncombe. The chiropractic therapeutics rest upon the doctrine that the way to get rid of such pinches is to climb upon a table and submit to an heroic pummeling by a retired piano mover. This, obviously, is buncombe doubly damned.

Both doctrines were launched upon the world by an old quack named Andrew T. Still, the father of osteopathy. For years his followers merchanted them, and made a lot of money at the trade. But as they grew opulent they grew ambitious, *i.e.*, they began to study anatomy and physiology. The result was a gradual abandonment of Papa Still's ideas. The high-toned osteopath of to-day is a sort of eclectic. He tries anything that promises to work, from tonsillectomy to the vibrations of the late Dr. Abrams. With four years' training behind him, he probably knows more anatomy than the average graduate of the Johns Hopkins Medical School, or, at all events, more osteology. Thus enlightened, he seldom has much to say about pinched nerves in the back. But as he abandoned the Still revelation it was seized by the chiropractors, led by another quack, one Palmer. This Palmer grabbed the pinched nerve nonsense and began teaching it to ambitious farm-hands and out-at-elbow Baptist preachers in a few easy lessons. To-day the backwoods swarm with chiropractors, and in most States they have been able to exert enough pressure on the rural politicians to get themselves licensed. Any lout with strong hands and arms is perfectly equipped to become a chiropractor. No education beyond the elements is necessary. The whole art and mystery may be imparted in a few months, and the graduate is then free to practice upon God's images. The takings are often high, and so the profession has attracted thousands of recruits—retired baseball players, plumbers, truck-drivers, longshoremen, bogus dentists, dubious preachers, village school superintendents. Now and then a quack doctor of some other school—say homeopathy—plunges into it. Hundreds of promising students come from the intellectual rank of hospital orderlies.

In certain States efforts have been made, sometimes by the medical fraternity, to make the practice of chiropractic unlawful. I am glad to be able to report that practically all of them have failed. Why should it be prohibited? I believe that every free-born man has a clear right, when he is ill, to seek any sort of treatment that he yearns for. If his mental processes are of such a character that the theory of chiropractic seems plausible to him, then he should be permitted to try chiropractic. And if it be granted that he has a right to do so, then it follows clearly that any stevedore privy to the technique of chiropractic has a right to treat him. To preach any contrary doctrine is to advocate despotism and slavery. The arguments for such despotism are all full of holes, and especially those that come from medical men who have been bitten by the public hygiene madness, *i.e.*, by the messianic delusion. Such fanatics infest every health department in the land. They assume glibly that the whole aim of civilization is to cut down the death-rate, and to attain that end they are willing to make a sacrifice of everything else imaginable, including their own sense of humor. There is, as a matter of fact, not the slightest reason to believe that cutting down the death-rate, in itself, is of much benefit to the human race. A people with an annual rate of 40 a thousand might still produce many Huxleys and Darwins, and one with a rate of but 8 or 9 might produce nothing but Coolidges and Billy Sundays. The former probability, in truth, is greater than the latter, for a low rate does not necessarily mean that more superior individuals are surviving; it may mean only that more of the inferior are surviving, and that the next generation will be burdened by their get.

Such quackeries as Christian Science, osteopathy and chiropractic work against the false humanitarianism of the hygienists and to excellent effect. They suck in the botched, and help them on to bliss eternal. When these botched fall into the hands of competent medical men they are very likely to be patched up and turned loose upon the world, to beget their kind. But massaged along the backbone to cure their lues, they quickly pass into the last stages, and so their pathogenic heritage perishes with them. What is too often forgotten is that nature obviously intends the botched to die, and that every interference with that benign process is full of dangers. Moreover, it is, like birth control, profoundly immoral. The chiropractors are innocent in both departments. That their labors tend to propagate epidemics and so menace the lives of all of us, as is alleged by their medical opponents—this I doubt. The fact is that most infectious diseases of any seriousness throw out such alarming symptoms and so quickly that no sane chiropractor is likely to monkey with them. Seeing his patient breaking out in pustules, or choking, or falling into a stupor, he takes to the woods at once, and leaves the business to the nearest medical man. His trade is mainly with ambulant patients; they must come to his studio for treatment. Most of them have lingering diseases; they tour all the neighborhood doctors before they reach him. His treatment, being entirely nonsensical, is in accord with the divine plan. It is seldom, perhaps, that he actually kills a patient, but at all events he keeps many a worthy soul from getting well.

Thus the multiplication of chiropractors in the Republic

gives me a great deal of pleasure. It is agreeable to see so many morons getting slaughtered, and it is equally agreeable to see so many other morons getting rich. The art and mystery of scientific medicine, for a decade or more past, has been closed to all save the sons of wealthy men. It takes a small fortune to go through a Class A medical college, and by the time the graduate is able to make a living for himself he is entering upon middle age, and is commonly so disillusioned that he is unfit for practice. Worse, his fees for looking at tongues and feeling pulses tend to be cruelly high. His predecessors charged fifty cents and threw in the pills; his own charges approach those of divorce lawyers, consulting engineers and the higher hetæræ. Even general practice, in our great Babylons, has become a sort of specialty, with corresponding emoluments. But the chiropractor, having no such investment in his training, can afford to work for more humane wages, and so he is getting more and more of the trade. Six weeks after he leaves his job at the filling-station or abandons the steering-wheel of his motor-truck he knows all the anatomy and physiology that he will ever learn in this world. Six weeks more, and he is an adept at all the half-Nelsons and left hooks that constitute the essence of chiropractic therapy. Soon afterward, having taken post-graduate courses in advertising, salesmanship and mental mastery, he is ready for practice. A sufficiency of patients, it appears, is always ready, too. I hear of no complaint from chiropractors of bad business. New ones are being turned out at a dizzy rate, but they all seem to find the pickings easy. Some time ago I heard of a chiropractor who, having once been a cornet-player, had abandoned chiropractic in despair, and gone back to cornet-playing. But investigation showed that he was really not a chiropractor at all, but an osteopath.

The osteopaths, I fear, are finding this new competition serious and unpleasant. As I have said, it was their Hippocrates, the late Dr. Still, who invented all of the thrusts, lunges, yanks, hooks and bounces that the lowly chiropractors now employ with such vast effect, and for years the osteopaths had a monopoly of them. But when they began to grow scientific and ambitious their course of training was lengthened until it took in all sorts of tricks and dodges borrowed from the regular doctors, or resurrection men, including plucking of tonsils, adenoids and appendices, the use of the stomach-pump, and even some of the legerdemain of psychiatry. They now harry their students furiously, and turn them out ready for anything from growing hair on a bald head to frying a patient with the *x*-rays. All this new striving, of course, quickly brought its inevitable penalties. The osteopathic graduate, having sweated so long, was no longer willing to take a case of sarcoma for $2, and in consequence he lost patients. Worse, very few aspirants could make the long grade. The essence of osteopathy itself could be grasped by any lively farm-hand or night watchman in a few weeks, but the borrowed magic baffled him. Confronted by the phenomenon of gastrulation, or by the curious behavior of heart muscle, or by any of the current theories of immunity, he commonly took refuge, like his brother of the orthodox faculty, in a gulp of laboratory alcohol, or fled the premises altogether. Thus he was lost to osteopathic science, and the chiropractors took him in; nay, they welcomed him. He was their meat. Borrowing that primitive part of osteopathy which was comprehensible to the meanest understanding, they threw the rest overboard, at the same time denouncing it as a sorcery invented by the Medical Trust. Thus they gathered in the garage mechanics, ash-men and decayed welter-weights, and the land began to fill with their graduates. Now there is a chiropractor at every cross-roads, and in such sinks of imbecility as Los Angeles they are as thick as bootleggers.

I repeat that it eases and soothes me to see them so prosperous, for they counteract the evil work of the so-called science of public hygiene, which now seeks to make morons immortal. If a man, being ill of a pus appendix, resorts to a shaved and fumigated longshoreman to have it disposed of, and submits willingly to a treatment that involved balancing him on McBurney's spot and playing on his vertebræ as on a concertina, then I am willing, for one, to believe that he is badly wanted in Heaven. And if that same man, having achieved lawfully a lovely babe, hires a blacksmith to cure its diphtheria by pulling its neck, then I do not resist the divine will that there shall be one less radio fan in 1967. In such matters, I am convinced, the laws of nature are far better guides than the fiats and machinations of the medical busybodies who now try to run us. If the latter gentlemen had their way, death, save at the hands of hangmen, Prohibition agents and other such legalized assassins, would be abolished altogether, and so the present differential in favor of the enlightened would disappear. I can't convince myself that that would work any good to the world. On the contrary, it seems to me that the current coddling of the half-witted should be stopped before it goes too far—if, indeed, it has not gone too far already. To that end nothing operates more cheaply and effectively than the prosperity of quacks. Every time a bottle of cancer specific goes through the mails *Homo americanus* is improved to that extent. And every time a chiropractor spits on his hands and proceeds to treat a gastric ulcer by stretching the backbone the same high end is achieved.

But chiropractic, of course, is not perfect. It has superb potentialities, but only too often they are not converted into concrete cadavers. The hygienists rescue many of its foreordained customers, and, turning them over to agents of the Medical Trust, maintained at the public expense, get them cured. Moreover, chiropractic itself is not certainly fatal: even an Iowan with diabetes may survive its embraces. Yet worse, I have a suspicion that it sometimes actually cures. For all I know (or any orthodox pathologist seems to know) it *may* be true that certain malaises are caused by the pressure of vagrom vertebræ upon the spinal nerves. And it *may* be true that a hearty ex-boilermaker, by a vigorous yanking and kneading, may be able to relieve that pressure. What is needed is a scientific inquiry into the matter, under rigid test conditions, by a committee of men learned in the architecture and plumbing of the body, and of a high and incorruptible sagacity. Let a thousand patients be selected, let a gang of selected chiropractors examine their backbones and determine what is the matter with them, and then let these diagnoses be checked up by the exact methods of scientific medicine. Then let the same chiropractors essay to cure the patients whose maladies have been determined. My guess is that the chiropractors' errors in diagnosis will run to at least 95% and that their failures in treatment will push 99%. But I am willing to be convinced.

Where is such a committee to be found? I undertake to nominate it at ten minutes' notice. The land swarms with men competent in anatomy and pathology, and yet not engaged as doctors. There are hundreds of roomy and well-heated hospitals, with endless clinical material. I offer to supply the committee with cigars and music during the test. I offer, further, to supply both the committee and the chiropractors with sound pre-war wet goods. I offer, finally, to give a bawdy banquet to the whole Medical Trust at the conclusion of the proceedings.

2
Criminology

The more I read the hand-books of the new criminology, the more I am convinced that it stands on a level with dogmatic theology, chiropractic and the New Thought—in brief, that it is mainly buncombe. That it has materially civilized punishment I do not, of course, deny; what I question is its doctrine as to the primary causes of crime. The average man, as every one knows, puts those causes in the domain of free will. The criminal, in his view, is simply a scoundrel who has deliberately chosen to break the law and injure his fellow-men. *Ergo*, he deserves to be punished swiftly and mercilessly. The new criminologists, in swinging away from that naïve view, have obviously gone too far in the other direction. They find themselves, in the end, embracing a determinism that is as childlike as the free will of the man in the street. Crime, as they depict it, becomes a sort of disease, either inherited or acquired by contagion, and as devoid of moral content or significance as smallpox. The criminal is no longer a black-hearted villain, to be put down by force, but a poor brother who has succumbed to the laws of Mendel and the swinish stupidity of society. The aim of punishment is not to make him sweat, but to dissuade and rehabilitate him. In every pickpocket there is a potential Good Man. All this, gradually gaining credit, has greatly ameliorated punishments. They have not only lost their old barbaric quality; they have also diminished quantitatively. Men do not sit in prison as long as they used to; the parole boards turn them out almost as fast as the cops shove them in. The result is a public discontent that must be manifest. Whenever a criminal of any eminence comes to trial there are loud bellows against any show of mercy to him, and demands that he be punished to the limit. One never hears complaints any more that the courts are too savage; one hears only complaints that they are too soft and sentimental.

I am a congenital disbeliever in laws, and have only the most formal respect for the juridic process and its learned protagonists; nevertheless, it seems to me that there is a certain reasonableness in this unhappiness. For what it indicates, basically, is simply the inability of the average man to grasp the determinism of the new criminologists. He cannot imagine an apparently voluntary act that is determined, or even materially conditioned, from without. He can think of crime only in terms of free will, and so thinking of it, he believes that it ought to be punished in the ancient Christian manner, *i.e.*, according to the damage flowing out of it, and not according to the temptations behind it. Certainly this is not an illogical ground to take. In all the other relations of life the average man sees free will accepted as axiomatic: he could not imagine a world in which it was denied. His religion is based squarely upon it: he knows, by the oath of his pastor, that his free acts can lift him to Heaven or cast him down to Hell. He works as a matter of free will, and is punished inevitably if he lags. His marriage, as he sees it, was a free will compact, and though he has some secret doubt, perhaps, that its issue came that way, he nevertheless orders his relations with his children on the same basis, and assumes it in judging them. In other words, he lives in a world in which free will is apparently omnipotent, and in which it is presumed even when there is no direct evidence for it. All his daily concerns are free will concerns. Well, what the criminologists ask him to do is to separate one special concern from the rest, and hand it over to determinism. They damn legislators for passing harsh laws, and judges and jailers for executing them—free will. They denounce society for "coercing" morons into crime—free will again. And then they argue that the criminals are no more than helpless victims of circumstance, like motes dancing along a sunbeam—determinism in its purest and sweetest form.

No wonder the plain man baulks! Suppose an analogous suspension of the usual rules were attempted in some other field. Suppose it were argued seriously that free will had nothing to do with, say, the execution of contracts. Suppose an employer who failed to pay his workmen on Saturday were excused on the ground that he was the helpless victim of an evil heredity or of the stupidity of society, and thus not to be blamed for dissipating his money on Ford parts, women, foreign missions, or drink? Suppose the workman who had got out a mechanic's lien against him and sought to levy on his assets were denounced as a cruel and medieval fellow, and at odds with human progress? Certainly there would be a horrible hullabaloo, and equally certainly it would be justified. For whatever the theoretical arguments for determinism—and I am prepared to go even further in granting them than the criminologists go—, it must be plain that the everyday affairs of the world are ordered on an assumption of free will, and that it is impossible, practically speaking, to get rid of it. Society itself, indeed, is grounded upon that assumption. Imagining it as determined is possible only to professional philosophers, whose other imaginings are surely not such as to give any authority to this one. The plain man simply gives up the effort as hopeless—and perhaps as also a bit anarchistic and un-Christian. So he is sniffish when the new criminologists begin to prattle their facile determinism, and when he observes it getting credit from the regular agents of the law he lets a loud whoop of protest. I do not believe he is naturally cruel and vindictive; on the contrary, he is very apt to be maudlinly sentimental. But sentiment is one thing, and what seems to him to be a palpably false philosophy is quite another. He no more favors letting criminals go on the ground that they can't help themselves than he favors giving money to foreign missions, or the Red Cross, or the Y.M.C.A. on the ground that it is his inescapable duty. In all of these cases he is willing to be persuaded, but in none of them is he willing to be dragooned.

Thus I fear that the criminologists of the new school only pile up trouble for themselves, and indirectly for their pets, when they attempt to revise so radically the immemorial human view of crime. If they kept quiet in the department of responsibility, they would be heard with far more attention and respect in the department of punishment, where they really have something apposite and useful to say. Their influence here, in fact, is already immense, and it works much good. Our prisons are no longer quite as sordid and demoralizing as they used to be. They are still bad enough, in all conscience, but they are not as bad as they were. Here there is room for yet more improvement, and it cries aloud to be made. The men to work out its details are the criminologists. They have studied the effects of the prevailing punishments, and know where those punishments succeed or fail. They are happily devoid of that proud ignorance which is one of the boasts of the average judge, and they lack the unpleasant zeal of district attorneys, jail wardens and other such professional blood-letters. They need only offer the proofs that this or that punishment is ineffective to see it abandoned for something better, or, at all events, less obviously bad. But when they begin to talk of criminals in terms of pathology, even of social pathology, they speak a language that the plain man cannot understand and doesn't want to hear. He believes that crime, in the overwhelming majority of cases, is a voluntary matter, and that it ought to pay its own way and bury its own dead. He is not bothered about curing criminals, or otherwise redeeming them. He is intent only upon punishing them, and the more swiftly and certainly that business is achieved the better he is satisfied. Every time it is delayed by theorizing about the criminal's heredity and environment, and the duty that society owes to him, the plain man breaks into indignation. Only too often that indignation has been wrecked upon criminology and the criminologists. More American States, of late, have gone back to capital punishment than have abandoned it. What set the tide to running that way was surely not mere blood-lust. It was simply a natural reaction against the doctrine that murder is mainly an accidental and unfortunate matter, and devoid of moral content, like slipping on an icy sidewalk or becoming the father of twins.

3
Eugenics

This great moral cause, like that of the criminologists, is much corrupted by blather. In none of the books of its master minds is there a clear definition of the superiority they talk about so copiously. At one time they seem to identify it with high intelligence, at another time with character, *i.e.*, moral stability, and at yet another time with mere fame, *i.e.*, luck.

Was Napoleon I a superior man, as I am privately inclined to believe, along with many of the eugenists? Then so was Aaron Burr, if in less measure. Was Paul of Tarsus? Then so was Brigham Young. Were the Gracchi? Then so were Karl Marx and William Jennings Bryan.

This matter of superiority, indeed, presents cruel and ineradicable difficulties. If it is made to run with service to the human race, the eugenist is soon mired, for many men held to be highly useful are obviously second-rate, and leave third-rate progeny behind them, for example, General Grant. And if it is made to run with intellectual brilliance and originality the troubles that loom up are just as serious, for men of that rare quality are generally felt to be dangerous, and sometimes they undoubtedly are. The case of Friedrich Wilhelm Nietzsche is in point. I suppose that no rational person to-day, not even an uncured Liberty Loan orator or dollar-a-year man, would argue seriously that Nietzsche was inferior. On the contrary, his extraordinary gifts are now unanimously admitted, save perhaps by the rev. clergy. But what of his value to the human race? And what of his eugenic fitness? It is not easy to answer these questions. Nietzsche, in fact, preached a gospel that to most human beings remains unbearable, and it will probably continue unbearable for centuries to come. Its adoption by Dr. Coolidge, by and with the advice and consent of the Senate, would plunge this Republic into dreadful woe. And Nietzsche himself was a chronic invalid who died insane—the sort of wreck who, had he lived into our time, would have been a customer of chiropractors. Worse, he suffered from a malady of a scandalous nature, and of evil effects upon the sufferer's offspring. Was it good or bad luck for the worth, eugenically speaking, that he died a bachelor?

But their vagueness about the exact nature of superiority is not the only thing that corrupts the fine fury of the eugenists. Even more dismaying is their gratuitous assumption that all of the socially useful and laudable qualities (whatever they may be) are the exclusive possession of one class of men, and that the other classes lack them altogether. This is plainly not true. All that may be truthfully said of such qualities is that they appear rather more frequently in one class than in another. But they are rare in all classes, and the difference in the frequency of their occurrence between this class and that one is not very great, and of little genuine importance. If all the biologists in the United States were hanged to-morrow (as has been proposed by the pastors and newspaper editors of Mississippi) and their children with them, we'd probably still have a sufficiency of biologists in the next generation. There might not be as many as we have to-day, but there would be enough. They would come out of the families of bricklayers and politicians, bootleggers and bond salesmen. Some of them, indeed, might even come out of the families of Mississippi editors and ecclesiastics. For the supply of such men, like the supply of synthetic gin, always tends to run with the demand. Whenever it is short, the demand almost automatically augments it. Every one knows that this is true on the lower levels. Before baseball was invented there were no Ty Cobbs and Babe Ruths; now they appear in an apparently endless series. Before the Wright brothers made their first flight there were no men skilled at aviation; now there are multitudes of highly competent experts. The eugenists forget that the same thing happens also on the higher levels. Whenever the world has stood in absolute need of a genius he has appeared. And though it is true that he has usually come out of the better half of humanity, it is also true that he has sometimes come out of the worse half. Beethoven was the grandson of a cook and the son of a drunkard, and Lincoln's forebears never lifted themselves above the level of village *prominenti*.

The fact is that the difference between the better sort of human beings and the lesser sort, biologically speaking, is very slight. There may be, at the very top, a small class of persons whose blood is decidedly superior and distinguished, and there may be, at the bottom, another class whose blood is almost wholly debased, but both are very small. The folks between are all pretty much alike. The baron has a great deal of peasant blood in him, and the peasant has some blood that is blue. The natural sinfulness of man is enough to make sure of that. No man in this world can ever be quite sure that he is the actual great-great-grandson of the great-great-grandfather whose memory he venerates. Thus, when the relatively superior and distinguished class ceases to be fecund (a phenomenon now visible everywhere in the world), natural selection comes to the rescue by selecting out and promoting individuals from the classes below. These individuals, in the main, are just as sound in blood as any one in the class they enter. Their sound blood has been concealed, perhaps for generations, but it has been there all the time. If Abraham Lincoln's ancestry were known with any certainty, it would probably be found to run back to manifestly able men. There are many more such hidden family-trees in the folk: the eugenists simply overlook them. They are also singularly blind to many familiar biological phenomena—for example, the appearance of mutations or sports. It is not likely that a commonplace family will produce a genius, but nevertheless it is by no means impossible: the thing has probably happened more than once. They forget, too, the influence of environment in human society. Mere environment, to be sure, cannot produce genius, but it can certainly help him enormously after he is born. If a potential Wagner were born to a Greek bootblack in New York City to-morrow, the chances of his coming to fruition and fame would be at least even. But if he were born to an Arab in the Libyan desert or to a Fundamentalist in Rhea county, Tennessee, the chances are that he would be a total loss.

The eugenists constantly make the false assumption that a healthy degree of human progress demands a large and steady supply of absolutely first-rate men. Here they succumb to the modern craze for mass production. Because a hundred policemen, or garbage men, or bootleggers are manifestly better than one they conclude absurdly that a hundred Beethovens would be better than one. But this is not true. The actual value of a genius often lies in his very singularity. If there had been a hundred Beethovens, the music of all of them would probably be very little known to-day, and so its civilizing effect would be appreciably less than it is. The number of first-rate men necessary to make a high civilization is really very small. If the United States could produce one Shakespeare or Newton or Bach or Michelangelo or Vesalius a century it would be doing better than any nation has ever done in history. Such culture as we have is due to a group of men so small that all of them alive at one time could be hauled in a single Pullman train. Once I went through "Who's Who in America," hunting the really first-rate men among its 27,000 names—that is, for the men who had really done something unique and difficult, and of unquestionable value to the human race. I found 200. The rest of the 27,000 were simply respectable blanks. Many of them (though certainly not all) were creditable members of society, but only the 200 had ever done anything useful that had not been done before.

An over-production of geniuses, indeed, would be very dangerous, for though they make for progress they also tend to disturb the peace. Imagine a country housing 100 head of Aristotles! It would be as unhappy as a city housing 100 head of Jesse Jameses. Even quasi-geniuses are a great burden upon society. There are, in the United States to-day, 1500 professional philosophers—that is, men who make their livings at the trade. The country would be far better off if all save two or three of them were driving taxicabs or serving with the Rum Fleet.

XI.
Life Under Bureaucracy

As the bureaucracy under which we all sweat and suffer gradually swells and proliferates in the Republic, life will become intolerable to every man save the one who has what is called influence, *i.e.*, the one who has access to the very privilege which the Fathers of the Republic hoped to abolish. It is, in fact, almost so already. The obscure and friendless man can exist unmolested in the United States only by being so obscure and friendless that the bureaucracy is quite unaware of him. The moment he emerges from complete anonymity its agents have at him with all the complex and insane laws and regulations that now crowd the statute-books, and unless he can find some more powerful person to aid him, either for cash in hand or in return for his vote, he may as well surrender himself at once to ruin and infamy. For if the job-holders don't fetch him with one law they will fetch him with another. Their one permanent purpose in life is to fetch him—by the heels if possible, and if not by the heels then at least by the ears.

Suppose, for example, he is one of the millions of Americans of foreign birth, duly naturalized but still unaccepted socially as a full-fledged citizen. He saves his money, and decides after awhile to make a visit to his birthplace, to show off his American watch and contemplate the tombs of his anthropoid ancestors. He must have, obviously, a passport, first to get out of the United States and then to get back. Well, procuring this passport is now so onerous and complicated a matter that to such a man, with no friendly 100% American to help him, it has become practically impossible. It takes him weeks, and in the end the chances are at least 10 to 1 that he will fail. Where does the blame lie, upon the laws or upon the bureaucracy? It lies upon the bureaucracy. The laws simply say that no man who is not actually a citizen shall have the passport. But the bureaucracy goes much further: it assumes that no man at all is a citizen. The moment he is heard of he is put down as an impostor, and thereafter the burden of proving that he is not is upon him. As a practical matter, it is often impossible for him to furnish the proof. Long before the bureaucracy is satisfied, he is worn out and in despair. Unless he can find some person of influence to help him he may as well give up before he begins.

It is the invariable habit of bureaucracies, at all times and everywhere, to assume in this way that every citizen is a criminal. There one apparent purpose, pursued with a relentless and furious diligence, is to convert the assumption into a fact. They hunt endlessly for proofs, and, when proofs are lacking, for mere suspicions. The moment they become aware of a definite citizen, John Doe, seeking what is his right under the law, they begin searching feverishly for an excuse for withholding it from him. A successful bureaucrat is simply one who is skilled at such withholdings. A failure is one who gives Mr. Doe what he is entitled to, without resistance and at once.

I have spoken of the poor hyphenate, the special mark and victim of our American bureaucracy. But the 100% Nordic, in his different way, suffers almost as cruelly. Consider, for example, his typical adventures with the bureaucrats of the Income Tax Bureau. To begin with, they give him a blank to fill out that not one man in a hundred, assuming that he has not had long training as an accountant, can understand. Its very complexity is a triumph of bureaucracy. It is made unintelligible deliberately, and by bureaucrats of the highest professional genius, expressly hired for the business. No ordinary man, filling it out, can conceivably avoid errors. Well, the minute it is deposited in the bureaucratic machine the taxpayer is assumed officially to be a criminal. His slightest slip is proof that he has tried to swindle the government. And how do the bureaucrats deal with him? By framing a definite accusation against him, and giving him his day in court, as provided by Articles V and VI of the Bill of Rights? Not at all. That would not be bureaucratic. They proceed by levying an additional (and often grossly excessive) tax upon him, and demanding that he pay it forthwith. He is now wholly in their net. The charge against him is no longer that he has deliberately falsified his return, which would be difficult to prove, but simply that he has failed to pay a tax lawfully levied, which is easy to prove. So he pays, and thereafter, for five or six years, he struggles to get his money back.

Not infrequently, it must be said, the bureaucrats finally give it to him. But only after a desperate resistance, made brilliant by innumerable demands for affidavits and endless conferences and hearings. All this hocus-pocus is of the very essence of the bureaucratic art and mystery. The bureaucrat, whatever his imbecilities otherwise, at least grasps clearly the central fact about government: he knows that it is the eternal enemy of the citizen. In his own eye he is an attorney employed to represent it in combats with citizens, and as a conscientious man he naturally tries to do the best he can for his client—legally if possible, but if not, then in any way feasible. His professional standing runs with his success. If he permits too many citizens to prevail against him, and so recover and preserve their rights, he loses caste, just as a surgeon loses caste when too many patients die upon the table, and his career is imperilled. The ideal bureaucrat is the one who beats the citizen every time.

Obviously, the realization of this ideal would make life almost impossible. We move steadily toward it, but so far we have not actually reached it. Many citizens, getting into the clutches of the bureaucracy, manage to escape. They achieve the business, commonly, by mustering up what is called influence. That is, they either demonstrate to the bureaucrats that they are themselves of such power and importance that oppressing them unduly would be dangerous, or they get the help of some other person of that sort. The fact explains the continued prosperity of political machines, despite the long effort to put them down. They offer even the humblest citizen an avenue of escape from the bureaucracy. In return for his vote they protect him. When the bureaucrats discover him and proceed to practice their art upon him, the machine brings pressure to bear upon their political superiors, and so hauls them off. This hauling off, as every one knows, is now the principal occupation of the inferior order of political hacks called Congressmen, and is fast becoming a crushing burden to them. In the early days of the Republic they spent their time at Washington (when not engaged in the bar-rooms and stews) debating the great problems of statecraft, often eloquently, and sometimes with what, on such modest levels of the human mind, passed for sense. But to-day, with the Federal laws enormously multiplied and the Federal bureaucracy glowing with professional skill and enterprise, they are forced to devote practically all of their energies to protecting their constituents. If a Congressman failed in that duty he would return home to find half of his constituents in jail and the rest fugitives from justice. So he has had to resign statecraft to a few leaders, mainly from remote and sparsely settled States. While they carry on the business of Congress he busies himself in the departments and bureaux, rescuing his customers from the clutches of the bureaucracy.

In this benign enterprise, alas, he fails far oftener than he succeeds. Only too often, indeed, his heart is not really in it, for as a professional feeder at the public crib he is something of a bureaucrat himself, and so his sympathies naturally run with the bureaucracy rather than with its victims. Here we come upon *esprit de corps*: there is a lot of it among the scoundrels who constitute the government of the United States: whatever their stupidities otherwise, they are at least bright enough to recognize the plain fact that they form a class separate from the general run of men, with interests opposed to those of the latter, and so they stand together resolutely whenever their common advantages are menaced. In a clash, before Congress, between the aspirations of the job-holders and the common weal, the aspirations of the job-holders nearly always prevail. And in a combat before the courts between a public official and a private citizen, the advantages of the public official are numerous and obvious. These advantages, rising beyond those lying naturally in friendly feeling and fellow interest, often show themselves, of late, in positive law. It was not by chance that Congress passed a statute providing that, when a Prohibition agent or other such chartered assassin is accused of murdering a citizen, the Federal district attorney of the district shall not prosecute him, but defend him. Here the job-holders of the legislative arm deliberately violated the ancient principle of equality before the law in order to give job-holders of the executive arm the full benefit of the natural prejudice in their favor among the district attorneys and judges of the judicial arm—appointees, as likely as not, of the same Anti-Saloon League which put them in their own jobs. In countless other ways the members of the prehensile oligarchy help one another to violate the common rights of the plain citizen. At every session of Congress there is a legislative assault upon the Bill of Rights for the benefit of some group or other of administrative bureaucrats, and save on very rare occasions the Federal courts always conjure up some sophistry to justify it. It causes considerable surprise, indeed, when they fail to do so. For whatever the adumbrations of theorists, the plain man is well aware that the interests of the shifting but compact group of self-seeking men constituting the so-called government of the nation are opposed, in the main, to his own interests—in brief, that the government, in its essence, is no more and no less than a gigantic conspiracy against his well-being.

Thus democracy turns upon and devours itself. Launched upon the world as a scheme for putting down privilege, it ends by making privilege absolutely essential to a safe and peaceful existence. The citizen who is too obscure to make a Congressman or some other such professional dealer in privilege want to help him, and too weak to help himself—this citizen, under our bureaucratic jurisprudence, now has no rights at all. He is, indeed, no longer a citizen; he is a subject, and his lord is the bureaucrat. He must do whatever he is ordered to do, or face dire and devastating penalties. All of his natural daily acts become converted into crimes. It is even a crime to-day, in certain situations, for him to criticize his oppressors. If, writhing under their oppressions, he appeals to their official superiors, he usually only makes his case worse, for one bureaucrat always supports all other bureaucrats. The only man who escapes is the man with a pull. The aim of every enlightened American is to get that pull.

XII.

In the Rolling Mills

ALMOST the only thing I believe in with a childlike and unquestioning faith, in this world of doubts and delusions, is free speech; nevertheless, I find it increasingly difficult to sympathize with the pedagogues who, ever and anon, are heaved out of some fresh-water college for trying to exercise it. Why? Mainly, perhaps, because I can't get rid of the suspicion that nothing a pedagogue ever says, as pedagogue, is worth hearing—that his avocation is as fatal to sense as that of an archbishop, a Federal judge, or one of the automata in Mr. Ford's great squirrel-cage at Detroit. But also, no doubt, because I am obsessed by the superstition that, assuming him miraculously to have sense, he is as much out of place in any ordinary American college as an archbishop would be in a bordello.

What ails all these bogus martyrs is a false theory of education. They seem to believe that its aim is to fill the pupil's head with a mass of provocative and conflicting ideas, to arouse his curiosity to incandescence and inspire him to inquiry and speculation—in the common phrase, to teach him how to think. But this is surely nonsense. If education really had any such aim its inevitable effect would be to reduce nine-tenths of its victims to insanity, and to convert most of the rest into anarchists. What it seeks to do is something quite different—something, in fact, almost the opposite. It is financed by the state and by private philanthropists, not to make lunatics and anarchists, but to make good citizens—in other words, to make citizens who are as nearly like all other citizens as possible. Its ideal product is not a boy or a girl full of novel ideas but one full of lawful and correct ideas—not one who thinks, but one who believes. If it actually graduated hordes of Platos and Nietzsches it would be closed by the Department of Justice, and quite properly.

One of the most amusing things in life to a bachelor is the horror that overcomes his married friends whenever one of their children turns out to be intelligent. They feel instinctively that the phenomenon offers a challenge to their parental dignity and authority, and when the child they suspect actually *is* intelligent it certainly does. For the first thing the youngster who has succumbed to the un-Christian vice of thinking attempts is a critical examination of its surroundings, and directly in the forefront of those surroundings stand the unfortunate composers of its being. The result, only too frequently, is turmoil and disaster at the domestic hearth. Children, as every one knows, are "ungrateful." So, argue judges and hangmen, are messieurs the condemned. Even the most intelligent agents and instruments of the Life Force are thus full of alarms when their progeny respond to Mendel's law: the very vigor and independence of judgment which they regard as their own most precious possession affrights them when it appears in their issue. I could tell some curious tales in point, but had better refrain. Suffice it to mention an old friend, extremely shrewd and realistic in all of his thinking, who was happily proud of his very intelligent daughter until, at the age of sixteen, she threatened to get a job in a shop if he sent her, as he proposed, to a finishing-school. Then he collapsed in horror, despite the plain fact that her ultimatum was an excellent proof of the intelligence that he was proud of. As man, he admired her differentiation from the mass. But as father he was made uneasy by her sharp departure from normalcy.

The great majority of American fathers, of course, have a great deal less fundamental sense than this one, who quickly recovered from his instinctive reaction, and ended, indeed, by boasting that his daughter had spurned the finishing-school at his advice. To this majority education can only mean the inculcation, by intensive torture, of all the superstitions and prejudices that they cherish themselves. When little Felix comes home to his patriotic and Christian home with the news that the Fathers of 1776 were a gang of smugglers and profiteers, and when his sister Flora follows with the news that Moses did not write his own obituary and that the baby, Gustave, was but recently indistinguishable from a tadpole, and later on from a nascent gorilla—when such subversive and astounding doctrines are brought home from the groves of learning there ensues inevitably a ringing of fire-bells, with a posse on the march against some poor pedagogue.

What I maintain is simply that the vigilantes are right and the pedagogue wrong. His error lies in assuming that taxpayers lay out their hard-earned money for the breeding of traitors and atheists; taxpayers actually lay out their money for the breeding of more taxpayers like themselves. And their natural desire that this program be followed strictly is supported by the overwhelming force of the state, which loses strength and authority in direct ratio as its citizens become heretics. What holds it up is not primarily brute force, as so many theorists argue; what holds it up is the fact that, on all really essential questions, the vast majority of its citizens think exactly alike—that there is never any general doubt of the fundamental communal superstitions. Once those superstitions are seriously challenged, the whole fabric of the state begins to crumble. The true function of the pedagogue is not to attack them, but to propagate them. His is a sort of priestly office. He is not paid to marshal doubts and weigh probabilities; he is paid to expound revelation. If he finds himself temperamentally unable to discharge that solemn and awful duty, then he should quit pedagogy and go into bootlegging or some other free craft. So long as he is publicly consecrated to the birch, he can no more depart from his text-book with seemliness than a Christian clergyman could depart from his sworn belief in witches.

Most of the current uproar in the colleges of the nation, I suspect, is due to a curse that I have often denounced in the past: the pestilential multiplication of Ph.D.'s. There was a time, before all the American universities began vomiting them forth by the thousand, when the whole annual produce of Ph.D.'s could be absorbed by the graduate-schools. In these graduate-schools, with all of the pupils of mature years and most of them already resolved to devote their lives to non-utilitarian and hence, by the national *mores*, subversive enterprises, it was safe enough to abandon the normal teaching process for a more or less free exchange of ideas. The teacher in such a school, having no authority to rattan his students, naturally had to submit to their cross-questioning criticism—sometimes, when they were intelligent, an embarrassing thing. In this atmosphere the Ph.D. could function unrestrained. Being compelled to suffer the doubts and even the derision of his students, he was free on his side to bombard them with all his vagaries, however unearthly and offensive. The result was not teaching, in any true sense, but a sort of learning in common. But when true yearly production of Ph.D.'s grew so large that the graduate-schools became glutted with them, and the profiteers who support all the higher institutions of learning began to yell "Enough!", many of them had to seek other situations. Some, as every one knows, took to the chautauquas. Others sat on public commissions, and drew up reports, or set up as executive secretaries or wowsers. Yet others began practice as experts in law-suits, *i.e.*, as professional perjurers. But great hordes remained, and these presently began to filter into the undergraduate-schools. In the old days the highest academic rank that a teacher in an undergraduate-school ever aspired to was that of M.A., but to-day most of them are Ph.D.'s, and an excess of Ph.D.'s, naturally of inferior quality, has emptied into the high-schools business colleges, correspondence schools and even grammar-schools.

It is these sick and wounded of the army of learning, I suspect, who are responsible for most of the academic Bolshevism that now fills the newspapers. Having been purged, by their superior education, of the fundamental communal superstitions —or, at all events, of a few of them—they get revenge upon the society that ill-uses them by inoculating the children of honest Rotarians with their own odd and often nonsensical heresies. These are the fellows who, at frequent intervals, commit *scandalum magnatum* by teaching that the American patriot infantry, at Bunker Hill, ran all the way down the hill, or that General Grant was a heavy lusher, or that the Bolsheviki have not really nationalized women, or that the world is older than the Bible says, or that the Nordic Blond, biologically, is no more than a bald chimpanzee. And these are the fellows who yell that they are undone when indignant trustees give them the gate.

It seems to me that those who protest against their thus getting the gate fall into the elemental error of assuming, only too often, that an American college is the exact equivalent of a European university. It is called a university, and so they accept it as one in fact. But it is really nothing of the kind. There has been but one genuine university in the United States in our time—the Johns Hopkins under Gilman—and it turned itself into a college with frantic haste the moment he died. The college student differs from a university student in a most important way: his formal education, when he matriculates, is not completed, but simply entering upon its last stage. That is to say, he has not yet taken in the whole of that body of correct and respectable ideas which all of us must somehow absorb before we are competent to think for ourselves—at all events, to any rational purpose and effect.

Only too often the fact is overlooked that even the most bold and talented of philosophers must suffer that stuffing before he is ready to go it alone. Aristotle, you may be sure, had the Greek alphabet rammed into him like any other Greek of his time, and studied the multiplication table, and learned the elements of Greek civics, and all that was then accepted about the nature of the Persians, the functions of the liver, and the aorist. Kant was grounded in Prussian history, the humoral pathology, and the Leibnitzian law of preëstablished harmony. Even Nietzsche had to master the grammar-book, the catechism and the Lutheran psalm-book, that he might be a good German and keep out of jail. Such training takes time, for children naturally resist it; it takes more time in America than elsewhere because our elementary-schools, in late years, devote themselves mainly to fol-de-rols borrowed from the Boy Scouts, Greenwich Village and Bernarr Macfadden. Thus the young American, when he enters college, is still only half-educated in the conventional sense. At least three of his four years are consumed in completing the lowly business of making him fit to vote, keep a check-book accurately, and understand what is in his newspaper. Every now and then some humorist subjects a class of freshmen to what is called a general information test. Four-fifths of them invariably turn out to be as ignorant as so many European schoolboys of ten or eleven.

Obviously, it is as imprudent to parade political heresies before such infants as it would be to lecture on obstetrics before girls of thirteen. When they are graduated at last, they are perhaps ripe for it, but when they are graduated they commonly depart the halls of learning for the bond business. The relatively few who remain seem to suffer no damage from such ideas as they encounter in the graduate-schools. At all events, there is never any complaint that they are being ruined, nor do they themselves complain that the notions of the salient anarchists are being withheld from them. Most of them, having no desire save to get their Ph.D.'s and settle down as pedagogues, are probably anæsthetic to whatever play of ideas goes on about them. A few, taking fire, afterward lecture scandalously in the prairie "universities" to which they are doomed, stir up the students to revolt against their colleagues, and so get themselves cashiered. But not many. Nor is the practical damage serious. There is always room enough for the minority of genuinely intelligent fellows in the graduate-schools whence they came. The spotlights of Babbitt do not bathe these schools, for his sons are not in them; thus they are quite free to monkey with ideas all they please, even with red-hot ones. What I have heard in my time from eminent ornaments of this higher faculty would make interesting news for both the Comstock Society and the Department of Justice. Antinomianism is rife among them, and seems to go unchallenged. So hands remain to carry on the torch.

I don't think the boy of lively mind is hurt much by going to college. If he encounters mainly jackasses, then he learns the useful lesson that this is a jackass world. The complaints come from fellows of small humor, which is to say, from fellows whose intelligence is like a glass of beer without foam. Nor, as I have hinted, am I greatly affected—certainly not to tears—by the grievance of the young professors. Do they complain bitterly that their superiors hobble the free play of their minds, and force them to teach doctrines that they don't believe in? Then examine, some day, the doctrines that they *do* believe in. You will find chiefly bilge—Liberalism and dish-water, the puerile heresies of the farm *bloc*, all the fly-blown fallacies of yesteryear. It is the dream of every such rambunctious Dr. Birch to crash the high gates of the *Atlantic Monthly* with a devilish essay entitled "A Plea for Necking." His goatishness passes with his youth. At forty he is lecturing docilely on the Lake School.

I am unable to discern any actual passion for the truth in such victims of the educational industrial system. What moves them more often, I suspect, is simply a desire to make a scandal and annoy their elders. The same martyr who argues that forbidding him to eulogize Lenin in class is an assault upon his sacred integrity—this same martyr is usually willing enough to teach that the late war was fought to save democracy, and that the United States played a chivalrous and honorable rôle in it. Is he heard against Fundamentalism to-day? Then why wasn't he heard against Prohibition eight or ten years ago—he or his predecessor? I don't cry him down; in his revolt, as in all revolts, there is something stimulating; he is at least not quite a clod. But his error, like that of his students, lies in mistaking the nature of the business he is engaged upon. It is a business that has very little, if anything, to do with the free play of ideas in this world. That goes on otherwise, and on a different level. His business is to polish the rough casts turned out by an inept and humorous God, that they may be as smooth and uniform as possible, and rub one another as little as possible.

XIII.
Ambrose Bierce

THE reputation of Ambrose Bierce, like that of Edgar Saltus, has always had an occult, artificial drug-store flavor. He has been hymned in a passionate, voluptuous, inordinate way by a small band of disciples, and he has been passed over altogether by the great majority of American critics, and no less by the great majority of American readers. Certainly it would be absurd to say that he is generally read, even by the *intelligentsia.* Most of his books, in fact, are out of print and almost unobtainable, and there is little evidence that his massive Collected Works, printed in twelve volumes between 1909 and 1912, have gone into anything even remotely approaching a wide circulation. I have a suspicion, indeed, that Bierce did a serious disservice to himself when he put those twelve volumes together. Already an old man at the time, he permitted his nostalgia for his lost youth to get the better of his critical faculty, never very powerful at best, and the result was a depressing assemblage of worn-out and fly-blown stuff, much of it quite unreadable. If he had boiled the collection down to four volumes, or even to six, it might have got him somewhere, but as it is, his good work is lost in a morass of bad and indifferent work. I doubt that any one save the Bierce fanatics aforesaid has ever plowed through the whole twelve volumes. They are filled with epigrams against frauds long dead and forgotten, and echoes of old and puerile newspaper controversies, and experiments in fiction that belong to a dark and expired age. But in the midst of all this blather there are some pearls—more accurately, there are two of them. One consists of the series of epigrams called "The Devil's Dictionary"; the other consists of the war stories, commonly called "Tales of Soldiers and Civilians." Among the latter are some of the best war stories ever written—things fully worthy to be ranged beside Zola's "L'Attaque du Moulin," Kipling's "The Taking of Lungtungpen," or Ludwig Thoma's "Ein Bayrischer Soldat." And among the former are some of the most gorgeous witticisms in the English language.

Bierce, I believe, was the first writer of fiction ever to treat war realistically. He antedated even Zola. It is common to say that he came out of the Civil War with a deep and abiding loathing of slaughter—that he wrote his war stories in disillusion, and as a sort of pacifist. But this is certainly not believed by any one who knew him, as I did in his last years. What he got out of his services in the field was not a sentimental horror of it, but a cynical delight in it. It appeared to him as a sort of magnificent *reductio ad absurdum* of all romance. The world viewed war as something heroic, glorious, idealistic. Very well, he would show how sordid and filthy it was—how stupid, savage and degrading. But to say this is not to say that he disapproved it. On the contrary, he vastly enjoyed the chance its discussion gave him to set forth dramatically what he was always talking about and gloating over: the infinite imbecility of man. There was nothing of the milk of human kindness in old Ambrose; he did not get the nickname of Bitter Bierce for nothing. What delighted him most in this life was the spectacle of human cowardice and folly. He put man, intellectually, somewhere between the sheep and the horned cattle, and as a hero somewhere below the rats. His war stories, even when they deal with the heroic, do not depict soldiers as heroes; they depict them as bewildered fools, doing things without sense, submitting to torture and outrage without resistance, dying at last like hogs in Chicago, the former literary capital of the United States. So far in this life, indeed, I have encountered no more thorough-going cynic than Bierce was. His disbelief in man went even further than Mark Twain's; he was quite unable to imagine the heroic, in any ordinary sense. Nor, for that matter, the wise. Man to him, was the most stupid and ignoble of animals. But at the same time the most amusing. Out of the spectacle of life about him he got an unflagging and Gargantuan joy. The obscene farce of politics delighted him. He was an almost amorous connoisseur of theology and theologians. He howled with mirth whenever he thought of a professor, a doctor or a husband. His favorites among his contemporaries were such zanies as Bryan, Roosevelt and Hearst.

Another character that marked him, perhaps flowing out of this same cynicism, was his curious taste for the macabre. All of his stories show it. He delighted in hangings, autopsies, dissecting-rooms. Death to him was not something repulsive, but a sort of low comedy—the last act of a squalid and rib-rocking buffoonery. When, grown old and weary, he departed for Mexico, and there—if legend is to be believed—marched into the revolution then going on, and had himself shot, there was certainly nothing in the transaction to surprise his acquaintances. The whole thing was typically Biercian. He died happy, one may be sure, if his executioners made a botch of dispatching him—if there was a flash of the grotesque at the end. Once I enjoyed the curious experience of going to a funeral with him. His conversation to and from the crematory was superb—a long series of gruesome but highly amusing witticisms. He had tales to tell of crematories that had caught fire and singed the mourners, of dead bibuli whose mortal remains had exploded, of widows guarding the fires all night to make sure that their dead husbands did not escape. The gentleman whose carcass we were burning had been a literary critic. Bierce suggested that his ashes be molded into bullets and shot at publishers, that they be presented to the library of the New York Lodge of Elks, that they be mailed anonymously to Ella Wheeler Wilcox. Later on, when he heard that they had been buried in Iowa, he exploded in colossal mirth. The last time I saw him he predicted that the Christians out there would dig them up and throw them over the State line. On his own writing desk, he once told me, he kept the ashes of his son. I suggested idly that the ceremental urn must be a formidable ornament. "Urn hell!" he answered. "I keep them in a cigar-box!"

There is no adequate life of Bierce, and I doubt if any will ever be written. His daughter, with some asperity, has forbidden the publication of his letters, and shows little hospitality to volunteer biographers. One of his disciples, the late George Sterling, wrote about him with great insight and affection, and another, Herman George Scheffauer, has greatly extended his fame abroad, especially in Germany. But Sterling is dead and Scheffauer seems indisposed to do him in grand manner, and I know of no one else competent to do so. He liked mystification, and there are whole stretches of his long life that are unaccounted for. His end had mystery in it too. It is assumed that he was killed in Mexico, but no eyewitness has ever come forward, and so the fact, if it is a fact, remains hanging in the air.

Bierce followed Poe in most of his short stories, but it is only a platitude to say that he wrote much better than Poe. His English was less tight and artificial; he had a far firmer grasp upon character; he was less literary and more observant. Unluckily, his stories seem destined to go the way of Poe's. Their influence upon the modern American short story, at least upon its higher levels, is almost nil. When they are imitated at all, it is by the lowly hacks who manufacture thrillers for the cheap magazines. Even his chief disciples, Sterling and Scheffauer, did not follow him. Sterling became a poet whose glowing romanticism was at the opposite pole to Bierce's cold realism, and Scheffauer, interested passionately in experiment, and strongly influenced by German example, has departed completely from the classicism of the master. Meanwhile, it remains astonishing that his wit is so little remembered. In "The Devil's Dictionary" are some of the most devastating epigrams ever written. "Ah, that we could fall into women's arms without falling into their hands": it is hard to find a match for that in Oscar himself. I recall another: "Opportunity: a favorable occasion for grasping a disappointment." Another: "Once: enough." A third: "Husband: one who, having dined, is charged with the care of the plate." A fourth: "Our vocabulary is defective: we give the same name to woman's lack of temptation and man's lack of opportunity." A fifth: "Slang is the speech of him who robs the literary garbage cans on their way to the dump."

But I leave the rest to your own exploration—if you can find a copy of "The Devil's Dictionary." It was never printed in full, save in the ghastly Collected Works that I have mentioned. A part of it, under the title of "The Cynic's Word-Book," was first published as a separate volume, but it is long out of print. The other first editions of Bierce are scarce, and begin to command high premiums. Three-fourths of his books were published by obscure publishers, some of them not too reputable. He spent his last quarter of a century in voluntary immolation on a sort of burning ghat, worshiped by his small band of zealots, but almost unnoticed by the rest of the human race. His life was a long sequence of bitter ironies. I believe that he enjoyed it.

XIV.

The Executive Secretary

SOME time ago, encountering an eminent bishop of my acquaintance, I found him suffering from a bad cold and what used to be called a fit of the vapors. The cause of his dual disorder soon became manifest. He was smarting under the slings and arrows of executive secretaries. By virtue of his lofty and transcendental office, he was naturally a man of wide influence in the land, and so they tried to enlist his interest in their multitudinous and often nefarious schemes. Every morning at 8 o'clock, just as he was rolling over for a last brief dream of Heaven, he was dragged to the telephone to hear their eloquent and lascivious night-letters, and there, on unlucky days, he stood for as much as half an hour, with his episcopal feet bare, and rage gradually mounting in his episcopal heart. Thus, on a cold morning, he had caught his cold, and thus he had acquired his bad humor.

This holy man, normally a most amiable fellow, told me that he believed the number of executive secretaries in the United States was increasing a the rate of at least a thousand a week. He said that he knew of 30,000 in the field of Christian and moral endeavor alone. There were, he told me, 8000 more engaged in running various pacifist societies, and more than 10,000 operating organizations for the detection and scotching of Bolsheviki. He estimated that the average number of dues-paying members behind each one did not run beyond half a dozen. Nine-tenths of them, he said, were supported by two or three well-heeled fanatics. These fanatics, mainly retired Babbitts and their wives, longed to make a noise in the world, and so escape oblivion. It was the essence of the executive secretary's art and mystery to show them how to do it. Chiefly it was done by discovering bugaboos and giving chase to them. But secondarily it was done by hauling poor ecclesiastics out of bed on frosty mornings, and making them listen to endless night-letters about the woes of the Armenians, the need of intensive missionary effort in Siam, the plot of

Moscow to set up soviets in Lowell, Mass., the high ideals of the Woodrow Wilson Foundation, and the absolute necessity of deeper waterways from the Lakes to the Atlantic.

The executive secretary is relatively new in the world. Like his colleague in well-paid good works, the Y.M.C.A. secretary, he has come into being since the Civil War. Compared to him, his predecessor of ante-bellum days was an amateur and an idiot. That predecessor had no comfortable office in a gaudy skyscraper, he got no lavish salary, and he had no juicy expense-account. On the contrary, he paid his own way, and, especially when he worked for Abolition, which was usually, he sometimes had to take a beating into the bargain. The executive secretary of to-day, as Perlmutter would say, is something else again. He belongs to the order of live wires. He speaks the language of up-and-coming men, and is not sparing with it at the sessions of Rotary and Kiwanis. In origin, not uncommonly, a shady and unsuccessful newspaper reporter or a press-agent out of a job, he quickly becomes, by virtue of his craft, a Man of Vision. The cause that he represents for cash in hand is not merely virtuous; it is, nine times out of ten, divinely inspired. If it fails, then civilization will also fail, and the heroic doings at Chateau Thierry and Hog Island will have been in vain.

It is a good job that he has—far better than legging it on the street for some gorilla of a city editor—far, far better than traversing the sticks ahead of a No. 4 company. There is no need to get up at 7 A.M. and there is no need to fume and strain after getting up. Once three or four—or maybe even only one or two—easy marks with sound bank accounts have been snared, the new "national"—or perhaps it is "international"—association is on its legs, and all that remains is to have brilliant stationary printed, put in an amiable and sightly stenographer, and begin deluging bishops, editors and the gullible generally with literature. The executive secretary, if he has any literary passion in him, may prepare this literature himself, but more often he employs experts to do it. Once a year he launches a drive. But it is only for publicity. The original suckers pay the freight. When they wear out the executive secretary starts a new "international" association.

Such sharks now swarm in every American city. The office-buildings are full of them. Their prosperity depends very largely upon the singular complaisance of the newspapers. The average American managing editor went through so dreadful a bath of propaganda during the late war, and was so thoroughly convinced that resisting it was a form of treason, that he is now almost unable to detect it from genuine news. Some time ago Mr. Stanley Walker, a New York journalist of sense and experience, examined a typical copy of one of the great New York dailies. He found that there were sixty-four items of local news in it—and that forty-two of them could be plainly traced to executive secretaries, and other such space-grabbers. The executive secretary, of course, does not have at his editors crudely. He seldom accompanies his item of "news" with any intimation that he is paid a good salary for planting it, and he discourages all inquires into the actual size, aims and personnel of his organization. Instead he commonly postures as the mere agent of men and women known to be earnest and altruistic philanthropists. These philanthropists are the suckers upon whom he feeds. They pay his salary, maintain his office, and keep up his respectability in newspaper offices. What do they get out of it themselves? In part, no doubt, an honest feeling that they are doing good: the executive secretary, in fact, has to convince them of it before he is in a position to tackle the newspapers at all. But in part, also, they enjoy the publicity—and maybe other usufructs too. In the United States, indeed, doing good has come to be, like patriotism, a favorite device of persons with something to sell. More than one great national organization for lifting up the fallen, especially in foreign lands, might be investigated to advantage. In such cases charity not infrequently gets its reward in the form of concessions.

Some time ago, sweating under this assault of executive secretaries, the editors of a great American newspaper hit upon a scheme of relief. It took the form of a questionnaire—something not seldom used, and to vast effect, by executive secretaries themselves. This questionnaire had a blank in which the executive secretary was asked to write his full name and address, and the amount of his annual salary. In other blanks there was room for putting down the total income and outgo of his association, with details of every item amounting to more than one per cent. of the whole, and for a full list of its contributors and employees, with the amount given by every one of the former contributing more than one per cent. and the salary received by every one of the latter getting more than one per cent. This simple questionnaire cut down the mail received from executive secretaries by at least one half. Many of them did not answer at all. Many others, answering, revealed the not surprising fact that their high-sounding national and international organizations were actually small clubs of a few men and women, and that they themselves consumed most of the revenues. It is a device that might be employed effectively by other American newspapers. When the executive secretaries return their answers by mail, which is usually the case, they are under pressure to answer truthfully, for answering otherwise is using the mails to obtain money by fraud, and many worthy men are jugged at Atlanta and Leavenworth for that offense.

I suggest this plan as a means of cutting down the present baleful activity of executive secretaries, but I am not so optimistic as to believe that it could conceivably dispose of them altogether. In the higher ranks of the profession are gentlemen so skillful that they no longer send out press-matter: they make actual news. To that aristocracy belong the adept executive secretaries who run such organizations as the Anti-Saloon League. These masters of the art do not beg for good-will in newspaper offices: they thrive upon ill-will quite as well as upon good-will. How are they to be got rid of? I am sure I don't know. In all probability the American people are doomed to suffer them forever, as they seem to be doomed to suffer Prohibition agents, revivalists, the radio and Congress.

XV.

Invitation to the Dance

WHAT this grand, gaudy, unapproachable country needs and lacks is an Ingersoll. It is, indeed, a wonder that the chautauquas do not spew one forth. Certainly there must be many a jitney Demosthenes on these lonely, dyspeptic circuits who tires mightily of the standard balderdash of his trade, and longs with a great longing to throw off the white chemise of Service and give the rustics a genuinely hot show. The old tricks begin to tire the steady customers, even in the heart of the Bible Belt. What made the rural Methodists of Iowa and South Carolina breathe hard and fast at the dawn of the century now only makes them shuffle their feet and yawn behind their hands. I have spies in all such horrible regions, and their reports all agree. The yokels no longer turn out to the last paralytic to gape at stereopticon pictures of the Holy Sepulchre and the Mount of Olives, or to see a genuine Hindu from Benares in his obscene native costume, or to listen to a sweating rhetorician flog "The Future of America." They sicken of the old stuff; more, they sicken of Service, Idealism, Vision. What ails them is that the village movie-parlor, the radio, the Ford sedan and the Ku Klux Klan have spoiled their primeval taste for simple, wholesome fare. They must have it hot now, or they don't want it at all. The master-minds of chautauqua try to meet the new demand, but cannot go all the way. They experiment gingerly with lectures on eugenics, the divorce evil, women in politics, and other such pornographic subjects, but that is not enough. They put on plays "direct from Broadway" —but have to omit the really tart ones. The horticulturists and their wives and issue pant for something more dreadful and shocking—something comparable, on the plane of ideas, to the tarring and feathering of the village fancy woman on the plane of manly sports. Their ears lie back and they hearken expectantly, and even somewhat impatiently. What they long for is a bomb.

My guess is that the one that would blow them highest, and

shake the most money out of them going up and coming down, is the big black bomb of Atheism. It has not been set off in the Federal Union, formally and with dramatic effect, since July 21, 1899, when Bob Ingersoll descended into Hell. Now it is loaded again, and ready to be fired, and the chautauquan who discovers it and fires it will be the luckiest mountebank heard of in these latitudes since Col. George B. M. Harvey thrust the halo on Woodrow's brow. For this favorite of fortune, unlike his fellows of the rustic big tops, will not have to drudge out all his days on the lonesome steppes, wrecking his stomach with fried beefsteak and saleratus biscuit and his limbs with travel on slow and bumpy trains. He will be able almost at once, like Ingersoll before him and the Rev. Billy Sunday in the last Golden Age, to horn into the big towns, or, at all events, into the towns, and there he will snore at ease of nights upon clean sheets, with his roll in his pantaloons pocket and a *Schluck* of genuine Scotch under his belt. The yokels, if they want to hear him, will have to come to Babylon in their Fords; he will be too busy and too prosperous to waste himself upon the cow-stable miasmas of the open spaces. Ingersoll, in one month, sometimes took in $50,000. It can be done again; it can be bettered. I believe that Dr. Jennings Bryan, if he had sold out God and gone over to Darwin and *Pongo pygmæus*, could have filled the largest hall in Nashville or Little Rock a month on end: he would have made the most profound sensation the country has known since the Breckenridge-Pollard case, nay, since Hannah and her amazing glands. And what Bryan could have done, any other chautauquan may now do, if not exactly in the same grand manner, then at least in a grand manner.

But this in a Christian country! *Soit!* But it was doubly a Christian country in the days of Bob the Hell-Cat. Bob faced a Babbittry that still went to church on Sunday as automatically as a Prohibition enforcement agent holds out his hand. No machinery for distracting it from that ancient practice had yet been invented. There was no baseball. There were no automobiles to take the whole family to green fields and wet roadhouses: the roads were too bad even for buggy-riding. There was no radio. There were no movies. There was no jazz. There were no Sunday comic supplements. There was no home-brewing. Moreover, a high tide of evangelistic passion was running: it was the day of Dwight L. Moody, of the Salvation Army, of prayer-meetings in the White House, of eager chapel-building on every suburban dump. Nevertheless, Bob hurled his challenge at the whole hierarchy of heaven, and within a few short years he had the Babbitts all agog, and after them the city proletariat, and then finally the yokels on the farms. He drew immense crowds; he became eminent; he planted seeds of infidelity that still sprout in Harvard and Yale. Thousands abandoned their accustomed places of worship to listen to his appalling heresies, and great numbers of them never went back. The evangelical churches, fifty years ago, were all prosperous and full of pious enterprise; the soul-snatching business was booming. Since then, despite the uproars that come from the Bible Belt, it has been declining steadily, in prosperity and in repute. The typical American ecclesiastic of 1880 was Henry Ward Beecher, a pet of Presidents and merchant princes. The typical American ecclesiastic of 1927 is the Rev. Dr. John Roach Straton, an inmate of the stable of Hearst.

In brief, the United States, despite its gallant resistance, has been swept along, to some extent at least, in the general current of human progress and increasing enlightenment. The proofs that it resists are only too often mistaken for proofs that it hasn't moved at all. For example, there is the matter of the Klan. Superficially, its appearance appears to indicate that whole areas of the Republic have gone over to Methodist voodooism with a bang, and that civilization has been barred out of them as effectively as the Bill of Rights is barred out of a Federal court. But actually all it indicates is that the remoter and more forlorn yokels have risen against their betters—and that their uprising is as hopeless as it is idiotic. Whenever the Klan wins, the fact is smeared all over the front pages of the great organs of intelligence: when it loses, which is at least three times as often, the news gets only a few lines. The truth is that the strength of the Klan, like the strength of the Anti-Saloon League, and that of the Methodist-Baptist bloc of moron churches, the pa of both of them, has always been greatly overestimated. Even in the most barbarous reaches of the South, where every village is bossed by a Baptist dervish, it met with vigorous challenge from the start, and there are not three Confederate States to-day in which, on a fair plebiscite, it could hope to prevail. The fact that huge hordes of Southern politicians jumped into night-shirts when it began is no proof that it was actually mighty; it is only proof that politicians are cowards and idiots. Of late all of them have been seeking to rid themselves of the tell-tale tar and feathers; they try to ride the very genuine wave of aversion and disgust as they tried to ride the illusory wave of popularity. As the Klan falls everywhere, the Anti-Saloon League tends to fall with it—and the evangelical churches are strapped tightly to both corpses.

This connection, when it was first denounced, was violently denied by the Baptist and Methodist ecclesiastics, but now every one knows that it was and is real. These ecclesiastics are responsible for the Anti-Saloon League and its swineries, and they are responsible no less for the Klan. In other words, they are responsible, directly and certainly, for all the turmoils and black hatreds that now rage in the bleak regions between the State roads—they are to blame for every witches' pot that now brews in the backwoods of the Union. They have sowed enmities that will last for years. They have divided neighbors, debauched local governments, and enormously multiplied lawlessness. They are responsible for more crime than even the wildest foes of the saloon ever laid to its discredit, and it is crime, in the main, that is infinitely more anti-social and dangerous. They have opposed every honest effort to compose the natural differences between man and man, and they have opposed every attempt to meet ignorance and prejudice with enlightenment. Alike in the name of God, they had advocated murder and they have murdered sense. Where they flourish no intelligent and well-disposed man is safe, and no sound and useful idea is safe. They have preached not only the bitter, savage morality of the Old Testament; they have also preached its childish contempt of obvious facts. Hordes of poor creatures have followed these appalling rogues and vagabonds of the cloth down their Gadarene hill: the result, in immense areas, is the conversion of Christianity into a machine for making civilized living impossible. It is wholly corrupt, rotten and abominable. It deserves no more respect than a pile of garbage.

What I contend is that hundreds of thousands of poor simpletons are beginning to be acutely aware of the fact—that they are not quite as stupid as they usually appear to be. In other words, I believe that they tire of the obscenity. One glances at such a State as Arkansas or such a town as Jackson, Miss., and sees only a swarm of bawling Methodists; only too easily one overlooks the fact that the bawling is far from unanimous. Logic is possible, in its rudiments, even to the *Simiidæ*. On the next step of the scale, in the suburbs, so to speak, of *Homo sapiens*, it flourishes intermittently and explosively. All that is needed to set it off is a suitable yell. The first chautauquan who looses such a yell against the True Faith will shake the Bible Belt like an earthquake, and, as they say, mop up. Half his work is already done for him. The True Faith, the only variety of the True Faith known to those hinds, is already under their rising distrust and suspicion. They look for the Ambassador of Christ, and they behold a Baptist elder in a mail-order suit, describing voluptuously the Harlot of Babylon. They yearn for consolation, and they are invited to a raid on bootleggers. Their souls reach out to the eternal mystery, and the evening's entertainment is the clubbing of a fancy woman. All they need is a leader. Christianity is sick all over this pious land, even in the South. The Christians have killed it. One blast upon a bugle horn, and the mob will be ready for the wake.

XVI.
Aubade

THE name of the man who first made a slave of fire, like the name of the original Franklin Pierce man, is unknown to historians: burrow and sweat as they will, their efforts to unearth it are always baffled. And no wonder! For isn't it easy to imagine how infamous that name must have been while it was still remembered, and how diligent and impassioned the endeavor to erase it from the tablets of the race? One pictures the indignation of the clergy when so vast an improvement upon their immemorial magic confronted them, and their herculean and unanimous struggle, first to put it down as unlawful and against God, and then to collar it for themselves. Bonfires were surely not unknown in the morning of the Pleistocene, for there were lightnings then as now, but the first one kindled by mortal hands must have shocked humanity. One pictures the news flashing from cave to cave and from tribe to tribe—out of Central Asia and then across the grasslands, and then around the feet of the glaciers into the gloomy, spook-haunted wilderness that is now Western Europe, and so across into Africa. Something new and dreadful was upon the human race, and by the time the *Ur*-Mississippians of the Neander Valley heard of it, you may be sure, the discoverer had sprouted horns and was in the pay of the Devil.

His fate at home, though his name is unknown, presents no difficulties to adepts at public psychology. The bad boys of the neighborhood, one may safely assume, got to the scene first of all and were delighted by the show, but upon their heels came the local pastor, and in two minutes he was bawling for the *Polizei*. The ensuing trial attracted such crowds that for weeks the saber-toothed tiger (*Machærodus neogæus*) and the woolly rhinoceros (*R. antiquitatus*) roamed the wilds unmolested, feasting upon colporteurs and wandering flint peddlers. The fellow stood confronted by his unspeakable and unparalleled felony, and could only beg for mercy. Publicly and without shame, he had performed a feat never performed by man before: *ergo*, it was as plain as day that he had engaged, anteriorly, in commerce with the powers of the air. So much, indeed, was elemental logic: even a lawyer could grasp it. But *what* powers? There the clergy certainly had something to say, and what they said must have been instantly damning. They were themselves the daily familiars of all reputable powers of the air, great and small. They knew precisely what could be done and what could not be done. Their professional skill and knowledge were admitted everywhere and by all. What they could not do was thus clearly irregular and disreputable: it issued out of an unlawful transaction with fiends. Any other theory would be laughable, and in plain contempt of court. One pictures the learned judge summing up, and one pictures the headsman spitting on his hands. That night there was a head on a pole in front of the episcopal cave of the ordinary of the diocese, and more than one ambitious cave hyena (*H. spelæa*) wore himself out trying to shin up.

But the secret did not pass with the criminal. He was dead, his relatives to the third degree were sold into slavery to the Chellean heathen down the river, and it was a capital offense, with preliminary tortures, to so much as mention his name. But in his last hours, one must bear in mind, he had a spiritual adviser, to hear his confession and give him absolution for his sorcery, and that spiritual adviser, it is reasonable to assume, had just as much natural curiosity as any other clergyman. So it is not hard to imagine that he wormed the trick out of the condemned, and later on, as in duty bound, conveyed it privately to his bishop. Nor is it hard to imagine its plans and specifications becoming generally known, *sotto voce*, to the adjacent clergy, nor some ingenious holy clerk, presently discovering that they could be carried out without bringing any fiends into the business. The lawful and laudable powers of the air, already sworn to the service of Holy Church, were quite as potent: a hint from the bishop was sufficient to set them to work. And so, if there is no flaw in my reasoning, the making of fire soon became one of the high privileges and prerogatives of the sacred office, forbidden to the laity upon penalty of the stone ax, and reserved in practice for high ceremonial uses and occasions. The ordination of a new rector, I suppose, was such an occasion. The consecration of a new cave was another. And among the uses were the laying of demons, the pursuit and scotching of dragons and other monsters, the abatement of floods and cyclones, the refutation of heresies, and the management of the sun, so that day always followed night and Spring came after Winter. I daresay fees were charged, for the clergy must live, but there was never any degradation of the new magic to sordid, secular uses. No one was allowed a fire to keep warm, and no one was allowed one to boil a bone.

It would be interesting to try to figure out, by the doctrine of probabilities, how long fire was thus reserved for sacramental purposes. The weather being, at this writing, too hot for mathematical exercises, I content myself with a guess, to wit, 10,000 years. It is probably over-moderate. The obvious usefulness of fire was certainly not enough to bring it into general use; it had to wait for the slow, tedious, extremely bloody growth of skepticism. No doubt there were heretics, even during the first two or three millennia, who set off piles of leaves far back in the woods, gingerly, cautiously and half expecting to be potted by thunderbolts. Perhaps there were even renegade clergymen who, unsettled in their faith by contemplation of *Pithecanthropus erectus* (the remote grandfather of the *P. biblicus* of our present Christian age), threw off the sacerdotal chemise, took to flight, and started forest fires. But the odds against such antinomians, for many centuries, must have been almost as heavy as the odds against a Unitarian in Tennessee to-day. They exited, but only as outlaws, with the ax waiting for them, and Hell beyond the ax. The unanimous sentiment of decent people was against them. It was plain to every one that a world in which they went unscotched would be a world resigned to sin and shame.

Nevertheless, they continued to exist, and what is worse, to increase gradually in numbers. Even when the regular force of police was augmented by bands of volunteer snouters, organized to search out unlawful fires in the deep woods and remote deserts, there were heretics who persisted in their contumacy, and even undertook to defend it with all the devices of sophistry. At intervals great crusades were launched against them, and they were rounded up and butchered by the hundred, and even by the thousand. The ordinary method of capital punishment prevailing in those times—to wit, decapitation with fifteen or twenty strokes of a stone ax—was found to be ineffective against such agents of the Devil, and so other and more rigorous methods were devised—chief among them, boiling to death in a huge pot set over a temple fire. More, the ordinary criminal procedure had to be changed to facilitate convictions, for the heretics were highly skilled at turning the safeguards of the law to their baleful uses. First, it was provided that a man accused of making fire should be tried, not before the judges who sat in common criminal cases, but before judges especially nominated for the purpose by the priests, or by the Anti-Fire League, an organization of citizens pledged to law and order. Then it was provided that no such prisoner should be permitted to consult counsel, or to enjoy the privilege of bail, or to call witnesses in his behalf. Finally, after all these half measures had failed, it was decided to abandon the whole sorry hocus-pocus of trial and judgment, and to hand the accused over to the public executioner at once, without any frivolous inquiry into the degree of his guilt.

This device seemed to work very well for a time. It worked very well, indeed, for nearly 5000 years. There were times during that long period when contraband fire-making seemed to be practically extinct in the world. Children grew up who had never seen a fire save in its proper place: a place of worship. Come to maturity, they begat children equally innocent, and so the thing went on for generations. But always, just as the fire heresy seemed about to disappear from human memory, some outlaw in the wilds revived it. These revivals sometimes spread as rapidly as their own flames. One year there would be complete peace everywhere and a spirit of obedience to the law; the next year bonfires would suddenly sparkle in the hills, and blasphemous whispers would go round. The heretics, at such times, made great play at the young. They would lure boys into the groves along the river-bottoms and teach them how to roast chestnuts. They would send in spies disguised as Chellean serving-maids to show little girls how much easier it was to do the family washing with hot water than with cold. The constituted authorities answered such defiances with vigorous campaigns of law enforcement. Fireleggers were taken by the thousand, and put to death at great public ceremonials. But always some escaped.

In the end (or, at all events, so I work it out by the device brought in by the new science of biometrics) enough escaped to make further proceedings against them dangerous and even impossible. No doubt it happened in what is now Southern France, in the region called the Dordogne. The fireleggers, taking to the hills, there organized a sort of outlaw state, and presently began passing laws of their own. The first of such laws, no doubt, converted fire-making from a crime into a patriotic act: it became the principal duty of every right-thinking citizen to keep a fire burning in front of his cave. Amendments soon followed. It became a felony to eat uncooked food, or to do the family washing in cold water. It became another to put out a fire, or to advocate putting it out, or to imagine putting it out.

Thus priests were barred from that outlaw state, and it became necessary to develop a new class of men skilled in public affairs, and privy to the desires of the gods. Nature responded with politicians. Anon these politicians became adept at all the arts that have distinguished them ever since. They invented new and more rigorous laws, they imposed taxes, they broke the fireleggers to military service. One day, having drilled a large army, they marched down into the plains, tackled the hosts of the orthodox, and overcame them. The next day the priests who had led these hosts were given a simple choice: either they could admit formally that fire-making for secular purposes was now lawful and even laudable, or they could submit to being burned alive upon their own sacramental pyres. Great numbers of them went heroically to the stake, firm in the hope of a glorious resurrection. The rest, retiring to their crypts and seeking divine guidance, emerged with the news that the gods were now in favor of universal fire-making. That night there was a cheerful blaze in front of every cave for miles around, and the priests themselves sat down to a hearty banquet of roast megatherium (*M. cuvieri*). Eight thousand years later a heretic who revived the primeval pagan habit of eating raw oysters was put to death for atheism.

XVII.
Appendix From Moronia

I
Note on Technic

HAVING made of late, after a longish hiatus, two separate attempts to sit through movie shows, I can only report that the so-called art of the film still eludes me. I was not chased out either time by the low intellectual content of the pictures on display. For one thing, I am anything but intellectual in my tastes, and for another thing the films I saw were not noticeably deficient in that direction. The ideas in them were simply the common and familiar ideas of the inferior nine-tenths of mankind. They were hollow and obvious, but they were not more hollow and obvious than the ideas one encounters in the theater every day, or in the ordinary run of popular novels, or, for that matter, in the discourses of the average American statesman or divine. Rotary, hearing worse once a week, still manages to preserve its idealism and digest carbohydrates.

What afflicts the movies is not unpalatable ideational content so much as an idiotic and irritating technic. The first moving-pictures, as I remember them thirty years ago, presented more or less continuous scenes. They were played like ordinary plays, and so one could follow them lazily and at ease. But the modern movie is no such organic whole; it is simply a maddening chaos of discrete fragments. The average scene, if the two shows I attempted were typical, cannot run for more than six or seven seconds. Many are far shorter, and very few are appreciably longer. The result is confusion horribly confounded. How can one work up any rational interest in a fable that changes its locale and its characters ten times a minute? Worse, this dizzy jumping about is plainly unnecessary: all it shows is the professional incompetence of the gilded pants-pressers, decayed actors and other such half-wits to whom the making of movies seems to be entrusted. Unable to imagine a sequence of coherent scenes, and unprovided with a sufficiency of performers capable of playing them if they were imagined, these preposterous mountebanks are reduced to the childish device of avoiding action altogether. Instead of it they present what is at bottom nothing but a poorly articulated series of meaningless postures and grimaces. One sees a ham cutting a face, and then one sees his lady co-star squeezing a tear—and so on, endlessly. These mummers cannot be said, in any true sense, to act at all. They merely strike attitudes—and are then whisked off. If, at the first attempt upon a scene, the right attitude is not struck, then all they have to do is to keep on trying until they strike it. On those terms a chimpanzee could play Hamlet, or even Juliet.

To most of the so-called actors engaged in the movies, I daresay, no other course would be possible. They are such obvious incompetents that they could no more play a rational scene, especially one involving any subtlety, than a cow could jump over the moon. They are engaged, not for their histrionic skill, but simply for their capacity to fill the heads of romantic virgins and neglected wives with the sort of sentiments that the Christian religion tries so hard to put down. It is, no doubt, a useful office, assuming that the human race must, should and will go on, but it has no more to do with acting, as an art, than being a Federal judge has with preserving the Constitution. The worst of it is that the occasional good actor, venturing into the movies, is brought down to the common level by the devices thus invented to conceal the incompetence of his inferiors. It is quite as impossible to present a plausible impersonation in a series of unrelated (and often meaningless) postures as it would be to make a sensible speech in a series of college yells. So the good actor, appearing in the films, appears to be almost as bad as the natural movie ham. One sees him only as one sees a row of telegraph poles, riding in a train. However skillful he may be, he is always cut off before, by any intelligible use of the device of his trade, he can make the fact evident.

In one of the pictures I saw lately a principal actor was George Bernard Shaw. The first scene showed him for fifteen or twenty seconds continuously, and it was at once plain that he had a great deal of histrionic skill—far more, indeed, than the average professional actor. He was seen engaged in a friendly argument with several other dramatists, among them Sir James M. Barrie and Sir Arthur Wing Pinero. Having admired all these notorious men for many years, and never having had the honor of meeting or even witnessing them, I naturally settled down with a grateful grunt to the pleasure of feasting my eyes upon them. But after that first scene all I saw of Shaw was a series of fifteen or twenty maddening flashes, none of them more than five seconds long. He would spring into view, leap upon Barrie or Pinero—and then disappear. Then he would spring back, his whiskers bristling—and disappear again. It was as maddening as the ring of the telephone.

There is, of course, a legitimate use for this off-again-on-again device in the movies: it may be used, at times, very effectively and even intelligently. The beautiful heroine, say, is powdering her nose, preparing to go out to her fatal dinner with her libidinous boss. Suddenly there flashes through her mind a prophylactic memory of the Sunday-school in her home town far away. An actress on the stage, with such a scene to play, faces serious technical difficulties: it is very hard for her—that is, it has been hard since Ibsen abolished the soliloquy—to convey the exact revolutions of her conscience to her audience. But the technic of the movies makes it very easy—in fact, so easy that it requires no skill at all. The director simply prepares a series of scenes showing what is going through the heroine's mind. There is the church on the hill, with the horde of unhappy children being driven into its basement by the town constable. There is the old maid teacher expounding the day's Golden Text, II Kings, II, 23–24. There is a flash of the two she-bears "taring" the "forty and two" little children. There is the heroine, in ringlets, clapping her hands in dutiful Presbyterian glee. There is a flash of the Sunday-school superintendent, his bald head shining, warning the scholars against the sins of simony, barratry and adultery. There is the collection, with the bad boy putting in the suspenders' button. There is the flash showing him, years later, as a bank president.

All this is ingenious. More, it is humane, for it prevents the star trying to act, and so saves the spectators pain. But it is manifestly a poor substitute for acting on the occasions when acting is actually demanded by the plot—that is, on the occasions when there must be cumulative action, and not merely a series of postures. Such occasions give rise to what the old-time dramatic theorists called *scènes à faire*, which is to say, scenes of action, crucial scenes, necessary scenes. In the movies they are dismembered, and so spoiled. Try to imagine the balcony scene from "Romeo and Juliet" in a string of fifty flashes —first Romeo taking his station and spitting on his hands, then Juliet with her head as big as a hay-wagon, then the two locked in a greasy kiss, then the Nurse taking a drink of gin, then Romeo rolling his eyes, and so on. If you can imagine it, then you ought to be in Hollywood, dodging bullets and amassing wealth.

If I were in a constructive mood I'd probably propose reforms, but that mood, I regret to say, is not on me. In any case, I doubt that proposing reforms would do any good. For this idiotic movie technic, as I have shown, has its origin in the incompetence of the clowns who perform in the great majority of movies, and it would probably be impossible to displace them with competent actors, for the customers of the movie-parlors appear to love them, and even to admire them. It is hard to believe, but it is obviously so. A successful movie mime is probably the most admired human being ever seen in the world. He is admired more than Napoleon, Lincoln or Beethoven; more, even, than Coolidge. The effects of this adulation, upon the mime himself and especially upon his clients, ought to be given serious study by competent psychiatrists, if any can be found. For there is nothing more corrupting to the human psyche, I believe, than the mean admiration of mean things. It produces a double demoralization, intellectual and spiritual. Its victim becomes not only a jackass, but also a bounder. The movie-parlors, I suspect, are turning out such victims by the million: they will, in the long run, so debauch the American proletariat that it will begin to put Coolidge above Washington, and Peaches Browning above Coolidge.

Meanwhile, they are ruining the ancient and noble art of the dramatist—an art that has engaged the talents of some of the greatest men the world has ever seen. And they are, at the same time, ruining the lesser but by no means contemptible art of the actor. It is no advantage to a movie ham to be a competent actor; on the contrary, it is a handicap. If he tried to act, as acting has been understood since the days of Æschylus, his director would shut him off instanter: what is wanted is simply aphrodisiacal posturing. And if, by any chance, his director were drunk and let him run on, the vast majority of movie morons would probably rush out of the house, bawling that the film was dull and cheap, and that they had been swindled.

2
Interlude in the Socratic Manner

Having completed your æsthetic researches at Hollywood, what is your view of the film art now?

I made no researches at Hollywood, and was within the corporate bounds of the town, in fact, only on a few occasions, and then for only a few hours. I spent my time in Los Angeles, studying the Christian pathology of that great city. When not so engaged I mainly devoted myself to quiet guzzling with Joe Hergesheimer, Jim Quirk, Johnny Hemphill, Jim Tully, Walter Wanger and other such literati. For the rest, I visited friends in the adjacent deserts, some of them employed in the pictures and some not. They treated me with immense politeness. With murderers as thick in the town as evangelists, nothing would have been easier than to have had me killed, but they let me go.

Did any of them introduce you to the wild night-life of the town?

The wildest night-life I encountered was at Sister Aimée McPherson's tabernacle. I saw no wildness among the movie-folk. They seemed to me, in the main, to be very serious and even gloomy people. And no wonder, for they are worked like Pullman porters or magazine editors. When they are engaged in posturing for a film and have finished their day's labor they are far too tired for any recreation requiring stamina. I encountered but two authentic souses in three weeks. One was a cowboy and the other was an author. I heard of a lady getting tight at a party, but I was not present. The news was a sensation in the town. Such are the sorrows of poor mummers: their most banal peccadilloes are magnified into horrors. Regard the unfortunate Chaplin. If he were a lime and cement dealer his latest divorce case would not have got two lines in the newspapers. But, as it was, he was placarded all over the front pages because he had had a banal disagreement with one of his wives. The world hears of such wild, frenzied fellows as Tully, and puts them down as typical of Hollywood. But Tully is not an actor; he eats actors. I saw him devour half a dozen of them on the half-shell in an hour. He wears a No. 30 collar and has a colossal capacity for wine-bibbing; I had to call up my last reserves to keep up with him. But the typical actor is a slim and tender fellow. What would be a mere apéritif for Tully or me would put him under the table, yelling for his pastor.

So you caught no glimpses of immorality?

Immorality? Oh, my God! Hollywood, despite the smell of patchouli and rattle of revolver fire, seemed to me to be one of the most respectable towns in America. Even Baltimore can't beat it. The notion that actors are immoral fellows is a delusion that comes down to us from Puritan days, just as the delusion that rum is a viper will go down to posterity from our days. There is no truth in it. The typical actor, at least in America, is the most upright of men: he always marries the girl. How many actors are bachelors? Not one in a thousand. The divorce rate is high among them simply because the marriage rate is so high. An actor, encountering a worthy girl, leaps from the couch to the altar almost as fast as a Baptist leaps from the altar to the couch. It is his incurable sentimentality that fetches him: if he was not born a romantic he is not an actor. Worse, his profession supports his natural weakness. In plays and movies he always marries the girl in the end, and so it seems to him to be the decent thing to do it in his private life. Actors always copy the doings of the characters they impersonate: no Oscar was needed to point out that nature always imitates art. I heard, of course, a great deal of gossip in Los Angeles, but all save a trivial part of it was excessively romantic. Nearly every great female star, it appeared, was desperately in love, either with her husband or with some pretty and well-heeled fellow, usually not an actor. And every male star was mooning over some coy and lovely miss. I heard more sweet love stories in three weeks than I had heard in New York in the previous thirty years. The whole place stank of orange-blossoms. Is honest love conducive to vice? Then one may argue that it is conducive to delirium tremens to be a Presbyterian elder. One of the largest industries in Hollywood is that of the florists. Next comes that of the traffickers in wedding silver. One beautiful lady star told me that buying such presents cost her $11,000 last year.

But the tales go round. Is there no truth in them at all?

To the best of my knowledge and belief, none. They are believed because the great masses of the plain people, though they admire movie actors, also envy them, and hence hate them. It is the old human story. Why am I hated by theologians? It is because I am an almost unparalleled expert in all branches of theology. Whenever they tackle me, my superior knowledge and talent floor them. In precisely the same way I hate such fellows as the movie Salvini, Jack Gilbert. Gilbert is an amiable and tactful young man, and treats me with the politeness properly due to my years and learning. But I heard in Culver City that no less than two thousand head of women, many of them rich, were mashed on him. Well, I can recall but fifteen or twenty women who have ever showed any sign of being flustered by me, and not one of them, at a forced sale, would have realized $200. Hence I hate Gilbert, and would rejoice unaffectedly to see him taken in some scandal that would stagger humanity. If he is accused of anything less than murdering his wife and eight children I shall be disappointed.

Then why do you speak for Mr. Chaplin?

Simply because he is not a handsome dog, as Gilbert is. The people who hate him do so because he is rich. It is the thought that his trouble will bust him that gives them delight. But I have no desire for money and so his prosperity does not offend me. I always have too much money; it is easy to get in New York, provided one is not a professing Christian. Gilbert, I suppose, is rich too; he wears very natty clothes. But it is not his wealth that bothers me: it is those two thousand head of women.

So, failing researches, you continue ignorant of the film art?

Ignorant? What a question! How could any man remain ignorant of the movies after three weeks in Los Angeles? As well continue ignorant of laparotomy after three weeks in a hospital sun-parlor! No, I am full of information about them, some of it accurate, for I heard them talked day and night, and by people who actually knew something about them. There was but one refuge from that talk, and that was La McPherson's basilica. Moreover, I have hatched some ideas of my own.

As for example?

That the movie folks, in so far as they are sentient at all, are on the hooks of a distressing dilemma. They have built their business upon a foundation of morons, and now they are paying for it. They seem to be unable to make a presentable picture without pouring out tons of money, and when they have made it they must either sell it to immense audiences of half-wits, or go broke. There seems to be very little ingenuity and resourcefulness in them. They are apparently quite unable, despite their melodramatic announcements of salary cuts, to solve the problem of making movies cheaply, and yet intelligently, so that civilized persons may visit the movie-parlors without pain. But soon or late some one will have to solve it. Soon or late the movies will have to split into two halves. There will be movies for the present mob, and there will be movies for the relatively enlightened minority. The former will continue idiotic; the latter, if competent men to make them are unearthed, will show sense and beauty.

Have you caught the scent of any such men?

Not yet. There are some respectable craftsmen in Hollywood. (I judged them by their talk: I have not seen many of their actual pictures.) They tackle the problems of their business in a more or less sensible manner. They have learned a lot from the Germans. But I think it would be stretching a point to say that there are any artists among them—as yet. They are adept, but not inspired. The movies need a first-rate artist—a man of genuine competence and originality. If he is in Hollywood to-day, he is probably bootlegging, running a pants pressing parlor, or grinding a camera crank. The movie magnates see him in literary directions. They pin their faith to novelists and playwrights. I presume to believe that this is bad medicine. The fact that a man can write a competent novel is absolutely no reason for assuming that he can write a competent film. The two things are as unlike as Pilsner and coca-cola. Even a sound dramatist is not necessarily a competent scenario-writer. What the movies need is a school of authors who will forget all dialogue and description, and try to set forth their ideas in terms of pure motion. It can be done, and it will be done. The German, Dr. Murnau, showed the way in certain scenes of "The Last Laugh." But the American magnates continue to buy bad novels and worse plays, and then put overworked hacks to the sorry job of translating them into movies. It is like hiring men to translate college yells into riddles. Æschylus himself would have been stumped by such a task.

When do you think the Shakespeare of the movies will appear? And where will he come from?

God knows. He may even be an American, as improbable as it may seem. One thing, only, I am sure of: he will not get much for his masterpieces. He will have to give them away, and the first manager who puts them on will lose money. The movies to-day are too rich to have any room for genuine artists. They produce a few passable craftsmen, but no artists. Can you imagine a Beethoven making $100,000 a year? If so, then you have a better imagination than Beethoven himself. No, the present movie folk, I fear, will never quite solve the problem, save by some act of God. They are too much under the heel of the East Side gorillas who own them. They think too much about money. They have allowed it to become too important to them, and believe they couldn't get along without it. This is an unfortunate delusion. Money is important to mountebanks, but not to artists. The first really great movie, when it comes at last, will probably cost less than $5000. A true artist is always a romantic. He doesn't ask what the job will pay; he asks if it will be interesting. In this way all the loveliest treasures of the human race have been fashioned—by careless and perhaps somewhat foolish men. The late Johann Sebastian Bach, compared to a movie star with nine automobiles, was simply a damned fool. But I cherish the feeling that a scientific inquiry would also develop other differences between them.

Are you against the star system?

I am neither for it nor against it. A star is simply a performer who pleases the generality of morons better than the average. Certainly I see no reason why such a performer should not be paid a larger salary than the average. The objection to swollen salaries should come from the stars themselves—that is, assuming them to be artists. The system diverts them from their proper business of trying to produce charming and amusing movies, and converts them into bogus society folk. What could be more ridiculous? And pathetic? I go further: it is tragic. As I have said in another place, nothing is more tragic in this world than for otherwise worthy people to meanly admire and imitate mean things. One may have some respect for the movie lady who buys books and sets up as an intellectual, for it is a creditable thing to want to be (or even simply to want to appear) well-informed and intelligent. But I can see nothing worthy in wanting to be mistaken for the president of a bank. Artists should sniff at such dull drudges, not imitate them. The movies will leap ahead the day some star in Hollywood organizes a string quartette and begins to study Mozart.

3
Valentino

By one of the chances that relieve the dullness of life and make it instructive, I had the honor of dining with this celebrated gentleman in New York, a week or so before his fatal illness. I had never met him before, nor seen him on the screen; the meeting was at his instance, and, when it was proposed, vaguely puzzled me. But soon its purpose became clear enough. Valentino was in trouble, and wanted advice. More, he wanted advice from an elder and disinterested man, wholly removed from the movies and all their works. Something that I had written, falling under his eye, had given him the notion that I was a judicious fellow. So he requested one of his colleagues, a lady of the films, to ask me to dinner at her hotel.

The night being infernally warm, we stripped off our coats, and came to terms at once. I recall that he wore suspenders of extraordinary width and thickness—suspenders almost strong enough to hold up the pantaloons of Chief Justice Taft. On so slim a young man they seemed somehow absurd, especially on a hot Summer night. We perspired horribly for an hour, mopping our faces with our handkerchiefs, the table napkins, the corners of the table-cloth, and a couple of towels brought in by the humane waiter. Then there came a thunder-storm, and we began to breathe. The hostess, a woman as tactful as she is charming, disappeared mysteriously and left us to commune.

The trouble that was agitating Valentino turned out to be very simple. The ribald New York papers were full of it, and that was what was agitating him. Some time before, out in

Chicago, a wandering reporter had discovered, in the men's wash-room of a gaudy hotel, a slot-machine selling talcum-powder. That, of course, was not unusual, but the color of the talcum-powder was. It was pink. The news made the town giggle for a day, and inspired an editorial writer on the eminent Chicago *Tribune* to compose a hot weather editorial. In it he protested humorously against the effeminization of the American man, and laid it light-heartedly to the influence of Valentino and his sheik movies. Well, it so happened that Valentino, passing through Chicago that day on his way east from the Coast, ran full tilt into the editorial, and into a gang of reporters who wanted to know what he had to say about it. What he had to say was full of fire. Throwing off his 100% Americanism and reverting to the *mores* of his fatherland, he challenged the editorial writer to a duel, and, when no answer came, to a fist fight. His masculine honor, it appeared, had been outraged. To the hint that he was less than he, even to the extent of one half of one per cent., there could be no answer save a bath of blood.

Unluckily, all this took place in the United States, where the word honor, save when it is applied to the structural integrity of women, has only a comic significance. One hears of the honor of politicians, of bankers, of lawyers even of the honor of the United States itself. Everyone naturally laughs. So New York laughed at Valentino. More, it ascribed his high dudgeon to mere publicity-seeking: he seemed a vulgar movie ham seeking space. The poor fellow, thus doubly beset, rose to dudgeons higher still. His Italian mind was simply unequal to the situation. So he sought counsel from the neutral, aloof and aged. Unluckily, I could only name the disease, and confess frankly that there was no remedy—none, that is, known to any therapeutics within my ken. He should have passed over the gibe of the Chicago journalist, I suggested, with a lofty snort —perhaps, better still, with a counter gibe. He should have kept away from the reporters in New York. But now, alas, the mischief was done. He was both insulted and ridiculous, but there was nothing to do about it. I advised him to let the dreadful farce roll along to exhaustion. He protested that it was infamous. Infamous? Nothing, I argued, is infamous that is not true. A man still has his inner integrity. Can he still look into the shaving-glass of a morning? Then he is still on his two legs in this world, and ready even for the Devil. We sweated a great deal, discussing these lofty matters. We seemed to get nowhere.

Suddenly it dawned upon me—I was too dull or it was too hot for me to see it sooner—that what we were talking about was really not what we were talking about at all. I began to observe Valentino more closely. A curiously naïve and boyish young fellow, certainly not much beyond thirty, and with a disarming air of inexperience. To my eye, at least, not handsome, but nevertheless rather attractive. There was an obvious fineness in him; even his clothes were not precisely those of his horrible trade. He began talking of his home, his people, his early youth. His words were simple and yet somehow very eloquent. I could still see the mime before me, but now and then, briefly and darkly, there was a flash of something else. That something else, I concluded, was what is commonly called, for want of a better name, a gentleman. In brief, Valentino's agony was the agony of a man of relatively civilized feelings thrown into a situation of intolerable vulgarity, destructive alike to his peace and to his dignity—nay, into a whole series of such situations. It was not that trifling Chicago episode that was riding him; it was the whole grotesque futility of his life. Had he achieved, out of nothing, a vast and dizzy success? Then that success was hollow as well as vast—a colossal and preposterous nothing. Was he acclaimed by yelling multitudes? Then every time the multitudes yelled he felt himself blushing inside. The old story of Diego Valdez once more, but with a new poignancy in it. Valdez, at all events, was High Admiral of Spain. But Valentino, with his touch of fineness in him—he had his commonness, too, but there was that touch of fineness—Valentino was only the hero of the rabble. Imbeciles surrounded him in a dense herd. He was pursued by women—but what women! (Consider the sordid comedy of his two marriages—the brummagem, star-spangled passion that invaded his very death-bed!) The thing, at the start, must have only bewildered him. But in those last days, unless I am a worse psychologist than even the professors of psychology, it was revolting him. Worse, it was making him afraid.

I incline to think that the inscrutable gods, in taking him off so soon and at a moment of fiery revolt, were very kind to him. Living, he would have tried inevitably to change his fame—if such it is to be called—into something closer to his heart's desire. That is to say, he would have gone the way of many another actor—the way of increasing pretension, of solemn artiness, of hollow hocus-pocus, deceptive only to himself. I believe he would have failed, for there was little sign of the genuine artist in him. He was essentially a highly respectable young man, which is the sort that never metamorphoses into an artist. But suppose he had succeeded? Then his tragedy, I believe, would have only become the more acrid and intolerable. For he would have discovered, after vast heavings and yearnings, that what he had come to was indistinguishable from what he had left. Was the fame of Beethoven any more caressing and splendid than the fame of Valentino? To you and me, of course, the question seems to answer itself. But what of Beethoven? He was heard upon the subject, *viva voce*, while he lived, and his answer survives, in all the freshness of its profane eloquence, in his music. Beethoven, too, knew what it meant to be applauded. Walking with Goethe, he heard something that was not unlike the murmur that reached Valentino through his hospital window. Beethoven walked away briskly. Valentino turned his face to the wall.

Here, after all, is the chiefest joke of the gods: that man must remain alone and lonely in this world, even with crowds surging about him. Does he crave approbation, with a sort of furious, instinctive lust? Then it is only to discover, when it comes, that it is somehow disconcerting—that its springs and motives offer an affront to his dignity. But do I sentimentalize the perhaps transparent story of a simple mummer? Then substitute Coolidge, or Mussolini, or any other poor devil that you can think of. Substitute Shakespeare, or Lincoln, or Goethe, or Beethoven, as I have. Sentimental or not, I confess that the predicament of poor Valentino touched me. It provided grist for my mill, but I couldn't quite enjoy it. Here was a young man who was living daily the dream of millions of other young men. Here was one who was catnip to women. Here was one who had wealth and fame. And here was one who was very unhappy.

CHRONOLOGY

NOTE ON THE TEXTS

NOTE ON THE ILLUSTRATIONS

NOTES

INDEX

Chronology

1880 Born Henry Louis Mencken on September 12, at what was then 380 West Lexington Street, Baltimore, Maryland, now 811 West Lexington Street; eldest child of August Mencken and Anna Abhau Mencken. (Grandfather Burkhardt Ludwig Mencken, born 1828 in Laas, Germany, landed in Baltimore, November 1848; was naturalized October 1852, and set up a tobacco business. Father, born June 16, 1854, established August Mencken & Bro. between 1873 and 1875, managing it with his brother Henry, and building it into one of the most successful cigar manufacturers along the South Atlantic coast. An agnostic and a high-tariff Republican, August was a loyal member of the Masonic order, also part owner of the major-league baseball club of Washington, D.C. Mother, Anna Abhau, born June 11, 1858, was the daughter of Carl Heinrich Abhau from Hesse, Germany. August and Anna were married on November 11, 1879.)

1882 Brother, Charles Edward, born May 16.

1883 Family moves to 1524 Hollins Street, in a prosperous German-American neighborhood in West Baltimore, facing Union Square.

1886 Mencken enrolls at F. Knapp's Institute, a private school, in September. Sister Anna Gertrude born November 17.

1888 Begins piano lessons. Receives a self-inking printing press for Christmas.

1889 Brother, August, born February 18. Reads Mark Twain's *Huckleberry Finn*, which makes a huge impact on him. Family begins spending summers in Ellicott City, Howard County, west of Baltimore (1889–1892), and Mt. Washington (1892–1899), then a northwestern suburb.

1892 Mencken enters Baltimore Polytechnic Institute, a public high school, on September 5.

1893 Mencken keenly interested in chemistry, photography, journalism, and literature. Visits the Enoch Pratt Free Library, reads four or five books a week, mostly English literature (including Dickens, Chaucer, Shakespeare, Herrick, Pepys, Addison, Steele, Pope, Swift, Johnson, Boswell, Fielding, Smollett, Sterne, Arnold, Macaulay, George Eliot, Tennyson, Swinburne, Thackeray, Kipling). Mencken will later call the library "my school"; his brother August will recall that Mencken "read like an athlete." Fire engulfs August Mencken & Bro. Cigar factory, causing $25,000 worth of damage, December 2.

1895 Reads Stephen Crane's *The Red Badge of Courage.*

1896 Graduates at age 15 from the Baltimore Polytechnic Institute, with highest grade point average yet recorded, June 23. Publishes a poem ("Ode to the Pennant on the Centerfield Pole") anonymously in the Baltimore *American*, summer. Tells his father that he plans to become a newspaper reporter, but is strongly dissuaded. Starts full-time work as clerk and salesman at August Mencken & Bro.

1898 Subscribes to *The Criterion* (New York) and is influenced by the work of James Gibbons Huneker, Percival Pollard, Ambrose Bierce, Oscar Wilde, George Bernard Shaw, and Friedrich Nietzsche. Becomes an admirer of the prose style and ideas of Thomas Henry Huxley. Studies books on journalism; enrolls in a correspondence school, the Associated Newspaper Bureau School of Journalism in New York, and states his career goal is "to begin as a reporter & after that trust to hard work and luck for something better." Resolves to quit working at August Mencken & Bro.; his father asks him to postpone the decision for at least another year. In a moment of despair, Mencken contemplates suicide. August Mencken, Sr., collapses unconscious with acute kidney infection, December 31. (Mencken writes later: "I remember well how . . . I kept saying to myself that if my father died I'd be free at last . . . I had got along with him very well, but I detested business and was frantic to get into newspaper work.")

1899 Father dies on January 13 and is buried at Loudon Park Cemetery. Two weeks later Mencken visits the offices of the Baltimore *Herald* and asks for a job. First story published February 24. Hired at $7 a week, the youngest (and first) cub reporter on the *Herald* to get paid a salary, July 2. A poem addressed to Rudyard Kipling appears in December 1899 issue of *Bookman* magazine. Quits working part-time for his Uncle Henry at August Mencken & Bro.

to devote himself to journalism, which he later calls "the maddest, gladdest, damnedest existence ever enjoyed by mortal youth."

1900 Reads Edward Kingsbury's editorials in the New York *Sun*, George Ade's *Fables in Slang*, the work of Émile Zola. Discovers Theodore Dreiser's *Sister Carrie*. Works twelve hours a day, seven days a week reporting for the *Herald*, writing short stories, poetry, and articles for out-of-town newspapers. Suffers from chronic bronchitis. Travels to Jamaica to recover, June. Gets third raise in salary, to $14 a week, August. Assigned to cover presidential election between William Jennings Bryan and William McKinley, November.

1901 Salary increased to $18 a week, February 1. Covers fire that devastated Jacksonville, Florida, in May. Becomes drama critic of the *Herald*, September, and editor of *Sunday Herald*, October (holds both positions until October 1903). Becomes an advocate of the work of playwrights Shaw and Ibsen.

1903 Becomes city editor of the *Morning Herald* in October 1903. Publication of *Ventures Into Verse*, a book of poetry modeled on Kipling. Begins subscribing to a service that provides clippings mentioning him or his books. (The clippings will fill more than 100 volumes during his lifetime.)

1904 Fire destroys more than 140 acres and 1,500 buildings in downtown Baltimore, February 7–8. The *Herald* is printed in Washington and Philadelphia and does not miss a single issue. Mencken attends the Republican National Convention in Chicago, June 19–24, and the Democratic National Convention in St. Louis, July 5–11. Made city editor of the Baltimore *Evening Herald*, August 25. Saturday Night Club established, a group of musicians who meet regularly, with Mencken at the piano.

1905 Promoted to managing editor of the *Herald*. Publication of *George Bernard Shaw: His Plays*, first book-length study of Shaw.

1906 The *Herald* ceases publication, June 17. Becomes editor of the Baltimore *Sunday Sun*, July 25. Makes sweeping changes in typography and content; introduces poetry, music criticism by John Philip Sousa; runs a twenty-four-part report on the city's health concerns and serializes work by popular authors (such as George Ade's revised history of slang). Circulation climbs steadily.

1908 Publication of *The Philosophy of Friedrich Nietzsche*, first book in English on the philosopher. Meets Theodore Dreiser. First trip to Europe, March; he visits England and Germany. Meets George Jean Nathan, theater critic, in New York in May. Assumes additional duties as editorial writer for the *Sun* papers. Begins monthly book reviews for *The Smart Set*, November (to be continued until December 1923), and praises the work of James Branch Cabell, Twain, Joseph Conrad, and Dreiser among others.

1909 Works (in collaboration with Holger A. Koppel, Danish consul in Baltimore) on notes and introductions to a new edition of Ibsen's *A Doll's House* and *Little Eyolf*, to be published as part of *The Player's Ibsen*. The volumes are a commercial failure, and the series is discontinued.

1910 Baltimore *Evening Sun* established, April 18, with Mencken as an editor. Ghostwrites *What You Ought to Know About Your Baby* with Leonard Hirshberg. Publication of *The Gist of Nietzsche* and of *Men Versus the Man* (a debate in letters with socialist Robert Rives La Monte).

1911 Becomes close friends with Percival Pollard, American writer who widens Mencken's understanding of German culture. Begins "The Free Lance," a satirical daily column in the Baltimore *Evening Sun*, May 8, addressing issues of local public health, the plight of the city's African Americans, the women's movement, the American language, and the pretensions of moralists, and featuring humorous pieces including the kernel of what would become his fictitious history of the bathtub. "Before it had gone on a year," he later notes, "I knew precisely where I was heading."

1912 Travels to Europe in April, visiting England, France, Switzerland, and Germany. Covers the Democratic National Convention in Baltimore, June 28. Publication of *The Artist: A Drama Without Words*.

1913 Meets publisher Alfred A. Knopf. Covers suffragist parade in Washington, D.C., March 3.

1914 Meets and becomes close friends with James Gibbons Huneker, influential American critic. Sails to Europe with George Jean Nathan and Willard Huntington Wright,

April. Publication of *Europe After 8:15* with Nathan and Wright. First World War begins, July 28–August 4. Mencken and Nathan become coeditors of *The Smart Set*, September. Publishes material from writers including F. Scott Fitzgerald, Edgar Lee Masters, Sherwood Anderson, Willa Cather, Ben Hecht, Eugene O'Neill, and Ezra Pound, as well as British and European writers such as Alexei Tolstoy, Anatole France, D. H. Lawrence, and James Joyce. The book reviews by Mencken, as well as the theater criticism by Nathan, attract wide attention.

1915 German sinking of the British liner *Lusitania* on May 7 increases anti-German sentiment in the United States. First issue of *Parisienne* magazine, edited anonymously with Nathan, is launched (last issue under their editorship will be October 1916). Mencken's pro-German stance becomes dominant in his increasingly controversial "Free Lance" column, as he scrutinizes the role of the press and examines stories of deliberate propaganda. "The Free Lance" ends abruptly, without explanation, on October 23.

1916 Dreiser's novel *The "Genius"* is suppressed when passages are deemed obscene by the New York Society for the Prevention of Vice. Mencken solicits the support of the Author's League of America for a petition in defense of the book (the novel remains out of circulation until 1922). Launches *Saucy Stories*, which (from August to October) he edits anonymously with Nathan. Publication of *A Book of Burlesques* and *A Little Book in C Major*. Resigns editorship at the *Sun*. Sails to England, December 28; travels to Germany to report on World War I.

1917 Germany commences unrestricted submarine warfare against neutral shipping on February 1. Mencken departs Germany to cover the Liberal revolt in Cuba against the U.S.-supported government of President García Menocal. Arrives in Havana, March 5, and returns to the U.S. on March 14. Stops writing for the *Sun* with publication of last dispatch, March 29. The United States declares war on Germany, April 6. Espionage Act goes into effect June 15. Writes for the New York *Evening Mail* from June 18 to July 8, 1918. Mencken meets James Weldon Johnson, begins to focus attention on African American and cultural issues. "The Sahara of the Bozart," an indictment of southern culture, published in the New York *Evening*

Mail, November 13. "A Neglected Anniversary," Mencken's invented history of the bathtub, published in the New York *Evening Mail*, December 28. Publication of *A Book of Prefaces*, and of *Pistols for Two*, written with Nathan under the joint pseudonym "Owen Hatteras."

1918 The editor of the New York *Evening Mail*, Edward Rumley, is arrested July 8 over allegations that the paper received secret German government funding; control then passes to pro-war individuals and Mencken stops writing for it. (Mencken later reflects, "I stopped writing and believed I was done with newspaper work forever.") German language eliminated from Baltimore public elementary schools, July; anti-German feeling rampant. The Bureau of Investigation (later the FBI) opens a case file on Mencken; his mail is opened and he is watched by agents. Mencken's *Damn! A Book of Calumny* is published by his close friend, Broadway producer Philip Goodman, who also publishes *In Defense of Women* (later editions published by Knopf beginning in 1919). Germany signs armistice, November 11.

1919 Publication of *The American Language* (first edition quickly sells out) and *Prejudices: First Series*, which also proves successful. With *Sun* publishers Paul Patterson and Harry Black, Mencken helps develop plan for expanded national coverage and an independent approach. Attorney General Mitchell Palmer orders mass arrests of radicals and foreigners. Mencken becomes increasingly frustrated by his work at *The Smart Set*, telling a friend: "We live, not in a literary age, but in a fiercely political age."

1920 Begins series of regular Monday columns in the Baltimore *Evening Sun* (they continue until January 31, 1938), regularly denouncing interference with free speech and calling for civil rights for all Americans. Reads manuscript of *Main Street* by Sinclair Lewis and encourages its publication. With Nathan, launches *Black Mask*, a mystery magazine, April. Publication of *Prejudices: Second Series.* Publication of *Heliogabalus* and *The American Credo*, both written with Nathan. Publication of *The Anti-Christ* by Nietzsche, translated with an introduction by Mencken.

1921 Becomes contributing editor of *The Nation*, May (until December 1932). Covers the naval disarmament conference in Washington, D.C., November–December. Publication of the second edition of *The American Language*.

1922 Travels to England and Germany, August–October. Publication of *Prejudices: Third Series.*

1923 On May 8, while lecturing at Baltimore's Goucher College, he meets Sara Powell Haardt (born March 1, 1898, in Montgomery, Alabama), a fiction writer and member of the English faculty. Mencken solicits manuscripts from American writers for a new magazine focusing exclusively on American cultural and political themes, summer. Mencken and Nathan resign as coeditors of *The Smart Set*, December. Publication of the third edition of *The American Language.*

1924 First issue of *The American Mercury* is published in January with Mencken and Nathan as coeditors. Contributors will include Countee Cullen, James Weldon Johnson, W.E.B. Du Bois, Dorothy Parker, Sherwood Anderson, George Schuyler, as well as bricklayers, hoboes, bishops, senators, lawyers, American Indians, prisoners. Its layout, typeface, buoyant tone, and sections "Americana" (items culled from newspapers and magazines across the country) and "Profiles" (portraits written by well-known writers about well-known subjects) are widely imitated. Covers Republican National Convention in Cleveland, June 9–13, and Democratic National Convention in New York City, June 23–29. Writes columns for the Chicago *Tribune* (until January 29, 1928). Publication of *Prejudices: Fourth Series.*

1925 Tension between Nathan and Mencken increases, with Mencken insisting on more social and political commentary in *The American Mercury* and Nathan favoring an equal emphasis on literature. Nathan withdraws as coeditor of *The American Mercury* in July. Mencken travels to Dayton, Tennessee, in July to cover trial of John Scopes, high school teacher arrested for teaching theory of evolution in contravention of newly passed state law. Mother, Anna Abhau Mencken, dies 6 P.M. December 13 and is buried at Loudon Park Cemetery. Publication of *Americana 1925.* The first two books about Mencken are published (*H. L. Mencken* by Ernest Boyd and *The Man Mencken: A Biographical and Critical Survey* by Isaac Goldberg). Breaks friendship with Dreiser because of a series of misunderstandings, among them Dreiser's seeming lack of sympathy concerning the death of Mencken's mother and Dreiser's callous treatment of women.

1926 Walter Lippmann calls Mencken "the most powerful personal influence on this whole generation of educated people." Through the influence of the New England Watch and Ward Society, the April issue of *The American Mercury* is banned in Boston because of Herbert Asbury's short story "Hatrack"; Mencken courts arrest by personally selling a copy to the Society's secretary; a judge declares the story not obscene and dismisses the complaint. Mencken tours the American South and arrives in California, October. Father's cigar firm, August Mencken & Bro., managed by Uncle Henry, goes bankrupt. Publication of *Notes on Democracy*, *Prejudices: Fifth Series*, and *Americana, 1926*.

1927 Publication of *Prejudices: Sixth Series* and *Selected Prejudices*.

1928 Travels to Havana, Cuba, to cover Pan American Conference, January. Covers Republican National Convention, Kansas City, June 11–16, and Democratic National Convention, Houston, June 23–29. Travels with Al Smith on campaign tour, October 12–30. Publication of *Menckeniana: A Schimpflexicon*, a humorous collection of anti-Mencken invective that had appeared in newspapers and magazines across the country. Circulation of *The American Mercury* reaches its height of 84,000. Begins courting Sara Powell Haardt on a steadier basis.

1929 Sara Powell Haardt undergoes surgery for the removal of a tubercular kidney, July 6.

1930 Covers London Naval Conference, January–February. Announces secret engagement to Sara Powell Haardt to family members, April. Marries Sara Powell Haardt August 27 at St. Stephen the Martyr Episcopal Church, Baltimore; they travel to Canada on their honeymoon. Moves to new residence, 704 Cathedral Street, Baltimore. Publication of *Treatise on the Gods*. Book sells well, but stirs controversy because of passage in which Mencken describes Jews as "plausibly the most unpleasant race ever heard of." (Passage is deleted in later editions.) In newspaper interview he denies he is an anti-Semite: "I don't like religious Jews. I don't like religious Catholics and Protestants." Begins writing a diary.

1931 Writes a series of controversial columns against lynching of Matthew Williams in Salisbury, Maryland, on December 4, causing a boycott of Baltimore businesses and the *Sun* papers by residents of the Eastern Shore. *The Nation* recognizes Mencken for "distinguished journalism in the face of personal danger," December.

1932 Mencken sails to the West Indies with Sara, January 9. Covers Republican National Convention in Chicago, June 13–18, and Democratic National Convention in Chicago, June 26–July 2. Franklin D. Roosevelt elected President, November. Publication of *Making a President*. Continues suggesting authors and ideas for books to his publisher, Alfred Knopf; elected board member of Knopf, Inc.

1933 Mencken becomes increasingly critical of the New Deal, directing most of his criticism against the "quacks" of the Brain Trust rather than the President himself. Writes controversial columns against lynching of George Arnwood in Princess Anne on Maryland's Eastern Shore, October 18 (last lynching in Maryland). With Mencken's popularity at a low ebb, circulation of *The American Mercury* sinks to 28,329; Mencken resigns as editor with the December issue.

1934 Travels on a two-month cruise to the Mediterranean with Sara, January–March, and is fascinated by his visit with Jewish colonists in Palestine; his writing on the subject for the *Evening Sun* is privately printed in a book entitled *Eretz Israel*. Writes series of articles on American English for the New York *American*, July 9–May 20, 1935. Joins Board of Directors of the A. S. Abell Company, October 15. Resumes friendship with Theodore Dreiser. Speaks before the Gridiron Club in Washington, D.C., December 8; his address is mildly critical of the New Deal, but when it is Roosevelt's turn to speak, he turns Mencken's commentary on journalists against him by quoting a passage from *Prejudices: Sixth Series*. Publication of *Treatise on Right and Wrong*. Last article for *The Nation*, December 12.

1935 Testifies in favor of the Costigan-Wagner Anti-Lynching Bill at Senate hearing, February 14. (Bill is later blocked by Senate filibuster.) Wife Sara Haardt Mencken dies of tubercular meningitis, May 31. Edits a compilation of her work, *Southern Album*; travels to England with his brother August, June 15.

1936 Returns to his family home at 1524 Hollins Street, which he calls "as much a part of me as my two hands." Begins to organize his papers and family archives. Publishes "Three Years of Dr. Roosevelt," a scathing attack on the president, whom he compares to "a snake-oil vendor at a village carnival," in *The American Mercury*, March. Publication of "The Ordeal of a Philosopher" in *The New Yorker*, April 11, which is later used as a chapter in *Happy Days*. Covers Republican National Convention, Cleveland, June 8–13, and Democratic National Convention, Philadelphia, June 22–28, as well as convention in support of the Townsend Plan (Cleveland, July 14–20) and Union Party convention organized by Father Charles Coughlin (Cleveland, August 13–18). Travels with Republican nominee Alf Landon on his campaign tour, August–October. Publication of the fourth edition of *The American Language*.

1937 Vacations in Daytona Beach, Florida, with his brother August, January. Publication of *The Sunpapers of Baltimore*, written with Frank R. Kent, Gerald W. Johnson, and Hamilton Owens. Publication of *The Charlatanry of the Learned*, edited by Mencken and translated from the Latin by Francis Litz; the book is a satirical attack on academic pretension, written by Mencken's ancestor, Leipzig scholar Johann Burkhard Mencke (1674–1732).

1938 Alarmed by what he sees as the Roosevelt administration's mastery at setting the agenda with the press, Mencken writes publisher Paul Patterson that "we confront a high development of government propaganda," and at Patterson's request becomes temporary editor of the Baltimore *Evening Sun*, January 24–May 9. Writes "Sunday Articles" for the Baltimore *Sun*, May 16–February 2, 1941. Appointed chairman of the *Sunpapers*' committee to negotiate with the Newspaper Guild, summer. Travels to Germany, June–July; refrains from reporting on any of his observations. Writes column, "Help for the Jews," proposing the United States open its doors to German Jewish refugees fleeing Nazi persecution, November 27, 1938.

1939 Convinced that America's security would depend on its abstention from European conflict, Mencken becomes increasingly isolationist. In a speech given before the American Society of Newspaper Editors, on April 20, Mencken reminds his audience of government censorship in 1917 and warns that war will once again pose a threat to freedom of the press. Suffers a minor stroke, "generalized arteriosclerosis," July 31. Hitler invades Poland, September 1. England declares war on Germany, September 3. With his brother August, begins taking photographs of West Baltimore. Completes *Happy Days*, September 18.

1940 Covers Republican National Convention in Philadelphia, June 22–29, and Democratic National Convention in Chicago, July 13–19. Travels with Wendell Wilkie on his campaign tour, August 16–November 3. Publication of *Happy Days: 1880–1892*, first of a series of memoirs, January 22. Death of best friend, Raymond Pearl, biometrician at the Johns Hopkins University School of Medicine.

1941 Resigns from the *Sun* papers, January 16, because of publishers' unease with his anti-Roosevelt and anti-war views. Begins writing memoir on his journalism career, "Thirty-Five Years of Newspaper Work" (published in 1994). Publication of *Newspaper Days: 1899–1906*, October 20, 1941. From 1941 to 1943 *The New Yorker* publishes Mencken's series "Days of Innocence," later revised and published as chapters in *Newspaper Days* and *Heathen Days.* Travels to Havana, April. Helps several Jewish refugees find asylum in the United States; pleads their case in person to the United States State Department, August 26. Japanese attack on Pearl Harbor brings the United States into war, December 7.

1942 Begins writing memoir that focuses on his literary career, "My Life as Author and Editor"; works on it periodically until 1948 (published 1993). Publication of *A New Dictionary of Quotations.*

1943 Testifies in October on behalf of *Esquire* magazine, which had lost its mailing privileges on charges of obscenity. Publication of *Heathen Days: 1890–1936*, March 1, published as an Armed Services Edition in September. Begins compiling lengthy typescripts of "Additions, Corrections, and Explanatory Notes" for each of the *Days* books.

1944 Publication of Armed Services Edition of *Happy Days*, February, which becomes a GI favorite. "That is the difference between a soldier and a civilian," remarks Mencken. "The letters you get from civilians are from those who don't like your books."

1945 Publication of *The American Language: Supplement I.* The end of World War II officially declared September 2. In the aftermath of Allied bombing, which had appalled him,

Mencken sends packages of food, shoes, and other necessities to friends in Berlin, copies of his books to correspondents in Japan. Theodore Dreiser dies, December 28.

1946 Publication of *Christmas Story*, a satirical account of a holiday feast among the homeless of Baltimore, and how the organizers impose their Puritanical morality among the crowd.

1947 Buoyed by news of Truman's plans to help the economic recovery of Europe, March; argues for immediate economic rehabilitation of Germany. In August suffers a minor stroke but recovers after a few days. The autobiographical trilogy is published in one volume as *The Days of H. L. Mencken*. Interviewed by Edgar Kemler and William Manchester, who are separately writing biographies of Mencken.

1948 Vacations in Florida with brother August, February. Rejoins *Sun* staff to cover Republican Party Convention, June 19–22; covers Democratic National Convention, July 10–15, and Progressive Party Convention, July 23–26, all held in Philadelphia. Revival of interest in Mencken's life and work demonstrated by cover story in *Newsweek* magazine, April 5. Records an interview for the Library of Congress, June 30. Publication of *The American Language, Supplement II*. Last public appearance, speaking before the American Philosophical Society, November 4. Writes series of articles for the *Sun*, August 1–November 9. Publication of last column, arguing against segregation, November 9. Suffers a massive stroke that prevents any further reading or writing for the remainder of his life, November 23. (In his remaining years he is cared for largely by his younger brother August.)

1949 Publication of *A Mencken Chrestomathy*, Mencken's selection from his writings. Spends remaining years helping his secretary organize his papers for posterity, well over 100,000 letters, as well as original manuscripts, memoirs, and books, dedicating the bulk of the collection to the Enoch Pratt Free Library, as well as to the New York Public Library and Dartmouth.

1950 Suffers heart attack, October 12. Members of the Saturday Night Club agree in December to disband permanently.

Spends five months in hospital, before he is discharged in March 1951.

1955 *Inherit the Wind*, play about the Scopes Trial by Jerome Lawrence and Robert E. Lee, featuring a character based on Mencken, opens in April. On Mencken's 75th birthday, Alistair Cooke's edition of *The Vintage Mencken* is published, selling out in two days. Secretary Rosalind Lorhfinck comes across an unpublished manuscript written by Mencken before his 1948 stroke (published posthumously the following year as *Minority Report: H. L. Mencken's Notebooks*).

1956 Dies in his sleep from a coronary occlusion, between 4 and 5 A.M. on January 29, leaving an estate valued at $300,000. Three-fourths of his estate is willed to the Enoch Pratt Free Library. He is cremated, and his ashes are interred at Loudon Park Cemetery, in West Baltimore, January 31.

Note on the Texts

This volume contains the complete texts of H. L. Mencken's *Prejudices: Fourth Series* (1924), *Prejudices: Fifth Series* (1926), and *Prejudices: Sixth Series* (1927). A Library of America companion volume, *Prejudices: The First, Second, and Third Series*, presents the complete contents of the three previous *Prejudices*, published in 1919, 1920, and 1922. The texts of the *Prejudices* have been taken from corrected later printings of the first editions of each collection, all published in New York by Alfred A. Knopf.

Mencken's relationship with Knopf was a congenial one, and he exercised an exceptional degree of control over the form in which his works appeared. He was also a careful proofreader of his own work, and encouraged Knopf (in a letter of March 24, 1921, noting some typographical errors in the first printing of *Prejudices: Second Series*), to "correct all such errors whenever the opportunity offers. Nothing looks worse than a dirty book. The English reviewers in particular, are very waspish about typographical errors." In the case of all of his *Prejudices*, Mencken's corrections to his proofs arrived too late to be incorporated into the first Knopf printings but were made in later printings. The present volume prints the texts of those printings that contain Mencken's final corrections: for *Prejudices: Fourth Series*, the third trade printing (issued in November 1924), for *Prejudices: Fifth Series*, the second trade printing (issued in December 1926), and for *Prejudices: Sixth Series*, the second state of a second limited printing (issued at an undetermined date, but soon after the October 1927 first printing, with Mencken's errata finally incorporated). All of Mencken's *Prejudices* contain material originally published in periodicals—including the Baltimore *Sun* papers, the *Smart Set*, and the *American Mercury*—and then extensively revised when he assembled his books. For a more detailed account of the periodical publication history of individual pieces in the *Prejudices*, see S. T. Joshi, *H. L. Mencken: An Annotated Bibliography* (Lanham, Maryland: Scarecrow Press, 2009).

This volume presents the texts of the printings and typescript chosen for inclusion, but it does not attempt to reproduce nontextual features of their typographic design. The texts are printed without change, except for the correction of typographical errors. Spelling, punctuation, and capitalization may be expressive features, and they are not altered, even when inconsistent or irregular. The following is a list of typographical errors corrected, cited by page and line number:

6.26, *non-sequiturs*; 31.40, beleagured; 33.9, *leit-motif*; 36.38, jucier; 70.33, themometer; 83.11, days; 105.7, statues; 143.22, that the; 150.27, Yoeman; 164.31, made a; 172.15, Brook; 174.32, Stationary; 184.26, *Ladies'*; 201.2, possesion; 212.17, Ashforth.; 219.33, as such; 227.27, T. T; 242.16, scioist; 247.36, white; 253.19, Browne, 257.5, Sinclair,; 260.28, extra-plaint; 275.29, Dr. Martin; 279.34, Apolliñaire's; 284.32, politics, 287.33, *legion*; 287.34, LL. D; 293.12, it it; 309. 6, Antonía,"; 309.6, "Hucklebery; 314.5, *Ladies'*; 314.33, Enforcemnt.; 323.9, venrated; 326.25, not they; 327.20, word; 332.39, resistence; 341.2, Gary,; 343.6, anthor; 391.7, spokesmen; 405.1, Scopes,; 417.1, 16; 418.17, Eric; 426.19, Calydon!"; 432.33, Cooglar,; 443.21, Poteet; 443.28, Sullen,; 445.23, reverence or; 359.10, Karlruhe; 468.8, months; 468.19, dietition; 492.33, ambulent; 494.31, treatment involved; 498.23, maudlingly.

Notes

In the notes below, the reference numbers denote page and line of this volume (the line count includes headings). No note is made for material included in standard desk-reference books. Quotations from Shakespeare are keyed to *The Riverside Shakespeare*, ed. G. Blakemore Evans (Boston: Houghton Mifflin, 1974). Biographical information beyond that included in the Chronology may be found in Marion Elizabeth Rodgers, *Mencken: The American Iconoclast* (Oxford, New York: Oxford University Press, 2005); Marion Elizabeth Rodgers, editor, *Mencken and Sara: A Life in Letters* (New York: McGraw-Hill, 1987); Marion Elizabeth Rodgers, editor, *The Impossible H. L. Mencken: A Selection of His Best Newspaper Stories* (New York: Anchor/Doubleday, 1991); Guy J. Forgue, editor, *Letters of H. L. Mencken* (New York: Knopf, 1961); Carl Bode, editor, *The New Mencken Letters* (New York: Dial Press, 1977); Thomas P. Riggio, editor, *Dreiser-Mencken Letters: The Correspondence of Theodore Dreiser and H. L. Mencken* (Philadelphia: University of Pennsylvania Press, 1986); Edward A. Martin, editor, *In Defense of Marion: The Love Letters of Marion Bloom and H. L. Mencken* (Athens: University of Georgia Press, 1996); Carl Bode, *Mencken* (Carbondale: Southern Illinois University Press, 1969); *Charles Scruggs, The Sage in Harlem: H. L. Mencken and the Black Writers of the 1920s* (Baltimore: Johns Hopkins University Press, 1984); Vincent Fitzpatrick, *H. L. Mencken* (Macon: Mercer University Press, 2004); Fred Hobson, *Mencken: A Life* (New York: Random House, 1994); William Manchester, *Disturber of the Peace: The Life of H. L. Mencken* (Amherst: University of Massachusetts Press, 1986); Terry Teachout, *The Skeptic: A Life of H. L. Mencken* (New York: HarperCollins, 2002); Charles A. Fecher, *Mencken: A Study of His Thought* (New York: Alfred A. Knopf, 1978); Richard J. Schrader, *H. L. Mencken: A Descriptive Bibliography* (Pittsburgh: University of Pittsburgh Press, 1998); and S. T. Joshi, *H. L. Mencken: An Annotated Bibliography* (Lanham, Maryland: Scarecrow Press, 2009).

PREJUDICES: FOURTH SERIES

3.4 William Crary Brownell] American literary critic (1851–1928), author of *American Prose Masters* (1909), *Standards* (1917), *The Genius of Style* (1924), and other books.

3.7 *Gelehrte*] Scholars.

3.12 George Creel] American journalist and publicity director (1876–1953), chairman of the Committee of Public Information (1917–19), created by Woodrow Wilson as a propaganda organization to enlist support for American participation entry in World War I. Thousands of paintings, cartoons, speeches, posters, pamphlets, press releases, news stories, and movies were created, promoting the President's war message.

3.13 Newell Dwight Hillis] Congregationalist clergyman (1858–1929), pastor of the Plymouth Congregational Church in Brooklyn, New York, from 1899 to 1924. He led a campaign against immorality in Broadway plays and subsequently wrote a number of books decrying alleged German atrocities in World War I.

3.14 James M. Beck] James Montgomery Beck (1861–1936), lawyer, Solicitor General of the United States (1921–1925), and member of the U.S. House of Representatives (1927–1934); author of *War and Humanity* (1916).

3.14 A. Mitchell Palmer] American statesman (1872–1936), U.S. attorney general, 1919–21. In November 1919 he initiated a series of raids directed against members of radical groups and others suspected of subversive activities; thousands were arrested, and ultimately 556 individuals were deported.

3.19 *os calcis*] Heel bone.

4.26 *vibrissae*] Thick hairs.

4.28 Doughty of Texas] Walter Francis Doughty (1873–1931), Texas state superintendent of public instruction, 1913–19.

4.35 Beers, of Yale] Henry Augustin Beers (1847–1926), professor of English literature at Yale, 1871–1926; author of studies of English romanticism.

4.38–39 Science and Health] *Science and Health with Key to the Scriptures* (1875) by Mary Baker Eddy (1821–1910), founder of the Christian Science movement.

4.40 Marie C. Stopes] Marie Carmichael Stopes (1880–1958), Scottish campaigner for women's rights and advocate of birth control. She was the author of *Married Love* (1918) and *Wise Parenthood* (1918).

5.4 Waldo Frank] American novelist and critic (1889–1967), founder and editor of the short-lived but influential magazine *The Seven Arts* (1916–17). His critical and travel writings included *Our America* (1919), *Salvos* (1924), *Virgin Spain* (1926), and *South American Journey* (1943).

5.7 *S4N*] Monthly magazine edited by Norman Fitts, published 1919–25; its contributors included Kenneth Burke, Waldo Frank, Hart Crane, E. E. Cummings, and others.

6.14 Brander Matthews] American scholar and playwright (1852–1929), known for his studies of dramatic literature including *The Development of the*

Drama (1904), *Shakspere as a Playwright* (1913), *A Book About the Theater* (1916), and *Principles of Playmaking* (1919).

6.15 Sherman] Stuart P. Sherman (1881–1926), literary critic and professor at the University of Illinois (1907–24), author of *Americans* (1922) and *The Genius of America* (1923).

6.16 Erskine] John Erskine (1879–1951), English professor at Columbia University, 1909–37; author of both scholarly and popular works, including the bestseller *The Private Life of Helen of Troy* (1925).

6.16 Boynton] Percy Holmes Boynton (1875–1946), professor of English at the University of Chicago, author of *American Poetry* (1918), *Some Contemporary Americans* (1924), *The Challenge of Modern Criticism* (1931), and other works.

6.33 Ernest Boyd] Ernest Augustus Boyd (1887–1946), Irish-born critic, essayist, and translator from French and German. He settled permanently in the United States in 1920. His books included *Contemporary Drama of Ireland* (1917) and *Appreciations and Depreciations* (1918). He published a study of Mencken in 1925.

7.7 Donald G. Mitchell] Donald Grant Mitchell (1822–1908), American author popularly known as Ik Marvel. His books included *Reveries of a Bachelor* (1850) and *Dream Life* (1851).

7.8 N. P. Willis] Nathaniel Parker Willis (1806–1867), poet and journalist. Founded the *American Monthly* (1829–31) in Boston and later became a prolific reporter on social matters in the U.S. and abroad for the *New-York Mirror.* His journalism was collected in numerous volumes such as *Pencillings by the Way* (1835) and *Dashes at Life with a Free Pencil* (1845).

7.8 J. G. Holland] Josiah Gilbert Holland (1819–1881), journalist and poet, editor of *Scribner's Monthly* and author of *Timothy Titcomb's Letters to Young People, Single and Married* (1858), *The Marble Prophecy* (1872), and *The Puritan's Guest* (1881).

7.8 Charles Dudley Warner] Essayist, novelist, and popular lecturer (1829–1900), author of *My Summer in a Garden* (1871), *My Winter on the Nile* (1876), *Fashions in Literature* (1902), and other works; co-author with Mark Twain of *The Gilded Age* (1873).

7.8–9 Mrs. Sigourney] Lydia Huntley Sigourney (1791–1865), prolific poet and essayist known abroad as "the American Hemans"; her collections included *Moral Pieces in Prose and Verse* (1815), *Traits of the Aborigines* (1822), and *The Voice of Flowers* (1846).

7.9 the Sweet Singer of Michigan] Julia A. Moore (1847–1920), author of *The Sentimental Song Book* (1876) and *A Few Choice Word to the Public* (1878). Her poetry was widely mocked in the press for its maudlin and inept character; she was satirized by Mark Twain as Emmeline Grangerford in *Adventures of Huckleberry Finn* (1885) and alluded to in *Following the Equator* (1897).

7.18–19 Bayard Taylor] Poet and travel writer (1825–1878), author of *Poems of the Orient* (1854), *Poems of Home and Travel* (1855), and such travel books as *Eldorado* (1850), *A Journey to Central Africa* (1854), and *Byways of Europe* (1869). His translation of *Faust* was published in two volumes, 1870–71.

7.31 Brandes] Georg Morris Cohen Brandes (1872–1927), preeminent Danish critic and scholar of his time, a leading proponent of realism, and a prolific commentator on literature, politics, religion, and philosophy. He was the author of many books including *Main Currents in the Literature of the Nineteenth Century* (1872–75) and monographs on Kierkegaard, Ibsen, Nietzsche, and Goethe, among others.

8.9 Griswold] Rufus Griswold (1815–1857), journalist, editor of literary anthologies including *The Poets and Poetry of America* (1842) and *The Female Poets of America* (1849). He quarreled with Edgar Allan Poe and, as Poe's literary executor, published a defamatory biography that had lingering influence.

8.19 Phelps of Yale] William Lyon Phelps (1865–1943), literary scholar and professor of English at Yale, who became popular as lecturer and columnist. Author of *Essays on Modern Novelists* (1910), *The Advance of the English Novel* (1916), and other works.

8.22 Van Wyck Brooks' "The Ordeal of Mark Twain"] Study (1920) by the critic and biographer (1886–1963).

8.29 Huneker] James Gibbons Huneker (1857–1921), critic of literature, music, and art, a friend of Mencken. He was founder of the magazine *M'lle New York* and musical editor of the New York *Sun*. His many books include *Chopin: The Man and His Music* (1900), *Iconoclasts, a Book of Dramatists* (1905), *Egoists: A Book of Supermen* (1909), *Ivory Apes and Peacocks* (1915), the memoirs *Old Fogy* (1913) and *Steeplejack* (1920), and the novel *Painted Veils* (1920).

8.30–31 Henry van Dyke] American clergyman, educator, and author (1852–1933), a prolific poet.

10.4 Madison Grant] Anthropologist and eugenicist (1865–1937), a campaigner for immigration restriction and antimiscegenation laws. His 1916 book *The Passing of the Great Race* argued for the superiority of the "Nordic" race and called for the segregation of other ethnic groups.

10.4 Gertrude Atherton] San Francisco-born novelist (1857–1948), author of *The Californians* (1898), *The Conqueror* (1902), *Rezánov* (1906), and *Black Oxen* (1923).

17.21 Omdurman] An Anglo-Egyptian army commanded by Sir Herbert

Kitchener defeated the Mahdist forces in the Sudan at Omdurman on September 2, 1898, killing almost 10,000 Sudanese, while losing only 47 men.

17.21 Manila Bay] At the Battle of Manila Bay (May 1, 1898), the American squadron sank or disabled all ten of the Spanish ships it faced without suffering any damage itself.

18.1 Tannenberg] The Russian 2nd Army was almost completely destroyed by the Germans at the Battle of Tannenberg (August 26–31, 1914), with 50,000 men killed or wounded and 92,000 Russians taken prisoner.

18.5 Verdun] In 1916 the French successfully defended the town of Verdun against a series of German offensives that began on February 21 and lasted until mid-July. The battle continued until December 18, 1916, as the French regained some of the ground they had earlier lost. In the ten months of fighting, 162,000 French and 143,000 German soldiers were killed.

18.15 the Turks . . . in 1922] The Turks decisively defeated the Greek army in Anatolia in 1922.

21.35 Edgar Guest] British-born American poet (1881–1959) whose light and sentimental verse was immensely popular. His collections included *A Heap o' Livin'* (1916), *Just Folks* (1917), and *When Day Is Done* (1921).

21.35 Frank Crane] American Methodist clergyman (1861–1928) whose syndicated inspirational newspaper column appeared across the country from 1909–1928. His writings were collected in ten volumes in *Four-Minute Essays* (1919).

22.6 *Lumbricus terrestris*] Earthworm.

23.10–11 *Bos taurus*] Cow.

24.7–8 *Laborantem agricolam oportet primum de fructibus percipere*] "The husbandman that laboureth must be first partaker of the fruits": 2 Timothy 2:6.

24.10–11 Mesmers] Franz Anton Mesmer (1734–1815), Austrian physician who induced trance states in patients through the power of what he called "animal magnetism."

24.11 Grimaldis] Joseph Grimaldi (1778–1837), famous English clown.

28.8 E. W. Howe] Edgar Watson Howe (1853–1937), Indiana journalist, editor and owner of *E. W. Howe's Monthly* (1911–1937), and author of *The Story of a Country Town* (1883), a realistic treatment of life in the Midwest.

29.36 Volstead Act] The National Prohibition Act of 1919, also known as the Volstead Act after its sponsor, U.S. Representative Andrew John Volstead (1860–1947; R-Minn, 1903–1923).

30.10 Mann Act] The White-Slave Traffic Act of 1910 prohibited the transportation of females across state lines for "immoral purposes." It was named after its sponsor, James Robert Mann (1856–1922), Republican congressman from Illinois.

31.11 Comstock Act] Law passed by Congress in 1873 which made it illegal to mail, transport, or deliver "obscene, lewd, or lascivious" information. It was named for Anthony Comstock (1844–1915), U.S. Postal Inspector who founded the New York Society for the Suppression of Vice.

32.13 *Eoanthropus*] Dawn Man.

32.36 *Sus scrofa*] Wild boar.

32.37 *Mephitis mephitis*] Skunk.

33.10 Bleases] Coleman Livingston Blease (1868–1942), governor of South Carolina (1911–15) and U.S. senator (1925–1931) known for his appeals to extreme populism and white supremacy.

36.20 Haeckel] Ernst Heinrich Haeckel (1834–1919), German biologist and philosopher who published many works helping to popularize evolutionary theory. His books include *The Riddle of the Universe* (1901), *Artforms of Nature* (1904), and *The History of Creation* (1914). He was the author of the subsequently contested formulation that "ontogeny recapitulates phylogeny," summarized here by Mencken as "the history of the individual rehearses the history of the species."

36.36–37 Richard Mansfield] Richard Mansfield (1854–1907), American actor, educated in England, who had his first major American success in the role of the brutal roué Baron Chevrial in A. M. Palmer's production *A Parisian Romance* (1883).

36.37 Schiller's play] *Don Carlos* (1787), historical tragedy by Johann Christoph Friedrich von Schiller.

38.23–24 the Henty books] Boy's historical adventure stories by the British novelist George Alfred Henty (1832–1902), including *Under Drake's Flag* (1883), *With Clive in India* (1884), and *With Wolfe in Canada* (1887).

45.5 *Biertisch*] Beer table.

49.9 Espionage Act] The Espionage Act, passed on June 15, 1917, included among its provisions severe penalties (up to $10,000 fine and twenty years' imprisonment) for persons found guilty of interfering with the draft or encouraging disloyalty to the United States. More than 1,500 persons were arrested for violating the act, including labor leader Eugene Debs and Socialist congressman Victor Berger, and several newspapers were barred from the mails, among them the *New York Call* and *Milwaukee Leader*.

50.5 Anti-Saloon League] Organization, founded in Ohio in 1893, that played a major role in lobbying for Prohibition.

51.9 Liberty Loan] One of a series of five bond issues floated by the U.S. Treasury Department that helped finance World War I.

51.22 the Chicago Socialist trials] On September 5, 1917, a raid was conducted by federal authorities on the national headquarters of the American Socialist Party in Chicago. Among those indicted under the provisions of the Espionage Act was Victor L. Berger, a congressman from Wisconsin. On February 20, 1919, Berger and four other members of the party were sentenced to twenty years in prison; their conviction was overturned by the Supreme Court on January 31, 1921.

51.26 Burleson] Albert S. Burleson (1863–1937), who served as U.S. postmaster general from 1913–21. During World War I he vigorously enforced the Espionage Act by attempting to bar radical and anti-war materials from the mails.

51.27 Hand, J.] In July 1917 federal district judge Billings Learned Hand (1872–1961) ruled in New York that *The Masses* should not be barred from the mail under the Espionage Act.

51.27 Rose, J.] John Carter Rose (1861–1927) was a federal district judge in Maryland, 1910–22, and a federal circuit judge, 1922–27.

52.22 judge who sentenced Debs] David C. Westenhaver (1865–1928), U. S. Federal judge in Cleveland, Ohio sentenced Socialist labor leader Eugene V. Debs (1855–1926) to ten years in prison for violating the Espionage Act, on the basis of a speech Debs made on June 16, 1918, in Canton, Ohio, in opposition to World War I. His sentence was commuted by President Harding in 1921.

61.40 "Way Down East"] Enormously successful play by Lottie Blair Parker, first produced by Florenz Ziegfeld in 1898.

61.40 Ben Hur] Dramatization by William W. Young, first produced in 1899, of Lew Wallace's novel *Ben-Hur: A Tale of the Christ* (1880).

62.4 Char-Freitag music] The Good Friday music in act 3, scene 1 of Richard Wagner's opera *Parsifal* (1882).

63.23 *Stammhalter*] Ancestor.

67.11 *Cavia Cobaya*] Guinea pig.

67.12–13 Hey-Rub-a-Dub-Dub] Essay (1918) by Theodore Dreiser, submitted to Mencken at *The Smart Set* but rejected.

67.29–30 Helmuth von Moltke] German field marshal (1800–1891), chief of staff of the Prussian army, 1857–87, during successful wars against Denmark (1864), Austria (1866), and France (1870–71).

67.35 Shonts, Yerkes, or Jim Fisk] Theodore P. Shonts (1856–1919), chairman of the Second Isthmian Canal Commission (1905–19) and president of the Interborough Rapid Transit Co., New York City (1907–19); Charles E. Yerkes (1839–1905), financier, model for the protagonist of Dreiser's novels *The Financier* and *The Titan*; James Fisk (1834–1872), stock-market speculator.

69.32 I.W.W.] Industrial Workers of the World, popularly known as "Wobblies," revolutionary international labor union founded in Chicago in 1905.

72.20 Babbitt] Conformist, middle-class booster, from George F. Babbitt, the protagonist of Sinclair Lewis's 1922 novel *Babbitt.*

72.29 *Katzenjammer*] Hangover.

73.7 Bishop Manning] William Thomas Manning (1866–1949), Episcopal bishop of New York, 1921–46.

73.7 John Roach Straton] American Baptist clergyman (1875–1929) who upheld fundamentalist and anti-evolutionist tenets in a series of debates with Charles Francis Potter, 1923–24, and published his remarks in *The Famous New York Fundamentalist Modernist Debates: The Orthodox Side* (1925). He led anti-Catholic opposition to the presidential candidacy of Al Smith.

77.4 Bela Kun] Béla Kun, Hungarian revolutionary and politician (1886–1938), founder (1918) of the Hungarian Communist Party and leader (March–August 1919) of the short-lived Hungarian Soviet Republic. Kun fled to Soviet Russia in 1920 and became a prominent figure in the Comintern. He was arrested in June 1937 during the Great Purge and shot in August 1938.

80.15 Henry H. Rogers] American financier and Standard Oil executive (1840–1909) who helped save Twain from financial ruin.

82.7 Harrison Anti-Narcotic Act] The Harrison Anti-Narcotic Act of 1914 imposed registration and record-keeping requirements to control the distribution of opiates and cocaine.

82.26 Joaquin Miller] Pseudonym of Cincinnatus Heine Miller (1837–1913), American poet and essayist, author of *Song of the Sierras* (1871).

84.2 *Totentanz*] Dance of the Dead.

91.6 Hansa towns] Refers to the Hanseatic League, a trade monopoly exercised by collusion between cities and guilds on Europe's northern coast.

92.21 Nick Carter and Old Sleuth] Dime novel detective heroes. Nick Carter first appeared in *The Old Detective's Pupil* (1886) and was then featured in his own magazine, *Nick Carter Weekly*; many of his adventures were first-person narratives published under the pseudonym Nick Carter. Old Sleuth, created by Harlan Halsey, made his first appearance in *Fireside Companion* in 1872, and later was featured in *Old Sleuth Library.*

93.12–13 Ned Buntline] Pseudonym of Edward Zane Carroll Judson (1823–1886), publisher and author of dime novels, among them those popularizing the exploits of "Buffalo Bill" Cody.

95.34 Anthony Comstock] See note 31.11.

98.40 *Todsäufer*] In *Happy Days* (1940), Mencken wrote: "A *Todsäufer* (literally, dead-drinker) was, and is a sort of brewer's customers' man. He is commonly called a collector, but his duties go far beyond collecting the bills owed to breweries by saloonkeepers. He is supposed to stand a general treat in the bar whenever he calls, to go to all weddings, birthday parties and funerals in the families of saloonkeepers, and to cultivate their wives and children with frequent presents . . . He is also one of the brewery's political agents, and must handle all the license difficulties of his clients."

99.13 Nicholas Murray Butler] American educator and diplomat (1862–1947), president of Columbia University, 1902–45, and president of the Carnegie Endowment for International Peace, 1925–45. He was active in various international peace conferences in the years preceding World War I.

103.9 *wie Gott im Frankreich*] *Leben wie Gott in Frankreich*: to live like a king.

106.12 Mr. Fall] Albert B. Fall (1861–1944), U.S. secretary of the interior, 1921–3. He resigned his office when it was disclosed that he had accepted bribes to transfer naval oil reserves (including the Teapot Dome reserve in Wyoming) to private oil operators in exchange for loans and without competitive bidding. Fall was convicted in 1929, and served a year in prison.

107.29 Denby, Secretary of the Navy] Edwin Denby (1870–1929), U. S. secretary of the navy, 1921–24), advised President Harding to transfer the administration of naval oil reserves (including those at Teapot Dome, Wyoming) to the Department of the Interior. Although not accused of corruption, Denby resigned on March 10, 1924.

108.3–4 Czolgosz] Leon Czolgosz (1873–1901), Detroit-born anarchist and assassin of President William McKinley.

109.40 Mr. Daugherty] Harry M. Daugherty (1860–1941), Republican party boss and U.S. attorney general under President Harding. He resigned in 1924 after coming under investigation for a kickback scheme, although he was eventually acquitted at trial.

116.2 *Veritas Odium Parit*] Truth begets hatred.

116.6 *et cognoscetis veritatem, et veritas liberabit vos*] And ye shall know the truth, and the truth shall make you free (John 8:32).

118.20 Lake Mohonk Conference] The Lake Mohonk Conference for International Arbitration, founded by Albert K. Smiley in 1895 to support the establishment of an international court. The annual conference took place in Lake Mohonk, New York from 1895 to 1916.

119.31–32 James Anthony Froude] English historian (1818–1894), author of *History of England from the Fall of Wolsey to the Defeat of the Spanish Armada* (1856–70), and biographer of Thomas Carlyle. His *The Knights Templars: Their Rise and Demise* was published in 1886.

120.5–6 *Schnorrer* and *Meshulachim*] Scroungers and charity collectors (sometimes perceived as fraudulent).

123.17 William McDougall] (1871–1938), professor of psychology at Harvard; he was interested in psychical research and eugenics, and diverged from orthodox Darwinian theory. He was the author of *The Group Mind* (1920).

133.15 Burns] William J. Burns (1861–1932), director of the Bureau of Investigation, 1921–24.

134.11 Stinnes] Hugo Stinnes (1870–1924), German industrialist and politician.

135.10–11 E. L. Godkin] Edwin Lawrence Godkin (1831–1902), founder and editor of *The Nation.*

135.11 Charles J. Bonaparte] Charles Joseph Bonaparte (1851–1921) served as Theodore Roosevelt's secretary of the navy (1905–1906) and U.S. attorney general (1906–09), in which capacity he founded the Bureau of Investigation.

136.26 Judge Gary] Elbert Henry Gary (1846–1927), president of U.S. Steel, 1901–27. Having served two terms as a county judge, 1884–92, he was commonly known as "Judge Gary."

141.37 "Atalanta in Calydon"] Verse drama (1865) by Algernon Charles Swinburne.

142.29–30 "Geschichten aus dem Wiener Wald"] *Tales from the Vienna Woods.*

146.20 Cosima Liszt-von Bülow] Cosima Wagner (1837–1930), daughter of Franz Liszt. Her first marriage to Hans von Bülow ended in divorce in 1869; she married Richard Wagner in 1870.

150.20 Admiral Gherardi] Rear Admiral Bancroft Gherardi (1832–1903).

150.23 Fighting Bob Evans] Robert Dunglison Evans (1846–1912), American naval officer.

150.23 Lillian Russell] American actress and singer (1861–1922), who became a star in the 1880s and retired from the stage in 1919.

150.25 Sampson-Schley controversy] The controversy involved credit for the American naval victory at the Battle of Santiago in July 1898; William T. Sampson was technically in command, but Commander Winfield S. Schley received popular credit for the victory.

150.29 Amos Rusie] Major League Baseball pitcher (1871–1942), known as the Hoosier Thunderbolt.

150.31 Admiral Sims] Rear Admiral William S. Sims (1858–1936).

151.27 Josephus Daniels] American journalist (1862–1948) and U. S. secretary of the navy, 1913–21.

153.14 Dwight L. Moody] American evangelist (1837–1899).

159.29 *Omnis homo mendax*] All men are liars.

168.1 Fergusson's "Capitol Hill,"] Novel (1923) by Harvey Fergusson (1890–1971), drawing on his experiences as a Washington reporter during the Taft and Wilson administrations.

168.12–13 Hamilton Wright Mabie] American essayist and lecturer (1846–1916), editor of the Christian magazine *The Outlook*; his books included *Books and Culture* (1896), *The Life of the Spirit* (1899), and *American Ideals, Character and Life* (1913).

168.18 Harriet Monroe] American poet (1860–1936), who founded *Poetry: A Magazine of Verse* in 1912, and edited it until her death. Contributors under her editorship included Ezra Pound, Wallace Stevens, Robert Frost, T. S. Eliot, Marianne Moore, Hart Crane, and many other major figures.

168.22 Augustus Thomas] Playwright (1857–1934) known for his use of American backgrounds in such plays as *Alabama* (1891), *In Mizzoura* (1893), *The Witching Hour* (1907), and *The Copperhead* (1918).

168.22–23 David Belasco] Playwright and theater producer (1853–1931), involved in more than a hundred Broadway productions. As a producer he was notable for technical advances in lighting and stage design. His plays included *Madame Butterfly* (1900) and *The Girl of the Golden West* (1905).

168.23 Clyde Fitch] Playwright (1865–1909) whose successes included *Barbara Frietchie* (1899), *The Climbers* (1901), and *Captain Jinks of the Horse Marines* (1901).

168.24 Hergesheimer] Joseph Hergesheimer (1880–1954), novelist whose many books, widely popular and in their time often critically acclaimed, included *The Three Black Pennys* (1917), *Java Head* (1919), and *Cytherea* (1922). He was a close friend of Mencken.

168.25 Cabell] James Branch Cabell (1878–1958), novelist whose works often explored a world of medieval fantasy. His books included *The Cream of the Jest* (1917), *Jurgen* (1919), which became a bestseller when it was denounced for obscenity, *Figures of Earth* (1921), and *The High Place* (1923).

168.28 Richard Harding Davis] Journalist and novelist (1864–1916). His novels included *Soldiers of Fortune* (1897); his war reporting was collected in many volumes including *Cuba in War Time* (1897), *The Cuban and Porto Rican Campaigns* (1898), *With Both Armies in South Africa* (1900), and *Notes of a War Correspondent* (1910).

168.28–29 Robert W. Chambers] Artist and bestselling author (1865–1933), best remembered for *The King in Yellow* (1895).

168.29 James Lane Allen] Novelist (1849–1925) best known for his local color stories set in Kentucky, including *A Kentucky Cardinal* (1894), *The Choir Invisible* (1897), and *The Mettle of the Pasture* (1903).

168.34 Paul Elmer More] Critic and philosopher (1864–1937) associated with the New Humanist movement. His *Shelburne Essays* were published in fourteen volumes (1904–36), and his other works included *Platonism* (1917), *The Religion of Plato* (1921), and *The Christ of the New Testament* (1924).

169.2 Hamlin Garland] Author (1860–1940) of fiction, memoirs, and poems, known for his realistic studies of farm life in Wisconsin. His early stories, collected in *Main-Travelled Roads* (1891) and *Boy Life on the Prairie* (1899), were followed by the autobiographies *A Son of the Middle Border* (1917) and *A Daughter of the Middle Border* (1921).

169.5 Mary Roberts Rinehart] Fiction writer and playwright (1876–1958), author of many mystery novels including *The Circular Staircase* (1908), *Where There's a Will* (1912), and *The Case of Jennie Brice* (1913). With Avery Hopwood she wrote the long-running mystery play *The Bat* (1920).

169.8 William Lyon Phelps] Literary scholar (1865–1943) and professor of English at Yale, who became popular as lecturer and columnist. Author of *Essays on Modern Novelists* (1910), *The Advance of the English Novel* (1916), and other works.

169.16 Edward E. Rose] Playwright (1862–1939) best known for his stage adaptations of popular novels, including *The Prisoner of Zenda* (1895), *David Harum* (1900), and *Richard Carvel* (1900).

169.27 Huneker] See note 8.29.

172.4 Winston Churchill] American novelist (1871–1947), author of historical novels including *Richard Carvel* (1899), *The Crisis* (1901), *The Crossing* (1904), and *Coniston* (1906).

172.4 Floyd Dell] Novelist and playwright (1887–1969), editor of *The Masses* (1914–17) and *The Liberator* (1918–24).

172.8 Charles W. Eliot] American academic (1834–1926) who began his long tenure as president of Harvard in 1869.

172.11 Fuller] Henry Blake Fuller (1857–1929), American novelist whose novels of Chicago included *The Cliff-Dwellers* (1893), *With the Procession* (1895), and *On the Stairs* (1918).

172.15 Otto Braun] The diaries, letters, and poems of Braun (1897–1918), a German soldier killed near Amiens in April 1918, were published in English in 1924.

175.34 Dunkards] Members of the German Baptist Brethren.

PREJUDICES: FIFTH SERIES

181.27 Volstead Act] See note 29.36.

183.31 Postal Act . . . Comstock] See note 31.11.

184.24 *Godey's Lady's Book*] American monthly magazine, 1830–98, influential on taste and fashion. It was published in Philadelphia by Louis A. Godey, and edited from 1837 to 1877 by Sarah Josepha Hale.

184.36 John S. Sumner] Sumner, a lawyer, succeeded Comstock as acting secretary of the Society for the Suppression of Vice in 1915.

185.2 "Three Weeks"] Novel (1907) by Elinor Glyn (1864–1943), about an affair between a Balkan queen and an English aristocrat.

186.21–22 Sylvanus Stall] Lutheran minister (1847–1915), author of books on sex such as *What A Young Boy Ought to Know* and *What a Young Woman Ought to Know*.

187.27 Jurgen] Novel (1919) by James Branch Cabell, which became a bestseller when it was denounced for obscenity.

187.28 The 'Genius'] Novel (1915) by Theodore Dreiser; it was withdrawn from sale by the publisher after the New York Society for the Suppression of Vice declared it lewd and profane.

187.28 Mlle. de Maupin] *Mademoiselle de Maupin*, novel (1835) by Théophile Gautier.

189.12 Anti-Saloon League] See note 50.5.

190.29–30 Leopold-Loeb trial] In 1924, Nathan Leopold (1904–1971) and Richard Loeb (1905–1936) were tried and convicted for the murder of Bobby Franks. Defense lawyer Clarence Darrow's summation asked that they be spared the death penalty; they each received a sentence of life imprisonment.

194.24 Venezuela episode] In a note sent to the British government on July 20, 1895, Secretary of State Richard Olney stated that the dispute between Great Britain and Venezuela over the boundary of British Guyana fell under the Monroe Doctrine and should be settled by arbitration. After Lord Salisbury, the British prime minister and foreign secretary, rejected arbitration, President Cleveland sent a message to Congress on December 17 in which he proposed the creation of a commission to determine the boundary and warned that the United States would treat a British refusal to accept the new boundary as an act of aggression. The resulting crisis lessened when Joseph Chamberlain, the British colonial secretary, described a possible Anglo-American war as "an absurdity" on January 24, 1896. Britain and Venezuela agreed on February 2, 1897, to submit the dispute to arbitration, and a settlement was reached in 1899.

196.34–35 *Hexentanz*] Witches' dance.

198.27–28 *durch componiert*] Through-composed.

199.12 Prof. Dr. Jadassohn] German composer and professor Salamon Jadassohn (1831–1902).

200.8–9 Benavente . . . Tagore] Jacinto Benavente y Martinez (1866–1954), Spanish dramatist (Nobel Prize, 1922); Verner von Heidenstam (1859–1940), Swedish poet (1916); Karl Adolph Gjellerup (1857–1919), Danish poet and novelist (1917); Rabindranath Tagore (1861–1941), Hindu poet (1913).

200.27 Hergesheimer] See note 168.24.

200.29–30 Lindley Murray] Scottish-American grammarian (1745–1826), author of grammar textbooks widely circulated in England and in the United States during the early 1800s.

203.1 La Belle Ettarre . . . Felix Kennaston] Characters in James Branch Cabell's *The Cream of the Jest* (1917).

205.5 Sam Slick] Humorous sketches collected in *The Clockmaker, or, The Sayings and Doings of Samuel Slick of Slickville* (1837) by Thomas Chandler Haliburton (1796–1865).

209.5 George H. Boker] George Henry Boker (1823–1890), poet and verse dramatist, author of *The Lessons of Life* (1848), *Poems of the War* (1864), and the play *Francesca da Rimini* (1855).

214.14 Peruna] Patent medicine marketed as a panacea by the Ohio physician Samuel Brubaker Hartman.

216.2 Mary Baker G. Eddy] See note 4.38–39.

216.2–3 Czolgosz] See note 108.3–4.

216.11 John W. Davis] Politician, lawyer, and diplomat (1873–1955), congressman from West Virginia (1911–13), solicitor general and ambassador to the United Kingdom under President Wilson, Democratic candidate for president in 1924.

216.14 Champ Clark] James Beauchamp Clark (1850–1921), U.S. congressman from Missouri who served as speaker of the house, 1911–19. He lost the Democratic presidential nomination in 1912 when William Jennings Bryan shifted his support to Woodrow Wilson.

217.27 Samuel Gompers] American union leader (1850–1924), founder of the American Federation of Labor.

217.35 Scopes case] John Scopes (1900–1970) was tried for violation of a recently passed Tennessee law against teaching the theory of evolution in tax-supported schools. The state's case was argued in court by William Jennings Bryan, while Scopes was represented by Clarence Darrow. Scopes was convicted and fined $100; the conviction was later reversed on technical grounds by the Tennessee supreme court.

224.24 Caliph Omar] In an account now regarded as apocryphal, Caliph Umar Ibn al-Khattab is said to have burned the Library of Alexandria in 640 on the grounds that if its contents agreed with the Koran they were superfluous and if they contradicted it they were heretical.

225.39 Ellis] Henry Havelock Ellis (1859–1939), English scientist and man of letters who studied the psychology and sociology of sex. His books included *The New Spirit* (1890), *Man and Woman* (1894), and the seven-volume *Studies in the Psychology of Sex* (1897–1928).

225.39 Moll] Albert Moll (1862–1939), German psychiatrist, a pioneer in the study of sexuality; author of *The Sexual Life of the Child* (1908).

227.23 Andy Gump] Protagonist of *The Gumps*, comic strip created by Sidney Smith in 1917.

228.17 Raffs] Joseph Joachim Raff (1822–1882), German-Swiss composer and pianist.

229.5 Korngolds] Erich Wolfgang Korngold (1897–1957), Austrian composer and conductor whose opera *Die Tote Stadt* premiered in 1920. Korngold later became an influential composer of Hollywood soundtracks.

229.21 Kulmbacher] German beer.

230.18–19 Bishop Manning] See note 73.7.

235.24 Graafian follicle] Fluid-filled cavity protecting the developing egg-cell in the ovary of a mammal.

237.31 *Veritas liberabit vos*!] The truth shall set you free (John 8:32).

242.6–7 Francis Asbury] Methodist Episcopal Bishop (1745–1816), a founder of the church in the United States, noted for the power of his preaching.

242.7 Jabez Bunting] English Wesleyan minister (1779–1858).

242.8 Robert Strawbridge] Irish immigrant who organized a Methodist church in Pipe Creek, Maryland, before the American Revolution.

242.15 *Blasmusik*] Brass music.

243.3 viewed from a tree] That is, seen from the viewpoint of Zacchaeus: a tax collector too short to see Jesus in the midst of a crowd, he climbed up a tree to do so (Luke 19:1–10).

244.5 Brisbane] Arthur Brisbane (1864–1936), influential editor and columnist for the Hearst newspapers.

244.5 Frank Crane] See note 21.35.

244.6 Mutt and Jeff] Daily comic strip created in 1907 by Bud Fisher (1885–1954).

244.24 Billy Sunday] American evangelist (1862–1935), who gave up a career as a professional baseball player to become one of the most influential preachers of the early twentieth century.

247.29 Bossuet] Jacques Bénigne Bossuet (1627–1704), bishop and renowned orator.

247.34 William Graham Sumner] American economist, sociologist and educator (1840–1910), author of *Folkways* (1907). *The Forgotten Man and Other Essays* was published in 1919. The title essay opens: "The type and formula of most schemes of philanthropy or humanitarianism is this: A and B put their heads together to decide what C shall be made to do for D. The radical vice of all these schemes, from a sociological point of view, is that C is not allowed a voice in the matter, and his position, character, and interests, as well as the ultimate effects on society through C's interests, are entirely overlooked. I call C the Forgotten Man."

252.37 Robert Andrews Millikans] Robert Andrews Millikan (1868–1953), experimental physicist, recipient of the 1923 Nobel Prize. He was a proponent of the need to reconcile science and religion.

253.24–25 John P. Altgeld] German-born American politician (1847–1902), governor of Illinois, 1892–97. He was a leader of the Progressive movement and a supporter of workplace and labor reforms.

253.27 Raisuli] Ahmed ibn-Muhammed Raisuli (1875?–1925), Berber insurgent who kidnapped several British and American citizens (including Ion Perdicaris and Walter Harris, correspondent for the London *Times*) in 1904. Theodore Roosevelt sent warships to Tangier and the slogan "Perdicaris Alive or Raisuli Dead" became a rallying cry for the Republican Party. Perdicaris was ultimately ransomed by the government of Morocco.

253.29 Wayne B. Wheeler] Wayne Bidwell Wheeler (1869–1927), general counsel of the Anti-Saloon League of America (1915–1927).

253.29 McNamara Brothers] James and John McNamara, members of the ironworkers union, were accused of bombing the offices of the anti-union *Los Angeles Times* in 1910, killing twenty-one employees. In 1911 James pled guilty to the newspaper bombing and was sentenced to life, while John received a sentence of 15 years after pleading guilty to the bombing of an iron works.

253.31 La Follette of 1917] Wisconsin Senator Robert Marion La Follette (1855–1925) was an outspoken opponent of American entry into World War I, military conscription, and the Espionage Act.

254.1 Charlie Ross] Charles Ross (born 1870) was abducted and held for ransom in Germantown, Pennsylvania, in 1874. Since he never was found, nor his remains recovered, rumors of sightings went on for years, and his name became a catchphrase.

254.5 *Gelehrte*] See note 3.7.

254.29 Chicago anarchists] In 1893 Governor John P. Altgeld pardoned three of the eight defendants convicted of the Haymarket bombing of May 1, 1886. Four other defendants had already been executed, and one had committed suicide in his cell.

254.34 Pullman strike] In 1894 President Cleveland sent 2,000 federal troops to Chicago to put down a strike of Pullman railcar workers led by Eugene V. Debs. Thirteen strikers were killed, fifty-seven were wounded, and Debs was imprisoned for defying a court injunction against the strike.

255.40 Dr. Crapsey] Algernon Sidney Crapsey (1847–1927), Episcopal clergyman from New York. He was convicted of heresy by an ecclesiastical court in 1906 after delivering a lecture stressing the humanity of Jesus in a fashion deemed contrary to literal Biblical interpretation.

256.26 *Stammvater*] Ancestor.

257.35 Beers] Henry A. Beers (1847–1926), an authority on English romanticism.

257.36 Matthews] See note 6.14.

259.35 Karl Ludwig] Carl Friedrich Wilhelm Ludwig (1816–1895), German physiologist, a pioneer in cardiovascular research.

259.35 Jowett] Benjamin Jowett (1817–1893), scholar and classicist, Master of Balliol College at Oxford. His commentary on the epistles of St. Paul (1855) stirred great controversy.

261.15 *Freiheitskrieg*] War of liberation.

270.12–13 Dr. La Follette's vaporous schemes] During the 1924 presidential campaign, Senator Robert M. La Follette, candidate for the Progressive Party, called for government ownership of railroads and utilities, cheap credit for farmers, an end to imperialism in Latin America, and the outlawing of child labor.

272.29 Harris Dickson] Lawyer and novelist (1868–1946), author of *The Black Wolf's Breed* (1899) and *Lady Resolute* (1902).

273.11 John Sharp Williams] Mississippi politician (1854–1932), U.S. senator, 1911–23.

274.12 Creel Press Bureau] See note 3.12.

275.26 ORISON SWETT MARDEN] American writer (1850–1924) associated with the New Thought movement, and author of self-help books emphasizing the power of positive thinking in order to achieve success, including *The Secret of Achievement* (1898), *Cheerfulness as a Life Power* (1899), and *The Hour of Opportunity* (1900).

275.29–30 Frank A. Munsey] American author and publisher (1854–1925), owner of the New York *Evening Sun* and *Evening Telegram*, *Munsey's Magazine*, and *Argosy All-Story Weekly*.

276.19 "Pushing to the Front"] *Pushing to the Front, or, Success Under Difficulties* was published in 1894.

276.31 James Oliver Curwood] Author of adventure stories (1878–1927), such as *The Courage of Captain Plum* (1908), *The Danger Trail* (1910), and *Back to God's Country* (1920).

277.10 Judge Elbert Gary] See note 136.26.

278.15 Matthew Josephson] American writer (1899–1978), author of *Zola and His Time* (1928) and other works; he edited the magazine *Secession* (1922–24), and was later a co-editor of *Broom*.

278.18–19 Ernest Boyd] See note 6.33.

278.23 *Broom*] Literary magazine established in Rome in 1921 by Harold Loeb and Alfred Kreymborg, and later edited in New York by Mathew Josephson, Slater Brown, and Malcolm Cowley. Its contributors included Sherwood Anderson, E. E. Cummings, William Carlos Williams, Conrad Aiken, and Jean Toomer.

278.23 *Little Review*] Literary quarterly, 1914–29, founded by Margaret Anderson and edited by her with Jane Heap. It was among the most influential magazines of its time, publishing W. B. Yeats, Ernest Hemingway, T. S. Eliot, Djuna Barnes, and Hart Crane. Its serialization of James Joyce's *Ulysses*, 1918–21, led to the editors being fined for obscenity.

278.25–26 Baroness Elsa von Freytag-Loringhoven] Poet and artist (1874–1927), born Elsa Hildegard Plötz in present-day Poland; she emigrated to the United States in 1910 and married the Baron von Freytag-Loringhoven in 1913. Her poems were published in *The Little Review* and other magazines; she became notorious for her outlandish appearance and extreme behavior. She returned to Europe in 1923 and died of asphyxiation in her Paris apartment three years later.

278.30–31 Paul Elmer More] See note 168.34.

278.33–34 Fred Lewis Pattee] Literary scholar (1863–1950), professor at Pennsylvania State College. His *History of American Literature Since 1870* appeared in 1915, followed by *The New American Literature, 1890–1930* (1930) and *The Feminine Fifties* (1940).

279.5 Eugène Sue] French novelist (1804–1857), author of long, serially published novels such as *The Mysteries of Paris* (1843) and *The Wandering Jew* (1845).

279.11 *Dial*] *The Dial*, major literary magazine of the 1920s, edited successively by Scofield Thayer and Marianne Moore; it published a wide range of international writers including D. H. Lawrence, T. S. Eliot, Ezra Pound, W. B. Yeats, Thomas Mann, and Sherwood Anderson.

279.30 Paul Morand] French writer and diplomat (1888–1976), author of fiction including *Open All Night* (1922) and *Closed All Night* (1923).

279.30 Harry Kemp] American poet and prose writer (1883–1960) who wrote about his travels as a hobo in *Tramping on Life* (1922) and other works.

279.31 André Salmon] French poet and art critic (1881–1969).

279.31 Maxwell Bodenheim] American poet and novelist (1893–1954).

281.19 Tupper] Martin Tupper (1810–1889) English author whose *Proverbial Philosophy* (1837), a collection of didactic and moral reflections, went through many editions in Great Britain and the United States.

285.5 Felicia Hemans] English poet (1793–1835) whose many volumes of verse included *The Forest Sanctuary* (1825) and *Songs of the Affections* (1830). She is best remembered for the poem "Casabianca."

285.5 Fanny Fern] Pseudonym of Sara Payson Willis (1811–1872), popular American writer of essays and children's books. Her books included *Fern Leaves from Fanny's Portfolio* (1853) and the novel *Ruth Hall* (1855).

286.30 *Aufklärung*] Enlightenment.

291.38 Edmund Clarence Stedman] Poet and critic (1833–1908). He edited *An American Anthology, 1787–1899* (1900), an influential survey of American poetry. He also co-edited, with Ellen M. Hutchinson, the eleven-volume *Library of American Literature 1880–1890* (1889–90) and, with George Woodberry, a ten-volume edition of Poe's works.

291.38 Richard Watson Gilder] Poet (1844–1909), editor of the *Century*, 1881–1909.

292.20 Max O'Rell] Pseudonym of Léon Paul Blouet (1848–1903), French writer best known for his travel books beginning with *John Bull and His Island* (1883).

292.20 Blasco Ibañez] Vicente Blasco-Ibáñez (1867–1928), Spanish novelist, author of *Blood and Sand* (1908) and *The Four Horsemen of the Apocalypse* (1916).

292.32–33 William C. Brownell] See note 3.4.

292.33 Augustus Thomas] See note 168.22.

292.33 Hamlin Garland] See note 169.2.

292.33–34 Owen Wister] Novelist (1860–1938), author of *The Virginian* (1902) as well as the memoir *Theodore Roosevelt: The Story of a Friendship* (1930).

292.34 Henry van Dyke] See note 8.30–31.

293.12 Henry Sydnor Harrison] Novelist (1880–1930), a frequent contributor to *Atlantic Monthly*. His works included *Queed* (1911), *V. V.'s Eyes* (1913), and *Angela's Business* (1915).

293.13 Clayton Hamilton] Critic, playwright, and producer (1881–1946), who wrote theatrical criticism for various magazines including *Bookman* (1910–18), *Everybody's Magazine* (1911–13) and *Vogue* (1912–20).

293.15 Robert W. Chambers] See note 168.28–29.

293.16 Herman Hagedorn] American author (1882–1964) whose poetry was collected in *A Troop of the Guard* (1909), *Poems and Ballads* (1912), and other volumes. He was a close friend of Theodore Roosevelt, of whom he published a biography in 1918. He also published the novels *Faces in the Dawn* (1914) and *Barbara Picks a Husband* (1918).

293.25 Gerhart Hauptmann] German playwright (1862–1946), author of *The Weavers* (1892), *The Beaver Coat* (1893), *The Sunken Bell* (1896), and many other works. He won the Nobel Prize for Literature in 1912.

293.27 A. Lawrence Lowell] Abbott Lawrence Lowell (1856–1943), professor of government at Harvard (1900–1909) and president of Harvard (1909–1933).

293.28 Otto Kahn] Investment banker and financier (1867–1934), a leading patron of the arts.

293.36 Nicholas Murray Butler] See note 99.13.

294.2 Tex Rickard] George Lewis Rickard (1871–1929), boxing promoter.

294.13 Frank Munsey] See note 275.29–30.

294.15 Max Eastman] Author and journalist (1883–1969), editor of *The Masses* (1913–1917) and *The Liberator* (1918–1922).

299.24–25 Terence V. Powderly] American labor leader (1849–1924), head of the Knights of Labor, 1879–93.

300.21 William Wrigley, Jr.] Industrialist (1861–1932), manufacturer of chewing gum and developer of Catalina Island off Los Angeles.

305.22–23 Alfred Kreymborg] American poet (1883–1966), editor of the magazine *Others* (1917–20). His poetry was collected in *Mushrooms* (1916), *Scarlet and Mellow* (1926), and other volumes, and his autobiography *Troubador* appeared in 1925. He later edited numerous anthologies including *The American Caravan* (1927–36) and *Lyric America* (1930).

306.3–4 Potash . . . One-Eye Feigenbaum] Characters from *Potash and Perlmutter* (1913) by Montague Glass; see note 309.34.

306.6 *Schnecken*] Snails.

306.23–24 *Schön ist die Jugendzeit; sie kommt nicht mehr!*] "Beautiful is youth; it will not return!": traditional German lyric.

309.6 Abraham Cahan] Novelist and editor (1860–1951). He was the longtime editor of the *Jewish Daily Forward* and author of *Yekl: a Tale of the New York Ghetto* (1896) and *The Rise of David Levinsky* (1917).

309.34 Montague Glass] English-born playwright and story writer (1877–1934), known for stories about Jewish businessmen dramatized as *Potash and Perlmutter* (1913), *Business Before Pleasure* (1917), and *His Honor Abe Potash* (1919).

310.15–16 Harvey Fergusson's "Capitol Hill"] See note 168.1.

312.3 William Z. Foster] Labor leader and politician (1881–1961). He organized the steelworkers' strike of 1919 and in 1921 joined the American Communist Party, serving as its general secretary, 1921–30, and chairman, 1945–56.

314.4 the Fox Sisters] Three sisters from Hydeville, New York, who beginning in the late 1840s acquired a reputation for mediumistic abilities manifested through mysterious rappings. At the height of their celebrity they attracted support from many prominent figures, notably Horace Greeley. In 1888 Margaret Fox published a confession (later recanted) that the rappings had been faked.

314.5 Dr. Munyon] James M. Munyon, manufacturer of patent medicines.

314.5 Godey of the *Lady's Book*] See note 184.24.

314.5–6 Daniel Drew] American financier, (1797–1879).

314.18–19 E. W. Howe's "The Story of a Country Town."] See note 28.8.

315.6 Wayne B. Wheeler] See note 253.29.

315.6 Billy Sunday] See note 244.24.

323.3 Barrett Wendell] American scholar (1855–1921), professor at Harvard and author of *A Literary History of America* (1900).

323.4 M. A. DeWolfe Howe] Mark Anthony DeWolfe Howe (1864–1960), prolific author, biographer of John Jay Chapman, Oliver Wendell Holmes, and other New England figures; editor of *Youth's Companion* and *Atlantic Monthly.*

325.8 Sir Arthur Quiller-Couch] English man of letters (1863–1944), sometimes known by the pen name "Q", author of many books including *On the Art of Reading* (1920).

325.39 Aldrich] Thomas Bailey Aldrich (1836–1907), American poet, novelist, editor, author of *The Story of a Bad Boy* (1870).

325.39 Blaine] James G. Blaine (1830–1893), American politician who served as congressman, senator, and secretary of state, and was a dominant figure in the Republican Party after the Civil War. He was defeated by Grover Cleveland in the 1884 presidential race.

327.11 Walter Prichard Eaton] Drama critic (1878–1957), author of *The American Stage of Today* (1908) and *Plays and Players* (1916).

331.12 E. L. Godkin] See note 135.10–11.

332.6 Villard] Oswald Garrison Villard (1872–1949), journalist, editor and owner of *The Nation*, 1918–32.

335.6 Mr. Secretary Denby] See note 107.29.

335.6–7 Falls and Dohenys] Fall, see note 106.12; Edward L. Doheny (1856–1935), California oilman implicated in the Teapot Dome Scandal.

335.7 Mr. Secretary Wilbur] Curtis Dwight Wilbur (1867–1954), U.S. secretary of the navy, 1924–29.

335.7–8 Josephus Daniels] See note 151.27.

336.30 Cathcart case] Vera, Countess of Cathcart, was denied entry into the United States in 1926 on grounds of adultery. (She had left her husband, the Earl of Cathcart, and taken up with the Earl of Craven.) A judge eventually ruled that she could stay in the United States; her play *Ashes of Love* had a brief run on Broadway in 1926.

339.22 John Roach Straton] See note 73.7.

343.2 Edgar Saltus] American writer (1855–1921), author of *The Philosophy of Disenchantment* (1885), *The Anatomy of Negation* (1886); novels including *Mr. Incoul's Misadventure* (1887), *The Truth about Tristrem Varick* (1888), *The Pace That Kills* (1889), *The Pomps of Satan* (1904), and *The Perfume of Eros* (1905); and works of popular history including *Mary Magdalen* (1891), *Imperial Purple* (1892), and *The Orgy* (1920, later retitled *Imperial Orgy*).

343.14 Percival Pollard] Joseph Percival Pollard (1869–1911), German-born literary critic, a close friend of Mencken; he was educated in England and emigrated with his family to the United States in 1885. He was a frequent contributor to *The Criterion* (New York). His books included *Their Day in Court* (1909) and *Masks and Minstrels of New Germany* (1911).

346.6 Gertrude Atherton] See note 10.4.

348.4 *Jack Ketch*] Public executioner during the reign of Charles II.

351.37 Col. Goethals] George Washington Goethals (1858–1928), chief engineer of the Panama Canal and governor of the Canal Zone until 1916; he was promoted to major general in 1915.

351.38 Col. Gorgas] William Crawford Gorgas (1854–1920), U.S. Army surgeon general; as chief sanitary officer of the Panama Canal Commission (1904–1913), helped suppress yellow fever so that the canal could be completed.

352.19 Bleases] See note 33.10.

352.19 Mayfields] Earle Bradford Mayfield (1881–1964), U.S. senator, 1923–29.

352.19 Slemps] Campbell Bascom Slemp (1870–1943), U.S. congressman from Virginia, 1907–22.

352.20 Peays] Austin Peay (1876–1927), governor of Tennessee, 1923–27.

352.20 Vardamans] James Kimble Vardaman (1861–1930), governor of Mississippi, 1904–8, and U.S. senator, 1913–19.

355.29 Hiram Johnson] American politician (1866–1945), governor of California, 1911–17, and U.S. senator, 1917–45.

355.30 Williams Gibbs MacAdoo] Lawyer and politician (1863–1941), secretary of the Treasury, 1913–18, and U.S. senator from California, 1933–38.

PREJUDICES: SIXTH SERIES

366.31 Johannes Müller] German physiologist and comparative anatomist (1801–1858).

368.31 Heywood Broun] American journalist (1888–1939), sportswriter, drama critic, and author of the syndicated column "It Seems to Me." He was the founder of the American Newspaper Guild.

368.33 Snyder trial] Ruth Brown Snyder (1895–1928) was tried, convicted, and executed, along with her lover Henry Judd Gray, for the 1927 murder of her husband Albert Snyder.

370.1–2 news from China in the early part of 1927] In March 1927 Chinese Nationalist troops in Nanjing attacked the British, American, and Japanese consulates, leading to the shelling of the city by British and American warships.

370.3 Miami hurricane of 1926] A hurricane devastated Miami, Florida during September 17–18, 1926, killing 373 people.

372.29 Cyrus H. K. Curtis] Cyrus Hermann Kotzschmar Curtis (1850–1933), American publisher, founder of the Curtis Publishing Co., publisher of *Ladies' Home Journal*, *The Country Gentleman*, and *The Saturday Evening Post.*

372.30 Frank A. Munsey] See note 275.29–30.

372.33 Hearst papers] By the end of 1922, newspaper publisher William Randolph Hearst (1863–1951) was the owner of twenty daily papers and eleven Sunday papers in thirteen of the largest American cities. He also owned two wire services, King Features (the largest of the comic strip syndicates), six American magazines, a newsreel (Hearst Metronome News), and a motion picture production company. His chain of newspapers included the San Francisco *Examiner*, Boston *American*, New York *American*, New York *Mirror*, and the New York *Journal*.

372.34 Scripps-Howard newspapers] Newspaper chain founded as the E. W. Scripps Company by Edward Willis Scripps (1854–1926).

373.11 Brisbane] See note 244.5.

373.15 Cox] James Middleton Cox (1857–1957), newspaper publisher and politician. He served as Ohio congressman and governor of Ohio (1913–15, 1917–21), and was the Democratic presidential nominee in 1920, losing to Warren G. Harding. He published the *Dayton Daily News* and founded the newspaper company Cox Enterprises.

381.17 Lady Cathcart] See note 336.30.

382.6 Whitney case] Charlotte Anita Whitney (1867–1955), suffragist and radical political organizer, a member of the Communist Labor Party, was charged with criminal syndicalism in 1919 after working to establish the American Communist Party. Her conviction was upheld by the Supreme Court in 1927.

382.6 Kollontai case] In November 1926 Secretary of State William Kellogg denied an entry visa to Alexandra Kollontai (1872–1952), the new Soviet ambassador to Mexico, because of her involvement with "the International Communist subversive movement." (The United States did not establish diplomatic relations with the Soviet Union until 1933.)

384.33 Thackeray's Louis XIV] See "Meditations at Versailles," *The Paris Sketch Book* (1840).

386.17 Senator Wheeler] In 1924, an investigation led by Senator Burton K. Wheeler of Montana (1882–1975) into Attorney General Harry Daugherty's failure to prosecute government officials in the Teapot Dome Scandal led to Daugherty's resignation. One month later, a federal grand jury in Montana indicted Senator Wheeler on charges involving his private law practice. Wheeler called for a Senate investigation of the charges, claiming an attempt by the Justice Department to discredit him; he was finally acquitted of all charges.

386.19 O'Leary case] Jeremiah O'Leary, editor of *The Bull*, an Irish Nationalist newspaper opposed to American participation in what it called "England's war," was indicted in 1918 under the Espionage Act for allegedly receiving funds from the German government. He was acquitted in March 1919.

386.21 Fatty Arbuckle] Roscoe Conkling "Fatty" Arbuckle (1887–1933), silent film comedian, was tried three times for manslaughter in the death of Virginia Rappe, whom he was accused of raping at a party he hosted in 1921. Although Arbuckle was eventually acquitted and received an apology from the jury for what they considered a gross injustice, his career was destroyed.

390.15–16 Professor Oppenheimer] Franz Oppenheimer (1864–1943), German sociologist and political economist, author of *The State* (1914) and *The Idolatry of the State* (1927).

397.16 Penrose] Senator Boise Penrose (1860–1921), Pennsylvania congressman 1897–1921, a champion of protective tariffs and pro-business legislation.

400.16 Rostand's "Chantecler."] Play (1910) by French dramatist Edmond Rostand (1868–1918).

400.32 Edgar Albert Guest] See note 21.35.

401.3 *Non in solo pane vivit homo.*] Man does not live by bread alone (Matthew 4:4).

404.3 January 16, 1920] The date when Prohibition went into effect.

405.1 "Only a Boy"] Erotic story attributed to the poet Eugene Field (1850–1895).

414.37 Sylvanus Stall] See note 186.21–22.

417.21–22 Upton Sinclair] Novelist (1878–1968) who became famous with the publication of *The Jungle*, an exposé of conditions in the Chicago stockyards, in 1906. (It was originally serialized in the Socialist newspaper *The Appeal to Reason.*) His many other books included *The Metropolis* (1908), *King Coal* (1917), *Oil!* (1927), and *The Wet Parade* (1931).

417.28 Albert Abrams] Self-proclaimed healer (1863–1924) who falsely claimed he had a medical degree from the University of Heidelberg and who marketed a machine called the Dynomizer which he asserted could diagnose any known disease. His defenders included Upton Sinclair and Arthur Conan Doyle. The American Medical Association mounted a successful campaign to debunk his claims.

417.39 A. Mitchell Palmer] See note 3.14.

418.36 the Single Tax] Economic theory propounded by Henry George (1839–1897) in *Progress and Poverty* (1879) and other works, advocating a tax on land. Hamlin Garland's novel *Jason Edwards: An Average Man* (1892) was written in support of the Single Tax.

419.10 Lucy Stone] American suffragist (1818–1893).

424.1 Vachel Lindsay] American poet (1879–1931), author of *General William Booth Enters into Heaven* (1913), *The Congo* (1914), *The Chinese Nightingale* (1917), and other collections.

424.11–12 James Weldon Johnson] Writer and diplomat (1871–1938), editor of *The Book of American Negro Poetry* (1921) and *The Book of American Negro Spirituals* (1925), author of *The Autobiography of an Ex-Colored Man* (1912), *God's Trombones* (1927), *Black Manhattan* (1930), and other works, including "Lift Every Voice and Sing."

429.22 Billy Sunday] See note 244.24.

429.23 John Roach Straton] See note 73.7.

430.12 Adam-Zad] See Rudyard Kipling's "The Truce of the Bear" (1898), in which the bear represents Russia: "Make ye no truce with Adam-zad—the Bear that walks like a man!"

430.22 Peckniff, Chadband or Elmer Gantry] Pecksniff, villain who makes a show of piety in Dickens' *Martin Chuzzlewit* (1843–44); Chadband, pompous and hypocritical clergyman in Dickens' *Bleak House* (1852–53); Elmer Gantry, barnstorming evangelist who is the title character of Sinclair Lewis's 1927 novel.

430.25 Charles Gallaudet Trumbull] American writer (1872–1941), author of *Anthony Comstock, Fighter: Some Impressions of a Lifetime of Adventure in Conflict with the Powers of Evil* (1913).

431.10–11 Frances E. Willard] Educator (1839–1898) who campaigned for temperance and suffrage.

431.11 Daniel Drew] See note 314.5–6.

431.17 C.E.M. Joad] Cyril Edwin Mitchinson Joad (1891–1953), British philosopher and pacifist, author of *Common Sense Ethics* (1921), *Common Sense Theology* (1922), and *Guide to Modern Thought* (1933).

431.21 Filippo G. Bruno] Giordano Bruno (1548–1600), Dominican friar who was burned at the stake for heresy by the Roman Inquisition. His many works on philosophy, cosmology, and mnemonics included *The Art of Memory* (1582), *The Ash Wednesday Supper* (1584), and *On the Infinite Universe and Worlds* (1584).

431.22 *Se non è vero, è ben trovato.*] If it is not true, it is a good invention.

431.33 J. Gordon Coogler] James Gordon Coogler (1865–1901), South Carolina-born poet, whose *Purely Original Verse* was published in five editions between 1891 and 1897.

432.28–29 Charlie Schwab] Charles Schwab (1862–1939), steel industry magnate, chief executive of Bethlehem Steel, known for his lavish spending.

433.13 Hamilton Wright Mabie] See note 168.12–13.

433.16–17 Gloria Swanson and Jack Gilbert] Gloria Swanson (1889–1983), silent movie star whose films included *Male and Female* (1919), *Manhandled* (1924), and *Sadie Thompson* (1928); John Gilbert, silent movie star who appeared frequently with Greta Garbo, in such films as *Flesh and the Devil* (1926) and *A Woman of Affairs* (1928).

433.31–32 Aimée Semple McPherson] Popular evangelist (1890–1944) who founded the International Church of the Foursquare Gospel in Los Angeles.

434.12–13 Montague Summers] English scholar (1880–1948), author of *Jane Austen, An Appreciation* (1919). His later works on demonology and related matters would include *The Vampire, His Kith and Kin* (1928), *The Black Mass* (1936), and *A Popular History of Witchcraft* (1937).

434.20 Robert Andrews Millikan] See note 252.37.

436.13–14 Bishop Manning] See note 73.7.

436.16 William N. Guthrie] Rector of St. Mark's-in-the-Bouwerie in New York.

436.32 Saorstát] Free state (Irish).

438.20–21 George B. M. Harvey] Journalist and publisher (1864–1928), editor of *The North American Review*, 1899–1926, and *Harper's Weekly*, 1901–13.

441.29 Mooney of Memphis] Charles Joseph Patrick Mooney (1865–1926), managing editor (1908–1923), then owner (1923–1924) of the Memphis *Commercial Appeal.* He won the 1923 Pulitzer Prize for his relentless editorializing against the Ku Klux Klan.

441.31–32 Hall of Montgomery] Grover Cleveland Hall (1888–1941), editor of the Montgomery (Alabama) *Advertiser*, who won the 1928 Pulitzer Prize for his editorials against racial intolerance

441.32 Wright of Columbia] R. Charlton Wright, editor of the Columbia (South Carolina) *Record.*

441.32 Jaffe of Norfolk] Louis I. Jaffe, editor of the Norfolk *Virginian-Pilot*, 1919–50.

441.33 Dabney of Richmond] Virginius Dabney (1901–1995), editor of the Richmond *Times-Dispatch.*

441.37 Johnson of Greensboro] Gerald White Johnson (1890–1980), journalist, editor, and novelist from North Carolina; Mencken enlisted him to write for the Baltimore *Evening Sun.*

441.38 Harris of Columbus, Ga.] Julian LaRose Harris (1874–1963) and his wife Julia Collier Harris (1875–1967) were owners and editors of the

Columbus (Georgia) *Enquirer-Sun*. It won the 1926 Pulitzer Prize for public service (the first small city daily to be so recognized) for their stance against lynching, the Ku Klux Klan, and legislation banning the teaching of evolution in Georgia schools.

442.2 Frances Newman] Novelist (1883–1928), author of *The Gold-Fish Bowl* (1921), *The Hard-Boiled Virgin* (1926) and *Dead Lovers Are Faithful Lovers* (1928). At the time of her death Newman was suffering from severe and painful vision problems.

442.2 Nell Battle Lewis] Lawyer (1893–1956) and newspaper columnist for the Raleigh *News and Observer.*

442.2–3 Sara Haardt] Sara Powell Haardt (1898–1935), short story writer from Montgomery, Alabama, who married H. L. Mencken in 1930.

442.10 Emily Clark] Emily Tapscott Clark (1893–1953), Virginia-born writer, author of *Stuffed Peacocks* (1927), and founder and editor of the literary magazine *The Reviewer.*

442.11 Mrs. Julia Peterkin] Julia M. Peterkin (1880–1961), fiction writer who wrote about the Gullah region of her native South Carolina. Her novels included *Black April* (1927) and *Scarlet Sister Mary* (1928), for which she won the Pulitzer Prize.

442.11 T. S. Stribling] Tennessee-born writer (1881–1965), author of *Birthright* (1921) and winner of the 1933 Pulitzer Prize for *The Store.*

442.12 Clement Wood] Alabama-born poet and novelist (1888–1950), author of *The Glory Road* (1936).

442.12 J. W. Krutch] Joseph Wood Krutch (1893–1970), esssayist and critic, author of *Edgar Allan Poe: A Study in Genius* (1926), *The Modern Temper* (1929), *The Measure of Man* (1954), and *The Desert Year* (1952).

442.26 John R. Neal] Controversial law professor at the University of Tennessee, who was one of seven professors dismissed in 1923 for, among other reasons, liberal views on evolution.

442.37 Peay] See note 352.20.

443.3 Walter Hines Page] American journalist and diplomat (1855–1918), U. S. ambassador to Britain, 1913–18.

443.4 William E. Dodd] Historian (1869–1940), author of *Woodrow Wilson and His Work* (1920) and editor, with Ray Stannard Baker, of *The Public Papers of Woodrow Wilson* (1924–26).

443.5 John Spencer Bassett] Historian (1867–1928), author of *The Life of Andrew Jackson* (1911), *A Short History of the United States* (1913), and *Our War with Germany* (1919).

443.5 W. P. Trent] Scholar (1862–1939), professor of English at Columbia University, author of *A History of American Literature, 1607–1865* (1903).

443.6 Ashby Jones] Professor at Atlanta University.

443.11 Gerald W. Johnson] See note 441.37.

443.12 Paul Y. Anderson] Reporter (1893–1938) for the St. Louis *Post-Dispatch*; his investigative stories helped expose the Teapot Dome Scandal during the Harding administration.

443.19–20 W. L. Poteat] William Louis Poteat (1856–1938), president of Wake Forest College in North Carolina (1905–1927), controversial for his acceptance of the theory of evolution.

443.20 John D. Wade] Georgia-born literary critic (1892–1963), a participant in the Vanderbilt Agrarian movement along with John Crowe Ransom, Allen Tate, and Robert Penn Warren; he was the author of *Augustus Baldwin Longstreet: A Study of the Development of Culture in the South* (1924).

443.20 Paul Green] North Carolina-born playwright (1894–1981), winner of 1927 Pulitzer prize for *In Abraham's Bosom.*

443.20 Howard W. Odum] Sociologist (1884–1954), founder of the journal *Social Forces* at Chapel Hill, and author of several novels.

443.27 Clark Howell] Journalist (1863–1936), editor in chief of the Atlanta *Journal Constitution.*

443.27 Douglas Freeman] Douglas Southall Freeman (1886–1953), editor of the Richmond *News Leader*, 1915–49, and author of multivolume biographies of Robert E. Lee and George Washington.

443.28 Sullens, of Mississippi] Frederick Sullens (1877–1957), editor of the Jackson (Mississippi) *Daily News* from 1904 on.

443.30–31 Bishop Candler] Warren Akin Candler (1857–1941), bishop of the Methodist Episcopal Church, president of Emory University, and author of *The History of Sunday Schools* (1880).

446.19 Albert Jay Nock] Social critic and political theorist (1873–1945), co-editor of *The Freeman*, 1920–24, and author of *The Myth of a Guilty Nation* (1922), *The Freeman Book* (1924), *Our Enemy, the State* (1935), and other works.

447.20 Alton B. Parker] Lawyer and judge (1852–1926), Democratic presidential nominee in 1904.

447.20 Jimmie Cox] See note 373.15.

447.21 W. G. McAdoo] See note 355.30.

447.21 Cole Blease] See note 33.10.

447.21 Ma and Pa Ferguson] Miriam Amanda Wallace "Ma" Ferguson (1875–1961), first female governor of Texas, 1924–27 and 1933–35. The unusual number of pardons granted during her first term led to accusations of bribes and kickbacks. Her husband, James Edward "Pa" Ferguson (1871–1944), Texas governor 1915–17, was removed from office by impeachment.

447.21–22 John W. Davis] See note 216.11.

447.22 Tom Taggart] Thomas Taggart (1856–1929), Democratic national committeeman, 1904–16.

449.25 Howard A. Kelly] Howard Atwood Kelly (1858–1925), professor of gynecology and obstetrics at Johns Hopkins and gynecological surgeon at Johns Hopkins Hospital. A strict religious fundamentalist, he kept a prayer book naming individuals whose souls he prayed for; topping the list was H. L. Mencken.

452.29 Paul Elmer More] See note 168.34.

452.30 Bliss Perry] Literary critic (1860–1954), teacher, and editor of the *Atlantic Monthly* (1899–1909).

452.32 Paul Shorey] Classical scholar (1857–1934), author of *The Idea of Good in Plato's Republic* (1895).

452.33 Brander Matthews] See note 6.14.

452.35 Henry van Dyke] See note 8.30–31.

453.1 Robert Underwood Johnson] Writer and diplomat (1853–1937), author of *The Winter Hour* (1891) and *Poems of War and Peace* (1916). He served as U.S. Ambassador to Italy, 1920–21.

453.3 William M. Sloane] Educator and historian (1850–1928), author of *The French War and the Revolution* (1893) and *The Life of Napoleon Bonaparte* (1896).

453.5 William Crary Brownell] See note 3.4.

453.30 *cabotin*] Ham actor.

453.31 George Arliss] English actor (1868–1946) whose stage career began in the 1880s. Among his best-known vehicles (later brought to the screen) were *Disraeli* and *The Green Goddess*.

453.32 Edith Wynne Matthison] English actress (1875–1955) who appeared in New York in the early 1900s in *Everyman* and *As You Like It*.

463.22 Ziehrer] Karl Michael Ziehrer (1843–1922), Austrian composer

463.23 Lincke] Paul Lincke (1866–1946), German composer.

476.5 an article] "A Neglected Anniversary."

476.10–11 *Stammvater*] Ancestor.

478.9–10 Hans Vaihinger] German philosopher (1852–1933), author of *The Philosophy of As If* (1911). He was a leading scholar of the work of Kant.

481.9 Mary Ware Dennett] American pacifist (1872–1947) and advocate of birth control, who was indicted in 1928 under the Comstock Law for distributing her pamphlet "The Sex Side of Life."

485.34 John Roach Straton] See note 73.7.

487.13–14 Felix Riesenberg's "East Side, West Side"] Novel (1927) by engineer Felix Riesenberg (1879–1939).

487.30 John Paleologus] Byzantine Emperor (1332–1391).

490.30 Andrew T. Still] Physician (1828–1917), founder of the American School of Osteopathy in 1892.

491.1 Dr. Abrams] See note 417.28.

491.7 Palmer] Daniel David Palmer (1845–1913), founder of the Palmer School of Chiropractic (1897).

513.25 Bernarr Macfadden] Publisher (1868–1955), a proponent of bodybuilding and nutritional diets.

516.3–4 Edgar Saltus] See note 343.3.

516.35 Ludwig Thoma] Bavarian novelist, story writer, and playwright (1867–1921).

518.23–24 Ella Wheeler Wilcox] American poet (1850–1919). Her poetry was collected in over twenty volumes including *Poems of Passion* (1883), *Poems of Pleasure* (1888), *Poems of Power* (1901), and *Poems of Sentiment* (1906). For some years she published a daily poem as a syndicated newspaper feature.

518.34–35 George Sterling] American poet (1869–1926), leader of an artistic and literary circle in Carmel, California; a close friend of Mencken. His books included *A Wine of Wizardry* (1909), *The House of Orchids* (1911), and *The Caged Eagle* (1916).

518.36 Herman George Scheffauer] San Francisco-born poet and playwright (1878–1927), an associate of Ambrose Bierce and George Sterling; his poetry collection *Looms of Life* was published in 1908. He moved to Germany in 1910 and committed suicide in 1927 after murdering his female secretary.

523.7 Stanley Walker] Journalist (1898–1962), author of *The Night Club Era* (1933).

526.4 Bob Ingersoll] Robert Greene Ingersoll (1833–1899), politician and orator, known as an advocate of agnosticism.

526.7–8 George B. M. Harvey] See note 438.20–21.

527.2 Dwight L. Moody] See note 153.14.

536.36 one of the pictures I saw lately] *Masks and Faces* (1918), of which the New York *Herald Tribune* wrote: "Never before has such an aggregation of notables been seen on the screen."

538.33 Peaches Browning] After a brief marriage, Manhattan teenager "Peaches" Browning, born Frances Belle Heenan (1910–1956), filed for divorce in January 1927 from her fifty-two-year-old husband, real-estate mogul Edward West Browning (1875–1934). The divorce proceedings brought to light his eccentric behavior and were widely publicized.

539.15–16 Joe Hergesheimer] See note 168.24.

539.16 Jim Quirk] James R. Quirk, publisher and editor of *Photoplay.*

539.16 Johnny Hemphill] John Mickle Hemphill (1891–1951) practiced as an attorney in Philadelphia; ran as a "wet" Democratic candidate for governor in 1930. His first cousin Dorothy (née Hemphill) was married to Mencken's friend Joseph Hergesheimer, who dedicated *The Three Black Pennys* to John.

539.16 Jim Tully] Hobo and writer (1891–1947), author of *Emmett Lawler* (1922) and *Beggars of Life* (1924); he was a frequent contributor to *The American Mercury.* He settled in California in 1912.

539.16–17 Walter Wanger] Hollywood producer (1894–1968) who after serving in World War I began working for Jesse Lasky at Paramount, and went on to produce films ranging from *The Cocoanuts* (1929) to *Cleopatra* (1963).

542.40 The Last Laugh] German silent film (1924), starring Emil Jannings and directed by Friedrich Wilhelm Murnau (1888–1931).

546.28 Diego Valdez] See Rudyard Kipling, "The Song of Diego Valdez" (1902).

Index

THE LIBRARY OF AMERICA SERIES

Library of America fosters appreciation of America's literary heritage by publishing, and keeping permanently in print, authoritative editions of America's best and most significant writing. An independent nonprofit organization, it was founded in 1979 with seed funding from the National Endowment for the Humanities and the Ford Foundation.

1. Herman Melville: Typee, Omoo, Mardi
2. Nathaniel Hawthorne: Tales & Sketches
3. Walt Whitman: Poetry & Prose
4. Harriet Beecher Stowe: Three Novels
5. Mark Twain: Mississippi Writings
6. Jack London: Novels & Stories
7. Jack London: Novels & Social Writings
8. William Dean Howells: Novels 1875–1886
9. Herman Melville: Redburn, White-Jacket, Moby-Dick
10. Nathaniel Hawthorne: Collected Novels
11 & 12. Francis Parkman: France and England in North America
13. Henry James: Novels 1871–1880
14. Henry Adams: Novels, Mont Saint Michel, The Education
15. Ralph Waldo Emerson: Essays & Lectures
16. Washington Irving: History, Tales & Sketches
17. Thomas Jefferson: Writings
18. Stephen Crane: Prose & Poetry
19. Edgar Allan Poe: Poetry & Tales
20. Edgar Allan Poe: Essays & Reviews
21. Mark Twain: The Innocents Abroad, Roughing It
22 & 23. Henry James: Literary Criticism
24. Herman Melville: Pierre, Israel Potter, The Confidence-Man, Tales & Billy Budd
25. William Faulkner: Novels 1930–1935
26 & 27. James Fenimore Cooper: The Leatherstocking Tales
28. Henry David Thoreau: A Week, Walden, The Maine Woods, Cape Cod
29. Henry James: Novels 1881–1886
30. Edith Wharton: Novels
31 & 32. Henry Adams: History of the U.S. during the Administrations of Jefferson & Madison
33. Frank Norris: Novels & Essays
34. W.E.B. Du Bois: Writings
35. Willa Cather: Early Novels & Stories
36. Theodore Dreiser: Sister Carrie, Jennie Gerhardt, Twelve Men
37. Benjamin Franklin: Writings (2 vols.)
38. William James: Writings 1902–1910
39. Flannery O'Connor: Collected Works
40, 41, & 42. Eugene O'Neill: Complete Plays
43. Henry James: Novels 1886–1890
44. William Dean Howells: Novels 1886–1888
45 & 46. Abraham Lincoln: Speeches & Writings
47. Edith Wharton: Novellas & Other Writings
48. William Faulkner: Novels 1936–1940
49. Willa Cather: Later Novels
50. Ulysses S. Grant: Memoirs & Selected Letters
51. William Tecumseh Sherman: Memoirs
52. Washington Irving: Bracebridge Hall, Tales of a Traveller, The Alhambra
53. Francis Parkman: The Oregon Trail, The Conspiracy of Pontiac
54. James Fenimore Cooper: Sea Tales
55 & 56. Richard Wright: Works
57. Willa Cather: Stories, Poems, & Other Writings
58. William James: Writings 1878–1899
59. Sinclair Lewis: Main Street & Babbitt
60 & 61. Mark Twain: Collected Tales, Sketches, Speeches, & Essays
62 & 63. The Debate on the Constitution
64 & 65. Henry James: Collected Travel Writings
66 & 67. American Poetry: The Nineteenth Century
68. Frederick Douglass: Autobiographies
69. Sarah Orne Jewett: Novels & Stories
70. Ralph Waldo Emerson: Collected Poems & Translations
71. Mark Twain: Historical Romances
72. John Steinbeck: Novels & Stories 1932–1937
73. William Faulkner: Novels 1942–1954
74 & 75. Zora Neale Hurston: Novels, Stories, & Other Writings
76. Thomas Paine: Collected Writings
77 & 78. Reporting World War II: American Journalism
79 & 80. Raymond Chandler: Novels, Stories, & Other Writings

81. Robert Frost: Collected Poems, Prose, & Plays
82 & 83. Henry James: Complete Stories 1892–1910
84. William Bartram: Travels & Other Writings
85. John Dos Passos: U.S.A.
86. John Steinbeck: The Grapes of Wrath & Other Writings 1936–1941
87, 88, & 89. Vladimir Nabokov: Novels & Other Writings
90. James Thurber: Writings & Drawings
91. George Washington: Writings
92. John Muir: Nature Writings
93. Nathanael West: Novels & Other Writings
94 & 95. Crime Novels: American Noir of the 1930s, 40s, & 50s
96. Wallace Stevens: Collected Poetry & Prose
97. James Baldwin: Early Novels & Stories
98. James Baldwin: Collected Essays
99 & 100. Gertrude Stein: Writings
101 & 102. Eudora Welty: Novels, Stories, & Other Writings
103. Charles Brockden Brown: Three Gothic Novels
104 & 105. Reporting Vietnam: American Journalism
106 & 107. Henry James: Complete Stories 1874–1891
108. American Sermons
109. James Madison: Writings
110. Dashiell Hammett: Complete Novels
111. Henry James: Complete Stories 1864–1874
112. William Faulkner: Novels 1957–1962
113. John James Audubon: Writings & Drawings
114. Slave Narratives
115 & 116. American Poetry: The Twentieth Century
117. F. Scott Fitzgerald: Novels & Stories 1920–1922
118. Henry Wadsworth Longfellow: Poems & Other Writings
119 & 120. Tennessee Williams: Collected Plays
121 & 122. Edith Wharton: Collected Stories
123. The American Revolution: Writings from the War of Independence
124. Henry David Thoreau: Collected Essays & Poems
125. Dashiell Hammett: Crime Stories & Other Writings
126 & 127. Dawn Powell: Novels
128. Carson McCullers: Complete Novels
129. Alexander Hamilton: Writings
130. Mark Twain: The Gilded Age & Later Novels
131. Charles W. Chesnutt: Stories, Novels, & Essays
132. John Steinbeck: Novels 1942–1952
133. Sinclair Lewis: Arrowsmith, Elmer Gantry, Dodsworth
134 & 135. Paul Bowles: Novels, Stories, & Other Writings
136. Kate Chopin: Complete Novels & Stories
137 & 138. Reporting Civil Rights: American Journalism
139. Henry James: Novels 1896–1899
140. Theodore Dreiser: An American Tragedy
141. Saul Bellow: Novels 1944–1953
142. John Dos Passos: Novels 1920–1925
143. John Dos Passos: Travel Books & Other Writings
144. Ezra Pound: Poems & Translations
145. James Weldon Johnson: Writings
146. Washington Irving: Three Western Narratives
147. Alexis de Tocqueville: Democracy in America
148. James T. Farrell: Studs Lonigan Trilogy
149, 150, & 151. Isaac Bashevis Singer: Collected Stories
152. Kaufman & Co.: Broadway Comedies
153. Theodore Roosevelt: Rough Riders, An Autobiography
154. Theodore Roosevelt: Letters & Speeches
155. H. P. Lovecraft: Tales
156. Louisa May Alcott: Little Women, Little Men, Jo's Boys
157. Philip Roth: Novels & Stories 1959–1962
158. Philip Roth: Novels 1967–1972
159. James Agee: Let Us Now Praise Famous Men, A Death in the Family, Shorter Fiction
160. James Agee: Film Writing & Selected Journalism
161. Richard Henry Dana Jr.: Two Years Before the Mast & Other Voyages
162. Henry James: Novels 1901–1902
163. Arthur Miller: Plays 1944–1961
164. William Faulkner: Novels 1926–1929
165. Philip Roth: Novels 1973–1977
166 & 167. American Speeches: Political Oratory
168. Hart Crane: Complete Poems & Selected Letters

169. Saul Bellow: Novels 1956–1964
170. John Steinbeck: Travels with Charley & Later Novels
171. Capt. John Smith: Writings with Other Narratives
172. Thornton Wilder: Collected Plays & Writings on Theater
173. Philip K. Dick: Four Novels of the 1960s
174. Jack Kerouac: Road Novels 1957–1960
175. Philip Roth: Zuckerman Bound
176 & 177. Edmund Wilson: Literary Essays & Reviews
178. American Poetry: The 17th & 18th Centuries
179. William Maxwell: Early Novels & Stories
180. Elizabeth Bishop: Poems, Prose, & Letters
181. A. J. Liebling: World War II Writings
182. American Earth: Environmental Writing Since Thoreau
183. Philip K. Dick: Five Novels of the 1960s & 70s
184. William Maxwell: Later Novels & Stories
185. Philip Roth: Novels & Other Narratives 1986–1991
186. Katherine Anne Porter: Collected Stories & Other Writings
187. John Ashbery: Collected Poems 1956–1987
188 & 189. John Cheever: Complete Novels & Collected Stories
190. Lafcadio Hearn: American Writings
191. A. J. Liebling: The Sweet Science & Other Writings
192. The Lincoln Anthology
193. Philip K. Dick: VALIS & Later Novels
194. Thornton Wilder: The Bridge of San Luis Rey & Other Novels 1926–1948
195. Raymond Carver: Collected Stories
196 & 197. American Fantastic Tales
198. John Marshall: Writings
199. The Mark Twain Anthology
200. Mark Twain: A Tramp Abroad, Following the Equator, Other Travels
201 & 202. Ralph Waldo Emerson: Selected Journals
203. The American Stage: Writing on Theater
204. Shirley Jackson: Novels & Stories
205. Philip Roth: Novels 1993–1995
206 & 207. H. L. Mencken: Prejudices
208. John Kenneth Galbraith: The Affluent Society & Other Writings 1952–1967
209. Saul Bellow: Novels 1970–1982
210 & 211. Lynd Ward: Six Novels in Woodcuts
212. The Civil War: The First Year
213 & 214. John Adams: Revolutionary Writings
215. Henry James: Novels 1903–1911
216. Kurt Vonnegut: Novels & Stories 1963–1973
217 & 218. Harlem Renaissance Novels
219. Ambrose Bierce: The Devil's Dictionary, Tales, & Memoirs
220. Philip Roth: The American Trilogy 1997–2000
221. The Civil War: The Second Year
222. Barbara W. Tuchman: The Guns of August, The Proud Tower
223. Arthur Miller: Plays 1964–1982
224. Thornton Wilder: The Eighth Day, Theophilus North, Autobiographical Writings
225. David Goodis: Five Noir Novels of the 1940s & 50s
226. Kurt Vonnegut: Novels & Stories 1950–1962
227 & 228. American Science Fiction: Nine Novels of the 1950s
229 & 230. Laura Ingalls Wilder: The Little House Books
231. Jack Kerouac: Collected Poems
232. The War of 1812
233. American Antislavery Writings
234. The Civil War: The Third Year
235. Sherwood Anderson: Collected Stories
236. Philip Roth: Novels 2001–2007
237. Philip Roth: Nemeses
238. Aldo Leopold: A Sand County Almanac & Other Writings
239. May Swenson: Collected Poems
240 & 241. W. S. Merwin: Collected Poems
242 & 243. John Updike: Collected Stories
244. Ring Lardner: Stories & Other Writings
245. Jonathan Edwards: Writings from the Great Awakening
246. Susan Sontag: Essays of the 1960s & 70s
247. William Wells Brown: Clotel & Other Writings
248 & 249. Bernard Malamud: Novels & Stories of the 1940s, 50s, & 60s
250. The Civil War: The Final Year
251. Shakespeare in America

252. Kurt Vonnegut: Novels 1976–1985
253 & 254. American Musicals 1927–1969
255. Elmore Leonard: Four Novels of the 1970s
256. Louisa May Alcott: Work, Eight Cousins, Rose in Bloom, Stories & Other Writings
257. H. L. Mencken: The Days Trilogy
258. Virgil Thomson: Music Chronicles 1940–1954
259. Art in America 1945–1970
260. Saul Bellow: Novels 1984–2000
261. Arthur Miller: Plays 1987–2004
262. Jack Kerouac: Visions of Cody, Visions of Gerard, Big Sur
263. Reinhold Niebuhr: Major Works on Religion & Politics
264. Ross Macdonald: Four Novels of the 1950s
265 & 266. The American Revolution: Writings from the Pamphlet Debate
267. Elmore Leonard: Four Novels of the 1980s
268 & 269. Women Crime Writers: Suspense Novels of the 1940s & 50s
270. Frederick Law Olmsted: Writings on Landscape, Culture, & Society
271. Edith Wharton: Four Novels of the 1920s
272. James Baldwin: Later Novels
273. Kurt Vonnegut: Novels 1987–1997
274. Henry James: Autobiographies
275. Abigail Adams: Letters
276. John Adams: Writings from the New Nation 1784–1826
277. Virgil Thomson: The State of Music & Other Writings
278. War No More: American Antiwar & Peace Writing
279. Ross Macdonald: Three Novels of the Early 1960s
280. Elmore Leonard: Four Later Novels
281. Ursula K. Le Guin: The Complete Orsinia
282. John O'Hara: Stories
283. The Unknown Kerouac: Rare, Unpublished & Newly Translated Writings
284. Albert Murray: Collected Essays & Memoirs
285 & 286. Loren Eiseley: Collected Essays on Evolution, Nature, & the Cosmos
287. Carson McCullers: Stories, Plays & Other Writings
288. Jane Bowles: Collected Writings
289. World War I and America: Told by the Americans Who Lived It
290 & 291. Mary McCarthy: The Complete Fiction
292. Susan Sontag: Later Essays
293 & 294. John Quincy Adams: Diaries
295. Ross Macdonald: Four Later Novels
296 & 297. Ursula K. Le Guin: The Hainish Novels & Stories
298 & 299. Peter Taylor: The Complete Stories
300. Philip Roth: Why Write? Collected Nonfiction 1960–2014
301. John Ashbery: Collected Poems 1991–2000
302. Wendell Berry: Port William Novels & Stories: The Civil War to World War II
303. Reconstruction: Voices from America's First Great Struggle for Racial Equality
304. Albert Murray: Collected Novels & Poems
305 & 306. Norman Mailer: The Sixties
307. Rachel Carson: Silent Spring & Other Writings on the Environment
308. Elmore Leonard: Westerns
309 & 310. Madeleine L'Engle: The Kairos Novels
311. John Updike: Novels 1959–1965
312. James Fenimore Cooper: Two Novels of the American Revolution
313. John O'Hara: Four Novels of the 1930s
314. Ann Petry: The Street, The Narrows
315. Ursula K. Le Guin: Always Coming Home
316 & 317. Wendell Berry: Collected Essays
318. Cornelius Ryan: The Longest Day, A Bridge Too Far
319. Booth Tarkington: Novels & Stories
320. Herman Melville: Complete Poems
321 & 322. American Science Fiction: Eight Classic Novels of the 1960s
323. Frances Hodgson Burnett: The Secret Garden, A Little Princess, Little Lord Fauntleroy
324. Jean Stafford: Complete Novels
325. Joan Didion: The 1960s & 70s
326. John Updike: Novels 1968–1975
327. Constance Fenimore Woolson: Collected Stories
328. Robert Stone: Dog Soldiers, Flag for Sunrise, Outerbridge Reach
329. Jonathan Schell: The Fate of the Earth, The Abolition, The Unconquerable World
330. Richard Hofstadter: Anti-Intellectualism in American Life, The Paranoid Style in American Politics, Uncollected Essays 1956–1965

Library of America, a nonprofit organization, champions our nation's cultural heritage by publishing America's greatest writing in authoritative new editions and providing resources for readers to explore this rich, living legacy.

H. L. MENCKEN

H. L. MENCKEN

PREJUDICES:
FIRST, SECOND, AND THIRD SERIES

Marion Elizabeth Rodgers, *editor*

THE LIBRARY OF AMERICA

H. L. MENCKEN: PREJUDICES: FIRST, SECOND, AND THIRD SERIES

Volume compilation, notes, and chronology copyright © 2010 by Literary Classics of the United States, Inc., New York, N.Y.
All rights reserved.
No part of this book may be reproduced in any manner whatsoever without the permission of the publisher, except in the case of brief quotations embodied in critical articles and reviews.

Published in the United States by Library of America.
Visit our website at www.loa.org.

Prejudices: First Series, Second Series, and Third Series copyright © 1919, 1920, 1922 by Alfred A. Knopf, Inc., renewed 1947, 1948, 1950 by H. L. Mencken. Reprinted by arrangement with Alfred A. Knopf, an imprint of The Knopf Doubleday Publishing Group, a division of Random House, Inc.

My Life as Author and Editor copyright © 1992 by Enoch Pratt Free Library.

Permission to quote H. L. Mencken has been granted by the Enoch Pratt Free Library, Baltimore, in accordance with the terms of the bequest of H. L. Mencken.

This paper exceeds the requirements of ANSI/NISO Z39.48–1992 (Permanence of Paper).

Distributed to the trade in the United States by Penguin Random House Inc. and in Canada by Penguin Random House Canada Ltd.

Library of Congress Control Number: 2010924448
ISBN 978-1-59853-074-2

Third Printing
The Library of America—206

Manufactured in the United States of America

H. L. Mencken's
Prejudices
is published with a gift in honor of

JAY CARL PENSKE

on his 30th birthday
from his parents,

Kathryn & Roger Penske

Contents

THIRD SERIES

PREJUDICES:
FIRST SERIES

I.
Criticism of Criticism of Criticism

EVERY now and then, a sense of the futility of their daily endeavors falling suddenly upon them, the critics of Christendom turn to a somewhat sour and depressing consideration of the nature and objects of their own craft. That is to say, they turn to criticizing criticism. What is it in plain words? What is its aim, exactly stated in legal terms? How far can it go? What good can it do? What is its normal effect upon the artist and the work of art?

Such a spell of self-searching has been in progress for several years past, and the critics of various countries have contributed theories of more or less lucidity and plausibility to the discussion. Their views of their own art, it appears, are quite as divergent as their views of the arts they more commonly deal with. One group argues, partly by direct statement and partly by attacking all other groups, that the one defensible purpose of the critic is to encourage the virtuous and oppose the sinful—in brief, to police the fine arts and so hold them in tune with the moral order of the world. Another group, repudiating this constabulary function, argues hotly that the arts have nothing to do with morality whatsoever—that their concern is solely with pure beauty. A third group holds that the chief aspect of a work of art, particularly in the field of literature, is its aspect as psychological document—that if it doesn't help men to know themselves it is nothing. A fourth group reduces the thing to an exact science, and sets up standards that resemble algebraic formulæ—this is the group of metrists, of contrapuntists and of those who gabble of light-waves. And so, in order, follow groups five, six, seven, eight, nine, ten, each with its theory and its proofs.

Against the whole corps, moral and æsthetic, psychological and algebraic, stands Major J. E. Spingarn, U.S.A. Major Spingarn lately served formal notice upon me that he had abandoned the life of the academic grove for that of the armed array, and so I give him his military title, but at the time he wrote his "Creative Criticism" he was a professor in Columbia University, and I still find myself thinking of him, not as a soldier extraordinarily literate, but as a professor in rebellion. For his notions, whatever one may say in opposition to them, are at least magnificently unprofessorial—they fly violently in the face of the principles that distinguish the largest and most influential group of campus critics. As witness: "To say that poetry is moral or immoral is as meaningless as to say that an equilateral triangle is moral and an isosceles triangle immoral." Or, worse: "It is only conceivable in a world in which dinner-table conversation runs after this fashion: 'This cauliflower would be good if it had only been prepared in accordance with international law.'" One imagines, on hearing such atheism flying about, the amazed indignation of Prof. Dr. William Lyon Phelps, with his discovery that Joseph Conrad preaches "the axiom of the moral law"; the "Hey, what's that!" of Prof. Dr. W. C. Brownell, the Amherst Aristotle, with his eloquent plea for standards as iron-clad as the Westminster Confession; the loud, patriotic alarm of the gifted Prof. Dr. Stuart P. Sherman, of Iowa, with his maxim that Puritanism is the official philosophy of America, and that all who dispute it are enemy aliens and should be deported. Major Spingarn, in truth, here performs a treason most horrible upon the reverend order he once adorned, and having achieved it, he straightway performs another and then another. That is to say, he tackles all the antagonistic groups of orthodox critics seriatim, and knocks them about unanimously—first the aforesaid agents of the sweet and pious; then the advocates of unities, meters, all rigid formulæ; then the experts in imaginary psychology; then the historical comparers, pigeonholers and makers of categories; finally, the professors of pure esthetic. One and all, they take their places upon his operating table, and one and all they are stripped and anatomized.

But what is the anarchistic ex-professor's own theory?—for a professor must have a theory, as a dog must have fleas. In brief, what he offers is a doctrine borrowed from the Italian, Benedetto Croce, and by Croce filched from Goethe—a doctrine anything but new in the world, even in Goethe's time, but nevertheless long buried in forgetfulness—to wit, the doctrine that it is the critic's first and only duty, as Carlyle once put it, to find out "what the poet's aim really and truly was, how the task he had to do stood before his eye, and how far, with such materials as were afforded him, he has fulfilled it." For poet, read artist, or, if literature is in question, substitute the Germanic word *Dichter*—that is, the artist in words, the creator of beautiful letters, whether in verse or in prose. Ibsen always called himself a *Digter*, not a *Dramatiker* or *Skuespiller*. So, I daresay, did Shakespeare. . . . Well, what is this generalized poet trying to do? asks Major Spingarn, and how has he done it? That, and no more, is the critic's quest. The morality of the work does not concern him. It is not his business to determine whether it heeds Aristotle or flouts Aristotle. He passes no judgment on its rhyme scheme, its length and breadth, its iambics, its politics, its patriotism, its piety, its psychological exactness, its good taste. He may note these things, but he may not protest about them—he may not complain if the thing criticized fails to fit into a pigeon-hole. Every sonnet, every drama, every novel is *sui generis*; it must stand on its own bottom; it must be judged by its own inherent intentions. "Poets," says Major Spingarn, "do not really write epics, pastorals, lyrics, however much they may be deceived by these false abstractions; they express *themselves, and this expression is their only form*. There are not, therefore, only three or ten or a hundred literary kinds; there are as many kinds as there are individual poets." Nor is there any valid appeal *ad hominem*. The character and background of the poet are beside the mark; the poem itself is the thing. Oscar Wilde, weak and swine-like, yet wrote beautiful prose. To reject that prose on the ground that Wilde had filthy habits is as absurd as to reject "What Is Man?" on the ground that its theology is beyond the intelligence of the editor of the New York *Times*.

This Spingarn-Croce-Carlyle-Goethe theory, of course, throws a heavy burden upon the critic. It presupposes that he is a civilized and tolerant man, hospitable to all intelligible ideas and capable of reading them as he runs. This is a demand that at once rules out nine-tenths of the grown-up sophomores who carry on the business of criticism in America. Their trouble is simply that they lack the intellectual resilience necessary for taking in ideas, and particularly new ideas. The only way they can ingest one is by transforming it into the nearest related formula—usually a harsh and devastating operation. This fact accounts for their chronic inability to understand all that is most personal and original and hence most forceful and significant in the emerging literature of the country. They can get down what has been digested and re-digested, and so brought into forms that they know, and carefully labeled by predecessors of their own sort—but they exhibit alarm immediately they come into the presence of the extraordinary. Here we have an explanation of Brownell's loud appeal for a tightening of standards—*i.e.*, a larger respect for precedents, patterns, rubber-stamps—and here we have an explanation of Phelps's inability to comprehend the colossal phenomenon of Dreiser, and of Boynton's childish nonsense about realism, and of Sherman's effort to apply the Espionage Act to the arts, and of More's querulous enmity to romanticism, and of all the fatuous pigeon-holing that passes for criticism in the more solemn literary periodicals.

As practiced by all such learned and diligent but essentially ignorant and unimaginative men, criticism is little more than a branch of homiletics. They judge a work of art, not by its clarity and sincerity, not by the force and charm of its ideas, not by the technical virtuosity of the artist, not by his originality and artistic courage, but simply and solely by his orthodoxy. If he is what is called a "right thinker," if he devotes himself to advocating the transient platitudes in a sonorous manner, then he is worthy of respect. But if he lets fall the slightest hint that he is in doubt about any of them, or, worse still, that he is indifferent, then he is a scoundrel, and hence, by their theory, a bad artist. Such pious piffle is horribly familiar among us. I do not exaggerate its terms. You will find it running through the critical writings of practically all the dull fellows who combine criticism with tutoring; in the words of many of them it is stated in the plainest way and defended with much heat, theological and pedagogical. In its baldest form it shows itself in the doctrine that it is scandalous for an artist—say a dramatist or a novelist—to depict vice as attractive. The fact that vice, more often than not, undoubtedly *is* attractive—else why should it ever gobble any of us?—is disposed of with a lofty gesture. What of it? say these birchmen. The artist is not a reporter, but a Great Teacher. It is not his business to depict the world as it is, but as it ought to be.

Against this notion American criticism makes but feeble headway. We are, in fact, a nation of evangelists; every third American devotes himself to improving and lifting up his fellow-citizens, usually by force; the messianic delusion is our national disease. Thus the moral *Privatdozenten* have the crowd on their side, and it is difficult to shake their authority; even the vicious are still in favor of crying vice down. "Here is a novel," says the artist. "Why didn't you write a tract?" roars the professor—and down the chute go novel and novelist. "This girl is pretty," says the painter. "But she has left off her undershirt," protests the head-master—and off goes the poor dauber's head. At its mildest, this balderdash takes the form of the late Hamilton Wright Mabie's "White List of Books"; at its worst, it is comstockery, an idiotic and abominable thing. Genuine criticism is as impossible to such inordinately narrow and cocksure men as music is to a man who is tone-deaf. The critic, to interpret his artist, even to understand his artist, must be able to get into the mind of his artist; he must feel and comprehend the vast pressure of the creative passion; as Major Spingarn says, "æsthetic judgment and artistic creation are instinct with the same vital life." This is why all the best criticism of the world has been written by men who have had within them, not only the reflective and analytical faculty of critics, but also the gusto of artists—Goethe, Carlyle, Lessing, Schlegel, Saint-Beuve, and, to drop a story or two, Hazlitt, Hermann Bahr, Georg Brandes and James Huneker. Huneker, tackling "Also sprach Zarathustra," revealed its content in illuminating flashes. But tackled by Paul Elmer More, it became no more than a dull student's exercise, ill-naturedly corrected. . . .

So much for the theory of Major J. E. Spingarn, U.S.A., late professor of modern languages and literatures in Columbia University. Obviously, it is a far sounder and more stimulating theory than any of those cherished by the other professors. It demands that the critic be a man of intelligence, of toleration, of wide information, of genuine hospitality to ideas, whereas the others only demand that he have learning, and accept anything as learning that has been said before. But once he has stated his doctrine, the ingenious ex-professor, professor-like, immediately begins to corrupt it by claiming too much for it. Having laid and hatched, so to speak, his somewhat stale but still highly nourishing egg, he begins to argue fatuously that the resultant flamingo is the whole mustering of the critical *Aves.* But the fact is, of course, that criticism, as humanly practiced, must needs fall a good deal short of this intuitive recreation of beauty, and what is more, it must go a good deal further. For one thing, it must be interpretation in terms that are not only exact but are also comprehensible to the reader, else it will leave the original mystery as dark as before—and once interpretation comes in, paraphrase and transliteration come in. What is recondite must be made plainer; the transcendental, to some extent at least, must be done into common modes of thinking. Well, what are morality, trochaics, hexameters, movements, historical principles, psychological maxims, the dramatic unities—what are all these save common modes of thinking, short cuts, rubber stamps, words of one syllable? Moreover, beauty as we know it in this world is by no means the apparition *in vacuo* that Dr. Spingarn seems to see. It has its social, its political, even its moral implications. The finale of Beethoven's C minor symphony is not only colossal as music; it is also colossal as revolt; it says something against something. Yet more, the springs of beauty are not within itself alone, nor even in genius alone, but often in things without. Brahms wrote his Deutsches Requiem, not only because he was a great artist, but also because he was a good German. And in Nietzsche there are times when the divine afflatus takes a back seat, and the *spirochaetae* have the floor.

Major Spingarn himself seems to harbor some sense of this limitation on his doctrine. He gives warning that "the poet's intention must be judged at the moment of the creative act"—which opens the door enough for many an ancient to creep in. But limited or not, he at least clears off a lot of moldy rubbish, and gets further toward the truth than any of his former colleagues. They waste themselves upon theories that only conceal the poet's achievement the more, the more diligently they are applied; he, at all events, grounds himself upon the sound notion that there should be free speech in art, and no protective tariffs, and no *a priori* assumptions, and no testing of ideas by mere words. The safe ground probably lies between the contestants, but nearer Spingarn. The critic who really illuminates starts off much as he starts off, but with a due regard for the prejudices and imbecilities of the world. I think the best feasible practice is to be found in certain chapters of Huneker, a critic of vastly more solid influence and of infinitely more value to the arts than all the prating pedagogues since Rufus Griswold. Here, as in the case of Poe, a sensitive and intelligent artist recreates the work of other artists, but there also comes to the ceremony a man of the world, and the things he has to say are apposite and instructive too. To denounce moralizing out of hand is to pronounce a moral judgment. To dispute the categories is to set up a new anti-categorical category. And to admire the work of Shakespeare is to be interested in his handling of blank verse, his social aspirations, his shot-gun marriage and his frequent concessions to the bombastic frenzy of his actors, and to have some curiosity about Mr. W. H. The really competent critic must be an empiricist. He must conduct his exploration with whatever means lie within the bounds of his personal limitation. He must produce his effects with whatever tools will work. If pills fail, he gets out his saw. If the saw won't cut, he seizes a club. . . .

Perhaps, after all, the chief burden that lies upon Major Spingarn's theory is to be found in its label. The word "creative" is a bit too flamboyant; it says what he wants to say, but it probably says a good deal more. In this emergency, I propose getting rid of the misleading label by pasting another over it. That is, I propose the substitution of "catalytic" for "creative," despite the fact that "catalytic" is an unfamiliar word, and suggests the dog-Latin of the seminaries. I borrow it from chemistry, and its meaning is really quite simple. A catalyzer, in chemistry, is a substance that helps two other substances to react. For example, consider the case of ordinary cane sugar and water. Dissolve the sugar in the water and nothing happens. But add a few drops of acid and the sugar changes into glucose and fructose. Meanwhile, the acid itself is absolutely unchanged. All it does is to stir up the reaction between the water and the sugar. The process is called catalysis. The acid is a catalyzer.

Well, this is almost exactly the function of a genuine critic of the arts. It is his business to provoke the reaction between the work of art and the spectator. The spectator, untutored, stands unmoved; he sees the work of art, but it fails to make any intelligible impression on him; if he were spontaneously sensitive to it, there would be no need for criticism. But now comes the critic with his catalysis. He makes the work of art live for the spectator; he makes the spectator live for the work of art. Out of the process comes understanding, appreciation, intelligent enjoyment—and that is precisely what the artist tried to produce.

II.
The Late Mr. Wells

THE man as artist, I fear, is extinct—not by some sudden and romantic catastrophe, like his own Richard Remington, but after a process of gradual and obscure decay. In his day he was easily the most brilliant, if not always the most profound, of contemporary English novelists. There were in him all of the requisites for the business and most of them very abundantly. He had a lively and charming imagination, he wrote with the utmost fluency and address, he had humor and eloquence, he had a sharp eye for the odd and intriguing in human character, and, most of all, he was full of feeling and could transmit it to the reader. That high day of his lasted, say, from 1908 to 1912. It began with "Tono-Bungay" and ended amid the last scenes of "Marriage," as the well-made play of Scribe gave up the ghost in the last act of "A Doll's House." There, in "Marriage," were the first faint signs of something wrong. Invention succumbed to theories that somehow failed to hang together, and the story, after vast heavings, incontinently went to pieces. One had begun with an acute and highly diverting study of monogamy in modern London; one found one's self, toward the close, gaping over an unconvincing fable of marriage in the Stone Age. Coming directly after so vivid a personage as Remington, Dr. Richard Godwin Trafford simply refused to go down. And his Marjorie, following his example, stuck in the gullet of the imagination. One ceased to believe in them when they set out for Labrador, and after that it was impossible to revive interest in them. The more they were explained and vivisected and drenched with theories, the more unreal they became.

Since then the decline of Wells has been as steady as his rise was rapid. Call the roll of his books, and you will discern a progressive and unmistakable falling off. Into "The Passionate Friends" there crept the first downright dullness. By this time his readers had become familiar with his machinery and his materials—his elbowing suffragettes, his tea-swilling London uplifters, his smattering of quasi-science, his intellectualized adulteries, his Thackerayan asides, his text-book paragraphs, his journalistic raciness—and all these things had thus begun to lose the blush of their first charm. To help them out he heaved in larger and larger doses of theory—often diverting enough, and sometimes even persuasive, but in the long run a poor substitute for the proper ingredients of character, situation and human passion. Next came "The Wife of Sir Isaac Harman," an attempt to rewrite "A Doll's House" (with a fourth act) in terms of ante-bellum 1914. The result was 500-odd pages of bosh, a flabby and tedious piece of work, Wells for the first time in the rôle of unmistakable bore. And then "Bealby," with its Palais Royal jocosity, its running in and out of doors, its humor of physical collision, its reminiscences of "A Trip to Chinatown" and "Peck's Bad Boy." And then "Boon," a heavy-witted satire, often incomprehensible, always incommoded by its disguise as a novel. And then "The Research Magnificent": a poor soup from the dry bones of Nietzsche. And then "Mr. Britling Sees It Through" . . .

Here, for a happy moment, there seemed to be something better—almost, in fact, a recrudescence of the Wells of 1910. But that seeming was only seeming. What confused the judgment was the enormous popular success of the book. Because it presented a fifth-rate Englishman in an heroic aspect, because it sentimentalized the whole reaction of the English proletariat to the war, it offered a subtle sort of flattery to other fifth-rate Englishmen, and, *per corollary*, to Americans of corresponding degree, to wit, the second. Thus it made a great pother, and was hymned as a masterpiece in such gazettes as the New York *Times*, as Blasco Ibáñez's "The Four Horsemen of the Apocalypse" was destined to be hymned three years later. But there was in the book, in point of fact, a great hollowness, and that hollowness presently begat an implosion that disposed of the shell. I daresay many a novel-reader returns, now and then, to "Tono-Bungay," and even to "Ann Veronica." But surely only a reader with absolutely nothing else to read would return to "Mr. Britling Sees It Through." There followed—what? "The Soul of a Bishop," perhaps the worst novel ever written by a serious novelist since novel-writing began. And then—or perhaps a bit before, or simultaneously

—an idiotic religious tract—a tract so utterly feeble and preposterous that even the Scotchman, William Archer, could not stomach it. And then, to make an end, came "Joan and Peter" —and the collapse of Wells was revealed at last in its true proportions.

This "Joan and Peter" I confess, lingers in my memory as unpleasantly as a summer cold, and so, in retrospect, I may perhaps exaggerate its intrinsic badness. I would not look into it again for gold and frankincense. I was at the job of reading it for days and days, endlessly daunted and halted by its laborious dullness, its flatulent fatuity, its almost fabulous inconsequentiality. It was, and is, nearly impossible to believe that the Wells of "Tono-Bungay" and "The History of Mr. Polly" wrote it, or that he was in the full possession of his faculties when he allowed it to be printed under his name. For in it there is the fault that the Wells of those days, almost beyond any other fictioneer of the time, was incapable of—the fault of dismalness, of tediousness—the witless and contagious coma of the evangelist. Here, for nearly six hundred pages of fine type, he rolls on in an intellectual cloud, boring one abominably with uninteresting people, pointless situations, revelations that reveal nothing, arguments that have no appositeness, expositions that expose naught save an insatiable and torturing garrulity. Where is the old fine address of the man? Where is his sharp eye for the salient and significant in character? Where is his instinct for form, his skill at putting a story together, his hand for making it unwind itself? These things are so far gone that it becomes hard to believe that they ever existed. There is not the slightest sign of them in "Joan and Peter." The book is a botch from end to end, and in that botch there is not even the palliation of an arduous enterprise gallantly attempted. No inherent difficulty is visible. The story is anything but complex, and surely anything but subtle. Its badness lies wholly in the fact that the author made a mess of the writing, that his quondam cunning, once so exhilarating, was gone when he began it.

Reviewing it at the time of its publication, I inclined momentarily to the notion that the war was to blame. No one could overestimate the cost of that struggle to the English, not only in men and money, but also and more importantly in the things of the spirit. It developed national traits that were greatly at odds with the old ideal of Anglo-Saxon character—an extravagant hysteria, a tendency to whimper under blows, political radicalism and credulity. It overthrew the old ruling caste of the land and gave over the control of things to upstarts from the lowest classes—shady Jews, snuffling Methodists, prehensile commercial gents, disgusting demagogues, all sorts of self-seeking adventurers. Worst of all, the strain seemed to work havoc with the customary dignity and reticence, and even with the plain commonsense of many Englishmen on a higher level, and in particular many English writers. The astounding bawling of Kipling and the no less astounding bombast of G. K. Chesterton were anything but isolated; there were, in fact, scores of other eminent authors in the same state of eruption, and a study of the resultant literature of objurgation will make a fascinating job for some sweating *Privatdozent* of to-morrow, say out of Göttingen or Jena. It occurred to me, as I say, that Wells might have become afflicted by this same demoralization, but reflection disposed of the notion. On the one hand, there was the plain fact that his actual writings on the war, while marked by the bitterness of the time, were anything but insane, and on the other hand there was the equally plain fact that his decay had been in progress a long while before the Germans made their fateful thrust at Liège.

The precise thing that ailed him I found at last on page 272 *et seq.* of the American edition of his book. There it was plainly described, albeit unwittingly, but if you will go back to the other novels since "Marriage" you will find traces of it in all of them, and even more vivid indications in the books of exposition and philosophizing that have accompanied them. What has slowly crippled him and perhaps disposed of him is his gradual acceptance of the theory, corrupting to the artist and scarcely less so to the man, that he is one of the Great Thinkers of his era, charged with a pregnant Message to the Younger Generation—that his ideas, rammed into enough skulls, will Save the Empire, not only from the satanic Nietzscheism of the Hindenburgs and post-Hindenburgs, but also from all those inner Weaknesses that taint and flabbergast its vitals, as the tapeworm with nineteen heads devoured Atharippus of Macedon. In brief, he suffers from a messianic delusion—and once a man begins to suffer from a messianic delusion his days as a serious artist are ended. He may yet serve the state with laudable devotion; he may yet enchant his millions; he may yet posture and gyrate before the world as a man of mark. But not in the character of artist. Not as a creator of sound books. Not in the separate place of one who observes the eternal tragedy of man with full sympathy and understanding, and yet with a touch of god-like remoteness. Not as Homer saw it, smiting the while his blooming lyre.

I point, as I say, to page 272 of "Joan and Peter," whereon, imperfectly concealed by jocosity, you will find Wells' private view of Wells—a view at once too flattering and libelous. What it shows is the absorption of the artist in the tin-pot reformer and professional wise man. A descent, indeed! The man impinged upon us and made his first solid success, not as a merchant of banal pedagogics, not as a hawker of sociological liver-pills, but as a master of brilliant and life-like representation, an evoker of unaccustomed but none the less deep-seated emotions, a dramatist of fine imagination and highly resourceful execution. It was the stupendous drama and spectacle of modern life, and not its dubious and unintelligible lessons, that drew him from his test-tubes and guinea-pigs and made an artist of him, and to the business of that artist, once he had served his apprenticeship, he brought a vision so keen, a point of view so fresh and sane and a talent for exhibition so lively and original that he straightway conquered all of us. Nothing could exceed the sheer radiance of "Tono-Bungay." It is a work that glows with reality. It projects a whole epoch with unforgettable effect. It is a moving-picture conceived and arranged, not by the usual ex-bartender or chorus man, but by an extremely civilized and sophisticated observer, alert to every detail of the surface and yet acutely aware of the internal play of forces, the essential springs, the larger, deeper lines of it. In brief, it is a work of art of the soundest merit, for it both represents accurately and interprets convincingly, and under everything is a current of feeling that co-ordinates and informs the whole.

But in the success of the book and of the two or three following it there was a temptation, and in the temptation a peril. The audience was there, high in expectation, eagerly demanding more. And in the ego of the man—a true proletarian, and hence born with morals, faiths, certainties, vasty gaseous hopes —there was an urge. That urge, it seems to me, began to torture him when he set about "The Passionate Friends." In the presence of it, he was dissuaded from the business of an artist,—made discontented with the business of an artist. It was not enough to display the life of his time with accuracy and understanding; it was not even enough to criticize it with a penetrating humor and sagacity. From the depths of his being, like some foul miasma, there arose the old, fatuous yearning to change it, to improve it, to set it right where it was wrong, to make it over according to some pattern superior to the one followed by the Lord God Jehovah. With this sinister impulse, as aberrant in an artist as a taste for legs in an archbishop, the instinct that had created "Tono-Bungay" and "The New Machiavelli" gave battle, and for a while the issue was in doubt. But with "Marriage," its trend began to be apparent—and before long the evangelist was triumphant, and his bray battered the ear, and in the end there was a quite different Wells before us, and a Wells worth infinitely less than the one driven off. To-day one must put him where he has begun to put himself—not among the literary artists of English, but among the brummagem prophets of England. His old rival was Arnold Bennett. His new rival is the Fabian Society, or maybe Lord Northcliffe, or the surviving Chesterton, or the later Hillaire Belloc.

The prophesying business is like writing fugues; it is fatal to every one save the man of absolute genius. The lesser fellow— and Wells, for all his cleverness, is surely one of the lesser fellows—is bound to come to grief at it, and one of the first signs of his coming to grief is the drying up of his sense of humor. Compare "The Soul of a Bishop" or "Joan and Peter" to "Ann Veronica" or "The History of Mr. Polly." One notices instantly the disappearance of the comic spirit, the old searching irony—in brief, of the precise thing that keeps the breath of life in Arnold Bennett. It was in "Boon," I believe, that this irony showed its last flare. There is a passage in that book which somehow lingers in the memory: a portrait of the United States as it arose in the mind of an Englishman reading the *Nation* of yesteryear: "a vain, garrulous and prosperous female of uncertain age, and still more uncertain temper, with unfounded pretensions to intellectuality and an idea of refinement of the most negative description . . . the Aunt Errant of Christendom." A capital whimsy—but blooming almost alone. A sense of humor, had it been able to survive the theology, would certainly have saved us from Lady Sunderbund, in "The Soul of a Bishop," and from Lady Charlotte Sydenham in "Joan and Peter." But it did not and could not survive. It always withers in the presence of the messianic delusion, like justice and the truth in front of patriotic passion. What takes its place is the oafish, witless buffoonishness of the chautauquas and the floor of Congress—for example, the sort of thing that makes an intolerable bore of "Bealby."

Nor are Wells' ideas, as he has so laboriously expounded them, worth the sacrifice of his old lively charm. They are, in fact, second-hand, and he often muddles them in the telling. In "First and Last Things" he preaches a flabby Socialism, and then, toward the end, admits frankly that it doesn't work. In "Boon" he erects a whole book upon an eighth-rate platitude, to wit, the platitude that English literature, in these latter times, is platitudinous—a three-cornered banality, indeed, for his own argument is a case in point, and so helps to prove what was already obvious. In "The Research Magnificent" he smouches an idea from Nietzsche, and then mauls it so badly that one begins to wonder whether he is in favor of it or against it. In "The Undying Fire" he first states the obvious, and then flees from it in alarm. In his war books he borrows right and left—from Dr. Wilson, from the British Socialists, from Romain Rolland, even from such profound thinkers as James M. Beck, Lloyd-George and the editor of the New York *Tribune*—and everything that he borrows is flat. In "Joan and Peter" he first argues that England is going to pot because English education is too formal and archaic, and then that Germany is going to pot because German education is too realistic and opportunist. He seems to respond to all the varying crazes and fallacies of the day; he swallows them without digesting them; he tries to substitute mere timeliness for reflection and feeling. And under all the rumble-bumble of bad ideas is the imbecile assumption of the jitney messiah at all times and everywhere: that human beings may be made over by changing the rules under which they live, that progress is a matter of intent and foresight, that an act of Parliament can cure the blunders and check the practical joking of God.

Such notions are surely no baggage for a serious novelist. A novelist, of course, must have a point of view, but it must be a point of view untroubled by the crazes of the moment, it must regard the internal workings and meanings of existence and not merely its superficial appearances. A novelist must view life from some secure rock, drawing it into a definite perspective, interpreting it upon an ordered plan. Even if he hold (as Conrad does, and Dreiser, and Hardy, and Anatole France) that it is essentially meaningless, he must at least display that meaninglessness with reasonable clarity and consistency. Wells shows no such solid and intelligible attitude. He is too facile, too enthusiastic, too eager to teach to-day what he learned yesterday. Van Wyck Brooks once tried to reduce the whole body of his doctrine to a succinct statement. The result was a little volume a great deal more plausible than any that Wells himself has ever written—but also one that probably surprised him now and then as he read it. In it all his contradictions were reconciled, all his gaps bridged, all his shifts ameliorated. Brooks did for him, in brief, what William Bayard Hale did for Dr. Wilson in "The New Freedom," and has lived to regret it, I daresay, or at all events the vain labor of it, in the same manner. . . .

What remains of Wells? There remains a little shelf of very excellent books, beginning with "Tono-Bungay" and ending with "Marriage." It is a shelf flanked on the one side by a long row of extravagant romances in the manner of Jules Verne, and on the other side by an even longer row of puerile tracts. But let us not underestimate it because it is in such uninviting company. There is on it some of the liveliest, most original, most amusing, and withal most respectable fiction that England has produced in our time. In that fiction there is a sufficient memorial to a man who, between two debauches of claptrap, had his day as an artist.

III.

Arnold Bennett

Of Bennett it is quite easy to conjure up a recognizable picture by imaging everything that Wells is not—that is, everything interior, everything having to do with attitudes and ideas, everything beyond the mere craft of arranging words in ingratiating sequences. As stylists, of course, they have many points of contact. Each writes a journalese that is extraordinarily fluent and tuneful; each is apt to be carried away by the rush of his own smartness. But in their matter they stand at opposite poles. Wells has a believing mind, and cannot resist the lascivious beckonings and eye-winkings of meretricious novelty; Bennett carries skepticism so far that it often takes on the appearance of a mere peasant-like suspicion of ideas, bellicose and unintelligent. Wells is astonishingly intimate and confidential; and more than one of his novels reeks with a shameless sort of autobiography; Bennett, even when he makes use of personal experience, contrives to get impersonality into it. Wells, finally, is a sentimentalist, and cannot conceal his feelings; Bennett, of all the English novelists of the day, is the most steadily aloof and ironical.

This habit of irony, in truth, is the thing that gives Bennett all his characteristic color, and is at the bottom of both his peculiar merit and his peculiar limitation. On the one hand it sets him free from the besetting sin of the contemporary novelist: he never preaches, he has no messianic delusion, he is above the puerile theories that have engulfed such romantic men as Wells, Winston Churchill and the late Jack London, and even, at times, such sentimental agnostics as Dreiser. But on the other hand it leaves him empty of the passion that is, when all is said and done, the chief mark of the true novelist. The trouble with him is that he cannot feel with his characters, that he never involves himself emotionally in their struggles against destiny, that the drama of their lives never thrills or dismays him—and the result is that he is unable to arouse in the reader that penetrating sense of kinship, that profound and instinctive sympathy, which in its net effect is almost indistinguishable from the understanding born of experiences actually endured and emotions actually shared. Joseph Conrad, in a memorable piece of criticism, once put the thing clearly. "My task," he said, "is, by the power of the written word, to make you hear, to make you feel—it is, above all, to make you *see*." Here seeing, it must be obvious, is no more than feeling put into physical terms; it is not the outward aspect that is to be seen, but the inner truth—and the end to be sought by that apprehension of inner truth is responsive recognition, the sympathy of poor mortal for poor mortal, the tidal uprush of feeling that makes us all one. Bennett, it seems to me, cannot evoke it. His characters, as they pass, have a deceptive brilliance of outline, but they soon fade; one never finds them haunting the memory as Lord Jim haunts it, or Carrie Meeber, or Huck Finn, or Tom Jones. The reason is not far to seek. It lies in the plain fact that they appear to their creator, not as men and women whose hopes and agonies are of poignant concern, not as tragic comedians in isolated and concentrated dramas, but as mean figures in an infinitely dispersed and unintelligible farce, as helpless nobodies in an epic struggle that transcends both their volition and their comprehension. Thus viewing them, he fails to humanize them completely, and so he fails to make their emotions contagious. They are, in their way, often vividly real; they are thoroughly accounted for; what there is of them is unfailingly life-like; they move and breathe in an environment that pulses and glows. But the attitude of the author toward them remains, in the end, the attitude of a biologist toward his laboratory animals. He does not *feel* with them—and neither does his reader.

Bennett's chief business, in fact, is not with individuals at all, even though he occasionally brings them up almost to life-size. What concerns him principally is the common life of large groups, the action and reaction of castes and classes, the struggle among societies. In particular, he is engrossed by the colossal and disorderly functioning of the English middle class—a division of mankind inordinately mixed in race, confused in ideals and illogical in ideas. It is a group that has had interpreters aplenty, past and present; a full half of the literature of the Victorian era was devoted to it. But never, I believe, has it had an interpreter more resolutely detached and relentless—never has it had one less shaken by emotional involvement. Here the very lack that detracts so much from Bennett's stature as a novelist in the conventional sense is converted into a valuable possession. Better than any other man of his time he has got upon paper the social anatomy and physiology of the masses of average, everyday, unimaginative Englishmen. One leaves the long series of Five Towns books with a sense of having looked down the tube of a microscope upon a huge swarm of infinitely little but incessantly struggling organisms—creatures engaged furiously in the pursuit of grotesque and unintelligible ends—helpless participants in and victims of a struggle that takes on, to their eyes, a thousand lofty purposes, all of them puerile to the observer above its turmoil. Here, he seems to say, is the middle, the average, the typical Englishman. Here is the fellow as he appears to himself—virtuous, laborious, important, intelligent, made in God's image. And here he is in fact—swinish, ineffective, inconsequential, stupid, a feeble parody upon his maker. It is irony that penetrates and devastates, and it is unrelieved by any show of the pity that gets into the irony of Conrad, or of the tolerant claim of kinship that mitigates that of Fielding and Thackeray. It is harsh and cocksure. It has, at its moments, some flavor of actual bounderism: one instinctively shrinks from so smart-alecky a pulling off of underclothes and unveiling of warts.

It is easy to discern in it, indeed, a note of distinct hostility, and even of disgust. The long exile of the author is not without its significance. He not only got in France something of the Frenchman's aloof and disdainful view of the English; he must have taken a certain distaste for the national scene with him in the first place, else he would not have gone at all. The same attitude shows itself in W. L. George, another Englishman smeared with Gallic foreignness. Both men, it will be recalled, reacted to the tremendous emotional assault of the war, not by yielding to it ecstatically in the manner of the unpolluted islanders, but by shrinking from it into a reserve that was naturally misunderstood. George has put his sniffs into "Blind Alley"; Bennett has got his into "The Pretty Lady." I do not say that either book is positively French; what I do say is that both mirror an attitude that has been somehow emptied of mere nationalism. An Italian adventure, I daresay, would have produced the same effect, or a Spanish, or Russian, or German. But it happened to be French. What the Bennett story attempts to do is what every serious Bennett story attempts to do: to exhibit dramatically the great gap separating the substance from the appearance in the English character. It seems to me that its prudent and self-centered G. J. Hoape is a vastly more real Englishman of his class, and, what is more, an Englishman vastly more useful and creditable to England, than any of the gaudy Bayards and Cids of conventional war fiction. Here, indeed, the irony somehow fails. The man we are obviously expected to disdain converts himself, toward the end, into a man not without his touches of the admirable. He is no hero, God knows, and there is no more brilliance in him than you will find in an average country squire or Parliament man, but he has the rare virtue of common sense, and that is probably the virtue that has served the English better than all others. Curiously enough, the English reading public recognized the irony but failed to observe its confutation, and so the book got Bennett into bad odor at home, and into worse odor among the sedulous apes of English ideas and emotions on this side of the water. But it is a sound work nevertheless—a sound work with a large and unescapable defect.

That defect is visible in a good many of the other things that Bennett has done. It is the product of his emotional detachment and it commonly reveals itself as an inability to take his own story seriously. Sometimes he pokes open fun at it, as in "The Roll-Call"; more often he simply abandons it before it is done, as if weary of a too tedious foolery. This last process is plainly visible in "The Pretty Lady." The thing that gives form and direction to that story is a simple enough problem in psychology, to wit: what will happen when a man of sound education and decent instincts, of sober age and prudent habit, of common sense and even of certain mild cleverness—what will happen, logically and naturally, when such a normal, respectable, cautious fellow finds himself disquietingly in love with a lady of no position at all—in brief, with a lady but lately of the town? Bennett sets the problem, and for a couple of hundred pages investigates it with the utmost ingenuity and address, exposing and discussing its sub-problems, tracing the gradual shifting of its terms, prodding with sharp insight into the psychological material entering into it. And then, as if suddenly tired of it—worse, as if suddenly convinced that the thing has gone on long enough, that he has given the public enough of a book for its money—he forthwith evades the solution altogether, and brings down his curtain upon a palpably artificial dénouement. The device murders the book. One is arrested at the start by a fascinating statement of the problem, one follows a discussion of it that shows Bennett at his brilliant best, fertile in detail, alert to every twist of motive, incisively ironical at every step—and then, at the end, one is incontinently turned out of the booth. The effect is that of being assaulted with an ice-pick by a hitherto amiable bartender, almost that of being bitten by a pretty girl in the midst of an amicable buss.

That effect, unluckily, is no stranger to the reader of Bennett novels. One encounters it in many of them. There is a tremendous marshaling of meticulous and illuminating observation, the background throbs with color, the sardonic humor is never failing, it is a capital show—but always one goes away from it with a sense of having missed the conclusion, always there is a final begging of the question. It is not hard to perceive the attitude of mind underlying this chronic evasion of issues. It is, in essence, agnosticism carried to the last place of decimals. Life itself is meaningless; therefore, the discussion of life is meaningless; therefore, why try futilely to get a meaning into it? The reasoning, unluckily, has holes in it. It may be sound logically, but it is psychologically unworkable. One goes to novels, not for the bald scientific fact, but for a romantic amelioration of it. When they carry that amelioration to the point of uncritical certainty, when they are full of "ideas" that click and whirl like machines, then the mind revolts against the childish naïveté of the thing. But when there is no organization of the spectacle at all, when it is presented as a mere formless panorama, when to the sense of its unintelligibility is added the suggestion of its inherent chaos, then the mind revolts no less. Art can never be simple representation. It cannot deal solely with precisely what is. It must, at the least, present the real in the light of some recognizable ideal; it must give to the eternal farce, if not some moral, then at all events some direction. For without that formulation there can be no clear-cut separation of the individual will from the general stew and turmoil of things, and without that separation there can be no coherent drama, and without that drama there can be no evocation of emotion, and without that emotion art is unimaginable. The field of the novel is very wide. There is room, on the one side, for a brilliant play of ideas and theories, provided only they do not stiffen the struggle of man with man, or of man with destiny, into a mere struggle of abstractions. There is room, on the other side, for the most complete agnosticism, provided only it be tempered by feeling. Joseph Conrad is quite as unshakable an agnostic as Bennett; he is a ten times more implacable ironist. But there is yet a place in his scheme for a sardonic sort of pity, and pity, however sardonic, is perhaps as good an emotion as another. The trouble with Bennett is that he essays to sneer, not only at the futile aspiration of man, but also at the agony that goes with it. The result is an air of affectation, of superficiality, almost of stupidity. The manner, on the one hand, is that of a highly skillful and profoundly original artist, but on the other hand it is that of a sophomore just made aware of Haeckel, Bradlaugh and Nietzsche.

Bennett's unmitigated skepticism explains two things that have constantly puzzled the reviewers, and that have been the cause of a great deal of idiotic writing about him—for him as well as against him. One of these things is his utter lack of anything properly describable as artistic conscience—his extreme readiness to play the star houri in the seraglio of the publishers; the other is his habit of translating platitudes into racy journalese and gravely offering them to the suburban trade as "pocket philosophies." Both crimes, it seems to me, have their rise in his congenital incapacity for taking ideas seriously, even including his own. "If this," he appears to say, "is the tosh you want, then here is another dose of it. Personally, I have little interest in that sort of thing. Even good novels—the best I can do—are no more than compromises with a silly convention. I am not interested in stories; I am interested in the anatomy of human melancholy; I am a descriptive sociologist, with overtones of malice. But if you want stories, and can pay for them, I am willing to give them to you. And if you prefer bad stories, then here is a bad one. Don't assume you can shame me by deploring my willingness. Think of what your doctors do every day, and your lawyers, and your men of God, and your stockbrokers, and your traders and politicians. I am surely no worse than the average. In fact, I am probably a good deal superior to the average, for I am at least not deceived by my own mountebankery—I at least know my sound goods from my shoddy." Such, I daresay, is the process of thought behind such hollow trade-goods as "Buried Alive" and "The Lion's Share." One does not need the man's own amazing confidences to hear his snickers at his audience, at his work and at himself.

The books of boiled-mutton "philosophy" in the manner of Dr. Orison Swett Marden and Dr. Frank Crane and the occasional pot-boilers for the newspapers and magazines probably have much the same origin. What appears in them is not a weakness for ideas that are stale and obvious, but a distrust of all ideas whatsoever. The public, with its mob yearning to be instructed, edified and pulled by the nose, demands certainties; it must be told definitely and a bit raucously that this is true and that is false. But there *are* no certainties. *Ergo*, one notion is as good as another, and if it happens to be utter flubdub, so much the better—for it is precisely flubdub that penetrates the popular skull with the greatest facility. The way is already made: the hole already gapes. An effort to approach the hidden and baffling truth would simply burden the enterprise with difficulty. Moreover, the effort is intrinsically laborious and ungrateful. Moreover, there is probably no hidden truth to be uncovered. Thus, by the route of skepticism, Bennett apparently arrives at his sooth-saying. That he actually believes in his own theorizing is inconceivable. He is far too intelligent a man to hold that any truths within the comprehension of the popular audience are sound enough to be worth preaching, or that it would do any good to preach them if they were. No doubt he is considerably amused *in petto* by the gravity with which his bedizened platitudes have been received by persons accustomed to that sort of fare, particularly in America. It would be interesting to hear his private view of the corn-fed critics who hymn him as a profound and impassioned moralist, with a mission to rescue the plain people from the heresies of such fellows as Dreiser.

So much for two of the salient symptoms of his underlying

skepticism. Another is to be found in his incapacity to be, in the ordinary sense, ingratiating; it is simply beyond him to say the pleasant thing with any show of sincerity. Of all his books, probably the worst are his book on the war and his book on the United States. The latter was obviously undertaken with some notion of paying off a debt. Bennett had been to the United States; the newspapers had hailed him in their side-show way; the women's clubs had pawed over him; he had, no doubt, come home a good deal richer. What he essayed to do was to write a volume on the republic that should be at once colorably accurate and discreetly agreeable. The enterprise was quite beyond him. The book not only failed to please Americans; it offended them in a thousand subtle ways, and from its appearance dates the decline of the author's vogue among us. He is not, of course, completely forgotten, but it must be plain that Wells now stands a good deal above him in the popular estimation—even the later Wells of bad novel after bad novel. His war book missed fire in much the same way. It was workmanlike, it was deliberately urbane, it was undoubtedly truthful—but it fell flat in England and it fell flat in America. There is no little significance in the fact that the British government, in looking about for English authors to uphold the British cause in America and labor for American participation in the war, found no usefulness in Bennett. Practically every other novelist with an American audience was drafted for service, but not Bennett. He was *non est* during the heat of the fray, and when at length he came forward with "The Pretty Lady" the pained manner with which it was received quite justified the judgment of those who had passed him over.

What all this amounts to may be very briefly put: in one of the requisite qualities of the first-rate novelist Bennett is almost completely lacking, and so it would be no juggling with paradox to argue that, at bottom, he is scarcely a novelist at all. His books, indeed,—that is, his serious books, the books of his better canon—often fail utterly to achieve the effect that one associates with the true novel. One carries away from them, not the impression of a definite transaction, not the memory of an outstanding and appealing personality, not the after-taste of a profound emotion, but merely the sense of having witnessed a gorgeous but incomprehensible parade, coming out of nowhere and going to God knows where. They are magnificent as representation, they bristle with charming detail, they radiate the humors of an acute and extraordinary man, they are entertainment of the best sort—but there is seldom anything in them of that clear, well-aimed and solid effect which one associates with the novel as work of art. Most of these books, indeed, are no more than collections of essays defectively dramatized. What is salient in them is not their people, but their backgrounds—and their people are forever fading into their backgrounds. Is there a character in any of these books that shows any sign of living as Pendennis lives, and Barry Lyndon, and Emma Bovary, and David Copperfield, and the George Moore who is always his own hero? Who remembers much about Sophia Baines, save that she lived in the Five Towns, or even about Clayhanger? Young George Cannon, in "The Roll-Call," is no more than an anatomical chart in a lecture on modern marriage. Hilda Lessways-Cannon-Clayhanger is not only inscrutable; she is also dim. The man and woman of "Whom God Hath Joined," perhaps the best of all the Bennett novels, I have so far forgotten that I cannot remember their names. Even Denry the Audacious grows misty. One remembers that he was the center of the farce, but now he is long gone and the farce remains.

This constant remainder, whether he be actually novelist or no novelist, is sufficient to save Bennett, it seems to me, from the swift oblivion that so often overtakes the popular fictioneer. He may not play the game according to the rules, but the game that he plays is nevertheless extraordinarily diverting and calls for an incessant display of the finest sort of skill. No writer of his time has looked into the life of his time with sharper eyes, or set forth his findings with a greater charm and plausibility. Within his deliberately narrow limits he had done precisely the thing that Balzac undertook to do, and Zola after him: he has painted a full-length portrait of a whole society, accurately, brilliantly and, in certain areas, almost exhaustively. The middle Englishman—not the individual, but the type—is there displayed more vividly than he is displayed anywhere else that I know of. The thing is rigidly held to its aim; there is no episodic descent or ascent to other fields. But within that one field every resource of observation, of invention and of imagination has been brought to bear upon the business—every one save that deep feeling for man in his bitter tragedy which is the most important of them all. Bennett, whatever his failing in this capital function of the artist, is certainly of the very highest consideration as craftsman. Scattered through his books, even his bad books, there are fragments of writing that are quite unsurpassed in our day—the shoe-shining episode in "The Pretty Lady," the adulterous interlude in "Whom God Hath Joined," the dinner party in "Paris Nights," the whole discussion of the Cannon-Ingram marriage in "The Roll-Call," the studio party in "The Lion's Share." Such writing is rare and exhilarating. It is to be respected. And the man who did it is not to be dismissed.

IV.

The Dean

AMERICANS, obsessed by the problem of conduct, usually judge their authors, not as artists, but as citizens, Christians, men. Edgar Allan Poe, I daresay, will never live down the fact that he was a periodical drunkard, and died in an alcoholic ward. Mark Twain, the incomparable artist, will probably never shake off Mark Twain, the after-dinner comedian, the flaunter of white dress clothes, the public character, the national wag. As for William Dean Howells, he gains rather than loses by this confusion of values, for, like the late Joseph H. Choate, he is almost the national ideal: an urbane and highly respectable old gentleman, a sitter on committees, an intimate of professors and the prophets of movements, a worthy vouched for by both the *Atlantic Monthly* and Alexander Harvey, a placid conformist. The result is his general acceptance as a member of the literary peerage, and of the rank of earl at least. For twenty years past his successive books have not been criticized, nor even adequately reviewed; they have been merely fawned over; the lady critics of the newspapers would no more question them than they would question Lincoln's Gettysburg speech, or Paul Elmer More, or their own virginity. The dean of American letters in point of years, and in point of published quantity, and in point of public prominence and influence, he has been gradually enveloped in a web of superstitious reverence, and it grates harshly to hear his actual achievement discussed in cold blood.

Nevertheless, all this merited respect for an industrious and inoffensive man is bound, soon or late, to yield to a critical examination of the artist within, and that examination, I fear, will have its bitter moments for those who naïvely accept the Howells legend. It will show, without doubt, a first-rate journeyman, a contriver of pretty things, a clever stylist—but it will also show a long row of uninspired and hollow books, with no more ideas in them than so many volumes of the *Ladies' Home Journal*, and no more deep and contagious feeling than so many reports of autopsies, and no more glow and gusto than so many tables of bond prices. The profound dread and agony of life, the surge of passion and aspiration, the grand crash and glitter of things, the tragedy that runs eternally under the surface—all this the critic of the future will seek in vain in Dr. Howells' elegant and shallow volumes. And seeking it in vain, he will probably dismiss all of them together with fewer words than he gives to "Huckleberry Finn." . . .

Already, indeed, the Howells legend tends to become a mere legend, and empty of all genuine significance. Who actually reads the Howells novels? Who even remembers their names? "The Minister's Charge," "An Imperative Duty," "The Unexpected Guests," "Out of the Question," "No Love Lost"—these titles are already as meaningless as a roll of Sumerian kings. Perhaps "The Rise of Silas Lapham" survives—but go read it if you would tumble downstairs. The truth about Howells is that he really has nothing to say, for all the charm he gets into saying it. His psychology is superficial, amateurish, often nonsensical; his irony is scarcely more than a polite facetiousness; his characters simply refuse to live. No figure even remotely comparable to Norris' McTeague or Dreiser's Frank Cowperwood is to be encountered in his novels. He is quite unequal to any such evocation of the race-spirit, of the essential conflict of forces among us, of the peculiar drift and color of American life. The world he moves in is suburban, caged, flabby. He could no more have written the last chapters of "Lord Jim" than he could have written the Book of Mark.

The vacuity of his method is well revealed by one of the books of his old age, "The Leatherwood God." Its composition, we are told, spread over many years; its genesis was in the days of his full maturity. An examination of it shows nothing but a suave piling up of words, a vast accumulation of nothings. The central character, one Dylks, is a backwoods evangelist who acquires a belief in his own buncombe, and ends by announcing that he is God. The job before the author was obviously that of tracing the psychological steps whereby this mountebank proceeds to that conclusion; the fact, indeed, is recognized in the canned review, which says that the book is "a study of American religious psychology." But an inspection of the text shows that no such study is really in it. Dr. Howells does not *show* how Dylks came to believe himself God; he merely *says* that he did so. The whole discussion of the process, indeed, is confined to two pages—172 and 173—and is quite infantile in its inadequacy. Nor do we get anything approaching a revealing look into the heads of the other converts—the saleratus-sodden, hell-crazy, half-witted Methodists and Baptists of a remote Ohio settlement of seventy or eighty years ago. All we have is the casual statement that they are converted, and begin to offer Dylks their howls of devotion. And when, in the end, they go back to their original bosh, dethroning Dylks overnight and restoring the gaseous vertebrate of Calvin and Wesley—when this contrary process is recorded, it is accompanied by no more illumination. In brief, the story is not a "study" at all, whether psychological or otherwise, but simply an anecdote, and without either point or interest. Its virtues are all negative ones: it is short, it keeps on the track, it deals with a religious maniac and yet contrives to offer no offense to other religious maniacs. But on the positive side it merely skims the skin.

So in all of the other Howells novels that I know. Somehow, he seems blissfully ignorant that life is a serious business, and full of mystery; it is a sort of college town *Weltanschauung* that one finds in him; he is an Agnes Repplier in pantaloons. In one of the later stories, "New Leaf Mills," he makes a faltering gesture of recognition. Here, so to speak, one gets at least a sniff of the universal mystery; Howells seems about to grow profound at last. But the sniff is only a sniff. The tragedy, at the end, peters out. Compare the story to E. W. Howe's "The Story of a Country Town," which Howells himself has intelligently praised, and you will get some measure of his own failure. Howe sets much the same stage and deals with much the same people. His story is full of technical defects—for one thing, it is overladen with melodrama and sentimentality. But nevertheless it achieves the prime purpose of a work of the imagination: it grips and stirs the emotions, it implants a sense of something experienced. Such a book leaves scars; one is not quite the same after reading it. But it would be difficult to point to a Howells book that produces any such effect. If he actually tries, like Conrad, "to make you hear, to make you feel—before all, to make you *see*," then he fails almost completely. One often suspects, indeed, that he doesn't really feel or see himself. . . .

As a critic he belongs to a higher level, if only because of his eager curiosity, his gusto in novelty. His praise of Howe I have mentioned. He dealt valiant licks for other débutantes: Frank Norris, Edith Wharton and William Vaughn Moody among them. He brought forward the Russians diligently and persuasively, albeit they left no mark upon his own manner. In his ingratiating way, back in the seventies and eighties, he made war upon the prevailing sentimentalities. But his history as a critic is full of errors and omissions. One finds him loosing a fanfare for W. B. Trites, the Philadelphia Zola, and praising Frank A. Munsey—and one finds him leaving the discovery of all the Shaws, George Moores, Dreisers, Synges, Galsworthys, Phillipses and George Ades to the Pollards, Meltzers and Hunekers. Busy in the sideshows, he didn't see the elephants go by. . . . Here temperamental defects handicapped him. Turn to his "My Mark Twain" and you will see what I mean. The Mark that is exhibited in this book is a Mark whose Himalayan outlines are discerned but hazily through a pink fog of Howells. There is a moral note in the tale—an obvious effort to palliate, to touch up, to excuse. The poor fellow, of course, was charming, and there was talent in him, but what a weakness he had for thinking aloud—and such shocking thoughts! What oaths in his speech! What awful cigars he smoked! How barbarous his contempt for the strict sonata form! It seems incredible, indeed, that two men so unlike should have found common denominators for a friendship lasting forty-four years. The one derived from Rabelais, Chaucer, the Elizabethans and Benvenuto—buccaneers of the literary high seas, loud laughers, law-breakers, giants of a lordlier day; the other came down from Jane Austen, Washington Irving and Hannah More. The one wrote English as Michelangelo hacked marble, broadly, brutally, magnificently; the other was a maker of pretty waxen groups. The one was utterly unconscious of the way he achieved his staggering effects; the other was the most toilsome, fastidious and self-conscious of craftsmen. . . .

What remains of Howells is his style. He invented a new harmony of "the old, old words." He destroyed the stately periods of the Poe tradition, and erected upon the ruins a complex and savory carelessness, full of naïvetés that were sophisticated to the last degree. He loosened the tightness of English, and let a blast of Elizabethan air into it. He achieved, for all his triviality, for all his narrowness of vision, a pungent and admirable style.

V.
Professor Veblen

TEN or twelve years ago, being engaged in a bombastic discussion with what was then known as an intellectual Socialist (like the rest of the *intelligentsia*, he succumbed to the first fife-corps of the war, pulled down the red flag, damned Marx as a German spy, and began whooping for Elihu Root, Otto Kahn and Abraham Lincoln), I was greatly belabored and incommoded by his long quotations from a certain Prof. Dr. Thorstein Veblen, then quite unknown to me. My antagonist manifestly attached a great deal of importance to these borrowed sagacities, for he often heaved them at me in lengths of a column or two, and urged me to read every word of them. I tried hard enough, but found it impossible going. The more I read them, in fact, the less I could make of them, and so in the end, growing impatient and impolite, I denounced this Prof. Veblen as a geyser of pishposh, refused to waste any more time upon his incomprehensible syllogisms, and applied myself to the other Socialist witnesses in the case, seeking to set fire to their shirts.

That old debate, which took place by mail (for the Socialist lived like a munitions patriot on his country estate and I was a wage-slave attached to a city newspaper), was afterward embalmed in a dull book, and made the mild pother of a day. The book, by name, "Men vs. the Man," is now as completely forgotten as Baxter's "Saint's Rest" or the Constitution of the United States. I myself, perhaps the only man who remembers it at all, have not looked into it for six or eight years, and all I can recall of my opponent's argument (beyond the fact that it not only failed to convert me to the nascent Bolshevism of the time, but left me a bitter and incurable scoffer at democracy in all its forms) is his curious respect for the aforesaid Prof. Dr. Thorstein Veblen, and his delight in the learned gentleman's long, tortuous and (to me, at least) intolerably flapdoodlish phrases.

There was, indeed, a time when I forgot even this—when

my mind was empty of the professor's very name. That was, say, from 1909 or thereabout to the middle of 1917. During those years, having lost all my old superior interest in Socialism, even as an amateur psychiatrist, I ceased to read its literature, and thus lost track of its Great Thinkers. The periodicals that I then gave an eye to, setting aside newspapers, were chiefly the familiar American imitations of the English weeklies of opinion, and in these the dominant Great Thinker was, first, the late Prof. Dr. William James, and, after his decease, Prof. Dr. John Dewey. The reign of James, as the illuminated will recall, was long and glorious. For three or four years running he was mentioned in every one of those American *Spectators* and *Saturday Reviews* at least once a week, and often a dozen times. Among the less somber gazettes of the republic, to be sure, there were other heroes: Maeterlinck, Rabindranath Tagore, Judge Ben B. Lindsey, the late Major-General Roosevelt, Tom Lawson and so on. Still further down the literary and intellectual scale there were yet others: Hall Caine, Brieux and Jack Johnson among them, with paper-bag cookery and the twilight sleep to dispute their popularity. But on the majestic level of the old *Nation*, among the white and lavender peaks of professorial ratiocination, there was scarcely a serious rival to James. Now and then, perhaps, Jane Addams had a month of vogue, and during one winter there was a rage for Bergson, and for a short space the unspeakable Bernstorff tried to set up Eucken (now damned with Wagner, Nietzsche and Ludendorff), but taking one day with another James held his own against the field. His ideas, immediately they were stated, became the ideas of every pedagogue from Harvard to Leland Stanford, and the pedagogues, laboring furiously at space rates, rammed them into the skulls of the lesser *cerebelli*. To have called James an ass, during the year 1909, would have been as fatal as to have written a sentence like this one without having used so many *haves*. He died a bit later, but his ghost went marching on: it took three or four years to interpret and pigeon-hole his philosophical remains and to take down and redact his messages (via Sir Oliver Lodge, Little Brighteyes, Wah-Wah the Indian Chief, and other gifted psychics) from the spirit world. But then, gradually, he achieved the ultimate, stupendous and irrevocable act of death, and there was a vacancy. To it Prof. Dr. Dewey was elected by the acclamation of all right-thinking and forward-looking men. He was an expert in pedagogics, metaphysics, psychology, ethics, logic, politics, pedagogical metaphysics, metaphysical psychology, psychological ethics, ethical logic, logical politics and political pedagogics. He was *Artium Magister*, *Philosophiæ Doctor* and twice *Legum Doctor*. He had written a book called "How to Think." He sat in a professor's chair and caned sophomores for blowing spit-balls. *Ergo*, he was the ideal candidate, and so he was nominated, elected and inaugurated, and for three years, more or less, he enjoyed a peaceful reign in the groves of sapience, and the inferior *umbilicarii* venerated him as they had once venerated James.

I myself greatly enjoyed and profited by the discourses of this Prof. Dewey and was in hopes that he would last. Born so recently as 1859 and a man of the highest bearable sobriety, he seemed likely to peg along until 1935 or 1940, a gentle and charming volcano of correct thought. But it was not, alas, to be. Under cover of pragmatism, that serpent's metaphysic, there was unrest beneath the surface. Young professors in remote and obscure universities, apparently as harmless as so many convicts in the death-house, were secretly flirting with new and red-hot ideas. Whole regiments and brigades of them yielded in stealthy privacy to rebellious and often incomprehensible yearnings. Now and then, as if to reveal what was brewing, a hell fire blazed and a Prof. Dr. Scott Nearing went sky-hooting through its smoke. One heard whispers of strange heresies—economic, sociological, even political. Gossip had it that pedagogy was hatching vipers, nay, was already brought to bed. But not much of this got into the home-made *Saturday Reviews* and Yankee *Athenæums*—a hint or two maybe, but no more. In the main they kept to their old resolute demands for a pure civil-service, the budget system in Congress, the abolition of hazing at the Naval Academy, an honest primary and justice to the Filipinos, with extermination of the Prussian serpent added after August, 1914. And Dr. Dewey, on his remote Socratic Alp, pursued the calm reënforcement of the philosophical principles underlying these and all other lofty and indignant causes. . . .

Then, of a sudden, Siss! Boom! Ah! Then, overnight, the

upspringing of the intellectual soviets, the headlong assault upon all the old axioms of pedagogical speculation, the nihilistic dethronement of Prof. Dewey—and rah, rah, rah for Prof. Dr. Thorstein Veblen! Veblen? Could it be—? Aye, it was! My old acquaintance! The *Doctor obscurus* of my half-forgotten bout with the so-called intellectual Socialist! The Great Thinker *redivivus*! Here, indeed, he was again, and in a few months—almost it seemed a few days—he was all over the *Nation*, the *Dial*, the *New Republic* and the rest of them, and his books and pamphlets began to pour from the presses, and the newspapers reported his every wink and whisper, and everybody who was anybody began gabbling about him. The spectacle, I do not hesitate to say, somewhat disconcerted me and even distressed me. On the one hand, I was sorry to see so learned and interesting a man as Dr. Dewey sent back to the insufferable dungeons of Columbia, there to lecture in imperfect Yiddish to classes of Grand Street Platos. And on the other hand, I shrunk supinely from the appalling job, newly rearing itself before me, of re-reading the whole canon of the singularly laborious and muggy, the incomparably tangled and unintelligible works of Prof. Dr. Thorstein Veblen. . . .

But if a sense of duty tortures a man, it also enables him to achieve prodigies, and so I managed to get through the whole infernal job. I read "The Theory of the Leisure Class," I read "The Theory of Business Enterprise," and then I read "The Instinct of Workmanship." An hiatus followed; I was racked by a severe neuralgia, with delusions of persecution. On recovering I tackled "Imperial Germany and the Industrial Revolution." Malaria for a month, and then "The Nature of Peace and the Terms of Its Perpetuation." What ensued was never diagnosed; probably it was some low infection of the mesentery or spleen. When it passed off, leaving only an asthmatic cough, I read "The Higher Learning in America," and then went to Mt. Clemens to drink the Glauber's salts. Eureka! the business was done! It had strained me, but now it was over. Alas, a good part of the agony had been needless. What I found myself aware of, coming to the end, was that practically the whole system of Prof. Dr. Veblen was in his first book and his last—that is, in "The Theory of the Leisure Class," and "The Higher Learning in America." I pass on the good news.

Read these two, and you won't have to read the others. And if even two daunt you, then read the first. Once through it, though you will have missed many a pearl and many a pain, you will have a fairly good general acquaintance with the gifted metaphysician's ideas.

For those ideas, in the main, are quite simple, and often anything but revolutionary in essence. What is genuinely remarkable about them is not their novelty, or their complexity, nor even the fact that a professor should harbor them; it is the astoundingly grandiose and rococo manner of their statement, the almost unbelievable tediousness and flatulence of the gifted headmaster's prose, his unprecedented talent for saying nothing in an august and heroic manner. There are tales of an actress of the last generation, probably Sarah Bernhardt, who could put pathos and even terror into a recitation of the multiplication table. The late Louis James did something of the sort; he introduced limericks into "Peer Gynt" and still held the yokelry agape. The same talent, raised to a high power, is in this Prof. Dr. Veblen. Tunnel under his great moraines and stalagmites of words, dig down into his vast kitchen-midden of discordant and raucous polysyllables, blow up the hard, thick shell of his almost theological manner, and what you will find in his discourse is chiefly a mass of platitudes—the self-evident made horrifying, the obvious in terms of the staggering. Marx, I daresay, said a good deal of it, and what Marx overlooked has been said over and over again by his heirs and assigns. But Marx, at this business, labored under a technical handicap: he wrote in German, a language he actually understood. Prof. Dr. Veblen submits himself to no such disadvantage. Though born, I believe, in These States, and resident here all his life, he achieves the effect, perhaps without employing the means, of thinking in some unearthly foreign language—say Swahili, Sumerian or Old Bulgarian—and then painfully clawing his thoughts into a copious but uncertain and book-learned English. The result is a style that affects the higher cerebral centers like a constant roll of subway expresses. The second result is a sort of bewildered numbness of the senses, as before some fabulous and unearthly marvel. And the third result, if I make no mistake, is the celebrity of the professor as a Great Thinker. In brief, he states his hollow nothings in such high, astounding terms that they must inevitably arrest and blister the right-thinking mind. He makes them mysterious. He makes them shocking. He makes them portentous. And so, flinging them at naïve and believing minds, he makes them stick and burn.

No doubt you think that I exaggerate—perhaps even that I lie. If so, then consider this specimen—the first paragraph of Chapter XIII of "The Theory of the Leisure Class":

> In an increasing proportion as time goes on, the anthropomorphic cult, with its code of devout observances, suffers a progressive disintegration through the stress of economic exigencies and the decay of the system of status. As this disintegration proceeds, there come to be associated and blended with the devout attitude certain other motives and impulses that are not always of an anthropomorphic origin, nor traceable to the habit of personal subservience. Not all of these subsidiary impulses that blend with the bait of devoutness in the later devotional life are altogether congruous with the devout attitude or with the anthropomorphic apprehension of sequence of phenomena. Their origin being not the same, their action upon the scheme of devout life is also not in the same direction. In many ways they traverse the underlying norm of subservience or vicarious life to which the code of devout observances and the ecclesiastical and sacerdotal institutions are to be traced as their substantial basis. Through the presence of these alien motives the social and industrial régime of status gradually disintegrates, and the canon of personal subservience loses the support derived from an unbroken tradition. Extraneous habits and proclivities encroach upon the field of action occupied by this canon, and it presently comes about that the ecclesiastical and sacerdotal structures are partially converted to other uses, in some measure alien to the purposes of the scheme of devout life as it stood in the days of the most vigorous and characteristic development of the priesthood.

Well, what have we here? What does this appalling salvo of rhetorical artillery signify? What is the sweating professor trying to say? What is his Message now? Simply that in the course of time, the worship of God is commonly corrupted by other enterprises, and that the church, ceasing to be a mere temple of adoration, becomes the headquarters of these other enterprises. More simply still, that men sometimes vary serving God by serving other men, which means, of course, serving themselves. This bald platitude, which must be obvious to any child who has ever been to a church bazaar or a parish house, is here tortured, worried and run through rollers until it is spread out to 241 words, of which fully 200 are unnecessary. The next paragraph is even worse. In it the master undertakes to explain in his peculiar dialect the meaning of "that non-reverent sense of æsthetic congruity with the environment which is left as a residue of the latter-day act of worship after elimination of its anthropomorphic content." Just what does he mean by this "non-reverent sense of æsthetic congruity"? I have studied the whole paragraph for three days, halting only for prayer and sleep, and I have come to certain conclusions. I may be wrong, but nevertheless it is the best that I can do. What I conclude is this: he is trying to say that many people go to church, not because they are afraid of the devil but because they enjoy the music, and like to look at the stained glass, the potted lilies and the rev. pastor. To get this profound and highly original observation upon paper, he wastes, not merely 241, but more than 300 words! To say what might be said on a postage stamp he takes more than a page in his book! . . .

And so it goes, alas, alas, in all his other volumes—a cent's worth of information wrapped in a bale of polysyllables. In "The Higher Learning in America" the thing perhaps reaches its damndest and worst. It is as if the practice of that incredibly obscure and malodorous style were a relentless disease, a sort of progressive intellectual diabetes, a leprosy of the horse sense. Words are flung upon words until all recollection that there must be a meaning in them, a ground and excuse for them, is lost. One wanders in a labyrinth of nouns, adjectives, verbs, pronouns, adverbs, prepositions, conjunctions and participles, most of them swollen and nearly all of them unable to walk. It is difficult to imagine worse English, within the limits of intelligible grammar. It is clumsy, affected, opaque, bombastic, windy, empty. It is without grace or distinction and it is often without the most elementary order. The learned professor gets himself enmeshed in his gnarled sentences like a bull trapped by barbed wire, and his efforts to extricate himself are quite as furious and quite as spectacular. He heaves, he leaps, he writhes; at times he seems to be at the point of yelling for the police. It is a picture to bemuse the vulgar and to give the judicious grief.

Worse, there is nothing at the bottom of all this strident

wind-music—the ideas it is designed to set forth are, in the overwhelming main, poor ideas, and often they are ideas that are almost idiotic. One never gets the thrill of sharp and original thinking, dexterously put into phrases. The concepts underlying, say, "The Theory of the Leisure Class" are simply Socialism and water; the concepts underlying "The Higher Learning in America" are so childishly obvious that even the poor drudges who write editorials for newspapers have often voiced them. When, now and then, the professor tires of this emission of stale bosh and attempts flights of a more original character, he straightway comes tumbling down into absurdity. What the reader then has to struggle with is not only intolerably bad writing, but also loose, flabby, cocksure and preposterous thinking. . . . Again I take refuge in an example. It is from Chapter IV of "The Theory of the Leisure Class." The problem before the author here has to do with the social convention which frowns upon the consumption of alcohol by women—at least to the extent to which men may consume it decorously. Well, then, what is his explanation of this convention? Here, in brief, is his process of reasoning:

1. The leisure class, which is the predatory class of feudal times, reserves all luxuries for itself, and disapproves their use by members of the lower classes, for this use takes away their charm by taking away their exclusive possession.

2. Women are chattels in the possession of the leisure class, and hence subject to the rules made for inferiors. "The patriarchal tradition . . . says that the woman, being a chattel, should consume only what is necessary to her sustenance, except so far as her further consumption contributes to the comfort or the good repute of her master."

3. The consumption of alcohol contributes nothing to the comfort or good repute of the woman's master, but "detracts sensibly from the comfort or pleasure" of her master. *Ergo*, she is forbidden to drink.

This, I believe, is a fair specimen of the Veblenian ratiocination. Observe it well, for it is typical. That is to say, it starts off with a gratuitous and highly dubious assumption, proceeds to an equally dubious deduction, and then ends with a platitude which begs the whole question. What sound reason is there for believing that exclusive possession is the hall-mark of luxury?

There is none that I can see. It may be true of a few luxuries, but it is certainly not true of the most familiar ones. Do I enjoy a decent bath because I know that John Smith cannot afford one—or because I delight in being clean? Do I admire Beethoven's Fifth Symphony because it is incomprehensible to Congressmen and Methodists—or because I genuinely love music? Do I prefer terrapin à la Maryland to fried liver because plowhands must put up with the liver—or because the terrapin is intrinsically a more charming dose? Do I prefer kissing a pretty girl to kissing a charwoman because even a janitor may kiss a charwoman—or because the pretty girl looks better, smells better and kisses better? Now and then, to be sure, the idea of exclusive possession enters into the concept of luxury. I may, if I am a bibliophile, esteem a book because it is a unique first edition. I may, if I am fond, esteem a woman because she smiles on no one else. But even here, save in a very small minority of cases, other attractions plainly enter into the matter. It pleases me to have a unique first edition, but I wouldn't care anything for a unique first edition of Robert W. Chambers or Elinor Glyn; the author must have my respect, the book must be intrinsically valuable, there must be much more to it than its mere uniqueness. And if, being fond, I glory in the exclusive smiles of a certain Miss —— or Mrs. ——, then surely my satisfaction depends chiefly upon the lady herself, and not upon my mere monopoly. Would I delight in the fidelity of the charwoman? Would it give me any joy to learn that, through a sense of duty to me, she had ceased to kiss the janitor?

Confronted by such considerations, it seems to me that there is little truth left in Prof. Dr. Veblen's theory of conspicuous consumption and conspicuous waste—that what remains of it, after it is practically applied a few times, is no more than a wraith of balderdash. In so far as it is true it is obvious. All the professor accomplishes with it is to take what every one knows and pump it up to such proportions that every one begins to doubt it. What could be plainer than his failure in the case just cited? He starts off with a platitude, and ends in absurdity. No one denies, I take it, that in a clearly limited sense, women occupy a place in the world—or, more accurately, aspire to a place in the world—that is a good deal like that of a chattel. Marriage, the goal of their only honest and permanent hopes, invades their individuality; a married woman becomes the function of another individuality. Thus the appearance she presents to the world is often the mirror of her husband's egoism. A rich man hangs his wife with expensive clothes and jewels for the same reason, among others, that he adorns his own head with a plug hat: to notify everybody that he can afford it—in brief, to excite the envy of Socialists. But he also does it, let us hope, for another and far better and more powerful reason, to wit, that she intrigues him, that he delights in her, that he loves her—and so wants to make her gaudy and happy. This reason may not appeal to Socialist sociologists. In Russia, according to an old scandal (officially endorsed by the British bureau for pulling Yankee noses) the Bolsheviki actually repudiated it as insane. Nevertheless, it continues to appeal very forcibly to the majority of normal husbands in the nations of the West, and I am convinced that it is a hundred times as potent as any other reason. The American husband, in particular, dresses his wife like a circus horse, not primarily because he wants to display his wealth upon her person, but because he is a soft and moony fellow and ever ready to yield to her desires, however preposterous. If any conception of her as a chattel were actively in him, even unconsciously, he would be a good deal less her slave. As it is, her vicarious practice of conspicuous waste commonly reaches such a development that her master himself is forced into renunciations—which brings Prof. Dr. Veblen's theory to self-destruction.

His final conclusion is as unsound as his premisses. All it comes to is a plain begging of the question. Why does a man forbid his wife to drink all the alcohol she can hold? Because, he says, it "detracts sensibly from his comfort or pleasure." In other words, it detracts from his comfort and pleasure because it detracts from his comfort and pleasure. Meanwhile, the real answer is so plain that even a professor should know it. A man forbids his wife to drink too much because, deep in his secret archives, he has records of the behavior of other women who drank too much, and is eager to safeguard his wife's self-respect and his own dignity against what he knows to be certain invasion. In brief, it is a commonplace of observation, familiar to all males beyond the age of twenty-one, that once a woman is drunk the rest is a mere matter of time and place: the girl is already there. A husband, viewing this prospect, perhaps shrinks from having his chattel damaged. But let us be soft enough to think that he may also shrink from seeing humiliation, ridicule and bitter regret inflicted upon one who is under his protection, and one whose dignity and happiness are precious to him, and one whom he regards with deep and (I surely hope) lasting affection. A man's grandfather is surely not his chattel, even by the terms of the Veblen theory, and yet I am sure that no sane man would let the old gentleman go beyond a discreet cocktail or two if a bout of genuine bibbing were certain to be followed by the complete destruction of his dignity, his chastity and (if a Presbyterian) his immortal soul. . . .

One more example of the Veblenian logic and I must pass on: I have other fish to fry. On page 135 of "The Theory of the Leisure Class" he turns his garish and buzzing search-light upon another problem of the domestic hearth, this time a double one. First, why do we have lawns around our country houses? Secondly, why don't we employ cows to keep them clipped, instead of importing Italians, Croatians and blackamoors? The first question is answered by an appeal to ethnology: we delight in lawns because we are the descendants of "a pastoral people inhabiting a region with a humid climate." True enough, there is in a well-kept lawn "an element of sensuous beauty," but that is secondary: the main thing is that our dolicho-blond ancestors had flocks, and thus took a keen professional interest in grass. (The Marx *motif*! The economic interpretation of history in E flat.) But why don't *we* keep flocks? Why do we renounce cows and hire Jugo-Slavs? Because "to the average popular apprehension a herd of cattle so pointedly suggests thrift and usefulness that their presence . . . would be intolerably cheap." With the highest veneration, Bosh! Plowing through a bad book from end to end, I can find nothing sillier than this. Here, indeed, the whole "theory of conspicuous waste" is exposed for precisely what it is: one per cent. platitude and ninety-nine per cent. nonsense. Has the genial professor, pondering his great problems, ever taken a walk in the country? And has he, in the course of that walk, ever crossed a pasture inhabited by a cow (*Bos taurus*)? And has he, making that crossing, ever passed astern of the cow herself? And has he, thus passing astern, ever stepped carelessly, and—

But this is not a medical work, and so I had better haul up. The cow, to me, symbolizes the whole speculation of this laborious and humorless pedagogue. From end to end you will find the same tedious torturing of plain facts, the same relentless piling up of thin and over-labored theory, the same flatulent bombast, the same intellectual strabismus. And always with an air of vast importance, always in vexed and formidable sentences, always in the longest words possible, always in the most cacophonous English that even a professor ever wrote. One visualizes him with his head thrown back, searching for cryptic answers in the firmament and not seeing the overt and disconcerting cow, not watching his step. One sees him as the pundit *par excellence*, infinitely earnest and diligent, infinitely honest and patient, but also infinitely humorless, futile and hollow. . . .

So much, at least for the present, for this Prof. Dr. Thorstein Veblen, head Great Thinker to the parlor radicals, Socrates of the intellectual Greenwich Village, chief star (at least transiently) of the American *Athanæums.* I am tempted to crowd in mention of some of his other astounding theories—for example, the theory that the presence of pupils, the labor of teaching, a concern with pedagogy, is necessary to the highest functioning of a scientific investigator—a notion magnificently supported by the examples of Flexner, Ehrlich, Metchnikoff, Loeb and Carrel! I am tempted, too, to devote a thirdly to the astounding materialism, almost the downright hoggishness, of his whole system—its absolute exclusion of everything approaching an æsthetic motive. But I must leave all these fallacies and absurdities to your own inquiry. More important than any of them, more important as a phenomenon than the professor himself and all his works, is the gravity with which his muddled and highly dubious ideas have been received. At the moment, I daresay, he is in decline; such Great Thinkers have a way of going out as quickly as they come in. But a year or so ago he dominated the American scene. All the reviews were full of his ideas. A hundred lesser sages reflected them. Every one of intellectual pretentions read his books. Veblenism was shining in full brilliance. There were Veblenists, Veblen clubs, Veblen remedies for all the sorrows of the world. There were even, in Chicago, Veblen Girls—perhaps Gibson girls grown middle-aged and despairing.

The spectacle, unluckily, was not novel. Go back through the history of America since the early nineties, and you will find a long succession of just such violent and uncritical enthusiasms. James had his day; Dewey had his day; Ibsen had his day; Maeterlinck had his day. Almost every year sees another intellectual Munyon arise, with his infallible peruna for all the current malaises. Sometimes this Great Thinker is imported. Once he was Pastor Wagner; once he was Bergson; once he was Eucken; once he was Tolstoi; once he was a lady, by name Ellen Key; again he was another lady, Signorina Montessori. But more often he is of native growth, and full of the pervasive cocksureness and superficiality of the land. I do not rank Dr. Veblen among the worst of these haruspices, save perhaps as a stylist; I am actually convinced that he belongs among the best of them. But that best is surely depressing enough. What lies behind it is the besetting intellectual sin of the United States—the habit of turning intellectual concepts into emotional concepts, the vice of orgiastic and inflammatory thinking. There is, in America, no orderly and thorough working out of the fundamental problems of our society; there is only, as one Englishman has said, an eternal combat of crazes. The things of capital importance are habitually discussed, not by men soberly trying to get at the truth about them, but by brummagem Great Thinkers trying only to get *kudos* out of them. We are beset endlessly by quacks—and they are not the less quacks when they happen to be quite honest. In all fields, from politics to pedagogics and from theology to public hygiene, there is a constant emotional obscuration of the true issues, a violent combat of credulities, an inane debasement of scientific curiosity to the level of mob gaping.

The thing to blame, of course, is our lack of an intellectual aristocracy—sound in its information, skeptical in its habit of mind, and, above all, secure in its position and authority. Every other civilized country has such an aristocracy. It is the natural corrective of enthusiasms from below. It is hospitable to ideas, but as adamant against crazes. It stands against the pollution of logic by emotion, the sophistication of evidence to the glory of God. But in America there is nothing of the sort. On the one hand there is the populace—perhaps more powerful here, more capable of putting its idiotic ideas into execution, than anywhere else—and surely more eager to follow platitudinous messiahs. On the other hand there is the ruling plutocracy—ignorant, hostile to inquiry, tyrannical in the exercise of its power, suspicious of ideas of whatever sort. In the middle ground there is little save an indistinct herd of intellectual eunuchs, chiefly professors—often quite as stupid as the plutocracy and always in great fear of it. When it produces a stray rebel he goes over to the mob; there is no place for him within his own order. This feeble and vacillating class, unorganized and without authority, is responsible for what passes as the well-informed opinion of the country—for the sort of opinion that one encounters in the serious periodicals—for what later on leaks down, much diluted, into the few newspapers that are not frankly imbecile. Dr. Veblen has himself described it in "The Higher Learning in America"; he is one of its characteristic products, and he proves that he is thoroughly of it by the timorousness he shows in that book. It is, in the main, only half-educated. It lacks experience of the world, assurance, the consciousness of class solidarity and security. Of no definite position in our national life, exposed alike to the clamors of the mob and the discipline of the plutocracy, it gets no public respect and is deficient in self-respect. Thus the better sort of men are not tempted to enter it. It recruits only men of feeble courage, men of small originality. Its sublimest flower is the American college president, well described by Dr. Veblen—a perambulating sycophant and platitudinarian, a gaudy mendicant and bounder, engaged all his life, not in the battle of ideas, the pursuit and dissemination of knowledge, but in the courting of rich donkeys and the entertainment of mobs. . . .

Nay, Veblen is not the worst. Veblen is almost the best. The worst is—but I begin to grow indignant, and indignation, as old Friedrich used to say, is foreign to my nature.

VI.
The New Poetry Movement

THE current pother about poetry, now gradually subsiding, seems to have begun about seven years ago—say in 1912. It was during that year that Harriet Monroe established *Poetry: A Magazine of Verse*, in Chicago, and ever since then she has been the mother superior of the movement. Other leaders have occasionally disputed her command—the bombastic Braithwaite, with his annual anthology of magazine verse; Amy Lowell, with her solemn pronunciamentos in the manner of a Harvard professor; Vachel Lindsay, with his nebulous vaporings and chautauqua posturings; even such cheap jacks as Alfred Kreymborg, out of Greenwich Village. But the importance of Miss Monroe grows more manifest as year chases year. She was, to begin with, clearly the pioneer. *Poetry* was on the stands nearly two years before the first Braithwaite anthology, and long before Miss Lowell had been lured from her earlier finishing-school doggerels by the Franco-British Imagists. It antedated, too, all the other salient documents of the movement—Master's "Spoon River Anthology," Frost's "North of Boston," Lindsay's "General William Booth Enters Heaven," the historic bulls of the Imagists, the frantic balderdash of the "Others" group. Moreover, Miss Monroe has always managed to keep on good terms with all wings of the heaven-kissed host, and has thus managed to exert a ponderable influence both to starboard and to port. This, I daresay, is because she is a very intelligent woman, which fact is alone sufficient to give her an austere eminence in a movement so beset by mountebanks and their dupes. I have read *Poetry* since the first number, and find it constantly entertaining. It has printed a great deal of extravagant stuff, and not a little downright nonsensical stuff, but in the main it has steered a safe and intelligible course, with no salient blunders. No other poetry magazine—and there have been dozens of them—has even remotely approached it in interest, or, for that matter, in genuine hospitality to ideas. Practically all of the others have been operated by passionate enthusiasts, often extremely ignorant and always narrow and humorless. But Miss Monroe has managed to retain a certain judicial calm in the midst of all the whooping and clapper-clawing, and so she has avoided running amuck, and her magazine has printed the very best of the new poetry and avoided much of the worst.

As I say, the movement shows signs of having spent its strength. The mere bulk of the verse that it produces is a great deal less than it was three or four years ago, or even one or two years ago, and there is a noticeable tendency toward the conservatism once so loftily disdained. I daresay the Knish-Morgan burlesque of Witter Bynner and Arthur Davison Ficke was a hard blow to the more fantastic radicals. At all events, they subsided after it was perpetrated, and for a couple of years nothing has been heard from them. These radicals, chiefly collected in what was called the "Others" group, rattled the slapstick in a sort of side-show to the main exhibition. They attracted, of course, all the more credulous and uninformed partisans of the movement, and not a few advanced professors out of one-building universities began to lecture upon them before bucolic women's clubs. They committed hari-kari in the end by beginning to believe in their own buncombe. When their leaders took to the chautauquas and sought to convince the peasantry that James Whitcomb Riley was a fraud the time was ripe for the lethal buffoonery of MM. Bynner and Ficke. That buffoonery was enormously successful—perhaps the best hoax in American literary history. It was swallowed, indeed, by so many magnificoes that it made criticism very timorous thereafter, and so did damage to not a few quite honest bards. To-day a new poet, if he departs ever so little from the path already beaten, is kept in a sort of literary delousing pen until it is established that he is genuinely sincere, and not merely another Bynner in hempen whiskers and a cloak to go invisible.

Well, what is the net produce of the whole uproar? How much actual poetry have all these truculent rebels against Stedman's Anthology and McGuffey's Sixth Reader manufactured? I suppose I have read nearly all of it—a great deal of it, as a magazine editor, in manuscript—and yet, as I look back, my memory is lighted up by very few flashes of any lasting brilliance. The best of all the lutists of the new school, I am inclined to think, are Carl Sandburg and James Oppenheim, and particularly Sandburg. He shows a great deal of raucous crudity, he is often a bit uncertain and wobbly, and sometimes he is downright banal—but, taking one bard with another, he is probably the soundest and most intriguing of the lot. Compare, for example, his war poems—simple, eloquent and extraordinarily moving—to the humorless balderdash of Amy Lowell, or, to go outside the movement, to the childish gush of Joyce Kilmer, Hermann Hagedorn and Charles Hanson Towne. Often he gets memorable effects by astonishingly austere means, as in his famous "Chicago" rhapsody and his "Cool Tombs." And always he is thoroughly individual, a true original, his own man. Oppenheim, equally eloquent, is more conventional. He stands, as to one leg, on the shoulders of Walt Whitman, and, as to the other, on a stack of Old Testaments. The stuff he writes, despite his belief to the contrary, is not American at all; it is absolutely Jewish, Levantine, almost Asiatic. But here is something criticism too often forgets: the Jew, intrinsically, is the greatest of poets. Beside his gorgeous rhapsodies the highest flights of any western bard seem feeble and cerebral. Oppenheim, inhabiting a brick house in New York, manages to get that sonorous Eastern note into his dithyrambs. They are often inchoate and feverish, but at their best they have the gigantic gusto of Solomon's Song.

Miss Lowell is the schoolmarm of the movement, and vastly more the pedagogue than the artist. She has written perhaps half a dozen excellent pieces in imitation of Richard Aldington and John Gould Fletcher, and a great deal of highfalutin bathos. Her "A Dome of Many-Colored Glass" is full of infantile poppycock, and though it is true that it was first printed in 1912, before she joined the Imagists, it is not to be forgotten that it was reprinted with her consent in 1915, after she had definitely set up shop as a foe of the *cliché*. Her celebrity, I fancy, is largely extra-poetical; if she were Miss Tilly Jones, of Fort Smith, Ark., there would be a great deal less rowing about her, and her successive masterpieces would be received less gravely. A literary craftsman in America, as I have already said once or twice, is never judged by his work alone. Miss Lowell has been helped very much by her excellent social position. The majority, and perhaps fully nine-tenths of the revolutionary poets are of no social position at all—newspaper reporters, Jews, foreigners of vague nationality, school teachers, lawyers, advertisement writers, itinerant lecturers, Greenwich Village posturers, and so on. I have a suspicion that it has subtly flattered such denizens of the *demi-monde* to find the sister of a president of Harvard in their midst, and that their delight has materially corrupted their faculties. Miss Lowell's book of exposition, "Tendencies in Modern American Poetry," is commonplace to the last degree. Louis Untermeyer's "The New Era in American Poetry" is very much better. And so is Prof. Dr. John Livingston Lowes' "Convention and Revolt in Poetry."

As for Edgar Lee Masters, for a short season the undisputed Homer of the movement, I believe that he is already extinct. What made the fame of "The Spoon River Anthology" was not chiefly any great show of novelty in it, nor any extraordinary poignancy, nor any grim truthfulness unparalleled, but simply the public notion that it was improper. It fell upon the country at the height of the last sex wave—a wave eternally ebbing and flowing, now high, now low. It was read, not as work of art, but as document; its large circulation was undoubtedly mainly among persons to whom poetry *qua* poetry was as sour a dose as symphonic music. To such persons, of course, it seemed something new under the sun. They were unacquainted with the verse of George Crabbe; they were quite innocent of E. A. Robinson and Robert Frost; they knew nothing of the *Ubi sunt* formula; they had never heard of the Greek Anthology. The roar of his popular success won Masters' case with the critics. His undoubted merits in detail—his half-wistful cynicism, his capacity for evoking simple emotions, his deft skill at managing the puny difficulties of *vers libre*—were thereupon pumped up to such an extent that his defects were lost sight of. Those defects, however, shine blindingly in his later books. Without the advantage of content that went with the anthology, they reveal themselves as volumes of empty doggerel, with now and then a brief moment of illumination. It would be difficult, indeed, to find poetry that is, in essence, less poetical. Most of the pieces are actually tracts, and many of them are very bad tracts.

Lindsay? Alas, he has done his own burlesque. What was

new in him, at the start, was an echo of the barbaric rhythms of the Jubilee Songs. But very soon the thing ceased to be a marvel, and of late his elephantine college yells have ceased to be amusing. His retirement to the chautauquas is self-criticism of uncommon penetration. Frost? A standard New England poet, with a few changes in phraseology, and the substitution of sour resignationism for sweet resignationism. Whittier without the whiskers. Robinson? Ditto, but with a politer bow. He has written sound poetry, but not much of it. The late Major-General Roosevelt ruined him by praising him, as he ruined Henry Bordeaux, Pastor Wagner, Francis Warrington Dawson and many another. Giovannitti? A forth-rate Sandburg. Ezra Pound? The American in headlong flight from America—to England, to Italy, to the Middle Ages, to ancient Greece, to Cathay and points East. Pound, it seems to me, is the most picturesque man in the whole movement—a professor turned fantee, Abelard in grand opera. His knowledge is abysmal; he has it readily on tap; moreover, he has a fine ear, and has written many an excellent verse. But now all the glow and gusto of the bard have been transformed into the rage of the pamphleteer: he drops the lute for the bayonet. One sympathizes with him in his choler. The stupidity he combats is actually almost unbearable. Every normal man must be tempted, at times, to spit on his hands, hoist the black flag, and begin slitting throats. But this business, alas, is fatal to the placid moods and fine other-worldliness of the poet. Pound gives a thrilling show, but—. . . . The remaining stars of the liberation need not detain us. They are the street-boys following the calliope. They have labored with diligence, but they have produced no poetry. . . .

Miss Monroe, if she would write a book about it, would be the most competent historian of the movement, and perhaps also its keenest critic. She has seen it from the inside. She knows precisely what it is about. She is able, finally, to detach herself from its extravagances, and to estimate its opponents without bile. Her failure to do a volume about it leaves Untermeyer's "The New Era in American Poetry" the best in the field. Prof. Dr. Lowes' treatise is very much more thorough, but it has the defect of stopping with the fundamentals—it has too little to say about specific poets. Untermeyer discusses all of them, and then throws in a dozen or two orthodox bards, wholly untouched by Bolshevism, for good measure. His criticism is often trenchant and always very clear. He thinks he knows what he thinks he knows, and he states it with the utmost address—sometimes, indeed, as in the case of Pound, with a good deal more address than its essential accuracy deserves. But the messianic note that gets into the bulls and ukases of Pound himself, the profound solemnity of Miss Lowell, the windy chautauqua-like nothings of Lindsay, the contradictions of the Imagists, the puerilities of Kreymborg *et al*—all these things are happily absent. And so it is possible to follow him amiably even when he is palpably wrong.

That is not seldom. At the very start, for example, he permits himself a lot of highly dubious rumble-bumble about the "inherent Americanism" and soaring democracy of the movement. "Once," he says, "the most exclusive and aristocratic of the arts, appreciated and fostered only by little *salons* and erudite groups, poetry has suddenly swung away from its self-imposed strictures and is expressing itself once more in terms of democracy." Pondering excessively, I can think of nothing that would be more untrue than this. The fact is that the new poetry is neither American nor democratic. Despite its remote grounding on Whitman, it started, not in the United States at all, but in France, and its exotic color is still its most salient characteristic. Practically every one of its practitioners is palpably under some strong foreign influence, and most of them are no more Anglo-Saxon than a samovar or a toccata. The deliberate strangeness of Pound, his almost fanatical anti-Americanism, is a mere accentuation of what is in every other member of the fraternity. Many of them, like Frost, Fletcher, H. D. and Pound, have exiled themselves from the republic. Others, such as Oppenheim, Sandburg, Giovannitti, Benét and Untermeyer himself, are palpably Continental Europeans, often with Levantine traces. Yet others, such as Miss Lowell and Masters, are little more, at their best, than translators and adapters—from the French, from the Japanese, from the Greek. Even Lindsay, superficially the most national of them all, has also his exotic smear, as I have shown. Let Miss Lowell herself be a witness. "We shall see them," she says at the opening of her essay on E. A. Robinson, "ceding more and more to the influence of other, alien, peoples. . . ." A glance is sufficient to show the correctness of this observation. There is no more "inherent Americanism" in the new poetry than there is in the new American painting and music. It lies, in fact, quite outside the main stream of American culture.

Nor is it democratic, in any intelligible sense. The poetry of Whittier and Longfellow was democratic. It voiced the elemental emotions of the masses of the people; it was full of their simple, rubber-stamp ideas; they comprehended it and cherished it. And so with the poetry of James Whitcomb Riley, and with that of Walt Mason and Ella Wheeler Wilcox. But the new poetry, grounded firmly upon novelty of form and boldness of idea, is quite beyond their understanding. It seems to them to be idiotic, just as the poetry of Whitman seemed to them to be idiotic, and if they could summon up enough interest in it to examine it at length they would undoubtedly clamor for laws making the confection of it a felony. The mistake of Untermeyer, and of others who talk to the same effect, lies in confusing the beliefs of poets and the subject matter of their verse with its position in the national consciousness. Oppenheim, Sandburg and Lindsay are democrats, just as Whitman was a democrat, but their poetry is no more a democratic phenomenon than his was, or than, to go to music, Beethoven's Eroica Symphony was. Many of the new poets, in truth, are ardent enemies of democracy, for example, Pound. Only one of them has ever actually sought to take his strophes to the vulgar. That one is Lindsay—and there is not the slightest doubt that the yokels welcomed him, not because they were interested in his poetry, but because it struck them as an amazing, and perhaps even a fascinatingly obscene thing, for a sane man to go about the country on any such bizarre and undemocratic business.

No sound art, in fact, could possibly be democratic. Tolstoi wrote a whole book to prove the contrary, and only succeeded in making his case absurd. The only art that is capable of reaching the *Homo Boobus* is art that is already debased and polluted—band music, official sculpture, Pears' Soap painting, the popular novel. What is honest and worthy of praise in the new poetry is Greek to the general. And, despite much nonsense, it seems to me that there is no little in it that is honest and worthy of praise. It has, for one thing, made an effective war upon the *cliché*, and so purged the verse of the nation of much of its old banality in subject and phrase. The elegant album pieces of Richard Henry Stoddard and Edmund Clarence Stedman are no longer in fashion—save, perhaps, among the democrats that Untermeyer mentions. And in the second place, it has substituted for this ancient conventionality an eager curiosity in life as men and women are actually living it—a spirit of daring experimentation that has made poetry vivid and full of human interest, as it was in the days of Elizabeth. The thing often passes into the grotesque, it is shot through and through with *héliogabalisme*, but at its high points it has achieved invaluable pioneering. A new poet, emerging out of the Baptist night of Peoria or Little Rock to-day, comes into an atmosphere charged with subtle electricities. There is a stimulating restlessness; ideas have a welcome; the art he aspires to is no longer a merely formal exercise, like practicing Czerny. When a Henry Van Dyke arises at some college banquet and begins to discharge an old-fashioned ode to *alma mater* there is a definite snicker; it is almost as if he were to appear in Congress gaiters or a beaver hat. An audience for such things, of course, still exists. It is, no doubt, an enormously large audience. But it has changed a good deal qualitatively, if not quantitatively. The relatively civilized reader has been educated to something better. He has heard a music that has spoiled his ear for the old wheezing of the melodeon. He weeps no more over what wrung him yesteryear.

Unluckily, the new movement, in America even more than in England, France and Germany, suffers from a very crippling lack, and that is the lack of a genuinely first-rate poet. It has produced many talents, but it has yet to produce any genius, or even the shadow of genius. There has been a general lifting of the plain, but no vasty and melodramatic throwing up of new peaks. Worse still, it has had to face hard competition from without—that is, from poets who, while also emerged from platitude, have yet stood outside it, and perhaps in some doubt of it. Untermeyer discusses a number of such poets in his book. There is one of them, Lizette Woodworth Reese, who has written more sound poetry, more genuinely eloquent and beautiful poetry, than all the new poets put together—more than a whole posse of Masterses and Lindsays, more than a hundred Amy Lowells. And there are others, Neihardt and John McClure among them—particularly McClure. Untermeyer, usually anything but an ass, once committed the unforgettable asininity of sneering at McClure. The blunder, I daresay, is already lamented; it is not embalmed in his book. But it will haunt him on Tyburn Hill. For this McClure, attempting the simplest thing in the simplest way, has done it almost superbly. He seems to be entirely without theories. There is no pedagogical passion in him. He is no reformer. But more than any of the reformers now or lately in the arena, he is a poet.

VII.
The Heir of Mark Twain

NOTHING could be stranger than the current celebrity of Irvin S. Cobb, an author of whom almost as much is heard as if he were a new Thackeray or Molière. One is solemnly told by various extravagant partisans, some of them not otherwise insane, that he is at once the successor to Mark Twain and the heir of Edgar Allan Poe. One hears of public dinners given in devotion to his genius, of public presentations, of learned degrees conferred upon him by universities, of other extraordinary adulations, few of them shared by such relatively puny fellows as Howells and Dreiser. His talents and sagacity pass into popular anecdotes; he has sedulous Boswells; he begins to take on the august importance of an actor-manager. Behind the scenes, of course, a highly dexterous publisher pulls the strings, but much of it is undoubtedly more or less sincere; men pledge their sacred honor to the doctrine that his existence honors the national literature. Moreover, he seems to take the thing somewhat seriously himself. He gives his *imprimatur* to various other authors, including Joseph Conrad; he engages himself to lift the literary tone of moving-pictures; he lends his name to movements; he exposes himself in the chautauquas; he takes on the responsibilities of a patriot and a public man. . . . Altogether, a curious, and, in some of its aspects, a caressingly ironical spectacle. One wonders what the graduate sophomores of to-morrow, composing their dull tomes upon American letters, will make of it. . . .

In the actual books of the man I can find nothing that seems to justify so much enthusiasm, nor even the hundredth part of it. His serious fiction shows a certain undoubted facility, but there are at least forty other Americans who do the thing quite as well. His public bulls and ukases are no more than clever journalism—superficial and inconsequential, first saying one thing and then quite another thing. And in his humor, which his admirers apparently put first among his products, I can discover, at best, nothing save a somewhat familiar aptitude for grotesque anecdote, and, at worst, only the laborious laugh-squeezing of Bill Nye. In the volume called "Those Times and These" there is an excellent comic story, to wit, "Hark, From the Tomb!" But it would surely be an imbecility to call it a masterpiece; too many other authors have done things quite as good; more than a few (I need cite only George Ade, Owen Johnson and Ring W. Lardner) have done things very much better. Worse, it lies in the book like a slice of Smithfield ham between two slabs of stale store-bread. On both sides of it are very stupid artificialities—stories without point, stories in which rustic characters try to talk like Wilson Mizner, stories altogether machine-made and depressing. Turn, now, to another book, vastly praised in its year—by name, "Cobb's Anatomy." One laughs occasionally—but precisely as one laughs over a comic supplement or the jokes in *Ayer's Almanac*. For example:

> There never was a hansom cab made that would hold a fat man comfortably unless he left the doors open, and that makes him feel undressed.

Again:

> Your hair gives you bother so long as you have it and more bother when it starts to go. You are always doing something for it and it is always showing deep-dyed ingratitude in return; or else the dye isn't deep enough, which is even worse.

Exactly; it is even worse. And then this:

> Once there was a manicure lady who wouldn't take a tip, but she is now no more. Her indignant sisters stabbed her to death with hatpins and nail-files.

I do not think I quote unfairly; I have tried to select honest specimens of the author's fancy. . . . Perhaps it may be well to glance at another book. I choose, at random, "Speaking of Operations—," a work described by the publisher as "the funniest yet written by Cobb" and "the funniest book we know of." In this judgment many other persons seem to have concurred. The thing was an undoubted success when it appeared as an article in the *Saturday Evening Post* and it sold thousands of copies between covers. Well, what is in it? In it, after a diligent reading, I find half a dozen mildly clever observations—and sixty odd pages of ancient and infantile wheezes, as flat to the taste as so many crystals of hyposulphite of soda. For example, the wheeze to the effect that in the days of the author's nonage "germs had not been invented yet." For example, the wheeze to the effect that doctors bury their mistakes. For example, the wheeze to the effect that the old-time doctor always prescribed medicines of abominably evil flavor. . . . But let us go into the volume more in detail, and so unearth all its gems.

On page 1, in the very first paragraph, there is the doddering old joke about the steepness of doctors' bills. In the second paragraph there is the somewhat newer but still fully adult joke about the extreme willingness of persons who have been butchered by surgeons to talk about it afterward. These two witticisms are all that I can find on page 1. For the rest, it consists almost entirely of a reference to MM. Bryan and Roosevelt—a reference well known by all newspaper paragraphists and vaudeville monologists to be as provocative of laughter as a mention of bunions, mothers-in-law or Pottstown, Pa. On page 2 Bryan and Roosevelt are succeeded by certain heavy stuff in the Petroleum V. Nasby manner upon the condition of obstetrics, pediatrics and the allied sciences among whales. Page 3 starts off with the old jocosity to the effect that people talk too much about the weather. It progresses or resolves, as the musicians say, into the wheeze to the effect that people like to dispute over what is the best thing to eat for breakfast. On page 4 we come to what musicians would call the formal statement of the main theme—that is, of the how-I-like-to-talk-of-my-operation motif. We have thus covered four pages.

Page 5 starts out with an enharmonic change: to wit, from the idea that ex-patients like to talk of their operations to the idea that patients in being like to swap symptoms. Following this there is a repetition of the gold theme—that is, the theme of the doctor's bill. On page 6 there are two chuckles. One springs out of a reference to "light housekeeping," a phrase which invariably strikes an American vaudeville audience as salaciously whimsical. The other is grounded upon the well-known desire of baseball fans to cut the umpire's throat. On page 6 there enters for the first time what may be called the second theme of the book. This is the whiskers motif. The whole of this page, with the exception of a sentence embodying the old wheeze about the happy times before germs were invented, is given over to variations of the whiskers joke. Page 8 continues this development section. Whiskers of various fantastic varieties are mentioned—trellis whiskers, bosky whiskers, ambush whiskers, loose, luxuriant whiskers, landscaped whiskers, whiskers that are winter quarters for pathogenic organisms. Some hard, hard squeezing, and the humor in whiskers is temporarily exhausted. Page 8 closes with the old joke about the cruel thumping which doctors perform upon their patients' clavicles.

Now for page 9. It opens with a third statement of the gold motif—"He then took my temperature and $15." Following comes the dentist's office motif—that is, the motif of reluctance, of oozing courage, of flight. At the bottom of the page the gold motif is repeated in the key of E minor. Pages 10 and 11 are devoted to simple description, with very little effort at humor. On page 12 there is a second statement, for the full brass choir, of the dentist's office motif. On page 13 there are more echoes from Petroleum V. Nasby, the subject this time being a man "who got his spleen back from the doctor's and now keeps it in a bottle of alcohol." On page 14 one finds the innocent bystander joke; on page 15 the joke about the terrifying effects of reading a patent medicine almanac. Also, at the bottom of the page, there is a third statement of the dentist's office joke. On page 16 it gives way to a restatement of the whiskers theme, in augmentation, which in turn yields to the third or fifth restatement of the gold theme.

Let us now jump a few pages. On page 19 we come to the old joke about the talkative barber; on page 22 to the joke about the book agent; on the same page to the joke about the fashionableness of appendicitis; on page 23 to the joke about the clumsy carver who projects the turkey's gizzard into the visiting pastor's eye; on page 28 to a restatement of the barber joke; on page 31 to another statement—is it the fifth or sixth? —of the dentist's office joke; on page 37 to the katzenjammer joke; on page 39 to the old joke about doctors burying their mistakes. . . . And so on. And so on and so on. And so on and so on and so on. On pages 48 and 49 there is a perfect riot of old jokes, including the *n*th variation of the whiskers joke and a fearful and wonderful pun about Belgian hares and heirs. . . .

On second thoughts I go no further. . . . This, remember, is the book that Cobb's publishers, apparently with his own *Nihil Obstat*, choose at his best. This is the official masterpiece of the "new Mark Twain." Nevertheless, even so laboriously flabby a farceur has his moments. I turn to Frank J. Wilstach's Dictionary of Similes and find this credited to him: "No more privacy than a goldfish." Here, at last, is something genuinely humorous. Here, moreover, is something apparently new.

VIII.
Hermann Sudermann

THE fact that Sudermann is the author of the most successful play that has come out of Germany since the collapse of the romantic movement is the most eloquent of all proofs, perhaps, of his lack of force and originality as a dramatist. "Heimat," Englished, Frenched and Italianized as "Magda," gave a new and gaudy leading rôle to all the middle-aged chewers of scenery; they fell upon it as upon a new Marguerite Gautier, and with it they coaxed the tears of all nations. That was in the middle nineties. To-day the piece seems almost as old-fashioned as "The Princess Bonnie," and even in Germany it has gone under the counter. If it is brought out at all, it is to adorn the death agonies of some doddering star of the last generation.

Sudermann was one of the first deer flushed by Arno Holz and Johannes Schlaf, the founders of German naturalism. He had written a couple of successful novels, "Frau Sorge" and "Der Katzensteg," before the *Uberbrettl'* got on its legs, and so he was a recruit worth snaring. The initial fruit of his enlistment was "Die Ehre," a *reductio ad absurdum* of Prussian notions of honor, as incomprehensible outside of Germany as Franz Adam Beyerlein's "Zapfenstreich" or Carl Bleibtreu's "Die Edelsten der Nation." Then followed "Sodoms Ende," and after it, "Heimat." Already the emptiness of naturalism was beginning to oppress Sudermann, as it was also oppressing Hauptmann. The latter, in 1892, rebounded from it to the unblushing romanticism of "Hanneles Himmelfahrt." As for Sudermann, he chose to temper the rigors of the Schlaf-Holz formula (by Ibsen out of Zola) with sardoodledum. The result was this "Heimat," in which naturalism was wedded to a mellow sentimentality, caressing to audiences bred upon the drama of perfumed adultery. The whole last scene of the play, indeed, was no more than an echo of Augier's "Le Mariage d'Olympe." It is no wonder that even Sarah Bernhardt pronounced it a great work.

Since then Sudermann has wobbled, and in the novel as well as in the drama. Lacking the uncanny versatility of Hauptmann, he has been unable to conquer the two fields of romance and reality. Instead he has lost himself between them, a rat without a tail. "Das hohe Lied," his most successful novel since "Frau Sorge," is anything but a first-rate work. Its opening chapter is a superlatively fine piece of writing, but after that he grows uncertain of his way, and toward the end one begins to wonder what it is all about. No coherent idea is in it; it is simply a sentimentalization of the unpleasant; if it were not for the naughtiness of some of the scenes no one would read it. An American dramatist has made a play of it—a shocker for the same clowns who were entranced by Brieux's "Les Avariés."

The trouble with Sudermann, here and elsewhere, is that he has no sound underpinnings, and is a bit uncertain about his characters and his story. He starts off furiously, let us say, as a Zola, and then dilutes Zolaism with romance, and then pulls himself up and begins to imitate Ibsen, and then trips and falls headlong into the sugar bowl of sentimentality. Lily Czepanek, in "Das hohe Lied," swoons at critical moments, like the heroine of a tale for chambermaids. It is almost as if Lord Jim should get converted at a gospel mission, or Nora Helmer let down her hair. . . . But these are defects in Sudermann the novelist and dramatist, and in that Sudermann only. In the short story they conceal themselves; he is done before he begins to vacillate. In this field, indeed, all his virtues—of brisk, incisive writing, of flashing observation, of dexterous stage management, of emotional fire and address—have a chance to show themselves, and without any wearing thin. The book translated as "The Indian Lily" contains some of the best short stories that German—or any other language, for that matter—can offer. They are mordant, succinct and extraordinarily vivid character studies, each full of penetrating irony and sardonic pity, each with the chill wind of disillusion blowing through it, each preaching that life is a hideous farce, that good and bad are almost meaningless words, that truth is only the lie that is easiest to believe. . . .

It is hard to choose between stories so high in merit, but surely "The Purpose" is one of the best. Of all the latter-day Germans, only Ludwig Thoma, in "Ein bayrischer Soldat," has ever got a more brilliant reality into a crowded space. Here, in less than fifteen thousand words, Sudermann rehearses the tragedy of a whole life, and so great is the art of the thing that one gets a sense of perfect completeness, almost of exhaustiveness. . . . Antonie Wiesner, the daughter of a country innkeeper, falls in love with Robert Messerschmidt, a medical student, and they sin the scarlet sin. To Robert, perhaps, the thing is a mere interlude of midsummer, but to Toni it is all life's meaning and glory. Robert is poor and his degree is still two years ahead; it is out of the question for him to marry. Very well, Toni will find a father for her child; she is her lover's property, and that property must be protected. And she will wait willingly, careless of the years, for the distant day of triumph and redemption. All other ideas and ideals drop out of her mind; she becomes an automaton moved by the one impulse, the one yearning. She marries one Wiegand, a decayed innkeeper; he, poor fool, accepts the parentage of her child. Her father, rich and unsuspicious, buys them a likely inn; they begin to make money. And then begins the second chapter of Toni's sacrifice. She robs her husband systematically and steadily; she takes commissions on all his goods; she becomes the houri of his bar, that trade may grow and pickings increase. Mark by mark, the money goes to Robert. It sees him through the university; it gives him his year or two in the hospitals; it buys him a practice; it feeds and clothes him, and his mother with him. The months and years pass endlessly—a young doctor's progress is slow. But finally the great day approaches. Soon Robert will be ready for his wife. But Wiegand—what of him? Toni thinks of half a dozen plans. The notion of poisoning him gradually formulates itself. Not a touch of horror stays her. She is, by this time, beyond all the common moralities—a monomaniac with no thought for anything save her great purpose. But an accident saves Wiegand. Toni, too elaborate in her plans, poisons herself by mischance, and comes near dying. Very well, if not poison, then some more subtle craft. She puts a barmaid into Wiegand's path; she manages the whole affair; before long she sees her victim safely enmeshed. A divorce follows; the inn is sold; her father's death makes her suddenly rich—at last she is off to greet her lord!

That meeting! . . . Toni waits in the little flat that she has rented in the city—she and her child, the child of Robert. Robert is to come at noon; as the slow moments pass the burden of her happiness seems too great to bear. And then suddenly the ecstatic climax—the ring at the door. . . . "A gentleman entered. A strange gentleman. Wholly strange. Had she met him on the street she would not have known him. He had grown old—forty, fifty, a hundred years. Yet his real age could not be over twenty-eight! . . . He had grown fat. He carried a little paunch around with him, round and comfortable. And the honorable scars gleamed in round, red cheeks. His eyes seemed small and receding. . . . And when he said: 'Here I am at last,' it was no longer the old voice, clear and a little resonant, which had echoed and reëchoed in her spiritual ear. He gurgled as though he had swallowed dumplings." An oaf without and an oaf within! Toni is for splendors, triumphs, the life; Robert has "settled down." His remote village, hard by the Russian border, is to his liking; he has made comfortable friends there; he is building up a practice. He is, of course, a man of honor. He will marry Toni—willingly and with gratitude, even with genuine affection. Going further, he will pay back to her every cent that ever came from Wiegand's till. He has kept a strict account. Here it is, in a little blue notebook—seven years of entries. As he reads them aloud the events of those seven years unroll themselves before Toni and every mark brings up its picture—stolen cash and trinkets, savings in railroad fares and food, commissions upon furniture and wines, profits of champagne debauches with the county councilor, sharp trading in milk and eggs, "suspense and longing, an inextricable web of falsification and trickery, of terror and lying without end. The memory of no guilt is spared her." Robert is an honest, an honorable man. He has kept a strict account; the money is waiting in bank. What is more, he will make all necessary confessions. He has not, perhaps, kept to the letter of fidelity. There was a waitress in Berlin; there was a nurse at the surgical clinic; there is even now a Lithuanian servant girl at his bachelor quarters. The last named, of course, will be sent away forthwith. Robert is a man of honor, a man sensitive to every requirement of the punctilio, a gentleman. He will order the announcement cards, consult a clergyman—and not forget to get rid of the Lithuanian and air the house. . . . Poor Toni stares at him as he departs. "Will he come back soon?" asks the child. "I scarcely think so," she answers. . . . "That night she broke the purpose of her life, the purpose that had become interwoven with a thousand others, and when the morning came she wrote a letter of farewell to the beloved of her youth."

A short story of rare and excellent quality. A short story—oh, miracle!—worth reading twice. It is not so much that its motive is new—that motive, indeed, has appeared in fiction many times, though usually with the man as the protagonist—as that its workmanship is superb. Sudermann here shows that, for all his failings elsewhere, he knows superlatively how to write. His act divisions are exactly right; his *scènes à faire* are magnificently managed; he has got into the thing that rhythmic ebb and flow of emotion which makes for great drama. And in most of the other stories in this book you will find much the same skill. No other, perhaps, is quite so good as "The Purpose," but at least one of them, "The Song of Death," is not far behind. Here we have the tragedy of a woman brought up rigorously, puritanically, stupidly, who discovers, just as it is too late, that love may be a wild dance, an ecstasy, an orgy. I can imagine no more grotesquely pathetic scene than that which shows this drab preacher's wife watching by her husband's death-bed—while through the door comes the sound of amorous delirium from the next room. And then there is a strangely moving Christmas story, "Merry Folk"—pathos with the hard iron in it. And there are "Autumn" and "The Indian Lily," elegies to lost youth—the first of them almost a fit complement to Joseph Conrad's great paean to youth triumphant. Altogether, a collection of short stories of the very first rank. Write off "Das hohe Lied," "Frau Sorge" and all the plays: a Sudermann remains who must be put in a high and honorable place, and will be remembered.

IX.

George Ade

WHEN, after the Japs and their vassals conquer us and put us to the sword, and the republic descends into hell, some literary don of Oxford or Mittel-Europa proceeds to the predestined autopsy upon our Complete Works, one of the things he will surely notice, reviewing our literary history, is the curious persistence with which the dons native to the land have overlooked its emerging men of letters. I mean, of course, its genuine men of letters, its salient and truly original men, its men of intrinsic and unmistakable distinction. The fourth-raters have fared well enough, God knows. Go back to any standard literature book of ten, or twenty, or thirty, or fifty years ago, and you will be amazed by its praise of shoddy mediocrities, long since fly-blown and forgotten. George William Curtis, now seldom heard of at all, save perhaps in the reminiscences of senile publishers, was treated in his day with all the deference due to a prince of the blood. Artemus Ward, Petroleum V. Nasby and half a dozen other such hollow buffoons were ranked with Mark Twain, and even above him. Frank R. Stockton, for thirty years, was the delight of all right-thinking reviewers. Richard Henry Stoddard and Edmund Clarence Stedman were eminent personages, both as critics and as poets. And Donald G. Mitchell, to make an end of dull names, bulked so grandly in the academic eye that he was snatched from his tear-jugs and his tea-pots to become a charter member of the National Institute of Arts and Letters, and actually died a member of the American Academy!

Meanwhile, three of the five indubitably first-rate artists that America has produced went quite without orthodox recognition at home until either foreign enthusiasm or domestic clamor from below forced them into a belated and grudging sort of notice. I need not say that I allude to Poe, Whitman and Mark Twain. If it ever occurred to any American critic of position, during Poe's lifetime, that he was a greater man than either Cooper or Irving, then I have been unable to find any trace of the fact in the critical literature of the time. The truth is that he was looked upon as a facile and somewhat dubious journalist, too cocksure by half, and not a man to be encouraged. Lowell praised him in 1845 and at the same time denounced the current over-praise of lesser men, but later on this encomium was diluted with very important reservations, and there the matter stood until Baudelaire discovered the poet and his belated fame came winging home. Whitman, as every one knows, fared even worse. Emerson first hailed him and then turned tail upon him, eager to avoid any share in his ill-repute among blockheads. No other critic of any influence gave him help. He was carried through his dark days of poverty and persecution by a few private enthusiasts, none of them with the ear of the public, and in the end it was Frenchmen and Englishmen who lifted him into the light. Imagine a Harvard professor lecturing upon him in 1865! As for Mark Twain, the story of his first fifteen years has been admirably told by Prof. Dr. William Lyon Phelps, of Yale. The dons were unanimously against him. Some sneered at him as a feeble mountebank; others refused to discuss him at all; not one harbored the slightest suspicion that he was a man of genius, or even one leg of a man of genius. Phelps makes merry over this academic attempt to dispose of Mark by putting him into Coventry—and himself joins the sanctimonious brethren who essay the same enterprise against Dreiser. . . .

I come by this route to George Ade—who perhaps fails to fit into the argument doubly, for on the one hand he is certainly not a literary artist of the first rank, and on the other hand he has long enjoyed a meed of appreciation and even of honor, for the National Institute of Arts and Letters elevated him to its gilt-edged purple in its first days, and he is still on its roll of men of "notable achievement in art, music or literature," along with Robert W. Chambers, Henry Sydnor Harrison, Oliver Herford, E. S. Martin and E. W. Townsend, author of "Chimmie Fadden." Nevertheless, he does not fall too far outside, after all, for if he is not of the first rank then he surely deserves a respectable place in the second rank, and if the National Institute broke the spell by admitting him then it was probably on the theory that he was a second Chambers or Herford, or maybe even a second Martin or Townsend. As for the text-book dons, they hold resolutely to the doctrine that he scarcely exists, and is not worth noticing at all. For example, there is Prof. Fred Lewis Pattee, author of "A History of American Literature Since 1870." Prof. Pattee notices Chambers, Marion Harland, Herford, Townsend, Amélie Rives, R. K. Munkittrick and many other such ornaments of the national letters, and even has polite bows for Gelett Burgess, Carolyn Wells and John Kendrick Bangs, but the name of Ade is missing from his index, as is that of Dreiser. So with the other pedagogues. They are unanimously shy of Ade in their horn-books for sophomores, and they are gingery in their praise of him in their innumerable review articles. He is commended, when at all, much as the late Joseph Jefferson used to be commended—that is, to the accompaniment of reminders that even a clown is one of God's creatures, and may have the heart of a Christian under his motley. The most laudatory thing ever said of him by any critic of the apostolic succession, so far as I can discover, is that he is clean—that he does not import the lewd buffooneries of the barroom, the smoking-car and the wedding reception into his books. . . .

But what are the facts? The facts are that Ade is one of the few genuinely original literary craftsmen now in practice among us; that he comes nearer to making literature, when he has full steam up, than any save a scant half-dozen of our current novelists, and that the whole body of his work, both in books and for the stage, is as thoroughly American, in cut and color, in tang and savor, in structure and point of view, as the work of Howells, E. W. Howe or Mark Twain. No single American novel that I can think of shows half the sense of nationality, the keen feeling for national prejudice and peculiarity, the sharp and pervasive Americanism of such Adean fables as "The Good Fairy of the Eighth Ward and the Dollar Excursion of the Steam-Fitters," "The Mandolin Players and the Willing Performer," and "The Adult Girl Who Got Busy Before They Could Ring the Bell on Her." Here, amid a humor so grotesque that it almost tortures the midriff, there is a startlingly vivid and accurate evocation of the American scene. Here, under all the labored extravagance, there are brilliant flashlight pictures of the American people, and American ways of thinking, and the whole of American *Kultur*. Here the veritable Americano stands forth, lacking not a waggery, a superstition, a snuffle or a wen.

Ade himself, for all his story-teller's pretense of remoteness, is as absolutely American as any of his prairie-town traders and pushers, Shylocks and Dogberries, beaux and belles. No other writer of our generation, save perhaps Howe, is more unescapably national in his every gesture and trick of mind. He is as American as buckwheat cakes, or the Knights of Pythias, or the chautauqua, or Billy Sunday, or a bull by Dr. Wilson. He fairly reeks of the national Philistinism, the national respect for respectability, the national distrust of ideas. He is a marcher, one fancies, in parades; he joins movements, and movements against movements; he knows no language save his own; he regards a Roosevelt quite seriously and a Mozart or an Ibsen as a joke; one would not be surprised to hear that, until he went off to his fresh-water college, he slept in his underwear and read the *Epworth Herald*. But, like Dreiser, he is a peasant touched by the divine fire; somehow, a great instinctive artist got himself born out there on that lush Indiana farm. He has the rare faculty of seeing accurately, even when the thing seen is directly under his nose, and he has the still rarer faculty of recording vividly, of making the thing seen move with life. One often doubts a character in a novel, even in a good novel, but who ever doubted Gus in "The Two Mandolin Players," or Mae in "Sister Mae," or, to pass from the fables, Payson in "Mr. Payson's Satirical Christmas"? Here, with strokes so crude and obvious that they seem to be laid on with a broom, Ade achieves what O. Henry, with all his ingenuity, always failed to achieve: he fills his bizarre tales with human beings. There is never any artfulness on the surface. The tale itself is never novel, or complex; it never surprises; often it is downright banal. But underneath there is an artfulness infinitely well wrought, and that is the artfulness of a story-teller who dredges his story out of his people, swiftly and skillfully, and does not squeeze his people into his story, laboriously and unconvincingly.

Needless to say, a moralist stands behind the comedian. He would teach; he even grows indignant. Roaring like a yokel at a burlesque show over such wild and light-hearted jocosities as "Paducah's Favorite Comedians" and "Why 'Gondola' Was

Put Away," one turns with something of a start to such things as "Little Lutie," "The Honest Money Maker" and "The Corporation Director and the Mislaid Ambition." Up to a certain point it is all laughter, but after that there is a flash of the knife, a show of teeth. Here a national limitation often closes in upon the satirist. He cannot quite separate the unaccustomed from the abominable; he is unable to avoid rattling his Philistine trappings a bit proudly; he must prove that he, too, is a right-thinking American, a solid citizen and a patriot, unshaken in his lofty rectitude by such poisons as aristocracy, adultery, *hors d'œuvres* and the sonata form. But in other directions this thorough-going nationalism helps him rather than hinders him. It enables him, for one thing, to see into sentimentality, and to comprehend it and project it accurately. I know of no book which displays the mooniness of youth with more feeling and sympathy than "Artie," save it be Frank Norris' forgotten "Blix." In such fields Ade achieves a success that is rare and indubitable. He makes the thing charming and he makes it plain.

But all these fables and other compositions of his are mere sketches, inconsiderable trifles, impromptus in bad English, easy to write and of no importance! Are they, indeed? Do not believe it for a moment. Fifteen or twenty years ago, when Ade was at the height of his celebrity as a newspaper Sganarelle, scores of hack comedians tried to imitate him—and all failed. I myself was of the number. I operated a so-called funny column in a daily newspaper, and like my colleagues near and far, I essayed to manufacture fables in slang. What miserable botches they were! How easy it was to imitate Ade's manner—and how impossible to imitate his matter! No; please don't get the notion that it is a simple thing to write such a fable as that of "The All-Night Seance and the Limit That Ceased to Be," or that of "The Preacher Who Flew His Kite, But Not Because He Wished to Do So," or that of "The Roystering Blades." Far from it! On the contrary, the only way you will ever accomplish the feat will be by first getting Ade's firm grasp upon American character, and his ability to think out a straightforward, simple, amusing story, and his alert feeling for contrast and climax, and his extraordinary talent for devising novel, vivid and unforgettable phrases. Those phrases of his sometimes wear the external vestments of a passing slang, but they are no more commonplace and vulgar at bottom than Gray's "mute, inglorious Milton" or the "somewheres East of Suez" of Kipling. They reduce an idea to a few pregnant syllables. They give the attention a fillip and light up a whole scene in a flash. They are the running evidences of an eye that sees clearly and of a mind that thinks shrewdly. They give distinction to the work of a man who has so well concealed a highly complex and efficient artistry that few have ever noticed it.

X.
The Butte Bashkirtseff

Of all the pseudo-rebels who have raised a tarletan black flag in These States, surely Mary MacLane is one of the most pathetic. When, at nineteen, she fluttered Vassar with "The Story of Mary MacLane," the truth about her was still left somewhat obscure; the charm of her flapperhood, so to speak, distracted attention from it, and so concealed it. But when, at thirty-five, she achieved "I, Mary MacLane," it emerged crystal-clear; she had learned to describe her malady accurately, though she still wondered, a bit wistfully, just what it was. And that malady? That truth? Simply that a Scotch Presbyterian with a soaring soul is as cruelly beset as a wolf with fleas, a zebra with the botts. Let a spark of the divine fire spring to life in that arid corpse, and it must fight its way to flame through a drum fire of wet sponges. A humming bird immersed in *Kartoffelsuppe*. Walter Pater writing for the London *Daily Mail*. Lucullus traveling steerage. . . . A Puritan wooed and tortured by the leers of beauty, Mary MacLane in a moral republic, in a Presbyterian diocese, in Butte. . . .

I hope my figures of speech are not too abstruse. What I mean to say is simply this: that the secret of Mary MacLane is simply this: that the origin of all her inchoate naughtiness is simply this: that she is a Puritan who has heard the call of joy and is struggling against it damnably. Remember so much, and the whole of her wistful heresy becomes intelligible. On the one hand the loveliness of the world enchants her; on the other hand the fires of hell warn her. This tortuous conflict accounts for her whole bag of tricks; her timorous flirtations with the devil, her occasional outbreaks of finishing-school rebellion, her hurried protestations of virginity, above all her incurable Philistinism. One need not be told that she admires the late Major General Roosevelt and Mrs. Atherton, that she wallows in the poetry of Keats. One knows quite as well that her phonograph plays the "Peer Gynt" suite, and that she is charmed by the syllogisms of G. K. Chesterton. She is, in brief, an absolutely typical American of the transition stage between Christian Endeavor and civilization. There is in her a definite poison of ideas, an æsthetic impulse that will not down—but every time she yields to it she is halted and plucked back by qualms and doubts, by the dominant superstitions of her race and time, by the dead hand of her kirk-crazy Scotch forebears.

It is precisely this grisly touch upon her shoulder that stimulates her to those naïve explosions of scandalous confidence which make her what she is. If there were no sepulchral voice in her ear, warning her that it is the mark of a hussy to be kissed by a man with "iron-gray hair, a brow like Apollo and a jowl like Bill Sykes," she would not confess it and boast of it, as she does on page 121 of "I, Mary MacLane." If it were not a Presbyterian axiom that a lady who says "damn" is fit only to join the white slaves, she would not pen a defiant Damniad, as she does on pages 108, 109 and 110. And if it were not held universally in Butte that sex passion is the exclusive infirmity of the male, she would not blab out in meeting that—but here I get into forbidden waters and had better refer you to page 209. It is not the godless voluptuary who patronizes leg-shows and the cabaret; it is the Methodist deacon with unaccustomed vine-leaves in his hair. It is not genuine artists, serving beauty reverently and proudly, who herd in Greenwich Village and bawl for art; it is precisely a mob of Middle Western Baptists to whom the very idea of art is still novel, and intoxicating, and more than a little bawdy. And to make an end, it is not cocottes who read the highly-spiced magazines which burden all the book-stalls; it is sedentary married women who, while faithful to their depressing husbands in the flesh, yet allow their imaginations to play furtively upon the charms of theoretical intrigues with such pretty fellows as Francis X. Bushman, Enrico Caruso and Vincent Astor.

An understanding of this plain fact not only explains the MacLane and her gingery carnalities of the *chair*; it also explains a good part of latter-day American literature. That literature is the self-expression of a people who have got only half way up the ladder leading from moral slavery to intellectual freedom. At every step there is a warning tug, a protest from below. Sometimes the climber docilely drops back; sometimes he emits a petulant defiance and reaches boldly for the next round. It is this occasional defiance which accounts for the periodical efflorescence of mere school-boy naughtiness in the midst of our oleaginous virtue—for the shouldering out of the *Ladies' Home Journal* by magazines of adultery all compact—for the provocative baring of calf and scapula by women who regard it as immoral to take Benedictine with their coffee—for the peopling of Greenwich Village by oafs who think it a devilish adventure to victual in cellars, and read Krafft-Ebing, and stare at the corset-scarred nakedness of decadent cloak-models.

I have said that the climber is but half way up the ladder. I wish I could add that he is moving ahead, but the truth is that he is probably quite stationary. We have our spasms of revolt, our flarings up of peekaboo waists, free love and "art," but a mighty backwash of piety fetches each and every one of them soon or late. A mongrel and inferior people, incapable of any spiritual aspiration above that of second-rate English colonials, we seek refuge inevitably in the one sort of superiority that the lower castes of men can authentically boast, to wit, superiority in docility, in credulity, in resignation, in morals. We are the most moral race in the world; there is not another that we do not look down upon in that department; our confessed aim and destiny as a nation is to inoculate them all with our incomparable rectitude. In the last analysis, all ideas are judged among us by moral standards; moral values are our only permanent tests of worth, whether in the arts, in politics, in philosophy or in life itself. Even the instincts of man, so intrinsically immoral, so innocent, are fitted with moral false-faces. That bedevilment by sex ideas which punishes continence, so abhorrent to nature, is converted into a moral frenzy, pathological in the end. The impulse to cavort and kick up one's legs, so healthy, so universal, is hedged in by incomprehensible taboos; it becomes stealthy, dirty, degrading. The desire to create and linger over beauty, the sign and touchstone of man's rise above the brute, is held down by doubts and hesitations; when it breaks through it must do so by orgy and explosion, half ludicrous and half pathetic. Our function, we choose to believe, is to teach and inspire the world. We are wrong. Our function is to amuse the world. We are the Bryan, the Henry Ford, the Billy Sunday among the nations. . . .

XI.
Six Members of the Institute

I
The Boudoir Balzac

THE late Percival Pollard was, in my nonage, one of my enthusiasms, and, later on, one of my friends. How, as a youngster, I used to lie in wait for the *Criterion* every week, and devour Pollard, Huneker, Meltzer and Vance Thompson! That was in the glorious middle nineties and savory pots were brewing. Scarcely a week went by without a new magazine of some unearthly *Tendenz* or other appearing on the stands; scarcely a month failed to bring forth its new genius. Pollard was up to his hips in the movement. He had a hand for every débutante. He knew everything that was going on. Polyglot, catholic, generous, alert, persuasive, forever oscillating between New York and Paris, London and Berlin, he probably covered a greater territory in the one art of letters than Huneker covered in all seven. He worked so hard as introducer of intellectual ambassadors, in fact, that he never had time to write his own books. One very brilliant volume, "Masks and Minstrels of New Germany," adequately represents him. The rest of his criticism, clumsily dragged from the files of the *Criterion* and *Town Topics*, is thrown together ineptly in "Their Day in Court." Death sneaked upon him from behind; he was gone before he could get his affairs in order. I shall never forget his funeral—no doubt a fit finish for a critic. Not one of the authors he had whooped and battled for was present—not one, that is, save old Ambrose Bierce. Bierce came in an elegant plug-hat and told me some curious anecdotes on the way to the crematory, chiefly of morgues, dissecting-rooms and lonely church-yards: he was the most gruesome of men. A week later, on a dark, sleety Christmas morning, I returned to the crematory, got the ashes, and shipped them West. Pollard awaits the Second Coming of his Redeemer in Iowa, hard by the birthplace of Prof. Dr. Stuart P. Sherman. Well, let us not repine. Huneker lives in Flatbush and was born in Philadelphia.

Cabell is a citizen of Richmond, Va. Willa Sibert Cather was once one of the editors of *McClure's Magazine*. Dreiser, before his annunciation, edited dime novels for Street & Smith, and will be attended by a Methodist friar, I daresay, on the gallows. . . .

Pollard, as I say, was a man I respected. He knew a great deal. Half English, half German and wholly cosmopolitan, he brought valuable knowledges and enthusiasms to the developing American literature of his time. Moreover, I had affection for him as well as respect, for he was a capital companion at the *Biertisch* and was never too busy to waste a lecture on my lone ear—say on Otto Julius Bierbaum (one of his friends), or Anatole France, or the technic of the novel, or the scoundrelism of publishers. It thus pains me to violate his tomb—but let his shade forgive me as it hopes to be forgiven! For it was Pollard, I believe, who set going the doctrine that Robert W. Chambers is a man of talent—a bit too commercial, perhaps, but still fundamentally a man of talent. You will find it argued at length in "Their Day in Court." There Pollard called the roll of the "promising young men" of the time, *circa* 1908. They were Winston Churchill, David Graham Phillips—and Chambers! Alas, for all prophets and their prognostications! Phillips, with occasional reversions to honest work, devoted most of his later days to sensational serials for the train-boy magazines, and when he died his desk turned out to be full of them, and they kept dribbling along for three or four years. Churchill, seduced by the uplift, has become an evangelist and a bore—a worse case, even, than that of H. G. Wells. And Chambers? Let the New York *Times* answer. Here, in all sobriety, is its description of the heroine of "The Moonlit Way," one of his latest pieces:

> She is a lovely and fascinating dancer who, before the war, held the attention of all Europe and incited a great many men who had nothing better to do to fall in love with her. She bursts upon the astonished gaze of several of the important characters of the story when she dashes into the ballroom of the German Embassy *standing upon a bridled ostrich*, which she compels to dance and go through its paces at her command. She is dressed, Mr. Chambers assures us, *in nothing but the skin of her virtuous youth, modified slightly by a yashmak and a zone of blue jewels about her hips and waist.*

The italics are mine. I wonder what poor Pollard would think of it. He saw the shoddiness in Chambers, the leaning toward "profitable pot-boiling," but he saw, too, a fundamental earnestness and a high degree of skill. What has become of these things? Are they visible, even as ghosts, in the preposterous serials that engaud the magazines of Mr. Hearst, and then load the department-stores as books? Were they, in fact, ever there at all? Did Pollard observe them, or did he merely imagine them? I am inclined to think that he merely imagined them—that his delight in what he described as "many admirable tricks" led him into a fatuity that he now has an eternity to regret. Chambers grows sillier and sillier, emptier and emptier, worse and worse. But was he ever more than a fifth-rater? I doubt it. Let us go back half a dozen years, to the days before the war forced the pot-boiler down into utter imbecility. I choose, at random, "The Gay Rebellion." Here is a specimen of the dialogue:

"It startled me. How did I know what it might have been? It might have been a bear—or a cow."

"You talk," said Sayre angrily, "like William Dean Howells! Haven't you *any* romance in you?"

"Not what *you* call romance. Pass the flapjacks." Sayre passed them.

"My attention," he said, "instantly became riveted upon the bushes. I strove to pierce them with a piercing glance. Suddenly—"

"Sure! 'Suddenly' always comes next."

"Suddenly . . . the leaves were stealthily parted, and—"

"A naked savage in full war paint—"

"Naked nothing! a young girl in—a perfectly fitting gown stepped noiselessly out."

"Out of what, you gink?"

"The bushes, dammit! . . . She looked at me; I gazed at her. Somehow—"

"In plainer terms, she gave you the eye. What?"

"That's a peculiarly coarse observation."

"Then tell it in your own way."

"I will. The sunlight fell softly upon the trees of the ancient wood."

"*Woodn't* that bark you!"

And so on, and so on, for page after page. Can you imagine more idiotic stuff—"pierce and piercing," "you gink," "she gave you the eye," "*woodn't* that bark you?" One is reminded of horrible things—the repartees of gas-house comedians in vaudeville, the whimsical editorials in *Life*, the forbidding ghouleries of Irvin Cobb among jokes pale and clammy in death. . . . But let us, you may say, go back a bit further—back to the days of the *Chap-Book*. There was then, perhaps, a far different Chambers—a fellow of sound talent and artistic self-respect, well deserving the confidence and encouragement of Pollard. Was there, indeed? If you think so, go read "The King in Yellow," *circa* 1895—if you can. I myself, full of hope, have tried it. In it I have found drivel almost as dull as that, say, in "Ailsa Page."

2
A Stranger on Parnassus

The case of Hamlin Garland belongs to pathos in the grand manner, as you will discover on reading his autobiography, "A Son of the Middle Border." What ails him is a vision of beauty, a seductive strain of bawdy music over the hills. He is a sort of male Mary MacLane, but without either Mary's capacity for picturesque blasphemy or her skill at plain English. The vision, in his youth, tore him from his prairie plow and set him to clawing the anthills at the foot of Parnassus. He became an elocutionist—what, in modern times, would be called a chautauquan. He aspired to write for the *Atlantic Monthly*. He fell under the spell of the Boston *aluminados* of 1885, which is as if one were to take fire from a June-bug. Finally, after embracing the Single Tax, he achieved a couple of depressing story-books, earnest, honest and full of indignation.

American criticism, which always mistakes a poignant document for æsthetic form and organization, greeted these moral volumes as works of art, and so Garland found himself an accepted artist and has made shift to be an artist ever since. No more grotesque miscasting of a diligent and worthy man is recorded in profane history. He has no more feeling for the intrinsic dignity of beauty, no more comprehension of it as a thing in itself, than a policeman. He is, and always has been, a moralist endeavoring ineptly to translate his messianic passion into æsthetic terms, and always failing. "A Son of the Middle Border," undoubtedly the best of all his books, projects his failure brilliantly. It is, in substance, a document of considerable value—a naïve and often highly illuminating contribution to the history of the American peasantry. It is, in form, a thoroughly third-rate piece of writing—amateurish, flat, banal, repellent. Garland gets facts into it; he gets the relentless sincerity of the rustic Puritan; he gets a sort of evangelical passion. But he doesn't get any charm. He doesn't get any beauty.

In such a career, as in such a book, there is something profoundly pathetic. One follows the progress of the man with a constant sense that he is steering by faulty compasses, that fate is leading him into paths too steep and rocky—nay, too dark and lovely—for him. An awareness of beauty is there, and a wistful desire to embrace it, but the confident gusto of the artist is always lacking. What one encounters in its place is the enthusiasm of the pedagogue, the desire to yank the world up to the soaring Methodist level, the hot yearning to displace old ideas with new ideas, and usually much worse ideas, for example, the Single Tax and spook-chasing. The natural goal of the man was the evangelical stump. He was led astray when those Boston Brahmins of the last generation, enchanted by his sophomoric platitudes about Shakespeare, set him up as a critic of the arts, and then as an imaginative artist. He should have gone back to the saleratus belt, taken to the chautauquas, preached his foreordained perunas, got himself into Congress, and so helped to save the republic from the demons that beset it. What a gladiator he would have made against the Plunderbund, the White Slave Traffic, the Rum Demon, the Kaiser! What a rival to the Hon. Claude Kitchin, the Rev. Dr. Newell Dwight Hillis!

His worst work, I daresay, is in some of his fiction—for example, in "The Forester's Daughter." But my own favorite among his books is "The Shadow World," a record of his communings with the gaseous precipitates of the departed. He takes great pains at the start to assure us that he is a man of alert intelligence and without prejudices or superstitions. He has no patience, it appears, with those idiots who swallow the buffooneries of spiritualist mediums too greedily. For him the scientific method—the method which examines all evidence cynically and keeps on doubting until the accumulated proof, piled mountain-high, sweeps down in an overwhelming avalanche. . . . Thus he proceeds to the haunted chamber and begins his dalliance with the banshees. They touch him with clammy, spectral hands; they wring music for him out of locked pianos; they throw heavy tables about the room; they give him messages from the golden shore and make him the butt of their coarse, transcendental humor. Through it all he sits tightly and solemnly, his mind open and his verdict up his sleeve. He is belligerently agnostic, and calls attention to it proudly. . . . Then, in the end, he gives himself away. One of his fellow "scientists," more frankly credulous, expresses the belief that real scientists will soon prove the existence of spooks. "I hope they will," says the agnostic Mr. Garland. . . .

Well, let us not laugh. The believing mind is a curious thing. It must absorb its endless rations of balderdash, or perish. . . . "A Son of the Middle Border" is less amusing, but a good deal more respectable. It is an honest book. There is some bragging in it, of course, but not too much. It tells an interesting story. It radiates hard effort and earnest purpose. . . . But what a devastating exposure of a member of the American Academy of Arts and Letters!

3
A Merchant of Mush

Henry Sydnor Harrison is thoroughly American to this extent: that his work is a bad imitation of something English. Find me a second-rate American in any of the arts and I'll find you his master and prototype among third, fourth or fifth-rate Englishmen. In the present case the model is obviously W. J. Locke. But between master and disciple there is a great gap. Locke, at his high points, is a man of very palpable merit. He has humor. He has ingenuity. He has a keen eye for the pathos that so often lies in the absurd. I can discover no sign of any of these things in Harrison's 100,000 word Christmas cards. They are simply sentimental bosh—huge gum-drops for fat women to snuffle over. Locke's grotesque and often extremely amusing characters are missing; in place of them there are the heroic cripples, silent lovers, maudlin war veterans and angelic grandams of the old-time Sunday-school books. The people of "V. V.'s Eyes" are preposterous and the thesis is too silly to be stated in plain words. No sane person would believe it if it were put into an affidavit. "Queed" is simply Locke diluted with vast drafts from "Laddie" and "Pollyanna." Queed, himself, long before the end, becomes a marionette without a toe on the ground; his Charlotte is incredible from the start. "Angela's Business" touches the bottom of the tear-jug; it would be impossible to imagine a more vapid story. Harrison, in fact, grows more mawkish book by book. He is touched, I should say, by the delusion that he has a mission to make life sweeter, to preach the Finer Things, to radiate Gladness. What! More Gladness? Another volt or two, and all civilized adults will join the Italians and Jugo-Slavs in their headlong hegira. A few more amperes, and the land will be abandoned to the Jews, the ex-Confederates and the Bolsheviki.

4
The Last of the Victorians

If William Allen White lives as long as Tennyson, and does not reform, our grandchildren will see the Victorian era gasping out its last breath in 1951. And eighty-three is no great age in Kansas, where sin is unknown. It may be, in fact, 1960, or even 1970, before the world hears the last of Honest Poverty, Chaste Affection and Manly Tears. For so long as White holds a pen these ancient sweets will be on sale at the department-store book-counters, and they will grow sweeter and sweeter, I daresay, as he works them over and over. In his very first book of fiction there was a flavor of chewing-gum and marshmallows. In "A Certain Rich Man" the intelligent palate detected saccharine. In "In the Heart of a Fool," his latest, the thing is carried a step further. If you are a forward-looker and a right-thinker, if you believe that God is in His heaven and all is for the best, if you yearn to uplift and like to sob, then the volume will probably affect you, in the incomparable phrase of Clayton Hamilton, like "the music of a million Easter-lilies leaping from the grave and laughing with a silver singing." But if you are a carnal fellow, as I am, with a stomach ruined by alcohol, it will gag you.

When I say that White is a Victorian I do not allude, of course, to the Victorianism of Thackeray and Tennyson, but to that of Felicia Hemens, of Samuel Smiles and of Dickens at his most maudlin. Perhaps an even closer relative is to be found in "The Duchess." White, like "The Duchess" is absolutely humorless, and, when he begins laying on the mayonnaise, absolutely shameless. I daresay the same sort of reader admires both: the high-school girl first seized by amorous tremors, the obese multipara in her greasy kimono, the remote and weepful farm-wife. But here a doubt intrudes itself: is it possible to imagine a woman sentimental enough to survive "In the Heart of a Fool"? I am constrained to question it. In women, once they get beyond adolescence, there is always a saving touch of irony; the life they lead infallibly makes cynics of them, though sometimes they don't know it. Observe the books they write—chiefly sardonic stuff, with heroes who are fools. Even their "glad" books, enormously successful among other women, stop far short of the sentimentality put between covers by men—for example, the aforesaid Harrison, Harold Bell Wright and the present White. Nay, it is the male sex that snuffles most and is easiest touched, particularly in America. The American man is forever falling a victim to his tender feelings. It was by that route that the collectors for the Y.M.C.A. reached him; it is thus that he is bagged incessantly by political tear-squeezers; it is precisely his softness that makes him the slave of his women-folk. What White gives him is exactly the sort of mush that is on tap in the chautauquas. "In the Heart of a Fool," like "A Certain Rich Man" is aimed deliberately and with the utmost accuracy at the delicate gizzard of the small-town yokel, the small-town yokel *male*, the horrible end-product of fifty years of Christian Endeavor, the little red school-house and the direct primary.

The White formula is simple to the verge of austerity. It is, in essence, no more than a dramatization of all the current political and sociological rumble-bumble, by Roosevelt out of Coxey's Army, with music by the choir of the First Methodist Church. On the one side are the Hell Hounds of Plutocracy, the Money Demons, the Plunderbund, and their attendant Bosses, Strike Breakers, Seducers, Nietzscheans, Free Lovers, Atheists and Corrupt Journalists. On the other side are the great masses of the plain people, and their attendant Uplifters, Good Samaritans, Honest Workingmen, Faithful Husbands,

Inspired Dreamers and tin-horn Messiahs. These two armies join battle, the Bad against the Good, and for five hundred pages or more the Good get all the worst of it. Their jobs are taken away from them, their votes are bartered, their mortgages are foreclosed, their women are debauched, their savings are looted, their poor orphans are turned out to starve. A sad business, surely. One wallows in almost unendurable emotions. The tears gush. It is as affecting as a movie. Even the prose rises to a sort of gospel-tent chant, like that of a Baptist Savonarola, with every second sentence beginning with *and*, *but* or *for*. . . . But we are already near the end, and no escape is in sight. Can it be that White is stumped, like Mark Twain in his mediæval romance—that Virtue will succumb to the Interests? Do not fear! In the third from the last chapter Hen Jackson, the stage-hand, returns from the Dutchman's at the corner and throws on a rose spot-light, and then an amber, and then a violet, and then a blue. One by one the rays of Hope begin to shoot across the stage, Dr. Hamilton's Easter-lilies leap from their tomb, the *dramatis personæ* (all save the local J. Pierpont Morgan!) begin "laughing with a silver singing," and as the curtain falls the whole scene is bathed in luminiferous ether, and the professor breaks into "Onward, Christian Soldiers!" on the cabinet-organ, and there is a happy, comfortable sobbing, and an upward rolling of eyes, and a vast blowing of noses. In brief, the finish of a chautauqua lecture on "The Grand Future of America, or, The Glory of Service." In brief, slobber. . . .

It would be difficult to imagine more saccharine writing or a more mawkish and preposterous point of view. Life, as White sees it, is a purely moral phenomenon, like living pictures by the Epworth League. The virtuous are the downtrodden; the up and doing are all scoundrels. It pays to be poor and pious. Ambition is a serpent. One honest Knight of Pythias is worth ten thousand Rockefellers. The pastor is always right. So is the *Ladies' Home Journal.* The impulse that leads a young yokel of, say, twenty-two to seek marriage with a poor working-girl of, say, eighteen, is the most elevating, noble, honorable and godlike impulse native to the human consciousness. . . . Not the slightest sign of an apprehension of life as the gaudiest and most gorgeous of spectacles—not a trace of healthy delight in the eternal struggle for existence—not the faintest suggestion of Dreiser's great gusto or of Conrad's penetrating irony! Not even in the massive fact of death itself—and, like all the other Victorians, this one from the Kansas steppes is given to wholesale massacres—does he see anything mysterious, staggering, awful, inexplicable, but only an excuse for a sentimental orgy.

Alas, what would you? It is ghastly drivel, to be sure, but isn't it, after all, thoroughly American? I have an uneasy suspicion that it is—that "In the Heart of a Fool" is, at bottom, a vastly more American book than anything that James Branch Cabell has done, or Vincent O'Sullivan, or Edith Wharton, or even Howells. It springs from the heart of the land. It is the æsthetic echo of thousands of movements, of hundreds of thousands of sentimental crusades, of millions of ecstatic gospel-meetings. This is what the authentic American public, unpolluted by intelligence, wants. And this is one of the reasons why the English sniff whenever they look our way. . . .

But has White no merit? He has. He is an honest and a respectable man. He is a patriot. He trusts God. He venerates what is left of the Constitution. He once wrote a capital editorial, "What's the Matter With Kansas?" He has the knack, when his tears are turned off, of writing a clear and graceful English. . . .

5
A Bad Novelist

As I have said, it is not the artistic merit and dignity of a novel, but often simply its content as document, that makes for its success in the United States. The criterion of truth applied to it is not the criterion of an artist, but that of a newspaper editorial writer; the question is not, Is it in accord with the profoundest impulses and motives of humanity? but Is it in accord with the current pishposh? This accounts for the huge popularity of such confections as Upton Sinclair's "The Jungle" and Blasco Ibáñez's "The Four Horsemen of the Apocalypse." Neither had much value as a work of art—at all events, neither was perceptibly superior to many contemporary novels that made no stir at all—but each had the advantage of reënforcing an emotion already aroused, of falling into step with the procession of the moment. Had there been no fever of muck-raking and trust busting in 1906, "The Jungle" would have died the death in the columns of the *Appeal to Reason*, unheard of by the populace in general. And had the United States been engaged against France instead of for France in 1918, there would have been no argument in the literary weeklies that Blasco was a novelist of the first rank and his story a masterpiece comparable to "Germinal."

Sinclair was made by "The Jungle" and has been trying his hardest to unmake himself ever since. Another of the same sort is Ernest Poole, author of "The Harbor." "The Harbor," judged by any intelligible æsthetic standard, was a bad novel. Its transactions were forced and unconvincing; its central character was shadowy and often incomprehensible; the manner of its writing was quite without distinction. But it happened to be printed at a time when the chief ideas in it had a great deal of popularity—when its vague grappling with insoluble sociological problems was the sport of all the weeklies and of half the more sober newspapers—when a nebulous, highfalutin Bolshevism was in the air—and so it excited interest and took on an aspect of profundity. That its discussion of those problems was superficial, that it said nothing new and got nowhere—all this was not an influence against its success, but an influence in favor of its success, for the sort of mind that fed upon the nebulous, professor-made politics and sociology of 1915 was the sort of mind that is chronically avid of half-truths and as chronically suspicious of forthright thinking. This has been demonstrated since that time by its easy *volte face* in the presence of emotion. The very ideas that Poole's vapid hero toyed with in 1915, to the delight of the novel-reading *intelligentsia*, would have damned the book as a pamphlet for the I.W.W., or even, perhaps, as German propaganda, three years later. But meanwhile, it had been forgotten, as novels are always forgotten, and all that remained of it was a general impression that Poole, in some way or other, was a superior fellow and to be treated with respect.

His subsequent books have tried that theory severely. "The Family" was grounded upon one of the elemental tragedies which serve a novelist most safely—the dismay of an aging man as his children drift away from him. Here was a subject full of poignant drama, and what is more, drama simple enough to develop itself without making any great demand upon the invention. Poole burdened it with too much background, and then killed it altogether by making his characters wooden. It began with a high air; it creaked and wobbled at the close; the catastrophe was quite without effect. "His Second Wife" dropped several stories lower. It turned out, on inspection, to be no more than a moral tale, feeble, wishy-washy and irritating. Everything in it—about the corrupting effects of money-lust and display, about the swinishness of cabaret "society" in New York, about the American male's absurd slavery to his women—had been said before by such gifted Balzacs as Robert W. Chambers and Owen Johnson, and, what is more, far better said. The writing, in fact, exactly matched the theme. It was labored, artificial, dull. In the whole volume there was not a single original phrase. Once it was put down, not a scene remained in the memory, or a character. It was a cheap, a hollow and, in places, almost an idiotic book. . . .

At the time I write, this is the whole product of Poole as novelist: three novels, bad, worse, worst.

6
A Broadway Brandes

I have hitherto, in discussing White de Kansas, presented a fragile dahlia from the rhetorical garden of Clayton Hamilton, M.A. (Columbia). I now print the whole passage:

> Whenever in a world-historic war the side of righteousness has triumphed, a great overflowing of art has followed soon upon the fact of victory. The noblest instincts of mankind—aroused in perilous moments fraught with intimations of mortality—have surged and soared, beneath the sunshine of a subsequent and dear-bought peace, into an immeasurable empyrean of heroic eloquence. Whenever right has circumvented might, Art has sprung alive into the world, with the music of a million Easter-lilies leaping from the grave and laughing with a silver singing.

With the highest respect for a *Magister Artium*, a pedagogue of Columbia University, a lecturer in Miss Spence's School and the Classical School for Girls, and a vice-president of the National Institute of Arts and Letters—Booh!

XII.
The Genealogy of Etiquette

BARRING sociology (which is yet, of course, scarcely a science at all, but rather a monkey-shine which happens to pay, like play-acting or theology), psychology is the youngest of the sciences, and hence chiefly guesswork, empiricism, hocus-pocus, poppycock. On the one hand, there are still enormous gaps in its data, so that the determination of its simplest principles remains difficult, not to say impossible; and, on the other hand, the very hollowness and nebulosity of it, particularly around its edges, encourages a horde of quacks to invade it, sophisticate it and make nonsense of it. Worse, this state of affairs tends to such confusion of effort and direction that the quack and the honest inquirer are often found in the same man. It is, indeed, a commonplace to encounter a professor who spends his days in the laborious accumulation of psychological statistics, sticking pins into babies and platting upon a chart the ebb and flow of their yells, and his nights chasing poltergeists and other such celestial fauna over the hurdles of a spiritualist's atelier, or gazing into a crystal in the privacy of his own chamber. The Binét test and the buncombe of mesmerism are alike the children of what we roughly denominate psychology, and perhaps of equal legitimacy. Even so ingenious and competent an investigator as Prof. Dr. Sigmund Freud, who has told us a lot that is of the first importance about the materials and machinery of thought, has also told us a lot that is trivial and dubious. The essential doctrines of Freudism, no doubt, come close to the truth, but many of Freud's remoter deductions are far more scandalous than sound, and many of the professed Freudians, both American and European, have grease-paint on their noses and bladders in their hands and are otherwise quite indistinguishable from evangelists and circus clowns.

In this condition of the science it is no wonder that we find it wasting its chief force upon problems that are petty and idle when they are not downright and palpably insoluble, and passing over problems that are of immediate concern to all of us, and that might be quite readily solved, or, at any rate, considerably illuminated, by an intelligent study of the data already available. After all, not many of us care a hoot whether Sir Oliver Lodge and the Indian chief Wok-a-wok-a-mok are happy in heaven, for not many of us have any hope or desire to meet them there. Nor are we greatly excited by the discovery that, of twenty-five freshmen who are hit with clubs, 17¾ will say "Ouch!" and 22⅕ will say "Damn!"; nor by a table showing that 38.2 per centum of all men accused of homicide confess when locked up with the carcasses of their victims, including 23.4 per centum who are innocent; nor by plans and specifications, by Cagliostro out of Lucrezia Borgia, for teaching poor, God-forsaken school children to write before they can read and to multiply before they can add; nor by endless disputes between half-witted pundits as to the precise difference between perception and cognition; nor by even longer feuds, between pundits even crazier, over free will, the subconscious, the endoneurium, the functions of the corpora quadrigemina, and the meaning of dreams in which one is pursued by hyenas, process-servers or grass-widows.

Nay; we do not bubble with rejoicing when such fruits of psychological deep-down-diving and much-mud-upbringing researches are laid before us, for after all they do not offer us any nourishment, there is nothing in them to engage our teeth, they fail to make life more comprehensible, and hence more bearable. What we yearn to know something about is the process whereby the ideas of everyday are engendered in the skulls of those about us, to the end that we may pursue a straighter and a safer course through the muddle that is life. Why do the great majority of Presbyterians (and, for that matter, of Baptists, Episcopalians, and Swedenborgians as well) regard it as unlucky to meet a black cat and lucky to find a pin? What are the logical steps behind the theory that it is indecent to eat peas with a knife? By what process does an otherwise sane man arrive at the conclusion that he will go to hell unless he is baptized by total immersion in water? What causes men to be faithful to their wives: habit, fear, poverty, lack of imagination, lack of enterprise, stupidity, religion? What is the psychological basis of commercial morality? What is the true nature of the vague pooling of desires that Rousseau called the social contract? Why does an American regard it as scandalous to wear dress clothes at a funeral, and a Frenchman regard it as equally scandalous *not* to wear them? Why is it that men trust one another so readily, and women trust one another so seldom? Why are we all so greatly affected by statements that we know are not true?—e.g. in Lincoln's Gettysburg speech, the Declaration of Independence and the CIII Psalm. What is the origin of the so-called double standard of morality? Why are women forbidden to take off their hats in church? What is happiness? Intelligence? Sin? Courage? Virtue? Beauty?

All these are questions of interest and importance to all of us, for their solution would materially improve the accuracy of our outlook upon the world, and with it our mastery of our environment, but the psychologists, busily engaged in chasing their tails, leave them unanswered, and, in most cases, even unasked. The late William James, more acute than the general, saw how precious little was known about the psychological inwardness of religion, and to the illumination of this darkness he addressed himself in his book, "The Varieties of Religious Experience." But life being short and science long, he got little beyond the statement of the problem and the marshaling of the grosser evidence—and even at this business he allowed himself to be constantly interrupted by spooks, hobgoblins, seventh sons of seventh sons and other such characteristic pets of psychologists. In the same way one Gustav le Bon, a Frenchman, undertook a psychological study of the crowd mind—and then blew up. Add the investigations of Freud and his school, chiefly into abnormal states of mind, and those of Lombroso and his school, chiefly quackish and for the yellow journals, and the idle romancing of such inquirers as Prof. Dr. Thorstein Veblen, and you have exhausted the list of contributions to what may be called practical and everyday psychology. The rev. professors, I daresay, have been doing some useful plowing and planting. All of their meticulous pin-sticking and measuring and chart-making, in the course of time, will enable their successors to approach the real problems of mind with more assurance than is now possible, and perhaps help to their solution. But in the meantime the public and social utility of psychology remains very small, for it is still unable to differentiate accurately between the true and the false, or to give us any effective protection against the fallacies, superstitions, crazes and hysterias which rage in the world.

In this emergency it is not only permissible but even laudable for the amateur to sniff inquiringly through the psychological pasture, essaying modestly to uproot things that the myopic (or, perhaps more accurately, hypermetropic) professionals have overlooked. The late Friedrich Wilhelm Nietzsche did it often, and the usufructs were many curious and daring guesses, some of them probably close to accuracy, as to the genesis of this, that or the other common delusion of man—*i.e.*, the delusion that the law of the survival of the fittest may be repealed by an act of Congress. Into the same field several very interesting expeditions have been made by Dr. Elsie Clews Parsons, a lady once celebrated by Park Row for her invention of trial marriage—an invention, by the way, in which the Nietzsche aforesaid preceded her by at least a dozen years. The records of her researches are to be found in a brief series of books: "The Family," "The Old-Fashioned Woman" and "Fear and Conventionality." Apparently they have wrung relatively little esteem from the learned, for I seldom encounter a reference to them, and Dr. Parsons herself is denied the very modest reward of mention in "Who's Who in America." Nevertheless, they are extremely instructive books, particularly "Fear and Conventionality." I know of no other work, indeed, which offers a better array of observations upon that powerful complex of assumptions, prejudices, instinctive reactions, racial emotions and unbreakable vices of mind which enters so massively into the daily thinking of all of us. The author does not concern herself, as so many psychologists fall into the habit of doing, with thinking as a purely laboratory phenomenon, a process in vacuo. What she deals with is thinking as it is done by men and women in the real world—thinking that is only half intellectual, the other half being as automatic and unintelligent as swallowing, blinking the eye or falling in love.

The power of the complex that I have mentioned is usually very much underestimated, not only by psychologists, but also by all other persons who pretend to culture. We take pride in the fact that we are thinking animals, and like to believe that our thoughts are free, but the truth is that nine-tenths of them are rigidly conditioned by the babbling that goes on around us from birth, and that the business of considering this babbling objectively, separating the true in it from the false, is an intellectual feat of such stupendous difficulty that very few men are ever able to achieve it. The amazing slanging which went on between the English professors and the German professors in the early days of the late war showed how little even cold and academic men are really moved by the bald truth and how much by hot and unintelligible likes and dislikes. The patriotic hysteria of the war simply allowed these eminent pedagogues to say of one another openly and to loud applause what they would have been ashamed to say in times of greater amenity, and what most of them would have denied stoutly that they believed. Nevertheless, it is probably a fact that before there was a sign of war the average English professor, deep down in his heart, thought that any man who ate sauerkraut, and went to the opera in a sackcoat, and intrigued for the appellation of *Geheimrat*, and preferred German music to English poetry, and venerated Bismarck, and called his wife "Mutter," was a scoundrel. He did not say so aloud, and no doubt it would have offended him had you accused him of believing it, but he believed it all the same, and his belief in it gave a muddy, bilious color to his view of German metaphysics, German electrochemistry and the German chronology of Babylonian kings. And by the same token the average German professor, far down in the ghostly recesses of his hulk, held that any man who read the London *Times*, and ate salt fish at first breakfast, and drank tea of an afternoon, and spoke of Oxford as a university was a *Schafskopf*, a *Schuft* and possibly even a *Schweinehund*.

Nay, not one of us is a free agent. Not one of us actually thinks for himself, or in any orderly and scientific manner. The pressure of environment, of mass ideas, of the socialized intelligence, improperly so called, is too enormous to be withstood. No American, no matter how sharp his critical sense, can ever get away from the notion that democracy is, in some subtle and mysterious way, more conducive to human progress and more pleasing to a just God than any of the systems of government which stand opposed to it. In the privacy of his study he may observe very clearly that it exalts the facile and specious man above the really competent man, and from this observation he may draw the conclusion that its abandonment would be desirable, but once he emerges from his academic seclusion and resumes the rubbing of noses with his fellow-men, he will begin to be tortured by a sneaking feeling that such ideas are heretical and unmanly, and the next time the band begins to play he will thrill with the best of them—or the worst. The actual phenomenon, in truth, was copiously on display during the war. Having myself the character among my acquaintances of one holding the democratic theory in some doubt, I was often approached by gentlemen who told me, in great confidence, that they had been seized by the same tremors. Among them were journalists employed daily in demanding that democracy be forced upon the whole world, and army officers engaged, at least theoretically, in forcing it. All these men, in reflective moments, struggled with ifs and buts. But every one of them, in his public capacity as a good citizen, quickly went back to *thinking* as a good citizen was then expected to think, and even to a certain inflammatory ranting for what, behind the door, he gravely questioned. . . .

It is the business of Dr. Parsons, in "Fear and Conventionality," to prod into certain of the ideas which thus pour into every man's mind from the circumambient air, sweeping away, like some huge cataract, the feeble resistance that his own powers of ratiocination can offer. In particular, she devotes herself to an examination of those general ideas which condition the thought and action of man as a social being—those general ideas which govern his everyday attitude toward his fellow-men and his prevailing view of himself. In one direction they lay upon us the bonds of what we call etiquette, *i.e.*, the duty of considering the habits and feelings of those around us—and in another direction they throttle us with what we call morality—*i.e.*, the rules which protect the life and property of those around us. But, as Dr. Parsons shows, the boundary between etiquette and morality is very dimly drawn, and it is often impossible to say of a given action whether it is downright immoral or merely a breach of the punctilio. Even when the moral law is plainly running, considerations of mere amenity and politeness may still make themselves felt. Thus, as Dr. Parsons points out, there is even an etiquette of adultery.

"The *ami de la famille* vows not to kiss his mistress in her husband's house"—not in fear, but "as an expression of conjugal consideration," as a sign that he has not forgotten the thoughtfulness expected of a gentleman. And in this delicate field, as might be expected, the differences in racial attitudes are almost diametrical. The Englishman, surprising his wife with a lover, sues the rogue for damages and has public opinion behind him, but for an American to do it would be for him to lose caste at once and forever. The plain and only duty of the American is to open upon the fellow with artillery, hitting him if the scene is south of the Potomac and missing him if it is above.

I confess to an endless interest in such puzzling niceties, and to much curiosity as to their origins and meaning. Why do we Americans take off our hats when we meet a flapper on the street, and yet stand covered before a male of the highest eminence? A Continental would regard this last as boorish to the last degree; in greeting any equal or superior, male or female, actual or merely conventional, he lifts his head-piece. Why does it strike us as ludicrous to see a man in dress clothes before 6 P.M.? The Continental puts them on whenever he has a solemn visit to make, whether the hour be six or noon. Why do we regard it as indecent to tuck the napkin between the waistcoat buttons—or into the neck!—at meals? The Frenchman does it without thought of crime. So does the Italian. So does the German. All three are punctilious men—far more so, indeed, than we are. Why do we snicker at the man who wears a wedding ring? Most Continentals would stare askance at the husband who didn't. Why is it bad manners in Europe and America to ask a stranger his or her age, and a friendly attention in China? Why do we regard it as absurd to distinguish a woman by her husband's title—*e.g.*, Mrs. Judge Jones, Mrs. Professor Smith? In Teutonic and Scandinavian Europe the omission of the title would be looked upon as an affront.

Such fine distinctions, so ardently supported, raise many interesting questions, but the attempt to answer them quickly gets one bogged. Several years ago I ventured to lift a sad voice against a custom common in America: that of married men, in speaking of their wives, employing the full panoply of "Mrs. Brown." It was my contention—supported, I thought, by logical considerations of the loftiest order—that a husband, in speaking of his wife to his equals, should say "my wife"—that the more formal mode of designation should be reserved for inferiors and for strangers of undetermined position. This contention, somewhat to my surprise, was vigorously combated by various volunteer experts. At first they rested their case upon the mere authority of custom, forgetting that this custom was by no means universal. But finally one of them came forward with a more analytical and cogent defense—the defense, to wit, that "my wife" connoted proprietorship and was thus offensive to a wife's *amour propre.* But what of "my sister" and "my mother"? Surely it is nowhere the custom for a man, addressing an equal, to speak of his sister as "Miss Smith." . . . The discussion, however, came to nothing. It was impossible to carry it on logically. The essence of all such inquiries lies in the discovery that there is a force within the liver and lights of man that is infinitely more potent than logic. His reflections, perhaps, may take on intellectually recognizable forms, but they seldom lead to intellectually recognizable conclusions.

Nevertheless, Dr. Parsons offers something in her book that may conceivably help to a better understanding of them, and that is the doctrine that the strange persistence of these rubber-stamp ideas, often unintelligible and sometimes plainly absurd, is due to fear, and that this fear is the product of a very real danger. The safety of human society lies in the assumption that every individual composing it, in a given situation, will act in a manner hitherto approved as seemly. That is to say, he is expected to react to his environment according to a fixed pattern, not necessarily because that pattern is the best imaginable, but simply because it is determined and understood. If he fails to do so, if he reacts in a novel manner—conducive, perhaps, to his better advantage or to what he thinks is his better advantage—then he disappoints the expectation of those around him, and forces them to meet the new situation he has created by the exercise of independent thought. Such independent thought, to a good many men, is quite impossible, and to the overwhelming majority of men, extremely painful. "To all of us," says Dr. Parsons, "to the animal, to the savage and to the civilized being, few demands are as uncomfortable, . . .

disquieting or fearful, as the call to innovate. . . . Adaptations we all of us dislike or hate. We dodge or shirk them as best we may." And the man who compels us to make them against our wills we punish by withdrawing from him that understanding and friendliness which he, in turn, looks for and counts upon. In other words, we set him apart as one who is anti-social and not to be dealt with, and according as his rebellion has been small or great, we call him a boor or a criminal.

This distrust of the unknown, this fear of doing something unusual, is probably at the bottom of many ideas and institutions that are commonly credited to other motives. For example, monogamy. The orthodox explanation of monogamy is that it is a manifestation of the desire to have and to hold property—that the husband defends his solitary right to his wife, even at the cost of his own freedom, because she is the pearl among his chattels. But Dr. Parsons argues, and with a good deal of plausibility, that the real moving force, both in the husband and the wife, may be merely the force of habit, the antipathy to experiment and innovation. It is easier and safer to stick to the one wife than to risk adventures with another wife—and the immense social pressure that I have just described is all on the side of sticking. Moreover, the indulgence of a habit automatically strengthens its bonds. What we have done once or thought once, we are more apt than we were before to do and think again. Or, as the late Prof. William James put it, "the selection of a particular hole to live in, of a particular mate, . . . a particular anything, in short, out of a possible multitude . . . carries with it an insensibility to *other* opportunities and occasions—an insensibility which can only be described physiologically as an inhibition of new impulses by the habit of old ones already formed. The possession of homes and wives of our own makes us strangely insensible to the charms of other people. . . . The original impulse which got us homes, wives, . . . seems to exhaust itself in its first achievements and to leave no surplus energy for reacting on new cases." Thus the benedict looks no more on women (at least for a while), and the post-honeymoon bride, as the late David Graham Phillips once told us, neglects the bedizenments which got her a man.

In view of the popular or general character of most of the

taboos which put a brake upon personal liberty in thought and action—that is to say, in view of their enforcement by people in the mass, and not by definite specialists in conduct—it is quite natural to find that they are of extra force in democratic societies, for it is the distinguishing mark of democratic societies that they exalt the powers of the majority almost infinitely, and tend to deny the minority any rights whatever. Under a society dominated by a small caste the revolutionist in custom, despite the axiom to the contrary, has a relatively easy time of it, for the persons whose approval he seeks for his innovation are relatively few in number, and most of them are already habituated to more or less intelligible and independent thinking. But under a democracy he is opposed by a horde so vast that it is a practical impossibility for him, without complex and expensive machinery, to reach and convince all of its members, and even if he could reach them he would find most of them quite incapable of rising out of their accustomed grooves. They cannot understand innovations that are genuinely novel and they don't want to understand them; their one desire is to put them down. Even at this late day, with enlightenment raging through the republic like a pestilence, it would cost the average Southern or Middle Western Congressman his seat if he appeared among his constituents in spats, or wearing a wrist-watch. And if a Justice of the Supreme Court of the United States, however gigantic his learning and his juridic rectitude, were taken in crim. con. with the wife of a Senator, he would be destroyed instanter. And if, suddenly revolting against the democratic idea, he were to propose, however gingerly, its abandonment, he would be destroyed with the same dispatch.

But how, then, explain the fact that the populace is constantly ravished and set aflame by fresh brigades of moral, political and sociological revolutionists—that it is forever playing the eager victim to new mountebanks? The explanation lies in the simple circumstance that these performers upon the public midriff are always careful to ladle out nothing actually new, and hence nothing incomprehensible, alarming and accursed. What they offer is always the same old panacea with an extra-gaudy label—the tried, tasted and much-loved dose, the colic cure that mother used to make. Superficially, the United States seems to suffer from an endless and astounding neophilism; actually all its thinking is done within the boundaries of a very small group of political, economic and religious ideas, most of them unsound. For example, there is the fundamental idea of democracy—the idea that all political power should remain in the hands of the populace, that its exercise by superior men is intrinsically immoral. Out of this idea spring innumerable notions and crazes that are no more, at bottom, than restatements of it in sentimental terms: rotation in office, direct elections, the initiative and referendum, the recall, the popular primary, and so on. Again, there is the primary doctrine that the possession of great wealth is a crime—a doctrine half a religious heritage and half the product of mere mob envy. Out of it have come free silver, trust-busting, government ownership, muck-raking, Populism, Bleaseism, Progressivism, the milder forms of Socialism, the whole gasconade of "reform" politics. Yet again, there is the ineradicable peasant suspicion of the man who is having a better time in the world—a suspicion grounded, like the foregoing, partly upon undisguised envy and partly upon archaic and barbaric religious taboos. Out of it have come all the glittering pearls of the uplift, from Abolition to Prohibition, and from the crusade against horse-racing to the Mann Act. The whole political history of the United States is a history of these three ideas. There has never been an issue before the people that could not be translated into one or another of them. What is more, they have also colored the fundamental philosophical (and particularly epistemological) doctrines of the American people, and their moral theory, and even their foreign relations. The late war, very unpopular at the start, was "sold" to them, as the advertising phrase has it, by representing it as a campaign for the salvation of democracy, half religious and wholly altruistic. So represented to them, they embraced it; represented as the highly obscure and complex thing it actually was, it would have been beyond their comprehension, and hence abhorrent to them.

Outside this circle of their elemental convictions they are quite incapable of rational thought. One is not surprised to hear of Bismarck, a thorough royalist, discussing democracy with calm and fairness, but it would be unimaginable for the

American people, or for any other democratic people, to discuss royalism in the same manner: it would take a cataclysm to bring them to any such violation of their mental habits. When such a cataclysm occurs, they embrace the new ideas that are its fruits with the same adamantine firmness. One year before the French Revolution, disobedience to the king was unthinkable to the average Frenchman; only a few daringly immoral men cherished the notion. But one year *after* the fall of the Bastille, obedience to the king was equally unthinkable. The Russian Bolsheviki, whose doings have furnished a great deal of immensely interesting material to the student of popular psychology, put the principle into plain words. Once they were in the saddle, they decreed the abolition of the old imperial censorship and announced that speech would be free henceforth—but only so long as it kept within the bounds of the Bolshevist revelation! In other words, any citizen was free to think and speak whatever he pleased—but only so long as it did not violate certain fundamental ideas. This is precisely the sort of freedom that has prevailed in the United States since the first days. It is the only sort of freedom comprehensible to the average man. It accurately reveals his constitutional inability to shake himself free from the illogical and often quite unintelligible prejudices, instincts and mental vices that condition ninety per cent. of all his thinking. . . .

But here I wander into political speculation and no doubt stand in contumacy of some statute of Congress. Dr. Parsons avoids politics in her very interesting book. She confines herself to the purely social relations, *e.g.*, between man and woman, parent and child, host and guest, master and servant. The facts she offers are vastly interesting, and their discovery and coördination reveal a tremendous industry, but of even greater interest are the facts that lie over the margin of her inquiry. Here is a golden opportunity for other investigators: I often wonder that the field is so little explored. Perhaps the Freudians, once they get rid of their sexual obsession, will enter it and chart it. No doubt the inferiority complex described by Prof. Dr. Alfred Adler will one day provide an intelligible explanation of many of the puzzling phenomena of mob thinking. In the work of Prof. Dr. Freud himself there is, perhaps, a clew to the origin and anatomy of Puritanism, that worst of intellectual nephritises. I live in hope that the Freudians will fall upon the business without much further delay. Why do otherwise sane men believe in spirits? What is the genesis of the American axiom that the fine arts are unmanly? What is the precise machinery of the process called falling in love? Why do people believe newspapers? . . . Let there be light!

XIII.

The American Magazine

IT is astonishing, considering the enormous influence of the popular magazine upon American literature, such as it is, that there is but one book in type upon magazine history in the republic. That lone volume is "The Magazine in America," by Prof. Dr. Algernon Tassin, a learned birchman of the great university of Columbia, and it is so badly written that the interest of its matter is almost concealed—almost, but fortunately not quite. The professor, in fact, puts English to paper with all the traditional dullness of his flatulent order, and, as usual, he is most horribly dull when he is trying most kittenishly to be lively. I spare you examples of his writing; if you know the lady essayists of the United States, and their academic imitators in pantaloons, you know the sort of arch and whimsical jocosity he ladles out. But, as I have hinted, there is something worth attending to in his story, for all the defects of its presentation, and so his book is not to be sniffed at. He has, at all events, brought together a great mass of scattered and concealed facts, and arranged them conveniently for whoever deals with them next. The job was plainly a long and laborious one, and rasping to the higher cerebral centers. The historian had to make his mole-like way through the endless files of old and stupid magazines; he had to read the insipid biographies and autobiographies of dead and forgotten editors, many of them college professors, preachers out of work, pre-historic uplifters and bad poets; he had to sort out the facts from the fancies of such incurable liars as Griswold; he had to hack and blast a path across a virgin wilderness. The thing was worth doing, and, as I say, it has been done with commendable pertinacity.

Considering the noisiness of the American magazines of today, it is rather instructive to glance back at the timorous and bloodless quality of their progenitors. All of the early ones, when they were not simply monthly newspapers or almanacs, were depressingly "literary" in tone, and dealt chiefly in stupid poetry, silly essays and artificial fiction. The one great fear of their editors seems to have been that of offending some one; all of the pioneer prospectuses were full of assurances that nothing would be printed which even "the most fastidious" could object to. Literature, in those days,—say from 1830 to 1860—was almost completely cut off from contemporary life. It mirrored, not the struggle for existence, so fierce and dramatic in the new nation, but the pallid reflections of poetasters, self-advertising clergymen, sissified "gentlemen of taste," and other such donkeys. Poe waded into these *literati* and shook them up a bit, but even after the Civil War the majority of them continued to spin pretty cobwebs. Edmund Clarence Stedman and Donald G. Mitchell were excellent specimens of the clan; its last survivor was the lachrymose William Winter. The "literature" manufactured by these tear-squeezers, though often enough produced in beer cellars, was frankly aimed at the Young Person. Its main purpose was to avoid giving offense; it breathed a heavy and oleaginous piety, a snug niceness, a sickening sweetness. It is as dead to-day as Baalam's ass.

The *Atlantic Monthly* was set up by men in revolt against this reign of mush, as *Putnam's* had been a few years before, but the business of reform proved to be difficult and hazardous, and it was a long while before a healthier breed of authors could be developed, and a public for them found. "There is not much in the *Atlantic*," wrote Charles Eliot Norton to Lowell in 1874, "that is likely to be read twice save by its writers, and this is what the great public likes. . . . You should hear Godkin express himself in private on this topic." *Harper's Magazine*, in those days, was made up almost wholly of cribbings from England; the *North American Review* had sunk into stodginess and imbecility; *Putnam's* was dead, or dying; the *Atlantic* had yet to discover Mark Twain; it was the era of *Godey's Lady's Book*. The new note, so long awaited, was struck at last by *Scribner's*, now the *Century* (and not to be confused with the *Scribner's* of to-day). It not only threw all the old traditions overboard; it established new traditions almost at once. For the first time a great magazine began to take notice of the daily life of the American people. It started off with a truly remarkable series of articles on the Civil War; it plunged into contemporary politics; it eagerly sought out and encouraged new writers; it began printing decent pictures instead of the old chromos; it forced itself, by the sheer originality and enterprise of its editing, upon the public attention. American literature owes more to the *Century* than to any other magazine, and perhaps American thinking owes almost as much. It was the first "literary" periodical to arrest and interest the really first-class men of the country. It beat the *Atlantic* because it wasn't burdened with the *Atlantic's* decaying cargo of Boston Brahmins. It beat all the others because it was infinitely and obviously better. Almost everything that is good in the American magazine of to-day, almost everything that sets it above the English magazine or the Continental magazine, stems from the *Century.*

At the moment, of course, it holds no such clear field; perhaps it has served its function and is ready for a placid old age. The thing that displaced it was the yellow magazine of the *McClure's* type—a variety of magazine which surpassed it in the race for circulation by exaggerating and vulgarizing all its merits. Dr. Tassin seems to think, with William Archer, that S. S. McClure was the inventor of this type, but the truth is that its real father was the unknown originator of the Sunday supplement. What McClure—a shrewd literary bagman—did was to apply the sensational methods of the cheap newspaper to a new and cheap magazine. Yellow journalism was rising and he went in on the tide. The satanic Hearst was getting on his legs at the same time, and I daresay that the muck-raking magazines, even in their palmy days, followed him a good deal more than they led him. McClure and the imitators of McClure borrowed his adept thumping of the tom-tom; Munsey and the imitators of Munsey borrowed his mush. *McClure's* and *Everybody's*, even when they had the whole nation by the ears, did little save repeat in solemn, awful tones what Hearst had said before. As for *Munsey's*, at the height of its circulation, it was little more than a Sunday "magazine section" on smooth paper, and with somewhat clearer half-tones than Hearst could print. Nearly all the genuinely original ideas of these Yankee Harmsworths of yesterday turned out badly. John Brisben Walker, with the *Cosmopolitan*, tried to make his magazine a sort of national university, and it went to pot. Ridgway, of

Everybody's, planned a weekly to be published in a dozen cities simultaneously, and lost a fortune trying to establish it. McClure, facing a situation to be described presently, couldn't manage it, and his magazine got away from him. As for Munsey, there are many wrecks behind him; he is forever experimenting boldly and failing gloriously. Even his claim to have invented the all-fiction magazine is open to caveat; there were probably plenty of such things, in substance if not in name, before the *Argosy*. Hearst, the teacher of them all, now openly holds the place that belongs to him He has galvanized the corpse of the old *Cosmopolitan* into a great success, he has distanced all rivals with *Hearst's*, he has beaten the English on their own ground with *Nash's*, and he has rehabilitated various lesser magazines. More, he has forced the other magazine publishers to imitate him. A glance at *McClure's* to-day offers all the proof that is needed of his influence upon his inferiors.

Dr. Tassin, apparently in fear of making his book too nearly good, halts his chronicle at its most interesting point, for he says nothing of what has gone on since 1900—and very much, indeed, has gone on since 1900. For one thing, the *Saturday Evening Post* has made its unparalleled success, created its new type of American literature for department store buyers and shoe drummers, and bred its school of brisk, business-like, high-speed authors. For another thing, the *Ladies' Home Journal*, once supreme in its field, has seen the rise of a swarm of imitators, some of them very prosperous. For a third thing, the all-fiction magazine of Munsey, Robert Bonner and Street & Smith has degenerated into so dubious a hussy that Munsey, a very moral man, must blush every time he thinks of it. For a fourth thing, the moving-picture craze has created an entirely new type of magazine, and it has elbowed many other types from the stands. And for a fifth thing, to make an end, the muck-raking magazine has blown up and is no more.

Why this last? Have all the possible candidates for the rake been raked? Is there no longer any taste for scandal in the popular breast? I have heard endless discussion of these questions and many ingenious answers, but all of them fail to answer. In this emergency I offer one of my own. It is this: that the muck-raking magazine came to grief, not because the public tired of muck-raking, but because the muck-raking that it began with succeeded. That is to say, the villains so long belabored by the Steffenses, the Tarbells and the Phillipses were either driven from the national scene or forced (at least temporarily) into rectitude. Worse, their places in public life were largely taken by nominees whose chemical purity was guaranteed by these same magazines, and so the latter found their occupation gone and their following with it. The great masses of the plain people, eager to swallow denunciation in horse-doctor doses, gagged at the first spoonful of praise. They chortled and read on when Aldrich, Boss Cox, Gas Addicks, John D. Rockefeller and the other bugaboos of the time were belabored every month, but they promptly sickened and went elsewhere when Judge Ben B. Lindsey, Francis J. Heney, Governor Folk and the rest of the bogus saints began to be hymned.

The same phenomenon is constantly witnessed upon the lower level of daily journalism. Let a vociferous "reform" newspaper overthrow the old gang and elect its own candidates, and at once it is in a perilous condition. Its stock in trade is gone. It can no longer give a good show—within the popular meaning of a good show. For what the public wants eternally —at least the American public—is rough work. It delights in vituperation. It revels in scandal. It is always on the side of the man or journal making the charges, no matter how slight the probability that the accused is guilty. The late Roosevelt, perhaps one of the greatest rabble-rousers the world has ever seen, was privy to this fact, and made it the corner-stone of his singularly cynical and effective politics. He was forever calling names, making accusations, unearthing and denouncing demons. Dr. Wilson, a performer of scarcely less talent, has sought to pursue the same plan, with varying fidelity and success. He was a popular hero so long as he confined himself to reviling men and things—the Hell Hounds of Plutocracy, the Socialists, the Kaiser, the Irish, the Senate minority. But the moment he found himself on the side of the defense, he began to wobble, just as Roosevelt before him had begun to wobble when he found himself burdened with the intricate constructive program of the Progressives. Roosevelt shook himself free by deserting the Progressives, but Wilson found it impossible to get rid of his League of Nations, and so, for awhile at least, he presented a quite typical picture of a muck-raker hamstrung by blows from the wrong end of the rake.

That the old appetite for bloody shows is not dead but only sleepeth is well exhibited by the recent revival of the weekly of opinion. Ten years ago the weekly seemed to be absolutely extinct; even the *Nation* survived only as a half-forgotten appendage of the *Evening Post*. Then, of a sudden, the alliance was broken, the *Evening Post* succumbed to Wall Street, the *Nation* started on an independent course—and straightway made a great success. And why? Simply because it began breaking heads—not the old heads of the *McClure's* era, of course, but nevertheless heads salient enough to make excellent targets. For years it had been moribund; no one read it save a dwindling company of old men; its influence gradually approached *nil*. But by the elementary device of switching from mild expostulation to violent and effective denunciation it made a new public almost over-night, and is now very widely read, extensively quoted and increasingly heeded. . . . I often wonder that so few publishers of periodicals seem aware of the psychological principle here exposed. It is known to every newspaper publisher of the slightest professional intelligence; all successful newspapers are ceaselessly querulous and bellicose. They never defend any one or anything if they can help it; if the job is forced upon them, they tackle it by denouncing some one or something else. The plan never fails. Turn to the moving-picture trade magazines: the most prosperous of them is given over, in the main, to bitter attacks upon new films. Come back to daily journalism. The New York *Tribune*, a decaying paper, well nigh rehabilitated itself by attacking Hearst, the cleverest muck-raker of them all. For a moment, apparently dismayed, he attempted a defense of himself—and came near falling into actual disaster. Then, recovering his old form, he began a whole series of counter attacks and cover attacks, and in six months he was safe and sound again. . . .

XIV.

The Ulster Polonius

A GOOD half of the humor of the late Mark Twain consisted of admitting frankly the possession of vices and weaknesses that all of us have and few of us care to acknowledge. Practically all of the sagacity of George Bernard Shaw consists of bellowing vociferously what every one knows. I think I am as well acquainted with his works, both hortatory and dramatic, as the next man. I wrote the first book ever devoted to a discussion of them, and I read them pretty steadily, even today, and with endless enjoyment. Yet, so far as I know, I have never found an original idea in them—never a single statement of fact or opinion that was not anteriorly familiar, and almost commonplace. Put the thesis of any of his plays into a plain proposition, and I doubt that you could find a literate man in Christendom who had not heard it before, or who would seriously dispute it. The roots of each one of them are in platitude; the roots of *every* effective stage-play are in platitude; that a dramatist is inevitably a platitudinarian is itself a platitude double damned. But Shaw clings to the obvious even when he is not hampered by the suffocating conventions of the stage. His Fabian tracts and his pamphlets on the war are veritable compendiums of the undeniable; what is seriously stated in them is quite beyond logical dispute. They have excited a great deal of ire, they have brought down upon him a great deal of amusing abuse, but I have yet to hear of any one actually controverting them. As well try to controvert the Copernican astronomy. They are as bullet-proof in essence as the multiplication table, and vastly more bullet-proof than the Ten Commandments or the Constitution of the United States.

Well, then, why does the Ulsterman kick up such a pother? Why is he regarded as an arch-heretic, almost comparable to Galileo, Nietzsche or Simon Magnus? For the simplest of reasons. Because he practices with great zest and skill the fine art of exhibiting the obvious in unexpected and terrifying lights—because he is a master of the logical trick of so matching two apparently safe premisses that they yield an incongruous and inconvenient conclusion—above all, because he is a fellow of the utmost charm and address, quick-witted, bold, limber-tongued, persuasive, humorous, iconoclastic, ingratiating—in brief, a true Kelt, and so the exact antithesis of the solemn Sassenachs who ordinarily instruct and exhort us. Turn to his "Man and Superman," and you will see the whole Shaw machine at work. What he starts out with is the self-evident fact, disputed by no one not idiotic, that a woman has vastly more to gain by marriage, under Christian monogamy, than a man. That fact is as old as monogamy itself; it was, I dare say, the admitted basis of the palace revolution which brought monogamy into the world. But now comes Shaw with an implication that the sentimentality of the world chooses to conceal—with a deduction plainly resident in the original proposition, but kept in safe silence there by a preposterous and hypocritical taboo—to wit, the deduction that women are well aware of the profit that marriage yields for them, and that they are thus much more eager to marry than men are, and ever alert to take the lead in the business. This second fact, to any man who has passed through the terrible years between twenty-five and forty, is as plain as the first, but by a sort of general consent it is not openly stated. Violate that general consent and you are guilty of *scandalum magnatum*. Shaw is simply one who is guilty of *scandalum magnatum* habitually, a professional criminal in that department. It is his life work to announce the obvious in terms of the scandalous.

What lies under the horror of such blabbing is the deepest and most widespread of human weaknesses, which is to say, intellectual cowardice, the craven appetite for mental ease and security, the fear of thinking things out. All men are afflicted by it more or less; not even the most courageous and frank of men likes to admit, in specific terms, that his wife is fat, or that she seduced him to the altar by a transparent trick, or that their joint progeny resemble her brother or father, and are thus cads. A few extraordinary heroes of logic and evidence may do it occasionally, but only occasionally. The average man never does it at all. He is eternally in fear of what he knows in his heart; his whole life is made up of efforts to dodge it and conceal it; he is always running away from what passes for his intelligence and taking refuge in what pass for his higher feelings, *i.e.*, his stupidities, his delusions, his sentimentalities. Shaw is devoted to the art of hauling this recreant fellow up. He is one who, for purposes of sensation, often for the mere joy of outraging the tender-minded, resolutely and mercilessly thinks things out—sometimes with the utmost ingenuity and humor, but often, it must be said, in the same muddled way that the average right-thinker would do it if he ever got up the courage. Remember this formula, and all of the fellow's alleged originality becomes no more than a sort of bad-boy audacity, usually in bad taste. He drags skeletons from their closet and makes them dance obscenely—but every one, of course, knew that they were there all the while. He would produce an excitement of exactly the same kind (though perhaps superior in intensity) if he should walk down the Strand bared to the waist, and so remind the shocked Londoners of the unquestioned fact (though conventionally concealed and forgotten) that he is a mammal, and has an umbilicus.

Turn to a typical play-and-preface of his later canon, say "Androcles and the Lion." Here the complete Shaw formula is exposed. On the one hand there is a mass of platitudes; on the other hand there is the air of a peep-show. On the one hand he rehearses facts so stale that even Methodist clergymen have probably heard of them; on the other hand he states them so scandalously that the pious get all of the thrills out of the business that would accompany a view of the rector in liquor in the pulpit. Here, for example, are some of his contentions:

(a) That the social and economic doctrines preached by Jesus were indistinguishable from what is now called Socialism.

(b) That the Pauline transcendentalism visible in the Acts and the Epistles differs enormously from the simple humanitarianism set forth in the Four Gospels.

(c) That the Christianity on tap to-day would be almost as abhorrent to Jesus, supposing Him returned to earth, as the theories of Nietzsche, Hindenburg or Clemenceau, and vastly more abhorrent than those of Emma Goldman.

(d) That the rejection of the Biblical miracles, and even of the historical credibility of the Gospels, by no means disposes of Christ Himself.

(e) That the early Christians were persecuted, not because their theology was regarded as unsound, but because their public conduct constituted a nuisance.

It is unnecessary to go on. Could any one imagine a more abject surrender to the undeniable? Would it be possible to reduce the German exegesis of a century and a half to a more depressing series of platitudes? But his discussion of the inconsistencies between the Four Gospels is even worse; you will find all of its points set forth in any elemental treatise upon New Testament criticism—even in so childish a tract as Ramsden Balmforth's. He actually dishes up, with a heavy air of profundity, the news that there is a glaring conflict between the genealogy of Jesus in Matthew i, 1–17, and the direct claim of divine paternity in Matthew i, 18. More, he breaks out with the astounding discovery that Jesus was a good Jew, and that Paul's repudiation of circumcision (now a cardinal article of the so-called Christian faith) would have surprised Him and perhaps greatly shocked Him. The whole preface, running to 114 pages, is made up of just such shop-worn stuff. Searching it from end to end with eagle eye, I have failed to find a single fact or argument that was not previously familiar to me, despite the circumstance that I ordinarily give little attention to the sacred sciences and thus might have been expected to be surprised by their veriest commonplaces.

Nevertheless, this preface makes bouncing reading—and therein lies the secret of the continued vogue of Shaw. He has a large and extremely uncommon capacity for provocative utterance; he knows how to get a touch of bellicosity into the most banal of doctrines; he is forever on tiptoe, forever challenging, forever *sforzando*. His matter may be from the public store, even from the public junk-shop, but his manner is always all his own. The tune is old, but the words are new. Consider, for example, his discussion of the personality of Jesus. The idea is simple and obvious: Jesus was not a long-faced prophet of evil, like John the Baptist, nor was He an ascetic, or a mystic. But here is the Shaw way of saying it: "He was . . . what we call an artist and a Bohemian in His manner of life." The fact remains unchanged, but in the extravagant statement of it there is a shock for those who have been confusing the sour donkey they hear of a Sunday with the tolerant, likable

Man they profess to worship—and perhaps there is even a genial snicker in it for their betters. So with his treatment of the Atonement. His objections to it are time-worn, but suddenly he gets the effect of novelty by pointing out the quite manifest fact that acceptance of it is apt to make for weakness, that the man who rejects it is thrown back upon his own courage and circumspection, and is hence stimulated to augment them. The first argument—that Jesus was of free and easy habits—is so commonplace that I have heard it voiced by a bishop. The second suggests itself so naturally that I myself once employed it against a chance Christian encountered in a Pullman smoking-room. This Christian was at first shocked as he might have been by reading Shaw, but in half an hour he was confessing that he had long ago thought of the objection himself, and put it away as immoral. I well remember his fascinated interest as I showed him how my inability to accept the doctrine put a heavy burden of moral responsibility upon me, and forced me to be more watchful of my conduct than the elect of God, and so robbed me of many pleasant advantages in finance, the dialectic and amour. . . .

A double jest conceals itself in the Shaw legend. The first half of it I have already disclosed. The second half has to do with the fact that Shaw is not at all the wholesale agnostic his fascinated victims see him, but an orthodox Scotch Presbyterian of the most cock-sure and bilious sort—in fact, almost the archetype of the blue-nose. In the theory that he is Irish I take little stock. His very name is as Scotch as haggis, and the part of Ireland from which he springs is peopled almost exclusively by Scots. The true Irishman is a romantic. He senses life as a mystery, a thing of wonder, an experience of passion and beauty. In politics he is not logical, but emotional. In religion his interest centers, not in the commandments, but in the sacraments. The Scot, on the contrary, is almost devoid of romanticism. He is a materialist, a logician, a utilitarian. Life to him is not a poem, but a series of police regulations. God is not an indulgent father, but a hanging judge. There are no saints, but only devils. Beauty is a lewdness, redeemable only in the service of morality. It is more important to get on in the world than to be brushed by angels' wings. Here Shaw runs exactly true to type. Read his critical writings from end to end, and you will not find the slightest hint that objects of art were passing before him as he wrote. He founded, in England, the superstition that Ibsen was no more than a tin-pot evangelist —a sort of brother to General Booth, Mrs. Pankhurst and the syndics of the Sex Hygiene Society. He turned Shakespeare into a bird of evil, croaking dismally in a rain-barrel. He even injected a moral content (by dint of herculean straining) into the music dramas of Richard Wagner—surely the most colossal sacrifices of moral ideas ever made on the altar of beauty! Always the ethical obsession, the hall-mark of the Scotch Puritan, is visible in him. His politics is mere moral indignation. His æsthetic theory is cannibalism upon æsthetics. And in his general writing he is forever discovering an atrocity in what was hitherto passed as no more than a human weakness; he is forever inventing new sins, and demanding their punishment; he always sees his opponent, not only as wrong, but also as a scoundrel. I have called him a Presbyterian. Need I add that he flirts with predestination under the quasi-scientific *nom de guerre* of determinism—that he seems to be convinced that, while men may not be responsible for their virtues, they are undoubtedly responsible for their offendings, and deserve to be clubbed therefor? . . .

And this is Shaw the revolutionist, the heretic! Next, perhaps, we shall be hearing of Benedict XV, the atheist. . . .

XV.

An Unheeded Law-Giver

ONE discerns, in all right-thinking American criticism, the doctrine that Ralph Waldo Emerson was a great man, but the specifications supporting that doctrine are seldom displayed with any clarity. Despite the vast mass of writing about him, he remains to be worked out critically; practically all the existing criticism of him is marked by his own mellifluous obscurity. Perhaps a good deal of this obscurity is due to contradictions inherent in the man's character. He was dualism ambulant. What he actually *was* was seldom identical with what he represented himself to be or what his admirers thought him to be. Universally greeted, in his own day, as a revolutionary, he was, in point of fact, imitative and cautious—an importer of stale German elixirs, sometimes direct and sometimes through the Carlylean branch house, who took good care to dilute them with buttermilk before merchanting them. The theoretical spokesman, all his life long, of bold and forthright thinking, of the unafraid statement of ideas, he stated his own so warily and so muggily that they were ratified on the one hand by Nietzsche and on the other hand by the messiahs of the New Thought, that lavender buncombe.

What one notices about him chiefly is his lack of influence upon the main stream of American thought, such as it is. He had admirers and even worshipers, but no apprentices. Nietzscheism and the New Thought are alike tremendous violations of orthodox American doctrine. The one makes a headlong attack upon egalitarianism, the corner-stone of American politics; the other substitutes mysticism, which is the notion that the true realities are all concealed, for the prevailing American notion that the only true realities lie upon the surface, and are easily discerned by Congressmen, newspaper editorial writers and members of the Junior Order of United American Mechanics. The Emerson cult, in America, has been an affectation from the start. Not many of the chautauqua orators, literary professors, vassarized old maids and other such bogus *intelligentsia* who devote themselves to it have any intelligible understanding of the Transcendentalism at the heart of it, and not one of them, so far as I can make out, has ever executed Emerson's command to "defer never to the popular cry." On the contrary, it is precisely within the circle of Emersonian adulation that one finds the greatest tendency to test all ideas by their respectability, to combat free thought as something intrinsically vicious, and to yield placidly to "some great decorum, some fetish of a government, some ephemeral trade, or war, or man." It is surely not unworthy of notice that the country of this prophet of Man Thinking is precisely the country in which every sort of dissent from the current pishposh is combated most ferociously, and in which there is the most vigorous existing tendency to suppress free speech altogether.

Thus Emerson, on the side of ideas, has left but faint tracks behind him. His quest was for "facts amidst appearances," and his whole metaphysic revolved around a doctrine of transcendental first causes, a conception of interior and immutable realities, distinct from and superior to mere transient phenomena. But the philosophy that actually prevails among his countrymen—a philosophy put into caressing terms by William James—teaches an almost exactly contrary doctrine: its central idea is that whatever satisfies the immediate need is substantially true, that appearance is the only form of fact worthy the consideration of a man with money in the bank, and the old flag floating over him, and hair on his chest. Nor has Emerson had any ponderable influence as a literary artist in the technical sense, or as the prophet of a culture—that is, at home. Despite the feeble imitations of campus critics, his manner has vanished with his matter. There is, in the true sense, no Emersonian school of American writers. Current American writing, with its cocksureness, its somewhat hard competence, its air of selling goods, is utterly at war with his loose, impressionistic method, his often mystifying groping for ideas, his relentless pursuit of phrases. In the same way, one searches the country in vain for any general reaction to the cultural ideal that he set up. When one casts about for salient men whom he moved profoundly, men who got light from his torch, one thinks first and last, not of Americans, but of such men as Nietzsche and Hermann Grimm, the Germans, and Tyndall and Matthew

Arnold, the Englishmen. What remains of him at home, as I have said, is no more than, on the one hand, a somewhat absurd affectation of intellectual fastidiousness, now almost extinct even in New England, and, on the other hand, a debased Transcendentalism rolled into pills for fat women with vague pains and inattentive husbands—in brief, the New Thought—in brief, imbecility. This New Thought, a decadent end-product of American superficiality, now almost monopolizes him. One hears of him in its preposterous literature and one hears of him in text-books for the young, but not often elsewhere. Allowing everything, it would surely be absurd to hold that he has colored and conditioned the main stream of American thought as Goethe colored and conditioned the thought of Germany, or Pushkin that of Russia, or Voltaire that of France. . . .

XVI.
The Blushful Mystery

I
Sex Hygiene

THE literature of sex hygiene, once so scanty and so timorous, now piles mountain high. There are at least a dozen formidable series of books of instruction for inquirers of all ages, beginning with "What Every Child of Ten Should Know" and ending with "What a Woman of Forty-five Should Know," and they all sell amazingly. Scores of diligent authors, some medical, some clerical and some merely shrewdly chautauqual, grow rich at the industry of composing them. One of these amateur Havelock Ellises had the honor, during the last century, of instructing me in the elements of the sacred sciences. He was then the pastor of a fourth-rate church in a decaying neighborhood and I was sent to his Sunday-school in response to some obscure notion that the agony of it would improve me. Presently he disappeared, and for a long while I heard nothing about him. Then he came into sudden prominence as the author of such a series of handbooks and as the chief stockholder, it would seem, in the publishing house printing them. By the time he died, a few years ago, he had been so well rewarded by a just God that he was able to leave funds to establish a missionary college in some remote and heathen land.

This holy man, I believe, was honest, and took his platitudinous compositions quite seriously. Regarding other contributors to the literature it may be said without malice that their altruism is obviously corrupted by a good deal of hocus-pocus. Some of them lecture in the chautauquas, peddling their books before and after charming the yokels. Others, being members of the faculty, seem to carry on medical practice on the side. Yet others are kept in profitable jobs by the salacious old men who finance vice crusades. It is hard to draw the line between the mere thrifty enthusiast and the downright fraud. So, too, with the actual vice crusaders. The books of the latter, like the sex hygiene books, are often sold, not as wisdom, but as pornography. True enough, they are always displayed in the show-window of the small-town Methodist Book Concern—but you will also find them in the back-rooms of dubious second-hand book-stores, side by side with the familiar scarlet-backed editions of Rabelais, Margaret of Navarre and Balzac's "Droll Tales." Some time ago, in a book advertisement headed "Snappy Fiction," I found announcements of "My Battles With Vice," by Virginia Brooks—and "Life of My Heart," by Victoria Cross. The former was described by the publisher as a record of "personal experiences in the fight against the gray wolves and love pirates of modern society." The book was offered to all comers by mail. One may easily imagine the effects of such an offer.

But even the most serious and honest of the sex hygiene volumes are probably futile, for they are all founded upon a pedagogical error. That is to say, they are all founded upon an attempt to explain a romantic mystery in terms of an exact science. Nothing could be more absurd: as well attempt to interpret Beethoven in terms of mathematical physics—as many a fatuous contrapuntist, indeed, has tried to do. The mystery of sex presents itself to the young, not as a scientific problem to be solved, but as a romantic emotion to be accounted for. The only result of the current endeavor to explain its phenomena by seeking parallels in botany is to make botany obscene. . . .

2
Art and Sex

One of the favorite notions of the Puritan mullahs who specialize in this moral pornography is that the sex instinct, if suitably repressed, may be "sublimated" into the higher sorts of idealism, and especially into aesthetic idealism. That notion is to be found in all their books; upon it they ground the theory that the enforcement of chastity by a huge force of spies, stool pigeons and police would convert the republic into a nation of incomparable uplifters, forward-lookers and artists. All this, of course, is simply pious fudge. If the notion were actually sound, then all the great artists of the world would come from the ranks of the hermetically repressed, *i.e.*, from the ranks of

Puritan old maids, male and female. But the truth is, as every one knows, that the great artists of the world are never Puritans, and seldom even ordinarily respectable. No virtuous man —that is, virtuous in the Y.M.C.A. sense—has ever painted a picture worth looking at, or written a symphony worth hearing, or a book worth reading, and it is highly improbable that the thing has ever been done by a virtuous woman. The actual effect of repression, lamentable though it may be, is to destroy idealism altogether. The Puritan, for all his pretensions, is the worst of materialists. Passed through his sordid and unimaginative mind, even the stupendous romance of sex is reduced to a disgusting transaction in physiology. As artist he is thus hopeless; as well expect an auctioneer to qualify for the Sistine Chapel choir. All he ever achieves, taking pen or brush in hand, is a feeble burlesque of his betters, all of whom, by his hog's theology, are doomed to hell.

3
A Loss to Romance

Perhaps the worst thing that this sex hygiene nonsense has accomplished is the thing mourned by Agnes Repplier in "The Repeal of Reticence." In America, at least, innocence has been killed, and romance has been sadly wounded by the same discharge of smutty artillery. The flapper is no longer naïve and charming; she goes to the altar of God with a learned and even cynical glitter in her eye. The veriest school-girl of to-day, fed upon Forel, Sylvanus Stall, Reginald Wright Kauffman and the Freud books, knows as much as the midwife of 1885, and spends a good deal more time discharging and disseminating her information. All this, of course, is highly embarrassing to the more romantic and ingenuous sort of men, of whom I have the honor to be one. We are constantly in the position of General Mitchener in Shaw's one-acter, "Press Cuttings," when he begs Mrs. Farrell, the talkative charwoman, to reserve her confidences for her medical adviser. One often wonders, indeed, what women now talk of to doctors. . . .

Please do not misunderstand me here. I do not object to this New Freedom on moral grounds, but on æsthetic grounds. In the relations between the sexes all beauty is founded upon romance, all romance is founded upon mystery, and all mystery is founded upon ignorance, or, failing that, upon the deliberate denial of the known truth. To be in love is merely to be in a state of perceptual anæsthesia—to mistake an ordinary young man for a Greek god or an ordinary young woman for a goddess. But how can this condition of mind survive the deadly matter-of-factness which sex hygiene and the new science of eugenics impose? How can a woman continue to believe in the honor, courage and loving tenderness of a man after she has learned, perhaps by affidavit, that his hæmoglobin count is 117%, that he is free from sugar and albumen, that his blood pressure is 112/79 and that his Wassermann reaction is negative? . . . Moreover, all this new-fangled "frankness" tends to dam up, at least for civilized adults, one of the principal well-springs of art, to wit, impropriety. What is neither hidden nor forbidden is seldom very charming. If women, continuing their present tendency to its logical goal, end by going stark naked, there will be no more poets and painters, but only dermatologists and photographers. . . .

4
Sex on the Stage

The effort to convert the theater into a forum of solemn sex discussion is another abhorrent by-product of the sex hygiene rumble-bumble. Fortunately, it seems to be failing. A few years ago, crowds flocked to see Brieux's "Les Avariés," but to-day it is forgotten, and its successors are all obscure. The movement originated in Germany with the production of Frank Wedekind's "Frühlings Erwachen." The Germans gaped and twisted in their seats for a season or two, and then abandoned sex as a horror and went back to sex as a comedy. This last is what it actually should be, at least in the theater. The theater is no place for painful speculation; it is a place for diverting representation. Its best and truest sex plays are not such overstrained shockers as "Le Mariage d'Olympe" and "Damaged Goods," but such penetrating and excellent comedies as "Much Ado About Nothing" and "The Taming of the Shrew." In "Much Ado" we have an accurate and unforgettable picture of the way in which the normal male of the human species is brought to the altar—that is, by the way of appealing to his hollow vanity, the way of capitalizing his native and ineradicable asininity. And in "The Taming of the Shrew" we have a picture of the way in which the average woman, having so snared him, is purged of her resultant vainglory and bombast, and thus reduced to decent discipline and decorum, that the marriage may go on in solid tranquillity.

The whole drama of sex, in real life, as well as on the stage, revolves around these two enterprises. One-half of it consists of pitting the native intelligence of women against the native sentimentality of men, and the other half consists of bringing women into a reasonable order, that their superiority may not be too horribly obvious. To the first division belong the dramas of courtship, and a good many of those of marital conflict. In each case the essential drama is not a tragedy but a comedy —nay, a farce. In each case the conflict is not between imperishable verities but between mere vanities and pretensions. This is the essence of the comic: the unmasking of fraud, its destruction by worse fraud. Marriage, as we know it in Christendom, though its utility is obvious and its necessity is at least arguable, is just such a series of frauds. It begins with the fraud that the impulse to it is lofty, unearthly and disinterested. It proceeds to the fraud that both parties are equally eager for it and equally benefited by it—which actually happens only when two Mondays come together. And it rests thereafter upon the fraud that what is once agreeable (or tolerable) remains agreeable ever thereafter—that I shall be exactly the same man in 1938 that I am to-day, and that my wife will be the same woman, and intrigued by the merits of the same man. This last assumption is so outrageous that, on purely evidential and logical grounds, not even the most sentimental person would support it. It thus becomes necessary to reënforce it by attaching to it the concept of honor. That is to say, it is held up, not on the ground that it is actually true, but on the ground that a recognition of its truth is part of the bargain made at the altar, and that a repudiation of this bargain would be dishonorable. Here we have honor, which is based upon a sense of the deepest and most inviolable truth, brought in to support something admittedly not true. Here, in other words, we have a situation in comedy, almost exactly parallel to that in which a colored bishop whoops "Onward, Christian Soldiers!" like a calliope in order to drown out the crowing of the rooster concealed beneath his chasuble.

In all plays of the sort that are regarded as "strong" and "significant" in Greenwich Village, in the finishing schools and by the newspaper critics, connubial infidelity is the chief theme. Smith, having a wife, Mrs. Smith, betrays her love and trust by running off with Miss Rabinowitz, his stenographer. Or Mrs. Brown, detecting her husband, Mr. Brown, in lamentable proceedings with a neighbor, the grass widow Kraus, forgives him and continues to be true to him in consideration of her children, Fred, Pansy and Little Fern. Both situations produce a great deal of eye-rolling and snuffling among the softies aforesaid. Yet neither contains the slightest touch of tragedy, and neither at bottom is even honest. Both, on the contrary, are based upon an assumption that is unsound and ridiculous —the assumption, to wit, that the position of the injured wife is grounded upon the highest idealism—that the injury she suffers is directed at her lofty and impeccable spirit—that it leaves her standing in an heroic attitude. All this, soberly examined, is found to be untrue. The fact is that her moving impulse is simply a desire to cut a good figure before her world—in brief, that plain vanity is what animates her.

This public expectation that she will endure and renounce is itself hollow and sentimental, and so much so that it can seldom stand much strain. If, for example, her heroism goes beyond a certain modest point—if she carries it to the extent of complete abnegation and self-sacrifice—her reward is not that she is thought heroic, but that she is thought weak and foolish. And if, by any chance, the external pressure upon her is removed and she is left to go on with her alleged idealism alone—if, say, her recreant husband dies and some new suitor enters to dispute the theory of her deathless fidelity—then it is regarded as down-right insane for her to continue playing her artificial part.

In frank comedy we see the situation more accurately dealt with and hence more honestly and more instructively. Instead of depicting one party as revolting against the assumption of eternal fidelity melodramatically and the other as facing the revolt heroically and tragically, we have both criticizing it by a good-humored flouting of it—not necessarily by act, but by attitude. This attitude is normal and sensible. It rests upon genuine human traits and tendencies. It is sound, natural and honest. It gives the comedy of the stage a high validity that the bombastic fustian of the stage can never show, all the sophomores to the contrary notwithstanding.

When I speak of infidelity, of course, I do not mean only the gross infidelity of "strong" sex plays and the divorce courts, but that lighter infidelity which relieves and makes bearable the burdens of theoretical fidelity—in brief, the natural reaction of human nature against an artificial and preposterous assumption. The assumption is that a sexual choice, once made, is irrevocable—more, that all desire to revoke it, even transiently, disappears. The fact is that no human choice can ever be of that irrevocable character, and that the very existence of such an assumption is a constant provocation to challenge it and rebel against it.

What we have in marriage actually—or in any other such contract—is a constant war between the impulse to give that rebellion objective reality and a social pressure which puts a premium on submission. The rebel, if he strikes out, at once collides with a solid wall, the bricks of which are made up of the social assumption of his docility, and the mortar of which is the frozen sentimentality of his own lost yesterday—his fatuous assumption that what was once agreeable to him would be always agreeable to him. Here we have the very essence of comedy—a situation almost exactly parallel to that of the pompous old gentleman who kicks a plug hat lying on the sidewalk, and stumps his toe against the cobblestone within.

Under the whole of the conventional assumption reposes an assumption even more foolish, to wit, that sexual choice is regulated by some transcendental process, that a mysterious accuracy gets into it, that it is limited by impenetrable powers, that there is for every man one certain woman. This sentimentality not only underlies the theory of marriage, but is also the chief apology for divorce. Nothing could be more ridiculous. The truth is that marriages in Christendom are determined, not by elective affinities, but by the most trivial accidents, and that the issue of those accidents is relatively unimportant. That is to say, a normal man could be happy with any one of at least two dozen women of his acquaintance, and a man specially fitted to accept the false assumptions of marriage could be happy with almost any presentable woman of his race, class and age. He is married to Marie instead of to Gladys because Marie definitely decided to marry him, whereas Gladys vacillated between him and some other. And Marie decided to marry him instead of some other, not because the impulse was irresistibly stronger, but simply because the thing seemed more feasible. In such choices, at least among women, there is often not even any self-delusion. They see the facts clearly, and even if, later on, they are swathed in sentimental trappings, the revelation is not entirely obliterated.

Here we have comedy double distilled—a combat of pretensions, on the one side, perhaps, risen to self-hallucination, but on the other side more or less uneasily conscious and deliberate. This is the true soul of high farce. This is something not to snuffle over but to roar at.

XVII.
George Jean Nathan

ONE thinks of Gordon Craig, not as a jester, but as a very serious and even solemn fellow. For a dozen years past all the more sober dramatic critics of America have approached him with the utmost politeness, and to the gushing old maids and autointoxicated professors of the Drama League of America he has stood for the last word in theatrical æstheticism. Moreover, a good deal of this veneration has been deserved, for Craig has done excellent work in the theater, and is a man of much force and ingenuity and no little originality. Nevertheless, there must be some flavor of low, bar-room wit in him, some echo of Sir Toby Belch and the Captain of Köpenick, for a year or so ago he shook up his admirers with a joke most foul. Need I say that I refer to the notorious Nathan affair? Imagine the scene: the campus Archers and Walkleys in ponderous conclave, perhaps preparing their monthly cablegram of devotion to Maeterlinck. Arrives now a messenger with dreadful news. Gordon Craig, from his far-off Italian retreat, has issued a bull praising Nathan! Which Nathan? George Jean, of course. What! The *Smart Set* scaramouche, the ribald fellow, the raffish mocker, with his praise of Florenz Ziegfeld, his naughty enthusiasm for pretty legs, his contumacious scoffing at Brieux, Belasco, Augustus Thomas, Mrs. Fiske? Aye; even so. And what has Craig to say of him? . . . In brief, that he is the *only* American dramatic critic worth reading, that he knows far more about the theater than all the honorary pallbearers of criticism rolled together, that he is immeasurably the superior, in learning, in sense, in shrewdness, in candor, in plausibility, in skill at writing, of—

But names do not matter. Craig, in fact, did not bother to rehearse them. He simply made a clean sweep of the board, and then deftly placed the somewhat disconcerted Nathan in the center of the vacant space. It was a sad day for the honest donkeys who, for half a decade, had been laboriously establishing Craig's authority in America, but it was a glad day for

Knopf, the publisher. Knopf, at the moment, had just issued Nathan's "The Popular Theater." At once he rushed to a job printer in Eighth avenue, ordered 100,000 copies of the Craig encomium, and flooded the country with them. The result was amusing, and typical of the republic. Nathan's previous books, when praised at all, had been praised faintly and with reservations. The fellow, it appeared, was too spoofish; he lacked the sobriety and dignity necessary to a True Critic; he was entertaining but not to be taken seriously. But now, with foreign backing, and particularly English backing, he suddenly began to acquire merit and even a certain vague solemnity—and "The Popular Theater" was reviewed more lavishly and more favorably than I have ever seen any other theater book reviewed, before or since. The phenomenon, as I say, was typical. The childish mass of superstitions passing for civilized opinion in America was turned inside out over-night by one authoritative foreign voice. I have myself been a figure in the same familiar process. All of my books up to "The American Language" were, in the main, hostilely noticed. "A Book of Prefaces," in particular, was manhandled by the orthodox reviewers. Then, just before "The American Language" was issued, the *Mercure de France* printed an article commending "A Book of Prefaces" in high, astounding terms. The consequence was that "The American Language," a far inferior work, was suddenly discovered to be full of merit, and critics of the utmost respectability, who had ignored all my former books, printed extremely friendly reviews of it. . . .

But to return to Nathan. What deceived the Drama Leaguers and other such imposing popinjays for so long, causing them to mistake him for a mere sublimated Alan Dale, was his refusal to take imbecilities seriously, his easy casualness and avoidance of pedagogics, his frank delight in the theater as a show-shop—above all, his bellicose iconoclasm and devastating wit. What Craig, an intelligent man, discerned underneath was his extraordinary capacity for differentiating between sham and reality, his catholic freedom from formulæ and prejudice, his astonishing acquaintance with the literature of the practical theater, his firm grounding in rational æsthetic theory—above all, his capacity for making the thing he writes of interesting, his uncommon craftsmanship. This craftsmanship had already got him a large audience; he had been for half a dozen years, indeed, one of the most widely read of American dramatic critics. But the traditional delusion that sagacity and dullness are somehow identical had obscured the hard and accurate thinking that made the show. What was so amusing seemed necessarily superficial. It remained for Craig to show that this appearance of superficiality was only an appearance, that the Nathan criticism was well planned and soundly articulated, that at the heart of it there was a sound theory of the theater, and of the literature of the theater no less.

And what was that theory? You will find it nowhere put into a ready formula, but the outlines of it must surely be familiar to any one who has read "Another Book on the Theater," "The Popular Theater" and "Mr. George Jean Nathan Presents." In brief, it is the doctrine preached with so much ardor by Benedetto Croce and his disciple, Dr. J. E. Spingarn, and by them borrowed from Goethe and Carlyle—the doctrine, to wit, that every work of art is, at bottom, unique, and that it is the business of the critic, not to label it and pigeon-hole it, but to seek for its inner intent and content, and to value it according as that intent is carried out and that content is valid and worth while. This is the precise opposite of the academic critical attitude. The professor is nothing if not a maker of card-indexes; he must classify or be damned. His masterpiece is the dictum that "it is excellent, but it is not a play." Nathan has a far more intelligent and hospitable eye. His criterion, elastic and undefined, is inimical only to the hollow, the meretricious, the fraudulent. It bars out the play of flabby and artificial sentiment. It bars out the cheap melodrama, however gaudily set forth. It bars out the moony mush of the bad imitators of Ibsen and Maeterlinck. It bars out all mere clap-trap and sensation-monging. But it lets in every play, however conceived or designed, that contains an intelligible idea well worked out. It lets in every play by a dramatist who is ingenious, and original, and genuinely amusing. And it lets in every other sort of theatrical spectacle that has an honest aim, and achieves that aim passably, and is presented frankly for what it is.

Bear this theory in mind, and you have a clear explanation of Nathan's actual performances—first, his merciless lampooning of the trade-goods of Broadway and the pifflings of the Drama

League geniuses, and secondly, his ardent championing of such widely diverse men as Avery Hopwood, Florenz Ziegfeld, Ludwig Thoma, Lord Dunsany, Sasha Guitry, Lothar Schmidt, Ferenz Molnar, Roberto Bracco and Gerhart Hauptmann, all of whom have one thing in common: they are intelligent and full of ideas and know their trade. In Europe, of course, there are many more such men than in America, and some of the least of them are almost as good as our best. That is why Nathan is forever announcing them and advocating the presentation of their works—not because he favors foreignness for its own sake, but because it is so often accompanied by sound achievement and by stimulating example to our own artists. And that is why, when he tackles the maudlin flubdub of the Broadway dons, he does it with the weapons of comedy, and even of farce. Does an Augustus Thomas rise up with his corn-doctor magic and Sunday-school platitudes, proving heavily that love is mightier than the sword, that a pure heart will baffle the electric chair, that the eye is quicker than the hand? Then Nathan proceeds against him with a slapstick, and makes excellent practice upon his pantaloons. Does a Belasco, thumb on forelock, posture before the yeomanry as a Great Artist, the evidence being a large chromo of a Childs' restaurant, and a studio like a Madison avenue antique-shop? Then Nathan flings a laugh at him and puts him in his place. And does some fat rhinoceros of an actress, unearthing a smutty play by a corn-fed Racine, loose its banal obscenities upon the vulgar in the name of Sex Hygiene, presuming thus to teach a Great Lesson, and break the Conspiracy of Silence, and carry on the Noble Work of Brieux and company, and so save impatient flappers from the Moloch's Sacrifice of the Altar—does such a bumptious and preposterous baggage fill the newspapers with her pishposh and the largest theater in Manhattan with eager dunderheads? Then the ribald Jean has at her with a flour-sack filled with the pollen of the *Ambrosia artemisiaefolia*, driving her from the scene to the tune of her own unearthly sneezing.

Necessarily, he has to lay on with frequency. For one honest play, honestly produced and honestly played, Broadway sees two dozen that are simply so much green-goods. To devote serious exposition to the badness of such stuff would be to descend to the donkeyish futility of William Winter. Sometimes, indeed, even ridicule is not enough; there must be a briefer and more dramatic display of the essential banality. Well, then, why not recreate it in the manner of Croce—but touching up a line here, a color there? The result is burlesque, but burlesque that is the most searching and illuminating sort of criticism. Who will forget Nathan's demonstration that a platitudinous play by Thomas would be better if played backward? A superb bravura piece, enormously beyond the talents of any other American writer on the theater, it smashed the Thomas legend with one stroke. In the little volume called "Bottoms Up" you will find many other such annihilating waggeries. Nathan does not denounce melodrama with a black cap upon his head, painfully demonstrating its inferiority to the drama of Ibsen, Scribe and Euripides; he simply sits down and writes a little melodrama so extravagantly ludicrous that the whole genus collapses. And he does not prove in four columns of a Sunday paper that French plays done into American are spoiled; he simply shows the spoiling in six lines.

This method, of course, makes for broken heads; it outrages the feelings of tender theatrical mountebanks; it provokes reprisals more or less furtive and behind the door. The theater in America, as in most other countries, is operated chiefly by bounders. Men so constantly associated with actors tend to take on the qualities of the actor—his idiotic vanity, his herculean stupidity, his chronic underrating of his betters. The miasma spreads to dramatists and dramatic critics; the former drift into charlatanery and the latter into a cowardly and disgusting dishonesty. Amid such scenes a man of positive ideas, of civilized tastes and of unshakable integrity is a stranger, and he must face all the hostility that the lower orders of men display to strangers. There is, so far as I know, no tripe-seller in Broadway who has not tried, at one time or another, to dispose of Nathan by *attentat*. He has been exposed to all the measures ordinarily effective against rebellious reviewers, and, resisting them, he has been treated to special treatment with infernal machines of novel and startling design. No writer for the theater has been harder beset, and none has been less incommoded by the onslaught. What is more, he has never made the slightest effort to capitalize this drum-fire—the invariable device of lesser men. So far as I am aware, and I have been in close association with him for ten years, it has had not the slightest effect upon him whatsoever. A thoroughgoing skeptic, with no trace in him of the messianic delusion, he has avoided timorousness on the one hand and indignation on the other. No man could be less a public martyr of the Metcalfe type; it would probably amuse him vastly to hear it argued that his unbreakable independence (and often somewhat high and mighty sniffishness) has been of any public usefulness. I sometimes wonder what keeps such a man in the theater, breathing bad air nightly, gaping at prancing imbeciles, sitting cheek by jowl with cads. Perhaps there is, at bottom, a secret romanticism —a lingering residuum of a boyish delight in pasteboard and spangles, gaudy colors and soothing sounds, preposterous heroes and appetizing wenches. But more likely it is a sense of humor—the zest of a man to whom life is a spectacle that never grows dull—a show infinitely surprising, amusing, buffoonish, vulgar, obscene. The theater, when all is said and done, is not life in miniature, but life enormously magnified, life hideously exaggerated. Its emotions are ten times as powerful as those of reality, its ideas are twenty times as idiotic as those of real men, its lights and colors and sounds are forty times as blinding and deafening as those of nature, its people are grotesque burlesques of every one we know. Here is diversion for a cynic. And here, it may be, is the explanation of Nathan's fidelity.

Whatever the cause of his enchantment, it seems to be lasting. To a man so fertile in ideas and so facile in putting them into words there is a constant temptation to make experiments, to plunge into strange waters, to seek self-expression in ever-widening circles. And yet, at the brink of forty years, Nathan remains faithful to the theater; of his half dozen books, only one does not deal with it, and that one is a very small one. In four or five years he has scarcely written of aught else. I doubt that anything properly describable as enthusiasm is at the bottom of this assiduity; perhaps the right word is curiosity. He is interested mainly, not in the staple fare of the playhouse, but in what might be called its fancy goods—in its endless stream of new men, its restless innovations, the radical overhauling that it has been undergoing in our time. I do not recall, in any of his books or articles, a single paragraph appraising the classics of the stage, or more than a brief note or two on their interpretation. His attention is always turned in a quite opposite direction. He is intensely interested in novelty of whatever sort, if it be only free from sham. Such experimentalists as Max Reinhardt, George Bernard Shaw, Sasha Guitry and the daring nobodies of the Grand Guignol, such divergent originals as Dunsany, Ziegfeld, George M. Cohan and Schnitzler, have enlisted his eager partisanship. He saw something new to our theater in the farces of Hopwood before any one else saw it; he was quick to welcome the novel points of view of Eleanor Gates and Clare Kummer; he at once rescued what was sound in the Little Theatre movement from what was mere attitudinizing and pseudo-intellectuality. In the view of Broadway, an exigent and even malignant fellow, wielding a pen dipped in *aqua fortis*, he is actually amiable to the last degree, and constantly announces pearls in the fodder of the swine. Is the new play in Forty-second Street a serious work of art, as the press-agents and the newspaper reviewers say? Then so are your grandmother's false teeth! Is Maeterlinck a Great Thinker? Then so is Dr. Frank Crane! Is Belasco a profound artist? Then so is the man who designs the ceilings of hotel dining rooms! But let us not weep too soon. In the play around the corner there is a clever scene. Next door, amid sickening dullness, there are two buffoons who could be worse: one clouts the other with a *Blutwurst* filled with mayonnaise. And a block away there is a girl in the second row with a very charming twist of the *vastus medialis*. Let us sniff the roses and forget the thorns!

What this attitude chiefly wars with, even above cheapness, meretriciousness and banality, is the fatuous effort to turn the theater, a place of amusement, into a sort of outhouse to the academic grove—the Maeterlinck-Brieux-Barker complex. No critic in America, and none in England save perhaps Walkley, has combated this movement more vigorously than Nathan. He is under no illusion as to the functions and limitations of the stage. He knows, with Victor Hugo, that the best it can do, in the domain of ideas, is to "turn thoughts into food for the crowd," and he knows that only the simplest and shakiest ideas may undergo that transformation. Coming upon the scene at the height of the Ibsen mania of half a generation ago, he ranged himself against its windy pretenses from the start. He saw at once the high merit of Ibsen as a dramatic craftsman and welcomed him as a reformer of dramatic technique, but he also saw how platitudinous was the ideational content of his plays and announced the fact in terms highly offensive to the Ibsenites. . . . But the Ibsenites have vanished and Nathan remains. He has survived, too, the Brieux hubbub. He has lived to preach the funeral sermon of the Belasco legend. He has himself sworded Maeterlinck and Granville Barker. He has done frightful execution upon many a poor mime. And meanwhile, breasting the murky tide of professorial buncombe, of solemn pontificating, of Richard-Burtonism, Clayton-Hamiltonism and other such decaying forms of William-Winterism, he has rescued dramatic criticism among us from its exile with theology, embalming and obstetrics, and given it a place among what Nietzsche called the gay sciences, along with war, fiddle-playing and laparotomy. He has made it amusing, stimulating, challenging, even, at times, a bit startling. And to the business, artfully concealed, he has brought a sound and thorough acquaintance with the heavy work of the pioneers, Lessing, Schlegel, Hazlitt, Lewes *et al*—and an even wider acquaintance, lavishly displayed, with every nook and corner of the current theatrical scene across the water. And to discharge this extraordinarily copious mass of information he has hauled and battered the English language into new and often astounding forms, and when English has failed he has helped it out with French, German, Italian, American, Swedish, Russian, Turkish, Latin, Sanskrit and Old Church Slavic, and with algebraic symbols, chemical formulæ, musical notation and the signs of the Zodiac. . . .

This manner, of course, is not without its perils. A man so inordinately articulate is bound to succumb, now and then, to the seductions of mere virtuosity. The average writer, and particularly the average critic of the drama, does well if he gets a single new and racy phrase into an essay; Nathan does well if he dilutes his inventions with enough commonplaces to enable the average reader to understand his discourse at all. He carries the avoidance of the *cliché* to the length of an *idée fixe*. It would be difficult, in all his books, to find a dozen of the usual rubber stamps of criticism; I daresay it would kill him, or, at all events, bring him down with cholera morbus, to discover that he had called a play "convincing" or found "authority" in the snorting of an English actor-manager. At best, this incessant flight from the obvious makes for a piquant and arresting style, a procession of fantastic and often highly pungent neologisms —in brief, for Nathanism. At worst, it becomes artificiality, pedantry, obscurity. I cite an example from an essay on Eleanor Gates' "The Poor Little Rich Girl," prefaced to the printed play:

> As against the not unhollow symbolic strut and gasconade of such over-pæaned pieces as, let us for example say, "The Blue Bird" of Maeterlinck, so simple and unaffected a bit of stage writing as this—of school dramatic intrinsically the same—cajoles the more honest heart and satisfies more plausibly and fully those of us whose thumbs are ever being pulled professionally for a native stage less smeared with the snobberies of empty, albeit high-sounding, nomenclatures from overseas.

Fancy that, Hedda!—and in praise of a "simple and unaffected bit of stage writing"! I denounced it at the time, *circa* 1916, and perhaps with some effect. At all events, I seem to notice a gradual disentanglement of the parts of speech. The old florid invention is still there; one encounters startling coinages in even the most casual of reviews; the thing still flashes and glitters; the tune is yet upon the E string. But underneath I hear a more sober rhythm than of old. The fellow, in fact, takes on a sedater habit, both in style and in point of view. Without abandoning anything essential, without making the slightest concession to the orthodox opinion that he so magnificently disdains, he yet begins to yield to the middle years. The mere shocking of the stupid is no longer as charming as it used to be. What he now offers is rather more *gemütlich*; sometimes it even verges upon the instructive. . . . But I doubt that Nathan will ever become a professor, even if he enjoys the hideously prolonged senility of a William Winter. He will be full of surprises to the end. With his last gasp he will make a phrase to flabbergast a dolt.

XVIII.

Portrait of an Immortal Soul

ONE day in Spring, six or eight years ago, I received a letter from a man somewhere beyond the Wabash announcing that he had lately completed a very powerful novel and hinting that my critical judgment upon it would give him great comfort. Such notifications, at that time, reached me far too often to be agreeable, and so I sent him a form-response telling him that I was ill with pleurisy, had just been forbidden by my oculist to use my eyes, and was about to become a father. The aim of this form-response was to shunt all that sort of trade off to other reviewers, but for once it failed. That is to say, the unknown kept on writing to me, and finally offered to pay me an honorarium for my labor. This offer was so unusual that it quite demoralized me, and before I could recover I had received, cashed and dissipated a modest check, and was confronted by an accusing manuscript, perhaps four inches thick, but growing thicker every time I glanced at it.

One night, tortured by conscience and by the inquiries and reminders arriving from the author by every post, I took up the sheets and settled down for a depressing hour or two of it. . . . No, I did *not* read all night. No, it was *not* a masterpiece. No, it has *not* made the far-off stranger famous. Let me tell the story quite honestly. I am, in fact, far too rapid a reader to waste a whole night on a novel; I had got through this one by midnight and was sound asleep at my usual time. And it was by no means a masterpiece; on the contrary, it was inchoate, clumsy, and, in part, artificial, insincere and preposterous. And to this day the author remains obscure. . . . But underneath all the amateurish writing, the striving for effects that failed to come off, the absurd literary self-consciousness, the recurrent falsity and banality—underneath all these stigmata of a neophyte's book there was yet a capital story, unusual in content, naïve in manner and enormously engrossing. What is more, the faults that it showed in execution were, most of them, not ineradicable. On page after page, as I read on, I saw chances to improve it—to get rid of its intermittent bathos, to hasten its action, to eliminate its spells of fine writing, to purge it of its imitations of all the bad novels ever written—in brief, to tighten it, organize it, and, as the painters say, tease it up.

The result was that I spent the next morning writing the author a long letter of advice. It went to him with the manuscript, and for weeks I heard nothing from him. Then the manuscript returned, and I read it again. This time I had a genuine surprise. Not only had the unknown followed my suggestions with much intelligence; in addition, once set up on the right track, he had devised a great many excellent improvements of his own. In its new form, in fact, the thing was a very competent and even dexterous piece of writing, and after re-reading it from the first word to the last with even keener interest than before, I sent it to Mitchell Kennerley, then an active publisher, and asked him to look through it. Kennerley made an offer for it at once, and eight or nine months later it was published with his imprint. The author chose to conceal himself behind the *nom de plume* of Robert Steele; I myself gave the book the title of "One Man." It came from the press—and straightway died the death. The only favorable review it received was mine in the *Smart Set.* No other reviewer paid any heed to it. No one gabbled about it. No one, so far as I could make out, even read it. The sale was small from the start, and quickly stopped altogether. . . . To this day the fact fills me with wonder. To this day I marvel that so dramatic, so penetrating and so curiously moving a story should have failed so overwhelmingly. . . .

For I have never been able to convince myself that I was wrong about it. On the contrary, I am more certain than ever, re-reading it after half a dozen years, that I was right—that it was and is one of the most honest and absorbing human documents ever printed in America. I have called it, following the author, a novel. It is, in fact, nothing of the sort; it is autobiography. More, it is autobiography unadorned and shameless, autobiography almost unbelievably cruel and betraying, autobiography that is as devoid of artistic sophistication as an operation for gall-stones. This so-called Steele is simply too stupid, too ingenuous, too moral to lie. He is the very reverse of an artist; he is a born and incurable Puritan—and in his alleged novel he draws the most faithful and merciless picture of an American Puritan that has ever got upon paper. There is never the slightest effort at amelioration; he never evades the ghastly horror of it; he never tries to palm off himself as a good fellow, a hero. Instead, he simply takes his stand in the center of the platform, where all the spotlights meet, and there calmly strips off his raiment of reticence—first his Sunday plug-hat, then his long-tailed coat, then his boiled shirt, then his shoes and socks, and finally his very B.V.D.'s. The closing scene shows the authentic *Mensch-an-sich*, the eternal blue-nose in the nude, with every wart and pimple glittering and every warped bone and flabby muscle telling its abhorrent tale. There stands the Puritan stripped of every artifice and concealment, like Thackeray's Louis XIV.

Searching my memory, I can drag up no recollection of another such self-opener of secret chambers and skeletonic closets. Set beside this pious babbler, the late Giovanni Jacopo Casanova de Seingalt shrinks to the puny proportions of a mere barroom boaster, a smoking-car Don Juan, an Eighteenth Century stock company leading man or whiskey drummer. So, too, Benvenuto Cellini: a fellow vastly entertaining, true enough, but after all, not so much a psychological historian as a liar, a yellow journalist. One always feels, in reading Benvenuto, that the man who is telling the story is quite distinct from the man about whom it is being told. The fellow, indeed, was too noble an artist to do a mere portrait with fidelity; he could not resist the temptation to repair a cauliflower ear here, to paint out a tell-tale scar there, to shine up the eyes a bit, to straighten the legs down below. But this Steele—or whatever his name may be—never steps out of himself. He is never describing the gaudy one he would *like* to be, but always the commonplace, the weak, the emotional, the ignorant, the third-rate Christian male that he actually is. He deplores himself, he distrusts himself, he plainly wishes heartily that he was not himself, but he never makes the slightest attempt to disguise and bedizen himself. Such as he is, cheap, mawkish, unæsthetic, conscience-stricken, he depicts himself with fierce and unrelenting honesty.

Superficially, the man that he sets before us seems to be a felonious fellow, for he confesses frankly to a long series of youthful larcenies, to a somewhat banal adventure in forgery (leading to a term in jail), to sundry petty deceits and breaches of trust, and to an almost endless chain of exploits in amour, most of them sordid and unrelieved by anything approaching romance. But the inner truth about him, of course, is that he is really a moralist of the moralists—that his one fundamental and all-embracing virtue is what he himself regards as his viciousness —that he is never genuinely human and likable save in those moments which lead swiftly to his most florid self-accusing. In brief, the history is that of a moral young man, the child of God-fearing parents, and its moral, if it has one, is that a strictly moral upbringing injects poisons into the system that even the most steadfast morality cannot resist. It is, in a way, the old story of the preacher's son turned sot and cutthroat.

Here we see an apparently sound and normal youngster converted into a sneak and rogue by the intolerable pressure of his father's abominable Puritanism. And once a rogue, we see him make himself into a scoundrel by the very force of his horror of his roguery. Every step downward is helped from above. It is not until he resigns himself frankly to the fact of his incurable degradation, and so ceases to struggle against it, that he ever steps out of it.

The external facts of the chronicle are simple enough. The son of a school teacher turned petty lawyer and politician, the hero is brought up under such barbaric rigors that he has already become a fluent and ingenious liar, in sheer self-protection, at the age of five or six. From lying he proceeds quite naturally to stealing: he lifts a few dollars from a neighbor, and then rifles a tin bank, and then takes to filching all sorts of small articles from the store-keepers of the vicinage. His harsh, stupid, Christian father, getting wind of these peccadilloes, has at him in the manner of a mad bull, beating him, screaming at him, half killing him. The boy, for all the indecent cruelty of it, is convinced of the justice of it. He sees himself as one lost; he accepts the fact that he is a disgrace to his family; in the end, he embraces the parental theory that there is something strange and sinister in his soul, that he couldn't be good if he tried. Finally, filled with some vague notion of taking his abhorrent self out of sight, he runs away from home. Brought back in the character of a felon, he runs away again. Soon he is a felon in fact. That is to say, he forges his father's name to a sheaf of checks, and his father allows him to go to prison.

This prison term gives the youngster a chance to think things out for himself, without the constant intrusion of his father's Presbyterian notions of right or wrong. The result is a measurably saner philosophy than that he absorbed at home, but there is still enough left of the old moral obsession to cripple him in all his thinking, and especially in his thinking about himself. His attitude toward women, for example, is constantly conditioned by puritanical misgivings and superstitions. He can never view them innocently, joyously, unmorally, as a young fellow of twenty or twenty-one should, but is always oppressed by Sunday-schoolish notions of his duty to them, and to society in general. On the one hand, he is appalled by his ready yielding to those hussies who have at him unofficially, and on the other hand he is filled with the idea that it would be immoral for him, an ex-convict, to go to the altar with a virgin. The result of these doubts is that he gives a good deal more earnest thought to the woman question than is good for him. The second result is that he proves an easy victim to the discarded mistress of his employer. This worthy working girl craftily snares him and marries him—and then breaks down on their wedding night, unwomaned, so to speak, by the pathetic innocence of the ass, and confesses to a choice roll of her past doings, ending with the news that she is suffering from what the vice crusaders mellifluously denominate a "social disease."

Naturally enough, the blow almost kills the poor boy—he is still, in fact, scarcely out of his nonage—and the problems that grow out of the confession engage him for the better part of the next two years. Always he approaches them and wrestles with them morally; always his search is for the way that the copybook maxims approve, not for the way that self-preservation demands. Even when a brilliant chance for revenge presents itself, and he is forced to embrace it by the sheer magnetic pull of it, he does so hesitatingly, doubtingly, ashamedly. His whole attitude to this affair, indeed, is that of an Early Christian Father. He hates himself for gathering rose-buds while he may; he hates the woman with a double hatred for strewing them so temptingly in his path. And in the end, like the moral and upright fellow that he is, he sells out the temptress for cash in hand, and salves his conscience by handing over the money to an orphan asylum. This after prayers for divine guidance. A fact! Don't miss the story of it in the book. You will go far before you get another such illuminating glimpse into a pure and righteous mind.

So in episode after episode. One observes a constant oscillation between a pharisaical piety and a hoggish carnality. The praying brother of yesterday is the night-hack roisterer of to-day; the roisterer of to-day is the snuffling penitent and pledge-taker of to-morrow. Finally, he is pulled both ways at once and suffers the greatest of all his tortures. Again, of course, a woman is at the center of it—this time a stenographer. He has no delusions about her virtue—she admits herself, in fact, that it is extinct—but all the same he falls head over heels in love with her, and is filled with an inordinate yearning to marry her and settle down with her. Why not, indeed? She is pretty and a nice girl; she seems to reciprocate his affection; she is naturally eager for the obliterating gold band; she will undoubtedly make him an excellent wife. But he has forgotten his conscience—and it rises up in revenge and floors him. What! Marry a girl with such a Past! Take a fancy woman to his bosom! Jealousy quickly comes to the aid of conscience. Will he be able to forget? Contemplating the damsel in the years to come, at breakfast, at dinner, across the domestic hearth, in the cold, blue dawn, will he ever rid his mind of those abhorrent images, those phantasms of men?

Here, at the very end, we come to the most engrossing chapter in this extraordinary book. The duelist of sex, thrust through the gizzard at last, goes off to a lonely hunting camp to wrestle with his intolerable problem. He describes his vacillations faithfully, elaborately, cruelly. On the one side he sets his honest yearning, his desire to have done with light loves, the girl herself. On the other hand he ranges his moral qualms, his sneaking distrusts, the sinister shadows of those nameless ones, his morganatic brothers-in-law. The struggle within his soul is gigantic. He suffers as Prometheus suffered on the rock; his very vitals are devoured; he emerges battered and exhausted. He decides, in the end, that he will marry the girl. She has wasted the shining dowry of her sex; she comes to him spotted and at second-hand; snickers will appear in the polyphony of the wedding music—but he will marry her nevertheless. It will be a marriage unblessed by Holy Writ; it will be a flying in the face of Moses; luck and the archangels will be against it—but he will marry her all the same, Moses or no Moses. And so, with his face made bright by his first genuine revolt against the archaic, barbaric morality that has dragged him down, and his heart pulsing to his first display of authentic, unpolluted charity, generosity and nobility, he takes his departure from us. May the fates favor him with their mercy! May the Lord God strain a point to lift him out of his purgatory at last! He has suffered all the agonies of belief. He has done abominable penance for the Westminster Catechism, and for the moral order of the world, and for all the despairing misery of back-street, black bombazine, Little Bethel goodness. He is Puritanism incarnate, and Puritanism become intolerable. . . .

I daresay any second-hand bookseller will be able to find a copy of the book for you: "One Man," by Robert Steele. There is some raciness in the detail of it. Perhaps, despite its public failure, it enjoys a measure of *pizzicato* esteem behind the door. The author, having achieved its colossal self-revelation, became intrigued by the notion that he was a literary man of sorts, and informed me that he was undertaking the story of the girl last-named—the spotted ex-virgin. But he apparently never finished it. No doubt he discovered, before he had gone very far, that the tale was intrinsically beyond him—that his fingers all turned into thumbs when he got beyond his own personal history. Such a writer, once he has told the one big story, is done for.

XIX.
Jack London

THE quasi-science of genealogy, as it is practiced in the United States, is directed almost exclusively toward establishing aristocratic descents for nobodies. That is to say, it records and glorifies decay. Its typical masterpiece is the discovery that the wife of some obscure county judge is the grandchild, infinitely removed, of Mary Queen of Scots, or that the blood of Geoffrey of Monmouth flows in the veins of a Philadelphia stockbroker. How much more profitably its professors might be employed in tracing the lineage of truly salient and distinguished men! For example, the late Jack London. Where did he get his hot artistic passion, his delicate feeling for form and color, his extraordinary skill with words? The man, in truth, was an instinctive artist of a high order, and if ignorance often corrupted his art, it only made the fact of his inborn mastery the more remarkable. No other popular writer of his time did any better writing than you will find in "The Call of the Wild," or in parts of "John Barleycorn," or in such short stories as "The Sea Farmer" and "Samuel." Here, indeed, are all the elements of sound fiction: clear thinking, a sense of character, the dramatic instinct, and, above all, the adept putting together of words—words charming and slyly significant, words arranged, in a French phrase, for the respiration and the ear. You will never convince me that this æsthetic sensitiveness, so rare, so precious, so distinctively aristocratic, burst into abiogenetic flower on a San Francisco sand-lot. There must have been some intrusion of an alien and superior strain, some *pianissimo* fillup from above; there was obviously a great deal more to the thing than a routine hatching in low life. Perhaps the explanation is to be sought in a Jewish smear. Jews were not few in the California of a generation ago, and one of them, at least, attained to a certain high, if transient, fame with the pen. Moreover, the name, London, has a Jewish smack; the Jews like to call themselves after great cities. I have, indeed, heard this possibility of an Old Testament descent put into an actual rumor. Stranger genealogies are not unknown in seaports. . . .

But London the artist did not live *a cappella*. There was also London the amateur Great Thinker, and the second often hamstrung the first. That great thinking of his, of course, took color from the sordid misery of his early life; it was, in the main, a jejune Socialism, wholly uncriticised by humor. Some of his propagandist and expository books are almost unbelievably nonsensical, and whenever he allowed any of his so-called ideas to sneak into an imaginative work the intrusion promptly spoiled it. Socialism, in truth, is quite incompatible with art; its cook-tent materialism is fundamentally at war with the first principle of the æsthetic gospel, which is that one daffodil is worth ten shares of Bethlehem Steel. It is not by accident that there has never been a book on Socialism which was also a work of art. Papa Marx's "Das Kapital" at once comes to mind. It is as wholly devoid of graces as "The Origin of Species" or "Science and Health"; one simply cannot conceive a reasonable man reading it without aversion; it is as revolting as a barrel organ. London, preaching Socialism, or quasi-Socialism, or whatever it was that he preached, took over this offensive dullness. The materialistic conception of history was too heavy a load for him to carry. When he would create beautiful books he had to throw it overboard as Wagner threw overboard democracy, the superman and free thought. A sort of temporary Christian created "Parsifal." A sort of temporary aristocrat created "The Call of the Wild."

Also in another way London's early absorption of social and economic nostrums damaged him as an artist. It led him into a socialistic exaltation of mere money; it put a touch of avarice into him. Hence his too deadly industry, his relentless thousand words a day, his steady emission of half-done books. The prophet of freedom, he yet sold himself into slavery to the publishers, and paid off with his soul for his ranch, his horses, his trappings of a wealthy cheese-monger. His volumes rolled out almost as fast as those of E. Phillips Oppenheim; he simply could not make them perfect at such a gait. There are books on his list—for example, "The Scarlet Plague" and "The Little Lady of the Big House"—that are little more than garrulous notes for books.

But even in the worst of them one comes upon sudden splashes of brilliant color, stray proofs of the adept penman, half-wistful reminders that London, at bottom, was no fraud. He left enough, I am convinced, to keep him in mind. There was in him a vast delicacy of perception, a high feeling, a sensitiveness to beauty. And there was in him, too, under all his blatancies, a poignant sense of the infinite romance and mystery of human life.

XX.
Among the Avatars

It may be, as they say, that we Americanos lie in the gutter of civilization, but all the while our eyes steal cautious glances at the stars. In the midst of the prevailing materialism—the thin incense of mysticism. As a relief from money drives, politics and the struggle for existence—Rosicrucianism, the Knights of Pythias, passwords, grips, secret work, the 33rd degree. In flight from Peruna, Mandrake Pills and Fletcherism—Christian Science, the Emmanuel Movement, the New Thought. The tendency already has its poets: Edwin Markham and Ella Wheeler Wilcox. It has acquired its romancer: Will Levington Comfort. . . .

This Comfort wields an easy pen. He has done, indeed, some capital melodramas, and when his ardor heats him up he grows downright eloquent. But of late the whole force of his æsthetic engines has been thrown into propaganda, by the Bhagavad-Gītā out of Victorian sentimentalism. The nature of this propaganda is quickly discerned. What Comfort preaches is a sort of mellowed mariolatry, a humorless exaltation of woman, a flashy effort to turn the inter-attraction of the sexes, ordinarily a mere cause of scandal, into something transcendental and highly portentous. Woman, it appears, is the beyond-man, the trans-mammal, the nascent angel; she is the Upward Path, the Way to Consecration, the door to the Third Lustrous Dimension; all the mysteries of the cosmos are concentrated in Mystic Motherhood, whatever that may be. I capitalize in the Comfortian (and New Thought) manner. On one page of "Fate Knocks at the Door" I find Voices, Pits of Trade, Woman, the Great Light, the Big Deep and the Twentieth Century Lie. On another are the Rising Road of Man, the Transcendental Soul Essence, the Way Uphill, the Sempiternal Mother. Thus Andrew Bedient, the spouting hero of the tale:

> I believe in the natural greatness of Woman; that through the spirit of Woman are born sons of strength; that only through the potential greatness of Woman comes the militant greatness of man.

I believe Mothering is the loveliest of the Arts; that great mothers are handmaidens of the Spirit, to whom are intrusted God's avatars; that no prophet is greater than his mother.

I believe when humanity arises to Spiritual evolution (as it once evolved through Flesh, and is now evolving through Mind) Woman will assume the ethical guiding of the race.

I believe that the Holy Spirit of the Trinity is Mystic Motherhood, and the source of the divine principle is Woman; that the prophets are the union of this divine principle and the higher manhood; that they are beyond the attractions of women of flesh, because unto their manhood has been added Mystic Motherhood. . . .

I believe that the way to Godhood is the Rising Road of Man.

I believe that, as the human mother brings a child to her husband, the father—so Mystic Motherhood, the Holy Spirit, is bringing the world to God, the Father.

The capitals are Andrew's—or Comfort's. I merely transcribe and perspire. This Andrew, it appears, is a sea cook who has been mellowed and transfigured by exhaustive study of the Bhagavad Gītā, one of the sacred nonsense books of the Hindus. He doesn't know who his father was, and he remembers his mother only as one dying in a strange city. When she finally passed away he took to the high seas and mastered marine cookery. Thus for many years, up and down the world. Then he went ashore at Manila and became chef to an army packtrain. Then he proceeded to China, to Japan. Then to India, where he entered the forestry service and plodded the Himalayan heights, always with the Bhagavad Gītā under his arm. At some time or other, during his years of culinary seafaring, he saved the life of a Yankee ship captain, and that captain, later dying, left him untold millions in South America. But it is long after all this is past that we have chiefly to do with him. He is now a young Monte Cristo at large in New York, a Monte Cristo worshiped and gurgled over by a crowd of mushy old maids, a hero of Uneeda-biscuit parties in God-forsaken studios, the madness and despair of senescent virgins.

But it is not Andrew's wealth that inflames these old girls, nor even his manly beauty, but rather his revolutionary and astounding sapience, his great gift for solemn and incomprehensible utterance, his skill as a metaphysician. They hang upon his every word. His rhetoric makes their heads swim. Once he gets fully under way, they almost swoon. . . . And what girls they are! Alas, what pathetic neck-stretching toward tinsel stars! What eager hearing of the soulful, gassy stuff! One of them has red hair and "wine dark eyes, now cryptic black, now suffused with red glows like the night sky above a prairie fire." Another is "tall and lovely in a tragic, flower-like way" and performs upon the violoncello. A third is "a tanned woman rather variously weathered," who writes stupefying epigrams about Whitman and Nietzsche—making the latter's name Nietschze, of course! A fourth is "the Gray One"—O mystic appellation! A fifth—but enough! You get the picture. You can imagine how Andrew's sagacity staggers these poor dears. You can see them fighting for him, each against all, with sharp, psychical excaliburs.

Arm in arm with all this exaltation of Woman, of course, goes a great suspicion of mere woman. The combination is as old as Christian mysticism, and Havelock Ellis has discussed its origin and nature at great length. On the one hand is the *Übermensch*; on the other hand is the temptress, the Lorelei. The Madonna and Mother Eve, the celestial virgins and the succubi! The hero of "Fate Knocks at the Door," for all his flaming words, still distrusts his goddess. His colleague of "Down Among Men" is poisoned by the same suspicions. Woman has led him up to grace, she has shown him the Upward Path, she has illuminated him with her Mystic Motherhood—but the moment she lets go his hand he takes to his heels. What is worse, he sends a friend to her (I forget her name, and his) to explain in detail how unfavorably any further communion with her would corrupt his high mission, *i.e.*, to save the downtrodden by writing plays that fail and books that not even Americans will read. An intellectual milk-toast! A mixture of Dr. Frank Crane and Mother Tingley, of Edward Bok and the Archangel Eddy! . . .

So far, not much of this ineffable stuff has got among the best-sellers, but I believe that it is on its way. Despite materialism and pragmatism, mysticism is steadily growing in fashion. I hear of paunchy Freemasons holding sacramental meetings on Maundy Thursday, of Senators in Congress railing against *materia medica*, of Presidents invoking divine intercession at Cabinet meetings. The New Thoughters march on; they have at least a dozen prosperous magazines, and one of them has a circulation comparable to that of any 20-cent repository of lingerie fiction. Such things as Karma, the Ineffable Essence and the Zeitgeist become familiar fauna, chained up in the cage of every woman's club. Thousands of American women know far more about the Subconscious than they know about plain sewing. The pungency of myrrh and frankincense is mingled with *odeur de femme*. Physiology is formally repealed and repudiated; its laws are all lies. No doubt the fleshly best-seller of the last decade, with its blushing amorousness, its flashes of underwear, its obstetrics between chapters, will give place to a more delicate piece of trade-goods to-morrow. In this New Thought novel the hero and heroine will seek each other out, not to spoon obscenely behind the door, but for the purpose of uplifting the race. Kissing is already unsanitary; in a few years it may be downright sacrilegious, a crime against some obscure avatar or other, a business libidinous and accursed.

XXI.
Three American Immortals

1
Aristotelean Obsequies

I TAKE the following from the Boston *Herald* of May 1, 1882:

> A beautiful floral book stood at the left of the pulpit, being spread out on a stand. . . . Its last page was composed of white carnations, white daisies and light-colored immortelles. On the leaf was displayed, in neat letters of purple immortelles, the word "Finis." This device was about two feet square, and its border was composed of different colored tea-roses. The other portion of the book was composed of dark and light-colored flowers. . . . The front of the large pulpit was covered with a mass of white pine boughs laid on loosely. In the center of this mass of boughs appeared a large harp composed of yellow jonquils. . . . Above this harp was a handsome bouquet of dark pansies. On each side appeared large clusters of calla lilies.

Well, what have we here? The funeral of a Grand Exalted Pishposh of the Odd Fellows, of an East Side Tammany leader, of an aged and much respected brothel-keeper? Nay. What we have here is the funeral of Ralph Waldo Emerson. It was thus that New England lavished the loveliest fruits of the Puritan æsthetic upon the bier of her greatest son. It was thus that Puritan *Kultur* mourned a philosopher.

2
Edgar Allan Poe

The myth that there is a monument to Edgar Allan Poe in Baltimore is widely believed; there are even persons who, stopping off in Baltimore to eat oysters, go to look at it. As a matter of fact, no such monument exists. All that the explorer actually finds is a cheap and hideous tombstone in the corner of a Presbyterian churchyard—a tombstone quite as bad as the worst in Père La Chaise. For twenty-six years after Poe's death there was not even this: the grave remained wholly unmarked.

Poe had surviving relatives in Baltimore, and they were well-to-do. One day one of them ordered a local stonecutter to put a plain stone over the grave. The stonecutter hacked it out and was preparing to haul it to the churchyard when a runaway freight-train smashed into his stoneyard and broke the stone to bits. Thereafter the Poes seem to have forgotten Cousin Edgar; at all events, nothing further was done.

The existing tombstone was erected by a committee of Baltimore schoolmarms, and cost about $1,000. It took the dear girls ten long years to raise the money. They started out with a "literary entertainment" which yielded $380. This was in 1865. Six years later the fund had made such slow progress that, with accumulated interest, it came to but $587.02. Three years more went by: it now reached $627.55. Then some anonymous Poeista came down with $100, two others gave $50 each, one of the devoted schoolmarms raised $52 in nickels and dimes, and George W. Childs agreed to pay any remaining deficit. During all this time not a single American author of position gave the project any aid. And when, finally, a stone was carved and set up and the time came for the unveiling, the only one who appeared at the ceremony was Walt Whitman. All the other persons present were Baltimore nobodies—chiefly schoolteachers and preachers. There were three set speeches—one by the principal of a local high school, the second by a teacher in the same seminary, and the third by a man who was invited to give his "personal recollections" of Poe, but who announced in his third sentence that "I never saw Poe but once, and our interview did not last an hour."

This was the gaudiest Poe celebration ever held in America. The poet has never enjoyed such august posthumous attentions as those which lately flattered the shade of James Russell Lowell. At his actual burial, in 1849, exactly eight persons were present, of whom six were relatives. He was planted, as I have said, in a Presbyterian churchyard, among generations of honest believers in infant damnation, but the officiating clergyman was a Methodist. Two days after his death a Baptist gentleman of God, the illustrious Rufus W. Griswold, printed a defamatory article upon him in the New York *Tribune*, and for years it set the tone of native criticism of him. And so he rests: thrust among Presbyterians by a Methodist and formally damned by a Baptist.

3
Memorial Service

Let us summon from the shades the immortal soul of James Harlan, born in 1820, entered into rest in 1899. In the year 1865 this Harlan resigned from the United States Senate to enter the cabinet of Abraham Lincoln as Secretary of the Interior. One of the clerks in that department, at $600 a year, was Walt Whitman, lately emerged from three years of hard service as an army nurse during the Civil War. One day, discovering that Whitman was the author of a book called "Leaves of Grass," Harlan ordered him incontinently kicked out, and it was done forthwith. Let us remember this event and this man; he is too precious to die. Let us repair, once a year, to our accustomed houses of worship and there give thanks to God that one day in 1865 brought together the greatest poet that America has ever produced and the damndest ass.

PREJUDICES: SECOND SERIES

I.
The National Letters

I
Prophets and Their Visions

It is convenient to begin, like the gentlemen of God, with a glance at a text or two. The first, a short one, is from Ralph Waldo Emerson's celebrated oration, "The American Scholar," delivered before the Phi Beta Kappa Society at Cambridge on August 31st, 1837. Emerson was then thirty-four years old and almost unknown in his own country, though he had already published "Nature" and established his first contacts with Landor and Carlyle. But "The American Scholar" brought him into instant notice at home, partly as man of letters but more importantly as seer and prophet, and the fame thus founded has endured without much diminution, at all events in New England, to this day. Oliver Wendell Holmes, giving words to what was undoubtedly the common feeling, hailed the address as the intellectual declaration of independence of the American people, and that judgment, amiably passed on by three generations of pedagogues, still survives in the literature books. I quote from the first paragraph:

> Our day of dependence, our long apprenticeship to the learning of other lands, draws to a close. . . . Events, actions arise, that must be sung, that will sing themselves. Who can doubt that poetry will revive and lead in a new age, as the star in the constellation Harp, which now flames in our zenith, astronomers announce, shall one day be the pole-star for a thousand years?

This, as I say, was in 1837. Thirty-three years later, in 1870, Walt Whitman echoed the prophecy in his even more famous "Democratic Vistas." What he saw in his vision and put into his gnarled and gasping prose was

> a class of native authors, literatuses, far different, far higher in grade, than any yet known, sacerdotal, modern, fit to cope with our occasions,

lands, permeating the whole mass of American morality, taste, belief, breathing into it a new breath of life, giving it decision, affecting politics far more than the popular superficial suffrage, with results inside and underneath the elections of Presidents or Congress—radiating, begetting appropriate teachers, schools, manners, and, as its grandest result, accomplishing, (what neither the schools nor the churches and their clergy have hitherto accomplished, and without which this nation will no more stand, permanently, soundly, than a house will stand without a substratum,) a religious and moral character beneath the political and productive and intellectual bases of the States.

And out of the vision straightway came the prognostication:

The promulgation and belief in such a class or order—a new and greater literatus order—its possibility, (nay, certainty,) underlies these entire speculations. . . . Above all previous lands, a great original literature is sure to become the justification and reliance, (in some respects the sole reliance,) of American democracy.

Thus Whitman in 1870, the time of the first draft of "Democratic Vistas." He was of the same mind, and said so, in 1888, four years before his death. I could bring up texts of like tenor in great number, from the years before 1837, from those after 1888, and from every decade between. The dream of Emerson, though the eloquence of its statement was new and arresting, embodied no novel projection of the fancy; it merely gave a sonorous *Waldhorn* tone to what had been dreamed and said before. You will find almost the same high hope, the same exuberant confidence in the essays of the elder Channing and in the "Lectures on American Literature" of Samuel Lorenzo Knapp, LL.D., the first native critic of beautiful letters—the primordial tadpole of all our later Mores, Brownells, Phelpses, Mabies, Brander Matthewses and other such grave and glittering fish. Knapp believed, like Whitman long after him, that the sheer physical grandeur of the New World would inflame a race of bards to unprecedented utterance. "What are the Tibers and Scamanders," he demanded, "measured by the Missouri and the Amazon? Or what the loveliness of Illysus or Avon by the Connecticut or the Potomack? Whenever a nation wills it, prodigies are born." That is to say, prodigies literary and ineffable as well as purely material—prodigies aimed, in his own words, at "the olympick crown" as well as at mere railroads, ships, wheat-fields, droves of hogs, factories and money. Nor were Channing and Knapp the first of the haruspices. Noah Webster, the lexicographer, who "taught millions to spell but not one to sin," had seen the early starlight of the same Golden Age so early as 1789, as the curious will find by examining his "Dissertations on the English Language," a work fallen long since into undeserved oblivion. Nor was Whitman, taking sober second thought exactly a century later, the last of them. Out of many brethren of our own day, extravagantly articulate in print and among the chautauquas, I choose one—not because his hope is of purest water, but precisely because, like Emerson, he dilutes it with various discreet whereases. He is Van Wyck Brooks, a young man far more intelligent, penetrating and hospitable to fact than any of the reigning professors—a critic who is sharply differentiated from them, indeed, by the simple circumstance that he has information and sense. Yet this extraordinary Mr. Brooks, in his "Letters and Leadership," published in 1918, rewrites "The American Scholar" in terms borrowed almost bodily from "Democratic Vistas"—that is to say, he prophesies with Emerson and exults with Whitman. First there is the Emersonian doctrine of the soaring individual made articulate by freedom and realizing "the responsibility that lies upon us, each in the measure of his own gift." And then there is Whitman's vision of a self-interpretative democracy, forced into high literary adventures by Joseph Conrad's "obscure inner necessity," and so achieving a "new synthesis adaptable to the unique conditions of our life." And finally there is the specific prediction, the grandiose, Adam Forepaugh mirage: "We shall become a luminous people, dwelling in the light and sharing our light." . . .

As I say, the roll of such soothsayers might be almost endlessly lengthened. There is, in truth, scarcely a formal discourse upon the national letters (forgetting, perhaps, Barrett Wendell's sour threnody upon the New England *Aufklärung*) that is without some touch of this previsional exultation, this confident hymning of glories to come, this fine assurance that American literature, in some future always ready to dawn, will burst into so grand a flowering that history will cherish its loveliest blooms even above such salient American gifts to culture as the moving-picture, the phonograph, the New Thought and the bichloride tablet. If there was ever a dissenter from the national optimism, in this as in other departments, it was surely Edgar Allan Poe—without question the bravest and most original, if perhaps also the least orderly and judicious, of all the critics that we have produced. And yet even Poe, despite his general habit of disgust and dismay, caught a flash or two of that engaging picture—even Poe, for an instant, in 1846, thought that he saw the beginnings of a solid and autonomous native literature, its roots deep in the soil of the republic—as you will discover by turning to his forgotten essay on J.G.C. Brainard, a thrice-forgotten doggereleer of Jackson's time. Poe, of course, was too cautious to let his imagination proceed to details; one feels that a certain doubt, a saving peradventure or two, played about the unaccustomed vision as he beheld it. But, nevertheless, he unquestionably beheld it. . . .

2
The Answering Fact

Now for the answering fact. How has the issue replied to these visionaries? It has replied in a way that is manifestly to the discomfiture of Emerson as a prophet, to the dismay of Poe as a pessimist disarmed by transient optimism, and to the utter collapse of Whitman. We have, as every one knows, produced no such "new and greater literatus order" as that announced by old Walt. We have given a gaping world no books that "radiate," and surely none intelligibly comparable to stars and constellations. We have achieved no prodigies of the first class, and very few of the second class, and not many of the third and fourth classes. Our literature, despite several false starts that promised much, is chiefly remarkable, now as always, for its respectable mediocrity. Its typical great man, in our own time, has been Howells, as its typical great man a generation ago was Lowell, and two generations ago, Irving. Viewed largely, its salient character appears as a sort of timorous flaccidity, an amiable hollowness. In bulk it grows more and more formidable, in ease and decorum it makes undoubted progress, and on the side of mere technic, of the bald capacity to write, it shows an ever-widening competence. But when one proceeds from such agencies and externals to the intrinsic substance, to the creative passion within, that substance quickly reveals itself as thin and watery, and that passion fades to something almost puerile. In all that mass of suave and often highly diverting writing there is no visible movement toward a distinguished and singular excellence, a signal national quality, a ripe and stimulating flavor, or, indeed, toward any other describable goal. What one sees is simply a general irresolution, a pervasive superficiality. There is no sober grappling with fundamentals, but only a shy sporting on the surface; there is not even any serious approach, such as Whitman dreamed of, to the special experiences and emergencies of the American people. When one turns to any other national literature—to Russian literature, say, or French, or German or Scandinavian—one is conscious immediately of a definite attitude toward the primary mysteries of existence, the unsolved and ever-fascinating problems at the bottom of human life, and of a definite preoccupation with some of them, and a definite way of translating their challenge into drama. These attitudes and preoccupations raise a literature above mere poetizing and tale-telling; they give it dignity and importance; above all, they give it national character. But it is precisely here that the literature of America, and especially the later literature, is most colorless and inconsequential. As if paralyzed by the national fear of ideas, the democratic distrust of whatever strikes beneath the prevailing platitudes, it evades all resolute and honest dealing with what, after all, must be every healthy literature's elementary materials. One is conscious of no brave and noble earnestness in it, of no generalized passion for intellectual and spiritual adventure, of no organized determination to think things out. What is there is a highly self-conscious and insipid correctness, a bloodless respectability, a submergence of matter in manner—in brief, what is there is the feeble, uninspiring quality of German painting and English music.

It was so in the great days and it is so to-day. There has always been hope and there has always been failure. Even the most optimistic prophets of future glories have been united, at all times, in their discontent with the here and now. "The mind of this country," said Emerson, speaking of what was currently visible in 1837, "is taught to aim at low objects. . . . There is no work for any but the decorous and the complaisant. . . . Books are written . . . by men of talent . . . . who start wrong, who set out from accepted dogmas, not from their own sight of principles." And then, turning to the way out: "The office of the scholar (*i.e.*, of Whitman's 'literatus') is to cheer, to raise and to guide men by showing them *facts amid appearances.*" Whitman himself, a full generation later, found that office still unfilled. "Our fundamental want to-day in the United States," he said, "with closest, amplest reference to present conditions, and to the future, is of a class, and the clear idea of a class, of native authors, literatuses, far different, far higher in grade, than any yet known"—and so on, as I have already quoted him. And finally, to make an end of the prophets, there is Brooks, with nine-tenths of his book given over, not to his prophecy—it is crowded, indeed, into the last few pages—but to a somewhat heavy mourning over the actual scene before him. On the side of letters, the æsthetic side, the side of ideas, we present to the world at large, he says, "the spectacle of a vast, undifferentiated herd of good-humored animals"—Knights of Pythias, Presbyterians, standard model Ph.D.'s, readers of the *Saturday Evening Post*, admirers of Richard Harding Davis and O. Henry, devotees of Hamilton Wright Mabie's "white list" of books, members of the Y.M.C.A. or the Drama League, weepers at chautauquas, wearers of badges, 100 per cent. patriots, children of God. Poe I pass over; I shall turn to him again later on. Nor shall I repeat the parrotings of Emerson and Whitman in the jeremiads of their innumerable heirs and assigns. What they all establish is what is already obvious: that American thinking, when it concerns itself with beautiful letters as when it concerns itself with religious dogma or political theory, is extraordinarily timid and superficial—that it evades the genuinely serious problems of life and art as if they were stringently taboo—that the outward virtues it undoubtedly shows are always the virtues, not of profundity, not of courage, not of originality, but merely those of an emasculated and often very trashy dilettantism.

3
The Ashes of New England

The current scene is surely depressing enough. What one observes is a literature in three layers, and each inordinately doughy and uninspiring—each almost without flavor or savor. It is hard to say, with much critical plausibility, which layer deserves to be called the upper, but for decorum's sake the choice may be fixed upon that which meets with the approval of the reigning Lessings. This is the layer of the novels of the late Howells, Judge Grant, Alice Brown and the rest of the dwindling survivors of New England *Kultur*, of the brittle, academic poetry of Woodberry and the elder Johnson, of the tea-party essays of Crothers, Miss Repplier and company, and of the solemn, highly judicial, coroner's inquest criticism of More, Brownell, Babbitt and their imitators. Here we have manner, undoubtedly. The thing is correctly done; it is never crude or gross; there is in it a faint perfume of college-town society. But when this highly refined and attenuated manner is allowed for what remains is next to nothing. One never remembers a character in the novels of these aloof and de-Americanized Americans; one never encounters an idea in their essays; one never carries away a line out of their poetry. It is literature as an academic exercise for talented grammarians, almost as a genteel recreation for ladies and gentlemen of fashion—the exact equivalent, in the field of letters, of eighteenth century painting and German *Augenmusik*.

What ails it, intrinsically, is a dearth of intellectual audacity and of æsthetic passion. Running through it, and characterizing the work of almost every man and woman producing it, there is an unescapable suggestion of the old Puritan suspicion of the fine arts as such—of the doctrine that they offer fit asylum for good citizens only when some ulterior and superior purpose is carried into them. This purpose, naturally enough, most commonly shows a moral tinge. The aim of poetry, it appears, is to fill the mind with lofty thoughts—not to give it joy, but to give it a grand and somewhat gaudy sense of virtue. The essay is a weapon against the degenerate tendencies of the age. The novel, properly conceived, is a means of uplifting the spirit; its aim is to inspire, not merely to satisfy the low curiosity of man in man. The Puritan, of course, is not entirely devoid of æsthetic feeling. He has a taste for good form; he responds to style; he is even capable of something approaching a purely æsthetic emotion. But he fears this æsthetic emotion as an insinuating distraction from his chief business in life: the sober consideration of the all-important problem of conduct. Art is a temptation, a seduction, a Lorelei, and the Good Man may safely have traffic with it only when it is broken to moral uses—in other words, when its innocence is pumped out of it, and it is purged of gusto. It is precisely this gusto that one misses in all the work of the New England school, and in all the work of the formal schools that derive from it. One observes in such a fellow as Dr. Henry Van Dyke an excellent specimen of the whole clan. He is, in his way, a genuine artist. He has a hand for pretty verses. He wields a facile rhetoric. He shows, in indiscreet moments, a touch of imagination. But all the while he remains a sound Presbyterian, with one eye on the devil. He is a Presbyterian first and an artist second, which is just as comfortable as trying to be a Presbyterian first and a chorus girl second. To such a man it must inevitably appear that a Molière, a Wagner, a Goethe or a Shakespeare was more than a little bawdy.

The criticism that supports this decaying caste of literary Brahmins is grounded almost entirely upon ethical criteria. You will spend a long while going through the works of such typical professors as More, Phelps, Boynton, Burton, Perry, Brownell and Babbitt before ever you encounter a purely æsthetic judgment upon an æsthetic question. It is almost as if a man estimating daffodils should do it in terms of artichokes. Phelps' whole body of "we churchgoers" criticism—the most catholic and tolerant, it may be said in passing, that the faculty can show—consists chiefly of a plea for correctness, and particularly for moral correctness; he never gets very far from "the axiom of the moral law." Brownell argues eloquently for standards that would bind an imaginative author as tightly as a Sunday-school superintendent is bound by the Ten Commandments and the Mann Act. Sherman tries to save Shakespeare for the right-thinking by proving that he was an Iowa Methodist—a member of his local Chamber of Commerce, a contemner of Reds, an advocate of democracy and the League of Nations, a patriotic dollar-a-year-man during the Armada scare. Elmer More devotes himself, year in and year out, to denouncing the Romantic movement, *i.e.*, the effort to emancipate the artist from formulæ and categories, and so make him free to dance with arms and legs. And Babbitt, to make an end, gives over his days and his nights to deploring Rousseau's anarchistic abrogation of "the veto power" over the imagination, leading to such "wrongness" in both art and life that it threatens "to wreck civilization." In brief, the alarms of schoolmasters. Not many of them deal specifically with the literature that is in being. It is too near to be quite nice. To More or Babbitt only death can atone for the primary offense of the artist. But what they preach nevertheless has its echoes contemporaneously, and those echoes, in the main, are woefully falsetto. I often wonder what sort of picture of These States is conjured up by foreigners who read, say, Crothers, Van Dyke, Babbitt, the later Winston Churchill, and the old maids of the Freudian suppression school. How can such a foreigner, moving in those damp, asthmatic mists, imagine such phenomena as Roosevelt, Billy Sunday, Bryan, the Becker case, the I.W.W., Newport, Palm Beach, the University of Chicago, Chicago itself—the whole, gross, glittering, excessively dynamic, infinitely grotesque, incredibly stupendous drama of American life?

As I have said, it is not often that the *ordentlichen Professoren* deign to notice contemporary writers, even of their own austere kidney. In all the Shelburne Essays there is none on Howells, or on Churchill, or on Mrs. Wharton; More seems to think of American literature as expiring with Longfellow and Donald G. Mitchell. He has himself hinted that in the department of criticism of criticism there enters into the matter something beyond mere aloof ignorance. "I soon learned (as editor of the pre-Bolshevik *Nation*)," he says, "that it was virtually impossible to get fair consideration for a book written by a scholar not connected with a university from a reviewer so connected." This class consciousness, however, should not apply to artists, who are admittedly inferior to professors, and it surely does not show itself in such men as Phelps and Spingarn, who seem to be very eager to prove that they are not professorial. Yet Phelps, in the course of a long work on the novel, pointedly omits all mention of such men as Dreiser, and Spingarn, as the aforesaid Brooks has said, "appears to be less inclined even than the critics with whom he is theoretically at war to play an active, public part in the secular conflict of darkness and light." When one comes to the *Privat-Dozenten* there is less remoteness, but what takes the place of it is almost as saddening. To Sherman and Percy Boynton the one aim of criticism seems to be the enforcement of correctness—in Emerson's phrase, the upholding of "some great decorum, some fetish of a government, some ephemeral trade, or war, or man"—*e.g.*, Puritanism, democracy, monogamy, the League of Nations, the Wilsonian piffle. Even among the critics who escape the worst of this schoolmastering frenzy there is some touch of the heavy "culture" of the provincial schoolma'm. For example, consider Clayton Hamilton, M.A., vice-president of the National Institute of Arts and Letters. Here are the tests he proposes for dramatic critics, *i.e.*, for gentlemen chiefly employed in reviewing such characteristic American compositions as the Ziegfeld Follies, "Up in Mabel's Room," "Ben-Hur" and "The Witching Hour":

1. Have you ever stood bareheaded in the nave of Amiens?
2. Have you ever climbed to the Acropolis by moonlight?
3. Have you ever walked with whispers into the hushed presence of the Frari Madonna of Bellini?

What could more brilliantly evoke an image of the eternal Miss Birch, blue veil flying and Baedeker in hand, plodding along faithfully through the interminable corridors and catacombs of the Louvre, the while bands are playing across the river, and young bucks in three-gallon hats are sparking the gals, and the Jews and harlots uphold the traditions of French *hig leef* at Longchamps, and American deacons are frisked and debauched up on martyrs' hill? The banality of it is really too exquisite to be borne; the lack of humor is almost that of a Fifth avenue divine. One seldom finds in the pronunciamentoes of these dogged professors, indeed, any trace of either Attic or Gallic salt. When they essay to be jocose, the result is usually simply an elephantine whimsicality, by the chautauqua out of the *Atlantic Monthly*. Their satire is mere ill-nature. One finds it difficult to believe that they have ever read Lewes, or Hazlitt, or, above all, Saintsbury. I often wonder, in fact, how Saintsbury would fare, an unknown man, at the hands of, say, Brownell or More. What of his iconoclastic gayety, his boyish weakness for tweaking noses and pulling whiskers, his obscene delight in slang? . . .

4
The Ferment Underground

So much for the top layer. The bottom layer is given over to the literature of Greenwich Village, and by Greenwich Village, of course, I mean the whole of the advanced wing in letters, whatever the scene of its solemn declarations of independence and forlorn hopes. Miss Amy Lowell is herself a fully-equipped and automobile Greenwich Village, domiciled in Boston amid the crumbling gravestones of the New England *intelligentsia*, but often in waspish joy-ride through the hinterland. Vachel Lindsay, with his pilgrim's staff, is another. There is a third in Chicago, with *Poetry: A Magazine of Verse* as its Exhibit A; it is, in fact, the senior of the Village fornenst Washington Square. Others you will find in far-flung factory towns, wherever there is a Little Theater, and a couple of local Synges and Chekovs to supply its stage. St. Louis, before Zoë Akins took flight, had the busiest of all these Greenwiches, and the most interesting. What lies under the whole movement is the natural revolt of youth against the pedagogical Prussianism of the professors. The oppression is extreme, and so the rebellion is extreme. Imagine a sentimental young man of the provinces, awaking one morning to the somewhat startling discovery that he is full of the divine afflatus, and nominated by the hierarchy of hell to enrich the literature of his fatherland. He seeks counsel and aid. He finds, on consulting the official treatises on that literature, that its greatest poet was Longfellow. He is warned, reading More and Babbitt, that the literatus who lets feeling get into his compositions is a psychic fornicator, and under German influences. He has formal notice from Sherman that Puritanism is the lawful philosophy of the country, and that any dissent from it is treason. He gets the news, plowing through the New York *Times Book Review*, the *Nation* (so far to the left in its politics, but hugging the right so desperately in letters!), the *Bookman*, the *Atlantic* and the rest, that the salient artists of the living generation are such masters as Robert Underwood Johnson, Owen Wister, James Lane Allen, George E. Woodberry, Hamlin Garland, William Roscoe Thayer and Augustus Thomas, with polite bows to Margaret Deland, Mary Johnston and Ellen Glasgow. It slowly dawns upon him that Robert W. Chambers is an academician and Theodore Dreiser isn't, that Brian Hooker is and George Sterling isn't, that Henry Sydnor Harrison is and James Branch Cabell isn't, that "Chimmie Fadden" Townsend is and Sherwood Anderson isn't.

Is it any wonder that such a young fellow, after one or two sniffs of that prep-school fog, swings so vastly backward that one finds him presently in corduroy trousers and a velvet jacket, hammering furiously upon a pine table in a Macdougal street cellar, his mind full of malicious animal magnetism against even so amiable an old maid as Howells, and his discourse full of insane hair-splittings about *vers libre*, futurism, spectrism, vorticism, *Expressionismus*, *héliogabalisme*? The thing, in truth, is in the course of nature. The Spaniards who were outraged by the Palmerism of Torquemada did not become members of the Church of England; they became atheists. The American colonists, in revolt against a bad king, did not set up a good king; they set up a democracy, and so gave every honest man a chance to become a rogue on his own account. Thus the young literatus, emerging from the vacuum of Ohio or Arkansas. An early success, as we shall see, tends to halt and moderate him. He finds that, after all, there is still a place for him, a sort of asylum for such as he, not over-populated or very warmly-heated, but nevertheless quite real. But if his sledding at the start is hard, if the corrective birch finds him while he is still tender, then he goes, as Andrew Jackson would say, the whole hog, and another voice is added to the raucous bellowing of the literary Reds.

I confess that the spectacle gives me some joy, despite the fact that the actual output of the Village is seldom worth noticing. What commonly engulfs and spoils the Villagers is their concern with mere technique. Among them, it goes without saying, are a great many frauds—poets whose yearning to write is unaccompanied by anything properly describable as capacity, dramatists whose dramas are simply Schnitzler and well-water, workers in prose fiction who gravitate swiftly and inevitably to the machine-made merchandise of the cheap magazines—in brief, American equivalents of the bogus painters of the Boul' Mich'. These pretenders, having no ideas, naturally try to make the most of forms. Half the wars in the Village are over form; content is taken for granted, or forgotten altogether. The extreme leftists, in fact, descend to a meaningless gibberish, both in prose and in verse; it is their last defiance to intellectualism. This childish concentration upon externals unfortunately tends to debauch the small minority that is of more or less genuine parts; the good are pulled in by the bad. As a result, the Village produces nothing that justifies all the noise it makes. I have yet to hear of a first-rate book coming out of it, or a short story of arresting quality, or even a poem of any solid distinction. As one of the editors of a magazine which specializes in the work of new authors I am in an exceptional position to report. Probably nine-tenths of the stuff written in the dark dens and alleys south of the arch comes to my desk soon or late, and I go through all of it faithfully. It is, in the overwhelming main, jejune and imitative. The prose is quite without distinction, either in matter or in manner. The verse seldom gets beyond a hollow audaciousness, not unlike that of cubist painting. It is not often, indeed, that even personality is in it; all of the Villagers seem to write alike. "Unless one is an expert in some detective method," said a recent writer in *Poetry*, "one is at a loss to assign correctly the ownership of much free verse—that is, if one plays fairly and refuses to look at the signature until one has ventured a guess. It is difficult, for instance, to know whether Miss Lowell is writing Mr. Bynner's verse, or whether he is writing hers." Moreover, this monotony keeps to a very low level. There is no poet in the movement who has produced anything even remotely approaching the fine lyrics of Miss Reese, Miss Teasdale and John McClure, and for all its war upon the *cliché* it can show nothing to equal the *cliché*-free beauty of Robert Loveman's "Rain Song." In the drama the Village has gone further. In Eugene O'Neill, Rita Wellman and Zoë Akins it offers dramatists who are obviously many cuts above the well-professored mechanicians who pour out of Prof. Dr. Baker's *Ibsenfabrik* at Cambridge. But here we must probably give the credit, not to any influence residing within the movement itself, but to mere acts of God. Such pieces as O'Neill's one-acters, Miss Wellman's "The Gentile Wife" and Miss Akins' extraordinary "Papa" lie quite outside the Village scheme of things. There is no sign of formal revolt in them. They are simply first-rate work, done miraculously in a third-rate land.

But if the rebellion is thus sterile of direct results, and, in more than one aspect, fraudulent and ridiculous, it is at all events an evidence of something not to be disregarded, and that something is the gradual formulation of a challenge to the accepted canons in letters and to the accepted canon lawyers. The first hoots come from a tatterdemalion horde of rogues and vagabonds without the gates, but soon or late, let us hope, they will be echoed in more decorous quarters, and with much greater effect. The Village, in brief, is an earnest that somewhere or other new seeds are germinating. Between the young tutor who launches into letters with imitations of his seminary chief's imitations of Agnes Repplier's imitations of Charles Lamb, and the young peasant who tries to get his honest exultations into free verse there can be no hesitant choice: the peasant is, by long odds, the sounder artist, and, what is more, the sounder American artist. Even the shy and somewhat stagey carnality that characterizes the Village has its high symbolism and its profound uses. It proves that, despite repressions unmatched in civilization in modern times, there is still a sturdy animality in American youth, and hence good health. The poet hugging his Sonia in a Washington square beanery, and so giving notice to all his world that he is a devil of a fellow, is at least a better man than the emasculated stripling in a Y.M.C.A. gospel-mill, pumped dry of all his natural appetites and the vacuum filled with double-entry book-keeping, business economics and autoerotism. In so foul a nest of imprisoned and fermenting sex as the United States, plain fornication becomes a mark of relative decency.

5
In the Literary Abattoir

But the theme is letters, not wickedness. The upper and lower layers have been surveyed. There remains the middle layer, the thickest and perhaps the most significant of the three. By the middle layer I mean the literature that fills the magazines and burdens the book-counters in the department-stores—the literature adorned by such artists as Richard Harding Davis, Rex Beach, Emerson Hough, O. Henry, James Whitcomb Riley, Augustus Thomas, Robert W. Chambers, Henry Sydnor Harrison, Owen Johnson, Cyrus Townsend Brady, Irvin Cobb and Mary Roberts Rinehart—in brief, the literature that pays like a bucket-shop or a soap-factory, and is thus thoroughly American. At the bottom this literature touches such depths of banality that it would be difficult to match it in any other country. The "inspirational" and patriotic essays of Dr. Frank Crane, Orison Swett Marden, Porter Emerson Browne, Gerald Stanley Lee, E. S. Martin, Ella Wheeler Wilcox and the Rev. Dr. Newell Dwight Hillis, the novels of Harold Bell Wright, Eleanor H. Porter and Gene Stratton-Porter, and the mechanical sentimentalities in prose and verse that fill the cheap fiction magazines—this stuff has a native quality that is as unmistakable as that of Mother's Day, Billy-Sundayism or the Junior Order of United American Mechanics. It is the natural outpouring of a naïve and yet half barbarous people, full of delight in a few childish and inaccurate ideas. But it would be a grave error to assume that the whole of the literature of the middle layer is of the same infantile quality. On the contrary, a great deal of it—for example, the work of Mrs. Rinehart, and that of Corra Harris, Gouverneur Morris, Harold MacGrath and the late O. Henry—shows an unmistakably technical excellence, and even a certain civilized sophistication in point of view. Moreover, this literature is constantly graduating adept professors into something finer, as witness Booth Tarkington, Zona Gale, Ring W. Lardner and Montague Glass. S. L. Clemens came out of it forty years ago. Nevertheless, its general tendency is distinctly in the other direction. It seduces by the power of money, and by the power of great acclaim no less. One constantly observes the collapse and surrender of writers who started out with aims far above that of the magazine nabob. I could draw up a long, long list of such victims: Henry Milner Rideout, Jack London, Owen Johnson, Chester Bailey Fernald, Hamlin Garland, Will Levington Comfort, Stephen French Whitman, James Hopper, Harry Leon Wilson, and so on. They had their forerunner, in the last generation, in Bret Harte. It is, indeed, a characteristic American phenomenon for a young writer to score a success with novel and meritorious work, and then to yield himself to the best-seller fever, and so disappear down the sewers. Even the man who struggles to emerge again is commonly hauled back. For example, Louis Joseph Vance, Rupert Hughes, George Bronson-Howard, and, to go back a few years, David Graham Phillips and Elbert Hubbard—all men flustered by high aspiration, and yet all pulled down by the temptations below. Even Frank Norris showed signs of yielding. The pull is genuinely powerful. Above lies not only isolation, but also a dogged and malignant sort of opposition. Below, as Morris has frankly admitted, there is the place at Aiken, the motor-car, babies, money in the bank, and the dignity of an important man.

It is a commonplace of the envious to put all the blame upon the *Saturday Evening Post*, for in its pages many of the Magdalens of letters are to be found, and out of its bulging coffers comes much of the lure. But this is simply blaming the bull for the sins of all the cows. The *Post*, as a matter of fact, is a good deal less guilty than such magazines as the *Cosmopolitan*, *Hearst's*, *McClure's* and the *Metropolitan*, not to mention the larger women's magazines. In the *Post* one often discerns an effort to rise above the level of shoe-drummer fiction. It is edited by a man who, almost alone among editors of the great periodicals of the country, is himself a writer of respectable skill. It has brought out (after lesser publications unearthed them) a member of authors of very solid talents, notably Glass, Lardner and E. W. Howe. It has been extremely hospitable to men not immediately comprehensible to the mob, for example, Dreiser and Hergesheimer. Most of all, it has avoided the Barnum-like exploitation of such native bosh-mongers as Crane, Hillis and Ella Wheeler Wilcox, and of such exotic mountebanks as D'Annunzio, Hall Caine and Maeterlinck. In brief, the *Post* is a great deal better than ever Greenwich Village and the Cambridge campus are disposed to admit. It is the largest of all the literary Hog Islands, but it is by no means the worst. Appealing primarily to the great masses of right-thinking and unintelligent Americans, it must necessarily print a great deal of preposterous tosh, but it flavors the mess with not a few things of a far higher quality, and at its worst it is seldom downright idiotic. In many of the other great magazines one finds stuff that it would be difficult to describe in any other words. It is gaudily romantic, furtively sexual, and full of rubber-stamp situations and personages—a sort of amalgam of the worst drivel of Marie Corelli, Elinor Glyn, E. Phillips Oppenheim, William Le Quex and Hall Caine. This is the literature of the middle layer—the product of the national Rockefellers and Duponts of letters. This is the sort of thing that the young author of facile pen is encouraged to manufacture. This is the material of the best sellers and the movies.

Of late it is the movies that have chiefly provoked its composition: the rewards they offer are even greater than those held out by the commercial book-publishers and the train-boy magazines. The point of view of an author responsive to such rewards was recently set forth very naïvely in the *Authors' League Bulletin*. This author undertook, in a short article, to refute the fallacies of an unknown who ventured to protest against the movies on the ground that they called only for bald plots, elementary and generally absurd, and that all the rest of a sound writer's equipment—"the artistry of his style, the felicity of his apt expression, his subtlety and thoroughness of observation and comprehension and sympathy, the illuminating quality of his analysis of motive and character, even the fundamental skillful development of the bare plot"—was disdained by the Selznicks, Goldfishes, Zukors and other such *entrepreneurs*, and by the overwhelming majority of their customers. I quote from the reply:

> There are some conspicuous word merchants who deal in the English language, but the general public doesn't clamor for their wares. They write for the "thinking class." The élite, the discriminating. As a rule, they scorn the crass commercialism of the magazines and movies and such catchpenny devices. However, literary masterpieces live because they have been and will be read, not by the few, but by the many. That was true in the time of Homer, and even to-day the first

move made by an editor when he receives a manuscript, or a gentle reader when he buys a book, or a T.B.M. when he sinks into an orchestra chair is to look around for John Henry Plot. If Mr. Plot is too long delayed in arriving or doesn't come at all, the editor usually sends regrets, the reader yawns and the tired business man falls asleep. It's a sad state of affairs and awful tough on art, but it can't be helped.

Observe the lofty scorn of mere literature—the superior irony at the expense of everything beyond the bumping of boobs. Note the sound judgment as to the function and fate of literary masterpieces, *e.g.*, "Endymion," "The Canterbury Tales," "Faust," "Typhoon." Give your eye to the chaste diction—"John Henry Plot," "T.B.M.," "awful tough," and so on. No doubt you will at once assume that this curious counterblast to literature was written by some former bartender now engaged in composing scenarios for Pearl White and Theda Bara. But it was not. It was written and signed by the president of the Authors' League of America.

Here we have, unconsciously revealed, the secret of the depressing badness of what may be called the staple fiction of the country—the sort of stuff that is done by the Richard Harding Davises, Rex Beaches, Houghs, McCutcheons, and their like, male and female. The worse of it is not that it is addressed primarily to shoe-drummers and shop-girls; the worst of it is that it is written by authors who *are*, to all intellectual intents and purposes, shoe-drummers and shop-girls. American literature, even on its higher levels, seldom comes out of the small and lonesome upper classes of the people. An American author with traditions behind him and an environment about him comparable to those, say, of George Moore, or Hugh Walpole, or E. F. Benson is and always has been relatively rare. On this side of the water the arts, like politics and religion, are chiefly in the keeping of persons of obscure origin, defective education and elemental tastes. Even some of the most violent upholders of the New England superstition are aliens to the actual New England heritage; one discovers, searching "Who's Who in America," that they are recent fugitives from the six-day sock and saleratus *Kultur* of the cow and hog States. The artistic merchandise produced by liberated yokels of that sort is bound to show its intellectual newness, which is to say, its deficiency in civilized culture and sophistication. It is, on the plane of letters, precisely what evangelical Christianity is on the plane of religion, to wit, the product of ill-informed, emotional and more or less pushing and oafish folk. Life, to such Harvardized peasants, is not a mystery; it is something absurdly simple, to be described with surety and in a few words. If they set up as critics their criticism is all a matter of facile labeling, chiefly ethical; find the pigeon-hole, and the rest is easy. If they presume to discuss the great problems of human society, they are equally ready with their answers: draw up and pass a harsh enough statute, and the corruptible will straightway put on incorruption. And if, fanned by the soft breath of beauty, they go into practice as creative artists, as poets, as dramatists, as novelists, then one learns from them that we inhabit a country that is the model and despair of other states, that its culture is coextensive with human culture and enlightenment, and that every failure to find happiness under that culture is the result of sin.

6
Underlying Causes

Here is one of the fundamental defects of American fiction —perhaps the one character that sets it off sharply from all other known kinds of contemporary fiction. It habitually exhibits, not a man of delicate organization in revolt against the inexplicable tragedy of existence, but a man of low sensibilities and elemental desires yielding himself gladly to his environment, and so achieving what, under a third-rate civilization, passes for success. To get on: this is the aim. To weigh and reflect, to doubt and rebel: this is the thing to be avoided. I describe the optimistic, the inspirational, the Authors' League, the popular magazine, the peculiarly American school. In character creation its masterpiece is the advertising agent who, by devising some new and super-imbecile boob-trap, puts his hook-and-eye factory "on the map," ruins all other factories, marries the daughter of his boss, and so ends as an eminent man. Obviously, the drama underlying such fiction—what Mr. Beach would call its John Henry Plot—is false drama, Sunday-school drama, puerile and disgusting drama. It is the sort of thing that awakens a response only in men who are essentially unimaginative, timorous and degraded—in brief, in democrats, bagmen, yahoos. The man of reflective habit cannot conceivably take any passionate interest in the conflicts it deals with. He doesn't want to marry the daughter of the owner of the hook-and-eye factory; he would probably burn down the factory itself if it ever came into his hands. What interests this man is the far more poignant and significant conflict between a salient individual and the harsh and meaningless fiats of destiny, the unintelligible mandates and vagaries of God. His hero is not one who yields and wins, but one who resists and fails.

Most of these conflicts, of course, are internal, and hence do not make themselves visible in the overt melodrama of the Beaches, Davises and Chamberses. A superior man's struggle in the world is not with exterior lions, trusts, margraves, policemen, rivals in love, German spies, radicals and tornadoes, but with the obscure, atavistic impulses within him—the impulses, weaknesses and limitations that war with his notion of what life should be. Nine times out of ten he succumbs. Nine times out of ten he must yield to the dead hand. Nine times out of ten his aspiration is almost infinitely above his achievement. The result is that we see him sliding downhill—his ideals breaking up, his hope petering out, his character in decay. Character in decay is thus the theme of the great bulk of superior fiction. One has it in Dostoievsky, in Balzac, in Hardy, in Conrad, in Flaubert, in Zola, in Turgenieff, in Goethe, in Sudermann, in Bennett, and, to come home, in Dreiser. In nearly all first-rate novels the hero is defeated. In perhaps a majority he is completely destroyed. The hero of the inferior—*i.e.*, the typically American—novel engages in no such doomed and fateful combat. His conflict is not with the inexplicable ukases of destiny, the limitations of his own strength, the dead hand upon him, but simply with the superficial desires of his elemental fellow men. He thus has a fair chance of winning—and in bad fiction that chance is always converted into a certainty. So he marries the daughter of the owner of the factory and eventually gobbles the factory itself. His success gives thrills to persons who can imagine no higher aspiration. He embodies their optimism, as the other hero embodies the pessimism of more introspective and idealistic men. He is the protagonist of that great majority which is so inferior that it is quite unconscious of its inferiority.

It is this superficiality of the inferior man, it seems to me, that is the chief hallmark of the American novel. Whenever one encounters a novel that rises superior to it the thing takes on a subtle but unmistakable air of foreignness—for example, Frank Norris' "Vandover and the Brute," Hergesheimer's "The Lay Anthony" and Miss Cather's "My Antonía," or, to drop to short stories, Stephen Crane's "The Blue Hotel" and Mrs. Wharton's "Ethan Frome." The short story is commonly regarded, at least by American critics, as a preëminently American form; there are even patriots who argue that Bret Harte invented it. It meets very accurately, in fact, certain characteristic demands of the American temperament: it is simple, economical and brilliantly effective. Yet the same hollowness that marks the American novel also marks the American short story. Its great masters, in late years, have been such cheese-mongers as Davis, with his servant-girl romanticism, and O. Henry, with his smoke-room and variety show smartness. In the whole canon of O. Henry's work you will not find a single recognizable human character; his people are unanimously marionettes; he makes Mexican brigands, Texas cowmen and New York cracksmen talk the same highly ornate Broadwayese. The successive volumes of Edward J. O'Brien's "Best Short-Story" series throw a vivid light upon the feeble estate of the art in the land. O'Brien, though his æsthetic judgments are ludicrous, at least selects stories that are thoroughly representative; his books are trade successes because the crowd is undoubtedly with him. He has yet to discover a single story that even the most naïve professor would venture to mention in the same breath with Joseph Conrad's "Heart of Darkness," or Andrieff's "Silence," or Sudermann's "Das Sterbelied," or the least considerable tale by Anatole France. In many of the current American makers of magazine short stories—for example, Gouverneur Morris—one observes, as I have said, a truly admirable technical skill. They have mastered the externals of the form. They know how to get their effects. But in content their work is as hollow as a jug. Such stuff has no imaginable relation to life as men live it in the world. It is as artificial as the heroic strut and romantic eyes of a moving-picture actor.

I have spoken of the air of foreignness that clings to certain exceptional American compositions. In part it is based upon a psychological trick—upon the surprise which must inevitably seize upon any one who encounters a decent piece of writing in so vast a desert of mere literacy. But in part it is grounded soundly enough on the facts. The native author of any genuine force and originality is almost invariably found to be under strong foreign influences, either English or Continental. It was so in the earliest days. Freneau, the poet of the Revolution, was thoroughly French in blood and traditions. Irving, as H. R. Haweis has said, "took to England as a duck takes to water," and was in exile seventeen years. Cooper, with the great success of "The Last of the Mohicans" behind him, left the country in disgust and was gone for seven years. Emerson, Bryant, Lowell, Hawthorne and even Longfellow kept their eyes turned across the water; Emerson, in fact, was little more than an importer and popularizer of German and French ideas. Bancroft studied in Germany; Prescott, like Irving, was enchanted by Spain. Poe, unable to follow the fashion, invented mythical travels to save his face—to France, to Germany, to the Greek isles. The Civil War revived the national consciousness enormously, but it did not halt the movement of *émigrés.* Henry James, in the seventies, went to England, Bierce and Bret Harte followed him, and even Mark Twain, absolutely American though he was, was forever pulling up stakes and setting out for Vienna, Florence or London. Only poverty tied Whitman to the soil; his audience, for many years, was chiefly beyond the water, and there, too, he often longed to be. This distaste for the national scene is often based upon a genuine alienness. The more, indeed, one investigates the ancestry of Americans who have won distinction in the fine arts, the more one discovers tempting game for the critical Know Nothings. Whitman was half Dutch, Harte was half Jew, Poe was partly German, James had an Irish grandfather, Howells was largely Irish and German, Dreiser is German and Hergesheimer is Pennsylvania Dutch. Fully a half of the painters discussed in John C. van Dyke's "American Painting and Its Tradition" were of mixed blood, with the Anglo-Saxon plainly recessive. And of the five poets singled out for encomium by Miss Lowell in "Tendencies in Modern American Poetry" one is a Swede, two are partly German, one was educated in the German language, and three of the five exiled themselves to England as soon as they got out of their nonage. The exiles are of all sorts: Frank Harris, Vincent O'Sullivan, Ezra Pound, Herman Scheffauer, T. S. Eliot, Henry B. Fuller, Stuart Merrill, Edith Wharton. They go to England, France, Germany, Italy—anywhere to escape. Even at home the literatus is perceptibly foreign in his mien. If he lies under the New England tradition he is furiously colonial—more English than the English. If he turns to revolt, he is apt to put on a French hat and a Russian red blouse. *The Little Review*, the organ of the extreme wing of *révoltés*, is so violently exotic that several years ago, during the plupatriotic days of the war, some of its readers protested. With characteristic lack of humor it replied with an American number—and two of the stars of that number bore the fine old Anglo-Saxon names of Ben Hecht and Elsa von Freytag-Loringhoven.

This tendency of American literature, the moment it begins to show enterprise, novelty and significance, to radiate an alien smell is not an isolated phenomenon. The same smell accompanies practically all other sorts of intellectual activity in the republic. Whenever one hears that a new political theory is in circulation, or a scientific heresy, or a movement toward rationalism in religion, it is always safe to guess that some discontented stranger or other has a hand in it. In the newspapers and on the floor of Congress a new heterodoxy is always denounced forthwith as a product of foreign plotting, and here public opinion undoubtedly supports both the press and the politicians, and with good reason. The native culture of the country—that is, the culture of the low caste Anglo-Saxons who preserve the national tradition—is almost completely incapable of producing ideas. It is a culture that roughly corresponds to what the culture of England would be if there were no universities over there, and no caste of intellectual individualists and no landed aristocracy—in other words, if the tone of the national thinking were set by the nonconformist industrials, the camorra of Welsh and Scotch political scoundrels, and the town and country mobs. As we shall see, the United States has not yet produced anything properly describable as an aristocracy, and so there is no impediment to the domination of the inferior orders. Worse, the Anglo-Saxon strain, second-rate at the start, has tended to degenerate steadily to lower levels—in New England, very markedly. The result is that there is not only a great dearth of ideas in the land, but also an active and relentless hostility to ideas. The chronic suspiciousness of the inferior man here has full play; never in modern history has there been another civilization showing so vast a body of prohibitions and repressions, in both conduct and thought. The second result is that intellectual experimentation is chiefly left to the immigrants of the later migrations, and to the small sections of the native population that have been enriched with their blood. For such a pure Anglo-Saxon as Cabell to disport himself in the field of ideas is a rarity in the United States—and no exception to the rule that I have just mentioned, for Cabell belongs to an aristocracy that is now almost extinct, and has no more in common with the general population than a Baltic baron has with the indigenous herd of Letts and Esthonians. All the arts in America are thoroughly exotic. Music is almost wholly German or Italian, painting is French, literature may be anything from English to Russian, architecture (save when it becomes a mere branch of engineering) is a maddening phantasmagoria of borrowings. Even so elemental an art as that of cookery shows no native development, and is greatly disesteemed by Americans of the Anglo-Saxon majority; any decent restaurant that one blunders upon in the land is likely to be French, and if not French, then Italian or German or Chinese. So with the sciences: they have scarcely any native development. Organized scientific research began in the country with the founding of the Johns Hopkins University, a bald imitation of the German universities, and long held suspect by native opinion. Even after its great success, indeed, there was rancorous hostility to its scheme of things on chauvinistic grounds, and some years ago efforts were begun to Americanize it, with the result that it is now sunk to the level of Princeton, Amherst and other such glorified high-schools, and is dominated by native savants who would be laughed at in any Continental university. Science, oppressed by such assaults from below, moves out of the academic grove into the freer air of the great foundations, where the pursuit of the shy fact is uncontaminated by football and social pushing. The greatest of these foundations is the Rockefeller Institute. Its salient men are such investigators as Flexner, Loeb and Carrel—all of them Continental Jews.

Thus the battle of ideas in the United States is largely carried on under strange flags, and even the stray natives on the side of free inquiry have to sacrifice some of their nationality when they enlist. The effects of this curious condition of affairs are both good and evil. The good ones are easily apparent. The racial division gives the struggle a certain desperate earnestness, and even bitterness, and so makes it the more inviting to lively minds. It was a benefit to the late D. C. Gilman rather than a disadvantage that national opinion opposed his traffic with Huxley and the German professors in the early days of the Johns Hopkins; the stupidity of the opposition stimulated him, and made him resolute, and his resolution, in the long run, was of inestimable cultural value. Scientific research in America, indeed, was thus set securely upon its legs precisely because the great majority of right-thinking Americans were violently opposed to it. In the same way it must be obvious that Dreiser got something valuable out of the grotesque war that was carried on against him during the greater war overseas because of his German name—a *jehad* fundamentally responsible for the suppression of "The 'Genius.'" The chief danger that he ran six or seven years ago was the danger that he might be accepted, explained away, and so seduced downward to the common level. The attack of professional patriots saved him from that calamity. More, it filled him with a keen sense of his isolation, and stirred up the vanity that was in him as it is in all of us, and so made him cling with new tenacity to the very peculiarities that differentiate him from his inferiors. Finally, it is not to be forgotten that, without this rebellion of immigrant iconoclasts, the whole body of the national literature would tend to sink to the 100% American level of such patriotic literary business men as the president of the Authors' League. In other words, we must put up with the æsthetic Bolshevism of the Europeans and Asiatics who rage in the land, for without them we might not have any literature at all.

But the evils of the situation are not to be gainsaid. One of them I have already alluded to: the tendency of the beginning literatus, once he becomes fully conscious of his foreign affiliations, to desert the republic forthwith, and thereafter view it from afar, and as an actual foreigner. More solid and various cultures lure him; he finds himself uncomfortable at home. Sometimes, as in the case of Henry James, he becomes a downright expatriate, and a more or less active agent of anti-American feeling; more often, he goes over to the outlanders without yielding up his theoretical citizenship, as in the cases of Irving, Harris, Pound and O'Sullivan. But all this, of course, works relatively light damage, for not many native authors are footloose enough to indulge in any such physical desertion of the soil. Of much more evil importance is the tendency of the cultural alienism that I have described to fortify the uncontaminated native in his bilious suspicion of all the arts, and particularly of all artists. The news that the latest poet to flutter the dovecotes is a Jew, or that the last novelist mauled by comstockery has a German or Scandinavian or Russian name, or that the critic newly taken in sacrilege is a partisan of Viennese farce or of the French moral code or of English literary theory—this news, among a people so ill-informed, so horribly well-trained in flight from bugaboos, and so savagely suspicious of the unfamiliar in ideas, has the inevitable effect of stirring up opposition that quickly ceases to be purely æsthetic objection, and so becomes increasingly difficult to combat. If Dreiser's name were Tompkins or Simpson, there is no doubt whatever that he would affright the professors a good deal less, and appear less of a hobgoblin to the *intelligentsia* of the women's clubs. If Oppenheim were less palpably levantine, he would come much nearer to the popularity of Edwin Markham and Walt Mason. And if Cabell kept to the patriotic business of a Southern gentleman, to wit, the praise of General Robert E. Lee, instead of prowling the strange and terrible fields of mediæval Provence, it is a safe wager that he would be sold openly over the counter instead of stealthily behind the door.

In a previous work I have discussed this tendency in America to estimate the artist in terms of his secular character. During the war, when all of the national defects in intelligence were enormously accentuated, it went to ludicrous lengths. There were then only authors who were vociferous patriots and thus geniuses, and authors who kept their dignity and were thus suspect and without virtue. By this gauge Chambers became the superior of Dreiser and Cabell, and Joyce Kilmer and Amy Lowell were set above Sandburg and Oppenheim. The test was even extended to foreigners: by it H. G. Wells took precedence of Shaw, and Blasco Ibáñez became a greater artist than Romain Rolland. But the thing is not peculiar to war times; when peace is densest it is to be observed. The man of letters, pure and simple, is a rarity in America. Almost always he is something else—and that something else commonly determines his public eminence. Mark Twain, with only his books to recommend him, would probably have passed into obscurity in middle age; it was in the character of a public entertainer, not unrelated to Coxey, Dr. Mary Walker and Citizen George Francis Train, that he wooed and won his country. The official criticism of the land denied him any solid literary virtue to the day of his death, and even to-day the campus critics and their journalistic valets stand aghast before "The Mysterious Stranger" and "What is Man?" Emerson passed through almost the same experience. It was not as a man of letters that he was chiefly thought of in his time, but as the prophet of a new cult, half religious, half philosophical, and wholly unintelligible to nine-tenths of those who discussed it. The first author of a handbook of American literature to sweep away the codfish Moses and expose the literary artist was the Polish Jew, Leon Kellner, of Czernowitz. So with Whitman and Poe—both hobgoblins far more than artists. So, even, with Howells: it was as the exponent of a dying culture that he was venerated, not as the practitioner of an art. Few actually read his books. His celebrity, of course, was real enough, but it somehow differed materially from that of a pure man of letters—say Shelley, Conrad, Hauptmann, Hardy or Synge. That he was himself keenly aware of the national tendency to judge an artist in terms of the citizen was made plain at the time of the Gorky scandal, when he joined Clemens in an ignominious desertion of Gorky, scared out of his wits by the danger of being manhandled for a violation of the national pecksniffery. Howells also refused to sign the Dreiser Protest.

The case of Frank Harris is one eloquently in point. Harris has written, among other books, perhaps the best biography ever done by an American. Yet his politics keep him in a sort of Coventry and the average American critic would no more think of praising him than of granting Treitschke any merit as an historian.

7
The Lonesome Artist

Thus falsely judged by standards that have no intelligible appositeness when applied to an artist, however accurately they may weigh a stockbroker or a Presbyterian elder, and forced to meet not only the hunkerous indifference of the dominant mob but also the bitter and disingenuous opposition of the classes to which he might look reasonably for understanding and support, the American author is forced into a sort of social and intellectual vacuum, and lives out his days, as Henry James said of Hawthorne, "an alien everywhere, an æsthetic solitary."

The wonder is that, in the face of so metallic and unyielding a front, any genuine artists in letters come to the front at all. But they constantly emerge; the first gestures are always on show; the prodigal and gorgeous life of the country simply forces a sensitive minority to make some attempt at representation and interpretation, and out of many trying there often appears one who can. The phenomenon of Dreiser is not unique. He had his forerunners in Fuller and Frank Norris and he has his *compagnons du voyage* in Anderson, Charles G. Norris and more than one other. But the fact only throws up his curious isolation in a stronger light. It would be difficult to imagine an artist of his sober purpose and high accomplishment, in any civilized country, standing so neglected. The prevailing criticism, when it cannot dispose of him by denying that he exists—in the two chief handbooks of latter-day literature by professors he is not even mentioned!—seeks to dispose of him by arraying the shoddy fury of the mob against him. When he was under attack by the Comstocks, more than one American critic gave covert aid to the common enemy, and it was with difficulty that the weight of the Authors' League was held upon his side. More help for him, in fact, came from England, and quite voluntarily, than could be drummed up for him at home. No public sense of the menace that the attack offered to free speech and free art was visible; it would have made a nine-days' sensation for any layman of public influence to have gone to his rescue, as would have certainly happened in France, England or Germany. As for the newspaper-reading mob, it probably went unaware of the business altogether. When Arnold Bennett, landing in New York some time previously, told the reporters that Dreiser was the American he most desired to meet, the news was quite unintelligible to perhaps nine readers out of ten: they had no more heard of Dreiser than their fathers had heard of Whitman in 1875.

So with all the rest. I have mentioned Harris. It would be difficult to imagine Rolland meeting such a fate in France or Shaw in England as he has met in the United States. O'Sullivan, during the war, came home with "A Good Girl" in his pocket. The book was republished here—and got vastly less notice than the latest piece of trade-goods by Kathleen Norris. Fuller, early in his career, gave it up as hopeless. Norris died vainly battling for the young Dreiser. An Abraham Cahan goes unnoticed. Miss Cather, with four sound books behind her, lingers in the twilight of an esoteric reputation. Cabell, comstocked, is apprehended by his country only as a novelist to be bought by stealth and read in private. When Hugh Walpole came to America a year or two ago he favored the newspapers, like Bennett before him, with a piece of critical news that must have puzzled all readers save a very small minority. Discussing the living American novelists worth heeding, he nominated three—and of them only one was familiar to the general run of novel-buyers, or had ever been mentioned by a native critic of the apostolic succession. Only the poets of the land seem to attract the notice of the professors, and no doubt this is largely because most of the more salient of them—notably Miss Lowell and Lindsay—are primarily press-agents. Even so, the attention that they get is seldom serious. The only professor that I know of who has discussed the matter in precise terms holds that Alfred Noyes is the superior of all of them. Moreover, the present extraordinary interest in poetry stops short with a few poets, and one of its conspicuous phenomena is its lack of concern with the poets outside the movement, some of them unquestionably superior to any within.

Nor is this isolation of the artist in America new. The contemporary view of Poe and Whitman was almost precisely like the current view of Dreiser and Cabell. Both were neglected by the Brahmins of their time, and both were regarded hostilely by the great body of right-thinking citizens. Poe, indeed, was the victim of a furious attack by Rufus W. Griswold, the Hamilton Wright Mabie of the time, and it set the tone of native criticism for years. Whitman, living, narrowly escaped going to jail as a public nuisance. One thinks of Hawthorne and Emerson as writers decently appreciated by their contemporaries, but it is not to be forgotten that the official criticism of the era saw no essential difference between Hawthorne and Cooper, and that Emerson's reputation, to the end of his life, was far more that of a theological prophet and ethical platitudinarian, comparable to Lyman Abbott or Frank Crane, than that of a literary artist, comparable to Tennyson or Matthew Arnold. Perhaps Carlyle understood him, but who in America understood him? To this day he is the victim of gross misrepresentation by enthusiasts who read into him all sorts of flatulent bombast, as Puritanism is read into the New Testament by Methodists. As for Hawthorne, his extraordinary physical isolation during his lifetime was but the symbol of a complete isolation of the spirit, still surviving. If his preference for the internal conflict as opposed to the external act were not sufficient to set him off from the main stream of American speculation, there would always be his profound ethical skepticism —a state of mind quite impossible to the normal American, at least of Anglo-Saxon blood. Hawthorne, so far as I know, has never had a single professed follower in his own country. Even his son, attempting to carry on his craft, yielded neither to his meticulous method nor to his detached point of view. In the third generation, with infinite irony, there is a grand-daughter who is a reviewer of books for the New York *Times*, which is almost as if Wagner should have a grand-daughter singing in the operas of Massenet.

Of the four indubitable masters thus named, Hawthorne, Emerson, Whitman and Poe, only the last two have been sufficiently taken into the consciousness of the country to have any effect upon its literature, and even here that influence has been exerted only at second-hand, and against very definite adverse pressure. It would certainly seem reasonable for a man of so forceful a habit of mind as Poe, and of such prodigal and arresting originality, to have founded a school, but a glance at the record shows that he did nothing of the sort. Immediately he was dead, the shadows of the Irving tradition closed around his tomb, and for nearly thirty years thereafter all of his chief ideas went disregarded in his own country. If, as the literature books argue, Poe was the father of the American short story, then it was a posthumous child, and had step-fathers who did their best to conceal its true parentage. When it actually entered upon the vigorous life that we know to-day Poe had been dead for a generation. Its father, at the time of its belated adolescence, seemed to be Bret Harte—and Harte's debt to Dickens was vastly more apparent, first and last, than his debt to Poe. What he got from Poe was essential; it was the inner structure of the modern short story, the fundamental devices whereby a mere glimpse at events could be made to yield brilliant and seemingly complete images. But he himself was probably largely unaware of this indebtedness. A man little given to critical analysis, and incompetent for it when his own work was under examination, he saw its externals much more clearly than he saw its intrinsic organization, and these externals bore the plain marks of Dickens. It remained for one of his successors, Ambrose Bierce, to bridge belatedly the space separating him from Poe, and so show the route that he had come. And it remained for foreign criticism, and particularly for French criticism, to lift Poe himself to the secure place that he now holds. It is true enough that he enjoyed, during his lifetime, a certain popular reputation, and that he was praised by such men as N. P. Willis and James Russell Lowell, but that reputation was considerably less than the fame of men who were much his inferiors, and that praise, especially in Lowell's case, was much corrupted by reservations. Not many native critics of respectable position, during the 50's and 60's, would have ranked him clearly above, say, Irving or Cooper, or even above Longfellow, his old enemy. A few partisans argued for him, but in the main, as Saintsbury has said, he was the victim of "extreme and almost incomprehensible injustice" at the hands of his countrymen. It is surely not without significance that it took ten years to raise money enough to put a cheap and hideous tombstone upon his neglected grave, that it was not actually set up until he had been dead twenty-six years, that no contemporary American writer took any part in furthering the project, and that the only one who attended the final ceremony was Whitman.

It was Baudelaire's French translation of the prose tales and Mallarmé's translation of the poems that brought Poe to Valhalla. The former, first printed in 1856, founded the Poe cult in France, and during the two decades following it flourished amazingly, and gradually extended to England and Germany. It was one of the well-springs, in fact, of the whole so-called decadent movement. If Baudelaire, the father of that movement, "cultivated hysteria with delight and terror," he was simply doing what Poe had done before him. Both, reacting against the false concept of beauty as a mere handmaiden of logical ideas, sought its springs in those deep feelings and inner experiences which lie beyond the range of ideas and are to be interpreted only as intuitions. Emerson started upon the same quest, but was turned off into mazes of contradiction and unintelligibility by his ethical obsession—the unescapable burden of his Puritan heritage. But Poe never wandered from the path. You will find in "The Poetic Principle" what is perhaps the clearest statement of this new and sounder concept of beauty that has ever been made—certainly it is clearer than any ever made by a Frenchman. But it was not until Frenchmen had watered the seed out of grotesque and vari-colored pots that it began to sprout. The tide of Poe's ideas, set in motion in France early in the second half of the century, did not wash England until the last decade, and in America, save for a few dashes of spray, it has yet to show itself. There is no American writer who displays the influence of this most potent and original of Americans so clearly as whole groups of Frenchmen display it, and whole groups of Germans, and even a good many Englishmen. What we have from Poe at first hand is simply a body of obvious yokel-shocking in the *Black Cat* manner, with the tales of Ambrose Bierce as its finest flower—in brief, an imitation of Poe's externals without any comprehension whatever of his underlying aims and notions. What we have from him at second-hand is a somewhat childish Maeterlinckism, a further dilution of Poe-and-water. This Maeterlinckism, some time ago, got itself intermingled with the Whitmanic stream flowing back to America through the channel of French Imagism, with results destructive to the sanity of earnest critics and fatal to the gravity of those less austere. It is significant that the critical writing of Poe, in which there lies most that was best in him, has not come back; no normal American ever thinks of him as a critic, but only as a poet, as a raiser of goose-flesh, or as an immoral fellow. The cause thereof is plain enough. The French, instead of borrowing his critical theory directly, deduced it afresh from his applications of it; it became criticism *of* him rather than *by* him. Thus his own speculations have lacked the authority of foreign approval, and have consequently made no impression. The weight of native opinion is naturally against them, for they are at odds, not only with its fundamental theories, but also with its practical doctrine that no criticism can be profound and respectable which is not also dull.

"Poe," says Arthur Ransome, in his capital study of the man and the artist, "was like a wolf chained by the leg among a lot of domestic dogs." The simile here is somewhat startling, and Ransome, in a footnote, tries to ameliorate it: the "domestic dogs" it refers to were magnificoes of no less bulk than Longfellow, Whittier, Holmes and Emerson. In the case of Whitman, the wolf was not only chained, but also muzzled. Nothing, indeed, could be more amazing than the hostility that surrounded him at home until the very end of his long life. True enough, it was broken by certain feeble mitigations. Emerson, in 1855, praised him—though later very eager to forget it and desert him, as Clemens and Howells, years afterward, deserted Gorky. Alcott, Thoreau, Lowell and even Bryant, during his brief Bohemian days, were polite to him. A group of miscellaneous enthusiasts gradually gathered about him, and out of this group emerged at least one man of some distinction, John Burroughs. Young adventurers of letters—for example, Huneker—went to see him and hear him, half drawn by genuine admiration and half by mere deviltry. But the general tone of the opinion that beat upon him, the attitude of domestic criticism, was unbrokenly inimical; he was opposed by misrepresentation and neglect. "The prevailing range of criticism on my book," he wrote in "A Backward Glance on My Own Road" in 1884, "has been either mockery or denunciation—and . . . I have been the marked object of two or three (to me pretty serious) official buffetings." "After thirty years of trial," he wrote in "My Book and I," three years later, "public criticism on the book and myself as author of it shows marked anger and contempt more than anything else." That is, at home. Abroad he was making headway all the while, and long years afterward, by way of France and England, he began to force his way into the consciousness of his countrymen. What could have been more ironical than the solemn celebrations of Whitman's centenary that were carried off in various American universities in 1919? One can picture the old boy rolling with homeric mirth in hell. Imagine the fate of a university don of 1860, or 1870, or 1880, or even 1890 who had ventured to commend "Leaves of Grass" to the young gentlemen of his seminary! He would have come to grief as swiftly as that Detroit pedagogue of day before yesterday who brought down the Mothers' Legion upon him by commending "Jurgen."

8
The Cultural Background

So far, the disease. As to the cause, I have delivered a few hints. I now describe it particularly. It is, in brief, a defect in the general culture of the country—one reflected, not only in the national literature, but also in the national political theory, the national attitude toward religion and morals, the national habit in all departments of thinking. It is the lack of a civilized aristocracy, secure in its position, animated by an intelligent curiosity, skeptical of all facile generalizations, superior to the sentimentality of the mob, and delighting in the battle of ideas for its own sake.

The word I use, despite the qualifying adjective, has got itself meanings, of course, that I by no means intend to convey. Any mention of an aristocracy, to a public fed upon democratic fustian, is bound to bring up images of stockbrokers' wives lolling obscenely in opera boxes, or of haughty Englishmen slaughtering whole generations of grouse in an inordinate and incomprehensible manner, or of Junkers with tight waists elbowing American schoolmarms off the sidewalks of German beer towns, or of perfumed Italians coming over to work their abominable magic upon the daughters of breakfast-food and bathtub kings. Part of this misconception, I suppose, has its roots in the gaudy imbecilities of the yellow press, but there is also a part that belongs to the general American tradition, along with the oppression of minorities and the belief in political panaceas. Its depth and extent are constantly revealed by the naïve assumption that the so-called fashionable folk of the large cities—chiefly wealthy industrials in the interior-decorator and country-club stage of culture—constitute an aristocracy, and by the scarcely less remarkable assumption that the peerage of England is identical with the gentry—that is, that such men as Lord Northcliffe, Lord Iveagh and even Lord Reading are English gentlemen, and of the ancient line of the Percys.

Here, as always, the worshiper is the father of the gods, and no less when they are evil than when they are benign. The inferior man must find himself superiors, that he may marvel at his political equality with them, and in the absence of recognizable superiors *de facto* he creates superiors *de jure*. The sublime principle of one man, one vote must be translated into terms of dollars, diamonds, fashionable intelligence; the equality of all men before the law must have clear and dramatic proofs. Sometimes, perhaps, the thing goes further and is more subtle. The inferior man needs an aristocracy to demonstrate, not only his mere equality, but also his actual superiority. The society columns in the newspapers may have some such origin: they may visualize once more the accomplished journalist's understanding of the mob mind that he plays upon so skillfully, as upon some immense and cacophonous organ, always going *fortissimo*. What the inferior man and his wife see in the sinister revels of those amazing first families, I suspect, is often a massive witness to their own higher rectitude—to their relative innocence of cigarette-smoking, poodle-coddling, child-farming and the more abstruse branches of adultery—in brief, to their firmer grasp upon the immutable axioms of

Christian virtue, the one sound boast of the nether nine-tenths of humanity in every land under the cross.

But this bugaboo aristocracy, as I hint, is actually bogus, and the evidence of its bogusness lies in the fact that it is insecure. One gets into it only onerously, but out of it very easily. Entrance is effected by dint of a long and bitter struggle, and the chief incidents of that struggle are almost intolerable humiliations. The aspirant must school and steel himself to sniffs and sneers; he must see the door slammed upon him a hundred times before ever it is thrown open to him. To get in at all he must show a talent for abasement—and abasement makes him timorous. Worse, that timorousness is not cured when he succeeds at last. On the contrary, it is made even more tremulous, for what he faces within the gates is a scheme of things made up almost wholly of harsh and often unintelligible taboos, and the penalty for violating even the least of them is swift and disastrous. He must exhibit exactly the right social habits, appetites and prejudices, public and private. He must harbor exactly the right political enthusiasms and indignations. He must have a hearty taste for exactly the right sports. His attitude toward the fine arts must be properly tolerant and yet not a shade too eager. He must read and like exactly the right books, pamphlets and public journals. He must put up at the right hotels when he travels. His wife must patronize the right milliners. He himself must stick to the right haberdashery. He must live in the right neighborhood. He must even embrace the right doctrines of religion. It would ruin him, for all opera box and society column purposes, to set up a plea for justice to the Bolsheviki, or even for ordinary decency. It would ruin him equally to wear celluloid collars, or to move to Union Hill, N.J., or to serve ham and cabbage at his table. And it would ruin him, too, to drink coffee from his saucer, or to marry a chambermaid with a gold tooth, or to join the Seventh Day Adventists. Within the boundaries of his curious order he is worse fettered than a monk in a cell. Its obscure conception of propriety, its nebulous notion that this or that is honorable, hampers him in every direction, and very narrowly. What he resigns when he enters, even when he makes his first deprecating knock at the door, is every right to attack the ideas that happen to prevail within. Such as they are, he must accept them without question. And as they shift and change in response to great instinctive movements (or perhaps, now and then, to the punished but not to be forgotten revolts of extraordinary rebels) he must shift and change with them, silently and quickly. To hang back, to challenge and dispute, to preach reforms and revolutions—these are crimes against the brummagen Holy Ghost of the order.

Obviously, that order cannot constitute a genuine aristocracy, in any rational sense. A genuine aristocracy is grounded upon very much different principles. Its first and most salient character is its interior security, and the chief visible evidence of that security is the freedom that goes with it—not only freedom in act, the divine right of the aristocrat to do what he jolly well pleases, so long as he does not violate the primary guarantees and obligations of his class, but also and more importantly freedom in thought, the liberty to try and err, the right to be his own man. It is the instinct of a true aristocracy, not to punish eccentricity by expulsion, but to throw a mantle of protection about it—to safeguard it from the suspicions and resentments of the lower orders. Those lower orders are inert, timid, inhospitable to ideas, hostile to changes, faithful to a few maudlin superstitions. All progress goes on on the higher levels. It is there that salient personalities, made secure by artificial immunities, may oscillate most widely from the normal track. It is within that entrenched fold, out of reach of the immemorial certainties of the mob, that extraordinary men of the lower orders may find their city of refuge, and breathe a clear air. This, indeed, is at once the hall-mark and the justification of an aristocracy—that it is beyond responsibility to the general masses of men, and hence superior to both their degraded longings and their no less degraded aversions. It is nothing if it is not autonomous, curious, venturesome, courageous, and everything if it is. It is the custodian of the qualities that make for change and experiment; it is the class that organizes danger to the service of the race; it pays for its high prerogatives by standing in the forefront of the fray.

No such aristocracy, it must be plain, is now on view in the United States. The makings of one were visible in the Virginia of the later eighteenth century, but with Jefferson and Washington the promise died. In New England, it seems to me, there was never any aristocracy, either in being or in nascency: there was only a theocracy that degenerated very quickly into a plutocracy on the one hand and a caste of sterile *Gelehrten* on the other—the passion for God splitting into a lust for dollars and a weakness for mere words. Despite the common notion to the contrary—a notion generated by confusing literacy with intelligence—New England has never shown the slightest sign of a genuine enthusiasm for ideas. It began its history as a slaughter-house of ideas, and it is to-day not easily distinguishable from a cold-storage plant. Its celebrated adventures in mysticism, once apparently so bold and significant, are now seen to have been little more than an elaborate hocus-pocus—respectable Unitarians shocking the peasantry and scaring the horned cattle in the fields by masquerading in the robes of Roscicrucians. The ideas that it embraced in those austere and far-off days were stale, and when it had finished with them they were dead: to-day one hears of Jakob Böhme almost as rarely as one hears of Allen G. Thurman. So in politics. Its glory is Abolition—an English invention, long under the interdict of the native plutocracy. Since the Civil War its six states have produced fewer political ideas, as political ideas run in the Republic, than any average county in Kansas or Nebraska. Appomattox seemed to be a victory for New England idealism. It was actually a victory for the New England plutocracy, and that plutocracy has dominated thought above the Housatonic ever since. The sect of professional idealists has so far dwindled that it has ceased to be of any importance, even as an opposition. When the plutocracy is challenged now, it is challenged by the proletariat.

Well, what is on view in New England is on view in all other parts of the nation, sometimes with ameliorations, but usually with the colors merely exaggerated. What one beholds, sweeping the eye over the land, is a culture that, like the national literature, is in three layers—the plutocracy on top, a vast mass of undifferentiated human blanks at the bottom, and a forlorn *intelligentsia* gasping out a precarious life between. I need not set out at any length, I hope, the intellectual deficiencies of the plutocracy—its utter failure to show anything even remotely resembling the makings of an aristocracy. It is badly educated, it is stupid, it is full of low-caste superstitions and indignations, it is without decent traditions or informing vision; above all, it is extraordinarily lacking in the most elemental independence and courage. Out of this class comes the grotesque fashionable society of our big towns, already described. Imagine a horde of peasants incredibly enriched and with almost infinite power thrust into their hands, and you will have a fair picture of its habitual state of mind. It shows all the stigmata of inferiority—moral certainty, cruelty, suspicion of ideas, fear. Never did it function more revealingly than in the late *pogrom* against the so-called Reds, *i.e.*, against humorless idealists who, like Andrew Jackson, took the platitudes of democracy quite seriously. The machinery brought to bear upon these feeble and scattered fanatics would have almost sufficed to repel an invasion by the united powers of Europe. They were hunted out of their sweat-shops and coffee-houses as if they were so many Carranzas or Ludendorffs, dragged to jail to the tooting of horns, arraigned before quaking judges on unintelligible charges, condemned to deportation without the slightest chance to defend themselves, torn from their dependent families, herded into prison-ships, and then finally dumped in a snow waste, to be rescued and fed by the Bolsheviki. And what was the theory at the bottom of all these astounding proceedings? So far as it can be reduced to comprehensible terms it was much less a theory than a fear—a shivering, idiotic, discreditable fear of a mere banshee—an overpowering, paralyzing dread that some extra-eloquent Red, permitted to emit his balderdash unwhipped, might eventually convert a couple of courageous men, and that the courageous men, filled with indignation against the plutocracy, might take to the highroad, burn down a nail-factory or two, and slit the throat of some virtuous profiteer. In order to lay this fear, in order to ease the jangled nerves of the American successors to the Hapsburgs and Hohenzollerns, all the constitutional guarantees of the citizen were suspended, the statute-books were burdened with laws that surpass anything heard of in the Austria of Maria Theresa, the country was handed over to a frenzied mob of detectives, informers and *agents provocateurs*—and the Reds departed laughing loudly, and were hailed by the Bolsheviki as innocents escaped from an asylum for the criminally insane.

Obviously, it is out of reason to look for any hospitality to ideas in a class so extravagantly fearful of even the most palpably absurd of them. Its philosophy is firmly grounded upon the thesis that the existing order must stand forever free from attack, and not only from attack, but also from mere academic criticism, and its ethics are as firmly grounded upon the thesis that every attempt at any such criticism is a proof of moral turpitude. Within its own ranks, protected by what may be regarded as the privilege of the order, there is nothing to take the place of this criticism. A few feeble platitudes by Andrew Carnegie and a book of moderate merit by John D. Rockefeller's press-agent constitute almost the whole of the interior literature of ideas. In other countries the plutocracy has often produced men of reflective and analytical habit, eager to rationalize its instincts and to bring it into some sort of relationship to the main streams of human thought. The case of David Ricardo at once comes to mind. There have been many others: John Bright, Richard Cobden, George Grote, and, in our own time, Walther von Rathenau. But in the United States no such phenomenon has been visible. There was a day, not long ago, when certain young men of wealth gave signs of an unaccustomed interest in ideas on the political side, but the most they managed to achieve was a banal sort of Socialism, and even this was abandoned in sudden terror when the war came, and Socialism fell under suspicion of being genuinely international —in brief, of being honest under the skin. Nor has the plutocracy of the country ever fostered an inquiring spirit among its intellectual valets and footmen, which is to say, among the gentlemen who compose headlines and leading articles for its newspapers. What chiefly distinguishes the daily press of the United States from the press of all other countries pretending to culture is not its lack of truthfulness or even its lack of dignity and honor, for these deficiencies are common to the newspapers everywhere, but its incurable fear of ideas, its constant effort to evade the discussion of fundamentals by translating all issues into a few elemental fears, its incessant reduction of all reflection to mere emotion. It is, in the true sense, never well-informed. It is seldom intelligent, save in the arts of the mob-master. It is never courageously honest. Held harshly to a rigid correctness of opinion by the plutocracy that controls it with less and less attempt at disguise, and menaced on all sides by censorships that it dare not flout, it sinks rapidly into formalism and feebleness. Its yellow section is perhaps its most respectable section, for there the only vestige of the old free journalist survives. In the more conservative papers one finds only a timid and petulant animosity to all questioning of the existing order, however urbane and sincere—a pervasive and ill-concealed dread that the mob now heated up against the orthodox hobgoblins may suddenly begin to unearth hobgoblins of its own, and so run amok. For it is upon the emotions of the mob, of course, that the whole comedy is played. Theoretically the mob is the repository of all political wisdom and virtue; actually it is the ultimate source of all political power. Even the plutocracy cannot make war upon it openly, or forget the least of its weaknesses. The business of keeping it in order must be done discreetly, warily, with delicate technique. In the main that business consists of keeping alive its deep-seated fears—of strange faces, of unfamiliar ideas, of unhackneyed gestures, of untested liberties and responsibilities. The one permanent emotion of the inferior man, as of all the simpler mammals, is fear—fear of the unknown, the complex, the inexplicable. What he wants beyond everything else is safety. His instincts incline him toward a society so organized that it will protect him at all hazards, and not only against perils to his hide but also against assaults upon his mind—against the need to grapple with unaccustomed problems, to weigh ideas, to think things out for himself, to scrutinize the platitudes upon which his everyday thinking is based. Content under kaiserism so long as it functions efficiently, he turns, when kaiserism falls, to some other and perhaps worse form of paternalism, bringing to its benign tyranny only the docile tribute of his pathetic allegiance. In America it is the newspaper that is his boss. From it he gets support for his elemental illusions. In it he sees a visible embodiment of his own wisdom and consequence. Out of it he draws fuel for his simple moral passion, his congenital suspicion of heresy, his dread of the unknown. And behind the newspaper stands the plutocracy, ignorant, unimaginative and timorous.

Thus at the top and at the bottom. Obviously, there is no aristocracy here. One finds only one of the necessary elements, and that only in the plutocracy, to wit, a truculent egoism. But where is intelligence? Where are ease and surety of manner? Where are enterprise and curiosity? Where, above all, is courage, and in particular, moral courage—the capacity for independent thinking, for difficult problems, for what Nietzsche called the joys of the labyrinth? As well look for these things in a society of half-wits. Democracy, obliterating the old aristocracy, has left only a vacuum in its place; in a century and a half it has failed either to lift up the mob to intellectual autonomy and dignity or to purge the plutocracy of its inherent stupidity and swinishness. It is precisely here, the first and favorite scene of the Great Experiment, that the culture of the individual has been reduced to the most rigid and absurd regimentation. It is precisely here, of all civilized countries, that eccentricity in demeanor and opinion has come to bear the heaviest penalties. The whole drift of our law is toward the absolute prohibition of all ideas that diverge in the slightest from the accepted platitudes, and behind that drift of law there is a far more potent force of growing custom, and under that custom there is a national philosophy which erects conformity into the noblest of virtues and the free functioning of personality into a capital crime against society.

9
Under the Campus Pump

But there remain the *intelligentsia*, the free spirits in the middle ground, neither as anæsthetic to ideas as the plutocracy on the one hand nor as much the slaves of emotion as the proletariat on the other. Have I forgotten them? I have not. But what actually reveals itself when this small brotherhood of the superior is carefully examined? What reveals itself, it seems to me, is a gigantic disappointment. Superficially, there are all the marks of a caste of learned and sagacious men—a great book-knowledge, a laudable diligence, a certain fine reserve and sniffishness, a plain consciousness of intellectual superiority, not a few gestures that suggest the aristocratic. But under the surface one quickly discovers that the whole thing is little more than play-acting, and not always very skillful. Learning is there, but not curiosity. A heavy dignity is there, but not much genuine self-respect. Pretentiousness is there, but not a trace of courage. Squeezed between the plutocracy on one side and the mob on the other, the *intelligentsia* face the eternal national problem of maintaining their position, of guarding themselves against challenge and attack, of keeping down suspicion. They have all the attributes of knowledge save the sense of power. They have all the qualities of an aristocracy save the capital qualities that arise out of a feeling of security, of complete independence, of absolute immunity to onslaught from above and below. In brief, the old bogusness hangs about them, as about the fashionable aristocrats of the society columns. They are safe so long as they are good, which is to say, so long as they neither aggrieve the plutocracy nor startle the proletariat. Immediately they fall into either misdemeanor all their apparent dignity vanishes, and with it all of their influence, and they become simply somewhat ridiculous rebels against a social order that has no genuine need of them and is disposed to tolerate them only when they are not obtrusive.

For various reasons this shadowy caste is largely made up of men who have official stamps upon their learning—that is, of professors, of doctors of philosophy; outside of academic circles it tends to shade off very rapidly into a half-world of isolated anarchists. One of those reasons is plain enough: the old democratic veneration for mere schooling, inherited from the Puritans of New England, is still in being, and the mob, always eager for short cuts in thinking, is disposed to accept a schoolmaster without looking beyond his degree. Another reason lies in the fact that the higher education is still rather a novelty in the country, and there have yet to be developed any devices for utilizing learned men in any trade save teaching. Yet other reasons will suggest themselves. Whatever the ramification of causes, the fact is plain that the pedagogues have almost a monopoly of what passes for the higher thinking in the land. Not only do they reign unchallenged in their own chaste grove; they also penetrate to all other fields of ratiocination, to the almost complete exclusion of unshrived rivals. They dominate the weeklies of opinion; they are to the fore in every review; they write nine-tenths of the serious books of the country; they begin to invade the newspapers; they instruct and exhort the yokelry from the stump; they have even begun to penetrate into the government. One cannot turn in the United States without encountering a professor. There is one on every municipal commission. There is one in every bureau of the federal government. There is one at the head of every intellectual movement. There is one to explain every new mystery. Professors appraise all works of art, whether graphic, tonal or literary. Professors supply the brain power for agriculture, diplomacy, the control of dependencies and the distribution of commodities. A professor was until lately sovereign of the country, and pope of the state church.

So much for their opportunity. What, now, of their achievement? I answer as one who has had thrown upon him, by the impenetrable operations of fate, the rather thankless duties of a specialist in the ways of pedagogues, a sort of professor of professors. The job has got me enemies. I have been accused of carrying on a defamatory *jehad* against virtuous and laborious men; I have even been charged with doing it in the interest of the Wilhelmstrasse, the White Slave Trust and the ghost of Friedrich Wilhelm Nietzsche. Nothing could be more absurd. All my instincts are on the side of the professors. I esteem a man who devotes himself to a subject with hard diligence; I esteem even more a man who puts poverty and a shelf of books above profiteering and evenings of jazz; I am naturally monkish. Moreover, there are more Ph.D.'s on my family tree than even a Boston bluestocking can boast; there was a whole century when even the most ignorant of my house was at least *Juris utriusque Doctor*. But such predispositions should not be permitted to color sober researches. What I have found, after long and arduous labors, is a state of things that is surely not altogether flattering to the *Gelehrten* under examination. What I have found, in brief, is that pedagogy turned to general public uses is almost as timid and flatulent as journalism—that the professor, menaced by the timid dogmatism of the plutocracy above him and the incurable suspiciousness of the mob beneath him, is almost invariably inclined to seek his own security in a mellifluous inanity—that, far from being a courageous spokesman of ideas and an apostle of their free dissemination, in politics, in the fine arts, in practical ethics, he comes close to being the most prudent and skittish of all men concerned with them—in brief, that he yields to the prevailing correctness of thought in all departments, north, east, south and west, and is, in fact, the chief exponent among us of the democratic doctrine that heresy is not only a mistake, but also a crime.

A philosophy is not put to much of a test in ordinary times, for in ordinary times philosophies are permitted to lie like sleeping dogs. When it shows its inward metal is when the band begins to play. The turmoils of the late lamentable war, it seems to me, provided for such a trying out of fundamental ideas and attitudes upon a colossal scale. The whole thinking of the world was thrown into confusion; all the worst fears and prejudices of ignorant and emotional men came to the front; it was a time, beyond all others in modem history, when intellectual integrity was subjected to a cruel strain. How did the *intelligentsia* of These States bear up under that strain? What was the reaction of our learned men to the challenge of organized hysteria, mob fear, incitement to excess, downright insanity? How did they conduct themselves in that universal whirlwind? They conducted themselves, I fear, in a manner that must leave a brilliant question mark behind their claim to independence and courage, to true knowledge and dignity, to ordinary self-respect—in brief, to every quality that belongs to the authentic aristocrat. They constituted themselves, not a restraining influence upon the mob run wild, but the loudest spokesmen of its worst imbecilities. They fed it with bogus history, bogus philosophy, bogus idealism, bogus heroics. They manufactured blather for its entertainment. They showed themselves to be as naïve as so many Liberty Loan orators, as emotional, almost, as the spy hunters, and as disdainful of the ordinary intellectual decencies as the editorial writers. I accumulated, in those great days, for the instruction and horror of posterity, a very large collection of academic arguments, expositions and pronunciamentos; it fills a trunk, and got me heavily into debt to three clipping-bureaux. Its contents range from solemn hymns of hate in the learned (and even the theological) reviews and such official donkeyisms as the formal ratification of the so-called Sisson documents down to childish harangues to student-bodies, public demands that the study of the enemy language and literature be prohibited by law, violent denunciations of all enemy science as negligible and fraudulent, vitriolic attacks upon enemy magnificos, and elaborate proofs that the American Revolution was the result of a foul plot hatched in the Wilhelmstrasse of the time, to the wanton injury of two loving bands of brothers. I do not exaggerate in the slightest. The proceedings of Mr. Creel's amazing corps of "twenty-five hundred American historians" went further than anything I have described. And in every far-flung college town, in every one-building "university" on the prairie, even the worst efforts of those "historians" were vastly exceeded.

But I am forgetting the like phenomena on the other side of the bloody chasm? I am overlooking the darker crimes of the celebrated German professors? Not at all. Those crimes against all reason and dignity, had they been committed in fact, would not be evidence in favor of the Americans in the dock: the principle of law is too well accepted to need argument. But I venture to deny them, and out of a very special and singular knowledge, for I seem to be one of the few Americans who has ever actually read the proclamations of the German professors: all the most indignant critics of them appear to have accepted second-hand accounts of their contents. Having suffered the onerous labor of reading them, I now offer sworn witness to their relative mildness. Now and then one encounters in them a disconcerting bray. Now and then one weeps with sore heart. Now and then one is bogged in German made wholly unintelligible by emotion. But taking them as they stand, and putting them fairly beside the corresponding documents of American vintage, one is at once struck by their comparative suavity and decorum, their freedom from mere rhetoric and fustian—above all, by their effort to appeal to reason, such as it is, rather than to emotion. No German professor, from end to end of the war, put his hand to anything as transparently silly as the Sisson documents. No German professor essayed to prove that the Seven Years' War was caused by Downing Street. No German professor argued that the study of English would corrupt the soul. No German professor denounced Darwin as an ignoramus and Lister as a scoundrel. Nor was anything of the sort done, so far as I know, by any French professor. Nor even by any reputable English professor. All such honorable efforts on behalf of correct thought in wartime were monopolized by American professors. And if the fact is disputed, then I threaten upon some future day, when the stealthy yearning to forget has arisen, to print my proofs in parallel columns—the most esteemed extravagances of the German professors in one column and the corresponding masterpieces of the American professors in the other.

I do not overlook, of course, the self-respecting men who, in the midst of all the uproar, kept their counsel and their dignity. A small minority, hard beset and tested by the fire! Nor do I overlook the few sentimental fanatics who, in the face of devastating evidence to the contrary, proceeded upon the assumption that academic freedom was yet inviolable, and so got themselves cashiered, and began posturing in radical circles as martyrs, the most absurd of men. But I think I draw a fair picture of the general. I think I depict with reasonable accuracy the typical response of the only recognizable *intelligentsia* of the land to the first great challenge to their aristocratic aloofness—the first test in the grand manner of their freedom alike from the bellicose imbecility of the plutocracy and the intolerable fears and childish moral certainties of the mob. That test exposed them shamelessly. It revealed their fast allegiance to the one thing that is the antithesis of all free inquiry, of all honest hospitality to ideas, of all intellectual independence and integrity. They proved that they were correct—and in proving it they threw a brilliant light upon many mysteries of our national culture.

10
The Intolerable Burden

Among others, upon the mystery of our literature—its faltering feebleness, its lack of genuine gusto, its dearth of salient personalities, its general air of poverty and imitation. What ails the beautiful letters of the Republic, I repeat, is what ails the general culture of the Republic—the lack of a body of sophisticated and civilized public opinion, independent of plutocratic control and superior to the infantile philosophies of the mob—a body of opinion showing the eager curiosity, the educated skepticism and the hospitality to ideas of a true aristocracy. This lack is felt by the American author, imagining him to have anything new to say, every day of his life. He can hope for no support, in ordinary cases, from the mob: it is too suspicious of all ideas. He can hope for no support from the spokesmen of the plutocracy: they are too diligently devoted to maintaining the intellectual *status quo*. He turns, then, to the *intelligentsia*—and what he finds is correctness! In his two prime functions, to represent the life about him accurately and to criticize it honestly, he sees that correctness arrayed against him. His representation is indecorous, unlovely, too harsh to be borne. His criticism is in contumacy to the ideals upon which the whole structure rests. So he is either attacked vigorously as an anti-patriot whose babblings ought to be put down by law, or enshrouded in a silence which commonly disposes of him even more effectively.

Soon or late, of course, a man of genuine force and originality is bound to prevail against that sort of stupidity. He will unearth an adherent here and another there; in the long run they may become numerous enough to force some recognition of him, even from the most immovable exponents of correctness. But the business is slow, uncertain, heart-breaking. It puts a burden upon the artist that ought not to be put upon him. It strains beyond reason his diligence and passion. A man who devotes his life to creating works of the imagination, a man who gives over all his strength and energy to struggling with problems that are essentially delicate and baffling and pregnant with doubt—such a man does not ask for recognition as a mere reward for his industry; he asks for it as a necessary *help* to his industry; he needs it as he needs decent subsistence and peace of mind. It is a grave damage to the artist and a grave loss to the literature when such a man as Poe has to seek consolation among his inferiors, and such a man as the Mark Twain of "What Is Man?" is forced to conceal his most profound beliefs, and such men as Dreiser and Cabell are exposed to incessant attacks by malignant stupidity. The notion that artists flourish upon adversity and misunderstanding, that they are able to function to the utmost in an atmosphere of indifference or hostility—this notion is nine-tenths nonsense. If it were true, then one would never hear of painters going to France or of musicians going to Germany. What the artist actually needs is comprehension of his aims and ideals by men he respects—not necessarily approval of his products, but simply an intelligent sympathy for him in the great agony of creation.

And that sympathy must be more than the mere fellow-feeling of other craftsmen; it must come, in large part, out of a connoisseurship that is beyond the bald trade interest; it must have its roots in the intellectual curiosity of an aristocracy of taste. Billroth, I believe, was more valuable to Brahms than even Schumann. His eager interest gave music-making a solid dignity. His championship offered the musician a visible proof that his labors had got for him a secure place in a civilized and stable society, and that he would be judged by his peers, and safeguarded against the obtuse hostility of his inferiors.

No such security is thrown about an artist in America. It is not that the country lacks the standards that Dr. Brownell pleads for; it is that its standards are still those of a primitive and timorous society. The excesses of Comstockery are profoundly symbolical. What they show is the moral certainty of the mob in operation against something that is as incomprehensible to it as the theory of least squares, and what they show even more vividly is the distressing lack of any automatic corrective of that outrage—of any firm and secure body of educated opinion, eager to hear and test all intelligible ideas and sensitively jealous of the right to discuss them freely. When "The Genius" was attacked by the Comstocks, it fell to my lot to seek assistance for Dreiser among the *intelligentsia*. I found them almost unanimously disinclined to lend a hand. A small number permitted themselves to be induced, but the majority held back, and not a few, as I have said, actually offered more or less furtive aid to the Comstocks. I pressed the matter and began to unearth reasons. It was, it appeared, dangerous for a member of the *intelligentsia*, and particularly for a member of the academic *intelligentsia*, to array himself against the mob inflamed—against the moral indignation of the sort of folk who devour vice reports and are converted by the Rev. Billy Sunday! If he came forward, he would have to come forward alone. There was no organized support behind him. No instinctive urge of class, no prompting of a great tradition, moved him to speak out for artistic freedom . . . England supplied the lack. Over there they have a mob too, and something akin to Comstockery, and a cult of hollow correctness—but they also have a caste that stands above all that sort of thing, and out of that caste came aid for Dreiser.

England is always supplying the lack—England, or France, or Germany, or some other country, but chiefly England. "My market and my reputation," said Prescott in 1838, "rest principally with England." To Poe, a few years later, the United States was "a literary colony of Great Britain." And there has been little change to this day. The English leisure class, says Prof. Dr. Veblen, is "for purposes of reputable usage the upper leisure class of this country." Despite all the current highfalutin about melting pots and national destinies the United States remains almost as much an English colonial possession, intellectually and spiritually, as it was on July 3, 1776. The American social pusher keeps his eye on Mayfair; the American literatus dreams of recognition by the London weeklies; the American don is lifted to bliss by the imprimatur of Oxford or Cambridge; even the American statesman knows how to cringe to Downing Street. Most of the essential policies of Dr. Wilson between 1914 and 1920—when the realistic English, finding him no longer useful, incontinently dismissed him—were, to all intents and purposes, those of a British colonial premier. He went into the Peace Conference willing to yield everything to English interests, and he came home with a treaty that was so extravagantly English that it fell an easy prey to the anti-English minority, ever alert for the makings of a bugaboo to scare the plain people. What lies under all this subservience is simple enough. The American, for all his braggadocio, is quite conscious of his intrinsic inferiority to the Englishman, on all cultural counts. He may put himself first as a man of business, as an adventurer in practical affairs or as a pioneer in the applied arts and sciences, but in all things removed from the mere pursuit of money and physical ease he well understands that he belongs at the second table. Even his recurrent attacks of Anglophobia are no more than Freudian evidences of his inferiority complex. He howls in order to still his inner sense of inequality, as he howls against imaginary enemies in order to convince himself that he is brave and against fabulous despotisms in order to prove that he is free. The Englishman is never deceived by this hocus-pocus. He knows that it is always possible to fetch the rebel back into camp by playing upon his elemental fears and vanities. A few dark threats, a few patronizing speeches, a few Oxford degrees, and the thing is done. More, the English scarcely regard it as hunting in the grand manner; it is a business of subalterns. When, during the early stages of the war, they had occasion to woo the American *intelligentsia*, what agents did they choose? Did they nominate Thomas Hardy, Joseph Conrad, George Moore and company? Nay, they nominated Conan Doyle, Coningsby Dawson, Alfred Noyes, Ian Hay, Chesterton, Kipling, Zangwill and company. In the choice there was high sagacity and no little oblique humor—as there was a bit later in the appointment of Lord Reading and Sir Auckland Geddes to Washington. The valuation they set upon the *aluminados* of the Republic was exactly the valuation they were in the habit of setting, at home, upon MM. of the Free Church Federation. They saw the eternal green-grocer beneath the master's gown and mortarboard. Let us look closely and we shall see him, too.

The essence of a self-reliant and autonomous culture is an unshakable egoism. It must not only regard itself as the peer of any other culture; it must regard itself as the superior of any other. You will find this indomitable pride in the culture of any truly first-rate nation: France, Germany or England. But you will not find it in the so-called culture of America. Here the decadent Anglo-Saxon majority still looks obediently and a bit wistfully toward the motherland. No good American ever seriously questions an English judgment on an æsthetic question, or even on an ethical, philosophical or political question. There is, in fact, seldom any rational reason why he should: it is almost always more mature, more tolerant, more intelligent than any judgment hatched at home. Behind it lies a settled scheme of things, a stable point of view, the authority of a free intellectual aristocracy, the pride of tradition and of power. The English are sure-footed, well-informed, persuasive. It is beyond their imagination that any one should seriously challenge them. In this overgrown and oafish colony there is no such sureness. The American always secretly envies the Englishman, even when he professes to flout him. The Englishman never envies the American.

The extraordinary colonist, moved to give utterance to the ideas bubbling within him, is thus vastly handicapped, for he must submit them to the test of a culture that, in the last analysis, is never quite his own culture, despite its dominance.

Looking within himself, he finds that he is different, that he diverges from the English standard, that he is authentically American—and to be authentically American is to be officially inferior. He thus faces dismay at the very start: support is lacking when he needs it most. In the motherland—in any motherland, in any wholly autonomous nation—there is a class of men like himself, devoted to translating the higher manifestations of the national spirit into ideas—men differing enormously among themselves, but still united in common cause against the lethargy and credulity of the mass. But in a colony that class, if it exists at all, lacks coherence and certainty; its authority is not only disputed by the inertia and suspiciousness of the lower orders, but also by the superior authority overseas; it is timorous and fearful of challenge. Thus it affords no protection to an individual of assertive originality, and he is forced to go as a suppliant to a quarter in which nothing is his by right, but everything must go by favor—in brief to a quarter where his very application must needs be regarded as an admission of his inferiority. The burden of proof upon him is thus made double. Obviously, he must be a man of very strong personality to surmount such obstacles triumphantly. Such strong men, of course, sometimes appear in a colony, but they always stand alone; their worst opposition is at home. For a colonial of less vigorous soul the battle is almost hopeless. Either he submits to subordination and so wears docilely the inferior badge of a praiseworthy and tolerated colonist, or he deserts the minority for the far more hospitable and confident majority, and so becomes a mere mob-artist.

Examples readily suggest themselves. I give you Poe and Whitman as men strong enough to weather the adverse wind. The salient thing about each of these men was this: that his impulse to self-expression, the force of his "obscure, inner necessity," was so powerful that it carried him beyond all ordinary ambitions and prudences—in other words, that the ego functioned so heroically that it quite disregarded the temporal welfare of the individual. Neither Poe nor Whitman made the slightest concession to what was the predominant English taste, the prevailing English authority, of his time. And neither yielded in the slightest to the maudlin echoes of English notions that passed for ideas in the United States; in neither will you find any recognizable reflection of the things that Americans were saying and doing all about them. Even Whitman, preaching democracy, preached a democracy that not one actual democrat in a hundred thousand could so much as imagine. What happened? *Imprimis*, English authority, at the start, dismissed them loftily; they were, at best, simply rare freaks from the colonies. Secondly, American stupidity, falling into step, came near overlooking them altogether. The accident that maintained them was an accident of personality and environment. They happened to be men accustomed to social isolation and of the most meager wants, and it was thus difficult to deter them by neglect and punishment. So they stuck to their guns—and presently they were "discovered," as the phrase is, by men of a culture wholly foreign to them and perhaps incomprehensible to them, and thereafter, by slow stages, they began to win a slow and reluctant recognition in England (at first only from rebels and iconoclasts), and finally even in America. That either, without French prompting, would have come to his present estate I doubt very much. And in support of that doubt I cite again the fact that Poe's high talents as a critic, not having interested the French, have never got their deserts either in England or at home.

It is lesser men that we chiefly have to deal with in this world, and it is among lesser men that the lack of a confident intellectual viewpoint in America makes itself most evident. Examples are numerous and obvious. On the one hand, we have Fenimore Cooper first making a cringing bow for English favor, and then, on being kicked out, joining the mob against sense; he wrote books so bad that even the Americans of 1830 admired them. On the other hand, we have Henry James, a deserter made by despair; one so depressed by the tacky company at the American first table that he preferred to sit at the second table of the English. The impulse was, and is common; it was only the forthright act that distinguished him. And in the middle ground, showing both seductions plainly, there is Mark Twain—at one moment striving his hardest for the English *imprimatur*, and childishly delighted by every favorable gesture; at the next, returning to the native mob as its premier clown—monkey-shining at banquets, cavorting in the newspapers, shrinking poltroonishly from his own ideas, obscenely eager to give no offense. A much greater artist than either Poe or Whitman, so I devoutly believe, but a good deal lower as a man. The ultimate passion was not there; the decent householder always pulled the ear of the dreamer. His fate has irony in it. In England they patronize him: he is, for an American, not so bad. In America, appalled by his occasional ascents to honesty, his stray impulses to be wholly himself, the dunderheads return him to arm's length, his old place, and one of the most eminent of them, writing in the New York *Times*, argues piously that it is impossible to imagine him actually believing the commonplace heresies he put into "What Is Man?"

II
Epilogue

I have described the disease. Let me say at once that I have no remedy to offer. I simply set down a few ideas, throw out a few hints, attempt a few modest inquiries into causes. Perhaps my argument often turns upon itself: the field is weed-grown and paths are hard to follow. It may be that insurmountable natural obstacles stand in the way of the development of a distinctively American culture, grounded upon a truly egoistic nationalism and supported by a native aristocracy. After all, there is no categorical imperative that ordains it. In such matters, when the conditions are right, nature often arranges a division of labor. A nation shut in by racial and linguistic isolation—a Sweden, a Holland or a France—is forced into autonomy by sheer necessity; if it is to have any intellectual life at all it must develop its own. But that is not our case. There is England to hold up the torch for us, as France holds it up for Belgium, and Spain for Latin America, and Germany for Switzerland. It is our function, as the younger and less confident partner, to do the simpler, rougher parts of the joint labor—to develop the virtues of the more elemental orders of men: industry, piety, docility, endurance, assiduity and ingenuity in practical affairs—the wood-hewing and water-drawing of the race. It seems to me that we do all this very well; in these things we are better than the English. But when it comes to those larger and more difficult activities which concern only the superior minority, and are, in essence, no more than products of its efforts to *demonstrate* its superiority—when it comes to the higher varieties of speculation and self-expression, to the fine arts and the game of ideas—then we fall into a bad second place. Where we stand, intellectually, is where the English non-conformists stand; like them, we are marked by a fear of ideas as disturbing and corrupting. Our art is imitative and timorous. Our political theory is hopelessly sophomoric and superficial; even English Toryism and Russian Bolshevism are infinitely more profound and penetrating. And of the two philosophical systems that we have produced, one is so banal that it is now imbedded in the New Thought, and the other is so shallow that there is nothing in it either to puzzle or to outrage a school-marm.

Nevertheless, hope will not down, and now and then it is supported by something rather more real than mere desire. One observes an under-current of revolt, small but vigorous, and sometimes it exerts its force, not only against the superficial banality but also against the fundamental, flabbiness, the intrinsic childishness of the Puritan *Anschauung*. The remedy for that childishness is skepticism, and already skepticism shows itself: in the iconoclastic political realism of Harold Stearns, Waldo Frank and company, in the grouping questions of Dreiser, Cabell and Anderson, in the operatic rebellions of the Village. True imagination, I often think, is no more than a function of this skepticism. It is the dull man who is always sure, and the sure man who is always dull. The more a man dreams, the less he believes. A great literature is thus chiefly the product of doubting and inquiring minds in revolt against the immovable certainties of the nation. Shakespeare, at a time of rising democratic feeling in England, flung the whole force of his genius against democracy. Cervantes, at a time when all Spain was romantic, made a headlong attack upon romance. Goethe, with Germany groping toward nationalism, threw his influences on the side of internationalism. The central trouble with America is conformity, timorousness, lack of enterprise and audacity. A nation of third-rate men, a land offering hospitality only to fourth-rate artists. In Elizabethan England they would have bawled for democracy, in the Spain of Cervantes they would have yelled for chivalry, and in the Germany of Goethe they would have wept and beat their breasts for the Fatherland. To-day, as in the day of Emerson, they set the tune. . . . But into the singing there occasionally enters a discordant note. On some dim to-morrow, perhaps, perchance, peradventure, they may be challenged.

II.
Roosevelt: An Autopsy

ONE thinks of Dr. Woodrow Wilson's biography of George Washington as of one of the strangest of all the world's books. Washington: the first, and perhaps also the last American gentleman. Wilson: the self-bamboozled Presbyterian, the right-thinker, the great moral statesman, the perfect model of the Christian cad. It is as if the Rev. Dr. Billy Sunday should do a biography of Charles Darwin—almost as if Dr. Wilson himself should dedicate his senility to a life of the Chevalier Bayard, or the Cid, or Christ. . . . But such phenomena, of course, are not actually rare in the republic; here everything happens that is forbidden by the probabilities and the decencies. The chief native critic of beautiful letters, for a whole generation, was a Baptist clergyman; he was succeeded by a literary Wall Street man, who gave way, in turn, to a soviet of ninth-rate pedagogues; this very curious apostolic succession I have already discussed. The dean of the music critics, even today, is a translator of grand opera libretti, and probably one of the worst that ever lived. Return, now, to political biography. Who can think of anything in American literature comparable to Morley's life of Gladstone, or Trevelyan's life of Macaulay, or Carlyle's Frederick, or even Winston Churchill's life of his father? I dredge my memory hopelessly; only William Graham Sumner's study of Andrew Jackson emerges—an extraordinarily astute and careful piece of work by one of the two most underestimated Americans of his generation, the other being Daniel Coit Gilman. But where is the first-rate biography of Washington—sound, fair, penetrating, honest, done by a man capable of comprehending the English gentry of the eighteenth century? And how long must we wait for adequate treatises upon Jefferson, Hamilton, Sam Adams, Aaron Burr, Henry Clay, Calhoun, Webster, Sumner, Grant, Sherman, Lee?

Even Lincoln is yet to be got vividly between the covers of a book. The Nicolay-Hay work is quite impossible; it is not a biography, but simply a huge storehouse of biographical raw materials; whoever can read it can also read the official Records of the Rebellion. All the other standard lives of old Abe—for instance, those of Lamon, Herndon and Weik, Stoddard, Morse and Miss Tarbell—fail still worse; when they are not grossly preachy and disingenuous they are trivial. So far as I can make out, no genuinely scientific study of the man has ever been attempted. The amazing conflict of testimony about him remains a conflict; the most elemental facts are yet to be established; he grows vaguer and more fabulous as year follows year. One would think that, by this time, the question of his religious views (to take one example) ought to be settled, but apparently it is not, for no longer than a year ago there came a reverend author, Dr. William E. Barton, with a whole volume upon the subject, and I was as much in the dark after reading it as I had been before I opened it. All previous biographers, it appeared by this author's evidence, had either dodged the problem, or lied. The official doctrine, in this as in other departments, is obviously quite unsound. One hears in the Sunday-schools that Abe was an austere and pious fellow, constantly taking the name of God in whispers, just as one reads in the school history-books that he was a shining idealist, holding all his vast powers by the magic of an inner and ineffable virtue. Imagine a man getting on in American politics, interesting and enchanting the boobery, sawing off the horns of other politicians, elbowing his way through primaries and conventions, by the magic of virtue! As well talk of fetching the mob by hawking exact and arctic justice! Abe, in fact, must have been a fellow highly skilled at the great democratic art of gum-shoeing. I like to think of him as one who defeated such politicians as Stanton, Douglas and Sumner with their own weapons—deftly leading them into ambuscades, boldly pulling their noses, magnificently ham-stringing and horn-swoggling them—in brief, as a politician of extraordinary talents, who loved the game for its own sake, and had the measure of the crowd. His official portraits, both in prose and in daguerreotype, show him wearing the mien of a man about to be hanged; one never sees him smiling. Nevertheless, one hears that, until he emerged from Illinois, they always put the women, children and clergy to bed when he got a few gourds of corn aboard, and it is a matter of unescapable record that his career in the State Legislature was indistinguishable from that of a Tammany Nietzsche.

But, as I say, it is hopeless to look for the real man in the biographies of him: they are all full of distortion, chiefly pious and sentimental. The defect runs through the whole of American political biography, and even through the whole of American history. Nearly all our professional historians are poor men holding college posts, and they are ten times more cruelly beset by the ruling politico-plutocratic-social oligarchy than ever the Prussian professors were by the Hohenzollerns. Let them diverge in the slightest from what is the current official doctrine, and they are turned out of their chairs with a ceremony suitable for the expulsion of a drunken valet. During the recent war a herd of two thousand and five hundred such miserable slaves was organized by Dr. Creel to lie for their country, and they at once fell upon the congenial task of rewriting American history to make it accord with the ideas of H. P. Davison, Admiral Sims, Nicholas Murray Butler, the Astors, Barney Baruch and Lord Northcliffe. It was a committee of this herd that solemnly pledged the honor of American scholarship to the authenticity of the celebrated Sisson documents. . . .

In the face of such acute military imbecility it is not surprising to discover that all of the existing biographies of the late Colonel Roosevelt—and they have been rolling off the presses at a dizzy rate since his death—are feeble, inaccurate, ignorant and preposterous. I have read, I suppose, at least ten of these tomes during the past year or so, and in all of them I have found vastly more gush than sense. Lawrence Abbott's "Impressions of Theodore Roosevelt" and William Roscoe Thayer's "Theodore Roosevelt" may well serve as specimens. Abbott's book is the composition, not of an unbiased student of the man, but of a sort of groom of the hero. He is so extremely eager to prove that Roosevelt was the perfect right-thinker, according to the transient definitions of right-thinking, that he manages to get a flavor of dubiousness into his whole chronicle. I find myself doubting him even when I know that he is honest and suspect that he is right. As for Thayer, all he offers is a hasty and hollow pot-boiler—such a work as might have been well within the talents of, say, the late Murat Halstead or the editor of the New York *Times.* This Thayer has been heavily praised of late as the Leading American Biographer, and one constantly hears that some new university has made him *Legum Doctor*, or that he has been awarded a medal by this or that learned society, or that the post has brought him a new ribbon from some literary potentate in foreign parts. If, in fact, he is actually the cock of the walk in biography, then all I have said against American biographers is too mild and mellow. What one finds in his book is simply the third-rate correctness of a Boston colonial. Consider, for example, his frequent discussions of the war—a necessity in any work on Roosevelt. In England there is the mob's view of the war, and there is the view of civilized and intelligent men, *e.g.*, Lansdowne, Loreburn, Austin Harrison, Morel, Keynes, Haldane, Hirst, Balfour, Robert Cecil. In New England, it would appear, the two views coalesce, with the first outside. There is scarcely a line on the subject in Thayer's book that might not have been written by Horatio Bottomley. . . .

Obviously, Roosevelt's reaction to the war must occupy a large part of any adequate biography of him, for that reaction was probably more comprehensively typical of the man than any other business of his life. It displayed not only his whole stock of political principles, but also his whole stock of political tricks. It plumbed, on the one hand, the depths of his sagacity, and on the other hand the depths of his insincerity. Fundamentally, I am convinced, he was quite out of sympathy with, and even quite unable to comprehend the body of doctrine upon which the Allies, and later the United States, based their case. To him it must have seemed insane when it was not hypocritical, and hypocritical when it was not insane. His instincts were profoundly against a new loosing of democratic fustian upon the world; he believed in strongly centralized states, founded upon power and devoted to enterprises far transcending mere internal government; he was an imperialist of the type of Cecil Rhodes, Treitschke and Delcassé. But the fortunes of domestic politics jockeyed him into the position of standing as the spokesman of an almost exactly contrary philosophy. The visible enemy before him was Wilson. What he wanted as a politician was something that he could get only by wresting it from Wilson, and Wilson was too cunning to yield it without making a tremendous fight, chiefly by chicane—whooping for peace while preparing for war, playing mob fear against mob fear, concealing all his genuine motives and desires beneath clouds of chautauqual rhetoric, leading a mad dance whose tune changed at every swing. Here was an opponent that more than once puzzled Roosevelt, and in the end flatly dismayed him. Here was a mob-master with a technique infinitely more subtle and effective than his own. So lured into an unequal combat, the Rough Rider got bogged in absurdities so immense that only the democratic anæsthesia to absurdity saved him. To make any progress at all he was forced into fighting against his own side. He passed from the scene bawling piteously for a cause that, at bottom, it is impossible to imagine him believing in, and in terms of a philosophy that was as foreign to his true faith as it was to the faith of Wilson. In the whole affair there was a colossal irony. Both contestants were intrinsically frauds.

The fraudulence of Wilson is now admitted by all save a few survivors of the old corps of official press-agents, most of them devoid of both honesty and intelligence. No unbiased man, in the presence of the revelations of Bullitt, Keynes and a hundred other witnesses, and of the Russian and Shantung performances, and of innumerable salient domestic phenomena, can now believe that the *Doctor dulcifluus* was ever actually in favor of any of the brummagem ideals he once wept for, to the edification of a moral universe. They were, at best, no more than ingenious *ruses de guerre*, and even in the day of their widest credit it was the Espionage Act and the Solicitor-General to the Postoffice, rather than any plausibility in their substance, that got them their credit. In Roosevelt's case the imposture is less patent; he died before it was fully unmasked. What is more, his death put an end to whatever investigation of it was under way, for American sentimentality holds that it is indecent to inquire into the weaknesses of the dead, at least until all the flowers have withered on their tombs. When, a year ago, I ventured in a magazine article to call attention to Roosevelt's philosophical kinship to the Kaiser I received letters of denunciation from all parts of the United States, and not a few forthright demands that I recant on penalty of lynch law. Prudence demanded that I heed these demands. We live in a curious and often unsafe country. Haled before a Roosevelt judge for speeding my automobile, or spitting on the sidewalk, or carrying a jug, I might have been railroaded for ten years under some constructive corollary of the Espionage Act. But there were two things that supported me in my contumacy to the departed. One was a profound reverence for and fidelity to the truth, sometimes almost amounting to fanaticism. The other was the support of my venerable brother in epistemology, the eminent Iowa right-thinker and patriot, Prof. Dr. S. P. Sherman. Writing in the *Nation*, where he survives from more seemly days than these, Prof. Dr. Sherman put the thing in plain terms. "With the essentials in the religion of the militarists of Germany," he said, "Roosevelt was utterly in sympathy."

Utterly? Perhaps the adverb is a bit too strong. There was in the man a certain instinctive antipathy to the concrete aristocrat and in particular to the aristocrat's private code—the product, no doubt, of his essentially *bourgeois* origin and training. But if he could not go with the Junkers all the way, he could at least go the whole length of their distrust of the third order—the undifferentiated masses of men below. Here, I daresay, he owed a lot to Nietzsche. He was always reading German books, and among them, no doubt, were "Also sprach Zarathustra" and "Jenseits von Gut und Böse." In fact, the echoes were constantly sounding in his own harangues. Years ago, as an intellectual exercise while confined to hospital, I devised and printed a give-away of the Rooseveltian philosophy in parallel columns—in one column, extracts from "The Strenuous Life"; in the other, extracts from Nietzsche. The borrowings were numerous and unescapable. Theodore had swallowed Friedrich as a peasant swallows Peruna—bottle, cork, label and testimonials. Worse, the draft whetted his appetite, and soon he was swallowing the Kaiser of the *Garde-Kavallerie*-mess and battleship-launching speeches—another somewhat defective Junker. In his palmy days it was often impossible to distinguish his politico-theological bulls from those of Wilhelm; during the war, indeed, I suspect that some of them were boldly lifted by the British press bureau, and palmed off as felonious imprudences out of Potsdam. Wilhelm was his model in *Weltpolitik*, and in sociology, exegetics, administration, law, sport and connubial polity no less. Both roared for doughty armies, eternally prepared—for the theory that the way to prevent war is to make all conceivable enemies think twice, thrice, ten times. Both dreamed of gigantic navies, with battleships as long as Brooklyn Bridge. Both preached incessantly the duty of the citizen to the state, with the soft pedal upon the duty of the state to the citizen. Both praised the habitually gravid wife. Both delighted in the armed pursuit of the lower fauna. Both heavily patronized the fine arts. Both were intimates of God, and announced His desires with authority. Both believed that all men who stood opposed to them were prompted by the devil and would suffer for it in hell.

If, in fact, there was any difference between them, it was all in favor of Wilhelm. For one thing, he made very much fewer speeches; it took some colossal event, such as the launching of a dreadnaught or the birthday of a colonel-general, to get him upon his legs; the Reichstag was not constantly deluged with his advice and upbraiding. For another thing, he was a milder and more modest man—one more accustomed, let us say, to circumstance and authority, and hence less intoxicated by the greatness of his state. Finally, he had been trained to think, not only of his own immediate fortunes, but also of the remote interests of a family that, in his most expansive days, promised to hold the throne for many years, and so he cultivated a certain prudence, and even a certain ingratiating suavity. He could, on occasion, be extremely polite to an opponent. But Roosevelt was never polite to an opponent; perhaps a gentleman, by American standards, he was surely never a gentle man. In a political career of nearly forty years he was never even fair to an opponent. All of his gabble about the square deal was merely so much protective coloration, easily explicable on elementary Freudian grounds. No man, facing Roosevelt in the heat of controversy, ever actually got a square deal. He took extravagant advantages; he played to the worst idiocies of the mob; he hit below the belt almost habitually. One never thinks of him as a duelist, say of the school of Disraeli, Palmerston and, to drop a bit, Blaine. One always thinks of him as a glorified longshoreman engaged eternally in cleaning out bar-rooms—and not too proud to gouge when the inspiration came to him, or to bite in the clinches, or to oppose the relatively fragile brass knuckles of the code with chair-legs, bung-starters, cuspidors, demijohns, and ice-picks.

Abbott and Thayer, in their books, make elaborate efforts to depict their hero as one born with a deep loathing of the whole Prussian scheme of things, and particularly of the Prussian technique in combat. Abbott even goes so far as to hint that the attentions of the Kaiser, during Roosevelt's historic tour of Europe on his return from Africa, were subtly revolting to him. Nothing could be more absurd. Prof. Dr. Sherman, in the article I have mentioned, blows up that nonsense by quoting from a speech made by the tourist in Berlin—a speech arguing for the most extreme sort of militarism in a manner that must have made even some of the Junkers blow their noses dubiously. The disproof need not be piled up; the America that Roosevelt dreamed of was always a sort of swollen Prussia, truculent without and regimented within. There was always a clank of the saber in his discourse; he could not discuss the tamest matter without swaggering in the best dragoon fashion. Abbott gets into yet deeper waters when he sets up the doctrine that the invasion of Belgium threw his darling into an instantaneous and tremendous fit of moral indignation, and that the curious delay in the public exhibition thereof, so much discussed since, was due to his (Abbott's) fatuous interference—a *faux pas* later regretted with much bitterness. Unluckily, the evidence he offers leaves me full of doubts. What the doctrine demands that one believe is simply this: that the man who, for mere commercial advantage and (in Frederick's famous phrase) "to make himself talked of in the world," tore up the treaty of 1848 between the United States and Colombia (*geb.* New Granada), whereby the United States forever guaranteed the "sovereignty and ownership" of the Colombians in the isthmus of Panama—that this same man, thirteen years later, was horrified into a fever when Germany, facing powerful foes on two fronts, tore up the treaty of 1832, guaranteeing, not the sovereignty, but the bald neutrality of Belgium—a neutrality already destroyed, according to the evidence before the Germans, by Belgium's own acts.

It is hard, without an inordinate strain upon the credulity, to believe any such thing, particularly in view of the fact that this instantaneous indignation of the most impulsive and vocal of men was diligently concealed for at least six weeks, with reporters camped upon his doorstep day and night, begging him to say the very thing that he left so darkly unsaid. Can one imagine Roosevelt, with red-fire raging within him and sky-rockets bursting in his veins, holding his peace for a month and a half? I have no doubt whatever that Abbott, as he says, desired to avoid embarrassing Dr. Wilson—but think of Roosevelt showing any such delicacy! For one, I am not equal to the feat. All that unprecedented reticence, in fact, is far more readily explicable on other and less lofty grounds. What really happened I presume to guess. My guess is that Roosevelt, like the great majority of other Americans, was *not* instantly and automatically outraged by the invasion of Belgium. On the contrary, he probably viewed it as a regrettable, but not unexpected or unparalleled device of war—if anything, as something rather thrillingly gaudy and effective—a fine piece of virtuosity, pleasing to a military connoisseur. But then came the deluge of Belgian atrocity stories, and the organized campaign to enlist American sympathies. It succeeded very quickly. By the middle of August the British press bureau was in full swing; by the beginning of September the country was flooded with inflammatory stuff; six weeks after the war opened it was already hazardous for a German in America to state his country's case. Meanwhile, the Wilson administration had declared for neutrality, and was still making a more or less sincere effort to practice it, at least on the surface. Here was Roosevelt's opportunity, and he leaped to it with sure instinct. On the one side was the adminstration that he detested, and that all his self-interest (*e.g.*, his yearning to get back his old leadership and to become President again in 1917) prompted him to deal a mortal blow, and on the other side was a ready-made issue, full of emotional possibilities, stupendously pumped up by extremely clever propaganda, and so far unembraced by any other rabble-rouser of the first magnitude. Is it any wonder that he gave a whoop, jumped upon his cayuse, and began screaming for war? In war lay the greatest chance of his life. In war lay the confusion and destruction of Wilson, and the melodramatic renaissance of the Rough Rider, the professional hero, the national Barbarossa.

In all this, of course, I strip the process of its plumes and spangles, and expose a chain of causes and effects that Roosevelt himself, if he were alive, would denounce as grossly contumelious to his native purity of spirit—and perhaps in all honesty. It is not necessary to raise any doubts as to that honesty. No one who has given any study to the development and propagation of political doctrine in the United States can have failed to notice how the belief in issues among politicians tends to run in exact ratio to the popularity of those issues. Let the populace begin suddenly to swallow a new panacea or to take fright at a new bugaboo, and almost instantly nine-tenths of the master-minds of politics begin to believe that the panacea is a sure cure for all the malaises of the republic, and the bugaboo an immediate and unbearable menace to all law, order and domestic tranquillity. At the bottom of this singular intellectual resilience, of course, there is a good deal of hard calculation; a man must keep up with the procession of crazes, or his day is swiftly done. But in it there are also considerations a good deal more subtle, and maybe less discreditable. For one thing, a man devoted professionally to patriotism and the wisdom of the fathers is very apt to come to a resigned sort of acquiescence in all the doctrinaire rubbish that lies beneath the national scheme of things—to believe, let us say, if not that the plain people are gifted with an infallible sagacity, then at least that they have an inalienable right to see their follies executed. Poll-parroting nonsense as a matter of daily routine, the politician ends by assuming that it is sense, even though he doesn't believe it. For another thing, there is the contagion of mob enthusiasm—a much underestimated murrain. We all saw what it could do during the war—college professors taking their tune from the yellow journals, the rev. clergy performing in the pulpit like so many Liberty Loan orators in five-cent moving-picture houses, hysteria grown epidemic like the influenza. No man is so remote and arctic that he is wholly safe from that contamination; it explains many extravagant phenomena of a democratic society; in particular, it explains why the mob leader is so often a victim to his mob.

Roosevelt, a perfectly typical politician, devoted to the trade, not primarily because he was gnawed by ideals, but because he frankly enjoyed its rough-and-tumble encounters and its gaudy rewards, was probably moved in both ways—and also by the hard calculation that I have mentioned. If, by any ineptness of the British press-agents, tear-squeezers and orphan-exhibitors, indignation over the invasion of Belgium had failed to materialize—if, worse still, some gross infringement of American rights by the English had caused it to be forgotten completely—if, finally, Dr. Wilson had been whooping for war with the populace firmly against him—in such event it goes without saying that the moral horror of Dr. Roosevelt would have stopped short at a very low amperage, and that he would have refrained from making it the center of his polity. But with things as they were, lying neatly to his hand, he permitted it to take on an extraordinary virulence, and before long all his old delight in German militarism had been converted into a lofty detestation of German militarism, and its chief spokesman on this side of the Atlantic became its chief opponent. Getting rid of that old delight, of course, was not easily achieved. The concrete enthusiasm could be throttled, but the habit of mind remained. Thus one beheld the curious spectacle of militarism belabored in terms of militarism—of the Kaiser arraigned in unmistakably *kaiserliche* tones.

Such violent swallowings and regurgitations were no novelties to the man. His whole political career was marked, in fact, by performances of the same sort. The issues that won him most votes were issues that, at bottom, he didn't believe in; there was always a mental reservation in his rhetoric. He got into politics, not as a tribune of the plain people, but as an amateur reformer of the snobbish type common in the eighties, by the *Nation* out of the Social Register. He was a young Harvard man scandalized by the discovery that his town was run by men with such names as Michael O'Shaunnessy and Terence Googan—that his social inferiors were his political superiors. His sympathies were essentially anti-democratic. He had a high view of his private position as a young fellow of wealth and education. He believed in strong centralization—the concentration of power in a few hands, the strict regimentation of the nether herd, the abandonment of democratic platitudes. His heroes were such Federalists as Morris and Hamilton; he made his first splash in the world by writing about them and praising them. Worse, his daily associations were with the old

Union League crowd of high-tariff Republicans—men almost apoplectically opposed to every movement from below—safe and sane men, highly conservative and suspicious men—the profiteers of peace, as they afterward became the profiteers of war. His early adventures in politics were not very fortunate, nor did they reveal any capacity for leadership. The bosses of the day took him in rather humorously, played him for what they could get out of him, and then turned him loose. In a few years he became disgusted and went West. Returning after a bit, he encountered catastrophe: as a candidate for Mayor of New York he was drubbed unmercifully. He went back to the West. He was, up to this time, a comic figure—an anti-politician victimized by politicians, a pseudo-aristocrat made ridiculous by the mob-masters he detested.

But meanwhile something was happening that changed the whole color of the political scene, and was destined, eventually, to give Roosevelt his chance. That something was a shifting in what might be called the foundations of reform. Up to now it had been an essentially aristocratic movement—superior, sniffish and anti-democratic. But hereafter it took on a strongly democratic color and began to adopt democratic methods. More, the change gave it new life. What Harvard, the Union League Club and the *Nation* had failed to accomplish, the plain people now undertook to accomplish. This invasion of the old citadel of virtue was first observed in the West, and its manifestations out there must have given Roosevelt a good deal more disquiet than satisfaction. It is impossible to imagine him finding anything to his taste in the outlandish doings of the Populists, the wild schemes of the pre-Bryan dervishes. His instincts were against all that sort of thing. But as the movement spread toward the East it took on a certain urbanity, and by the time it reached the seaboard it had begun to be quite civilized. With this new brand of reform Roosevelt now made terms. It was full of principles that outraged all his pruderies, but it at least promised to work. His entire political history thereafter, down to the day of his death, was a history of compromises with the new forces—of a gradual yielding, for strategic purposes, to ideas that were intrinsically at odds with his congenital prejudices. When, after a generation of that sort of compromising, the so-called Progressive party was organized and he seized the leadership of it from the Westerners who had founded it, he performed a feat of wholesale englutination that must forever hold a high place upon the roll of political prodigies. That is to say, he swallowed at one gigantic gulp, and out of the same herculean jug, the most amazing mixture of social, political and economic perunas ever got down by one hero, however valiant, however athirst—a cocktail made up of all the elixirs hawked among the boobery in his time, from woman suffrage to the direct primary, and from the initiative and referendum to the short ballot, and from prohibition to public ownership, and from trust-busting to the recall of judges.

This homeric achievement made him the head of the most tatterdemalion party ever seen in American politics—a party composed of such incompatible ingredients and hung together so loosely that it began to disintegrate the moment it was born. In part it was made up of mere disordered enthusiasts—believers in anything and everything, pathetic victims of the credulity complex, habitual followers of jitney messiahs, incurable hopers and snufflers. But in part it was also made up of rice converts like Roosevelt himself—men eager for office, disappointed by the old parties, and now quite willing to accept any aid that half-idiot doctrinaires could give them. I have no doubt that Roosevelt himself, carried away by the emotional storms of the moment and especially by the quasi-religious monkey-shines that marked the first Progressive convention, gradually convinced himself that at least some of the doctrinaires, in the midst of all their imbecility, yet preached a few ideas that were workable, and perhaps even sound. But at bottom he was against them, and not only in the matter of their specific sure cures, but also in the larger matter of their childish faith in the wisdom and virtue of the plain people. Roosevelt, for all his fluent mastery of democratic counter-words, democratic gestures and all the rest of the armamentarium of the mob-master, had no such faith in his heart of hearts. He didn't believe in democracy; he believed simply in government. His remedy for all the great pangs and longings of existence was not a dispersion of authority, but a hard concentration of authority. He was not in favor of unlimited experiment; he was in favor of a rigid control from above, a despotism of inspired prophets and policemen. He was not for democracy as his followers understood democracy, and as it actually is and must be; he was for a paternalism of the true Bismarckian pattern, almost of the Napoleonic or Ludendorffian pattern—a paternalism concerning itself with all things, from the regulation of coal-mining and meat-packing to the regulation of spelling and marital rights. His instincts were always those of the property-owning Tory, not those of the romantic Liberal. All the fundamental objects of Liberalism—free speech, unhampered enterprise, the least possible governmental interference—were abhorrent to him. Even when, for campaign purposes, he came to terms with the Liberals his thoughts always ranged far afield. When he tackled the trusts the thing that he had in his mind's eye was not the restoration of competition but the subordination of all private trusts to one great national trust, with himself at its head. And when he attacked the courts it was not because they put their own prejudice before the law but because they refused to put *his* prejudices before the law.

In all his career no one ever heard him make an argument for the rights of the citizen; his eloquence was always expended in expounding the duties of the citizen. I have before me a speech in which he pleaded for "a spirit of kindly justice toward every man and woman," but that seems to be as far as he ever got in that direction—and it was the gratuitous justice of the absolute monarch that he apparently had in mind, not the autonomous and inalienable justice of a free society. The duties of the citizen, as he understood them, related not only to acts, but also to thoughts. There was, to his mind, a simple body of primary doctrine, and dissent from it was the foulest of crimes. No man could have been more bitter against opponents, or more unfair to them, or more ungenerous. In this department, indeed, even so gifted a specialist in dishonorable controversy as Dr. Wilson has seldom surpassed him. He never stood up to a frank and chivalrous debate. He dragged herrings across the trail. He made seductive faces at the gallery. He capitalized his enormous talents as an entertainer, his rank as a national hero, his public influence and consequence. The two great law-suits in which he was engaged were screaming burlesques upon justice. He tried them in the newspapers before ever they were called; he befogged them with irrelevant issues; his appearances in court were not the appearances of a witness standing on a level with other witnesses, but those of a comedian sure of his crowd. He was, in his dealings with concrete men as in his dealings with men in the mass, a charlatan of the very highest skill—and there was in him, it goes without saying, the persuasive charm of the charlatan as well as the daring deviousness, the humanness of naïveté as well as the humanness of chicane. He knew how to woo—and not only boobs. He was, for all his ruses and ambuscades, a jolly fellow.

It seems to be forgotten that the current American theory that political heresy should be put down by force, that a man who disputes whatever is official has no rights in law or equity, that he is lucky if he fares no worse than to lose his constitutional benefits of free speech, free assemblage and the use of the mails—it seems to be forgotten that this theory was invented, not by Dr. Wilson, but by Roosevelt. Most Liberals, I suppose, would credit it, if asked, to Wilson. He has carried it to extravagant lengths; he is the father superior of all the present advocates of it; he will probably go down into American history as its greatest prophet. But it was first clearly stated, not in any Wilsonian bull to the right-thinkers of all lands, but in Roosevelt's proceedings against the so-called Paterson anarchists. You will find it set forth at length in an opinion prepared for him by his Attorney-General, Charles J. Bonaparte, another curious and almost fabulous character, also an absolutist wearing the false whiskers of a democrat. Bonaparte furnished the law, and Roosevelt furnished the blood and iron. It was an almost ideal combination; Bonaparte had precisely the touch of Italian finesse that the Rough Rider always lacked. Roosevelt believed in the Paterson doctrine—in brief, that the Constitution does not throw its cloak around heretics—to the end of his days. In the face of what he conceived to be contumacy to revelation his fury took on a sort of lyrical grandeur. There was nothing too awful for the culprit in the dock. Upon his head were poured denunciations as violent as the wildest interdicts of a mediæval pope.

The appearance of such men, of course, is inevitable under a democracy. Consummate showmen, they arrest the wonder of the mob, and so put its suspicions to sleep. What they actually believe is of secondary consequence; the main thing is what they say; even more, the way they say it. Obviously, their activity does a great deal of damage to the democratic theory, for they are standing refutations of the primary doctrine that the common folk choose their leaders wisely. They damage it again in another and more subtle way. That is to say, their ineradicable contempt for the minds they must heat up and bamboozle leads them into a fatalism that shows itself in a cynical and opportunistic politics, a deliberate avoidance of fundamentals. The policy of a democracy thus becomes an eternal improvisation, changing with the private ambitions of its leaders and the transient and often unintelligible emotions of its rank and file. Roosevelt, incurably undemocratic in his habits of mind, often found it difficult to gauge those emotional oscillations. The fact explains his frequent loss of mob support, his periodical journeys into Coventry. There were times when his magnificent talents as a public comedian brought the proletariat to an almost unanimous groveling at his feet, but there were also times when he puzzled and dismayed it, and so awakened its hostility. When he assaulted Wilson on the neutrality issue, early in 1915, he made a quite typical mistake. That mistake consisted in assuming that public indignation over the wrongs of the Belgians would maintain itself at a high temperature—that it would develop rapidly into a demand for intervention. Roosevelt made himself the spokesman of that demand, and then found to his consternation that it was waning—that the great masses of the plain people, prospering under the Wilsonian neutrality, were inclined to preserve it, at no matter what cost to the Belgians. In 1915, after the *Lusitania* affair, things seemed to swing his way again, and he got vigorous support from the British press bureau. But in a few months he found himself once more attempting to lead a mob that was fast slipping away. Wilson, a very much shrewder politician, with little of Roosevelt's weakness for succumbing to his own rhetoric, discerned the truth much more quickly and clearly. In 1916 he made his campaign for reëlection on a flatly anti-Roosevelt peace issue, and not only got himself reëlected, but also drove Roosevelt out of the ring.

What happened thereafter deserves a great deal more careful study than it will ever get from the timorous eunuchs who posture as American historians. At the moment, it is the official doctrine in England, where the thing is more freely discussed than at home, that Wilson was forced into the war by an irresistible movement from below—that the plain people compelled him to abandon neutrality and move reluctantly upon the Germans. Nothing could be more untrue. The plain people, at the end of 1916, were in favor of peace, and they believed that Wilson was in favor of peace. How they were gradually worked up to complaisance and then to enthusiasm and then to hysteria and then to acute mania—this is a tale to be told in more leisurely days and by historians without boards of trustees on their necks. For the present purpose it is sufficient to note that the whole thing was achieved so quickly and so neatly that its success left Roosevelt surprised and helpless. His issue had been stolen from directly under his nose. He was left standing daunted and alone, a boy upon a burning deck. It took him months to collect his scattered wits, and even then his attack upon the administration was feeble and ineffective. To the plain people it seemed a mere ill-natured snapping at a successful rival, which in fact it was, and so they paid no heed to it, and Roosevelt found himself isolated once more. Thus he passed from the scene in the shadows, a broken politician and a disappointed man.

I have a notion that he died too soon. His best days were probably not behind him, but ahead of him. Had he lived ten years longer, he might have enjoyed a great rehabilitation and exchanged his old false leadership of the inflammatory and fickle mob for a sound and true leadership of the civilized minority. For the more one studies his mountebankeries as mob-master, the more one is convinced that there was a shrewd man beneath the motley, and that his actual beliefs were anything but nonsensical. The truth of them, indeed, emerges more clearly day by day. The old theory of a federation of free and autonomous states has broken down by its own weight, and we are moved toward centralization by forces that have long been powerful and are now quite irresistible. So with the old theory of national isolation: it, too, has fallen to pieces. The United States can no longer hope to lead a separate life in the world, undisturbed by the pressure of foreign aspirations. We came out of the war to find ourselves hemmed in by hostilities that no longer troubled to conceal themselves, and if they are not as close and menacing today as those that have hemmed in Germany for centuries they are none the less plainly there and plainly growing. Roosevelt, by whatever route of reflection or intuition, arrived at a sense of these facts at a time when it was still somewhat scandalous to state them, and it was the capital effort of his life to reconcile them, in some dark way or other, to the prevailing platitudes, and so get them heeded. To-day no one seriously maintains, as all Americans once maintained, that the states can go on existing together as independent commonwealths, each with its own laws, its own legal theory and its own view of the common constitutional bond. And to-day no one seriously maintains, as all Americans once maintained, that the nation may safely potter on without adequate means of defense. However unpleasant it may be to contemplate, the fact is plain that the American people, during the next century, will have to fight to maintain their place in the sun.

Roosevelt lived just long enough to see his notions in these directions take on life, but not long enough to see them openly adopted. To the extent of his prevision he was a genuine leader of the nation, and perhaps in the years to come, when his actual ideas are disentangled from the demagogic fustian in which he had to wrap them, his more honest pronunciamentoes will be given canonical honors, and he will be ranked among the prophets. He saw clearly more than one other thing that was by no means obvious to his age—for example, the inevitability of frequent wars under the new world-system of extreme nationalism; again, the urgent necessity, for primary police ends, of organizing the backward nations into groups of vassals, each under the hoof of some first-rate power; yet again, the probability of the breakdown of the old system of free competition; once more, the high social utility of the Spartan virtues and the grave dangers of sloth and ease; finally, the incompatibility of free speech and democracy. I do not say that he was always quite honest, even when he was most indubitably right. But in so far as it was possible for him to be honest and exist at all politically, he inclined toward the straightforward thought and the candid word. That is to say, his instinct prompted him to tell the truth, just as the instinct of Dr. Wilson prompts him to shift and dissimulate. What ailed him was the fact that his lust for glory, when it came to a struggle, was always vastly more powerful than his lust for the eternal verities. Tempted sufficiently, he would sacrifice anything and everything to get applause. Thus the statesman was debauched by the politician, and the philosopher was elbowed out of sight by the popinjay.

Where he failed most miserably was in his remedies. A remarkably penetrating diagnostician, well-read, unprejudiced and with a touch of genuine scientific passion, he always stooped to quackery when he prescribed a course of treatment. For all his sensational attacks upon the trusts, he never managed to devise a scheme to curb them—and even when he sought to apply the schemes of other men he invariably corrupted the business with timorousness and insincerity. So with his campaign for national preparedness. He displayed the disease magnificently, but the course of medication that he proposed was vague and unconvincing; it was not, indeed, without justification that the plain people mistook his advocacy of an adequate army for a mere secret yearning to prance upon a charger at the head of huge hordes. So, again, with his eloquent plea for national solidarity and an end of hyphenism. The dangers that he pointed out were very real and very menacing, but his plan for abating them only made them worse. His objurgations against the Germans surely accomplished nothing; the hyphenate of 1915 is still a hyphenate in his heart —with bitter and unforgettable grievances to support him. Roosevelt, very characteristically, swung too far. In denouncing German hyphenism so extravagantly he contrived to give an enormous impetus to English hyphenism, a far older and more perilous malady. It has already gone so far that a large and influential party endeavors almost openly to convert the United States into a mere vassal state of England's. Instead of national solidarity following the war, we have only a revival of Know-Nothingism; one faction of hyphenates tries to exterminate another faction. Roosevelt's error here was one that he was always making. Carried away by the ease with which he could heat up the mob, he tried to accomplish instantly and by *force majeure* what could only be accomplished by a long and complex process, with more good will on both sides than ever so opinionated and melodramatic a pseudo-Junker was capable of. But though he thus made a mess of the cure, he was undoubtedly right about the disease.

The talented Sherman, in the monograph that I have praised, argues that the chief contribution of the dead gladiator to American life was the example of his gigantic gusto, his delight in toil and struggle, his superb aliveness. The fact is plain. What he stood most clearly in opposition to was the superior pessimism of the three Adams brothers—the notion that the public problems of a democracy are unworthy the thought and effort of a civilized and self-respecting man—the sad error that lies in wait for all of us who hold ourselves above the general. Against this suicidal aloofness Roosevelt always hurled himself with brave effect. Enormously sensitive and resilient, almost pathological in his appetite for activity, he made it plain to every one that the most stimulating sort of sport imaginable was to be obtained in fighting, not for mere money, but for ideas. There was no aristocratic reserve about him. He was not, in fact, an aristocrat at all, but a quite typical member of the upper *bourgeoisie*; his people were not *patroons* in New Amsterdam, but simple traders; he was himself a social pusher, and eternally tickled by the thought that he had had a Bonaparte in his cabinet. The marks of the thoroughbred were simply not there. The man was blatant, crude, overly confidential, devious, tyrannical, vainglorious, sometimes quite childish. One often observed in him a certain pathetic wistfulness, a reaching out for a grand manner that was utterly beyond him. But the sweet went with the bitter. He had all the virtues of the fat and complacent burgher. His disdain of affectation and prudery was magnificent. He hated all pretension save his own pretension. He had a sound respect for hard effort, for loyalty, for thrift, for honest achievement.

His worst defects, it seems to me, were the defects of his race and time. Aspiring to be the leader of a nation of third-rate men, he had to stoop to the common level. When he struck out for realms above that level he always came to grief: this was the "unsafe" Roosevelt, the Roosevelt who was laughed at, the Roosevelt retired suddenly to cold storage. This was the Roosevelt who, in happier times and a better place, might have been. Well, one does what one can.

III.

The Sahara of the Bozart

Alas, for the South! Her books have grown fewer—
She never was much given to literature.

IN the lamented J. Gordon Coogler, author of these elegaic lines, there was the insight of a true poet. He was the last bard of Dixie, at least in the legitimate line. Down there a poet is now almost as rare as an oboe-player, a dry-point etcher or a metaphysician. It is, indeed, amazing to contemplate so vast a vacuity. One thinks of the interstellar spaces, of the colossal reaches of the now mythical ether. Nearly the whole of Europe could be lost in that stupendous region of fat farms, shoddy cities and paralyzed cerebrums: one could throw in France, Germany and Italy, and still have room for the British Isles. And yet, for all its size and all its wealth and all the "progress" it babbles of, it is almost as sterile, artistically, intellectually, culturally, as the Sahara Desert. There are single acres in Europe that house more first-rate men than all the states south of the Potomac; there are probably single square miles in America. If the whole of the late Confederacy were to be engulfed by a tidal wave to-morrow, the effect upon the civilized minority of men in the world would be but little greater than that of a flood on the Yang-tse-kiang. It would be impossible in all history to match so complete a drying-up of a civilization.

I say a civilization because that is what, in the old days, the South had, despite the Baptist and Methodist barbarism that reigns down there now. More, it was a civilization of manifold excellences—perhaps the best that the Western Hemisphere has ever seen—undoubtedly the best that These States have ever seen. Down to the middle of the last century, and even beyond, the main hatchery of ideas on this side of the water was across the Potomac bridges. The New England shopkeepers and theologians never really developed a civilization; all they ever developed was a government. They were, at their best, tawdry and tacky fellows, oafish in manner and devoid of imagination; one searches the books in vain for mention of a salient Yankee gentleman; as well look for a Welsh gentleman. But in the south there were men of delicate fancy, urbane instinct and aristocratic manner—in brief, superior men—in brief, gentry. To politics, their chief diversion, they brought active and original minds. It was there that nearly all the political theories we still cherish and suffer under came to birth. It was there that the crude dogmatism of New England was refined and humanized. It was there, above all, that some attention was given to the art of living—that life got beyond and above the state of a mere infliction and became an exhilarating experience. A certain noble spaciousness was in the ancient southern scheme of things. The *Ur*-Confederate had leisure. He liked to toy with ideas. He was hospitable and tolerant. He had the vague thing that we call culture.

But consider the condition of his late empire today. The picture gives one the creeps. It is as if the Civil War stamped out every last bearer of the torch, and left only a mob of peasants on the field. One thinks of Asia Minor, resigned to Armenians, Greeks and wild swine, of Poland abandoned to the Poles. In all that gargantuan paradise of the fourth-rate there is not a single picture gallery worth going into, or a single orchestra capable of playing the nine symphonies of Beethoven, or a single opera-house, or a single theater devoted to decent plays, or a single public monument (built since the war) that is worth looking at, or a single workshop devoted to the making of beautiful things. Once you have counted Robert Loveman (an Ohioan by birth) and John McClure (an Oklahoman) you will not find a single southern poet above the rank of a neighborhood rhymester. Once you have counted James Branch Cabell (a lingering survivor of the *ancien régime*: a scarlet dragonfly imbedded in opaque amber) you will not find a single southern prose writer who can actually write. And once you have—but when you come to critics, musical composers, painters, sculptors, architects and the like, you will have to give it up, for there is not even a bad one between the Potomac mud-flats and the Gulf. Nor an historian. Nor a sociologist. Nor a philosopher. Nor a theologian. Nor a scientist. In all these fields the south is an awe-inspiring blank—a brother to Portugal, Serbia and Esthonia.

Consider, for example, the present estate and dignity of Virginia—in the great days indubitably the premier American state, the mother of Presidents and statesmen, the home of the first American university worthy of the name, the *arbiter elegantiarum* of the western world. Well, observe Virginia to-day. It is years since a first-rate man, save only Cabell, has come out of it; it is years since an idea has come out of it. The old aristocracy went down the red gullet of war; the poor white trash are now in the saddle. Politics in Virginia are cheap, ignorant, parochial, idiotic; there is scarcely a man in office above the rank of a professional job-seeker; the political doctrine that prevails is made up of hand-me-downs from the bumpkinry of the Middle West—Bryanism, Prohibition, vice crusading, all that sort of filthy claptrap; the administration of the law is turned over to professors of Puritanism and espionage; a Washington or a Jefferson, dumped there by some act of God, would be denounced as a scoundrel and jailed over-night. Elegance, *esprit*, culture? Virginia has no art, no literature, no philosophy, no mind or aspiration of her own. Her education has sunk to the Baptist seminary level; not a single contribution to human knowledge has come out of her colleges in twenty-five years; she spends less than half upon her common schools, *per capita*, than any northern state spends. In brief, an intellectual Gobi or Lapland. Urbanity, *politesse*, chivalry? Go to! It was in Virginia that they invented the device of searching for contraband whiskey in women's underwear. . . . There remains, at the top, a ghost of the old aristocracy, a bit wistful and infinitely charming. But it has lost all its old leadership to fabulous monsters from the lower depths; it is submerged in an industrial plutocracy that is ignorant and ignominious. The mind of the state, as it is revealed to the nation, is pathetically naïve and inconsequential. It no longer reacts with energy and elasticity to great problems. It has fallen to the bombastic trivialities of the camp-meeting and the chautauqua. Its foremost exponent—if so flabby a thing may be said to have an exponent—is a stateman whose name is synonymous with empty words, broken pledges and false pretenses. One could no more imagine a Lee or a Washington in the Virginia of to-day than one could imagine a Huxley in Nicaragua.

I choose the Old Dominion, not because I disdain it, but precisely because I esteem it. It is, by long odds, the most civilized of the southern states, now as always. It has sent a host of creditable sons northward; the stream kept running into our own time. Virginians, even the worst of them, show the effects of a great tradition. They hold themselves above other southerners, and with sound pretension. If one turns to such a commonwealth as Georgia the picture becomes far darker. There the liberated lower orders of whites have borrowed the worst commercial bounderism of the Yankee and superimposed it upon a culture that, at bottom, is but little removed from savagery. Georgia is at once the home of the cotton-mill sweater and of the most noisy and vapid sort of chamber of commerce, of the Methodist parson turned Savonarola and of the lynching bee. A self-respecting European, going there to live, would not only find intellectual stimulation utterly lacking; he would actually feel a certain insecurity, as if the scene were the Balkans or the China Coast. The Leo Frank affair was no isolated phenomenon. It fitted into its frame very snugly. It was a natural expression of Georgian notions of truth and justice. There is a state with more than half the area of Italy and more population than either Denmark or Norway, and yet in thirty years it has not produced a single idea. Once upon a time a Georgian printed a couple of books that attracted notice, but immediately it turned out that he was little more than an amanuensis for the local blacks—that his works were really the products, not of white Georgia, but of black Georgia. Writing afterward *as* a white man, he swiftly subsided into the fifth rank. And he is not only the glory of the literature of Georgia; he is, almost literally, the whole of the literature of Georgia—nay, of the entire art of Georgia.

Virginia is the best of the south to-day, and Georgia is perhaps the worst. The one is simply senile; the other is crass, gross, vulgar and obnoxious. Between lies a vast plain of mediocrity, stupidity, lethargy, almost of dead silence. In the north, of course, there is also grossness, crassness, vulgarity. The north, in its way, is also stupid and obnoxious. But nowhere in the north is there such complete sterility, so depressing a lack of all civilized gesture and aspiration. One would find it difficult to unearth a second-rate city between the Ohio and the

Pacific that isn't struggling to establish an orchestra, or setting up a little theater, or going in for an art gallery, or making some other effort to get into touch with civilization. These efforts often fail, and sometimes they succeed rather absurdly, but under them there is at least an impulse that deserves respect, and that is the impulse to seek beauty and to experiment with ideas, and so to give the life of every day a certain dignity and purpose. You will find no such impulse in the south. There are no committees down there cadging subscriptions for orchestras; if a string quartet is ever heard there, the news of it has never come out; an opera troupe, when it roves the land, is a nine days' wonder. The little theater movement has swept the whole country, enormously augmenting the public interest in sound plays, giving new dramatists their chance, forcing reforms upon the commercial theater. Everywhere else the wave rolls high—but along the line of the Potomac it breaks upon a rock-bound shore. There is no little theater beyond. There is no gallery of pictures. No artist ever gives exhibitions. No one talks of such things. No one seems to be interested in such things.

As for the cause of this unanimous torpor and doltishness, this curious and almost pathological estrangement from everything that makes for a civilized culture, I have hinted at it already, and now state it again. The south has simply been drained of all its best blood. The vast blood-letting of the Civil War half exterminated and wholly paralyzed the old aristocracy, and so left the land to the harsh mercies of the poor white trash, now its masters. The war, of course, was not a complete massacre. It spared a decent number of first-rate southerners—perhaps even some of the very best. Moreover, other countries, notably France and Germany, have survived far more staggering butcheries, and even showed marked progress thereafter. But the war not only cost a great many valuable lives; it also brought bankruptcy, demoralization and despair in its train—and so the majority of the first-rate southerners that were left, broken in spirit and unable to live under the new dispensation, cleared out. A few went to South America, to Egypt, to the Far East. Most came north. They were fecund; their progeny is widely dispersed, to the great benefit of the north. A southerner of good blood almost always does well in the north. He finds, even in the big cities, surroundings fit for a man of condition. His peculiar qualities have a high social value, and are esteemed. He is welcomed by the codfish aristocracy as one palpably superior. But in the south he throws up his hands. It is impossible for him to stoop to the common level. He cannot brawl in politics with the grandsons of his grandfather's tenants. He is unable to share their fierce jealousy of the emerging black—the cornerstone of all their public thinking. He is anæsthetic to their theological and political enthusiasms. He finds himself an alien at their feasts of soul. And so he withdraws into his tower, and is heard of no more. Cabell is almost a perfect example. His eyes, for years, were turned toward the past; he became a professor of the grotesque genealogizing that decaying aristocracies affect; it was only by a sort of accident that he discovered himself to be an artist. The south is unaware of the fact to this day; it regards Woodrow Wilson and Col. John Temple Graves as much finer stylists, and Frank L. Stanton as an infinitely greater poet. If it has heard, which I doubt, that Cabell has been hoofed by the Comstocks, it unquestionably views that assault as a deserved rebuke to a fellow who indulges a lewd passion for fancy writing, and is a covert enemy to the Only True Christianity.

What is needed down there, before the vexatious public problems of the region may be intelligently approached, is a survey of the population by competent ethnologists and anthropologists. The immigrants of the north have been studied at great length, and any one who is interested may now apply to the Bureau of Ethnology for elaborate data as to their racial strains, their stature and cranial indices, their relative capacity for education, and the changes that they undergo under American *Kultur*. But the older stocks of the south, and particularly the emancipated and dominant poor white trash, have never been investigated scientifically, and most of the current generalizations about them are probably wrong. For example, the generalization that they are purely Anglo-Saxon in blood. This I doubt very seriously. The chief strain down there, I believe, is Celtic rather than Saxon, particularly in the hill country. French blood, too, shows itself here and there, and so does Spanish, and so does German. The last-named entered from the northward, by way of the limestone belt just east of the

Allegheníes. Again, it is very likely that in some parts of the south a good many of the plebeian whites have more than a trace of negro blood. Interbreeding under concubinage produced some very light half-breeds at an early day, and no doubt appreciable numbers of them went over into the white race by the simple process of changing their abode. Not long ago I read a curious article by an intelligent negro, in which he stated that it is easy for a very light negro to pass as white in the south on account of the fact that large numbers of southerners accepted as white have distinctly negroid features. Thus it becomes a delicate and dangerous matter for a train conductor or a hotel-keeper to challenge a suspect. But the Celtic strain is far more obvious than any of these others. It not only makes itself visible in physical stigmata—*e.g.*, leanness and dark coloring—but also in mental traits. For example, the religious thought of the south is almost precisely identical with the religious thought of Wales. There is the same naïve belief in an anthropomorphic Creator but little removed, in manner and desire, from an evangelical bishop; there is the same submission to an ignorant and impudent sacerdotal tyranny, and there is the same sharp contrast between doctrinal orthodoxy and private ethics. Read Caradoc Evans' ironical picture of the Welsh Wesleyans in his preface to "My Neighbors," and you will be instantly reminded of the Georgia and Carolina Methodists. The most booming sort of piety, in the south, is not incompatible with the theory that lynching is a benign institution. Two generations ago it was not incompatible with an ardent belief in slavery.

It is highly probable that some of the worst blood of western Europe flows in the veins of the southern poor whites, now poor no longer. The original strains, according to every honest historian, were extremely corrupt. Philip Alexander Bruce (a Virginian of the old gentry) says in his "Industrial History of Virginia in the Seventeenth Century" that the first native-born generation was largely illegitimate. "One of the most common offenses against morality committed in the lower ranks of life in Virginia during the seventeenth century," he says, "was bastardy." The mothers of these bastards, he continues, were chiefly indentured servants, and "had belonged to the lowest class in their native country." Fanny Kemble Butler, writing of the Georgia poor whites of a century later, described them as "the most degraded race of human beings claiming an Anglo-Saxon origin that can be found on the face of the earth—filthy, lazy, ignorant, brutal, proud, penniless savages." The Sunday-school and the chautauqua, of course, have appreciably mellowed the descendants of these "savages," and their economic progress and rise to political power have done perhaps even more, but the marks of their origin are still unpleasantly plentiful. Every now and then they produce a political leader who puts their secret notions of the true, the good and the beautiful into plain words, to the amazement and scandal of the rest of the country. That amazement is turned into downright incredulity when news comes that his platform has got him high office, and that he is trying to execute it.

In the great days of the south the line between the gentry and the poor whites was very sharply drawn. There was absolutely no intermarriage. So far as I know there is not a single instance in history of a southerner of the upper class marrying one of the bondwomen described by Mr. Bruce. In other societies characterized by class distinctions of that sort it is common for the lower class to be improved by extra-legal crosses. That is to say, the men of the upper class take women of the lower class as mistresses, and out of such unions spring the extraordinary plebeians who rise sharply from the common level, and so propagate the delusion that all other plebeians would do the same thing if they had the chance—in brief, the delusion that class distinctions are merely economic and conventional, and not congenital and genuine. But in the south the men of the upper classes sought their mistresses among the blacks, and after a few generations there was so much white blood in the black women that they were considerably more attractive than the unhealthy and bedraggled women of the poor whites. This preference continued into our own time. A southerner of good family once told me in all seriousness that he had reached his majority before it ever occurred to him that a white woman might make quite as agreeable a mistress as the octaroons of his jejune fancy. If the thing has changed of late, it is not the fault of the southern white man, but of the southern mulatto women. The more sightly yellow girls of the region, with improving economic opportunities, have gained self-respect, and so they are no longer as willing to enter into concubinage as their grand-dams were.

As a result of this preference of the southern gentry for mulatto mistresses there was created a series of mixed strains containing the best white blood of the south, and perhaps of the whole country. As another result the poor whites went unfertilized from above, and so missed the improvement that so constantly shows itself in the peasant stocks of other countries. It is a commonplace that nearly all negroes who rise above the general are of mixed blood, usually with the white predominating. I know a great many negroes, and it would be hard for me to think of an exception. What is too often forgotten is that this white blood is not the blood of the poor whites but that of the old gentry. The mulatto girls of the early days despised the poor whites as creatures distinctly inferior to negroes, and it was thus almost unheard of for such a girl to enter into relations with a man of that submerged class. This aversion was based upon a sound instinct. The southern mulatto of to-day is a proof of it. Like all other half-breeds he is an unhappy man, with disquieting tendencies toward anti-social habits of thought, but he is intrinsically a better animal than the pure-blooded descendant of the old poor whites, and he not infrequently demonstrates it. It is not by accident that the negroes of the south are making faster progress, economically and culturally, than the masses of the whites. It is not by accident that the only visible æsthetic activity in the south is wholly in their hands. No southern composer has ever written music so good as that of half a dozen white-black composers who might be named. Even in politics, the negro reveals a curious superiority. Despite the fact that the race question has been the main political concern of the southern whites for two generations, to the practical exclusion of everything else, they have contributed nothing to its discussion that has impressed the rest of the world so deeply and so favorably as three or four books by southern negroes.

Entering upon such themes, of course, one must resign one's self to a vast misunderstanding and abuse. The south has not only lost its old capacity for producing ideas; it has also taken on the worst intolerance of ignorance and stupidity. Its prevailing mental attitude for several decades past has been that of its own hedge ecclesiastics. All who dissent from its orthodox doctrines are scoundrels. All who presume to discuss its ways realistically are damned. I have had, in my day, several experiences in point. Once, after I had published an article on some phase of the eternal race question, a leading southern newspaper replied by printing a column of denunciation of my father, then dead nearly twenty years—a philippic placarding him as an ignorant foreigner of dubious origin, inhabiting "the Baltimore ghetto" and speaking a dialect recalling that of Weber & Fields—two thousand words of incandescent nonsense, utterly false and beside the point, but exactly meeting the latter-day southern notion of effective controversy. Another time, I published a short discourse on lynching, arguing that the sport was popular in the south because the backward culture of the region denied the populace more seemly recreations. Among such recreations I mentioned those afforded by brass bands, symphony orchestras, boxing matches, amateur athletic contests, shoot-the-chutes, roof gardens, horse races, and so on. In reply another great southern journal denounced me as a man "of wineshop temperament, brass-jewelry tastes and pornographic predilections." In other words, brass bands, in the south, are classed with brass jewelry, and both are snares of the devil! To advocate setting up symphony orchestras is pornography! . . . Alas, when the touchy southerner attempts a greater urbanity, the result is often even worse. Some time ago a colleague of mine printed an article deploring the arrested cultural development of Georgia. In reply he received a number of protests from patriotic Georgians, and all of them solemnly listed the glories of the state. I indulge in a few specimens:

> Who has not heard of Asa G. Candler, whose name is synonymous with Coca-Cola, a Georgia product?
>
> The first Sunday-school in the world was opened in Savannah.
>
> Who does not recall with pleasure the writings of . . . Frank L. Stanton, Georgia's brilliant poet?
>
> Georgia was the first state to organize a Boys' Corn Club in the South—Newton county, 1904.
>
> The first to suggest a common United Daughters of the Confederacy badge was Mrs. Raynes, of Georgia.

The first to suggest a state historian of the United Daughters of the Confederacy was Mrs. C. Helen Plane (Macon convention, 1896).

The first to suggest putting to music Heber's "From Greenland's Icy Mountains" was Mrs. F. R. Goulding, of Savannah.

And so on, and so on. These proud boasts came, remember, not from obscure private persons, but from "Leading Georgians"—in one case, the state historian. Curious sidelights upon the ex-Confederate mind! Another comes from a stray copy of a negro paper. It describes an ordinance lately passed by the city council of Douglas, Ga., forbidding any trousers presser, on penalty of forfeiting a $500 bond, to engage in "pressing for both white and colored." This in a town, says the negro paper, where practically all of the white inhabitants have "their food prepared by colored hands," "their babies cared for by colored hands," and "the clothes which they wear right next to their skins washed in houses where negroes live"—houses in which the said clothes "remain for as long as a week at a time." But if you marvel at the absurdity, keep it dark! A casual word, and the united press of the south will be upon your trail, denouncing you bitterly as a scoundrelly Yankee, a Bolshevik Jew, an agent of the Wilhelmstrasse. . . .

Obviously, it is impossible for intelligence to flourish in such an atmosphere. Free inquiry is blocked by the idiotic certainties of ignorant men. The arts, save in the lower reaches of the gospel hymn, the phonograph and the chautauqua harangue, are all held in suspicion. The tone of public opinion is set by an upstart class but lately emerged from industrial slavery into commercial enterprise—the class of "hustling" business men, of "live wires," of commercial club luminaries, of "drive" managers, of forward-lookers and right-thinkers—in brief, of third-rate southerners inoculated with all the worst traits of the Yankee sharper. One observes the curious effects of an old tradition of truculence upon a population now merely pushful and impudent, of an old tradition of chivalry upon a population now quite without imagination. The old repose is gone. The old romanticism is gone. The philistinism of the new type of town-boomer southerner is not only indifferent to the ideals of the old south; it is positively antagonistic to them. That philistinism regards human life, not as an agreeable adventure, but as a mere trial of rectitude and efficiency. It is overwhelmingly utilitarian and moral. It is inconceivably hollow and obnoxious. What remains of the ancient tradition is simply a certain charming civility in private intercourse—often broken down, alas, by the hot rages of Puritanism, but still generally visible. The southerner, at his worst, is never quite the surly cad that the Yankee is. His sensitiveness may betray him into occasional bad manners, but in the main he is a pleasant fellow—hospitable, polite, good-humored, even jovial. . . . But a bit absurd. . . . A bit pathetic.

IV.

The Divine Afflatus

THE suave and œdematous Chesterton, in a late effort to earn the honorarium of a Chicago newspaper, composed a thousand words of labored counterblast to what is called inspiration in the arts. The thing itself, he argued, has little if any actual existence; we hear so much about it because its alleged coyness and fortuitousness offer a convenient apology for third-rate work. The man taken in such third-rate work excuses himself on the ground that he is a helpless slave of some power that stands outside him, and is quite beyond his control. On days when it favors him he teems with ideas and creates masterpieces, but on days when it neglects him he is crippled and impotent—a fiddle without a bow, an engine without steam, a tire without air. All this, according to Chesterton, is nonsense. A man who can really write at all, or paint at all, or compose at all should be able to do it at almost any time, provided only "he is not drunk or asleep."

So far Chesterton. The formula of the argument is simple and familiar: to dispose of a problem all that is necessary is to deny that it exists. But there are plenty of men, I believe, who find themselves unable to resolve the difficulty in any such cavalier manner—men whose chief burden and distinction, in fact, is that they do not employ formulæ in their thinking, but are thrown constantly upon industry, ingenuity and the favor of God. Among such men there remains a good deal more belief in what is vaguely called inspiration. They know by hard experience that there are days when their ideas flow freely and clearly, and days when they are dammed up damnably. Say a man of that sort has a good day. For some reason quite incomprehensible to him all his mental processes take on an amazing ease and slickness. Almost without conscious effort he solves technical problems that have badgered him for weeks. He is full of novel expedients, extraordinary efficiencies, strange cunnings. He has a feeling that he has suddenly and unaccountably broken through a wall, dispersed a fog, got himself out of the dark. So he does a double or triple stint of the best work that he is capable of—maybe of far better work than he has ever been capable of before—and goes to bed impatient for the morrow. And on the morrow he discovers to his consternation that he has become almost idiotic, and quite incapable of any work at all.

I challenge any man who trades in ideas to deny that he has this experience. The truth is that he has it constantly. It overtakes poets and contrapuntists, critics and dramatists, philosophers and journalists; it may even be shared, so far as I know, by advertisement writers, chautauqua orators and the rev. clergy. The characters that all anatomists of melancholy mark in it are the irregular ebb and flow of the tides, and the impossibility of getting them under any sort of rational control. The brain, as it were, stands to one side and watches itself pitching and tossing, full of agony but essentially helpless. Here the man of creative imagination pays a ghastly price for all his superiorities and immunities; nature takes revenge upon him for dreaming of improvements in the scheme of things. Sitting there in his lonely room, gnawing the handle of his pen, racked by his infernal quest, horribly bedevilled by incessant flashes of itching, toothache, eye-strain and evil conscience—thus tortured, he makes atonement for his crime of being intelligent. The normal man, the healthy and honest man, the good citizen and householder—this man, I daresay, knows nothing of all that travail. It is reserved especially for artists and metaphysicians. It is the particular penalty of those who pursue strange butterflies into dark forests, and go fishing in enchanted and forbidden streams.

Let us, then, assume that the fact is proved: the nearest poet is a witness to it. But what of the underlying mystery? How are we to account for that puckish and inexplicable rise and fall of inspiration? My questions, of course, are purely rhetorical. Explanations exist; they have existed for all time; there is always a well-known solution to every human problem—neat, plausible, and wrong. The ancients, in the case at bar, laid the blame upon the gods: sometimes they were remote and surly, and sometimes they were kind. In the Middle Ages lesser powers took a hand in the matter, and so one reads of works of art inspired by Our Lady, by the Blessed Saints, by the souls of the departed, and even by the devil. In our own day there are explanations less supernatural but no less fanciful—to wit, the explanation that the whole thing is a matter of pure chance, and not to be resolved into any orderly process—to wit, the explanation that the controlling factor is external circumstance, that the artist happily married to a dutiful wife is thereby inspired—finally, to make an end, the explanation that it is all a question of Freudian complexes, themselves lurking in impenetrable shadows. But all of these explanations fail to satisfy the mind that is not to be put off with mere words. Some of them are palpably absurd; others beg the question. The problem of the how remains, even when the problem of the why is disposed of. What is the precise machinery whereby the cerebrum is bestirred to such abnormal activity on one day that it sparkles and splutters like an arclight, and reduced to such feebleness on another day that it smokes and gutters like a tallow dip?

In this emergency, having regard for the ages-long and unrelieved sufferings of artists great and small, I offer a new, simple, and at all events not ghostly solution. It is supported by the observed facts, by logical analogies and by the soundest known principles of psychology, and so I present it without apologies. It may be couched, for convenience, in the following brief terms: that inspiration, so-called, is a function of metabolism, and that it is chiefly conditioned by the state of the intestinal flora—in larger words, that a man's flow of ideas is controlled and determined, both quantitatively and qualitatively, not by the whims of the gods, nor by the terms of his armistice with his wife, nor by the combinations of some transcendental set of dice, but by the chemical content of the blood that lifts itself from his liver to his brain, and that this chemical content is established in his digestive tract, particularly south of the pylorus. A man may write great poetry when he is drunk, when he is cold and miserable, when he is bankrupt, when he has a black eye, when his wife glowers at him across the table, when his children lie dying of smallpox; he may even write it during an earthquake, or while crossing the English channel, or in the midst of a Methodist revival, or in New York. But I am so far gone in materialism that I am disposed to deny flatly and finally, and herewith do deny flatly and finally, that there has lived a poet in the whole history of the world, ancient or modern, near or far, who ever managed to write great poetry, or even passably fair and decent poetry, at a time when he was suffering from stenosis at any point along the thirty-foot *via dolorosa* running from the pylorus to the sigmoid flexure. In other words, when he was—

But perhaps I had better leave your medical adviser to explain. After all, it is not necessary to go any further in this direction; the whole thing may be argued in terms of the blood stream—and the blood stream is respectable, as the duodenum is an outcast. It is the blood and the blood only, in fact, that the cerebrum is aware of; of what goes on elsewhere it can learn only by hearsay. If all is well below, then the blood that enters the brain through the internal carotid is full of the elements necessary to bestir the brain-cells to their highest activity; if, on the contrary, anabolism and katabolism are going on ineptly, if the blood is not getting the supplies that it needs and not getting rid of the wastes that burden it, then the brain-cells will be both starved and poisoned, and not all the king's horses and all the king's men can make them do their work with any show of ease and efficiency. In the first case the man whose psyche dwells in the cells will have a moment of inspiration—that is, he will find it a strangely simple and facile matter to write his poem, or iron out his syllogism, or make his bold modulation from F sharp minor to C major, or get his flesh-tone, or maybe only perfect his swindle. But in the second case he will be stumped and helpless. The more he tries, the more vividly he will be conscious of his impotence. Sweat will stand out in beads upon his brow, he will fish patiently for the elusive thought, he will try coaxing and subterfuge, he will retire to his ivory tower, he will tempt the invisible powers with black coffee, tea, alcohol and the alkaloids, he may even curse God and invite death—but he will not write his poem, or iron out his syllogism, or find his way into C major, or get his flesh-tone, or perfect his swindle.

Fix your eye upon this hypothesis of metabolic inspiration, and at once you will find the key to many a correlative mystery. For one thing, it quickly explains the observed hopelessness of trying to pump up inspiration by mere hard industry—the essential imbecility of the 1,000 words a day formula. Let there be stenosis below, and not all the industry of a Hercules will suffice to awaken the lethargic brain. Here, indeed, the harder the striving, the worse the stagnation—as every artist knows only too well. And why not? Striving in the face of such an interior obstacle is the most cruel of enterprises—a business more nerve-wracking and exhausting than reading a newspaper or watching a bad play. The pain thus produced, the emotions thus engendered, react upon the liver in a manner scientifically displayed by Dr. George W. Crile in his "Man: An Adaptive Mechanism," and the result is a steady increase in the intestinal demoralization, and a like increase in the pollution of the blood. In the end the poor victim comes to a familiar pass; beset on the one hand by impotence and on the other hand by an impatience grown pathological, he gets into a state indistinguishable from the frantic. It is at such times that creative artists suffer most atrociously. It is then that they writhe upon the sharp spears and red-hot hooks of a jealous and unjust Creator for their invasion of His monopoly. It is then that they pay a grisly supertax upon their superiority to the great herd of law-abiding and undistinguished men. The men of this herd never undergo any comparable torture; the agony of the artist is quite beyond their experience and even beyond their imagination. No catastrophe that could conceivably overtake a lime and cement dealer, a curb broker, a lawyer, a plumber or a Presbyterian is to be mentioned in the same breath with the torments that, to the most minor of poets, are familiar incidents of his professional life, and, to such a man as Poe, or Beethoven, or Brahms, are the commonplaces of every day. Beethoven suffered more during the composition of the Fifth symphony than all the judges on the supreme benches of the world have suffered jointly since the time of the Gerousia.

Again, my hypothesis explains the fact that inspiration, save under extraordinary circumstances, is never continuous for more than a relatively short period. A banker, a barber or a manufacturer of patent medicines does his work day after day without any noticeable rise or fall of efficiency; save when he is drunk, jailed or ill in bed the curve of his achievement is flattened out until it becomes almost a straight line. But the curve of an artist, even of the greatest of artists, is frightfully zigzagged. There are moments when it sinks below the bottom of the chart, and immediately following there may be moments when it threatens to run off the top. Some of the noblest passages written by Shakespeare are in his worst plays, cheek by jowl with padding and banality; some of the worst music of Wagner is in his finest music dramas. There is, indeed, no such thing as a flawless masterpiece. Long labored, it may be gradually enriched with purple passages—the high inspirations of widely separated times crowded together—, but even so it will remain spotty, for those purple passages will be clumsily joined, and their joints will remain as apparent as so many false teeth. Only the most elementary knowledge of psychology is needed to show the cause of the zig-zagging that I have mentioned. It lies in the elemental fact that the chemical constitution of the blood changes every hour, almost every minute. What it is at the beginning of digestion is not what it is at the end of digestion, and in both cases it is enormously affected by the nature of the substances digested. No man, within twenty-four hours after eating a meal in a Pennsylvania Railroad dining-car, could conceivably write anything worth reading. A tough beefsteak, I daresay, has ditched many a promising sonnet, and bad beer, as every one knows, has spoiled hundreds of sonatas. Thus inspiration rises and falls, and even when it rises twice to the same height it usually shows some qualitative difference—there is the inspiration, say, of Spring vegetables and there is the inspiration of Autumn fruits. In a long work the products of greatly differing inspirations, of greatly differing streams of blood, are hideously intermingled, and the result is the inevitable spottiness that I have mentioned. No one but a maniac argues that "Die Meistersinger" is *all* good. One detects in it days when Wagner felt, as the saying goes, like a fighting cock, but one also detects days when he arose in the morning full of acidosis and despair—days when he turned heavily from the Pierian spring to castor oil.

Moreover, it must be obvious that the very conditions under which works of art are produced tend to cause great aberrations in metabolism. The artist is forced by his calling to be a sedentary man. Even a poet, perhaps the freest of artists, must spend a good deal of time bending over a desk. He may conceive his poems in the open air, as Beethoven conceived his music, but the work of reducing them to actual words requires diligent effort in camera. Here it is a sheer impossibility for him to enjoy the ideal hygienic conditions which surround the farmhand, the curb-broker and the sailor. His viscera are congested; his eyes are astrain; his muscles are without necessary exercise. Furthermore, he probably breathes bad air and goes without needed sleep. The result is inevitably some disturbance of metabolism, with a vitiated blood supply and a starved cerebrum. One is always surprised to encounter a poet who is ruddy and stout; the standard model is a pale and flabby stenotic, kept alive by patent medicines. So with the painter, the musical composer, the sculptor, the artist in prose. There is no more confining work known to man than instrumentation. The composer who has spent a day at it is invariably nervous and ill. For hours his body is bent over his music-paper, the while his pen engrosses little dots upon thin lines. I have known composers, after a week or so of such labor, to come down with auto-intoxication in its most virulent forms. Perhaps the notorious ill health of Beethoven, and the mental break-downs of Schumann, Tschaikowsky and Hugo Wolf had their origin in this direction. It is difficult, going through the history of music, to find a single composer in the grand manner who was physically and mentally up to par.

I do not advance it as a formal corollary, but no doubt this stenosis hypothesis also throws some light upon two other immemorial mysteries, the first being the relative æsthetic sterility of women, and the other being the low æsthetic development of certain whole classes, and even races of men, *e.g.*, the Puritans, the Welsh and the Confederate Americans. That women suffer from stenosis far more than men is a commonplace of internal medicine; the weakness is chiefly to blame, rather than the functional peculiarities that they accuse, for their liability to headache. A good many of them, in fact, are habitually in the state of health which, in the artist, is accompanied by an utter inability to work. This state of health, as I have said, does not inhibit *all* mental activity. It leaves the powers of observation but little impaired; it does not corrupt common sense; it is not incompatible with an intelligent discharge of the ordinary duties of life. Thus a lime and cement dealer, in the midst of it, may function almost as well as when his metabolic processes are perfectly normal, and by the same token a woman chronically a victim to it may yet show all the sharp mental competence which characterizes her sex. But here the thing stops. To go beyond—to enter the realm of constructive thinking, to abandon the mere application of old ideas and essay to invent new ideas, to precipitate novel and intellectual concepts out of the chaos of memory and perception—this is quite impossible to the stenotic. *Ergo*, it is unheard of among classes and races of men who feed grossly and neglect personal hygiene; the pill-swallower is the only artist in such groups. One may thus argue that the elder Beecham saved poetry in England, as the younger Beecham saved music. . . . But, as I say, I do not stand behind the hypothesis in this department, save, perhaps, in the matter of women. I could amass enormous evidences in favor of it, but against them there would always loom the disconcerting contrary evidence of the Bulgarians. Among them, I suppose, stenosis must be unknown—but so are all the fine arts.

"La force et la foiblesse de l'esprit," said Rochefoucauld, "sont mal nommées; elles ne sont, en effect, que la bonne ou la mauvaise des organes du corps." Science wastes itself hunting in the other direction. We are flooded with evidences of the effects of the mind on the body, and so our attention is diverted from the enormously greater effects of the body on the mind. It is rather astonishing that the Wassermann reaction has not caused the latter to be investigated more thoroughly. The first result of the general employment of that great diagnostic device was the discovery that thousands of cases of so-called mental disease were really purely physical in origin—that thousands of patients long supposed to have been crazed by seeing ghosts, by love, by grief, or by reverses in the stock-market were actually victims of the small but extremely enterprising *spirochaete pallida*. The news heaved a bomb into psychiatry, but it has so far failed to provoke a study of the effects of other such physical agents. Even the effects of this one agent remain to be inquired into at length. One now knows that it may cause insanity, but what of the lesser mental aberrations that it produces? Some of these aberrations may be actually beneficial. That is to say, the mild toxemia accompanying the less virulent forms of infection may stimulate the brain to its highest functioning, and so give birth to what is called genius—a state of mind long recognized, by popular empiricism, as a sort of half-way station on the road to insanity. Beethoven, Nietzsche and Schopenhauer suffered from such mild toxemias, and there is not the slightest doubt that their extraordinary mental activity was at least partly due to the fact. That tuberculosis, in its early stages, is capable of the same stimulation is a commonplace of observation. The consumptive may be weak physically, but he is usually very alert mentally. The history of the arts, in fact, shows the names of hundreds of inspired consumptives.

Here a physical infirmity produces a result that is beneficial, just as another physical infirmity, the stenosis aforesaid, produces a result that is baleful. The artist often oscillates horribly between the two effects; he is normally anything but a healthy animal. Perfect health, indeed, is a boon that very few men above the rank of clodhoppers ever enjoy. What health means is a degree of adaptation to the organism's environment so nearly complete that there is no irritation. Such a state, it must be obvious, is not often to be observed in organisms of the highest complexity. It is common, perhaps, in the earthworm. This elemental beast makes few demands upon its environment, and is thus subject to few diseases. It seldom gets out of order until the sands of its life are run, and then it suffers one grand illness and dies forthwith. But man is forever getting out of order, for he is enormously complicated—and the higher he rises in complexity, the more numerous and the more serious are his derangements. There are whole categories of diseases, *e.g.*, neurasthenia and hay-fever, that afflict chiefly the more civilized and delicate ranks of men, leaving the inferior orders unscathed. Good health in man, indeed, is almost invariably a function of inferiority. A professionally healthy man, *e.g.*, an acrobat, an osteopath or an ice-wagon driver, is always stupid. In the Greece of the great days the athletes we hear so much about were mainly slaves. Not one of the eminent philosophers, poets or statesmen of Greece was a good high-jumper. Nearly all of them, in fact, suffered from the same malaises which afflict their successors of to-day, as you will quickly discern by examining their compositions. The æsthetic impulse, like the thirst for truth, might almost be called a disease. It seldom if ever appears in a perfectly healthy man.

But we must take the aloes with the honey. The artist suffers damnably, but there is compensation in his dreams. Some of his characteristic diseases cripple him and make his whole life a misery, but there are others that seem to help him. Of the latter, the two that I have mentioned carry with them concepts of extreme obnoxiousness. Both are infections, and one is associated in the popular mind with notions of gross immorality. But these concepts of obnoxiousness should not blind us to the benefits that apparently go with the maladies. There are, in fact, maladies much more obnoxious, and they carry no compensating benefits. Cancer is an example. Perhaps the time will come when the precise effects of these diseases will be worked out accurately, and it will be possible to gauge in advance their probable influence upon this or that individual. If that time ever comes the manufacture of artists will become a feasible procedure, like the present manufacture of soldiers, capons, right-thinkers and doctors of philosophy. In those days the promising young men of the race, instead of being protected from such diseases at all hazards, will be deliberately infected with them, as soils are now inoculated with nitrogen-liberating bacteria. . . . At the same time, let us hope, some progress will be made against stenosis. It is, after all, simply a question of technique, like the artificial propagation of the race by the device of Dr. Jacques Loeb. The poet of the future, come upon a period of doldrums, will not tear his hair in futile agony. Instead, he will go to the nearest clinic, and there get his rasher of Bulgarian bacilli, or an injection of some complex organic compound out of a ductless gland, or an order on a masseur, or a diet list, or perchance a barrel of Russian oil.

V.
Scientific Examination of a Popular Virtue

An old *Corpsbruder*, assaulting my ear lately with an abstruse tale of his sister's husband's brother's ingratitude, ended by driving me quite out of his house, firmly resolved to be his acquaintance no longer. The exact offense I heard inattentively, and have already partly forgotten—an obscure tort arising out of a lawsuit. My ex-friend, it appears, was appealed to for help in a bad case by his grapevine relative, and so went on the stand for him and swore gallantly to some complex and unintelligible lie. Later on, essaying to cash in on the perjury, he asked the fellow to aid him in some domestic unpleasantness, and was refused on grounds of morals. Hence his indignation—and my spoiled evening. . . .

What is one to think of a man so asinine that he looks for gratitude in this world, or so puerilely egotistical that he enjoys it when found? The truth is that the sentiment itself is not human but doggish, and that the man who demands it in payment for his doings is precisely the sort of man who feels noble and distinguished when a dog licks his hand. What a man says when he expresses gratitude is simply this: "You did something for me that I could not have done myself. *Ergo*, you are my superior. Hail, *Durchlaucht*!" Such a confession, whether true or not, is degrading to the confessor, and so it is very hard to make, at all events for a man of self-respect. That is why such a man always makes it clumsily and with many blushes and hesitations. It is hard for him to put so embarrassing a doctrine into plain words. And that is why the business is equally uncomfortable to the party of the other part. It distresses him to see a human being of decent instincts standing before him in so ignominious a position. He is as flustered as if the fellow came in handcuffs, or in rags, or wearing the stripes of a felon. Moreover, his confusion is helped out by his inward knowledge—very clear if he is introspective, and plain enough even if he is not—that he really deserves no such tribute to his high mightiness; that the altruism for which he is being praised was really bogus; that he did the thing behind the gratitude which now assails him, not for any grand and lofty reason, but for a purely selfish and inferior reason, to wit, for the reason that it pleases all of us to show what we can do when an appreciative audience is present; that we delight to exercise our will to power when it is safe and profitable. This is the primary cause of the benefits which inspire gratitude, real and pretended. This is the fact at the bottom of altruism. Find me a man who is always doing favors for people and I will show you a man of petty vanity, forever trying to get fuel for it in the cheapest way. And find me a man who is notoriously grateful in habit and I'll show you a man who is essentially third rate and who is conscious of it at the bottom of his heart. The man of genuine self-respect—which means the man who is more or less accurately aware, not only of his own value, but also and more importantly, of his own limitations—tries to avoid entering either class. He hesitates to demonstrate his superiority by such banal means, and he shrinks from confessing an inferiority that he doesn't believe in.

Nevertheless, the popular morality of the world, which is the creation, not of its superior men but of its botches and half-men—in brief, of its majorities—puts a high value on gratitude and denounces the withholding of it as an offense against the proprieties. To be noticeably ungrateful for benefits—that is, for the by-products of the egotism of others—is to be disliked. To tell a tale of ingratitude is to take on the aspect of a martyr to the defects of others, to get sympathy in an affliction. All of us are responsive to such ideas, however much we may resent them logically. One may no more live in the world without picking up the moral prejudices of the world than one will be able to go to hell without perspiring. . . .

Let me recall a case within my own recent experience. One day I received a letter from a young woman I had never heard of before, asking me to read the manuscripts of two novels that she had written. She represented that she had venerated my critical parts for a long while, and that her whole future career in letters would be determined by my decision as to her talents. The daughter of a man apparently of some consequence in some sordid business or other, she asked me to meet her at her father's office, and there to impart to her, under socially aseptic conditions, my advice. Having a standing rule against meeting women authors, even in their fathers' banks and soap factories, I pleaded various imaginary engagements, but finally agreed, after a telephone debate, to read her manuscripts. They arrived promptly and I found them to be wholly without merit—in fact, the veriest twaddle. Nevertheless I plowed through them diligently, wasted half an hour at the job, wrote a polite letter of counsel and returned the manuscripts to her house, paying a blackamoor 50 cents to haul them.

By all ordinary standards, an altruistic service and well deserving some show of gratitude. Had she knitted me a pair of pulse-warmers it would have seemed meet and proper. Even a copy of the poems of Alfred Noyes would not have been too much. At the very least I expected a note of thanks. Well, not a word has ever reached me. For all my laborious politeness and disagreeable labor my reward is exactly nil. The lady is improved by my counsel—and I am shocked by her gross ingratitude. . . . That is, conventionally, superficially, as a member of society in good standing. But when on sour afternoons I roll the affair in my mind, examining, not the mere surface of it but the inner workings and anatomy of it, my sense of outrage gradually melts and fades away—the inevitable recompense of skepticism. What I see clearly is that I was an ass to succumb to the blandishments of this discourteous miss, and that she was quite right in estimating my service trivially, and out of that clear seeing comes consolation, and amusement, and, in the end, even satisfaction. I got exactly what I deserved. And she, whether consciously or merely instinctively, measured out the dose with excellent accuracy.

Let us go back. Why did I waste two hours, or maybe three, reading those idiotic manuscripts? Why, in the first place, did I answer her opening request—the request, so inherently absurd, that I meet her in her father's office? For a very plain reason: she accompanied it with flattery. What she said, in effect, was that she regarded me as a critic of the highest talents, and this ludicrous cajolery—sound, I dare say, in substance, but reduced to naught by her obvious obscurity and stupidity—was quite enough to fetch me. In brief, she assumed that, being a man, I was vain to the point of imbecility, and this assumption was correct, as it always is. To help out, there was the concept of romantic adventure vaguely floating in my mind. Her voice, as I heard it by telephone, was agreeable; her appearance, since she seemed eager to show herself, I probably judged (subconsciously) to be at least not revolting. Thus curiosity got on its legs, and vanity in another form. Am I fat and half decrepit, a man seldom noticed by cuties? Then so much the more reason why I should respond. The novelty of an apparently comely and respectable woman desiring to witness me finished what the primary (and very crude) appeal to my vanity had begun. I was, in brief, not only the literary popinjay but also the eternal male—and hard at the immemorial folly of the order.

Now turn to the gal and her ingratitude. The more I inspect it the more I became convinced that it is not discreditable to her, but highly creditable—that she demonstrates a certain human dignity, despite her imbecile writings, by exhibiting it. Would a show of gratitude put her in a better light? I doubt it. That gratitude, considering the unfavorable report I made on her manuscripts, would be doubly invasive of her *amour propre*. On the one hand it would involve a confession that my opinion of her literary gifts was better than her own, and that I was thus her superior. And on the other hand it would involve a confession that my own actual writings (being got into print without aid) were better than hers, and that I was thus her superior again. Each confession would bring her into an attitude of abasement, and the two together would make her position intolerable. Moreover, both would be dishonest: she would privately believe in neither doctrine. As for my opinion, its hostility to her aspiration is obviously enough to make her ego dismiss it as false, for no organism acquiesces in its own destruction. And as for my relative worth as a literary artist, she must inevitably put it very low, for it depends, in the last analysis, upon my dignity and sagacity as a man, and she has proved by experiment, and quite easily, that I am almost as susceptible to flattery as a moving picture actor, and hence surely no great shakes.

Thus there is not the slightest reason in the world why the fair creature should knit me a pair of pulse-warmers or send me the poems of Noyes, or even write me a polite note. If she did any of these things, she would feel herself a hypocrite and hence stand embarrassed before the mirror of her own thoughts.

Confronted by a choice between this sort of shame and the incomparably less uncomfortable shame of violating a social convention and an article of popular morals, secretly and without danger of exposure, she very sensibly chooses the more innocuous of the two. At the very start, indeed, she set up barriers against gratitude, for her decision to ask a favor of me was, in a subtle sense, a judgment of my inferiority. One does not ask favors, if it can be avoided, of persons one genuinely respects; one puts such burdens upon the naïve and colorless, upon what are called the good natured; in brief, upon one's inferiors. When that girl first thought of me as a possible aid to her literary aspiration she thought of me (perhaps vaguely, but none the less certainly) as an inferior fortuitously outfitted with a body of puerile technical information and competence, of probable use to her. This unfavorable view was immediately reënforced by her discovery of my vanity.

In brief, she showed and still shows the great instinctive sapience of her sex. She is female, and hence far above the nonsensical delusions, vanities, conventions and moralities of men.

VI.
Exeunt Omnes

ONE of the hardest jobs that faces an American magazine editor in this, the one-hundred-and-forty-fifth year of the Republic, is that of keeping the minnesingers of the land from filling his magazine with lugubrious dithyrambs to, on and against somatic death. Of spiritual death, of course, not many of them ever sing. Most of them, in fact, deny its existence in plain terms; they are all sure of the immortality of the soul, and in particular they are absolutely sure of the immortality of their own souls, and of those of their best girls. In this department the most they ever allow to the materialism of the herds that lie bogged in prose is such a benefit of the half doubt as one finds in Christina Rossetti's "When I am Dead." But when it comes to somatic death, the plain brutal death of coroners' inquests and vital statistics, their optimism vanishes, and, try as they may, they can't get around the harsh fact that on such and such a day, often appallingly near, each and every one of us will heave a last sigh, roll his eyes despairingly, turn his face to the wall and then suddenly change from a proud and highly complex mammal, made in the image of God, to a mere inert aggregate of disintegrating colloids, made in the image of a stale cabbage.

The inevitability of it seems to fascinate them. They write about it more than they write about anything else save love. Every day my editorial desk is burdened with their manuscripts —poems in which the poet serves notice that, when his time comes, he will die bravely and even a bit insolently; poems in which he warns his mistress that he will wait for her on the roof of the cosmos and keep his harp in tune; poems in which he asks her grandly to forget him, and, above all, to avoid torturing herself by vain repining at his grave; poems in which he directs his heirs and assigns to bury him in some lonely, romantic spot, where the whippoorwills sing; poems in which he hints that he will not rest easily if Philistines are permitted to begaud his last anchorage with *couronnes des perles*; poems in which he speaks jauntily of making a rendezvous with death, as if death were a wench; poems in which—

But there is no need to rehearse the varieties. If you read the strophes that are strung along the bottoms of magazine pages you are familiar with all of them; even in the great moral periodical that I help to edit, despite my own excessive watchfulness and Dr. Nathan's general theory that both death and poetry are nuisances and in bad taste, they have appeared multitudinously, no doubt to the disgust of the *intelligentsia*. As I say, it is almost impossible to keep the minnesingers off the subject. When my negro flops the morning bale of poetry manuscripts upon my desk and I pull up my chair to have at them, I always make a bet with myself that, of the first dozen, at least seven will deal with death—and it is so long since I lost that I don't remember it. Periodically I send out a circular to all the recognized poets of the land, begging them in the name of God to be less mortuary, but it never does any good. More, I doubt that it ever will—or any other sort of appeal. Take away death and love and you would rob poets of both their liver and their lights; what would remain would be little more than a feeble gurgle in an illimitable void. For the business of poetry, remember, is to set up a sweet denial of the harsh facts that confront all of us—to soothe us in our agonies with emollient words—in brief, to lie sonorously and reassuringly. Well, what is the worst curse of life? Answer: the abominable magnetism that draws unlikes and incompatibles into delirious and intolerable conjunction—the kinetic over-stimulation called love. And what is the next worst? Answer: the fear of death. No wonder the poets give so much attention to both! No other foe of human peace and happiness is one-half so potent, and hence none other offers such opportunities to poetry, and, in fact, to all art. A sonnet designed to ease the dread of bankruptcy, even if done by a great master, would be banal, for that dread is itself banal, and so is bankruptcy. The same may be said of the old fear of hell, now no more. There was a day when this latter raged in the breast of nearly every man—and in that day the poets produced antidotes that were very fine poems. But to-day only the elect and anointed of God fear hell, and so there is no more production of sound poetry in that department.

As I have hinted, I tire of reading so much necrotic verse in manuscript, and wish heartily that the poets would cease to assault me with it. In prose, curiously enough, one observes a corresponding shortage. True enough, the short story of commerce shows a good many murders and suicides, and not less than eight times a day I am made privy to the agonies of a widower or widow who, on searching the papers of his wife or her husband immediately after her or his death, discovers that she or he had a lover or a mistress. But I speak of serious prose: not of trade balderdash. Go to any public library and look under "Death: Human" in the card index, and you will be surprised to find how few books there are on the subject. Worse, nearly all the few are by psychical researchers who regard death as a mere removal from one world to another or by New Thoughters who appear to believe that it is little more than a sort of illusion. Once, seeking to find out what death was physiologically—that is, to find out just what happened when a man died—I put in a solid week without result. There seemed to be nothing whatever on the subject even in the medical libraries. Finally, after much weariness, I found what I was looking for in Dr. George W. Crile's "Man: An Adaptive Mechanism"—incidentally, a very solid and original work, much less heard of than it ought to be. Crile said that death was acidosis—that it was caused by the failure of the organism to maintain the alkalinity necessary to its normal functioning—and in the absence of any proofs or even arguments to the contrary I accepted his notion forthwith and have held to it ever since. I thus think of death as a sort of deleterious fermentation, like that which goes on in a bottle of Château Margaux when it becomes corked. Life is a struggle, not against sin, not against the Money Power, not against malicious animal magnetism, but against hydrogen ions. The healthy man is one in whom those ions, as they are dissociated by cellular activity, are immediately fixed by alkaline bases. The sick man is one in whom the process has begun to lag, with the hydrogen ions getting ahead. The dying man is one in whom it is all over save the charges of fraud.

But here I get into chemical physics, and not only run afoul of revelation but also reveal, perhaps, a degree of ignorance verging upon intellectual coma. The thing I started out to do was to call attention to the only full-length and first-rate treatise on death that I have ever encountered or heard of, to wit, "Aspects of Death and Correlated Aspects of Life," by Dr. F. Parkes Weber, a fat, hefty and extremely interesting tome, the fruit of truly stupendous erudition. What Dr. Weber has attempted is to bring together in one volume all that has been said or thought about death since the time of the first human records, not only by poets, priests and philosophers, but also by painters, engravers, soldiers, monarchs and the populace generally. The author, I take it, is primarily a numismatist, and he apparently began his work with a collection of inscriptions on coins and medals. But as it stands it covers a vastly wider area. One traces, in chapter after chapter, the ebb and flow of human ideas upon the subject, of the human attitude to the last and greatest mystery of them all—the notion of it as a mere transition to a higher plane of life, the notion of it as a benign panacea for all human suffering, the notion of it as an incentive to this or that way of living, the notion of it as an impenetrable enigma, inevitable and inexplicable. Few of us quite realize how much the contemplation of death has colored human thought throughout the ages. There have been times when it almost shut out all other concerns; there has never been a time when it has not bulked enormously in the racial consciousness. Well, what Dr. Weber does in his book is to detach and set forth the salient ideas that have emerged from all that consideration and discussion—to isolate the chief theories of death, ancient and modern, pagan and Christian, scientific and mystical, sound and absurd.

The material thus digested is appallingly copious. If the learned author had confined himself to printed books alone, he would have faced a labor fit for a new Hercules. But in addition to books he has given his attention to prints, to medals, to paintings, to engraved gems and to monumental inscriptions. His authorities range from St. John on what is to happen at the Day of Judgment to Sir William Osler on what happens upon the normal human death-bed, and from Socrates on the relation of death to philosophy to Havelock Ellis on the effects of Christian ideas of death upon the mediæval temperament. The one field that Dr. Weber has overlooked is that of music, a somewhat serious omission. It is hard to think of a great composer who never wrote a funeral march, or a requiem, or at least a sad song to some departed love. Even old Papa Haydn had moments when he ceased to be merry, and let his thought turn stealthily upon the doom ahead. To me, at all events, the slow movement of the Military Symphony is the saddest of music—an elegy, I take it, on some young fellow who went out in the incomprehensible wars of those times and got himself horribly killed in a far place. The trumpet blasts towards the end fling themselves over his hasty grave in a remote cabbage field; one hears, before and after them, the honest weeping of his comrades into their wine-pots. In truth, the shadow of death hangs over all the music of Haydn, despite its lightheartedness. Life was gay in those last days of the Holy Roman Empire, but it was also precarious. If the Turks were not at the gate, then there was a peasant rising somewhere in the hinterland, or a pestilence swept the land. Beethoven, a generation later, growled at death surlily, but Haydn faced it like a gentleman. The romantic movement brought a sentimentalization of the tragedy; it became a sort of orgy. Whenever Wagner dealt with death he treated it as if it were some sort of gaudy tournament—a thing less dreadful than ecstatic. Consider, for example, the *Char-Freitag* music in "Parsifal"—death music for the most memorable death in the history of the world. Surely no one hearing it for the first time, without previous warning, would guess that it had to do with anything so gruesome as a crucifixion. On the contrary, I have a notion that the average auditor would guess that it was a musical setting for some lamentable fornication between a Bayreuth baritone seven feet in height and a German soprano weighing at least three hundred pounds.

But if Dr. Weber thus neglects music, he at least gives full measure in all other departments. His book, in fact, is encyclopædic; he almost exhausts the subject. One idea, however, I do not find in it: the conception of death as the last and worst of all the practical jokes played upon poor mortals by the gods. That idea apparently never occurred to the Greeks, who thought of almost everything, but nevertheless it has an ingratiating plausibility. The hardest thing about death is not that men die tragically, but that most of them die ridiculously. If it were possible for all of us to make our exits at great moments, swiftly, cleanly, decorously, and in fine attitudes, then the experience would be something to face heroically and with high and beautiful words. But we commonly go off in no such gorgeous, poetical way. Instead, we die in raucous prose—of arterio-sclerosis, of diabetes, of toxemia, of a noisome perforation in the ileo-cæcal region, of carcinoma of the liver. The abominable acidosis of Dr. Crile sneaks upon us, gradually paralyzing the adrenals, flabbergasting the thyroid, crippling the poor old liver, and throwing its fog upon the brain. Thus the ontogenetic process is recapitulated in reverse order, and we pass into the mental obscurity of infancy, and then into the blank unconsciousness of the prenatal state, and finally into the condition of undifferentiated protoplasm. A man does not die quickly and brilliantly, like a lightning stroke; he passes out by inches, hesitatingly and, one may almost add, gingerly. It is hard to say just when he is fully dead. Long after his heart has ceased to beat and his lungs have ceased to swell him up with the vanity of his species, there are remote and obscure parts of him that still live on, quite unconcerned about the central catastrophe. Dr. Alexis Carrel has cut them out and kept them alive for months. The hair keeps on growing for a long while. Every time another one of the corpses of Barbarossa or King James I is examined it is found that the hair is longer than it was the last time. No doubt there are many parts of the body, and perhaps even whole organs, which wonder what it is all about when they find that they are on the way to the crematory. Burn a man's mortal remains, and you inevitably burn a good portion of him alive, and no doubt that portion sends alarmed messages to the unconscious brain, like dissected tissue under anæsthesia, and the resultant shock brings the deceased before the hierarchy of heaven in a state of collapse, with his face white, sweat bespangling his forehead and a great thirst upon him. It would not be pulling the nose of reason to argue that many a cremated Sunday-school superintendent thus confronting the ultimate tribunal in the aspect of a man taken with the goods, has been put down as suffering from an uneasy conscience when what actually ailed him was simply surgical shock. The cosmic process is not only incurably idiotic; it is also indecently unjust.

But here I become medico-legal. What I had in mind when

I began was this: that the human tendency to make death dramatic and heroic has little excuse in the facts. No doubt you remember the scene in the last act of "Hedda Gabler," in which Dr. Brack comes in with the news of Lövborg's suicide. Hedda immediately thinks of him putting the pistol to his temple and dying instantly and magnificently. The picture fills her with romantic delight. When Brack tells her that the shot was actually through the breast she is disappointed, but soon begins to romanticise even *that*. "The breast," she says, "is also a good place. . . . There is something beautiful in this!" A bit later she recurs to the charming theme, "In the breast—ah!" Then Brack tells her the plain truth—in the original, thus: *"Nej,—det traf ham i underlivet!"* . . . Edmund Gosse, in his first English translation of the play, made the sentence: "No—it struck him in the abdomen." In the last edition William Archer makes it "No—in the bowels!" Abdomen is nearer to *underlivet* than bowels, but belly would probably render the meaning better than either. What Brack wants to convey to Hedda is the news that Lövborg's death was not romantic in the least—that he went to a brothel, shot himself, not through the cerebrum or the heart, but through the duodenum or perhaps the jejunum, and is at the moment of report awaiting autopsy at the Christiania *Allgemeine-krankenhaus.* The shock floors her, but it is a shock that all of us must learn to bear. Men upon whom we lavish our veneration reduce it to an absurdity at the end by dying of chronic cystitis, or by choking upon marshmallows or dill pickles, or as the result of getting cut by dirty barbers. Women whom we place upon pedestals worthy of the holy saints come down at last with mastoid abscesses or die obscenely of hiccoughs. And we ourselves? Let us not have too much hope. The chances are that, if we go to war, eager to leap superbly at the cannon's mouth, we'll be finished on the way by an ingrowing toenail or by being run over by an army truck driven by a former Greek bus-boy and loaded with imitation Swiss cheeses made in Oneida, N.Y. And that if we die in our beds, it will be of measles or albuminuria.

The aforesaid Crile, in one of his smaller books, "A Mechanistic View of War and Peace," has a good deal to say about death in war, and in particular, about the disparity between the glorious and inspiring passing imagined by the young soldier and the messy finish that is normally in store for him. He shows two pictures of war, the one ideal and the other real. The former is the familiar print, "The Spirit of '76," with the three patriots springing grandly to the attack, one of them with a neat and romantic bandage around his head—apparently, to judge by his liveliness, to cover a wound no worse than an average bee-sting. The latter picture is what the movie folks call a close-up of a French soldier who was struck just below the mouth by a German one-pounder shell—a soldier suddenly converted into the hideous simulacrum of a cruller. What one notices especially is the curious expression upon what remains of his face—an expression of the utmost surprise and indignation. No doubt he marched off to the front firmly convinced that, if he died at all, it would be at the climax of some heroic charge, up to his knees in blood and with his bayonet run clear through a Bavarian at least four feet in diameter. He imagined the clean bullet through the heart, the stately last gesture, the final words: "Thérèse! Sophie! Olympe! Marie! Suzette! Odette! Dénise! Julie! . . . France!" Go to the book and see what he got. . . . Dr. Crile, whose experience of war has soured him against it, argues that the best way to abolish it would be to prohibit such romantic prints as "The Spirit of '76" and substitute therefor a series of actual photographs of dead and wounded men. The plan is plainly of merit. But it would be expensive. Imagine a war getting on its legs before the conversion of the populace had become complete. Think of the huge herds of spy-chasers, letter-openers, pacifist-hounds, burlesons and other such operators that it would take to track down and confiscate all those pictures! . . .

Even so, the vulgar horror of death would remain, for, as Ellen La Motte well says in her little book, "The Backwash of War," the finish of a civilian in a luxurious hospital, with trained nurses fluttering over him and his pastor whooping and heaving for him at the foot of his bed, is often quite as terrible as any form of exitus witnessed in war. It is, in fact, always an unpleasant business. Let the poets disguise it all they may and the theologians obscure the issue with promises of post-mortem felicity, the plain truth remains that it gives one pause to reflect that, on some day not far away, one must yield supinely to acidosis, sink into the mental darkness of an idiot, and so suffer a withdrawal from these engaging scenes. "No. 8," says the nurse in faded pink, tripping down the corridor with a hooch of rye for the diabetic in No. 2, "has just passed out." "Which is No. 8?" asks the new nurse. "The one whose wife wore that awful hat this afternoon?" . . . But all the authorities, it is pleasant to know, report that the final scene is placid enough. Dr. Weber quotes many of them. The dying man doesn't struggle much and he isn't much afraid. As his alkalies give out he succumbs to a blest stupidity. His mind fogs. His will power vanishes. He submits decently. He scarcely gives a damn.

VII.
The Allied Arts

I
On Music-Lovers

Of all forms of the uplift, perhaps the most futile is that which addresses itself to educating the proletariat in music. The theory behind it is that a taste for music is an elevating passion, and that if the great masses of the plain people could be inoculated with it they would cease to herd into the moving-picture theaters, or to listen to Socialists, or to beat their wives and children. The defect in this theory lies in the fact that such a taste, granting it to be elevating, simply cannot be implanted. Either it is born in a man or it is not born in him. If it is, then he will get gratification for it at whatever cost—he will hear music if hell freezes over. But if it isn't, then no amount of education will ever change him—he will remain stone deaf until the last sad scene on the gallows.

No child who has this congenital taste ever has to be urged or tempted or taught to love music. It takes to tone inevitably and irresistibly; nothing can restrain it. What is more, it always tries to *make* music, for the delight in sounds is invariably accompanied by a great desire to make them. I have never encountered an exception to this rule. All genuine music-lovers try to make music. They may do it badly, and even absurdly, but nevertheless they do it. Any man who pretends to a delight in the tone-art and yet has never learned the scale of C major—any and every such man is a fraud. The opera-houses of the world are crowded with such liars. You will even find hundreds of them in the concert-halls, though here the suffering they have to undergo to keep up their pretense is almost too much for them to bear. Many of them, true enough, deceive themselves. They are honest in the sense that they credit their own buncombe. But it is buncombe none the less.

Music, of course, has room for philanthropy. The cost of giving an orchestral concert is so great that ordinary music-lovers could not often pay for it. Here the way is open for rich backers, most of whom have no more ear for music than so many Chinamen. Nearly all the opera of the world is so supported. A few rich cads pay the bills, their wives posture obscenely in the boxes, and the genuine music-lovers upstairs and down enjoy the more or less harmonious flow of sound. But this business doesn't *make* music-lovers. It merely gives pleasure to music-lovers who already exist. In twenty-five years, I am sure, the Metropolitan Opera Company hasn't converted a single music-lover. On the contrary, it has probably disgusted and alienated many thousands of faint-hearted quasi-music-lovers, *i.e.*, persons with no more than the most nebulous taste for music—so nebulous that one or two evenings of tremendous gargling by fat tenors was enough to kill it altogether.

In the United States the number of genuine music-lovers is probably very low. There are whole states, *e.g.*, Alabama, Arkansas and Idaho, in which it would be difficult to muster a hundred. In New York, I venture, not more than one person in every thousand of the population deserves to be counted. The rest are, to all intents and purposes, tone-deaf. They can not only sit through the infernal din made by the current jazz-bands; they actually like it. This is precisely as if they preferred the works of The Duchess to those of Thomas Hardy, or the paintings of the men who make covers for popular novels to those of El Greco. Such persons inhabit the sewers of the bozart. No conceivable education could rid them of their native ignobility of soul. They are born unspeakable and incurable.

2
Opera

Opera, to a person genuinely fond of aural beauty, must inevitably appear tawdry and obnoxious, if only because it presents aural beauty in a frame of purely visual gaudiness, with overtones of the grossest sexual provocation. The most successful opera singers of the female sex, at least in America, are not those whom the majority of auditors admire most as singers but those whom the majority of male spectators desire most as mistresses. Opera is chiefly supported in all countries by the same sort of wealthy sensualists who also support musical comedy. One finds in the directors' room the traditional stock company of the stage-door alley. Such vermin, of course, pose in the newspapers as devout and almost fanatical partisans of art; they exhibit themselves at every performance; one hears of their grand doings, through their press agents, almost every day. But one has merely to observe the sort of opera they think is good to get the measure of their actual artistic discrimination.

The genuine music-lover may accept the carnal husk of opera to get at the kernel of actual music within, but that is no sign that he approves the carnal husk or enjoys gnawing through it. Most musicians, indeed, prefer to hear operatic music outside the opera house; that is why one so often hears such things as "The Ride of the Valkyrie" in the concert hall. "The Ride of the Valkyrie" has a certain intrinsic value as pure music; played by a competent orchestra it may give civilized pleasure. But as it is commonly performed in an opera house, with a posse of flat beldames throwing themselves about the stage, it can only produce the effect of a dose of ipecacuanha. The sort of person who actually delights in such spectacles is the sort of person who delights in plush furniture. Such half-wits are in a majority in every opera house west of the Rhine. They go to the opera, not to hear music, not even to hear bad music, but merely to see a more or less obscene circus. A few, perhaps, have a further purpose; they desire to assist in that circus, to show themselves in the capacity of fashionables, to enchant the yokelry with their splendor. But the majority must be content with the more lowly aim. What they get for the outrageous prices they pay for seats is a chance to feast their eyes upon glittering members of the superior *demi-monde*, and to abase their groveling souls before magnificoes on their own side of the footlights. They esteem a performance, not in proportion as true music is on tap, but in proportion as the display of notorious characters on the stage is copious, and the exhibition of wealth in the boxes is lavish. A soprano who can gargle her way up to G sharp in alto is more to such simple souls than a whole drove of Johann Sebastian Bachs; her one real rival, in the entire domain of art, is the contralto who has a pension from a grand duke and is reported to be *enceinte* by several profiteers. Heaven visualizes itself as an opera house with forty-eight Carusos, each with forty-eight press agents. . . . On the Continent, where frankness is unashamed, the opera audience often reveals its passion for tone very naïvely. That is to say, it arises on its hind legs, turns its back upon the stage and gapes at the boxes in charming innocence.

The music that such ignobles applaud is usually quite as shoddy as they are themselves. To write a successful opera a knowledge of harmony and counterpoint is not enough; one must also be a sort of Barnum. All the first-rate musicians who have triumphed in the opera house have been skillful mountebanks as well. I need cite only Richard Wagner and Richard Strauss. The business, indeed, has almost nothing to do with music. All the actual music one finds in many a popular opera —for example, "Thaïs"—mounts up to less than one may find in a pair of Gung'l waltzes. It is not this mild flavor of tone that fetches the crowd; it is the tinpot show that goes with it. An opera may have plenty of good music in it and fail, but if it has a good enough show it will succeed.

Such a composer as Wagner, of course, could not write even an opera without getting some music into it. In nearly all of his works, even including "Parsifal," there are magnificent passages, and some of them are very long. Here his natural genius overcame him, and he forgot temporarily what he was about. But these magnificent passages pass unnoticed by the average opera audience. What it esteems in his music dramas is precisely what is cheapest and most mountebankish—for example, the more lascivious parts of "Tristan und Isolde." The sound music it dismisses as tedious. The Wagner it venerates is not the musician, but the showman. That he had a king for a backer and was seduced by Liszt's daughter—these facts, and not the fact of his stupendous talent, are the foundation stones of his fame in the opera house.

Greater men, lacking his touch of the quack, have failed where he succeeded—Beethoven, Schubert, Schumann, Brahms, Bach, Haydn, Haendel. Not one of them produced a genuinely successful opera; most of them didn't even try. Imagine Brahms writing for the diamond horseshoe! Or Bach! Or Haydn! Beethoven attempted it, but made a mess of it; "Fidelio" survives to-day chiefly as a set of concert overtures.

Schubert wrote more actual music every morning between 10 o'clock and lunch time than the average opera composer produces in 250 years, and yet he always came a cropper in the opera house.

3
The Music of To-morrow

Viewing the current musical scene, Carl Van Vechten finds it full of sadness. Even Debussy bores him; he heard nothing interesting from that quarter for a long while before the final scene. As for Germany, he finds it a desert, with Arnold Schoenberg behind the bar of its only inviting *Gasthaus.* Richard Strauss? Pooh! Strauss is an exploded torpedo, a Zeppelin brought to earth; "he has nothing more to say." (Even the opening of the Alpine symphony, it would appear, is mere stick-candy.) England? Go to! Italy? Back to the barrel-organ! Where, then, is the tone poetry of to-morrow to come from? According to Van Vechten, from Russia. It is the steppes that will produce it—or, more specifically, Prof. Igor Strawinsky, author of "The Nightingale" and of various revolutionary ballets. In the scores of Strawinsky, says Van Vechten, music takes a vast leap forward. Here, at last, we are definitely set free from melody and harmony; the thing becomes an ineffable complex of rhythms; "all rhythms are beaten into the ears."

New? Of the future? I have not heard all of the powerful shiverings and tremblings of M. Strawinsky, but I presume to doubt it none the less. "The ancient Greeks," says Van Vechten, "accorded rhythm a higher place than either melody or harmony." Well, what of it? So did the ancient Goths and Huns. So do the modern Zulus and New Yorkers. The simple truth is that the accentuation of mere rhythm is a proof, not of progress in music, but of a reversion to barbarism. Rhythm is the earliest, the underlying element. The African savage, beating his tom-tom, is content to go no further; the American composer of fox trots is with him. But music had scarcely any existence as an art-form until melody came to rhythm's aid, and its fruits were little save dullness until harmony began to support melody. To argue that mere rhythm, unsupported by anything save tone-color, may now take their place is to argue something so absurd that its mere statement is a sufficient answer to it.

The rise of harmony, true enough, laid open a dangerous field. Its exploration attracted meticulous minds; it was rigidly mapped in hard, geometrical forms; in the end, it became almost unnavigable to the man of ideas. But no melodramatic rejection of all harmony is needed to work a reform. The business, indeed, is already gloriously under way. The dullest conservatory pupil has learned how to pull the noses of the old-time schoolmasters. No one cares a hoot any more about the ancient laws of preparation and resolution. (The rules grow so loose, indeed, that I may soon be tempted to write a tone-poem myself). But out of this chaos new laws will inevitably arise, and though they will not be as rigid as the old ones, they will still be coherent and logical and intelligible. Already, in fact, gentlemen of professorial mind are mapping them out; one needs but a glance at such a book as René Lenormand's to see that there is a certain order hidden in even the wildest vagaries of the moment. And when the boiling in the pot dies down, the truly great musicians will be found to be, not those who have been most daring, but those who have been most discreet and intelligent—those who have most skillfully engrafted what is good in the new upon what was sound in the old. Such a discreet fellow is Richard Strauss. His music is modern enough—but not too much. One is thrilled by its experiments and novelties, but at the same time one can enjoy the thing as music.

Haydn, Mozart, Beethoven and Wagner belonged to the same lodge. They were by no means the wildest revolutionaries of their days, but they were the best musicians. They didn't try to improve music by purging it of any of the elements that made it music; they tried, and with success, to give each element a new force and a new significance. Berlioz, I dare say, knew more about the orchestra than Wagner; he surely went further than Wagner in reaching out for new orchestral effects. But nothing he ever wrote has a fourth of the stability and value of "Die Meistersinger." He was so intrigued by his tone-colors that he forgot his music.

4
Tempo di Valse

Those Puritans who snort against the current dances are quite right when they argue that the tango and the shimmie are violently aphrodisiacal, but what they overlook is the fact that the abolition of such provocative wriggles would probably revive something worse, to wit, the Viennese waltz. The waltz never quite goes out of fashion; it is always just around the corner; every now and then it comes back with a bang. And to the sore harassment and corruption, I suspect, of chemical purity, the ideal of all right-thinkers. The shimmie and the tango are too gross to be very dangerous to civilized human beings; they suggest drinking beer out of buckets; the most elemental good taste is proof enough against them. But the waltz! Ah, the waltz, indeed! It is sneaking, insidious, disarming, lovely. It does its work, not like a college-yell or an explosion in a munitions plant, but like the rustle of the trees, the murmur of the illimitable sea, the sweet gurgle of a pretty girl. The jazz-band fetches only vulgarians, barbarians, idiots, pigs. But there is a mystical something in "Weiner Blut" or "Künstler Leben" that fetches even philosophers.

The waltz, in fact, is magnificently improper—the art of tone turned bawdy. I venture to say that the compositions of one man alone, Johann Strauss II, have lured more fair young creatures to lamentable complaisance than all the hyperdermic syringes of all the white slave scouts since the fall of the Western Empire. There is something about a waltz that is simply irresistible. Try it on the fattest and sedatest or even upon the thinnest and most acidulous of women, and she will be ready, in ten minutes, for a stealthy kiss behind the door—nay, she will forthwith impart the embarrassing news that her husband misunderstands her, and drinks too much, and cannot appreciate Maeterlinck, and is going to Cleveland, O., on business to-morrow. . . .

I often wonder that the Comstocks have not undertaken a crusade against the waltz. If they suppress "The 'Genius'" and "Jurgen," then why do they overlook "Rosen aus dem Süden"? If they are so hot against "Madame Bovary" and the Decameron, then why the immunity of "Wein, Weib und Gesang"?

. . . I throw out the suggestion and pass on. Nearly all the great waltzes of the world, incidently, were written by Germans—or Austrians. A waltz-pogrom would thus enlist the American Legion and the Daughters of the Revolution. Moreover, there is the Public Health Service: it is already engaged upon a campaign to enforce virginity in both sexes by statute and artillery. Imagine such an enterprise with every band free to play "Wiener Mad'l"!

5
The Puritan as Artist

The saddest thing that I have ever heard in the concert hall is Herbert K. Hadley's overture, "In Bohemia." The title is a magnificent piece of profound, if unconscious irony. One looks, at least, for a leg flung in the air, a girl kissed, a cork popped, a flash of drawer-ruffles. What one encounters is a meeting of the Lake Mohonk Conference. Such prosy correctness and hollowness, in music, is almost inconceivable. It is as if the most voluptuous of the arts were suddenly converted into an abstract and austere science, like comparative grammar or astro-physics. "Who's Who in America" says that Hadley was born in Somerville, Mass., and "studied violin and other branches in Vienna." A prodigy thus unfolds itself: here is a man who lived in Vienna, and yet never heard a Strauss waltz! This, indeed, is an even greater feat than being born an artist in Somerville.

6
The Human Face

Probably the best portrait that I have ever seen in America is one of Theodore Dreiser by Bror Nordfeldt. Who this Bror Nordfeldt may be I haven't the slightest notion—a Scandinavian, perhaps. Maybe I have got his name wrong; I can't find any Nordfeldt in "Who's Who in America." But whatever his name, he has painted Dreiser in a capital manner. The portrait not only shows the outward shell of the man; it also conveys something of his inner spirit—his simple-minded wonder at the mystery of existence, his constant effort to argue himself out of a despairing pessimism, his genuine amazement before life as a spectacle. The thing is worth a hundred Sargents, with their slick lying, their childish facility, their general hollowness and tackiness. Sargent should have been a designer of candy-box tops. The notion that he is a great artist is one of the astounding delusions of Anglo-Saxondom. What keeps it going is the patent fact that he is a very dexterous craftsman—one who understands thoroughly how to paint, just as a good plumber knows how to plumb. But of genuine æsthetic feeling the man is almost as destitute as the plumber. His portrait of the four Johns Hopkins professors is probably the worst botch ever palmed off on a helpless committee of intellectual hay and feed dealers. But Nordfeldt, in his view of Dreiser, somehow gets the right effect. It is rough painting, but real painting. There is a knock-kneed vase in the foreground, and a bunch of flowers apparently painted with a shaving-brush—but Dreiser himself is genuine. More, he is made interesting. One sees at once that he is no common man.

The artist himself seems to hold the portrait in low esteem. Having finished it, he reversed the canvas and used the back for painting a vapid snow scene—a thing almost bad enough to go into a Fifth Avenue show-window. Then he abandoned both pictures. I discovered the portrait by accidentally knocking the snow scene off a wall. It has never been framed. Drieser himself has probably forgotten it. . . . No, I do *not* predict that it will be sold to some Pittsburgh nail manufacturer, in 1950, for $100,000. If it lasts two or three more years, unframed and disesteemed, it will be running in luck. When Dreiser is hanged, I suppose, relic-hunters will make a search for it. But by that time it will have died as a doormat.

7
The Cerebral Mime

Of all actors, the most offensive to the higher cerebral centers is the one who pretends to intellectuality. His alleged intelligence, of course, is always purely imaginary: no man of genuinely superior intelligence has ever been an actor. Even supposing a young man of appreciable mental powers to be lured upon the stage, as philosophers are occasionally lured into bordellos, his mind would be inevitably and almost immediately destroyed by the gaudy nonsense issuing from his mouth every night. That nonsense enters into the very fiber of the actor. He becomes a grotesque boiling down of all the preposterous characters that he has ever impersonated. Their characteristics are seen in his manner, in his reactions to stimuli, in his point of view. He becomes a walking artificiality, a strutting dummy, a thematic catalogue of imbecilities.

There are, of course, plays that are not wholly nonsense, and now and then one encounters an actor who aspires to appear in them. This aspiration almost always overtakes the so-called actor-manager—that is to say, the actor who has got rich and is thus ambitious to appear as a gentleman. Such aspirants commonly tackle Shakespeare, and if not Shakespeare, then Shaw, or Hauptmann, or Rostand, or some other apparently intellectual dramatist. But this is seldom more than a passing madness. The actor-manager may do that sort of thing once in a while; but in the main he sticks to his garbage. Consider, for example, the late Henry Irving. He posed as an intellectual and was forever gabbling about his high services to the stage, and yet he appeared constantly in such puerile things as "The Bells," beside which the average newspaper editorial or college yell was literature. So with the late Mansfield. His pretension, deftly circulated by press-agents, was that he was a man of brilliant and polished mind. Nevertheless, he spent two-thirds of his life in the theater playing such abominable drivel as "A Parisian Romance" and "Dr. Jekyll and Mr. Hyde."

It is commonly urged in defense of certain actors that they are forced to appear in that sort of stuff by the public demand for it—that appearing in it painfully violates their secret pruderies. This defense is unsound and dishonest. An actor never disdains anything that gets him applause and money; he is almost completely devoid of that æsthetic conscience which is the chief mark of the genuine artist. If there were a large public willing to pay handsomely to hear him recite limericks, or to blow a cornet, or to strip off his underwear and dance a polonaise stark naked, he would do it without hesitation—and then convince himself that such buffooning constituted a difficult and elevated art, fully comparable to Wagner's or Dante's. In brief, the one essential, in his sight, is the chance to shine, the fat part, the applause. Who ever heard of an actor declining a fat part on the ground that it invaded his intellectual integrity? The thing is simply unimaginable.

VIII.
The Cult of Hope

Of all the sentimental errors which reign and rage in this incomparable republic, the worst, I often suspect, is that which confuses the function of criticism, whether æsthetic, political or social, with the function of reform. Almost invariably it takes the form of a protest: "The fellow condemns without offering anything better. Why tear down without building up?" So coo and snivel the sweet ones: so wags the national tongue. The messianic delusion becomes a sort of universal murrain. It is impossible to get an audience for an idea that is not "constructive"—*i.e.*, that is not glib, and uplifting, and full of hope, and hence capable of tickling the emotions by leaping the intermediate barrier of the intelligence.

In this protest and demand, of course, there is nothing but a hollow sound of words—the empty babbling of men who constantly mistake their mere feelings for thoughts. The truth is that criticism, if it were thus confined to the proposing of alternative schemes, would quickly cease to have any force or utility at all, for in the overwhelming majority of instances no alternative scheme of any intelligibility is imaginable, and the whole object of the critical process is to demonstrate it. The poet, if the victim is a poet, is simply one as bare of gifts as a herring is of fur: no conceivable suggestion will ever make him write actual poetry. The cancer cure, if one turns to popular swindles, is wholly and absolutely without merit—and the fact that medicine offers us no better cure does not dilute its bogusness in the slightest. And the plan of reform, in politics, sociology or what not, is simply beyond the pale of reason; no change in it or improvement of it will ever make it achieve the downright impossible. Here, precisely, is what is the matter with most of the notions that go floating about the country, particularly in the field of governmental reform. The trouble with them is not only that they won't and don't work; the trouble with them, more importantly, is that the thing they propose to accomplish is intrinsically, or at all events most probably, beyond accomplishment. That is to say, the problem they are ostensibly designed to solve is a problem that is insoluble. To tackle them with a proof of that insolubility, or even with a colorable argument of it, is sound criticism; to tackle them with another solution that is quite as bad, or even worse, is to pick the pocket of one knocked down by an automobile.

Unluckily, it is difficult for a certain type of mind to grasp the concept of insolubility. Thousands of poor dolts keep on trying to square the circle; other thousands keep pegging away at perpetual motion. The number of persons so afflicted is far greater than the records of the Patent Office show, for beyond the circle of frankly insane enterprise there lie circles of more and more plausible enterprise, and finally we come to a circle which embraces the great majority of human beings. These are the optimists and chronic hopers of the world, the believers in men, ideas and things. These are the advocates of leagues of nations, wars to make the world safe for democracy, political mountebanks, "clean-up" campaigns, laws, raids, Men and Religion Forward Movements, eugenics, sex hygiene, education, newspapers. It is the settled habit of such credulous folk to give ear to whatever is comforting; it is their settled faith that whatever is desirable will come to pass. A caressing confidence—but one, unfortunately, that is not borne out by human experience. The fact is that some of the things that men and women have desired most ardently for thousands of years are not nearer realization to-day than they were in the time of Rameses, and that there is not the slightest reason for believing that they will lose their coyness on any near to-morrow. Plans for hurrying them on have been tried since the beginning; plans for forcing them overnight are in copious and antagonistic operation to-day; and yet they continue to hold off and elude us, and the chances are that they will keep on holding off and eluding us until the angels get tired of the show, and the whole earth is set off like a gigantic bomb, or drowned, like a sick cat, between two buckets.

But let us avoid the grand and chronic dreams of the race and get down to some of the concrete problems of life under the Christian enlightenment. Let us take a look, say, at the so-called drink problem, a small sub-division of the larger problem of saving men from their inherent and incurable hoggishness. What is the salient feature of the discussion of the drink problem, as one observes it going on eternally in These States? The salient feature of it is that very few honest and intelligent men ever take a hand in the business—that the best men of the nation, distinguished for their sound sense in other fields, seldom show any interest in it. On the one hand it is labored by a horde of obvious jackasses, each confident that he can dispose of it overnight. And on the other hand it is sophisticated and obscured by a crowd of oblique fellows, hired by interested parties, whose secret desire is that it be kept unsolved. To one side, the professional gladiators of Prohibition; to the other side, the agents of the brewers and distillers. But why do all neutral and clear-headed men avoid it? Why does one hear so little about it from those who have no personal stake in it, and can thus view it fairly and accurately? Is it because they are afraid? Is it because they are not intrigued by it? I doubt that it would be just to accuse them in either way. The real reason why they steer clear of the gabble is simpler and more creditable. It is this: that none of them—that no genuinely thoughtful and prudent man—can imagine any solution which meets the tests of his own criticism—that no genuinely intelligent man believes the thing is soluble at all.

Here, of course, I generalize a bit heavily. Honest and intelligent men, though surely not many of them, occasionally come forward with suggestions. In the midst of so much debate it is inevitable that even a man of critical mind should sometimes lean to one side or the other—that some salient imbecility should make him react toward its rough opposite. But the fact still remains that not a single complete and comprehensive scheme has ever come from such a man, that no such man has ever said, in so many words, that he thought the problem could be solved, simply and effectively. All such schemes come from idiots or from sharpers disguised as idiots to win the public confidence. The whole discussion is based upon assumptions that even the most casual reflection must reject as empty balderdash.

And as with the drink problem, so with most of the other great questions that harass and dismay the helpless human race. Turn, for example, to the sex problem. There is no half-baked ecclesiastic, bawling in his galvanized-iron temple on a suburban lot, who doesn't know precisely how it ought to be dealt with. There is no fantoddish old suffragette, sworn to get her revenge on man, who hasn't a sovereign remedy for it. There is not a shyster of a district attorney, ambitious for higher office, who doesn't offer to dispose of it in a few weeks, given only enough help from the city editors. And yet, by the same token, there is not a man who has honestly studied it and pondered it, bringing sound information to the business, and understanding of its inner difficulties and a clean and analytical mind, who doesn't believe and hasn't stated publicly that it is intrinsically and eternally insoluble. I can't think of an exception, nor does a fresh glance through the literature suggest one. The latest expert to tell the disconcerting truth is Dr. Maurice Parmelee, the criminologist. His book, "Personality and Conduct," is largely devoted to demonstrating that the popular solutions, for all the support they get from vice crusaders, complaisant legislators and sensational newspapers, are unanimously imbecile and pernicious—that their only effect in practice is to make what was bad a good deal worse. His remedy is—what? An alternative solution? Not at all. His remedy, in brief, is to abandon all attempts at a solution, to let the whole thing go, to cork up all the reformers and try to forget it.

And in this proposal he merely echoes Havelock Ellis, undoubtedly the most diligent and scientific student of the sex problem that the world has yet seen—in fact, the one man who, above all others, has made a decorous and intelligent examination of it possible. Ellis' remedy is simply a denial of all remedies. He admits that the disease is bad, but he shows that the medicine is infinitely worse, and so he proposes going back to the plain disease, and advocates bearing it with philosophy, as we bear colds in the head, marriage, the noises of the city, bad cooking and the certainty of death. Man is inherently vile —but he is never so vile as when he is trying to disguise and deny his vileness. No prostitute was ever so costly to a community as a prowling and obscene vice crusader, or as the dubious legislator or prosecuting officer who jumps as he pipes.

Ellis, in all this, falls under the excommunication of the sentimentalists. He demolishes one scheme without offering an alternative scheme. He tears down without making any effort to build up. This explains, no doubt, his general unpopularity;

into mouths agape for peruna, he projects only paralyzing streams of ice-water. And it explains, too, the curious fact that his books, the most competent and illuminating upon the subject that they discuss, are under the ban of the Comstocks in both England and America, whereas the hollow treatises of ignorant clerics and smutty old maids are merchanted with impunity, and even commended from the sacred desk. The trouble with Ellis is that he tells the truth, which is the unsafest of all things to tell. His crime is that he is a man who prefers facts to illusions, and knows what he is talking about. Such men are never popular. The public taste is for merchandise of a precisely opposite character. The way to please is to proclaim in a confident manner, not what is true, but what is merely comforting. This is what is called building up. This is constructive criticism.

IX.
The Dry Millennium

I
The Holy War

THE fact that the enforcement of Prohibition entails a host of oppressions and injustices—that it puts a premium upon the lowest sort of spying, affords an easy livelihood to hordes of professional scoundrels, subjects thousands of decent men to the worst sort of blackmail, violates the theoretical sanctity of domicile, and makes for bitter and relentless enmities,—this fact is now adduced by its ever-hopeful foes as an argument for the abandonment of the whole disgusting crusade. By it they expect to convert even a large minority of the drys, apparently on the theory that the latter got converted emotionally and hastily, and that an appeal to their sense of justice and fair-dealing will debamboozle them.

No hope could be more vain. What all the current optimists overlook is that the illogical and indefensible persecutions certain to occur in increasing number under the Prohibition Amendment constitute the chief cause of its popularity among the sort of men who are in favor of it. The typical Prohibitionist, in other words, is a man full of religious excitement, with the usual sadistic overtones. He delights in persecution for its own sake. He likes to see the other fellow jump and to hear him yell. This thirst is horribly visible in all the salient mad mullahs of the land—that is, in all the genuine leaders of American culture. Such skillful boob-bumpers as the Rev. Dr. Billy Sunday know what that culture is; they know what the crowd wants. Thus they convert the preaching of the alleged Word of God into a rough-and-tumble pursuit of definite sinners—saloon-keepers, prostitutes, Sabbath-breakers, believers in the Darwinian hypothesis, German exegetes, hand-books, poker-players, adulterers, cigarette-smokers, users of profanity. It is the chase that heats up the great mob of Methodists, not the

Word. And the fact that the chase is unjust only tickles them the more, for to do injustice with impunity is a sign of power, and power is the thing that the inferior man always craves most violently.

Every time the papers print another account of a Prohibitionist agent murdering a man who resists him, or searching some woman's underwear, or raiding a Vanderbilt yacht, or blackmailing a Legislature, or committing some other such inordinate and anti-social act, they simply make a thousand more votes for Prohibition. It is precisely that sort of entertainment that makes Prohibition popular with the boobery. It is precisely because it is unjust, imbecile, arbitrary and tyrannical that they are so hot for it. The incidental violation of even the inferior man's liberty is not sufficient to empty him of delight in the chase. The victims reported in the newspapers are commonly his superiors; he thus gets the immemorial democratic satisfaction out of their discomfiture. Besides, he has no great rage for liberty himself. He is always willing to surrender it at demand. The most popular man under a democracy is not the most democratic man, but the most despotic man. The common folk delight in the exactions of such a man. They like him to boss them. Their natural gait is the goose-step.

It was predicted by romantics that the arrival of Prohibition would see the American workingman in revolt against its tyranny, with mills idle and industry paralyzed. Certain boozy labor leaders even went so far as to threaten a general strike. No such strike, of course, materialized. Not a single American workingman uttered a sound. The only protests heard of came from a few barbarous foreigners, and these malcontents were quickly beaten into submission by the *Polizei*. In a week or two all the reserve stocks of beer were exhausted, and every jug of authentic hard liquor was emptied. Since then, save for the ghastly messes that he has brewed behind locked doors, the American workingman has been dry. Worse, he has also been silent. Not a sound has come out of him. . . . But his liver is full of bile? He nourishes an intolerable grievance? He will get his revenge, soon or late, at the polls? All moonshine! He will do nothing of the sort. He will actually do what he always does—that is, he will make a virtue of his necessity, and straightway begin believing that he *likes* Prohibition, that it is doing him a lot of good, that he wouldn't be without it if he could. This is the habitual process of thought of inferior men, at all times and everywhere. This is the sturdy common sense of the plain people.

2
The Lure of Babylon

One of the ultimate by-products of Prohibition and the allied Puritanical barbarities will probably be an appreciable slackening in the present movement of yokels toward the large cities. The thing that attracted the peasant youth to our gaudy Sodoms and Ninevehs, in the past, was not, as sociologists have always assumed, the prospect of less work and more money. The country boy, in point of fact—that is, the average country boy, the normal country boy—had to work quite as hard in the city as he ever worked in the country, and his wages were anything but princely. Unequipped with a city trade, unprotected by a union, and so forced into competition with the lowest types of foreign labor, he had to be content with monotonous, uninspiring and badly-paid jobs. He did not become a stock-broker, or even a plumber; until the war gave him a temporary chance at its gigantic swag, he became a car conductor, a porter or a wagon-driver. And it took him many years to escape from that sordid fate, for the city boy, with a better education and better connections, was always a lap or two ahead of him. The notion that yokels always succeed in the cities is a great delusion. The overwhelming majority of our rich men are city-born and city-bred. And the overwhelming majority of our elderly motormen, forlorn corner grocerymen, neighborhood carpenters and other such blank cartridges are country-bred.

No, it was not money that lured the adolescent husbandman to the cities, but the gay life. What he dreamed of was a more spacious and stimulating existence than the farm could offer—an existence crowded with intriguing and usually unlawful recreations. A few old farmers may have come in now and then to buy gold bricks or to hear the current Henry Ward Beechers, but these oldsters were mere trippers—they never thought of settling down—the very notion of it would have appalled them. The actual settlers were all young, and what brought them on was less an economic impulse than an æsthetic one. They wanted to live magnificently, to taste the sweets that drummers talked of, to sample the refined divertisements described in such works as "The Confessions of an Actress," "Night Life in Chicago" and "What Every Young Husband Should Know." Specifically, they yearned for a semester or two in the theaters, the saloons and the bordellos—particularly, the saloons and bordellos. It was this gorgeous bait that dragged them out of their barn-yards. It was this bait that landed a select few in Wall street and the United States Senate—and millions on the front seats of trolley-cars, delivery-wagons and ash-carts.

But now Puritanism eats the bait. In all our great cities the public stews are closed, and the lamentable irregularities they catered to are thrown upon an individual initiative that is quite beyond the talents and enterprise of a plow-hand. Now the saloons are closed too, and the blind-pigs begin to charge such prices that no peasant can hope to pay them. Only the theater remains—and already the theater loses its old lavish devilishness. True enough, it still deals in pornography, but that pornography becomes exclusive and even esoteric: a yokel could not understand the higher farce, nor could he afford to pay for a seat at a modern leg-show. The cheap burlesque house of other days is now incurably moral; I saw a burlesque show lately which was almost a dramatization of a wall-card by Dr. Frank Crane. There remains the movie, but the peasant needn't come to the city to see movies—there is one in every village. What remains, then, of the old lure? What sane youth, comfortably housed on a farm, with Theda Bara performing at the nearest cross-roads, wheat at $2.25 a bushel and milkers getting $75 a month and board—what jejune rustic, not downright imbecile, itches for the city to-day?

3
Cupid and Well-Water

In the department of amour, I daresay, the first effect of Prohibition will be to raise up impediments to marriage. It was alcohol, in the past, that was the primary cause of perhaps a majority of alliances among civilized folk. The man, priming himself with cocktails to achieve boldness, found himself suddenly bogged in sentimentality, and so yielded to the ancient tricks of the lady. Absolutely sober men will be harder to snare. Coffee will never mellow them sufficiently. Thus I look for a fall in the marriage rate.

But only temporarily. In the long run, Prohibition will make marriage more popular, at least among the upper classes, than it has ever been in the past, and for the plain reason that, once it is in full effect, the life of a civilized bachelor will become intolerable. In the past he went to his club. But a club without a bar is as hideously unattractive as a beautiful girl without hair or teeth. No sane man will go into it. In two years, in fact, nine out of ten clubs will be closed. The only survivors will be a few bleak rookeries for senile widowers. The bachelor of less years, unable to put up with the society of such infernos, will inevitably decide that if he must keep sober he might just as well have a charming girl to ease his agonies, and so he will expose himself in society, and some fair one or other will nab him.

At the moment, observing only the first effect of Prohibition, the great majority of intelligent women are opposed to it. But when the secondary effect begins to appear they will become in favor of it. They now have the vote. I see no hope.

4
The Triumph of Idealism

Another effect of Prohibition will be that it will gradually empty the United States of its present small minority of civilized men. Almost every man that one respects is now casting longing eyes across the ocean. Some of them talk frankly of emigrating, once Europe pulls itself together. Others merely propose to go abroad every year and to stay there as long as possible, visiting the United States only at intervals, as a Russian nobleman, say, used to visit his estates in the Ukraine. Worse, Prohibition will scare off all the better sort of immigrants from the other side. The lower order of laborers may continue to come in small numbers—each planning to get all the money he can and then escape, as the Italians are even now escaping. But no first-rate man will ever come—no Stephen Girard, or William Osler, or Carl Schurz, or Theodore

Thomas, or Louis Agassiz, or Edwin Klebs, or Albert Gallatin, or Alexander Hamilton. It is not Prohibition *per se* that will keep them away; it is the whole complex of social and political attitudes underlying Prohibition—the whole clinical picture of Puritanism rampant. The United States will become a sort of huge Holland—fat and contented, but essentially undistinguished. Its superior men will leave it automatically, as nine-tenths of all superior Hollanders leave Holland.

But all this, from the standpoint of Prohibitionists, is no argument against Prohibition. On the contrary, it is an argument in favor of Prohibition. For the men the Prohibitionist—*i.e.*, the inferior sort of Puritan—distrusts and dislikes most intensely is precisely what the rest of humanity regards as the superior man. You will go wrong if you imagine that the honest yeomen of, say, Mississippi deplore the fact that in the whole state there is not a single distinguished man. They actually delight in it. It is a source of genuine pride to them that no such irreligious scoundrel as Balzac lives there, and no such scandalous adulterer as Wagner, and no scoundrelly atheist as Huxley, and no such rambunctious piano-thumper as Beethoven, and no such German spy as Nietzsche. Such men, settling there, would be visited by a Vigilance Committee and sharply questioned. The Puritan Commonwealth, now as always, has no traffic with heretics.

X.
Appendix on a Tender Theme

I
The Nature of Love

WHATEVER the origin (in the soul, the ductless glands or the convolutions of the cerebrum) of the thing called romantic love, its mere phenomenal nature may be very simply described. It is, in brief, a wholesale diminishing of disgusts, primarily based on observation, but often, in its later stages, taking on an hallucinatory and pathological character. Friendship has precisely the same constitution, but the pathological factor is usually absent. When we are attracted to a person and find his or her proximity agreeable, it means that he or she disgusts us less than the average human being disgusts us—which, if we have delicate sensibilities, is a good deal more than is comfortable. The elemental man is not much oppressed by this capacity for disgust; in consequence, he is capable of falling in love with almost any woman who seems sexually normal. But the man of a higher type is vastly more sniffish, and so the majority of women whom he meets are quite unable to interest him, and when he succumbs at last it is always to a woman of special character, and often she is also one of uncommon shrewdness and enterprise.

Because human contacts are chiefly superficial, most of the disgusts that we are conscious of are physical. We are never honestly friendly with a man who is dirtier than we are ourselves, or who has table manners that are cruder than our own (or merely noticeably different), or who laughs in a way that strikes us as gross, or who radiates some odor that we do not like. We never conceive a romantic passion for a woman who employs a toothpick in public, or who suffers from acne, or who offers the subtle but often quite unescapable suggestion that she has on soiled underwear. But there are also psychical disgusts. Our friends, in the main, must be persons who think substantially as we do, at least about all things that actively concern us, and who have the same general tastes. It is impossible to imagine a Brahmsianer being honestly fond of a man who enjoys jazz, or a man who admires Joseph Conrad falling in love with a woman who reads Rex Beach. By the same token, it is impossible to imagine a woman of genuine refinement falling in love with a Knight of Pythias, a Methodist or even a chauffeur; either the chauffeur is a Harvard aviator in disguise or the lady herself is a charwoman in disguise. Here, however, the force of aversion may be greatly diminished by contrary physical attractions; the body, as usual, is enormously more potent than the so-called mind. In the midst of the bitterest wars, with every man of the enemy held to be a fiend in human form, women constantly fall in love with enemy soldiers who are of pleasant person and wear attractive uniforms. And many a fair agnostic, as every one knows, is on good terms with a handsome priest. . . .

Imagine a young man in good health and easy circumstances, entirely ripe for love. The prompting to mate and beget arises within his interstitial depths, traverses his lymphatic system, lifts his blood pressure, and goes whooping through his *meatus auditorium externus* like a fanfare of slide trombones. The impulse is very powerful. It staggers and dismays him. He trembles like a stag at bay. Why, then, doesn't he fall head over heels in love with the first eligible woman that he meets? For the plain reason that the majority of women that he meets offend him, repel him, disgust him. Often it is in some small, inconspicuous and, at first glance, unanalyzable way. She is, in general, a very pretty girl—but her ears stand out too much. Or her hair reminds him of oakum. Or her mouth looks like his aunt's. Or she has beer-keg ankles. Here very impalpable things, such as bodily odors, play a capital part; their importance is always much underestimated. Many a girl has lost a husband by using the wrong perfume, or by neglecting to have her hair washed. Many another has come to grief by powdering her nose too much or too little, or by shrinking from the paltry pain of having some of her eyebrows pulled, or by employing a lip-salve with too much purple in it, or by patronizing a bad dentist, or by speaking incautiously of chilblains. . . .

But eventually the youth finds his love—soon or late the angel foreordained comes along. Who is this prodigy? Simply the *first* girl to sneak over what may be called the threshold of his disgusts—simply the *first* to disgust him so little, at first glance, that the loud, insistent promptings of the Divine Schadchen have a chance to be heard. If he muffs this first, another will come along, maybe soon, maybe late. For every normal man there are hundreds of thousands in Christendom, thousands in his own town, scores within his own circle of acquaintance. This normal man is not too delicate. His fixed foci of disgust are neither very numerous nor very sensitive. For the rest, he is swayed by fashion, by suggestion, by transient moods. Anon a mood of cynicism is upon him and he is hard to please, but anon he succumbs to sentimentality and is blind to everything save the grossest offendings. It is only the man of extraordinary sensitiveness, the man of hypertrophied delicacy, who must search the world for his elective affinity.

Once the threshold is crossed emotion comes to the aid of perception. That is to say, the blind, almost irresistible mating impulse, now fortuitously relieved from the contrary pressure of active disgusts, fortifies itself by manufacturing illusions. The lover sees with an eye that is both opaque and out of focus. Thus he begins the familiar process of editing and improving his girl. Features and characteristics that, observed in cold blood, might have quickly aroused his most active disgust are now seen through a rose-tinted fog, like drabs in a musical comedy. The lover ends by being almost anæsthetic to disgust. While the spell lasts his lady could shave her head or take to rubbing snuff, or scratch her leg at a communion service, or smear her hair with bear's grease, and yet not disgust him. Here the paralysis of the faculties is again chiefly physical—a matter of obscure secretions, of shifting pressure, of metabolism. Nature is at her tricks. The fever of love is upon its victim. His guard down, he is little more than a pathetic automaton. The shrewd observer of gaucheries, the sensitive sniffer, the erstwhile cynic, has become a mere potential papa.

This spell, of course, doesn't last forever. Marriage cools the fever and lowers the threshold of disgust. The husband begins to observe what the lover was blind to, and often his discoveries affect him as unpleasantly as the treason of a trusted friend. And not only is the fever cooled: the opportunities for exact observation are enormously increased. It is a commonplace of juridical science that the great majority of divorces have their origin in the connubial chamber. Here intimacy is so extreme that it is fatal to illusion. Both parties, thrown into the closest human contact that either has suffered since their unconscious days *in utero*, find their old capacity for disgust reviving, and then suddenly flaming. The girl who was perfect in her wedding gown becomes a ghastly caricature in her *robe de nuit*; the man who was a Chevalier Bayard as a wooer becomes a snuffling, shambling, driveling nuisance as a husband—a fellow offensive to eyes, ears, nose, touch and immortal soul. A learned judge of my acquaintance, constantly hearing divorce actions and as constantly striving to reconcile the parties, always tries to induce plaintiff and defendant to live apart for a while, or, failing that, to occupy separate rooms, or, failing that, to at least dress in separate rooms. According to this jurist, a husband who shaves in his wife's presence is either an idiot or a scoundrel. The spectacle, he argues, is intrinsically disgusting, and to force it upon a refined woman is either to subject her to the most exquisite torture or to degrade her gradually to the insensate level of an *Abortfrau*.

The day is saved, as every one knows, by the powerful effects of habit. The acquisition of habit is the process whereby disgust is overcome in daily life—the process whereby one may cease to be disgusted by a persistent noise or odor. One suffers horribly at first, but after a bit one suffers less, and in the course of time one scarcely suffers at all. Thus a man, when his marriage enters upon the stage of regularity and safety, gets used to his wife as he might get used to a tannery next door, and *vice versa*. I think that women, in this direction, have the harder row to hoe, for they are more observant than men, and vastly more sensitive in small ways. But even women succumb to habit with humane rapidity, else every marriage would end in divorce. Disgusts pale into mere dislikes, disrelishes, distastes. They cease to gag and torture. But though they thus shrink into the shadow, they are by no means disposed of. Deep down in the subconscious they continue to lurk, and some accident may cause them to flare up at any time, and so work havoc. This flaring up accounts for a familiar and yet usually very mystifying phenomenon—the sudden collapse of a marriage, a friendship or a business association after years of apparent prosperity.

2
The Incomparable Buzzsaw

The chief (and perhaps the only genuine) charm of women is seldom mentioned by the orthodox professors of the sex. I refer to the charm that lies in the dangers they present. The allurement that they hold out to men is precisely the allurement that Cape Hatteras holds out to sailors: they are enormously dangerous and hence enormously fascinating. To the average man, doomed to some banal and sordid drudgery all his life long, they offer the only grand hazard that he ever encounters. Take them away and his existence would be as flat and secure as that of a milch-cow. Even to the unusual man, the adventurous man, the imaginative and romantic man, they offer the adventure of adventures. Civilization tends to dilute and cheapen all other hazards. War itself, once an enterprise stupendously thrilling, has been reduced to mere caution and calculation; already, indeed, it employs as many press-agents, letter-openers, and chautauqua orators as soldiers. On some not distant tomorrow its salient personality may be Potash, and if not Potash, then Perlmutter. But the duel of sex continues to be fought in the Berserker manner. Whoso approaches women still faces the immemorial dangers. Civilization has not made them a bit more safe than they were in Solomon's time; they are still inordinately barbarous and menacing, and hence inordinately provocative, and hence inordinately charming and romantic. . . .

The most disgusting cad in the world is the man who, on grounds of decorum and morality, avoids the game of love. He is one who puts his own ease and security above the most laudable of philanthropies. Women have a hard time of it in this world. They are oppressed by man-made laws, man-made social customs, masculine egoism, the delusion of masculine superiority. Their one comfort is the assurance that, even though it may be impossible to prevail against man, it is always possible to enslave and torture a man. This feeling is fostered when one makes love to them. One need not be a great beau, a seductive catch, to do it effectively. Any man is better than none. No woman is ever offended by admiration. The wife of a millionaire notes the reverent glance of a head-waiter. To withhold that devotion, to shrink poltroonishly from giving so much happiness at such small expense, to evade the business on the ground that it has hazards—this is the act of a puling and tacky fellow.

3
Women as Spectacles

Women, when it comes to snaring men, through the eye, bait a great many hooks that fail to fluster the fish. Nine-tenths of their primping and decorating of their persons not only doesn't please men; it actually repels men. I often pass two days running without encountering a single woman who is charmingly dressed. Nearly all of them run to painful color schemes, absurd designs and excessive over-ornamentation. One seldom observes a man who looks an absolute guy, whereas such women are very numerous; in the average theater audience they constitute a majority of at least nine-tenths. The reason is not far to seek. The clothes of men are plain in design and neutral in hue. The only touch of genuine color is in the florid blob of the face, the center of interest—exactly where it ought to be. If there is any other color at all, it is a faint suggestion in the cravat—adjacent to the face, and so leading the eye toward it. It is color that kills the clothes of the average woman. She runs to bright spots that take the eye away from her face and hair. She ceases to be woman clothed and becomes a mere piece of clothing womaned.

Even at the basic feminine art of pigmenting their faces very few women excel. The average woman seems to think that she is most lovely when her sophistication of her complexion is most adroitly concealed—when the *poudre de riz* is rubbed in so hard that it is almost invisible, and the penciling of eyes and lips is perfectly realistic. This is a false notion. Most men of appreciative eye have no objection to artificiality *per se*, so long as it is intrinsically sightly. The marks made by a lip-stick may be very beautiful; there are many lovely shades of scarlet, crimson and vermilion. A man with eyes in his head admires them for themselves; he doesn't have to be first convinced that they are non-existent, that what he sees is not the mark of a lip-stick at all, but an authentic lip. So with the eyes. Nothing could be more charming than an eye properly reënforced; the naked organ is not to be compared to it; nature is an idiot when it comes to shadows. But it must be admired as a work of art, not as a miraculous and incredible eye. . . . Women, in this important and venerable art, stick too closely to crude representation. They forget that men do not admire the technique, but the result. What they should do is to forget realism for a while, and concentrate their attention upon composition, chiaroscuro and color.

4
Woman and the Artist

Much gabble is to be found in the literature of the world upon the function of woman as inspiration, stimulant and *agente provocateuse* to the creative artist. The subject is a favorite one with sentimentalists, most of whom are quite beyond anything properly describable as inspiration, either with or without feminine aid. I incline to think, as I hint, that there is little if any basis of fact beneath the theory. Women not only do not inspire creative artists to high endeavor; they actually stand firmly against every high endeavor that a creative artist initiates spontaneously. What a man's women folks almost invariable ask of him is that he be respectable—that he do something generally approved—that he avoid yielding to his aberrant fancies—in brief, that he sedulously eschew showing any sign of genuine genius. Their interest is not primarily in the self-expression of the individual, but in the well-being of the family organization, which means the safety of themselves. No sane woman would want to be the wife of such a man, say, as Nietzsche or Chopin. His mistress perhaps, yes—for a mistress can always move on when the weather gets too warm. But not a wife. I here speak by the book. Both Nietzsche and Chopin had plenty of mistresses, but neither was ever able to get a wife.

Shakespeare and Ann Hathaway, Wagner and Minna Planer,

Molière and Armande Béjart—one might multiply instances almost endlessly. Minna, at least in theory, knew something of music; she was thus what romance regards as an ideal wife for Wagner. But instead of helping him to manufacture his incomparable masterpieces, she was for twenty-five years the chief impediment to their manufacture. "Lohengrin" gave her the horrors; she begged Richard to give up his lunacies and return to the composition of respectable cornet music. In the end he had to get rid of her in sheer self-defense. Once free, with nothing worse on his hands than the illicit affection of Cosima Liszt von Bülow, he produced music drama after music drama in rapid succession. Then, married to Cosima, he descended to the anticlimax of "Parsifal," a truly tragic mixture of the stupendous and the banal, of work of genius and *sinfonia domestica*—a great man dying by inches, smothered by the smoke of French fried potatoes, deafened by the wailing of children, murdered in his own house by the holiest of passions.

Sentimentalists always bring up the case of Schumann and his Clara in rebuttal. But does it actually rebut? I doubt it. Clara, too, perpetrated her *attentat* against art. Her fair white arms, lifting from the keyboard to encircle Robert's neck, squeezed more out of him than mere fatuous smirks. He had the best head on him that music had seen since Beethoven's day; he was, on the cerebral side, a colossus; he might have written music of the very first order. Well, what he *did* write was piano music—some of it imperfectly arranged for orchestra. The sad eyes of Clara were always upon him. He kept within the limits of her intelligence, her prejudices, her wifely love. No grand experiments with the orchestra. No superb leapings and cavortings. No rubbing of sandpaper over critical ears. Robert lived and died a respectable musical *Hausvater*. He was a man of genuine genius—but he didn't leave ten lines that might not have been passed by old Prof. Jadassohn.

The truth is that, no matter how great the domestic concord and how lavish the sacrifices a man makes for his women-folk, they almost always regard him secretly as a silly and selfish fellow, and cherish the theory that it would be easily possible to improve him. This is because the essential interests of men and women are eternally antithetical. A man may yield over and over again, but in the long run he must occasionally look out for himself—and it is these occasions that his women-folk remember. The typical domestic situation shows a woman trying to induce a man to do something that he doesn't want to do, or to refrain from something that he does want to do. This is true in his bachelor days, when his mother or his sister is his antagonist. It is pre-eminently true just before his marriage, when the girl who has marked him down is hard at the colossal job of overcoming his reluctance. And after marriage it is so true that there is hardly need to state it. One of the things every man discovers to his disquiet is that his wife, after the first play-acting is over, regards him essentially as his mother used to regard him—that is, as a self-worshiper who needs to be policed and an idiot who needs to be protected. The notion that women *admire* their men-folks is pure moonshine. The most they ever achieve in that direction is to pity them. When a woman genuinely loves a man it is a sign that she regards him much as a healthy man regards a one-armed and epileptic soldier.

5
Martyrs

Nearly the whole case of the birth-controllers who now roar in Christendom is grounded upon the doctrine that it is an intolerable outrage for a woman to have to submit to motherhood when her private fancies may rather incline to automobiling, shopping or going to the movies. For this curse the husband is blamed; the whole crime is laid to his swinish lasciviousness. With the highest respect, nonsense! My private suspicion, supported by long observation, copious prayer and the most laborious cogitation, is that no woman delights in motherhood so vastly as this woman who theoretically abhors it. She experiences, in fact, a double delight. On the one hand, there is the caressing of her vanity—a thing enjoyed by every woman when she achieves the banality of viable offspring. And on the other hand, there is the fine chance it gives her to play the martyr—a chance that every woman seeks as diligently as a man seeks ease. All these so-called unwilling mothers wallow in their martyrdom. They revel in the opportunity to be pitied, made much over and envied by other women.

6
The Burnt Child

The fundamental trouble with marriage is that it shakes a man's confidence in himself, and so greatly diminishes his general competence and effectiveness. His habit of mind becomes that of a commander who has lost a decisive and calamitous battle. He never quite trusts himself thereafter.

7
The Supreme Comedy

Marriage, at best, is full of a sour and inescapable comedy, but it never reaches the highest peaks of the ludicrous save when efforts are made to escape its terms—that is, when efforts are made to loosen its bonds, and so ameliorate and denaturize it. All projects to reform it by converting it into a free union of free individuals are inherently absurd. The thing is, at bottom, the most rigid of existing conventionalities, and the only way to conceal the fact and so make it bearable is to submit to it docilely. The effect of every revolt is merely to make the bonds galling, and, what is worse, poignantly obvious. Who are happy in marriage? Those with so little imagination that they cannot picture a better state, and those so shrewd that they prefer quiet slavery to hopeless rebellion.

8
A Hidden Cause

Many a woman, in order to bring the man of her choice to the altar of God, has to fight him with such relentless vigilance and ferocity that she comes to hate him. This, perhaps, explains the unhappiness of many marriages. In particular, it explains the unhappiness of many marriages based upon what is called "love."

9
Bad Workmanship

The essential slackness and incompetence of women, their congenital incapacity for small expertness, already descanted upon at length in my psychological work, "In Defense of Women," is never more plainly revealed than in their manhandling of the primary business of their sex. If the average woman were as competent at her trade of getting a husband as the average car conductor is at his trade of robbing the fare-box, then a bachelor beyond the age of twenty-five would be so rare in the world that yokels would pay ten cents to gape at him. But women, in this fundamental industry, pursue a faulty technique and permit themselves to be led astray by unsound principles. The axioms into which they have precipitated their wisdom are nearly all untrue. For example, the axiom that the way to capture a man is through his stomach—which is to say, by feeding him lavishly. Nothing could be more absurd. The average man, at least in England and America, has such rudimentary tastes in victualry that he doesn't know good food from bad. He will eat anything set before him by a cook that he likes. The true way to fetch him is with drinks. A single bottle of drinkable wine will fill more men with the passion of love than ten sides of beef or a ton of potatoes. Even a *Seidel* of beer, deftly applied, is enough to mellow the hardest bachelor. If women really knew their business, they would have abandoned cooking centuries ago, and devoted themselves to brewing, distilling and bartending. It is a rare man who will walk five blocks for a first-rate meal. But it is equally a rare man who, even in the old days of freedom, would *not* walk five blocks for a first-rate cocktail. To-day he would walk five miles.

Another unsound feminine axiom is the one to the effect that the way to capture a man is to be distant—to throw all the burden of the courtship upon him. This is precisely the way to lose him. A man face to face with a girl who seems reserved and unapproachable is not inspired thereby to drag her off in the manner of a caveman; on the contrary, he is inspired to thank God that here, at last, is a girl with whom it is possible to have friendly doings without getting into trouble—that here is one not likely to grow mushy and make a mess. The average man does not marry because some marble fair one challenges his enterprise. He marries because chance throws into his way a fair one who repels him less actively than most, and because his delight in what he thus calls her charm is reënforced by a growing suspicion that she has fallen in love with him. In brief, it is chivalry that undoes him. The girl who infallibly gets a husband—in fact, *any* husband that she wants—is the one who tracks him boldly, fastens him with sad eyes, and then, when his conscience has begun to torture him, throws her arms around his neck, bursts into maidenly tears on his shoulder, and tells him that she fears her forwardness will destroy his respect for her. It is only a colossus who can resist such strategy. But it takes only a man of the intellectual grade of a Y.M.C.A. secretary to elude the girl who is afraid to take the offensive.

A third bogus axiom I have already discussed, to wit, the axiom that a man is repelled by palpable cosmetics—that the wise girl is the one who effectively conceals her sophistication of her complexion. What could be more untrue? The fact is that very few men are competent to distinguish between a layer of talc and the authentic epidermis, and that the few who have the gift are quite free from any notion that the latter is superior to the former. What a man seeks when he enters the society of women is something pleasing to the eye. That is all he asks. He does not waste any time upon a chemical or spectroscopic examination of the object observed; he simply determines whether it is beautiful or not beautiful. Has it so long escaped women that their husbands, when led astray, are usually led astray by women so vastly besmeared with cosmetics that they resemble barber-poles more than human beings? Are they yet blind to the superior pull of a French maid, a chorus girl, a stenographer begauded like a painter's palette? . . . And still they go on rubbing off their varnish, brushing the lampblack from their eyelashes, seeking eternally the lip-stick that is so depressingly purple that it will deceive! Alas, what a folly!

PREJUDICES:
THIRD SERIES

I.
On Being an American

I

APPARENTLY there are those who begin to find it disagreeable—nay, impossible. Their anguish fills the Liberal weeklies and every ship that puts out from New York carries a groaning cargo of them, bound for Paris, London, Munich, Rome and way points—anywhere to escape the great curses and atrocities that make life intolerable for them at home. Let me say at once that I find little to cavil at in their basic complaints. In more than one direction, indeed, I probably go a great deal further than even the Young Intellectuals. It is, for example, one of my firmest and most sacred beliefs, reached after an inquiry extending over a score of years and supported by incessant prayer and meditation, that the government of the United States, in both its legislative arm and its executive arm, is ignorant, incompetent, corrupt, and disgusting—and from this judgment I except no more than twenty living lawmakers and no more than twenty executioners of their laws. It is a belief no less piously cherished that the administration of justice in the Republic is stupid, dishonest, and against all reason and equity—and from this judgment I except no more than thirty judges, including two upon the bench of the Supreme Court of the United States. It is another that the foreign policy of the United States—its habitual manner of dealing with other nations, whether friend or foe—is hypocritical, disingenuous, knavish, and dishonorable—and from this judgment I consent to no exceptions whatever, either recent or long past. And it is my fourth (and, to avoid too depressing a bill, final) conviction that the American people, taking one with another, constitute the most timorous, sniveling, poltroonish, ignominious mob of serfs and goose-steppers ever gathered under one flag in Christendom since the end of the Middle Ages, and that they grow more timorous, more sniveling, more poltroonish, more ignominious every day.

So far I go with the fugitive Young Intellectuals—and into the Bad Lands beyond. Such, in brief, are the cardinal articles of my political faith, held passionately since my admission to citizenship and now growing stronger and stronger as I gradually disintegrate into my component carbon, oxygen, hydrogen, phosphorus, calcium, sodium, nitrogen and iron. This is what I believe and preach, *in nomine Domini*, Amen. Yet I remain on the dock, wrapped in the flag, when the Young Intellectuals set sail. Yet here I stand, unshaken and undespairing, a loyal and devoted Americano, even a chauvinist, paying taxes without complaint, obeying all laws that are physiologically obeyable, accepting all the searching duties and responsibilities of citizenship unprotestingly, investing the sparse usufructs of my miserable toil in the obligations of the nation, avoiding all commerce with men sworn to overthrow the government, contributing my mite toward the glory of the national arts and sciences, enriching and embellishing the native language, spurning all lures (and even all invitations) to get out and stay out—here am I, a bachelor of easy means, forty-two years old, unhampered by debts or issue, able to go wherever I please and to stay as long as I please—here am I, contentedly and even smugly basking beneath the Stars and Stripes, a better citizen, I daresay, and certainly a less murmurous and exigent one, than thousands who put the Hon. Warren Gamaliel Harding beside Friedrich Barbarossa and Charlemagne, and hold the Supreme Court to be directly inspired by the Holy Spirit, and belong ardently to every Rotary Club, Ku Klux Klan, and Anti-Saloon League, and choke with emotion when the band plays "The Star-Spangled Banner," and believe with the faith of little children that one of Our Boys, taken at random, could dispose in a fair fight of ten Englishmen, twenty Germans, thirty Frogs, forty Wops, fifty Japs, or a hundred Bolsheviki.

Well, then, why am I still here? Why am I so complacent (perhaps even to the point of offensiveness), so free from bile, so little fretting and indignant, so curiously happy? Why did I answer only with a few academic "Hear, Hears" when Henry James, Ezra Pound, Harold Stearns and the *emigrés* of Greenwich Village issued their successive calls to the corn-fed *intelligentsia* to flee the shambles, escape to fairer lands, throw off the curse forever? The answer, of course, is to be sought in the nature of happiness which tempts to metaphysics. But let me keep upon the ground. To me, at least (and I can only follow my own nose) happiness presents itself in an aspect that is tripartite. To be happy (reducing the thing to its elementals) I must be:

a. Well-fed, unhounded by sordid cares, at ease in Zion.
b. Full of a comfortable feeling of superiority to the masses of my fellow-men.
c. Delicately and unceasingly amused according to my taste.

It is my contention that, if this definition be accepted, there is no country on the face of the earth wherein a man roughly constituted as I am—a man of my general weaknesses, vanities, appetites, prejudices, and aversions—can be so happy, or even one-half so happy, as he can be in these free and independent states. Going further, I lay down the proposition that it is a sheer physical impossibility for such a man to live in These States and *not* be happy—that it is as impossible to him as it would be to a schoolboy to weep over the burning down of his school-house. If he says that he isn't happy here, then he either lies or is insane. Here the business of getting a living, particularly since the war brought the loot of all Europe to the national strong-box, is enormously easier than it is in any other Christian land—so easy, in fact, that an educated and forehanded man who fails at it must actually make deliberate efforts to that end. Here the general average of intelligence, of knowledge, of competence, of integrity, of self-respect, of honor is so low that any man who knows his trade, does not fear ghosts, has read fifty good books, and practices the common decencies stands out as brilliantly as a wart on a bald head, and is thrown willy-nilly into a meager and exclusive aristocracy. And here, more than anywhere else that I know of or have heard of, the daily panorama of human existence, of private and communal folly—the unending procession of governmental extortions and chicaneries, of commercial brigandages and throat-slittings, of theological buffooneries, of æsthetic ribaldries, of legal swindles and harlotries, of miscellaneous rogueries, villainies, imbecilities, grotesqueries, and extravagances—is so inordinately gross and preposterous, so perfectly brought up to the highest conceivable amperage, so steadily enriched with an almost fabulous daring and originality, that only the man who was born with a petrified diaphragm can fail to laugh himself to sleep every night, and to awake every morning with all the eager, unflagging expectation of a Sunday-school superintendent touring the Paris peep-shows.

A certain sough of rhetoric may be here. Perhaps I yield to words as a chautauqua lecturer yields to them, belaboring and fermenting the hinds with his Message from the New Jerusalem. But fundamentally I am quite as sincere as he is. For example, in the matter of attaining to ease in Zion, of getting a fair share of the national swag, now piled so mountainously high. It seems to me, sunk in my Egyptian night, that the man who fails to do this in the United States to-day is a man who is somehow stupid—maybe not on the surface, but certainly deep down. Either he is one who cripples himself unduly, say by setting up a family before he can care for it, or by making a bad bargain for the sale of his wares, or by concerning himself too much about the affairs of other men; or he is one who endeavors fatuously to sell something that no normal American wants. Whenever I hear a professor of philosophy complain that his wife has eloped with some moving-picture actor or bootlegger who can at least feed and clothe her, my natural sympathy for the man is greatly corrupted by contempt for his lack of sense. Would it be regarded as sane and laudable for a man to travel the Soudan trying to sell fountain-pens, or Greenland offering to teach double-entry bookkeeping or counterpoint? Coming closer, would the judicious pity or laugh at a man who opened a shop for the sale of incunabula in Little Rock, Ark., or who demanded a living in McKeesport, Pa., on the ground that he could read Sumerian? In precisely the same way it seems to me to be nonsensical for a man to offer generally some commodity that only a few rare and dubious Americans want, and then weep and beat his breast because he is not patronized. One seeking to make a living in a country must pay due regard to the needs and tastes of that country. Here in the United States we have no jobs for grand dukes, and none for *Wirkliche Geheimräte*, and none for palace eunuchs, and none for masters of the buckhounds, and none (any more) for brewery *Todsaufer*—and very few for oboe-players, metaphysicians, astrophysicists, assyriologists, watercolorists, stylites and epic poets. There was a time when the *Todsaufer* served a public need and got an adequate reward, but it is no more. There may come a time when the composer of string quartettes is paid as much as a railway conductor, but it is not yet. Then why practice such trades—that is, as trades? The man of independent means may venture into them prudently; when he does so, he is seldom molested; it may even be argued that he performs a public service by adopting them. But the man who has a living to make is simply silly if he goes into them; he is like a soldier going over the top with a coffin strapped to his back. Let him abandon such puerile vanities, and take to the uplift instead, as, indeed, thousands of other victims of the industrial system have already done. Let him bear in mind that, whatever its neglect of the humanities and their monks, the Republic has never got half enough bond salesmen, quack doctors, ward leaders, phrenologists, Methodist evangelists, circus clowns, magicians, soldiers, farmers, popular song writers, moonshine distillers, forgers of gin labels, mine guards, detectives, spies, snoopers, and *agents provocateurs.* The rules are set by Omnipotence; the discreet man observes them. Observing them, he is safe beneath the starry bed-tick, in fair weather or foul. The *boobus Americanus* is a bird that knows no closed season—and if he won't come down to Texas oil stock, or one-night cancer cures, or building lots in Swampshurst, he will always come down to Inspiration and Optimism, whether political, theological, pedagogical, literary, or economic.

The doctrine that it is *infra dignitatem* for an educated man to take a hand in the snaring of this goose is one in which I see nothing convincing. It is a doctrine chiefly voiced, I believe, by those who have tried the business and failed. They take refuge behind the childish notion that there is something honorable about poverty *per se*—the Greenwich Village complex. This is nonsense. Poverty may be an unescapable misfortune, but that no more makes it honorable than a cocked eye is made honorable by the same cause. Do I advocate, then, the ceaseless, senseless hogging of money? I do not. All I advocate—and praise as virtuous—is the hogging of enough to provide security and ease. Despite all the romantic superstitions to the contrary, the artist cannot do his best work when he is oppressed by unsatisfied wants. Nor can the philosopher. Nor can the man of science. The best and clearest thinking of the world is done and the finest art is produced, not by men who are hungry, ragged and harassed, but by men who are well-fed, warm and easy in mind. It is the artist's first duty to his art to achieve that tranquility for himself. Shakespeare tried to achieve it; so did Beethoven, Wagner, Brahms, Ibsen and Balzac. Goethe, Schopenhauer, Schumann and Mendelssohn were born to it. Joseph Conrad, Richard Strauss and Anatole France have got it for themselves in our own day. In the older countries, where competence is far more general and competition is thus more sharp, the thing is often cruelly difficult, and sometimes almost impossible. But in the United States it is absurdly easy, given ordinary luck. Any man with a superior air, the intelligence of a stockbroker, and the resolution of a hat-check girl—in brief, any man who believes in himself enough, and with sufficient cause, to be called a journeyman—can cadge enough money, in this glorious commonwealth of morons, to make life soft for him.

And if a lining for the purse is thus facilely obtainable, given a reasonable prudence and resourcefulness, then balm for the ego is just as unlaboriously got, given ordinary dignity and decency. Simply to exist, indeed, on the plane of a civilized man is to attain, in the Republic, to a distinction that should be enough for all save the most vain; it is even likely to be too much, as the frequent challenges of the Ku Klux Klan, the American Legion, the Anti-Saloon League, and other such vigilance committees of the majority testify. Here is a country in which all political thought and activity are concentrated upon the scramble for jobs—in which the normal politician, whether he be a President or a village road supervisor, is willing to renounce any principle, however precious to him, and to adopt any lunacy, however offensive to him, in order to keep his place at the trough. Go into politics, then, without seeking or wanting office, and at once you are as conspicuous as a red-haired blackamoor—in fact, a great deal more conspicuous, for red-haired blackamoors have been seen, but who has ever seen or heard of an American politician, Democrat or

Republican, Socialist or Liberal, Whig or Tory, who did not itch for a job? Again, here is a country in which it is an axiom that a business man shall be a member of a Chamber of Commerce, an admirer of Charles M. Schwab, a reader of the *Saturday Evening Post*, a golfer—in brief, a vegetable. Spend your hours of escape from *Geschäft* reading Remy de Gourmont or practicing the violoncello, and the local Sunday newspaper will infallibly find you out and hymn the marvel—nay, your banker will summon you to discuss your notes, and your rivals will spread the report (probably truthful) that you were pro-German during the war. Yet again, here is a land in which women rule and men are slaves. Train your women to get your slippers for you, and your ill fame will match Galileo's or Darwin's. Once more, here is the Paradise of back-slappers, of democrats, of mixers, of go-getters. Maintain ordinary reserve, and you will arrest instant attention—and have your hand kissed by multitudes who, despite democracy, have all the inferior man's unquenchable desire to grovel and admire.

Nowhere else in the world is superiority more easily attained or more eagerly admitted. The chief business of the nation, as a nation, is the setting up of heroes, mainly bogus. It admired the literary style of the late Woodrow; it respects the theological passion of Bryan; it venerates J. Pierpont Morgan; it takes Congress seriously; it would be unutterably shocked by the proposition (with proof) that a majority of its judges are ignoramuses, and that a respectable minority of them are scoundrels. The manufacture of artificial *Durchlauchten, k.k. Hoheiten* and even gods goes on feverishly and incessantly; the will to worship never flags. Ten iron-molders meet in the back-room of a near-beer saloon, organize a lodge of the Noble and Mystic Order of American Rosicrucians, and elect a wheelwright Supreme Worthy Whimwham; a month later they send a notice to the local newspaper that they have been greatly honored by an official visit from that Whimwham, and that they plan to give him a jeweled fob for his watch-chain. The chief national heroes—Lincoln, Lee, and so on—cannot remain mere men. The mysticism of the mediæval peasantry gets into the communal view of them, and they begin to sprout haloes and wings. As I say, no intrinsic merit—at least, none commensurate with the mob estimate—is needed to come to such august dignities. Everything American is a bit amateurish and childish, even the national gods. The most conspicuous and respected American in nearly every field of endeavor, saving only the purely commercial (I exclude even the financial) is a man who would attract little attention in any other country. The leading American critic of literature, after twenty years of diligent exposition of his ideas, has yet to make it clear what he is in favor of, and why. The queen of the *haut monde*, in almost every American city, is a woman who regards Lord Reading as an aristocrat and her superior, and whose grandfather slept in his underclothes. The leading American musical director, if he went to Leipzig, would be put to polishing trombones and copying drum parts. The chief living American military man—the national heir to Frederick, Marlborough, Wellington, Washington and Prince Eugene—is a member of the Elks, and proud of it. The leading American philosopher (now dead, with no successor known to the average pedagogue) spent a lifetime erecting an epistemological defense for the national æsthetic maxim: "I don't know nothing about music, but I know what I like." The most eminent statesman the United States has produced since Lincoln was fooled by Arthur James Balfour, and miscalculated his public support by more than 5,000,000 votes. And the current Chief Magistrate of the nation—its defiant substitute for czar and kaiser—is a small-town printer who, when he wishes to enjoy himself in the Executive Mansion, invites in a homeopathic doctor, a Seventh Day Adventist evangelist, and a couple of moving-picture actresses.

2

All of which may be boiled down to this: that the United States is essentially a commonwealth of third-rate men—that distinction is easy here because the general level of culture, of information, of taste and judgment, of ordinary competence is so low. No sane man, employing an American plumber to repair a leaky drain, would expect him to do it at the first trial, and in precisely the same way no sane man, observing an American Secretary of State in negotiation with Englishmen and Japs, would expect him to come off better than second best. Third-rate men, of course, exist in all countries, but it is only here that they are in full control of the state, and with it of all the national standards. The land was peopled, not by the hardy adventurers of legend, but simply by incompetents who could not get on at home, and the lavishness of nature that they found here, the vast ease with which they could get livings, confirmed and augmented their native incompetence. No American colonist, even in the worst days of the Indian wars, ever had to face such hardships as ground down the peasants of Central Europe during the Hundred Years War, nor even such hardships as oppressed the English lower classes during the century before the Reform Bill of 1832. In most of the colonies, indeed, he seldom saw any Indians at all: the one thing that made life difficult for him was his congenital dunderheadedness. The winning of the West, so rhetorically celebrated in American romance, cost the lives of fewer men than the single battle of Tannenberg, and the victory was much easier and surer. The immigrants who have come in since those early days have been, if anything, of even lower grade than their forerunners. The old notion that the United States is peopled by the offspring of brave, idealistic and liberty loving minorities, who revolted against injustice, bigotry and mediævalism at home—this notion is fast succumbing to the alarmed study that has been given of late to the immigration of recent years. The truth is that the majority of non-Anglo-Saxon immigrants since the Revolution, like the majority of Anglo-Saxon immigrants before the Revolution, have been, not the superior men of their native lands, but the botched and unfit: Irishmen starving to death in Ireland, Germans unable to weather the *Sturm und Drang* of the post-Napoleonic reorganization, Italians weed-grown on exhausted soil, Scandinavians run to all bone and no brain, Jews too incompetent to swindle even the barbarous peasants of Russia, Poland and Roumania. Here and there among the immigrants, of course, there may be a bravo, or even a superman—*e.g.*, the ancestors of Volstead, Ponzi, Jack Dempsey, Schwab, Daugherty, Debs, Pershing—but the average newcomer is, and always has been simply a poor fish.

Nor is there much soundness in the common assumption, so beloved of professional idealists and wind-machines, that the people of America constitute "the youngest of the great peoples." The phrase turns up endlessly; the average newspaper editorial writer would be hamstrung if the Postoffice suddenly interdicted it, as it interdicted "the right to rebel" during the war. What gives it a certain specious plausibility is the fact that the American Republic, compared to a few other existing governments, is relatively young. But the American Republic is not necessarily identical with the American people; they might overturn it to-morrow and set up a monarchy, and still remain the same people. The truth is that, as a distinct nation, they go back fully three hundred years, and that even their government is older than that of most other nations, *e.g.*, France, Italy, Germany, Russia. Moreover, it is absurd to say that there is anything properly describable as youthfulness in the American outlook. It is not that of young men, but that of old men. All the characteristics of senescence are in it: a great distrust of ideas, an habitual timorousness, a harsh fidelity to a few fixed beliefs, a touch of mysticism. The average American is a prude and a Methodist under his skin, and the fact is never more evident than when he is trying to disprove it. His vices are not those of a healthy boy, but those of an ancient paralytic escaped from the *Greisenheim*. If you would penetrate to the causes thereof, simply go down to Ellis Island and look at the next shipload of immigrants. You will not find the spring of youth in their step; you will find the shuffling of exhausted men. From such exhausted men the American stock has sprung. It was easier for them to survive here than it was where they came from, but that ease, though it made them feel stronger, did not actually strengthen them. It left them what they were when they came: weary peasants, eager only for the comfortable security of a pig in a sty. Out of that eagerness has issued many of the noblest manifestations of American *Kultur*: the national hatred of war, the pervasive suspicion of the aims and intents of all other nations, the short way with heretics and disturbers of the peace, the unshakable belief in devils, the implacable hostility to every novel idea and point of view.

All these ways of thinking are the marks of the peasant—more, of the peasant long ground into the mud of his wallow, and determined at last to stay there—the peasant who has definitely renounced any lewd desire he may have ever had to gape at the stars. The habits of mind of this dull, sempiternal *fellah*—the oldest man in Christendom—are, with a few modifications, the habits of mind of the American people. The peasant has a great practical cunning, but he is unable to see any further than the next farm. He likes money and knows how to amass property, but his cultural development is but little above that of the domestic animals. He is intensely and cocksurely moral, but his morality and his self-interest are crudely identical. He is emotional and easy to scare, but his imagination cannot grasp an abstraction. He is a violent nationalist and patriot, but he admires rogues in office and always beats the tax-collector if he can. He has immovable opinions about all the great affairs of state, but nine-tenths of them are sheer imbecilities. He is violently jealous of what he conceives to be his rights, but brutally disregardful of the other fellow's. He is religious, but his religion is wholly devoid of beauty and dignity. This man, whether city or country bred, is the normal Americano—the 100 per cent. Methodist, Odd Fellow, Ku Kluxer, and Know Nothing. He exists in all countries, but here alone he rules—here alone his anthropoid fears and rages are accepted gravely as logical ideas, and dissent from them is punished as a sort of public offense. Around every one of his principal delusions—of the sacredness of democracy, of the feasibility of sumptuary law, of the incurable sinfulness of all other peoples, of the menace of ideas, of the corruption lying in all the arts—there is thrown a barrier of taboos, and woe to the anarchist who seeks to break it down!

The multiplication of such taboos is obviously not characteristic of a culture that is moving from a lower plane to a higher—that is, of a culture still in the full glow of its youth. It is a sign, rather, of a culture that is slipping downhill—one that is reverting to the most primitive standards and ways of thought. The taboo, indeed, is the trade-mark of the savage, and wherever it exists it is a relentless and effective enemy of civilized enlightenment. The savage is the most meticulously moral of men; there is scarcely an act of his daily life that is not conditioned by unyielding prohibitions and obligations, most of them logically unintelligible. The mob-man, a savage set amid civilization, cherishes a code of the same draconian kind. He believes firmly that right and wrong are immovable things—

that they have an actual and unchangeable existence, and that any challenge of them, by word or act, is a crime against society. And with the concept of wrongness, of course, he always confuses the concept of mere differentness—to him the two are indistinguishable. Anything strange is to be combatted; it is of the Devil. The mob-man cannot grasp ideas in their native nakedness. They must be dramatized and personalized for him, and provided with either white wings or forked tails. All discussion of them, to interest him, must take the form of a pursuit and scotching of demons. He cannot think of a heresy without thinking of a heretic to be caught, condemned, and burned.

The Fathers of the Republic, I am convinced, had a great deal more prevision than even their most romantic worshipers give them credit for. They not only sought to create a governmental machine that would be safe from attack without; they also sought to create one that would be safe from attack within. They invented very ingenious devices for holding the mob in check, for protecting the national polity against its transient and illogical rages, for securing the determination of all the larger matters of state to a concealed but none the less real aristocracy. Nothing could have been further from the intent of Washington, Hamilton and even Jefferson than that the official doctrines of the nation, in the year 1922, should be identical with the nonsense heard in the chautauqua, from the evangelical pulpit, and on the stump. But Jackson and his merry men broke through the barbed wires thus so carefully strung, and ever since 1825 *vox populi* has been the true voice of the nation. To-day there is no longer any question of statesmanship, in any real sense, in our politics. The only way to success in American public life lies in flattering and kowtowing to the mob. A candidate for office, even the highest, must either adopt its current manias *en bloc*, or convince it hypocritically that he has done so, while cherishing reservations *in petto*. The result is that only two sorts of men stand any chance whatever of getting into actual control of affairs—first, glorified mob-men who genuinely believe what the mob believes, and secondly, shrewd fellows who are willing to make any sacrifice of conviction and self-respect in order to hold their jobs. One finds perfect examples of the first class in Jackson and Bryan.

One finds hundreds of specimens of the second among the politicians who got themselves so affectingly converted to Prohibition, and who voted and blubbered for it with flasks in their pockets. Even on the highest planes our politics seems to be incurably mountebankish. The same Senators who raised such raucous alarms against the League of Nations voted for the Disarmament Treaty—a far more obvious surrender to English hegemony. And the same Senators who pleaded for the League on the ground that its failure would break the heart of the world were eloquently against the treaty. The few men who maintained a consistent course in both cases, voting either for or against both League and treaty, were denounced by the newspapers as deliberate marplots, and found their constituents rising against them. To such an extent had the public become accustomed to buncombe that simple honesty was incomprehensible to it, and hence abhorrent!

As I have pointed out in a previous work, this dominance of mob ways of thinking, this pollution of the whole intellectual life of the country by the prejudices and emotions of the rabble, goes unchallenged because the old landed aristocracy of the colonial era has been engulfed and almost obliterated by the rise of the industrial system, and no new aristocracy has arisen to take its place, and discharge its highly necessary functions. An upper class, of course, exists, and of late it has tended to increase in power, but it is culturally almost indistinguishable from the mob: it lacks absolutely anything even remotely resembling an aristocratic point of view. One searches in vain for any sign of the true *Junker* spirit in the Vanderbilts, Astors, Morgans, Garys, and other such earls and dukes of the plutocracy; their culture, like their aspiration, remains that of the pawnshop. One searches in vain too, for the aloof air of the don in the official *intelligentsia* of the American universities; they are timorous and orthodox, and constitute a reptile Congregatio de Propaganda Fide to match Bismarck's *Reptilienpresse*. Everywhere else on earth, despite the rise of democracy, an organized minority of aristocrats survives from a more spacious day, and if its personnel has degenerated and its legal powers have decayed it has at least maintained some vestige of its old independence of spirit, and jealously guarded its old right to be heard without risk of penalty. Even in England, where the peerage has been debauched to the level of a political baptismal fount for Jewish money-lenders and Wesleyan soap-boilers, there is sanctuary for the old order in the two ancient universities, and a lingering respect for it in the peasantry. But in the United States it was paralyzed by Jackson and got its death blow from Grant, and since then no successor to it has been evolved. Thus there is no organized force to oppose the irrational vagaries of the mob. The legislative and executive arms of the government yield to them without resistance; the judicial arm has begun to yield almost as supinely, particularly when they take the form of witch-hunts; outside the official circle there is no opposition that is even dependably articulate. The worst excesses go almost without challenge. Discussion, when it is heard at all, is feeble and superficial, and girt about by the taboos that I have mentioned. The clatter about the so-called Ku Klux Klan, two or three years ago, was typical. The astounding program of this organization was discussed in the newspapers for months on end, and a committee of Congress sat in solemn state to investigate it, and yet not a single newspaper or Congressman, so far as I am aware, so much as mentioned the most patent and important fact about it, to wit, that the Ku Klux was, to all intents and purposes, simply the secular arm of the Methodist Church, and that its methods were no more than physical projections of the familiar extravagances of the Anti-Saloon League. The intimate relations between church and Klan, amounting almost to identity, must have been plain to every intelligent American, and yet the taboo upon the realistic consideration of ecclesiastical matters was sufficient to make every public soothsayer disregard it completely.

I often wonder, indeed, if there would be any intellectual life at all in the United States if it were not for the steady importation in bulk of ideas from abroad, and particularly, in late years, from England. What would become of the average American scholar if he could not borrow wholesale from English scholars? How could an inquisitive youth get beneath the surface of our politics if it were not for such anatomists as Bryce? Who would show our statesmen the dotted lines for their signatures if there were no Balfours and Lloyd-Georges? How could our young professors formulate æsthetic judgments, especially in the field of letters, if it were not for such gifted English mentors as Robertson Nicoll, Squire and Clutton-Brock? By what process, finally, would the true style of a visiting card be determined, and the *höflich* manner of eating artichokes, if there were no reports from Mayfair? On certain levels this naïve subservience must needs irritate every self-respecting American, and even dismay him. When he recalls the amazing feats of the English war propagandists between 1914 and 1917—and their even more amazing confessions of method since—he is apt to ask himself quite gravely if he belongs to a free nation or to a crown colony. The thing was done openly, shamelessly, contemptuously, cynically, and yet it was a gigantic success. The office of the American Secretary of State, from the end of Bryan's grotesque incumbency to the end of the Wilson administration, was little more than an antechamber of the British Foreign Office. Dr. Wilson himself, in the conduct of his policy, differed only legally from such colonial premiers as Hughes and Smuts. Even after the United States got into the war it was more swagger for a Young American blood to wear the British uniform than the American uniform. No American ever seriously questions an Englishman or Englishwoman of official or even merely fashionable position at home. Lord Birkenhead was accepted as a gentleman everywhere in the United States; Mrs. Asquith's almost unbelievable imbecilities were heard with hushed fascination; even Lady Astor, an American married to an expatriate German-American turned English viscount, was greeted with solemn effusiveness. During the latter part of 1917, when New York swarmed with British military missions, I observed in *Town Topics* a polite protest against a very significant habit of certain of their gallant members: that of going to dances wearing spurs, and so macerating the frocks and heels of the fawning fair. The protest, it appears, was not voiced by the hosts and hostesses of these singular officers: they would have welcomed their guests in trench boots. It was left to a dubious weekly, and it was made very gingerly.

The spectacle, as I say, has a way of irking the American touched by nationalistic weakness. Ever since the day of Lowell —even since the day of Cooper and Irving—there have been denunciations of it. But however unpleasant it may be, there is no denying that a chain of logical causes lies behind it, and that they are not to be disposed of by objecting to them. The average American of the Anglo-Saxon majority, in truth, is simply a second-rate Englishman, and so it is no wonder that he is spontaneously servile, despite all his democratic denial of superiorities, to what he conceives to be first-rate Englishmen. He corresponds, roughly, to an English Nonconformist of the better-fed variety, and he shows all the familiar characters of the breed. He is truculent and cocksure, and yet he knows how to take off his hat when a bishop of the Establishment passes. He is hot against the dukes, and yet the notice of a concrete duke is a singing in his heart. It seems to me that this inferior Anglo-Saxon is losing his old dominance in the United States—that is, biologically. But he will keep his cultural primacy for a long, long while, in spite of the overwhelming inrush of men of other races, if only because those newcomers are even more clearly inferior than he is. Nine-tenths of the Italians, for example, who have come to these shores in late years have brought no more of the essential culture of Italy with them than so many horned cattle would have brought. If they become civilized at all, settling here, it is the civilization of the Anglo-Saxon majority that they acquire, which is to say, the civilization of the English second table. So with the Germans, the Scandinavians, and even the Jews and Irish. The Germans, taking one with another, are on the cultural level of green-grocers. I have come into contact with a great many of them since 1914, some of them of considerable wealth and even of fashionable pretensions. In the whole lot I can think of but a score or two who could name offhand the principal works of Thomas Mann, Otto Julius Bierbaum, Ludwig Thoma or Hugo von Hofmannsthal. They know much more about Mutt and Jeff than they know about Goethe. The Scandinavians are even worse. The majority of them are mere clods, and they are sucked into the Knights of Pythias, the chautauqua and the Methodist Church almost as soon as they land; it is by no means a mere accident that the national Prohibition Enforcement Act bears the name of a man theoretically of the blood of Gustavus Vasa, Svend of the Forked Beard, and Eric the Red. The Irish in the United States are scarcely touched by the revival of Irish culture, despite their melodramatic concern with

Irish politics. During the war they supplied diligent and dependable agents to the Anglo-Saxon White Terror, and at all times they are very susceptible to political and social bribery. As for the Jews, they change their names to Burton, Thompson and Cecil in order to qualify as true Americans, and when they are accepted and rewarded in the national coin they renounce Moses altogether and get themselves baptized in St. Bartholomew's Church.

Whenever ideas enter the United States from without they come by way of England. What the London *Times* says to-day, about Ukranian politics, the revolt in India, a change of ministry in Italy, the character of the King of Norway, the oil situation in Mesopotamia, will be said week after next by the *Times* of New York, and a month or two later by all the other American newspapers. The extent of this control of American opinion by English news mongers is but little appreciated in the United States, even by professional journalists. Fully four-fifths of all the foreign news that comes to the American newspapers comes through London, and most of the rest is supplied either by Englishmen or by Jews (often American-born) who maintain close relations with the English. During the years 1914–1917 so many English agents got into Germany in the guise of American correspondents—sometimes with the full knowledge of their Anglomaniac American employers—that the Germans, just before the United States entered the war, were considering barring American correspondents from their country altogether. I was in Copenhagen and Basel in 1917, and found both towns—each an important source of war news—full of Jews representing American journals as a side-line to more delicate and confidential work for the English department of press propaganda. Even to-day a very considerable proportion of the American correspondents in Europe are strongly under English influences, and in the Far East the proportion is probably still larger. But these men seldom handle really important news. All that is handled from London, and by trustworthy Britons. Such of it as is not cabled directly to the American newspapers and press associations is later clipped from English newspapers, and printed as bogus letters or cablegrams.

The American papers accept such very dubious stuff, not

chiefly because they are hopelessly stupid or Anglomaniac, but because they find it impossible to engage competent American correspondents. If the native journalists who discuss our domestic politics avoid the fundamentals timorously, then those who venture to discuss foreign politics are scarcely aware of the fundamentals at all. We have simply developed no class of experts in such matters. No man comparable, say to Dr. Dillon, Wickham Steed, Count zu Reventlow or Wilfrid Scawen Blunt exists in the United States. When, in the Summer of 1920, the editors of the Baltimore *Sun* undertook plans to cover the approaching Disarmament Conference at Washington in a comprehensive and intelligent manner, they were forced, willy-nilly, into employing Englishmen to do the work. Such men as Brailsford and Bywater, writing from London, three thousand miles away, were actually better able to interpret the work of the conference than American correspondents on the spot, few of whom were capable of anything beyond the most trivial gossip. During the whole period of the conference not a professional Washington correspondent—the flower of American political journalism—wrote a single article upon the proceedings that got further than their surface aspects. Before the end of the sessions this enforced dependence upon English opinion had an unexpected and significant result. Facing the English and the Japs in an unyielding alliance, the French turned to the American delegation for assistance. The issue specifically before the conference was one on which American self-interest was obviously identical with French self-interest. Nevertheless, the English had such firm grip upon the machinery of news distribution that they were able, in less than a week, to turn American public opinion against the French, and even to set up an active Francophobia. No American, not even any of the American delegates, was able to cope with their propaganda. They not only dominated the conference and pushed through a set of treaties that were extravagantly favorable to England; they even established the doctrine that all opposition to those treaties was immoral!

When Continental ideas, whether in politics, in metaphysics or in the fine arts, penetrate to the United States they nearly always travel by way of England. Emerson did not read Goethe; he read Carlyle. The American people, from the end of 1914 to the end of 1918, did not read first-handed statements of the German case; they read English interpretations of those statements. In London is the clearing house and transformer station. There the latest notions from the mainland are sifted out, carefully diluted with English water, and put into neat packages for the Yankee trade. The English not only get a chance to ameliorate or embellish; they also determine very largely what ideas Americans are to hear of at all. Whatever fails to interest them, or is in any way obnoxious to them, is not likely to cross the ocean. This explains why it is that most literate Americans are so densely ignorant of many Continentals who have been celebrated at home for years, for example, Huysmans, Hartleben, Vaihinger, Merezhkovsky, Keyserling, Snoilsky, Mauthner, Altenberg, Heidenstam, Alfred Kerr. It also explains why they so grossly overestimate various third-raters, laughed at at home, for example, Brieux. These fellows simply happen to interest the English *intelligentsia*, and are thus palmed off upon the gaping colonists of Yankeedom. In the case of Brieux the hocus-pocus was achieved by one man, George Bernard Shaw, a Scotch blue-nose disguised as an Irish patriot and English soothsayer. Shaw, at bottom, has the ideas of a Presbyterian elder, and so the moral frenzy of Brieux enchanted him. Whereupon he retired to his chamber, wrote a flaming Brieuxiad for the American trade, and founded the late vogue of the French Dr. Sylvanus Stall on this side of the ocean.

This wholesale import and export business in Continental fancies is of no little benefit, of course, to the generality of Americans. If it did not exist they would probably never hear of many of the salient Continentals at all, for the obvious incompetence of most of the native and resident introducers of intellectual ambassadors makes them suspicious even of those who, like Boyd and Nathan, are thoroughly competent. To this day there is no American translation of the plays of Ibsen; we use the William Archer Scotch-English translations, most of them atrociously bad, but still better than nothing. So with the works of Nietzsche, Anatole France, Georg Brandes, Turgeniev, Dostoyevsky, Tolstoi, and other moderns after their kind. I can think of but one important exception: the work of Gerhart Hauptmann, done into English by and under the supervision of Ludwig Lewisohn. But even here Lewisohn used a number of English translations of single plays: the English were still ahead of him, though they stopped half way. He is, in any case, a very extraordinary American, and the Department of Justice kept an eye on him during the war. The average American professor is far too dull a fellow to undertake so difficult an enterprise. Even when he sports a German Ph.D. one usually finds on examination that all he knows about modern German literature is that a *Mass* of Hofbräu in Munich used to cost 27 *Pfennig* downstairs and 32 *Pfennig* upstairs. The German universities were formerly very tolerant of foreigners. Many an American, in preparation for professing at Harvard, spent a couple of years roaming from one to the other of them without picking up enough German to read the *Berliner Tageblatt.* Such frauds swarm in all our lesser universities, and many of them, during the war, became eminent authorities upon the crimes of Nietzsche and the errors of Treitschke.

3

In rainy weather, when my old wounds ache and the four humors do battle in my spleen, I often find myself speculating sourly as to the future of the Republic. Native opinion, of course, is to the effect that it will be secure and glorious; the superstition that progress must always be upward and onward will not down; in virulence and popularity it matches the superstition that money can accomplish anything. But this view is not shared by most reflective foreigners, as any one may find out by looking into such a book as Ferdinand Kürnberger's "Der Amerikamüde," Sholom Asch's "America," Ernest von Wolzogen's "Ein Dichter in Dollarica," W. L. George's "Hail, Columbia!", Annalise Schmidt's "Der Amerikanische Mensch" or Sienkiewicz's "After Bread," or by hearkening unto the confidences, if obtainable, of such returned immigrants as Georges Clemenceau, Knut Hamsun, George Santayana, Clemens von Pirquet, John Masefield and Maxim Gorky, and, via the ouija board, Antonin Dvořák, Frank Wedekind and Edwin Klebs. The American Republic, as nations go, has led a safe and easy life, with no serious enemies to menace it, either within or without, and no grim struggle with want. Getting a living here has always been easier than anywhere else in Christendom; getting a secure foothold has been possible to whole classes of men who would have remained submerged in Europe, as the character of our plutocracy, and no less of our *intelligentsia* so brilliantly shows. The American people have never had to face such titanic assults as those suffered by the people of Holland, Poland and half a dozen other little countries; they have not lived with a ring of powerful and unconscionable enemies about them, as the Germans have lived since the Middle Ages; they have not been torn by class wars, as the French, the Spaniards and the Russians have been torn; they have not thrown their strength into far-flung and exhausting colonial enterprises, like the English. All their foreign wars have been fought with foes either too weak to resist them or too heavily engaged elsewhere to make more than a half-hearted attempt. The combats with Mexico and Spain were not wars; they were simply lynchings. Even the Civil War, compared to the larger European conflicts since the invention of gunpowder, was trivial in its character and transient in its effects. The population of the United States, when it began, was about 31,500,000—say 10 per cent. under the population of France in 1914. But after four years of struggle, the number of men killed in action or dead of wounds, in the two armies, came but 200,000—probably little more than a sixth of the total losses of France between 1914 and 1918. Nor was there any very extensive destruction of property. In all save a small area in the North there was none at all, and even in the South only a few towns of any importance were destroyed. The average Northerner passed through the four years scarcely aware, save by report, that a war was going on. In the South the breath of Mars blew more hotly, but even there large numbers of men escaped service, and the general hardship everywhere fell a great deal short of the hardships suffered by the Belgians, the French of the North, the Germans of East Prussia, and the Serbians and Rumanians in the World War. The agonies of the South have been much exaggerated in popular romance; they were probably more severe during Reconstruction, when they were chiefly psychical, than they were during the actual war. Certainly General Robert E. Lee was in a favorable position to estimate the military achievement of the Confederacy. Well, Lee was of the opinion that his army was very badly supported by the civil population, and that its final disaster was largely due to that ineffective support.

Coming down to the time of the World War, one finds precious few signs that the American people, facing an antagonist of equal strength and with both hands free, could be relied upon to give a creditable account of themselves. The American share in that great straggle, in fact, was marked by poltroonery almost as conspicuously as it was marked by knavery. Let us consider briefly what the nation did. For a few months it viewed the struggle idly and unintelligently, as a yokel might stare at a sword-swallower at a county fair. Then, seeing a chance to profit, it undertook with sudden alacrity the ghoulish office of *Kriegslieferant*. One of the contestants being debarred, by the chances of war, from buying, it devoted its whole energies, for two years, to purveying to the other. Meanwhile, it made every effort to aid its customer by lending him the cloak of its neutrality—that is, by demanding all the privileges of a neutral and yet carrying on a stupendous wholesale effort to promote the war. On the official side, this neutrality was fraudulent from the start, as the revelations of Mr. Tumulty have since demonstrated; popularly it became more and more fraudulent as the debts of the customer contestant piled up, and it became more and more apparent—a fact diligently made known by his partisans—that they would be worthless if he failed to win. Then, in the end, covert aid was transformed into overt aid. And under what gallant conditions! In brief, there stood a nation of 65,000,000 people, which, without effective allies, had just closed two and a half years of homeric conflict by completely defeating an enemy state of 135,000,000 and two lesser ones of more than 10,000,000 together, and now stood at bay before a combination of at least 140,000,000. Upon this battle-scarred and war-weary foe the Republic of 100,000,000 freemen now flung itself, so lifting the odds to 4 to 1. And after a year and a half more of struggle it emerged triumphant—a knightly victor surely!

There is no need to rehearse the astounding and unprecedented swinishness that accompanied this glorious business—

the colossal waste of public money, the savage persecution of all opponents and critics of the war, the open bribery of labor, the half-insane reviling of the enemy, the manufacture of false news, the knavish robbery of enemy civilians, the incessant spy hunts, the floating of public loans by a process of blackmail, the degradation of the Red Cross to partisan uses, the complete abandonment of all decency, decorum and self-respect. The facts must be remembered with shame by every civilized American; lest they be forgotten by the generations of the future I am even now engaged with collaborators upon an exhaustive record of them, in twenty volumes folio. More important to the present purpose are two things that are apt to be overlooked, the first of which is the capital fact that the war was "sold" to the American people, as the phrase has it, not by appealing to their courage, but by appealing to their cowardice—in brief, by adopting the assumption that they were not warlike at all, and certainly not gallant and chivalrous, but merely craven and fearful. The first selling point of the proponents of American participation was the contention that the Germans, with gigantic wars still raging on both fronts, were preparing to invade the United States, burn down all the towns, murder all the men, and carry off all the women—that their victory would bring staggering and irresistible reprisals for the American violation of the duties of a neutral. The second selling point was that the entrance of the United States would end the war almost instantly—that the Germans would be so overwhelmingly outnumbered, in men and guns, that it would be impossible for them to make any effective defense—above all, that it would be impossible for them to inflict any serious damage upon their new foes. Neither argument, it must be plain, showed the slightest belief in the warlike skill and courage of the American people. Both were grounded upon the frank theory that the only way to make the mob fight was to scare it half to death, and then show it a way to fight without risk, to stab a helpless antagonist in the back. And both were mellowed and reënforced by the hint that such a noble assault, beside being safe, would also be extremely profitable—that it would convert very dubious debts into very good debts, and dispose forever of a diligent and dangerous competitor for trade, especially in Latin America. All the idealist nonsense emitted by Dr. Wilson and company was simply icing on the cake. Most of it was abandoned as soon as the bullets began to fly, and the rest consisted simply of meaningless words—the idiotic babbling of a Presbyterian evangelist turned prophet and seer.

The other thing that needs to be remembered is the permanent effect of so dishonest and cowardly business upon the national character, already far too much inclined toward easy ventures and long odds. Somewhere in his diaries Wilfrid Scawen Blunt speaks of the marked debasement that showed itself in the English spirit after the brutal robbery and assassination of the South African Republics. The heroes that the mob followed after Mafeking Day were far inferior to the heroes that it had followed in the days before the war. The English gentleman began to disappear from public life, and in his place appeared a rabble-rousing bounder obviously almost identical with the American professional politician—the Lloyd-George, Chamberlain, F. E. Smith, Isaacs-Reading, Churchill, Bottomley, Northcliffe type. Worse, old ideals went with old heroes. Personal freedom and strict legality, says Blunt, vanished from the English tables of the law, and there was a shift of the social and political center of gravity to a lower plane. Precisely the same effect is now visible in the United States. The overwhelming majority of conscripts went into the army unwillingly, and once there they were debauched by the twin forces of the official propaganda that I have mentioned and a harsh, unintelligent discipline. The first made them almost incapable of soldierly thought and conduct; the second converted them into cringing goose-steppers. The consequences display themselves in the amazing activities of the American Legion, and in the rise of such correlative organizations as the Ku Klux Klan. It is impossible to fit any reasonable concept of the soldierly into the familiar proceedings of the Legion. Its members conduct themselves like a gang of Methodist vice-crusaders on the loose, or a Southern lynching party. They are forever discovering preposterous burglars under the national bed, and they advance to the attack, not gallantly and at fair odds, but cravenly and in overwhelming force. Some of their enterprises, to be set forth at length in the record I have mentioned, have been of almost unbelievable baseness—the mobbing of harmless Socialists, the prohibition of concerts by musicians of enemy nationality, the mutilation of cows designed for shipment abroad to feed starving children, the roughing of women, service as strike-breakers, the persecution of helpless foreigners, regardless of nationality.

During the last few months of the war, when stories of the tyrannical ill-usage of conscripts began to filter back to the United States, it was predicted that they would demand the punishment of the guilty when they got home, and that if it was not promptly forthcoming they would take it into their own hands. It was predicted, too, that they would array themselves against the excesses of Palmer, Burleson and company, and insist upon a restoration of that democratic freedom for which they had theoretically fought. But they actually did none of these things. So far as I know, not a single martinet of a lieutenant or captain has been manhandled by his late victims; the most they have done has been to appeal to Congress for revenge and damages. Nor have they thrown their influence against the mediæval despotism which grew up at home during the war; on the contrary, they have supported it actively, and if it has lessened since 1919 the change has been wrought without their aid and in spite of their opposition. In sum, they show all the stigmata of inferior men whose natural inferiority has been made worse by oppression. Their chief organization is dominated by shrewd ex-officers who operate it to their own ends—politicians in search of jobs, Chamber of Commerce witch-hunters, and other such vermin. It seems to be wholly devoid of patriotism, courage, or sense. Nothing quite resembling it existed in the country before the war, not even in the South. There is nothing like it anywhere else on earth. It is a typical product of two years of heroic effort to arouse and capitalize the worst instincts of the mob, and it symbolizes very dramatically the ill effects of that effort upon the general American character.

Would men so degraded in gallantry and honor, so completely purged of all the military virtues, so submerged in baseness of spirit—would such pitiful caricatures of soldiers offer the necessary resistance to a public enemy who was equal, or perhaps superior in men and resources, and who came on with confidence, daring and resolution—say England supported by

Germany as *Kriegslieferant* and with her inevitable swarms of Continental allies, or Japan with the Asiatic hordes behind her? Against the best opinion of the chatauquas, of Congress and of the patriotic press I presume to doubt it. It seems to me quite certain, indeed, that an American army fairly representing the American people, if it ever meets another army of anything remotely resembling like strength, will be defeated, and that defeat will be indistinguishable from rout. I believe that, at any odds less than two to one, even the exhausted German army of 1918 would have defeated it, and in this view, I think, I am joined by many men whose military judgment is far better than mine—particularly by many French officers. The changes in the American character since the Civil War, due partly to the wearing out of the old Anglo-Saxon stock, inferior to begin with, and partly to the infusion of the worst elements of other stocks, have surely not made for the fostering of the military virtues. The old cool head is gone, and the old dogged way with difficulties. The typical American of to-day has lost all the love of liberty that his forefathers had, and all their distrust of emotion, and pride in self-reliance. He is led no longer by Davy Crocketts; he is led by cheer leaders, press agents, word-mongers, uplifters. I do not believe that such a faint-hearted and inflammatory fellow, shoved into a war demanding every resource of courage, ingenuity and pertinacity, would give a good account of himself. He is fit for lynching-bees and heretic-hunts, but he is not fit for tight corners and desperate odds.

Nevertheless, his docility and pusillanimity may be overestimated, and sometimes I think that they *are* overestimated by his present masters. They assume that there is absolutely no limit to his capacity for being put on and knocked about—that he will submit to any invasion of his freedom and dignity, however outrageous, so long as it is depicted in melodious terms. He permitted the late war to be "sold" to him by the methods of the grind-shop auctioneer. He submitted to conscription without any of the resistance shown by his brother democrats of Canada and Australia. He got no further than academic protests against the brutal usage he had to face in the army. He came home and found Prohibition foisted on him, and contented himself with a few feeble objurgations. He is a pliant slave of capitalism, and ever ready to help it put down fellow-slaves who venture to revolt. But this very weakness, this very credulity and poverty of spirit, on some easily conceivable to-morrow, may convert him into a rebel of a peculiarly insane kind, and so beset the Republic from within with difficulties quite as formidable as those which threaten to afflict it from without. What Mr. James N. Wood calls the corsair of democracy —that is, the professional mob-master, the merchant of delusions, the pumper-up of popular fears and rages—is still content to work for capitalism, and capitalism knows how to reward him to his taste. He is the eloquent statesman, the patriotic editor, the fount of inspiration, the prancing milch-cow of optimism. He becomes public leader, Governor, Senator, President. He is Billy Sunday, Cyrus K. Curtis, Dr. Frank Crane, Charles E. Hughes, Taft, Wilson, Cal Coolidge, General Wood, Harding. His, perhaps, is the best of trades under democracy—but it has its temptations! Let us try to picture a master corsair, thoroughly adept at pulling the mob nose, who suddenly bethought himself of that Pepin the Short who found himself mayor of the palace and made himself King of the Franks. There were lightnings along that horizon in the days of Roosevelt; there were thunder growls when Bryan emerged from the Nebraska steppes. On some great day of fate, as yet unrevealed by the gods, such a professor of the central democratic science may throw off his employers and set up a business for himself. When that day comes there will be plenty of excuse for black type on the front pages of the newspapers.

I incline to think that military disaster will give him his inspiration and his opportunity—that he will take the form, so dear to democracies, of a man on horseback. The chances are bad to-day simply because the mob is relatively comfortable—because capitalism has been able to give it relative ease and plenty of food in return for its docility. Genuine poverty is very rare in the United States, and actual hardship is almost unknown. There are times when the proletariat is short of phonograph records, silk shirts and movie tickets, but there are very few times when it is short of nourishment. Even during the most severe business depression, with hundreds of thousands out of work, most of these apparent sufferers, if they are willing, are able to get livings outside their trades. The cities may be choked with idle men, but the country is nearly always short of labor. And if all other resources fail, there are always public agencies to feed the hungry: capitalism is careful to keep them from despair. No American knows what it means to live as millions of Europeans lived during the war and have lived, in some places, since: with the loaves of the baker reduced to half size and no meat at all in the meatshop. But the time may come and it may not be far off. A national military disaster would disorganize all industry in the United States, already sufficiently wasteful and chaotic, and introduce the American people, for the first time in their history, to genuine want—and capital would be unable to relieve them. The day of such disaster will bring the savior foreordained. The slaves will follow him, their eyes fixed ecstatically upon the newest New Jerusalem. Men bred to respond automatically to shibboleths will respond to this worst and most insane one. Bolshevism, said General Foch, is a disease of defeated nations.

But do not misunderstand me: I predict no revolution in the grand manner, no melodramatic collapse of capitalism, no repetition of what has gone on in Russia. The American proletarian is not brave and romantic enough for that; to do him simple justice, he is not silly enough. Capitalism, in the long run, will win in the United States, if only for the reason that every American hopes to be a capitalist before he dies. Its roots go down to the deepest, darkest levels of the national soil; in all its characters, and particularly in its antipathy to the dreams of man, it is thoroughly American. To-day it seems to be immovably secure, given continued peace and plenty, and not all the demagogues in the land, consecrating themselves desperately to the one holy purpose, could shake it. Only a cataclysm will ever do that. But is a cataclysm conceivable? Isn't the United States the richest nation ever heard of in history, and isn't it a fact that modern wars are won by money? It is not a fact. Wars are won to-day, as in Napoleon's day, by the largest battalions, and the largest battalions, in the next great struggle, may not be on the side of the Republic. The usurious profits it wrung from the last war are as tempting as negotiable securities hung on the wash-line, as pre-Prohibition Scotch stored in open cellars. Its knavish ways with friends and foes alike have left it only foes. It is plunging ill-equipped into a competition for a living in the world that will be to the death. And the late Disarmament Conference left it almost hamstrung. Before the conference it had the Pacific in its grip, and with the Pacific in its grip it might have parleyed for a fair half of the Atlantic. But when the Japs and the English had finished their operations upon the Feather Duster, Popinjay Lodge, Master-Mind Root, Vacuum Underwood, young Teddy Roosevelt and the rest of their so-willing dupes there was apparent a baleful change. The Republic is extremely insecure to-day on both fronts, and it will be more insecure to-morrow. And it has no friends.

However, as I say, I do not fear for capitalism. It will weather the storm, and no doubt it will be the stronger for it afterward. The inferior man hates it, but there is too much envy mixed with his hatred, in the land of the theoretically free, for him to want to destroy it utterly, or even to wound it incurably. He struggles against it now, but always wistfully, always with a sneaking respect. On the day of Armageddon he may attempt a more violent onslaught. But in the long run he will be beaten. In the long run the corsairs will sell him out, and hand him over to his enemy. Perhaps—who knows?—the combat may raise that enemy to genuine strength and dignity. Out of it may come the superman.

4

All the while I have been forgetting the third of my reasons for remaining so faithful a citizen of the Federation, despite all the lascivious inducements from expatriates to follow them beyond the seas, and all the surly suggestions from patriots that I succumb. It is the reason which grows out of my mediæval but unashamed taste for the bizarre and indelicate, my congenital weakness for comedy of the grosser varieties. The United States, to my eye, is incomparably the greatest show on earth. It is a show which avoids diligently all the kinds of clowning which tire me most quickly—for example, royal ceremonials, the tedious hocus-pocus of *haut politique*, the taking of politics seriously—and lays chief stress upon the kinds which delight me unceasingly—for example, the ribald combats of demagogues, the exquisitely ingenious operations of master rogues, the pursuit of witches and heretics, the desperate struggles of inferior men to claw their way into Heaven. We have clowns in constant practice among us who are as far above the clowns of any other great state as a Jack Dempsey is above a paralytic—and not a few dozen or score of them, but whole droves and herds. Human enterprises which, in all other Christian countries, are resigned despairingly to an incurable dullness—things that seem devoid of exhilarating amusement by their very nature—are here lifted to such vast heights of buffoonery that contemplating them strains the midriff almost to breaking. I cite an example: the worship of God. Everywhere else on earth it is carried on in a solemn and dispiriting manner; in England, of course, the bishops are obscene, but the average man seldom gets a fair chance to laugh at them and enjoy them. Now come home. Here we not only have bishops who are enormously more obscene than even the most gifted of the English bishops; we have also a huge force of lesser specialists in ecclesiastical mountebankery—tin-horn Loyolas, Savonarolas and Xaviers of a hundred fantastic rites, each performing untiringly and each full of a grotesque and illimitable whimsicality. Every American town, however small, has one of its own: a holy clerk with so fine a talent for introducing the arts of jazz into the salvation of the damned that his performance takes on all the gaudiness of a four-ring circus, and the bald announcement that he will raid Hell on such and such a night is enough to empty all the town blind-pigs and bordellos and pack his sanctuary to the doors. And to aid him and inspire him there are traveling experts to whom he stands in the relation of a wart to the Matterhorn—stupendous masters of theological imbecility, contrivers of doctrines utterly preposterous, heirs to the Joseph Smith, Mother Eddy and John Alexander Dowie tradition—Bryan, Sunday, and their like. These are the eminences of the American Sacred College. I delight in them. Their proceedings make me a happier American.

Turn, now, to politics. Consider, for example, a campaign for the Presidency. Would it be possible to imagine anything more uproariously idiotic—a deafening, nerve-wracking battle to the death between Tweedledum and Tweedledee, Harlequin and Sganarelle, Gobbo and Dr. Cook—the unspeakable, with fearful snorts, gradually swallowing the inconceivable? I defy any one to match it elsewhere on this earth. In other lands, at worst, there are at least intelligible issues, coherent ideas, salient personalities. Somebody says something, and somebody replies. But what did Harding say in 1920, and what did Cox reply? Who was Harding, anyhow, and who was Cox? Here, having perfected democracy, we lift the whole combat to symbolism, to transcendentalism, to metaphysics. Here we load a pair of palpably tin cannon with blank cartridges charged with talcum powder, and so let fly. Here one may howl over the show without any uneasy reminder that it is serious, and that some one may be hurt. I hold that this elevation of politics to the plane of undiluted comedy is peculiarly American, that nowhere else on this disreputable ball has the art of the sham-battle been developed to such fineness. Two experiences are in point. During the Harding-Cox combat of bladders an article of mine, dealing with some of its more melodramatic phases, was translated into German and reprinted by a Berlin paper. At the head of it the editor was careful to insert a preface explaining to his readers, but recently delivered to democracy, that such contests were not taken seriously by intelligent Americans, and warning them solemnly against getting into sweats over politics. At about the same time I had dinner with an Englishman. From cocktails to bromo seltzer he bewailed the political lassitude of the English populace—its growing indifference to the whole partisan harlequinade. Here were two typical foreign attitudes: the Germans were in danger of making politics too harsh and implacable, and the English were in danger of forgetting politics altogether. Both attitudes, it must be plain, make for bad shows. Observing a German campaign, one is uncomfortably harassed and stirred up; observing an English campaign (at least in times of peace), one falls asleep. In the United States the thing is done better. Here politics is purged of all menace, all sinister quality, all genuine significance, and stuffed with such gorgeous humors, such inordinate farce that one comes to the end of a campaign with one's ribs loose, and ready for "King Lear," or a hanging, or a course of medical journals.

But feeling better for the laugh. *Ridi si sapis*, said Martial. Mirth is necessary to wisdom, to comfort, above all, to happiness. Well, here is the land of mirth, as Germany is the land of metaphysics and France is the land of fornication. Here the buffoonery never stops. What could be more delightful than the endless struggle of the Puritan to make the joy of the minority unlawful and impossible? The effort is itself a greater joy to one standing on the side-lines than any or all of the carnal joys that it combats. Always, when I contemplate an uplifter at his hopeless business, I recall a scene in an old-time burlesque show, witnessed for hire in my days as a dramatic critic. A chorus girl executed a fall upon the stage, and Rudolph Krausemeyer, the Swiss comedian, rushed to her aid. As he stooped painfully to succor her, Irving Rabinovitz, the Zionist comedian, fetched him a fearful clout across the cofferdam with a slap-stick. So the uplifter, the soul-saver, the Americanizer, striving to make the Republic fit for Y.M.C.A. secretaries. He is the eternal American, ever moved by the best of intentions, ever running *à la* Krausemeyer to the rescue of virtue, and ever getting his pantaloons fanned by the Devil. I am naturally sinful, and such spectacles caress me. If the slap-stick were a sash-weight the show would be cruel, and I'd probably complain to the *Polizei*. As it is, I know that the uplifter is not really hurt, but simply shocked. The blow, in fact, does him good, for it helps to get him into Heaven, as exegetes prove from Matthew v, 11: *Heureux serez-vous, lorsqu'on vous outragera, qu'on vous persécutera*, and so on. As for me, it makes me a more contented man, and hence a better citizen. One man prefers the Republic because it pays better wages than Bulgaria. Another because it has laws to keep him sober and his daughter chaste. Another because the Woolworth Building is higher than the cathedral at Chartres. Another because, living here, he can read the New York *Evening Journal*. Another because there is a warrant out for him somewhere else. Me, I like it because it amuses me to my taste. I never get tired of the show. It is worth every cent it costs.

That cost, it seems to me is very moderate. Taxes in the United States are not actually high. I figure, for example, that my private share of the expense of maintaining the Hon. Mr. Harding in the White House this year will work out to less than 80 cents. Try to think of better sport for the money: in New York it has been estimated that it costs $8 to get comfortably tight, and $17.50, on an average, to pinch a girl's arm.

The United States Senate will cost me perhaps $11 for the year, but against that expense set the subscription price of the *Congressional Record*, about $15, which, as a journalist, I receive for nothing. For $4 less than nothing I am thus entertained as Solomon never was by his hooch dancers. Col. George Brinton McClellan Harvey costs me but 25 cents a year; I get Nicholas Murray Butler free. Finally, there is young Teddy Roosevelt, the naval expert. Teddy costs me, as I work it out, about 11 cents a year, or less than a cent a month. More, he entertains me doubly for the money, first as naval expert, and secondly as a walking *attentat* upon democracy, a devastating proof that there is nothing, after all, in that superstition. We Americans subscribe to the doctrine of human equality—and the Rooseveltii reduce it to an absurdity as brilliantly as the sons of Veit Bach. Where is your equal opportunity now? Here in this Eden of clowns, with the highest rewards of clowning theoretically open to every poor boy—here in the very citadel of democracy we found and cherish a clown *dynasty*!

II.
Huneker: A Memory

THERE was a stimulating aliveness about him always, an air of living eagerly and a bit recklessly, a sort of defiant resiliency. In his very frame and form something provocative showed itself—an insolent singularity, obvious to even the most careless glance. That Caligulan profile of his was more than simply unusual in a free republic, consecrated to good works; to a respectable American, encountering it in the lobby of the Metropolitan or in the smoke-room of a *Doppelschrauben-schnellpostdampfer*, it must have suggested inevitably the dark enterprises and illicit metaphysics of a Heliogabalus. More, there was always something rakish and defiant about his hat—it was too white, or it curled in the wrong way, or a feather peeped from the band—, and a hint of antinomianism in his cravat. Yet more, he ran to exotic tastes in eating and drinking, preferring occult goulashes and risi-bisis to honest American steaks, and great floods of Pilsner to the harsh beverages of God-fearing men. Finally, there was his talk, that cataract of sublime trivialities: gossip lifted to the plane of the gods, the unmentionable bedizened with an astounding importance, and even profundity.

In his early days, when he performed the tonal and carnal prodigies that he liked to talk of afterward, I was at nurse, and too young to have any traffic with him. When I encountered him at last he was in the high flush of the middle years, and had already become a tradition in the little world that critics inhabit. We sat down to luncheon at one o'clock; I think it must have been at Lüchow's, his favorite refuge and rostrum to the end. At six, when I had to go, the waiter was hauling in his tenth (or was it twentieth?) *Seidel* of Pilsner, and he was bringing to a close *prestissimo* the most amazing monologue that these ears (up to that time) had ever funnelled into this consciousness. What a stew, indeed! Berlioz and the question of the clang-tint of the viola, the psychopathological causes of the suicide of Tschaikowsky, why Nietzsche had to leave Sils

Maria between days in 1887, the echoes of Flaubert in Joseph Conrad (then but newly dawned), the precise topography of the warts of Liszt, George Bernard Shaw's heroic but vain struggles to throw off Presbyterianism, how Frau Cosima saved Wagner from the libidinous Swedish baroness, what to drink when playing Chopin, what Cézanne thought of his disciples, the defects in the structure of "Sister Carrie," Anton Seidl and the musical union, the complex love affairs of Gounod, the early days of David Belasco, the varying talents and idiosyncrasies of Lillian Russell's earlier husbands, whether a girl educated at Vassar could ever really learn to love, the exact composition of chicken paprika, the correct tempo of the Vienna waltz, the style of William Dean Howells, what George Moore said about German bathrooms, the true inwardness of the affair between D'Annunzio and Duse, the origin of the theory that all oboe players are crazy, why Löwenbräu survived exportation better than Hofbräu, Ibsen's loathing of Norwegians, the best remedy for Rhine wine *Katzenjammer*, how to play Brahms, the degeneration of the Bal Bullier, the sheer physical impossibility of getting Dvořák drunk, the genuine last words of Walt Whitman. . . .

I left in a sort of fever, and it was a couple of days later before I began to sort out my impressions, and formulate a coherent image. Was the man allusive in his books—so allusive that popular report credited him with the actual manufacture of authorities? Then he was ten times as allusive in his discourse—a veritable geyser of unfamiliar names, shocking epigrams in strange tongues, unearthly philosophies out of the backwaters of Scandinavia, Transylvania, Bulgaria, the Basque country, the Ukraine. And did he, in his criticism, pass facilely from the author to the man, and from the man to his wife, and to the wives of his friends? Then at the *Biertisch* he began long beyond the point where the last honest wife gives up the ghost, and so, full tilt, ran into such complexities of adultery that a plain sinner could scarcely follow him. I try to give you, ineptly and grotesquely, some notion of the talk of the man, but I must fail inevitably. It was, in brief, chaos, and chaos cannot be described. But it was chaos made to gleam and corruscate with every device of the seven arts—chaos drenched in all the colors imaginable, chaos scored for an orchestra which made the great band of Berlioz seem like a fife and drum corps. One night a few months before the war, I sat in the Paris Opera House listening to the first performance of Richard Strauss's "Josef's Legend," with Strauss himself conducting. On the stage there was a riot of hues that swung the eyes 'round and 'round in a crazy mazurka; in the orchestra there were such volleys and explosions of tone that the ears (I fall into a Hunekeran trope) began to go pale and clammy with surgical shock. Suddenly, above all the uproar, a piccolo launched into a new and saucy tune—in an unrelated key! . . . Instantly and quite naturally, I thought of the incomparable James. When he gave a show at Lüchow's he never forgot that anarchistic passage for the piccolo.

I observe a tendency since his death to estimate him in terms of the content of his books. Even Frank Harris, who certainly should know better, goes there for the facts about him. Nothing could do him worse injustice. In those books, of course, there is a great deal of perfectly sound stuff; the wonder is, in truth, that so much of it holds up so well to-day—for example, the essays on Strauss, on Brahms and on Nietzsche, and the whole volume on Chopin. But the real Huneker never got himself formally between covers, if one forgets "Old Fogy" and parts of "Painted Veils." The volumes of his regular canon are made up, in the main, of articles written for the more intellectual magazines and newspapers of their era, and they are full of a conscious striving to qualify for respectable company. Huneker, always curiously modest, never got over the notion that it was a singular honor for a man such as he—a mere diurnal scribbler, innocent of academic robes—to be published by so austere a publisher as Scribner. More than once, anchored at the beer-table, we discussed the matter at length, I always arguing that all the honor was enjoyed by Scribner. But Huneker, I believe in all sincerity, would not have it so, any more than he would have it that he was a better music critic than his two colleagues, the pedantic Krehbiel and the nonsensical Finck. This illogical modesty, of course, had its limits; it made him cautious about expressing himself, but it seldom led him into downright assumptions of false personality. Nowhere in all his books will you find him doing the things that every right-thinking Anglo-Saxon critic is supposed to do—the Middleton Murry, Paul Elmer More, Clutton-Brock sort of puerility—solemn essays on Coleridge and Addison, abysmal discussions of the relative merits of Schumann and Mendelssohn, horrible treatises upon the relations of Goethe to the Romantic Movement, dull scratchings in a hundred such exhausted and sterile fields. Such enterprises were not for Hunker; he kept himself out of that black coat. But I am convinced that he always had his own raiment pressed carefully before he left Lüchow's for the temple of Athene—and maybe changed cravats, and put on a boiled shirt, and took the feather out of his hat. The simon-pure Huneker, the Huneker who was the true essence and prime motor of the more courtly Huneker—remained behind. This real Huneker survives in conversations that still haunt the rafters of the beer-halls of two continents, and in a vast mass of newspaper impromptus, thrown off too hastily to be reduced to complete decorum, and in two books that stand outside the official canon, and yet contain the man himself as not even "Iconoclasts" or the Chopin book contains him, to wit, the "Old Fogy" aforesaid and the "Painted Veils" of his last year. Both were published, so to speak, out of the back door—the former by a music publisher in Philadelphia and the latter in a small and expensive edition for the admittedly damned. There is a chapter in "Painted Veils" that is Huneker to every last hitch of the shoulders and twinkle of the eye—the chapter in which the hero soliloquizes on art, life, immortality, and women—especially women. And there are half a dozen chapters in "Old Fogy"—superficially buffoonery, but how penetrating! how gorgeously flavored! how learned!—that come completely up to the same high specification. If I had to choose one Huneker book and give up all the others, I'd choose "Old Fogy" instantly. In it Huneker is utterly himself. In it the last trace of the pedagogue vanishes. Art is no longer, even by implication, a device for improving the mind. It is wholly a magnificent adventure.

That notion of it is what Huneker brought into American criticism, and it is for that bringing that he will be remembered. No other critic of his generation had a tenth of his influence. Almost single-handed he overthrew the æsthetic theory that had flourished in the United States since the death of Poe, and set up an utterly contrary æsthetic theory in its place. If the younger men of to-day have emancipated themselves from the Puritan æsthetic, if the schoolmaster is now palpably on the defensive, and no longer the unchallenged assassin of the fine arts that he once was, if he has already begun to compromise somewhat absurdly with new and sounder ideas, and even to lift his voice in artificial hosannahs, then Huneker certainly deserves all the credit for the change. What he brought back from Paris was precisely the thing that was most suspected in the America of those days: the capacity for gusto. Huneker had that capacity in a degree unmatched by any other critic. When his soul went adventuring among masterpieces it did not go in Sunday broadcloth; it went with vine leaves in its hair. The rest of the appraisers and criers-up—even Howells, with all his humor—could never quite rid themselves of the professorial manner. When they praised it was always with some hint of ethical, or, at all events, of cultural purpose; when they condemned that purpose was even plainer. The arts, to them, constituted a sort of school for the psyche; their aim was to discipline and mellow the spirit. But to Huneker their one aim was always to make the spirit glad—to set it, in Nietzsche's phrase, to dancing with arms and legs. He had absolutely no feeling for extra-æsthetic valuations. If a work of art that stood before him was honest, if it was original, if it was beautiful and thoroughly alive, then he was for it to his last corpuscle. What if it violated all the accepted canons? Then let the accepted canons go hang! What if it lacked all purpose to improve and lift up? Then so much the better! What if it shocked all right-feeling men, and made them blush and tremble? Then damn all men of right feeling forevermore.

With this ethical atheism, so strange in the United States and so abhorrent to most Americans, there went something that was probably also part of the loot of Paris: an insatiable curiosity about the artist as man. This curiosity was responsible for two of Huneker's salient characters: his habit of mixing even the most serious criticism with cynical and often scandalous gossip, and his pervasive foreignness. I believe that it is almost literally true to say that he could never quite make up his mind about a new symphony until he had seen the composer's mistress, or at all events a good photograph of her. He thought of Wagner, not alone in terms of melody and harmony, but also in terms of the Tribschen idyl and the Bayreuth tragi-comedy. Go through his books and you will see how often he was fascinated by mere eccentricity of personality. I doubt that even Huysmans, had he been a respectable French Huguenot, would have interested him; certainly his enthusiasm for Verlaine, Villiers de l'Isle Adam and other such fantastic fish was centered upon the men quite as much as upon the artists. His foreignness, so often urged against him by defenders of the national tradition, was grounded largely on the fact that such eccentric personalities were rare in the Republic—rare, and well watched by the *Polizei*. When one bobbed up, he was alert at once—even though the newcomer was only a Roosevelt. The rest of the American people he dismissed as a horde of slaves, goose-steppers, cads, Methodists; he could not imagine one of them be coming a first-rate artist, save by a miracle. Even the American executant was under his suspicion, for he knew very well that playing the fiddle was a great deal more than scraping four strings of copper and catgut with a switch from a horse's tail. What he asked himself was how a man could play Bach decently, and then, after playing, go from the hall to a soda-fountain, or a political meeting, or a lecture at the Harvard Club. Overseas there was a better air for artists, and overseas Huneker looked for them.

These fundamental theories of his, of course, had their defects. They were a bit too simple, and often very much too hospitable. Huneker, clinging to them, certainly did his share of whooping for the sort of revolutionist who is here to-day and gone tomorrow; he was fugleman, in his time, for more than one cause that was lost almost as soon as it was stated. More, his prejudices made him somewhat anæsthetic, at times, to the new men who were not brilliant in color but respectably drab, and who tried to do their work within the law. Particularly in his later years, when the old gusto began to die out and all that remained of it was habit, he was apt to go chasing after strange birds and so miss seeing the elephants go by. I could put together a very pretty list of frauds that he praised. I could concoct another list of genuine *arrivés* that he overlooked. But all that is merely saying that there were human limits to him; the professors, on their side, have sinned far worse, and in both directions. Looking back over the whole of his work, one must needs be amazed by the general soundness of his judgments. He discerned, in the main, what was good and he described it in terms that were seldom bettered afterward. His successive heroes, always under fire when he first championed them, almost invariably moved to secure ground and became solid men, challenged by no one save fools—Ibsen, Nietzsche, Brahms, Strauss, Cézanne, Stirner, Synge, the Russian composers, the Russian novelists. He did for this Western world what Georg Brandes was doing for Continental Europe—sorting out the new comers with sharp eyes, and giving mighty lifts to those who deserved it. Brandes did it in terms of the old academic bombast; he was never more the professor than when he was arguing for some hobgoblin of the professors. But Huneker did it with verve and grace; he made it, not schoolmastering, but a glorious deliverance from schoolmastering. As I say, his influence was enormous. The fine arts, at his touch, shed all their Anglo-American lugubriousness, and became provocative and joyous. The spirit of senility got out of them and the spirit of youth got into them. His criticism, for all its French basis, was thoroughly American—vastly more American, in fact, than the New England ponderosity that it displaced. Though he was an Easterner and a cockney of the cockneys, he picked up some of the Western spaciousness that showed itself in Mark Twain. And all the young men followed him.

A good many of them, I daresay, followed him so ardently that they got a good distance ahead of him, and often, perhaps, embarrassed him by taking his name in vain. For all his enterprise and iconoclasm, indeed, there was not much of the Berserker in him, and his floutings of the national æsthetic tradition seldom took the form of forthright challenges. Here the strange modesty that I have mentioned always stayed him as a like weakness stayed Mark Twain. He could never quite rid himself of the feeling that he was no more than an amateur among the gaudy doctors who roared in the reviews, and that it would be unseemly for him to forget their authority. I have a notion that this feeling was born in the days when he stood almost alone, with the whole faculty grouped in a pained circle around him. He was then too miserable a worm to be noticed at all. Later on, gaining importance, he was lectured somewhat severely for his violation of decorum; in England even Max Beerbohm made an idiotic assault upon him. It was the Germans and the French, in fact, who first praised him intelligently —and these friends were too far away to help a timorous man in a row at home. This sensation of isolation and littleness, I suppose, explains his fidelity to the newspapers, and the otherwise inexplicable joy that he always took in his forgotten work for the *Musical Courier*, in his day a very dubious journal. In such waters he felt at ease. There he could disport without thought of the dignity of publishers and the eagle eyes of campus reviewers. Some of the connections that he formed were full of an ironical inappropriateness. His discomforts in his *Puck* days showed themselves in the feebleness of his work; when he served the *Times* he was as well placed as a Cabell at a colored ball. Perhaps the *Sun*, in the years before it was munseyized, offered him the best berth that he ever had, save it were his old one on *Mlle. New York*. But whatever the flag, he served it loyally, and got a lot of fun out of the business. He liked the pressure of newspaper work; he liked the associations that it involved, the gabble in the press-room of the Opera House, the exchanges of news and gossip; above all, he liked the relative ease of the intellectual harness. In a newspaper article he could say whatever happened to pop into his mind, and if it looked thin the next day, then there was, after all, no harm done. But when he sat down to write a book—or rather to compile it, for all of his volumes were reworked magazine (and sometimes newspaper) articles—he became self-conscious, and so knew uneasiness. The tightness of his style, its one salient defect, was probably the result of this weakness. The corrected clippings that constituted most of his manuscripts are so beladen with revisions and rerevisions that they are almost indecipherable.

Thus the growth of Huneker's celebrity in his later years filled him with wonder, and never quite convinced him. He was certainly wholly free from any desire to gather disciples about him and found a school. There was, of course, some pride of authorship in him, and he liked to know that his books were read and admired; in particular, he was pleased by their translation into German and Czech. But it seemed to me that he shrank from the bellicosity that so often got into praise of them—that he disliked being set up as the opponent and superior of the professors whom he always vaguely respected and the rival newspaper critics whose friendship he esteemed far above their professional admiration, or even respect. I could never draw him into a discussion of these rivals, save perhaps a discussion of their historic feats at beer-guzzling. He wrote vastly better than any of them and knew far more about the arts than most of them, and he was undoubtedly aware of it in his heart, but it embarrassed him to hear this superiority put into plain terms. His intense gregariousness probably accounted for part of this reluctance to pit himself against them; he could not imagine a world without a great deal of easy comradeship in it, and much casual slapping of backs. But under it all was the chronic underestimation of himself that I have discussed—his fear that he had spread himself over too many arts, and that his equipment was thus defective in every one of them. "Steeplejack" is full of this apologetic timidity. In its very title, as he explains it, there is a confession of inferiority that is almost maudlin: "Life has been the Barmecide's feast to me," and so on. In the book itself he constantly takes refuge in triviality from the harsh challenges of critical parties, and as constantly avoids facts that would shock the Philistines. One might reasonably assume, reading it from end to end, that his early days in Paris were spent in the fashion of a Y.M.C.A. secretary. A few drinking bouts, of course, and a love affair in the manner of Dubuque, Iowa—but where are the wenches?

More than once, indeed, the book sinks to downright equivocation—for example, in the Roosevelt episodes. Certainly no one who knew Huneker in life will ever argue seriously that he was deceived by the Roosevelt buncombe, or that his view of life was at all comparable to that of the great demagogue. He stood, in fact, at the opposite pole. He saw the world, not as a moral show, but as a sort of glorified Follies. He was absolutely devoid of that obsession with the problem of conduct which was Roosevelt's main virtue in the eyes of a stupid and superstitious people. More, he was wholly against Roosevelt on many concrete issues—the race suicide banality, the Panama swindle, the war. He was far too much the realist to believe in the American case, either before or after 1917, and the manner in which it was urged, by Roosevelt and others, violated his notions of truth, honor and decency. I assume nothing here; I simply record what he told me himself. Nevertheless, the sheer notoriety of the Rough Rider—his picturesque personality and talent as a mountebank—had its effect on Huneker, and so he was a bit flattered when he was summoned to Oyster Bay, and there accepted gravely the nonsense that was poured into his ear, and even repeated some of it without a cackle in his book. To say that he actually believed in it would be to libel him. It was precisely such hollow tosh that he stood against in his rôle of critic of art and life; it was by exposing its hollowness that he lifted himself above the general. The same weakness induced him to accept membership in the National Institute of Arts and Letters. The offer of it to a man of his age and attainments, after he had been passed over year after year in favor of all sorts of cheapjack novelists and tenth-rate compilers of college textbooks, was intrinsically insulting; it was almost as if the Musical Union had offered to admit a Brahms. But with the insult went a certain gage of respectability, a certain formal forgiveness for old frivolities, a certain abatement of old doubts and self-questionings and so Huneker accepted. Later on, reviewing the episode in his own mind, he found it the spring of doubts that were even more uncomfortable. His last letter to me was devoted to the matter. He was by then eager to maintain that he had got in by a process only partly under his control, and that, being in, he could discover no decorous way of getting out.

But perhaps I devote too much space to the elements in the man that worked against his own free development. They were, after all, grounded upon qualities that are certainly not to be deprecated—modesty, good-will to his fellow-men, a fine sense of team-work, a distaste for acrimonious and useless strife. These qualities gave him great charm. He was not only humorous; he was also good-humored; even when the crushing discomforts of his last illness were upon him his amiability never faltered. And in addition to humor there was wit, a far rarer thing. His most casual talk was full of this wit, and it bathed everything that he discussed in a new and brilliant light. I have never encountered a man who was further removed from dullness; it seemed a literal impossibility for him to open his mouth without discharging some word or phrase that arrested the attention and stuck in the memory. And under it all, giving an extraordinary quality to the verbal fire-works, there was a solid and apparently illimitable learning. The man knew as much as forty average men, and his knowledge was well-ordered and instantly available. He had read everything and had seen everything and heard everything, and nothing that he had ever read or seen or heard quite passed out of his mind.

Here, in three words, was the main virtue of his criticism—its gigantic richness. It had the dazzling charm of an ornate and intricate design, a blazing fabric of fine silks. It was no mere pontifical statement of one man's reactions to a set of ideas; it was a sort of essence of the reactions of many men—of all the men, in fact, worth hearing. Huneker discarded their scaffolding, their ifs and whereases, and presented only what was important and arresting in their conclusions. It was never a mere *pastiche*; the selection was made delicately, discreetly, with almost unerring taste and judgment. And in the summing up there was always the clearest possible statement of the whole matter. What finally emerged was a body of doctrine that came, I believe, very close to the truth. Into an assembly of national critics who had long wallowed in dogmatic puerilities, Huneker entered with a taste infinitely surer and more civilized, a learning infinitely greater, and an address infinitely more engaging. No man was less the reformer by inclination, and yet he became a reformer beyond compare. He emancipated criticism in America from its old slavery to stupidity, and with it he emancipated all the arts themselves.

III.

Footnote on Criticism

NEARLY all the discussions of criticism that I am acquainted with start off with a false assumption, to wit, that the primary motive of the critic, the impulse which makes a critic of him instead of, say, a politician, or a stockbroker, is pedagogical—that he writes because he is possessed by a passion to advance the enlightenment, to put down error and wrong, to disseminate some specific doctrine: psychological, epistemological, historical, or æsthetic. This is true, it seems to me, only of bad critics, and its degree of truth increases in direct ratio to their badness. The motive of the critic who is really worth reading—the only critic of whom, indeed, it may be said truthfully that it is at all possible to read him, save as an act of mental discipline—is something quite different. That motive is not the motive of the pedagogue, but the motive of the artist. It is no more and no less than the simple desire to function freely and beautifully, to give outward and objective form to ideas that bubble inwardly and have a fascinating lure in them, to get rid of them dramatically and make an articulate noise in the world. It was for this reason that Plato wrote the "Republic," and for this reason that Beethoven wrote the Ninth Symphony, and it is for this reason, to drop a million miles, that I am writing the present essay. Everything else is afterthought, mock-modesty, messianic delusion—in brief, affectation and folly. Is the contrary conception of criticism widely cherished? Is it almost universally held that the thing is a brother to jurisprudence, advertising, laparotomy, chautauqua lecturing and the art of the schoolmarm? Then certainly the fact that it is so held should be sufficient to set up an overwhelming probability of its lack of truth and sense. If I speak with some heat, it is as one who has suffered. When, years ago, I devoted myself diligently to critical pieces upon the writings of Theodore Dreiser, I found that practically every one who took any notice of my proceedings at all fell into either one of two assumptions about my underlying purpose: (*a*) that I had a fanatical devotion for Mr. Dreiser's ideas and desired to propagate them, or (*b*) that I was an ardent patriot, and yearned to lift up American literature. Both assumptions were false. I had then, and I have now, very little interest in many of Mr. Dreiser's main ideas; when we meet, in fact, we usually quarrel about them. And I am wholly devoid of public spirit, and haven't the least lust to improve American literature; if it ever came to what I regard as perfection my job would be gone. What, then, was my motive in writing about Mr. Dreiser so copiously? My motive, well known to Mr. Dreiser himself and to every one else who knew me as intimately as he did, was simply and solely to sort out and give coherence to the ideas of Mr. Mencken, and to put them into suave and ingratiating terms, and to discharge them with a flourish, and maybe with a phrase of pretty song, into the dense fog that blanketed the Republic.

The critic's choice of criticism rather than of what is called creative writing is chiefly a matter of temperament—perhaps, more accurately of hormones—with accidents of education and environment to help. The feelings that happen to be dominant in him at the moment the scribbling frenzy seizes him are feelings inspired, not directly by life itself, but by books, pictures, music, sculpture, architecture, religion, philosophy—in brief, by some other man's feelings about life. They are thus, in a sense, secondhand, and it is no wonder that creative artists so easily fall into the theory that they are also second-rate. Perhaps they usually are. If, indeed, the critic continues on this plane—if he lacks the intellectual agility and enterprise needed to make the leap from the work of art to the vast and mysterious complex of phenomena behind it—then they *always* are, and he remains no more than a fugleman or policeman to his betters. But if a genuine artist is concealed within him—if his feelings are in any sense profound and original, and his capacity for self-expression is above the average of educated men—then he moves inevitably from the work of art to life itself, and begins to take on a dignity that he formerly lacked. It is impossible to think of a man of any actual force and originality, universally recognized as having those qualities, who spent his whole life appraising and describing the work of other men. Did Goethe, or Carlyle, or Matthew Arnold, or Sainte-Beuve, or Macaulay, or even, to come down a few pegs, Lewes, or

Lowell, or Hazlitt? Certainly not. The thing that becomes most obvious about the writings of all such men, once they are examined carefully, is that the critic is always being swallowed up by the creative artist—that what starts out as the review of a book, or a play, or other work of art, usually develops very quickly into an independent essay upon the theme of that work of art, or upon some theme that it suggests—in a word, that it becomes a fresh work of art, and only indirectly related to the one that suggested it. This fact, indeed, is so plain that it scarcely needs statement. What the pedagogues always object to in, for example, the *Quarterly* reviewers is that they forgot the books they were supposed to review, and wrote long papers —often, in fact, small books—expounding ideas suggested (or not suggested) by the books under review. Every critic who is worth reading falls inevitably into the same habit. He cannot stick to his task: what is before him is always infinitely less interesting to him than what is within him. If he is genuinely first-rate—if what is within him stands the test of type, and wins an audience, and produces the reactions that every artist craves—then he usually ends by abandoning the criticism of specific works of art altogether, and setting up shop as a general merchant in general ideas, *i.e.*, as an artist working in the materials of life itself.

Mere reviewing, however conscientiously and competently it is done, is plainly a much inferior business. Like writing poetry, it is chiefly a function of intellectual immaturity. The young literatus just out of the university, having as yet no capacity for grappling with the fundamental mysteries of existence, is put to writing reviews of books, or plays, or music, or painting. Very often he does it extremely well; it is, in fact, not hard to do well, for even decayed pedagogues often do it, as such graves of the intellect as the New York *Times* bear witness. But if he continues to do it, whether well or ill, it is a sign to all the world that his growth ceased when they made him *Artium Baccalaureus.* Gradually he becomes, whether in or out of the academic grove, a professor, which is to say, a man devoted to diluting and retailing the ideas of his superiors—not an artist, not even a bad artist, but almost the antithesis of an artist. He is learned, he is sober, he is painstaking and accurate—but he is as hollow as a jug. Nothing is in him save the ghostly echoes of other men's thoughts and feelings. If he were a genuine artist he would have thoughts and feelings of his own, and the impulse to give them objective form would be irresistible. An artist can no more withstand that impulse than a politician can withstand the temptations of a job. There are no mute, inglorious Miltons, save in the hallucinations of poets. The one sound test of a Milton is that he functions as a Milton. His difference from other men lies precisely in the superior vigor of his impulse to self-expression, not in the superior beauty and loftiness of his ideas. Other men, in point of fact, often have the same ideas, or perhaps even loftier ones, but they are able to suppress them, usually on grounds of decorum, and so they escape being artists, and are respected by right-thinking persons, and die with money in the bank, and are forgotten in two weeks.

Obviously, the critic whose performance we are commonly called upon to investigate is a man standing somewhere along the path leading from the beginning that I have described to the goal. He has got beyond being a mere cataloguer and valuer of other men's ideas, but he has not yet become an autonomous artist—he is not yet ready to challenge attention with his own ideas alone. But it is plain that his motion, in so far as he is moving at all, must be in the direction of that autonomy—that is, unless one imagines him sliding backward into senile infantilism: a spectacle not unknown to literary pathology, but too pathetic to be discussed here. Bear this motion in mind, and the true nature of his aims and purposes becomes clear; more, the incurable falsity of the aims and purposes usually credited to him becomes equally clear. He is not actually trying to perform an impossible act of arctic justice upon the artist whose work gives him a text. He is not trying with mathematical passion to find out exactly what was in that artist's mind at the moment of creation, and to display it precisely and in an ecstasy of appreciation. He is not trying to bring the work discussed into accord with some transient theory of æsthetics, or ethics, or truth, or to determine its degree of departure from that theory. He is not trying to lift up the fine arts, or to defend democracy against sense, or to promote happiness at the domestic hearth, or to convert sophomores into right-thinkers, or to serve God. He is not trying to fit a group of novel phenomena into the orderly process of history. He is not even trying to discharge the catalytic office that I myself, in a romantic moment, once sought to force upon him. He is, first and last, simply trying to express himself. He is trying to arrest and challenge a sufficient body of readers, to make them pay attention to him, to impress them with the charm and novelty of his ideas, to provoke them into an agreeable (or shocked) awareness of him, and he is trying to achieve thereby for his own inner ego the grateful feeling of a function performed, a tension relieved, a *katharsis* attained which Wagner achieved when he wrote "Die Walküre," and a hen achieves every time she lays an egg.

Joseph Conrad is moved by that necessity to write romances; Bach was moved to write music; poets are moved to write poetry; critics are moved to write criticism. The form is nothing; the only important thing is the motive power, and it is the same in all cases. It is the pressing yearning of every man who has ideas in him to empty them upon the world, to hammer them into plausible and ingratiating shapes, to compel the attention and respect of his equals, to lord it over his inferiors. So seen, the critic becomes a far more transparent and agreeable fellow than ever he was in the discourses of the psychologists who sought to make him a mere appraiser in an intellectual customs house, a gauger in a distillery of the spirit, a just and infallible judge upon the cosmic bench. Such offices, in point of fact, never fit him. He always bulges over their confines. So labelled and estimated, it inevitably turns out that the specific critic under examination is a very bad one, or no critic at all. But when he is thought of, not as pedagogue, but as artist, then he begins to take on reality, and, what is more, dignity. Carlyle was surely no just and infallible judge; on the contrary, he was full of prejudices, biles, naïvetés, humors. Yet he is read, consulted, attended to. Macaulay was unfair, inaccurate, fanciful, lyrical—yet his essays live. Arnold had his faults too, and so did Sainte-Beauve, and so did Goethe, and so did many another of that line—and yet they are remembered to-day, and all the learned and conscientious critics of their time, laboriously concerned with the precise intent of the artists under review, and passionately determined to set it forth with god-like care and to relate it exactly to this or that great stream of ideas—all these pedants are forgotten. What saved Carlyle, Macaulay and company is as plain as day. They were first-rate artists. They could make the thing charming, and that is always a million times more important than making it true.

Truth, indeed, is something that is believed in completely only by persons who have never tried personally to pursue it to its fastnesses and grab it by the tail. It is the adoration of second-rate men—men who always receive it at second-hand. Pedagogues believe in immutable truths and spend their lives trying to determine them and propagate them; the intellectual progress of man consists largely of a concerted effort to block and destroy their enterprise. Nine times out of ten, in the arts as in life, there is actually no truth to be discovered; there is only error to be exposed. In whole departments of human inquiry it seems to me quite unlikely that the truth ever *will* be discovered. Nevertheless, the rubber-stamp thinking of the world always makes the assumption that the exposure of an error is identical with the discovery of the truth—that error and truth are simple opposites. They are nothing of the sort. What the world turns to, when it has been cured of one error, is usually simply another error, and maybe one worse than the first one. This is the whole history of the intellect in brief. The average man of to-day does not believe in precisely the same imbecilities that the Greek of the fourth century before Christ believed in, but the things that he *does* believe in are often quite as idiotic. Perhaps this statement is a bit too sweeping. There is, year by year, a gradual accumulation of what may be called, provisionally, truths—there is a slow accretion of ideas that somehow manage to meet all practicable human tests, and so survive. But even so, it is risky to call them absolute truths. All that one may safely say of them is that no one, as yet, has demonstrated that they are errors. Soon or late, if experience teaches us anything, they are likely to succumb too. The profoundest truths of the Middle Ages are now laughed at by schoolboys. The profoundest truths of democracy will be laughed at, a few centuries hence, even by school-teachers.

In the department of æsthetics, wherein critics mainly disport themselves, it is almost impossible to think of a so-called truth that shows any sign of being permanently true. The most profound of principles begins to fade and quiver almost as soon as it is stated. But the work of art, as opposed to the theory behind it, has a longer life, particularly if that theory be obscure and questionable, and so cannot be determined accurately. "Hamlet," the Mona Lisa, "Faust," "Dixie," "Parsifal," "Mother Goose," "Annabel Lee," "Huckleberry Finn"—these things, so baffling to pedagogy, so contumacious to the categories, so mysterious in purpose and utility—these things live. And why? Because there is in them the flavor of salient, novel and attractive personality, because the quality that shines from them is not that of correct demeanor but that of creative passion, because they pulse and breathe and speak, because they are genuine works of art. So with criticism. Let us forget all the heavy effort to make a science of it; it is a fine art, or nothing. If the critic, retiring to his cell to concoct his treatise upon a book or play or what-not, produces a piece of writing that shows sound structure, and brilliant color, and the flash of new and persuasive ideas, and civilized manners, and the charm of an uncommon personality in free function, then he has given something to the world that is worth having, and sufficiently justified his existence. Is Carlyle's "Frederick" true? Who cares? As well ask if the Parthenon is true, or the C Minor Symphony, or "Wiener Blut." Let the critic who is an artist leave such necropsies to professors of æsthetics, who can no more determine the truth than he can, and will infallibly make it unpleasant and a bore.

It is, of course, not easy to practice this abstention. Two forces, one within and one without, tend to bring even a Hazlitt or a Huneker under the campus pump. One is the almost universal human susceptibility to messianic delusions—the irresistible tendency of practically every man, once he finds a crowd in front of him, to strut and roll his eyes. The other is the public demand, born of such long familiarity with pedagogical criticism that no other kind is readily conceivable, that the critic teach something as well as say something—in the popular phrase, that he be constructive. Both operate powerfully against his free functioning, and especially the former. He finds it hard to resist the flattery of his customers, however little he may actually esteem it. If he knows anything at all, he knows that his following, like that of every other artist in ideas, is chiefly made up of the congenitally subaltern type of man and woman—natural converts, lodge joiners, me-toos, stragglers after circus parades. It is precious seldom that he ever gets a positive idea out of them; what he usually gets is mere unintelligent ratification. But this troop, despite its obvious failings, corrupts him in various ways. For one thing, it enormously reënforces his belief in his own ideas, and so tends to make him stiff and dogmatic—in brief, precisely everything that he ought not to be. And for another thing, it tends to make him (by a curious contradiction) a bit pliant and politic: he begins to estimate new ideas, not in proportion as they are amusing or beautiful, but in proportion as they are likely to please. So beset, front and rear, he sometimes sinks supinely to the level of a professor, and his subsequent proceedings are interesting no more. The true aim of a critic is certainly not to make converts. He must know that very few of the persons who are susceptible to conversion are worth converting. Their minds are intrinsically flabby and parasitical, and it is certainly not sound sport to agitate minds of that sort. Moreover, the critic must always harbor a grave doubt about most of the ideas that they lap up so greedily—it must occur to him not infrequently, in the silent watches of the night, that much that he writes is sheer buncombe. As I have said, I can't imagine any idea—that is, in the domain of æsthetics—that is palpably and incontrovertibly sound. All that I am familiar with, and in particular all that I announce most vociferously, seem to me to contain a core of quite obvious nonsense. I thus try to avoid cherishing them too lovingly, and it always gives me a shiver to see any one else gobble them at one gulp. Criticism, at bottom, is indistinguishable from skepticism. Both launch themselves, the one by æsthetic presentations and the other by logical presentations, at the common human tendency to accept whatever is approved, to take in ideas ready-made, to be responsive to mere rhetoric and gesticulation. A critic who believes in anything absolutely is bound to that something quite as helplessly as a Christian is bound to the Freudian garbage in the Book of Revelation. To that extent, at all events, he is unfree and unintelligent, and hence a bad critic.

The demand for "constructive" criticism is based upon the same false assumption that immutable truths exist in the arts, and that the artist will be improved by being made aware of them. This notion, whatever the form it takes, is always absurd—as much so, indeed, as its brother delusion that the critic, to be competent, must be a practitioner of the specific art he ventures to deal with, *i.e.*, that a doctor, to cure a belly-ache, must have a belly-ache. As practically encountered, it is disingenuous as well as absurd, for it comes chiefly from bad artists who tire of serving as performing monkeys, and crave the greater ease and safety of sophomores in class. They demand to be taught in order to avoid being knocked about. In their demand is the theory that instruction, if they could get it, would profit them—that they are capable of doing better work than they do. As a practical matter, I doubt that this is ever true. Bad poets never actually grow any better; they invariably grow worse and worse. In all history there has never been, to my knowledge, a single practitioner of any art who, as a result of "constructive" criticism, improved his work. The curse of all the arts, indeed, is the fact that they are constantly invaded by persons who are not artists at all—persons whose yearning to express their ideas and feelings is unaccompanied by the slightest capacity for charming expression—in brief, persons with absolutely nothing to say. This is particularly true of the art of letters, which interposes very few technical obstacles to the vanity and garrulity of such invaders. Any effort to teach them to write better is an effort wasted, as every editor discovers for himself; they are as incapable of it as they are of jumping over the moon. The only sort of criticism that can deal with them to any profit is the sort that employs them frankly as laboratory animals. It cannot cure them, but it can at least make an amusing and perhaps edifying show of them. It is idle to argue that the good in them is thus destroyed with the bad. The simple answer is that there *is* no good in them. Suppose Poe had wasted his time trying to dredge good work out of Rufus Dawes, author of "Geraldine." He would have failed miserably—and spoiled a capital essay, still diverting after three-quarters of a century. Suppose Beethoven, dealing with Gottfried Weber, had tried laboriously to make an intelligent music critic of him. How much more apt, useful and durable the simple note: "Arch-ass! Double-barrelled ass!" Here was absolutely sound criticism. Here was a judgment wholly beyond challenge. Moreover, here was a small but perfect work of art.

Upon the low practical value of so-called constructive criticism I can offer testimony out of my own experience. My books are commonly reviewed at great length, and many critics devote themselves to pointing out what they conceive to be my errors, both of fact and of taste. Well, I cannot recall a case in which any suggestion offered by a constructive critic has helped me in the slightest, or even actively interested me. Every such wet-nurse of letters has sought fatuously to make me write in a way differing from that in which the Lord God Almighty, in His infinite wisdom, impels me to write—that is, to make me write stuff which, coming from me, would be as false as an appearance of decency in a Congressman. All the benefits I have ever got from the critics of my work have come from the destructive variety. A hearty slating always does me good, particularly if it be well written. It begins by enlisting my professional respect; it ends by making me examine my ideas coldly in the privacy of my chamber. Not, of course, that I usually revise them, but I at least examine them. If I decide to hold fast to them, they are all the dearer to me thereafter, and I expound them with a new passion and plausibility. If, on the contrary, I discern holes in them, I shelve them in a *pianissimo* manner, and set about hatching new ones to take their place. But constructive criticism irritates me. I do not object to being denounced, but I can't abide being school-mastered, especially by men I regard as imbeciles.

I find, as a practicing critic, that very few men who write books are even as tolerant as I am—that most of them, soon or late, show signs of extreme discomfort under criticism, however polite its terms. Perhaps this is why enduring friendships between authors and critics are so rare. All artists, of course, dislike one another more or less, but that dislike seldom rises to implacable enmity, save between opera singer and opera singer, and creative author and critic. Even when the latter two keep up an outward show of good-will, there is always bitter antagonism under the surface. Part of it, I daresay, arises out of the impossible demands of the critic, particularly if he be tinged with the constructive madness. Having favored an author with his good opinion, he expects the poor fellow to live up to that good opinion without the slightest compromise or faltering, and this is commonly beyond human power. He feels that any let-down compromises *him*—that his hero is stabbing him in the back, and making him ridiculous—and this feeling rasps his vanity. The most bitter of all literary quarrels are those between critics and creative artists, and most of them arise in just this way. As for the creative artist, he on his part naturally resents the critic's air of pedagogical superiority and he resents it especially when he has an uneasy feeling that he has fallen short of his best work, and that the discontent of the critic is thus justified. Injustice is relatively easy to bear; what stings is justice. Under it all, of course, lurks the fact that I began with: the fact that the critic is himself an artist, and that his creative impulse, soon or late, is bound to make him neglect the punctilio. When he sits down to compose his criticism, his artist ceases to be a friend, and becomes mere raw material for his work of art. It is my experience that artists invariably resent this cavalier use of them. They are pleased so long as the critic confines himself to the modest business of interpreting them—preferably in terms of their own estimate of themselves—but the moment he proceeds to adorn their theme with variations of his own, the moment he brings new ideas to the enterprise and begins contrasting them with their ideas, that moment they grow restive. It is precisely at this point, of course, that criticism becomes genuine criticism; before that it was mere reviewing. When a critic passes it he loses his friends. By becoming an artist, he becomes the foe of all other artists.

But the transformation, I believe, has good effects upon him: it makes him a better critic. Too much *Gemütlichkeit* is as fatal to criticism as it would be to surgery or politics. When it rages unimpeded it leads inevitably either to a dull professorial sticking on of meaningless labels or to log-rolling, and often it leads to both. One of the most hopeful symptoms of the new *Aufklärung* in the Republic is the revival of acrimony in criticism—the renaissance of the doctrine that æsthetic matters are important, and that it is worth the while of a healthy male to take them seriously, as he takes business, sport and amour. In the days when American literature was showing its first vigorous growth, the native criticism was extraordinarily violent and even vicious; in the days when American literature swooned upon the tomb of the Puritan *Kultur* it became flaccid and childish. The typical critic of the first era was Poe, as the typical critic of the second was Howells. Poe carried on his critical jehads with such ferocity that he often got into law-suits, and sometimes ran no little risk of having his head cracked. He regarded literary questions as exigent and momentous. The lofty aloofness of the don was simply not in him. When he encountered a book that seemed to him to be bad, he attacked it almost as sharply as a Chamber of Commerce would attack a fanatic preaching free speech, or the corporation of Trinity Church would attack Christ. His opponents replied in the same Berserker manner. Much of Poe's surviving ill-fame, as a drunkard and dead-beat, is due to their inordinate denunciations of him. They were not content to refute him; they constantly tried to dispose of him altogether. The very ferocity of that ancient row shows that the native literature, in those days, was in a healthy state. Books of genuine value were produced. Literature always thrives best, in fact, in an atmosphere of hearty strife. Poe, surrounded by admiring professors, never challenged, never aroused to the emotions of revolt, would probably have written poetry indistinguishable from the hollow stuff of, say, Prof. Dr. George E. Woodberry. It took the persistent (and often grossly unfair and dishonorable) opposition of Griswold *et al* to stimulate him to his highest endeavors. He needed friends, true enough, but he also needed enemies.

To-day, for the first time in years, there is strife in American criticism, and the Paul Elmer Mores and Hamilton Wright Mabies are no longer able to purr in peace. The instant they fall into stiff professorial attitudes they are challenged, and often with anything but urbanity. The *ex cathedra* manner thus passes out, and free discussion comes in. Heretics lay on boldly, and the professors are forced to make some defense. Often, going further, they attempt counterattacks. Ears are bitten off. Noses are bloodied. There are wallops both above and below the belt. I am, I need not say, no believer in any magical merit in debate, no matter how free it may be. It certainly does not necessarily establish the truth; both sides, in fact, may be wrong, and they often are. But it at least accomplishes two important effects. On the one hand, it exposes all the cruder fallacies to hostile examination, and so disposes of many of them. And on the other hand, it melodramatizes the business of the critic, and so convinces thousands of bystanders, otherwise quite inert, that criticism is an amusing and instructive art, and that the problems it deals with are important. What men will fight for seems to be worth looking into.

IV.
Das Kapital

AFTER a hearty dinner of *potage créole*, planked Chesapeake shad, Guinea hen *en casserole* and some respectable salad, with two or three cocktails made of two-thirds gin, one-third Martini-Rossi vermouth and a dash of absinthe as *Vorspiel* and a bottle of Ruhländer 1903 to wash it down, the following thought often bubbles up from my subconscious: that many of the acknowledged evils of capitalism, now so horribly visible in the world, are not due primarily to capitalism itself but rather to democracy, that universal murrain of Christendom.

What I mean, in brief, is that capitalism, under democracy, is constantly under hostile pressure and often has its back to the wall, and that its barbaric manners and morals, at least in large part, are due to that fact—that they are, in essence, precisely the same manners and morals that are displayed by any other creature or institution so beset. Necessity is not only the mother of invention; it is also the mother of every imaginable excess and infamy. A woman defending her child is notoriously willing to go to lengths that even a Turk or an agent of the Department of Justice would regard as inordinate, and so is a Presbyterian defending his hell, or a soldier defending his fatherland, or a banker defending his gold. It is only when there is no danger that the average human being is honorable, just as it is only when there *is* danger that he is virtuous. He would commit adultery every day if it were safe, and he would commit murder every day if it were necessary.

The essential thing about democracy, as every one must know, is that it is a device for strengthening and heartening the have-nots in their eternal war upon the haves. That war, as every one knows again, has its psychological springs in envy pure and simple—envy of the more fortunate man's greater wealth, the superior pulchritude of his wife or wives, his larger mobility and freedom, his more protean capacity for and command of happiness—in brief, his better chance to lead a bearable life in this worst of possible worlds. It follows that under democracy, which gives a false power and importance to the have-nots by counting every one of them as the legal equal of George Washington or Beethoven, the process of government consists largely, and sometimes almost exclusively, of efforts to spoil that advantage artificially. Trust-busting, free silver, direct elections, Prohibition, government ownership and all the other varieties of American political quackery are but symptoms of the same general rage. It is the rage of the have-not against the have, of the farmer who must drink hard cider and forty-rod against the city man who may drink Burgundy and Scotch, of the poor fellow who must stay at home looking at a wife who regards the lip-stick as lewd and lascivious against the lucky fellow who may go to Atlantic City or Palm Beach and ride up and down in a wheelchair with a girl who knows how to make up and has put away the fear of God.

The ignobler sort of men, of course, are too stupid to understand various rare and exhilarating sorts of superiority, and so they do not envy the happiness that goes with them. If they could enter into the mind of a Wagner or a Brahms and begin to comprehend the stupendous joy that such a man gets out of the practice of his art, they would pass laws against it and make a criminal of him, as they have already made criminals, in the United States, of the man with a civilized taste for wines, the man so attractive to women that he can get all the wives he wants without having to marry them, and the man who can make pictures like Félicien Rops, or books like Flaubert, Zola, Dreiser, Cabell or Rabelais. Wagner and Brahms escape, and their arts with them, because the great masses of men cannot understand the sort of thing they try to do, and hence do not envy the man who does it well, and gets joy out of it. It is much different with, say, Rops. Every American Congressman, as a small boy, covered the fence of the Sunday-School yard with pictures in the manner of Rops. What he now remembers of the business is that the pictures were denounced by the superintendent, and that he was cowhided for making them; what he hears about Rops, when he hears at all, is that the fellow is vastly esteemed, and hence probably full of a smug æsthetic satisfaction. In consequence, it is unlawful in the United States to transmit the principal pictures of Rops by mail, or, indeed, "to have and possess" them. The man who owns them must conceal them from the *okhrána* of the Department of Justice just as carefully as he conceals the wines and whiskeys in his cellar, or the poor working girl he transports from the heat and noise of New York to the salubrious calm of the Jersey coast, or his hand-tooled library set of the "Contes Drôlatiques," or his precious first edition of "Jurgen."

But, as I say, the democratic pressure in such directions is relatively feeble, for there are whole categories of more or less æsthetic superiority and happiness that the democrat cannot understand at all, and is in consequence virtually unaware of. It is far different with the varieties of superiority and happiness that are the functions of mere money. Here the democrat is extraordinarily alert and appreciative. He can not only imagine hundreds of ways of getting happiness out of money; he devotes almost the whole of his intellectual activity, such as it is, to imagining them, and he seldom if ever imagines anything else. Even his sexual fancies translate themselves instantly into concepts of dollars and cents; the thing that confines him so miserably to one wife, and to one, alas, so unappetizing and depressing, is simply his lack of money; if he only had the wealth of Diamond Jim Brady he too would be the glittering Don Giovanni that Jim was. All the known species of democratic political theory are grounded firmly upon this doctrine that money, and money only, makes the mare go—that all the conceivable varieties of happiness are possible to the man who has it. Even the Socialists, who profess to scorn money, really worship it. Socialism, indeed, is simply the degenerate capitalism of bankrupt capitalists. Its one genuine object is to get more money for its professors; all its other grandiloquent objects are afterthoughts, and most of them are bogus. The democrats of other schools pursue the same single aim—and adorn it with false pretenses even more transparent. In the United States the average democrat, I suppose, would say that the establishment and safeguarding of liberty was the chief purpose of democracy. The theory is mere wind. The average American democrat really cares nothing whatever for liberty, and is always willing to sell it for money. What he actually wants, and strives to get by his politics, is more money. His fundamental political ideas nearly all contemplate restraints and raids upon capital, even when they appear superficially to be quite free from economic flavor, and most of the political banshees and bugaboos that alternately freeze and boil his blood have dollar marks written all over them. There is no need to marshal a long catalogue of examples from English and American political history: I simply defy any critic of my doctrine to find a single issue of genuine appeal to the populace, at any time during the past century, that did not involve a more or less obvious scheme for looting a minority—the slave-owners, Wall Street, the railroads, the dukes, or some other group representing capital. Even the most affecting idealism of the plain people has a thrifty basis. In the United States, during the early part of the late war, they were very cynical about the Allied cause; it was not until the war orders of the Allies raised their wages that they began to believe in the noble righteousness of Lloyd-George and company. And after Dr. Wilson had jockeyed the United States itself into the war, and the cost of living began to increase faster than wages, he faced a hostile country until he restored altruism by his wholesale bribery of labor.

It is my contention that the constant exposure of capitalism to such primitive lusts and forays is what makes it so lamentably extortionate and unconscionable in democratic countries, and particularly in the United States. The capitalist, warned by experience, collars all he can while the getting is good, regardless of the commonest honesty and decorum, because he is haunted by an uneasy feeling that his season will not be long. His dominating passion is to pile up the largest amount of capital possible, by fair means or foul, so that he will have ample reserves when the next raid comes, and he has to use part of it to bribe one part of the proletariat against the other. In the long run, of course, he always wins, for this bribery is invariably feasible; in the United States, indeed, every fresh struggle leaves capital more secure than it was before. But though the capitalist thus has no reason to fear actual defeat and disaster, he is well aware that victory is always expensive, and his natural prudence causes him to discount the cost in advance, even when he has planned to shift it to other shoulders. I point, in example, to the manner in which capital dealt with the discharged American soldiers after the war. Its first effort was to cajole them into its service, as they had been cajoled by the politicians after the Civil War. To this end, it borrowed the machine erected by Dr. Wilson and his agents for debauching the booboisie during the actual war, and by the skillful use of that machine it quickly organized the late conscripts into the American Legion, alarmed them with lies about a Bolshevist scheme to make slaves of them (*i.e.*, to cut off forever their hope of getting money), and put them to clubbing and butchering their fellow proletarians. The business done, the conscripts found themselves out of jobs: their gallant war upon Bolshevism had brought down wages, and paralysed organized labor. They now demanded pay for their work, and capital had to meet the demand. It did so by promising them a bonus—*i.e.*, loot—out of the public treasury, and by straightway inventing a scheme whereby the ultimate cost would fall chiefly upon poor folk.

Throughout the war, indeed, capital exhibited an inordinately extortionate spirit, and thereby revealed its underlying dread. First it robbed the Allies in the manner of bootleggers looting a country distillery, then it swindled the plain people at home by first bribing them with huge wages and then taking away all their profits and therewith all their savings, and then it seized and made away with the impounded property of enemy nationals—property theoretically held in trust for them, and the booty, if it was booty at all, of the whole American people. This triple burglary was excessive, to be sure, but who will say that it was not prudent? The capitalists of the Republic are efficient, and have foresight. They saw some lean and hazardous years ahead, with all sorts of raids threatening. They took measures to fortify their position. To-day their prevision is their salvation. They are losing some of their accumulation, of course, but they still have enough left to finance an effective defense of the remainder. There was never any time in the history of any country, indeed, when capital was so securely intrenched as it is to-day in the United States. It has divided the proletariat into two bitterly hostile halves, it has battered and crippled unionism almost beyond recognition, it has a firm grip upon all three arms of the government, and it controls practically every agency for the influencing of public opinion, from the press to the church. Had it been less prudent when times were good, and put its trust in God alone, the I.W.W. would have rushed it at the end of the war.

As I say, I often entertain the thought that it would be better, in the long run, to make terms with a power so hard to resist, and thereby purge it of its present compulsory criminality. I doubt that capitalists, as a class, are naturally vicious; certainly they are no more vicious than, say, lawyers and politicians—upon whom the plain people commonly rely, in their innocence, to save them. I have known a good many men of great wealth in my time, and most of them have been men showing all the customary decencies. They deplore the harsh necessities of their profession quite as honestly as a judge deplores the harsh necessities of his. You will never convince me that the average American banker, during the war, got anything properly describable as professional satisfaction out of selling Liberty bonds at 100 to poor stenographers, and then buying them back at 83. He knew that he'd need his usurious profit against the blue day when the boys came home, and so he took it, but it would have given him ten times as much pleasure if it had come from the reluctant gizzard of some other banker. In brief, there is a pride of workmanship in capitalists, just as there is in all other men above the general. They get the same spiritual lift out of their sordid swindles that Swinburne got out of composing his boozy dithyrambs, and I often incline to think that it is quite as worthy of respect. In a democratic society, with the arts adjourned and the sciences mere concubines of money, it is chiefly the capitalists, in fact, who keep pride of workmanship alive. In their principal enemies, the trades-unionists, it is almost extinct. Unionism seldom, if ever, uses such power as it has to insure better work; almost always it devotes a large part of that power to safeguarding bad work. A union man who, moved by professional pride, put any extra effort into his job would probably be punished by his union as a sort of scab. But a capitalist is still able to cherish some of the old spirit of the guildsman. If he invents a new device for corralling the money of those who have earned it, or operates an old device in some new and brilliant way, he is honored and envied by his colleagues. The late J. Pierpont Morgan was thus honored and envied, not because he made more actual money than any other capitalist of his time—in point of fact, he made a good deal less than some, and his own son, a much inferior man, has made more since his death than he did during his whole life—but because his operations showed originality, daring, coolness, and imagination—in brief, because he was a great virtuoso in the art he practiced.

What I contend is that the democratic system of government would be saner and more effective in its dealings with capital if it ceased to regard all capitalists as criminals *ipso facto,* and thereby ceased to make their armed pursuit the chief end of practical politics—if it gave over this vain effort to put them down by force, and tried to bring them to decency by giving greater play and confidence to the pride of workmanship that I have described. They would be less ferocious and immoderate, I think, if they were treated with less hostility, and put more upon their conscience and honor. No doubt the average democrat, brought up upon the prevailing superstitions and prejudices of his faith, will deny at once that they are actually capable of conscience or honor, or that they have any recognizable pride of workmanship. Well, let him deny it. He will make precisely the same denial with respect to kings. Nevertheless, it must be plain to every one who has read history attentively that the majority of the kings of the past, even when no criticism could reach them, showed a very great pride of workmanship—that they tried to be good kings even when it was easier to be bad ones. The same thing is true of the majority of capitalists—the kings of to-day. They are criminals by our democratic law, but their criminality is chiefly artificial and theoretical, like that of a bootlegger. If it were abolished by repealing the laws which create it—if it became legally just as virtuous to organize and operate a great industrial corporation, or to combine and rehabilitate railroads, or to finance any other such transactions as it is to organize a trades-union, a *Bauverein,* or a lodge of Odd Fellows—then I believe that capitalists would forthwith abandon a great deal of the scoundrelism which now marks their proceedings, that they could be trusted to police their order at least as vigilantly as physicians or lawyers police theirs, and that the activities of those members of it who showed no pride of workmanship at all would be effectively curbed.

The legal war upon them under democracy is grounded upon the false assumption that it would be possible, given laws enough, to get rid of them altogether. The *Ur*-Americanos, who set the tone of our legislation and provided examples for the legislation of every other democratic country, were chiefly what would be called Bolsheviki to-day. They dreamed of a republic wholly purged of capitalism—and taxes. They were have-nots of the most romantic and ambitious variety, and saw Utopia before them. Every man of their time who thought capitalistically—that is, who believed that things consumed had to be paid for—was a target for their revilings: for example, Alexander Hamilton. But they were wrong, and their modern heirs and assigns are wrong just as surely. That wrongness of theirs, in truth, has grown enormously since it was launched, for the early Americans were a pastoral people, and could get along with very little capital, whereas the Americans of to-day lead a very complex life, and need the aid of capitalism at almost every breath they draw. Most of their primary necessities—the railroad, the steamship lines, the trolley car, the telephone, refrigerated meats, machine-made clothes, phonograph records, moving-picture shows, and so on—are wholly unthinkable save as the products of capital in large aggregations. No man of to-day can imagine doing without them, or getting them without the aid of such aggregations. The most even the wildest Socialist can think of is to take the capital away from the capitalists who now have it and hand it over to the state—in other words, to politicians. A century ago there were still plenty of men who, like Thoreau, proposed to abolish it altogether. But now even the radicals of the extreme left assume as a matter of course that capital is indispensible, and that abolishing it or dispersing it would cause a collapse of civilization.

What ails democracy, in the economic department, is that it proceeds upon the assumption that the contrary is true—that it seeks to bring capitalism to a state of innocuous virtue by grossly exaggerating its viciousness—that it penalizes ignorantly what is, at bottom, a perfectly natural and legitimate aspiration, and one necessary to society. Such penalizings, I need not argue, never destroy the impulse itself; surely the American experience with Prohibition should make even a democrat aware of that. What they do is simply to make it evasive, intemperate, and relentless. If it were legally as hazardous in the United States to play a string quartette as it is to build up a great bank or industrial enterprise—if the performers, struggling with their parts, had to watch the windows in constant fear that a Bryan, a Roosevelt, a Lloyd-George or some other such predatory mountebank would break in, armed with a club and followed by a rabble—then string quartette players would become as devious and anti-social in their ways as the average American capitalist is today, and when, by a process of setting one part of the mob against the rest, they managed to get a chance to play quartettes in temporary peace, despite the general mob hatred of them, they would forget the lovely music of Haydn and Mozart altogether, and devote their whole time to a *fortissimo* playing of the worst musical felonies of Schönberg, Ravel and Strawinsky.

V.
Ad Imaginem Dei Creavit Illum

1
The Life of Man

THE old anthropomorphic notion that the life of the whole universe centers in the life of man—that human existence is the supreme expression of the cosmic process—this notion seems to be on its way toward the Sheol of exploded delusions. The fact is that the life of man, as it is more and more studied in the light of general biology, appears to be more and more empty of significance. Once apparently the chief concern and masterpiece of the gods, the human race now begins to bear the aspect of an accidental by-product of their vast, inscrutable and probably nonsensical operations. A blacksmith making a horse-shoe produces something almost as brilliant and mysterious—the shower of sparks. But his eye and thought, as we know, are not on the sparks, but on the horse-shoe. The sparks, indeed, constitute a sort of disease of the horse-shoe; their existence depends upon a wasting of its tissue. In the same way, perhaps, man is a local disease of the cosmos—a kind of pestiferous eczema or urethritis. There are, of course, different grades of eczema, and so are there different grades of men. No doubt a cosmos afflicted with nothing worse than an infection of Beethovens would not think it worth while to send for the doctor. But a cosmos infested by prohibitionists, Socialists, Scotsmen and stockbrokers must suffer damnably. No wonder the sun is so hot and the moon is so diabetically green!

2
The Anthropomorphic Delusion

As I say, the anthropomorphic theory of the world is made absurd by modern biology—but that is not saying, of course, that it will ever be abandoned by the generality of men. To the contrary, they will cherish it in proportion as it becomes more and more dubious. To-day, indeed, it is cherished as it was never cherished in the Ages of Faith, when the doctrine that man was god-like was at least ameliorated by the doctrine that woman was vile. What else is behind charity, philanthropy, pacifism, Socialism, the uplift, all the rest of the current sentimentalities? One and all, these sentimentalities are based upon the notion that man is a glorious and ineffable animal, and that his continued existence in the world ought to be facilitated and insured. But this notion is obviously full of fatuity. As animals go, even in so limited a space as our world, man is botched and ridiculous. Few other brutes are so stupid or so cowardly. The commonest yellow dog has far sharper senses and is infinitely more courageous, not to say more honest and dependable. The ants and the bees are, in many ways, far more intelligent and ingenious; they manage their government with vastly less quarreling, wastefulness and imbecility. The lion is more beautiful, more dignified, more majestic. The antelope is swifter and more graceful. The ordinary house-cat is cleaner. The horse, foamed by labor, has a better smell. The gorilla is kinder to his children and more faithful to his wife. The ox and the ass are more industrious and serene. But most of all, man is deficient in courage, perhaps the noblest quality of them all. He is not only mortally afraid of all other animals of his own weight or half his weight—save a few that he has debased by artificial inbreeding—; he is even mortally afraid of his own kind—and not only of their fists and hooves, but even of their sniggers.

No other animal is so defectively adapted to its environment. The human infant, as it comes into the world, is so puny that if it were neglected for two days running it would infallibly perish, and this congenital infirmity, though more or less concealed later on, persists until death. Man is ill far more than any other animal, both in his savage state and under civilization. He has more different diseases and he suffers from them oftener. He is easier exhausted and injured. He dies more horribly and usually sooner. Practically all the other higher vertebrates, at least in their wild state, live longer and retain their faculties to a greater age. Here even the anthropoid apes are far beyond their human cousins. An orang-outang marries at the age of seven or eight, raises a family of seventy or eighty children, and is still as hale and hearty at eighty as a European at forty-five.

All the errors and incompetencies of the Creator reach their climax in man. As a piece of mechanism he is the worst of them all; put beside him, even a salmon or a staphylococcus is a sound and efficient machine. He has the worst kidneys known to comparative zoölogy, and the worst lungs, and the worst heart. His eye, considering the work it is called upon to do, is less efficient than the eye of an earthworm; an optical instrument maker who made an instrument so clumsy would be mobbed by his customers. Alone of all animals, terrestrial, celestial or marine, man is unfit by nature to go abroad in the world he inhabits. He must clothe himself, protect himself, swathe himself, armor himself. He is eternally in the position of a turtle born without a shell, a dog without hair, a fish without fins. Lacking his heavy and cumbersome trappings, he is defenseless even against flies. As God made him he hasn't even a tail to switch them off.

I now come to man's one point of unquestionable natural superiority: he has a soul. This is what sets him off from all other animals, and makes him, in a way, their master. The exact nature of that soul has been in dispute for thousands of years, but regarding its function it is possible to speak with some authority. That function is to bring man into direct contact with God, to make him aware of God, above all, to make him resemble God. Well, consider the colossal failure of the device! If we assume that man actually does resemble God, then we are forced into the impossible theory that God is a coward, an idiot and a bounder. And if we assume that man, after all these years, does *not* resemble God, then it appears at once that the human soul is as inefficient a machine as the human liver or tonsil, and that man would probably be better off, as the chimpanzee undoubtedly *is* better off, without it.

Such, indeed, is the case. The only practical effect of having a soul is that it fills man with anthropomorphic and anthropocentric vanities—in brief with cocky and preposterous superstitions. He struts and plumes himself because he has this soul—and overlooks the fact that it doesn't work. Thus he is the supreme clown of creation, the *reductio ad absurdum* of animated nature. He is like a cow who believed that she could jump over the moon, and ordered her whole life upon that theory. He is like a bullfrog boasting eternally of fighting lions, of flying over the Matterhorn, and of swimming the Hellespont. And yet this is the poor brute we are asked to venerate as a gem in the forehead of the cosmos! This is the worm we are asked to defend as God's favorite on earth, with all its millions of braver, nobler, decenter quadrupeds— its superb lions, its lithe and gallant leopards, its imperial elephants, its honest dogs, its courageous rats! This is the insect we are besought, at infinite trouble, labor and expense, to reproduce!

3
Meditation on Meditation

Man's capacity for abstract thought, which most other mammals seem to lack, has undoubtedly given him his present mastery of the land surface of the earth—a mastery disputed only by several hundred species of microscopic organisms. It is responsible for his feeling of superiority, and under that feeling there is undoubtedly a certain measure of reality, at least within narrow limits. But what is too often overlooked is that the capacity to perform an act is by no means synonymous with its salubrious exercise. The simple fact is that most of man's thinking is stupid, pointless, and injurious to him. Of all animals, indeed, he seems the least capable of arriving at accurate judgments in the matters that most desperately affect his welfare. Try to imagine a rat, in the realm of rat ideas, arriving at a notion as violently in contempt of plausibility as the notion, say, of Swedenborgianism, or that of homeopathy, or that of infant damnation, or that of mental telepathy. Try to think of a congregation of educated rats gravely listening to such disgusting intellectual rubbish as was in the public bulls of Dr. Woodrow Wilson. Man's natural instinct, in fact, is never toward what is sound and true; it is toward what is specious and false. Let any great notion of modern times be confronted by two conflicting propositions, the one grounded upon the utmost probability and reasonableness and the other upon the most glaring error, and it will almost invariably embrace the latter. It is so in politics, which consists wholly of a succession of unintelligent crazes, many of them so idiotic that they exist only as battle-cries and shibboleths and are not reducible to logical statement at all. It is so in religion, which, like poetry, is simply a concerted effort to deny the most obvious realities. It is so in nearly every field of thought. The ideas that conquer the race most rapidly and arouse the wildest enthusiasm and are held most tenaciously are precisely the ideas that are most insane. This has been true since the first "advanced" gorilla put on underwear, cultivated a frown and began his first lecture tour in the first chautauqua, and it will be so until the high gods, tired of the farce at last, obliterate the race with one great, final blast of fire, mustard gas and streptococci.

No doubt the imagination of man is to blame for this singular weakness. That imagination, I daresay, is what gave him his first lift above his fellow primates. It enabled him to visualize a condition of existence better than that he was experiencing, and bit by bit he was able to give the picture a certain crude reality. Even to-day he keeps on going ahead in the same manner. That is, he thinks of something that he would like to be or to get, something appreciably better than what he is or has, and then, by the laborious, costly method of trial and error, he gradually moves toward it. In the process he is often severely punished for his discontent with God's ordinances. He mashes his thumb, he skins his shin; he stumbles and falls; the prize he reaches out for blows up in his hands. But bit by bit he moves on, or, at all events, his heirs and assigns move on. Bit by bit he smooths the path beneath his remaining leg, and achieves pretty toys for his remaining hand to play with, and accumulates delights for his remaining ear and eye.

Alas, he is not content with this slow and sanguinary progress! Always he looks further and further ahead. Always he imagines things just over the sky-line. This body of imaginings constitutes his stock of sweet beliefs, his corpus of high faiths and confidences—in brief, his burden of errors. And that burden of errors is what distinguishes man, even above his capacity for tears, his talents as a liar, his excessive hypocrisy and poltroonery, from all the other orders of mammalia. Man is the yokel *par excellence*, the booby unmatchable, the king dupe of the cosmos. He is chronically and unescapably deceived, not only by the other animals and by the delusive face of nature herself, but also and more particularly by himself—by his incomparable talent for searching out and embracing what is false, and for overlooking and denying what is true.

The capacity for discerning the essential truth, in fact, is as rare among men as it is common among crows, bullfrogs and mackerel. The man who shows it is a man of quite extraordinary quality—perhaps even a man downright diseased. Exhibit a new truth of any natural plausibilty before the great masses of men, and not one in ten thousand will suspect its existence, and not one in a hundred thousand will embrace it without a ferocious resistance. All the durable truths that have come into the world within historic times have been opposed as bitterly as if they were so many waves of smallpox, and every individual who has welcomed and advocated them, absolutely without exception, has been denounced and punished as an enemy of the race. Perhaps "absolutely without exception" goes too far. I substitute "with five or six exceptions." But who were the five or six exceptions? I leave you to think of them; myself, I can't. . . . But I think at once of Charles Darwin and his associates, and of how they were reviled in their time. This reviling, of course, is less vociferous than it used to be, chiefly because later victims are in the arena, but the underlying hostility remains. Within the past two years the principal Great Thinker of Britain, George Bernard Shaw, has denounced the hypothesis of natural selection to great applause, and a three-times candidate for the American Presidency, William Jennings Bryan, has publicly advocated prohibiting the teaching of it by law. The great majority of Christian ecclesiastics in both English-speaking countries, and with them the great majority of their catachumens, are still committed to the doctrine that Darwin was a scoundrel, and Herbert Spencer another, and Huxley a third—and that Nietzsche is to the three of them what Beelzebub himself is to a trio of bad boys. This is the reaction of the main body of respectable folk in two puissant and idealistic Christian nations to the men who will live in history as the intellectual leaders of the Nineteenth Century. This is the immemorial attitude of men in the mass, and of their chosen prophets, to whatever is honest, and important, and most probably true.

But if truth thus has hard sledding, error is given a loving welcome. The man who invents a new imbecility is hailed gladly, and bidden to make himself at home; he is, to the great masses of men, the *beau ideal* of mankind. Go back through the history of the past thousand years and you will find that nine-tenths of the popular idols of the world—not the heroes of small sects, but the heroes of mankind in the mass—have been merchants of palpable nonsense. It has been so in politics, it has been so in religion, and it has been so in every other department of human thought. Every such hawker of the not-true has been opposed, in his time, by critics who denounced and refuted him; his contention has been disposed of immediately it was uttered. But on the side of every one there has been the titanic force of human credulity, and it has sufficed in every case to destroy his foes and establish his immortality.

4
Man and His Soul

Of all the unsound ideas thus preached by great heroes and accepted by hundreds of millions of their eager dupes, probably the most patently unsound is the one that is most widely held, to wit, the idea that man has an immortal soul—that there is a part of him too ethereal and too exquisite to die. Absolutely the only evidence supporting this astounding notion lies in the hope that it is true—which is precisely the evidence underlying the late theory that the Great War would put an end to war, and bring in an era of democracy, freedom, and peace. But even archbishops, of course, are too intelligent to be satisfied permanently by evidence so unescapably dubious; in consequence, there have been efforts in all ages to give it logical and evidential support. Well, all I ask is that you give some of that corroboration your careful scrutiny. Examine, for example, the proofs amassed by five typical witnesses in five widely separated ages: St. John, St. Augustine, Martin Luther, Emanuel Swedenborg and Sir Oliver Lodge. Approach these proofs prayerfully, and study them well. Weigh them in the light of the probabilities, the ordinary intellectual decencies. And then ask yourself if you could imagine a mud-turtle accepting them gravely.

5
Coda

To sum up:

1. The cosmos is a gigantic fly-wheel making 10,000 revolutions a minute.

2. Man is a sick fly taking a dizzy ride on it.

3. Religion is the theory that the wheel was designed and set spinning to give him the ride.

VI.

Star-Spangled Men

I OPEN the memoirs of General Grant, Volume II, at the place where he is describing the surrender of General Lee, and find the following:

> I was without a sword, as I usually was when on horseback on (*sic*) the field, and wore a soldier's blouse for a coat, with the shoulder straps of my rank to indicate to the army who I was.

Anno 1865. I look out of my window and observe an officer of the United States Army passing down the street. Anno 1922. Like General Grant, he is without a sword. Like General Grant, he wears a sort of soldier's blouse for a coat. Like General Grant, he employs shoulder straps to indicate to the army who he is. But there is something more. On the left breast of this officer, apparently a major, there blazes so brilliant a mass of color that, as the sun strikes it and the flash bangs my eyes, I wink, catch my breath and sneeze. There are two long strips, each starting at the sternum and disappearing into the shadows of the axillia—every hue in the rainbow, the spectroscope, the kaleidoscope—imperial purples, *sforzando* reds, wild Irish greens, romantic blues, loud yellows and oranges, rich maroons, sentimental pinks, all the half-tones from ultra-violet to infra-red, all the vibrations from the impalpable to the unendurable. A gallant *Soldat,* indeed! How he would shame a circus ticketwagon if he wore all the medals and badges, the stars and crosses, the pendants and lavallières, that go with those ribbons! . . . I glance at his sleeves. A simple golden stripe on the one—six months beyond the raging main. None on the other—the Kaiser's cannon missed him.

Just what all these ribbons signify I am sure I don't know; probably they belong to campaign medals and tell the tale of butcheries in foreign and domestic parts—mountains of dead Filipinos, Mexicans, Haitians, Dominicans, West Virginia miners, perhaps even Prussians. But in addition to campaign medals and the Distinguished Service Medal there are now certainly enough foreign orders in the United States to give a distinct brilliance to the national scene, viewed, say, from Mars. The Frederician tradition, borrowed by the ragged Continentals and embodied in Article I, Section 9, of the Constitution, lasted until 1918, and then suddenly blew up; to mention it to-day is a sort of indecorum, and to-morrow, no doubt, will be a species of treason. Down with Frederick; up with John Philip Sousa! Imagine what General Pershing would look like at a state banquet of his favorite American order, the Benevolent and Protective one of Elks, in all the Byzantine splendor of his casket of ribbons, badges, stars, garters, sunbursts and cockades—the lordly Bath of the grateful motherland, with its somewhat disconcerting "Ich dien"; the gorgeous tricolor baldrics, sashes and festoons of the Légion d'Honneur; the grand cross of SS. Maurizio e Lazzaro of Italy; the sinister Danilo of Montenegro, with its cabalistic monogram of Danilo I and its sinister hieroglyphics; the breastplate of the Paulownia of Japan, with its rising sun of thirty-two white rays, its blood-red heart, its background of green leaves and its white ribbon edged with red; the mystical St. Saviour of Greece, with its Greek motto and its brilliantly enameled figure of Christ; above all, the Croix de Guerre of Czecho-Slovakia, a new one and hence not listed in the books, but surely no shrinking violet! Alas, Pershing was on the wrong side—that is, for one with a fancy for gauds of that sort. The most blinding of all known orders is the Medijie of Turkey, which not only entitles the holder to four wives, but also absolutely requires him to wear a red fez and a frozen star covering his whole façade. I was offered this order by Turkish spies during the war, and it wabbled me a good deal. The Alexander of Bulgaria is almost as seductive. The badge consists of an eight-pointed white cross, with crossed swords between the arms and a red Bulgarian lion over the swords. The motto is "Za Chrabrost!" Then there are the Prussian orders—the Red and Black Eagles, the Pour le Mérite, the Prussian Crown, the Hohenzollern and the rest. And the Golden Fleece of Austria—the noblest of them all. Think of the Golden Fleece on a man born in Linn County, Missouri! . . . I begin to doubt that the General would have got it, even supposing him to have taken the other side. The Japs, I note, gave him only the grand cordon of the Paulownia, and the Belgians and Montenegrins were similarly cautious. There are higher classes. The highest of the Paulownia is only for princes, which is to say, only for non-Missourians.

Pershing is the champion, with General March a bad second. March is a K.C.M.G., and entitled to wear a large cross of white enamel bearing a lithograph of the Archangel Michael and the motto, "Auspicium Melioris Aevi," but he is not a K.C.B. Admirals Benson and Sims are also grand crosses of Michael and George, and like most other respectable Americans, members of the Legion of Honor, but they seem to have been forgotten by the Greeks, the Montenegrins, the Italians and the Belgians. The British-born and extremely Anglomaniacal Sims refused the Distinguished Service Medal of his adopted country, but is careful to mention in "Who's Who in America" that his grand cross of Michael and George was conferred upon him, not by some servile gold-stick, but by "King George of England"; Benson omits mention of His Majesty, as do Pershing and March. It would be hard to think of any other American officer, real or bogus, who would refuse the D.S.M., or, failing it, the grand decoration of chivalry of the Independent Order of Odd Fellows. I once saw the latter hung, with ceremonies of the utmost magnificence, upon a bald-headed tinner who had served the fraternity long and faithfully; as he marched down the hall toward the throne of the Supreme Exalted Pishposh a score of little girls, the issue of other tinners, strewed his pathway with roses, and around the stem of each rose was a piece of glittering tinfoil. The band meanwhile played "The Rosary," and, at the conclusion of the spectacle, as fried oysters were served, "Wien Bleibt Wien."

It was, I suspect, by way of the Odd Fellows and other such gaudy heirs to the Deutsche Ritter and Rosicrucians that the lust to gleam and jingle got into the arteries of the American people. For years the austere tradition of Washington's day served to keep the military bosom bare of spangles, but all the while a weakness for them was growing in the civil population. Rank by rank, they became Knights of Pythias, Odd Fellows, Red Men, Nobles of the Mystic Shrine, Knights Templar, Patriarchs Militant, Elks, Moose, Woodmen of the World, Foresters, Hoo-Hoos, Ku Kluxers—and in every new order there were thirty-two degrees, and for every degree there was a badge, and for every badge there was a yard of ribbon. The Nobles of the Mystic Shrine, chiefly paunchy wholesalers of the Rotary Club species, are not content with swords, baldrics, stars, garters and jewels; they also wear red fezes. The Elks run to rubies. The Red Men array themselves like Sitting Bull. The patriotic ice-wagon drivers and Methodist deacons of the Ku Klux Klan carry crosses set with incandescent lights. An American who is forced by his profession to belong to many such orders—say a life insurance solicitor, a bootlegger or a dealer in Oklahoma oil stock—accumulates a trunk full of decorations, many of them weighing a pound. There is an undertaker in Hagerstown, Md., who has been initiated eighteen times. When he robes himself to plant a fellow joiner he weighs three hundred pounds and sparkles and flashes like the mouth of hell itself. He is entitled to bear seven swords, all jeweled, and to hang his watch chain with the golden busts of nine wild animals, all with precious stones for eyes. Put beside this lowly washer of the dead, Pershing newly polished would seem almost like a Trappist.

But even so the civil arm is robbed of its just dues in the department of gauds and radioactivity, no doubt by the direct operation of military vanity and jealousy. Despite a million proofs (and perhaps a billion eloquent arguments) to the contrary, it is still the theory at the official ribbon counter that the only man who serves in a war is the man who serves in uniform. This is soft for the Bevo officer, who at least has his service stripes and the spurs that gnawed into his desk, but it is hard upon his brother Irving, the dollar-a-year man, who worked twenty hours a day for fourteen months buying soap-powder, canned asparagus and raincoats for the army of God. Irving not only labored with inconceivable diligence; he also faced hazards of no mean order, for on the one hand was his natural prejudice in favor of a very liberal rewarding of commercial enterprise, and on the other hand were his patriotism and his fear of Atlanta Penitentiary. I daresay that many and many a time, after working his twenty hours, he found it difficult to sleep the remaining four hours. I know, in fact, survivors of that obscure service who are far worse wrecks to-day than Pershing is. Their reward is—what? Winks, sniffs, innuendos.

If they would indulge themselves in the now almost universal American yearning to go adorned, they must join the Knights of Pythias. Even the American Legion fails them, for though it certainly does not bar non-combatants, it insists that they shall have done their non-combatting in uniform.

What I propose is a variety of the Distinguished Service Medal for civilians,—perhaps, better still, a distinct order for civilians, closed to the military and with badges of different colors and areas, to mark off varying services to democracy. Let it run, like the Japanese Paulownia, from high to low—the lowest class for the patriot who sacrificed only time, money and a few nights' sleep; the highest for the great martyr who hung his country's altar with his dignity, his decency and his sacred honor. For Irving and his nervous insomnia, a simple rosette, with an iron badge bearing the national motto, "Safety First"; for the university president who prohibited the teaching of the enemy language in his learned grove, heaved the works of Goethe out of the university library, cashiered every professor unwilling to support Woodrow for the first vacancy in the Trinity, took to the stump for the National Security League, and made two hundred speeches in moving picture theaters—for this giant of loyal endeavor let no 100 per cent. American speak of anything less than the grand cross of the order, with a gold badge in polychrome enamel and stained glass, a baldric of the national colors, a violet plug hat with a sunburst on the side, the privilege of the floor of Congress, and a pension of $10,000 a year. After all, the cost would not be excessive; there are not many of them. Such prodigies of patriotism are possible only to rare and gifted men. For the grand cordons of the order, *e.g.*, college professors who spied upon and reported the seditions of their associates, state presidents of the American Protective League, alien property custodians, judges whose sentences of conscientious objectors mounted to more than 50,000 years, members of Dr. Creel's herd of 2,000 American historians, the authors of the Sisson documents, etc.—pensions of $10 a day would be enough, with silver badges and no plug hats. For the lower ranks, bronze badges and the legal right to the title of "the Hon.," already every true American's by courtesy.

Not, of course, that I am insensitive to the services of the gentlemen of those lower ranks, but in such matters one must go by rarity rather than by intrinsic value. If the grand cordon or even the nickel plated eagle of the third class were given to every patriot who bored a hole through the floor of his flat to get evidence against his neighbors, the Krausmeyers, and to every one who visited the Hofbräuhaus nightly, denounced the Kaiser in searing terms, and demanded assent from Emil and Otto, the waiters, and to every one who notified the catchpolls of the Department of Justice when the wireless plant was open in the garret of the Arion Liedertafel, and to all who took a brave and forward part in slacker raids, and to all who lent their stenographers funds at 6 per cent. to buy Liberty bonds at 4¼ per cent., and to all who sold out at 99 and then bought in again at 83.56 and to all who served as jurors or perjurers in cases against members and ex-members of the I.W.W., and to the German-American members of the League for German Democracy, and to all the Irish who snitched upon the Irish—if decorations were thrown about with any such lavishness, then there would be no nickel left for our bathrooms. On the civilian side as on the military side the great rewards of war go, not to mere dogged industry and fidelity, but to originality—to the unprecedented, the arresting, the bizarre. The New York *Tribune* liar who invented the story about the German plant for converting the corpses of the slain into soap did more for democracy and the Wilsonian idealism, and hence deserves a more brilliant recognition, than a thousand uninspired hawkers of atrocity stories supplied by Viscount Bryce and his associates. For that great servant of righteousness the grand cordon, with two silver badges and the chair of history at Columbia, would be scarcely enough; for the ordinary hawkers any precious metal would be too much.

Whether or not the Y.M.C.A. has decorated its chocolate pedlars and soul-snatchers I do not know; since the chief Y.M.C.A. lamassary in my town of Baltimore became the scene of a homo-sexual scandal I have ceased to frequent evangelical society. If not, then there should be some governmental recognition of those highly characteristic heroes of the war for democracy. The veterans of the line, true enough, dislike them excessively, and have a habit of denouncing them obscenely when the corn-juice flows. They charged too much for cigarettes; they tried to discourage the amiability of the ladies of France; they had a habit of being absent when the shells burst in air. Well, some say this and some say that. A few, at least, of the pale and oleaginous brethren must have gone into the Master's work because they thirsted to save souls, and not simply because they desired to escape the trenches. And a few, I am told, were anything but unpleasantly righteous, as a round of Wassermanns would show. If, as may be plausibly argued, these Soldiers of the Double Cross deserve to live at all, then they surely deserve to be hung with white enameled stars of the third class, with gilt dollar marks superimposed. Motto: "Glory, glory, hallelujah!"

But what of the vaudeville actors, the cheer leaders, the doughnut fryers, the camp librarians, the press agents? I am not forgetting them. Let them be distributed among all the classes from the seventh to the eighth, according to their sufferings for the holy cause. And the agitators against Beethoven, Bach, Brahms, Wagner, Richard Strauss, all the rest of the cacophonous Huns? And the specialists in the crimes of the German professors? And the collectors for the Belgians, with their generous renunciation of all commissions above 80 per cent.? And the pathologists who denounced Johannes Müller as a fraud, Karl Ludwig as an imbecile, and Ehrlich as a thief? And the patriotic chemists who discovered arsenic in dill pickles, ground glass in pumpernickel, bichloride tablets in Bismarck herring, pathogenic organisms in aniline dyes? And the inspired editorial writers of the New York *Times* and *Tribune*, the Boston *Transcript*, the Philadelphia *Ledger*, the Mobile *Register*, the Jones Corners *Eagle*? And the headline writers? And the Columbia, Yale and Princeton professors? And the authors of books describing how the Kaiser told them the whole plot in 1913, while they were pulling his teeth or shining his shoes? And the ex-ambassadors? And the *Nietzschefresser*? And the chautauqua orators? And the four-minute men? And the Methodist pulpit pornographers who switched so facilely from vice-crusading to German atrocities? And Dr. Newell Dwight Hillis? And Dr. Henry Van Dyke? And the master minds of the *New Republic*? And Tumulty? And the Vigilantes? Let no grateful heart forget them!

Palmer and Burleson I leave for special legislation. If mere university presidents, such as Nicholas Murray Butler, are to have the grand cross, then Palmer deserves to be rolled in malleable gold from head to foot, and polished until he blinds the cosmos—then Burleson must be hung with diamonds like Mrs. Warren and bathed in spotlights like Gaby Deslys. . . . Finally, I reserve a special decoration, to be conferred in camera and worn only in secret chapter, for husbands who took chances and refused to read anonymous letters from Paris: the somber badge of the Ordre de la Cuculus Canorus, first and only class.

VII.

The Poet and His Art

I

"A GOOD prose style," says Prof. Dr. Otto Jespersen in his great work, "Growth and Structure of the English Language," "is everywhere a late acquirement, and the work of whole generations of good authors is needed to bring about the easy flow of written prose." The learned *Sprachwissenschaftler* is here speaking of Old English, or, as it used to be called when you and I were at the breast of enlightenment, Anglo-Saxon. An inch or so lower down the page he points out that what he says of prose is by no means true of verse—that poetry of very respectable quality is often written by peoples and individuals whose prose is quite as crude and graceless as that, say of the Hon. Warren Gamaliel Harding—that even the so-called Anglo-Saxons of Beowulf's time, a race as barbarous as the modern Jugo-Slavs or Mississippians, were yet capable, on occasion, of writing dithyrambs of an indubitable sweet gaudiness.

The point needs no laboring. A glance at the history of any literature will prove its soundness. Moreover, it is supported by what we see around us every day—that is, if we look in literary directions. Some of the best verse in the modern movement, at home and abroad, has been written by intellectual adolescents who could no more write a first-rate paragraph in prose then they could leap the Matterhorn—girls just out of Vassar and Newnham, young army officers, chautauqua orators, New England old maids, obscure lawyers and doctors, newspaper reporters, all sorts of hollow dilettanti, male and female. Nine-tenths of the best poetry of the world has been written by poets less than thirty years old; a great deal more than half of it has been written by poets under twenty-five. One always associates poetry with youth, for it deals chiefly with the ideas that are peculiar to youth, and its terminology is quite as youthful as its content. When one hears of a poet past thirty-five, he seems somehow unnatural and even a trifle obscene; it is as if one encountered a graying man who still played the Chopin waltzes and believed in elective affinities. But prose, obviously, is a sterner and more elderly matter. All the great masters of prose (and especially of English prose, for its very resilience and brilliance make it extraordinarily hard to write) have had to labor for years before attaining to their mastery of it. The early prose of Abraham Lincoln was remarkable only for its badness; it was rhetorical and bombastic, and full of supernumerary words; in brief, it was a kind of poetry. It took years and years of hard striving for Abe to develop the simple and exquisite prose of his last half-decade. So with Thomas Henry Huxley, perhaps the greatest virtuoso of plain English who has ever lived. His first writings were competent but undistinguished; he was almost a grandfather before he perfected his superb style. And so with Anatole France, and Addison, and T. B. Macaulay, and George Moore, and James Branch Cabell, and Æ., and Lord Dunsany, and Nietzsche, and to go back to antiquity, Marcus Tullius Cicero. I have been told that the average age of the men who made the Authorized Version of the Bible was beyond sixty years. Had they been under thirty they would have made it lyrical; as it was, they made it colossal.

The reason for all this is not far to seek. Prose, however powerful its appeal to the emotions, is always based primarily upon logic, and is thus scientific; poetry, whatever its so-called intellectual content is always based upon mere sensation and emotion, and is thus loose and disorderly. A man must have acquired discipline over his feelings before he can write sound prose; he must have learned how to subordinate his transient ideas to more general and permanent ideas; above all, he must have acquired a good head for words, which is to say, a capacity for resisting their mere lascivious lure. But to write acceptable poetry, or even good poetry, he needs none of these things. If his hand runs away with his head it is actually a merit. If he writes what every one knows to be untrue, in terms that no sane adult would ever venture to use in real life, it is proof of his divine afflation. If he slops over and heaves around in a manner never hitherto observed on land or sea, the fact proves his originality. The so-called forms of verse and the rules of rhyme and rhythm do not offer him difficulties; they offer him refuges. Their purpose is not to keep him in order, but simply to give him countenance by providing him with a formal orderliness when he is most out of order. Using them is like swimming with bladders. The first literary composition of a quick-minded child is always some sort of jingle. It starts out with an inane idea—half an idea. Sticking to prose, it could go no further. But to its primary imbecility it now adds a meaningless phrase which, while logically unrelated, provides an agreeable concord in mere sound—and the result is the primordial tadpole of a sonnet. All the sonnets of the world, save a few of miraculous (and perhaps accidental) quality, partake of this fundamental nonsensicality. In all of them there are ideas that would sound idiotic in prose, and phrases that would sound clumsy and uncouth in prose. But the rhyme scheme conceals this nonsensicality. As a substitute for the missing logical plausibility it provides a sensuous harmony. Reading the thing, one gets a vague effect of agreeable sound, and so the logical feebleness is overlooked. It is, in a sense, like observing a pretty girl, competently dressed and made up, across the footlights. But translating the poem into prose is like meeting and marrying her.

II

Much of the current discussion of poetry—and what, save Prohibition, is more discussed in America?—is corrupted by a fundamental error. That error consists in regarding the thing itself as a simple entity, to be described conveniently in a picturesque phrase. "Poetry," says one critic, "is the statement of overwhelming emotional values." "Poetry," says another, "is an attempt to purge language of everything except its music and its pictures." "Poetry," says a third, "is the entering of delicately imaginative plateaus." "Poetry," says a fourth, "is truth carried alive into the heart by a passion." "Poetry," says a fifth, "is compacted of what seems, not of what is." "Poetry," says a sixth, "is the expression of thought in musical language." "Poetry," says a seventh, "is the language of a state of crisis." And so on, and so on. *Quod est poetica?* They all answer, and yet they all fail to answer. Poetry, in fact, is two quite distinct things. It may be either or both. One is a series of words that are intrinsically musical, in clang-tint and rhythm, as the single word *cellar-door* is musical. The other is a series of ideas, false in themselves, that offer a means of emotional and imaginative escape from the harsh realities of everyday. In brief, (I succumb, like all the rest, to phrase-making), poetry is a comforting piece of fiction set to more or less lascivious music—a slap on the back in waltz time—a grand release of longings and repressions to the tune of flutes, harps, sackbuts, psalteries and the usual strings.

As I say, poetry may be either the one thing or the other—caressing music or caressing assurance. It need not necessarily be both. Consider a familiar example from "Othello":

> Not poppy, nor mandragora,
> Nor all the drowsy syrups of the world
> Shall ever medicine thee to that sweet sleep
> Which thou owed'st yesterday.

Here the sense, at best, is surely very vague. Probably not one auditor in a hundred, hearing an actor recite those glorious lines, attaches any intelligible meaning to the archaic word *owed'st*, the cornerstone of the whole sentence. Nevertheless, the effect is stupendous. The passage assaults and benumbs the faculties like Schubert's "Ständchen" or the slow movement of Schumann's Rhenish symphony; hearing it is a sensuous debauch; the man anæsthetic to it could stand unmoved before Rheims cathedral or the Hofbräuhaus at Munich. One easily recalls many other such bursts of pure music, almost meaningless but infinitely delightful—in Poe, in Swinburne, in Marlowe, even in Joaquin Miller. Two-thirds of the charm of reading Chaucer (setting aside the Rabelaisian comedy) comes out of the mere burble of the words; the meaning, to a modern, is often extremely obscure, and sometimes downright undecipherable. The whole fame of Poe, as a poet, is based upon five short poems. Of them, three are almost pure music. Their intellectual content is of the vaguest. No one would venture to reduce them to plain English. Even Poe himself always thought of them, not as statements of poetic ideas, but as simple utterances of poetic *(i.e.,* musical) sounds.

It was Sidney Lanier, himself a competent poet, who first showed the dependence of poetry upon music. He had little to say, unfortunately, about the clang-tint of words; what concerned him almost exclusively was rhythm. In "The Science of English Verse," he showed that the charm of this rhythm could be explained in the technical terms of music—that all the old gabble about dactyls and spondees was no more than a dog Latin invented by men who were fundamentally ignorant of the thing they discussed. Lanier's book was the first intelligent work ever published upon the nature and structure of the sensuous content of English poetry. He struck out into such new and far paths that the professors of prosody still lag behind him after forty years, quite unable to understand a poet who was also a shrewd critic and a first-rate musician. But if, so deeply concerned with rhythm, he marred his treatise by forgetting clang-tint, he marred it still more by forgetting content. Poetry that is all music is obviously relatively rare, for only a poet who is also a natural musician can write it, and natural musicians are much rarer in the world than poets. Ordinary poetry, average poetry, thus depends in part upon its ideational material, and perhaps even chiefly. It is the *idea* expressed in a poem, and not the mellifluousness of the words used to express it, that arrests and enchants the average connoisseur. Often, indeed, he disdains this mellifluousness, and argues that the idea ought to be set forth without the customary pretty jingling, or, at most, with only the scant jingling that lies in rhythm—in brief, he wants his ideas in the altogether, and so advocates *vers libre.*

It was another American, this time Prof. Dr. F. C. Prescott, of Cornell University, who first gave scientific attention to the intellectual content of poetry. His book is called "Poetry and Dreams." Its virtue lies in the fact that it rejects all the customary mystical and romantic definitions of poetry, and seeks to account for the thing in straightforward psychological terms. Poetry, says Prescott, is simply the verbal materialization of a day-dream, the statement of a Freudian wish, an attempt to satisfy a subconscious longing by saying that it is satisfied. In brief, poetry represents imagination's bold effort to escape from the cold and clammy facts that hedge us in—to soothe the wrinkled and fevered brow with beautiful balderdash. On the precise nature of this beautiful balderdash you can get all the information you need by opening at random the nearest book of verse. The ideas you will find in it may be divided into two main divisions. The first consists of denials of objective facts; the second of denials of subjective facts. Specimen of the first sort:

> God's in His heaven,
> All's well with the world.

Specimen of the second:

> I am the master of my fate;
> I am the captain of my soul.

It is my contention that all poetry (forgetting, for the moment, its possible merit as mere sound) may be resolved into either the one or the other of these frightful imbecilities—that its essential character lies in its bold flouting of what every reflective adult knows to be the truth. The poet, imagining him to be sincere, is simply one who disposes of all the horrors of life on this earth, and of all the difficulties presented by his own inner weaknesses no less, by the childish device of denying them. Is it a well-known fact that love is an emotion that is almost as perishable as eggs—that it is biologically impossible for a given male to yearn for a given female more than a few brief years? Then the poet disposes of it by assuring his girl that he will nevertheless love her forever—more, by pledging his word of honor that he believes that *she* will love *him* forever. Is it equally notorious that there is no such thing as justice in the world—that the good are tortured insanely and the evil go free and prosper? Then the poet composes a piece crediting God with a mysterious and unintelligible theory of jurisprudence, whereby the torture of the good is a sort of favor conferred upon them for their goodness. Is it of almost equally widespread report that no healthy man likes to contemplate his own inevitable death—that even in time of war, with a vast pumping up of emotion to conceal the fact, every soldier hopes and believes that he, personally, will escape? Then the poet, first carefully introducing himself into a bomb-proof, achieves strophes declaring that he is free from all such weakness—that he will deliberately seek a rendezvous with death, and laugh ha-ha when the bullet finds him.

The precise nature of the imbecility thus solemnly set forth depends, very largely, of course, upon the private prejudices and yearnings of the poet, and the reception that is given it depends, by the same token, upon the private prejudices and yearnings of the reader. That is why it is often so difficult to get any agreement upon the merits of a definite poem, *i.e.*, to get any agreement upon its capacity to soothe. There is the man who craves only the animal delights of a sort of Moslem-Methodist paradise: to him "The Frost is on the Pumpkin" is a noble poem. There is the man who yearns to get out of the visible universe altogether and tread the fields of asphodel: for him there is delight only in the mystical stuff of Crashaw, Thompson, Yeats and company. There is the man who revolts against the sordid Christian notion of immortality—an eternity to be spent flapping wings with pious greengrocers and oleaginous Anglican bishops; he finds *his* escape in the gorgeous blasphemies of Swinburne. There is, to make an end of examples, the man who, with an inferiority complex eating out his heart, is moved by a great desire to stalk the world in heroic guise: he may go to the sonorous swanking of Kipling, or he may go to something more subtle, to some poem in which the boasting is more artfully concealed, say Christina Rossetti's "When I am Dead." Many men, many complexes, many secret yearnings! They collect, of course, in groups; if the group happens to be large enough the poet it is devoted to becomes famous. Kipling's great fame is thus easily explained. He appeals to the commonest of all types of men, next to the sentimental type—which is to say, he appeals to the bully and braggart type, the chest-slapping type, the patriot type. Less harshly described, to the boy type. All of us have been Kiplingomaniacs at some time or other. I was myself a very ardent one at 17, and wrote many grandiloquent sets of verse in the manner of "Tommy Atkins" and "Fuzzy-Wuzzy." But if the gifts of observation and reflection have been given to us, we get over it. There comes a time when we no longer yearn to be heroes, but seek only peace—maybe even hope for quick extinction. Then we turn to Swinburne and "The Garden of Proserpine"—more false assurances, more mellifluous play-acting, another tinkling make-believe—but how sweet on blue days!

III

One of the things to remember here (too often it is forgotten, and Dr. Prescott deserves favorable mention for stressing it) is that a man's conscious desires are not always identical with his subconscious longings; in fact, the two are often directly antithetical. No doubt the real man lies in the depths of the subconscious, like a carp lurking in mud. His conscious personality is largely a product of his environment—the reaction of his subconscious to the prevailing notions of what is meet and seemly. Here, of course, I wander into platitude, for the news that all men are frauds was already stale in the days of Hammurabi. The ingenious Freud simply translated the fact into pathological terms, added a bedroom scene, and so laid the foundations for his psychoanalysis. Incidentally, it has always seemed to me that Freud made a curious mistake when he brought sex into the foreground of his new magic. He was, of course, quite right when he set up the doctrine that, in civilized societies, sex impulses were more apt to be suppressed than any other natural impulses, and that the subconscious thus tended to be crowded with their ghosts. But in considering sex impulses, he forgot sex imaginings. Digging out, by painful cross-examination in a darkened room, some startling tale of carnality in his patient's past, he committed the incredible folly of assuming it to be literally true. More often than not, I believe, it was a mere piece of boasting, a materialization of desire—in brief, a poem. It is astonishing that this possibility never occurred to the venerable professor; it is more astonishing that it has never occurred to any of his disciples. He should have psychoanalyzed a few poets instead of wasting all his time upon psychopathic women with sclerotic husbands. He would have dredged amazing things out of their subconsciouses, heroic as well as amorous. Imagine the billions of Boers, Germans, Irishmen and Hindus that Kipling would have confessed to killing!

But here I get into morbid anatomy, and had better haul up. What I started out to say was that a man's preferences in poetry constitute an excellent means of estimating his inner cravings and credulities. The music disarms his critical sense, and he confesses to chershing ideas that he would repudiate with indignation if they were put into plain words. I say he cherishes those ideas. Maybe he simply tolerates them unwillingly; maybe they are no more than inescapable heritages from his barbarous ancestors, like his vermiform appendix. Think of the poems you like, and you will come upon many such intellectual fossils—ideas that you by no means subscribe to openly, but that nevertheless give you a strange joy. I put myself on the block as Exhibit A. There is my delight in Lizette Woodworth Reese's sonnet, "Tears." Nothing could do more violence to my conscious beliefs. Put into prose, the doctrine in the poem would exasperate and even enrage me. There is no man in Christendom who is less a Christian than I am. But here the dead hand grabs me by the ear. My ancestors were converted to Christianity in the year 1535, and remained of that faith until near the middle of the eighteenth century. Observe, now, the load I carry; more than two hundred years of Christianity, and perhaps a thousand years (maybe even two, or three thousand years) of worship of heathen gods before that—at least twelve hundred years of uninterrupted belief in the immortality of the soul. Is it any wonder that, betrayed by the incomparable music of Miss Reese's Anglo-Saxon monosyllables, my conscious faith is lulled to sleep, thus giving my subconscious a chance to wallow in its immemorial superstition?

Even so, my vulnerability to such superstitions is very low, and it tends to grow less as I increase in years and sorrows. As I have said, I once throbbed to the drum-beat of Kipling; later on, I was responsive to the mellow romanticism of Tennyson; now it takes one of the genuinely fundamental delusions of the human race to move me. But progress is not continuous; it has interludes. There are days when every one of us experiences a sort of ontogenetic back-firing, and returns to an earlier stage of development. It is on such days that grown men break down and cry like children; it is then that they play games, or cheer the flag, or fall in love. And it is then that they are in the mood for poetry, and get comfort out of its asseverations of the obviously not true. A truly civilized man, when he is wholly himself, derives no pleasure from hearing a poet state, as Browning stated, that this world is perfect. Such tosh not only does not please him; it definitely offends him, as he is offended by an idiotic article in a newspaper; it roils him to encounter so much stupidity in Christendom. But he may like it when he is drunk, or suffering from some low toxemia, or staggering beneath some great disaster. Then, as I say, the ontogenetic process reverses itself, and he slides back into infancy. Then he goes to poets, just as he goes to women, "glad" books, and dogmatic theology. The very highest orders of men, perhaps, never suffer from such malaises of the spirit, or, if they suffer from them, never succumb to them. These are men who are so thoroughly civilized that even the most severe attack upon the emotions is not sufficient to dethrone their reason. Charles Darwin was such a man. There was never a moment in his life when he sought religious consolation, and there was never a moment when he turned to poetry; in fact, he regarded all poetry as silly. Other first-rate men, more sensitive to the possible music in it, regard it with less positive aversion, but I have never heard of a truly first-rate man who got any permanent satisfaction out of its content. The Browning Societies of the latter part of the nineteenth century (and I choose the Browning Societies because Browning's poetry was often more or less logical in content, and thus above the ordinary intellectually) were not composed of such men as Huxley, Spencer, Lecky, Buckle and Trevelyan, but of third-rate schoolmasters, moony old maids, candidates for theosophy, literary vicars, collectors of Rogers groups, and other such Philistines. The chief propagandist for Browning in the United States was not Henry Adams, or William Summer, or Daniel C. Gilman, but an obscure professor of English who was also an ardent spook-chaser. And what is thus true ontogenetically is also true phylogenetically. That is to say, poetry is chiefly produced and esteemed by peoples that have not yet come to maturity. The Romans had a dozen poets of the first talent before they had a single prose writer of any skill whatsoever. So did the English. So did the Germans. In our own day we see the negroes of the South producing religious and secular verse of such quality that it is taken over by the whites, and yet the number of negroes who show a decent prose style is still very small, and there is no sign of it increasing. Similarly, the white authors of America, during the past ten or fifteen years, have produced a great mass of very creditable poetry, and yet the quality of our prose remains very low, and the Americans with prose styles of any distinction could be counted on the fingers of two hands.

IV

So far I have spoken chiefly of the content of poetry. In its character as a sort of music it is plainly a good deal more respectable, and makes an appeal to a far higher variety of reader, or, at all events, to a reader in a state of greater mental clarity. A capacity for music—by which I mean melody, harmony and clang-tint—comes late in the history of every race. The savage can apprehend rhythm, but he is quite incapable of carrying a tune in any intelligible scale. The negro roustabouts of our own South, who are commonly regarded as very musical, are actually only rhythmical; they never invent melodies, but only rhythms. And the whites to whom their barbarous dance-tunes chiefly appeal are in their own stage of culture. When one observes a room full of well-dressed men and women swaying and wriggling to the tune of some villainous mazurka from the Mississippi levees, one may assume very soundly that they are all the sort of folk who play golf and bridge, and prefer "The Sheik" to "Heart of Darkness" and believe in the League of Nations. A great deal of superficial culture is compatible with that pathetic barbarism, and even a high degree of æsthetic sophistication in other directions. The Greeks who built the Parthenon knew no more about music than a hog knows of predestination; they were almost as ignorant in that department as the modern Iowans or New Yorkers. It was not, indeed, until the Renaissance that music as we know it appeared in the world, and it was not until less than two centuries ago that it reached a high development. In Shakespeare's day music was just getting upon its legs in England; in Goethe's day it was just coming to full flower in Germany; in France and America it is still in the savage state. It is thus the youngest of the arts, and the most difficult, and hence the noblest. Any sane young man of twenty-two can write an acceptable sonnet, or design a habitable house or draw a horse that will not be mistaken for an automobile, but before he may write even a bad string quartet he must go through a long and arduous training, just as he must strive for years before he may write prose that is instantly recognizable as prose, and not as a string of mere words.

The virtue of such great poets as Shakespeare does not lie in the content of their poetry, but in its music. The content of the Shakespearean plays, in fact, is often puerile, and sometimes quite incomprehensible. No scornful essays by George Bernard Shaw and Frank Harris were needed to demonstrate the fact; it lies plainly in the text. One snickers sourly over the spectacle of generations of pedants debating the question of Hamlet's mental processes; the simple fact is that Shakespeare gave him no more mental processes than a Fifth avenue rector has, but merely employed him as a convenient spout for some of the finest music ever got into words. Assume that he has all the hellish sagacity of a Nietzsche, and that music remains unchanged; assume that he is as idiotic as a Grand Worthy Flubdub of the Freemasons, and it still remains unchanged. As it is intoned on the stage by actors, the poetry of Shakespeare commonly loses content altogether. One cannot make out what the *cabotin* is saying; one can only observe that it is beautiful. There are whole speeches in the Shakespearean plays whose meaning is unknown even to scholars—and yet they remain favorites, and well deserve to. Who knows, again, what the sonnets are about? Is the bard talking about the inn-keeper's wife at Oxford, or about a love affair of a pathological, Y.M.C.A. character? Some say one thing, and some say the other. But all who have ears must agree that the sonnets are extremely beautiful stuff—that the English language reaches in them the topmost heights of conceivable beauty. Shakespeare thus ought to be ranked among the musicians, along with Beethoven. As a philosopher he was a ninth-rater—but so was old Ludwig. I wonder what he would have done with prose? I can't make up my mind about it. One day I believe that he would have written prose as good as Dryden's, and the next day I begin to fear that he would have produced something as bad as Swinburne's. He had the ear, but he lacked the logical sense. Poetry has done enough when it charms, but prose must also convince.

I do not forget, of course, that there is a borderland in which it is hard to say, of this or that composition, whether it is prose or poetry. Lincoln's Gettysburg speech is commonly reckoned as prose, and yet I am convinced that it is quite as much poetry as the Queen Mab speech or Marlowe's mighty elegy on Helen of Troy. More, it is so read and admired by the great masses of the American people. It is an almost perfect specimen of a comforting but unsound asseveration put into rippling and hypnotizing words; done into plain English, the statements of fact in it would make even a writer of school history-books laugh. So with parts of the Declaration of Independence. No one believes seriously that they are true, but nearly everyone agrees that it would be a nice thing if they *were* true—and meanwhile Jefferson's eighteenth century rhetoric, by Johnson out of John Lyly's "Euphues," completes the enchantment. In the main, the test is to be found in the audience rather than in the poet. If it is naturally intelligent and in a sober and critical mood, demanding sense and proofs, then nearly all poetry becomes prose; if, on the contrary, it is congenitally maudlin, or has a few drinks aboard, or is in love, or is otherwise in a soft and believing mood, then even the worst of prose, if it has a touch of soothing sing-song in it, becomes moving poetry—for example, the diplomatic and political gospel-hymns of the late Dr. Wilson, a man constitutionally unable to reason clearly or honestly, but nevertheless one full of the burbling that caresses the ears of simple men. Most of his speeches, during the days of his divine appointment, translated into intelligible English, would have sounded as idiotic as a prose version of "The Blessed Damozel." Read by his opponents, they sounded so without the translation.

But at the extremes, of course, there are indubitable poetry and incurable prose, and the difference is not hard to distinguish. Prose is simply a form on writing in which the author intends that his statements shall be accepted as conceivably true, even when they are about imaginary persons and events; its appeal is to the fully conscious and alertly reasoning man. Poetry is a form of writing in which the author attempts to disarm reason and evoke emotion partly by presenting images that awaken a powerful response in the subconscious and partly by the mere sough and blubber of words. Poetry is not distinguished from prose, as Prof. Dr. Lowes says in his "Convention and Revolt in Poetry," by an exclusive phraseology, but by a peculiar attitude of mind—an attitude of self-delusion, of fact-denying, of saying what isn't true. It is essentially an effort to elude the bitter facts of life, whereas prose is essentially a means of unearthing and exhibiting them. The gap is bridged by sentimental prose, which is half prose and half poetry—Lincoln's Gettysburg speech, the average sermon, the prose of an erotic novelette. Immediately the thing acquires a literal meaning it ceases to be poetry; immediately it becomes capable of convincing an adult and perfectly sober man during the hours between breakfast and luncheon it is indisputably prose.

This quality of untruthfulness pervades all poetry, good and bad. You will find it in the very best poetry that the world has so far produced, to wit, in the sonorous poems of the Jewish Scriptures. The ancient Jews were stupendous poets. Moreover, they were shrewd psychologists, and so knew the capacity of poetry, given the believing mind, to convince and enchant—in other words, its capacity to drug the auditor in such a manner that he accepts it literally, as he might accept the baldest prose. This danger in poetry, given auditors impressionable enough, is too little estimated and understood. It is largely responsible for the persistence of sentimentality in a world apparently designed for the one purpose of manufacturing cynics. It is probably chiefly responsible for the survival of Christianity, despite the hard competition that it has met with from other religions. The theology of Christianity—*i.e.*, its prose—is certainly no more convincing than that of half a dozen other religions that might be named; it is, in fact, a great deal less convincing than the theology of, say, Buddhism. But the poetry of Christianity is infinitely more lush and beautiful than that of any other religion ever heard of. There is more lovely poetry in one of the Psalms than in all of the Non-Christian scriptures of the world taken together. More, this poetry is in both Testaments, the New as well as the Old. Who could imagine a more charming poem than that of the Child in the manger? It has enchanted the world for nearly two thousand years. It is simple, exquisite and overwhelming. Its power to arouse emotion is so great that even in our age it is at the bottom of fully a half of the kindliness, romanticism and humane sentimentality that survive in Christendom. It is worth a million syllogisms.

Once, after plowing through sixty or seventy volumes of bad verse, I described myself as a poetry-hater. The epithet was and is absurd. The truth is that I enjoy poetry as much as the next man—when the mood is on me. But what mood? The mood, in a few words, of intellectual and spiritual fatigue, the mood of revolt against the insoluble riddle of existence, the mood of disgust and despair. Poetry, then, is a capital medicine. First its sweet music lulls, and then its artful presentation of the beautifully improbable soothes and gives surcease. It is an escape from life, like religion, like enthusiasm, like glimpsing a pretty girl. And to the mere sensuous joy in it, to the mere low delight in getting away from the world for a bit, there is added, if the poetry be good, something vastly better, something reaching out into the realm of the intelligent, to wit, appreciation of good workmanship. A sound sonnet is almost as pleasing an object as a well-written fugue. A pretty lyric, deftly done, has all the technical charm of a fine carving. I think it is craftsmanship that I admire most in the world. Brahms enchants me because he knew his trade perfectly. I like Richard Strauss because he is full of technical ingenuities, because he is a master-workman. Well, who ever heard of a finer craftsman than William Shakespeare? His music was magnificent, he played superbly upon all the common emotions—and he did it magnificently, he did it with an air. No, I am no poetry-hater. But even Shakespeare I most enjoy, not on brisk mornings when I feel fit for any deviltry, but on dreary evenings when my old wounds are troubling me, and some fickle one has just sent back the autographed set of my first editions, and bills are piled up on my desk, and I am too sad to work. Then I mix a stiff dram—and read poetry.

VIII.
Five Men at Random

I
Abraham Lincoln

THE backwardness of the art of biography in These States is made shiningly visible by the fact that we have yet to see a first-rate life of either Lincoln or Whitman. Of Lincolniana, of course, there is no end, nor is there any end to the hospitality of those who collect it. Some time ago a publisher told me that there are four kinds of books that never, under any circumstances, lose money in the United States—first, detective stories; secondly, novels in which the heroine is forcibly debauched by the hero; thirdly, volumes on spiritualism, occultism and other such claptrap, and fourthly, books on Lincoln. But despite all the vast mass of Lincolniana and the constant discussion of old Abe in other ways, even so elemental a problem as that of his religious faith—surely an important, matter in any competent biography—is yet but half solved. Here, for example, is the Rev. William E. Barton, grappling with it for more than four hundred large pages in "The Soul of Abraham Lincoln." It is a lengthy inquiry—the rev. pastor, in truth, shows a good deal of the habitual garrulity of his order—but it is never tedious. On the contrary, it is curious and amusing, and I have read it with steady interest, including even the appendices. Unluckily, the author, like his predecessors, fails to finish the business before him. Was Lincoln a Christian? Did he believe in the Divinity of Christ? I am left in doubt. He was very polite about it, and very cautious, as befitted a politician in need of Christian votes, but how much genuine conviction was in that politeness? And if his occasional references to Christ were thus open to question, what of his rather vague avowals of belief in a personal God and in the immortality of the soul? Herndon and some of his other close friends always maintained that he was an atheist, but Dr. Barton argues that this atheism was simply disbelief in the idiotic Methodist and Baptist dogmas of his time—that nine Christian churches out of ten, if he were alive to-day, would admit him to their high privileges and prerogatives without anything worse than a few warning coughs. As for me, I still wonder.

The growth of the Lincoln legend is truly amazing. He becomes the American solar myth, the chief butt of American credulity and sentimentality. Washington, of late years, has been perceptibly humanized; every schoolboy now knows that he used to swear a good deal, and was a sharp trader, and had a quick eye for a pretty ankle. But meanwhile the varnishers and veneerers have been busily converting Abe into a plaster saint, thus making him fit for adoration in the chautauquas and Y.M.C.A.'s. All the popular pictures of him show him in his robes of state, and wearing an expression fit for a man about to be hanged. There is, so far as I know, not a single portrait of him showing him smiling—and yet he must have cackled a good deal, first and last: who ever heard of a story-teller who didn't? Worse, there is an obvious effort to pump all his human weaknesses out of him, and so leave him a mere moral apparition, a sort of amalgam of John Wesley and the Holy Ghost. What could be more absurd? Lincoln, in point of fact, was a practical politician of long experience and high talents, and by no means cursed with inconvenient ideals. On the contrary, his career in the Illinois Legislature was that of a good organization man, and he was more than once denounced by reformers. Even his handling of the slavery question was that of a politician, not that of a fanatic. Nothing alarmed him more than the suspicion that he was an Abolitionist. Barton tells of an occasion when he actually fled town to avoid meeting the issue squarely. A genuine Abolitionist would have published the Emancipation Proclamation the day after the first battle of Bull Run. But Lincoln waited until the time was more favorable—until Lee had been hurled out of Pennsylvania, and, more important still, until the political currents were safely running his way. Always he was a wary fellow, both in his dealings with measures and in his dealings with men. He knew how to keep his mouth shut.

Nevertheless, it was his eloquence that probably brought him to his great estate. Like William Jennings Bryan, he was a dark horse made suddenly formidable by fortunate rhetoric. The Douglas debate launched him, and the Cooper Union speech got him the presidency. This talent for emotional utterance, this gift for making phrases that enchanted the plain people, was an accomplishment of late growth. His early speeches were mere empty fireworks—the childish rhodomontades of the era. But in middle life he purged his style of ornament and it became almost baldly simple—and it is for that simplicity that he is remembered to-day. The Gettysburg speech is at once the shortest and the most famous oration in American history. Put beside it, all the whoopings of the Websters, Sumners and Everetts seem gaudy and silly. It is eloquence brought to a pellucid and almost child-like perfection—the highest emotion reduced to one graceful and irresistible gesture. Nothing else precisely like it is to be found in the whole range of oratory. Lincoln himself never even remotely approached it. It is genuinely stupendous.

But let us not forget that it is oratory, not logic; beauty, not sense. Think of the argument in it! Put it into the cold words of everyday! The doctrine is simply this: that the Union soldiers who died at Gettysburg sacrificed their lives to the cause of self-determination—"that government of the people, by the people, for the people," should not perish from the earth. It is difficult to imagine anything more untrue. The Union soldiers in that battle actually fought against self-determination; it was the Confederates who fought for the right of their people to govern themselves. What was the practical effect of the battle of Gettysburg? What else than the destruction of the old sovereignty of the States, *i.e.*, of the people of the States? The Confederates went into battle an absolutely free people; they came out with their freedom subject to the supervision and vote of the rest of the country—and for nearly twenty years that vote was so effective that they enjoyed scarcely any freedom at all. Am I the first American to note the fundamental nonsensicality of the Gettysburg address? If so, I plead my æsthetic joy in it in amelioration of the sacrilege.

2
Paul Elmer More

Nothing new is to be found in the latest volume of Paul Elmer More's Shelburne Essays. The learned author, undismayed by the winds of anarchic doctrine that blow down his Princeton stovepipe, continues to hold fast to the notions of his earliest devotion. He is still the gallant champion sent against the Romantic Movement by the forces of discipline and decorum. He is still the eloquent fugleman of the Puritan ethic and æsthetic. In so massive a certainty, so resolute an immovability there is something almost magnificent. These are somewhat sad days for the exponents of that ancient correctness. The Goths and the Huns are at the gate, and as they batter wildly they throw dead cats, perfumed lingerie, tracts against predestination, and the bound files of the *Nation*, the *Freeman* and the *New Republic* over the fence. But the din does not flabbergast Dr. More. High above the blood-bathed battlements there is a tower, of ivory within and solid ferro-concrete without, and in its austere upper chamber he sits undaunted, solemnly composing an elegy upon Jonathan Edwards, "the greatest theologian and philosopher yet produced in this country."

Magnificent, indeed—and somehow charming. On days when I have no nobler business I sometimes join the barbarians and help them to launch their abominable bombs against the embattled blue-noses. It is, in the main, fighting that is too easy, too Anglo-Saxon to be amusing. Think of the decayed professors assembled by Dr. Franklin for the *Profiteers' Review*; who could get any genuine thrill out of dropping *them*? They come out on crutches, and are as much afraid of what is behind them as they are of what is in front of them. Facing all the horrible artillery of Nineveh and Tyre, they arm themselves with nothing worse than the pedagogical birch. The janissaries of Adolph Ochs, the Anglo-Saxon supreme archon, are even easier. One has but to blow a *shofar*, and down they go. Even Prof. Dr. Stuart P. Sherman is no antagonist to delight a hard-boiled heretic. Sherman is at least honestly American, of course, but the trouble with him is that he is *too* American. The Iowa hayseed remains in his hair; he can't get rid of the smell of the chautauqua; one inevitably sees in him a sort of *reductio ad absurdum* of his fundamental theory—to wit, the theory that the test of an artist is whether he hated the Kaiser in 1917, and plays his honorable part in Christian Endeavor, and prefers Coca-Cola to Scharlachberger 1911, and has taken to heart the great lessons of sex hygiene. Sherman is game, but he doesn't offer sport in the grand manner. Moreover, he has been showing sad signs of late of a despairing heart: he tries to be ingratiating, and begins to hug in the clinches.

The really tempting quarry is More. To rout him out of his armored tower, to get him out upon the glacis for a duel before both armies, to bring him finally to the wager of battle—this would be an enterprise to bemuse the most audacious and give pause to the most talented. More has a solid stock of learning in his lockers; he is armed and outfitted as none of the pollyannas who trail after him is armed and outfitted; he is, perhaps, the nearest approach to a genuine scholar that we have in America, God save us all! But there is simply no truculence in him, no flair for debate, no lust to do execution upon his foes. His method is wholly *ex parte*. Year after year he simply iterates and reiterates his misty protests, seldom changing so much as a word. Between his first volume and his last there is not the difference between Gog and Magog. Steadily, ploddingly, vaguely, he continues to preach the gloomy gospel of tightness and restraint. He was against "the electric thrill of freer feeling" when he began, and he will be against it on that last gray day—I hope it long post-dates my own hanging—when the ultimate embalmer sneaks upon him with velvet tread, and they haul down the flag to half-staff at Princeton, and the readers of the New York *Evening Journal* note that an obscure somebody named Paul E. More is dead.

3
Madison Cawein

A vast and hefty tome celebrates this dead poet, solemnly issued by his mourning friends in Louisville. The editor is Otto A. Rothert, who confesses that he knew Cawein but a year or two, and never read his poetry until after his death. The contributors include such local *literati* as Reuben Post Halleck, Leigh Gordon Giltner, Anna Blanche McGill and Elvira S. Miller Slaughter. Most of the ladies gush over the departed in the manner of high-school teachers paying tribute to Plato, Montaigne or Dante Alighieri. His young son, seventeen years old, contributes by far the most vivid and intelligent account of him; it is, indeed, very well written, as, in a different way, is the contribution of Charles Hamilton Musgrove, an old newspaper friend. The ladies, as I hint, simply swoon and grow lyrical. But it is a fascinating volume, all the same, and well worth the room it takes on the shelf. Mr. Rothert starts off with what he calls a "picturography" of Cawein—the poet's father and mother in the raiment of 1865, the coat-of-arms of his mother's great-grandfather's uncle, the house which now stands on the site of the house in which he was born, the rock spring from which he used to drink as a boy, a group showing him with his three brothers, another showing him with one brother and their cousin Fred, Cawein himself with sideboards, the houses he lived in, the place where he worked, the walks he liked around Louisville, his wife and baby, the hideous bust of him in the Louisville Public Library, the church from which he was buried, his modest grave in Cave Hill Cemetery—in brief, all the photographs that collect about a man as he staggers through life, and entertain his ribald grandchildren after he is gone. Then comes a treatise on the ancestry and youth of the poet, then a collection of newspaper clippings about him, then a gruesomely particular account of his death, then a fragment of autobiography, then a selection from his singularly dull letters, then some prose pieces from his pen, then the aforesaid tributes of his neighbors, and finally a bibliography of his works, and an index to them.

As I say, a volume of fearful bulk and beam, but nevertheless full of curious and interesting things. Cawein, of course, was not a poet of the first rank, nor is it certain that he has any secure place in the second rank, but in the midst of a great deal of obvious and feeble stuff he undoubtedly wrote some nature lyrics of excellent quality. The woods and the fields were his delight. He loved to roam through them, observing the flowers, the birds, the tall trees, the shining sky overhead, the green of Spring, the reds and browns of Autumn, the still whites of Winter. There were times when he got his ecstasy into words—when he wrote poems that were sound and beautiful. These poems will not be forgotten; there will be no history of American literature written for a hundred years that does not mention Madison Cawein. But what will the literary historians make of the man himself: How will they explain his possession, however fitfully, of the divine gift—his genuine kinship with Wordsworth and Shelley? Certainly no more unlikely candidate for the bays ever shinned up Parnassus. His father was a quack doctor; his mother was a professional spiritualist; he himself, for years and years, made a living as cashier in a gambling-house! Could anything be more grotesque? Is it possible to imagine a more improbable setting for a poet? Yet the facts are the facts, and Mr. Rothert makes no attempt whatever to conceal them. Add a final touch of the bizarre: Cawein fell over one morning while shaving in his bathroom, and cracked his head on the bathtub, and after his death there was a row over his life insurance. Mr. Rothert presents all of the documents. The autopsy is described; the death certificate is quoted. . . . A strange, strange tale, indeed!

4
Frank Harris

Though, so far as I know, this Harris is a perfectly reputable man, fearing God and obeying the laws, it is not to be gainsaid that a certain flavor of the sinister hangs about his aspect. The first time I ever enjoyed the honor of witnessing him, there bobbed up in my mind (instantly put away as unworthy and unseemly) a memory of the handsome dogs who used to chain shrieking virgins to railway tracks in the innocent, pre-Ibsenish dramas of my youth, the while a couple of stage hands imitated the rumble of the Empire State Express in the wings. There was the same elegance of turn-out, the same black mustachios, the same erect figure and lordly air, the same agate glitter in the eyes, the same aloof and superior smile. A sightly fellow, by all the gods, and one who obviously knew how to sneer. That afternoon, in fact, we had a sneering match, and before it was over most of the great names in the letters and politics of the time, *circa* 1914, had been reduced to faint hisses and ha-has. . . . Well, a sneerer has his good days and his bad days. There are times when his gift gives him such comfort that it can be matched only by God's grace, and there are times when it launches upon him such showers of darts that he is bound to feel a few stings. Harris got the darts first, for the year that he came back to his native land, after a generation of exile, was the year in which Anglomania rose to the dignity of a national religion—and what he had to say about the English, among whom he had lived since the early 80's, was chiefly of a very waspish and disconcerting character. Worse, he not only said it, twirling his mustache defiantly; he also wrote it down, and published it in a book. This book was full of shocks for the rapt worshippers of the Motherland, and particularly for the literary *Kanonendelicatessen* who followed the pious leadership of Woodrow and Ochs, Putnam and Roosevelt, Wister and Cyrus Curtis, young Reid and Mrs. Jay. So they called a special meeting of the American Academy of Arts and Letters, sang "God Save the King," kissed the Union Jack, and put Harris into Coventry. And there he remained for five or six long years. The literary reviews never mentioned him. His books were expunged from the minutes. When he was heard of at all, it was only in whispers, and the general burden of those whispers was that he was in the pay of the Kaiser, and plotting to garrot the Rev. Dr. William T. Manning. . . .

So down to 1921. Then the English, with characteristic lack of delicacy, played a ghastly trick upon all those dutiful and well-meaning colonists. That is to say, they suddenly forgave Harris his criminal refusal to take their war buncombe seriously, exhumed him from his long solitude among the Anglo-Ashkenazim, and began praising him in rich, hearty terms as a literary gentleman of the first water, and even as the chief adornment of American letters! The English notices of his "Contemporary Portraits: Second Series" were really quite amazing. The London *Times* gave him two solid columns, and where the *Times* led, all the other great organs of English literary opinion followed. The book itself was described as something extraordinary, a piece of criticism full of shrewdness and originality, and the author was treated with the utmost politeness. . . . One imagines the painful sensation in the New York *Times* office, the dismayed groups around far-flung campus pumps, the special meetings of the Princeton, N.J., and Urbana, Ill., American Legions, the secret conference between the National Institute of Arts and Letters and the Ku Klux Klan. But though there was tall talk by hot heads, nothing could be done. Say "Wo!" and the dutiful jackass turns to the right; say "Gee!" and he turns to the left. It is too much, of course, to ask him to cheer as well as turn—but he nevertheless turns. Since 1921 I have heard no more whispers against Harris from professors and Vigilantes. But on two or three occasions, the subject coming up, I have heard him sneer his master sneer, and each time my blood has run cold.

Well, what is in him? My belief, frequently expressed, is that there is a great deal. His "Oscar Wilde" is, by long odds, the best literary biography ever written by an American—an astonishingly frank, searching and vivid reconstruction of character—a piece of criticism that makes all ordinary criticism seem professorial and lifeless. The Comstocks, I need not say, tried to suppress it; a brilliant light is thrown upon Harris by the fact that they failed ignominiously. All the odds were in favor of the Comstocks; they had patriotism on their side and the help of all the swine who flourished in those days; nevertheless, Harris gave them a severe beating, and scared them half to death. In brief, a man of the most extreme bellicosity, enterprise and courage—a fellow whose ideas are expressed absolutely regardless of tender feelings, whether genuine or bogus. In "The Man Shakespeare" and "The Women of Shakespeare" he tackled the whole body of academic English critics *en masse*—and routed them *en masse*. The two books, marred perhaps by a too bombastic spirit, yet contain some of the soundest, shrewdest and most convincing criticism of Shakespeare that has ever been written. All the old hocus-pocus is thrown overboard. There is an entirely new examination of the materials, and to the business is brought a knowledge of the plays so ready and so vast that that of even the most learned don begins to seem a mere smattering. The same great grasp of facts and evidences is visible in the sketches which make up the three volumes of "Contemporary Portraits." What one always gets out of them is a feeling that the man knows the men he is writing about—that he not only knows what he sets down, but a great deal more. There is here nothing of the cold correctness of the usual literary "estimate." Warts are not forgotten, whether of the nose or of the immortal soul. The subject, beginning as a political shibboleth or a row of books, gradually takes on all the colors of life, and then begins to move, naturally and freely. I know of no more brilliant evocations of personality in any literature—and most of them are personalities of sharp flavor, for Harris, in his day, seems to have known almost everybody worth knowing, and whoever he knew went into his laboratory for vivisection.

The man is thus a first rate critic of his time, and what he has written about his contemporaries is certain to condition the view of them held in the future. What gives him his value in this difficult field is, first of all and perhaps most important of all, his cynical detachment—his capacity for viewing men and ideas objectively. In his life, of course, there have been friendships and some of them have been strong and long-continued, but when he writes it is with a sort of surgical remoteness, as if the business in hand were vastly more important than the man. He was lately protesting violently that he was and is quite devoid of malice. Granted. But so is a surgeon. To write of George Moore as he has written may be writing devoid of malice, but nevertheless the effect is precisely that which would follow if some malicious enemy were to drag poor George out of his celibate couch in the dead of night, and chase him naked down Shaftsbury avenue. The thing is appallingly revelatory—and I believe that it is true. The Moore that he depicts may not be absolutely the real Moore, but he is unquestionably far nearer to the real Moore than the Moore of the Moore books. The method, of course, has its defects. Harris is far more interested, fundamentally, in men than in their ideas: the catholic sweep of his "Contemporary Portraits" proves it. In consequence his judgments of books are often colored by his opinions of their authors. He dislikes Mark Twain as his own antithesis: a trimmer and poltroon. *Ergo*, "A Connecticut Yankee" is drivel, which leads us, as Euclid hath it, to absurdity. He once had a row with Dreiser. *Ergo*, "The Titan" is nonsense, which is itself nonsense. But I know of no critic who is wholly free from that quite human weakness. In the academic bunkophagi it is everything; they are willing to swallow anything so long as the author is sound upon the League of Nations. It seems to me that such aberrations are rarer in Harris than in most. He may have violent prejudices, but it is seldom that they play upon a man who is honest.

I judge from his frequent discussions of himself—he is happily free from the vanity of modesty—that the pets of his secret heart are his ventures into fiction, and especially, "The Bomb" and "Montes the Matador." The latter has been greatly praised by Arnold Bennett, who has also praised Leonard Merrick. I have read it four or five times, and always with enjoyment. It is a powerful and adept tale; well constructed and beautifully written; it recalls some of the best of the shorter stories of Thomas Hardy. Alongside it one might range half a dozen other Harris stories—all of them carefully put together, every one the work of a very skillful journeyman. But despite Harris, the authentic Harris is not the story-writer: he has talents, of course, but it would be absurd to put "Montes the Matador" beside "Heart of Darkness." In "Love in Youth" he descends to unmistakable fluff and feebleness. The real Harris is the author of the Wilde volumes, of the two books about Shakespeare, of the three volumes of "Contemporary Portraits." Here there is stuff that lifts itself clearly and brilliantly above the general—criticism that has a terrific vividness and plausibility, and all the gusto that the professors can never pump up. Harris makes his opinions not only interesting, but important. What he has to say always seems novel, ingenious, and true. Here is the chief lifework of an American who, when all values are reckoned up, will be found to have been a sound artist and an extremely intelligent, courageous and original man—and infinitely the superior of the poor dolts who once tried so childishly to dispose of him.

5
Havelock Ellis

If the test of the personal culture of a man be the degree of his freedom from the banal ideas and childish emotions which move the great masses of men, then Havelock Ellis is undoubtedly the most civilized Englishman of his generation. He is a man of the soundest and widest learning, but it is not his positive learning that gives him distinction; it is his profound and implacable skepticism, his penetrating eye for the transient, the disingenuous, and the shoddy. So unconditioned a skepticism, it must be plain, is not an English habit. The average Englishman of science, though he may challenge the Continentals within his speciality, is only too apt to sink to the level of a politician, a green grocer, or a suburban clergyman outside it. The examples of Wallace, Crookes, and Lodge are anything but isolated. Scratch an English naturalist and you are likely to discover a spiritualist; take an English metaphysician to where the band is playing, and if he begins to snuffle patriotically you need not be surprised. The late war uncovered this weakness in a wholesale manner. The English *Gelehrten*, as a class, not only stood by their country; they also stood by the Hon. David Lloyd George, the *Daily Mail*, and the mob in Trafalgar Square. Unluckily, the asinine manifestations ensuing —for instance, the "proofs" of the eminent Oxford philologist that the Germans had never contributed anything to philology—are not to be described with good grace by an American, for they were far surpassed on this side of the water. England at least had Ellis, with Bertrand Russell, Wilfrid Scawen Blunt, and a few others in the background. We had, on that plane, no one.

Ellis, it seems to me, stood above all the rest, and precisely because his dissent from the prevailing imbecilities was quite devoid of emotion and had nothing in it of brummagen moral purpose. Too many of the heretics of the time were simply orthodox witch-hunters off on an unaccustomed tangent. In their disorderly indignation they matched the regular professors; it was only in the objects of their ranting that they differed. But Ellis kept his head throughout. An Englishman of the oldest native stock, an unapologetic lover of English scenes and English ways, an unshaken believer in the essential soundness and high historical destiny of his people, he simply stood aside from the current clown-show and waited in patience for sense and decency to be restored. His "Impressions and Comments," the record of his war-time reflections, is not without its note of melancholy; it was hard to look on without depression. But for the man of genuine culture there were at least some resources remaining within himself, and what gives this volume its chief value is its picture of how such a man made use of them. Ellis, facing the mob unleashed, turned to concerns and ideas beyond its comprehension—to the humanism that stands above all such sordid conflicts. There is something almost of Renaissance dignity in his chronicle of his speculations. The man that emerges is not a mere scholar immured in a cell, but a man of the world superior to his race and his time—a philosopher viewing the childish passion of lesser men disdainfully and yet not too remote to understand it, and even to see in it a certain cosmic use. A fine air blows through the book. It takes the reader into the company of one whose mind is a rich library and whose manner is that of a gentleman. He is the complete anti-Kipling. In him the Huxleian tradition comes to full flower.

His discourse ranges from Beethoven to Comstockery and from Spanish architecture to the charm of the English village. The extent of the man's knowledge is really quite appalling. His primary work in the world has been that of a psychologist, and in particular he has brought a great erudition and an extraordinarily sound judgment to the vexatious problems of the psychology of sex, but that professional concern, extending over so many years, has not prevented him from entering a dozen other domains of speculation, nor has it dulled his sensitiveness to beauty nor his capacity to evoke it. His writing was never better than in this volume. His style, especially towards the end, takes on a sort of glowing clarity. It is English that is as transparent as a crystal, and yet it is English that is full of fine colors and cadences. There could be no better investiture for the questionings and conclusions of so original, so curious, so learned, and, above all, so sound and hearty a man.

IX.

The Nature of Liberty

EVERY time an officer of the constabulary, in the execution of his just and awful powers under American law, produces a compound fracture of the occiput of some citizen in his custody, with hemorrhage, shock, coma and death, there comes a feeble, falsetto protest from specialists in human liberty. Is it a fact without significance that this protest is never supported by the great body of American freemen, setting aside the actual heirs and creditors of the victim? I think not. Here, as usual, public opinion is very realistic. It does not rise against the policeman for the plain and simple reason that it does not question his right to do what he has done. Policemen are not given night-sticks for ornament. They are given them for the purpose of cracking the skulls of the recalcitrant plain people, Democrats and Republicans alike. When they execute that high duty they are palpably within their rights.

The specialists aforesaid are the same fanatics who shake the air with sobs every time the Postmaster-General of the United States bars a periodical from the mails because its ideas do not please him, and every time some poor Russian is deported for reading Karl Marx, and every time a Prohibition enforcement officer murders a bootlegger who resists his levies, and every time agents of the Department of Justice throw an Italian out of the window, and every time the Ku Klux Klan or the American Legion tars and feathers a Socialist evangelist. In brief, they are Radicals, and to scratch one with a pitchfork is to expose a Bolshevik. They are men standing in contempt of American institutions and in enmity to American idealism. And their evil principles are no less offensive to right-thinking and red-blooded Americans when they are United States Senators or editors of wealthy newspapers than when they are degraded I.W.W.'s throwing dead cats and infernal machines into meetings of the Rotary Club.

What ails them primarily is the ignorant and uncritical monomania that afflicts every sort of fanatic, at all times and everywhere. Having mastered with their limited faculties the theoretical principles set forth in the Bill of Rights, they work themselves into a passionate conviction that those principles are identical with the rules of law and justice, and ought to be enforced literally, and without the slightest regard for circumstance and expediency. It is precisely as if a High Church rector, accidentally looking into the Book of Chronicles, and especially Chapter II, should suddenly issue a mandate from his pulpit ordering his parishioners, on penalty of excommunication and the fires of hell, to follow exactly the example set forth, to wit: "And Jesse begat his first born Eliab, and Abinadab the second, and Shimma the third, Netheneel the fourth, Raddai the fifth, Ozen the sixth, David the seventh," and so on. It might be very sound theoretical theology, but it would surely be out of harmony with modern ideas, and the rev. gentleman would be extremely lucky if the bishop did not give him 10 days in the diocesan hoosegow.

So with the Bill of Rights. As adopted by the Fathers of the Republic, it was gross, crude, inelastic, a bit fanciful and transcendental. It specified the rights of a citizen, but it said nothing whatever about his duties. Since then, by the orderly processes of legislative science and by the even more subtle and beautiful devices of juridic art, it has been kneaded and mellowed into a far greater pliability and reasonableness. On the one hand, the citizen still retains the great privilege of membership in the most superb free nation ever witnessed on this earth. On the other hand, as a result of countless shrewd enactments and sagacious decisions, his natural lusts and appetites are held in laudable check, and he is thus kept in order and decorum. No artificial impediment stands in the way of his highest aspiration. He may become anything, including even a policeman. But once a policeman, he is protected by the legislative and judicial arms in the peculiar rights and prerogatives that go with his high office, including especially the right to jug the laity at his will, to sweat and mug them, to subject them to the third degree, and to subdue their resistance by beating out their brains. Those who are unaware of this are simply ignorant of the basic principles of American jurisprudence, as they have been exposed times without number by the courts of first instance and ratified in lofty terms by the

Supreme Court of the United States. The one aim of the controlling decisions, magnificently attained, is to safeguard public order and the public security, and to substitute a judicial process for the inchoate and dangerous interaction of discordant egos.

Let us imagine an example. You are, say, a peaceable citizen on your way home from your place of employment. A police sergeant, detecting you in the crowd, approaches you, lays his hand on your collar, and informs you that you are under arrest for killing a trolley conductor in Altoona, Pa., in 1917. Amazed by the accusation, you decide hastily that the officer has lost his wits, and take to your heels. He pursues you. You continue to run. He draws his revolver and fires at you. He misses you. He fires again and fetches you in the leg. You fall and he is upon you. You prepare to resist his apparently maniacal assault. He beats you into insensibility with his espantoon, and drags you to the patrol box.

Arrived at the watch house you are locked in a room with five detectives, and for six hours they question you with subtle art. You grow angry—perhaps robbed of your customary politeness by the throbbing in your head and leg—and answer tartly. They knock you down. Having failed to wring a confession from you, they lock you in a cell, and leave you there all night. The next day you are taken to police headquarters, your photograph is made for the Rogues' Gallery, and a print is duly deposited in the section labeled "Murderers." You are then carted to jail and locked up again. There you remain until the trolley conductor's wife comes down from Altoona to identify you. She astonishes the police by saying that you are not the man. The actual murderer, it appears, was an Italian. After holding you a day or two longer, to search your house for stills, audit your income tax returns, and investigate the premarital chastity of your wife, they let you go.

You are naturally somewhat irritated by your experience and perhaps your wife urges you to seek redress. Well, what are your remedies? If you are a firebrand, you reach out absurdly for those of a preposterous nature: the instant jailing of the sergeant, the dismissal of the Police Commissioner, the release of Mooney, a fair trial for Sacco and Vanzetti, free trade with Russia, One Big Union. But if you are a 100 per cent. American and respect the laws and institutions of your country, you send for your solicitor—and at once he shows you just how far your rights go, and where they end. You cannot cause the arrest of the sergeant, for you resisted him when he attempted to arrest you, and when you resisted him he acquired an instant right to take you by force. You cannot proceed against him for accusing you falsely, for he has a right to make summary arrests for felony, and the courts have many times decided that a public officer, so long as he cannot be charged with corruption or malice, is not liable for errors of judgment made in the execution of his sworn duty. You cannot get the detectives on the mat, for when they questioned you you were a prisoner accused of murder, and it was their duty and their right to do so. You cannot sue the turnkey at the watch house or the warden at the jail for locking you up, for they received your body, as the law says, in a lawful and regular manner, and would have been liable to penalty if they had turned you loose.

But have you no redress whatever, no rights at all? Certainly you have a right, and the courts have jealously guarded it. You have a clear right, guaranteed to you under the Constitution, to go into a court of equity and apply for a mandamus requiring the *Polizei* to cease forthwith to expose your portrait in the Rogues' Gallery among the murderers. This is your inalienable right, and no man or men on earth can take it away from you. You cannot prevent them cherishing your portrait in their secret files, but you can get an order commanding them to refrain forever from exposing it to the gaze of idle visitors, and if you can introduce yourself unseen into their studio and prove that they disregard that order, you can have them haled into court for contempt and fined by the learned judge.

Thus the law, statute, common and case, protects the free American against injustice. It is ignorance of that subtle and perfect process and not any special love of liberty *per se* that causes radicals of anti-American kidney to rage every time an officer of the *gendarmerie*, in the simple execution of his duty, knocks a citizen in the head. The *gendarme* plainly has an inherent and inalienable right to knock him in the head: it is an essential part of his general prerogative as a sworn officer of the public peace and a representative of the sovereign power of the state. He may, true enough, exercise that prerogative in a manner liable to challenge on the ground that it is imprudent and lacking in sound judgment. On such questions reasonable men may differ. But it must be obvious that the sane and decorous way to settle differences of opinion of that sort is not by public outcry and florid appeals to sentimentality, not by ill-disguised playing to class consciousness and antisocial prejudice, but by an orderly resort to the checks and remedies superimposed upon the Bill of Rights by the calm deliberation and austere logic of the courts of equity.

The law protects the citizen. But to get its protection he must show due respect for its wise and delicate processes.

X.
The Novel

An unmistakable flavor of effeminacy hangs about the novel, however heroic its content. Even in the gaudy tales of a Rex Beach, with their bold projections of the Freudian dreams of go-getters, ice-wagon drivers, Ku Kluxers, Rotary Club presidents and other such carnivora, there is a subtle something that suggests water-color painting, lip-sticks and bon-bons. Well, why not? When the novel, in the form that we know to-day, arose in Spain toward the end of the sixteenth century, it was aimed very frankly at the emerging women of the Castilian seraglios—women who were gradually emancipating themselves from the *Küche-Kinder-Kirche* darkness of the later Middle Ages, but had not yet come to anything even remotely approaching the worldly experience and intellectual curiosity of men. They could now read and they liked to practice the art, but the grand literature of the time was too profound for them, and too somber. So literary confectioners undertook stuff that would be more to their taste, and the modern novel was born. A single plot served most of these confectioners; it became and remains one of the conventions of the form. Man and maid meet, love, and proceed to kiss—but the rest must wait. The buss remains chaste through long and harrowing chapters; not until the very last scene do fate and Holy Church license anything more. This plot, as I say, still serves, and Arnold Bennett is authority for the doctrine that it is the safest known. Its appeal is patently to the feminine fancy, not to the masculine. Women like to be wooed endlessly before they loose their girdles and are wooed no more. But a man, when he finds a damsel to his taste, is eager to get through the preliminary hocus-pocus as soon as possible.

That women are still the chief readers of novels is known to every book clerk: Joseph Hergesheimer, a little while back, was bemoaning the fact as a curse to his craft. What is less often noted is that women themselves, as they have gradually become fully literate, have forced their way to the front as makers of the stuff they feed on, and that they show signs of ousting the men, soon or late, from the business. Save in the department of lyrical verse, which demands no organization of ideas but only fluency of feeling, they have nowhere else done serious work in literature. There is no epic poem of any solid value by a woman, dead or alive; and no drama, whether comedy or tragedy; and no work of metaphysical speculation; and no history; and no basic document in any other realm of thought. In criticism, whether of works of art or of the ideas underlying them, few women have ever got beyond the *Schwärmerei* of Madame de Staël's "L'Allemagne." In the essay, the most competent woman barely surpasses the average Fleet Street *causerie* hack or Harvard professor. But in the novel the ladies have stood on a level with even the most accomplished men since the day of Jane Austen, and not only in Anglo-Saxondom, but also everywhere else—save perhaps in Russia. To-day it would be difficult to think of a contemporary German novelist of sounder dignity than Clara Viebig, Helene Böhlau or Ricarda Huch, or a Scandinavian novelist clearly above Selma Lagerlöf, or an Italian above Mathilda Serao, or, for that matter, more than two or three living Englishmen above May Sinclair, or more than two Americans equal to Willa Cather. Not only are women writing novels quite as good as those written by men—setting aside, of course, a few miraculous pieces by such fellows as Joseph Conrad: most of them not really novels at all, but metaphysical sonatas disguised as romances—; they are actually surpassing men in their experimental development of the novel form. I do not believe that either Evelyn Scott's "The Narrow House" or May Sinclair's "Life and Death of Harriet Frean" has the depth and beam of, say, Dreiser's "Jennie Gerhardt" or Arnold Bennett's "Old Wives' Tale," but it is certainly to be argued plausibly that both books show a far greater venturesomeness and a far finer virtuosity in the novel form—that both seek to free that form from artificialities which Dreiser and Bennett seem to be almost unaware of. When men exhibit any discontent with those artificialities it usually takes the shape of a vain and uncouth revolt against the whole inner spirit of the novel—that is, against the characteristics which make it what it is. Their lusher imagination tempts them to try to convert it into something that it isn't—for example, an epic, a political document, or a philosophical work. This fact explains, in one direction, such dialectical parables as Dreiser's "The 'Genius,'" H. G. Wells' "Joan and Peter" and Upton Sinclair's "King Coal," and, in a quite different direction, such rhapsodies as Cabell's "Jurgen," Meredith's "The Shaving of Shagpat" and Jacob Wassermann's "The World's Illusion." These things are novels only in the very limited sense that Beethoven's "Vittoria" and Goldmark's "Landliche Hochzeit" are symphonies. Their chief purpose is not that of prose fiction; it is either that of argumentation or that of poetry. The women novelists, with very few exceptions, are far more careful to remain within the legitimate bounds of the form; they do not often abandon representation to exhort or exult. Miss Cather's "My Ántonia" shows a great deal of originality in its method; the story it tells is certainly not a conventional one, nor is it told in a conventional way. But it remains a novel none the less, and as clearly so, in fact, as "The Ordeal of Richard Feverel" or "Robinson Crusoe."

Much exertion of the laryngeal and respiratory muscles is wasted upon a discussion of the differences between realistic novels and romantic novels. As a matter of fact, every authentic novel is realistic in its method, however fantastic it may be in its fable. The primary aim of the novel, at all times and everywhere, is the representation of human beings at their follies and villainies, and no other art form clings to that aim so faithfully. It sets forth, not what might be true, or what ought to be true, but what actually *is* true. This is obviously not the case with poetry. Poetry is the product of an effort to invent a world appreciably better than the one we live in; its essence is not the representation of the facts, but the deliberate concealment and denial of the facts. As for the drama, it vacillates, and if it touches the novel on one side it also touches the epic on the other. But the novel is concerned solely with human nature as it is practically revealed and with human experience as men actually know it. If it departs from that representational fidelity ever so slightly, it becomes to that extent a bad novel; if it departs violently it ceases to be a novel at all. Cabell, who shows all the critical deficiencies of a sound artist, is one who has spent a good deal of time questioning the uses of realism. Yet it is a plain fact that his own stature as an artist depends almost wholly upon his capacity for accurate observation and realistic representation. The stories in "The Line of Love," though they may appear superficially to be excessively romantic, really owe all of their charm to their pungent realism. The pleasure they give is the pleasure of recognition; one somehow delights in seeing a mediæval baron acting precisely like a New York stockbroker. As for "Jurgen," it is as realistic in manner as Zola's "La Terre," despite its grotesque fable and its burden of political, theological and epistemological ideas. No one not an idiot would mistake the dialogue between Jurgen and Queen Guinevere's father for romantic, in the sense that Kipling's "Mandalay" is romantic; it is actually as mordantly realistic as the dialogue between Nora and Helmer in the last act of "A Doll's House."

It is my contention that women succeed in the novel—and that they will succeed even more strikingly as they gradually throw off the inhibitions that have hitherto cobwebbed their minds—simply because they are better fitted for this realistic representation than men—because they see the facts of life more sharply, and are less distracted by mooney dreams. Women seldom have the pathological faculty vaguely called imagination. One doesn't often hear of them groaning over colossal bones in their sleep, as dogs do, or constructing heavenly hierarchies or political utopias, as men do. Their concern is always with things of more objective substance—roofs, meals, rent, clothes, the birth and upbringing of children. They are, I believe, generally happier than men, if only because the demands they make of life are more moderate and less romantic. The chief pain that a man normally suffers in his progress through this vale is that of disillusionment; the chief pain that a woman suffers is that of parturition. There is enormous significance in the difference. The first is artificial and self-inflicted the second is natural and unescapable. The psychological history of the differentiation I need not go into here: its springs lie obviously in the greater physical strength of man and his freedom from child-bearing, and in the larger mobility and capacity for adventure that go therewith. A man dreams of utopias simply because he feels himself free to construct them; a woman must keep house. In late years, to be sure, she has toyed with the idea of escaping that necessity, but I shall not bore you with arguments showing that she never will. So long as children are brought into the world and made ready for the trenches, the sweatshops and the gallows by the laborious method ordained of God she will never be quite as free to roam and dream as man is. It is only a small minority of her sex who cherish a contrary expectation, and this minority, though anatomically female, is spiritually male. Show me a woman who has visions comparable, say, to those of Swedenborg, Woodrow Wilson, Strindberg or Dr. Ghandi, and I'll show you a woman who is a very powerful anaphrodisiac.

Thus women, by their enforced preoccupation with the harsh facts of life, are extremely well fitted to write novels, which must deal with the facts or nothing. What they need for the practical business, in addition, falls under two heads. First, they need enough sense of social security to make them free to set down what they see. Secondly, they need the modest technical skill, the formal mastery of words and ideas, necessary to do it. The latter, I believe, they have had ever since they learned to read and write, say three hundred years ago; it comes to them more readily than to men, and is exercised with greater ease. The former they are fast acquiring. In the days of Aphra Behn and Ann Radcliffe it was almost as scandalous for a woman to put her observations and notions into print as it was for her to show her legs; even in the days of Jane Austen and Charlotte Brontë the thing was regarded as decidedly unladylike. But now, within certain limits, she is free to print whatever she pleases, and before long even those surviving limits will be obliterated. If I live to the year 1950 I expect to see a novel by a women that will describe a typical marriage under Christianity, from the woman's standpoint, as realistically as it is treated from the man's standpoint in Upton Sinclair's "Love's Pilgrimage." That novel, I venture to predict, will be a cuckoo. At one stroke it will demolish superstitions that have prevailed in the Western World since the fall of the Roman Empire. It will seem harsh, but it will be true. And, being true, it will be a good novel. There can be no good one that is not true.

What ailed the women novelists, until very recently, was a lingering ladyism—a childish prudery inherited from their mothers. I believe that it is being rapidly thrown off; indeed, one often sees a concrete woman novelist shedding it. I give you two obvious examples: Zona Gale and Willa Cather. Miss Gale started out by trying to put into novels the conventional prettiness that is esteemed along the Main Streets of her native Wisconsin. She had skill and did it well, and so she won a good deal of popular success. But her work was intrinsically as worthless as a treatise on international politics by the Hon. Warren Gamaliel Harding or a tract on the duties of a soldier and a gentleman by a state president of the American Legion. Then, of a sudden, for some reason quite unknown to the deponent, she threw off all that flabby artificiality, and began describing the people about her as they really were. The result was a second success even more pronounced than her first, and on a palpably higher level. The career of Miss Cather has covered less ground, for she began far above Main Street. What she tried to do at the start was to imitate the superficial sophistication of Edith Wharton and Henry James—a deceptive thing, apparently realistic in essence, but actually as conventional as table manners or the professional buffooneries of a fashionable rector. Miss Cather had extraordinary skill as a writer, and so her imitation was scarcely to be distinguished from the original, but in the course of time she began to be aware of its hollowness. Then she turned to first-hand representation—to pictures of the people she actually knew. There ensued a series of novels that rose step by step to the very distinguished quality of "My Ántonia." That fine piece is a great deal more than simply a good novel. It is a document in the history of American literature. It proves, once and for all time, that accurate representation is not, as the campus critics of Dreiser seem to think, inimical to beauty. It proves, on the contrary, that the most careful and penetrating representation is itself the source of a rare and wonderful beauty. No romantic novel ever written in America, by man or woman, is one-half so beautiful as "My Ántonia."

As I have said, the novel, in the United States as elsewhere, still radiates an aroma of effeminacy, in the conventional sense. Specifically, it deals too monotonously with the varieties of human transactions which chiefly interest the unintelligent women who are its chief patrons and the scarcely less intelligent women who, until recently, were among its chief commercial manufacturers, to wit, the transactions that revolve around the ensnarement of men by women—the puerile tricks and conflicts of what is absurdly called romantic love. But I believe that the women novelists, as they emerge into the fullness of skill, will throw overboard all that old baggage, and leave its toting to such male artisans as Chambers, Beach, Coningsby Dawson and Emerson Hough, as they have already left the whole flag-waving and "red-blooded" buncombe. True enough, the snaring of men will remain the principal business of women in this world for many generations, but it would be absurd to say that intelligent women, even to-day, view it romantically—that is, as it is viewed by bad novelists. They see it realistically, and they see it, not as an end in itself, but as a means to other ends. It is, speaking generally, after she has got her man that a woman begins to live. The novel of the future, I believe, will show her thus living. It will depict the intricate complex of forces that conditions her life and generates her ideas, and it will show, against a background of actuality, her conduct in the eternal struggle between her aspiration and her destiny. Women, as I have argued, are not normally harassed by the grandiose and otiose visions that inflame the gizzards of men, but they too discover inevitably that life is a conflict, and that it is the harsh fate of *Homo sapiens* to get the worst of it. I should like to read a "Main Street" by an articulate Carol Kennicott, or a "Titan" by one of Cowperwood's mistresses, or a "Cytherea" by a Fanny Randon—or a Savina Grove! It would be sweet stuff, indeed. . . . And it will come.

XI.
The Forward-Looker

WHEN the history of the late years in America is written, I suspect that their grandest, gaudiest gifts to *Kultur* will be found in the incomparable twins: the right-thinker, and the forward-looker. No other nation can match them, at any weight. The right-thinker is privy to all God's wishes, and even whims; the forward-looker is the heir to all His promises to the righteous. The former is never wrong; the latter is never despairing. Sometimes the two are amalgamated into one man, and we have a Bryan, a Wilson, a Dr. Frank Crane. But more often there is a division: the forward-looker thinks wrong, and the right-thinker looks backward. I give you Upton Sinclair and Nicholas Murray Butler as examples. Butler is an absolute masterpiece of correct thought; in his whole life, so far as human records show, he has not cherished a single fancy that might not have been voiced by a Fifth Avenue rector or spread upon the editorial page of the New York *Times.* But he has no vision, alas, alas! All the revolutionary inventions for lifting up humanity leave him cold. He is against them all, from the initiative and referendum to birth control, and from Fletcherism to osteopathy. Now turn to Sinclair. He believes in every one of them, however daring and fantoddish; he grasps and gobbles all the new ones the instant they are announced. But the man simply cannot think right. He is wrong on politics, on economics, and on theology. He glories in and is intensely vain of his wrongness. Let but a new article of correct American thought get itself stated by the constituted ecclesiastical and secular authorities—by Bishop Manning, or Judge Gary, or Butler, or Adolph Ochs, or Dr. Fabian Franklin, or Otto Kahn, or Dr. Stephen S. Wise, or Roger W. Babson, or any other such inspired omphalist—and he is against it almost before it is stated.

On the whole, as a neutral in such matters, I prefer the forward-looker to the right-thinker, if only because he shows more courage and originality. It takes nothing save lack of humor to believe what Butler, or Ochs, or Bishop Manning believes, but it takes long practice and a considerable natural gift to get down the beliefs of Sinclair. I remember with great joy the magazine that he used to issue during the war. In the very first issue he advocated Socialism, the single tax, birth control, communism, the League of Nations, the conscription of wealth, government ownership of coal mines, sex hygiene and free trade. In the next issue he added the recall of judges, Fletcherism, the Gary system, the Montessori method, paper-bag cookery, war gardens and the budget system. In the third he came out for sex hygiene, one big union, the initiative and referendum, the city manager plan, chiropractic and Esperanto. In the fourth he went to the direct primary, fasting, the Third International, a federal divorce law, free motherhood, hot lunches for school children, Prohibition, the vice crusade, *Expressionismus*, the government control of newspapers, deep breathing, international courts, the Fourteen Points, freedom for the Armenians, the limitation of campaign expenditures, the merit system, the abolition of the New York Stock Exchange, psychoanalysis, crystal-gazing, the Little Theater movement, the recognition of Mexico, *vers libre*, old age pensions, unemployment insurance, coöperative stores, the endowment of motherhood, the Americanization of the immigrant, mental telepathy, the abolition of grade crossings, federal labor exchanges, profit-sharing in industry, a prohibitive tax on Poms, the clean-up-paint-up campaign, relief for the Jews, osteopathy, mental mastery, and the twilight sleep. And so on, and so on. Once I had got into the swing of the Sinclair monthly I found that I could dispense with at least twenty other journals of the uplift. When he abandoned it I had to subscribe for them anew, and the gravel has stuck in my craw ever since.

In the first volume of his personal philosophy, "The Book of Life: Mind and Body," he is estopped from displaying whole categories of his ideas, for his subject is not man the political and economic machine, but man and mammal. Nevertheless, his characteristic hospitality to new revelations is abundantly visible. What does the mind suggest? The mind suggests its dark and fascinating functions and powers, some of them very recent. There is, for example, psychoanalysis. There is mental telepathy. There is crystal-gazing. There is double personality. Out of each springs a scheme for the uplift of the race—in each there is something for a forward-looker to get his teeth into. And if mind, then why not also spirit? Here even a forward-looker may hesitate; here, in fact, Sinclair himself hesitates. The whole field of spiritism is barred to him by his theological heterodoxy; if he admits that man has an immortal soul, he may also have to admit that the soul can suffer in hell. Thus even forward-looking may turn upon and devour itself. But if the meadow wherein spooks and poltergeists disport is closed, it is at least possible to peep over the fence. Sinclair sees materializations in dark rooms, under red, satanic lights. He is, perhaps, not yet convinced, but he is looking pretty hard. Let a ghostly hand reach out and grab him, and he will be over the fence! The body is easier. The new inventions for dealing with it are innumerable and irresistible; no forward-looker can fail to succumb to at least some of them. Sinclair teeters dizzily. On the one hand he stoutly defends surgery—that is, provided the patient is allowed to make his own diagnosis!—on the other hand he is hot for fasting, teetotalism, and the avoidance of drugs, coffee and tobacco, and he begins to flirt with osteopathy and chiropractic. More, he has discovered a new revelation in San Francisco—a system of diagnosis and therapeutics, still hooted at by the Medical Trust, whereby the exact location of a cancer may be determined by examining a few drops of the patient's blood, and syphilis may be cured by vibrations, and whereby, most curious of all, it can be established that odd numbers, written on a sheet of paper, are full of negative electricity, and even numbers are full of positive electricity.

The book is written with great confidence and address, and has a good deal of shrewdness mixed with its credulities; few licensed medical practitioners could give you better advice. But it is less interesting than its author, or, indeed, than forward-lookers in general. Of all the known orders of men they fascinate me the most. I spend whole days reading their pronunciamentos, and am an expert in the ebb and flow of their singularly bizarre ideas. As I have said, I have never encountered one who believed in but one sure cure for all the sorrows of the world, and let it go at that. Nay, even the most timorous of them gives his full faith and credit to at least two. Turn, for example, to the official list of eminent single taxers issued by the Joseph Fels Fund. I defy you to find one solitary man on it who stops with the single tax. There is David Starr Jordan: he is also one of the great whales of pacifism. There is B. O. Flower: he is the emperor of anti-vaccinationists. There is Carrie Chapman Catt: she is hot for every peruna that the suffragettes brew. There is W. S. U'Ren: he is in general practise as a messiah. There is Hamlin Garland: he also chases spooks. There is Jane Addams: vice crusader, pacifist, suffragist, settlement worker. There is Prof. Dr. Scott Nearing: Socialist and martyr. There is Newt Baker: heir of the Wilsonian idealism. There is Gifford Pinchot: conservationist, Prohibitionist, Bull Moose, and professional Good Citizen. There is Judge Ben B. Lindsey: forward-looking's Jack Horner, forever sticking his thumb into new pies. I could run the list to columns, but no need. You know the type as well as I do. Give the forward-looker the direct primary, and he demands the short ballot. Give him the initiative and referendum, and he bawls for the recall of judges. Give him Christian Science, and he proceeds to the swamis and yogis. Give him the Mann Act, and he wants laws providing for the castration of fornicators. Give him Prohibition, and he launches a new crusade against cigarettes, coffee, jazz, and custard pies.

I have a wide acquaintance among such sad, mad, glad folks, and know some of them very well. It is my belief that the majority of them are absolutely honest—that they believe as fully in their baroque gospels as I believe in the dishonesty of politicians—that their myriad and amazing faiths sit upon them as heavily as the fear of hell sits upon a Methodist deacon who has degraded the vestry-room to carnal uses. All that may be justly said against them is that they are chronically full of hope, and hence chronically uneasy and indignant—that they belong to the less sinful and comfortable of the two grand divisions of the human race. Call them the tender-minded, as the late William James used to do, and you have pretty well described them. They are, on the one hand, pathologically sensitive to the sorrows of the world, and, on the other hand, pathologically susceptible to the eloquence of quacks. What seems to lie in all of them is the doctrine that evils so vast as those they see about them *must* and *will* be laid—that it would be an insult to a just God to think of them as permanent and irremediable. This notion, I believe, is at the bottom of much of the current pathetic faith in Prohibition. The thing itself is obviously a colossal failure—that is, when viewed calmly and realistically. It has not only not cured the rum evil in the United States; it has plainly made that evil five times as bad as it ever was before. But to confess that bald fact would be to break the forward-looking heart: it simply refuses to harbor the concept of the incurable. And so, being debarred by the legal machinery that supports Prohibition from going back to any more feasible scheme of relief, it cherishes the sorry faith that somehow, in some vague and incomprehensible way, Prohibition will yet work. When the truth becomes so horribly evident that even forward-lookers are daunted, then some new quack will arise to fool them again, with some new and worse scheme of super-Prohibition. It is their destiny to wobble thus endlessly between quack and quack. One pulls them by the right arm and one by the left arm. A third is at their coat-tail pockets, and a fourth beckons them over the hill.

The rest of us are less tender-minded, and, in consequence, much happier. We observe quite clearly that the world, as it stands, is anything but perfect—that injustice exists, and turmoil, and tragedy, and bitter suffering of ten thousand kinds—that human life, at its best, is anything but a grand, sweet song. But instead of ranting absurdly against the fact, or weeping over it maudlinly, or trying to remedy it with inadequate means, we simply put the thought of it out of our minds, just as a wise man puts away the thought that alcohol is probably bad for his liver, or that his wife is a shade too fat. Instead of mulling over it and suffering from it, we seek contentment by pursuing the delights that are so strangely mixed with the horrors—by seeking out the soft spots and endeavoring to avoid the hard spots. Such is the intelligent habit of practical and sinful men, and under it lies a sound philosophy. After all, the world is not our handiwork, and we are not responsible for what goes on in it, save within very narrow limits. Going outside them with our protests and advice tends to become contumacy to the celestial hierarchy. Do the poor suffer in the midst of plenty? Then let us thank God politely that we are not that poor. Are rogues in offices? Well, go call a policeman, thus setting rogue upon rogue. Are taxes onerous, wasteful, unjust? Then let us dodge as large a part of them as we can. Are whole regiments and army corps of our fellow creatures doomed to hell? Then let them complain to the archangels, and, if the archangels are too busy to hear them, to the nearest archbishop.

Unluckily for the man of tender mind, he is quite incapable of any such easy dismissal of the great plagues and conundrums of existence. It is of the essence of his character that he is too sensitive and sentimental to put them ruthlessly out of his mind: he cannot view even the crunching of a cockroach without feeling the snapping of his own ribs. And it is of the essence of his character that he is unable to escape the delusion of duty—that he can't rid himself of the notion that, whenever he observes anything in the world that might conceivably be improved, he is commanded by God to make every effort to improve it. In brief, he is a public-spirited man, and the ideal citizen of democratic states. But Nature, it must be obvious, is opposed to democracy—and whoso goes counter to nature must expect to pay the penalty. The tender-minded man pays it by hanging forever upon the cruel hooks of hope, and by fermenting inwardly in incessant indignation. All this, perhaps, explains the notorious ill-humor of uplifters—the wowser touch that is in even the best of them. They dwell so much upon the imperfections of the universe and the weaknesses of man that they end by believing that the universe is altogether out of joint and that every man is a scoundrel and every woman a vampire. Years ago I had a combat with certain eminent reformers of the sex hygiene and vice crusading species, and got out of it a memorable illumination of their private minds. The reform these strange creatures were then advocating was directed against sins of the seventh category, and they proposed to put them down by forcing through legislation of a very harsh and fantastic kind—statutes forbidding any woman, however forbidding, to entertain a man in her apartment without the presence of a third party, statutes providing for the garish lighting of all dark places in the public parks, and so on. In the course of my debates with them I gradually jockeyed them into abandoning all of the arguments they started with, and so brought them down to their fundamental doctrine, to wit, that no woman, without the aid of the police, could be trusted to protect her virtue. I pass as a cynic in Christian circles, but this notion certainly gave me pause. And it was voiced by men who were the fathers of grown and unmarried daughters!

It is no wonder that men who cherish such ideas are so ready to accept any remedy for the underlying evils, no matter how grotesque. A man suffering from hay-fever, as every one knows, will take any medicine that is offered to him, even though he knows the compounder to be a quack; the infinitesimal chance that the quack may have the impossible cure gives him a certain hope, and so makes the disease itself more bearable. In precisely the same way a man suffering from the conviction that the whole universe is hell-bent for destruction—that the government he lives under is intolerably evil, that the rich are growing richer and the poor poorer, that no man's word can be trusted and no woman's chastity, that another and worse war is hatching, that the very regulation of the weather has fallen into the hands of rogues—such a man will grab at anything, even birth control, osteopathy or the Fourteen Points, rather than let the foul villainy go on. The apparent necessity of finding a remedy without delay transforms itself, by an easy psychological process, into a belief that the remedy has been found; it is almost impossible for most men, and particularly for tender-minded men, to take in the concept of the insoluble. Every problem that remains unsolved, including even the problem of evil, is in that state simply because men of strict virtue and passionate altruism have not combined to solve it—because the business has been neglected by human laziness and rascality. All that is needed to dispatch it is the united effort of enough pure hearts: the accursed nature of things will yield inevitably to a sufficiently desperate battle; mind (usually written Mind) will triumph over matter (usually written Matter —or maybe Money Power, or Land Monopoly, or Beef Trust, or Conspiracy of Silence, or Commercialized Vice, or Wall Street, or the Dukes, or the Kaiser), and the Kingdom of God will be at hand. So, with the will to believe in full function, the rest is easy. The eager forward-looker is exactly like the man with hay-fever, or arthritis, or nervous dyspepsia, or diabetes. It takes time to try each successive remedy—to search it out, to take it, to observe its effects, to hope, to doubt, to shelve it. Before the process is completed another is offered; new ones are always waiting before their predecessors have been discarded. Here, perhaps, we get a glimpse of the causes behind the protean appetite of the true forward-looker—his virtuosity in credulity. He is in all stages simultaneously—just getting over the initiative and referendum, beginning to have doubts about the short ballot, making ready for a horse doctor's dose of the single tax, and contemplating an experimental draught of Socialism tomorrow.

What is to be done for him? How is he to be cured of his great thirst for sure-cures that do not cure, and converted into a contented and careless backward-looker, peacefully snoozing beneath his fig tree while the oppressed bawl for succor in forty abandoned lands, and injustice stalks the world, and taxes mount higher and higher, and poor working-girls are sold into white slavery, and Prohibition fails to prohibit, and cocaine is hawked openly, and jazz drags millions down the primrose way, and the trusts own the legislatures of all Christendom, and judges go to dinner with millionaires, and Europe prepares for another war, and children of four and five years work as stevedores and locomotive firemen, and guinea pigs and dogs are vivisected, and Polish immigrant women have more children every year, and divorces multiply, and materialism rages, and the devil runs the cosmos? What is to be done to save the forward-looker from his torturing indignation, and set him in paths of happy dalliance? Answer: nothing. He was born that way, as men are born with hare lips or bad livers, and he will remain that way until the angels summon him to eternal rest. Destiny has laid upon him the burden of seeing unescapably what had better not be looked at, of believing what isn't so. There is no way to help him. He must suffer vicariously for the carnal ease of the rest of us. He must die daily that we may live in peace, corrupt and contented.

As I have said, I believe fully that this child of sorrow is honest—that his twinges and malaises are just as real to him as those that rack the man with arthritis, and that his trusting faith in quacks is just as natural. But this, of course, is not saying that the quacks themselves are honest. On the contrary, their utter dishonesty must be quite as obvious as the simplicity of their dupes. Trade is good for them in the United States, where hope is a sort of national vice, and so they flourish here more luxuriously than anywhere else on earth. Some one told me lately that there are now no less than 25,000 national organizations in the United States for the uplift of the plain people and the snaring and shaking down of forward-lookers—societies for the Americanization of immigrants, for protecting poor working-girls against Jews and Italians, for putting Bibles into the bedrooms of week-end hotels, for teaching Polish women how to wash their babies, for instructing school-children in ring-around-a-rosy, for crusading against the cigarette, for preventing accidents in rolling-mills, for making street-car conductors more polite, for testing the mentality of Czecho-Slovaks, for teaching folk-songs, for restoring the United States to Great Britain, for building day-nurseries in the devastated regions of France, for training deaconesses, for fighting the house-fly, for preventing cruelty to mules and Tom-cats, for forcing householders to clean their backyards, for planting trees, for saving the Indian, for sending colored boys to Harvard, for opposing Sunday movies, for censoring magazines, for God knows what else. In every large American city such organizations swarm, and every one of them has an executive secretary who tries incessantly to cadge space in the newspapers. Their agents penetrate to the remotest hamlets in the land, and their circulars, pamphlets and other fulminations swamp the mails. In Washington and at every state capital they have their lobbyists, and every American legislator is driven half frantic by their innumerable and preposterous demands. Each of them wants a law passed to make its crusade official and compulsory; each is forever hunting for forward-lookers with money.

One of the latest of these uplifting vereins to score a ten-strike is the one that sponsored the so-called Maternity Bill. That measure is now a law, and the over-burdened American taxpayer, at a cost of $3,000,000 a year, is supporting yet one more posse of perambulating gabblers and snouters. The influences behind the bill were exposed in the Senate by Senator Reed, of Missouri, but to no effect: a majority of the other Senators, in order to get rid of the propagandists in charge of it, had already promised to vote for it. Its one intelligible aim, as Senator Reed showed, is to give government jobs at good salaries to a gang of nosey old maids. These virgins now traverse the country teaching married women how to have babies in a ship-shape and graceful manner, and how to keep them alive after having them. Only one member of the corps has ever been married herself; nevertheless, the old gals are authorized to go out among the Italian and Yiddish women, each with ten or twelve head of kids to her credit, and tell them all about it. According to Senator Reed, the ultimate aim of the forward-lookers who sponsored the scheme is to provide for the official registration of expectant mothers, that they may be warned what to eat, what movies to see, and what midwives to send for when the time comes. Imagine a young bride going down to the County Clerk's office to report herself! And imagine an elderly and anthropopagous spinster coming around next day to advise her! Or a boozy political doctor!

All these crazes, of course, are primarily artificial. They are set going, not by the plain people spontaneously, nor even by the forward-lookers who eventually support them, but by professionals. The Anti-Saloon League is their archetype. It is owned and operated by gentlemen who make excellent livings stirring up the tender-minded; if their salaries were cut off to-morrow, all their moral passion would ooze out, and Prohibition would be dead in two weeks. So with the rest of the uplifting camorras. Their present enormous prosperity, I believe, is due in large part to a fact that is never thought of, to wit, the fact that the women's colleges of the country, for a dozen years past, have been turning out far more graduates than could be utilized as teachers. These supernumerary lady Ph.D's almost unanimously turn to the uplift—and the uplift saves them. In the early days of higher education for women in the United States, practically all the graduates thrown upon the world got jobs as teachers, but now a good many are left over. Moreover, it has been discovered that the uplift is easier than teaching, and that it pays a great deal better. It is a rare woman professor who gets more than $5,000 a year, but there are plenty of uplifting jobs at $8,000 and $10,000 a year, and in the future there will be some prizes at twice as much. No wonder the learned girls fall upon them so eagerly!

The annual production of male Ph.D's is also far beyond the

legitimate needs of the nation, but here the congestion is relieved by the greater and more varied demand for masculine labor. If a young man emerging from Columbia or Ohio Wesleyan as *Philosophiæ Doctor* finds it impossible to get a job teaching he can always go on the road as a salesman of dental supplies, or enlist in the marines, or study law, or enter the ministry, or go to work in a coal-mine, or a slaughter-house, or a bucket-shop, or begin selling Oklahoma mine-stock to widows and retired clergymen. The woman graduate faces far fewer opportunities. She is commonly too old and too worn by meditation to go upon the stage in anything above the grade of a patent-medicine show, she has been so poisoned by instruction in sex hygiene that she shies at marriage, and most of the standard professions and grafts of the world are closed to her. The invention of the uplift came as a godsend to her. Had not some mute, inglorious Edison devised it at the right time, humanity would be disgraced to-day by the spectacle of hordes of Lady Ph.D's going to work in steam-laundries, hooch shows and chewing-gum factories. As it is, they are all taken care of by the innumerable societies for making the whole world virtuous and happy. One may laugh at the aims and methods of many such societies—for example, at the absurd vereins for Americanizing immigrants, *i.e.*, degrading them to the level of the native peasantry. But one thing, at least, they accomplish: they provide comfortable and permanent jobs for hundreds and thousands of deserving women, most of whom are far more profitably employed trying to make Methodists out of Sicilians than they would be if they were trying to make husbands out of bachelors. It is for this high purpose also that the forward-looker suffers.

XII.
Memorial Service

WHERE is the grave-yard of dead gods? What lingering mourner waters their mounds? There was a day when Jupiter was the king of the gods, and any man who doubted his puissance was *ipso facto* a barbarian and an ignoramus. But where in all the world is there a man who worships Jupiter to-day? And what of Huitzilopochtli? In one year—and it is no more than five hundred years ago—50,000 youths and maidens were slain in sacrifice to him. To-day, if he is remembered at all, it is only by some vagrant savage in the depths of the Mexican forest. Huitzilopochtli, like many other gods, had no human father; his mother was a virtuous widow; he was born of an apparently innocent flirtation that she carried on with the sun. When he frowned, his father, the sun, stood still. When he roared with rage, earthquakes engulfed whole cities. When he thirsted he was watered with 10,000 gallons of human blood. But to-day Huitzilopochtli is as magnificently forgotten as Allen G. Thurman. Once the peer of Allah, Buddha and Wotan, he is now the peer of General Coxey, Richmond P. Hobson, Nan Patterson, Alton B. Parker, Adelina Patti, General Weyler and Tom Sharkey.

Speaking of Huitzilopochtli recalls his brother, Tezcatilpoca. Tezcatilpoca was almost as powerful: he consumed 25,000 virgins a year. Lead me to his tomb: I would weep, and hang a *couronne des perles.* But who knows where it is? Or where the grave of Quitzalcoatl is? Or Tialoc? Or Chalchihuitlicue? Or Xiehtecutli? Or Centeotl, that sweet one? Or Tlazolteotl, the goddess of love? Or Mictlan? Or Ixtlilton? Or Omacatl? Or Yacatecutli? Or Mixcoatl? Or Xipe? Or all the host of Tzitzimitles? Where are their bones? Where is the willow on which they hung their harps? In what forlorn and unheard-of hell do they await the resurrection morn? Who enjoys their residuary estates? Or that of Dis, whom Cæser found to be the chief god of the Celts? Or that of Tarves, the bull? Or that of Moccos, the pig? Or that of Epona, the mare? Or that of Mullo, the celestial jack-ass? There was a time when the Irish revered all these gods as violently as they now hate the English. But to-day even the drunkest Irishman laughs at them.

But they have company in oblivion: the hell of dead gods is as crowded as the Presbyterian hell for babies. Damona is there, and Esus, and Drunemeton, and Silvana, and Dervones, and Adsalluta, and Deva, and Belisama, and Axona, and Vintios, and Taranuous, and Sulis, and Cocidius, and Adsmerius, and Dumiatis, and Caletos, and Moccus, and Ollovidius, and Albiorix, and Leucitius, and Vitucadrus, and Ogmios, and Uxellimus, and Borvo, and Grannos, and Mogons. All mighty gods in their day, worshiped by millions, full of demands and impositions, able to bind and loose—all gods of the first class, not dilettanti. Men labored for generations to build vast temples to them—temples with stones as large as hay-wagons. The business of interpreting their whims occupied thousands of priests, wizards, archdeacons, evangelists, haruspices, bishops, archbishops. To doubt them was to die, usually at the stake. Armies took to the field to defend them against infidels: villages were burned, women and children were butchered, cattle were driven off. Yet in the end they all withered and died, and to-day there is none so poor to do them reverence. Worse, the very tombs in which they lie are lost, and so even a respectful stranger is debarred from paying them the slightest and politest homage.

What has become of Sutekh, once the high god of the whole Nile Valley? What has become of:

Resheph	Baal
Anath	Astarte
Ashtoreth	Hadad
El	Addu
Nergal	Shalem
Nebo	Dagon
Ninib	Sharrab
Melek	Yau
Abijah	Amon-Re
Isis	Osiris
Ptah	Sebek
Anubis	Molech?

All these were once gods of the highest eminence. Many of them are mentioned with fear and trembling in the Old Testament. They ranked, five or six thousand years ago, with Jahveh himself; the worst of them stood far higher than Thor. Yet they have all gone down the chute, and with them the following:

Bilé
Lêr
Arianrod
Morrigu
Govannon
Gunfled
Sokk-mimi
Memetona
Dagda
Kerridwen
Pwyll
Ogyrvan
Dea Dia
Ceros
Vaticanus
Edulia
Adeona
Iuno Lucina
Saturn
Furrina
Vediovis
Consus
Cronos
Enki
Engurra
Belus
Dimmer
Mu-ul-lil
Ubargisi
Ubilulu
Gasan-lil
U-dimmer-an-kia
Enurestu
U-sab-sib

Gwydion
Manawyddan
Nuada Argetlam
Tagd
Goibniu
Odin
Llaw Gyffes
Lleu
Ogma
Mider
Rigantona
Marzin
Mars
Jupiter
Cunina
Potina
Statilinus
Diana of Ephesus
Robigus
Pluto
Ops
Meditrina
Vesta
Tilmun
Zer-panitu
Merodach
U-ki
Dauke
Gasan-abzu
Elum
U-Tin-dir ki
Marduk
Nin-lil-la
Nin

U-Mersi	Persephone
Tammuz	Istar
Venus	Lagas
Bau	U-urugal
Mulu-hursang	Sirtumu
Anu	Ea
Beltis	Nirig
Nusku	Nebo
Ni-zu	Samas
Sahi	Ma-banba-anna
Aa	En-Mersi
Allatu	Amurru
Sin	Assur
Abil Addu	Aku
Apsu	Beltu
Dagan	Dumu-zi-abzu
Elali	Kuski-banda
Isum	Kaawanu
Mami	Nin-azu
Nin-man	Lugal-Amarada
Zaraqu	Qarradu
Suqamunu	Ura-gala
Zagaga	Ueras

You may think I spoof. That I invent the names. I do not. Ask the rector to lend you any good treatise on comparative religion: you will find them all listed. They were gods of the highest standing and dignity—gods of civilized peoples—worshipped and believed in by millions. All were theoretically omnipotent, omniscient and immortal. And all are dead.

XIII.
Education

I

NEXT to the clerk in holy orders, the fellow with the worst job in the world is the schoolmaster. Both are underpaid, both fall steadily in authority and dignity, and both wear out their hearts trying to perform the impossible. How much the world asks of them, and how little they can actually deliver! The clergyman's business is to save the human race from hell: if he saves one-eighth of one per cent., even within the limits of his narrow flock, he does magnificently. The schoolmaster's is to spread the enlightenment, to make the great masses of the plain people intelligent—and intelligence is precisely the thing that the great masses of the plain people are congenitally and eternally incapable of.

Is it any wonder that the poor birchman, facing this labor that would have staggered Sisyphus Æolusohn, seeks refuge from its essential impossibility in a Chinese maze of empty technic? The ghost of Pestalozzi, once bearing a torch and beckoning toward the heights, now leads down stairways into black and forbidding dungeons. Especially in America, where all that is bombastic and mystical is most esteemed, the art of pedagogics becomes a sort of puerile magic, a thing of preposterous secrets, a grotesque compound of false premises and illogical conclusions. Every year sees a craze for some new solution of the teaching enigma, at once simple and infallible—manual training, playground work, song and doggerel lessons, the Montessori method, the Gary system—an endless series of flamboyant arcanums. The worst extravagances of *privatdozent* experimental psychology are gravely seized upon; the uplift pours in its ineffable principles and discoveries; mathematical formulæ are worked out for every emergency; there is no sure-cure so idiotic that some superintendent of schools will not swallow it.

A couple of days spent examining the literature of the New Thought in pedagogy are enough to make the judicious weep.

Its aim seems to be to reduce the whole teaching process to a sort of automatic reaction, to discover some master formula that will not only take the place of competence and resourcefulness in the teacher but that will also create an artificial receptivity in the child. The merciless application of this formula (which changes every four days) now seems to be the chief end and aim of pedagogy. Teaching becomes a thing in itself, separable from and superior to the thing taught. Its mastery is a special business, a transcendental art and mystery, to be acquired in the laboratory. A teacher well grounded in this mystery, and hence privy to every detail of the new technic (which changes, of course, with the formula), can teach anything to any child, just as a sound dentist can pull any tooth out of any jaw.

All this, I need not point out, is in sharp contrast to the old theory of teaching. By that theory mere technic was simplified and subordinated. All that it demanded of the teacher told off to teach, say, geography, was that he master the facts in the geography book and provide himself with a stout rattan. Thus equipped, he was ready for a test of his natural pedagogical genius. First he exposed the facts in the book, then he gilded them with whatever appearance of interest and importance he could conjure up, and then he tested the extent of their transference to the minds of his pupils. Those pupils who had ingested them got apples; those who had failed got fanned with the rattan. Followed the second round, and the same test again, with a second noting of results. And then the third, and fourth, and the fifth, and so on until the last and least pupil had been stuffed to his subnormal and perhaps moronic brim.

I was myself grounded in the underlying delusions of what is called knowledge by this austere process, and despite the eloquence of those who support newer ideas, I lean heavily in favor of it, and regret to hear that it is no more. It was crude, it was rough, and it was often not a little cruel, but it at least had two capital advantages over all the systems that have succeeded it. In the first place, its machinery was simple; even the stupidest child could understand it; it hooked up cause and effect with the utmost clarity. And in the second place, it tested the teacher as and how he ought to be tested—that is, for his actual capacity to teach, not for his mere technical virtuosity.

There was, in fact, no technic for him to master, and hence none for him to hide behind. He could not conceal a hopeless inability to impart knowledge beneath a correct professional method.

That ability to impart knowledge, it seems to me, has very little to do with technical method. It may operate at full function without any technical method at all, and contrariwise, the most elaborate of technical methods, whether out of Switzerland, Italy or Gary, Ind., cannot make it operate when it is not actually present. And what does it consist of? It consists, first, of a natural talent for dealing with children, for getting into their minds, for putting things in a way that they can comprehend. And it consists, secondly, of a deep belief in the interest and importance of the thing taught, a concern about it amounting to a sort of passion. A man who knows a subject thoroughly, a man so soaked in it that he eats it, sleeps it and dreams it—this man can always teach it with success, no matter how little he knows of technical pedagogy. That is because there is enthusiasm in him, and because enthusiasm is almost as contagious as fear or the barber's itch. An enthusiast is willing to go to any trouble to impart the glad news bubbling within him. He thinks that it is important and valuable for to know; given the slightest glow of interest in a pupil to start with, he will fan that glow to a flame. No hollow formalism cripples him and slows him down. He drags his best pupils along as fast as they can go, and he is so full of the thing that he never tires of expounding its elements to the dullest.

This passion, so unordered and yet so potent, explains the capacity for teaching that one frequently observes in scientific men of high attainments in their specialties—for example, Huxley, Ostwald, Karl Ludwig, Virchow, Billroth, Jowett, William G. Sumner, Halsted and Osler—men who knew nothing whatever about the so-called science of pedagogy, and would have derided its alleged principles if they had heard them stated. It explains, too, the failure of the general run of high-school and college teachers—men who are undoubtedly competent, by the professional standards of pedagogy, but who nevertheless contrive only to make intolerable bores of the things they presume to teach. No intelligent student ever learns much from the average drover of undergraduates; what he actually carries away has come out of his textbooks, or is the fruit of his own reading and inquiry. But when he passes to the graduate school, and comes among men who really understand the subjects they teach, and, what is more, who really love them, his store of knowledge increases rapidly, and in a very short while, if he has any intelligence at all, he learns to think in terms of the thing he is studying.

So far, so good. But an objection still remains, the which may be couched in the following terms: that in the average college or high school, and especially in the elementary school, most of the subjects taught are so bald and uninspiring that it is difficult to imagine them arousing the passion I have been describing—in brief that only an ass could be enthusiastic about them. In witness, think of the four elementals: reading, penmanship, arithmetic and spelling. This objection, at first blush, seems salient and dismaying, but only a brief inspection is needed to show that it is really of very small validity. It is made up of a false assumption and a false inference. The false inference is that there is any sound reason for prohibiting teaching by asses, if only the asses know how to do it, and do it well. The false assumption is that there are no asses in our schools and colleges to-day. The facts stand in almost complete antithesis to these notions. The truth is that the average schoolmaster, on all the lower levels, is and always must be essentially an ass, for how can one imagine an intelligent man engaging in so puerile an avocation? And, the truth is that it is precisely his inherent asininity, and not his technical equipment as a pedagogue, that is responsible for whatever modest success he now shows.

I here attempt no heavy jocosity, but mean exactly what I say. Consider, for example, penmanship. A decent handwriting, it must be obvious, is useful to all men, and particularly to the lower orders of men. It is one of the few things capable of acquirement in school that actually helps them to make a living. Well, how is it taught to-day? It is taught, in the main, by schoolmarms so enmeshed in a complex and unintelligible technic that, even supposing them able to write clearly themselves, they find it quite impossible to teach their pupils. Every few years sees a radical overhauling of the whole business. First the vertical hand is to make it easy; then certain curves are the favorite magic; then there is a return to slants and shadings. No department of pedagogy sees a more hideous cavorting of quacks. In none is the natural talent and enthusiasm of the teacher more depressingly crippled. And the result? The result is that our American school children write abominably—that a clerk or stenographer with a simple, legible hand becomes almost as scarce as one with Greek.

Go back, now, to the old days. Penmanship was then taught, not mechanically and ineffectively, by unsound and shifting formulæ, but by passionate penmen with curly patent-leather hair and far-away eyes—in brief, by the unforgettable professors of our youth, with their flourishes, their heavy downstrokes and their lovely birds-with-letters-in-their-bills. You remember them, of course. Asses all! Preposterous popinjays and numskulls! Pathetic idiots! But they loved penmanship, they believed in the glory and beauty of penmanship, they were fanatics, devotees, almost martyrs of penmanship—and so they got some touch of that passion into their pupils. Not enough, perhaps, to make more flourishers and bird-blazoners, but enough to make sound penmen. Look at your old writing book; observe the excellent legibility, the clear strokes of your "Time is money." Then look at your child's.

Such idiots, despite the rise of "scientific" pedagogy, have not died out in the world. I believe that our schools are full of them, both in pantaloons and in skirts. There are fanatics who love and venerate spelling as a tom-cat loves and venerates catnip. There are grammatomaniacs; schoolmarms who would rather parse than eat; specialists in an objective case that doesn't exist in English; strange beings, otherwise sane and even intelligent and comely, who suffer under a split infinitive as you or I would suffer under gastro-enteritis. There are geography cranks, able to bound Mesopotamia and Beluchistan. There are zealots for long division, experts in the multiplication table, lunatic worshipers of the binomial theorem. But the system has them in its grip. It combats their natural enthusiam diligently and mercilessly. It tries to convert them into mere technicians, clumsy machines. It orders them to teach, not by the process of emotional osmosis which worked in the days gone by, but by formulæ that are as baffling to the pupil as they are paralyzing to the teacher. Imagine what would happen to one of them who stepped to the blackboard, seized a piece of chalk, and engrossed a bird that held the class spell-bound—a bird with a thousand flowing feathers, wings bursting with parabolas and epicycloids, and long ribbons streaming from its bill! Imagine the fate of one who began "Honesty is the best policy" with an H as florid and—to a child—as beautiful as the initial of a mediæval manuscript! Such a teacher would be cashiered and handed over to the secular arm; the very enchantment of the assembled infantry would be held as damning proof against him. And yet it is just such teachers that we should try to discover and develop. Pedagogy needs their enthusiasm, their naïve belief in their own grotesque talents, their capacity for communicating their childish passion to the childish.

But this would mean exposing the children of the Republic to contact with monomaniacs, half-wits, defectives? Well, what of it? The vast majority of them are already exposed to contact with half-wits in their own homes; they are taught the word of God by half-wits on Sundays; they will grow up into Knights of Pythias, Odd Fellows, Red Men and other such half-wits in the days to come. Moreover, as I have hinted, they are already face to face with half-wits in the actual schools, at least in three cases out of four. The problem before us is not to dispose of this fact, but to utilize it. We cannot hope to fill the schools with persons of high intelligence, for persons of high intelligence simply refuse to spend their lives teaching such banal things as spelling and arithmetic. Among the teachers male we may safely assume that 95 per cent. are of low mentality, else they would depart for more appetizing pastures. And even among the teachers female the best are inevitably weeded out by marriage, and only the worst (with a few romantic exceptions) survive. The task before us, as I say, is not to make a vain denial of this cerebral inferiority of the pedagogue, nor to try to combat and disguise it by concocting a mass of technical hocus-pocus, but to search out and put to use the value lying concealed in it. For even stupidity, it must be plain, has its uses in the world, and some of them are uses that intelligence cannot meet. One would not tell off a Galileo or a Pasteur to drive an ash-cart or an Ignatius Loyola to be a stockbroker, or a Brahms to lead the orchestra in a Broadway cabaret. By the same token, one would not ask a Herbert Spencer or a Duns Scotus to instruct sucklings. Such men would not only be wasted at the job; they would also be incompetent. The business of dealing with children, in fact, demands a certain childishness of mind. The best teacher, until one comes to adult pupils, is not the one who knows most, but the one who is most capable of reducing knowledge to that simple compound of the obvious and the wonderful which slips easiest into the infantile comprehension. A man of high intelligence, perhaps, may accomplish the thing by a conscious intellectual feat. But it is vastly easier to the man (or woman) whose habits of mind are naturally on the plane of a child's. The best teacher of children, in brief, is one who is essentially childlike.

I go so far with this notion that I view the movement to introduce female bachelors of arts into the primary schools with the utmost alarm. A knowledge of Bergsonism, the Greek aorist, sex hygiene and the dramas of Percy MacKaye is not only no help to the teaching of spelling, it is a positive handicap to the teaching of spelling, for it corrupts and blows up that naïve belief in the glory and portentousness of spelling which is at the bottom of all successful teaching of it. If I had my way, indeed, I should expose all candidates for berths in the infant grades to the Binet-Simon test, and reject all those who revealed the mentality of more than fifteen years. Plenty would still pass. Moreover, they would be secure against contamination by the new technic of pedagogy. Its vast wave of pseudo-psychology would curl and break against the hard barrier of their innocent and passionate intellects—as it probably does, in fact, even now. They would know nothing of cognition, perception, attention, the sub-conscious and all the other half-fabulous fowl of the pedagogic aviary. But they would see in reading, writing and arithmetic the gaudy charms of profound and esoteric knowledge, and they would teach these ancient branches, now so abominably in decay, with passionate gusto, and irresistible effectiveness, and a gigantic success.

II

Two great follies corrupt the present pedagogy, once it gets beyond the elementals. One is the folly of overestimating the receptivity of the pupil; the other is the folly of overestimating the possible efficiency of the teacher. Both rest upon that tendency to put too high a value upon mere schooling which characterizes democratic and upstart societies—a tendency born of the theory that a young man who has been "educated," who has "gone through college," is in some subtle way more capable of making money than one who hasn't. The nature of the schooling on tap in colleges is but defectively grasped by the adherents of the theory. They view it, I believe, as a sort of extension of the schooling offered in elementary schools—that is, as an indefinite multiplication of training in such obviously valuable and necessary arts as reading, writing and arithmetic. It is, of course, nothing of the sort. If the pupil, as he climbs the educational ladder, is fortunate enough to come into contact with a few Huxleys or Ludwigs, he may acquire a great deal of extremely sound knowledge, and even learn how to think for himself. But in the great majority of cases he is debarred by two things: the limitations of his congenital capacity and the limitations of the teachers he actually encounters. The latter is usually even more brilliantly patent than the former. Very few professional teachers, it seems to me, really know anything worth knowing, even about the subjects they essay to teach. If you doubt it, simply examine their contributions to existing knowledge. Several years ago, while engaged upon my book, "The American Language," I had a good chance to test the matter in one typical department, that of philology. I found a truly appalling condition of affairs. I found that in the whole United States there were not two dozen teachers of English philology—in which class I also include the innumerable teachers of plain grammar—who had ever written ten lines upon the subject worth reading. It was not that they were indolent or illiterate: in truth, they turned out to be enormously diligent. But as I plowed through pyramid after pyramid of their doctrines and speculations, day after day and week after week, I discovered little save a vast laboring of the obvious, with now and then a bold flight into the nonsensical. A few genuinely original philologians revealed themselves—pedagogues capable of observing accurately and reasoning clearly. The rest simply wasted time and paper. Whole sections of the field were unexplored, and some of them appeared to be even unsuspected. The entire life-work of many an industrious professor, boiled down, scarcely made a footnote in my book, itself a very modest work.

This tendency to treat the superior pedagogue too seriously —to view him as, *ipso facto*, a learned man, and one thus capable of conveying learning to others—is supported by the circumstance that he so views himself, and is, in fact, very pretentious and even bombastic. Nearly all discussions of the educational problem, at least in the United States, are carried on by schoolmasters or ex-schoolmasters—for example, college presidents, deans, and other such magnificoes—and so they assume it to be axiomatic that such fellows are genuine bearers of the enlightenment, and hence capable of transmitting it to others. This is true sometimes, as I have said, but certainly not usually. The average high-school or college pedagogue is not one who has been selected because of his uncommon knowledge; he is simply one who has been stuffed with formal ideas and taught to do a few conventional intellectual tricks. Contact with him, far from being inspiring to any youth of alert mentality, is really quite depressing; his point of view is commonplace and timorous; his best thought is no better than that of any other fourth-rate professional man, say a dentist or an advertisement writer. Thus it is idle to talk of him as if he were a Socrates, an Aristotle, or even a Leschetizky. He is actually much more nearly related to a barber or a lieutenant of marines. A worthy man, industrious and respectable—but don't expect too much of him. To ask him to struggle out of his puddle of safe platitudes and plunge into the whirlpool of surmise and speculation that carries on the fragile shallop of human progress—to do this is as absurd as to ask a neighborhood doctor to undertake major surgery.

In the United States his low intellectual status is kept low, not only by the meager rewards of his trade in a country where money is greatly sought and esteemed, but also by the democratic theory of education—that is, by the theory that mere education can convert a peasant into an intellectual aristocrat, with all of the peculiar superiorities of an aristocrat—in brief, that it is possible to make purses out of sow's ears. The intellectual collapse of the American *Gelehrten* during the late war —a collapse so nearly unanimous that those who did not share it attained to a sort of immortality overnight—was perhaps largely due to this error. Who were these bawling professors, so pathetically poltroonish and idiotic? In an enormous number of cases they were simply peasants in frock coats—oafs from the farms and villages of Iowa, Kansas, Vermont, Alabama, the Dakotas and other such backward states, horribly stuffed with standardized learning in some freshwater university, and then set to teaching. To look for a civilized attitude of mind in such Strassburg geese is to look for honor in a valet; to confuse them with scholars is to confuse the Knights of Pythias with the Knights Hospitaller. In brief, the trouble with them was that they had no sound tradition behind them, that they had not learned to think clearly and decently, that they were not gentlemen. The youth with a better background behind him, passing through an American university, seldom acquires any yearning to linger as a teacher. The air is too thick for him; the rewards are too trivial; the intrigues are too old-maidish and degrading. Thus the chairs, even in the larger universities, tend to be filled more and more by yokels who have got themselves what is called an education only by dint of herculean effort. Exhausted by the cruel process, they are old men at 26 or 28, and so, hugging their Ph.D's, they sink into convenient instructorships, and end at 60 as *ordentliche Professoren*. The social status of the American pedagogue helps along the process. Unlike in Europe, where he has a secure and honorable position, he ranks, in the United States, somewhere between a Methodist preacher and a prosperous brickyard owner—certainly clearly below the latter. Thus the youth of civilized upbringings feels that it would be stooping a bit to take up the rattan. But the plow-hand obviously makes a step upward, and is hence eager for the black gown. Thereby a vicious circle is formed. The plow-hand, by entering the ancient guild, drags it down still further, and so makes it increasingly difficult to snare apprentices from superior castes.

A glance at "Who's Who in America" offers a good deal of support for all this theorizing. There was a time when the typical American professor came from a small area in New England—for generations the seat of a high literacy, and even of a certain austere civilization. But to-day he comes from the region of silos, revivals, and saleratus. Behind him there is absolutely no tradition of aristocratic aloofness and urbanity, or even of mere civilized decency. He is a hind by birth, and he carries the smell of the dunghill into the academic grove—and not only the smell, but also some of the dung itself. What one looks for in such men is dullness, superficiality, a great credulity, an incapacity for learning anything save a few fly-blown rudiments, a passionate yielding to all popular crazes, a malignant distrust of genuine superiority, a huge megalomania. These are precisely the things that one finds in the typical American pedagogue of the new dispensation. He is not only a numskull; he is also a boor. In the university president he reaches his heights. Here we have a so-called learned man who spends his time making speeches before chautauquas, chambers of commerce and Rotary Clubs, and flattering trustees who run both universities and street-railways, and cadging money from such men as Rockefeller and Carnegie.

III

The same educational fallacy which fills the groves of learning with such dunces causes a huge waste of energy and money on lower levels—those, to wit, of the secondary schools. The theory behind the lavish multiplication of such schools is that they outfit the children of the mob with the materials of reasoning, and inculcate in them a habit of indulging in it. I have never been able to discover any evidence in support of that theory. The common people of America—at least the white portion of them—are rather above the world's average in literacy, but there is no sign that they have acquired thereby any capacity for weighing facts or comparing ideas. The school statistics show that the average member of the American Legion can read and write after a fashion, and is able to multiply eight by seven after four trials, but they tell us nothing about his actual intelligence. The returns of the Army itself, indeed, indicate that he is stupid almost beyond belief—that there is at least an even chance that he is a moron. Is such a fellow appreciably superior to the villein of the Middle Ages? Sometimes I am tempted to doubt it. I suspect, for example, that the belief in witchcraft is still almost as widespread among the plain people of the United States, at least outside the large cities, as it was in Europe in the year 1500. In my own state of Maryland all of the negroes and mulattoes believe absolutely in witches, and so do most of the whites. The belief in ghosts penetrates to quite high levels. I know very few native-born Americans, indeed, who reject it without reservation. One constantly comes upon grave defenses of spiritism in some form or other by men theoretically of learning; in the two houses of Congress it would be difficult to muster fifty men willing to denounce the thing publicly. It would not only be politically dangerous for them to do so; it would also go against their consciences.

What is always forgotten is that the capacity for knowledge of the great masses of human blanks is very low—that, no matter how adroitly pedagogy tackles them with its technical sorceries, it remains a practical impossibility to teach them anything beyond reading and writing, and the most elementary arithmetic. Worse, it is impossible to make any appreciable improvement in their congenitally ignoble tastes, and so they devote even the paltry learning that they acquire to degrading uses. If the average American read only the newspapers, as is frequently alleged, it would be bad enough, but the truth is that he reads only the most imbecile *parts* of the newspapers. Nine-tenths of the matter in a daily paper of the better sort is almost as unintelligible to him as the theory of least squares. The words lie outside his vocabulary; the ideas are beyond the farthest leap of his intellect. It is, indeed, a sober fact that even an editorial in the New York *Times* is probably incomprehensible to all Americans save a small minority—and not, remember, on the ground that it is too nonsensical but on the ground that it is too subtle. The same sort of mind that regards Rubinstein's Melody in F as too "classical" to be agreeable is also stumped by the most transparent English.

Like most other professional writers I get a good many letters from my customers. Complaints, naturally, are more numerous than compliments; it is only indignation that can induce the average man to brave the ardors of pen and ink. Well, the complaint that I hear most often is that my English is unintelligible—that it is too full of "hard" words. I can imagine nothing more astounding. My English is actually almost as bald and simple as the English of a college yell. My sentences are short and plainly constructed: I resolutely cultivate the most direct manner of statement; my vocabulary is deliberately composed of the words of everyday. Nevertheless, a great many of my readers in my own country find reading me an uncomfortably severe burden upon their linguistic and intellectual resources. These readers are certainly not below the American average in intelligence; on the contrary, they must be a good deal above the average, for they have at least got to the point where they are willing to put out of the safe harbor of the obvious and respectable, and to brave the seas where more or less novel ideas rage and roar. Think of what the ordinary newspaper reader would make of my compositions! There is, in fact, no need to think; I have tried them on him. His customary response, when, by mountebankish devices, I forced him to read—or, at all events, to try to read—, was to demand resolutely that the guilty newspaper cease printing me, and to threaten to bring the matter to the attention of the *Polizei*. I do not exaggerate in the slightest; I tell the literal truth.

It is such idiots that the little red schoolhouse operates upon, in the hope of unearthing an occasional first-rate man. Is that hope ever fulfilled? Despite much testimony to the effect that it is, I am convinced that it really isn't. First-rate men are never begotten by Knights of Pythias; the notion that they sometimes are is due to an optical delusion. When they appear in obscure and ignoble circles it is no more than a proof that only an extremely wise sire knows his own son. Adultery, in brief, is one of nature's devices for keeping the lowest orders of men from sinking to the level of downright simians: sometimes for a few brief years in youth, their wives and daughters are comely—and now and then the baron drinks more than he ought to. But it is foolish to argue that the gigantic machine of popular education is needed to rescue such hybrids from their environment. The truth is that all the education rammed into the average pupil in the average American public school could be acquired by the larva of any reasonably intelligent man in no more than six weeks of ordinary application, and that where schools are unknown it actually *is* so acquired. A bright child, in fact, can learn to read and write without any save the most casual aid a great deal faster than it can learn to read and write in a classroom, where the difficulties of the stupid retard it enormously and it is further burdened by the crazy formulæ, invented by pedagogues. And once it can read and write, it is just as well equipped to acquire further knowledge as nine-tenths of the teachers it will subsequently encounter in school or college.

IV

I know a good many men of great learning—that is, men born with an extraordinary eagerness and capacity to acquire knowledge. One and all, they tell me that they can't recall learning anything of any value in school. All that schoolmasters managed to accomplish with them was to test and determine the amount of knowledge that they had already acquired independently—and not infrequently the determination was made clumsily and inaccurately. In my own nonage I had a great desire to acquire knowledge in certain limited directions, to wit, those of the physical sciences. Before I was ever permitted, by the regulations of the secondary seminary I was penned in, to open a chemistry book I had learned a great deal of chemistry by the simple process of reading the texts and then going through the processes described. When, at last, I was introduced to chemistry officially, I found the teaching of it appalling. The one aim of that teaching, in fact, seemed to be to first purge me of what I already knew and then refill me with the same stuff in a formal, doltish, unintelligible form. My experience with physics was even worse. I knew nothing about it when I undertook its study in class, for that was before the days when physics swallowed chemistry. Well, it was taught so abominably that it immediately became incomprehensible to me, and hence extremely distasteful, and to this day I know nothing about it. Worse, it remains unpleasant to me, and so I am shut off from the interesting and useful knowledge that I might otherwise acquire by reading.

One extraordinary teacher I remember who taught me something: a teacher of mathematics. I had a dislike for that science, and knew little about it. Finally, my neglect of it brought me to bay: in transferring from one school to another I found that I was hopelessly short in algebra. What was needed, of course, was not an actual knowledge of algebra, but simply the superficial smattering needed to pass an examination. The teacher that I mention, observing my distress, generously offered to fill me with that smattering after school hours. He got the whole year's course into me in exactly six lessons of half an hour each. And how? More accurately, why? Simply because he was an algebra fanatic—because he believed that algebra was not only a science of the utmost importance, but also one of the greatest fascination. He was the penmanship professor of years ago, lifted to a higher level. A likable and plausible man, he convinced me in twenty minutes that ignorance of algebra was as calamitous, socially and intellectually, as ignorance of table manners—that acquiring its elements was as necessary as washing behind the ears. So I fell upon the book and gulped it voraciously, greatly to the astonishment of my father, whose earlier mathematical teaching had failed to set me off because it was too pressing—because it bombarded me, not when I was penned in a school and so inclined to make the best of it, but when I had got through a day's schooling, and felt inclined to play. To this day I comprehend the binomial theorem, a very rare accomplishment in an author. For many years, indeed, I was probably the only American newspaper editor who knew what it was.

Two other teachers of that school I remember pleasantly as fellows whose pedagogy profitted me—both, it happens, were drunken and disreputable men. One taught me to chew tobacco, an art that has done more to give me an evil name, perhaps, than even my Socinianism. The other introduced me to Shakespeare, Congreve, Wycherly, Marlowe and Sheridan, and so filled me with that taste for coarseness which now offends so many of my customers, lay and clerical. Neither ever came to a dignified position in academic circles. One abandoned pedagogy for the law, became involved in causes of a dubious nature, and finally disappeared into the shades which engulf third-rate attorneys. The other went upon a fearful drunk one Christmastide, got himself shanghaied on the water-front and is supposed to have fallen overboard from a British tramp, bound east for Cardiff. At all events, he has never been heard from since. Two evil fellows, and yet I hold their memories in affection, and believe that they were the best teachers I ever had. For in both there was something a good deal more valuable than mere pedagogical skill and diligence, and even more valuable than correct demeanor, and that was a passionate love of sound literature. This love, given reasonably receptive soil, they knew how to communicate, as a man can nearly always communicate whatever moves him profoundly. Neither ever made the slightest effort to "teach" literature, as the business is carried on by the usual idiot schoolmaster. Both had a vast contempt for the text-books that were official in their school, and used to entertain the boys by pointing out the nonsense in them. Both were full of derisory objections to the principal heroes of such books in those days: Scott, Irving, Pope, Jane Austen, Dickens, Trollope, Tennyson. But both, discoursing in their disorderly way upon heroes of their own, were magnificently eloquent and persuasive. The boy who could listen to one of them intoning Whitman and stand unmoved was a dull fellow indeed. The boy who could resist the other's enthusiasm for the old essayists was intellectually deaf, dumb and blind.

I often wonder if their expoundings of their passions and prejudices would have been half so charming if they had been wholly respectable men, like their colleagues of the school faculty. It is not likely. A healthy boy is in constant revolt against the sort of men who surround him at school. Their puerile pedantries, their Christian Endeavor respectability, their sedentary pallor, their curious preference for the dull and uninteresting, their general air of so many Y.M.C.A. secretaries—these things infallibly repel the youth who is above milksoppery. In every boys' school the favorite teacher is one who occasionally swears like a cavalryman, or is reputed to keep a jug in his room, or is known to receive a scented note every morning. Boys are good judges of men, as girls are good judges of women. It is not by accident that most of them, at some time or other, long to be cowboys or ice-wagon drivers, and that none of them, not obviously diseased in mind, ever longs to be a Sunday-school superintendent. Put that judgment to a simple test. What would become of a nation in which all of the men were, at heart, Sunday-school superintendents—or Y.M.C.A. secretaries, or pedagogues? Imagine it in conflict with a nation of cowboys and ice-wagon drivers. Which would be the stronger, and which would be the more intelligent, resourceful, enterprising and courageous?

XIV.
Types of Men

I
The Romantic

THERE is a variety of man whose eye inevitably exaggerates, whose ear inevitably hears more than the band plays, whose imagination inevitably doubles and triples the news brought in by his five senses. He is the enthusiast, the believer, the romantic. He is the sort of fellow who, if he were a bacteriologist, would report the streptoccocus pyogenes to be as large as a St. Bernard dog, as intelligent as Socrates, as beautiful as Beauvais Cathedral and as respectable as a Yale professor.

2
The Skeptic

No man ever quite believes in any other man. One may believe in an idea absolutely, but not in a man. In the highest confidence there is always a flavor of doubt—a feeling, half instinctive and half logical, that, after all, the scoundrel *may* have something up his sleeve. This doubt, it must be obvious, is always more than justified, for no man is worthy of unlimited reliance—his treason, at best, only waits for sufficient temptation. The trouble with the world is not that men are too suspicious in this direction, but that they tend to be too confiding—that they still trust themselves too far to other men, even after bitter experience. Women, I believe, are measurably less sentimental, in this as in other things. No married woman ever trusts her husband absolutely, nor does she ever act as if she *did* trust him. Her utmost confidence is as wary as an American pickpocket's confidence that the policeman on the beat will stay bought.

3
The Believer

Faith may be defined briefly as an illogical belief in the occurrence of the improbable. Or, psychoanalytically, as a wish neurose. There is thus a flavor of the pathological in it; it goes beyond the normal intellectual process and passes into the murky domain of transcendental metaphysics. A man full of faith is simply one who has lost (or never had) the capacity for clear and realistic thought. He is not a mere ass: he is actually ill. Worse, he is incurable, for disappointment, being essentially an objective phenomenon, cannot permanently affect his subjective infirmity. His faith takes on the virulence of a chronic infection. What he usually says, in substance, is this: "Let us trust in God, *who has always fooled us in the past.*"

4
The Worker

All democratic theories, whether Socialistic or bourgeois, necessarily take in some concept of the dignity of labor. If the have-not were deprived of this delusion that his sufferings in the sweat-shop are somehow laudable and agreeable to God, there would be little left in his ego save a belly-ache. Nevertheless, a delusion is a delusion, and this is one of the worst. It arises out of confusing the pride of workmanship of the artist with the dogged, painful docility of the machine. The difference is important and enormous. If he got no reward whatever, the artist would go on working just the same; his actual reward, in fact, is often so little that he almost starves. But suppose a garment-worker got nothing for his labor: would he go on working just the same? Can one imagine him submitting voluntarily to hardship and sore want that he might express his soul in 200 more pairs of pantaloons?

5
The Physician

Hygiene is the corruption of medicine by morality. It is impossible to find a hygienist who does not debase his theory of the healthful with a theory of the virtuous. The whole hygienic art, indeed, resolves itself into an ethical exhortation, and, in the sub-department of sex, into a puerile and belated advocacy of asceticism. This brings it, at the end, into diametrical conflict with medicine proper. The aim of medicine is surely not to make men virtuous; it is to safeguard and rescue them from the consequences of their vices. The true physician does not preach repentance; he offers absolution.

6
The Scientist

The value the world sets upon motives is often grossly unjust and inaccurate. Consider, for example, two of them: mere insatiable curiosity and the desire to do good. The latter is put high above the former, and yet it is the former that moves some of the greatest men the human race has yet produced: the scientific investigators. What animates a great pathologist? Is it the desire to cure disease, to save life? Surely not, save perhaps as an afterthought. He is too intelligent, deep down in his soul, to see anything praiseworthy in such a desire. He knows by life-long observation that his discoveries will do quite as much harm as good, that a thousand scoundrels will profit to every honest man, that the folks who most deserve to be saved will probably be the last to be saved. No man of self-respect could devote himself to pathology on such terms. What actually moves him is his unquenchable curiosity—his boundless, almost pathological thirst to penetrate the unknown, to uncover the secret, to find out what has not been found out before. His prototype is not the liberator releasing slaves, the good Samaritan lifting up the fallen, but the dog sniffing tremendously at an infinite series of rat-holes. And yet he is one of the greatest and noblest of men. And yet he stands in the very front rank of the race.

7
The Business Man

It is, after all, a sound instinct which puts business below the professions, and burdens the business man with a social inferiority that he can never quite shake off, even in America. The business man, in fact, acquiesces in this assumption of his inferiority, even when he protests against it. He is the only man who is forever apologizing for his occupation. He is the only one who always seeks to make it appear, when he attains the object of his labors, *i.e.*, the making of a great deal of money, that it was not the object of his labors.

8
The King

Perhaps the most valuable asset that any man can have in this world is a naturally superior air, a talent for sniffishness and reserve. The generality of men are always greatly impressed by it, and accept it freely as a proof of genuine merit. One need but disdain them to gain their respect. Their congenital stupidity and timorousness make them turn to any leader who offers, and the sign of leadership that they recognize most readily is that which shows itself in external manner. This is the true explanation of the survival of monarchism, which invariably lives through its perennial deaths. It is the popular theory, at least in America, that monarchism is a curse fastened upon the common people from above—that the monarch saddles it upon them without their consent and against their will. The theory is without support in the facts. Kings are created, not by kings, but by the people. They visualize one of the ineradicable needs of all third-rate men, which means of nine men out of ten, and that is the need of something to venerate, to bow down to, to follow and obey.

The king business begins to grow precarious, not when kings reach out for greater powers, but when they begin to resign and renounce their powers. The czars of Russia were quite secure upon the throne so long as they ran Russia like a reformatory, but the moment they began to yield to liberal ideas, *i.e.*, by emancipating the serfs and setting up constitutionalism, their doom was sounded. The people saw this yielding as a sign of weakness; they began to suspect that the czars, after all, were not actually superior to other men. And so they turned to other and antagonistic leaders, all as cock-sure as the czars had once been, and in the course of time they were stimulated to rebellion. These leaders, or, at all events, the two or three most resolute and daring of them, then undertook to run the country in the precise way that it had been run in the palmy days of the monarchy. That is to say, they seized and exerted irresistible power and laid claim to infallible wisdom. History will date their downfall from the day they began to ease their pretensions. Once they confessed, even by implication, that they were merely human, the common people began to turn against them.

9
The Average Man

It is often urged against the so-called scientific Socialists, with their materialistic conception of history, that they overlook certain spiritual qualities that are independent of wage scales and metabolism. These qualities, it is argued, color the aspirations and activities of civilized man quite as much as they are colored by his material condition, and so make it impossible to consider him simply as an economic machine. As examples, the anti-Marxians cite patriotism, pity, the æsthetic sense and the yearning to know God. Unluckily, the examples are ill-chosen. Millions of men are quite devoid of patriotism, pity and the æsthetic sense, and have no very active desire to know God. Why don't the anti-Marxians cite a spiritual quality that is genuinely universal? There is one readily to hand. I allude to cowardice. It is, in one form or other, visible in every human being; it almost serves to mark off the human race from all the other higher animals. Cowardice, I believe, is at the bottom of the whole caste system, the foundation of every organized society, including the most democratic. In order to escape going to war himself, the peasant was willing to give the warrior certain privileges—and out of those privileges has grown the whole structure of civilization. Go back still further. Property arose out of the fact that a few relatively courageous men were able to accumulate more possessions than whole hordes of cowardly men, and, what is more, to retain them after accumulating them.

10

The Truth-Seeker

The man who boasts that he habitually tells the truth is simply a man with no respect for it. It is not a thing to be thrown about loosely, like small change; it is something to be cherished and hoarded, and disbursed only when absolutely necessary. The smallest atom of truth represents some man's bitter toil and agony; for every ponderable chunk of it there is a brave truth-seeker's grave upon some lonely ash-dump and a soul roasting in hell.

11

The Pacifist

Nietzsche, in altering Schopenhauer's will-to-live to will-to-power, probably fell into a capital error. The truth is that the thing the average man seeks in life is not primarily power, but peace; all his struggle is toward a state of tranquillity and equilibrium; what he always dreams of is a state in which he will have to do battle no longer. This dream plainly enters into his conception of Heaven; he thinks of himself, *post mortem*, browsing about the celestial meadows like a cow in a safe pasture. A few extraordinary men enjoy combat at all times, and all men are inclined toward it at orgiastic moments, but the race as a race craves peace, and man belongs among the more timorous, docile and unimaginative animals, along with the deer, the horse and the sheep. This craving for peace is vividly displayed in the ages-long conflict of the sexes. Every normal woman wants to be married, for the plain reason that marriage offers her security. And every normal man avoids marriage as long as possible, for the equally plain reason that marriage invades and threatens *his* security.

12

The Relative

The normal man's antipathy to his relatives, particularly of the second degree, is explained by psychologists in various tortured and improbable ways. The true explanation, I venture, is a good deal simpler. It lies in the plain fact that every man sees in his relatives, and especially in his cousins, a series of grotesque caricatures of himself. They exhibit his qualities in disconcerting augmentation or diminution; they fill him with a disquieting feeling that this, perhaps, is the way he appears to the world and so they wound his *amour propre* and give him intense discomfort. To admire his relatives whole-heartedly a man must be lacking in the finer sort of self-respect.

13
The Friend

One of the most mawkish of human delusions is the notion that friendship should be eternal, or, at all events, life-long, and that any act which puts a term to it is somehow discreditable. The fact is that a man of active and resilient mind outwears his friendships just as certainly as he outwears his love affairs, his politics and his epistemology. They become threadbare, shabby, pumped-up, irritating, depressing. They convert themselves from living realities into moribund artificialities, and stand in sinister opposition to freedom, self-respect and truth. It is as corrupting to preserve them after they have grown fly-blown and hollow as it is to keep up the forms of passion after passion itself is a corpse. Every act and attitude that they involve thus become an act of hypocrisy, an attitude of dishonesty. . . . A prudent man, remembering that life is short, gives an hour or two, now and then, to a critical examination of his friendships. He weighs them, edits them, tests the metal of them. A few he retains, perhaps with radical changes in their terms. But the majority he expunges from his minutes and tries to forget, as he tries to forget the cold and clammy loves of year before last.

XV.
The Dismal Science

EVERY man, as the Psalmist says, to his own poison, or poisons, as the case may be. One of mine, following hard after theology, is political economy. What! Political economy, that dismal science? Well, why not? Its dismalness is largely a delusion, due to the fact that its chief ornaments, at least in our own day, are university professors. The professor must be an obscurantist or he is nothing; he has a special and unmatchable talent for dullness; his central aim is not to expose the truth clearly, but to exhibit his profundity, his esotericity—in brief, to stagger sophomores and other professors. The notion that German is a gnarled and unintelligible language arises out of the circumstance that it is so much written by professors. It took a rebel member of the clan, swinging to the antipodes in his unearthly treason, to prove its explicitness, its resiliency, its downright beauty. But Nietzsches are few, and so German remains soggy, and political economy continues to be swathed in dullness. As I say, however, that dullness is only superficial. There is no more engrossing book in the English language than Adam Smith's "The Wealth of Nations"; surely the eighteenth century produced nothing that can be read with greater ease to-day. Nor is there any inherent reason why even the most technical divisions of its subject should have gathered cobwebs with the passing of the years. Taxation, for example, is eternally lively; it concerns nine-tenths of us more directly than either smallpox or golf, and has just as much drama in it; moreover, it has been mellowed and made gay by as many gaudy, preposterous theories. As for foreign exchange, it is almost as romantic as young love, and quite as resistent to formulæ. Do the professors make an autopsy of it? Then read the occasional treatises of some professor of it who is not a professor, say, Garet Garrett or John Moody.

Unluckily, Garretts and Moodys are almost as rare as Nietzsches, and so the amateur of such things must be content to wrestle with the professors, seeking the violet of human interest beneath the avalanche of their graceless parts of speech. A hard business, I daresay, to one not practiced, and to its hardness there is added the disquiet of a doubt. That doubt does not concern itself with the doctrine preached, at least not directly. There may be in it nothing intrinsically dubious; on the contrary, it may appear as sound as the binomial theorem, as well supported as the dogma of infant damnation. But all the time a troubling question keeps afloat in the air, and that is briefly this: What would happen to the learned professors if they took the other side? In other words, to what extent is political economy, as professors expound and practice it, a free science, in the sense that mathematics and physiology are free sciences? At what place, if any, is speculation pulled up by a rule that beyond lies treason, anarchy and disaster? These questions, I hope I need not add, are not inspired by any heterodoxy in my own black heart. I am, in many fields, a flouter of the accepted revelation and hence immoral, but the field of economics is not one of them. Here, indeed, I know of no man who is more orthodox than I am. I believe that the present organization of society, as bad as it is, is better than any other that has ever been proposed. I reject all the sure cures in current agitation, from government ownership to the single tax. I am in favor of free competition in all human enterprises, and to the utmost limit. I admire successful scoundrels, and shrink from Socialists as I shrink from Methodists. But all the same, the aforesaid doubt pursues me when I plow through the solemn disproofs and expositions of the learned professors of economics, and that doubt will not down. It is not logical or evidential, but purely psychological. And what it is grounded on is an unshakable belief that no man's opinion is worth a hoot, however well supported and maintained, so long as he is not absolutely free, if the spirit moves him, to support and maintain the exactly contrary opinion. In brief, human reason is a weak and paltry thing so long as it is not wholly free reason. The fact lies in its very nature, and is revealed by its entire history. A man may be perfectly honest in a contention, and he may be astute and persuasive in maintaining it, but the moment the slightest compulsion to maintain it is laid upon him, the moment the slightest external reward goes with his partisanship or the slightest penalty with its abandonment, then there appears a defect in his ratiocination that is more deep-seated than any error in fact and more destructive than any conscious and deliberate bias. He may seek the truth and the truth only, and bring up his highest talents and diligence to the business, but always there is a specter behind his chair, a warning in his ear. Always it is safer and more hygienic for him to think one way than to think another way, and in that bald fact there is excuse enough to hold his whole chain of syllogisms in suspicion. He may be earnest, he may be honest, but he is not free, and if he is not free, he is not anything.

Well, are the reverend professors of economics free? With the highest respect, I presume to question it. Their colleagues of archeology may be reasonably called free, and their colleagues of bacteriology, and those of Latin grammar and sidereal astronomy, and those of many another science and mystery, but when one comes to the faculty of political economy one finds that freedom as plainly conditioned, though perhaps not as openly, as in the faculty of theology. And for a plain reason. Political economy, so to speak, hits the employers of the professors where they live. It deals, not with ideas that affect those employers only occasionally or only indirectly or only as ideas, but with ideas that have an imminent and continuous influence upon their personal welfare and security, and that affect profoundly the very foundations of that social and economic structure upon which their whole existence is based. It is, in brief, the science of the ways and means whereby they have come to such estate, and maintain themselves in such estate, that they are able to hire and boss professors. It is the boat in which they sail down perilous waters—and they must needs yell, or be more or less than human, when it is rocked. Now and then that yell duly resounds in the groves of learning. One remembers, for example, the trial, condemnation and execution of Prof. Dr. Scott Nearing at the University of Pennsylvania, a seminary that is highly typical, both in its staff and in its control. Nearing, I have no doubt, was wrong in his notions—honestly, perhaps, but still wrong. In so far as I heard them stated at the time, they seemed to me to be hollow and of no validity. He has since discharged them from the chautauquan stump, and at the usual hinds. They have been chiefly accepted and celebrated by men I regard as asses. But Nearing was not thrown out of the University of Pennsylvania, angrily and ignominiously, because he was honestly wrong, or because his errors made him incompetent to prepare sophomores for their examinations; he was thrown out because his efforts to get at the truth disturbed the security and equanimity of the rich ignoranti who happened to control the university, and because the academic slaves and satellites of these shopmen were restive under his competition for the attention of the student-body. In three words, he was thrown out because he was not safe and sane and orthodox. Had his aberration gone in the other direction, had he defended child labor as ardently as he denounced it and denounced the minimum wage as ardently as he defended it, then he would have been quite as secure in his post, for all his cavorting in the newspapers, as Chancellor Day was at Syracuse.

Now consider the case of the professors of economics, near and far, who have *not* been thrown out. Who will say that the lesson of the Nearing *débâcle* has been lost upon them? Who will say that the potency of the wealthy men who command our universities—or most of them—has not stuck in their minds? And who will say that, with this sticking remembered, their arguments against Nearing's so-called ideas are as worthy of confidence and respect as they would be if they were quite free to go over to Nearing's side without damage? Who, indeed, will give them full credit, even when they are right, so long as they are hamstrung, nose-ringed and tied up in gilded pens? It seems to me that these considerations are enough to cast a glow of suspicion over the whole of American political economy, at least in so far as it comes from college economists. And, in the main, it has that source, for, barring a few brilliant journalists, all our economists of any repute are professors. Many of them are able men, and most of them are undoubtedly honest men, as honesty goes in the world, but over practically every one of them there stands a board of trustees with its legs in the stock-market and its eyes on the established order, and that board is ever alert for heresy in the science of its being, and has ready means of punishing it, and a hearty enthusiasm for the business. Not every professor, perhaps, may be sent straight to the block, as Nearing was, but there are plenty of pillories and guardhouses on the way, and every last pedagogue must be well aware of it.

Political economy, in so far as it is a science at all, was not pumped up and embellished by any such academic clients and ticket-of-leave men. It was put on its legs by inquirers who were not only safe from all dousing in the campus pump, but who were also free from the mental timorousness and conformity which go inevitably with school-teaching—in brief, by men of the world, accustomed to its free air, its hospitality to originality and plain speaking. Adam Smith, true enough, was once a professor, but he threw up his chair to go to Paris, and there he met, not more professors, but all the current enemies of professors—the Nearings and Henry Georges and Karl Marxes of the time. And the book that he wrote was not orthodox, but revolutionary. Consider the others of that bulk and beam: Bentham, Ricardo, Mill and their like. Bentham held no post at the mercy of bankers and tripesellers; he was a man of independent means, a lawyer and politician, and a heretic in general practice. It is impossible to imagine such a man occupying a chair at Harvard or Princeton. He had a hand in too many pies: he was too rebellious and contumacious: he had too little respect for authority, either academic or worldly. Moreover, his mind was too wide for a professor; he could never remain safely in a groove; the whole field of social organization invited his inquiries and experiments. Ricardo? Another man of easy means and great worldly experience—by academic standards, not even educated. To-day, I daresay, such meager diplomas as he could show would not suffice to get him an instructor's berth in a freshwater seminary in Iowa. As for Mill, he was so well grounded by his father that he knew more, at eighteen, than any of the universities could teach him, and his life thereafter was the exact antithesis of that of a cloistered pedagogue. Moreover, he was a heretic in religion and probably violated the Mann act of those days—an offense almost as heinous, in a college professor of economics, as giving three cheers for Prince Kropotkin.

I might lengthen the list, but humanely refrain. The point is that these early English economists were all perfectly free men, with complete liberty to tell the truth as they saw it, regardless of its orthodoxy or lack of orthodoxy. I do not say that the typical American economist of to-day is not as honest, nor even that he is not as diligent and competent, but I do say that he is not as free—that penalties would come upon him for stating ideas that Smith or Ricardo or Bentham or Mill, had he so desired, would have been free to state without damage. And in that menace there is an ineradicable criticism of the ideas that he does state, and it lingers even when they are plausible and are accepted. In France and Germany, where the universities and colleges are controlled by the state, the practical effect of such pressure has been frequently demonstrated. In the former country the violent debate over social and economic problems during the quarter century before the war produced a long list of professors cashiered for heterodoxy, headed by the names of Jean Jaures and Gustave Herve. In Germany it needed no Nietzsche to point out the deadening produced by this state control. Germany, in fact, got out of it an entirely new species of economist—the state Socialist who flirted with radicalism with one eye and kept the other upon his chair, his salary and his pension.

The Nearing case and the rebellions of various pedagogues elsewhere show that we in America stand within the shadow of a somewhat similar danger. In economics, as in the other sciences, we are probably producing men who are as good as those on view in any other country. They are not to be surpassed for learning and originality, and there is no reason to believe that they lack honesty and courage. But honesty and courage, as men go in the world, are after all merely relative values. There comes a point at which even the most honest man considers consequences, and even the most courageous looks before he leaps. The difficulty lies in establishing the position of that point. So long as it is in doubt, there will remain, too, the other doubt that I have described. I rise in meeting, I repeat, not as a radical, but as one of the most hunkerous of the orthodox. I can imagine nothing more dubious in fact and wobbly in logic than some of the doctrines that amateur economists, chiefly Socialists, have set afloat in this country during the past dozen years. I have even gone to the trouble of writing a book against them; my convictions and instincts are all on the other side. But I should be a great deal more comfortable in those convictions and instincts if I were convinced that the learned professors were really in full and absolute possession of academic freedom—if I could imagine them taking the other tack now and then without damnation to their jobs, their lecture dates, their book sales and their hides.

XVI.
Matters of State

I
Le Contrat Social

ALL government, in its essence, is a conspiracy against the superior man: its one permanent object is to police him and cripple him. If it be aristocratic in organization, then it seeks to protect the man who is superior only in law against the man who is superior in fact; if it be democratic, then it seeks to protect the man who is inferior in every way against both. Thus one of its primary functions is to regiment men by force, to make them as much alike as possible and as dependent upon one another as possible, to search out and combat originality among them. All it can see in an original idea is potential change, and hence an invasion of its prerogatives. The most dangerous man, to any government, is the man who is able to think things out for himself, without regard to the prevailing superstitions and taboos. Almost inevitably he comes to the conclusion that the government he lives under is dishonest, insane and intolerable, and so, if he is romantic, he tries to change it. And even if he is not romantic personally he is very apt to spread discontent among those who are. Ludwig van Beethoven was certainly no politician. Nor was he a patriot. Nor had he any democratic illusions in him: he held the Viennese in even more contempt than he held the Hapsburgs. Nevertheless, I am convinced that the sharp criticism of the Hapsburg government that he used to loose in the cafés of Vienna had its effects—that some of his ideas of 1818, after a century of germination, got themselves translated into acts in 1918. Beethoven, like all other first-rate men, greatly disliked the government he lived under. I add the names of Goethe, Heine, Wagner and Nietzsche, to keep among Germans. That of Bismarck might follow: he admired the Hohenzollern idea, as Carlyle did, not the German people or the German administration. In his "Errinerungen," whenever he discusses the government that he was a part of, he has difficulty keeping his contempt within the bounds of decorum.

Nine times out of ten, it seems to me, the man who proposes a change in the government he lives under, no matter how defective it may be, is romantic to the verge of sentimentality. There is seldom, if ever, any evidence that the kind of government he is unlawfully inclined to would be any better than the government he proposes to supplant. Political revolutions, in truth, do not often accomplish anything of genuine value; their one undoubted effect is simply to throw out one gang of thieves and put in another. After a revolution, of course, the successful revolutionists always try to convince doubters that they have achieved great things, and usually they hang any man who denies it. But that surely doesn't prove their case. In Russia, for many years, the plain people were taught that getting rid of the Czar would make them all rich and happy, but now that they have got rid of him they are poorer and unhappier than ever before. The Germans, with the Kaiser in exile, have discovered that a shoemaker turned statesman is ten times as bad as a Hohenzollern. The Alsatians, having become Frenchmen again after 48 years' anxious wait, have responded to the boon by becoming extravagant Germanomaniacs. The Tyrolese, though they hated the Austrians, now hate the Italians enormously more. The Irish, having rid themselves of the English after 700 years of struggle, instantly discovered that government by Englishmen, compared to government by Irishmen, was almost paradisiacal. Even the American colonies gained little by their revolt in 1776. For twenty-five years after the Revolution they were in far worse condition as free states than they would have been as colonies. Their government was more expensive, more inefficient, more dishonest, and more tyrannical. It was only the gradual material progress of the country that saved them from starvation and collapse, and that material progress was due, not to the virtues of their new government, but to the lavishness of nature. Under the British hoof they would have got on just as well, and probably a great deal better.

The ideal government of all reflective men, from Aristotle to Herbert Spencer, is one which lets the individual alone—one which barely escapes being no government at all. This ideal, I believe, will be realized in the world twenty or thirty centuries after I have passed from these scenes and taken up my home in Hell.

2
On Minorities

It is a commonplace of historical science that the forgotten worthies who framed the Constitution of the United States had no belief in democracy. Prof. Dr. Beard, in a slim, sad book, has laboriously proved that most obvious of obviousities. Two prime objects are visible in the Constitution, beautifully enshrouded in disarming words: to protect property and to safeguard minorities—in brief, to hold the superior few harmless against the inferior many. The first object is still carried out, despite the effort of democratic law to make capital an outlaw. The second, alas, has been defeated completely. What is worse, it has been defeated in the very holy of holies of those who sought to attain it, which is to say, in the funereal chamber of the Supreme Court of the United States. Bit by bit this great bench of master minds has gradually established the doctrine that a minority in the Republic has no rights whatever. If they still exist theoretically, as fossils surviving from better days, there is certainly no machinery left for protecting and enforcing them. The current majority, if it so desired tomorrow, could add an amendment to the Constitution prohibiting the ancient Confederate vice of chewing the compressed leaves of the tobacco plant (*Nicotiana tabacum*); the Supreme Court, which has long since forgotten the Bill of Rights, would promptly issue a writ of *nihil obstat*, with a series of moral reflections as *lagniappe*. More, the Supreme Court would as promptly uphold a law prohibiting the chewing of gum (*Achras sapota*)—on the ground that any unnecessary chewing, however harmless in itself, might tempt great hordes of morons to chew tobacco. This is not a mere torturing of sardonic theory: the thing has been actually done in the case of Prohibition. The Eighteenth Amendment prohibits the sale of intoxicating beverages; the Supreme Court has decided plainly that, in order to enforce it, Congress also has the right to prohibit the sale of beverages that are admittedly *not* intoxicating. It could, indeed, specifically prohibit near-beer tomorrow, or any drink containing malt or hops, however low in alcohol; the more extreme Prohibitionists actually demand that it do so forthwith.

Worse, a minority not only has no more inalienable rights in the United States; it is not even lawfully entitled to be heard. This was well established by the case of the Socialists elected to the New York Assembly. What the voters who elected these Socialists asked for was simply the privilege of choosing spokesmen to voice their doctrines in a perfectly lawful and peaceable manner,—nothing more. This privilege was denied them. In precisely the same way, the present national House of Representatives, which happens to be Republican in complexion, might expel all of its Democratic members. The voters who elected them would have no redress. If the same men were elected again, or other men of the same views, they might be expelled again. More, it would apparently be perfectly constitutional for the majority in Congress to pass a statute denying the use of the mails to the minority—that is, for the Republicans to bar all Democratic papers from the mails. I do not toy with mere theories. The thing has actually been done in the case of the Socialists. Under the present law, indeed—upheld by the Supreme Court—the Postmaster-General, without any further authority from Congress, might deny the mails to all Democrats. Or to all Catholics. Or to all single-taxers. Or to all violoncellists.

Yet more, a citizen who happens to belong to a minority is not even safe in his person: he may be put into prison, and for very long periods, for the simple offense of differing from the majority. This happened, it will be recalled, in the case of Debs. Debs by no means advised citizens subject to military duty, in time of war, to evade that duty, as the newspapers of the time alleged. On the contrary, he advised them to meet and discharge that duty. All he did was to say that, even in time of war, he was against war—that he regarded it as a barbarous method of settling disputes between nations. For thus differing from the majority on a question of mere theory he was sentenced to ten years in prison. The case of the three young Russians arrested in New York was even more curious. These poor idiots were jailed for the almost incredible crime of circulating purely academic protests against making war upon a country with which the United States was legally at peace, to wit, Russia. For this preposterous offense two of them were sent to prison for fifteen years, and one, a girl, for ten years, and the Supreme Court upheld their convictions. Here was a plain case of proscription and punishment for a mere opinion. There was absolutely no contention that the protest of the three prisoners could have any practical result—that it might, for example, destroy the *morale* of American soldiers 6,000 miles away, and cut off from all communication with the United States. The three victims were ordered to be punished in that appalling manner simply because they ventured to criticise an executive usurpation which happened, at the moment, to have the support of public opinion, and particularly of the then President of the United States and of the holders of Russian government securities.

It must be obvious, viewing such leading cases critically—and hundreds like them might be cited—that the old rights of the free American, so carefully laid down by the Bill of Rights, are now worth nothing. Bit by bit, Congress and the State Legislatures have invaded and nullified them, and today they are so flimsy that no lawyer not insane would attempt to defend his client by bringing them up. Imagine trying to defend a man denied the use of the mails by the Postmaster-General, without hearing or even formal notice, on the ground that the Constitution guarantees the right of free speech! The very catchpolls in the courtroom would snicker. I say that the legislative arm is primarily responsible for this gradual enslavement of the Americano; the truth is, of course, that the executive and judicial arms are responsible to a scarcely less degree. Our law has not kept pace with the development of our bureaucracy; there is no machinery provided for curbing its excesses. In Prussia, in the old days, there were special courts for the purpose, and a citizen oppressed by the police or by any other public official could get relief and redress. The guilty functionary could be fined, mulcted in damages, demoted, cashiered, or even jailed. But in the United States to-day there are no such tribunals. A citizen attacked by the Postmaster-General simply has no redress whatever; the courts have refused, over and over again, to interfere save in cases of obvious fraud. Nor is there, it would seem, any remedy for the unconstitutional acts of Prohibition agents. Some time ago, when Senator Stanley, of Kentucky, tried to have a law passed forbidding them to break into a citizen's house in violation of the Bill of Rights, the Prohibitionists mustered up their serfs in the Senate against him, and he was voted down.

The Supreme Court, had it been so disposed, might have put a stop to all this sinister buffoonery long ago. There was a time, indeed, when it was alert to do so. That was during the Civil War. But since then the court has gradually succumbed to the prevailing doctrine that the minority has no rights that the majority is bound to respect. As it is at present constituted, it shows little disposition to go to the rescue of the harassed freeman. When property is menaced it displays a laudable diligence, but when it comes to the mere rights of the citizen it seems hopelessly inclined to give the prosecution the benefit of every doubt. Two justices commonly dissent—two out of nine. They hold the last switch-trench of the old constitutional line. When they depart to realms of bliss the Bill of Rights will be buried with them.

XVII.
Reflections on the Drama

THE drama is the most democratic of the art forms, and perhaps the only one that may legitimately bear the label. Painting, sculpture, music and literature, so far as they show any genuine æsthetic or intellectual content at all, are not for crowds, but for selected individuals, mostly with bad kidneys and worse morals, and three of the four are almost always enjoyed in actual solitude. Even architecture and religious ritual, though they are publicly displayed, make their chief appeal to man as individual, not to man as mass animal. One goes into a church as part of a crowd, true enough, but if it be a church that has risen above mere theological disputation to the beauty of ceremonial, one is, even in theory, alone with the Lord God Jehovah. And if, passing up Fifth Avenue in the 5 o'clock throng, one pauses before St. Thomas's to drink in the beauty of that archaic facade, one's drinking is almost sure to be done *a cappella*; of the other passers-by, not one in a thousand so much as glances at it.

But the drama, as representation, is inconceivable save as a show for the mob, and so it has to take on protective coloration to survive. It must make its appeal, not to individuals as such, nor even to individuals as units in the mob, but to the mob as mob—a quite different thing, as Gustav Le Bon long ago demonstrated in his "Psychologie des Foules." Thus its intellectual content, like its æsthetic form, must be within the mental grasp of the mob, and what is more important, within the scope of its prejudices. *Per corollary*, anything even remotely approaching an original idea, or an unpopular idea, is foreign to it, and if it would make any impression at all, abhorrent to it. The best a dramatist can hope to do is to give poignant and arresting expression to an idea so simple that the average man will grasp it at once, and so banal that he will approve it in the next instant. The phrase "drama of ideas" thus becomes a mere phrase. What is actually meant by it is "drama of platitudes."

So much for the theory. An appeal to the facts quickly substantiates it. The more one looks into the so-called drama of ideas of the last age—that is, into the acting drama—the more one is astounded by the vacuity of its content. The younger Dumas' "La Dame aux Camélias," the first of all the propaganda plays (it raised a stupendous pother in 1852, the echoes of which yet roll), is based upon the sophomoric thesis that a prostitute is a human being like you and me, and suffers the slings and arrows of the same sorrows, and may be potentially quite as worthy of heaven. Augier's "La Mariage d'Olympe" (1854), another sensation-making pioneer, is even hollower; its four acts are devoted to rubbing in the revolutionary discovery that it is unwise for a young man of good family to marry an elderly cocotte. Proceed now to Ibsen. Here one finds the same tasteless platitudes—that it is unpleasant for a wife to be treated as a doll; that professional patriots and town boomers are frauds; that success in business is often grounded upon a mere willingness to do what a man of honor is incapable of; that a woman who continues to live with a debauched husband may expect to have unhealthy children; that a joint sorrow tends to bring husband and wife together; that a neurotic woman is apt to prefer death to maternity; that a man of 55 is an ass to fall in love with a flapper of 17. Do I burlesque? If you think so, turn to Ibsen's "Nachgelassene Schriften" and read his own statements of the ideas in his social dramas—read his own succinct summaries of their theses. You will imagine yourself, on more than one page, in the latest volume of mush by Orison Swett Marden. Such "ideas" are what one finds in newspaper editorials, speeches before Congress, sermons by evangelical divines—in brief, in the literature expressly addressed to those persons whose distinguishing mark is that ideas never enter their heads.

Ibsen himself, an excellent poet and a reflective man, was under no delusions about his "dramas of ideas." It astounded him greatly when the sentimental German middle-classes hailed "Ein Puppenheim" as a revolutionary document; he protested often and bitterly against being mistaken for a prophet of feminism. His own interest in this play and in those that followed it was chiefly technical; he was trying to displace the well-made play of Scribe and company with something simpler, more elastic and more hospitable to character. He wrote "Ghosts" to raise a laugh against the fools who had seen something novel and horrible in the idea of "A Doll's House"; he wanted to prove to them that that idea was no more than a platitude. Soon afterward he became thoroughly disgusted with the whole "drama of ideas." In "The Wild Duck" he cruelly burlesqued it, and made a low-comedy Ibsenist his chief butt. In "Hedda Gabler" he played a joke on the Ibsen fanatics by fashioning a first-rate drama out of the oldest, shoddiest materials of Sardou, Feuillet, and even Meilhac and Halévy. And beginning with "Little Eyolf" he threw the "drama of ideas" overboard forever, and took to mysticism. What could be more comical than the efforts of critical talmudists to read a thesis into "When We Dead Awaken"? I have put in many a gay hour perusing their commentaries. Ibsen, had he lived, would have roared over them—as he roared over the effort to inject portentous meanings into "The Master Builder," at bottom no more than a sentimental epitaph to a love affair that he himself had suffered at 60.

Gerhart Hauptmann, another dramatist of the first rank, has gone much the same road. As a very young man he succumbed to the "drama of ideas" gabble, and his first plays showed an effort to preach this or that in awful tones. But he soon discovered that the only ideas that would go down, so to speak, on the stage were ideas of such an austere platitudinousness that it was beneath his artistic dignity to merchant them, and so he gave over propaganda altogether. In other words, his genius burst through the narrow bounds of mob ratiocination, and he began appealing to the universal emotions—pity, religious sentiment, patriotism, amorousness. Even in his first play, "Vor Sonnenaufgang," his instinct got the better of his mistaken purpose, and reading it to-day one finds that the sheer horror of it is of vastly more effect than its nebulous and unimportant ideas. It really says nothing; it merely makes us dislike some very unpleasant people.

Turn now to Shaw. At once one finds that the only plays from his pen which contain actual ideas have failed dismally on the stage. These are the so-called "discussions"—*e.g.*, "Getting Married." The successful plays contain no ideas; they contain only platitudes, balderdash, buncombe that even a suffragette might think of. Of such sort are "Man and Superman," "Arms and the Man," "Candida," "Androcles and the Lion," and their like. Shaw has given all of these pieces a specious air of profundity by publishing them hooked to long and garrulous prefaces and by filling them with stage directions which describe and discuss the characters at great length. But as stage plays they are almost as empty as "Hedda Gabler." One searches them vainly for even the slightest novel contribution to the current theories of life, joy and crime. Shaw's prefaces, of course, have vastly more ideational force and respectability than his plays. If he fails to get any ideas of genuine savor into them it is not because the preface form bars them out but because he hasn't any to get in. By attaching them to his plays he converts the latter into colorable imitations of novels, and so opens the way for that superior reflectiveness which lifts the novel above the play, and makes it, as Arnold Bennett has convincingly shown, much harder to write. A stage play in the modern realistic manner—that is, without soliloquies and asides—can seldom rise above the mere representation of some infinitesimal episode, whereas even the worst novel may be, in some sense, an interpretation as well. Obviously, such episodes as may be exposed in 20,000 words—the extreme limit of the average play—are seldom significant, and not often clearly intelligible. The author has a hard enough job making his characters recognizable as human beings; he hasn't time to go behind their acts to their motives, or to deduce any conclusions worth hearing from their doings. One often leaves a "social drama," indeed, wondering what the deuce it is all about; the discussion of its meaning offers endless opportunities for theorists and fanatics. The Ibsen symbolists come to mind again. They read meanings into such plays as "Rosmersholm" and "The Wild Duck" that aroused Ibsen, a peaceful man, to positive fury. In the same way the suffragettes collared "A Doll's House." Even "Peer Gynt" did not escape. There is actually an edition of it edited by a theosophist, in the preface to which it is hymned as a theosophical document. Luckily for Ibsen, he died before this edition was printed. But one may well imagine how it would have made him swear.

The notion that there are ideas in the "drama of ideas," in truth, is confined to a special class of illuminati, whose chief visible character is their capacity for ingesting nonsense—Maeterlinckians, uplifters, women's clubbers, believers in all the sure cures for all the sorrows of the world. To-day the Drama League carries on the tradition. It is composed of the eternally young—unsuccessful dramatists who yet live in hope, young college professors, psychopathic old maids, middle-aged ladies of an incurable jejuneness, the innumerable caravan of the ingenuous and sentimental. Out of the same intellectual *Landsturm* comes the following of Bergson, the parlor metaphysician; and of the third-rate novelists praised by the newspapers; and of such composers as Wolf-Ferrari and Massenet. These are the fair ones, male and female, who were ecstatically shocked by the platitudes of "Damaged Goods," and who regard Augustus Thomas as a great dramatist, and what is more, as a great thinker. Their hero, during a season or two, was the Swedish John the Baptist, August Strindberg—a lunatic with a gift for turning the preposterous into the shocking. A glance at Strindberg's innumerable volumes of autobiography reveals the true horse-power of his so-called ideas. He believed in everything that was idiotic, from transcendentalism to witchcraft. He believed that his enemies were seeking to destroy him by magic; he spent a whole winter trying to find the philosopher's stone. Even among the clergy, it would be difficult to find a more astounding ass than Strindberg. But he had, for all his folly, a considerable native skill at devising effective stage-plays—a talent that some men seem to be born with—and under cover of it he acquired his reputation as a thinker. Here he was met half-way by the defective powers of observation and reflection of his followers, the half-wits aforesaid; they mistook their enjoyment of his adept technical trickery for an appreciation of ideas. Turn to the best of his plays, "The Father." Here the idea—that domestic nagging can cause insanity—is an almost perfect platitude, for on the one hand it is universally admitted and on the other hand it is not true. But as a stage play pure and simple, the piece is superb—a simple and yet enormously effective mechanism. So with "Countess Julie." The idea here is so vague and incomprehensible that no two commentators agree in stating it, and yet the play is so cleverly written, and appeals with such a sure touch to the universal human weakness for the obscene, that it never fails to enchant an audience. The. case of "Hedda Gabler" is parallel. If the actresses playing Hedda in this country made up for the part in the scandalous way their sisters do in Germany (that is, by wearing bustles in front), it would be as great a success here as it is over there. Its general failure among us is due to the fact that it is not made indelicate enough. This also explains the comparative failure of the rest of the Ibsen plays. The crowd has been subtly made to believe that they are magnificently indecent—and is always dashed and displeased when it finds nothing to lift the diaphragm. I well remember the first production of "Ghosts" in America—a business in which I had a hand. So eager was the audience for the promised indecencies that it actually read them into the play, and there were protests against it on the ground that Mrs. Alving was represented as trying to seduce her own son! Here comstockery often helps the "drama of ideas." If no other idea is visible, it can always conjure up, out of its native swinishness, some idea that is offensively sexual, and hence pleasing to the mob.

That mob rules in the theater, and so the theater remains infantile and trivial—a scene, not of the exposure of ideas, nor even of the exhibition of beauty, but one merely of the parading of mental and physical prettiness and vulgarity. It is at its worst when its dramatists seek to corrupt this function by adding a moral or intellectual purpose. It is at its best when it confines itself to the unrealities that are its essence, and swings amiably from the romance that never was on land or sea to the buffoonery that is at the bottom of all we actually know of human life. Shakespeare was its greatest craftsman: he wasted no tortured ratiocination upon his plays. Instead, he filled them with the gaudy heroes that all of us see ourselves becoming on some bright tomorrow, and the lowly frauds and clowns we are to-day. No psychopathic problems engaged him; he took love and ambition and revenge and braggadocio as he found them. He held no clinics in dingy Norwegian apartment-houses: his field was Bohemia, glorious Rome, the Egypt of the scene-painter, Arcady. . . . But even Shakespeare, for all the vast potency of his incomparable, his stupefying poetry, could not long hold the talmudists out in front from their search for invisible significances. Think of all the tomes that have been written upon the profound and revolutionary "ideas" in the moony musings of the diabetic sophomore, Hamlet von Dänemark!

XVIII.
Advice to Young Men

I
To Him That Hath

THE most valuable of all human possessions, next to a superior and disdainful air, is the reputation of being well to do. Nothing else so neatly eases one's way through life, especially in democratic countries. There is in ninety-nine per cent. of all democrats an irresistible impulse to crook the knee to wealth, to defer humbly to the power that goes with it, to see all sorts of high merits in the man who has it, or is said to have it. True enough, envy goes with the pliant neck, but it is envy somehow purged of all menace: the inferior man is afraid to do evil to the man with money in eight banks; he is even afraid to *think* evil of him—that is, in any patent and offensive way. Against capital as an abstraction he rants incessantly, and all of the laws that he favors treat it as if it were criminal. But in the presence of the concrete capitalist he is singularly fawning. What makes him so is easy to discern. He yearns with a great yearning for a chance to tap the capitalist's purse, and he knows very well, deep down in his heart, that he is too craven and stupid to do it by force of arms. So he turns to politeness, and tries to cajole. Give out the news that one has just made a killing in the stock market, or robbed some confiding widow of her dower, or swindled the government in some patriotic enterprise, and at once one will discover that one's shabbiness is a charming eccentricity, and one's judgment of wines worth hearing, and one's politics worthy of attention and respect. The man who is thought to be poor never gets a fair chance. No one wants to listen to him. No one gives a damn what he thinks or knows or feels. No one has any active desire for his good opinion.

I discovered this principle early in life, and have put it to use ever since. I have got a great deal more out of men (and women) by having the name of being a well-heeled fellow than I have ever got by being decent to them, or by dazzling them with my sagacity, or by hard industry, or by a personal beauty that is singular and ineffable.

2
The Venerable Examined

The older I grow the more I distrust the familiar doctrine that age brings wisdom. It is my honest belief that I am no wiser to-day than I was five or ten years ago; in fact, I often suspect that I am appreciably *less* wise. Women can prevail over me to-day by devices that would have made me hoof them out of my studio when I was thirty-five. I am also an easier mark for male swindlers than I used to be; at fifty I'll probably be joining clubs and buying Mexican mine stock. The truth is that every man goes up-hill in sagacity to a certain point, and then begins sliding down again. Nearly all the old fellows that I know are more or less balmy. Theoretically, they should be much wiser than younger men, if only because of their greater experience, but actually they seem to take on folly faster than they take on wisdom. A man of thirty-five or thirty-eight is almost woman-proof. For a woman to marry him is a herculean feat. But by the time he is fifty he is quite as easy as a Yale sophomore. On other planes the same decay of the intelligence is visible. Certainly it would be difficult to imagine any committee of relatively young men, of thirty or thirty-five, showing the unbroken childishness, ignorance and lack of humor of the Supreme Court of the United States. The average age of the learned justices must be well beyond sixty, and all of them are supposed to be of finished and mellowed sagacity. Yet their knowledge of the most ordinary principles of justice often turns out to be extremely meager, and when they spread themselves grandly upon a great case their reasoning powers are usually found to be precisely equal to those of a respectable Pullman conductor.

3
Duty

Some of the loosest thinking in ethics has duty for its theme. Practically all writers on the subject agree that the individual owes certain unescapable duties to the race—for example, the duty of engaging in productive labor, and that of marrying and begetting offspring. In support of this position it is almost always argued that if *all* men neglected such duties the race would perish. The logic is hollow enough to be worthy of the college professors who are guilty of it. It simply confuses the conventionality, the pusillanimity, the lack of imagination of the majority of men with the duty of *all* men. There is not the slightest ground for assuming, even as a matter of mere argumentation, that *all* men will ever neglect these alleged duties. There will always remain a safe majority that is willing to do whatever is ordained—that accepts docilely the government it is born under, obeys its laws, and supports its theory. But that majority does not comprise the men who render the highest and most intelligent services to the race; it comprises those who render nothing save their obedience.

For the man who differs from this inert and well-regimented mass, however slightly, there are no duties *per se.* What he is spontaneously inclined to do is of vastly more value to all of us than what the majority is willing to do. There is, indeed, no such thing as duty-in-itself; it is a mere chimera of ethical theorists. Human progress is furthered, not by conformity, but by aberration. The very concept of duty is thus a function of inferiority; it belongs naturally only to timorous and incompetent men. Even on such levels it remains largely a self-delusion, a soothing apparition, a euphemism for necessity. When a man succumbs to duty he merely succumbs to the habit and inclination of other men. Their collective interests invariably pull against his individual interests. Some of us can resist a pretty strong pull—the pull, perhaps, of thousands. But it is only the miraculous man who can withstand the pull of a whole nation.

4
Martyrs

"History," says Henry Ford, "is bunk." I inscribe myself among those who dissent from this doctrine; nevertheless, I am often hauled up, in reading history, by a feeling that I am among unrealities. In particular, that feeling comes over me when I read about the religious wars of the past—wars in which thousands of men, women and children were butchered on account of puerile and unintelligible disputes over transubstantiation, the atonement, and other such metaphysical banshees. It does not surprise me that the majority murdered the minority; the majority, even to-day, does it whenever it is possible. What I can't understand is that the minority went voluntarily to the slaughter. Even in the worst persecutions known to history—say, for example, those of the Jews of Spain—it was always possible for a given member of the minority to save his hide by giving public assent to the religious notions of the majority. A Jew who was willing to be baptized, in the reign of Ferdinand and Isabella, was practically unmolested; his descendants today are 100% Spaniards. Well, then, why did so many Jews refuse? Why did so many prefer to be robbed, exiled, and sometimes murdered?

The answer given by philosophical historians is that they were a noble people, and preferred death to heresy. But this merely begs the question. Is it actually noble to cling to a religious idea so tenaciously? Certainly it doesn't seem so to me. After all, no human being really *knows* anything about the exalted matters with which all religions deal. The most he can do is to match his private guess against the guesses of his fellow-men. For any man to say absolutely, in such a field, that this or that is wholly and irrefragably true and this or that is utterly false is simply to talk nonsense. Personally, I have never encountered a religious idea—and I do not except even the idea of the existence of God—that was instantly and unchallengeably convincing, as, say, the Copernican astronomy is instantly and unchallengeably convincing. But neither have I ever encountered a religious idea that could be dismissed offhand as palpably and indubitably false. In even the worst nonsense of such theological mountebanks as the Rev. Dr. Billy Sunday, Brigham Young and Mrs. Eddy there is always enough lingering plausibility, or, at all events, possibility, to give the judicious pause. Whatever the weight of the probabilities against it, it nevertheless *may* be true that man, on his decease, turns into a gaseous vertebrate, and that this vertebrate, if its human larva has engaged in embezzlement, bootlegging, profanity or adultery on this earth, will be boiled for a million years in a cauldron of pitch. My private inclination, due to my defective upbringing, is to doubt it, and to set down any one who believes it as an ass, but it must be plain that I have no means of disproving it.

In view of this uncertainty it seems to me sheer vanity for any man to hold his religious views too firmly, or to submit to any inconvenience on account of them. It is far better, if they happen to offend, to conceal them discreetly, or to change them amiably as the delusions of the majority change. My own views in this department, being wholly skeptical and tolerant, are obnoxious to the subscribers to practically all other views; even atheists sometimes denounce me. At the moment, by an accident of American political history, these dissenters from my theology are forbidden to punish me for not agreeing with them. But at any succeeding moment some group or other among them may seize such power and proceed against me in the immemorial manner. If it ever happens, I give notice here and now that I shall get converted to their nonsense instantly, and so retire to safety with my right thumb laid against my nose and my fingers waving like wheat in the wind. I'd do it even to-day, if there were any practical advantage in it. Offer me a case of Rauenthaler 1903, and I engage to submit to baptism by any rite ever heard of, provided it does not expose my gothic nakedness. Make it ten cases, and I'll agree to be both baptized and confirmed. In such matters I am broad-minded. What, after all, is one more lie?

5
The Disabled Veteran

The science of psychological pathology is still in its infancy. In all its literature in three languages, I can't find a line about the permanent ill effects of acute emotional diseases—say, for example, love affairs. The common assumption of the world is that when a love affair is over it is over—that nothing remains behind. This is probably grossly untrue. It is my belief that every such experience leaves scars upon my psyche, and that they are quite as plain and quite as dangerous as the scars left on the neck by a carbuncle. A man who has passed through a love affair, even though he may eventually forget the lady's very name, is never quite the same thereafter. His scars may be small, but they are permanent. The sentimentalist, exposed incessantly, ends as a psychic cripple; he is as badly off as the man who has come home from the wars with shell-shock. The precise nature of the scars remains to be determined. My own notion is that they take the form of large yellow patches upon the self-esteem. Whenever a man thinks of one of his dead love affairs, and in particular whenever he allows his memory to dredge up an image of the woman he loved, he shivers like one taken in some unmanly and discreditable act. Such shivers, repeated often enough, must inevitably shake his inner integrity off its base. No man can love, and yet remain truly proud. It is a disarming and humiliating experience.

6
Patriotism

Patriotism is conceivable to a civilized man in times of stress and storm, when his country is wobbling and sore beset. His country then appeals to him as any victim of misfortune appeals to him—say, a street-walker pursued by the police. But when it is safe, happy and prosperous it can only excite his loathing. The things that make countries safe, happy and prosperous—a secure peace, an active trade, political serenity at home—are all intrinsically corrupting and disgusting. It is as impossible for a civilized man to love his country in good times as it would be for him to respect a politician.

XIX.
Suite Américaine

I
Aspiration

POLICE sergeants praying humbly to God that Jews will start poker-rooms on their posts, and so enable them to educate their eldest sons for holy orders. . . . Newspaper reporters resolving firmly to work hard, keep sober and be polite to the city editor, and so be rewarded with jobs as copy-readers. . . . College professors in one-building universities on the prairie, still hoping, at the age of sixty, to get their whimsical essays into the *Atlantic Monthly*. . . . Car-conductors on lonely suburban lines, trying desperately to save up $500 and start a Ford garage. . . . Pastors of one-horse little churches in decadent villages, who, whenever they drink two cups of coffee at supper, dream all night that they have been elected bishops. . . . Movie actors who hope against hope that the next fan letter will be from Bar Harbor. . . . Delicatessen dealers who spend their whole lives searching for a cheap substitute for the embalmed veal used in chicken-salad. . . . Italians who wish that they were Irish. . . . Mulatto girls in Georgia and Alabama who send away greasy dollar bills for bottles of Mme. Celestine's Infallible Hair-Straightener. . . . Ash-men who pull wires to be appointed superintendents of city dumps. . . . Mothers who dream that the babies in their cradles will reach, in the mysterious after years, the highest chairs in the Red Men and the Maccabees. . . . Farmers who figure that, with good luck, they will be able to pay off their mortgages by 1943. . . . Contestants for the standing broad-jump championship of the Altoona, Pa., Y.M.C.A. . . . Editorial writers who essay to prove mathematically that a war between England and the United States is unthinkable. . . .

2
Virtue

Pale druggists in remote towns of the Epworth League and flannel nightgown belts, endlessly wrapping up bottles of Peruna. . . . Women hidden away in the damp kitchens of unpainted houses along the railroad tracks, frying tough beefsteaks. . . . Lime and cement dealers being initiated into the Knights of Pythias, the Red Men or the Woodmen of the World. . . . Watchmen at lonely railroad crossings in Iowa, hoping that they'll be able to get off to hear the United Brethren evangelist preach. . . . Ticket-choppers in the subway, breathing sweat in its gaseous form. . . . Family doctors in poor neighborhoods, faithfully relying upon the therapeutics taught in their Eclectic Medical College in 1884. . . . Farmers plowing sterile fields behind sad meditative horses, both suffering from the bites of insects. . . . Greeks tending all-night coffee-joints in the suburban wildernesses where the trolley-cars stop. . . . Grocery-clerks stealing prunes and ginger-snaps, and trying to make assignations with soapy servant-girls. . . . Women confined for the ninth or tenth time, wondering helplessly what it is all about. . . . Methodist preachers retired after forty years of service in the trenches of God, upon pensions of $600 a year. . . . Wives and daughters of Middle Western country bankers, marooned in Los Angeles, going tremblingly to swami séances in dark, smelly rooms. . . . Chauffeurs in huge fur coats waiting outside theaters filled with folks applauding Robert Edeson and Jane Cowl. . . . Decayed and hopeless men writing editorials at midnight for leading papers in Mississippi, Arkansas and Alabama. . . . Owners of the principal candy-stores in Green River, Neb., and Tyrone, Pa. . . . Presidents of one-building universities in the rural fastnesses of Kentucky and Tennessee. . . . Women with babies in their arms weeping over moving-pictures in the Elks' Hall at Schmidtsville, Mo. . . . Babies just born to the wives of milk-wagon drivers. . . . Judges on the benches of petty county courts in Virginia, Vermont and Idaho. . . . Conductors of accommodation trains running between Kokomo, Ind., and Logansport. . . .

3
Eminence

The leading Methodist layman of Pottawattamie county, Iowa. . . . The man who won the limerick contest conducted by the Toomsboro, Ga., *Banner*. . . . The secretary of the Little Rock, Ark., Kiwanis Club. . . . The president of the Johann Sebastian Bach *Bauverein* of Highlandtown, Md. . . . The girl who sold the most Liberty Bonds in Duquesne, Pa. . . . The captain of the champion basket-ball team at the Gary, Ind., Y.M.C.A. . . . The man who owns the best bull in Coosa county, Ala. . . . The tallest man in Covington, Ky. . . . The oldest subscriber to the Raleigh, N.C., *News and Observer*. . . . The most fashionable milliner in Bucyrus, O. . . . The business agent of the Plasterers' Union of Somerville, Mass. . . . The author of the ode read at the unveiling of the monument to General Robert E. Lee at Valdosta, Ga. . . . The original Henry Cabot Lodge man. . . . The owner of the champion Airedale of Buffalo, N.Y. . . . The first child named after the Hon. Warren Gamaliel Harding. . . . The old lady in Wahoo, Neb., who has read the Bible 38 times. . . . The boss who controls the Italian, Czecho-Slovak and Polish votes in Youngstown, O. . . . The professor of chemistry, Greek, rhetoric and piano at the Texas Christian University, Fort Worth, Tex. . . . The boy who sells 225 copies of the *Saturday Evening Post* every week in Cheyenne, Wyo. . . . The youngest murderer awaiting hanging in Chicago. . . . The leading dramatic critic of Pittsburgh. . . . The night watchman in Penn Yan, N.Y., who once shook hands with Chester A. Arthur. . . . The Lithuanian woman in Bluefield, W. Va., who has had five sets of triplets. . . . The actor who has played in "Lightning" 1,600 times. . . . The best horsedoctor in Oklahoma. . . . The highest-paid church-choir soprano in Knoxville, Tenn. . . . The most eligible bachelor in Cheyenne, Wyo. . . . The engineer of the locomotive which pulled the train which carried the Hon. A. Mitchell Palmer to the San Francisco Convention. . . . The girl who got the most votes in the popularity contest at Egg Harbor, N.J. . . .

APPENDIX

from

MY LIFE AS AUTHOR AND EDITOR

from

My Life as Author and Editor

MY second large enterprise of 1919 was the launching of my "Prejudices" series, the first volume of which came out in September. The idea of this series was rather obvious, for my periodical writings, and especially my *Smart Set* reviews, were getting more and more notice, but rather strangely it did not occur to either Knopf or me. Knopf, indeed, was against it when he first heard it proposed. Its originator was a bookseller in Cleveland named Richard Laukhuff, and in a letter of April 23, 1943 he told me the story, which Knopf corroborated. Thus:

> During the days of the *Smart Set* I collected your book reviews and placed them in folders for easy reference by people coming to the shop. I found them much to the point, and thought others might, so I kept them lying around. People did pick them up and read them, and most lively discussions were started and people discovered books. One day Mr. Knopf, who in those days was his own salesman, came to the store. He invited suggestions. Among other ideas, I suggested publication of some of your reviews.
>
> Mr. Knopf: Nobody would buy them.
>
> Laukhuff: Many people will buy them.
>
> The next Knopf catalog had the announcement of "Prejudices."

I was myself rather dubious about the project, for it was common publishing experience that reprinted reviews did not sell. Moreover, I was full of plans in those days for editing a history of the American share in World War I—not the military history, but the record of the spy-hunting, profiteering and patrioteering at home—and was eager to get to work on it. I had conceived it on a large scale, and figured that it would run to 25 or 30 volumes, and perhaps more—one, for example, to be devoted to the record of the American clergy in the war, another to the wholesale stealing of German property, a third to the war-mongering in the colleges, a fourth to the Liberty loan campaigns, a fifth to the part played by the newspapers and so on and so on. Such an enterprise, of course, was beyond the capacity of one man, so I counted on getting together a committee of like-minded persons, raising a fund to finance the writing and printing, and perhaps setting a mob of nascent Ph.D.'s to work at the amassing of materials. This amassing would involve an examination of all the principal American newspapers from 1914 to date, and of many minor ones, and it would also take a great deal of traveling. Unhappily, I soon found that executing the scheme on anything approaching an adequate scale would cost at least $1,000,000, and inasmuch as I could find no one willing to put up so much money I had to abandon it. But while I cherished it it entertained me pleasantly, and I accumulated myself a great mass of newspaper clippings and other documents. They nearly filled the loft of the little pony-stable in Hollins street, and there they remained until I returned to the old house in 1936, when I called in a colored trash man and presented the whole lot to him as waste-paper. The history of the American share in World War I has not been written to this day, and I doubt that it ever will be. The academic historians adopted the official view of it, and only a few of them—for example, Sidney B. Fay of Harvard*—have ever made any effort, however slight, to unearth and print the extremely discreditable facts. The same thing is now happening (1945) in the case of World War II, and I suppose the American people will continue to be fed balderdash until the end of the chapter. It is always possible, however, that some foreigner—say an Englishman—will attempt some day to tell the truth, but I should add at once that it is not likely. I often wonder whether the history of the remoter past is any more reliable. It has been investigated at enormous length by earnest and diligent men, and some of the delusions that once prevailed have been exploded, but in the main what we believe about it is probably quite as dubious as what Americans believe about World War I.

Following Laukhuff's plan, "Prejudices: First Series" was mainly made up of things that had been printed in the *Smart Set*, but I did some painstaking rewriting, and also added material from my articles in other magazines and in newspapers, and some stuff written especially for the book. On September 6, 1919 I wrote to Fielding H. Garrison: "It is full of rough stuff, perhaps too cruel—but, after all, it is foolish to be polite

*His Origins of the World War was published in 1928.

to frauds". And on September 28: "It is light stuff, chiefly rewritten from the *Smart Set*, but with now and then a blast from the lower woodwind. It will outrage the umbilicari, if that is the way to spell it. Such books are mere stinkpots, heaved occasionally to keep the animals perturbed. The real artillery fire will begin a bit later".* How many copies of the first edition Knopf printed I do not recall, but he had sold 1678 by December 31—a very pleasant surprise to both of us. The second printing was already on the press, and it came out in January, 1920. A third followed in April, 1920, and a fourth in March, 1921. There was a fifth in December, and a sixth in March, 1923, and in February of the latter year Knopf issued a reprint in his Borzoi Pocket Books. Reprints in this series and in the regular edition followed in 1924, 1926 and 1929, and the book remained in print until 1933, when the plates were at last melted. Jonathan Cape took 500 sheets for England, but had sold only 296 copies by November, 1921. In the United States it did much better. Though it was overtaken by "Prejudices: Second Series" in October, 1920, it sold 1052 copies in that year. It kept on selling steadily until 1931, eleven years after its first publication, when there was a drop, and Knopf and I began to discuss letting it go out of print. When the plates were melted in 1933 about 300 copies remained in stock. They were finally disposed of by 1942, and "Prejudices: First Series" perished from this earth. The total sales by that time, if I calculate correctly, were 15,712, and counting in the small fees paid by Cape for the English rights and the sums received from reprint rights, my receipts from it amounted altogether to $3222.33. This was certainly good pay for a book that I had compounded out of clippings in no more than a few weeks of intermittent labor. Requests for reprint rights still occasionally come in.† After the first edition was published Knopf told me that he thought he should adopt a standard format for all of my books, and we decided upon dark blue cloth with gilt stamping, and my coat-of-arms in blind stamping on the front

*This is a reference, of course, to my projected history of the war.

†The copy from which Prejudices I was set up is in a volume entitled Prejudices: First Series—Original Typescript—1919, in the Mencken collection at the Pratt Library, Baltimore.

cover. This was first used for the second printing, and was retained for my books thereafter, though not invariably.*

My description of "Prejudices: First Series" as a stinkpot designed "to keep the animals perturbed" was not altogether inept, for if that was not the fundamental purpose of the book, then it was certainly its effect. Most of the contents were not new, for they had been printed before in the *Smart Set*, but their impact, coming out in small instalments, had been much less than their impact in one blast. I made a deliberate effort to lay as many quacks as possible, and chose my targets, not only from the great names of the past, but also from the current company of favorites. Thus butcheries of some of the elder demigods were accompanied by onslaughts upon some of the reigning favorites of 1919, ranging from H. G. Wells, William Dean Howells and George Bernard Shaw down to Henry Van Dyke, William Allen White, Irvin Cobb, Henry Sydnor Harrison, Hamlin Garland, Amy Lowell, Ernest Poole, Thorstein Veblen, Will Levington Comfort and Joyce Kilmer. Some of these attacks drew blood, and their victims never recovered afterward, notably Veblen, Poole, Garland, Comfort, Harrison and Cobb.† Nor did I spare, in my laying about, men with whom I was on good terms personally, and in whom I saw, mixed with fustian, some sound merit—for example, Edgar Lee Masters, Vachel Lindsay, Ezra Pound and Robert Frost. My book, of course, was not all abuse, for I had friendly words in it for all these men, and also for Arnold Bennett, Jack London, George Ade, Elsie Clews Parsons, Hermann Sudermann,

*It was still used for my Supplement I to The American Language, 1945.

†After Veblen's death in 1929 a biography of him appeared, and I was somewhat upset to learn from it that my *reductio ad absurdum* of his pompous pseudo-philosophy had greatly disconcerted him, and in fact thrown him into despair. Before I tackled him he had been the favorite sage of all the advanced thinkers of the time, and the *New Republic* whooped him up in terms fit for Aristotle, but a little while afterward he was abandoned for an even worse quack, John Dewey. I regretted his sufferings, but I still believe that my denunciation of him was deserved. Garland attempted to strike back at me in one of his volumes of autobiography, published in his later years, but this riposte was too transparent to be effective, and he was by that time pretty well frayed. He died in 1940. Comfort, Harrison, Cobb and Poole were never taken seriously after 1919. Comfort died in 1932, Harrison in 1930 and Cobb in 1944. Poole is still living (1945), but all his books since those I excoriated have fallen flat.

George Jean Nathan* and many others. Also, I gave over several chapters to less personal themes—for example, the uproar over sex, then in full blast; the psychology of Puritanism, and the general state of civilization in the United States. On the latter theme, though the Treaty of Versailles was but three months old, I had this to say:

> A mongrel and inferior people, incapable of any spiritual aspiration above that of second-rate English colonials, we seek refuge inevitably in the one sort of superiority that the lower castes of men can authentically boast, to wit, superiority in docility, in credulity, in resignation, in morals. We are the most moral race in the world; there is not another that we do not look down upon in that department; our confessed aim and destiny as a nation is to inoculate them all with our incomparable rectitude. In the last analysis, all ideas are judged among us by moral standards; moral values are our only permanent tests of worth, whether in the arts, in politics, in philosophy or in life itself. Even the instincts of man, so intrinsically immoral, so innocent, are fitted with moral false-faces. That bedevilment by sex ideas which punishes continence, so abhorrent to nature, is converted into a moral frenzy, pathological in the end. The impulse to cavort and kick up one's legs, so healthy, so universal, is hedged in by incomprehensible taboos; it becomes stealthy, dirty, degrading. The desire to create and linger over beauty, the sign and touchstone of man's rise above the brute, is held down by doubts and hesitations; when it breaks through it must do so by orgy and explosion, half ludicrous and half pathetic. Our function, we choose to believe, is to teach and inspire the world. We are wrong. Our function is to amuse the world.

This sort of thing naturally alarmed many of the book reviewers, so they dealt with "Prejudices: First Series" in a rather gingery fashion, avoiding too particular an account of its contents and tempering their approval with caution. This was true, for example, of Philip Littell, who gave it a generally favorable notice in the *New Republic* for January 21, 1920, but

*Some of the reviewers professed to be surprised and amused by my notion that Nathan was a better dramatic critic than any of the others then practising in New York, for example, Clayton Hamilton, whom I derided as a jackass, but it must be manifest today (1945) that I was right. I did not believe then, and do not believe now, that writing notices of current theatrical exhibitions is a very lofty branch of the literary art, but such as it is Nathan carried it on with wit, sound information and plenty of acumen. No other New York dramatic critic of his day, or of any other day, has been better.

saved himself with many prudent whereases and howevers. It was true, likewise, of many newspaper reviews, for example, those of the Indianapolis *News*, the Detroit *News* (D. Kenneth Laub),* the Binghampton (N.Y.) *Sun*, the San Francisco *Bulletin* (who led off with "Everybody is reading Mencken"), the Pittsburgh *Press*, the New York *World*, the Brooklyn *Eagle*, the Newark *News*, the Toledo *Blade* and the New York *Sun*. The book puzzled and disquieted these poor dolts. They saw that it was far more than a collection of book reviews, and were inclined to treat it seriously, but they shied at its fundamental doctrine, not only as aesthetes of the current model but also as patriotic Americans. A common way out for them was to allege that I was not in earnest—that the whole thing was only a buffoonish play to the galleries, full of exaggerations and conscious falsifications. But just what galleries I was playing to they did not explain. This warning note was struck by the reviewers of the Hartford *Courant*, the New York *Evening Sun*, the Boston *Herald*, the Springfield *Republican*, the Springfield *Union*,† the Baltimore *Sun*,‡ and the New York *Tribune*. But the author of the last-named, signing himself W.H.C., admitted some merit in the book, despite its obnoxious Nietzschean flavor. It was, he said, "a tremendously successful experiment in the revaluation of American critical values" (a Nietzschean phrase, borrowed in spite of himself), and the author was "one of the few men who redeem American criticism from the charge of hopeless mediocrity". The downright excoriations were rather more amusing. The most violent of them was Stuart Pratt Sherman's, printed in the New York *Times* for December 7, 1919 under the title of "Mr. Mencken and the Jeune Fille".§ I had used Sherman harshly in the first chapter of my

*Laub was one of the innumerable young literati of the time who showed some promise, but never came to anything.

†The author of the *Union* review was A.L.S. Wood, a frustrated Taine who is dealt with on p. 501 of this chronicle.

‡The *Sun's* review, printed Nov. 1, 1919, was signed Malcolm Meiklejohn, a pseudonym. The identity of the author I do not know. No one in the *Sun* office today (1945) remembers him. He spoke sadly of my "alcohol-saturated stomach," my "uncivilized moral standards," and my "Nietzschean obsession," and described me as having "no sympathy with the ignoble feelings of pity, compassion, tenderness and sacrifice."

§This was reprinted in Sherman's book, American; New York, 1922, with book, and on sundry other occasions, and he came back, characteristically, with the hint that I was somehow connected with the German spy system. Another appeal to the prevailing fears was made by the reviewer of the Los Angeles *Times* (shades of Willard Wright!)* on November 30. He spoke of me as *Herr* Mencken, and declared that I had "a complete *Kultur*, but no culture whatever".

But there were also some friendly reviews, notably those in the San Francisco *Bulletin*, the New York *American*, the San Francisco *Argonaut*, the *Dial* (by Winthrop Parkhurst), the Richmond *Times-Dispatch* and the Albany *Knickerbocker-Press* (by Belford Forrest). The Chicago *News* printed a review by the Montana pythoness, Mary Maclane, who was dealt with in the book under the title of the Butte Bashkirtseff—Chapter X.† The Boston *Transcript* reviewed the book no less than three times. The first notice, published October 8, 1919, appeared anonymously in the department headed "The Librarian," and was full of patriotic tremors. It began "Mr. H. L. Mencken is fully ninety per cent Prussian in all his utterances, and proud of it. His most malignant and persistent sneers are reserved for any American who was active in enmity to Germany and Austria". But even this anonymous granted that there are some true hits in the book—for example, in the chapters on Thorstein Veblen and the sex hygiene racket—and toward the end of his diatribe he mellowed considerably. There must have been some sharp dissent from his general position in the *Transcript* office, for the two reviews that followed were both predominantly friendly. On November 1, 1919, over the initials H.T.S., I was dealt with as follows:

Considered altogether, Mr. Mencken has about the sanest views on literature of any well known critic in the country. He has a way of brushing aside all cobwebby traditions and dogmas and pointing

---

the title expanded to Mr. Mencken, the Jeune Fille, and the New Spirit in Letters.

*See p. 382 of this chronicle.

†See my Thirty-five Years of Newspaper Work, 1906–41, pp. 266–67. See also a note on La Maclane by Miriam deFord in *American Notes and Queries*, Jan., 1945, p. 155. Her letters to me, not many, are in my letter-file, to go to the New York Public Library at my death.

unerringly to the truth of whatever matter he decides to discuss, and he doesn't care whom he offends when he is about it. He has no reverence and no fear. His style is little short of fascinating, smacking a little of Shaw, for whom he appears to entertain a mingled admiration and contempt. "Prejudices" is a book full of sound, hard sense.

The third *Transcript* review was printed on December 27 and signed D.L.M. It was altogether favorable, though somewhat pedantic and even spinsterish. The English notices, save that of the Manchester *Guardian*, which has always sneered at my books, were friendly. The *Guardian's* reviewer, who signed himself B.S., apparently unaware of the American significance of the letters, objected strongly to my way of writing, and had this to say of it:

> He has absorbed a sham-comedy, swashbuckling style in some backwater of provincial journalism, and he has never reflected that ears of the shape and size a critic must catch hold of before they will attend to him are by nature impervious to critical distinctions. Slang and slapdash will not do for the work of the literary critic, and readers who want that kind of thing must be left to find it where it belongs. And there is another consideration: the manner is bad in itself, and also it has no general currency. English is understood in the four quarters of the globe, but Mr. Mencken's comic cuts are merely doleful for people whose patois is not the same as his.

The London *Times*, dissenting from all this, credited me with "a fine style" and called "Prejudices" "a lively book to dip into". The London *Athenaeum* printed three notices, the first of which described the book as "refreshing" and "delightful," but added: "Mr. Mencken writes brightly, perhaps too brightly: the brilliance of his style suggests the flash of the best American dentistry". The second notice, signed A.L.H.,* ran in part as follows:

> Mr. Mencken turns a pair of civilized eyes on the extraordinary and fantastic spectacle which is contemporary American life. It passes before him, a circus parade—vast ponderous elephants, lions, shy gazelles, apes, performing horses—and he comments upon it, laughingly, in that brilliant, masterfully vulgar style of which he knows the strange secret. All the animals interest him, graceful and ugly alike, noble and repulsive; but by preference he lingers, fascinated no doubt

*This was Aldous Huxley, as will appear a bit later on.

by the fabulous grotesqueness of their swollen shapes, among the solemn mammoths of stupidity, mountain-bodied and mouse-brained, slow-moving, prehistoric. They exist everywhere, these monsters, but it is surely in America that they reach their greatest growth. Puritanism there swells into Comstockism; our harmless little European uplift becomes a sinister, rapacious philanthropic beast; religions pullulate, strange and improbable as the saurians of the Mesozoic age. Mr. Mencken contemplates them with a civilized man's astonishment and horror, then sets his pen in rest and charges upon them. His pen is sharp, his aim unerring, and the punctured monsters collapse with a dolorous whistling of escaping gas. It is a wonderful display. Admiring his skill, one thinks of what Dryden said of himself in his Essay on Satire: "There is still a vast difference between the slovenly butchering of a man and the fineness of a stroke that separates the head from the body and leaves it standing in its place. A man may be capable, as Jack Ketch's wife said of his servant, of a plain piece of work, a bare hanging; but to make a malefactor die sweetly was only belonging to her husband". Mr. Mencken is a worthy apprentice of this great Jack Ketch of literature. . . . We should welcome his appearance among us here, for we have sore need of critics who hate humbug, who are not afraid of putting out their tongues at pretentiousness, however noble an aspect it may wear, who do not mind being vulgar at need, and who, finally, know not only how to make us think, but how to make us laugh as well.

This notice, which appeared on January 2, 1920, undoubtedly colored some of the later discussions of the earlier "Prejudices" books, for American criticism is always extremely responsive to English leading. It was supported by reviews in the London *New Statesman*, the London *New Witness* (by Vincent O'Sullivan) and other English journals and by high praise in a number of British colonial publications, for example, the *Triad* of Sydney, Australia, the Sydney *Sunday Times* and the Toronto *Saturday Night*. Also, it was supported by a blast in the *Mercure de France*, printed before the appearance of "Prejudices: First Series," in which "A Book of Prefaces" was described as "the best and most free criticism of literature that has appeared in the United States since Poe". This *Mercure* judgment was quoted in a number of the American notices of "Prejudices," and it obviously had some influence upon them. Nor was there any encouragement to the aroused and alarmed patriots when Hugh Walpole, the English novelist, landed in

New York late in 1919, and announced that the four American authors who interested him most were Willa Cather, Hergesheimer, Cabell and myself. Of me he said in an interview:

> Mencken is an extraordinarily keen and effective critic. He puts things with amazing honesty and force. Such a change, you know, from the stupid blurb and indiscriminate praise that so generally passes for criticism over here. I should think that Mencken will do a lot of good for your literature.*

The discussion of "Prejudices: First Series" went far beyond the reviews. It continued, in fact, for months after the book came out, and was participated in by columnists, editorial

*Philadelphia *Press* (magazine section), Nov. 2, 1919, p. 3. Walpole came to Baltimore to see me, and we had a pleasant session on Nov. 20. The next day I wrote to Blanche Knopf: "At the end of it Janvier, the local Pirie MacDonald, made a couple of pictures of us sitting together on an old sofa, gazing into each other's eyes. I doubt that the pictures will be fit to show. I had a bleary eye and Walpole snickered. The result will probably be a Portrait of Two Souses. I'll send you a clipping of the halftone from the *Police Gazette*". A print of this photograph is in a book entitled Photographs and Other Portraits —H. L. Mencken—1881–1936, to go to the Pratt Library, Baltimore, at my death. In 1922 I paid Walpole a return visit in London, and had lunch with him in his luxurious house at 24 York Terrace, Regent's Park, served by a butler out of an English society play. The place was very charming, with a garden behind it and all the rooms within crowded with books and manuscripts, including some of Sir Walter Scott. In 1925, in response to my frequent charge that the English reviewers neglected American novels and devoted too much time to log-rolling for their fellow-nationals, he wrote me an open letter that was published in the *Bookman*, then edited by John Farrar. I replied soon afterward, and my reply was printed as a pamphlet by the George H. Doran Company, under the title of My dear Walpole. I never saw him after 1922, and our correspondence soon dropped off. In 1923 or thereabout Joseph Hergesheimer told me that Walpole was a homosexual, and had actually made an attempt upon him (Hergesheimer) when on a visit to West Chester. He gave no evidence of this when I met him myself, but maybe that was because homosexuals always avoid me. Reports to the same effect reached me from other sources during the years following. Walpole was knighted in 1937 and died in 1944. I reviewed his The Gods and Mr. Perrin very favorably in the *Smart Set* for Feb., 1912, but after that I began to have doubts about him, and in Dec., 1914 I described The Duchess of Wrexe as a bore, which it undoubtedly was. Of his later novels, which were numerous, I reviewed only The Green Mirror (March, 1918), The Thirteenth Traveler (Jan., 1922) and The Cathedral (March, 1923). I treated The Cathedral politely, but dismissed the other two without ceremony.

writers and a miscellany of other sages.* Indeed, it launched that debate over my ideas—and, by an easy transition, my objects and motives—which roared on for years afterward, and produced so vast a crop of invective that in 1928 I was moved to gather some of its pearls in "Menckeniana: A Schimpflexikon". All of the discussion of me printed before the end of 1917 found room in little more than a single volume of the 300-odd-page scrapbooks that I set up in that year, but 1918 needed more than 150 pages and 1919 more than 200, and after that there were many years that filled two or three whole volumes. I am now (August, 1945) in Volume 89, and the flood still continues.†

It had been my plan to bring out a volume of "Prejudices" every two years, for they were to be made up largely of selections from my magazine stuff, and I wanted as wide a range of choice as possible, but the pother raised by Series I suggested to Knopf that we had better schedule Series II for 1920 instead of 1921. "I have discovered something," he said to me one day. "It is that H. L. Mencken has become a good property". "Prejudices: Second Series" was accordingly published in October, 1920, and had already sold 1853 copies by the end of the year. The first printing was 3000 copies, and Knopf was reprinting in June. There were other reprintings in February, 1922; February‡ and December, 1923; and October and December, 1924, making seven in all. By 1927 the sales as a single volume began

*I also received a great many letters from readers, most of them friendly. On September 29, 1919 Fielding H. Garrison wrote to me: "It certainly is a ripsnorter—a cyclone of vigorous thinking and common sense, expressed in language that is *strepitoso e veloce*. I know nothing of many of the people you excoriate and from what you say of them I am glad I don't. But the chapters on the Dean, Veblen, Ade, Shaw, London et al are stone-fences and corpse-reviewers".

†The incoming clippings are entered by Mrs. C. F. Lappin of Minneapolis, once my secretary. When she married and left Baltimore she said she would like to go on handling them, and she has been doing it ever since. There are, of course, many gaps in the collection, for clipping bureaus are far from infallible. Moreover, large numbers of clippings have been diverted from these books to my collecteana on the American language, and enough to fill a pushcart went into The "Hatrack" Case 1926–27, now in the Pratt Library, Baltimore.

‡In this reprinting I made many corrections in the book.

to bog down, but it continued to sell as a part of three different sets of "Prejudices," one of the first four series, one of the first five, and the other of all six. It went out of print finally in 1933, by which time, disregarding these sets, it had sold a little short of 8000 copies, and earned me about $2400. Like "Prejudices: First Series," it was published by Jonathan Cape in London, bound in staring yellow cloth that made the gaudiest effort of Knopf seem pale. In 1925 some extracts from it were printed in various fonts of small type by Dr. E. F. Darling, a New York oculist, and used by him for testing the eyes of his patients.* The book had "Prejudices: First Series" but thirteen months ahead of it, and thus faced stiff competition in its own house. The sets of "Prejudices" that I have mentioned were issued in boxes for gift purposes, and the first of them, embracing the first four volumes, did pretty well, for it sold 768 sets and brought me in $1152. The second with five volumes sold 261 sets and earned me nearly $500. The third, including all six volumes, sold only 25 copies, and earned me but $156.25. "Selected Prejudices," brought out in 1927, was made up of chapters from the first five volumes. It sold 2246 copies and brought me $872.04. It was not Knopf's idea, but Cape's. Cape, who was an enterprising and resourceful publisher and very friendly to me, had found it impossible to work up a satisfactory sale for the successive volumes of "Prejudices" in England, despite the extensive newspaper notice they got there, so he suggested that it might be worth while to try a volume of selections, made up of the stuff most likely to interest Englishmen. I fell in with the plan willingly, selected things that seemed to meet that specification, and undertook to translate them from American into English. The result was "Selected Prejudices," a little volume of 256 pages, published by Cape in his charming Traveller's Library in 1926. It was an immediate success, and a year later it was followed by a second volume. These two books of selections remained in print for years; indeed, I receive occasional small royalties on them from Cape to this day (1945). In 1929 Régis Michaud made a French trans-

*His little pamphlet consisted of twelve pages, 2⅞ by 4⅛ inches, and was bound in gray paper.

lation on the same plan, and it was published by Furne, Boivin & Cie in Paris. It came out in two forms, one of them an edition of 25 copies on vellum.

"Prejudices: Second Series" followed the plan of the first series closely. It opened with a 93–page blast entitled "The National Letters," mainly made up of reworkings of my *Smart Set* reviews and my contributions to "Répétition Générale," but it also included some surplus material left out of the 1922 revision of "In Defense of Women," under way in 1921, and some revisions of newspaper articles, for example, "The Sahara of the Bozart," from the New York *Evening Mail* of November 13, 1917 and "The Divine Afflatus" from the same paper of November 16. "Exeunt Omnes" came from the *Smart Set* for December, 1919, and "Roosevelt: an Autopsy" was mainly lifted from my book article in the issue for March, 1920.* "The National Letters" was based upon an article called "The National Literature" which I contributed to the *Yale Review* for June, 1920, but there was material in it from "Observations Upon the National Letters" in the *Smart Set* for July of the

*I wrote to Fielding H. Garrison on Nov. 4: "The formula of the 'Prejudices' books is simple: a fundamental structure of serious argument, with enough personal abuse to engage the general, and one or two Rabelaisian touches. The Roosevelt chapter will get more attention than any other. The Roosevelt family, having tasted the preliminary blast in the *Smart Set*, is furious. In particular, the doctrine that Theodore was not an aristocrat is offensive to his heirs and assigns". Theodore, Jr., denounced me violently in his book of reminiscences, All in the Family, published in 1929, but cooled off afterward, and on Sept. 7, 1934 he wrote me a cordial letter about an article I had written for *Liberty* discussing crime and punishment. We presently became friends, and he visited me more than once in Baltimore. I had met his sister Alice in 1928. See my Thirty-five Years of Newspaper Work, 1906–41, p. 521. Both Alice and young Teddy were bitterly opposed to Franklin D. Roosevelt's efforts to horn into World War II, and so delighted in my articles on the subject in the Baltimore *Sun* down to Jan., 1941. One day Teddy said to me: "Franklin will make the war, but it is our branch of the family that will fight in it". As a reserve officer he was called up for service before Pearl Harbor, and was soon promoted to brigadier-general. He died of pneumonia in France. He was a considerable boozer, and when tight loved to recite poetry. His memory was amazing, and he specialized in dramatic recitations of the longer Kipling poems. He bought stock in the publishing firm of Doubleday, Doran & Co. in 1935 and was active in its management. My last letter from him was dated Aug. 28, 1941. He was then in camp at Fort Devens, Mass., in command of the 26th Infantry. He often invited me to visit him at Oyster Bay, but I never did so.

same year, "Notes and Queries" in the issue for September, and various other book articles. From this time forward I kept the "Prejudices" books in mind in all my magazine and newspaper work, and not infrequently an idea that was first tried out in the Baltimore *Evening Sun* was later expanded and embellished in the *Smart Set* or some other magazine, and then finally polished for book form. This preparedness made the putting together of the successive "Prejudices" relatively easy. I did, of course, a good deal of rewriting but I also did a lot of mere pasting in, and my scissors and pot were worked almost as hard as my typewriter.* From the first volume onward I provided each of the "Prejudices" books with an adequate index. Making it was tedious work, but I believed that that work was well expended.

The reviews of "Prejudices: Second Series" paid relatively little attention to the contents of the book, but were devoted mainly to discussions of the author. I had suddenly become, by the end of 1920, a sort of symbol of all the disillusionment following World War I, and was credited with a leadership in dissent that I did not want, and tried constantly to avoid. The messianic passion was simply not in me, then or afterward; indeed, it is probable that no articulate American ever lived who had less taste for the shroud of the evangelist. It was thus somewhat disconcerting for me to discover that I was becoming the text of all sorts of manifestos and homilies by propagandists of a score of warring sects, and the frequent theme of editorials by the dull idiots who write such things, and a favorite subject of debate in the colleges and women's clubs.†

*Nevertheless, constant interruptions sometimes greatly incommoded the business. On April 3, 1920 I wrote to a correspondent in New York: "The second volume of Prejudices is giving me hell, and I am in a fearful humor. The bloody thing has to be delivered June 1, and I haven't two chapters written. Worse, editorial nuisances are driving me crazy. My next address will be Matteawan". On May 13 I wrote to Fielding H. Garrison: "Still at work on Prejudices II and still cursing the Lord God Jehovah".

†So far as I can make out by a somewhat sketchy examination of my early clipping-books, the first women's club to wrestle with me was that of Helena, Mont., on May 19, 1919. The programme of the meeting, published in the year-book of the club for 1918–19 (Clippings—H. L. Mencken—Vol. III, p. 329), shows that two members were appointed to expound me to the others. The first was a Mrs. Le Lano, whose theme was "His View-point in Criticism,"

The pedagogues of the land of course, were against me almost to a man, and tried their best to stem the rising tide of interest in me among the youth they afflicted. I responded by picking out one of them anon and anon, and subjected him to a third degree worse than any ever staged by a police lieutenant. For example, a poor ass named T. E. Rankin, Kansas born and educated at Princeton, who professed rhetoric at the University of Michigan. When he printed the first edition of a work called "American Authorship of the Present Day" in 1918 I missed it, but when a second edition followed in 1920 I fell upon it with all arms in the *Smart Set* for May, 1921.* The book was an almost incredible exhibition of academic imbecility, for in it the author whooped up Ernest Poole, F. Marion Crawford, Cale Young Rice and other such quacks, cried down Huneker, Dreiser and Carl Sandburg and passed over altogether Cabell, Miss Cather, Sherwood Anderson, Eugene O'Neill and George Ade. I gave a long summary of his curiously idiotic judgments, and then went on:

What interests me is the effect upon the poor yokels who strive heroically for a "liberal" education at such universities as Michigan, and are then belabored and stupified with such balderdash. Can you imagine the thirst for enlightenment that must be in some of those candidates for the arts degree, and the vast sacrifices that must stand behind their candidacy—remote farmers sweating like slaves for year after year that their sons and daughters may be "educated," farmwives wearing out their lives in miserable drudgery and loneliness, pennies saved one by one, thousands of little deprivations, hopes

---

and the other was a Miss Mosher, who undertook a review of "A Book of Prefaces". The ensuing discussion was led by a Mrs. Plum. My name was spelled Menken on the programme, and there was a quotation from Mrs. Wiggs of the Cabbage Patch, to the effect that "the way to get cheerful is to smile when you feel bad, to think about somebody else's headache when your own is most bustin', to keep on believin' the sun is shinin' when the clouds are thick enough to cut". The spy who sent me the programme reported that La Mosher was "big of bust and short of waist and brains," and that she bucked at the last minute and her job fell to another member, unnamed.

*Born in 1872, Rankin at first dallied with divinity, but in 1901 took to the rattan. Michigan fired him in 1929 and he went to Carleton College, a one-horse seminary maintained by the Congregationalists at Northfield, Minn. There it still survives. He has a Phi Beta Kappa key and is a member of the Authors' Club of London, a famous boob-trap for American suckers.

cherished through whole generations? And then the result—a bath of bosh. If a professor writes a text-book, I assume that it is for his students: who else would want to read it? Well, imagine a young man or woman outfitted with such a notion of literature of the country as one finds in the tome of Prof. Rankin! Think of raising chickens and milking cows for twenty years to pay for such an education! I am surely not one to laugh at the spectacle. To me it seems to be tragic.

The aim here, of course, was to brush off the yokel students as well as the yokel professor, but unhappily it failed. The campus newspaper, the *Michigan Daily*, printed a dutiful denunciation of my review on April 24, 1921, but it was so feeble that it opened the way for a vigorous riposte by a student signing himself Menckenite, three days later.* Indeed, after reading the two I began to suspect that the former may have been only a plant for the latter.† Thus I found myself a champion of the students against their professors, and this unwilling rôle afflicted me for fifteen years afterward. I became, on the one hand, a constant point of reference in the campus revolts that then went on throughout the American colleges, and on the other hand I was besought with great frequency to come to this or that campus and harangue the rebels on the issues of the hour. Having, as I have said, no taste for saving humanity, and being, moreover, averse to making speeches, I refused all these invitations. In all my life, in fact, I talked to college boys but once, and that violation of my rules was forced on me in 1926, when the Harvard students staged a demonstration in my support when I tackled the Boston wowsers on Boston Common.‡ But the invitations came on pouring in, and sometimes they were underwritten by the sassier faction of young tutors. Unhappily, I preserved none of these invitations, for I have always made a practise to destroy mail of no permanent interest. But there have been times since when I have doubted that such letters were as little interesting as I thought they

*He was, I heard afterward, one Bob Sage.

†The controversy raged for a month, in the *Michigan Chimes* as well as in the *Daily*. The former, in its May issue, took my side flatfootedly, and heaped scorn upon the *Daily*.

‡This was at the time of the attempt to suppress the *American Mercury* because of its publication of Hatrack. The episode will be described in its proper chronological place.

were when they came in. If I had them today they would throw an illuminating light upon the play of opinion on American campuses in the 1920's.

Of the things that went into "Prejudices: Second Series," as opposed to my current *Smart Set* stuff, the one that made the greatest uproar was my revision and expansion of "The Sahara of the Bozart". When it appeared originally in the New York *Evening Mail*, which had only a small circulation outside New York City, it seems to have been missed by the sub-Potomac editorial writers, but now they all became suddenly and painfully aware of it, and many of them had at me with great ferocity. The Nashville *Tennessean* led off on November 28, 1920, with the now familiar hints that I was the American front for Nietzsche and the other German enemies of the true, the good and the beautiful, and the usual loud boast that the Southern whites were the purest Anglo-Saxons in the Western world, and hence models of patriotism, piety and intelligence. My criticism of the post-Confederate *Kultur*, it argued hotly, was marked by ignorance and wickedness, and all I knew of the subject had been "gained by making a ten-day Cook's tour of the Potomac river". From Tennessee the conflagration spread to other States, and soon it was roaring fiercest in Arkansas. Here the principal defenders of the outraged South were the *Daily News* and *Arkansas Democrat* of Little Rock, but they got gallant support from the Little Rock *Trade Record*, the organ of the State Babbitts, and the *Arkansas Writer*, a strange monthly operated by one Clio Harper, a member of the *Smart Set* Rejection-Slip Association. The stuff these heroes printed was so amusing that I decided to throw some gasoline upon their flames, and in the *Smart Set* for August, 1921, I printed "The South Begins to Mutter". In this article, under cover of praising three Southern magazines that showed some impatience with the circumambient imbecility—*All's Well*, published by Charles J. Finger at Fayetteville, Ark.; the *Double-Dealer*, published at New Orleans by a small group of young intellectuals, nearly all of them Jews; and the *Reviewer*, set up at Richmond, Va., in February, 1921, by a rebellious young woman named Emily Clark, with the imprimatur of James Branch Cabell*—,

*The first issue appeared on Feb. 15, 1921. In it Miss Clark's a chief associate,

I piled insult on insult. Save for a few walled towns, I declared, the South was so far steeped in savagry that civilized men not only refused to live in it, but even avoided visiting it. "I know New Yorkers," I said, "who have been in Cochin China, Kafristan, Paraguay, Somaliland and West Virginia, but not one who has ever penetrated the miasmatic jungles of Arkansas".

This device worked very effectively, and the second wave of denunciation was ten times as violent as the first. Harper had at me with especial violence in the *Arkansas Writer*, describing me as "an imported scion of German *Schrecklichkeit*," a "self-appointed emissary of the Wilhelmstrasse," and "an insufferable excrescence on the body of American literature". "Even Sing Sing and Matteawan," he went on, "would be contaminated by such as he," and he concluded by calling upon "every prominent newspaper and civic organization throughout the South . . . to see if there is not some recourse in law to banish him as a pestilent nuisance from the country he has so contumaciously insulted, and whose soil his presence contaminates". This call was answered by the Hon. Virgil C. Pettie, president of the Arkansas Advancement Association, who petitioned "the Arkansas members of Congress to call all other Southern Congressmen into conference to see what action can be taken against H. L. Mencken," and went about the State recruiting support from the Rotarians, Kiwanians, Lions and other such idealists, and also from chambers of commerce and women's clubs. Unhappily, this campaign came to nothing, for some of the statesmen consulted must have discovered that I was a native American and the son of native Americans, and let fall a warning that the main postulate of the Harper-Pettie holy war was libellous, legally speaking. On August 26, 1921, after printing all of the current denunciations of *Herr* Mencken at length, the *Arkansas Democrat* prudently sought cover in a news article headed

---

Hunter T. Stagg, had a cautious but generally favorable review of Prejudices: Second Series. He quoted from The Sahara of the Bozart, and after protesting that some of it was "unjust, some merely unsound," admitted that "the main outline of the argument, the outstanding deductions, are so true that it were petty to cavil at the weaknesses". It was The Sahara of the Bozart, in fact, that inspired the setting up of the *Reviewer*. There is more about it and Miss Clark later on.

MENCKEN IS NATIVE
OF BALTIMORE, MD.
Editor of *Smart Set*, Who
Attacked South, Not
a Native of Germany

The *Democrat* put all the blame on the Arkansas Advance Association, and made a somewhat painful effort, probably inspired by its lawyer, to clear its skirts.* Thus I lost the pleasant experience of being investigated by a committee of Southern congressmen, and though the uproar continued for months longer it soon lost its steam, for the German spy note had to be avoided. Meanwhile, a number of the more intelligent Southern newspapers—for example, the New Orleans *Picayune*, the Miami *Herald*, and the Greensboro (N. C.) *Record*—took to discussing my allegations with some rationality and tolerance, and even with mild approval. This heretical party gradually gained recruits, and in the course of time the theory began to be heard that "The Sahara of the Bozart" had really done the South a valuable service, and was responsible for the resuscitation of its literature. I have since read many an article, written by a Southerner and printed in the South, which credited me formally with having set off such Southern authors of the new generation as Erskine Caldwell, William Faulkner, Frances Newman,† and even Thomas Wolfe. Thus I became once more a prophet in spite of myself.

*I kept banging away at Arkansas until 1931, when I had a bout in the grand manner with one of its former Governors, Charles H. Brough. But this went on in the Baltimore *Evening Sun*. See my Thirty-five Years of Newspaper Work, 1906–41, p. 638. I received more one threat that if I ever showed myself in Arkansas I'd be lynched, but this did not incommode me, for I was barred by similar threats from other areas, including the lower Eastern Shore of my native Maryland. As a matter of fact, I visited the Ozark region of Arkansas in the Summer of 1928, on my way by automobile from the Republican National Convention in Kansas City to the Democratic Convention in Houston, and no one offered me any affront.

†Frances Newman was a member of one of the first families of Atlanta, and joined the staff of the Carnegie Library there in 1912. She wrote a weekly column of literary news for one of the Atlanta papers, and reviewed Prejudices: Second Series in it. Her review was very cautious. Soon afterward she came to New York and I met her. She was an extraordinarily homely woman, but very

In the North the reviews of "Prejudices: Second Series" were evenly divided between praise and denunciation, and most of them were discussions of me rather than of the book. A good many of the reviewers tried to account for and dispose of me by labelling me, and I was likened variously to George Bernard Shaw, Nietzsche, Brann the iconoclast and Elbert Hubbard! A few papers—for example, the Chicago *Tribune*—came out for me without qualification, but the majority were more cautious, and not a few expressed the opinion, plainly born of a hope, that Stuart P. Sherman had finished me, once and for all time. The debate over my ideas throughout the country had curious repercussions in Baltimore, where the notion that a local newspaper man could become a national figure caused astonishment, and even a kind of resentment. In the Baltimore *Evening Sun* for November 27, 1920, Samuel C. Chew* thus described the situation:

---

amusing. In 1924 she published her first book, The Short Story's Mutations. It showed an immense range of reading, but was chaotic and overwritten. Two years later she came to me with a novel, and I found a good deal of merit in it. Unhappily, she proposed to call it, absurdly, The Hard-Boiled Virgin, and her publisher, Horace Liveright, supported her. I argued against so gratuitously sensational a title, but she persisted, and her book was denounced by many reviewers who never read it. Her highly respectable family was grossly outraged. In May, 1924 she contributed a short story to the *American Mercury*, Rachel and Her Children, which was adjudged the best story of the year by the judges in the annual O. Henry contest. Frances's extreme lack of pulchritude was a sore affliction to her, for her sisters were all beautiful women. She became more and more depressed, and on Oct. 22, 1928 she committed suicide at the Algonquin Hotel by swallowing veronal. She had some talent, but was unbridled and without judgment. If she had lived ten years longer, and settled down a bit, she might have come to something.

*Chew was a Baltimorean himself, and the son of a once famous medical consultant of the same given names, called at the time of my father's last illness in 1899. After taking his Ph.D. at the Johns Hopkins young Chew became a schoolmaster, and in 1914 joined the faculty of Bryn Mawr College, where he is now professor of English (1945). He has published the usual definitive editions of a diligent pedagogue, but his original writings are of small importance. He was in the 1920 era, a friend of Harry C. Black, and was recruited by Black to write for the *Sunpapers.* In 1918 he fell in love from his academic pulpit with one of the students, Lucy Evans, and presently married her. She was a very pretty girl. I have not seen or heard from him for years.

There must be enlightened souls here who realize the worth and significance of Mr. Mencken. . . . but most prominent Baltimoreans. . . . imagine that they have disposed of this extraordinary person when they have said: "Oh, it's only Mencken," or, "It's just Mencken," or, more laconically, "Mencken". They are totally unconscious of the fact that saving always his Eminence,* the author of "Prejudices" is the most truly prominent citizen the town possesses. When he dies it will take ten years to raise funds for a tombstone, and even then the memorial will be cheap and hideous, like Poe's. He must content himself meanwhile with the applause of the *Athenaeum*, the *New Statesman* and the *Mercure de France*. New York doesn't say "It's just Mencken" when he drops into town. There he is "the Baltimore critic," "the Baltimore philosopher," "the Sage of Baltimore".

On July 13, 1921 the Cincinnati *Times-Star* printed a dispatch from its London correspondent headed "Mencken's Fame Growing Apace" and saying:

The remarkable growth in England and continental Europe of the fame of Henry L. Mencken, the Baltimore author, is one of the curious literary phenomena of the time. A series of articles in the London *Times* on current American literature is largely devoted to his work, and nearly all his estimates of contemporary American authors are accepted. J. C. Squire and other English critics have been writing about him meanwhile in other English journals. He has been the subject of several extensive articles in German reviews, and many of his essays have been translated and published. In France, too, his work is being translated, particularly his political writings. In Australia he is constantly discussed, and even in South America he has a number of eager disciples.

The reception given to the first two series of "Prejudices," when Cape brought them out in England, was generally favorable, but there were some sharp dissents and many of the reviewers attempted straddles in the manner of their American colleagues. But the reviews were at least numerous, and many of them were long, so that they covered altogether, counting only those that reached me, more than twelve feet of column space. Several papers printed more than one notice. The London *Times*, having given the American edition of "Prejudices: First Series," a very cordial welcome, now began to develop

**i.e.*, James, Cardinal Gibbons (1834–1921), archbishop of Baltimore from 1877 until his death.

doubts, and its two reviews, on June 16 and July 14, showed an increasing coldness, but it gave space in May and June to five long articles by C. E. Bechhofer (just mentioned in the Cincinnati *Times-Star* dispatch) in which I was treated politely indeed.* Contrariwise, the Manchester *Guardian* became more friendly, and its two reviews, on July 24 and December 21, showed more amiability than it was ever to exhibit in noticing my books thereafter. Thomas Moult went to the bat for me in two reviews, one in *John o' London's Weekly* and the other in the Christmas *Bookman*, and John C. Squire had his say, which was far from enthusiastic, in the *Observer*.† The London *Morning Post*, the *Saturday Review*, the *Publishers' Circular*, the *Tatler*, the *Daily Graphic* and even the Edinburgh *Scotsman* were friendly, but the Liverpool *Post*, the *New Statesman*, the London *Telegraph* (Arthur Waugh), *Eve*, the *Daily Herald* (Alan Porter), the *Illustrated London News*, the *Athenaeum* (by now absorbed by the *Nation*), the *Westminster Gazette*, the *Daily News* (R. Ellis Roberts), *Country Life*, the Glasgow *Herald*, the *Daily Express* (S. P. Mais) and the *Spectator* were cool,‡ and the *Pall Mall Gazette*, the Liverpool *Daily Post* and the *Sunday Times* (H. C. Minchin) were hostile.

*These articles were printed on May 26, and June 9, 16, 23 and 30. Bechhofer reprinted them in 1923, considerably expanded, as The Literary Renaissance in America. He was a London Jew who had spent some time in youth in the United States. I met him in London in 1922, and we had a couple of boozy evenings together. He hung about the fringes of English letters for many years, but never got very far. He also held various minor political jobs and tried his hand as a newspaper correspondent in Russia. In 1936 he brought out an extraordinarily vituperative biography of Stanley Baldwin. Some time after World War I he attached his mother's surname to his own, and became C. E. Bechhofer-Roberts. Later on he dropped the hyphen and became Carl Eric Bechhofer Roberts.

†My only encounter with Squire was in London in 1922. He was then editor of the London *Mercury*. His position in the London literary world was curious. There was little in his numerous books in prose and verse that was of any moment, but he was, by a sort of general consent, the spokesman for literature on public occasions, much as Howells had been in the United States, and in that capacity was a frequent speaker at public dinners. In 1933 he was knighted for this heroic service. Squire was a heavy boozer, and in the later 1930's began to fade out.

‡But the *Spectator*, on June 18, 1931, listed Prejudices: First Series among seven contemporary Books Worth Reading, along with volumes by Benedetto Croce, Bertrand Russell and Sir T. Clifford Allbutt.

Meanwhile, articles on the two "Prejudices" appeared in various languages other than English—for example, in *Das literarische Echo* of Berlin, *El Porvenit* (the future) of Cartagena, Colombia, the *Frankfurter Zeitung*, *Die Neue Zeit* (Berlin), and *El Universal* (Caracas, Venezuela)*—and news came from Paris, where Charles Cestre had just been appointed professor of American literature and civilization at the Sorbonne, that he was putting my books in a collection being gathered to instruct his students. At home extensive articles on me were published by Frank Harris in *Pearson's Magazine* for May, 1921,† S. K. Ratcliffe (an Englishman) in the *New Republic* for April 13, F. Scott Fitzgerald in the *Bookman*, William McFee in the same for December, 1921, Edmund Wilson, Jr., in the *New Republic* for June 1, and Ernest A. Boyd in the *Freeman* for February 2. Cape, in London, brought out a pamphlet entitled "The New American Literary Movement," in which he whooped up Edgar Lee Masters, Dorothy Canfield, Sherwood Anderson, Henry G. Aikman‡ and myself, all recent recruits to his list, and Knopf, in New York, issued on March 22, 1921 a press sheet quoting encomiums on my work from papers in four foreign countries. On December 4, 1920 the Baltimore *Evening Sun* reported that "Prejudices: Second Series" was a best-seller in Baltimore, and on July 30, 1921 the London correspondent of the *Publishers' Weekly* reported that it was a best-seller there, along with Shaw's "Back to Methuselah". In

*All this notice naturally led to the publication of translations from my books and articles. So far as my records show, the first was of a group of epigrams, done by Herman George Scheffauer (1878–1927), and published in *Jugend*, Nov. 28, 1920 under the title of Amerikanisches. My first appearance in Spanish seems to have been in *La Revista Mexicana* in 1921. I got into French the same year, into Italian the year following, into Russian in 1928, and into Swedish in 1930. There will be more about Scheffauer hereafter.

†Reprinted in his Contemporary Portraits: Fourth Series, 1923.

‡Aikman was one of the many promising authors of the period who quickly blew up. His first novel, The Groper, was published by Liveright in 1919 and I reviewed it favorably in the *Smart Set* for October of that year. In 1920 he wrote a second called Zell and brought the MS. to me. I liked it so well that I induced Knopf to take him over. The book got very good notices, including mine in the *Smart Set* for March, 1921, and Cape liked it so much that he added Aikman to his list. But it was the last thing of any significance to come from its author. He kept on writing for some years, but never did anything else worth reading.

1920 I saw books of mine listed, for the first time, in an antiquarian bookseller's catalogue. The bookseller was Meredith Janvier of Baltimore,* and he asked $6 for "Pistols For Two" and $20 for an autographed first edition of "The American Language," then only a year old. I was so delighted that I gave him the typescripts of two chapters, "Roosevelt: an Autopsy" and "The Sahara of the Bozart," in "Prejudices: Second Series". Soon afterward he was offering the first for $25 and the second for $15.† In September, 1921, the booksellers' trade-journal, *Biblio*, reported that, during the three months ending August 30, my books ranked eighth among the American first editions advertised for. In October they went up to third place, and that place they also held in November. On June 11, 1921 the New York *Evening Mail* listed Nathan and me among persons who need "no press-agents," along with Margot Asquith, Lloyd-George, William J. Bryan, Andrew Volstead and Babe Ruth.

*A strange fellow who started out as a lawyer, became famous as a strong man, took to professional photography, and ended as a dealer in old books and prints. See my Thirty-five Years of Newspaper Work, 1906–41, p. 821; also p. 777 of the present record.

†At the sale of the Charles Romm collection in New York, early in 1921, four of my books and a copy of Pistols For Two sold for $25. At the same sale forty-eight books by Brander Matthews also fetched $25. In both cases all of the items were autographed. See Book Prices Current (editorial), Chicago *Post*, May 27, 1921.

CHRONOLOGY

NOTE ON THE TEXTS

NOTE ON THE ILLUSTRATIONS

NOTES

INDEX

Chronology

1880 Born Henry Louis Mencken on September 12, at what was then 380 West Lexington Street, Baltimore, Maryland, now 811 West Lexington Street; eldest child of August Mencken and Anna Abhau Mencken. (Grandfather Burkhardt Ludwig Mencken, born 1828 in Laas, Germany, landed in Baltimore, November 1848; was naturalized October 1852, and set up a tobacco business. Father, born June 16, 1854, established August Mencken & Bro. between 1873 and 1875, managing it with his brother Henry, and building it into one of the most successful cigar manufacturers along the South Atlantic coast. An agnostic and a high-tariff Republican, August was a loyal member of the Masonic order, also part owner of the major-league baseball club of Washington, D.C. Mother, Anna Abhau, born June 11, 1858, was the daughter of Carl Heinrich Abhau from Hesse, Germany. August and Anna were married on November 11, 1879.)

1882 Brother, Charles Edward, born May 16.

1883 Family moves to 1524 Hollins Street, in a prosperous German-American neighborhood in West Baltimore, facing Union Square.

1886 Mencken enrolls at F. Knapp's Institute, a private school, in September. Sister Anna Gertrude born November 17.

1888 Begins piano lessons. Receives a self-inking printing press for Christmas.

1889 Brother, August, born February 18. Reads Mark Twain's *Huckleberry Finn*, which makes a huge impact on him. Family begins spending summers in Ellicott City, Howard County, west of Baltimore (1889–1892), and Mt. Washington (1892–1899), then a northwestern suburb.

1892 Mencken enters Baltimore Polytechnic Institute, a public high school, on September 5.

1893 Mencken keenly interested in chemistry, photography, journalism, and literature. Visits the Enoch Pratt Free Library, reads four or five books a week, mostly English literature (including Dickens, Chaucer, Shakespeare, Herrick, Pepys, Addison, Steele, Pope, Swift, Johnson, Boswell, Fielding, Smollett, Sterne, Arnold, Macaulay, George Eliot, Tennyson, Swinburne, Thackeray, Kipling). Mencken will later call the library "my school"; his brother August will recall that Mencken "read like an athlete." Fire engulfs August Mencken & Bro. Cigar factory, causing $25,000 worth of damage, December 2.

1895 Reads Stephen Crane's *The Red Badge of Courage.*

1896 Graduates at age 15 from the Baltimore Polytechnic Institute, with highest grade point average yet recorded, June 23. Publishes a poem ("Ode to the Pennant on the Centerfield Pole") anonymously in the Baltimore *American*, summer. Tells his father that he plans to become a newspaper reporter, but is strongly dissuaded. Starts full-time work as clerk and salesman at August Mencken & Bro.

1898 Subscribes to *The Criterion* (New York) and is influenced by the work of James Gibbons Huneker, Percival Pollard, Ambrose Bierce, Oscar Wilde, George Bernard Shaw, and Friedrich Nietzsche. Becomes an admirer of the prose style and ideas of Thomas Henry Huxley. Studies books on journalism; enrolls in a correspondence school, the Associated Newspaper Bureau School of Journalism in New York, and states his career goal is "to begin as a reporter & after that trust to hard work and luck for something better." Resolves to quit working at August Mencken & Bro.; his father asks him to postpone the decision for at least another year. In a moment of despair, Mencken contemplates suicide. August Mencken, Sr., collapses unconscious with acute kidney infection, December 31. (Mencken writes later: "I remember well how . . . I kept saying to myself that if my father died I'd be free at last . . . I had got along with him very well, but I detested business and was frantic to get into newspaper work.")

1899 Father dies on January 13 and is buried at Loudon Park Cemetery. Two weeks later Mencken visits the offices of the Baltimore *Herald* and asks for a job. First story published February 24. Hired at $7 a week, the youngest (and first) cub reporter on the *Herald* to get paid a salary, July 2. A poem addressed to Rudyard Kipling appears in December 1899 issue of *Bookman* magazine. Quits working part-time for his Uncle Henry at August Mencken & Bro.

to devote himself to journalism, which he later calls "the maddest, gladdest, damnedest existence ever enjoyed by mortal youth."

1900 Reads Edward Kingsbury's editorials in the New York *Sun*, George Ade's *Fables in Slang*, the work of Émile Zola. Discovers Theodore Dreiser's *Sister Carrie*. Works twelve hours a day, seven days a week reporting for the *Herald*, writing short stories, poetry, and articles for out-of-town newspapers. Suffers from chronic bronchitis. Travels to Jamaica to recover, June. Gets third raise in salary, to $14 a week, August. Assigned to cover presidential election between William Jennings Bryan and William McKinley, November.

1901 Salary increased to $18 a week, February 1. Covers fire that devastated Jacksonville, Florida, in May. Becomes drama critic of the *Herald*, September, and editor of *Sunday Herald*, October (holds both positions until October 1903). Becomes an advocate of the work of playwrights Shaw and Ibsen.

1903 Becomes city editor of the *Morning Herald* in October 1903. Publication of *Ventures Into Verse*, a book of poetry modeled on Kipling. Begins subscribing to a service that provides clippings mentioning him or his books. (The clippings will fill more than 100 volumes during his lifetime.)

1904 Fire destroys more than 140 acres and 1,500 buildings in downtown Baltimore, February 7–8. The *Herald* is printed in Washington and Philadelphia and does not miss a single issue. Mencken attends the Republican National Convention in Chicago, June 19–24, and the Democratic National Convention in St. Louis, July 5–11. Made city editor of the Baltimore *Evening Herald*, August 25. Saturday Night Club established, a group of musicians who meet regularly, with Mencken at the piano.

1905 Promoted to managing editor of the *Herald*. Publication of *George Bernard Shaw: His Plays*, first book-length study of Shaw.

1906 The *Herald* ceases publication, June 17. Becomes editor of the Baltimore *Sunday Sun*, July 25. Makes sweeping changes in typography and content; introduces poetry, music criticism by John Philip Sousa; runs a twenty-four-part report on the city's health concerns and serializes work by popular authors (such as George Ade's revised history of slang). Circulation climbs steadily.

1908 Publication of *The Philosophy of Friedrich Nietzsche*, first book in English on the philosopher. Meets Theodore Dreiser. First trip to Europe, March; he visits England and Germany. Meets George Jean Nathan, theater critic, in New York in May. Assumes additional duties as editorial writer for the *Sun* papers. Begins monthly book reviews for *The Smart Set*, November (to be continued until December 1923), and praises the work of James Branch Cabell, Twain, Joseph Conrad, and Dreiser among others.

1909 Works (in collaboration with Holger A. Koppel, Danish consul in Baltimore) on notes and introductions to a new edition of Ibsen's *A Doll's House* and *Little Eyolf*, to be published as part of *The Player's Ibsen*. The volumes are a commercial failure, and the series is discontinued.

1910 Baltimore *Evening Sun* established, April 18, with Mencken as an editor. Ghostwrites *What You Ought to Know About Your Baby* with Leonard Hirshberg. Publication of *The Gist of Nietzsche* and of *Men Versus the Man* (a debate in letters with socialist Robert Rives La Monte).

1911 Becomes close friends with Percival Pollard, American writer who widens Mencken's understanding of German culture. Begins "The Free Lance," a satirical daily column in the Baltimore *Evening Sun*, May 8, addressing issues of local public health, the plight of the city's African Americans, the women's movement, the American language, and the pretensions of moralists, and featuring humorous pieces including the kernel of what would become his fictitious history of the bathtub. "Before it had gone on a year," he later notes, "I knew precisely where I was heading."

1912 Travels to Europe in April, visiting England, France, Switzerland, and Germany. Covers the Democratic National Convention in Baltimore, June 28. Publication of *The Artist: A Drama Without Words.*

1913 Meets publisher Alfred A. Knopf. Covers suffragist parade in Washington, D.C., March 3.

1914 Meets and becomes close friends with James Gibbons Huneker, influential American critic. Sails to Europe with George Jean Nathan and Willard Huntington Wright,

April. Publication of *Europe After 8:15* with Nathan and Wright. First World War begins, July 28–August 4. Mencken and Nathan become coeditors of *The Smart Set*, September. Publishes material from writers including F. Scott Fitzgerald, Edgar Lee Masters, Sherwood Anderson, Willa Cather, Ben Hecht, Eugene O'Neill, and Ezra Pound, as well as British and European writers such as Alexei Tolstoy, Anatole France, D. H. Lawrence, and James Joyce. The book reviews by Mencken, as well as the theater criticism by Nathan, attract wide attention.

1915 German sinking of the British liner *Lusitania* on May 7 increases anti-German sentiment in the United States. First issue of *Parisienne* magazine, edited anonymously with Nathan, is launched (last issue under their editorship will be October 1916). Mencken's pro-German stance becomes dominant in his increasingly controversial "Free Lance" column, as he scrutinizes the role of the press and examines stories of deliberate propaganda. "The Free Lance" ends abruptly, without explanation, on October 23.

1916 Dreiser's novel *The "Genius"* is suppressed when passages are deemed obscene by the New York Society for the Prevention of Vice. Mencken solicits the support of the Author's League of America for a petition in defense of the book (the novel remains out of circulation until 1922). Launches *Saucy Stories*, which (from August to October) he edits anonymously with Nathan. Publication of *A Book of Burlesques* and *A Little Book in C Major*. Resigns editorship at the *Sun*. Sails to England, December 28; travels to Germany to report on World War I.

1917 Germany commences unrestricted submarine warfare against neutral shipping on February 1. Mencken departs Germany to cover the Liberal revolt in Cuba against the U.S.-supported government of President García Menocal. Arrives in Havana, March 5, and returns to the U.S. on March 14. Stops writing for the *Sun* with publication of last dispatch, March 29. The United States declares war on Germany, April 6. Espionage Act goes into effect June 15. Writes for the New York *Evening Mail* from June 18 to July 8, 1918. Mencken meets James Weldon Johnson, begins to focus attention on African American and cultural issues. "The Sahara of the Bozart," an indictment of southern culture, published in the New York *Evening*

Mail, November 13. "A Neglected Anniversary," Mencken's invented history of the bathtub, published in the New York *Evening Mail*, December 28. Publication of *A Book of Prefaces*, and of *Pistols for Two*, written with Nathan under the joint pseudonym "Owen Hatteras."

1918 The editor of the New York *Evening Mail*, Edward Rumley, is arrested July 8 over allegations that the paper received secret German government funding; control then passes to pro-war individuals and Mencken stops writing for it. (Mencken later reflects, "I stopped writing and believed I was done with newspaper work forever.") German language eliminated from Baltimore public elementary schools, July; anti-German feeling rampant. The Bureau of Investigation (later the FBI) opens a case file on Mencken; his mail is opened and he is watched by agents. Mencken's *Damn! A Book of Calumny* is published by his close friend, Broadway producer Philip Goodman, who also publishes *In Defense of Women* (later editions published by Knopf beginning in 1919). Germany signs armistice, November 11.

1919 Publication of *The American Language* (first edition quickly sells out) and *Prejudices: First Series*, which also proves successful. With *Sun* publishers Paul Patterson and Harry Black, Mencken helps develop plan for expanded national coverage and an independent approach. Attorney General Mitchell Palmer orders mass arrests of radicals and foreigners. Mencken becomes increasingly frustrated by his work at *The Smart Set*, telling a friend: "We live, not in a literary age, but in a fiercely political age."

1920 Begins series of regular Monday columns in the Baltimore *Evening Sun* (they continue until January 31, 1938), regularly denouncing interference with free speech and calling for civil rights for all Americans. Reads manuscript of *Main Street* by Sinclair Lewis and encourages its publication. With Nathan, launches *Black Mask*, a mystery magazine, April. Publication of *Prejudices: Second Series*. Publication of *Heliogabalus* and *The American Credo*, both written with Nathan. Publication of *The Anti-Christ* by Nietzsche, translated with an introduction by Mencken.

1921 Becomes contributing editor of *The Nation*, May (until December 1932). Covers the naval disarmament conference in Washington, D.C., November–December. Publication of the second edition of *The American Language*.

1922 Travels to England and Germany, August–October. Publication of *Prejudices: Third Series.*

1923 On May 8, while lecturing at Baltimore's Goucher College, he meets Sara Powell Haardt (born March 1, 1898, in Montgomery, Alabama), a fiction writer and member of the English faculty. Mencken solicits manuscripts from American writers for a new magazine focusing exclusively on American cultural and political themes, summer. Mencken and Nathan resign as coeditors of *The Smart Set*, December. Publication of the third edition of *The American Language.*

1924 First issue of *The American Mercury* is published in January with Mencken and Nathan as coeditors. Contributors will include Countee Cullen, James Weldon Johnson, W.E.B. Du Bois, Dorothy Parker, Sherwood Anderson, George Schuyler, as well as bricklayers, hoboes, bishops, senators, lawyers, American Indians, prisoners. Its layout, typeface, buoyant tone, and sections "Americana" (items culled from newspapers and magazines across the country) and "Profiles" (portraits written by well-known writers about well-known subjects) are widely imitated. Covers Republican National Convention in Cleveland, June 9–13, and Democratic National Convention in New York City, June 23–29. Writes columns for the Chicago *Tribune* (until January 29, 1928). Publication of *Prejudices: Fourth Series.*

1925 Tension between Nathan and Mencken increases, with Mencken insisting on more social and political commentary in *The American Mercury* and Nathan favoring an equal emphasis on literature. Nathan withdraws as coeditor of *The American Mercury* in July. Mencken travels to Dayton, Tennessee, in July to cover trial of John Scopes, high school teacher arrested for teaching theory of evolution in contravention of newly passed state law. Mother, Anna Abhau Mencken, dies 6 P.M. December 13 and is buried at Loudon Park Cemetery. Publication of *Americana 1925*. The first two books about Mencken are published (*H. L. Mencken* by Ernest Boyd and *The Man Mencken: A Biographical and Critical Survey* by Isaac Goldberg). Breaks friendship with Dreiser because of a series of misunderstandings, among them Dreiser's seeming lack of sympathy concerning the death of Mencken's mother and Dreiser's callous treatment of women.

1926 Walter Lippmann calls Mencken "the most powerful personal influence on this whole generation of educated people." Through the influence of the New England Watch and Ward Society, the April issue of *The American Mercury* is banned in Boston because of Herbert Asbury's short story "Hatrack"; Mencken courts arrest by personally selling a copy to the Society's secretary; a judge declares the story not obscene and dismisses the complaint. Mencken tours the American South and arrives in California, October. Father's cigar firm, August Mencken & Bro., managed by Uncle Henry, goes bankrupt. Publication of *Notes on Democracy*, *Prejudices: Fifth Series*, and *Americana, 1926*.

1927 Publication of *Prejudices: Sixth Series* and *Selected Prejudices*.

1928 Travels to Havana, Cuba, to cover Pan American Conference, January. Covers Republican National Convention, Kansas City, June 11–16, and Democratic National Convention, Houston, June 23–29. Travels with Al Smith on campaign tour, October 12–30. Publication of *Menckeniana: A Schimpflexicon*, a humorous collection of anti-Mencken invective that had appeared in newspapers and magazines across the country. Circulation of *The American Mercury* reaches its height of 84,000. Begins courting Sara Powell Haardt on a steadier basis.

1929 Sara Powell Haardt undergoes surgery for the removal of a tubercular kidney, July 6.

1930 Covers London Naval Conference, January–February. Announces secret engagement to Sara Powell Haardt to family members, April. Marries Sara Powell Haardt August 27 at St. Stephen the Martyr Episcopal Church, Baltimore; they travel to Canada on their honeymoon. Moves to new residence, 704 Cathedral Street, Baltimore. Publication of *Treatise on the Gods*. Book sells well, but stirs controversy because of passage in which Mencken describes Jews as "plausibly the most unpleasant race ever heard of." (Passage is deleted in later editions.) In newspaper interview he denies he is an anti-Semite: "I don't like religious Jews. I don't like religious Catholics and Protestants." Begins writing a diary.

1931 Writes a series of controversial columns against lynching of Matthew Williams in Salisbury, Maryland, on December 4, causing a boycott of Baltimore businesses and the *Sun* papers by residents of the Eastern Shore. *The Nation* recognizes Mencken for "distinguished journalism in the face of personal danger," December.

1932 Mencken sails to the West Indies with Sara, January 9. Covers Republican National Convention in Chicago, June 13–18, and Democratic National Convention in Chicago, June 26–July 2. Franklin D. Roosevelt elected President, November. Publication of *Making a President*. Continues suggesting authors and ideas for books to his publisher, Alfred Knopf; elected board member of Knopf, Inc.

1933 Mencken becomes increasingly critical of the New Deal, directing most of his criticism against the "quacks" of the Brain Trust rather than the President himself. Writes controversial columns against lynching of George Arnwood in Princess Anne on Maryland's Eastern Shore, October 18 (last lynching in Maryland). With Mencken's popularity at a low ebb, circulation of *The American Mercury* sinks to 28,329; Mencken resigns as editor with the December issue.

1934 Travels on a two-month cruise to the Mediterranean with Sara, January–March, and is fascinated by his visit with Jewish colonists in Palestine; his writing on the subject for the *Evening Sun* is privately printed in a book entitled *Eretz Israel*. Writes series of articles on American English for the New York *American*, July 9–May 20, 1935. Joins Board of Directors of the A. S. Abell Company, October 15. Resumes friendship with Theodore Dreiser. Speaks before the Gridiron Club in Washington, D.C., December 8; his address is mildly critical of the New Deal, but when it is Roosevelt's turn to speak, he turns Mencken's commentary on journalists against him by quoting a passage from *Prejudices: Sixth Series*. Publication of *Treatise on Right and Wrong*. Last article for *The Nation*, December 12.

1935 Testifies in favor of the Costigan-Wagner Anti-Lynching Bill at Senate hearing, February 14. (Bill is later blocked by Senate filibuster.) Wife Sara Haardt Mencken dies of tubercular meningitis, May 31. Edits a compilation of her work, *Southern Album*; travels to England with his brother August, June 15.

1936 Returns to his family home at 1524 Hollins Street, which he calls "as much a part of me as my two hands." Begins to organize his papers and family archives. Publishes "Three Years of Dr. Roosevelt," a scathing attack on the president, whom he compares to "a snake-oil vendor at a village carnival," in *The American Mercury*, March. Publication of "The Ordeal of a Philosopher" in *The New Yorker*, April 11, which is later used as a chapter in *Happy Days*. Covers Republican National Convention, Cleveland, June 8–13, and Democratic National Convention, Philadelphia, June 22–28, as well as convention in support of the Townsend Plan (Cleveland, July 14–20) and Union Party convention organized by Father Charles Coughlin (Cleveland, August 13–18). Travels with Republican nominee Alf Landon on his campaign tour, August–October. Publication of the fourth edition of *The American Language*.

1937 Vacations in Daytona Beach, Florida, with his brother August, January. Publication of *The Sunpapers of Baltimore*, written with Frank R. Kent, Gerald W. Johnson, and Hamilton Owens. Publication of *The Charlatanry of the Learned*, edited by Mencken and translated from the Latin by Francis Litz; the book is a satirical attack on academic pretension, written by Mencken's ancestor, Leipzig scholar Johann Burkhard Mencke (1674–1732).

1938 Alarmed by what he sees as the Roosevelt administration's mastery at setting the agenda with the press, Mencken writes publisher Paul Patterson that "we confront a high development of government propaganda," and at Patterson's request becomes temporary editor of the Baltimore *Evening Sun*, January 24–May 9. Writes "Sunday Articles" for the Baltimore *Sun*, May 16–February 2, 1941. Appointed chairman of the *Sunpapers*' committee to negotiate with the Newspaper Guild, summer. Travels to Germany, June–July; refrains from reporting on any of his observations. Writes column, "Help for the Jews," proposing the United States open its doors to German Jewish refugees fleeing Nazi persecution, November 27, 1938.

1939 Convinced that America's security would depend on its abstention from European conflict, Mencken becomes increasingly isolationist. In a speech given before the American Society of Newspaper Editors, on April 20, Mencken reminds his audience of government censorship in 1917 and warns that war will once again pose a threat to freedom of the press. Suffers a minor stroke, "generalized arteriosclerosis," July 31. Hitler invades Poland, September 1. England declares war on Germany, September 3. With his brother August, begins taking photographs of West Baltimore. Completes *Happy Days*, September 18.

1940 Covers Republican National Convention in Philadelphia, June 22–29, and Democratic National Convention in Chicago, July 13–19. Travels with Wendell Wilkie on his campaign tour, August 16–November 3. Publication of *Happy Days: 1880–1892*, first of a series of memoirs, January 22. Death of best friend, Raymond Pearl, biometrician at the Johns Hopkins University School of Medicine.

1941 Resigns from the *Sun* papers, January 16, because of publishers' unease with his anti-Roosevelt and anti-war views. Begins writing memoir on his journalism career, "Thirty-Five Years of Newspaper Work" (published in 1994). Publication of *Newspaper Days: 1899–1906*, October 20, 1941. From 1941 to 1943 *The New Yorker* publishes Mencken's series "Days of Innocence," later revised and published as chapters in *Newspaper Days* and *Heathen Days.* Travels to Havana, April. Helps several Jewish refugees find asylum in the United States; pleads their case in person to the United States State Department, August 26. Japanese attack on Pearl Harbor brings the United States into war, December 7.

1942 Begins writing memoir that focuses on his literary career, "My Life as Author and Editor"; works on it periodically until 1948 (published 1993). Publication of *A New Dictionary of Quotations.*

1943 Testifies in October on behalf of *Esquire* magazine, which had lost its mailing privileges on charges of obscenity. Publication of *Heathen Days: 1890–1936*, March 1, published as an Armed Services Edition in September. Begins compiling lengthy typescripts of "Additions, Corrections, and Explanatory Notes" for each of the *Days* books.

1944 Publication of Armed Services Edition of *Happy Days*, February, which becomes a GI favorite. "That is the difference between a soldier and a civilian," remarks Mencken. "The letters you get from civilians are from those who don't like your books."

1945 Publication of *The American Language: Supplement I.* The end of World War II officially declared September 2. In the aftermath of Allied bombing, which had appalled him,

Mencken sends packages of food, shoes, and other necessities to friends in Berlin, copies of his books to correspondents in Japan. Theodore Dreiser dies, December 28.

1946 Publication of *Christmas Story*, a satirical account of a holiday feast among the homeless of Baltimore, and how the organizers impose their Puritanical morality among the crowd.

1947 Buoyed by news of Truman's plans to help the economic recovery of Europe, March; argues for immediate economic rehabilitation of Germany. In August suffers a minor stroke but recovers after a few days. The autobiographical trilogy is published in one volume as *The Days of H. L. Mencken*. Interviewed by Edgar Kemler and William Manchester, who are separately writing biographies of Mencken.

1948 Vacations in Florida with brother August, February. Rejoins *Sun* staff to cover Republican Party Convention, June 19–22; covers Democratic National Convention, July 10–15, and Progressive Party Convention, July 23–26, all held in Philadelphia. Revival of interest in Mencken's life and work demonstrated by cover story in *Newsweek* magazine, April 5. Records an interview for the Library of Congress, June 30. Publication of *The American Language, Supplement II*. Last public appearance, speaking before the American Philosophical Society, November 4. Writes series of articles for the *Sun*, August 1–November 9. Publication of last column, arguing against segregation, November 9. Suffers a massive stroke that prevents any further reading or writing for the remainder of his life, November 23. (In his remaining years he is cared for largely by his younger brother August.)

1949 Publication of *A Mencken Chrestomathy*, Mencken's selection from his writings. Spends remaining years helping his secretary organize his papers for posterity, well over 100,000 letters, as well as original manuscripts, memoirs, and books, dedicating the bulk of the collection to the Enoch Pratt Free Library, as well as to the New York Public Library and Dartmouth.

1950 Suffers heart attack, October 12. Members of the Saturday Night Club agree in December to disband permanently.

Spends five months in hospital, before he is discharged in March 1951.

1955 *Inherit the Wind*, play about the Scopes Trial by Jerome Lawrence and Robert E. Lee, featuring a character based on Mencken, opens in April. On Mencken's 75th birthday, Alistair Cooke's edition of *The Vintage Mencken* is published, selling out in two days. Secretary Rosalind Lorhfinck comes across an unpublished manuscript written by Mencken before his 1948 stroke (published posthumously the following year as *Minority Report: H. L. Mencken's Notebooks*).

1956 Dies in his sleep from a coronary occlusion, between 4 and 5 A.M. on January 29, leaving an estate valued at $300,000. Three-fourths of his estate is willed to the Enoch Pratt Free Library. He is cremated, and his ashes are interred at Loudon Park Cemetery, in West Baltimore, January 31.

Note on the Texts

This volume contains the complete texts of H. L. Mencken's *Prejudices: First Series* (1919), *Prejudices: Second Series* (1920), and *Prejudices: Third Series* (1922), along with an excerpt from Mencken's unfinished autobiography, *My Life as Author and Editor* (written 1942–48), in which he discusses the composition and reception of the first two series of *Prejudices.* A Library of America companion volume, *Prejudices: Fourth, Fifth, and Sixth Series*, presents the complete contents of the three subsequent *Prejudices*, published in 1924, 1926, and 1927. The texts of the *Prejudices* have been taken from the corrected second printings of the first editions of each collection, all published in New York by Alfred A. Knopf. The text of *My Life as Author and Editor* has been taken from Mencken's hand-corrected typescript, now in the Mencken Collection at the Enoch Pratt Free Library in Baltimore.

By Mencken's account, the initial suggestion that he gather his periodical writings in book form came from Richard Laukhuff, a Cleveland bookseller, who proposed such a collection to Mencken's publisher. *Prejudices: First Series* was assembled largely out of articles from the *Smart Set*, to which Mencken had been contributing since 1908; he also drew on his writing in newspapers, including the New York *Evening Mail* and the Baltimore *Evening Sun.*

Setting the pattern for all of his *Prejudices*, he revised these original articles extensively—rewriting, and adding new material—before he sent his finished work to Knopf. Mencken's subsequent *Prejudices* also began, though to a lesser extent, with contributions to the *Smart Set* and *The American Mercury*; for a more detailed account of the periodical publication history of individual pieces in the *Prejudices*, see S. T. Joshi, *H. L. Mencken: An Anotated Bibliography* (Lanham, Maryland: Scarecrow Press, 2009).

Mencken's relationship with Knopf was a congenial one, and he exercised an exceptional degree of control over the form in which his works appeared. He was also a careful proofreader of his own work, and encouraged Knopf (in a letter of March 24, 1921, noting some typographical errors in the first printing of *Prejudices: Second Series*) to "correct all such errors whenever the opportunity offers. Nothing looks worse than a dirty book. The English reviewers, in particular, are very waspish about typographical errors." In the case of all of his *Prejudices*, Mencken's final textual corrections were not incorporated in the first Knopf printings, where they are listed separately as errata (for *Prejudices: Second Series* through *Prejudices: Sixth Series*), or not noted (in *Prejudices: First Series*). No evidence has been found for Mencken's further correction or revision of his texts in subsequent printings and editions of the *Prejudices* in the United States or in England, though he did permit minor changes to be made, for the benefit of English readers, in two English editions: *Prejudices* (London: Jonathan Cape, 1925), and *Selected Prejudices: Second Series* (London: Jonathan Cape, 1927). The present volume prints the texts of the corrected second printings of the Knopf first editions, issued in January 1920 (*Prejudices: First Series*), June 1921 (*Prejudices: Second Series*), and November 1922 (*Prejudices: Third Series*).

Mencken began writing *My Life as Author and Editor* in November 1942 and continued—with interruptions to finish *The American Language: Supplement 1* (1945) and *The American Language: Supplement 2* (1948)—until November 1948, when a stroke left him permanently disabled. Afterwards, he donated his unfinished corrected typescript to the Enoch Pratt Free Library in Baltimore, with the instruction that it not be accessible until 1980 or thirty-five years after his death, whichever came later.

In 1992, Alfred A. Knopf published a substantial portion of Mencken's work (which runs to almost 2000 pages, including appendices, in the original typescript) as *My Life as Author and Editor* (Jonathan Yardley, ed.). The present volume includes an excerpt from the autobiography in which Mencken discusses his first and second series of *Prejudices*. The text printed here has been taken from Mencken's typescript.

This volume presents the texts of the printings and typescript chosen for inclusion, but it does not attempt to reproduce nontextual features of their typographic design. The texts are printed without change, except for the correction of typographical errors. Spelling, punctuation, and capitalization may be expressive features, and they are not altered, even when inconsistent or irregular. The following is a list of typographical errors corrected, cited by page and line number: 14.23, Liége.; 74.34, chair; 99.9, Bastile,; 147.4, Aristotolean; 163.38, letters!); 167.17, Sweet; 167.36, of forty; 175.13, Russion; 178.35, Provençe,; 191.23, astouning; 195.2, on on; 210.3, Weil; 211.23, miliary; 218.6, developement; 250.7, or gross; 256.2, one-hundred-and forty-fifth; 274.28, drival; 276.7, condems; 282.5, Prohibionist; 305.30, *digitatem*; 313.5, incurable; 313.31, too for; 316.14, biologically But; 332.5, that; 332.16, *a la*; 346.30, fugelman; 383.4, Jerpersen; 387.40, get all in the; 389.22, Rosetti's; 392.22, Travelyn; 394.22, ever; 404.3, Shelly; 418.8, Goldmarck's; 418.14, "My Antonía" (and *passim*); 427.24, life at; 430.34, contented,; 433.9, women; 438.29, *privat dozent*; 453.24, sedentery; 461.16, it downright; 469.21, years; 477.35, collared,; 482.8, appreciable; 482.32, [no "4"]; 493.20, "Prejudices"; 496.37, reposte; 497.18, fitter; 498.20, last-named signing; 498.24, phrases,; 502.37, Perrin"; 502.39, Wrex; 504.1, difference; 510.39, to setting; 512.35, jointed; 514.18, *Westminister*.

Notes

In the notes below, the reference numbers denote page and line of this volume (the line count includes headings). No note is made for material included in standard desk-reference books. Quotations from Shakespeare are keyed to *The Riverside Shakespeare*, ed. G. Blakemore Evans (Boston: Houghton Mifflin, 1974). Biographical information beyond that included in the Chronology may be found in Marion Elizabeth Rodgers, *Mencken: The American Iconoclast* (Oxford, New York: Oxford University Press, 2005); Marion Elizabeth Rodgers, editor, *Mencken and Sara: A Life in Letters* (New York: McGraw-Hill, 1987); Marion Elizabeth Rodgers, editor, *The Impossible H. L. Mencken: A Selection of His Best Newspaper Stories* (New York: Anchor/Doubleday, 1991); Guy J. Forgue, editor, *Letters of H. L. Mencken* (New York: Knopf, 1961); Carl Bode, editor, *The New Mencken Letters* (New York: Dial Press, 1977); Thomas P. Riggio, editor, *Dreiser-Mencken Letters: The Correspondence of Theodore Dreiser and H. L. Mencken* (Philadelphia: University of Pennsylvania Press, 1986); Edward A. Martin, editor, *In Defense of Marion: The Love Letters of Marion Bloom and H. L. Mencken* (Athens: University of Georgia Press, 1996); Carl Bode, *Mencken* (Carbondale: Southern Illinois University Press, 1969); *Charles Scruggs, The Sage in Harlem: H. L. Mencken and the Black Writers of the 1920s* (Baltimore: Johns Hopkins University Press, 1984); Vincent Fitzpatrick, *H. L. Mencken* (Macon: Mercer University Press, 2004); Fred Hobson, *Mencken: A Life* (New York: Random House, 1994); William Manchester, *Disturber of the Peace: The Life of H. L. Mencken* (Amherst: University of Massachusetts Press, 1986); Terry Teachout, *The Skeptic: A Life of H. L. Mencken* (New York: HarperCollins, 2002); Charles A. Fecher, *Mencken: A Study of His Thought* (New York: Alfred A. Knopf, 1978); Richard J. Schrader, *H. L. Mencken: A Descriptive Bibliography* (Pittsburgh: University of Pittsburgh Press, 1998); and S. T. Joshi, *H. L. Mencken: An Annotated Bibliography* (Lanham, Maryland: Scarecrow Press, 2009).

PREJUDICES: FIRST SERIES

3.33 Major J. E. Spingarn] Joel Elias Spingarn (1875–1939), professor of comparative literature at Columbia and literary critic. His books included *The New Criticism* (1911) and *Creative Criticism* (1917).

4.14–15 William Lyon Phelps] Literary scholar (1865–1943) and professor of English at Yale, who became popular as lecturer and columnist. Author of *Essays on Modern Novelists* (1910), *The Advance of the English Novel* (1916), and other works.

4.17 W. C. Brownell] William Crary Brownell (1851–1928), literary critic, author of *American Prose Masters* (1909), *Standards* (1917), *The Genius of Style* (1924), and other books.

4.19–20 Stuart P. Sherman] Stuart Pratt Sherman (1881–1926), literary critic and professor at the University of Illinois (1907–24). In 1917 Sherman charged Mencken with being unpatriotic and a defender of licentious literature, using Theodore Dreiser as an example. Mencken ridiculed Sherman in his article, "The Dreiser Bugaboo," published in *Seven Arts* (August 1917), and Sherman responded with a negative review of *A Book of Prefaces* in *The Nation* (November 1917).

5.29 "What Is Man?"] Essay (1906) by Mark Twain.

6.14 Espionage Act] The Espionage Act, passed on June 15, 1917, included among its provisions severe penalties (up to $10,000 fine and twenty years' imprisonment) for persons found guilty of interfering with the draft or encouraging disloyalty to the United States. Some newspapers were barred from the mails, notably the *New York Call* and *Milwaukee Leader*. More than 1500 persons were arrested, among them labor leaders Eugene Debs and Victor Berger.

7.7 *Privatdozenten*] German academic title corresponding roughly to associate professor.

7.15 Hamilton Wright Mabie's "White List of Books"] Mabie (1846–1916), essayist, lecturer, and editor of the Christian magazine *The Outlook*; his books included *Books and Culture* (1896), *The Life of the Spirit* (1899), and *American Ideals, Character and Life* (1913). His "White List" itemized works suitable for Christian homes and the perusal of children.

7.28–29 Hermann Bahr] Austrian playwright, novelist, and critic (1863–1934).

7.29 Georg Brandes] Georg Morris Cohen Brandes (1872–1927), preeminent Danish critic and scholar of his time, a leading proponent of realism and a prolific commentator on literature, politics, religion, and philosophy. He was the author of many books including *Main Currents in the Literature of the Nineteenth Century* (1872–75) and monographs on Kierkegaard, Ibsen, Nietzsche, and Goethe, among others.

7.29 James Huneker] James Gibbons Huneker (1857–1921), critic of literature, music, and art. He was founder of the magazine *M'lle New York* and musical editor of the New York *Sun*. His many books include *Chopin: The Man and His Music* (1900), *Iconoclasts, a Book of Dramatists* (1905), *Egoists:*

A Book of Supermen (1909), *Ivory Apes and Peacocks* (1915), the memoirs *Old Fogy* (1913) and *Steeplejack* (1920), and the novel *Painted Veils* (1920).

7.31 Paul Elmer More] Critic and philosopher (1864–1937) associated with the New Humanist movement. His *Shelburne Essays* were published in fourteen volumes (1904–36), and his other works included *Platonism* (1917), *The Religion of Plato* (1921), and *The Christ of the New Testament* (1924).

9.7–8 Rufus Griswold] Journalist and editor (1815–1857) of literary anthologies including *The Poets and Poetry of America* (1842) and *The Female Poets of America* (1849). He quarreled with Edgar Allan Poe and as Poe's literary executor published a defamatory biography that had lingering influence.

9.17 Mr. W. H.] Unidentified dedicatee of Shakespeare's sonnets ("the onlie begetter of these insuing sonnets"), subject of Oscar Wilde's speculative story "The Portrait of Mr. W. H." (1889).

11.2 Mr. Wells] H. G. Wells (1866–1946), English novelist whose later works, discussed by Mencken, included *Tono-Bungay* (1909), *Ann Veronica* (1909), *The History of Mr. Polly* (1910), *The New Machiavelli* (1911), *Marriage* (1912), *The Passionate Friends* (1913), *The Wife of Sir Isaac Harman* (1914), *Bealby: A Holiday* (1915), *Boon* (1915), *The Research Magnificent* (1916), *Mr. Britling Sees It Through* (1917), *The Soul of a Bishop* (1917), *Joan and Peter: The Story of an Education* (1918), and *The Undying Fire* (1919). *First and Last Things* (1908) was a book of essays intended, in Wells's words, "to put down what I believe."

11.4–5 Richard Remington] Protagonist of Wells's novel *The New Machiavelli* (1911).

11.16 Scribe] Eugène Scribe (1791–1861), French playwright, author of hundreds of plays alone or in collaboration, noted for his mastery of stagecraft and plot construction. His plays included *Le Mariage de raison* (1826), *Le Mariage d'argent* (1828), *Une Chaîne* (1841), and *Le Verre d'eau* (1842).

12.15 A Trip to Chinatown] Long-running musical comedy (1891), by Charles H. Hoyt (1859–1900).

12.15 Peck's Bad Boy] Series of books written by George Wilbur Peck (1840–1916), beginning with *Peck's Bad Boy and His Pa* (1883).

12.30–31 The Four Horsemen of the Apocalypse] Novel (1916) by Spanish novelist Vicente Blasco Ibáñez (1867–1928).

13.2 William Archer] Scottish dramatic critic (1886–1924) and translator of Henrik Ibsen's plays. (The Ibsen translations were published in eleven volumes, 1906–8.) *The Old Drama and the New*, a defense of modern playwriting, appeared in 1923.

14.15–16 *Privatdozenten*] See note 7.7.

16.23–24 Fabian Society] British socialist movement founded in 1884, and favoring incremental rather than revolutionary change. Among its early members were George Bernard Shaw, H. G. Wells, and Beatrice and Sidney Webb.

16.24 Lord Northcliffe] Alfred Charles William Harmsworth, 1st Viscount Northcliffe (1865–1922), British newspaper and publishing magnate, proprietor of the London *Times* and the *Daily Mail*; appointed Director of Propaganda during World War I.

17.27 Dr. Wilson] Woodrow Wilson (1856–1924), president of the United States (1913–1921).

17.27 British Socialists] British Socialist Party, Marxist political movement established in England in 1911, a predecessor to the Communist Party of Great Britain (founded 1920).

17.27–28 Romain Rolland] French man of letters (1866–1941), author of biographical and critical studies of Beethoven, Michelangelo, and Tolstoy, plays, political tracts, and novels including the ten-volume *Jean-Christophe*; winner of the Nobel Prize in Literature in 1915.

17.28 James M. Beck] James Montgomery Beck (1861–1936), lawyer, Solicitor General of the United States (1921–1925), and member of the U.S. House of Representatives (1927–1934).

18.15 Van Wyck Brooks] Critic and literary biographer (1886–1963), author of *America's Coming-of-Age* (1915), *The Ordeal of Mark Twain* (1920), *The Flowering of New England* (1936), and many other works. His study *The World of H. G. Wells* was published in 1915.

18.21 William Bayard Hale] American journalist (1869–1924). An Episcopal minister, he became editor of *Cosmopolitan* in 1900 and wrote the campaign biography *Woodrow Wilson: The Story of His Life* (1912). Wilson's 1913 volume *The New Freedom: A Call for the Emancipation of the Generous Energies of a People* was edited by Hale from the president's campaign speeches. Hale was subsequently a propaganda advisor to the German government before America's entry into the war, and in 1915 published *American Rights and British Pretension on the Seas*, an attack on Britain's blockade of German shipping. After the war he was an object of public denunciation and spent the remainder of his life in Europe.

21.32 W. L. George] Walter Lionel George (1882–1926), French-born English novelist best known for *A Bed of Roses* (1911), about the life of a prostitute.

21.37–38 Blind Alley] Novel (1919) by W. L. George.

21.38 The Pretty Lady] Novel (1918) by Arnold Bennett (1867–1931).

22.10 Bayards and Cids] Pierre LeVieux, seigneur de Bayard (1473–

1524), French soldier lauded in his lifetime as an emblem of chivalry, *le chevalier sans peur et sans reproche*; Rodrigo Diaz de Bivar (1040?-1099), known as El Cid, Castilian military leader commemorated in the twelfth-century poem *Cantar de Mio Cid*.

22.28 The Roll-Call] The fourth volume (1918) of Arnold Bennett's series of novels about the Clayhanger family.

24.20 Haeckel] Ernst Heinrich Haeckel (1834–1919), German biologist and philosopher who published many works helping to popularize evolutionary theory. His books include *The Riddle of the Universe* (1901), *Artforms of Nature* (1904), and *The History of Creation* (1914). He was the author of the subsequently contested formulation that "ontogeny recapitulates phylogeny."

24.20 Bradlaugh] Charles Bradlaugh (1833–1891), English political activist and atheist, a founder of the National Secular Society in 1866. Elected to Parliament in 1880, he was denied his seat because of his refusal to swear the religious Oath of Allegiance, initiating a long controversy not resolved until 1886. His books include *A Plea for Atheism* (1864) and *Humanity's Gain from Unbelief* (1889).

25.7–8 Buried Alive . . . The Lion's Share] Novels by Arnold Bennett, published respectively in 1908 and 1918.

25.12 Dr. Orison Swett Marden] American writer (1850–1924) associated with the New Thought movement, and author of self-help books emphasizing the power of positive thinking in order to achieve success, including *The Secret of Achievement* (1898), *Cheerfulness as a Life Power* (1899), and *The Hour of Opportunity* (1900).

25.12 Dr. Frank Crane] American Methodist clergyman (1861–1928) whose syndicated inspirational newspaper column appeared across the country from 1909–1928. His writings were collected in ten volumes in *Four-Minute Essays* (1919).

27.19 Whom God Hath Joined] Novel (1906) by Arnold Bennett.

28.9 Paris Nights] Novel (1914) by Arnold Bennett.

29.11–12 Joseph H. Choate] Joseph Hodges Choate (1832–1917), lawyer and diplomat. He played a major role in the prosecution of the Tweed Ring in New York and represented the Standard Oil Company in antitrust cases, and also served as U.S. Ambassador to Great Britain (1899–1905) and head of the U.S. Delegation of the International Peace Conference at the Hague (1907).

29.15 Alexander Harvey] Editor and author (1868–1949), associated with *Literary Digest*, *Current Opinion*, and *The Atlantic Monthly*. His study *William Dean Howells* appeared in 1917.

30.12–14 The Minister's Charge . . . The Leatherwood God] *The*

Minister's Charge (1887), *An Imperative Duty* (1893), *The Unexpected Guests* (1893), *Out of the Question* (1877), *No Love Lost* (1869), *The Leatherwood God* (1916), novels and plays by William Dean Howells.

31.24 Agnes Repplier] Philadelphia-born essayist (1855–1950) whose works were collected in many volumes including *Books and Men* (1888), *Points of View* (1891), *Essays in Idleness* (1893), and *The Fireside Sphinx* (1901).

31.25 New Leaf Mills] Memoir (1913) by William Dean Howells describing a childhood year spent living with his family in a Utopian commune at Eureka Mills, Ohio.

31.29–30 E. W. Howe's "The Story of a Country Town"] Novel (1883) by Edgar Watson Howe (1853–1937), a realistic treatment of life in a Midwestern town.

32.13 W. B. Trites] William Budd Trites, author of the novels *John Cave* (1909) and *Barbara Gwynne: Life* (1913).

32.13–14 Frank A. Munsey] Frank Andrew Munsey (1854–1925), publisher, owner of the New York *Evening Sun* and *Evening Telegram*, *Munsey's Magazine*, and *Argosy All-Story Weekly*.

32.15–16 Phillpses] Stephen Phillips (1864–1915), English poet and playwright, noted for his attempts to revive verse drama.

32.16 Pollards] Joseph Percival Pollard (1869–1911), German-born literary critic, a close friend of Mencken; he was educated in England and emigrated with his family to the United States in 1885. He was a frequent contributor to *The Criterion*. His books included *Their Day in Court* (1909) and *Masks and Minstrels of New Germany* (1911).

32.16 Meltzers] Charles Henry Meltzer (1853–1936), English music critic and translator, later resident in the United States.

32.33 Hannah More] English playwright (1745–1833), who in later life devoted herself to religious writing. She participated with William Wilberforce in the antislavery movement. The Religious Tract Society was founded to carry on her work.

34.7 Elihu Root] Lawyer and statesman (1845–1937), U.S. Secretary of War under Presidents McKinley and Roosevelt (1899–1904) and Secretary of State under President Roosevelt (1905–1909). He was a supporter of the League of Nations and founding chairman of the Council on Foreign Relations.

34.8 Otto Kahn] Otto Hermann Kahn (1867–1934), investment banker and financier, and patron of the arts.

34.10 Thorstein Veblen] Norwegian-American sociologist and economist (1857–1929), author of *The Theory of the Leisure Class* (1899), *The Theory of Business Enterprise* (1904), *The Instinct of Workmanship* (1914), *Imperial Germany and the Industrial Revolution* (1915), *The Higher Learning in America* (1918), *The Vested Interests and the State of the Industrial Arts* (1919), *An Inquiry into the Nature of Peace and the Terms of Its Perpetuation* (1919), and other works.

34.25 "Men Versus the Man"] *Men Versus the Man: A Correspondence Between Rives La Monte, Socialist, and H. L. Mencken, Individualist*, published in 1910.

34.26 Baxter's "Saint's Rest"] *The Saint's Everlasting Rest: or, Treatise on the Blessed State of the Saints and Their Enjoyment of God in Heaven* (1672) by English Puritan theologian Richard Baxter (1615–1691).

35.16 Judge Ben B. Lindsey] Benjamin Barr Lindsey (1869–1943), judge of the juvenile court of Colorado (1900–27), which became a model for the rest of the country. He was recognized as an authority on juvenile delinquency; his writings included *Problems of the Children* (1903) and *The Revolt of Modern Youth* (1925).

35.16 The late Major-General Roosevelt] President Theodore Roosevelt (1858–1924).

35.16–17 Tom Lawson] Thomas William Lawson (1857–1925), American stockbroker and author of *Frenzied Finance* (1902), about stock market operations in copper.

35.18 Hall Caine] English novelist (1853–1931), author of *The Shadow of a Crime* (1885), *The Deemster* (1887), and *The Manxman* (1894).

35.18 Brieux] Eugène Brieux (1858–1932), French playwright whose best-known works included *The Red Robe* (1900) and *Damaged Goods* (1901).

35.23 Jane Addams] American social reformer (1860–1935), founder in 1889 of Hull House in Chicago, the first settlement house in the United States. She was active as a pacifist during World War I and received the Nobel Peace Prize in 1931.

35.25 Bernstorff] Johann Heinrich von Bernstorff (1862–1939), German ambassador to the United States, 1908–17. After 1914 he was involved in secret efforts to promote sabotage of American industrial targets to aid the German war effort.

35.26 Eucken] Rudolph Christian Eucken (1846–1926), German philosopher, winner of the 1908 Nobel Prize in Literature. His books included *The Struggle for a Spiritual Content of Life* (1896), *The Truth of Religion* (1901), and *The Meaning and Value of Life* (1908).

35.26–27 Ludendorff] Erich Friedrich Wilhelm Ludendorff (1865–1937), German army officer who (with Paul von Hindenburg) directed the German army during World War I from August 1916 until his resignation in October

1918. Following the armistice he fled to Sweden and while in exile wrote books and articles propounding the idea that Germany had been defeated from within. He returned to Germany in 1920.

35.37 Sir Oliver Lodge] British physicist and inventor (1851–1940) who in later life devoted himself to the study of telepathy, mediums, and the afterlife.

36.26 Scott Nearing] American writer and radical political activist (1883–1983), who over the course of his long career advocated pacifism and a return to natural agrarian living. His many books include *Social Religion* (1910), *Poverty and Riches* (1916), *The Menace of Militarism* (1917), *The American Empire* (1921), *Must We Starve?* (1932), *The Revolution of Our Times* (1947), and *The Making of a Radical: A Political Autobiography* (1972).

38.16 Louis James] American actor (1842–1910), known for his touring Shakespearean company.

42.19 Robert W. Chambers] Artist and bestselling author (1865–1933), best remembered for *The King in Yellow* (1895).

42.20 Elinor Glyn] British novelist (1864–1943) who became famous for the scandalous bestseller *Three Weeks* (1907). Many of her works were filmed; the title story of *"It" and Other Stories* (1927) became a vehicle for Clara Bow.

45.26 Flexner] Abraham Flexner (1866–1955), educator, author of *The American College* (1908) and *Medical Education in the United States and Canada* (1910). He was associated with the cause of medical education reform and later was a founder of the Institute of Advanced Studies at Princeton.

45.26 Ehrlich] Eugen Ehrlich (1862–1922), Austrian legal scholar, author of *Fundamental Principles of the Sociology of Law* (1913).

45.26 Metchnikoff] Ilya Ilyich Mechnikov (1845–1916), Russian microbiologist who received the Nobel Prize in Medicine in 1908. He did pioneering research on the immune system.

45.27 Loeb] Jacques Loeb (1859–1924), German-American physiologist, known for his work on animal tropisms. His most famous experiment induced artificial parthenogenesis in sea urchins. He taught at Bryn Mawr and the Universities of Chicago and California before becoming a member of the Rockefeller Institute for Medical Research in 1910.

45.27 Carrel] Alexis Carrel (1873–1944), French biologist and proponent of eugenics. He received the Nobel Prize in 1912.

46.14 Ellen Key] Swedish feminist writer (1849–1926), author of *The Century of the Child* (1909), *Love and Marriage* (1911), and *The Woman Movement* (1912).

46.14 Signorina Montessori] Maria Montessori (1870–1952), Italian physician and educator, founder of the Montessori method of education for children.

48.8–9 Braithwaite] William Stanley Braithwhite (1878–1962), African American poet and anthologist, author of *Lyrics of Life and Love* (1904) and *Essayists and Critics of Today* (1920). From 1913 to 1929 he published the annual collection *Anthology of Magazine Verse*. He was a literary editor and columnist for the *Boston Evening Transcript*, 1906–31.

48.13 Alfred Kreymborg] American poet (1883–1966), editor of the magazine *Others* (1917–20). His poetry was collected in *Mushrooms* (1916), *Scarlet and Mellow* (1926), and other volumes. His autobiography *Troubador* appeared in 1925. He later edited numerous anthologies including *The American Caravan* (1927–36) and *Lyric America* (1930).

48.23 "Others" group] Poets published in Alfred Kreymborg's *Others* included William Carlos Williams, Wallace Stevens, Marianne Moore, T. S. Eliot, Mina Loy, and Carl Sandburg.

49.11–12 Knish-Morgan burlesque] *Spectra: A Book of Poetic Experiments* (1916), a collection of mock-modernist poems of the "Spectrist" school, written by Witter Bynner and Arthur Davison Ficke under the pseudonyms Emanuel Morgan and Anne Knish. The hoax was revealed in 1918.

49.12 Witter Bynner] American poet (1881–1968) whose many collections included *The Beloved Stranger* (1919), *A Canticle of Pan* (1920), and *Indian Earth* (1929).

49.12 Arthur Davison Ficke] American poet (1883–1945), author of many books including *The Breaking of Bonds* (1910), *The Man on the Hilltop* (1915), and *Selected Poems* (1926).

49.24 James Whitcomb Riley] American poet (1849–1916) whose humorous poems of Indiana life made him immensely popular. A six-volume edition of his complete works was published in 1913.

49.37 Stedman's anthology] Edmund Clarence Stedman (1833–1908), American poet and critic. He edited *An American Anthology, 1787–1899* (1900), an influential survey of American poetry. He also co-edited, with Ellen M. Hutchinson, the eleven–volume *Library of American Literature 1880–1890* (1889–90), and, with George Woodberry, a ten-volume edition of Poe's works.

49.37 McGuffey's Sixth Reader] The series of readers edited by William Holmes McGuffey (1800–1873) began appearing in 1836. The Sixth Reader, designed for the most advanced level, was edited by his brother Alexander McGuffey in the 1840s. The series was widely used and remains in print.

50.2 James Oppenheim] American poet and novelist (1882–1932). He was editor of the influential little magazine *The Seven Arts.* His poem "Bread and Roses" (1911) became a rallying point for labor activists.

50.10 Hermann Hagedorn] American author (1882–1964). His poetry was collected in *A Troop of the Guard* (1909), *Poems and Ballads* (1912), and other volumes. He was a close friend of Theodore Roosevelt, of whom he published a biography in 1918. He also published the novels *Faces in the Dawn* (1914) and *Barbara Picks a Husband* (1918).

50.10–11 Charles Hanson Towne] Poet (1877–1949), author of *The Quiet Singer* (1908), *Manhattan* (1909), and other volumes. He was an editor for *The Smart Set, McClure's Magazine, Harper's Bazaar*, and other publications, and later a columnist for the *New York American.*

50.28 Richard Aldington] English poet and novelist (1892–1962). He married the American poet H.D. (Hilda Doolittle) in 1911; the marriage broke up long before their divorce in 1938. He fought in World War I, an experience which provided the basis for some of his poetry and for the novel *Death of a Hero* (1929).

50.29 John Gould Fletcher] American poet (1886–1950) associated with the Imagist group; his collections included *Irradiations* (1915), *Sand and Spray* (1915), and *Goblins and Pagodas* (1916).

51.9 Tendencies in Modern Poetry] Critical study (1917) by Amy Lowell.

51.10–11 Louis Untermeyer] American poet, critic, and editor (1885–1977). His *The New Era in American Poetry* appeared in 1919. He was a prolific anthologist, responsible for the frequently revised *Modern American and British Poetry* (first published in 1919).

51.12 John Livingston Lowes] American scholar, critic, and educator (1867–1945), author of *Convention and Revolt in Poetry* (1919), *The Road to Xanadu* (first edition, 1927), and other works.

51.27 *Ubi sunt*] Literally "Where are"; a convention of medieval Latin poetry, imitated by François Villon (in his *Où sont les neiges d'antan?*—"Where are the snows of yesteryear?") and others.

52.2 Jubilee Songs] Spirituals, as collected in *Jubilee Songs as Sung by the Jubilee Singers of Fisk University* (1872).

52.11 Henry Bordeaux] French novelist (1870–1963). His *George Guynemer: Knight of the Air* (1918) was published with a preface by Theodore Roosevelt.

52.11 Pastor Wagner] Charles Wagner (1852–1916), French clergyman, author of *The Simple Life* (1904). He was admired by Theodore Roosevelt and invited to preach at the White House.

52.11 Francis Warrington Dawson] Novelist (1878–1962), author of *The*

Scourge (1908) and *The Scar* (1910). When working as a reporter for the United Press Dawson was invited by Theodore Roosevelt to accompany him on an African safari; he later published *Opportunity and Theodore Roosevelt* (1924).

52.12 Giovannitti] Arturo Giovannitti (1884–1959), poet and political activist. He was born in Italy and immigrated to the United States in 1902. He was a member of the IWW, and spent ten months in jail following his participation in the Lawrence, Massachusetts, textile strike of 1912.

52.17 fantee] Amok; gone native.

53.32 Benét] William Rose Benét (1886–1950), American poet, author of *Merchants from Cathay* (1913) and *The Great White Wall* (1916). He was a founder of the *Saturday Review of Literature* and won the Pulitzer Prize in 1942.

54.11 Walt Mason] Humorist and poet (1862–1939); his prose poems were syndicated in more than 200 newspapers and collected in *Uncle Walt: The Poet Philosopher* (1911). He was a colleague of William Allen White on the *Emporia Gazette.*

54.12 Ella Wheeler Wilcox] American poet (1850–1919); her poetry was collected in over twenty volumes including *Poems of Passion* (1883), *Poems of Pleasure* (1888), *Poems of Power* (1901), and *Poems of Sentiment* (1906). For some years she published a daily poem as a syndicated newspaper feature.

55.5 Richard Henry Stoddard] American critic and poet (1825–1903), author of *Poems* (1852) and *Songs of Summer* (1857).

55.19 Henry Van Dyke] American clergyman, educator, and author (1852–1933), a prolific poet.

55.40 Lizette Woodworth Reese] Poet (1856–1935), born in Maryland. She worked as a schoolteacher in the Baltimore area. Her poetry was collected in *A Branch of May* (1887), *A Handful of Lavendar* (1891), *A Quiet Road* (1896), and other volumes. Her sonnet "Tears," published in 1899, became especially popular.

56.4 Neihardt] John G. Neihardt (1881–1973), American poet, specialized in themes of religion and the history of the American West. In 1913 he began publishing his long poetic sequence *A Cycle of the West* (collected in a single volume in 1949). He collaborated with the Sioux shaman Black Elk on *Black Elk Speaks* (1932).

56.5 John McClure] American lyric poet (1893–1956), author of *Airs and Ballads* (1918). His work appeared frequently in *The Smart Set.*

57.4 Irvin S. Cobb] Humorous writer (1876–1944), born in Kentucky and later a New York journalist. His books included *Cobb's Anatomy* (1912), *Cobb's Bill of Fare* (1913), and *Old Judge Priest* (1915).

58.2 Bill Nye] Edgar Wilson Nye (1850–1896), American humorist and popular lecturer, known for his comic sketches about the Wyoming Territory.

58.6–7 Owen Johnson] Novelist and short story writer (1878–1952), author of *The Varmint* (1910), *Stover at Yale* (1911), *The Salamander* (1913), and other works.

58.11 Wilson Mizner] Playwright and screenwriter (1876–1933) who after an early career as confidence man and adventurer became widely known as entrepreneur and raconteur.

58.15–16 *Ayer's Almanac*] Patent medicine catalogue published annually in the late nineteenth and early twentieth centuries by J. C. Ayer & Co. of Lowell, Massachusetts.

59.22 Petroleum V. Nasby] Pseudonym of David Ross Locke (1833–1888), journalist and political satirist. His writings were collected in many volumes, beginning with *The Nasby Papers* (1864).

62.2 *Hermann Sudermann*] German novelist and playwright (1857–1928). His novels included *Frau Sorge* (*Dame Care*, 1887), *Der Katzensteg* (*Cats' Bridge*, 1889), and *Das Hohe Lied* (*The Song of Songs*, 1908). He turned to the stage with *Die Ehre* (*Honor*, 1889) and followed it with *Sodoms Ende* (*Sodom's End*, 1890), *Heimat* (*Homeland*, 1893), and other plays.

62.9–10 Marguerite Gautier] Tragic protagonist of *The Lady of the Camellias* (1848) by Alexandre Dumas fils.

62.12 The Princess Bonnie] Operetta (1893) with words and music by Willard Spenser.

62.16 Arno Holz] German poet, playwright, and critic (1863–1929), a leading proponent of Naturalism.

62.17 Johannes Schlaf] German novelist and playwright (1862–1941). He collaborated in his youth with Arno Holz.

62.19 *Uberbrettl'*] The Überbrettl, artistic cabaret established in Berlin in 1901; see also note 320.29–30.

62.23 Franz Adam Beyerlein] German novelist and playwright (1871–1949). *Zapfenstreich* (1903) concerns military life.

62.23 Carl Bleibtreu] German novelist and historian (1859–1928). His comedy *Die Edelsten der Nation* was published in 1901.

62.28 Hanneles Himmelfahrt] *Hannele's Trip to Heaven*, play (1893) by Gerhart Hauptmann, which after a realistic opening scene veers into the world of dreams.

62.30 sardoodledum] Style of internationally popular theater associated with Victorien Sardou (1831–1908), whose plays included *La Perle Noire* (1862), *Fédora* (1882), *La Tosca* (1887), and *Madame Sans-Gêne* (1893).

62.34–35 Augier's "Le Mariage d'Olympe"] *The Marriage of Olympia* (1855) by Emile Augier (1820–1889), play about a scheming courtesan.

63.13 Brieux's "Les Avariés"] Play (1901) on the social ravages of syphilis, by Eugène Brieux. It was translated into English as *Damaged Goods.*

63.40 Ludwig Thoma] Bavarian novelist, story writer, and playwright (1867–1921).

66.13 *scènes à faire*] Theatrically obligatory scenes, in the nineteenth-century tradition of the well-made play.

67.15–16 George William Curtis] Popular essayist and travel writer (1824–1892), editor of *Harper's Weekly* from 1863. His books included *Niles Notes of a Howadji* (1851), *Lotus-Eating* (1852), and *The Potiphar Papers* (1853).

67.18 Artemus Ward] Pseudonym of Charles Farrar Browne (1834–1867), Maine-born humorous writer who became internationally popular.

67.19 Petroleum V. Nasby] See note 59.22.

67.21 Frank R. Stockton] Novelist and humorist (1834–1902), best known for his short story "The Lady, or the Tiger?" published in *Century* magazine in 1882.

67.22 Richard Henry Stoddard] See note 55.5

67.22–23 Edmund Clarence Stedman] See note 49.37.

67.24 Donald G. Mitchell] Donald Grant Mitchell (1822–1908), American author popularly known as Ik Marvel, whose books included *Reveries of a Bachelor* (1850) and *Dream Life* (1851).

68.18 William Lyon Phelps] See note 4.14–15.

68.33 Robert W. Chambers] See note 42.19.

68.33 Henry Sydnor Harrison] American novelist (1880–1930), a frequent contributor to *The Atlantic Monthly.* His works included *Queed* (1911), *V. V.'s Eyes* (1913), and *Angela's Business* (1915).

68.34 Oliver Herford] English-born American humorist (1863–1935), whose works included *A Child's Primer of Natural History* (1899), *Rubaiyat of a Persian Kitten* (1904), and *A Little Book of Bores* (1906).

68.34 E. S. Martin] Edward Sandford Martin (1856–1939), editor and writer. He was a founder of *The Harvard Lampoon* (1876) and *Life* (1883), and contributed columns to *Scribner's Magazine* and *Harper's Weekly.*

68.34 E. W. Townsend] Edward Waterman Townsend (1855–1942), politician and journalist, served as a Congressman from New Jersey, 1911–15. His sketches of life on New York's Bowery were collected in *Chimmie Fadden, Major Max, and Other Stories* (1895) and *Chimmie Fadden Explains* (1895).

69.3 Fred Lewis Pattee] Literary scholar (1863–1950), professor at Pennsylvania State College. His *History of American Literature Since 1870* appeared in 1915, followed by *The New American Literature, 1890–1930* (1930) and *The Feminine Fifties* (1940).

69.5 Marion Harland] Pseudonym of Mary Virginia Hawes Terhune (1830–1922), prolific author of novels including *Alone* (1854), *The Hidden Path* (1855), and *Sunnybank* (1866), along with travel books, cookbooks, and books of household advice such as *Common Sense in the Household: A Manual of Practical Housewifery* (1871)

69.5 Amélie Rives] Novelist, poet, and playwright (1863–1945), author of *The Quick or the Dead?* (1888) and *Barbara Dering* (1892). She was the wife of Prince Pierre Troubetzkoy, Russian artist.

69.6 R. K. Munkittrick] Richard Kendall Munkittrick (1853–1911), humorist, editor of the comic magazine *Judge*, and author of *New Jersey Arabian Nights* (1893) and *The Acrobatic Muse* (1896).

67.2 George Ade] Indiana-born humorist and playwright (1866–1944), author of *Fables in Slang* (1899), *People You Know* (1903), *Hand-Made Fables* (1920), and many other books. His plays included *The College Widow* (1904) and *The Fair Co-ed* (1908).

69.7 Gelett Burgess] American humorist, illustrator, and poet (1866–1951). He edited the literary magazine *The Lark* (1895–97), in which he published the poem "The Purple Cow." His later books included *Goops and How To Be Them* (1900), *Are You a Bromide?* (1907), and *Burgess Unabridged: A New Dictionary of Words You Have Always Needed* (1914).

69.8 Carolyn Wells] Writer of fiction and light verse (1869–1942). She edited popular anthologies including *The Nonsense Anthology* (1902), *A Parody Anthology* (1904), and *A Satire Anthology* (1905). She wrote many detective novels and children's novels.

69.8 John Kendrick Bangs] Popular author (1862–1922), known especially for his humorous and fantastic fiction. He worked at various times as editor of *Life*, *Harper's Magazine*, *Munsey's Magazine*, and *Puck*.

69.13 Joseph Jefferson] American actor (1829–1905), known especially for his starring role in his adaptation of *Rip Van Winkle*, which he first played in 1858 and repeated countless times for the rest of his life.

70.9 Billy Sunday] Evangelist (1862–1935), who gave up a career as a major league baseball player to become one of the most influential preachers of the early twentieth century.

71.17 Blix] Novel (1899) by Frank Norris.

71.22 Sganarelle] Stock comic character in various plays by Molière.

72.2 "mute, inglorious Milton"] See Thomas Gray, "Elegy Written in a Country Churchyard," stanza 15.

72.2 "somewheres East of Suez"] See Rudyard Kipling, "Mandalay," stanza 6.

73.2 Bashkirtseff] Marie Bashkirtseff (1858–1884), diarist and artist. An abridged edition of her diary (begun at age 13) was published in English as *The Journal of Marie Bashkirtseff* (1890); a complete edition runs to sixteen volumes.

73.4 Mary MacLane] Canadian-born American writer (1881–1929), whose memoir, *The Story of Mary MacLane*, became a bestseller in 1902. It was followed by *I, Mary MacLane: A Diary of Human Days* (1917).

73.17 *Kartoffelsuppe*] Potato soup.

73.33 Mrs. Atherton] Gertrude Atherton (1857–1948), San Francisco-born novelist, author of *The Californians* (1898), *The Conqueror* (1902), *Rezánov* (1906), and *Black Oxen* (1923).

74.12 Bill Sykes] Bill Sikes, brutal criminal in Dickens' *Oliver Twist* (1838).

74.31–32 Francis X. Bushman] Movie actor (1883–1966), best known for his portrayal of Messala in *Ben-Hur* (1925). He appeared in some 200 films.

74.32 Vincent Astor] Businessman and philanthropist (1891–1959), who inherited a large fortune in 1912 when his father went down with the *Titanic.*

75.8 Krafft-Ebing] Richard von Krafft-Ebing (1840–1902), German psychiatrist, author of *Psychopathia Sexualis* (1886), a compendium of case histories of sexual perversion.

76.5 Percival Pollard] See note 32.16.

76.7 Criterion] *The Criterion* (not to be confused with the English magazine of the same name) originated in St. Louis as *Life* before changing its name and moving to New York in 1897. It published articles on George Bernard Shaw, Henrik Ibsen, George Moore, and other modern authors. It ceased publication in 1905.

76.8 Vance Thompson] Critic, novelist, and poet (1863–1925), co-editor with James Huneker of *M'lle New York* (1895–99) and author of *French Portraits: Being Appreciations of the Writers of Young France* (1900).

76.23 Town Topics] Scandalous gossip magazine founded by Colonel William Mann before the turn of the century. It ceased publication in 1932.

76.35 Stuart P. Sherman] See note 4.19–20.

77.1 Cabell] James Branch Cabell (1878–1958), novelist whose works often explored a world of medieval fantasy. His books included *The Cream of the Jest* (1917), *Jurgen* (1919), which became a bestseller when it was denounced for obscenity, *Figures of Earth* (1921), and *The High Place* (1923).

77.12 Otto Julius Bierbaum] German poet, novelist, and literary editor (1865–1910).

77.21 Winston Churchill] American novelist (1871–1947), author of historical novels including *Richard Carvel* (1899), *The Crisis* (1901), *The Crossing* (1904), and *Coniston* (1906).

77.21 David Graham Phillips] American novelist and muckraking journalist (1867–1911), author of *The Cost* (1904), *The Plum Tree* (1905), *The Fortune Hunter* (1906), and *The Second Generation* (1907). He was murdered by a music teacher convinced that his family had been defamed in Phillips's most recent novel.

79.5 *Chap-Book*] Small literary magazine (1894–98) that published work by Stephen Crane, Hamlin Garland, William Dean Howells, George Santayana, and others.

79.9–10 The King in Yellow] Collection of linked fantasy stories (1895) by Robert W. Chambers.

79.12 Ailsa Page] Novel *Alisa Paige* (1910) by Robert W. Chambers.

79.14 Hamlin Garland] Author (1860–1940) of fiction, memoirs, and poems, known for his realistic studies of farm life in Wisconsin. His early stories, collected in *Main-Travelled Roads* (1891) and *Boy Life on the Prairie* (1899), were followed by the autobiographies *A Son of the Middle Border* (1917) and *A Daughter of the Middle Border* (1921). Of other works cited by Mencken, *The Shadow World* appeared in 1908 and *The Forester's Daughter* in 1914.

79.26 The Single Tax] Economic theory propounded by Henry George (1839–1897) in *Progress and Poverty* (1879) and other works, advocating a tax on land. Hamlin Garland's novel *Jason Edwards: An Average Man* (1892) was written in support of the Single Tax.

80.23 saleratus belt] The American Midwest; Mencken sometimes also employed the phrases "silo and saleratus belt" and "saleratus and hog cholera belt."

80.24 perunas] Peruna was a patent medicine marketed as a panacea.

80.26–27 Plunderbund] Moneyed interests; the term was evidently coined by Arthur McEwen, chief editorial writer the *New York American*, during William Randolph Hearst's 1906 campaign for governor of New York.

80.28 Claude Kitchin] American politician (1869–1923), North Carolina congressman, 1900–20. He campaigned vigorously in favor of depriving

African Americans of voting rights, and resisted American entry into World War I.

80.28–29 Newell Dwight Hillis] Congregationalist clergyman (1858–1929), pastor of the Plymouth Congregational Church in Brooklyn, New York, from 1899 to 1924. He led a campaign against immorality in Broadway plays and subsequently wrote a number of books decrying alleged German atrocities in World War I.

81.23 Henry Sydnor Harrison] See note 68.33.

81.27–28 W. J. Locke] William John Locke (1863–1930), British novelist whose bestselling romantic novels included *The Beloved Vagabond* (1906) and *Stella Maris* (1913).

82.3 Laddie] *Laddie: A True Blue Story* (1913), novel by Gene Stratton-Porter; see also note 167.20–21.

82.3 Pollyanna] Novel (1913) by Eleanor H. Porter; see also note 167.20.

82.17 William Allen White] Journalist (1868–1944), owner and editor of the Emporia (Kansas) *Gazette.* His 1896 anti-Populist editorial "What's the Matter with Kansas?" made him famous. He published many books on politics and public affairs, and also wrote novels including *A Certain Rich Man* (1909) and *In the Heart of a Fool* (1918).

82.32 Clayton Hamilton] American critic, playwright and producer (1881–1946), who wrote theatrical criticism for various magazines including *Bookman* (1910–18), *Everybody's Magazine* (1911–13) and *Vogue* (1912–20).

83.1 Felicia Hemens] Felicia Hemans, English poet (1793–1835), whose many volumes of verse included *The Forest Sanctuary* (1825) and *Songs of the Affections* (1830). She is best remembered for the poem "Casabianca."

83.1 Samuel Smiles] Scottish biographer and essayist (1812–1904) whose immensely popular *Self-Help: With Illustrations of Character and Conduct* (1859) was followed by similar works on *Character* (1871), *Thrift* (1875), and *Duty* (1880).

83.3 "The Duchess"] Margaret Wolfe Hungerford (1855–1897), prolific Irish novelist whose works were published in the United States as by "The Duchess." Her novels included *Phyllis* (1877), *Molly Bawn* (1878), and *A Mental Struggle* (1886). The line "Beauty is in the eye of the beholder" comes from *Molly Bawn.*

83.17 Harold Bell Wright] Novelist (1872–1944) whose books included *The Shepherd of the Hills* (1907) and *The Winning of Barbara Worth* (1911).

83.34 Coxey's Army] Protest march of unemployed men, led by Populist politician Jacob Coxey (1854–1951), that headed to Washington D.C. during the economic depression of March 1894, to demand job creation. Coxey also led a later march in 1914.

84.31 Epworth League] Organization formed in 1889 by the Methodist Episcopal Church in Cleveland, Ohio, to encourage and train young people in churchmanship and religious life.

85.11 Vincent O'Sullivan] Poet, essayist, and fiction writer (1868–1940). He was born in New York but spent much of his life in Europe, and was a friend of Oscar Wilde and Aubrey Beardsley. His books included *Poems* (1896), *The Houses of Sin* (1897), *Human Affairs* (1907), and *Sentiment and Other Stories* (1913).

85.33 Upton Sinclair] Novelist (1878–1968) who became famous with the publication of *The Jungle*, an exposé of conditions in the Chicago stockyards, in 1906. (It was originally serialized in the Socialist newspaper *The Appeal to Reason.*) His many other books included *The Metropolis* (1908), *King Coal* (1917), *Oil!* (1927), and *The Wet Parade* (1931).

86.11 Ernest Poole] Novelist (1880–1950), author of *The Voice of the Street* (1906), *The Harbor* (1915), *The Family* (1917), *His Second Wife* (1918), and many other books. He was a war correspondent in Germany, France, and Russia during World War I.

86.31 I.W.W.] Industrial Workers of the World, popularly known as "Wobblies," international labor union founded in Chicago in 1905 and reaching its peak of influence in the 1920s.

88.21 Binét test] Intelligence test devised by Alfred Binet (1857–1911), French psychologist, along with Theodore Simon (1873–1961), to evaluate child development. The Simon-Binet scale became the standard intelligence test used in the United States during the 1920s, with their term "I.Q." ("intelligence quotient") entering the vocabulary.

89.4–5 Sir Oliver Lodge] See note 35.37.

89.13 Cagliostro] Count Alessandro di Cagliostro, pseudonym of Giuseppe Balsamo (1743–1795), Italian adventurer posing as a freemason, physician, and alchemist. He engaged in many intrigues and sold amulets and elixirs of youth throughout Europe before being arrested by the Inquisition in 1789. He died in prison.

90.27 Gustav le Bon] Gustave Le Bon, French sociologist (1841–1931), author of *La Psychologie des foules* (*The Crowd: A Study of the Popular Mind*, 1895).

91.15–16 Elsie Clews Parsons] Anthropologist and sociologist (1875–1941), whose studies of Native American cultures included *Hopi and Zuni Ceremonialism* (1933) and *Pueblo Indian Religion* (1939). Her earlier works included *The Family* (1906), *The Old-Fashioned Woman* (1913), *Fear and Conventionality* (1914), *Social Freedom* (1915), and *Social Rule* (1916).

92.19 *Geheimrat*] German court title equivalent to privy councillor.

98.15 Bleaseism] Extreme populism and white supremacism of the sort identified with Coleman Livingston Blease (1868–1942), South Carolina governor (1910–14) and later senator.

98.23 The Mann Act] The White-Slave Traffic Act of 1910 addressed human trafficking for prostitution and prohibited the transportation of females across state lines for "immoral purposes." It was named after its sponsor, James Robert Mann (1856–1922), Republican congressman from Illinois.

99.38 Alfred Adler] Viennese psychologist (1870–1937), a member of Freud's circle who subsequently broke away to form his own school. His books include *The Theory and Practice of Individual Psychology* (1918).

101.28 Griswold] See note 9.7–8.

102.12–13 Edmund Clarence Stedman] See note 49.37.

102.13 Donald G. Mitchell] See note 67.24.

102.14–15 William Winter] Drama critic (1836–1917), reviewer for the *New York Tribune* from 1865 to 1909. His writings were collected in *Other Days* (1908), *Old Friends* (1909), *Shakespeare on the Stage* (1911–13), and *The Wallet of Time* (1913).

102.19–20 Baalam's ass] See Numbers 22:1–35.

102.26 Charles Eliot Norton] Author and educator (1827–1908), professor of art history at Harvard, 1873–97. He was a founder of *The Nation* (1865) and a frequent contributor to *The Atlantic Monthly* and other publications. He was a translator of Dante and wrote prolifically on art and literature.

102.29 Godkin] Edwin Lawrence Godkin (1831–1902), founder and editor of *The Nation.*

102.34 *Godey's Lady's Book*] American monthly magazine, 1830–98, influential on taste and fashion. It was edited from 1837 to 1877 by Sarah Josepha Hale.

103.18 *McClure's*] Literary and political magazine founded in 1884 by muckraking journalist Samuel Sidney McClure (1857–1949) and John Sanborn Philips (1861–1949). Its contributors included Jack London, O. Henry, Lincoln Steffens, and Ida Tarbell. It ceased publication in 1929.

103.31–32 *Everybody's*] Popular American magazine, 1899–1928.

103.34 *Munsey's*] See note 32.13–14.

103.38–39 John Brisben Walker . . . *Cosmopolitan*] Walker (1847–1931) purchased *Cosmopolitan* (originally a conservative family publication) in 1889 and began publishing work by well-known authors such as Mark Twain, Henry James, Rudyard Kipling, Willa Cather, and Theodore Dreiser. Walker sold the magazine in 1905 to William Randolph Hearst.

104.9 Argosy] Frank Munsey founded *Argosy* in December 1882, and by 1894 had begun to transform it into what was later recognized as the first of the pulp magazines. In 1920 it merged with another Munsey publication to become *Argosy All-Story Weekly.*

104.27–28 Street & Smith] New York publisher eventually specializing in pulp novels and magazines, founded in 1855.

105.3 Steffenses] Lincoln Steffens (1866–1936), American journalist and editor at *McClure's* (1902–06), and both *American* and *Everybody's* (1906–11). He wrote *The Shame of the Cities* (1904), *The Struggle for Self-Government* (1906), and *The Autobiography of Lincoln Steffens* (1931).

105.3 Tarbells] Ida Minerva Tarbell (1857–1944), journalist and editor who worked at *McClure's* (1894–1906) and *American* (1906–1915). She was best known for her exposé *The History of the Standard Oil Company* (1904).

105.3 Phillipses] Magazine publisher John S. Phillips (1861–1949), co-founder with S. S. McClure of *McClure's* and with Ida Tarbell of *American*, which he edited from 1906 to 1915.

105.11 Aldrich] Nelson Wilmarth Aldrich (1841–1915), financier and politician. He served as Republican senator from Rhode Island, 1881–1911, and exerted great influence on all matters of financial and monetary policy.

105.11 Boss Cox] George Barnsedale Cox (1853–1916), political boss and saloon keeper in Cincinatti, Ohio, known as "Boss Cox." Elected to the city council in 1879, he served two terms, and in 1884 became executive chairman of the local chapter of the Republican Party, in which position he was able to control elections and award state jobs between 1888 and 1910.

105.11 Gas Addicks] John Edward Addicks (1841–1919), industrialist who became wealthy in the natural gas business. His struggle with Henry DuPont for political power in Delaware was marked by bribery and corruption.

105.14 Ben B. Lindsey] See note 35.16.

105.14 Francis J. Heney] Lawyer (1859–1937); as deputy district attorney of San Francisco, secured the conviction of the mayor for corruption in 1908.

105.14 Governor Folk] Joseph Wingate Folk (1869–1923), lawyer and politician, nicknamed "Holy Joe" for his exposure of municipal corruption while serving as prosecutor in St. Louis, Missouri. He served as governor of Missouri, 1905–9.

107.33 Simon Magnus] More usually Simon Magus, he appears as Simon in Acts 8:9–24, and was regarded in some early Christian sources as the founder of all heresies.

108.24 *scandalum magnatum*] In early English law, defamation of high personages of the realm.

110.9–10 Ramsden Balmforth] English Unitarian minister active in South Africa; he was the author of *The New Reformation and Its Relation to Moral and Social Problems* (1893) and *The New Testament in the Light of the Higher Criticism* (1905).

112.4 General Booth] William Booth, known as General Booth (1829–1912), English religious leader and founder of the Salvation Army.

112.4 Mrs. Pankhurst] Emmeline Pankhurst (1858–1928), English suffragist, founder of the Women's Social and Political Union in 1898, which became notorious for its violent tactics.

114.40 Hermann Grimm] Scholar and critic (1828–1901), author of studies of Michelangelo and Goethe.

114.40 Tyndall] John Tyndall (1820–1893), British physicist.

115.6 the New Thought] Spiritual movement originating in the U.S. in the late nineteenth century, emphasizing positive thinking, healing, and personal power.

116.13 Havelock Ellises] Henry Havelock Ellis (1859–1939), English scientist and man of letters who studied the psychology and sociology of sex. His books included *The New Spirit* (1890), *Man and Woman* (1894), and the seven-volume *Studies in the Psychology of Sex* (1897–1928).

117.6 Margaret of Navarre] Queen of Navarre (1492–1549), a patron of Humanism in arts and letters, and author of the story collection *The Heptameron*, published in 1559.

117.6–7 Balzac's "Droll Tales"] *Contes drôlatiques* (1832–37), collection of ribald stories by Honore de Balzac, written in a pastiche of medieval French.

118.20–21 "The Repeal of Reticence"] Essay by Agnes Repplier, published in the *Atlantic Monthly*, March 1914; Repplier objected to "the obsession of sex."

118.26 Forel] Auguste Henri Forel (1848–1941), Swiss entomologist, neurologist, and psychiatrist; he contributed the early sexological studies *The Sexual Question* (1905) and *Sexual Ethics* (1906).

118.26 Sylvanus Stall] Lutheran minister (1847–1915), author of books on sex such as *What A Young Boy Ought to Know* and *What a Young Woman Ought to Know*.

118.26 Reginald Wright Kauffman] American journalist and author (1877–1959). His books included *The House of Bondage* (1910), *The Girl That Goes Wrong* (1911), and other works.

118.32 Press Cuttings] Play (1909) by George Bernard Shaw.

119.25 Brieux's "Les Avariés"] See note 63.13.

119.27–28 Frank Wedekind's "Frühlings Erwachen"] *Spring's Awakening* (1891) by Frank Wedekind (1864–1918), on the theme of youthful sexuality; see also note 320.36.

119.34–35 Le Mariage d'Olympe . . . Damaged Goods] See notes 62.34–35 and 63.13.

124.2 George Jean Nathan] Drama critic (1882–1958), co-editor with Mencken of *The Smart Set*, 1914–24, and in 1924 co-founder with Mencken of *The American Mercury*, of which he was co-editor until 1930. His many books included *Another Book on the Theater* (1915), *Mr. George Jean Nathan Presents* (1917), *Bottoms Up: An Application of the Slapstick to Satire* (1917), *The Popular Theatre* (1918), *The Critic and the Drama* (1922), *Art of the Night* (1928), *Testament of a Critic* (1931), and *Encyclopaedia of the Theatre* (1940).

124.7–8 Drama League of America] Organization founded in Chicago in 1910 to stimulate interest in drama and support worthy plays. By 1926, thirty-seven local chapters existed across the country.

124.13 Captain of Köpenick] Friedrich Wilhelm Voigt (1848-1922), German impostor who masqueraded as a Prussian officer in a 1906 incident which became internationally famous.

124.19 Gordon Craig] Edward Henry Gordon Craig (1872–1966), English theater designer whose theories exerted great influence on the British and American stage. He was founder and editor of the journal *The Mask*, and author of *The Art of the Theater* (1905).

124.16 Archers] See note 13.2.

124.16 Walkleys] Arthur Bingham Walkley (1855–1926), English drama critic for the London *Times* and other publications. His books included *Playhouse Impressions* (1892) and *Dramatic Criticism* (1903).

124.18 Maeterlinck] Maurice Maeterlinck (1862–1949), Belgian poet and playwright associated with the Symbolist movement. His plays included *The Intruder* (1890), *Pelléas and Mélisande* (1892), *Monna Vanna* (1902), and *The Blue Bird* (1909).

124.22 Florenz Ziegfeld] American theatrical impresario (1867–1932) famous for his series of revues *The Ziegfeld Follies* (1907–31).

124.24 Belasco] David Belasco (1853–1931), American playwright and theater producer involved in more than a hundred Broadway productions. As a producer he was notable for technical advances in lighting and stage design. His plays included *Madame Butterfly* (1900) and *The Girl of the Golden West* (1905).

124.24 Augustus Thomas] American playwright (1857–1934) known for his use of American backgrounds in such plays as *Alabama* (1891), *In Mizzoura* (1893), *The Witching Hour* (1907), and *The Copperhead* (1918).

124.24 Mrs. Fiske] Minnie Maddern Fiske (1865–1932), American actress who promoted realism and Ibsen's plays on the New York stage.

125.30 Alan Dale] Pseudonym of Alfred J. Cohen (1861–1928), English-born writer who became drama critic for the New York *Journal* and the New York *American*. He was known for his interviews with theatrical celebrities.

126.16 Benedetto Croce] Italian philosopher (1866–1952), author of *Aesthetics* (1912).

126.16 J. E. Spingarn] See note 3.33.

127.2 Avery Hopwood] Broadway playwright (1882–1928) whose works included *The Gold Diggers* (1919) and *Getting Gertie's Garter* (1921, with Wilson Collison).

127.3 Ludwig Thoma] See note 63.40.

127.3 Lord Dunsany] Edward John Moreton Drax Plunkett, known as Lord Dunsany (1878–1957), Irish poet, dramatist, and story writer. His plays included *The Glittering Gate* (1909), *The Gods of the Mountain* (1909), and *A Night at an Inn* (1916).

127.3 Sasha Guitry] Sacha Guitry (1885–1957), French actor and dramatist who later wrote and produced motion pictures.

127.3 Lothar Schmidt] German playwright best known for *Only a Dream* (1909), filmed twice by Ernst Lubitsch as *The Marriage Circle* (1924) and *One Hour with You* (1932).

127.4 Ferenz Molnar] Ferenc Molnar (1878–1952), Hungarian playwright and fiction writer. His plays included *Liliom* (1909), *The Guardsman* (1910), *The Swan* (1920), and *The Play's the Thing* (1926).

127.4 Roberto Bracco] Italian playwright and novelist (1862–1943), author of *The Hidden Spring* (1907).

127.4 Gerhart Hauptmann] German playwright (1862–1946), author of *The Weavers* (1892), *The Beaver Coat* (1893), *The Sunken Bell* (1896), and many other works. He won the Nobel Prize in Literature in 1912.

127.34 *Ambrosia artemisiaefolia*] Ragweed.

127.40 William Winter] See note 102.14–15.

129.5 Metcalfe] James S. Metcalfe, drama critic for *Life*. He brought a lawsuit against the Theatre Managers' Assocation in 1906, claiming he had been barred from their theaters.

130.4–5 Max Reinhardt] Theatrical producer (1873–1943) who achieved fame in Berlin and Vienna for his elaborate anti-naturalistic style. His production of *The Miracle* played in New York in 1923, and he emigrated to the United States in 1937.

130.10–11 Eleanor Gates] American writer (1875–1951), author of the play and novel *The Poor Little Rich Girl* (1913).

130.11 Clare Kummer] American playwright and lyricist (1873–1943), author of *The Opera Ball* (1912), *A Successful Calamity* (1917), *The Rescuing Angel* (1917), and other comedies and musicals.

130.20 Dr. Frank Crane] See note 25.12.

131.9 Granville Barker] Harley Granville-Barker (1877–1946), English theater manager, actor, and playwright, author of *The Voysey Inheritance* (1904) and *The Madras House* (1910).

131.12 Richard Burtonism] Richard Eugene Burton (1861–1940), poet and critic, author of *From the Book of Life* (1909) and *Masters of the British Novel* (1909).

134.15 Mitchell Kennerley] American publisher (1878–1950).

134.20 One Man] Novel by Robert Steele (pseudonym of R. A. Lindsay), based on the author's experiences as a convicted criminal, published in 1915.

135.14 Thackeray's Louis XIV] See "Meditations at Versailles," *The Paris Sketch Book* (1840).

141.18 Science and Health] *Science and Health with Key to the Scriptures* (1875) by Mary Baker Eddy.

141.36 E. Phillips Oppenheim] English novelist (1866–1946), prolific author of thrillers and adventure stories such as *Enoch Strone* (1901), *The Malefactor* (1906), and *The Great Impersonation* (1920).

141.38–39 The Scarlet Plague . . . The Little Lady of the Big House] Novels by Jack London, published in 1912 and 1916 respectively.

143.9 Peruna] See note 80.24.

143.9 Mandrake Pills] Nineteenth-century patent medicine for the alleviation of liver complaints and other conditions, introduced in 1836 by Dr. Joseph H. Schenck.

143.9 Fletcherism] Named after Horace Fletcher (1849–1919), American nutritionist who touted the health benefits of the thorough mastication of food.

143.10 The Emmanuel Movement] Practice of medical psychotherapy or religious healing introduced in 1906 by the Emmanuel Church in Boston, Massachusetts.

143.10 the New Thought] See note 115.6.

143.11 Edwin Markham] American poet (1852–1940), author of *The Man with the Hoe* (1899), *Lincoln and Other Poems* (1901), and *The Star of Araby* (1937). He was an adherent in the 1870s of Thomas Lake Harris's spiritualist movement, the Brotherhood of the New Life.

143.11–12 Ella Wheeler Wilcox] See note 54.12.

143.12–13 Will Levington Comfort] American novelist (1880–1932), author of adventure novels such as *Routledge Rides Alone* (1910); his theosophical speculations were expounded in *The Will Levington Comfort Letters* (1920–21).

145.32 Mother Tingley] Katherine Augusta Tingley (1847–1929), spiritualist leader in New York City, later head of the Universal Brotherhood, a theosophical movement.

145.33 Edward Bok] Dutch-born American writer and journalist (1863–1930), editor of *The Ladies' Home Journal*, 1889–1919. He won the Pulitzer Prize for his autobiography *The Americanization of Edward Bok* (1920).

145.33 the Archangel Eddy] Mary Baker Eddy (1821–1910), founder of Christian Science.

148.37 Rufus W. Griswold] See note 9.7–8.

149.5–6 James Harlan] Politician (1820–1899), U.S. senator from Iowa and Secretary of the Interior, 1865–66.

PREJUDICES: SECOND SERIES

154.24 *Waldhorn*] Hunting horn.

154.26 the elder Channing] William Ellery Channing (1780–1842), Unitarian minister whose sermons and writing had wide intellectual influence. His *Remarks on American Literature* appeared in 1830.

154.27–28 Samuel Lorenzo Knapp] American writer (1783–1838), author of *Lectures on American Literature, with Remarks on Some Passages in American History* (1829).

154.29 Mores] See note 7.31.

154.29 Brownells] See note 4.17.

154.29 Phelpses] See note 4.14–15.

154.30 Mabies] See note 7.15.

154.30 Brander Mathewses] American scholar and playwright (1852–

1929), known for his studies of dramatic literature including *The Development of the Drama* (1904), *Shakspere as a Playwright* (1913), *A Book About the Theater* (1916), and *Principles of Playmaking* (1919).

155.13 Van Wyck Brooks] Literary critic (1886–1963), author of *America's Coming-of-Age* (1916), *Letters and Leadership* (1918), *The Ordeal of Mark Twain* (1920), *The Pilgrimage of Henry James* (1925), and many other studies.

155.29 Adam Forepaugh] American entrepreneur (1831–1890) who operated a circus from 1865 to 1890.

155.33–34 Barrett Wendell] American scholar (1855–1921), professor at Harvard and author of *A Literary History of America* (1900).

155.34 *Aufklärung*] Enlightenment.

156.10–11 J. G. Brainard] John Gardiner Brainard (1795–1828), New England lawyer, editor and poet. Poe's essay, "A Few Words About Brainard," appeared in *Graham's Magazine* in 1842.

158.21 Richard Harding Davis] Journalist and novelist (1864–1916). His novels included *Soldiers of Fortune* (1897). His war reporting was collected in many volumes including *Cuba in War Time* (1897), *The Cuban and Porto Rican Campaigns* (1898), *With Both Armies in South Africa* (1900), and *Notes of a War Correspondent* (1910).

158.22 Hamilton Wright Mabie's "white list"] See note 7.15.

159.10 Judge Grant] Robert Grant (1852–1940), jurist and author. His novels, often centered on social issues, included *An Average Man* (1883), *Unleavened Bread* (1900), *The Undercurrent* (1904), and *The High Priestess* (1915). He served in 1927 on the commission which ruled that the trial of Sacco and Vanzetti had been fairly conducted.

159.10 Alice Brown] New Hampshire-born writer (1857–1948), author of *Fools of Nature* (1887), *The Rose of Hope* (1896), *The Mannerings* (1906), and many other books.

159.12 Woodberry] George Edward Woodberry (1855–1930), Massachusetts-born poet and scholar, author of *The North Shore Watch* (1890) and other volumes of verse; his *Collected Poems* appeared in 1903. He was the author of numerous literary studies including *Makers of Literature* (1900) and *Nathaniel Hawthorne* (1902).

159.12 the elder Johnson] Robert Underwood Johnson (1853–1937), American man of letters, author of *The Winter Hour* (1891) and *Poems of War and Peace* (1916). He served as U.S. Ambassador to Italy, 1920–21. His son Owen McMahon Johnson (1878–1952) wrote novels and short stories.

159.13 Crothers] Samuel McChord Crothers (1857–1927), Unitarian Universalist minister whose essays were collected in numerous volumes, among them *The Understanding Heart* (1903), *By the Christmas Fire* (1908), and *Humanly Speaking* (1912).

159.13 Miss Repplier] See note 31.24.

159.15 Babbitt] Irving Babbitt (1865–1933), American scholar who, with Paul Elmer More, founded the New Humanism movement; he was the author of *The New Laokoön* (1910), *The Masters of Modern French Criticism* (1912), *Rousseau and Romanticism* (1919), and other works.

159.26 *Augenmusik*] "Eye music": presentation of a musical score in symbolic fashion (i.e., a love song in which the staves are heart-shaped), seen only by the performer.

160.13 Henry Van Dyke] See note 55.19.

160.26 Boynton] Percy Holmes Boynton (1875–1946), professor of English at the University of Chicago, author of *American Poetry* (1918), *Some Contemporary Americans* (1924), *The Challenge of Modern Criticism* (1931), and other works.

160.26 Perry] Bliss Perry (1860–1954), professor of English at Williams, Princeton, and Harvard, and editor of *The Atlantic Monthly*, 1899–1909. He published many literary studies including biographies of Whitman, Whittier, and Emerson.

161.20 the Becker case] Charles Becker (1870–1915), a New York City police officer, was tried, convicted, and executed for ordering the murder of the gambler Herman Rosenthal. He was the first American police officer to receive the death penalty. Some later writers have suggested that he was wrongly convicted.

161.25–26 *ordentlichen Professoren*] Full professors.

161.27 Shelburne Essays] See note 7.31.

161.30 Donald G. Mitchell] See note 67.24.

162.5 *Privat-Dozenten*] See note 7.7.

162.19 Up in Mabel's Room] Farce (1919) by Wilson Collison and Otto Harbach.

162.19 Ben-Hur] Dramatization by William W. Young, first produced in 1899, of Lew Wallace's novel *Ben-Hur: A Tale of the Christ* (1880).

162.20 The Witching Hour] Play (1907) by Augustus Thomas involving the themes of telepathy and hypnosis.

162.39 Lewes] George Henry Lewes (1817–1878), English philosopher and literary and dramatic critic who founded and edited *The Fortnightly Review*. He was the author of *Physiology of Common Life* (1859), *The Problems of Life and Mind* (1874–79), and *Actors and Acting* (1875).

163.2 Saintsbury] George Saintsbury (1845–1933), English critic and journalist. His many books included *Short History of French Literature* (1882), *Essays in English Literature* (1890–95), *History of Nineteenth Century Literature* (1896), *History of English Prose Rhythm* (1912), and *The English Novel* (1913).

163.21 Zoë Akins] (1886–1958) American poet and playwright. Her plays included *Déclassée* (1919), *Papa* (1919), *Daddy's Gone A-Hunting* (1921), and *The Greeks Had a Word for It* (1930). She won the Pulitzer Prize for *The Old Maid* (1935), based on Edith Wharton's novella.

163.34 Sherman] See note 4.19–20.

164.2–3 Robert Underwood Johnson] See note 159.12.

164.3 Owen Wister] Novelist (1860–1938), author of *The Virginian* (1902).

164.3 James Lane Allen] Novelist (1849–1925), best known for his local color stories set in Kentucky, including *A Kentucky Cardinal* (1894) and *The Choir Invisible* (1897).

164.3–4 George E. Woodberry] See note 159.12.

164.4 William Roscoe Thayer] American author (1859–1923) of *Theodore Roosevelt: An Intimate Biography* (1919) and works on Italian history.

164.5 Margaret Deland] Novelist (1857–1945) whose work evoked life in a small Pennsylvania town; author of *The Awakening of Helena Richie* (1906), *The Iron Woman* (1911), and *The Rising Tide* (1916).

164.5–6 Mary Johnston] American author (1870–1936) of romantic fiction set against the backdrop of Virginia history; best known for *To Have and to Hold* (1900).

164.8 Brian Hooker] American academic and poet (1880–1946), noted for his 1923 translation of Edmond Rostand's *Cyrano de Bergerac.*

164.8 George Sterling] American poet (1869–1926), leader of an artistic and literary circle in Carmel, California; a close friend of Mencken. His books included *A Wine of Wizardry* (1909), *The House of Orchids* (1911), and *The Caged Eagle* (1916).

164.9–10 "Chimmie Fadden" Townsend] See note 68.34.

164.18 *héliogabalisme*] A favorite term of Mencken's. In *In Defense of Women* (1922) he defines it as "the fascination of what is strange, the charm of the unlike."

164.20 Palmerism of Torquemada] A. Mitchell Palmer (1872–1936), U.S. attorney general, 1919–21, initiated in November 1919 a series of raids directed against members of radical groups and others suspected of subversive activities; thousands were arrested, and ultimately 556 individuals were deported.

Tomás de Torquemada (1420–1498), a Dominican friar, was Inquisitor General of Spain, 1483–98.

164.40 Schnitzler] Arthur Schnitzler (1862–1931), Austrian dramatist and novelist, author of the plays *Anatol* (1893), *Liebelei* (1895), and *Reigen* (1900).

165.33 Miss Reese] See note 55.40.

165.33 Miss Teasdale] American poet (1884–1933), author of *Rivers to the Sea* (1915), *Love Songs* (1917), *Flame and Shadow* (1920), and *Dark of the Moon* (1926). Following her suicide her late poems were collected in *Strange Victory* (1933).

165.33 John McClure] See note 56.5.

165.35 Robert Loveman] American poet (1864–1923) whose poem "The Rain Song" ("It isn't raining rain to me, / It's raining daffodils") was widely anthologized.

165.37 Rita Wellman] Playwright (1890–1965), a member of the Provincetown Players. Her plays included *Barbarians* (1916), *The Rib-Person* (1917), and *The Gentile Wife* (1919).

165.39 Dr. Baker's *Ibsenfabrik*] George Pierce Baker (1866–1935) founded the Harvard Dramatic Club in 1908 and the 47 Workshop (his "Ibsen factory") dedicated to performing plays by his students. He moved to Yale in 1925, where he was instrumental in founding the Yale School of Drama. Baker's students included Eugene O'Neill, George Abbott, Thomas Wolfe, and Sidney Howard.

166.18 Agnes Repplier] See note 31.24.

167.9 Rex Beach] Novelist (1877–1949), author of adventure stories including *The Spoilers* (1906) and *The Iron Trail* (1913).

167.9 Emerson Hough] Novelist and journalist (1857–1923), author of *The Mississippi Bubble* (1902), *The Sagebrusher* (1919), and *The Covered Wagon* (1922). He wrote many articles on national parks and wildlife preservation.

167.11–12 Cyrus Townsend Brady] Novelist (1861–1920), author of many historical romances and popular histories including *Indian Fights and Fighters* (1904) and *Three Daughters of the Confederacy* (1905).

167.12 Mary Roberts Rinehart] American fiction writer and playwright (1876–1958), author of many mystery novels including *The Circular Staircase* (1908), *Where There's a Will* (1912), and *The Case of Jennie Brice* (1913). With Avery Hopwood she wrote the long-running mystery play *The Bat* (1920).

167.17 Dr. Frank Crane] See note 25.12.

167.17 Orison Swett Marden] See note 25.12.

167.17–18 Porter Emerson Browne] Playwright (1879–1934), author of *A Fool There Was* (1908) and *The Spendthrift* (1910).

167.18 Gerald Stanley Lee] Clergyman, lecturer, and writer (1862–1944), author of *The Lost Art of Reading* (1902), *Crowds: A Moving-Picture of Democracy* (1915), and *Seven Studies in Self-Command* (1921).

167.18 E. S. Martin] See note 68.34.

167.18–19 Ella Wheeler Wilcox] See note 54.12.

167.19 Newell Dwight Hillis] See note 80.28–29.

167.20 Harold Bell Wright] See note 83.17.

167.20 Eleanor H. Porter] Novelist (1868–1920), author of *Cross Currents* (1907), *Pollyanna* (1913), and *Pollyanna Grows Up* (1915).

167.20–21 Gene Stratton-Porter] Novelist and naturalist (1868–1924), author of such books as *The Song of the Cardinal* (1902), *Freckles* (1904), *A Girl of the Limberlost* (1909), and *Friends in Feathers* (1917).

167.30 Corra Harris] Corra White Harris (1869–1935), Georgia writer best known for her novel *A Circuit Rider's Wife* (1910).

167.30–31 Gouverneur Morris] Novelist and screenwriter (1876–1953), author of *The Pagan's Progress* (1904), *The Penalty* (1913), and other works.

167.31 Harold MacGrath] Novelist (1871–1932), author of popular romances such as *Arms and the Woman* (1899), *Hearts and Masks* (1905), and *Half a Rogue* (1906). He wrote the scenario of the silent serial *The Perils of Pauline.*

167.35 Zona Gale] Wisconsin writer (1874–1938) known for stories collected in *Friendship Village* (1908) and *Yellow Gentians and Blue* (1927), and for novels including *Birth* (1918) and *Miss Lulu Bett* (1920).

167.36 Montague Glass] English-born playwright and story writer (1877–1934), known for stories about Jewish businessmen dramatized as *Potash and Perlmutter* (1913), *Business Before Pleasure* (1917), and *His Honor Abe Potash* (1919).

168.3 Henry Milner Rideout] Maine-born novelist (1877–1927), author of *Admiral's Light* (1907), *Dragon's Blood* (1909), *The Twisted Foot* (1910), and other works.

168.4 Chester Bailey Fernald] Fiction writer (1869–1938), author of the story collections *The Cat and the Cherub* (1896) and *Chinatown Stories* (1899), both set in San Francisco's Chinatown.

168.4–5 Will Levington Comfort] See note 143.12–13.

168.5 Stephen French Whitman] Novelist (1880–1950), author of *Predes-*

tined: A Novel of New York Life (1910), *The Isle of Life* (1913), and other works.

168.5 James Hopper] Novelist and journalist (1876–1956) who settled in Carmel, California.

168.6 Harry Leon Wilson] Fiction writer (1867–1939) best known for *Ruggles of Red Gap* (1915) and *Merton of the Movies* (1922). He was editor of *Puck*, 1896–1902.

168.12 Louis Joseph Vance] Novelist (1879–1933), best known for *The Lone Wolf* (1914) and other novels of intrigue featuring the series character Michael Lanyard.

168.12 Rupert Hughes] Historian, novelist, playwright, and filmmaker (1872–1956), author of many novels including *Excuse Me!* (1911), *Souls for Sale* (1922), and *Destiny* (1925). He was the uncle of Howard Hughes.

168.13 George Bronson-Howard] Writer and journalist (1844–1922), reporter for the Baltimore *American* and other newspapers, author of novels including *Scars of the Southern Seas* (1907) and *Norroy, Diplomatic Agent* (1920), and plays including *The Only Law* (1909, with Wilson Mizner). He committed suicide in Los Angeles where he was working as a scenarist for Universal.

168.13–14 David Graham Phillips] See note 77.21.

168.14 Elbert Hubbard] Writer and publisher (1856–1915), founder of the Roycroft Press, an active figure in the Arts and Crafts movement, and editor of *The Philistine*, a monthly magazine in which he published humorous and philosophical musings. He died in the sinking of the *Lusitania* on May 7, 1915.

169.11 Marie Corelli] Pseudonym of Mary Mackay (1855–1924), immensely popular English writer, whose bestselling novels, sometimes on spiritualist themes, included *A Romance of Two Worlds* (1886), *The Soul of Lilith* (1892), *The Sorrows of Satan* (1895), and *The Master Christian* (1900).

169.11 Elinor Glyn] See note 42.20.

169.11–12 E. Phillips Oppenheim] See note 141.36.

169.12 William Le Quex] William Le Queux (1864–1927), Anglo-French journalist and author of thrillers and futuristic fantasies, including *The Great War in England in 1897* (1894) and *The Invasion of 1910* (1906).

169.12 Hall Caine] See note 35.18.

169.31 Selznicks, Goldfishes, Zukors] Movie moguls Lewis J. Selznick (1870–1933), Samuel Goldwyn (1882–1974), who was known until 1918 by his given name Samuel Goldfish, and Adolph Zukor (1873–1976).

170.15 Pearl White] Silent movie actress (1889–1938) whose starring role in the cliffhanging serial *The Perils of Pauline* (1914) was followed by similar roles in *The Exploits of Elaine* (1915), *The Iron Claw* (1916), and *The Fatal Ring* (1917).

170.15 Theda Bara] Silent movie actress (1855–1955), born Theodosia Burr Goodman, and known as The Vamp following her starring role in *A Fool There Was* (1915). Her other films included *Carmen* (1915), *Cleopatra* (1917), and *Madame Du Barry* (1918).

170.21 McCutcheons] George Barr McCutcheon (1866–1928), American newspaper editor and writer of popular novels including *Brewster's Millions* (1902) and *A Fool and His Money* (1913).

170.29 George Moore] Irish author (1852–1933), author of *A Mummer's Wife* (1885), *Confessions of a Young Man* (1886), *Esther Waters* (1896), and many other realist novels.

170.29 Hugh Walpole] English novelist (1884–1941) whose many books included *Fortitude* (1913), *The Dark Forest* (1916), *The Cathedral* (1922), and *Rogue Herries* (1930).

170.30 E. F. Benson] Edward Frederic Bensen (1867–1940), novelist and story writer, author of works variously satiric, melodramatic, and fantastic, including the series of comic novels featuring Miss Mapp and Lucia, beginning with *Queen Lucia* (1920).

170.37 saleratus] See note 80.23.

173.33–34 Andrieff's "Silence"] Novella by Leonid Andreyev (1871–1919), published in English translation in 1910.

173.34 Sudermann's "Das Sterbelied"] "The Song of Death," short story by Hermann Sudermann (1857–1928).

174.12 Freneau] Philip Freneau (1752–1832), American poet of French Huguenot descent, author of *A Poem on the Rising Glory of America* (1772), *American Liberty* (1775), and *The British Prison-Ship* (1781), a long poem based on his wartime imprisonment by the British. Many further collections followed, including *The Poems of Philip Freneau* (1786) and *A Collection of Poems on American Affairs* (1815).

174.14 H. R. Haweis] Hugh Reginald Haweis (1838–1901), English clergyman and writer.

174.21 Bancroft] George Bancroft (1800–1891), American historian, studied in Heidelburg, Göttingen, and Berlin, and later returned to Germany as U.S. ambassador, 1867–74. His multivolume *History of the United States* was published between 1834 and 1874.

174.40 John C. van Dyke] John Charles van Dyke (1856–1932), American art historian, author of *Principles of Art* (1887), *How to Judge a Picture*

(1888), *Art for Art's Sake* (1893), *A History of Painting* (1894), and other works. *American Painting and Its Tradition* was publishing in 1919.

175.7 Frank Harris] British-born American author (1854–1931) whose books included *The Bomb* (1908), a novel; *The Man Shakespeare and His Tragic Love Story* (1909); *The Women of Shakespeare* (1911); *Contemporary Portraits* (1915–27); *Oscar Wilde, His Life and Confessions* (1916); and the long-banned autobiography *My Life and Loves* (1922–27).

175.7 Vincent O'Sullivan] See note 85.11.

175.7–8 Herman Scheffauer] Herman George Scheffauer (1878–1927), San Francisco-born poet and playwright, an associate of Ambrose Bierce and George Sterling. His poetry collection *Looms of Life* was published in 1908. He moved to Germany in 1910 and committed suicide in 1927 after murdering his female secretary.

175.8 Henry B. Fuller] Henry Blake Fuller (1857–1929), American novelist whose novels of Chicago included *The Cliff-Dwellers* (1893), *With the Procession* (1895), and *On the Stairs* (1918).

175.8 Stuart Merrill] American poet (1863–1915) educated and later resident in France; most of his work was written in French, including the collections *Les Fastes* (1891), *Une Voix dans la Foule* (1909), and *Poèmes 1887–1897*. He was associated with the literary circle of Stéphane Mallarmé.

175.14 *The Little Review*] Literary quarterly, 1914–29, founded by Margaret Anderson and edited by her with Jane Heap. It was among the most influential magazines of its time, publishing W. B. Yeats, Ernest Hemingway, T. S. Eliot, Djuna Barnes, and Hart Crane. Its serialization of James Joyce's *Ulysses*, 1918–21, led to the editors being fined for obscenity.

175.19 Ben Hecht] Writer and journalist (1894–1964), a reporter for the *Chicago Daily News* (1914–1923), and author of *Erik Dorn* (1921), *1001 Afternoons in Chicago* (1923), and *Count Bruga* (1926). He wrote the play *The Front Page* (1928) with Charles MacArthur and had a long and successful career as a Hollywood screenwriter, his credits including *Scarface* (1932), *Nothing Sacred* (1937), *Wuthering Heights* (1939), and *Notorious* (1946).

175.19–20 Elsa von Freytag-Loringhoven] Poet and artist (1874–1927), born Elsa Hildegard Plötz in present-day Poland; she emigrated to the United States in 1910 and married the Baron von Freytag-Loringhoven in 1913. Her poems were published in *The Little Review* and other magazines; she became notorious for her outlandish appearance and extreme behavior. She returned to Europe in 1923 and died of asphyxiation in her Paris apartment three years later.

177.5 Flexner] See note 45.26.

177.5 Loeb] See note 45.27.

177.6 Carrel] See note 45.27.

177.14 D. C. Gilman] Daniel Coit Gilman (1831–1908), American educator and first president of Johns Hopkins, 1875–1901, and the Carnegie Institution in Washington D.C., 1901–4.

177.26 The 'Genius'] Novel (1915) by Dreiser; it was withdrawn from sale by the publisher after the New York Society for the Suppression of Vice declared it lewd and profane. A review of the book by Stuart P. Sherman in *The Nation* attributed its defects in part to Dreiser's German heritage.

179.5 Joyce Kilmer] American poet (1886–1918), author of *Trees and Other Poems* (1914); he enlisted to fight in World War I and was killed near Seringes, France.

179.16 Coxey] See note 87.34.

179.16 Dr. Mary Walker] Mary Edwards Walker (1832–1919), American physician and advocate of women's rights.

179.16–17 George Francis Train] Businessman and author (1829–1904), promoter of the Union Pacific Railroad who became embroiled in the Crédit Mobilier scandal of 1872. He referred to himself as "Citizen Train" and was noted for his eccentric behavior and espousal of a number of causes. His books included *Young America Abroad* (1857) and *Championship of Women* (1868).

179.28 Leon Kellner] Author (1859–1928), professor of English in Vienna. His history of American literature was published in German in 1913.

179.37 the Gorky scandal] In April 1906, during a trip to raise funds for revolutionary activities, the novelist and playwright Maxim Gorky was asked to leave the Manhattan hotel where he was staying when it was revealed in the press that his companion was not his wife, as stated in the hotel register, but his mistress.

179.40 the Dreiser Protest] Petition protesting the suppression of *The "Genius"*, organized by Mencken.

180.5 Treitschke] Heinrich von Treitschke (1834–1896), German historian and politician of strong nationalist and anti-Semitic views.

180.25 Charles G. Norris] Novelist (1881–1945), brother of Frank Norris. His books, often dealing with social problems, included *The Amateur* (1915), *Salt* (1917), and *Brass* (1921).

180.34 the Comstocks] Pro-censorship forces associated with Anthony Comstock (1844–1915), U.S. Postal Inspector who founded the New York Society for the Suppression of Vice. In 1873 Congress passed the Comstock Law, which made it illegal to mail, transport, or deliver "obscene, lewd, and/or lascivious" information.

180.17 A Good Girl] Novel (1916) by Vincent O'Sullivan.

180.19 Kathleen Norris] Novelist (1880–1966), wife of Charles G. Norris. Her many books included *Mother* (1911), *Saturday's Child* (1914), and *The Sea Gull* (1927).

180.21 Abraham Cahan] Novelist and editor (1860–1951). He was the longtime editor of the *Jewish Daily Forward* and author of *Yekl, a Tale of the New York Ghetto* (1896) and *The Rise of David Levinsky* (1917).

181.39 Alfred Noyes] English poet (1880–1958), best known for his ballad "The Highwayman."

182.9 Rufus W. Griswold] See note 9.7–8.

182.18 Lyman Abbott] Congregational clergyman (1835–1922) who joined Henry Ward Beecher in editorship of the weekly *Christian Union*, before succeeding him as editor; his many books included *The Evolution of Christianity* (1896), *Problems of Life* (1900), and *The Spirit of Democracy* (1910).

182.18 Frank Crane] See note 25.12.

182.33 his son] Julian Hawthorne (1846–1934), novelist and journalist, author of *Idolatry: A Romance* (1874), *Archibald Malmaison* (1879), and numerous other novels and works of popular history.

182.35 a grand-daughter] Hildegarde Hawthorne (1871–1952), poet and journalist, author of *Old Seaport Towns of New England* (1916).

183.33 N. P. Willis] Nathaniel Parker Willis (1806–1867), poet and journalist. Founded the *American Monthly* (1829–31) in Boston and later became a prolific reporter on social matters in the U.S. and abroad for the *New-York Mirror*. His journalism was collected in numerous volumes such as *Pencillings by the Way* (1835) and *Dashes at Life with a Free Pencil* (1845).

185.2 Maeterlinckism] See note 124.18.

185.21 Arthur Ransome] English author (1884–1967). His study of Poe appeared in 1910.

185.37 John Burroughs] American naturalist (1837–1921), a close friend of Walt Whitman, John Muir, and Theodore Roosevelt. His many books included *Notes on Walt Whitman as Poet and Person* (1867), *Wake Robin* (1871), *Birds and Poets* (1877), *Ways of Nature* (1905), and *Camping and Tramping with Roosevelt* (1907).

186.22 Jurgen] See note 77.1.

187.17 Lord Northcliffe] See note 16.24.

187.17 Lord Iveagh] Edward Cecil (1847–1927), 1st earl of Iveagh, chairman of the Guinness Brewery at Dublin, who contributed large sums to slum clearance and endowed the Lister Institute for bacteriological research.

187.17–18 Lord Reading] Rufus Daniel Isaacs (1860–1935), lst Marquis of Reading, first British attorney general to be a member of the cabinet; special envoy to the United States, 1918–19.

190.3 *Gelehrten*] Scholars.

190.17 Jakob Böhme] German mystic and theologian (1575–1624), author of *Aurora, oder die Morgenröte im Aufgang* (1612, published 1634), *Of the Earthly and of the Heavenly Mystery* (1620), *The Signature of All Things* (1621), *The Mysterium Magnum* (1623), and other treatises.

190.18 Allen G. Thurman] Democratic politician (1813–1895), congressman and senator from Ohio, and Grover Cleveland's running mate in his unsuccessful 1888 presidential run.

191.16 Carranzas] Venustiano Carranza (1859–1920), Mexican revolutionary leader, president of Mexico from 1917 until his assassination in May 1920.

191.16–17 Ludendorffs] See note 35.26–27.

192.16–17 David Ricardo] English economist (1772–1823), author of *Principles of Political Economy and Taxation* (1817).

192.18 John Bright] English orator and reformist statesman (1811–1889), with Richard Cobden a founder of the Anti-Corn Law League. He was an advocate of free trade and religious freedom.

192.18 Richard Cobden] English statesman and economist (1804–1865) known as "The Apostle of Free Trade," who succeeded in forcing repeal of corn laws, and was a promoter of peace and reduced armaments.

192.18 George Grote] English historian (1794–1871), author of *A History of Greece* (1846–56).

192.19 Walther von Rathenau] German industrialist and politician (1867–1922) who was appointed foreign minister of the Weimar Republic in 1922. In that capacity he insisted that Germany pay its war reparations while at the same time working toward a revision of the terms of the Versailles treaty; he also negotiated a treaty with the Soviet Union. As a prominent German-Jewish figure, he advocated assimilation and opposed Zionism, and despite his ardent German nationalism was a target for extremist right-wing groups. He was assassinated by a right-wing army faction.

196.27 *Juris utriusque Doctor*] Doctor of Canon and Civil Law.

198.4 Mr. Creel] George Creel (1876–1953), journalist and publicity director; chairman of the Committee of Public Information (1917–19), created by Woodrow Wilson as a propaganda organization to enlist support for American entry into World War I.

198.31 Sisson documents] Documents, now believed to have been mostly forged, obtained in 1918 by Edgar Sisson, the Petrograd representative for the U.S. Committee on Public Information, purporting to show that Trotsky, Lenin, and other Bolsheviks were paid agents of the German government during World War I.

201.5 Billroth] Theodor Billroth (1829–1894), German surgeon and pianist; a close friend of Brahms, he pioneered the application of scientific methods to musicology.

201.12 Dr. Brownell] See note 4.17.

201.14 Comstockery] See note 180.34.

203.6–7 Coningsby Dawson] English writer (1883–1959), author of *The Garden Without Walls* (1913) and *Living Bayonets* (1919). He served with the Canadian army in World War I and later lectured throughout the United States on the aftereffects of the war.

203.7 Ian Hay] Pseudonym of John Hay Beith (1876–1952), Scottish novelist and playwright. His experiences in World War I are recounted in *The First Hundred Thousand* (1915).

203.7–8 Zangwill] Israel Zangwill (1864–1926), English novelist and playwright whose works included the plays *The Melting Pot* (1908), *The War God* (1911), and *We Moderns* (1924), and the novels *Children of the Ghetto* (1892) and *The King of Schnorrers* (1894).

203.10 Sir Auckland Geddes] British diplomat (1879–1954) who served as ambassador to the United States during 1920–24.

203.13 Free Church Federation] Association of British Nonconformist churches founded in the late nineteenth century. The movement, dedicated to religious social work, broadened to become international in scope.

207.22 Harold Stearns] American writer (1891–1943), author of *America and the Young Intellectual* (1921) and *The Street I Know* (1935).

207.23 Waldo Frank] American novelist and critic (1889–1967), founder and editor of the short-lived but influential magazine *The Seven Arts* (1916–17). His critical and travel writings included *Our America* (1919), *Salvos* (1924), *Virgin Spain* (1926), and *South American Journey* (1943).

209.10–11 Chevalier Bayard] See note 22.10.

209.22 Morley's life of Gladstone] *The Life of William Ewart Gladstone* (1903) by John Morley, Viscount Morley of Blackburn (1838–1923).

209.22 Trevelyan's life of Macaulay] *The Life and Letters of Lord*

Macaulay (1876) by Sir George Otto Trevelyan (1838–1928), who was Macaulay's nephew.

209.23 Carlyle's Frederick] *History of Friedrich II of Prussia, Called Frederick the Great* (1858–65) by Thomas Carlyle.

209.23–24 Winston Churchill's life of his father] *Lord Randolph Churchill* (1906).

209.24–25 William Graham Sumner's study of Andrew Jackson] *Andrew Jackson as a Public Man* (1882).

209.28 Daniel Coit Gilman] See note 177.14.

209.35 The Nicolay-Hay work] *Abraham Lincoln: A History*, published in ten volumes in 1890.

210.3–4 those of Lamon . . . and Miss Tarbell] *Life of Abraham Lincoln from His Birth to His Inauguration as President* (1872) by Ward Hill Lamon; *Herndon's Lincoln: The True Story of a Great Life* (1889) by William Henry Herndon (1818–1891, with Jesse W. Weik); *Abraham Lincoln: The True Story of a Great Life* (1885) by William Osborn Stoddard; *Abraham Lincoln* (1893) by John T. Morse, Jr.; *The Life of Abraham Lincoln* (1920) by Ida M. Tarbell.

210.13 William E. Barton] Congregational clergyman (1861–1930), author of *The Soul of Abraham Lincoln* (1920), among other books about him.

211.15 Dr. Creel] See note 198.4.

211.18 H. P. Davison] American banker (1867–1922), chairman of the American Red Cross Council during World War I.

211.18 Admiral Sims] William Sims (1858–1936), commander of naval operations in European waters, 1917–19.

211.19 Nicholas Murray Butler] American educator and diplomat (1862–1947), president of Columbia University, 1902–45, and president for Carnegie Endowment for International Peace, 1925–45. He was active in various international peace conferences in the years preceding World War I.

211.20 Barney Baruch] Bernard Baruch (1870–1965), American businessman and statesman, appointed by President Wilson to Advisory Commission of the Council for National Defense (1916); he served as chairman of the War Industries Board (1918–19), and was a member of the American peace commission in 1919.

211.29–30 Lawrence Abbott's "Impressions of Theodore Roosevelt"] Published in 1919. Abbott (1859–1933) was Roosevelt's secretary during his 1909–10 tour of Europe and Africa and editor of his *African and European Addresses* (1910).

211.30–31 William Roscoe Thayer's "Theodore Roosevelt"] *Theodore Roosevelt: An Intimate Biography* (1919).

212.1 Murat Halstead] American journalist and author (1829–1908), editor of the Cincinnati *Gazette* and author of a biography of President McKinley.

212.14 Lansdowne] Henry Charles Keith Petty-Fitzmaurice, 5th Marquess of Lansdowne (1845–1927), who served as governor general of Canada, 1883–88; viceroy of India, 1888–94; secretary of state for war, 1895–1900; and secretary of state for foreign affairs, 1900–5. In a letter published in November 1917, he called for a negotiated settlement with Germany.

212.14–15 Loreburn] Robert Reid, 1st Earl of Loreburn (1846–1923).

212.15 Austin Harrison] British journalist (1873–1928), editor of *The English Review*, 1909–23. He favored lenient peace terms for Germany after World War I.

212.15 Morel] E. D. Morel (1873–1924), French-born British journalist who was a leader of the pacifist movement during World War I.

212.15 Keynes] John Maynard Keynes (1883–1946), English economist and representative at the Paris Peace Conference in 1919.

212.15 Haldane] Richard Burdon, Viscount Haldane (1856–1928), British statesman and philosopher. Prior to World War I he implemented a set of reforms aimed at preparing the British army for a war in Europe. In 1915 he was forced to resign as Lord Chancellor after being accused of pro-German sympathies.

212.15 Hirst] Francis W. Hirst (1873–1953), English economist and author of *Political Economy of War* (1915). He was editor of *The Economist*, 1907–15.

212.15–16 Balfour] Arthur James Balfour (1848–1930), British statesman who served as prime minister, 1902–5. He was the author of the Balfour Declaration of 1917, favoring the establishment of a Jewish homeland in Palestine.

212.16 Robert Cecil] 1st Viscount Cecil of Chelwood (1864–1958), British statesman and an architect of the League of Nations.

212.19 Horatio Bottomley] British financier and journalist (1860–1933), founded *The Financial Times* in 1888 and *John Bull* in 1906. After 1914 he called for the extermination of the German nation and the trial for treason of anti-war English politicians. In 1921 he was convicted of financial fraud and perjury and served five years in prison.

212.36 Treitschke] See note 180.5.

212.36 Delcassé] Théophile Delcassé (1852–1923), French statesman and minister of foreign affairs. He played a leading role in French colonial expansion and was strongly anti-German in his policy views.

213.5 chautauqual rhetoric] Following the New York Chatauqua Assembly of 1874, the term *chatauqua* was widely used to denote adult summer camps bringing education and entertainment to rural areas.

213.22 Bullitt] William Christian Bullitt (1891–1967), American diplomat who worked for Woodrow Wilson at the Paris Peace Conference of 1919.

213.23 Shantung] At the Paris Peace Conference, special privileges that had been exercised by Germany in the Chinese province of Shantung were transferred to Japan, provoking Chinese nationalist sentiment.

214.24–25 Also sprach Zarathustra . . . Jenseits von Gut und Böse] *Thus Spoke Zarathustra* (1883–85) and *Beyond Good and Evil* (1886).

214.29–30 The Strenuous Life] Speech given by Theodore Roosevelt in Chicago, Illinois on April 10, 1899, in which he declared, "I wish to preach, not the doctrine of ignoble ease, but the doctrine of the strenuous life, the life of toil and effort, of labor and strife."

215.38 Blaine] James G. Blaine (1830–1893), American politician who served as congressman, senator, and secretary of state, and was a dominant figure in the Republican Party in the period after the Civil War. He was defeated by Grover Cleveland in the 1884 presidential race.

217.40 Barbarossa] Frederick I (1122–1190), Holy Roman Emperor.

218.32 Liberty Loan] Series of five bond issues floated by the U.S. Treasury Department that helped finance World War I.

221.21 rice converts] The term refers to persons converting nominally to Christianity in order to receive rice and other material benefits from missionaries.

223.22–23 Paterson anarchists] In 1900 an Italian anarchist resident in Paterson, New Jersey, traveled to Italy and assassinated King Umberto. Following the assassination of President McKinley in 1901, Theodore Roosevelt called for strong action against international anarchists, stating: "Anarchy is a crime against the whole human race; and all mankind should band against the anarchist."

223.24 Charles J. Bonaparte] Charles Joseph Bonaparte (1851–1921) served as Roosevelt's Secretary of the Navy (1905–1906) and U.S. Attorney General (1906–09), in which capacity he founded the Bureau of Investigation.

229.5 J. Gordon Coogler] South Carolina-born poet (1865–1901), whose *Purely Original Verse* was published in five editions between 1891 and 1897.

230.27 Robert Loveman] See note 165.35.

230.28 John McClure] See note 56.5.

232.18 Leo Frank affair] In 1913, Leo Frank (1884–1915), the Jewish manager of a pencil factory in Atlanta, Georgia, was accused of the rape and murder of Mary Phagan, a thirteen-year-old worker in his employ. Frank was found guilty but in 1915 Georgia governor John Slaton, convinced of his innocence, commuted his sentence to life imprisonment. Frank was abducted from prison by a group including a former governor and the son of a state senator, and lynched on August 17, 1915.

234.17 John Temple Graves] Journalist and lecturer (1856–1925), editor of the *Atlanta Journal* and the *Atlanta Georgian*, a strident spokesman for white supremacism and an open apologist for lynching.

234.18 Frank L. Stanton] Georgia-born poet (1857–1927) whose poems appeared regularly in the *Atlanta Constitution*.

235.22 Caradoc Evans] Welsh fiction writer (1878–1945), author of *My People* (1915), *My Neighbors* (1919), *Taffy* (1923), and other books.

235.32–33 Philip Alexander Bruce] American historian (1856–1933), a specialist in the history of Virginia.

235.40 Fanny Kemble Butler] Fanny Kemble (1809–95), English actress who came to America in 1832 and left the stage two years later to marry Pierce Butler, a Georgia plantation-owner. The marriage ended in 1846. Her *Journal of a Residence on a Georgian Plantation* (1868), written 1838–39, was a highly critical account of the culture of slavery.

238.11 Weber & Fields] Joe Weber (1867–1942) and Lew Fields (1867–1941), team of comedians known for their German and Yiddish dialect routines; their many successful shows included *Helter Skelter* (1899) and *Whoop-dee-doo*.

247.19 Hugo Wolf] Austrian composer (1860–1903) of over two hundred *Lieder*.

248.10 the elder Beecham] Thomas Beecham (1820–1907), creator of Beecham's Pills, a laxative that he began selling around 1847.

248.11 the younger Beecham] Sir Thomas Beecham (1879–1961), English conductor and impresario. He founded the London Philharmonic and Royal Philharmonic orchestras, conducted the first English performances of Richard Strauss's *Elektra* and *Salome*, and accompanied the Ballets Russes at Covent Garden and elsewhere.

248.18–19 "La force et la foiblesse . . . des organes du corps"] The strength and weakness of the mind are misnamed; they are only, in effect, the good or poor condition of the physical organs.

248.32 *spirochaete pallida*] Causative agent of syphilis.

250.24 Dr. Jacques Loeb] See note 45.27.

251.23 *Durchlaucht*] Serene Highness.

256.36 *couronnes des perles*] Crowns of pearls.

258.21 George W. Crile] American surgeon (1864–1943), author of studies including *Hemorrhage and Transfusion* (1909), *Origin and Nature of the Emotions* (1915), *A Mechanistic View of War and Peace* (1915), and *Man: An Adaptive Mechanism* (1916).

259.3–4 F. Parkes Weber] Physician and numismatist (1863–1962).

259.35 Sir William Osler] Canadian-born physician and medical administrator (1849–1919), first chief of staff of the Johns Hopkins Hospital. From 1905 he held the Regius Chair of Medicine at Oxford.

260.22 *Char-Freitag*] Good Friday.

261.20 Dr. Alexis Carrel] See note 45.27.

262.13 Edmund Gosse] British literary critic, poet and biographer (1849–1928), author of the autobiography *Father and Son* (1907).

262.15–16 William Archer] See note 13.2.

262.23 *Allgemeine-krankenhaus*] General hospital.

263.31 Ellen La Motte] American journalist (1873–1961) who served as a nurse in France during World War I. Her book *The Backwash of War: The Human Wreckage of the Battlefield as Witnessed by an American Hospital Nurse* (1916) was adapted from her journals.

266.22 The Duchess] See note 83.3.

268.14 Thaïs] Opera (1894) by Jules Massenet, based on the novel by Anatole France.

268.15 Gung'l] Josef Gung'l (1810–1889), Hungarian composer.

269.7 Carl Van Vechten] Novelist and critic (1880–1964). Early in his career he was music critic for the *New York Times.*

270.18–19 René Lenormand] French composer (1846–1932), author of *A Study of Modern Harmony* (1915).

271.20 Wiener Blut . . . Künstler Leben] "Vienna Blood" and "Artists' Life," waltzes by Johann Strauss II.

271.37–39 Rosen aus dem Süden . . . Wein, Weib und Gesang] "Roses from the South" and "Wine, Women, and Song," waltzes by Johann Strauss II.

272.8 Wiener Mad'l] "Vienna Girls," waltz by Carl Michael Ziehrer.

272.12 Herbert K. Hadley . . . In Bohemia] American composer (1871–1937). "In Bohemia" was his Concert Overture, Op. 28.

272.29 Bror Nordfeldt] Bror Julius Olsson Nordfeldt (1878–1955), artist who emigrated to the United States from Sweden in 1891 and first drew attention with solo exhibits in Chicago, 1911–12. He later settled in New Mexico.

274.21–24 Henry Irving . . . The Bells] English actor-manager (1838–1905) who dominated the London stage for many decades. His celebrated melodramatic vehicle *The Bells* was adapted by Leopold Lewis from Erckmann-Chatrian's *Le Juif Polonais.* The play opened in New York in 1883.

274.25–29 the late Mansfield . . . Dr. Jekyll and Mr. Hyde] Richard Mansfield (1854–1907), American actor, educated in England, who had his first major American success in the role of the brutal roué Baron Chevrial in A. M. Palmer's production *A Parisian Romance* (1883). Mansfield's production of *Dr. Jekyll and Mr. Hyde* opened in 1887.

279.13–14 Maurice Parmelee] American sociologist (1882–1969), author of *Personality and Conduct* (1918), *Criminology* (1918), *The Science of Human Behavior* (1924), and *The New Gymnosophy* (1927), a defense of nudism.

280.4 the Comstocks] See note 180.34.

284.25–26 Dr. Frank Crane] See note 25.12.

284.29 Theda Bara] See note 170.15.

285.37–38 Stephen Girard] French-born banker and philanthropist (1750–1831) who saved the U.S. government from financial collapse during the War of 1812 and helped found the Second Bank of the United States (1816). He left most of his fortune to charitable institutions in Philadelphia and New Orleans.

285.38–286.1 Theodore Thomas] German-born conductor (1835–1905) of the Chicago Symphony.

286.1 Edwin Klebs] German-Swiss pathologist (1834–1913) known for work on infectious diseases. He taught at Rush Medical College in Chicago, 1896–1900.

288.5 Rex Beach] See note 167.9.

288.22 *meatus auditorium externus*] Auditory canal.

290.22 *Abortfrau*] Cleaning woman.

293.38 Minna Planer] Christine Wilhelmine Planer (1809–1866), first wife of Richard Wagner. They were married in 1836 and separated in 1857.

294.1 Armande Béjart] French actress (1642–1700), wife of Molière from 1662 until his death in 1673.

294.10–11 Cosima Liszt von Bülow] Cosima Wagner (1837–1930), daughter of Franz Liszt. Her first marriage to Hans von Bülow ended in divorce in 1869; she married Richard Wagner in 1870.

PREJUDICES: THIRD SERIES

302.30 Anti-Saloon League] Organization, founded in Ohio in 1893, that played a major role in lobbying for Prohibition.

302.40 Harold Stearns] See note 207.22.

304.40 *Wirkliche Geheimräte*] Privy Councilors.

305.2 *Todsaufer*] In his memoir *Happy Days* (1940), Mencken writes: "A *Todsäufer* (literally, dead-drinker) was, and is, a sort of brewer's customers' man. He is commonly called a collector, but his duties go far beyond collecting the bills owed to breweries by saloonkeepers. He is supposed to stand a general treat in the bar whenever he calls, to go to all weddings, birthday parties and funerals in the families of saloonkeepers, and to cultivate their wives and children with frequent presents. . . . He is also one of the brewery's political agents, and must handle all the license difficulties of his clients."

307.4 Charles M. Schwab] Steel industry magnate (1862–1939), chief executive of Bethlehem Steel, known for his lavish spending.

307.6 *Geschäft*] Business.

307.6 Remy de Gourmont] French poet, novelist, and critic (1858–1915), author of *The Natural Philosophy of Love* (1904) and *A Night in the Luxembourg* (1906).

307.27–28 *Durchlauchten, k.k. Hoheiten*] German forms of royal address.

308.9 Lord Reading] See note 187.17–18.

308.15 Prince Eugene] Francois Eugène de Savoy-Carignan, Prince of Savoy (1633–1736), Austrian military commander.

308.21–22 Arthur James Balfour] See note 212.14–15.

309.12 Reform Bill of 1832] Act of Parliament that introduced major changes to the electoral system of the United Kingdom, increasing the size of the electorate by as much as 80 percent.

309.16 Volstead] Minnesota congressman Andrew John Volstead (1860–1947), sponsor of The National Prohibition Act of 1919, also known as the Volstead Act.

309.16 Ponzi] Charles Ponzi (1882–1949), financial swindler whose method of paying early investors with money from later investors originated the term "Ponzi scheme."

309.16 Jack Dempsey] Boxer (1895–1983), heavy-weight champion 1919–26.

309.16 Daugherty] Harry M. Daugherty (1860–1914), Republican Party boss and U.S. Attorney General under President Harding.

309.16 Debs] Eugene Victor Debs (1855–1926), American socialist leader and founder of the Social Democratic Party. Debs was arrested under the Espionage Act for an anti-war speech made in 1918.

310.11 *Greisenheim*] Old People's Home.

313.29 Garys] Elbert Henry Gary (1846–1927), president of U.S. Steel, 1901–27. Having served two terms as a county judge, 1884–92, he was commonly known as "Judge Gary."

313.33–34 Congregatio de Propaganda Fide] Congregation for the Propagation of the Faith.

313.34 Bismarck's *Reptilienpresse*] Newspapers bribed by Otto von Bismarck to publish articles favorable to the government; they were paid out of a secret "reptile fund," so-called because it was created to counter opponents Bismarck described as "reptiles."

314.37–38 Bryce] James Bryce (1838–1922), English politician and historian, author of *The American Commonwealth* (1888).

315.2 Robertson Nicoll] Sir William Roberston Nicoll (1851–1923), Scottish minister and journalist, founder of the literary monthly *The Bookman* in 1891. His *History of English Literature* appeared in 1906.

315.2 Squire] Sir John Collings Squire (1884–1958), poet and critic. He was editor of the *London Mercury*, 1919–34. His books included *Books in General* (1918–21) and *Life and Letters* (1920).

315.2–3 Clutton-Brock] Arthur Clutton-Brock (1868–1924), English essayist and critic, a frequent contributor to the *Times Literary Supplement*. His books included *Shelley: The Man and the Poet* (1909) and *Essays on Art* (1918).

315.23 Birkenhead] Frederick Birkenhead (1872–1930), British attorney general (1915) and lord chancellor (1919–1922).

315.29 *Town Topics*] See note 76.23.

316.30 Otto Julius Bierbaum] German poet and critic (1865–1910).

316.30 Ludwig Thoma] See note 63.40.

318.7–8 Dr. Dillon] Emile Joseph Dillon (1854–1933), journalist and philologist.

318.8 Wickham Steed] English journalist (1871–1956), foreign editor (1914–19) and editor (1920–22) of the London *Times*. His books included *The Hapsburg Monarchy* (1913) and *The Antecedents of Post-War Europe* (1932).

318.8 Count zu Reventlow] Ernst zu Reventlow (1869–1943), German journalist who wrote on military and political matters; he founded the newspaper *Der Reichswart*, which he published until his death. He joined the Nazi party in 1927.

318.8 Wilfrid Scawen Blunt] English poet and essayist (1840–1922). Aside from collections of verse, his books included *The Future of Islam* (1882), *India under Ripon* (1909), and *The Land War in Ireland* (1912).

318.11 Disarmament Conference] Also called the Washington Naval Conference, held in Washington D.C. November 12, 1921–February 6, 1922. The primary aim of the conference was to restrain the expansion of the Japanese Navy.

318.14 Brailsford] Henry Noel Brailsford (1873–1958), British journalist.

318.14 Bywater] Hector Charles Bywater (1884–1940), British journalist and writer on military and naval subjects, author of *Sea Power in the Pacific: A Study of the American-Japanese Naval Problem* (1921).

318.25–26 The issue . . . before the conference] Mencken refers to the question of allowed capital ship tonnage for each signatory to the treaty.

319.13 Huysmans] Joris Karl Huysmans (1848–1907), French novelist, author of *The Vatard Sisters* (1879), *Against the Grain* (1884), and *Down There* (1891).

319.13 Hartleben] Otto Erich Hartleben (1864–1905), German writer of poetry, fiction, and plays.

319.13 Vaihinger] Hans Vaihinger (1852–1933), German philosopher, author of *The Philosophy of As If* (1911). He was a leading scholar of the work of Kant.

319.13 Merezhkovsky] Dmitri Sergeyevich Merezhkovski (1865–1941), Russian novelist and poet, a leader of the Russian Symbolist movement. His fictional trilogy *Christ and Antichrist* was comprised of *The Death of the Gods* (1896), *The Romance of Leonardo da Vinci* (1902), and *Peter and Alexis* (1905).

319.13 Keyserling] Count Hermann Alexander Keyserling (1880–1946), German social philosopher from an aristocratic Estonian family. Following World War I he founded the Society for Free Philosophy at Darmstadt. His book *The Travel Diary of a Philosopher* (1919), recounting his 1911 world tour, was an international bestseller.

319.14 Snoilsky] Count Carl Snoilsky (1841–1903), Swedish lyric poet.

319.14 Mauthner] Fritz Mauthner (1849–1923), German novelist and philosopher.

319.14 Altenberg] Peter Altenberg (1859–1919), author of essays and sketches.

319.14 Heidenstam] Verner von Heidenstam (1859–1940), Swedish poet, awarded the Nobel Prize in Literature in 1916.

319.14 Alfred Kerr] German drama critic (1867–1948), an advocate of Naturalism. He emigrated to London in 1933.

319.16 Brieux] See note 35.18.

319.25 Dr. Sylvanus Stall] See note 118.26.

319.35 Boyd] Ernest Augustus Boyd (1887–1946), Irish-born critic, essayist, and translator from French and German. He settled permanently in the United States in 1920. His books included *Contemporary Drama of Ireland* (1917) and *Appreciations and Depreciations* (1918). He published a study of Mencken in 1925.

319.35 Nathan] See note 124.2.

319.37 William Archer] See note 13.2.

319.37 Georg Brandes] See note 7.29.

319.40 Gerhart Hauptmann] See note 127.4.

320.1 Ludwig Lewisohn] German-born American writer (1882–1955). His books included the autobiographies *Upstream* (1922) and *Mid-Channel* (1929), and many novels including *The Case of Mr. Crump* (1926) and *The Island Within* (1928).

320.29 Der Amerikamüde] Novel (1855) by the Austrian writer Ferdinand Kürnberger (1829–1879).

320.29 America] Novel (1911) by Sholem Asch (1880–1957), Polish-born American dramatist and novelist.

320.29–30 Ernst von Wolzogen] German author of satirical plays and fiction (1855–1934), founder of the Berlin cabaret Das Überbrettl.

320.30–31 Hail Columbia!] "Hail, Columbia! Random Impressions of a Conservative Radical" (1921); for W. L. George, see note 21.32.

320.31 Annalise Schmidt's "Der Amerikanische Mensch"] Study of "the American individual" published in 1920.

320.32 Sienkiewicz's "After Bread"] Novel (1880) by Polish writer Henryk Sienkiewicz (1846–1916), published in America in 1897 as *After Bread: A Story of Polish Emigrant Life to America*. Sienkiewicz's other novels included *With Fire and Sword* (1884) and *Quo Vadis* (1896).

320.35 Clemens von Pirquet] Austrian scientist and pediatrician (1874–1929) who did major work in immunological research. He declined an invitation to teach at Johns Hopkins University in 1909.

320.35 John Masefield] English poet (1878–1967), author of *Salt Water*

Poems and Ballads (1916), which included the poem "Sea-Fever." Named Poet Laureate in 1930, he lived briefly in New York in his youth.

320.36 Frank Wedekind] German playwright (1864–1918), author of *Spring's Awakening* (1891), *Earth Spirit* (1895), and *Pandora's Box* (1904).

320.36–37 Edwin Klebs] See note 286.1.

322.15 *Kriegslieferant*] War supplier.

324.18 Chamberlain] Joseph Chamberlain (1836–1914), British statesman.

324.18 F. E. Smith] Frederick Edwin Smith, lst Earl of Birkenhead (1872–1930), English lawyer and statesman; Lord Chancellor, 1919–22.

324.18 Isaacs-Reading] See note 187.17–18.

324.19 Bottomley] See note 212.18.

324.19 Northcliffe] See note 16.24.

325.12 Palmer] See note 164.20.

325.12 Burleson] Albert S. Burleson (1863–1937) served as U.S. postmaster general from 1913–21. During World War I he vigorously enforced the Espionage Act by attempting to bar radical and anti-war materials from the mails.

327.7 James M. Wood] Author of *Democracy and the Will to Power* (1921). The book contained an introduction by Mencken.

327.14 Billy Sunday] See note 70.9.

327.14 Cyrus K. Curtis] Cyrus Hermann Kotzschmar Curtis (1850–1933), American publisher, founder of the Curtis Publishing Co., publisher of *Ladies' Home Journal*, *The Country Gentleman*, and *The Saturday Evening Post*.

327.14 Dr. Frank Crane] See note 25.12.

327.15 Charles E. Hughes] Charles Evans Hughes (1862–1948), governor of New York, 1907–10; associate justice of the U.S. Supreme Court, 1910–16; Republican nominee for president (1916). He served as secretary of state, 1921–25, and as chief justice of the U.S. Supreme Court from 1930 until his retirement in 1941.

327.15 General Wood] Leonard Wood (1860–1927), physician and army officer. He helped Theodore Roosevelt in raising and organizing the Rough Riders, and later became chief of staff of the U.S. Army, 1910–14.

329.6 the Feather Duster] Charles Evans Hughes; see note 327.15.

329.6 Popinjay Lodge] Henry Cabot Lodge (1850–1924), legislator and author; member of the U.S. House of Representatives, 1887–93, and U.S.

Senate, 1893–1924. He led opposition to the Peace Treaty of 1919 and the Covenant of the League of Nations.

329.7 Master-Mind Root] Elihu Root (1845–1937), lawyer and statesman, secretary of war under McKinley and Theodore Roosevelt; he was appointed secretary of state following the death of John Hay. He received the Nobel Peace Prize in 1912. He later served as senator from New York, 1909–14, and as president of the Carnegie Endowment for International Peace, 1910–25.

329.7 Vacuum Underwood] Oscar Wilder Underwood (1862–1929), lawyer and politician; represented Alabama in the U.S. House of Representatives, 1896–1915, and U.S. Senate, 1915–27.

330.31 Mother Eddy] See note 145.33.

330.32 John Alexander Dowie] Scottish-born evangelist and faith healer (1847–1907) who in 1896 founded the Christian Catholic Apostolic Church in Zion. In 1900 he established the city of Zion, Illinois, forty-two miles from Chicago.

331.5 Cox] James Middleton Cox (1870–1957), newspaper publisher and politician. He served as governor of Ohio (1913–15, 1917–21) and was Democratic nominee for president in 1920.

331.38 *Ridi si sapis*] Laugh if you are wise.

332.23–24 Matthew v, 11] "Blessed are ye, when men revile you, and persecute you, and say all manner of evil against you falsely, for my sake."

334.2 Huneker] See note 7.29.

334.10–11 *Doppelschraubenschnellpostdampfer*] Fast ocean liner.

334.36–335.1 Sils Maria] Nietzsche spent many summers in Sils Maria, near St. Moritz in Switzerland.

335.4 Frau Cosima] See note 294.10–11.

335.7 Anton Seidel] Anton Seidl (1850–1898), Hungarian conductor who led the New York Philharmonic from 1891 to 1898.

335.9 David Belasco] See note 124.24.

335.10 Lillian Russell] The American singer and actress (1861–1922) was married four times.

335.13 George Moore] See note 170.29.

335.15 D'Annunzio and Duse] Gabriele D'Annunzio (1863–1938), Italian poet and playwright; Eleanora Duse (1859–1924), Italian actress.

335.19 Bal Bullier] Celebrated Paris dance hall.

336.4 Josef's Legend] *Josephslegende*, Opus 63, ballet music composed in 1914.

336.15 Frank Harris] See note 175.7.

336.20–21 essays on Strauss . . . Chopin] See "The Music of the Future," "Richard Strauss and Nietzsche," and "The Greater Chopin" in *Mezzotints in Modern Music* (1899); "Richard Strauss" and "Nietzsche the Rhapsodist" in *Over Tones* (1904); "Phases of Nietzsche" in *Egoists: A Book of Supermen* (1909); "Richard Strauss at Stuttgart" in *Ivory Apes and Peacocks* (1915); "Brahmsody" and "The Classic Chopin" in *Unicorns* (12917); "Phases of the Greater Chopin" in *Variations* (1922); and *Chopin: The Man and His Music* (1900). See also *Essays by James Huneker* (1929), edited by Mencken.

336.35 Krehbiel] Henry Edward Krehbiel (1854–1923), American music critic, music editor of the *New York Tribune*. His books included *Studies in the Wagnerian Drama* (1891), *How to Listen to Music* (1897), and *Afro-American Folksongs: A Study in Racial and National Music* (1914).

336.36 Finck] Henry Theophilus Finck (1854–1926), American musical critic, musical editor of the *New York Evening Post* and writer for *The Nation*. He published, among other books, *Wagner and His Works* (1891), *Anton Seidl* (1899), and *Edward Grieg* (1905).

337.1 Middleton Murry] John Middleton Murry (1889–1957), English critic, author of *The Evolution of an Intellectual* (1920), *The Problem of Style* (1922), *D. H. Lawrence* (1930), and many other books.

337.1 Paul Elmer More] See note 7.31.

337.1–2 Clutton-Brock] See note 315.2–3.

340.10 Georg Brandes] See note 7.29.

341.2–3 Max Beerbohm] English essayist and caricaturist (1872–1956), a frequent contributor to *The Yellow Book* (1894–97) and *The Saturday Review*, where he succeeded George Bernard Shaw as dramatic critic. His books included *The Happy Hypocrite* (1897), *Zuleika Dobson* (1911), and *Seven Men* (1919).

341.16–18 *Sun . . . Mlle. New York*] Under the editorship (1868–97) of Charles H. Dana, the New York *Sun* (1833–1950) was known for its lively criticism. *M'lle New York*, founded by Vance Thompson in 1895, helped introduce French symbolist poetry, Nietzsche, and other modern European intellectual and artistic trends to American readers.

351.20 Carlyle's "Frederick"] See note 209.23.

353.33–34 Rufus Dawes] Massachusetts-born poet and dramatist (1803–1859). His *Geraldine, Athenia of Damascus, and Miscellaneous Poems* was published in 1839.

353.36–37 Gottfried Weber] German writer on music (1779–1839), editor of the influential periodical *Cäcilia*, 1824–39, and author of *Theory of Musical Composition* (1817–21).

355.35 *Aufklärung*] Enlightenment.

356.23 George E. Woodberry] See note 159.12.

356.29–30 Hamilton Wright Mabie] See note 7.15.

358.6 *Vorspiel*] Prelude.

359.26 Félicien Rops] Belgian artist (1833–1898) associated with writers including Baudelaire, Gautier, and Mallarmé; noted for the erotic and supposedly blasphemous elements of his work.

360.21 Diamond Jim Brady] James Buchanan Brady (1856–1917), American financier famous for his vast appetite and lavish lifestyle.

364.34 *Bauverein*] Building Society.

367.2 *Ad Imaginem Dei Creavit Illum*] Genesis 1:27 in the Latin Vulgate version: "In the Divine image he created him."

373.33 Sir Oliver Lodge] See note 35.37.

379.32 American Protective League] Private organization active during World War I, whose aim was to work with federal agencies to combat radicals, anti-war activists, and left-wing political groups.

379.34 Dr Creel] See note 198.4.

380.10 Arion Liedertafel] German singing group.

381.22–23 Johannes Müller] German physiologist (1801–1858).

381.23 Karl Ludwig] German astronomer (1765–1834).

381.23 Ehrlich] German scientist (1854–1915) who won the Nobel Prize in Medicine in 1908. He developed the cure for syphilis.

381.36–37 Newell Dwight Hillis] See note 80.28–29.

381.37 Henry Van Dyke] See note 55.19.

381.40 Palmer and Burleson] See notes 164.20 and 325.12.

382.5 Gaby Deslys] French dancer and actress (1881–1920).

383.4 Otto Jespersen] Danish linguist (1860–1943), founder of the International Phonetic Association. *Growth and Structure of the English Language* appeared in 1905.

384.17 Æ] Pseudonym of George William Russell (1867–1935), Irish poet.

384.17 Lord Dunsany] See note 127.3.

386.13–16 Not poppy . . . thou owed'st yesterday.] *Othello* III.iii.330–333.

386.28 Joaquin Miller] Pseudonym of Cincinnatus Heine Miller (1837–1913), American poet and essayist, author of *Song of the Sierras* (1871).

386.38 Sidney Lanier] Georgia-born poet (1842–1881), whose prosodical study *The Science of English Verse* appeared in 1880.

387.27 F. C. Prescott] Prescott (1871–1957) published *Poetry and Dreams* in 1912.

388.5–6 God's in . . . with the world.] cf. Robert Browning, song from *Pippa Passes* (1841): "God's in his Heaven — / All's right with the world!"

388.8–9 I am the . . . captain of my soul.] William Ernest Henley, "Invictus," lines 15–16.

389.8 "The Frost is on the Pumpkin"] "When the Frost is on the Punkin," poem by James Whitcomb Riley (1849–1916).

389.11 Crashaw] Richard Crashaw (1613–1649), English metaphysical poet.

389.12 Thompson] Francis Thompson (1889–1907), English poet best known for the religious allegory "The Hound of Heaven" (1893).

389.32 "Tommy Atkins" and "Fuzzy-Wuzzy"] Poems from Kipling's collection *Barrack-Room Ballads* (1892).

391.8–9 Lizette Woodworth Reese] See note 55.40.

392.22 Lecky] William Hartpole Lecky (1838–1903), Irish historian, author of *History of Rationalism in Europe* (1865) and *History of European Morals from Augustus to Charlemagne* (1869).

392.22 Buckle] Henry Thomas Buckle (1821–1862), English historian, author of the unfinished *History of Civilization in England.*

392.24 Rogers groups] Clay and plaster statue groups created by the English sculptor John Rogers (1829–1904) that were widely collected in late nineteenth-century America.

392.26 William Sumner] William Graham Sumner (1840–1910), American economist, sociologist and educator, author of *Folkways* (1907).

392.26 Daniel C. Gilman] See note 177.14.

393.19–20 The Sheik] Novel (1919) by Edith Maude Hull, filmed in 1921 with Rudolph Valentino in the title role.

394.20 *cabotin*] Ham.

395.27 "The Blessed Damozel"] Poem (1850) by Dante Gabriel Rossetti.

395.39–40 John Livingston Lowes] See note 51.12.

398.19 Barton] See note 210.13.

400.36 *Paul Elmer More*] See note 7.31.

401.24 Dr. Franklin . . . *Profiteers' Review*] Dr. Fabian Franklin, Hungarian-born journalist (1853–1939), associate editor of *The New York Evening Post* and founder in 1919 of *The Review.*

401.32 Stuart P. Sherman] See note 4.19–20.

402.29 *Madison Cawein*] Kentucky-born poet (1865–1914), author of many volumes of verse including *Lyrics and Idyls* (1890), *The Garden of Dreams* (1896), *Weeds by the Wall* (1901), and *Minions of the Moon* (1913).

403.3 Charles Hamilton Musgrove] Kentucky-born poet, author of *The Dream Beautiful* (1898) and *Pan and Æolus* (1913).

404.17 *Frank Harris*] See note 175.7.

408.3 Leonard Merrick] English novelist (1864–1939), author of *The Man Who Was Good* (1892), *Conrad in Quest of His Youth* (1903), and other works.

408.27 Havelock Ellis] See note 116.13.

409.2 Wallace] Alfred Russel Wallace (1823–1913), English scientist and naturalist who developed an independent theory of evolution by natural selection. He later became involved in political activism and spiritualism.

409.2 Crookes] Sir William Crookes (1832–1919), English physicist and chemist, pioneer of vacuum tubes. He later became interested in spiritualism and joined the Society for Psychic Research.

409.2 Lodge] See note 35.37.

409.15 Wilfrid Scawen Blunt] See note 318.8.

413.39 Mooney] Thomas Mooney (1882–1942), American labor leader tried and convicted for the bombing that killed nine and wounded forty during a Preparedness Parade in San Francisco on July 22, 1916. His death sentence was commuted to life imprisonment in 1918, and became the object of a worldwide campaign to free him. He was pardoned in 1938.

413.40 One Big Union] Slogan of the IWW.

416.5 Rex Beach] See note 167.9.

416.13 *Küche-Kinder-Kirche*] Children, kitchen, church: German slogan defining the traditional role of women.

416.33 Joseph Hergesheimer] American novelist (1880–1954) whose many books, widely popular and in their time often critically acclaimed, included *The Three Black Pennys* (1917) and *Java Head* (1919).

417.10 *Schwärmerei*] Excessive enthusiasm.

417.11 L'Allemagne] *De l'Allemagne* (1810–13) by the French writer Anne Louise Germaine Necker, Madame de Staël (1766–1817), a study of German culture that became a crucial work for the Romantic movement.

417.18 Clara Viebig] German naturalistic novelist (1860–1952), author of *Our Daily Bread* (1902), *The Watch on the Rhine* (1902), and other works.

417.18 Helene Böhlau] German writer of naturalistic novels and stories (1859–1940), author of *Ratsmädelgeschichten* (1888), *Der Rangierbahnhof* (1895), and other works.

417.18–19 Ricarda Huch] German author (1864–1947) of poetry, plays, novels and literary criticism, whose works included *The Last Summer* (1910) and *The Deruda Trial* (1917).

417.19 Selma Lagerlöf] Swedish novelist and poet (1858–1940), recipient of 1909 Nobel Prize in Literature.

417.20 Mathilda Serao] Matilda Serao (1856–1927), Italian novelist and journalist. She was founder and editor of *Il Mattino* and *Il Giorno.*

417.21 May Sinclair] English novelist (1866–1952), author of *Divine Fire* (1904), *Mary Oliver* (1919), *The Life and Death of Harriet Frean* (1922), and other works.

417.28–29 Evelyn Scott's "The Narrow House"] Scott (1893–1963) published *The Narrow House* in 1921. It was followed by *Narcissus* (1922), *The Golden Door* (1923), *Escapade* (1923), *The Wave* (1929), and other books.

418.5–6 Meredith's "The Shaving of Shagpat"] *The Shaving of Shagpat: An Arabian Entertainment* (1856) by George Meredith (1828–1909).

418.6 Jacob Wasserman's "The World Illusion"] *Christian Wannschaffe* (1919), internationally popular novel by Jakob Wasserman (1873–1934).

418.8 Beethoven's "Vittoria"] Orchestral fantasia "Wellington's Victory, or The Battle of Vittoria," Opus 91 (1813).

418.8 Goldmarck's "Landliche Hochzeit"] "Rustic Wedding Symphony," Opus 26 (1876), by Hungarian composer Karl Goldmark (1830–1915).

418.18 The Ordeal of Richard Feverel] Novel (1859) by George Meredith.

419.2 The Line of Love] A series of linked stories (1905) by James Branch Cabell. It was reissued in 1921 with a preface by Mencken.

419.8 Zola's "La Terre"] *The Earth* (1887), the fifteenth novel in Emile Zola's *Rougon-Macquart* series.

420.22 Aphra Behn] Playwright and novelist (1640–1689), considered the first English professional woman writer. Her works included the play *The Rover* (1681) and the novel *Oroonoko* (1688).

420.32 Love Pilgrimage] Novel (1911) by Upton Sinclair.

421.2 Zona Gale] See note 167.35.

422.6 Chambers] See note 42.19.

422.7 Coningsby Dawson] See note 203.6–7.

422.7 Emerson Hough] See note 167.9.

423.29 Bishop Manning] William Thomas Manning (1866–1949), Episcopal bishop of New York, 1921–46.

423.29 Judge Gary] See note 313.29.

423.30 Dr. Fabian Franklin] See note 401.24.

423.31 Dr. Stephen S. Wise] American Reform rabbi and Zionist leader (1874–1949).

423.31 Roger W. Babson] Entrepreneur and author of books on business theory (1875–1967); founder of Babson College.

424.9 the Gary system] Innovative educational approach fostered by the public school system of Gary, Indiana, in the 1920s.

424.27 twilight sleep] Drug-induced state advocated as a means of painless childbirth, developed in Germany and popular in the United States following the publication of Hanna Rion's *The Truth About Twilight Sleep* (1915).

426.3 David Starr Jordan] Eugenicist and peace activist (1851–1931).

426.4–5 B. O. Flower] Benjamin Orange Flower (1858–1918), journalist, editor of *The Arena* (1889–1909).

426.7 W. S. U'Ren] William Simon U'Ren (1859–1949), progressive Oregon politician, an advocate of Henry George's single tax.

426.9 Jane Addams] See note 35.23.

426.10 Dr. Scott Nearing] See note 36.26.

426.11 Newt Baker] Newton Baker (1871–1937), American politician who served as secretary of war, 1916–21.

426.12 Gifford Pinchot] American statesman (1865–1946), who was first chief of the United States Forest Service (1905–10).

426.13–14 Judge Ben B. Lindsey] See note 35.16.

431.32 vereins] Associations.

434.19 Allen G. Thurman] See note 190.18.

434.20 General Coxey] See note 87.34.

434.20–21 Richmond P. Hobson] Rear admiral and U.S. congressman from Alabama (1870–1937).

434.21 Nan Patterson] Showgirl, a member of the Florodora Girls, who at nineteen stood trial in 1905 for the murder of her lover Caesar Young, a bookmaker, who was killed by gunshot while the two were riding together in a hansom cab. Patterson claimed that Young had committed suicide; she was released after two mistrials.

434.21 Alton B. Parker] Lawyer and judge (1852–1926), Democratic presidential nominee in 1904.

434.21–22 General Weyler] Spanish army officer (1838–1930) who served in Cuba and the Philippines.

434.22 Tom Sharkey] Boxer (1873–1953) whose career ran from 1893 to 1904.

444.17 Percy MacKaye] Poet and playwright (1875–1956) who attempted to revive verse drama.

446.24 Leschetizky] Theodor Leschetizky (1830–1915), Polish pianist and composer.

461.33 Garet Garrett or John Moody] Garrett (1878–1954), American journalist, author of *The Driver* (1922); *Moody* (1868–1958), financial analyst.

465.36 Prince Kropotkin] Prince Pyotr Alekseyevich Kropotkin (1842–1921), Russian social philosopher, a leading advocate of anarchism.

466.15 Gustave Herve] Gustave Hervé (1871–1944), French politician who was imprisoned in 1910 for pacifist activities and upon his release changed his position to one of ultranationalism, forming the protofascist Parti Socialiste Nationale.

470.9 Dr. Beard] Charles A. Beard (1874–1948), historian, author of *An Economic Interpretation of the Constitution* (1911).

474.24 Gustav le Bon] See note 90.27.

475.5 La Dame aux Camélias] *The Lady of the Camellias*, play adapted by Alexandre Dumas fils from his 1848 novel; it became the basis for Verdi's *La Traviata*.

475.10 Le Mariage d'Olympe] See note 62.34–35.

475.24 Nachgelassene Schriften] Unpublished writings.

475.36 Ein Puppenheim] *A Doll's House*.

476.10 Meilhac and Halévy] Henri Meilhac (1831–1897) and Ludovic Halévy (1834–1908), popular team of French playwrights and opera librettists, whose plays were collected in twelve volumes, 1900–2.

476.20 Gerhart Hauptmann] See note 127.4.

478.4 Maeterlinckians] See note 124.18.

478.13 Wolf-Ferrari] Ermanno Wolf-Ferrari (1876–1948), Italian composer of comic operas such as *Il Segreto di Susanna* (1909).

478.13 Massenet] Jules Emile Frederic Massenet (1842–1912), French composer whose operas included *Manon* (1884), *Werther* (1892), and *Thaïs* (1894).

478.15 Damaged Goods] See note 35.18.

478.16 Augustus Thomas] See note 124.24.

484.32 Reverend Billy Sunday] See note 70.9.

484.33 Mrs. Eddy] See note 145.33.

from MY LIFE AS AUTHOR AND EDITOR

493.8 Knopf] Alfred A. Knopf (1892–1984), publisher.

494.18 Sidney B. Fay] American historian (1876–1967).

494.37 Fielding H. Garrison] Medical historian and bibliographer (1870–1935), a close friend of Mencken.

497.32 Philip Littell] Literary critic (1868–1943), author of *Books and Things* (1919).

498.35 p. 501] The reference is to an earlier page of Mencken's manuscript.

501.16 Jack Ketch] Public executioner during the reign of Charles II.

502.14 Pirie MacDonald] Portrait photographer (1867–1942).

507.13 Ernest Poole] See note 86.11.

507.13 F. Marion Crawford] American fiction writer (1854–1909), author of *Dr. Claudius* (1883), *A Roman Singer* (1884), *Zoroaster* (1885), and many other novels.

507.14 Cale Young Rice] Kentucky-born poet and playwright (1872–1943), author of *Nirvana Days* (1908) and *The Immortal Lure* (1911).

510.10 *Schrecklichkeit*] "Frightfulness," German military doctrine of harsh measures designed to suppress civilian resistance in Belgium and elsewhere during World War I.

511.24 Frances Newman] Novelist (1883–1928), author of *The Gold-Fish Bowl* (1921), *The Hard-Boiled Virgin* (1926) and *Dead Lovers Are Faithful Lovers* (1928). At the time of her death Newman was suffering from severe and painful vision problems.

512.6 Brann the iconoclast] William Cowper Brann (1855–1898), owner and editor of *The Iconoclast*, published in Waco, Texas. He was shot to death by a reader angry over a published attack on Baylor University; Brann mortally wounded his attacker.

512.6 Elbert Hubbard] See note 168.14.

514.9 Thomas Moult] English poet and journalist (1893–1974).

515.18 Dorothy Canfield] Novelist and social activist (1879–1958) who later published as Dorothy Canfield Fisher.

515.19 Henry G. Aikman] Novelist and short story writer (1884–1979).

Index

THE LIBRARY OF AMERICA SERIES

Library of America fosters appreciation of America's literary heritage by publishing, and keeping permanently in print, authoritative editions of America's best and most significant writing. An independent nonprofit organization, it was founded in 1979 with seed funding from the National Endowment for the Humanities and the Ford Foundation.

1. Herman Melville: Typee, Omoo, Mardi
2. Nathaniel Hawthorne: Tales & Sketches
3. Walt Whitman: Poetry & Prose
4. Harriet Beecher Stowe: Three Novels
5. Mark Twain: Mississippi Writings
6. Jack London: Novels & Stories
7. Jack London: Novels & Social Writings
8. William Dean Howells: Novels 1875–1886
9. Herman Melville: Redburn, White-Jacket, Moby-Dick
10. Nathaniel Hawthorne: Collected Novels

11 & 12. Francis Parkman: France and England in North America

13. Henry James: Novels 1871–1880
14. Henry Adams: Novels, Mont Saint Michel, The Education
15. Ralph Waldo Emerson: Essays & Lectures
16. Washington Irving: History, Tales & Sketches
17. Thomas Jefferson: Writings
18. Stephen Crane: Prose & Poetry
19. Edgar Allan Poe: Poetry & Tales
20. Edgar Allan Poe: Essays & Reviews
21. Mark Twain: The Innocents Abroad, Roughing It

22 & 23. Henry James: Literary Criticism

24. Herman Melville: Pierre, Israel Potter, The Confidence-Man, Tales & Billy Budd
25. William Faulkner: Novels 1930–1935

26 & 27. James Fenimore Cooper: The Leatherstocking Tales

28. Henry David Thoreau: A Week, Walden, The Maine Woods, Cape Cod
29. Henry James: Novels 1881–1886
30. Edith Wharton: Novels

31 & 32. Henry Adams: History of the U.S. during the Administrations of Jefferson & Madison

33. Frank Norris: Novels & Essays
34. W.E.B. Du Bois: Writings
35. Willa Cather: Early Novels & Stories
36. Theodore Dreiser: Sister Carrie, Jennie Gerhardt, Twelve Men
37. Benjamin Franklin: Writings (2 vols.)
38. William James: Writings 1902–1910
39. Flannery O'Connor: Collected Works

40, 41, & 42. Eugene O'Neill: Complete Plays

43. Henry James: Novels 1886–1890
44. William Dean Howells: Novels 1886–1888

45 & 46. Abraham Lincoln: Speeches & Writings

47. Edith Wharton: Novellas & Other Writings
48. William Faulkner: Novels 1936–1940
49. Willa Cather: Later Novels
50. Ulysses S. Grant: Memoirs & Selected Letters
51. William Tecumseh Sherman: Memoirs
52. Washington Irving: Bracebridge Hall, Tales of a Traveller, The Alhambra
53. Francis Parkman: The Oregon Trail, The Conspiracy of Pontiac
54. James Fenimore Cooper: Sea Tales

55 & 56. Richard Wright: Works

57. Willa Cather: Stories, Poems, & Other Writings
58. William James: Writings 1878–1899
59. Sinclair Lewis: Main Street & Babbitt

60 & 61. Mark Twain: Collected Tales, Sketches, Speeches, & Essays

62 & 63. The Debate on the Constitution

64 & 65. Henry James: Collected Travel Writings

66 & 67. American Poetry: The Nineteenth Century

68. Frederick Douglass: Autobiographies
69. Sarah Orne Jewett: Novels & Stories
70. Ralph Waldo Emerson: Collected Poems & Translations
71. Mark Twain: Historical Romances
72. John Steinbeck: Novels & Stories 1932–1937
73. William Faulkner: Novels 1942–1954

74 & 75. Zora Neale Hurston: Novels, Stories, & Other Writings

76. Thomas Paine: Collected Writings

77 & 78. Reporting World War II: American Journalism

79 & 80. Raymond Chandler: Novels, Stories, & Other Writings

81. Robert Frost: Collected Poems, Prose, & Plays
82 & 83. Henry James: Complete Stories 1892–1910
84. William Bartram: Travels & Other Writings
85. John Dos Passos: U.S.A.
86. John Steinbeck: The Grapes of Wrath & Other Writings 1936–1941
87, 88, & 89. Vladimir Nabokov: Novels & Other Writings
90. James Thurber: Writings & Drawings
91. George Washington: Writings
92. John Muir: Nature Writings
93. Nathanael West: Novels & Other Writings
94 & 95. Crime Novels: American Noir of the 1930s, 40s, & 50s
96. Wallace Stevens: Collected Poetry & Prose
97. James Baldwin: Early Novels & Stories
98. James Baldwin: Collected Essays
99 & 100. Gertrude Stein: Writings
101 & 102. Eudora Welty: Novels, Stories, & Other Writings
103. Charles Brockden Brown: Three Gothic Novels
104 & 105. Reporting Vietnam: American Journalism
106 & 107. Henry James: Complete Stories 1874–1891
108. American Sermons
109. James Madison: Writings
110. Dashiell Hammett: Complete Novels
111. Henry James: Complete Stories 1864–1874
112. William Faulkner: Novels 1957–1962
113. John James Audubon: Writings & Drawings
114. Slave Narratives
115 & 116. American Poetry: The Twentieth Century
117. F. Scott Fitzgerald: Novels & Stories 1920–1922
118. Henry Wadsworth Longfellow: Poems & Other Writings
119 & 120. Tennessee Williams: Collected Plays
121 & 122. Edith Wharton: Collected Stories
123. The American Revolution: Writings from the War of Independence
124. Henry David Thoreau: Collected Essays & Poems
125. Dashiell Hammett: Crime Stories & Other Writings
126 & 127. Dawn Powell: Novels
128. Carson McCullers: Complete Novels
129. Alexander Hamilton: Writings
130. Mark Twain: The Gilded Age & Later Novels
131. Charles W. Chesnutt: Stories, Novels, & Essays
132. John Steinbeck: Novels 1942–1952
133. Sinclair Lewis: Arrowsmith, Elmer Gantry, Dodsworth
134 & 135. Paul Bowles: Novels, Stories, & Other Writings
136. Kate Chopin: Complete Novels & Stories
137 & 138. Reporting Civil Rights: American Journalism
139. Henry James: Novels 1896–1899
140. Theodore Dreiser: An American Tragedy
141. Saul Bellow: Novels 1944–1953
142. John Dos Passos: Novels 1920–1925
143. John Dos Passos: Travel Books & Other Writings
144. Ezra Pound: Poems & Translations
145. James Weldon Johnson: Writings
146. Washington Irving: Three Western Narratives
147. Alexis de Tocqueville: Democracy in America
148. James T. Farrell: Studs Lonigan Trilogy
149, 150, & 151. Isaac Bashevis Singer: Collected Stories
152. Kaufman & Co.: Broadway Comedies
153. Theodore Roosevelt: Rough Riders, An Autobiography
154. Theodore Roosevelt: Letters & Speeches
155. H. P. Lovecraft: Tales
156. Louisa May Alcott: Little Women, Little Men, Jo's Boys
157. Philip Roth: Novels & Stories 1959–1962
158. Philip Roth: Novels 1967–1972
159. James Agee: Let Us Now Praise Famous Men, A Death in the Family, Shorter Fiction
160. James Agee: Film Writing & Selected Journalism
161. Richard Henry Dana Jr.: Two Years Before the Mast & Other Voyages
162. Henry James: Novels 1901–1902
163. Arthur Miller: Plays 1944–1961
164. William Faulkner: Novels 1926–1929
165. Philip Roth: Novels 1973–1977
166 & 167. American Speeches: Political Oratory
168. Hart Crane: Complete Poems & Selected Letters

169. Saul Bellow: Novels 1956–1964
170. John Steinbeck: Travels with Charley & Later Novels
171. Capt. John Smith: Writings with Other Narratives
172. Thornton Wilder: Collected Plays & Writings on Theater
173. Philip K. Dick: Four Novels of the 1960s
174. Jack Kerouac: Road Novels 1957–1960
175. Philip Roth: Zuckerman Bound
176 & 177. Edmund Wilson: Literary Essays & Reviews
178. American Poetry: The 17th & 18th Centuries
179. William Maxwell: Early Novels & Stories
180. Elizabeth Bishop: Poems, Prose, & Letters
181. A. J. Liebling: World War II Writings
182. American Earth: Environmental Writing Since Thoreau
183. Philip K. Dick: Five Novels of the 1960s & 70s
184. William Maxwell: Later Novels & Stories
185. Philip Roth: Novels & Other Narratives 1986–1991
186. Katherine Anne Porter: Collected Stories & Other Writings
187. John Ashbery: Collected Poems 1956–1987
188 & 189. John Cheever: Complete Novels & Collected Stories
190. Lafcadio Hearn: American Writings
191. A. J. Liebling: The Sweet Science & Other Writings
192. The Lincoln Anthology
193. Philip K. Dick: VALIS & Later Novels
194. Thornton Wilder: The Bridge of San Luis Rey & Other Novels 1926–1948
195. Raymond Carver: Collected Stories
196 & 197. American Fantastic Tales
198. John Marshall: Writings
199. The Mark Twain Anthology
200. Mark Twain: A Tramp Abroad, Following the Equator, Other Travels
201 & 202. Ralph Waldo Emerson: Selected Journals
203. The American Stage: Writing on Theater
204. Shirley Jackson: Novels & Stories
205. Philip Roth: Novels 1993–1995
206 & 207. H. L. Mencken: Prejudices
208. John Kenneth Galbraith: The Affluent Society & Other Writings 1952–1967
209. Saul Bellow: Novels 1970–1982
210 & 211. Lynd Ward: Six Novels in Woodcuts
212. The Civil War: The First Year
213 & 214. John Adams: Revolutionary Writings
215. Henry James: Novels 1903–1911
216. Kurt Vonnegut: Novels & Stories 1963–1973
217 & 218. Harlem Renaissance Novels
219. Ambrose Bierce: The Devil's Dictionary, Tales, & Memoirs
220. Philip Roth: The American Trilogy 1997–2000
221. The Civil War: The Second Year
222. Barbara W. Tuchman: The Guns of August, The Proud Tower
223. Arthur Miller: Plays 1964–1982
224. Thornton Wilder: The Eighth Day, Theophilus North, Autobiographical Writings
225. David Goodis: Five Noir Novels of the 1940s & 50s
226. Kurt Vonnegut: Novels & Stories 1950–1962
227 & 228. American Science Fiction: Nine Novels of the 1950s
229 & 230. Laura Ingalls Wilder: The Little House Books
231. Jack Kerouac: Collected Poems
232. The War of 1812
233. American Antislavery Writings
234. The Civil War: The Third Year
235. Sherwood Anderson: Collected Stories
236. Philip Roth: Novels 2001–2007
237. Philip Roth: Nemeses
238. Aldo Leopold: A Sand County Almanac & Other Writings
239. May Swenson: Collected Poems
240 & 241. W. S. Merwin: Collected Poems
242 & 243. John Updike: Collected Stories
244. Ring Lardner: Stories & Other Writings
245. Jonathan Edwards: Writings from the Great Awakening
246. Susan Sontag: Essays of the 1960s & 70s
247. William Wells Brown: Clotel & Other Writings
248 & 249. Bernard Malamud: Novels & Stories of the 1940s, 50s, & 60s
250. The Civil War: The Final Year
251. Shakespeare in America

252. Kurt Vonnegut: Novels 1976–1985
253 & 254. American Musicals 1927–1969
255. Elmore Leonard: Four Novels of the 1970s
256. Louisa May Alcott: Work, Eight Cousins, Rose in Bloom, Stories & Other Writings
257. H. L. Mencken: The Days Trilogy
258. Virgil Thomson: Music Chronicles 1940–1954
259. Art in America 1945–1970
260. Saul Bellow: Novels 1984–2000
261. Arthur Miller: Plays 1987–2004
262. Jack Kerouac: Visions of Cody, Visions of Gerard, Big Sur
263. Reinhold Niebuhr: Major Works on Religion & Politics
264. Ross Macdonald: Four Novels of the 1950s
265 & 266. The American Revolution: Writings from the Pamphlet Debate
267. Elmore Leonard: Four Novels of the 1980s
268 & 269. Women Crime Writers: Suspense Novels of the 1940s & 50s
270. Frederick Law Olmsted: Writings on Landscape, Culture, & Society
271. Edith Wharton: Four Novels of the 1920s
272. James Baldwin: Later Novels
273. Kurt Vonnegut: Novels 1987–1997
274. Henry James: Autobiographies
275. Abigail Adams: Letters
276. John Adams: Writings from the New Nation 1784–1826
277. Virgil Thomson: The State of Music & Other Writings
278. War No More: American Antiwar & Peace Writing
279. Ross Macdonald: Three Novels of the Early 1960s
280. Elmore Leonard: Four Later Novels
281. Ursula K. Le Guin: The Complete Orsinia
282. John O'Hara: Stories
283. The Unknown Kerouac: Rare, Unpublished & Newly Translated Writings
284. Albert Murray: Collected Essays & Memoirs
285 & 286. Loren Eiseley: Collected Essays on Evolution, Nature, & the Cosmos
287. Carson McCullers: Stories, Plays & Other Writings
288. Jane Bowles: Collected Writings
289. World War I and America: Told by the Americans Who Lived It
290 & 291. Mary McCarthy: The Complete Fiction
292. Susan Sontag: Later Essays
293 & 294. John Quincy Adams: Diaries
295. Ross Macdonald: Four Later Novels
296 & 297. Ursula K. Le Guin: The Hainish Novels & Stories
298 & 299. Peter Taylor: The Complete Stories
300. Philip Roth: Why Write? Collected Nonfiction 1960–2014
301. John Ashbery: Collected Poems 1991–2000
302. Wendell Berry: Port William Novels & Stories: The Civil War to World War II
303. Reconstruction: Voices from America's First Great Struggle for Racial Equality
304. Albert Murray: Collected Novels & Poems
305 & 306. Norman Mailer: The Sixties
307. Rachel Carson: Silent Spring & Other Writings on the Environment
308. Elmore Leonard: Westerns
309 & 310. Madeleine L'Engle: The Kairos Novels
311. John Updike: Novels 1959–1965
312. James Fenimore Cooper: Two Novels of the American Revolution
313. John O'Hara: Four Novels of the 1930s
314. Ann Petry: The Street, The Narrows
315. Ursula K. Le Guin: Always Coming Home
316 & 317. Wendell Berry: Collected Essays
318. Cornelius Ryan: The Longest Day, A Bridge Too Far
319. Booth Tarkington: Novels & Stories
320. Herman Melville: Complete Poems
321 & 322. American Science Fiction: Eight Classic Novels of the 1960s
323. Frances Hodgson Burnett: The Secret Garden, A Little Princess, Little Lord Fauntleroy
324. Jean Stafford: Complete Novels
325. Joan Didion: The 1960s & 70s
326. John Updike: Novels 1968–1975
327. Constance Fenimore Woolson: Collected Stories
328. Robert Stone: Dog Soldiers, Flag for Sunrise, Outerbridge Reach
329. Jonathan Schell: The Fate of the Earth, The Abolition, The Unconquerable World
330. Richard Hofstadter: Anti-Intellectualism in American Life, The Paranoid Style in American Politics, Uncollected Essays 1956–1965